The Good Pub Guide

The Good Pub Guide 1986

Edited by Alisdair Aird

Assistant editor: Fiona May

PUBLISHED BY CONSUMERS' ASSOCIATION
AND HODDER & STOUGHTON

First published in Great Britain by
Consumers' Association
14 Buckingham Street, London WC2N 6DS and
Hodder & Stoughton Ltd
47 Bedford Square, London WC1B 3DP

Designed by Trevor Vincent
Illustrations by Trevor Vincent from photographs by the editor
Cover artwork by John Holder
Maps by Eugene Fleury

The Good Pub Guide.—1986.
    1. Hotels, taverns, etc.—Great Britain—
    Directories   2. Restaurants, lunchrooms etc.
    —Great Britain—Directories
    I. Aird, Alisdair   II. Consumers' Association
    647'.9541'05   TX910.G7

ISBN 0 340 38202 3

Typeset by Foremost Typesetting Limited, London EC4
Printed and bound in The Netherlands
by Rotatie Boekendruk B.V., Krommenie

Contents

Introduction

This year, many pubs are facing a crisis of identity. The breweries, which between them own about 60 per cent of all pubs, have seen beer sales fall by about 12 per cent during the 1980s. People are going to pubs less often. Apart from drinking and driving, the main things that have put them off are smoke, crowds and too few seats, and above all the high price of pub drinks. Other problems identified by the brewers include women disliking pubs, people with families seeing pubs as being hostile to children, video films keeping people at home, pub licensing hours being too restrictive, the great boom in wine drinking leaving pubs behind (70 per cent of wine is drunk at home), and people going out for the evening choosing to eat out rather than spending their time in the boozer. All this can be summed up as general tackiness, poor value for money, and a failure to move with the times.

Naturally, the breweries – seeing their profits threatened – have reacted strongly. Along with their pub tenants, the hotel and restaurant trade, tourist boards, and the Campaign for Real Ale, they've mounted a vigorous campaign to have the licensing laws changed so that pubs can stay open all day. But even more importantly, they've geared up for a colossal spending spree to improve the image of their pubs, earmarking an average of some £40,000 to invest in upgrading each pub over the next two or three years. And ironically that – along with a string of regional takeovers and some 15 major brewery closures in the last few years – is what has precipitated this crisis of identity.

In a hunt for how to invest most wisely, the breweries have turned to science. Some of the results have been apparently straightforward. Detailed market research and project development analysis has confirmed what readers of this *Guide* could have told the breweries years ago – there's money to be made from food (and from wine – four times as powerful a market factor now as it was 10 years ago). The chairman of the Brewers' Society has said that a substantial part of breweries' investment will be devoted to the catering side. But some of what has come up is altogether more esoteric.

Several of the big breweries – Watneys has so far been the most striking example – have set about analysing the social structure of each area in which they trade, using the computerised postcode-area population breakdowns that have become available since the last census. This gives them, for example, an idea of how many big-earning courting couples there are within walking distance of a particular pub, or how many car-owning families with young children and a particular income level there are in an area. These are simple examples; the analysis is very much more complex. What comes out of it all is a series of novel predictions: that a particular area where, for instance, that brewery owns seven quite ordinary pubs could profitably support, say, one romantic late-night rendezvous with regular discos, two clean-living family-style pub-restaurants, two video-game and fruit machine dens with loud pop music, and one traditional and nostalgic thatched inn with old-fashioned English food.

That, in our simplistic example, is a total of six potentially profitable pubs. The brewery sells the seventh, and it becomes a free house (the proportion of free houses – not tied to any brewery, often privately owned – has risen by nearly 50 per cent during the last decade). The architects, designers and marketing men move into the other six pubs. Typically, they have a portfolio of a dozen or two more or less standardised new pub styles. The ones that match the demographic breakdown of the area best are chosen, so that in this case the Rising Sun is turned into a 1920s-style softly lit bar called Kisses & Cream, the George IV acquires a Mistress Martha Family Eatery, the Ship blossoms into the Happy Galleon hamburger and Mexican taco restaurant, the Green Man becomes Greens and the Rams Head becomes Chances (both full of games and decibels), and a couple of tons of synthetic straw and plastic oak turn the Black Cat into Ye Olde Blacke Catte, with Farmer Tom's Country Kitchen attached.

These precisely targeted pub themes (the brewers talk of 'product styles') often have umbrella names, such as Barnaby's (Watneys cheery family fixed-price carvery restaurants), Pub 80 (Watneys' idea of what young people, especially young women, want), Cavalier Inns (Ind Coope/Allied Breweries steakhouses), Country Inns and White Rose Taverns (Allied Breweries again, for older people with traditional tastes), Roast Inns (Whitbreads food pubs for people who like Beefeater steakhouses – another Whitbreads style – but want to spend less), not-dissimilar two-tier approaches to pub eating from Bass and Courage (respectively, Toby Pantries and Vintage Inns, and Harvesters and Falstaff Inns), Drummonds (Bass café-bars serving wine and interesting food, designed to appeal to women), or Calendars (the Watford prototype for yet another Allied Breweries chain is a big bar-restaurant with a Cadillac hanging from the ceiling and American-Mexican as well as British food).

This idea of kitting out pubs in more or less off-the-peg theme outfits can work wonders. By and large, the 'branded' pub restaurant chains are very popular: people know what they can expect, and the breweries have taken a great deal of trouble developing the original concepts so that customers are happy with them. But sometimes the facelift is a bit of a Frankenstein's monster. A pub may *look* like an art deco café, or something from the heyday of the Raj, or a rustic tavern, but it doesn't *feel* like it. We've been into pubs that a year or two ago were grubby nonentities and have since been fitted out as smart cocktail bars: the gear and glitter's all there, but so is the original lack-lustre atmosphere – and even the same bored faces that went with it before the changes.

Over three years or so, the breweries are pouring some £2,000 million into pub refurbishment. But we fear that some of the money is being wasted. What attracts people to pubs, besides good food, good drink and well kept surroundings, is a natural warmth and individuality – genuine character. An ordinary high-street pub suddenly billed as Al Capone's or The Merrie Days of Yore or whatever is a bit like an ordinary high-street bloke deluding himself that he's Napoleon. And that's the identity crisis we mentioned at the beginning. Are all these pubs really restaurants? Are they wine bars? Cocktail bars? Speakeasies? Amusement arcades? All too often, the answer is that they don't really know *what* they are.

A large part of the problem is that you cannot impose the qualities that people look for in a good pub from above – they have to develop naturally and genuinely within the pub itself. They depend heavily on the people who actually run the pub. Often, they are found in the tenants and sometimes managers of pubs tied to the breweries. Hundreds of very good brewery-tied pubs, with bags of genuine character and true personality, are included as main entries in this *Guide*. Perhaps even more often, it's the free house that scores (of the seven pubs in our fanciful example above, we're most optimistic about the seventh – the one sold off by the brewery as a free house). But always, it's the stamp of true individuality that makes a pub worth travelling to. (And, incidentally, the EEC has this last year given pub individuality a useful boost. Tied pubs can now buy spirits, soft drinks, crisps and so forth from sources other than their parent brewery, as well as beers that differ in 'taste, appearance and composition' from the breweries' own – that usually means real ales, Guinness and unusual or foreign bottled beers.)

It is in this quite small minority of truly genuine pubs that we are seeing a remarkable flowering of pub quality. For every 30 or so pubs content to remain unambitious locals, and 30 more that now seem to be floundering in uncertainty about what they are and who they're for, there are perhaps one or two that are confidently stepping forward in absolute certainty about their own identity. These are the pubs where – usually at prices representing outstanding value for money, when compared with similar quality in a restaurant – you will find really good individual food (not some catering blueprint), genuine furnishings and decoration (instead of pictures bought by the yard and chairs and tables identical to those in a thousand other pubs), interesting drinks, proper gardens (not the Number Six, Size Four Patio Installation with Thatched Wishing Well), and above all a real human landlord, landlady and staff (not the identikit wheel-ins that we suspect are concocted in the deep slurries of some redundant brewery, and which actually charged one reader 20p for a glass of water to have with his curry on the grumpy grounds that they had to wash the glass didn't they).

And – does it now need to be said? – these are the pubs that fill the pages of this book. Which brings us to some scraps of news about the book itself. This is the *Guide*'s fourth year. Since its first edition it has changed a lot – far more pubs, more detail on individual pubs (particularly about food), and the inclusion of thousands of extra Lucky Dip pubs, recommended and described briefly by readers. This year, after good-natured complaints from readers that they now needed a trailer to cart such a fat book around with them, or that holding it open was wearing out the muscles in their drinking arm, (and some understandably less good-natured ones about the binding falling apart), we've tried to save some page space by revising the layout a bit, and reducing the type size of the Lucky Dip entries.

Another important change is that this year the *Guide* has taken on as part-time Assistant Editor Fiona May (previously one of our more enthusiastic reporters, and someone with long experience of similar work on *Holiday Which?*). And that means that – if you take us up on the guarded invitation that we repeat from previous editions – there are now two of us for you to come and meet. If you're passing the *Guide* office (134 Lots Road, London SW10 – just off the King's Road, near World's End), why not drop in for a drink? Since we moved into this office, no less than two new pubs have opened almost on the doorstep, one of them brewing its own beer. So if we're in and not tied up, and especially if you're one of the readers who so magnificently fuel our work with reports on pubs, we might buy you a drink! (And who knows, he mutters hopefully, you might feel like buying us one instead. . . .)

Alisdair Aird

What is a Good Pub?

The more than 1,400 pubs chosen as main entries in this book have been through a two-stage sifting process. First of all, some 2,000 regular correspondents keep in touch with us about the pubs they visit. They keep us up to date about pubs included in previous editions – it's their alarm signals that warn us when a pub's standards have dropped (after a change of management, say), and it's their continuing approval that reassures us about keeping a pub as a main entry for another year. Very important, though, are the reports they send us on pubs we don't know at all. It's from these new discoveries that we make up a shortlist, to be considered for possible inclusion as new main entries. The more people who report favourably on a new pub, the more likely it is to win a place on this shortlist – especially if some of the reporters belong to our hard core of about 200 trusted correspondents whose judgement we have learned to rely on. These are people who have each given us detailed comments on dozens of pubs, and shown that (when we ourselves know some of these pubs too) their judgement is closely in line with our own.

This brings us to the acid test. Each pub, before inclusion as a main entry, is inspected anonymously by the Editor in person. The Editor has to find some special quality that would make strangers enjoy visiting it. What often marks the pub out for special attention is good value food (and that might mean anything from a well made sandwich, with good fresh ingredients at a low price, to imaginative cooking outclassing most restaurants in the area). Maybe the drinks are out of the ordinary (pubs with over 300 whiskies, with remarkable wine lists, with home-made country wines or good beer or cider made on the premises, with a wide range of well kept real ales or bottled beers from all over the world). Perhaps there's a special appeal about it as a place to stay, with good bedrooms and obliging service. Maybe it's the building itself (from centuries-old parts of monasteries to extravagant Victorian gin-palaces), or its surroundings (lovely countryside, attractive waterside, an extensive well kept garden), or what's in it (charming furnishings, extraordinary collections of bric-à-brac).

Above all, though, what makes a good pub is its atmosphere – you should be able to feel at home there, and feel not just that *you're* glad you've come but that *they're* glad you've come.

It follows from this that a great many ordinary locals, perfectly good in their own right, don't earn a place in the book. What makes them attractive to their regular customers (an almost clubby chumminess) may even make strangers feel rather out of place.

Another important point is that there's not necessarily any link between charm and luxury – though we like our creature comforts as much as anyone. A basic unspoilt tavern in a woodland village, with hard seats and a flagstone floor, may be worth travelling miles to find, while a deluxe pub-restaurant may not be worth crossing the street for. Landlords can't buy the Good Pub accolade by spending thousands on thickly padded banquettes, soft music and luxuriously shrimpy sauces for their steaks – they can only win it, by having a genuinely personal concern for both their customers and their pub.

How to use the Guide

THE COUNTIES

England has been split alphabetically into counties, mainly to make it easier for people scanning through the book to find pubs near them. Each chapter starts by picking out pubs that are specially attractive for one reason or another.

Occasionally, counties have been lumped together into a single chapter, and metropolitan areas have been included in the counties around them – for example, Merseyside in Lancashire. When there's any risk of confusion, we have put a note about where to find a county at the place in the book where you'd probably look for it. But check the Contents if in doubt.

Scotland and Wales have each been covered in single chapters, and London appears immediately before them at the end of England. We have split London into Central, North, South, East and West, and listed pubs alphabetically in each of those areas. In all other counties, pubs are listed alphabetically under the name of the town or village where they are. If the village is so small that you probably wouldn't find it on a road map, we've listed it under the name of the nearest sizeable village or town instead. The maps use the same town and village names.

We always list pubs in their true locations – so if a pub's village is actually in the county of Buckinghamshire, say, we list it under Buckinghamshire even if its postal address is via some town in Oxfordshire.

STARS

Specially good pubs are picked out with a star after their name. In a few cases, pubs have two stars: these are the aristocrats among pubs, really worth going out of your way to find. And just a small handful have three stars – the tops. The stars do *not* signify extra luxury or specially good food. The detailed description of each pub shows what its special appeal is, and it's that that the stars refer to.

RECOMMENDERS

At the end of each main entry we include the names of readers who have recommended that pub (unless they've asked us not to). Important note: the description of the pub and the comments on it are our own and *not* the recommenders'; they are based on our own personal inspections and on later verification of facts with each pub. As some recommenders' names appear quite often, you can get an extra idea of what a pub is like by seeing which other pubs those recommenders have approved.

LUCKY DIPS

At the end of each county chapter we include brief descriptions of pubs that have been recommended by readers, with the readers' names in brackets. The initials LYM among the recommenders mean that the pub was in a previous edition of the *Guide*. The usual reason that it's no longer a main entry is that, although we've heard nothing really condemnatory about it, we've not had enough favourable reports to be sure that it's still ahead of the local competition. In this case, the description is our own. The initials BB mean that, although the pub has never been a main entry, we have inspected it, found nothing against it, and reckon it's useful to know of – and perhaps worth a closer look.

The Lucky Dips are under consideration for inspection for a future edition, so please let us have any comments you can make on them. You can use the report forms at the end of the book, the report card which should be included in it, or just write direct (no stamp needed if posted in the UK). Our address is *The Good Pub Guide*, FREEPOST, London SW10 0BR.

MAP REFERENCES

This year we have given four-figure map references for all pubs listed, including the Lucky Dips. On the main entries, it looks like this: SX5678 Map 1. Map 1 means that it's on the first map at the end of the book. SX means it's in the square labelled SX on that map. The first figure, 5, tells you to look along the grid at the top and bottom of the SX square for the figure 5. The *third* figure, 7, tells you to look down the grid at the side of the square to find the figure 7. Imaginary lines drawn down and across the square from these figures should intersect near the pub itself.

The second and fourth figures, the 6 and the 8, are for more precise pin-pointing, and are really for use with larger-scale maps such as road atlases or the Ordnance Survey 1:50,000 maps, which use exactly the same map reference system. On the relevant Ordnance Survey map, instead of finding the 5 marker on the top grid you'd find the 56 one; instead of the 7 on the side grid you'd look for the 78 marker. This makes it very easy to locate even the smallest village.

Where a pub is exceptionally difficult to find, we include a six-figure reference in the directions, such as OS Sheet 102 reference 654783. This refers to Sheet 102 of the Ordnance Survey 1:50,000 maps, which explain how to use the six-figure references to pinpoint a pub to the nearest 100 metres.

MOTORWAY PUBS

If a pub is within four or five miles of a motorway junction, and reaching it doesn't involve much slow traffic, we give special directions for finding it from the motorway. And the Special Interest lists at the end of the book include a list of these pubs, motorway by motorway.

PRICES AND OTHER FACTUAL DETAILS

The *Guide* went to press during the summer of 1985. As late as possible before that, each pub was sent a checking sheet to provide us with up-to-date food, drink and bedroom prices and other factual information. Not every pub returned the sheet to us, and in some cases those that did omitted some prices. In such cases we ourselves were often able to gather the information – especially prices – anyway. But where details are missing, that is the explanation. And we should say that in a few cases in which pubs had previously failed to co-operate with us – and the question of including them in this new edition was in the balance – we left those pubs out altogether, partly because we see that failure as a rather poor reflection on either their friendliness or their standards of management.

Real ale is used by us to mean beer that has been maturing naturally in its cask. We do not count as real ale beer which has been pasteurised or filtered to remove its natural yeasts. If it is kept under a blanket of carbon dioxide ('blanket pressure') to preserve it, we don't normally call it real ale, but do generally mention the beer by name in the text – as long as the pressure is too light for you to notice any extra fizz, it's hard to tell the difference. So many pubs now stock one of the main brands of draught cider that we normally mention cider only if the pub keeps quite a range, or one of the less common farm-made ciders.

Wines and spirits are mentioned only if there's an unusual range; you can reckon to get wine by the glass in virtually all but the simplest of the pubs in the book. If we mention country wines, we mean traditional elderberry-type wines.

Meals refers to what is sold in the bar, not in any separate restaurant. It means that pub sells food in its bar substantial enough to do as a proper meal – something you'd sit down to with knife and fork. It doesn't necessarily mean you can get three separate courses.

Snacks means sandwiches, ploughman's, pies and so forth, rather than pork scratchings or packets of crisps. We always mention sandwiches in the text if we know that a pub does them – if you don't see them mentioned, assume you can't get them.

The food listed in the description of each pub is an example of the sort of thing you'd find there on a normal day. We try to indicate any difference we know of between different days of the week, and between summer and winter (on the whole stressing summer food more). In winter, many pubs tend to have a more restricted range, particularly of salads, and tend then to do more in the way of filled baked potatoes, casseroles and hot pies. We always mention barbecues if we know a pub does them.

Unless we say otherwise, you can generally assume that bar food is served at normal lunch and supper times (which of course may vary from region to region). Though we note days when pubs have told us they don't do food, experience suggests that you should play safe on Sundays and check first with any pub before planning an expedition that depends on getting a meal there. Also, out-of-the-way pubs often cut down on cooking during the week if they're quiet – as they tend to be, except at holiday times. Please let us know if you find anything different from what we say!

Any separate restaurant is normally mentioned, and may be briefly described. But in general all comments on the type of food served, and in particular all the details about meals and snacks at the end of each entry, relate to the pub food and not to the restaurant food.

Children under 14 are now allowed in to at least some part of most of the pubs included in this *Guide*. As we went to press, we asked pubs a series of detailed questions about their rules. *Children welcome* means the pub has told us that it simply lets them come in, with no special restrictions. In other cases we report exactly what arrangements pubs say they make for children. And even if we don't mention children at all, it is worth asking: one or two pubs told us frankly that they do welcome children but don't want to advertise the fact for fear of being penalised. All but one or two pubs (we mention them in the text) allow children in their garden or on their terrace, if they have one.

Parking is not mentioned if we believe that you should normally be able to park outside the pub, or in a private car park, without difficulty. But if we know that parking space is limited or metered, we say so.

Dogs and cats are mentioned in the text, if we or readers have noticed them in a pub – readers seem almost equally divided between those who like them and those who don't (or are allergic to them).

Opening hours are for summer weekdays. If these show a pub stays open until 11pm, it will close at 10.30pm in winter unless we say *all year*. And in winter some pubs open an hour or so later, too; we mention this where we know of it. In the country, many pubs may open rather later and close earlier than their details show unless there are plenty of customers around (if you come across this, please let us know – with details). Unless we say otherwise for a particular county or pub, pubs generally stay open until 11pm on Friday and Saturday evenings. Pubs that are licensed to stay open all day are listed at the back of the book.

Sunday hours are standard for all English and Welsh pubs that open on that day: 12–2, 7–10.30. In Scotland, a few pubs close on Sundays (we specify those that we know of); most are open 12.30–2.30 and 6.30–11, and some stay open all day. If we know of a pub closing for any day of the week or part of the year, we say so. The few pubs that we specify as closed on Monday open on bank holiday Mondays.

Bedroom prices normally include full English breakfasts (if these are available, which they usually are), VAT and any automatic service charge that we know about. If we give just one price, it is the total price for two people sharing a double or twin-bedded room for one night. A capital 'B' against the price means that it includes a private bath or shower. ('S' means we know there's only a shower). A '/' means that the pub has told us it can put up single people: prices before the '/' are for single occupancy, prices after it for double. As all this coding packs in quite a lot of information, some examples may help to explain it:

£20 on its own means that's the total bill for two people sharing a twin or double room without private bath; the pub has no rooms with private bath, and a single person might have to pay that full price

£20B means exactly the same – but all the rooms have private bath or shower

£20 (£24B) means rooms with private baths cost £4 extra

£15/£20 (£24B) means the same as the last example, but also shows that there are single rooms for £15, none of which have private bathrooms

If there's a choice of rooms at different prices, we normally give the cheapest. If there are seasonal price variations, we give the summer price (the highest). This winter – 1985–6 – many inns, particularly in the country, will have special cheaper rates. And at other times, especially in holiday areas, you will often find prices cheaper if you stay for several nights. On weekends inns that aren't in obvious weekending areas often have bargain rates for two- or three-night stays.

Changes are inevitable during the course of the year. Landlords change, and so do their policies. And, as we've said, not all returned our fact-checking sheets. We very much hope that you will find everything just as we say. But if you find anything different, please let us know. You don't need a stamp: the address is *The Good Pub Guide*, FREEPOST, London SW10 0BR.

Author's acknowledgements

We should like to thank the publicans who have taken such trouble over filling in our very detailed fact sheets – and thank them, too, for making and running so many friendly and attractive places.

We owe a great deal to the many hundreds of readers who report, often regularly, on pubs – thanks to you all. Particular thanks to the people who have given most help to this new edition, in rough order of the number of reports they've sent us this year, are due to: Tim Halstead, Philip Asquith, Keith Myers, Paul West, S V Bishop, William Meadon, Richard Steel, my uncle W T Aird, Dr A K Clarke, Sue and Len Beattie, Steve and Carolyn Harvey, Gwen and Peter Andrews, Lee Goulding, Jane English, Gordon and Daphne, Flt Lt A Darroch Harkness, Jon Dewhirst, Martyn Quinn, T Mansell, Ian Clay, Heather Sharland, Howard Gascoyne, Robert Aitken, Jeff Cousins, MGBD, G L Archer, Dave Butler, Les Storey, Tim and Ann Bracey, Andy Jones and the P A Club, David Regan, Frank Cummins, H K R, P T Young, Mr and Mrs Philip Denison, Michael and Alison Sandy, Peter Hitchcock and D A Angless.

England

Avon *see* Somerset

Bedfordshire *see* Cambridgeshire

Berkshire

This edition of the Guide sees a few interesting newcomers to the Berkshire chapter. One, with perhaps the least attractive name we've come across so far – the Slug & Lettuce at Winkfield Row – has good food, not too expensive at lunchtime, and well kept real ales in attractively old-fashioned surroundings. The landlord of another, the Bird in Hand at Knowl Hill, has been selling real ales since long before CAMRA came on the scene – but his pub's forte is now good food, very reasonably priced for the area, served in the civilised lounge bar. The Crown at Bray is another with good food in comfortable surroundings, bouncing back into this edition in fine form. Perhaps the best pub food in the county is now to be found at the Royal Oak in Yattendon, a fine old inn which this year gains a star award for its consistently high standards; and at the Bear in Hungerford (bar snacks not always available there), which also gains a star for its civilised and old-fashioned atmosphere and good cooking. Indeed, the county does stand out for the relatively large number of places where quite high prices allow the survival of old-fashioned standards and an old-fashioned atmosphere: these include the

The Bell, Waltham St Lawrence

*Hind's Head at Bray, Bel & the Dragon in Cookham (a
particular favourite for a leisurely evening of people-
watching), the White Hart in Sonning and the Swan at
Streatley (these last two have lovely Thames-side gardens).
Among country pubs, we'd pick out particularly the Bell on
the Downs in Aldworth, the thatched Blue Boar at Chieveley
(comfortable bedrooms and good food), the unspoilt rustic
Old Hatch Gate at Cockpole Green, the Pot Kiln at Frilsham
and Dew Drop lost in the woods above Hurley (both these
two are idyllic on a summer's day), and the Cricketers facing
its cricket ground at Littlewick Green. Food is a strong point
in the Little Angel, Remenham (seafood), Dundas Arms in
Kintbury (its good restaurant has a remarkable choice of
clarets; also a nice place to stay), and, more simply, at the
Crown & Horns in East Ilsley, friendly Five Bells in Wickham
(a good value place to stay) and New Inn in Hampstead
Norreys. Beer prices are in general high in Berkshire: this last
pub, and the Old Hatch Gate at Cockpole Green, Pot Kiln
near Frilsham, Five Bells at Wickham and Nut & Bolt near
Yattendon were less pricey than most. We found the best
range of real ales at the Crown & Horns in East Ilsley,
Cricketers at Littlewick Green, and Rising Sun at
Woolhampton.*

ALDWORTH · SU5579 Map 2

Bell ★

Benches are built around the panelled walls and in to the gaps left by
a big disused fireplace and bread oven (though there's still a wood-
burning stove), and there are beams in the shiny ochre ceiling, in this
busy and cheerful small-roomed country pub. The atmosphere is
friendly and old-fashioned, and perfectly kept Arkells BBB and
Kingsdown, Badger Best and Morlands Mild (all on handpump) are
handed through a small hatch in the central servery. Fresh hot crusty
rolls are filled with Cheddar (45p), ham, pâté or Stilton (50p) and
turkey or tongue (60p); darts, shove-ha'penny, dominoes, cribbage,
chess and Aunt Sally (the local single-pin version of skittles). At
Christmas time local mummers perform in the road outside, by the
ancient well-head (the shaft is sunk 400 feet through the chalk), and
steaming jugs of hot punch and mince pies are handed round. In
summer, the quiet garden at the side is full of roses, mallows and
lavender. The path by the pub joins the nearby Ridgeway.
(Recommended by Jane English, MHG, Gordon and Daphne)

*Free house · Licensee H E Macaulay · Real ale · Snacks (not Mon) · Children in
tap-room · Open 11–2.30, 6–10.30; closed Mon and 25 Dec*

BINFIELD SU8471 Map 2

Victoria Arms

4½ miles from M4 junction 10; take A329(M) towards Wokingham, turn left on A329 towards Bracknell and Binfield, left again at Binfield signpost, and straight on into Terrace Road North

The open-plan layout here has cleverly combined space and airiness with the snug atmosphere and variety of a number of distinct areas, separated by short railed wooden dividers. You can choose between low-ceilinged intimacy and a lofty pitched wooden ceiling (which has shelves of unusual beer bottles below it) or simple country chairs and trestle tables on a tiled floor (this bit has sensibly placed darts, shove-ha'penny, dominoes, and even a red telephone box built in to one wall). There is a winter fire in the central bare-brick chimney. Reasonably priced lunchtime bar food includes freshly cut sandwiches, home-made fish pâté, a choice of ploughman's, summer salads including home-cooked meats and prawns, pizzas, cider-baked ham and beef Stroganoff. In the evenings a slightly different choice includes kebabs in pitta bread, scampi and steaks. In summer there are barbecues in the quiet back garden, which has picnic-table sets among roses. Well kept Fullers Chiswick, London Pride and ESB on handpump. *(Recommended by C P Price, Mr and Mrs Luciano Gristina; more reports please)*

Fullers · Licensee Mick Whelan · Real ale · Meals and snacks (not Sun) Children's room · Open 10.30–2.30, 5.30–11

BRAY   SU9079   Map 2
Crown

1¾ miles from M4 junction 9; A308 towards Windsor, then left at Bray signpost on to B3028

The flagstoned courtyard behind this fourteenth-century timbered house is very attractive, with tables and benches in a flagstoned vine arbour. In summer they play Aunt Sally and have Sunday lunchtime barbecues in the big back garden, where there are tables under cocktail parasols. Indoors, soft lighting, low beams, panelling, and old timbers, conveniently left at elbow height where walls have been knocked through, combine with the comfortable leather-backed seats around tables set with red gingham tablecloths and with the attractive service, to make for a relaxed atmosphere. Good bar food includes a choice of well filled rolls (50p), ploughman's (£2.50) and main dishes such as summer salads, cheese and asparagus flan (£2.50), steak and kidney pie, chilli con carne, lasagne or a curry (all £3). Readers like the food served in the evenings in the separate dining area, such as home-made liver pâté (£1.50), smoked trout or salmon mousse (£2), six Mediterranean prawns (£4.50), chicken suprême and garlic (£6.50), half a roast duck with orange sauce (£8), honey-baked rack of lamb (£8.50) and fillet steak (£9.50). Courage Best tapped from the cask, and a fair choice of wines. The walls are decorated with guns, pistols, stuffed animals, and caricatures by Spy and his competitors. *(Recommended by Doreen and Toby Carrington, J W Tomlinson, R K Whitehead)*

Courage · Licensee Hugh Whitton · Real ale · Meals (not Sat lunchtime, or Sun, except for barbecues Sun lunchtime in summer) and snacks (lunchtime, not Sat) · Children in restaurant · Open 10.30–2.30, 5.30–11

Hind's Head

1¾ miles from M4 junction 9; A308 towards Windsor, then left at Bray signpost

This beautifully kept establishment, with leather armchairs and high-backed settles under early Tudor beams, has mementoes of royal visits on the oak-panelled walls. In the words of one reader, instant nostalgia here, where you can almost see your reflection in the glossy woodblock floor. The friendly barman mixes good cocktails, and Courage Directors is tapped straight from the cask. Outside a nice touch is the provision of tablecloths for the tables in a small front courtyard. There is a handsome restaurant upstairs. (Recommended by Heather Sharland, Doreen and Toby Carrington; more reports please)

Courage · Licensee Marguerite Tinker · Real ale · Open 10.30–2.30, 6–10.30

CHADDLEWORTH   SU4177   Map 2

Ibex

From A338 pass church and follow signs to Brightwalton

The relaxed, friendly atmosphere and good value food continue to draw readers to this well kept flint village pub. The carpeted lounge has prints on the cream walls, fresh flowers on its refectory-style tables, old-fashioned bench seating, and a big winter log fire. Quickly served bar food includes white or brown bread sandwiches (from 65p, rare beef 95p, prawn £1.30; crusty French bread about 25p extra), home-made soup (70p), ploughman's (from £1.35), pizza (£1.90), salads (smoked peppered mackerel £2.50, smoked salmon £3.50), fresh sardines (£2.50), gammon with egg or pineapple (£2.90), prawns in garlic butter (£3), home-made steak, kidney and mushroom pie (£3), eight-ounce rump steak (£5.50) and dishes of the day such as quiches (£2.50), vegetable lasagne (£2.75), Bobotie (£2.95), chicken and mushroom pie (£2.95), seafood pie (£3) and puddings such as treacle tart, bread and butter pudding and fresh fruit pies and crumbles (£1). On Sundays there is a three-course lunch (£5.95). More tables are set for evening meals in the chintz-curtained sun-lounge and in a snug little dining-room which has plates on its walls and an antique oak corner cupboard. Well kept Courage Best and Directors on handpump; maybe piped music. The public bar has darts, cribbage and a fruit machine. There are tables out on a sheltered lawn, and a terrace is being built alongside the dining area. (Recommended by John Hill, MHG, Julian Lewis, T Doyne-Ditman)

Courage · Licensees Sheila and Peter Houser · Real ale · Meals and snacks (not Sun evening) · Children in special area overlooking garden · Open 10.30–2.30, 6–11

CHIEVELEY   SU4774   Map 2

Blue Boar   [illustrated on page 38]

3½ miles from M4 junction 13: A34 towards Newbury, first right, then right again on to B4494

This sixteenth-century thatched inn – quite alone on the Downs – has a cheerful and friendly atmosphere in the attractively furnished beamed bar, with old-fashioned high-backed settles and Windsor chairs. There is a big brick inglenook fireplace, and the walls are hung with cart-horse harness and hunting prints. One of the sturdy wooden tables, in a sunny bow window, has a fine view over the rolling fields to the distant M4. Food includes sandwiches (made to order at the bar), soup (85p), pâté (£1.50), garlic mussels with French bread or deep-fried Camembert (£1.75), a choice of ploughman's with good cheeses (from £1.50), cod (£2.75), chicken or beef curry (£2.95), strongly recommended home-made eight-ounce burgers topped with Brie or a fried egg and hot Bratwurst (£3.50), chicken Kiev, grilled salmon steak or wiener Schnitzel (£5.50), sirloin steak (£6.75) and three daily specials; home-made puddings (£1). There is also a separate restaurant. Well kept Arkells, Courage, Morlands, Ushers Best and Wadworths 6X on handpump, and friendly and obliging service; maybe piped music. The bedrooms have changed somewhat since Oliver Cromwell stayed here in 1694 and are now well equipped. There are tables among tubs and beds of flowers on the rough front cobbles, by the picturesquely stunted ancient oak which carries the inn sign. (Recommended by Patrick Stapley, RAB, S N Johnson, Iain Baillie, Glyn Edmunds)

Free house · Licensee Noel Morton · Real ale · Meals and snacks · Children in bar eating area · Open 10.30–2.30, 5.30–11 (11–2.30, 6–11 in winter); closed 25 Dec · Bedrooms tel Chieveley (063 521) 236; £20B/£25 (£28B)

COCKPOLE GREEN   SU7981   Map 2
Old Hatch Gate
Village signposted from A423 and A321

A splendidly unspoilt rustic pub with comfortable easy chairs in a carpeted saloon, and – for the best atmosphere – a beamed and partly panelled tap-room with a comfortable leatherette built-in bench and a flagstoned floor. Well kept and very reasonably priced Brakspears Mild, SB or Old ale. You can sit out by the car park, where there are slides, a climbing frame, and ducks and hens. (Recommended by W T Aird; more reports please)

Brakspears · Licensee Bill Mitchell · Real ale · Snacks · Open 10.30–2.30, 6–10.30

COOKHAM   SU8884   Map 2
Bel & the Dragon ★   [illustrated on page 32]
High Street; B4447

The atmosphere in the three communicating lounge rooms of this old pub is quietly civilised – oak panelling, pewter tankards hanging from heavy Tudor beams, leather chairs and old oak settles. A gravely friendly red-coated barman behind the very low zinc-topped bar counter serves well kept Brakspears and Youngs, wines including decent ports and champagne, and all the ingredients necessary for proper cocktails; not a cheap place, but worth every penny particularly if you like people-watching. Freshly cut sandwiches to order, and usually free peanuts and so forth. There is a smart separate restaurant. The Stanley Spencer Gallery is almost opposite. *(Recommended by Doug Kennedy, Heather Sharland; more reports please)*

Free house · Licensee F E Stuber · Real ale · Meals (restaurant only) and snacks Open 11–2.30, 6–10.30

King's Arms

This handsome old pub has a lovely garden with a spacious and sheltered lawn, a fountain and goldfish pool, and terraces and balustrades winding among flowerbeds and bushy cypresses. Its restaurant has been very popular with readers. Since our last edition the pub has been completely re-vamped inside as a Beefeater Steak House, and until we get approving reports from readers we are provisionally keeping it in as a full entry chiefly on the strength of its charming garden. They will be doing sandwiches, salads and home-cooked hot snacks (£2.25) as well as grills. *(More reports please)*

Wethereds (Whitbreads) · Licensee Gordon Atkins · Real ale · Meals and snacks · Children in eating area of bar and in restaurant · Open 10–2.30, 6–11 (11–2.30, 6–10.30 in winter)

EAST ILSLEY   SU4981   Map 2
Crown & Horns

The pretty paved stable-yard of this rambling old house has lots of tables under two chestnut trees, and is enlivened by brass-band concerts, music hall, puppet and clown shows and the occasional poetry reading. This is horse-training country: the beamed and partly panelled main bar's walls are hung with racing prints and photographs, and its stocks include a fine collection of 160 whiskies from all over the world – Moroccan, Korean, Japanese, Chinese, Spanish and New Zealand, say. There is an excellent and sensibly priced range of real ales which at any one time might include Arkells BBB, Badger Best, Devenish Wessex, Morlands, Ringwood Old Thumper, Ushers Best and Wadworths 6X, all on handpump. Bar food includes sandwiches, ploughman's (from £1.40), pâté (£1.45), taramosalata, a Stilton, port and celery pâté or mushrooms à la grecque (from £1.95), home-made pies such as steak, mutton and apple or chicken and mushroom (£1.85–£2.25). There is also a separate restaurant, and on fine summer days barbecues, grills and picnic-style lunches are served outside. The public bar has bar billiards, and there is a skittle alley. Fruit machine, juke box and piped music. Bypassed by the A34, the village is very peaceful. *(Recommended by MHG, C P Price; more reports please)*

Free house · Licensee Noel Bennett · Real ale · Meals and snacks (not Sun evening) · Children welcome · Occasional music hall, jazz and poetry readings Open 10.30–2.30, 6–11 (11–2, 6–11 in winter)

Meal times are generally the normal times at which people eat in the region. But they tend to vary from day to day and with the season, depending on how busy the pub hopes to be. We don't specify them as our experience shows you can't rely on them.

FRILSHAM   SU5473 Map 2
Pot Kiln

From Yattendon follow Frilsham signpost, but just after crossing motorway go
straight on towards Bucklebury where Frilsham is signposted right

This friendly and simple country pub is surrounded by wooded hills
and peaceful pastures, with sun-trap tables and folding garden chairs
outside – idyllic in fine weather on a quiet weekday. Generous
helpings of good value bar food include filled hot rolls (50p–65p),
ploughman's (£1.20), cottage pie or lasagne (£1.90), big pizzas, and,
in season, pheasant and even rook pie. Well kept Arkells BBB,
Morlands and Theakstons XB, all on handpump, are served from a
hatch in the panelled entrance lobby – which just has room for one
bar stool. On either side are a simply furnished lounge bar with log
fire to warm its traditional built-in wall benches, and a small bare-
board public bar with darts, dominoes, shove-ha'penny and cribbage.
(Recommended by Jane English, Gordon and Daphne; more reports please)

*Free house · Licensee Philip Gent · Real ale · Meals (not Sun) and snacks
Children welcome if well behaved · Folk singing Sun · Open 12–2.30, 6–11*

GREAT SHEFFORD   SU3875 Map 2
Swan

2 miles from M4 junction 14; on A338 towards Wantage

As we went to press this pub was undergoing major refurbishment,
though it's still run by the same people – we look forward to receiving
readers' up-to-date comments. The friendly and welcoming
atmosphere, good food and the fact that it's close to the M4 make it a
popular place for lunch. The bar menu was due for changes too, but
at lunchtime you can get sandwiches, ploughman's (£1.30) and a
smorgasbord (£2.95). Except on Sunday or Monday evenings you
can book tables in the newly renovated back dining-room, which
looks out on the clear River Lambourn; it has a daily changing menu
(£8–£10). Well kept Courage Best and Directors on handpump. The
public bar has darts, pool, cribbage, a fruit machine and a juke box.
A barbecue area is being built to cater for parties, and there are tables
on a terrace by a big willow and sycamore overhanging the stream,
with more on an attractive quiet lawn with a swing. *(Recommended by
E O Stephens, J M M Hill, W T Aird; more reports please)*

*Courage · Licensee Mike Lovett · Real ale · Meals and snacks (not Sun or Mon
evening); reservations tel Great Shefford (048 839) 271 · Children welcome
Open 10.30–2.30, 6–11*

HAMPSTEAD NORREYS   SU5376 Map 2
New Inn

Yattendon Road

The excellent bar food and friendly atmosphere continue to attract
readers to this unpretentious and well kept pub. The comfortable
back lounge has a log fire, horse brasses on the low black beams,
pictures of horses and reproduction coaching prints, and maybe the

licensees' Great Dane. Well kept Morlands Mild, Bitter and Best on handpump, and food ranging from sandwiches (65p for cheese to £1.50 for prawn), baked potatoes (from 60p), toasties (from 70p, with onion or tomato 10p extra), pâté (£1) or ploughman's (£1.25–£1.45), to basket meals (from £1, basket of chips 50p), home-made cottage pie, curry or savoury Chinese spring rolls (£1.25), fishburger (£1.35), salads (from £1.60), plaice dippers (£1.95), lasagne (£2.30), moussaka (£2.50), seafood platter (£3.25), and an eight-ounce rump steak (£5). The lively and simply furnished public bar, decorated with early 1950s local photographs, has darts, dominoes, cribbage, juke box, space game and a fruit machine. There is a sheltered terrace, and beyond that a big lawn with a swing, children's play area and goldfish pond with a fountain, and well spaced seats among roses, conifers and fruit trees; there are Shetland ponies in the paddock beyond a post-and-rails fence. (Recommended by J M M Hill, P F and T Dilnot, Gordon and Daphne, Mrs Lynda Myers, Mr and Mrs E N Reid)

Morlands · Licensees Ken and Gloria Vivash · Real ale · Meals and snacks (not Tues evening) · Children may be allowed in at landlords' discretion · Open 10–2.30, 5.30–11 all year · Bedrooms tel Hermitage (0635) 201301; £9/£18

HUNGERFORD   SU3368   Map 2

Bear ★

3 miles from M4 junction 14; town signposted at junction

Although the style of food has recently changed, the old-fashioned and spacious bar remains the same with civilised touches like the day's newspapers (including the FT, Sporting Life and Herald Tribune) hanging on reading sticks, spirits served in quarter-gill measures (instead of the usual sixth of a gill) and properly mixed Kir. Big French windows open on to a charming enclosed courtyard with pergola and fountain. Well kept Arkells BBB and Kingsdown and Morlands on handpump. The menu has steered away from bar snacks – though they do a beef granary roll (£2.50) – and meals are brought to your table. The food is good: for starters (though you can just order this one course) there is a home-made soup of the day (95p) as well as fish soup flavoured with saffron (£1.55), avocado salad (£1.85) or Stilton and walnut pâté (£1.95); main courses include lasagne with green salad, Alderton ham with melon or stuffed chicken legs with noodles (all £3.95), Hungerford trout (£4.75 – Pepys, staying in 1668, mentioned the 'very good trouts, eels and crayfish' to be had here), Scotch sirloin steak with café de Paris butter (£6.15) and fillet of beef in a cream and paprika sauce (£6.35). Puddings include fresh fruit salad and Guernsey cream or chocolate and orange slice (£1.35) and iced nougat with raspberry sauce (£1.45). A separate restaurant also. There is a pleasantly rambling and well kept garden, with a terrace where the River Dun splashes over a little weir. No dogs. (Recommended by Roy McIsaac, Dave Butler and Lesley Storey, GBH, K J Salway, W T Aird)

Free house · Licensee Roy Tudor Hughes · Real ale · Meals and lunchtime snacks · Children in the Kennet Room · Open 10.30–2.30, 6–10.30 Bedrooms tel Hungerford (0488) 82512; £33.75 (£37.75B)/£42 (£48.50B)

nr HURLEY   SU8283   Map 2
Dew Drop

Just W of Hurley on A423 turn left up Honey Lane, signposted Grassland
Research Institute; at small red post-box after large farm, fork right – the pub
is down a right-hand turn-off at the first cluster of little houses

Although it's quite a struggle to find this friendly pub it really is
worth it. The inside is simply furnished and very cosy – especially in
winter – and the generously served food is reasonably priced;
sandwiches, ploughman's, soup, cottage pie, ham and other salads,
gammon, egg and chips and seafood platter. Well kept Brakspears PA
and Old on handpump and some good malt whiskies. But the chief
point is that the surrounding countryside is completely unspoilt; seats
in the sloping and attractively wildish garden look down to where
white doves strut on the pub's red tiles, above tubs of bright flowers.
(Recommended by J H DuBois, Iain Maclean, C P Price, G Keen)

*Brakspears · Licensee M J Morris · Real ale · Snacks (not Mon or Sun evening)
Open 11–2.30, 6–11*

HURST   SU7972   Map 2
Green Man

Hinton Road: off A321 Twyford–Wokingham, turning NE just S of filling
station in village centre

This is the sort of pub that Brakspears do really well: unspoilt but
wholly civilised. Once through the low door, you find dark oak
beams hung with horse brasses, black standing timbers, an open fire
at both ends (neatly closed off in summer by black and brass folding
doors), wheelback chairs and tapestried wall seats around brass-
topped tables on the red carpet, lots of alcoves and country pictures,
and a warmly welcoming and thoroughly relaxed atmosphere. There
are some black japanned milkchurns as seats around the servery,
which dispenses well kept Brakspears PA and SB straight from the
barrel. Gentle piped music; good simple lunchtime food, including
sandwiches; a pleasant back garden. *(Recommended by Gordon and
Daphne, W T Aird)*

*Brakspears · Licensee Allen Hayward · Real ale · Meals and snacks (lunchtime,
not Sun) · Open 11–2.30, 6–11 all year*

KINTBURY   SU3866   Map 2
Dundas Arms

The position of this pub is especially lovely in warm weather when
you can sit by a quiet pool of the River Kennet on one side, or by the
Kennet and Avon Canal itself on the other – there is an attractive lock
just the other side of the hump-backed bridge. The partly panelled
carpeted bar has a remarkable collection of blue and white plates on
one cream wall, a juke box with rather a nostalgic repertoire, and a
fruit machine. Good value bar food here includes home-made soup
(80p), sandwiches (all 80p), toasted sandwiches (£1), country pâté
(£1), ploughman's with a choice of cheeses (£1.50), pork and rabbit

terrine (£1.30), smoked salmon quiche (£1.65), smoked salmon pâté or crab au gratin (£1.70), hot Cornish pasty (£1.75), chicken curry (£2.20), avocado and prawn salad (£2.35), clam fries or gammon, egg and chips (both £2.50) and rump steak (£4.90). Well kept Morlands and Ushers Best on handpump. (Arkells BBB kept under CO_2 blanket.) In the evening a separate restaurant has excellent food and a remarkable range of clarets. Comfortable bedrooms have French windows opening on to a secluded waterside terrace. *(Recommended by J M M Hill, Doug Kennedy)*

Free house · Licensee David Dalzell-Piper · Real ale · Meals and snacks (lunchtime, not Sun) · Children welcome · Open 11–2.30, 6–10.30 Bedrooms tel Kintbury (0488) 58263; £32B/£38B

KNOWL HILL   SU8279   Map 2
Bird in Hand

A4

Mr Shone has been here for 27 years now, and has always been a real-ale enthusiast – serving well kept Brakspears PA and Old, Courage Directors and Youngs Special from handpump. The food too gains from his enthusiasm for the genuine – nothing is bought in, and on our visit we found an excellent buffet (£3.50 for as much as we wanted), with good cold salt beef, salami, ham, three other cold meats, four or five fish and shellfish dishes, and no less than 19 fresh and imaginative salads such as apple, celery and peanut, or carrot and leek strips in a lemon-juice dressing. His lady chef likes to try out two or three new ones each day – popular acclaim then gets her best efforts a place in the main repertoire. There's also soup (£1), uncommonly good bread, a couple of hot dishes such as pheasant casserole or steak and kidney pudding (also £3.50), and good puddings. A restaurant serves full meals (three courses £8.75, four courses £10). The spacious main bar has cosy alcoves, red Turkey carpet on polished oak parquet, dark brown panelling with a high shelf of willow pattern plates, logs burning in the big brick fireplace, ceiling beams and some attractive Victorian stained glass in one big bow window. A centuries-older side bar, quarry-tiled, has darts, and there's a snug, well-padded back cocktail bar. Efficient helpful service; a few good malt whiskies, including the Macallan. There are tables in the roomy and neatly kept tree-sheltered side garden. *(Recommended by W T Aird)*

Free house · Licensee Jack Shone · Real ale · Meals (not Sat evening) and snacks Children in eating area and restaurant · Open 11–3, 5.30–11 all year; closed evening 25 Dec

LITTLEWICK GREEN   SU8379   Map 2
Cricketers

3¾ miles from M4 junction 9: A423(M) then left on to M4, from which village is signposted on left

This old tiled pub, among tubs of brightly flowering plants, faces an attractive village green where, in summer, it runs two cricket teams (matches every weekend, some weekdays). There are cricketing prints and cartoons in the comfortable carpeted lounge, which boasts an enormous old factory clocking-in clock. The communicating public bar, also carpeted, and warmed by a wood-burning stove in winter, has darts, cribbage and a fruit machine. Good simple bar food here includes sandwiches, filled rolls served with salad and freshly made coleslaw (from 90p), hamburgers (from £1.10), a choice of ploughman's (from £2), ham off the bone with egg and chips, or chilli con carne (£2.50), fried scampi or fried calamari (£3); there are also various dishes of the day. Adnams, Badger Best, Barnstormer, North Country Riding, Old Tradition, Ruddles County and Theakstons XB served from handpumps at a perfect temperature, with some interesting bottled beers; maybe piped music. The National Trust's Maidenhead Thicket, just east on the A4, and the woods along the A404 towards Marlow, have good walks. (*Recommended by MHG, W T Aird; more reports please*)

Free house · Licensees Ray and Maureen Batty · Real ale · Meals and snacks (not Mon evening) · Open 10.30–2.30, 5.30–11

Shire Horse

3 miles from M4, junction 9; A423(M), then left on to A4

Courage's adjoining Shire Horse Centre, which has a pet's corner as well as an excellently presented display of the prize-winning shire horses in action, is open from March to October, and makes a good family outing. That's why we're including this pub, which does have a comfortable and well kept open-plan lounge bar – decorated with pictures, trophies and equipment to do with the horses. We regret that we can give no information about food as the licensee feels he can't spare the time to tell us. The Courage Best and Directors on handpump is well kept; piped music, and a games area with a fruit machine and a space game (also dominoes and cribbage). The pub is set well back from the road, with a children's slide and playhouse and plenty of seats among fruit trees on a big side lawn. There is a separate tea house, and a restaurant on Saturday evenings. (*More reports please*)

Courage · Real ale · Children in eating area and restaurant · Open 10.30–2.30, 6–10.30

NEWBURY   SU4666   Map 2
Old Waggon & Horses

Market Place

Two special bonuses here – not usually found in a town pub – are the sunny flower-filled back terrace by the canalised River Kennet, and the huge upstairs family Riverside Bar where quickly served lunchtime food includes reasonably priced sandwiches, salads, and four home-made dishes of the day such as steak and kidney pie, casseroles and curries. The more straightforwardly pubby front part has Courage Best, Directors and Simonds on handpump, darts, a fruit machine and a juke box. There may be piped music. (*More reports please*)

Courage · Real ale · Meals lunchtimes and snacks (lunchtime, not Sun)
Children in Riverside Bar · Jazz every second Sunday · Open 10.30–2.30,
6.00–11 all year

REMENHAM   SU7683   Map 2
Little Angel

A423, just over bridge E of Henley

The main attraction here is the wide choice of food (which is even
wider if you eat in the restaurant where there is a £5 minimum
charge). The bar menu might typically include a dozen or so starter or
main course dishes, with half a dozen puddings and a good cheese
board; home-made soup (£1.50), home-made pâté (£1.70), baked
potato and chilli or vegetarian platter (£2.95), cold gammon and
prawn mayonnaise, fisherman's pie, open seafood sandwich or Parma
ham, melon and prawn salad (all £3.95), farmer's steak pie, roast
lamb or Scotch smoked salmon salad (£4.95), Mediterranean prawns
or rump steak (£6.95) and seafood platter (£8.50); home-made
sweets (£2 and £2.50), cheeseboard and grapes (£1.75–£2.50). The
restaurant is particularly strong on seafood and includes home-made
lobster soup (£2.50), smoked salmon terrine with Norwegian prawns
(£2.95), fresh Cornish crab (£3.25), giant scallops cooked with herbs,

Bel & The Dragon, Cookham

garlic and cream in a pastry case (£3.95), a seafood salad selected from Billingsgate daily (£5.75), prime fillets of Dover sole with mango and kumquat marmalade (£6.95) and jumbo scampi flamed with calvados and cream and served with asparagus (£7.50). They also have quite a number of special events such as a champagne and seafood evening, a carnival of seafood fortnight and several menus for the Henley Regatta. The main part of the bar has a deep glossy red ceiling – like the walls – which matches the little red tiles of the bar counter and autumnal reddish carpet. There are big bay window seats here, and some built-in cushioned black wall seats: it can get very crowded at peak times (when even the big car park overflows into a tricky narrow side lane). The high-ceilinged back part, with cosy alcoves and candlelight, is more given over to eating, and the restaurant is behind. A wide range of attractive and reasonably priced wines, as well as Brakspears PA and SB on handpump. This was one of the six finalists in the 1985 Egon Ronay Pub of the Year competition. *(Recommended by Susan Grossman; more reports please)*

Brakspears · Licensees Paul and June Southwood · Real ale · Meals and snacks Children in eating area of bar and restaurant · Open 10.30–3, 6–11 all year

SINDLESHAM   SU7768 Map 2
Walter Arms

Bearwood Road; signposted Sindlesham from B3349, or signposted Barkham 2 from mini-roundabout on B3030 just S of Winnersh

There's a good welcoming atmosphere here, with friendly and efficient service even on a really crowded evening, when the heavy green velvet curtains help a lot to damp down the noise level. Three rooms open together, with a collection of old plates in one, hunting prints on the cream walls in another, and comfortable stools, chairs and wall banquettes. Get here early to be sure of a table: people crowd in at lunchtime and – at least towards the end of the week – in the evening too, for the generous helpings of good value bar food, which includes soup (50p), ham sandwiches (75p), pâté (£1.05), pizza (£1.15), ploughman's (£1.25), cannelloni or spaghetti (£1.40), salads such as home-baked ham (£1.90), chicken curry (£2.30), country pie (£2.50), Alabama chicken (£2.60), pork goulash (£2.60) and beef bourguignonne (£3.05). A choice of puddings includes good treacle tart (80p) and various gateaux (£1), and dishes such as game pie, rabbit casserole and Scotch salmon turn up in season. Well kept Courage Best and Directors on handpump; maybe piped music. You can sit outside in the attractive garden, kept as neatly as the pub itself. The pub is named after John Walter III of *The Times*, whose huge Victorian mansion nearby, in its vast estate, is now Bearwood College. *(Recommended by W T Aird; more reports please)*

Courage · Licensee Bill Cox · Real ale · Meals and snacks · Open 11–2.30, 6–11 all year · Bedrooms tel Wokingham (0734) 780260; £14 (£16S)/£25 (£28S)

Post office address codings confusingly give the impression that some pubs are in Berkshire when they're really in Oxfordshire or Hampshire – which is where we list them.

SONNING   SU7575   Map 2

Bull

Off B478, in village

This black and white timbered pub, covered with wistaria, has a
charming courtyard between it and the churchyard, with tubs of
flowers and a rose pergola. (Unfortunately at busy times you may find
it packed with cars.) If you bear left through the churchyard opposite
(taken over by Russian ivy), then turn left along the bank of the River
Thames, you come to a very pretty lock. The pub's two
communicating rooms each have an inglenook fireplace, and there
are heavy beams in the low ceilings, cushioned antique settles, snug
alcoves, and even a penny-farthing. Lunchtime bar food includes a
good cold buffet with salads such as pork pie and mixed meats;
Wethereds and SPA on handpump. A separate restaurant is open in
the evenings. *(Recommended by Miss U Ostermann, Jane English,
Iain Maclean, S J Grundell)*

*Wethereds (Whitbread) · Real ale · Meals (lunchtime, not Sun) · Children in
restaurant · Open 10–2.30, 6–10.30*

White Hart

B478

The main bar of this white Thames-side hotel is an atmospheric
heavily timbered room with cushioned oak settles, small armchairs
and bow-window seats on its Turkey carpet, winter log fires in a
handsome stone fireplace, and an old-fashioned oak-partitioned
serving counter with Brakspears and Wethereds SPA on handpump.
A small plush bar by a nicely re-created hall with panelled stairway
provides any cocktails to order. Another bar serves sandwiches at
lunchtime (£2; £4 for smoked salmon) and does a carvery, also at
lunchtime, which includes beef, lamb or pork (£3.95); a cold buffet is
the same price. There is a third small plush cocktail bar. A well kept
and spacious lawn – the inn's particular attraction in summer – runs
down towards the Thames, with white tables and chairs here and
there on crazy paving or among the cedar, weeping willows and neat
rosebeds. A spacious separate restaurant looks over this riverside
garden. *(Recommended by C P Scott-Malden; more reports please)*

*Free house · Licensee M C Mogford · Real ale · Snacks (lunchtime) · Children in
restaurant and lounge · Open 11–2.30, 6–10.30 · Bedrooms tel Reading
(0734) 692277; £45B/£57B*

STANFORD DINGLEY   SU5771   Map 2

Old Boot

There are tables in front of this quietly friendly beamed pub and more
on a secluded back terrace by a sloping country garden. The inside
has been carefully decorated with thoughtfully chosen pictures,
attractive fabrics for the old-fashioned wooden-ring curtains and
lovely old furniture – pews, settles, country chairs and tables with
bunches of fresh flowers. The inglenook fireplace and soft lighting

make for a cosy atmosphere in the evenings. A good choice of bar food includes home-made soup (£1.25), pâté (£2.60), ploughman's (£2.50), cottage pie (£3), steak and kidney pie or lasagne (£3.50), garlic mussels (served in pots from Provence, £3.25), prime Scotch steaks (10-ounce sirloin £6.50) and (in season, on Thursdays) moules marinière (£4). There are Sunday roast lunches (£5); also a small separate restaurant (Wednesday to Saturday evenings, with a supper licence extension). Well kept Arkells BBB, Everards Tiger, Fullers London Pride and Ruddles County on handpump, also Kir; darts, dominoes, liar dice, shut-the-box and a fruit machine. *(Recommended by Doug Kennedy; more reports please)*

Free house · Licensees John and Eliane Pratt · Real ale · Children in restaurant Open 11–2.30, 6–10.30

STREATLEY   SU5980   Map 2
Swan

The smart and elegant lounge of this substantial Thames-side hotel, with its hunting prints on pale panelled walls, has big windows overlooking the river and splendid gardens. Below the lawns, terraces and paths winding among rose pergolas and well kept herbaceous borders floats a restored Oxford college state barge, used as a bar – you can also eat light evening meals there (not Sundays). Bar food includes ploughman's and good fresh salads (by no means cheap – but given the surroundings that could hardly be expected), with friendly service. They were installing real ales as we went to press. In summer, weather permitting, barbecues are arranged on Saturday and Sunday lunchtimes; there is a separate restaurant. Many of the very comfortably furnished bedrooms have river views and their own terraces. *(Recommended by HKR, Michael Sandy, Mrs A M Arnold, C P Scott-Malden)*

Free house · Licensee John Robson · Real ale ·Meals (lunchtime) · Open 11–2.30, 6–10.30 · Bedrooms tel Goring-on-Thames (0491) 873737; £45B/£67.50B

WALTHAM ST LAWRENCE   SU8276   Map 2
Bell   [illustrated on page 21]

You step back 50 or more years when you enter this heavily timbered black and white ancient pub. Inside, both of the friendly and civilised beamed bars have attractive features. The lounge has finely carved oak panelling and a good antique oak settle among more modern furniture. In the public bar – which has darts – there is an attractive seat in the deep window recess, and some unusual and colourful highly glazed tiles set in to the floor. Well kept Arkells BBB and Brakspears PA and Mild on handpump, with Brakspears Old tapped from the cask; food is good and simple with filled rolls and hot bar snacks, also a separate restaurant. There are some heavy tables on the well kept back lawn, sheltered by a thatched barn and shaded by small trees and flowering shrubs. *(Recommended by W T Aird; more reports please)*

Free house · Real ale · Snacks · Open 11–2.30, 6–11

WARGRAVE   SU7878   Map 2

White Hart

High Street

This former coaching-inn has a low-beamed and extensive lounge bar
with a long L-shaped serving counter presided over by friendly and
welcoming hosts. There are copper warming pans, pistols, small old-
fashioned prints and antique enamel jar tops above the black half-
panelling. A few eighteenth-century-style settles join crowds of smart
little red plush dining-chairs around the many tables – warmed in
winter by a good open fire. Hot and cold snacks include daily
'specials' and a traditional Sunday roast beef lunch. Soup (70p),
sandwiches (from 75p – steak sandwich £1.50), ploughman's
(£1.30), pâté (£1.35), basket meals (such as plaice £1.95, chicken
£2.35 or scampi £2.65), spaghetti milanese (£2.25), chilli con carne
(£2.30), lasagne (£2.50), salads (from £2.50), seafood platter (£2.65)
and sirloin steak (£4.95). Well kept Wethereds, SPA, Flowers
Original and (in winter) Winter Royal on handpump; piped music,
and a fruit machine away at the back. The restaurant is open on
Tuesday to Saturday evenings, and at lunchtimes Monday to Friday.
(Recommended by Simon Porter, W T Aird; more reports please)

Wethereds (Whitbreads) · Licensees Richard and Chris Barnwell · Real ale
Meals and snacks · Children in restaurant · Open 10.30–2.30, 6–11

WICKHAM   SU3971   Map 2

Five Bells

3 miles from M4 junction 14; A338 towards Wantage, then first right on to
B4000

Quite a few of the pub's regulars are involved with racehorses, and
that often seems to guarantee comfortable furnishings, including a
sofa on the unusually thick carpet and winter fires at both ends of the
long low-ceilinged room. This is also home to two winning darts
teams and to Welford Park cricket team. The sandwiches (from 75p)
are specially good, and other home-made bar food includes egg
mayonnaise (85p), soup (95p), smoked mackerel (£1.25),
ploughman's with a choice of cheeses or ham (£1.50), pâté (£1.50),
avocado and prawns (£2.25), breaded cod or plaice (£2), pizza
(£2.50), steak and kidney pie (£3), gammon with egg or pineapple
(£3.25), seafood platter or scampi (£3.25), a large choice of salads
(from £3.75, avocado and prawn or smoked salmon salad £4.50),
grilled steak (£5.50) and a choice of puddings (£1.25). The
traditional Sunday lunch is very popular, and there are summer
barbecue parties in the garden (which has plenty of room for more
tables, games and even a swimming pool). Another mark of a pub in
racehorse country is the separate TV room, to keep up with the latest
racing; a pool-table has recently been added. Well kept Ushers PA
and Best on handpump, relatively cheap for the area (the servery is
squeezed picturesquely under the sloping beams that support the low
thatched roof); darts, dominoes and piped music. Booking is essential
for the separate evening restaurant. (Recommended by Mark Stocker,
Dr B W Marsden, Commander J C Taylor; more reports please)

Ushers (Watneys) · Licensee Mrs Dorothy Channing-Williams · Real ale
Meals and snacks · Children welcome · Open 10.30–2.30, 5.30–11
Bedrooms tel Boxford (048 838) 242; £17/£25

WINKFIELD   SU9272 Map 2
White Hart

Church Road (A330)

This well kept and neatly modernised Tudor pub must have been a
chilly place for the prisoners locked up here when what is now the
restaurant used to be the area courthouse – it's in the path of an
underground watercourse, which does keep the Courage Best and
Directors at a pleasantly fresh temperature even in hot weather. The
bar was once the village bakery, and you can still see the back of one
of the old ovens, where the dark panelling meets the white paintwork
of the walls. It's now a comfortable place, with a big open fireplace,
cushioned Windsor chairs and upholstered modern settles on the red
patterned carpet and pewter tankards hanging by the bar counter.
Bar food includes sandwiches, home-made soup (90p), pâté (£1.90),
quiche of the day (£1.90), seafood pancake (£2.50), various salads,
gammon and home-made steak and kidney pie (£2.90); puddings
such as home-made blackcurrant and apple pie (£1.20). There is a
restaurant at weekends; piped music. Outside the tiled and timbered
house there are tables among the fruit-trees on the sizeable side lawn
– the field next to it has a small flock of Soay sheep, and across the
road is a quiet cedar-shaded churchyard. *(More reports please)*

Courage · Licensees Ron and Pauline Haywood · Real ale · Meals (not Sun)
Children in area set aside for them · Open 10.30–2.30, 6–11 all year

WINKFIELD ROW   SU8971 Map 2
Slug & Lettuce

Lovel Road; A330 just W of junction with B3034, turning off at Fleur-de-lis

Deftly stripped back to herringbone timbered brickwork, brick-tiled
floor and standing black oak timbers, this well kept cottagey pub has
low beams, plain wooden chairs and benches by sturdy deal tables,
latticed windows, log-effect gas fires, pastelly seascapes, a snug tête-à-
tête alcove for two, and a quiet corner room with tapestried wall
benches and a wall of leather book-backs. Good bar lunches include
taramosalata (£1.20), home-made carrot soup (£1.35), quiche
(£2.25), baked ham salad (£2.50), steak and kidney pie (£3), smoked
salmon salad (£4.50) and steaks (£6.75). Vegetables are crispy,
puddings said to be lovely. In the evening, when a pretty little pink-
walled side restaurant area comes into its own, food includes a wide
choice of starters such as avocado, prawns with dips, and smoked
salmon, and main dishes such as duck, scampi (£6.50) and steaks
(from £7.70 – the chateaubriand is highly praised). Well kept
Brakspears, Friary Meux, Gales HSB and Timothy Taylors Landlord
on handpump (with take-home flagons hanging over the servery), and
local white wine; good atmosphere. A seat in front is sheltered by the
overhanging upper floor, and in summer they do barbecues in the

garden. The large stuffed crocodile on the back roof must have given some people a nasty late-night turn. *(Recommended by Jane English, Miss G Nutton, C D Jacobs)*

Free house · Licensee A R Murray · Real ale · Meals and snacks · Open 10.30–2.30, 6–11 all year

WOOLHAMPTON   SU5767   Map 2

Rising Sun

A4, nearly a mile E of village

This small and friendly pub (which is useful for the A4) has a good range of real ales such as Adnams Best, Badger Best, Morlands, North Country Riding, Ringwood Old Thumper, Ruddles County and Theakstons XB on handpump, and they do change regularly. The red and black lounge is decorated with small reproduction coaching prints. Readers praise the food which includes sandwiches (from 60p), filled jacket potatoes (from 95p), lasagne (£1.40), home-made pies (£1.50), chicken curry (£1.65), salads (£1.80–£2.75), scampi and chips (£2.35), gammon (£2.90), rainbow trout (£3.15), pork chop (£3.25) and steaks (from £4.75). There is a separate restaurant. The public bar has darts, dominoes, cribbage, a fruit machine and

The Blue Boar, Chieveley

piped music. You can sit out behind, where there's a swing.
(Recommended by P J Lambert; more reports please)

*Free house · Licensees Peter and Paula Head · Real ale · Meals and snacks
Children in restaurant · Open 11.30–2.30, 6–11 all year*

Rowbarge

Turn S off A4 opposite the Angel (may be signposted Station)

The bay windows have built-in seats and one wall has an aquarium
(visible in the little adjoining panelled family room) in this friendly
beamed bar with flowery cushions on its chairs and fresh flowers on
the tables. A fearsome stuffed pike dominates the small deep-green
snug, partly partitioned off from the main bar. The pub has recently
been taken over by new owners, but as far as we know there are no
plans to change the sort of food and drink which has been popular
here in the past – including sandwiches and other bar food such as
home-made rissoles, Lancashire hot-pot and home-made steak and
veal pie. The big French-windowed deep-green dining-room, looking
out on the back garden, serves full meals. There are tables in a side
cottage garden with flowers and a rose rambling up one of the fruit-
trees, and on the other side, beyond a towpath and a couple of low
fences, is the canal. *(Recommended by Doreen and Toby Carrington,
Gordon and Daphne; up-to-date reports please)*

*Free house · Meals and snacks (not Sun evening, limited Sun lunchtime)
Children in family room · Open 11–2.30, 6–10.30*

YATTENDON   SU5574   Map 2
Nut & Bolt

Burnt Hill; from Yattendon head towards Pangbourne and take third turn
right (after about a mile), signposted Bradfield and Burnt Hill

The atmosphere in this cottagey little country inn is very relaxed, and
there are daily newspapers at the bar, simple country chairs and
Windsors, a variety of settles, Liberty-style curtains and an open fire;
also darts, dominoes, cribbage and a fruit machine. Reasonably
priced home-made food includes soup, pâté, ploughman's with
warmed fresh bread and mature Cheddar or Stilton (from £1.25), a
good choice of filled baked potatoes – such as turkey and sweetcorn,
chilli, curry and prawn cocktail (from £1.25), cottage pie, chilli con
carne or curry (£1.75), moussaka or lasagne (£2.25) and steak
(£3.95). Though there is no separate restaurant, you can arrange a
full meal or a buffet supper – it means booking well ahead, as
everything is bought and cooked to order. There is a good range of
fairly priced real ales on handpump: Fullers ESB and London Pride,
Morlands Bitter and Best, and Ruddles Bitter and County. There are
teak benches outside on a terrace by honeysuckle, with more seats on
grass among roses. *(Recommended by Jane English, W T Aird; more reports
please)*

*Free house · Licensees Gerry and Jane Campkin · Real ale · Meals and snacks;
bookings tel Hermitage (0635) 201496 · Open 12–2.30, 6.30–11 all year
Bedrooms tel Hermitage (0635) 201496; £17.50/£22*

Royal Oak ★

This elegant inn was chosen Pub of the Year in 1985 by Egon Ronay – moreover, it's his local, lucky man. As we forecast last year on the basis of their previous record in good London restaurants, the new owners have quickly established an enthusiastic following for their extensive choice of imaginative bar food. Moreover, the atmosphere is extremely pleasant, with a comfortable and stylishly old-fashioned lounge and a prettily decorated panelled bar, warmed by a good log fire in winter. The extensive choice of food changes daily and includes home-made soups such as creamy carrot or gazpacho (£1.75), herrings with brown bread (£2), ploughman's with a selection of cheeses (£2.25), deep-fried mushrooms with avocado and garlic sauce or smoked haddock and scrambled eggs (£2.25), warm baguettes with cheese or ham and salad (£2.50), smoked sprats with warm potato salad (£2.95), cold smoked mackerel or casserole of monkfish and prawns with saffron (£3.10), shallow fried fillets of lemon sole with tarragon butter (£3.50), casserole of fresh seafood with saffron (£3.75), grilled calf's liver and bacon (£4.75), rump steak and rösti or lamb steak with grainy mustard and rosemary (both £5.25); puddings such as meringues and Guernsey cream (£1.25) or apple, raspberry and blackcurrant crumble (£1.50). Well kept Bass Charringtons IPA and Wadworths 6X on handpump; dominoes and cribbage. The charming separate restaurant, outside our pubby purview, sounds good (closed two weeks in January to February). You can reserve a table in the bar or restaurant. The pretty garden is primarily for the use of residents and restaurant guests, but is available on busy days for those in the bar. A nice place to stay, and this village – where Robert Bridges lived for many years – is very attractive. (*Recommended by W T Aird, A J Triggle; more reports please*)

Free house · Licensees Richard and Kate Smith · Real ale · Meals and snacks Children welcome · Open 10.30–2.30, 6–11 · Bedrooms tel Hermitage (0635) 201325; £32.50B/£48B

Lucky Dip

Besides the fully inspected pubs, you might like to try these Lucky Dips recommended and described by readers (if you do, please send us reports):

ASCOT [High Street; SU9268], *Stag*: filled baked potatoes, wide range of sandwiches and other snacks; well kept Friary Meux served from old-fashioned heavy wooden bar; walls covered with regal and horsy Edwardiana *(Tony Gayfer)*
ASTON [SU7884], *Flower Pot*: sandwiches! Few minutes' stroll from river; big garden, outdoor bar in summer *(S J Tims)*
BARKHAM [SU7866], *Bull*: bar snacks and excellent restaurant in recently reopened pub: very comfortable, retaining original old character; well kept beer *(Mrs J P Neuhofer)*
BINFIELD [SU8471], *Jack o' Newbury*: Whitbreads pub with well kept beers, friendly landlord, darts, discreet juke box, nicely placed tables so doesn't feel overcrowded; good weekday food, slightly curtailed at weekends; lovely garden *(W T Aird)*
BURCHETTS GREEN [SU8381], *Crown*: simple, small local, friendly and well run, reasonably priced well kept Courage ales *(W T Aird)*

CHEAPSIDE [Cheapside Road; SU9469], *Thatched Tavern*: food in restaurant excellent, reasonably priced; general atmosphere pleasant, service efficient *(Theresa Grove)*

CHIEVELEY [SU4774], *Hare & Hounds*: food in quantity, good Ushers beer in pleasant bar; nice front garden *(David Ellis)*; *Red Lion*: food and beer good in friendly and attractive old pub used mainly by locals *(E L Sturgeon, Gordon and Daphne)*

CIPPENHAM [Cippenham Lane; SU9480], *Long Barn*: free house which has just started its own brewery, in medieval barn; good choice of food *(C Elliott)*

COOKHAM [SU8884], *Ferry*: splendid riverside position with big terrace, walk-in windows for waterside bar with stripped décor, upstairs restaurant, much older original pub behind, choice of real ales; food and service hiccups in 1984 – more reports please *(J Madley, LYM)*

CRAZIES HILL [SU7980], *Horn*: exceptional mainly oriental cuisine in simply furnished, well kept old pub, Brakspears real ales *(W T Aird)*

ETON [SU9678], *Christopher*: useful for the area *(Doreen and Toby Carrington)*; [Bridge Street] *Watermans Arms*: cheerful and neighbourly pub close to Thames, by Eton College rowing club *(LYM)*

FARLEY HILL [SU7565], *Fox and Hounds*: nothing fancy in this village local with very cheerful welcoming landlord; far views over heavily wooded country; darts in bar, pool in separate room; good Morlands *(Gordon and Daphne)*

FIFIELD [SU9076], *White Hart*: well run, recently refurbished; games bar with bar billiards and darts, Turkey carpeted lounge; weekday carvery lunches, Friday and Saturday cooked meals including evening steaks, Saturday and Sunday evening seafood special *(David Regan)*

FINCHAMPSTEAD [Church Lane; SU7963], *Queens Oak*: very pleasant well kept pub in big beer garden *(C Elliott)*

HARE HATCH [SU8077], *Queen Victoria*: good local atmosphere in well kept pubby place; lots of games, good value simple food; splendid landlord *(M Ryan, M B Flavell, BB)*

HERMITAGE [SU5073], *Fox*: recent change of ownership for pub with attractive garden and extended terrace; bar food and well kept real ales; handy for M4 junction 13 *(Gordon Mair, Elaine and Gavin Walkinshaw, W T Aird, LYM)*

HOLYPORT [SU9176], *Belgian Arms*: friendly welcome, good snacks and sandwiches, well kept Brakspears, garden, no music or bandits; children if well behaved *(W T Aird)*; [The Green] *George*: friendly, clean, well run pub with ancient beams on attractive village green; good choice of home-cooked food at honest prices, congenial; well kept drinks including wines *(J A Stein, Frank Withey)*

HUNGERFORD [Bridge Street; SU3368], *John o' Gaunt*: old inn, recently refurbished, with friendly atmosphere, obliging service and good food; bedrooms *(Elinor Goodman, LYM)*; [Charnham Street] *Red Lion*: friendly service, good food in warm, comfortable bar, good bar games; dogs allowed on leads; bedrooms *(GBH, Gordon and Daphne)*; [High Street] *Three Swans*: pleasant relaxed atmosphere, good beer and food including choice of well filled pizzas; friendly bar staff and regulars; bedrooms *(R V Cossins, Gordon and Daphne)*

HURLEY [SU8283], *Black Boy*: comfortable beamed Brakspears pub with bar food, and tables on lawn by paddock *(LYM)*; *Olde Bell*: civilised and old-fashioned bar in handsome timbered inn with Norman doorway and window; garden, restaurant, bedrooms *(Rosemary and Brian Wilmot, LYM)*

KNOWL HILL [SU8279], *New Inn*: good food and friendly atmosphere, with choice of real ales; bedrooms; handy for M4 junction 8/9 *(E O Stephens)*; *Seven Stars*: well run and friendly Brakspears pub with good simple food *(W T Aird, LYM)*

MAIDENHEAD [Queen Street; SU8783], *Jack of Both Sides*: food at lunchtime includes very good value dish of the day, home-made soup and tasty puddings; real ale; a favourite local for lunch *(Bruce Powell)*

nr MAIDENHEAD [Pinkneys Green; SU8882], *Golden Ball*: rural Wethereds pub with reasonably priced food, and lawn by green *(LYM)*

MAIDENS GREEN [SU8972], *Pheasant Plucker*: low-beamed cottagey pub with soft lighting, friendly atmosphere, and controversial new name – used to be The Cottage *(LYM)*

MAPLEDURHAM [SU6576], *Pack Horse*: good Gales beers and abundance of country wines, comfortably friendly atmosphere, pleasant décor, winter log fire, big garden *(Jane English, G Parry-Jones)*

MARSH BENHAM [SU4267], *Red House*: big pub with wide food choice; nice garden with extensive model railway *(Dr A K Clarke, J M M Hill)*

MIDGHAM [SU5567], *Coach & Horses*: comfortably refurbished Wethereds pub with wide range of bar food; back garden *(A Saunders, BB)*

PALEY STREET [SU8675], *Bridge*: nice pub with good choice of food and splendid service even when crowded; low prices; good parking; spacious garden; near Touchen End *(W T Aird)*

READING [West Street; SU7272], *Admiral*: unusual, with lunching area and second bar stepped down from main drinking area; Halls Harvest; well run *(W T Aird)*; [Eldon Terrace] *Eldon Arms*: food outstanding and cheap, in pleasant pub with excellently kept Wadworths IPA and 6X (rare here), pleasant relaxed atmosphere, good service, usually no piped music *(Gwyn Parry-Jones)*; [Kennetside] *Jolly Anglers*: lots of character and friendly landlord in small pub quietly placed on the Kennet *(A W Wells)*; [Friar Street] *Travellers Rest*: very good staff in friendly and roomy local with nice little shady patio; Morlands decently priced, good simple lunch menu and wide range of sandwiches *(W T Aird)*; [London Road] *Turks Head*: staff friendly and attentive, good choice of simple food; handy for university *(Gwyn Parry-Jones)*

nr SHIPLAKE [Henley Road; SU7476], *Flowing Spring*: pleasant location with big garden, stream and swans; Fullers ales, friendly landlord, nice atmosphere (for pub location see OS Sheet 175 reference 746768) *(Jill Atkinson, Richard Entwistle)*

STREATLEY [SU5980], *Bull*: pleasant ancient pub on busy crossroads with comfortable beamy bar and dining-room; nice relaxing shady back garden *(Gordon and Daphne)*

TILEHURST [City Road; SU6673], *Fox & Hounds*: friendly landlord and landlady, good food at reasonable prices, garden with swings and slides *(PF)*

TUTTS CLUMP [SU5771], *Travellers Rest*: in attractive countryside *(LYM)*

UPPER BASILDON [SU5976], *Beehive*: friendly and lively pub with excellent choice of baked potatoes; bar billiards, open fire, real ale and very wide range of wines *(Jane English)*; *Red Lion*: good simple bar food, well kept Courage Directors; smart lounge and spartan public bar with darts, bar billiards, juke box and a fruit machine; very pleasant rural pub with large quiet garden *(D J Penny)*

WALTHAM ST LAWRENCE [West End; SU8276], *Plough*: pleasant and civilised décor in old-fashioned country pub with quiet seats outside and neat little dining-room with good food, but service could be more helpful *(C P Price, J W Tomlinson, W T Aird, LYM)*

WARGRAVE [High Street; SU7878], *Bull*: pleasant sheltered terrace behind comfortable and friendly Brakspears inn with pleasant service and good value food; bedrooms *(Mrs M A Beck, LYM)*

WEST ILSLEY [SU4782], *Harrow*: good bar food including home-made rabbit pie in country pub with cosy lounge and friendly public bar; tables outside *(R V Cossins)*

WINDSOR [Thames Street; SU9676], *Adam & Eve*: bustling young people's pub by theatre; occasional barbecues in little back yard *(LYM)*; *Donkey House*: the only true riverside pub in Windsor *(Doreen and Toby Carrington)*; [Thames Street; SU9676] *Old House*: superb garden by Thames, and interesting Christopher Wren entrance hall; bedrooms *(LYM)*; [Crimp Hill, Old Windsor; SU9676] *Oxford Blue*: wide choice of food including pizzas, fry-ups and cold dishes, in trim and friendly pub with horsy décor, military badges and cheerful barmaids; garden with picnic benches, swings and slide *(Doreen and Toby Carrington)*; [Park Street] *Two Brewers*: small pub with a lot of atmosphere, friendly and well kept *(G A Wright, Doreen and Toby Carrington)*

WINKFIELD [SU9272], *Hernes Oak*: welcoming and friendly well run local with enterprising choice of spirits; children in back room; meals and snacks *(Mrs A Hammond, LYM)*
WINKFIELD ROW [SU8971], *Old Hatchet*: free house with Brakspears, and Woodman brewed on the premises; good bar food, also restaurant; service good even though busy; pleasant garden *(S J Tims)*
WOKINGHAM [Gardeners Green; SU8068], *Crooked Billet*: unusual white weatherboarded country pub, cosy inside, open fire and beams, three rooms; good basic food, Brakspears ales, warm atmosphere; don't try the ford in winter – it's deep! (For pub location see OS Sheet 175 reference 826668) *(Jill Atkinson, Richard Entwistle, Gordon and Daphne)*; [The Terrace] *Queens Head*: low-ceilinged bar in warm and friendly Morlands pub, unusually cottagey for Wokingham and one of its best locals *(Gordon and Daphne, W T Aird)*; [Denmark Street] *Raglan Arms*: fine lounge, nice public bar with bar billiards, juke box and darts all well spaced; good lunch food, well kept Morlands; popular small town pub *(W T Aird)*; [centre] *Ship*: now good Fullers pub, good salads *(W T Aird)*; [Holme Green] *White horse*: friendly country atmosphere, good food, especially sandwiches and unusual specials, well kept Morlands, overlooking pastures (OS sheet 175 reference 825676) *(W T Aird)*
WOODSIDE [SU9270], *Rose & Crown*: pretty and comfortable pub on quiet lane with good garden; Morlands on handpump; fairly close to Windsor Park *(BB)*
WRAYSBURY [TQ0174], *Perseverance*: cosy and friendly *(R A Corbett)*

Buckinghamshire

This year there has been an unusual amount of change among the pubs we list here. For a start, opening hours have altered in many of the pubs – most commonly giving later evening closing, occasionally earlier morning opening, but sometimes involving rather shorter hours. But that's probably the most superficial difference. More fundamentally, a much higher proportion of these Buckinghamshire pubs than usual have changed hands. When we have had good news of the new owners or have had some other good reason, we have kept them in as main entries, but the change of management has usually meant important alterations in style and character. For example, the attractive Swan at Astwood (now bypassed) has new owners who have redecorated it, brought in a new range of real ales, and started folk-band sessions. New licensees at the Swan in Denham, which still has a lovely garden (especially for children), have had it carefully restored to bring out all the antique features, are concentrating on home cooking, and have started jazz nights there. The civilised old Chequers at Fingest has been taken over by Bryan

The King's Arms, Amersham

Heasman – popular with readers of previous editions for the
way he ran the Grenadier in central London – and we've had
warm reports on the food and the welcome there. New
licensees at the Two Brewers in Marlow have spruced it up
and broken into an altogether new line of food. There have
been changes of ownership or management at the Old Red
Lion, Great Brickhill (notable for the staggering views from
its garden), the Stag & Huntsman in Hambleden (in lovely
countryside, with bedrooms and a pretty garden), the
attractively placed Cock & Rabbit at The Lee, the Crown at
Penn (a civilised old pub, again with good views – under the
new regime the food has quickly become very popular), the
Kings Arms at Skirmett (given a star rating in previous
editions for its atmosphere – now food's the important thing
here too, and early reports are promising; the bedrooms have
been attractively refurbished) and the Cock in Stony Stratford.
And there have been notable changes at pubs whose owners
stay the same. The Lions of Bledlow, with such a fine view
from its civilised lounge bar, has opened a new help-yourself
salad bar. The Peacock at Bolter End has continued to
develop its food, which is now definitely worth tracking
down. The Five Bells at Botley, popular for its wide range of
real ales in a remote country setting, has been completely
refurbished, and there's a new food policy (on which we await
readers' reports). The Walnut Tree at Fawley, a particular
favourite for its relaxed atmosphere and enterprising food,
has started cook-it-yourself barbecues – and not just your
ordinary old bangers, either. The Fox at Ibstone has been
refurbished, and again its range of food, gaining popularity
with readers, has been developed and extended. The Rising
Sun up in the Chilterns at Little Hampden has closed its
restaurant, allowing greater concentration on its bar food –
and more room in which to eat it; the changes here have
earned it a star this year. The Old Crown at Skirmett has won
very much more vigorous praise for its good, interesting food
and warm welcome – and also gains a star this year. The
owner of the beautifully situated and friendly Bull & Butcher
in Turville has given up his other pub and is concentrating his
attention here: the simple food and good atmosphere now
bring people back time and again – this too gains a star
award. And of course there are some splendid pubs that go on
more or less as before, earning continuing praise from readers:
the Fox at Dunsmore (simple and traditional, with a charming
old-fashioned garden), the Full Moon right on Hawridge
Common, the Nags Head in Northend (a friendly little inn to
stay at, with a lovely garden), the Old Swan near The Lee
(civilised and comfortable, with good food), the marvellous
old Royal Standard at Forty Green (the county's most

*interesting pub), the friendly little Ship in Marlow
(remarkably cheap simple food), the civilised old stone
Greyhound in Marsh Gibbon (good food, and good beers
brewed on the premises), and the George & Dragon in West
Wycombe (an ancient inn in a National Trust village). Drinks
prices are generally rather high in the area: we found them
highest at the Stony Stratford and, particularly, Forty Green
entries, and relatively low at the Walnut Tree in Fawley and
Old Crown in Skirmett.*

AKELEY   SP7037   Map 4

Bull & Butcher

The Square; just off A413

Readers praise the buffet lunches in this friendly village pub.
Supervised by the landlord's wife, they include generous slices of
good ham quiche, freshly made pies and interesting salads (£2–
£3.50). They are served in a long open-plan room, divided into
separate areas by a vast central stone chimney: this has two coal fires
in winter, and there's a third down at one end which is wood-floored
– most of the room is carpeted in red, with comfy red button-back
banquettes, and drawings of famous customers on the walls. Well
kept Hook Norton Best, Marstons Pedigree and one guest beer on
handpump, also good value wines by the bottle; shove-ha'penny,
sensibly placed darts, dominoes, cribbage, and Sunday bridge parties.
There may be piped music. In the evening there are full meals with for
example scampi, gammon steak or steak as a main course (a three-
course meal costs around £6.50–£10); separate restaurant.
(Recommended by Sqn Ldr D J Gilbert, M Lawrence; more reports please)

*Free house · Licensee Harold Dyson · Real ale · Children in eating area and
restaurant · Meals (not Mon evening or Sun) · Open 12–2.30, 6–11 all year*

AMERSHAM   SU9597   Map 4

King's Arms   [*illustrated on page 44*]

High Street; A413

Readers confirm that this handsome rambling place is still the best
pub in the vicinity, and it has recently won an award from its brewery
for its catering standards. The popular bar food includes individual
sausages (50p), soup (80p), sandwiches (from 75p, toasted 90p),
ploughman's (from £1.20), a choice of pizzas (from £1.65), prawns
with mayonnaise (half-pint £1.80), hot dishes such as cottage pie,
fisherman's pie or chilli con carne (£2.05) and ham, turkey or beef
salads (from £2.50). At lunchtime the heavily beamed bar is filled
with cheerful bustle, but the efficient and friendly service copes
admirably. This room has high-backed antique settles and quaint old-
fashioned chairs as well as other seats on its oak block floor, subdued
lighting (candles in the evening), a big inglenook fireplace, and plenty
of snug alcoves; there's also a civilised and relaxing coffee lounge.
The popular restaurant (closed Sunday evening and Monday,

otherwise booking recommended) serves a changing lunch menu with a daily special, and in the evenings such things as seafood kebab, braised pigeon with port, and pork chop stuffed with apricot, almonds and raisins. Benskins and Ind Coope Burton on handpump, with Ind Coope Bitter tapped from the cask behind the bar counter. A tree-sheltered back lawn behind the coachyard car park has sturdy rustic tables and a rope climbing-frame; there's also a very attractive little flower-filled courtyard, and at the front the black and white Tudor façade is very striking. *(Recommended by David Regan, Mrs Rosemary Wilmot, John Kemp, Martyn Quinn, T N de Bray)*

Benskins (Ind Coope) · Licensee John Jennison · Real ale · Meals and snacks; restaurant reservations tel Amersham (024 03) 6333 · Children in restaurant Open 11–2.30, 6–11 all year

ASTWOOD SP9547 Map 4
Swan

Main Road; village signposted from A422

New licensees have refurbished this partly thatched pub, carpeting the bars but stripping away plaster to show all the low ceiling beams and putting in more antique seats and tables among the other old-fashioned furnishings – which suits the character of the pub, with its handsome early seventeenth-century inglenook fireplace. They are keeping up the pub's reputation for a good range of well kept real ales, stocking guest beers as well as Adnams, Courage Best and Directors, Marstons Pedigree, Sam Smiths OB, Tetleys and Youngers Scotch, all on handpump. Food changes frequently, and besides sandwiches might typically include home-made oxtail soup (75p), home-made venison pâté (£1.10), harvest pie (£2), meat salads (£2.25–£3), home-made steak and kidney pie (£2.25), scampi (£3) and sirloin steak (£6); they now do a traditional Sunday lunch, and there's a separate restaurant (with licensing extensions to 3pm and midnight). The games and machines have been taken out now; piped music. The quiet lawn at the back has tables. *(More reports please)*

Free house · Licensee Brian Clemson · Real ale · Meals and snacks (not Sun evening); restaurant reservations tel North Crawley (023 065) 272 · Children in eating area and restaurant · Folk band Sun lunchtime and first Thurs of month · Open 11–2.30, 6–11 all year

BLEDLOW SP7702 Map 4
Lions of Bledlow ★

From B4009 from Chinnor towards Princes Risborough, the first right turn about 1 mile outside Chinnor goes straight to the pub; from the second, wider right turn, turn right through village

As we went to press, this civilised and well kept pub, so popular with readers both for its lovely position and for its reliable food, was opening a new salad bar: home-made pies such as seafood or pork (£2.25) and cold meats (£2.50), the prices including a range of help-yourself salads. They still serve other bar food, such as sandwiches (from 75p, prawn £1.25), good ploughman's (£1.25), home-cooked seafood platter (£2.75) and sirloin steak (£6.75). The bar has lots of low and heavy beams, a big brick inglenook fireplace, an old settle and more modern attractive oak stalls built in to one partly panelled wall, seats in a good bay window, plenty of tables on the gleaming old tiled floor, and a couple of unusual rather cottagey rooms opening off – one with sensibly placed darts, pool, shove-ha'penny, dominoes, cribbage, and a fruit machine. Well kept local Chiltern Beechwood, Courage Directors, Wadworths 6X and Youngs on handpump. There is a separate restaurant (closed Sunday evening). The low, mossy-tiled old building faces a small, quiet green, and has marvellous views out from this steep slope of the Chilterns. Behind it there are tables on a sheltered crazy-paved terrace, separated by a rockery from a series of small sloping lawns (and from the very large car park). From here there is a track straight up to the hills and the steep beechwoods. (*Recommended by Jack Taylor, HKR, H L McDougall, Doug Kennedy, H G and C J McCafferty and others*)

Free house · Licensee F J McKeown · Real ale · Meals and snacks (not Sun evening); restaurant reservations tel Princes Risborough (084 44) 3345 Children in games room or front bar · Open 11–2.30, 6–11 all year

BOLTER END   SU7992   Map 4
Peacock

Just over 4 miles from M40 junction 5; A40 to Stokenchurch, then B482

Consistently good food attracts many return visits to this friendly and well run pub: besides sandwiches and at least one changing dish of the day, the growing choice includes ploughman's (£1.70), enormous local sausages (£1.70 in French bread, with chips), five-ounce steak sandwich (£2.50), home-made pies such as steak and kidney and coq au vin (£2.50), scampi (£2.75), salads such as home-cooked ham (£2.95), prawn and mushroom provençale served on good Basmati rice (£2.95) and steaks (from eight-ounce sirloin, £5.25). A series of comfortably furnished separate bar areas and alcoves, with rugs on the polished brick and tile floor, rambles up and down steps, with a welcoming log fire in winter; well kept ABC, Bass and Chiltern Beechwood on handpump; darts, dominoes, cribbage, maybe piped music. In summer there are tables on the grass in front. (*Recommended by David Regan, PLC, HKR, Bob Rendle*)

Aylesbury (Ind Coope) · Licensee Peter Hodges · Real ale · Meals and snacks (not Sun evening) · Open 11–2.30, 6–10.30 all year

BOTLEY   SP9702   Map 4
Five Bells

Tylers Hill Road; coming from Chesham, the first right turn on entering Botley, opposite the Hen and Chickens

Since last year this friendly and remote family-run country pub has been redecorated throughout; the seating has been renewed, but keeps to the previous attractive simplicity. There are two fine beamed inglenook fireplaces. In the evenings people come from far and wide for the lively, cheerful atmosphere and above all for the good range of well kept real ales – now no less than nine on the go at a time (they ring the changes so often that there isn't much point in giving a list), as well as quite a few foreign lagers. The lunchtime bar food (for which we have not yet had recommendations) includes sandwiches (from 60p), a choice of ploughman's (£1.70), burgers (from £1.60), pizza (£1.85), egg and bacon (£2.75), scampi (£3) and rainbow trout (£3.50); children's half-portions of most things. If you order the day before, Mrs Pearman will do her best to provide other dishes, which may then go on the menu for other customers too, for that day only. Sensibly placed darts, shove-ha'penny, dominoes, cribbage, a fruit machine and a loud juke box (or maybe piped music). There are seats outside this small house, which has attractive views: tracks lead off into the woods. (Recommended by Tim Bracey, T N de Bray, Mrs S V Oldroyd; more reports please)

Free house · Licensees Thomas and David Pearman · Real ale · Meals and snacks (lunchtime, cold only on Sun); food orders tel High Wycombe (0494) 775042 · Children in eating area · Open 10–2.30, 6–11 all year; closed evening 25 Dec

CHALFONT ST PETER   SU9990   Map 2

Greyhound

High Street; A413

A stroll through from the shopping centre, this well run old inn has a little riverside lawn with a climbing-frame and slide, and tables among tubs of geraniums on the tarmac front court, sheltered by its two creeper-covered wings. Inside, the friendly and comfortable main bar is partly panelled, with low beams and a handsome open fireplace. There's a usefully long serving counter, with Courage Best and Directors on handpump; though it's service with a 'Sir' here, they still manage to preserve a friendly and informal atmosphere – it's easy to feel at home. Bar food includes sandwiches (from 60p), shepherd's pie (£1.50), plaice (£1.60), salads such as cold meats, egg, quiche or prawns (£1.80–£3.50), lasagne (£1.90), a good value mixed grill (£2.80), scampi (£2.95), trout (£3.50) and sirloin steak (£4.90). A high-ceilinged plush restaurant serves evening meals. (Recommended by R and S Houghton, Monica Darlington, T N de Bray; more reports please)

Courage · Licensee Mrs C I Scott · Real ale · Meals and snacks · Children in eating area or restaurant · Open 10.30–2.30, 5.30–11 all year · Bedrooms tel Gerrards Cross (028 13) 883404; £20.50/£32.30

DENHAM   TQ0486   Map 3

Swan

¾ mile from M40 junction 1; follow Denham Village signs

The new licensees have recently had this fine old pub completely restored, to reveal its oak beams, open fireplaces and attractive brickwork; it has been furnished to match in dark wood, and the space game has been replaced by more traditional pastimes (see below). All this goes well, too, with the lovely garden, floodlit at night: a sheltered terrace by the pub itself, then – through a honeysuckle arch – a rose garden, then a more spacious lawn with picnic-table sets and a sturdy Wendy house, perhaps with donkeys looking over the post-and-rails fence of the adjoining paddock. In summer, depending on the weather, they have barbecues out here on most nights. The regular bar food includes sandwiches (from 75p, toasted from £1), home-made soup (85p) baked potatoes (85p), pâté (£1.35), garlic prawns or mushrooms on toast (£1.50), ploughman's (from £1.70), plaice (£2), scampi (£3.20), seafood platter (£3.50) and steaks (rump £6, T-bone £8.50), with a slimmers' table (£1.30) and daily specials (from £1.75). Well kept Courage Best and Directors on handpump; darts, dominoes, cribbage, a fruit machine and maybe piped music. The pub is in a quiet and charming village street. (*Recommended by Simon Cattley, R G Brown; more reports please*)

Courage · Licensee Peter Martin · Real ale · Meals and snacks · Traditional jazz Tues · Open 10.30–2.30, 5.30–11 all year

DOWNLEY SU8594 Map 2
Le De Spencer

Follow unmarked track from NW corner of village (on High Wycombe's NW outskirts) as far as you can; OS Sheet 165 reference 849960

Quite hidden away, this unpretentious pub is worth finding almost just for the satisfaction of tracking it down behind its protecting belt of rough common and bramble bushes. But once there, you'll be warmly welcomed both by the staff and by the local regulars. It's a plainly furnished brick and flint house, with leatherette wall seats, stools and benches around sturdy wooden tables, and some horse brasses on the beams that divide the two main room areas; in summer the nicest place to sit is the fairy-lit loggia, overlooking the lawn (which has tables and seats on its changing levels). The bar food is simple but wholesome (they're very generous with the ham in their sandwiches). Sensibly placed darts, fruit machine, juke box. (*Recommended by Oliver Knox, David Regan, T N de Bray*)

Wethereds (Whitbreads) · Licensee Vivian Busby · Snacks · Open 11–2.30, 5.30–11 all year

DUNSMORE SP8605 Map 4
Fox ★

Village signposted W of A413, 1½ miles S of Wendover; then turn right at Village Only sign

In the heart of the Chilterns, and quite close to Chequers, this earns its star for its unaffected simplicity and its lovely old-fashioned garden: splendidly peaceful at lunchtime during the week, with its verandah, sturdy wooden seats, stone cherubs, mossy urn and clipped box and hawthorn hedges. There is a climbing-frame on the side lawn. At weekends, though, and on some evenings, it does get very busy – when you may expect to queue. Inside is thoroughly homely and simple, with plain country seats and settles under the low ceilings of the two little rooms, a log-effect electric fire in the old brick hearth, and photographs of the champion dachshunds which the owners bred in the 1950s. Well kept ABC is tapped from the cask in a back room; freshly cut sandwiches; a fruit machine. *(Recommended by Doug Kennedy, MHG, T N de Bray)*

Aylesbury (Ind Coope) · Licensee Edward Fox · Real ale · Snacks · Open 10–2.30, 6–11 all year

FAWLEY   SU7586   Map 2
Walnut Tree ★

Food is what marks this pub out as special – as is the Hardings' determination to preserve it predominantly as a pub rather than a restaurant. The restaurant area has been usefully extended, but there's no question of the Walnut Tree losing its relaxed and easy-going pub atmosphere – with splendidly friendly service, and that ready welcome for walkers that so many other Chilterns pubs seem to think themselves above. This last year a new departure has been the provision of a cook-your-own barbecue with smoked sausages, marinated shark steaks, smoked chump chops, venison burgers, hamburgers and steaks; indoors, the remarkably wide choice of food includes at least two soups, one usually vegetarian (90p), ploughman's (from £1.50), cottage pie (£1.60), three pâtés (£1.95), baked egg in cream with tarragon mint and tomato (£2.10), deep-fried Camembert with gooseberry relish (£2.30), cottage cheese cooked with spinach in a pastry envelope (£2.30), baked avocado with prawns (£2.50), honey-baked ham in a wine sauce (£3.95), lamb chops provençale (£4.75) and chicken suprême stuffed with ground walnuts and liver pâté, wrapped in bacon, with mushroom sauce (£4.95). That's just a choice from the main menu: a subsidiary blackboard shows the results of their early morning forays into the London markets, with maybe nut-stuffed mushrooms and garlic mayonnaise (£2.30), leg of lamb in hay with mint and tarragon sauce (£4.75), rock lobster in garlic and tarragon (£5.10) or baked scallops in cream and herbs with garlic bread and salad (£6.10). The puddings (£1.10) are always popular with readers, too, and if they're not too busy they'll cut sandwiches. The restaurant has the same menu and prices as the simply furnished comfortable bars. Well kept Brakspears PA and SB on handpump, with Old Ale in the cold season; darts, dominoes, cribbage and other card games, a fruit machine and a juke box. The big lawn around the gravel car park in front of the plain brick house has well spaced tables and there are seats in a covered verandah. *(Recommended by John DuBois, HKR, David Regan)*

Brakspears · Licensees Frank and Alexandra Harding · Real ale · Meals and snacks · Children in eating area and restaurant · Open 11–2.30, 6–11 all year

FINGEST   SU7791   Map 2
Chequers

Readers report the warmest of welcomes from Mr Heasman, who previously made the Grenadier in central London so popular, and who since our last edition has taken over this civilised and pleasantly old-fashioned pub, across the road from an unusual double-towered

Norman church. An inner room has eighteenth-century box settles, guns in a rack over the fireplace, and china in a corner cupboard as well as on a high shelf under the beams. A modernised food bar and a sunny lounge with easy chairs have French windows opening on to a spacious garden with lots of tables on the grass between rosebeds and a herbaceous border, below quiet pasture sloping up towards the beech woods (this garden is lovely on a summer's evening). The food bar works efficiently, serving generous helpings of salads and taking orders for sandwiches, and good hot dishes such as curried prawns or steak and kidney pie: cheapest snacks around £1, prices up to £4.50 for main dishes; well kept Brakspears PA, SB and in season Old Ale on handpump; dominoes, cribbage, backgammon. A separate restaurant serves full meals, including a £7.50 business lunch. *(Recommended by Colin McLaren, Gordon Hewitt, HKR, Hilary Rubinstein, Dennis Royles, Doug Kennedy, J P Berryman)*

Brakspears · Licensee Bryan Heasman · Real ale · Meals (not Sun evening) and snacks (limited Sun evening) · Children in eating area · Open 11–2.30, 6–11 all year

FORTY GREEN   SU9292   Map 2

Royal Standard of England ★ ★

3½ miles from M40 junction 2, via A40 to Beaconsfield, then follow signs to Forty Green, off B474 ¾ mile N of New Beaconsfield

If you go at the weekend, be sure of getting there early: this dimly lit and intriguing warren of rambling rooms – not to mention the good value simple food and good real ales – do attract masses of people even in winter. The pub is a treasury of oak settles, old rifles, powder-flasks and bugles, ancient pewter and pottery tankards, lots of brass and copper, needlework samplers, stained glass, and fine decorated iron firebacks for the open fires – including one from Edmund Burke's old home nearby. The nicest room is perhaps the one with great black ship's timbers, finely carved antique oak panelling, and a massive settle apparently built to fit the curved transom of an Elizabethan galleon. The pub is one of the best within reach of London to show foreign visitors. It got its name after the Battle of Worcester in 1651, when Charles II hid in the high rafters of what is now its food bar. This great hall, which has a vast inglenook fireplace, has a fine display of some two dozen cheeses (the cold buffet is not cheap), and other food here includes avocado filled with crabmeat (£1.10), sausages (£2.75), home-made chicken pie (£3.50), and plaice, chicken, scampi or fritto misto. Well kept Huntsman Royal Oak, Marstons Pedigree and Owd Rodger and Sam Smiths OB on handpump. There are seats outside in a neatly hedged front rose garden, or in the shade of a tree. *(Recommended by Mrs Rosemary Wilmot, D J Penny, Paul A Smith, Michael and Alison Sandy, MHG, Dennis Royles, T N de Bray)*

Free house · Licensees Philip Eldridge and Alan Wainwright · Real ale · Meals and snacks · Children in area alongside Candle Bar · Open 10.30–2.30, 5.30–11 all year

---

Pubs with outstanding views are listed at the back of the book.

GREAT BRICKHILL   SP9030   Map 4
Old Red Lion

We are sad to report that the Crowthers – so welcoming to readers of
previous editions – have decided to leave this village pub, which in
their hands has pleasantly preserved traditional values. We
understand that the brewers plan a major revamp, but one firm
reason for keeping it in the *Guide* as a main entry, at least
provisionally, is the superb view over Buckinghamshire and far
beyond, from the back garden which hangs over steeply falling
ground. This has white tables and chairs among roses, stocks and
sweet-williams (alas, the guinea pigs which poddled about so sociably
will probably have left with the Crowthers, too). *(Recommended by
J Dennaford, Monica Darlington; up-to-date reports please)*

*Whitbreads · Real ale · Meals and snacks (no details yet on timing) · Open
10.30–2.30, 5.30–11 all year*

HAMBLEDEN   SU7886   Map 2
Stag & Huntsman

Village centre signposted from A4155

Since the *Guide*'s last edition, a new licensee has taken over this quiet
inn, set on the far edge of one of the prettiest Chilterns villages. But
readers will be relieved to hear that little has changed. There's still a
fine range of real ales, now comprising Brakspears PA and SPA,
Flowers Original, Huntsman Royal Oak, Wadworths 6X and
Wethereds, all well kept on handpump. Bar food includes onion and
cider soup (£1.10), ploughman's (from £1.20), deep-fried
mushrooms, smoked mackerel or pâté (£1.75), smoked eel or smoked

The Crown, Penn

salmon pâté (£1.95), home-made quiches (£1.95), smoked chicken salad (£2.30), home-made steak and kidney or chicken and mushroom pie (£2.50), and home-made apple pie and cream or blackcurrant cheesecake (95p). There is some variation from morning to evening, when the menu also includes steaks from the village butcher (£6.50). They no longer do sandwiches. The carpeted back lounge, opening on to the garden, has red leatherette bucket seats, a low ochre ceiling, and pale gold wallpaper. There's also a little bow-windowed front snug, simple public bar (with darts, shove-ha'penny, dominoes, cribbage, fruit machine and a space game) and a small restaurant (closed Sunday evening). The lawn has tables among tubs of flowers, roses, apple-trees and some fairy lights at night, and backs on to the woods of the Chilterns. *(Recommended by Jonathan Mindell; more reports please)*

Free house · Licensee David Vidgen · Real ale · Meals and snacks · Children in restaurant · Open 11–2.30, 6–11 all year · Bedrooms tel Henley (0491) 571227; £18/£27 (£29S)

HAWRIDGE COMMON   SP9505   Map 4
Full Moon

Lane 2 miles N of Chesham

The snug little low-beamed rambling rooms of this pretty red-tiled white Chilterns pub have comfortably cushioned settles in their snug alcoves, flagstones as well as carpets, and in winter a log fire in the big inglenook fireplace. From sturdy tables among fruit-trees on the spacious side lawn (with roses along its low flint wall) you can watch the riders on the common. Bar food includes sandwiches (from 60p), ploughman's (from £1.30), salads (£2), and in winter home-made soups and pies; Wethereds Bitter and Special on handpump, with Winter Royal when it's available; darts, table skittles, dominoes, cribbage. A good place to start a walk – or maybe a better place to finish one. *(More reports please)*

Wethereds (Whitbreads) · Licensee Walter Pope · Real ale · Meals (weekday lunchtimes in winter, not Tues) and snacks (lunchtime only, not Tues or Sun) Open 11.30–2.30, 6–11 all year

IBSTONE   SU7593   Map 4
Fox

1¾ miles from M40 junction 5: unclassified lane leading S from motorway exit roundabout; pub is on Ibstone Common

Recent refurbishments have if anything emphasised the traditional qualities of this village-common pub, with its low seventeenth-century oak beams, traditional high-backed settles and other country seats, and winter log fires. In summer there are cook-it-yourself barbecues outside, where tables (lit by old lamps) look beyond the neat rose garden to the wilder common, which leads eventually to rolling fields and the Chiltern oak and beech woods. Food you can cook out here includes a choice of sausages (90p for three), pork chop (£1.25), large lamb chop (£1.35) or eight-ounce sirloin steak (£2.75).

Indoors, popular home-made food – developed quite a bit since last year – includes sandwiches, ploughman's, steak and mushroom pie (£2.95), chicken and prawns with rice (£3.25), mixed grill (£3.50), game pie (£4.50), Swiss-style chicken (£5.25), scampi thermidor (£5.30) and trout en croûte (£5.95). Puddings (from £1) are traditional: treacle tart, bread and butter pudding, chocolate and ginger fudge and so forth. The woodblock-floored public bar has darts, shove-ha'penny, dominoes, cribbage and a fruit machine, and there may be piped music; well kept Flowers Original, Wethereds and SPA and Sam Whitbreads on handpump, and in season Winter Royal. *(Recommended by David Regan, HKR)*

Free house · Licensees Ann and David Banks · Real ale · Meals and snacks Children in eating area · Open 11–2.30, 6–11 all year

LITTLE HAMPDEN   SP8503   Map 4

Rising Sun ★

At end of village lane

This beautifully placed pub earns a star this year, through the warm praise which many readers with quite different tastes have given its atmosphere, its position and its good food. This avoids the common problem of over-much choice by concentrating on a handful of tried favourites, such as Cheddar, Stilton or pâté ploughman's (£1.40), baked potato filled with cottage cheese and fruit (£1.50), smoked mackerel (£1.90), lasagne, a herb and sausagemeat pie with delicious pastry (£2.50), prawns (£3) and charcoal-grilled Scotch steaks (ten-ounce sirloin £4.70, eight-ounce fillet £5.70). It's served in the Turkey-carpeted lounge, which has plenty of tables with comfortable seats, as well as an extra dining area (made available since the restaurant here stopped functioning as a separate entity), and in a quarry-tiled front bar with a fine inglenook fireplace. Well kept Adnams, Brakspears SB, Greene King Abbot and Sam Smiths OB on handpump; darts, shove-ha'penny, dominoes and cribbage in the public bar; maybe piped music. No walking boots inside. A pretty back garden slopes up behind, and there are tables on the terrace by the sloping front grass. The pub is splendidly placed for walkers (who tend to leave their cars sprawled up and down the lane, which peters out here), with bridle paths leading on through the woods both to Coombe Hill (National Trust, with fine views) and to Dunsmore (about a mile away – see our entry for that village). *(Recommended by Tim Bracey, Jane English, T N de Bray, Oliver Knox)*

Free house · Licensee Casson Binns · Real ale · Meals and snacks · Open 12–2.30, 6–11 all year (opens 7 in winter)

LITTLEWORTH COMMON   SU9487   Map 2

Jolly Woodman

2 miles from M40 junction 2; follow Littleworth Common signs off A355

Included for its fine position alone in the forest edge of Burnham Beeches, this cottagey pub serves filled rolls, ploughman's with a choice of cheeses and pâté, filled baked potatoes, cottage pie, steak and kidney pie, lasagne, salads and so forth. It's simply furnished, and has benches under a lime-tree in front, and more in its small beer garden. Well kept Wethereds and SPA on handpump, with Winter Royal from October to March; darts, dominoes, cribbage and a fruit machine. *(More reports please)*

Wethereds (Whitbreads) · Licensee D E Oliver · Real ale · Meals (lunchtime, not Sat or Sun) and snacks (lunchtime, not Sun) · Open 10.30–2.30, 5.30–11 all year

MARLOW   SU8586   Map 2
Ship

West Street (A4155 towards Henley)

Almost anywhere, this pub's food prices would strike you as low – in this relatively high-priced area, they are really quite remarkable. The food includes sandwiches (from 50p), toasted sandwiches (60p), ploughman's (80p), various salads such as cheese, meat or prawns (£1.20) and a daily special, served with a baked potato, such as lasagne, humble pie or spicy pie (£1.20); gateaux and ices are only 45p. There are two cosy communicating rooms, one small and square, the other long and thin, with Windsor armchairs and mustard-coloured leatherette seats built in to partly panelled walls. There are very low beams, and an interesting collection of warship photographs. Well kept Wethereds and SPA on handpump, with Winter Royal when it's available; a fruit machine, space game and piped pop music. A longish paved courtyard at the back, with a fruiting vine along one wall, has tables among tubs of flowers, and beyond it is a boules pitch. There is a separate restaurant. *(Recommended by Bob Rendle; more reports please)*

Wethereds (Whitbreads) · Licensee Julian Hammond · Real ale · Meals and snacks · Nearby parking may be difficult · Open 10.30–2.30, 6–11 all year

Two Brewers

Peter Street; at double roundabout approaching bridge turn into Station Road, then first right

New owners have spruced up this friendly pub, giving a maritime theme to its T-shaped bar, which has low black beams and some black panelling. They've also rejuvenated the food, and in particular have found their shellfish counter so popular that, from being an occasional event, it has already become a regular thing, supported by twice-weekly trips to the London fish markets. It includes cockles, mussels, whelks and so forth (sold by the plate, 30p), jellied eels, and good value prawns (only £1.20 a pint). Other food includes sandwiches (from 80p), baked potatoes with a choice of fillings which changes each day (£2.20), around eight daily-changing hot dishes such as shepherd's pie (£2.50), macaroni cheese (£2.60), chilli con carne, scampi or steak and kidney pie (£2.90), a salad counter including pork and chestnut pie (£2.80) and turkey and cranberry pie or cold meats (£3) and steaks (from eight-ounce sirloin, £5.20). Well kept Wethereds on handpump. A courtyard behind has sturdy rustic

seats, and benches outside in the quiet street give a glimpse of the
Thames: the tow-path is just a few yards away. *(More reports please)*

*Wethereds (Whitbreads) · Licensee F W Boxall · Real ale · Meals and snacks
Open 10–2.30, 6–11 all year*

MARSH GIBBON   SP6423   Map 4
Greyhound ★

Back road about 4 miles E of Bicester; pub SW of village, towards
A41 and Blackthorn

A special attraction in this charmingly civilised old pub is the beer
produced in the pub's own brewhouse (which you can view):
Heritage and the stronger Ailrics Old Ale, both good value. They also
keep traditional cider. The friendly bar has walls stripped back to
golden-grey stone, traditional heavy seats with arms, brightened up
with patchwork leather cushions, arranged on its hexagonal stone
flooring-tiles, a finely ornamented iron stove, and beams in the
yellowing ceiling; the pub, originally Tudor, was largely rebuilt in
1740 after a 'terable fire'. Good bar food is entirely home made, and
includes soup (75p), a choice of ploughman's (from £1.50), pies such
as savoury mince, leek and bacon (£1.50), steak and kidney (£1.75)
or venison (£1.95), salads (mackerel £2, ham £3, beef £3.75) and a
substantially garnished dish of the day such as Cumberland sausage,
lamb cutlets Reform or goulash (£3). They keep a pot of fresh herbs
from their big herb garden, for you to add yourself to food or drink.
There is also an attractive separate restaurant, dimly lit and low
beamed (booking advisable). There is a traditional pub games-table
which includes drop out, as well as shove-ha'penny; also table
skittles, dominoes, cribbage and a fruit machine. A small but
attractive front garden has stone-topped tables, and behind the big
car park there's a large lawn with more tables, swings, a climbing-
frame, a pony and a donkey called Marcus. *(Recommended by Col G D
Stafford, MHG, A Saunders)*

*Own brew · Licensee Henry Phillips · Real ale · Meals and snacks (evenings in
summer only); restaurant reservations tel Stratton Audley (086 97) 365
Children in eating area · Open 10–2.30, 6.30–11 all year; closed Mon
lunchtime*

NORTHEND   SU7392   Map 4
White Hart

This mossy-tiled white inn has a snug and cosy carpeted bar, with
Windsor chairs, comfortable window seats, very low handsomely
carved beams, some panelling, and an outsize fireplace with a big log
fire in winter. Bar food includes splendid pork pies – a local legend –
sent down specially from Yorkshire each week (52p, with salad
£1.65), sandwiches, toasted sandwiches (96p), ploughman's in
variety (£1.65), quiche or meat salads (£1.70); for the moment they
aren't doing hot food. Well kept Brakspears PA, SB or sometimes Old
ale on handpump. The sheltered garden is lovely in summer, with
flowers, fruit-trees and high hedges, and the inn is very well placed for

walks in the surrounding beech woods. *(Recommended by HKR; more reports please)*

Brakspears · Licensee Frank Douglas · Real ale · Snacks (not Tues evening) Children in eating area · Open 11–2.30, 6–11 all year · Two bedrooms tel *Turville Heath (049 163) 353; £11/£22*

PENN   SU9193 Map 4

Crown   [*illustrated on page 53*]

B474

The comfortable lounge of this neatly kept pub looks out over a pretty rose garden opposite the village church (which has a fine medieval painting of the Last Judgement). Another low-ceilinged bar has ancient polished brick flooring-tiles, and the Wheelwrights Bar was once a coffin-maker's workshop. Bar food includes filled rolls, Stilton ploughman's (£1.30), turkey curry (£2), peppered smoked mackerel salad (£2.20) and Scotch beef salad (£3); there is a separate restaurant. The good choice of well kept real ales consists of Brakspears SB, Trumans Bitter, Best and Sampson, and Websters Yorkshire on handpump, with Brakspears PA and Old tapped from the cask; darts, bar billiards, shove-ha'penny, dominoes, cribbage, a fruit machine and a space game. Outside there are slides, swings, climbing-frames and a wooden horse and cart for children; the tables set among tubs of flowers just behind the creeper-covered tiled brick house have fine views over rolling pastures and woodland. This ridge is over 500 feet high, and from the fourteenth-century church tower you are supposed to be able to see 12 counties. *(Recommended by Brian and Rosemary Wilmot, Mark Medcalf, D R Mather)*

Trumans · Licensee Nick King · Real ale · Meals and snacks · Children in eating area, restaurant and Wheelwrights Bar at lunchtime · Open 11–2.30, 5.30–11 all year

SKIRMETT   SU7790 Map 2

Kings Arms

New owners have made extensive changes here, turning what used to be the snooker and games bar on the right into a small Italian-style restaurant specialising in fish and vegetarian dishes as well as pasta, with traditional Sunday lunches (closed Sunday evening, Monday and Tuesday); the rib of beef (£15.50 for two) is mouthwatering. They've kept the lofty-raftered side bistro (with a good spread of help-yourself cold meats and salads on a buffet table, and other food – in generous helpings – such as sandwiches, home-made soup with garlic bread, excellent filled baked potatoes, and puddings). The central bar has cushioned Windsor armchairs and an inglenook fireplace, with jugs, flagons and tankards hanging from the high black beams. Well kept Flowers Original, Wethereds and SPA and Sam Whitbreads on handpump, and a sensible range of wines; maybe piped music. There is a fruit machine in a room at the side. The new owners – who used to run a London hairdressers' – have attractively redecorated the bedrooms, with Liberty prints and so forth. There are seats on the side lawn by a weeping ash, and on the narrow terrace in front of this steep-tiled old brick house, which stands alone by a quiet lane through a pretty valley. (*Recommended by Mrs Rosemary Wilmot, HKR; more reports on the new regime please, to confirm whether or not the star rating awarded in previous editions should be reinstated*)

Free house · Licensees Henry Were and John Waddingham · Real ale · Meals and snacks (not Sun evening) · Children in bistro and restaurant · Open 11–2.30, 6–11 all year · Bedrooms tel Turville Heath (049 163) 247; £18/£30 (£32B)

Old Crown ★

In the main village (if that's not too grand a word for this friendly little cluster of houses), this charming old pub has been winning increasingly firm support from readers, both for its very warmly welcoming atmosphere and for its unusual – and uncommonly wide – choice of good food. On the strength of that, it gains a star award this year. The food includes sandwiches (from 75p), soup which might be Cheddar and onion (95p), herby giant sausage with French bread (£1), ploughman's with a choice of cheeses (from £1.25, full salad 50p more), home-made pork brawn, mussels in Parmesan sauce, spring lamb rolls or stuffed aubergines (£2), Stilton and pork pâté with white peaches (£2.25), gravlax with dill sauce (£3), beech-smoked chicken (£4.75), game pie (£5), marinated lamb kebabs (£5.50), eight-ounce sirloin steak (£6), with lots of puddings such as brown Betty or rhubarb crumble with custard (£1). The small central room and a larger one leading off (the village shop when we first knew this pub) are comfortably furnished with Windsor chairs on a neat carpet, and tankards hanging from beams. Well kept Brakspears PA, SB, Mild and Old ale are tapped from casks in a still-room, and served through a hatch. A small white-painted room at the side has an old-fashioned settle by its coal fire, and Windsor chairs around trestle tables. Darts, dominoes, cribbage and quoits. There are picnic-table sets under cocktail parasols on the big back lawn. (*Recommended by Mrs R Wilmot, HKR, Tim and Ann Bracey, Dennis Royles*)

Brakspears · Licensee Leon Banks · Real ale · Meals and snacks · Children in eating area and barn · Folk night Tues · Open 10.30–2.30, 6–11 all year

STONY STRATFORD SP7840 Map 4
Cock

72 High Street

This old coaching-inn, with its neighbour the Bull, is supposed to have been the origin of 'cock and bull stories', because of the extraordinarily garbled news brought here by coaching passengers in the Napoleonic Wars. The civilised lounge bar has a Regency-style décor, with numbered elm armchairs, soft lighting, an elegant dividing arch, and French windows looking out on the sheltered back lawn, which has picnic-table sets by a rockery. Waitress-served bar food includes sandwiches (sometimes special open ones), changing home-made soups (85p), lasagne or Johnson's Temptation (with potatoes and anchovies, £1.85), mussels in white wine (£1.95), stews, haddock, steak and kidney pie (£2), and good well hung rump steak (£5). Well kept Adnams and Hook Norton Best on handpump; maybe piped music. There is also a cheery bistro at the front (weekday lunchtimes), and a separate restaurant. *(Recommended by D A Angless, C P Price; more reports please)*

Free house · Licensee James Higgins · Real ale · Meals and snacks (not Sun evening, nor 25 and 26 Dec) · Children in eating areas · Open 10.30–2.30, 5.30–11 all year · Bedrooms tel Milton Keynes (0908) 562109; £23 (£30B)/ £34 (£40B)

THE LEE   SP8904   Map 4
Cock & Rabbit

Back roads 2½ miles N of Great Missenden, about 1½ miles E of A413

As we went to press we heard that this pub was being sold. We have kept it in as a main entry, as readers have enjoyed it most for its attractive location and pleasant layout. It's on the edge of the village green – a quiet village, in pleasant Chilterns countryside. There is quite a cluster of quaint inn signs outside – and lots of seats, on a side terrace or a lawn, on a crazy-paved courtyard facing the green, out on rougher grass by the paddock, or in the shelter of a verandah. There is a spacious plush lounge with good big windows, a plainer public bar with sensibly placed darts and shove-ha'penny, a little front family room, and a restaurant. In the past the pub has kept a good range of real ales. *(Recommended by HKR, T N de Bray and others; up-to-date reports please)*

Free house · Real ale · Meals and snacks · Children have been welcome · Open 12–2.30, 6–11 all year

nr THE LEE   SP8904   Map 4
Old Swan ★

Swan Bottom; back road ¾ mile N of The Lee; OS Sheet 165 reference 902055

The reasonably priced, good home-made bar food in this attractively restored Chilterns pub changes each day, and besides soup (£1), sandwiches (from £1, crab £1.30, smoked salmon £1.80) and ploughman's (£1.75) might typically include seafood pancakes (£2.75), good salads such as smoked trout and dressed crab, rabbit, pheasant or pigeon pie (£3), steak and kidney pudding (£3.25) and honey-roast ham (£3.50). The four low-beamed interconnecting rooms have a friendly and welcoming atmosphere, and service is efficient even when they're busy (they often are during the week, but readers have been pleased to find plenty of room even on a fine July Saturday). There are some high-backed old-fashioned settles, leatherette window seats, a wall clock with cheerful chimes, and ancient floor-tiles in front of a wood-burning open cooking range in one attractive inglenook fireplace. Well kept Adnams, Brakspears PA and SB and Morlands on handpump; shove-ha'penny, maybe piped music. There is a popular separate restaurant open evenings too. They run summer weekend barbecues on the spacious back lawns (which have a children's play area), and there are more seats in front of this pretty tiled white pub. Muddy boots are unwelcome. *(Recommended by Hope Chenhalls, Doug Kennedy, T N de Bray and others; more reports please)*

Free house · Licensees S C and K E Michaelson-Yeates · Real ale · Meals and snacks (lunchtime, not Sun); restaurant reservations tel The Lee (024 020) 239 Children in eating areas · Open 12–2.30, 6–11 all year

TURVILLE   SU7690 Map 2
Bull & Butcher ★

Since the landlord gave up his other pub (the Chequers in Fingest) to concentrate his attention undividedly on this one, there has been a marked increase in the flow and warmth of readers' approving reports – hence our award this year of a star. Food has been coming in for particular praise recently: virtually all home made, it includes soup (90p), pâtés such as venison and smoked mackerel (from £1.50), shrimps in garlic or a choice of ploughman's (£1.70), fresh prawns (£2.40), lasagne (£2.50), salads including ham off the bone, Scotch beef and prawns (£2.50–£3.50), excellent seafood platters, vegetarian dishes such as hazelnut bake (£2.80) and steak and kidney pie (£3.50). The wide range of filled baked potatoes is particularly popular in winter. The landlord has been a racing driver, and under the low shiny ochre ceiling the bar's walls are covered with racing and rallying photographs – their subjects actually wander in from time to time. Partly divided into two areas, it's comfortable and cheerful, with cushioned wall settles, an old-fashioned high-backed settle by the open fire, and well kept Brakspears PA and SB on handpump, with Old ale tapped from the cask. There's the sort of atmosphere that makes you stay much longer than you'd meant to. Charmingly set among old cottages sheltering in a wooded Chilterns valley – you might recognise the setting from one film or another – the black and white timbered house has tables outside on a neat lawn by fruit-trees and an umbrella-shaped hawthorn-tree. *(Recommended by Colin McLaren, Gordon Hewitt, Brian and Rosemary Wilmot, J W Tomlinson, Iain Maclean, HKR, Tim and Ann Bracey, BWJ, D A Haines)*

Brakspears · Licensee Jim Cowles · Real ale · Meals and snacks · Children in eating area · Open 11–2.30, 6–11 all year

WEST WYCOMBE   SU8394 Map 4
George & Dragon
A40

Dating from the fifteenth century, this handsome inn has massive oak beams, sloping walls, a fine staircase up to the bedrooms, and an unusual lead inn sign with heavy iron supports. Its big open-plan bar has been cheerfully modernised, with Windsor chairs and comfortable wall seats around its many wood- or copper-topped tables. Home-cooked bar food includes sandwiches (from 55p), soup (75p), ploughman's with a choice of cheeses (£1.45), spinach and blue-cheese pancakes (£1.95), sole and grape pie or ham and mushroom in a tomato and cheese sauce (£2.25), and two or three changing daily specials such as liver and bacon casserole or rabbit pie; Courage Best and Directors on handpump. There is a separate restaurant. Through the arched and cobbled coach entry (and the car park) there's a beer garden. This village is owned by the National Trust, and nearby you can visit the splendidly furnished West Wycombe Park with its classical landscaped grounds, the Hellfire Club's caves half way up the hill, and at the top of the hill the grandiose church with the tower-top golden ball in which the Club sometimes dined. There's a tale that Sukie, an attractive barmaid here, was stoned to death in the caves by people jealous of her affair with one of the inn's customers, and has come back to haunt the inn. *(Recommended by H L McDougall, Martyn Quinn; more reports please)*

Courage · Licensee Philip Todd · Real ale · Meals (not Sun) and snacks (not Sun evening) · Children in separate room, lunchtime only · Open 11–2.30, 5.30–11 all year · Bedrooms tel High Wycombe (0494) 23602; £20.50 (£23B)/£30.50 (£33B)

Lucky Dip

Besides the fully inspected pubs, you might like to try these Lucky Dips recommended and described by readers (if you do, please send us reports):

ADSTOCK [SP7330], *Old Thatched Inn*: beams and flagstones in comfortably modernised thatched pub with good ploughman's and other snacks, and choice of well kept real ales; sheltered back garden *(J W Gibson, LYM)*
AMERSHAM [SU9597], *Boot & Slipper*: excellent Courage Directors in local which has had music Tuesday and Sunday lunchtime; garden *(T N de Bray)*; *Saracens Head*: range of real ales, one changing guest beer, good moderately priced bistro, bedrooms; juke box, popular with young people *(T N de Bray, LYM)*
nr AMERSHAM [Wheilden Gate; SU9597], *Queens Head*: good Benskins and Ind Coope Burton on handpump, restricted choice of cheap but good bar food; back garden (for pub location see OS Sheet 165 reference 941957) *(T N de Bray)*
ASHERIDGE [SP9404], *Blue Moon*: good country pub *(T N de Bray)*; *Bull*: first-class bar food at reasonable prices *(Anon)*
AYLESBURY [Gibraltar; SP7510], *Bottle & Glass*: good food in thatched pub with low ceilings; cheese and pâté only for Saturday lunch; sandwiches only on Saturday and Sunday night (for pub location see OS sheet 165 reference 758108) *(David Regan)*; [SP8213] *Dark Lantern*: well furnished; food, good Ind Coope Burton on handpump; like a village pub though in the middle of town *(Colin McLaren)*
BEACONSFIELD [SU9490], *Beech Tree*: excellent Wethereds Bitter, Mild and in season Winter Royal *(T N de Bray)*; *George*: civilised old-fashioned inn specialising in seafood with weekly run to Yarmouth, well kept Ind Coope real ales; bedrooms *(Martyn Quinn, T N de Bray, LYM)*; *Royal Saracen's Head*: modernised open-plan plush bar in striking timbered building with pleasant courtyard terrace *(LYM, T N de Bray)*; *Swan*: busy and friendly; Wethereds, open fire, bar meals and popular restaurant *(Martyn Quinn, T N de Bray)*
BOURNE END [SU8985], *Heart in Hand*: comfortable pub with well kept Wethereds and good value food; old-fashioned verandah *(I Clark, LYM)*
BRADENHAM [SU8297], *Red Lion*: friendly, good service and varied choice of bar meals, in period flint building *(Miss J I Olivier)*
CASTLETHORPE [SP7944], *Navigation*: renovated canalside pub with excellent Hook Norton and steak and kidney pie *(LYM and others)*

Waterside pubs are listed at the back of the book.

CHALFONT COMMON [TQ0092], *Dumb Bell*: comfortably refurbished country pub with good value simple food and well kept Courage; welcoming landlord *(Gwen and Peter Andrews, T N de Bray, LYM)*

CHALFONT ST GILES [SU9893], *Feathers*: friendly homely local with warm atmosphere and well kept Wethereds real ale; near Milton's cottage *(Nick Dowson, Alison Hayward, T N de Bray, LYM)*; [Silver Hill; SU9893] *Fox & Hounds*: old low-ceilinged ivy-covered village pub with good value lunchtime food; congenial licensees, beer garden *(Chris Grundy, H Upson)*; *Ivy House*: recently re-opened; won one of Benskins' Gold Circle Food Awards *(David Regan)*; *Pheasant*: friendly pub with very comical and jovial landlord, good bar food; huge garden for children, with barbecues in summer; popular restaurant *(Mrs Rosemary Wilmot)*

CHALFONT ST PETER [Copthall Lane; SU9990], *Waggon & Horses*: cleanly kept pub with home-cooked food and well kept real ales; pretty terrace *(Anon)*

CHESHAM [SP9501], *Queens Head*: well kept Brakspears beer in nice pub with good atmosphere *(Wayne Rossiter, T N de Bray)*

COLESHILL [High Street; SU9495], *Red Lion*: food includes lovely barbecues in summer (nice big grassy area at the back with slide and swings for children); open fire in winter with very large helpings of ploughman's and other food in the two small bars *(Mrs R Wilmot)*

CRYERS HILL [SU8796], *White Lion*: friendly local with well kept Courage real ales and good value food; roomy games-room, and garden *(R G Brown, LYM)*

CUDDINGTON [SP7311], *Crown*: food very good, with generous helpings and reasonable prices, in nice welcoming thirteenth-century thatched pub with log fire and real ale *(Mrs E D Sherwood)*; *Red Lion*: good choice of game and fish at reasonable prices; attentive landlord and family create a welcoming atmosphere *(Ronald Arthur Corbett)*

DENHAM [TQ0486], *Falcon*: old one-bar local with good snacks, well kept beer, open fires *(B R Shiner)*; *Green Man*: likeable new Merseyside licensees doing home-cooked food and well kept Courage ales in small stone-floored village pub *(Simon Cattley)*

FARNHAM COMMON [SU9684], *Royal Oak*: delightful Green Belt pub with very good beer and snacks and excellent service – in an area where GPG pubs are a little thin on the ground *(Capt F A Bland)*

FLACKWELL HEATH [SU8988], *Heath Wine Bar*: used to be Rogues Retreat; name and management changed, but still pleasant *(David Regan)*

nr FLACKWELL HEATH [SU8988], *Crooked Billet*: flint country pub with pretty garden, good simple food and autumn scrumpy as well as Whitbreads real ale *(T N de Bray, LYM)*

FRIETH [SU7990], *Yew Tree*: good range of beers and food, and several Australian wines by the glass or bottle, in recently renovated pub *(Bob Rendle, David Regan)*

FULMER [Windmill Road; SU9985], *Black Horse*: lovely garden outside white-painted listed building which is cosy and old-fashioned inside, with good food and well kept Courage ales; attractive village *(Simon Cattley)*

GAYHURST [SP8446], *Sir Francis Drake*: curious pinnacled Gothick lodge converted into small plush pub with good choice of whiskies *(LYM)*

GREAT LINFORD [SP8542], *Black Horse*: simply furnished cheerful pub with real ales, garden and playground below canal embankment *(LYM)*

GREAT MISSENDEN [SP8900], *Black Horse*: good food in pleasant and civilised pub *(J W Tomlinson)*; *George*: some concentration on home-made food in fifteenth-century pub with real ales including Aylesbury, Bass, Everards Tiger, home-mulled wine *(reports please)*; *Green Man, Nags Head, Red Lion*: all are worth a visit *(T N de Bray)*

HAWRIDGE [The Vale; SP9505], *Rose & Crown*: excellent range of real ales, remarkable whiskies (up to 45 years old) and good food in fine well kept pub with one roomy bar; friendly landlord (for pub location see OS Sheet 165 reference 963045) *(A Foxman, C Wolbold, H E Cox, Wayne Rossiter)*

Pubs brewing their own beers are listed at the back of the book.

HEDGERLEY [SU9686], *One Pin*: ivy-clad village local with friendly and efficient service, freshly made food, well kept Courage beer, small terrace *(R and S Houghton)*

HIGH WYCOMBE [SU8593], *Bell*: small cosy Fullers pub with beer garden overlooking multi-storey car park *(Wayne Rossiter)*; *Roundabout*: modern, covered with pub mirrors, separate rooms for different groups; good range of real ales *(Wayne Rossiter)*; *White Lions*: good value food, even in the evenings; friendly staff and good service *(E O Stephens)*

HOLMER GREEN [SU9097], *Earl Howe*: pleasant low-ceilinged small village pub, homely with good fire, Courage Best and Directors *(Nicolas Dowson, Alison Hayward)*

HYDE HEATH [SU9399], *Plough*: small friendly country pub with open fires, fresh flowers, real welcome from staff, good food including vegetarian dishes, Benskins real ale; get there early as it can get very crowded *(David Regan, J W Tomlinson, Brian Huggett)*

KINGSWOOD [SP6919], *Crooked Billet*: friendly and old-fashioned roadside pub near Waddesdon Manor *(LYM)*

LACEY GREEN [Parslow's Hillock; SP8100], *Pink & Lily*: friendly and unspoilt Chilterns pub with Rupert Brooke connections (for pub location see OS Sheet 165 reference 826019) *(LYM, Richard Gibbs, Dennis Royles)*

LANE END [SU7991], *Old Sun*: archetypal local with good beer and good conversation, off the beaten track *(Colin McLaren)*

LEY HILL [SP9802], *Swan*: good small pub on common *(T N de Bray)*

LITTLE HORWOOD [SP7930], *Shoulder of Mutton*: rambling and attractively simple open-plan bar in ancient pub by church *(LYM)*

LONG CRENDON [Bicester Road; SP6808], *Chandos Arms*: good atmosphere in smart thatched pub; Buttery Bar nice and quiet, but enough noise seeps through from the 'Lower End' for it to feel like a lively night out in spirit, but a restful, relaxing drink in body; very well kept Wethereds *(Michael Sandy)*

MARLOW [Causeway; SU8586], *George & Dragon*: good bar food in pleasant surroundings, friendly service *(Helen Wood)*; [Station Road] *Marlow Donkey*: food good lunchtime and evening (with a certain charm in the eating alcove), in recently modernised pub which has kept its atmosphere; choice of ales and wines *(David Regan)*

MARSWORTH [SP9114], *Red Lion*: unspoilt village near canal; food (not Sun), real ale and cider *(G R Brown)*; *White Lion*: good food in busy canalside pub *(G R Brown)*

MEDMENHAM [SU8084], *Dog & Badger*: sandwiches and other bar food in modernised Wethereds pub 10 minutes' stroll from the Thames *(S J Tims, BB)*

MENTMORE [SP9119], *Stag*: good food and service in well run pub with separate restaurant *(Anon)*

MILTON KEYNES [Mount Farm Industrial Estate; SP8938], *Beacon*: brand new and stands out from other pubs here; very good position by pleasant lake; food includes giant sausages *(Monica Darlington)*; [Heelands, Saxon Street; SP8938] *Suffolk Punch*: new Tolly Cobbold pub with pleasant décor; bookable tables in two sittings for good value well organised carvery (as much as you like), with efficient service *(Anon)*

NAPHILL [SU8497], *Black Lion*: RAF Strike Command local; good filled baked potatoes and well kept Courage *(BWJ, Richard Gibbs, LYM)*

NORTHEND [SU7392], *Nags Head*: small pub included in previous editions for its neat and cosy atmosphere and good value food, now under new owners *(news please)*

PADBURY [SP7130], *Robin Hood*: clean and comfortable longish room with settles and wheelbacks; good value home-cooked food, Charles Wells real ale *(T A V Meikle)*

PENN STREET [SU9295], *Hit or Miss*: comfortably modernised low-ceilinged, three-room pub with own cricket ground and good value food *(T N de Bray, LYM)*

PRINCES RISBOROUGH [Whiteleaf; SP8003], *Red Lion*: friendly atmosphere, good meals and snacks, Brakspears and Morlands real ale and good value wines; open fire and warm welcome in cosy pub at foot of Chilterns; attractive garden (for pub location see OS Sheet 165 reference 817040) *(HKR, Wg Cdr D C Hencken)*; [Market Square] *Whiteleaf Cross*: good food and well kept Morlands in clean and well refurbished seventeenth-century house *(HKR, Wg Cdr D C Hencken)*

SAUNDERTON [SU8198], *Rose & Crown*: increasing concentration on food in pub well placed by Chilterns *(HKR)*;[SP7901] *Three Horseshoes*: old-fashioned pub with verandahs and garden, nice on summer evenings *(H L McDougall, LYM)*

SLAPTON [SP9320], *Carpenters Arms*: good Sunday lunches in very friendly old country pub, half a mile from canal *(G R Brown)*

SPEEN [SU8399], *Old Plow*: seventeenth-century cottagey inn, completely refurbished in old-fashioned style and recently reopened after long closure, in attractive walking countryside; restaurant, bedrooms being redecorated *(P McAtharney, LYM)*

STEEPLE CLAYDON [SP6926], *Phoenix*: thatched and timbered village pub, traditionally run; near Claydon House (a rococo stately home with Florence Nightingale museum and antique musical instruments) *(LYM)*

STOKE GOLDINGTON [SP8348], *White Hart*: thatched pub with beams and quarry tiles in saloon, comfortable plush lounge and lively public bar; enterprising choice of drinks, sheltered back lawn *(LYM)*

STOKE GREEN [SU9882], *Red Lion*: rambling New Zealand-run old-fashioned bar with comfortable no-smoking bar, good food including excellent ploughman's, and good drinks including a choice of winter hot toddies *(David Regan, Marilynne Blyth, LYM)*

STOKENCHURCH [SU7695], *Kings Arms*: recently extended accommodation, very reasonable bar meals, good restaurant (sometimes used for functions), Wethereds real ales, occasional live music *(David Regan, Bob Rendle)*; *Royal Oak*: recent extensions; superb beer selection *(Bob Rendle)*

STONY STRATFORD [High Street; SP7840], *Bull*: back-to-basics Vaults Bar with real ales and simple bar food, also plusher hotel bars; bedrooms *(LYM)*

THORNBOROUGH [SP7433], *Lone Tree*: food in wide choice at reasonable prices, pleasant and attractive pub, good ABC real ale *(N F Mackley)*

WAVENDON [SP9137], *Plough*: good cheap food in picturesque pub popular with Open University staff *(Monica Darlington)*

WEEDON [SP8118], *Five Elms*: attractive old pub, a favourite of many visitors *(T N de Bray)*

WENDOVER DENE [SP8607], *Halfway House*: well kept Fullers, if a trifle expensive; bedrooms *(T N de Bray)*

WESTON TURVILLE [Church Lane; SP8510], *Chequers*: good food in restaurant *(Dr D G Wray)*

WHEELEREND COMMON [SU8093], *Brickmakers Arms*: nicely furnished traditional pub with good food, open fireplace; bedrooms *(H L McDougall, R L Bowerman)*

WINCHMORE HILL [SU9394], *Potters Arms*: friendly, recently done up *(T N de Bray)*

WINSLOW [SP7627], *Bell*: tiny old-fashioned snug parlour and comfortable modernised lounge with good choice of real ales; bedrooms *(Richard Gibbs, LYM)*

WOBURN SANDS [SP9235], *Fir Tree*: simple inn with reasonably priced steaks and other food; handy for Milton Keynes and M1 junction 13; bedrooms good value *(S V Sherwood, LYM and others)*; *Weathercock*: good reasonably priced food *(Monica Darlington)*

WOOBURN COMMON [Wooburn Common Road; SU9387], *Royal Standard*: brightly redecorated pub, handy for M40 junction 2, has been popular for simple bar food and well kept Wethereds real ales; up-to-date reports please *(T N de Bray, LYM)*

WOOLSTONE [SP8738], *Cross Keys*: old bargee pub with generous helpings of particularly good food *(Monica Darlington)*

WOUGHTON [SP8737], *Old Swan*: ancient pub with good (if not very cheap) food and big, pleasant garden, often used for community events *(Monica Darlington)*

Cambridgeshire and Bedfordshire

After last year's exceptionally large influx of new main entries, we haven't this year added any further ones. So we do hope for reports on the Lucky Dip entries at the end of the chapter to help us select from these strong contenders for inspection as potential main entries in future editions. Among these Lucky Dips there are some that sound particularly promising (curiously, almost all are in Cambridgeshire rather than in Bedfordshire): the Spade & Becket (good riverside terrace) and new Ancient Druids (brewing its own beer) in Cambridge itself, the Blue Bell at Dogsthorpe (for atmosphere), the Horse & Jockey near Dunstable (very large garden, lots for children to do, and a very recent quarter-million-pound refurbishment), the White Horse in Eaton Socon (a main entry in previous editions – we heard about what sound like very good refurbishments under new licensees just too late for us to reinspect this fine old inn for this one), the King William IV in Heydon (masses of rustic decoration), the Great Northern in Peterborough (a rather gracious railway hotel), the Bell in Stilton (famous for 'discovering' Stilton cheese, and very recently successfully refurbished after a longish time in the doldrums), and Wicken Hall at Wicken (a fourteenth-century manor in large grounds, recently opened as an inn). Among the main entries, some important changes include new

The Three Tuns, Fen Drayton

licensees at several pubs (the lively Three Tuns in Biddenham, now doing a lot for children; the ancient Three Tuns in Fen Drayton; the Live & Let Live at Hexton, with its attractive garden just below the Chilterns; and the attractively placed Red Lion at Studham, handy for Whipsnade). Food has been coming in for warmer praise than before at the Kings Head on the green at Dullingham, the charming old Green Man not far from the river in Grantchester, the distinguished but friendly Haycock at Wansford (with a fine old-fashioned garden), the good value Black Horse just around the corner from the Abbey in Woburn, and, particularly, the Pheasant at Keyston. The Swan in Old Weston, always reliable for its good food, has opened a new dining area and branched out into a new style of cooking, and the Olde White Hart in Ufford has just figured prominently in a national competition to find Britain's best steak and kidney pie. Other pubs where the food is good value include the bustling Trinity Foot, Swavesey, the stylish Chequers at Fowlmere, the Three Horseshoes at Madingley (especially in summer, for its good buffet and attractive garden), the nicely furnished George & Dragon at Elsworth, the cheerful Chequers in Keysoe, the John o' Gaunt in Sutton (with a Finnish-style cold table as well as hot dishes), and — a special favourite — the pleasantly old-fashioned Plough & Fleece in Horningsea. The cheerful Locomotive, near Sandy, has a splendidly large garden, as does the White Horse at Southill — which also has a miniature steam railway. Good riverside pubs include the Bridge Hotel at Clayhithe, the atmospheric and ancient Olde Ferry Boat at Holywell, the Pike & Eel with its peaceful marina near Needingworth (you can stay at all these three places), and the Anchor at Tempsford (one of the best places for children in the area). No beer drinker should miss the Salisbury Arms in Cambridge, which has a splendid range of well kept real ales. Cambridge, incidentally, has a wealth of good pubs, with no less than five main entries as well as several good Lucky Dips. To round off this shortlist, a good all-rounder not yet mentioned is the Three Fyshes in Turvey: plenty of character, friendly, good beer and simple food. And you should certainly consider trying the Tickell Arms in Whittlesford, a uniquely unclassifiable pub that you might love.

Entries for these two counties are grouped together partly because quite a few entries lie so close to the boundary that they'd otherwise confuse all except earnest topographers, but chiefly because the number of entries for Bedfordshire alone is not large.

Post Office address codings confusingly give the impression that some pubs are in Cambridgeshire, when they're really in the Leicestershire or Midlands groups of counties – which is where we list them.

ARRINGTON (Cambs)   TL3250   Map 5

Hardwicke Arms

A14

This quaint old coaching-inn, which is covered with Virginia creeper, has a high-ceilinged bar with upholstered tub chairs around copper-topped tables, seats in its tall windows, and a long serving counter. The hospitable landlord and landlady offer good bar food which includes sandwiches, soup, home-made pâté, ploughman's, turkey hot-pot or chilli con carne, moussaka, steak and kidney pudding and salads, including trout and a choice of home-cooked meats. There is also a separate restaurant. Adnams, Greene King Abbot and IPA on handpump, and quite a few malt whiskies; piped music. Down steps is a quieter, beamed and oak-panelled room, and there is also a separate small games room, with darts, shove-ha'penny, dominoes, cribbage and a space game. There are tables on the grass beside the pub, which is next door to Wimpole Hall, a very grand eighteenth-century National Trust house with a fine park. *(Recommended by D J Penny, Howard Gascoyne)*

Free house · Licensees Graham and Pauline Burford · Real ale · Meals and snacks · Children in restaurant and room beside bar · Open 12–2.30, 6–11 all year; closed 25 Dec · Bedrooms tel Cambridge (0223) 207243; £15 (£18B)/£27B

BARRINGTON (Cambs)   TL3949   Map 5

Royal Oak

This thatched and timbered fourteenth-century pub faces the attractive and unusually long village green, where you can sit under cocktail parasols in summer. Inside, the rambling rooms, with openings knocked between them, are heavily beamed and timbered and decorated with brass, copper, antlers and harness. The huge central chimney (which has some fine Tudor brickwork above one mantelbeam) has also been knocked through, and is now a sort of connecting lobby. Waitress-served bar food includes sandwiches, soup, ploughman's, toasted steak sandwich, omelettes, salads, beef curry, chicken, steak and kidney pie, and eight-ounce steaks; well kept Adnams and Greene King IPA and Abbot on handpump; fruit machine and piped music. There is a separate restaurant. *(Recommended by Howard Gascoyne, Charlie Salt; more reports please)*

Free house · Licensee Robert Nicholls · Real ale · Meals and snacks · Open 11.30–2.30, 6.30–11 all year

BIDDENHAM (Beds)   TL0249   Map 5

Three Tuns

57 Main Road; village signposted from A428 just W of Bedford

This attractive and friendly pub is under new tenancy – early reports suggest that all is going well, and that the lively public bar hasn't changed: you're still quite likely to find a vigorous game of table skittles in progress, as well as darts, dominoes, a fruit machine and space game. The food, too, remains good, with 27 different dishes on the menu including sandwiches (from 60p, double-deckers 80p), home-made soup (65p), curried eggs or pâté (£1), ploughman's with a choice of Cheddar, Lymeswold, ham, smoked mackerel or sausage (£1), hamburgers (from £2), salads (£2) and various hot dishes such as quiche, lasagne or chilli con carne (£2) and home-made duck, apricot and walnut pie or steak and kidney pie (£2.20); there is a children's menu, both for food (from 60p) and fruit cocktails (from 35p). Well kept Greene King IPA and Abbot on handpump. The comfortable lounge has a little jungle of pot plants in its stone fireplace and country paintings on the walls. The big garden is good for families. (Recommended by Dr M V Jones, Peter Wright; more reports please)

Greene King · Licensees Alan and Tina Wilkins · Real ale · Meals and snacks (not Sun) · Children in eating area · Open 11.30–2.30, 6–11 all year

CAMBRIDGE   TL45 Map 5

The attractions of this city are too well known to repeat here, but you will certainly need a street map (free from tourist offices) to find these pubs and the many alternative Lucky Dips suggested at the end of this chapter.

Cambridge Arms

King Street

The spacious and comfortable back lounge bar is a fairly recent conversion of what until 1925 was the Scales Brewery (another of our entries here, the Fort St George, was one of its handful of local pubs). Big windows show tables out in a neat and sheltered brick-floored yard, and an expanse of plummy carpet winds through arches of bare brick and up and down steps: you can look up through what used to be the opening housing the great mash tun to the old brewing floor. The menu is split into sections – starters (which can be treated as a light snack) such as home-made soup (90p), egg mayonnaise (£1.25), two sorts of pâté (£1.60) and avocado with prawns (£1.80); hot main meals cooked to order from trout in almonds (£2.75), escalope of chicken cooked in cider (£3.45) and steak chasseur (£4.50); cold buffet dishes like home-made quiche (£1.95) to topside of beef (£3); hot and tasty curries, chillies or goulash (£2) and specialities like daily specials (£1.50), savoury stuffed pancakes (£1.75) and moules marinière (£1.90); also sandwiches (to order) and ploughman's (£1.75). Well kept Greene King IPA and Abbot on handpump; piped music. The friendly and simple public bar has bar billiards, darts, shove-ha'penny, cribbage and a fruit machine. (Recommended by T Mansell, David Symes, Howard Gascoyne)

Greene King · Real ale · Meals and snacks · Children in eating area of bar · Jazz Sun, Mon and Tues · Open 10.30–2.30, 6–11 all year

In next year's edition, as well as star ratings we hope to use a special rating to show pubs that either have specially good food or are specially nice to stay at. Please tell us if you think any pub – in the *Guide* or not – deserves one of these 'Food Awards' or 'Stay Awards'. No stamp needed: *The Good Pub Guide*, FREEPOST, London SW10 0BR.

Eagle

Bene't Street

The main bar of this sixteenth-century inn has a high, dark red ceiling that has been left unpainted since the Second World War to preserve the signatures of British and American airmen worked in with 'Zippo' lighters, candle smoke and lipstick. The smaller smoke room has more old-fashioned sturdy furniture, and there is a separate family room set with tables for eating. Bar food includes a choice of ploughman's (£1.60–£1.80), good value salads (£1.60–£2.25), and a choice of hot daily specials such as pork creole (£2.10), minted lamb casserole, or beef in strong Suffolk ale (£2.25); traditional Sunday lunch is £2.35. Well kept Greene King Abbot, IPA and XX Mild on handpump. A summer attraction is the cobbled and galleried coachyard, hidden behind a sturdy gate, with heavy wooden seats and tables. *(Recommended by T Mansell, Paul West, Stephen Brough, Howard Gascoyne)*

Greene King · Licensee John A Wiseman · Real ale · Meals and snacks (not Sun evening) · Children in family room · No car park nearby, but not far from Lion Yard multi-storey car park · Open 11–2.30, 6–11 all year

Fort St George

Midsummer Common, off Victoria Avenue: to park, turn down Ferry Path (actually a road) from Chesterton Road, and cross footbridge by junction of Pretoria Road and Aylestone Road

The original core of this Tudor pub is cosy and interesting, with high-backed settles, log fires and pewter hanging from the beams, and an airily attractive partly no-smoking extension, furnished to match, overlooks the river (as does an outside terrace). Home-made food includes pasties and Scotch eggs, Brie or Stilton served with granary bread, vegetarian dishes such as cauliflower cheese, and steak and kidney pie; well kept Greene King IPA and Abbot on handpump, and welcoming service. The public bar, decorated with oars and rowing photographs, has a juke box, space game, fruit machine and ring the bull. *(Recommended by Paul West, Susie Boulton)*

Greene King · Licensees Alan and Helen Winfield-Chislett · Real ale · Meals and snacks · Children in eating area only · Open 11–2.30, 6–11 all year

Free Press

Prospect Row

Though many pubs in Cambridge sport oars and rowing photographs, this has the perfect right to them, as it's the only one here – or indeed anywhere – which is registered as a boat club. This unspoilt local, well off the tourist track, used to be the city's smallest pub, and has managed to stay snug and friendly even after being extended into the house next door – and even when it's crowded. Though the licensees have just taken over a second pub in the town (see the Cambridge Blue in the Lucky Dip at the end of this chapter), the atmosphere here seems unchanged. Popular bar food includes soup (60p), cold dishes with three salads such as cheese (£1.10–£1.65), pâté (£1.20–£1.35), Scotch egg or quiche (£1.70), meat pies (£1.70–£2.20), smoked ham (£2.10) and smoked mackerel (£2.25); hot dishes such as Cornish pasties (£1.75), African pork, chicken à la king or moussaka (£1.85), and vegetarian curry (£2). Well kept Greene King IPA and Abbot on handpump; dominoes and cribbage. One room is served from a hatch, and furnishings are traditional throughout. *(Recommended by T Mansell, Brian Williams, Gwen and Peter Andrews, Howard Gascoyne, Paul West, David Symes, Susie Boulton)*

Greene King · Licensee Christopher Lloyd · Real ale · Meals and snacks (lunchtime only) · Children in snug · Open 12–2.30, 6–11.30

Salisbury Arms

Tenison Road

The reputation of this pub as a place for serious beer drinkers, with a dozen or so different real ales on sale at a time, still attracts crowds of customers to the large high-ceilinged back lounge. You can usually find a seat in the calmer side areas, which are decorated with reproductions of old posters relating to beers and brewing, and the much smaller front bar is sometimes a haven of relative quiet. Bar food includes ploughman's with granary bread and a choice of cheeses or pâté, a hot dish such as chilli con carne, and a cold table; darts, dominoes, ring the bull, a pin-table and fruit machine; they also keep farmhouse cider. *(Recommended by T Mansell, Susie Boulton, Paul West, Brian Williams, Gwen and Peter Andrews, Howard Gascoyne, David Symes)*

Free house · Real ale · Snacks (lunchtime) · Open 11–2.30, 6–11 all year

CASTOR (Cambs)   TL1298   Map 5

Royal Oak

24 Peterborough Road (A47, north side)

This thatched eighteenth-century listed building, with a friendly and unspoilt atmosphere, is often quiet and very relaxed during the week, but can get crowded at weekends – partly for the evening meals, which local readers particularly like. There are three cosy carpeted rooms, with antique chests (one used as a piano stool), low and gnarled rustic tables, soft brocaded seats, a collection of soup ladles and rose-covered plates, black beams in dark red or shiny wooden ceilings, open fires in winter, an earnest cribbage school, and well kept Ind Coope Bitter and Burton on handpump. *(Recommended by Derek Gibson, T Mansell; more reports please)*

Ind Coope · Real ale · Meals and snacks · Open 10.30–2.30, 6.30–11 all year

CLAYHITHE   TL5064   Map 5

Bridge Hotel

The pretty gardens of this white riverside hotel make it a popular place in summer, with a lazy view of the boats and the humpy bridge.

The generous log fire makes the bar attractive in winter too; there are original beams in its high yellowing ceiling, some timbering, one or two easy chairs as well as Windsor armchairs on the carpeted floor, and a serving counter built of old wooden doors. The staff are friendly and attentive. The food includes a popular cold buffet with various meats and quiches (£3) as well as ploughman's or pâté, home-made steak and kidney pie, plaice, gammon and sirloin steak; well kept Everards Tiger on handpump; maybe piped music. A restaurant with picture windows overlooks the river. The bedrooms are in a modern motel-style extension. (*Recommended by Howard Gascoyne, Gwen and Peter Andrews; more reports please*)

Free house · Real ale · Meals and snacks (lunchtime) · Open 11–2.30, 6–11 all year · Bedrooms tel Cambridge (0223) 860252; £20 (£24B)/£30 (£36B)

DULLINGHAM (Cambs)   TL6357 Map 5
Kings Head

50 Station Road

The very popular and freshly made bar food here includes sandwiches (65p–95p), ploughman's (£1.15), various omelettes such as prawn and mushroom (£1.99), grilled ham bake or chicken (£1.95), poached chickens' livers with orange and thyme (£2.28), scampi (£2.35) and schnitzel (£3.50); they also do daily specials such as lasagne, chilli con carne, fresh plaice or shepherd's pie (£1.75–£1.95), a vegetarian dish such as tagliatelle (£1.95) and a slimmer's menu (salad niçoise £1.95); the chips are good, and puddings include waffles with maple syrup and ice-cream. Friendly and courteous staff; well kept Tolly Bitter and Original on handpump. There is a relaxed old-fashioned atmosphere in the two connecting carpeted rooms (except when Newmarket racegoers crowd in) with small buttonback leatherette bucket seats, hunting prints, Windsor chairs, some more private booths around sturdy wooden tables, and a coal fire at each end in winter. There's also a separate restaurant, and a family/function room called the Loose Box. There are sheltered seats under fairy lights on grass above the car park and on a terrace overlooking the big sloping village green; also swings. (*Recommended by Frank W Gadbois, Mr and Mrs J Wilmore, W T Aird, D B Hughes, B R Woodcraft*)

Tolly · Licensee Erich Kettenacker · Real ale · Meals and snacks · Children in eating area, restaurant and Loose Box · Open 10.30–2.30, 6–11 all year

ELSWORTH (Cambs)   TL3163 Map 5
George & Dragon

On road out to Boxworth

Elegant cane chairs around tables in a back area by the garden make this a pleasant place to eat: the food includes home-made soup (85p), open French bread sandwiches (from £1), home-made pâté (£1.25), omelettes (£2.20), lasagne or moussaka (£2.60), a variety of chicken dishes – curried, Mexican or fricassée (£2.75) – trout or fried clams (£2.95), salads (from £2.50, home-cooked ham £2.95), steak and kidney pie (£2.95) and steaks (from £5.25), with several extra dishes of the day such as prawns in garlic butter and poached salmon. There is also a separate restaurant. The panelled main bar has winged high-backed settles, roomy old chairs and cast-iron-framed tables, and is decorated with earthenware jugs, copper, and a large pike above the winter log fire. Tolly and Original on handpump; a good range of spirits and cocktails, including non-alcoholic ones (a fruit juice dispenser does generous measures); darts, piped music. There are attractive terraces, and swings, a slide and so forth in the back garden. (*Recommended by Susie Boulton; more reports please*)

Tolly Cobbold · Licensees Malcolm and Sheilah Brownlie · Real ale · Meals and snacks · Children in garden room and restaurant · Open 10.30–2.30, 7–11 all year

ELTISLEY (Cambs)   TL2659   Map 5
Leeds Arms   [*illustrated on page 77*]
The Green; village signposted off A45

The welcoming, beamed lounge bar in this tall white brick house is basically two rooms knocked together, with red corduroy stools and pew-like cushioned wall benches set around a huge winter log fire. A third room down some steps has several tables, and there are more in the simple little separate dining-room. A good range of bar food includes sandwiches (from 85p, crab £1.75), soup (90p), ploughman's (from £1.10), pâté (£1.25), curry or steak and kidney pie (£2.75), scampi (£3) and eight-ounce sirloin steak (£4.95). Greene King IPA on handpump; darts, a fruit machine sensibly set aside in an alcove, dominoes and piped music. There are picnic-table sets, swings and a slide set among the silver birches on the lawn. (*Recommended by Alan Neale, Glyn Edmunds; more reports please*)

Free house · Licensee George Cottrell · Meals and snacks · Children in dining-room · Open 11.30–2.20, 6.30–11.30 all year · Bedrooms tel Croxton (048 087) 283; £20B/£27.50B

FEN DRAYTON (Cambs)   TL3368   Map 5
Three Tuns   [*illustrated on page 66*]

As we went to press new tenants were moving into this ancient pub. However, as people have liked it for the old-fashioned character of its structure and layout, we are provisionally keeping it in as a main entry. It has finely carved heavy ceiling beams, close-set wall timbers, inglenook fireplaces, old farm tools, and some antique chairs and settles among the more modern Windsor chairs. A dining area is separated from the main bar by a heavy velvet curtain. Bar food has included sandwiches, ploughman's, shepherd's pie, lasagne, steaks, and that sort of thing. It's likely that the full range of Greene King beers will continue to be kept under light top pressure; piped music, and sensibly placed darts, dominoes, cribbage, and a fruit machine. There are tables under cocktail parasols on the neat flower-edged lawn behind this partly thatched house, with apple and flowering

If you're interested in real ale, the CAMRA *Good Beer Guide* – no relation to us – lists thousands of pubs where you can get it.

cherry trees. *(Recommended by Mrs I Stickland, M D Hare, D J Fawthrop, Howard Gascoyne, Miss S L Terry; more reports please)*

Greene King · Meals and snacks · Open 11–2.30, 6.30–11 all year; closed 25 Dec

FOWLMERE (Cambs)   TL4245   Map 5

Chequers

B1368

Good bar food in this luxuriously restored old pub includes soups such as chicken and thyme or onion (£1.60) which can be served with garlic bread (50p), pâtés and terrines such as Stilton with walnut, champagne and garlic, rabbit (all £2.40) or duck with a full salad (£3.45), monkfish and stem ginger (£3.40), turkey and ham pancake (£3.60), tacos (£3.50), venison served in interesting ways from sausage to a tasty curried pancake (£4.20), crab au gratin flavoured with whisky (£4.20), and a trolley of excellent puddings (£1.90). Besides Tolly on handpump, there is usually a choice of vintage and late-bottled ports by the glass, and an excellent range of fine brandies and liqueurs. Soft lighting, upholstered wall banquettes and leather stools and chairs contribute to the quiet atmosphere in the two communicating bar rooms. The lower room has prints and photographs of Spitfires and Mustangs flown from Fowlmere aerodrome, and the upper – which has beams and some wall timbering – has some notable moulded plasterwork above the fireplace. If you ask, they will point out to you the priest's hole above the bar. Waitress service extends to the white tables under cocktail parasols among the flowers and shrub roses of the attractive and neatly kept garden. There is also an elegantly beamed and timbered restaurant, candlelit at night, which serves good, imaginative food (main courses around £7.50), and an extensive summer cold table. One of Ivo Vannocci's Poste Hotels. *(Recommended by Barnaby Marder, Dr J H Newton, A Saunders, D A Angless, Susie Boulton)*

Tolly Cobbold · Licensees Norman and Pauline Rushton · Real ale · Meals and snacks · Children welcome · Open 12–2.30, 6–11 all year; closed 25 and 26 Dec

GRANTCHESTER (Cambs)   TL4355   Map 5

Green Man

This small pub, low-beamed and dimly lit, has always been popular for its friendly and restful atmosphere, with snug corners in the narrow rooms that angle around the serving counter, some stripped panelling, and in winter an open fire and a wood-burning stove. But we've recently also had a growing chorus of approval for the freshly made bar food (you can eat in the bar or in a more spacious dining extension). This includes sandwiches (from 95p), mushrooms à la grecque (£1.45), smoked mackerel pâté (£1.75), pieces of duck deep fried in batter and served with sweet-and-sour sauce (£2.25), baked potatoes with various fillings (from £1.45), ploughman's with a choice of cheeses (£2.25), grilled fresh sardines with a tomato, onion and garlic sauce (£2.75), cannelloni (£2.85), deep-fried goujons of plaice (£2.95), kidneys in a red wine sauce (£3.45) and sirloin steak (£6.50). Well kept Tolly and Original on handpump. On the terrace in front of the small tiled white house there are a few tables, with more among wild roses in the narrow garden, from which you can walk down to the river. The quiet village and its setting of riverside meadows is famously beautiful. *(Recommended by Frank Cummins, Prof P M Deane, Susie Boulton, Paul West, Jonquil Lowe)*

Tolly · Licensee Norman Adamson · Real ale · Meals and snacks · Children in dining area · Small car park · Open 11–2.30, 6–11 all year

Red Lion

Behind this big white thatched pub, built just before the Second World War, is a sheltered terrace with picnic-table sets among roses, then more tables on a good-sized stretch of grass under fruit trees. A hutch here has white rabbits, and there are Shetland ponies over the fence: a number of families bring children in summer. Inside, it's comfortable and spacious, with a busy food counter: sandwiches (£1), ploughman's (£2.50), dishes of the day such as lasagne or cannelloni (£2.50–£3), help-yourself salads with cold pies and quiche (£3), scampi, pizza or plaice (£3), hot or cold home-made pies, like ham and mushroom or poacher's (£3.25) and sirloin steak (£5.95). There is also quite a large separate restaurant. Greene King ales under pressure; fruit machine, space game and rather grand piped music. *(Recommended by David Surridge, Jonquil Lowe; more reports please)*

Greene King · Licensees D W Gration and L C Barker · Meals and snacks Children in eating area and restaurant · Open 11–2.30, 6–11 all year

GREAT CHISHILL (Cambs)   TL4238   Map 5
Pheasant

Follow Heydon signpost from B1039 in village

This is an unpretentious and interestingly furnished little pub with a stuffed pheasant on the mantelpiece, a few plates on the timbered walls and some elaborately carved though modern seats and settles. There are dining-chairs around the tables at one end, and bar stools with decent backs. Bar food includes sandwiches (from 65p, smoked salmon £1.50), ploughman's (£1.10), beef casserole (£1.95), prawn salad (£2.95), scampi (£3.30), Dover sole (£6.50) and steaks from local beef (£5.50–£6.15). Well kept Greene King IPA and Tolly Original on handpump; faint piped music. The pretty back garden, on rising ground behind the pub, has stout teak seats among flowering cherries and a weeping willow. There is quiet farmland beyond the back rose hedge. *(More reports please)*

Free house · Licensees Denis and Marshella Ryan · Real ale · Children over 5 in eating area (lunchtime only) · Meals and snacks (not Sun lunchtime, nor Mon) Open 11.30–2.30, 6–11 all year; closed Mon lunchtime

---

We checked prices with the pubs as we went to press in summer 1985. They should hold until around spring 1986, when our experience suggests that you can expect an increase of around 10p in the £.

nr HEXTON (Beds)   TL1030 Map 5

Live & Let Live

Pegsdon; B655 Hitchin—Barton-le-Clay, 1 mile E of Hexton

Sadly, Don and Dot Stott who preserved such a charmingly old-fashioned atmosphere here have just retired. But this pub's special charm – it's position – stays on. It huddles snugly under the Chilterns, with a track leading straight up almost opposite, and has a pretty garden, with tables among fruit trees, roses and other flowers, and at either end an attractive inn-sign making play on the pub's name. Inside, two rooms open off a little red-tiled panelled taproom where the Greene King ales are served. There have been sensibly placed darts, dominoes, cribbage and a fruit machine. *(Recommended by Dennis Royles; up-to-date reports please)*

Greene King · Meals and snacks · Open 11–2.30, 6.30–11 all year

HOLYWELL (Cambs)   TL3370 Map 5

Olde Ferry Boat

Village and pub both signposted (keep your eyes skinned!) off A1123 in Needingworth

Originally, this was a monastic ferry house for the river, and there's been a building here for over 1,000 years – even the ghost is said to be some 900 years old. There is a splendidly old-fashioned atmosphere in the softly lit bar that wanders up and down steps between timbered or panelled walls. There are two open fires – one huge, and one with a fish and an eel among rushes moulded on its chimney-beam. A medley of seats includes red leather settees, river-view window seats and a pretty little carved settle. They buy fresh produce from the big London markets every Friday: bar food includes home-made soup (85p), sandwiches (from 85p), ploughman's (£1.50), home-made pâté (£1.65), omelettes (from £1.95), fruity curried chicken on toast (£1.95), chicken con carne or plaice (both £2.70), home-made steak and kidney pie (£2.85), seafood pancake (£3.20) and steaks (from £6.10). Well kept Bass, Greene King Abbot and IPA, and now Gibbs Mew Wiltshire, on handpump; piped music; also a separate restaurant. There are tables under cocktail parasols on a side rose lawn, and more on a flower-edged front terrace by the wistaria-covered thatched house, which is situated along the edge of the Great Ouse. *(Recommended by Noel Gifford, J H DuBois, Howard Gascoyne, D R Crafts)*

Free house · Licensee Mrs Joyce Edwards · Real ale · Meals and snacks Children in eating areas · Open 11–2.30, 6–11 all year; closed 24 and 31 Dec Bedrooms tel St Ives (0480) 63227; £25B/£35B

HORNINGSEA (Cambs)   TL4962 Map 5

Plough & Fleece ★

The friendly public bar in this small village pub has plain wooden tables including the regulars' favourite, an enormously long slab of elm (with an equally long pew to match it), black beams in the red ceiling, butter-yellow walls, a stuffed parrot on the black fireplace, and high-backed settles and plain seats on the red tiled floor. The popular and home-cooked good food, often using imaginatively recast antique recipes, includes soup (95p), chicken liver pâté (£1.50), devilled crab or smoked mackerel (£1.60), cottage pie (£1.85), omelettes (£2.40), good salads (£2.50), ham hot-pot (£2.75), uncommonly good fish pie (£3.40), steak and kidney pie (£3.70), honey-roast guinea-fowl (£4.50), steaks (£6.25) and beef Wellington (£6.50). In the evenings, when the menu also includes hot garlic cockles (£1.50) and giant prawns (£4.75), these hot dishes all cost about 70p extra, and are served with extra vegetables. At lunchtimes only there are also sandwiches (from 80p, toasties from 95p), ploughman's (£1.40), hot snacks such as sausage and bacon flan (£1.40), home-cooked ham and egg (£2.10), and omelettes (£2.40). Good puddings include Norfolk treacle tart or ginger and brandy ice-cream (£1.15) and a potent chocolate pudding (£1.25). There is a comfortable lounge. Well kept Greene King IPA, Abbot and Mild on handpump; dominoes and cribbage. There are picnic-table sets (with table service) beyond the car park, and beyond a herbaceous border is a children's play area with a rope ladder climbing into an old pear tree. *(Recommended by Noel Gifford, Paul West, Nick Alexander, Susie Boulton)*

Greene King · Licensees Mr and Mrs Kenneth Grimes · Real ale · Meals and snacks (snacks only Sun lunchtime, not Mon evening) · Open 11.30–2.30, 7–11 all year

HOUGHTON (Cambs)   TL2872 Map 5
Three Horseshoes

In the friendly snug bar of this steeply tiled old pub, the big inglenook makes for a warm atmosphere even when RAF Wyton aren't crowding

The Leeds Arms, Eltisley

under its low black beams. There's also a spacious lounge – since our last edition refurbished, and extended with an additional bar – which has French windows opening on to the sunny terrace. There are seats out here and in the sheltered garden (which has a children's play area). Bar food includes sandwiches, a cold buffet at lunchtime, with a help-yourself salad bar (£2.95), home-made specials such as steak and kidney pie (£2.95) and rump steak (£4.95); the details below show when food should normally be available (one reader found he couldn't actually get bar snacks on a Saturday). Well kept Manns IPA and Watneys Stag on handpump; sensibly placed darts, shove-ha'penny, fruit machine and piped music. Houghton Mill, a restored National Trust watermill, is nearby. *(Recommended by Howard Gascoyne; more reports please)*

Manns (Watneys) · Licensee Malcolm Holmes · Real ale · Meals and snacks (not Sun evening) · Open 11–2.30, 6–11 all year

HUNTINGDON (Cambs)   TL2371 Map 5
George

The elegant and spacious Georgian lounge bar of this handsome inn is popular at lunchtime for its food, which includes sandwiches (from 65p, prawns £1.50; double deckers from 95p), soup (90p), ploughman's with cheese or pâté (£1.80, also served in the evenings), quiche (£2.10), prawns with a tangy dip (£2.50), a daily casserole (£2.75), and a good cold table (£3.05); in the evenings, crêpe with meat sauce (£2.50), or seafood (£2.95), lasagne (£2.95), pork kebab (£3.25) and scampi (£3.75); also a separate restaurant. Greene King IPA and Abbot are kept under light top pressure. During the last fortnight or so of June a Shakespeare play is performed in the appropriate period setting of the galleried central inn yard here (you can book a bedroom to overlook the stage). *(More reports please)*

Free house (THF) · Meals and snacks · Children welcome · Open 10–2.30, 6–11 all year · Bedrooms tel Huntingdon (0480) 53096; £34B/£42B

KEYSOE (Beds)   TL0762 Map 5
Chequers

B660

An unusual stone-pillared log fireplace divides the two beamed and carpeted rooms in this modernised and comfortable village pub, but the chief attraction here is the good home-made food. This includes sandwiches (75p) and a range of hot dishes such as plaice (£1.90), chilli con carne (£1.95), omelettes and lasagne (£2), steak pie (£2.95), trout (£3.95) and steaks (£5.95), good puddings (£1), and children's dishes such as fish fingers. Well kept Adnams, Badger Best, Tanglefoot and Wethereds are served from handpumps on the stone bar counter; darts, a fruit machine, space game and piped music. A big dining area at the back is sometimes used for functions. There are tables outside on the small front lawn among flowers, and more on

---

Pubs shown as closing at 11 do so in the summer but close earlier – normally 10.30 – in winter unless we specify 'all year'.

the grass around the car park behind; since last year, a fairy-tale play tree has been added to the other swings and slides. *(Recommended by Paul West, K J Staples, R J Bates; more reports please)*

Free house · Licensee Jeffrey Kearns · Real ale · Meals and snacks · Children welcome · Open 11–2.30, 6.30–11 all year

KEYSTON (Cambs) TL0475 Map 5
Pheasant
Village loop road

Recent reports have been going overboard about the food in this comfortably modernised old village pub – now among the best in the county: sandwiches, soup with croûtons (95p), pâté (£1.45), fried squid with garlic rolls (£2.25), home-made lasagne (£2.85), home-made steak pies or swordfish steaks (both £3.25), créole Jambalaya (£3.45), sweet-and-sour chicken, beef curry, or turkey and mushroom pie (£3.65), shark steak (£3.85), grilled trout (£3.95) and lemon sole (£4.20). In season local pheasant is used in pâtés and casseroles. There is also a separate restaurant, with a good choice of dishes in the set-price meals (£9.75). A room leading off the comfortable and low-beamed main bar was once the village smithy, and has high rafters hung with heavy-horse harness and an old horse-drawn harrow. It's furnished with leather slung stools and a heavily carved wooden armchair among the Windsor chairs. Ruddles Bitter and County and Tolly on handpump; table skittles. The tables under cocktail parasols in front of this attractive thatched white house are laid with tablecloths – a pleasant, quiet spot. One of Ivo Vannocci's Poste Hotels. *(Recommended by J M M Hill, Rita Horridge, R J Bates and others)*

Free house · Licensee Steven Klamer · Meals and snacks · Children welcome Open 10.30–2.30, 6–11 all year

LEIGHTON BROMSWOLD (Cambs)   TL1175 Map 5
Green Man

The more or less open-plan sitting areas of this mossy-tiled village pub have been neatly modernised, though they still ramble about through the various low and heavy beams, festooned with hundreds of good horse brasses. Bar food at lunchtime includes sandwiches and ploughman's, home-made cream of leek soup (85p), smoked mackerel (£1.20), quiche with salad or sausage with onion rings (both £1.95), home-made pies (£2.75), scampi (£2.85), cold roast pork (£3.20) and lamb chop with garlic butter and piquant stuffing (£4.20); the evening menu has, in addition, open prawn sandwiches (£2.85), lemon sole Mornay (£4.20), chicken provençale (£4.50) and several steaks (from £6.50), and old-fashioned English puddings like rhubarb crumble and bread-and-butter pudding (90p). There are modern Windsor chairs among older seats and settles (not to mention a grand piano), and sensibly segregated space has been found for darts, pool, table skittles, a fruit machine and space game; there is also shove-ha'penny and dominoes. Well kept Tolly Original on handpump, maybe piped music. *(Recommended by J M Haddon; more reports please)*

Free house · Licensee Moira Macdonald · Real ale · Meals and snacks (not Sun evening) · Children in eating area · Piano Fri and Sat · Open 11–2.30, 6.30–11 all year

MADINGLEY (Cambs) TL3960 Map 5

Three Horseshoes

In summer an excellent refrigerated cold buffet brings droves of people from Cambridge to this neat and well run thatched white pub, and the smart canopied terrace restaurant overlooking the attractive garden is very popular then. The cold buffet includes cold meats, pâté, trout, prawns, crab and salmon (£3–£7); other bar food includes home-made soup (£1.35), deep-fried ploughman's (£3.50), home-made pies (£3.95), lasagne (£4.15) and steaks (£6.15); Tolly and Original on handpump. There are tables on the lawn, which is ringed by roses, flowering shrubs and trees. *(Recommended by Paul West, D A Haines, Susie Boulton; more reports please)*

Free house · Licensee Ivo Vannocci · Real ale · Meals and snacks · Children in eating area · Open 11–2.30, 6–11 all year

nr NEEDINGWORTH (Cambs)   TL3472 Map 5

Pike & Eel

Overcote Lane; pub signposted from A1123 in Needingworth

A couple of beamy older-fashioned small parlours leading off the more modern and spacious main bar date back some 350 years to the time when there was an important chain ferry here (and there had been some sort of an inn here for a good couple of hundred years before that). The big terrace is both peaceful and pretty, with baskets of flowers hanging from its Perspex roof, and honeysuckle covering the sturdy pillars; spacious lawns stretch down to the inn's own marina on a very quiet stretch of the Great Ouse, making this a charming place in summer. Inside, it's friendly and neat, with corduroy easy chairs and red plush upright seats around well spaced copper-topped tables in the main open-plan bar area, and gentle piped music. Bar food includes soup, whitebait, cod, plaice, steak and kidney pie, toasted steak sandwiches, gammon and salads, with specials such as grilled sea-trout in season (from £2.50–£3.50); also a separate restaurant. Well kept Adnams, Bass, Greene King Abbot and IPA on handpump; several malt whiskies too. A peaceful place to stay. *(Recommended by Noel Gifford, Gwen and Peter Andrews, G H Theaker, Howard Gascoyne)*

Free house · Real ale · Meals and snacks · Children in area set aside for them Organ and piano in restaurant Saturday nights · Open 10.30–2.30, 6–11 all year; closed evening 25 Dec · Bedrooms tel Huntingdon (0480) 63336; £20 (£24B)/£28 (£32B)

Sunday opening in Wales is 12–2 and 7–10.30; but pubs in Ceredigion (Cardigan to the mouth of the Dovey) and the Lleyn Peninsula are not allowed to open at all on that day.

NEWTON (Cambs) TL4349 Map 5

Queens Head

2½ miles from M11 junction 11; A10 towards Royston, then left on to B1368

This pretty brick village house, with its strikingly tall chimney, is decidedly simple and traditional inside: bare wooden benches and high settles built in to the walls and bow windows of the main bar, rugs on its yellow tiled floor, a loudly ticking clock and paintings on its cream walls. The little carpeted saloon is broadly similar but more cosy. Bar food is unpretentious, too: soup (75p), a good choice of freshly cut sandwiches (from 60p) including banana, jacket potatoes filled with buttered cheese (75p), and plates of farmhouse Cheddar, Brie, Stilton or pâté (£1.25), ham (£1.60) and beef or smoked salmon (£1.80) with granary bread and butter, tomato and cucumber. Adnams tapped from the cask, with Old ale in winter; darts in a side room, with shove-ha'penny, table skittles, dominoes, cribbage, nine men's morris and a fruit machine. *(Recommended by G S Crockett, Gordon Hewitt, Susie Boulton)*

Free house · Licensee David Short · Real ale · Snacks (lunchtime only)
Children in darts room · Open 11.30–2.30, 6–11 all year; closed 25 Dec

OLD WESTON (Cambs) TL0977 Map 5

Swan

B660

The highly praised food in this neatly kept old pub has taken two new directions – *nouvelle cuisine* and a move into a new dining-room (where the good value, three-course Sunday lunch is now served: £5.75). Bar snacks include sandwiches (from 65p), baked potatoes (55p–75p), Normandy onion soup (£1.10), various ploughman's (from £1.25), home-made pâté (£1.30), moules marinière (£2 when available), quiche (£2), salads (from £2.25), seafood platter (£2.40), escalope of veal (£2.80) and steak (£3.85). The comfortable low-ceilinged main lounge has elegant balustrading above the curved button-back banquette, and interesting horse brasses on the chimney-beam of its big stone inglenook fireplace. Well kept Adnams, Greene King Abbot and Marstons Pedigree on handpump. *(Recommended by J M M Hill, Rita Horridge, R Ongley, FB)*

Free house · Licensees Albert and Gary Oliver · Real ale · Meals and snacks
Children in eating areas · Open 11.30–2.30, 6.30–11 all year; closed evening 25 Dec

RIDGMONT (Beds) SP9736 Map 4

Rose and Crown

2½ miles from M1 junction 13: towards Woburn Sands, then left towards Ampthill on A418; in High Street

Readers are fond of this pretty roadside pub for its good food and warm, welcoming atmosphere. The low-ceilinged public bar has well cushioned settles below the harness on its walls, and maybe a couple of dogs in front of the open fire; there's also a smartly decorated lounge bar. Bar food includes sandwiches (from 60p, home-cooked beef or ham 80p, open steak sandwich (£2.15), ploughman's with Cheddar or Stilton (£1.25), beef or ham (£1.50), home-cooked pies such as steak and kidney, chicken and mushroom or poacher's (£1.95), seafood platter or scampi (£2.50) and steaks (from £4.50). There is a separate restaurant. Well kept Charles Wells Eagle and Bombardier on handpump; darts, pool, shove-ha'penny, dominoes, cribbage, fruit machine, space game and piped music. The old stables have a children's room which is open in summer and at weekends in winter. There is an attractive back garden, which has rabbits and a nude statue as well as flowers and shrubs. You can also sit in front of the old brick house, which has pretty hanging baskets. (Recommended by H P Gregory, Brian Clemens; more reports please)

Charles Wells · Licensee Neil McGregor · Real ale · Meals and snacks Children in eating area of bar and sometimes stable room · Open 10–2.30, 6–11 all year

nr SANDY (Beds)   TL1749   Map 5
Locomotive
Deepdale; B1042 towards Potton and Cambridge

This friendly and relaxed pub is particularly handy for people visiting the nearby RSPB headquarters and bird reserve. The smallish lounge has a big log fire, open on two sides, and has pewter and plates with the pictures above its cushioned wall banquettes. Good value bar food includes home-made soup (60p), sandwiches (75p), pâté (80p–95p), ploughman's with a choice of Cheddar, Stilton or Brie (95p), pizza (£1), smoked mackerel or grilled trout (£1.25), scampi or fisherman's platter (£2) and salads (from £2, dressed crab £2.50); several 'specials' such as pork steak in 'Locamotive' sauce, beef Stroganoff, roast pheasant in sherry sauce, and steaks (£5.75 including vegetables). A small dining area with an à la carte menu is shortly to be built. Well kept Charles Wells Eagle and Bombardier on handpump; piped music. There are Emett locomotive cartoons, and another open fire in the public bar, with sensibly placed darts, dominoes, cribbage and a fruit machine. Behind the pub, a spacious and attractive garden, floodlit at night, in summer has a big barbecue and outdoor drinks servery. (Recommended by Michael Sandy; more reports please)

Charles Wells · Licensee Clive Billings · Real ale · Meals (not Mon evening or Sun) and snacks (not Sun or Mon evenings) · Children in eating area · Open 12–2.30, 6–11 all year

SOUTHILL (Beds)   TL1542   Map 5
White Horse

As the pub is more or less alone in quiet countryside, and handy for the Shuttleworth Collection of old cars and early aeroplanes, it's an obvious possibility for family outings; even more so since the extended garden includes a garden shop, a children's games and play area, and, most importantly, a 7½-inch gauge railway with both steam and diesel engines. Children's rides are 20p, and steam enthusiasts are encouraged to bring their own locomotives. Inside, it's well run and comfortable, with country prints on the cream walls of the main lounge, which is popular for food: filled rolls and sandwiches (from 65p), quiche (£1.30), burgers (£1.45), basket meals such as cod (£1.60) and scampi (£2.50) and a Sunday roast lunch (£5.25). There is a separate restaurant. There are plain seats and settles in front of a big log fire in the smaller public bar, and pictures of vintage aeroplanes among the harness on the terracotta-coloured walls. Wethereds and Whitbreads Castle Eden on handpump, kept under light blanket pressure; darts, dominoes, cribbage, fruit machine and piped music.

Whitbreads · Licensees E M and M J Herbert · Meals and snacks (not Sun evening) · Children welcome (not public bar) · Open 11–2.30, 6–11 all year

STUDHAM (Beds)   TL0215   Map 5
Red Lion

Over the last year or so this pub has had its ups and downs, with management changes and so forth: we hope things will be settling down now under new licensees. In any event, this old tiled house is worth knowing about for its position. Sitting under the fruit trees on the sheltered side lawn, or in front of the house, you look up to a grassy common: Whipsnade Zoo is just a couple of miles away. The airy open-plan bar has Windsor chairs, plush wall banquettes, and flagstones in front of its reconstructed inglenook fireplace. Food includes home-made soup (70p), sandwiches (75p–£1.20 for beef), ploughman's (£1.50–£1.60), dishes of the day, such as lasagne (£1.95–£2.50), steak and kidney pie (£2.50) and scampi (£2.75). Well kept Adnams, Charringtons IPA, Marstons and Sam Smiths on handpump; dominoes, sensibly placed darts, fruit machine and space game. *(Recommended by Miss H R Morgan, Tim and Ann Bracey, Jonathan Rowe; more reports please)*

Free house · Real ale · Meals and snacks · Open 11–2.30, 6–10.30

SUTTON (Beds)   TL2247   Map 5
John o' Gaunt

This pink-washed tiled pub is just past a hump-backed fourteenth-century packhorse bridge (you drive through a shallow ford). The cosy lounge bar has Windsor chairs around copper-topped tables, low settles, and stuffed pheasants and pictures of birds of prey under the low beams. Good value bar food includes plain or toasted sandwiches (from 50p, smoked salmon £1.35), ploughman's (from 85p), chilli con carne or curry (£1.60), trout with sauté potatoes and salad (£1.80), gammon or king prawns in garlic butter (£2.95) and rump steak (£4.70); the Scandinavian meat and fish buffet – an innovation of the landlord's Finnish wife – is worth trying (£2.60). Well kept Greene King IPA on handpump. The public bar has sensibly placed darts, bar billiards, shove-ha'penny, dominoes, cribbage, a fruit machine and juke box. There is a large, well sheltered garden with picnic-table sets; swings for children are set well off the road. *(Recommended by D A Angless, MHG and others; more reports please)*

Greene King · Licensee L E Ivall · Meals and snacks (lunchtime only, not Sun) Children in eating area · Open 11.30–2.30, 7–11 all year

SWAVESEY (Cambs)   TL3668   Map 5
Trinity Foot

A604, N side; to reach it from the westbound carriageway, take Swavesey, Fen Drayton turnoff

This friendly and bustling place is a popular trunk road stop-off for family meals, quickly serving a wide choice of food that includes sandwiches (from 50p), ploughman's or pâté (£1.50), plain or curried chicken (£2.75), lamb cutlets (£3.25), mixed grill (£4) and daily specials which on our visit included oysters (£4 the half-dozen) as well as steak and kidney pie (£3). Well kept Wethereds and Flowers Original; a good big lawn, with a few flowers and roses and a belt of tall trees. Though the pub actually dates mainly from 1957, it is named after the foot-followers of Trinity College's beagles, which hunted here from the 1880s. *(Recommended by S V Bishop, B R Woodcraft)*

Whitbreads · Licensee Herbert John Mole · Real ale · Meals and snacks (not Sun evening) · Children in eating area · Open 10.30–2.30, 6.30–11 all year

TEMPSFORD (Beds)   TL1652   Map 5
Anchor

A1

The pub makes a welcome break from the Great North Road, with its spacious sheltered garden alongside the River Ouse. Children are well catered for, with free magic and puppet shows on Sunday evenings (at 7.45, from mid-May to early September), a children's room, and a large adventure playground. Inside, the long bar has quite a modern feel, though there are beams, flagstones, bare brick, and a big free-standing stove to go with the button-back banquettes and the high-ceilinged Scandinavian-style end section, which has tall curved windows looking out on the garden. Bar food includes sandwiches, salads, three 'specials', usually a pasta dish and steaks; Ushers Founders, Wilsons and Trumans kept on handpump; piped music, dominoes, fruit machine, space game and table football. There is a carvery restaurant (children's helpings available). Outdoor chess or draughts, pétanque and fishing. *(More reports please)*

Watneys · Licensees Roger and Cherry Wells · Real ale · Meals and snacks Children in area set aside for them · Open 10.30–2.30, 5.30–11 all year

TURVEY (Beds)   SP9452   Map 4
Three Fyshes

A428 NW of Bedford; pub at W end of village

This cheerfully old-fashioned pub has a good range of real ales on handpump: Adnams, Bass, Marstons Pedigree and Owd Rodger, guest beers and now Three Fyshes Bitter brewed for the pub (also Bland's or another farm cider). Food includes French onion soup (70p), giant crusty rolls (from 75p; £1.90 for a 'dynamic'), a good choice of ploughman's (£1.85–£2.20), lasagne or quiche (£2.25), fisherman's platter, scampi or chilli con carne (all £2.50), trout (£3.50) and steaks (£5.25). The heavy-beamed main bar has a stone inglenook fireplace, a big window seat and quite an assortment of other seats around the close-set tables on its carpet-and-flagstone floor, and is linked by a charming squint-walled stone corridor (which has a fruit machine) to the cosy flagstoned public bar. This room has another big inglenook, and sensibly placed darts, table skittles and dominoes; piped music. There is a garden room by the small back garden, close to the River Ouse, which now has summer barbecues. (Recommended by Roger Danes; more reports please)

Free house · Licensee Charles Wincott · Real ale · Meals and snacks · Children welcome · Open 11.30–2.30, 5.30–11 all year

UFFORD (Cambs)   TF0904 Map 5
Olde White Hart

The home-made steak and kidney pie here (£2.95) won this attractive old village inn a place in the finals of the 1985 Pub Steak and Kidney competition, sponsored by the trade magazine Pub Caterer. Other dishes from a separate food counter include home-made soup (95p), home-made quiche (£1.85), barbecued spare ribs (£2.50), chicken royal (£3.50) and pork and apricot tiffin (£3.50). The neatly furnished lounge bar has wheelback chairs around dark tripod tables, a grandfather clock in an alcove by the stone chimney which divides the room into two, and pewter tankards hanging from the beam over the bar counter. The simple public bar is popular with locals; darts, shove-ha'penny, dominoes and cribbage; friendly staff. There's a sunny terrace and pretty garden, and the surroundings – the pub is half way up the only hill for miles – are pleasant. (Recommended by Steve Coley, Derek Gibson; more reports please)

Home · Licensee Nigel Adams · Real ale · Meals (not Sat, Sun or Mon) and snacks (not Sat, Sun or Mon evenings) · Open 10.30–2.30, 6–11 all year

WANSFORD (Cambs)   TL0799 Map 5
Haycock ★

Heading N on A1, follow village signposts; from other directions follow Elton signpost from village centre

This imposing seventeenth-century inn manages to combine a civilised yet wholly relaxed atmosphere with friendly and welcoming service. Beyond the flagstoned entry hall is the main bar, opening on one side to a lively panelled room overlooking a cobbled courtyard surrounded by steeply tiled golden stone buildings, and on the other to a quieter lounge with wallpaper to match the flowery curtains, plush easy chairs and steeplechasing prints. Though you can eat here, it's another lounge, overlooking the attractive and spacious formal garden, which has the buffet table. This, spick and span with gleaming copper on clean white linen, has a delicious range of cold meats and salads (£3.65 for home-made turkey and pork pie, £5.65 for poached salmon and £7.50 for a half crawfish). Other waitress-served home-made food includes sandwiches to order, soup (£1.50), good chicken liver pâté (£2.75), seafood pancake, lasagne or crab puff with a cheese and wine sauce (all £3.45), vegetarian vegetable pie (£3.65), slices of sauté pork in a spicy tomato sauce or prawns and mushrooms cooked in a creamy curry sauce (both £3.95), and a cheese fondue for two (£7.50); also home-made puddings (£1.85). Weather permitting, there is a barbecue with beefy sausages (£4.95), a minute steak (£5.50) or a mixture (£6.95). Well kept Adnams, Bass and Ruddles County on handpump, with a good range of other drinks extending to mature vintage ports by the glass. The well run restaurant has good food (and civilised breakfasts). The walled garden opens on to the inn's own cricket field by the Nene; it also has pétanque and fishing. One of Ivo Vannocci's Poste Hotels; a nice place to stay. (*Recommended by David Perrott, Rachel Waterhouse, Mrs R Horridge, Tony Gayfer, Dr H B Cardwell, C P Price, W T Aird*)

Tolly Cobbold · Licensee Richard Neale · Real ale · Meals and snacks Children welcome · Open 10.30–2.30, 6–11 all year; closed evenings 24 and 25 Dec · Bedrooms tel Stamford (0780) 782223; £28 (£39.50B)/ £42.50 (£52B)

WHITTLESFORD (Cambs) TL4748 Map 5
Tickell Arms ★

1 mile from M11 junction 10; village signposted from A505 towards Newmarket; no pub sign – look for a vividly blue rose-covered house with a big gravel drive on W side of road

As we said in the last edition, the highly idiosyncratic character of this pub is so overwhelmingly strong that – while it charms many people, decidedly including us – it is bound to produce some very negative reactions, and some readers' reports indicate a feeling that some of that energy might be better diverted into practical matters of housekeeping. The Tickell Arms is so different from other pubs, though, that we think it would be a great shame to miss experiencing it. Perhaps a general rule might be: go if you like Wagner but think twice if you reckon opera is over-rated (let alone worry about value for money in the Dress Circle Bar). It is unique, as much for the larger-than-life personality of its vivid owner as for its theatrical décor and atmosphere. He tells us that he won't serve people in T-shirts, collarless shirts, or with jacketless braces or waistcoats, men in earrings or 'long-haired lefties'. The main room (no smoking) is shadowy and Gothick, with good solid furniture, candlelit alcoves, dark blue walls and well reproduced loud opera or ballet music. A big conservatory with pews on its flagstone floor opens on to a very neat garden with flower-filled stone urns and a long formal lily-pool with a fountain. From quite a wide choice of food we'd recommend the unusual locally smoked meats such as quail or pike (£1.95–£2.85), cheese or pâté with good bread, and game casseroles and pies (£4.45).

There is good punch, and mulled wine in winter (they also have Adnams and Greene King Abbot on handpump). *(Recommended by M M Lindley, Gordon Hewitt, Peter Hitchcock, Mrs R Horridge, Stuart Barker, A Saunders, Susie Boulton, Ianthe Brownrigg)*

Free house · Licensees J H de la T Tickell and Siegfried Fischer · Real ale Meals and snacks · Children over 12 years old · Open 10–2, 7–11 all year

WOBURN (Beds)   SP9433   Map 4
Black Horse

This friendly old pub naturally attracts tourists, being so close to Woburn Abbey, but it's popular with local people too – always a good sign. The good and efficiently served food includes soup (50p), toasted sandwiches (from 75p), ploughman's and pâté (£1), shepherd's or steak and kidney pie, quiche with salad and jacket potato, roast beef or lamb, gammon with pineapple, and kidneys in red wine (all around £1.60), American-style beefburger (£1.90), salads (from £1.95), chicken escalope (£2.15) and steaks (from £3.40). The many neat tables are divided between the carefully decorated L-shaped main bar, which has sporting prints above its terracotta-coloured half-panelling, and a back room, which has Liberty prints and stripped pine. There is a range of wines by the glass, and well kept Marstons Burton and Youngs Special on handpump. You can have a three-course meal including half a bottle of wine for under £7 a head in the separate restaurant (evenings only). Through the coach entry there are several tables in a sheltered, gravelled garden looking down to a small lawn and then the church. *(Recommended by Philip Denison, Dennis Royles, C P Price; more reports please)*

Free house · Licensee Thomas Aldous · Real ale · Meals and snacks · Children in eating areas · Open 10.30–2.30, 6–11 all year

---

Lucky Dip

Besides the fully inspected pubs, you might like to try these Lucky Dips recommended and described by readers (if you do, please send us reports):

ABBOTSLEY [TL2356], *Eight Bells*: neat friendly pub with welcoming off-beat atmosphere in pretty village *(A G Neale)*
ABINGTON PIGOTTS [TL3044], *Darby & Joan*: excellent example of true English village local; free house with five real ales and dozens of malt whiskies, good bar food, and period restaurant with adventurous cooking by landlord's wife *(D S Millar, Donald Turner)*
ALCONBURY [TL1875], *Crown*: nice pub with friendly service *(Tina Chattell)*; *Manor House*: fast, friendly service, good cosy atmosphere, good value food and choice of drinks; beer garden *(T Newman, Tina Chattell)*; *Mill*: good value home-made soup, pizzas and so forth in pleasant pub with unusual twin-backed bar stools; plenty to do *(Tina Chattell, Eirlys Roberts)*; *Saddle* [Alconbury Motel]: good drinks and very good Friday discos *(Tina Chattell)*; *White Hart*: food and drinks good, very friendly atmosphere *(Brian Chattell)*
AMPTHILL [Bedford Street; TL0337], *Prince of Wales*: smart and plushly comfortable, with quiet lounge, good beer, good value bar meals, attractive garden up hill *(Michael and Alison Sandy)*

BALSHAM [High Street; TL5850], *Black Bull*: attractive old thatched pub with bar meals and restaurant, central island servery giving three distinct areas, lots of cosy corners, brass and beams, well kept Adnams, Greene King IPA and Mauldons *(Howard Gascoyne)*

BEDFORD [St Mary's Street TL0449], *Kings Arms*: well kept open-plan town-centre pub, with good Greene King real ales, lunchtime bar meals *(LYM)*; [Park Avenue] *Park*: food includes a superb lunchtime choice of cheeses and home-made pies with locally baked bread; dark wood décor, Charles Wells beers, good wine, restaurant, small garden *(Roger Danes)*

BOLNHURST [TL0859], *Olde Plough*: 500-year-old listed building which the relatively new licensees have sympathetically extended and plan to make into Bedfordshire's prettiest free house *(Anon)*

BROMHAM [TL0050], *Swan*: food includes wide range of bar dishes, well kept beer; popular *(E A George)*

CAMBRIDGE [TL4658], *Ancient Druids*: new pub with own brewhouse (passers-by can watch brewing from street) producing good value Kite and Druids Special *(Anon)*; [Gwydir Street] *Cambridge Blue*: opened by the good licensees of the Free Press (see main entry) in spring 1985; at times even more atmospheric – first-class drinkers' pub *(Gwen and Peter Andrews, David Surridge)*; [Gwydir Street] *Dewdrop*: basic, simple, friendly, back-street pub with well kept Tolly Bitter and Original on handpump (plus Old Strong in winter) *(David Symes)*; [Newnham Road] *Granta*: food good in restaurant-style pub with good views over river (especially from its terrace and wooden verandah), landing stage for punts, and Greene King ales *(T Mansell, Dr A K Clarke, Howard Gascoyne, David Symes)*; [King Street] *Horse & Groom*: pleasant back-street pub, well kept Greene King IPA straight from the cask *(David Symes)*; [Trumpington Street] *Little Rose*: comfortable but busy – more room than first meets the eye – with well kept Bass, Charrington IPA and Paines XXX *(David Symes)*; [Park Street] *Maypole*: good food and well kept Tolly in comfortable lounge and small, friendly bar with bar billiards and sporting prints; piped music *(T Mansell, DJC)*; [Northampton Street] *Merton Arms*: limited choice of home-cooked food, Greene King ales and good atmosphere in friendly pub with comfortable cane furniture and piped music; open fires in winter *(T Mansell, DJC)*; [Chesterton Road] *Old Spring*: good bar lunches, especially tuna and pepper quiche; tables outside *(D J Fawthrop)*; [Panton Street] *Panton Arms*: simple, pleasant back-street pub, good Greene King beer *(David Symes)*; [Thompsons Lane] *Spade & Becket*: good choice of reasonably priced food and well kept Tolly ales served by friendly staff in pub with robust wooden furnishings; pretty riverside beer garden, close to park; can get crowded with students in term-time; river walk direct from Magdalene Bridge *(T Mansell, Howard Gascoyne, Gerhard Bauer)*; [James Street] *Zebra*: friendly, large lounge, small comfortable bar; Greene King ales and reasonably priced good food; can get crowded at weekends *(T Mansell, David Symes)*

CASTOR [TL1298], *Prince of Wales*: recently modernised but not overdone; typical village pub with Manns bitter, piano and traditional entertainments as well as pool-table and fruit machine *(John Armstrong)*

CATWORTH [TL0873], *Racehorse*: friendly service and wide range of good food, some unusual, in lounge bar, over 80 whiskies, skittles and darts in public bar, restaurant in style of a theatre, with photographs of stars, and so on *(J M Haddon, Mr and Mrs E Usher, D Fluck, Mrs C Reynolds)*

CLOPHILL [TL0837], *Stone Jug*: good choice of beers such as Courage Directors, Everards and Shefford, friendly atmosphere and good value food in unpretentious old stone pub *(Michael and Alison Sandy, Steve Lawrence)*

COTON [TL4058], *Plough*: fish especially good among other good bar food in popular pub with well kept beer *(E A George)*

DOGSTHORPE [TF1901], *Blue Bell*: plenty of atmosphere in fine dark-panelled room with Elgood ales; very popular (including off-duty firemen from station opposite) *(John Armstrong)*

nr DUNSTABLE (on A5 southbound; TL0221], *Horse & Jockey*: a £250,000 facelift and the eight-acre garden with large play area make this roadside pub well worth a try *(Wayne Rossiter, LYM; more reports please)*; *Packhorse*: welcoming pub, handy for A5 S of town *(Jonathan Rowe)*

DUNTON [High Street; TL2344], *March Hare*: food includes a good value range of burgers/steaks and more exotic cooking, Brakspears, Flowers and Whitbreads real ale, in comfortable and friendly village pub with open fire *(Roger Danes)*

DUXFORD [TL4745], *John Barleycorn*: good food, beer and décor in very well kept seventeenth-century ex-coaching inn *(D R Mather, Robin Taylor)*

EAST HYDE [TL1217], *Leather Bottle*: good value food, especially steaks and seafood, well kept Whitbreads ales *(M G McKenzie)*

EATON SOCON [Great North Road; TL1658], *White Horse*: recently renovated old coaching-inn, part thirteenth-century, comfortably old-fashioned bars with small alcoves, log fire, antique settles, good freshly cooked food, very friendly service, restaurant *(D S Millar, Howard Gascoyne, R Heeks)*

ETTON [TF1406], *Golden Pheasant*: warm fire in winter in comfortable lounge of elegant Georgian building, helpful landlord, Adnams and Ruddles real ale *(John Armstrong)*

FEN DITTON [TL4860], *Plough*: big unspoilt riverside lawn outside friendly pub with good value simple food *(LYM)*

GRANTCHESTER [The Broadway; TL4455], *Blue Ball*: good, not touristy, friendly and lively *(Jonquil Lowe)*; *Rupert Brooke*: friendly staff in comfortable and stylishly renovated beamed pub with good bar food – especially seafood pie – and restaurant *(J M Gowers)*

GREAT STUKELEY [TL2274], *Three Horseshoes*: nice drinks, good atmosphere, very friendly service *(Tina Chattell)*

HARLTON [TL3852], *Hare & Hounds*: comfortable and friendly, out of the way, well kept Charles Wells real ales, good ploughman's *(David Symes)*

HELPSTON [TF1204], *Bluebell*: John Clare born next door in 1793 and worked here until whisked off to fame when his first book was published *(Anon)*

HEYDON [TL4340], *King William IV*: fascinating village pub packed with intricate display of old horse brasses, country artefacts, riding tackle, brass pots hanging everywhere possible, big fires, good bar food, Adnams and Greene King, restaurant *(Steve Lawrence, C J Waldron)*

HILDERSHAM [TL5448], *Pear Tree*: friendly, jolly landlord in pleasant country pub with tables hung from ceiling by chains, unusual traditional beer dispensing system, garden *(Howard Gascoyne)*

HUNTINGDON [TL2371], *Falcon*: friendly service, good drinks and food, tea and coffee too *(Brian Chattell)*; *Old Bridge*: very good hotel bar overlooks the Ouse; bedrooms *(J M M Hill)*; *Three Tuns*: good atmosphere, darts *(Brian Chattell)*; *Victoria*: good value home-cooked food, especially daily specials, in friendly and unpretentious pub, relatively undiscovered *(A G Neale)*

LEIGHTON BUZZARD [Appenine Way; SP9225], *Clay Pipe*: friendly cheery staff in delightful town pub with good range of lunchtime food, well kept beers and interesting décor *(M G McKenzie)*

LINSLADE [Leighton Road; SP9225], *Locks Bar*: good food and atmosphere, good entertainment including jazz *(Miss J Kerr)*

LINTON [TL5646], *Bell*: good range of bar meals, separate restaurant, Greene King real ales in fifteenth-century timbered pub with panelled, beamed lounge, log fire, armchairs and settees; dress rules – smart casual but ties not necessary *(Howard Gascoyne)*

LITTLE STUKELEY [TL2075], *Three Horseshoes*: good restaurant food and beer garden *(T Newman)*

LUTON [TL0921], *Cock*: friendly, warm and comfortable central pub, well refurbished, Wethereds and guest ales *(Michael Sandy)*; [Castle Street] *Vine*: good choice of drinks in friendly free house with adult-orientated juke box *(M G McKenzie)*

nr LUTON [Farley Hill; TL0921], *Barn Owl*: roomy, well done mock-up of rural pub with real woodwork, lots of farm tools, good value food, unusually well

kept Wethereds, big garden, on edge of park, close to real country
(Michael Sandy)

MELCHBOURNE [Knotting Road; TL0265], *St John Arms*: friendly rambling country pub with bar food, well kept Greene King real ales, hood skittles, peaceful cottagey garden *(LYM, Nicholas Swan)*

MOGGERHANGER [TL1449], *Guinea*: nice friendly attractive pub with good professional service, real ale *(Peter Harding)*

ORWELL [Town Green Road; TL3650], *Chequers*: food good, service excellent, cheerful landlord and real ales in very comfortable pub, garden *(JDF)*

PERRY [TL1467], *Wheatsheaf*: well kept Greene King ales in inn with family room, bedrooms, big garden, near Grafham Water *(Nigel Pritchard)*

PETERBOROUGH [Oundle Road; TL1999], *Botolph Arms*: food good value in converted family house in country setting, good range of beers, garden, games room *(Derek Gibson, T Mansell)*; [Station Approach] *Great Northern*: Poacher Bar of this large railway hotel of some character fronts main approach to station; sumptuous settees on wall-to-wall carpet make it a very comfortable lounge indeed; interesting taxidermy in glass cases, Elgoods and Hereward both well kept; bedrooms *(John Armstrong)*; [Cumbergate] *Still*: good unpretentious pub with well kept Marstons Pedigree *(John Armstrong)*

ST IVES [Ramsey Road; TL3171], *Slepe Hall*: free house with good choice of bar food and restaurant, Tolly ale, bedrooms *(G H Theaker)*

SAWTRY [TL1683], *Bell*: good atmosphere, friendly service *(Brian Chattell)*

STILTON [TL1689], *Bell*: old coaching-inn which made the cheese famous, recently completely refurbished; good beer including Greene King, Hereward and Ruddles, interesting history, pleasant atmosphere, helpful owner *(C Elliot, J K Pepper, Robin Taylor, John Armstrong)*

SHILLINGTON [TL1234], *Crown*: nice atmosphere, good well-worn-in feeling, food (not Sunday) good, attractive garden with children's play area *(Michael and Alison Sandy)*

SUTTON GAULT [TL4279], *Anchor*: food good in this riverside pub with very friendly landlord; Tolly on draught; has recently been sensitively redecorated, open fire *(T J Daum)*

TEMPSFORD [Church Street; TL1652], *Wheatsheaf*: friendly and well kept village local *(Anon)*

UPPER DEAN [TL0467], *Three Compasses*: food good and simple, well kept beer (straight from the barrel if you want), friendly landlord in popular and attractively refurbished pub *(Keith Garley)*

UPWARE [TL5370], *Five Miles From Anywhere*: spacious modern riverside free house – its name means what it says *(LYM)*

WHIPSNADE [TL0117], *Old Hunters Lodge*: friendly service and reasonable prices in comfortable pub with good bar food and well kept beer; nice garden, separate restaurant; close to Zoo *(J P Rowe)*

WICKEN [TL5670], *Wicken Hall*: fourteenth-century manor in lovely tree-filled grounds with duck-pond, recently opened as inn: big comfortable beamed lounge, log fires, TV lounge, Ind Coope beers, good salads and separate dining-room, bedrooms *(Noel Giffard)*

Cheshire

Interesting newcomers to this edition are the Shroppie Fly on the canal in Audlem, the Harrington Arms at Gawsworth (an utterly unspoilt farmhouse pub), the Swan With Two Nicks in Little Bollington (full of interesting bric-à-brac), the Roebuck in Mobberley (unusual for its French landlord), the Crown in Nantwich (a lovely Elizabethan façade), the Ring of Bells in Overton (a small-roomed relaxed pub, kept charmingly old-fashioned), the Shady Oak near Tiverton (canalside, in lovely countryside) and the Ferry Inn outside Warrington (a pleasant family pub in surprisingly remote riverside country). The county's outstanding pub is the Bells of Peover in Lower Peover: old-fashioned civilised comfort in a lovely tranquil setting. In its own quite different way, the much simpler Holly Bush in Little Leigh also takes one back several decades, and the thatched and timbered White Lion in the beautiful village of Barthomley has a warmly old-fashioned welcome. Cheshire's top pub – in terms of sheer height, that is – is the Cat & Fiddle near Macclesfield: Britain's second highest. Two other hill pubs have notable views over the Cheshire Plain – the simple Cheshire View in Mow Cop, and the Highwayman at Rainow, perched high above Macclesfield and one of Cheshire's nicest pubs. This has good home cooking, and for food we can also particularly recommend the Crown at Goostrey. If you like distinguished and ancient pubs you should certainly see the award-winning restoration of the fine

The White Lion, Barthomley

*old Falcon in Chester, and at Brereton Green the Bears Head
attractively blends modern comfort in the bedroom block
with old-fashioned quaint charm in its bar. Other pubs here
with a rather similar combination of modern comfort and
efficiency and old-fashioned surroundings include the Smoker
at Plumley, Cock o' Barton at Barton and Bickerton Poacher
(which has particularly enterprising weekend barbecues).
Prices of drinks are in general quite low here – particularly so
at the Harrington Arms in Gawsworth, Holly Bush in Little
Leigh, Cheshire View in Mow Cop and Crown at Goostrey,
with the Falcon in Chester cheap for its area. (The Cock o'
Barton and Bears Head at Brereton Green have relatively high
prices.) The Mow Cop in the village of that name is owned by
Clive Winkle who brews Winkles Saxon Cross beers, and the
charming Swettenham Arms is owned by his parents – both
excellent places for trying the family ales.*

BARTHOMLEY SJ7752 Map 7
White Lion [illustrated on page 91]

A particular favourite of many readers with a taste for the unspoilt,
this black and white timbered and thatched pub is one of the nicest
buildings in a most attractive village. It dates from 1614, and one of
the heavy oak beams in its low ceilings is big enough to house quite a
collection of plates. The simply furnished main room has latticed
windows and attractively moulded black panelling, and is decorated
with Cheshire watercolours and prints. A second room, up steps,
with more oak panelling, a high-backed winged settle and a paraffin
lamp hinged to the wall, has sensibly placed darts, shove-ha'penny
and dominoes. Cheap bar snacks include hot pies, well filled ham,
beef or cheese salad rolls, and soup at lunchtime; well kept
Burtonwood Bitter and Mild on handpump; friendly service. Tables
under the yew tree at one side or on the front cobbles have a peaceful
view of village cottages and the early fifteenth-century red sandstone
church of St Bertiline just opposite. *(Recommended by Anthony Lewis
Furreddu, Mr and Mrs Michael Parrott, William Meadon, Richard Steel,
P J Taylor, Dennis Royles)*

*Burtonwood · Licensee Eric Critchlow · Real ale · Snacks (not Sun evening)
Children at lunchtime only · Open 11–3, 6–10.30*

AUDLEM SJ6644 Map 7
Shroppie Fly

Audlem Wharf; turn off A525 at Bridge Inn

Named after the horse-drawn narrow boats of the Shropshire Union
Canal, this friendly and comfortably converted canal warehouse
looks out on brightly painted boats negotiating the long flight of
locks that passes the village. It has good black and white local canal
photographs on its walls, and a couple of cases filled with the brightly
painted china and bric-à-brac that bargees collected. The three

communicating rooms have well made modern settles – some high-backed, with wings – as well as wheelback chairs around their dark wooden tables; most of the floor is carpeted, some parts with quarry tiles or crazy-paved flagstones. Popular food includes sandwiches (70p), ploughman's or other salads (£1.95), burgers or giant sausages (£1.95, children's helpings £1.30), deep-fried chicken (£2.25), trout (£3.25), chicken stuffed with mushrooms and cream (£3.60), eight-ounce rump steak (£4.50) and mixed grill (£5.25). There is also a small dining-room. Tea or coffee, as well as well kept Springfield on handpump; sensibly placed darts, a juke box and a fruit machine at one end, another fruit machine and a space game by the entrance; also dominoes, cribbage, pool. There are picnic-table sets on the lockside terrace. *(Recommended by R Davies, P J Taylor)*

Free house · Licensee Malcolm Roy Goodwin · Real ale · Meals and snacks Children in room off bar and restaurant · Pop music duo Fri in summer · Open 11.30–3, 6–11 (12–2, 7–11 in winter)

BARTON SJ4554 Map 7
Cock o' Barton

A534 E of Farndon

Very neat and friendly, this handsome sandstone pub has been carefully modernised, keeping old-fashioned furnishings (including high-backed built-in cushioned settles) in the separate snug areas of its more or less open-plan bar. There are log fires, black beams and joists, old prints of ornamental fowls and newer ones of game birds on the bobbly white walls, green Turkey carpet in the most spacious area (closest to the entry), and carpet squares on the ancient black slate tiles of the older small-roomed part. One mystery that readers may be able to help us clear up concerns their Mild, on electric pump. Can anyone tell us who brews it? One reader was told McEwans, but surely not . . . and the pub – ex-directory, so we can't ring them – hasn't returned our fact-checking sheet! Also well kept McEwans 80/– on handpump, Youngers Scotch on electric. Bar food includes sandwiches (from 60p), ploughman's £1.50, lasagne (£1.85), gammon (£2.40) and eight-ounce rump steak (£4.50), and at lunchtime on Tuesdays to Fridays a much wider choice including some imaginative main dishes. There are some teak seats by a little lily-pool in a dwarf shrubbery. One reader found the pub recommended in an 1899 guidebook, and people have actually been coming here for 600 years. *(Recommended by Dr B W Marsden, P J Taylor)*

Free house · Real ale · Meals and snacks · Open 12–2.15, 7.30–10.30; closed Mon lunchtime

BICKERTON SJ5052 Map 7
Bickerton Poacher

A534 just E of junction with A41

Recommended as a typical Cheshire pub by one reader who has known it for 50 years, this friendly place has certainly kept up with

93

the times. Sturdy tables around its cleverly designed barbecue courtyard are protected by teahouse-style tiled roofs, and from May to September barbecues are held here on Friday and Saturday evenings and Sunday lunchtimes (until 3 pm, with children's menus and free orange squash); there's usually live music or an evening disco – maybe with half-price drinks. All sorts of special events here include frog races, pig weighing, vintage car shows, attempts on the world fondu-eating record. Inside, the several connecting rooms conjure up much older times, with a big kitchen range in the back room, hunting and 1930s humorous prints over the low panelling, a sofa and rocking chair as well as the front lounge's built-in banquettes and captain's chairs, and red-tiled or carpeted floors. Bar food includes home-made soup (65p), sandwiches (£1), pâté (£1.20), sausages (£1.75), home-made quiche (£1.75), ploughman's (£1.95), steak and kidney pie (£1.95), salads (£2) and several daily specials such as lamb hot-pot with red cabbage (£1.50), Arbroath smokie pie (£2) or steak (£3.95); well kept Border on handpump; darts, dominoes, a fruit machine, and piped music. A separate bistro-style restaurant opens in the evening (not Sunday) and on Sunday lunchtime, and a skittle alley is open on Mondays and Tuesdays (this and the barbecue park may be booked for private parties). The pub is handy for the wooded walks of the Peckforton Hills and Bickerton Hill. (*Recommended by E G Parish, P J Taylor*)

Free house · Licensee Mrs Johanna Jackson · Real ale · Meals and snacks Children welcome · Frequent live entertainment, particularly Fri–Sat evening, and Sun lunchtime in summer (such as Punch and Judy); skittle alley and barbecue park bookings tel Cholmondeley (082 922) 226 · Open 11–3, 6–11 all year (opens 7 in winter)

The Bears Head, Brereton Green

BRERETON GREEN SJ7864 Map 7
Bears Head [*illustrated on page 94*]

1¾ miles from M6, junction 17; fork left from Congleton road almost immediately, then left on to A50; also from junction 18 via Holmes Chapel

Immaculate white-coated Italian bar staff set the tone in the civilised and neatly kept lounge bar of this quaint black and white timbered inn. It is a series of open-plan communicating rooms with masses of heavy black beams and timbers, corner cupboards, horse brasses, antique settles, big Windsor armchairs and rush seats with scatter-cushions, and a large brick inglenook fireplace full of gleaming copper pots (with a coal fire in winter). Good bar food includes home-made soup (75p), sandwiches (from £1, including a good toasted steak and onion), pâtés (from £1.25) and salads or hot dishes such as well presented gammon with pineapple (from £3). There is a big softly lit communicating restaurant, with similar nooks and alcoves (lunch around £6.45). Well kept Bass and Springfield on handpump; fruit machine, soothing piped music and a pleasantly relaxed atmosphere. A pretty side terrace, with big black cast-iron lamp clusters and a central fountain, is sheltered by a small balconied brick block: the comfortable and well equipped bedrooms are in a modern extension. (*Recommended by Mr and Mrs Michael Parrott, Hazel Green, E G Parish, N Lawson, Brian and Anna Marsden, P J Taylor*)

Free house · Licensee Roberto Tarquini · Real ale · Meals (lunchtime) and snacks (not Sun evening) · Children in restaurant · Open 11–3, 6–11 all year Bedrooms tel Holmes Chapel (0477) 35251; £29.50B/£39B

CHESTER SJ4166 Map 7
Falcon

Lower Bridge Street

This splendidly ornamental timbered building dates mainly from around 1600, though the massive stone blocks of the base and the cellars go back some 700 years or more. It has been carefully restored and furnished unfussily, with traditional built-in benches, white walls with some black panelling, softly toned carpets and matching curtains; upstairs a second airy bar has a fine range of latticed windows looking over the street (it's available for functions in the early part of the week). Food includes open sandwiches (£1.40–£2.50), salads such as quiche, ham, prawn, game or turkey and ham pie and smoked mackerel (£1.65–£2.50), and daily hot dishes (£1.95–£2.60); well kept Sam Smiths Tadcaster and OB on handpump; fruit machine, mainstream piped music. This whole area of Chester has been well restored and brought back to life – earning the city a Europa Nostra civic conservation medal. (*Recommended by Mr and Mrs Michael Parrott, Dennis Royles*)

Sam Smiths · Licensee Frank Margrave · Real ale · Meals and snacks (lunchtime, not Sun) · Parking may be difficult · Open 11–3, 5–10.30

Post Office address codings confusingly give the impression that some pubs are in Cheshire, when they're really in Derbyshire (and therefore included in this book under that chapter) or in Greater Manchester (see the Lancashire chapter).

Olde Boot

Eastgate Row North

Long a favourite of readers, this pub opens off one of the first-floor
balconied arcades which are such a striking seventeenth-century
feature of the city centre. Things to see more or less within walking
distance include the lively British Heritage Museum, cathedral,
Roman remains and the fine riverside. The pub's unusual layout (you
go down a long corridor into the bar, itself long, narrow and cosy) is
always an attraction, as is the big side settle which curls right round
on itself to shelter people sitting in it. Sam Smiths Tadcaster and OB
on electric pump have this year taken over from the Border ales which
used to be on handpump; there's the same relaxed atmosphere, with
both lighting and piped music subdued. Reasonably priced lunchtime
snacks include good home-made soup (usually based on a ham bone
stock with lentils), split peas and leeks, hot filled rolls, pasties and
gala pie; in the evening the staff will do what they can about food. A
separate restaurant has a lunchtime help-yourself cold buffet (closed
Saturday, Sunday and Monday). The attractively landscaped zoo to
the north of the city is good. (*Recommended by Dennis Royles, C Elliott,
W T Aird*)

*Free house · Licensee Mrs Noreen Beadle · Real ale · Snacks (see above)
No nearby parking · Open 11.30–3, 5.30–10.30; closed 25 Dec*

GAWSWORTH SJ8969 Map 7

Harrington Arms

Congleton Road, off A536 S of Macclesfield; coming S through Warren go
straight past the big signpost to Gawsworth Hall on your left, then take the
next real left turning, unmarked, about ½ mile beyond Warren

A sign outside the handsome three-storey brick house advertises
potatoes for sale: this delightfully old-fashioned pub is part of a farm.
The serving counter is in a narrow space on your right as you go in,
with regular customers leaning on it and filling the bench opposite;
leading off are several individually numbered companionable rooms
simply furnished with old-fashioned settles, and one of the rooms is
served from the central bar through a curtained hatch. The pub is
notable for its very relaxed atmosphere, charmingly welcoming
service, and well kept Robinsons Best and Best Mild on handpump –
at low prices. The lane – to the left, if you've come by the route
suggested above – leads to one of Cheshire's prettiest villages, with a
fine black and white timbered Hall and Old rectory. (*Recommended by
William Meadon, Richard Steel*)

*Robinsons · Licensee Marjorie Bayley · Real ale · Snacks · Open 11–3,
5.30–10.30*

Pubs brewing their own beers are listed at the back of the book.

Real ale may be served from handpumps, electric pumps (not just the on-off
switches used for keg beer) or – common in Scotland – tall taps called founts
(pronounced 'fonts') where a separate pump pushes the beer up under air
pressure. With all pumps, the landlord can adjust the force of the flow – a tight
spigot gives the good creamy head that Yorkshire lads like.

GOOSTREY   SJ7870   Map 7

Crown

111 Main Road; village signposted from A50 and A535

Though the menu in this comfortable village pub is not extensive, the freshly prepared food is excellent value for money, luring readers back time and again. It includes sandwiches (75p), a choice of combination toasties such as ham and pineapple, cheese and onion or chicken, ham and mushroom (80p), pizza (£1.40), ploughman's (£1.45), pâté (£1.55), open prawn sandwich (£2.25), salads such as dressed crab with seasonal vegetables (£2.25), and hot dishes such as scampi (£2.75). The day's lunchtime special (£2.40) is said to be always worth a try, and in the evening extra dishes such as Barnsley chop (£4.85) or sirloin steak (£4.95) are available from the back bistro dining-room. Chips are done to a turn, and the cheeses and puddings are particularly popular. Well kept Marstons Burton, Mild and Pedigree on handpump. The building was originally a farmhouse, and the two communicating rooms of the lounge bar are comfortably furnished, with cushioned settles and a chaise-longue as well as more conventional seats: get there reasonably early to be sure of a place, particularly towards the end of the week. Decorations include a couple of Lowry prints – not the usual ones. The smaller and brighter tap-room is plain and traditional, with darts and dominoes; also pool. An upstairs room can be booked for dinner parties, preferably not on Saturdays, and is otherwise available for diners. Seats on the front terrace face the village road. *(Recommended by Mr and Mrs Michael Parrott, G W Crowther, Dennis Royles, Sue Cowan)*

Marstons · Licensee Peter McGrath · Real ale · Meals (not Mon, not Sun evening) and snacks (not Mon); dinner parties tel Holmes Chapel (0477) 32128 · Children in back bistro · Open 11.30–3, 5.30–11 all year

Olde Red Lion

Main Road; closer to A535

White tables on a small lawn at the bottom of an attractively planted steep dell make the pretty garden of this comfortably modernised pub a popular draw in summer. At almost any time of the year a special feature is the way that fresh Pacific oysters are sold over the bar (75p each), and other fresh seafood includes prawns (half-pint £1.30, pint £2.50), grilled sardines (£1.95), prawn and smoked salmon open sandwich (£2.50), cod in a herb batter (£2.65), and (when available) mussels. There is also home-made soup (75p), sandwiches (from 80p), ploughman's (£1.95), basket meals such as chicken (£2.65), sirloin steak (£5.50) and daily hot specials. The open-plan bar has red-cushioned banquettes built in against the cream swirly-plastered walls, dimpled copper tables, and easy chairs at the back. Tetleys and Walkers Best on handpump; darts, a fruit machine, space game, maybe piped music. There is a separate restaurant (evenings Tuesday

---

Most pubs in the *Guide* sell draught cider. We mention it specifically only if they have unusual farm-produced scrumpy or specialise in it (as some pubs do in Bristol, say).

to Saturday and bank holidays, Sunday lunch). *(Recommended by Mr and Mrs Michael Parrott, S Mason)*

Tetleys (Ind Coope) · Licensee Peter Yorke · Real ale · Meals and snacks; restaurant tel Holmes Chapel (0477) 32033 · Children in room by restaurant reception · Open 11.30–3, 5.30–11 all year

nr LANGLEY   SJ9471   Map 7
Hanging Gate

Higher Sutton; follow Langley singpost from A54 beside Fourways Motel, and that road passes the pub; from Macclesfield, turn off A523 at Langley, Wincle signpost and follow Langley signs until Church House Inn, then take Wildboarclough road, turning sharp right at steep hairpin bend; OS Sheet 118 reference 952696

Window seats in the snug little low-beamed rooms of this friendly country pub look out beyond a patchwork of valley pastures to distant moors (and the tall Sutton Common transmitter above them). The pub, first licensed nearly 300 years ago (but built much earlier), is simply furnished with small seats and modern settles by the big coal fires, and has some attractive old photographs of Cheshire towns. Down stone steps an airier garden room has a picture window for the view, and a juke box and sitting space game; there's also a fruit machine. Reasonably priced bar food includes a pair of sausages on a stick (50p), soup (60p), sandwiches (85p, toasted 95p), basket meals such as lasagne (£2), chicken (£2.25) or scampi (£2.50), salads (£3), local trout (£3) and sirloin steak (£4.50); well kept Chesters Best, Marstons Burton, Pedigree and Owd Rodger on handpump, with mulled wine in winter; maybe piped radio. There is a crazy-paved terrace outside. *(Recommended by P J Taylor; more reports please)*

Free house · Licensee Daniel Campbell · Real ale · Children in garden room or upper small room · Open 12–3, 7–10.30

LITTLE BOLLINGTON   SJ7286   Map 7
Swan With Two Nicks

Park Lane; off A56 at Stamford Arms, W of Altrincham

Close to the Bridgewater Canal and the River Bollin, this cosy pub has lots of snug alcoves. Its beams are festooned with brass and copper pots, miners' lamps and ornaments, and the walls are decorated richly with pictures, horse brasses, superannuated brass fire-extinguishers and hose nozzles, and shelves of china. The front part has little wheelback armchairs and upholstered wall seats around its dimpled copper tables; the back includes antiques such as cushioned oak settles and a fine chair-table of the sort dealers call a monk's seat (on our visit a cat was sleeping here). There's a stag's head above the log fire. Good home-cooked lunchtime bar food includes toasted sandwiches (from 60p), farmer's lunch (£1.80), plaice or chilli con carne (£2.10) and steak and kidney pie or salads (£2.35); well kept Chesters Best, Best Mild and Whitbread Trophy on handpump from the old-fashioned wood-enclosed central servery. There are traditional white slatted seats and tables on a crazy-paved terrace by the pretty creeper-covered old house. The quiet lane past here stops at a foot-bridge over the River Bollin, for a short walk to Dunham Hall's deer park (National Trust). *(Recommended by Andrew Rice, Dennis Royles)*

Whitbreads · Licensees Denis and Yvonne O'Neill · Real ale · Meals (lunchtime Weds – Sat) and snacks (lunchtime, not Sun) · Open 11–3, 5.30–10.30

LITTLE LEIGH   SJ6276   Map 7
Holly Bush

4½ miles from M56 junction 10: A49 towards Northwich, pub just S of A533 junction

If you long for a return to the sort of atmosphere that in most places died out about 50 years ago, make a bee-line for this unspoilt country tavern. From the word go, you're firmly in the past. No gaudy brewery advertising outside: you have to keep your eyes skinned for the timber-framed thatched cottage (its sign is almost hidden in a holly tree), and the closest approach to a car park is the yard of the farm that surrounds the pub. Inside, the heavy-beamed parlour has varnished wall benches around waxed and polished country tables, a warm open fire, and a quite unspoilt atmosphere. Well kept Greenalls and Mild (on handpump) is served from the open doorway of a little back tap-room, and there are hot or cold pies and pasties (40p) and sandwiches (40p–60p); darts, dominoes. There's a friendly welcome from the licensees and the local regulars (half of them, it seems, traction-engine enthusiasts), and there always seems to be somewhere to sit, even mid-evening at the weekend. A separate overflow room has much more space, but less atmosphere; you can also sit outside. *(Recommended by Mr and Mrs Michael Parrott, Brian and Anna Marsden, Dennis Royles, BOB)*

Greenalls · Licensee Albert Cowap · Real ale · Snacks · Children in small snug Open 11–3, 5.30–10.30

LOWER PEOVER   SJ7474   Map 7
Bells of Peover ★★

From B5081 take short cobbled lane signposted to church

The sheltered crazy-paved terrace in front of this wistaria-covered pub faces a beautiful black and white timbered church (mainly fourteenth-century, with lovely woodwork inside; the stone tower is sixteenth-century). A spacious lawn beyond the old coachyard at the side spreads down through trees and rose pergolas to a little stream. It is largely this tranquil setting which makes the pub so special, but inside, its civilised and old-fashioned atmosphere has a long record of approval from readers – including one who, as he says, has liked it man and boy for over 40 years. The main Turkey-carpeted lounge has groups of people chatting quietly on its well cushioned seats, which include several antique settles, high-backed Windsor armchairs, a large window seat and a brass fender of the sort you can perch on, by the fire. It is decorated with lots of pictures and a substantial dresser filled with china, and has a long-case clock. The bar counter, with side hatches, is out in a small tiled room with wall seats under masses of toby jugs and prints from Victorian magazines. Well garnished home-cooked meat, farmhouse Cheshire cheese or smoked salmon sandwiches (also a separate stylish and popular restaurant); well kept Greenalls Best on handpump. *(Recommended by Colin McLaren, Andrew Parffrey, William Meadon, Richard Steel, George Jonas, G M Crowther, Mrs V Somervell, Dr B W Marsden, H G and C J McCafferty, R K Whitehead, P J Taylor, Dennis Royles)*

Greenalls · Licensee James Goodier Fisher · Real ale · Snacks (not every Mon) Children in area away from bar only · Open 11–3, 5.30–11 all year

nr MACCLESFIELD   SJ9273   Map 7
Cat & Fiddle

A537 (actually several miles from Macclesfield and closer to Buxton – but really miles from anywhere!); OS Sheet 119 reference 001719

At 1,690 feet this isolated pub is the second highest in Britain (for the highest, see Tan Hill, Yorkshire), and is surrounded by spectacular moorland and fine walking country. Inside it surprises you with all the facilities you'd expect of a lowland pub on an equally busy trunk road, and in the last year the kitchen has been completely refurbished. Bar food now includes sandwiches, home-made soup (75p), pears with cheese or savoury crab on toast in fingers (£1), filled baked potatoes, ploughman's or smoked mackerel (£1.95), scampi (£2.35), pizza (£2.50), salads, chicken (from £2.50) and steaks (from £4.75). The spacious lounge has upright rush seats and some easy chairs, and the public bar (also roomy) has darts, pool, dominoes, cribbage, a fruit machine and a juke box. Robinsons Best, Best Mild and Old Tom on electric pump; piped light music. Handy for the Goyt Valley. *(Recommended by D A Haines, P J Taylor)*

Robinsons · Licensees Peter and Doreen Robinson · Real ale · Meals and snacks (not Mon evening) · Children in family room · Open 11–3, 5.30–10.30

MOBBERLEY   SJ7879   Map 7
Roebuck

Town Lane; down hill from the sharp bend on B5085, at E edge of 30 mph limit

The popular French licensee (who has a Cheshire wife) runs a very neat house here. In the spacious open-plan main room the richly coloured close-set floorboards have been recycled from an old mill, and the comfortably cushioned long dark wooden pews were rescued from a redundant Welsh chapel. Bar food, served generously, includes filled barm cakes or French bread (from 55p, giant sausage 85p, rare beef £1.10), soups such as chicken and vegetable (60p), four-ounce burger (75p), salads (from £1.50), chilli con carne or lasagne (£1.50), daily specials such as beef bourguignonne (£2.20) or barbecued spare ribs (£2.50), and evening grills such as trout (£2.75) and eight-ounce sirloin steak (£4.75). Well kept Wilsons Bitter and Mild served from handpumps on the handsome bar counter (which has high stools and a good brass footrail); a wide choice of cocktails;

quite loud, well reproduced pop music. There is a cobbled courtyard, and picnic-table sets by the car park. The Bulls Head mentioned in the Lucky Dip is just across the quiet lane; a pleasant conjunction on a summer evening when they're playing bowls. (Recommended by David Guthrie)

Wilsons (Watneys) · Licensee Philippe Elissalde · Real ale · Meals and snacks Children in eating area · Open 12–3, 5.30–10.30

MOW COP SJ8557 Map 7
Cheshire View

Station Road; village signposted from A34; OS Sheet 118 reference 854574

This friendly and simply furnished stone pub has a superb view over the Cheshire Plain. Because the hillside is so steep, the view of the flat plain is startlingly clear – almost like looking down from an aeroplane, with microscopic Friesian cows in tiny green pastures, and villages almost small enough to pick up. Big picture windows make the most of the view from the lounge extension – a simple white-walled room with neat little leatherette chairs on its carpet. Bar food includes sandwiches, cottage pie with red cabbage (80p), sausages with baked beans and chips (£1.20), plaice (£1.50) and scampi (£2.20); well kept Marstons Burton and Pedigree on handpump. There are seats out on a small terrace by the car park, and the public bar has darts, pool, dominoes and cribbage; also a juke box or background music. (Recommended by G W Crowther, R Davies)

Marstons · Licensee Philip Kirkham · Real ale · Meals and snacks (lunchtime) Open 11–3, 7–10.30

Mow Cop

Mow Cop Road, on the corner with Castle Road

The knocked-through bar of this small stone village pub still keeps the shapes of its original separate rooms. It has blue plush stools and upholstered wall seats around cast-iron-framed tables on its Turkey carpet. Clive Winkle, the friendly landlord, has a small brewery near Buxton supplying his Castle Bitter, Saxon Cross and Mild (well kept here) to quite a few pubs – including his parents' (see Swettenham entry). Simple bar food includes home-made shepherd's or steak and kidney pie (80p, with chips £1.25) and chicken, cod or scampi (£1.60–£2); space game and a fruit machine. The steep road beside the pub leads to the Old Man of Mow, owned by the National Trust, with walks and magnificent views. (Recommended by A J Melville)

Free house · Licensee Clive Winkle · Real ale · Meals and snacks · Open 11–3, 7–10.30

NANTWICH SJ6552 Map 7
Crown

High Street; in pedestrian-only centre, close to church; free public parking behind the inn

The black and white Elizabethan timbered façade is so strikingly quaint, with its overhanging upper galleries and uncertain perpendiculars and horizontals, that it's hard to resist wandering inside. There are beams and timbered walls in the rambling bar, but it has been comfortably modernised, with cushioned settles, button-back leather sofas, red plush banquettes and round stools, tripod tables, Turkey carpet. Bar food includes sandwiches (70p), soup (75p), open sandwiches (from £1.05, for beef or ham), pâté (£1.25), filled baked potatoes (from £1.05), toasted club sandwiches (£1.35), ploughman's (£1.95), pizza (£1.95), chicken casserole (£1.95), scampi (£2.25), lamb kebab (£3) and sirloin steak (£5.10), with vegetarian dishes such as cheese and walnut burgers. There is a newly opened upstairs restaurant (three-course lunch £6). Well kept Ind Coope Burton and Tetleys on handpump; fruit machine; on our visit, loud, well reproduced pop music. *(Recommended by P J Taylor)*

Free house · Licensee Philip John Martin · Real ale · Meals and snacks Children welcome · Live music monthly · Open 11–3, 5.30–10.30 · Bedrooms tel *Nantwich (0270) 628047; £16(£22B)/£29(£33B)*

OVERTON   SJ5277   Map 7
Ring o' Bells

2 Bellemonte Road; just over 2 miles from M56, junction 12 – from A56 in Frodsham take B5152 and turn right (uphill) at Parish Church signpost

Several small snug rooms ramble around the old-fashioned hatch-like central servery of this early seventeenth-century pub: a couple have red plush seats with windows giving a view past the stone church to the Mersey far below; one at the back has some antique settles, brass and leather fender seats by the log fire, and old hunting prints on its butter-coloured walls; yet another small room, with beams, antique dark oak panelling and stained-glass, leads through to a darts room (there's also cribbage and dominoes) liberally adorned with pictures of naked ladies. Lunchtime bar food includes soup (60p), sandwiches (from 75p, toasted from 80p), pâté or ploughman's (£1.20), steak sandwich with chips (£1.40), chilli con carne, lasagne, quiche or steak and mushroom pie (£1.80), plaice or cod (£1.90), scampi (£2.10) and prawn salad (£2.10). Well kept Greenalls Traditional and Original on electric pump; charming, relaxed atmosphere – including the strolling Siamese cat. *(Recommended by Andrew Rice)*

Greenalls · Licensee Shirley Wroughton-Craig · Real ale · Meals and snacks (lunchtime) · Children welcome · Open 11–3, 5.30–10.30

PLUMLEY   SJ7175   Map 7
Smoker

2½ miles from M6 junction 19: A556 towards Northwich and Chester

The leisured atmosphere of this well run traditional thatched pub makes it a relaxing motorway break – or, as one reader notes, a good stop on the way to Oulton Park motor races. An Edwardian print by Goodwin Kilburne of a hunt meeting outside this pub, named after a favourite racehorse of the Prince Regent, shows that it has hardly changed at least in this century. Its three communicating carpeted rooms have sofas, well cushioned settles, Windsor chairs and some rush-seat dining-chairs, with military prints on dark panelling in one room. Good value bar food includes wholemeal sandwiches such as freshly cooked chicken (85p), steak and kidney pie, curries, lasagne, chicken casserole and salads, and there's a separate restaurant. Robinsons Best and Best Mild on electric pump. Outside is kept as neatly as inside, with the quite spacious side lawn prettily broken up by roses and flowerbeds. *(Recommended by C McDowall, Colin McLaren, Dr B W Marsden, P J Taylor, Dennis Royles, R K Whitehead)*

Robinsons · Licensee Jorge Masso · Meals (not Sat evening or Sun lunchtime) and snacks; restaurant tel Lower Peover (056 581) 2338 · Open 11–3, 5.30–10.30

RAINOW   SJ9576   Map 7
Highwayman ★

Above village, a mile along A5002 towards Whaley Bridge

The Cheshire Plain, picturesquely framed by nearby hills, stretches out in a splendid panorama below this early seventeenth-century moorland pub. There are fine views both from the terrace outside and from the small windows in its series of snug and warmly welcoming little rooms. These have low beams, some antique settles as well as simpler cushioned seats around rustic wooden tables, abundant open fires in winter, and a high copper-covered bar counter serving well kept Thwaites from handpump. Good value food includes sandwiches and filled barm cakes with home-cooked meats (from 70p, steak canadien 80p), home-made soup (75p), black pudding (£1.20), savoury pancake rolls (£1.50), a choice of half a dozen freshly made pizzas (£1.50, with salad £2), breaded plaice (£1.60), freshly roasted chicken and scampi; darts, fruit machine. Parking nearby may not be easy on fine summer evenings or weekends (when the pub is very popular). *(Recommended by Gordon and Daphne; more reports please)*

Thwaites · Licensee Frank Jones · Real ale · Meals and snacks · Children in snug · Open 12–3, 6–10.30

SWETTENHAM   SJ8067   Map 7
Swettenham Arms ★

Should be signposted from A535 in Twemlow Green and B5392 in Withington; or turn off A54 just W of Congleton into Chelford Road (blue sign Axle Weight Limit Eight Tons, No Track Laying Vehicles, by white metal fence above low stone wall); however you come, mind the very sharp hairpin bend at the village

Sitting on the neat side lawn or on the flagstones out in front of this stone-tiled and shuttered white house, you hear nothing much beyond birds singing, cocks crowing, or perhaps the bells of the village church beyond the bushy cypresses screening the big car park. The beamed bar is open-plan, divided by the stubs of brown stone walls. It has been carefully restored, with leather slung stools and highly polished antique settles and tables on the Turkey carpet; there's a good aquarium. From the long bar counter the friendly licensees serve their son's Saxon Cross Bitter and Mild, kept well on handpump. Good bar food includes sandwiches such as Cheshire cheese or home-boiled ham (85p), home-made pâté or whitebait (£1.50), quiche or cod (£2.10), home-made chilli con carne (£2.20), scampi (£2.40), rainbow trout (£2.60), gammon or half-chicken (£3.20), home-made steak and kidney pie (£3.30), sirloin steak (£4.50) and home-made puddings such as apple pie (85p). The pub can get crowded at weekends, which can slow down the service. *(Recommended by William Meadon, Richard Steel, Dr B W Marsden, Dennis Royles, P J Taylor)*

Free house · Licensees Donald and Vera Winkle · Real ale · Meals and snacks Children in room away from bar · Open 11.30–3, 7–11 all year; usually closed lunchtime in winter; tel Holmes Chapel (0477) 71283

TARPORLEY   SJ5563   Map 7
Swan
High Street; A49

The flagstoned back bar used to be the kitchen in the days when this was a grand Georgian coaching-inn: you can still see the bread oven beside the log fire in the bare brick wall. This heavy-beamed room is now thoroughly civilised (the barman may wear a smart black bow tie), and comfortably furnished with Windsor armchairs, easy chairs and two or three softly cushioned antique oak settles. Bar food changes each day, and might include home-made soup (65p), sandwiches to order, omelettes (from £1.90), cod with mushy peas and chips (£2.35) and home-made steak and kidney pie (£2.45). Greenalls Local on handpump; unobtrusive music. There is a separate restaurant in the more stately main building. *(More reports please)*

Greenalls · Licensee Bernard McQueen · Real ale · Meals and snacks (not Sat evening, Sun lunchtime) · Children in eating area and restaurant · Open 11.30–3, 5.30–10.30; closed 25–26 Dec · Bedrooms tel Tarporley (082 93) 2411; £18/£28

TIVERTON   SJ5560   Map 7
Shady Oak
Bates Mill Lane; from A49 S of Tarporley follow Tiverton, Huxley, Tattersall signpost, then turn left at Beeston signpost; OS Sheet 117 reference 532603

This well kept and enthusiastically run canalside pub has splendid views over to Beeston and Peckforton castles on their dourly wooded sandstone crags. The attractively modernised carpeted lounge is airy and neatly kept, with house plants in the windows. It has sturdy cushioned seats around its tables, a white pitched ceiling, and French windows opening on to a flagstone terrace and lawn by the Shropshire Union Canal, with longboats moored alongside. Beside plenty of old-fashioned teak slatted seats and picnic-table sets out here, there is a tyre swing, slide and see-saw, and they hold barbecues twice a week in summer. A nice touch is having glass-cased large-scale maps and tourist information sheets by the car park. Bar food includes French onion soup (75p), sandwiches, filled baked potatoes (from £1), pâté (£1.25), a good choice of salads, pizza (£1.50), lasagne or beef and claret pie (£3), scampi (£3.10), trout with almonds (£3.75) and sirloin steak (£4.95), also children's dishes. Well kept Wilsons Original and Mild on handpump; a friendly and efficient young licensee; juke box; one fruit machine up the steps in a lobby, another in the quarry-tiled back public bar (which has darts, dominoes and cribbage). *(Recommended by Dr M V Jones)*

Wilsons (Watneys) · Licensee Andy Luccock · Real ale · Meals and snacks Children in area partly set aside · Weekend disco · Open 11.30–3, 5.30–10.30 (opens 7 in winter)

nr WARRINGTON SJ6188 Map 7
Ferry

Fiddlers Ferry; leaving Warrington on A562 Widnes road, keep eyes open as you pass Harris Carpets in Penketh; turn left beside Red Lion Cavalier Restaurant (Tetleys), and in Tannery Lane turn left again into Station Road; park by the railway and walk across – 50 yards or so; OS Sheet 108 reference 560863

Between the Manchester Ship Canal and the wide winding Mersey, this pretty and pleasantly isolated country pub was in the nineteenth century rated 'quite comfortable for visitors of a mildly adventurous mind' – and we'd agree today. There are old-fashioned easy chairs, an antique high-backed winged settle and a sofa in the pink-carpeted bar, as well as more modern seats; steps lead down to a brick-floored area with a good river view; and there are plenty of low beams, toby jugs, country pictures, nautical brassware such as an engine-room telegraph, even a figurehead. Well kept Wilsons Original on handpump (the bar counter has dated plaques showing Mersey floodwater heights); hot and cold dishes from the buffet counter (salads from £1.80); darts and juke box or piped music; picnic-table sets with cocktail parasols on a side terrace, in front and on the grass by the river. *(Recommended by Dr M V Jones, Andrew Rice)*

Wilsons (Watneys) · Licensee Gerald David Hewitt · Real ale · Meals and snacks (not Sun or Mon evenings) · Children in eating area · Live music Weds Open 11–3, 7–10.30

WILDBOARCLOUGH SJ9868 Map 7
Crag Inn

Village signposted from A54; pub S of village towards Wincle

Sheltering in a lush valley filled with rhododendrons and beech woods, this secluded little stone house is actually surrounded by high moors. The L-shaped bar has Windsor chairs, red brocade seats, antique flowery-cushioned settles, and a couple of coal fires in cool weather. Bar food includes sandwiches (from 75p, toasties 85p, home-roast beef 90p), home-made soup (75p), chicken chasseur, scampi or trout (£3.50), duck (£5.95) and steaks; there is also a separate restaurant, and a family dining-room. Apart from the usual drinks, they have a good range of non-alcoholic ones; darts in a side room. The crazy-paved terrace outside is surrounded by lilacs, old-fashioned roses and other flowers, and is raised a little above the quiet lane. *(More reports please)*

Free house · Licensees John and Helen Burgess · Meals (not Mon lunchtime)
Children in restaurant or dining-room · Open 12–3, 7–10.30

Lucky Dip

Besides the fully inspected pubs, you might like to try these Lucky Dips recommended and described by readers (if you do, please send us reports):

ACTON BRIDGE [SJ5975], *Maypole*: comfortably refurbished and well run spacious village pub with well kept Wilsons real ales and soft music *(G W Crowther, BB)*

ALSAGER [Sandbach Road, N; SJ7956], *Wilbraham Arms*: food good with excellent puddings; spacious, with pleasant service *(P C Goodwin)*

ASHTON [SJ5169] *Golden Lion*: bar snacks and Sunday lunchtime cold table in friendly country pub, never too crowded even in summer *(Andrew Rice)*

BARBRIDGE [SJ6156], *Barbridge*: by canal, moorings, good sized garden; Boddingtons, very varied menu, roomy inside *(D W Roberts)*

BOLLINGTON [SJ7286], *Olde No 3*: canal boats tie up at night behind it – used to be third stop on old London–York run, said to be haunted; warm and friendly, bar snacks, John Smiths *(Andrew Rice)*

BUNBURY [SJ5758]. *Dysart Arms*: food reasonably priced and beer good in honest-to-goodness village local, good atmosphere, children welcome *(John Prescott)*

BURTONWOOD [Alder Lane; SJ5692], *Fiddle i'th' Bag*: sign shows eighteenth-century seed-sowing fiddle; bar has one with original canvas bag. Bar snacks, basket meals, side restaurant, summer beer garden with outside bar *(Andrew Rice)*

CHESTER [Lower Bridge Street; SJ4166], *Bear & Billet*: well kept half-timbered pub dating from 1664 *(C Elliott)*; [The Groves] *Boathouse*: friendly licensees, plush River Bar with terrace, moorings; locals' Dee Bar has pool, darts, dominoes, juke box, TV; Youngers No 3 and Scotch on handpump, reasonably priced food, live music two or three nights a week *(D Watson)*

COMBERBACH [SJ6477], *Spinner & Bergamot*: food good, pleasant ambience *(E Knott)*

CROWTON [SJ5875], *Hare & Hounds*: Cheshire Hunt pub with lively local following *(G W Crowther)*

DANEBRIDGE [SJ9665], *Ship*: welcoming and friendly; relaxed *(Janet Williams)*

DISLEY [SJ9784], *White Horse*: friendly little local, clean and snug, with tiny back bar, good helpings of delicious home-cooked food *(Gordon and Daphne)*

DODLESTON [SJ3661], *Red Lion*: food good, generous helpings, attractively presented (especially salads and omelettes), reasonable prices; cheerful, quick service in neat, clean lounge and bar, always well patronised *(PJC)*

FRODSHAM [SJ5278], *Bears Paw*: old sandstone inn with small cobbled back car park where horses were once kept; inside decorated with horse brasses, and nice welcoming fire on cold evenings *(Andrew Rice)*

HASSALL GREEN [SJ7858], *Romping Donkey*: pleasant country pub, handy for M6 junction 16 *(Jack Taylor, LYM)*

HIGHER WHITLEY [Northwich Road; SJ6280], *Birch & Bottle*: warm friendly atmosphere in old pub with lots of brassware, antique prints and guns; well kept Greenalls, reasonably priced food, darts, entertaining antique one-armed bandit *(Dennis Royles)*

KELSALL [SJ5268], *Morris Dancers*: food basic but excellent and cheap; real ale (Greenalls) in low-beamed pub with log fire and weekend folk music *(F T and A K Hargreaves)*

LOWER WHITLEY [SJ6179], *Chetwode Arms*: unspoilt traditional country pub with comfortable lounge, good open fires, old-fashioned snug and tap-room, Greenalls real ales, bowling green *(Dennis Royles)*

MACCLESFIELD [Mill Street; SJ9273], *Bear*: food excellent, with various delicious cheeses, also pâtés and salads; Ind Coope Burton, pleasant environment *(Juliet and Richard Keen);* [27 Churchwallgate] *Castle*: quaint friendly old pub in ancient cobbled lane, good atmosphere *(Janet Williams)*

nr MACCLESFIELD [Sutton Lane Ends; SJ9273], *Sutton Hall*: food good, and well kept Bass and Stones on handpump, in small hotel serving also as local pub, in converted manor house; for pub location see OS Sheet 118 reference 925715 *(R L D Cochrane)*

MOBBERLEY [SJ7879], *Bird in Hand*: eighteenth-century building with four or five rooms leading off the bar via alcoves; very friendly service and regulars; snacks such as peanuts and cocktail biscuits on the bar *(David Guthrie);* [Town Lane] *Bulls Head*: friendly and comfortable low-beamed village pub with soft lighting, well kept Tetleys real ale, folk-singing landlord and own immaculate bowling green *(David Guthrie, B B)*

NANTWICH [Hospital Street; SJ6552], *Lamb*: good bar snacks and good traditional restaurant in cool elegant eighteenth-century coaching-inn, refined but unpretentious; real ale *(P J Taylor)*

NORLEY [SJ5773], *Tigers Head*: good food, especially home-baked steak and kidney pie, small selection of other dishes; well kept Burtonwood beer, in biggish village pub with excellent views *(Jim Brown)*

PARKGATE [Boathouse Lane; SJ2878], *Parkgate Hotel*: refurbished pub with real ale served in unusual pint glasses, lots of atmosphere; bedrooms *(R L Wilson)*

PLUMLEY [Lower Peover Road; SJ7175], *Golden Pheasant*: large friendly pub with good value Lees real ale and food, separate dining area and games room *(Dr B W Marsden)*

PUDDINGTON [A540; SJ3373], *Yacht*: good choice of beers and bar food in popular attractively decorated pub with good atmosphere *(David Regan)*

SANDBACH [Newcastle Road; SJ7661], *Old Hall*: charming pub/hotel with good bar food, quick friendly service, Jacobean panelling, handsome restaurant *(E G Parish)*

SANDIWAY [SJ6071], *Bluecap*: friendly pub with excellent reasonably priced Sunday lunch, good beer, restaurant and nightclub at weekends *(N M Pickford)*

TARPORLEY [High Street; SJ5563], *Rising Sun*: good food and service, well kept Robinsons; charming comfortable low-ceilinged building with open log fires *(Simon Evans)*

TARVIN [SJ4967], *Village Green*: fully refurbished in art deco style: now a roomy and comfortable 'venue pub' with attractive lighting, bistro-type bar meals, cocktails, reasonable wine list, TV, good terrace *(EK)*

THELWALL [SJ6587], *Pickering Arms*: coal fire and lots of old beams covered with brass ornaments and horse brasses; friendly village atmosphere, good bar snacks, Greenalls ales *(Andrew Rice)*

WESTON [SJ7352], *White Lion*: attractive half-timbered seventeenth-century country pub; cosy inside with low beams, open fires and good food – even turbot and bass for Sunday lunch *(Gareth Ratcliffe, A K Grice, William Meadon, Richard Steel)*

WHITELEY GREEN [SJ9278], *Windmill*: friendly landlord and good range of real ales in big open-plan free house; good bar food, big garden and picnic area near Macclesfield Canal; for pub location see OS Sheet 118 reference 924789 *(Dr B W Marsden)*

WINCHAM [SJ6775], *Black Greyhound*: good choice of reasonably priced food in very friendly pub *(Jon Brown)*

WINCLE [SU9666], *Wild Boar*: good range of reasonably priced food and well kept Robinsons ales in comfortable main-road country pub near moors *(LYM)*

Cornwall

This year's new entries in Cornwall include one that jumps straight in with a star – the Bush at Morwenstow, a charmingly old-fashioned country pub which is close to some of Cornwall's finest cliffs and has some claim to be one of the oldest pubs in Britain. Others on or near the sea include two more new entries: the friendly Blue Peter just above Polperro's pretty harbour, and the Mill House at Trebarwith (a converted watermill close to a fine secluded beach); also the Pandora near Mylor Bridge (an atmospheric pub right on the water), Port Gaverne Hotel near Port Isaac (a nice place to stay, almost alone by a National Trust cove), the Cobweb at Boscastle (gains a star this year for its cheerful, relaxed atmosphere and delightful village setting), Old Ferry above the Fowey at Bodinnick (good food, a nice place to stay), Shipwrights Arms in Helford (barbecues on a palm-shaded terrace), Lamorna Wink (a splendid collection of nautical memorabilia, a stroll away from a beautiful shell-sand cove), Rashleigh Inn in Polkerris (isolated by a handsomely rebuilt jetty and terrace), and the Rising Sun in St Mawes (a comfortable small hotel with waterfront terrace), with many others to choose from. Prices are attractive here: bed and breakfast is often less than £10 a head even in high season, pasties at 65p can be big enough to make a meal of, and beer in the average pub tends to be cheaper than in another

The Miners Arms, Mithian

county's cheapest pubs. Even so, there is a wide range in drinks prices here, with pubs selling the local Devenish and St Austell beers – not to mention brewing their own, like the atmospheric old Blue Anchor in Helston, which is up to 25 per cent cheaper than ones selling beers from further away. The cheapest we found for drinks were the recently refurbished Dolphin in Penzance (Captain Hawkins' HQ before the Armada) and the well run Logan Rock at Treen (good value food in a warmly old-fashioned atmosphere), while the Blue Peter in Polperro and the Port Gaverne Hotel stood out for selling national brews at low prices for the area. The Market Inn in Truro has really cheap food, and you can eat very well in the Maltsters Arms by the green in Chapel Amble (a new entry this year), the unspoilt St Kew Inn (another new entry, very popular for its evening steaks), the friendly Miners Arms in Mithian, the civilised and attractive New Inn in Manaccan and the charming flower-filled Roseland in Philleigh. Besides pubs already mentioned, places to stay include the welcoming old Carpenters Arms in Metherell, the comfortable Weary Friar in Pillaton, the stylish and well run Jubilee in Pelynt, the Coachmakers Arms in Callington (yet another new entry) and – specially useful for the north coast – the Cornish Arms in Pendoggett.

In winter most pubs close half an hour earlier in the evening than stated here, and may open later too.

BODINNICK   SX1352   Map 1
Old Ferry Inn

The good restaurant and residents' lounge of this cosy old inn have superb views across the River Fowey. The public rooms are stepped back from here, following the steep slope of the hillside – at the back, a games room (with darts, shove-ha'penny, dominoes and a fruit machine) is actually cut into the rock itself. The comfortable lounge bar has a 'Parliament' clock, aquarium, and sea photographs and prints, and behind that there's a traditionally furnished public bar – a friendly room, with sea photographs on the panelled walls and a very large stuffed salmon. Barfood includes home-made pasties (58p), sandwiches, ploughman's (£1.40), smoked mackerel (£1.55) and home-cooked ham salad (£2); Flowers Original and St Austell Tinners on handpump; bar billiards played in winter. Make sure your brakes work well if you park on the steep lane outside. *(More reports please)*

Free house · Licensee Kenneth Farr · Real ale · Snacks · Children in eating area and games room · Open 10.30–2.30, 6–11 (11–2.30, 7–10.30 in winter) Bedrooms tel Polruan (072 687) 237; £16.50 (£18.50B)/£33 (£37B)

If you enjoy your visit to a pub please tell the publican. They work extraordinarily long hours, and when people show their appreciation it makes it all seem worthwhile.

CORNWALL

BOSCASTLE   SX0990 Map 1
Cobweb ★
On B3263, just E of harbour

Just right after a three-hour spell on the Cornish Coast Path, say
readers: a lively place, roomy in winter but crowded in summer, with
a flagstone floor, two or three curved high-backed winged settles
against its dark stone walls, a few leatherette dining-chairs, heavy
beams hung with hundreds of old bottles, and a log fire in cool
weather. Bar food includes rolls and sandwiches (from 70p – Danish
open sandwiches with local prawns and crab are a speciality), locally
made pasties (80p), ploughman's (from £1.30), basket meals from
pasty or hamburger (£1.30) upwards, salads (from £1.70), with a
daily hot special (roasts on Sunday) and children's meals; also a
restaurant upstairs, praised by readers. Well kept St Austell Tinners,
HSD and Wadworths 6X on handpump, with a guest beer tapped
from the cask. There's a good juke box, darts, dominoes, a pool-table
(keen players here) and a fruit machine, with a space game in the big
communicating family room – which has an enormous armchair
carved out of a tree trunk as well as more conventional Windsor
armchairs, and another cosy winter fire. Opening off this, a good-
sized children's room has a second pool-table and more machines.
The tiny steeply cut harbour nearby is very attractive, as is the main
village climbing up above. (Recommended by Dr N A Hedger, Julia Hoyle)

*Free house · Licensee Alfred Bright · Real ale · Meals and snacks · Children in
restaurant, family room and children's room · Live music Sat, sometimes Weds
Open 10.30–2.30, 5.30–11*

Napoleon
High Street; just off B3266 by Bottreaux House Hotel, entering village from
Camelford

This sixteenth-century cosy white cottage is up at the top of the steep,
quaint village – well worth the walk from our other entry here, with
splendid views on the way. Several little flagstoned rooms ramble
around: one has comfortable red leatherette easy chairs facing a big
log fire in its massive stone fireplace; another has a large aquarium set
into its wall, and a good collection of Napoleon prints including
many uncommon ones (there's a well lit pool-table in here). Food,
mainly home-cooked, includes soup (80p), sandwiches (plain from
60p, toasted from 70p), pasty (70p), fresh-caught cod (£1.40), T-
bone steak (£4.25) – there's also a separate restaurant; well kept
Bass, St Austell HSD and Tinners tapped from the cask, Inch's cider;
darts sensibly placed in a side room; also a space game, fruit machine
and piped pop music. There are seats out on a small sheltered terrace,
with fairy lights strung around a huge fatsia. (Recommended by
M Buxton)

*Free house · Licensee Allan Dogan · Real ale · Meals and snacks · Children in
eating area and restaurant · Folk music Weds and Fri · Open 11–2.30, 6–11
(opens noon in winter)*

It's against the law for bar staff to smoke while handling food or drink.

CALLINGTON   SX3669 Map 1
Coachmakers Arms

Newport Square (A388 towards Launceston)

Handy for its good value simple food (served in unusually generous helpings) and comfortable bedrooms, this inn has an enthusiastic local following. The long irregularly shaped bar has black beams, timbered butter-coloured walls decorated with reproductions of old local advertisements (particularly for coaching and coachbuilding), little winged settles and stools made from polished brass-bound casks; one comfortably carpeted end has a log-effect electric fire in its stone fireplace. The food includes soup, often gamey (75p), liver pâté (£1.40), hot savoury crab (£1.95), omelettes (from £2.65), salads (from £2.95), plaice (£3), chicken (£3.25) and gammon grilled with various accompaniments (£4.45), with daily specials such as crab pâté, smoked salmon mousse (£1.95) and beef and vegetable curry (£2). Puddings come with lots of clotted cream, and there's a local belief that the only people who can actually get through three courses here are Commandos straight in from a day's training on the Moor. Fruit machine, and on our visit – with luck put right by now – rather a lot of noise from the cooler (the beers are keg). *(Recommended by Carol Swan, Adrian Burnett, Mrs M Smith, Debbie and Ian Trotman)*

Free house · Licensees Ken and Sheila Hadfield · Snacks (winter) and meals Open 11–2.30, 6–11 · Bedrooms tel Liskeard (0579) 82567; £17.50B/£27B

CHAPEL AMBLE   SW9975 Map 1
Maltsters Arms

Village signposted from A39 NE of Wadebridge; and from B3314

Good home-cooked bar food in this attractive sixteenth-century village pub includes soup (70p), ploughman's (£1.35), salads (from £1.80), plaice (£1.90), beef curry (£2), trout with almonds (£2.85) and sirloin steak (£4.85), with daily specials such as hotpot (£1.60), salad quiche (£1.85) and chicken and mushroom or turkey and ham pie (£1.95). Even the simplest things, say sausage and chips (£1.50), are praised by readers. There's a warm welcome in the attractively opened-up rooms of the busy main bar, which has bared stone walls with some panelling, black oak joists in the white ceiling, a capacious stone fireplace, and heavy wooden tables on the partly carpeted big flagstones. Besides an upstairs restaurant (the Sunday lunches are reported to be specially good value), there is a family room, and a side room with Windsor chairs. Well kept St Austell Tinners on handpump; in winter, darts and pool. Benches outside in a sheltered sunny corner of the pub overlook the village green. *(Recommended by Peter and Rose Flower, Miss G B Austen, A A Worthington, Mrs Joan Harris, Mrs Hilary Hyde, Linda and Alex Christison)*

Free house · Licensee Dudley Hugh Dines · Real ale · Meals and snacks Children in restaurant and family room · Open 10.30–2.30, 5.30–11

Cribbage is a card game using a block of wood with holes for matchsticks or special pins with which to keep the score; regulars in cribbage pubs are usually happy to teach strangers how to play.

Chain Locker (Marine Restaurant)

Custom House Quay; off Church Street – the main shopping street, parallel to waterfront

Seats in the big corner windows of the bar and picnic-table sets outside on the quay have a fine view of fishing boats and the old St Denys steam tug a few feet away in Falmouth's small central harbour. Wood floor, plank ceiling hung with ship's pennants and wheels, strip-panelled walls and a collection of ship models, marine photographs and general chandlery reinforce the nautical atmosphere, and many people working with boats use this as their local – it strongly supports the local lifeboat. A bigger communicating inner room has a good separate darts alley. Well kept Devenish and Cornish Best on handpump; substantial and well garnished sandwiches (from 75p, crab (£1.40), ploughman's (£1.50), a buffet table with salads such as home-made pork pie, quiche, ham, beef, crab and prawn (£2.45–£3.25), and in winter hot dishes too; separate restaurant; darts, fruit machine, piped music. (*Recommended by Gwen and Peter Andrews, Howard Gascoyne, D A McLellan*)

Devenish · Licensee Terence Kelwin · Real ale · Meals and snacks (not Sun evening) · Parking may be difficult · Children in eating area and restaurant Open 10.30–2.30, 6–11

King's Head

Church Street; the main shopping street, parallel to the waterfront

The long central servery of this friendly town pub divides it into two: on the left, a series of rooms with pews, high-backed settles, tubby little casks, old plates and engravings on partly panelled walls, stuffed fish and a winter log fire; on the other side, a narrower area with lots of mirrors down the wall. Though it gets crowded at lunchtime, people do make room for you – and even when he's busy the landlord takes trouble to draw his well kept Devenish and Cornish Best carefully. Bar food includes filled rolls (80p), sandwiches, hot dishes such as shepherd's pie or beef casserole (around £1.25–£2) and home-cooked cold meats with a choice of individually priced salads. There is a separate restaurant upstairs. In the evening the clientele is much younger; table skittles, fruit machine. *(Recommended by Gwen and Peter Andrews)*

Devenish · Licensee Richard Stiles · Real ale · Meals and snacks (lunchtime) Children at back of lounge · Folk guitarist Weds or Thurs · Parking may be difficult · Open 11–2.30, 6.30–11

HELFORD   SW7526 Map 1
Shipwrights Arms ★

A combination of good value food, splendid friendly service and the lovely waterside position make this well worth visiting – especially on summer evenings, when you can have eight-ounce burgers (£2.95), veal chops, fish or prawns (£4.95) and steaks (from £5.75) barbecued out on the terraces, which drop down among flowers and even palm trees to the water's edge. The top part of the terrace is roofed over with Perspex. Inside, snacks include home-made pasties (80p), ploughman's (£1.75; with crab £2.95) and open sandwiches, with salads such as home-baked ham (£2.95) and crab (£3.95) from the lunchtime buffet. Winter dishes include home-made soup (90p), crab claws with garlic mayonnaise (£1.50) and local scallops in white wine (£5.50). There are lots of ship models and lamps, drawings of lifeboat coxswains, and sea pictures, with yachtsmen congregating under the low shiny ochre ceiling by the bar counter. At the other end there are oak settles and tables in a dining area with waitress service; there is an open fire in winter. John Devenish and Cornish Best on tap, under light blanket pressure; dominoes, cribbage, euchre, piped music. *(Recommended by Gwen and Peter Andrews, A M Simmons, David Hills, Mrs M E Sanders-Hewett, Flt Lt A D Harkness, Heather Sharland)*

Devenish · Licensees Brandon and Susan Flynn · Real ale · Meals and snacks tel Manaccan (032 623) 235 · Children in dining area · Parking only right outside village in summer · Open 11–2.30, 6–11

HELSTON   SW6527 Map 1
Blue Anchor

50 Coinagehall Street

This thatched medieval town pub – once a monks' hospice – has a series of small, snug rooms opening off the central corridor, with flagstone floors, low beams, interesting old prints, some bared stone walls, simple old-fashioned furniture, and in one room a fine inglenook fireplace. The Blue Anchor was right at the forefront of the trend for the revival of own brews, and still uses its ancient brewhouse to produce Medium, Best, 'Spingo' Special and Extra Special ales. A family room has several space games and a fruit machine. Past the brewhouse, and an old stone bench in the sheltered little garden, is a skittle alley which has its own bar at busy times (when the pub does get crowded). The nearby Cornwall Aero Park has a lot of family attractions, and Godolphin House is well worth visiting. (*Recommended by Steve and Carolyn Harvey, Mr and Mrs R Houghton*)

Own brew · Licensees Patricia and Sidney Cannon · Real ale · Snacks Children in family room · Parking sometimes difficult · Open 10.30–2.30, 6–11

KILKHAMPTON   SS2511   Map 1
New Inn
A39 N of Bude

A warm welcome for strangers in this spacious and well kept local. The bar rambles back through a series of communicating rooms: the first is carpeted, with winged high-backed settles, pews, a cushioned window seat and a big log fire; the next has cushioned wall seats and crazy-paved flagstones; then, under a high pitched ceiling, there are blond spindleback chairs, a pew, a cushioned wicker settee, a fine wood-burning stove with fat stainless-steel chimney, a good juke box and sitting space game; finally, behind a glass panel, there is a spacious stone-walled games room with darts, a fruit machine, skittles and pool. Bar food includes sandwiches, pasties or beefburgers (65p), ploughman's with cheese (£1.30) or with ham (£1.40), curries (£1.95), cod or chicken (£2) and scampi (£2.20); well kept Bass on handpump. (*Recommended by D Lloyd, R Gorzynski, Mr and Mrs S Crossingham*)

Free house · Licensee Christopher Pearce · Real ale · Meals and snacks Children in games room · Open 11–2.30, 7–11

LAMORNA   SW4424   Map 1
Lamorna Wink ★

The collection of warship mementoes, sea photographs and nautical brassware in this simply furnished beamed pub is one of the best in the country. This is a friendly and neatly kept place, with flowers on the tables and bar food that includes superb home-made quiches (£1.50) and fruit pies with Cornish cream (80p) as well as sandwiches (from 60p, local crab £1.30), ploughman's (£1.50) and salads such as crab (£4). John Devenish and Cornish Best tapped from the cask; darts, pool, dominoes, cribbage, a fruit machine, space game and a juke box – readers like the way the games are out in a connected, but quite separate, building. Sitting on the front benches, you can just hear the sound of the sea in the attractive sandy cove down the lane (a fine place to search for seashells); it joins the birdsong and the burble of the stream behind, where you can catch trout. The 'wink' of the name used to be the secret sign you had to give when ordering, if you wanted something stronger than the ale originally covered by this pub's licence. *(Recommended by Gwen and Peter Andrews, Andy Jones and the PA Club, Prof David Brokensha, Elizabeth Haigh, John and Lucy Roots, Richard Gibbs)*

Devenish · Licensee Bob Drennan · Real ale · Meals and snacks (lunchtime) Children in games room · Open 10.30–2.30, 6–11

MALPAS   SW8442 Map 1
Heron

Village signposted from A39 at main Truro roundabout

The long rectangular bar is friendly and comfortable, with maps and plates over the wall banquettes, and outside, a sunny slate-paved terrace has a good view over the wooded creek far below. A wide choice of quickly served food includes generously filled open sandwiches such as crab, tongue or ham, ploughman's or smoked mackerel, and hot dishes such as cheese and asparagus flan, pizza, curry or plaice. Evening meals include a good range of salads and more solid dishes such as pork Marsala and beef Stroganoff (main dishes around £5). Well kept St Austell Tinners and HSD on handpump; fruit machine, space game, maybe piped music. *(Recommended by Jack Davey, R G Bentley, Patrick Young; more reports please)*

St Austell · Licensee Calvin Kneebone · Real ale · Meals and snacks · Children in eating area · Open 11–2.30, 6–11

MANACCAN   SW7625 Map 1
New ★

Down hill signposted to Gillan and St Keverne

This friendly and civilised pub combines charming furnishings and atmosphere with good food. It concentrates on home-cooked locally caught fish, from simple kedgeree or crab salad to sea bass, monk-fish provençale, John Dory in parsley butter, langoustines and so on (depending on availability), with home-made soup, sandwiches and steaks (evenings), and changing specials such as devilled kidneys, beef and prawn hash or Chinese liver casserole. There are two rooms with beam-and-plank ceilings and traditional built-in wall seats, and nice touches such as oriental rugs, individually chosen chairs, freshly cut flowers or heavy embroidered cloths on the tables; squeezed into a converted hearth, with plates decorating its chimney-piece, are some seats and a table. Devenish and Cornish Best tapped from the cask, and farm cider. A sheltered lawn slopes up behind the old thatched house. *(Recommended by A Darroch Harkness, J P Berryman, Gwen and Peter Andrews, George Jonas)*

Devenish · Licensee Patrick Cullinan · Real ale · Meals (not Tues evening) and snacks · Children welcome · Parking may be difficult in summer Open 11–2.30, 6–11

MARHAMCHURCH   SS2203   Map 1
Bullers Arms

The entertaining landlord makes sure of a friendly atmosphere in the L-shaped bar of this big village inn. Little settles form booths around its walls, local hunting trophies are mounted above the stone fireplace, and a good long bar counter supplies well kept St Austell Tinners and HSD on handpump, or tapped from casks in a back still-room. The widest choice of bar food is at lunchtime, including omelettes, home-cured ham salad, lasagne, home-made steak and turkey or steak and kidney pie, and grilled Tamar trout; most main dishes are around £2.50–£3, some are around £8 (such as a big T-bone steak or lobster salad); there is also a separate evening dining room. Juke box, with darts and fruit machine in a flagstone-floored back part; beyond that a separate pool-room with a space game; also shuffleboard, and a spacious functions room and skittle alley which in summer becomes an overflow family bar. The simply furnished modern bedrooms are comfortable and have bath and colour TV. Opposite where the village road joins the A39, a mile-long footpath leads to the cliffy coves just north of Widemouth Sand. *(Recommended by Gwen and Peter Andrews, Prof A N Black)*

Free house · Licensee Bill Kneebone · Real ale · Meals and snacks · Children in bar eating area and games room · Open 11–2.30, 6–11 · Country and western and ballads Thurs and Sat · Bedrooms tel Widemouth Bay (028 885) 277; £12B/£24B

METHERELL   SX4069   Map 1
Carpenters Arms

Village signposted from Honicombe, which is signposted from St Ann's Chapel, just W of Gunnislake on A390; pub signposted in village, OS Sheet 201 reference 408694

Tiny windows, huge polished flagstones, massive stone walls and heavy black beams suggest the age of this village inn – actually some

The Pandora, nr Mylor Bridge

500 years. Its bar is a friendly place, with winged high-backed red leatherette settles in its various alcoves, brasses, lots of succulent plants, and a large slowly ticking clock. There are easy chairs in the simply furnished separate lounge. We'd like more reports on the food served by the new licensees, which includes pasties (from 52p), sandwiches (from 75p), home-made soup (75p), ploughman's with cheese or ham (from £1.40), salads (from £1.80), kebabs (pork £2.10), omelettes (from £2.20), vegetarian dishes (£2.50), beef bourguignonne (£4.10) and steaks (from six-ounce sirloin at £4.95). Well kept Bass and guest beers tapped from casks behind the bar, and Flowers Original on handpump; gently piped music; sensibly placed darts, shove-ha'penny, dominoes and a fruit machine. Outside, near an old well, tables are sheltered by the building and by a balcony of the neatly harmonising upstairs bedroom extension. Cotehele, the lovely National Trust Tudor house by the head of the Tamar estuary, is a couple of miles further on through these narrow lanes. *(Recommended by Carol Swan)*

Free house · Licensees Doug and Jill Brace · Real ale · Meals and snacks Children in lounge · Open 11.30–2.30, 7–11 · Bedrooms tel Liskeard (0579) 50242; £9.50/£19

MITCHELL   SW8654 Map 1
Plume of Feathers

The L-shaped carpeted bar of this friendly roadside pub is decorated with lots of army hats, helmets and guns. Reasonably priced simple bar food includes pasties and filled rolls, ploughman's, chicken, plaice, salads and scampi, and with well kept John Devenish and Cornish Best on handpump, this is a useful break from the busy A30. It is comfortably furnished with captain's chairs, traditional winged settles built in to its walls, a shelf full of toby jugs and a winter log fire. Fruit machine, gentle piped music, and in winter darts and euchre; space game in one of the two family rooms. There are tables on a raised lawn behind the car park. *(Recommended by Robin Anderson, Flt Lt A D Harkness; more reports please)*

Devenish · Licensee John Dart · Real ale · Meals and snacks · Children in family room · Open 11–2.30, 6–11

MITHIAN   SW7450 Map 1
Miners Arms ★   [*illustrated on page 108*]

Since last year this well run and welcoming pub's comfortable main lounge bar has been enlarged; there is also a cellar lounge and darts room, and a little back bar with bags of character and a good fire in cool weather. Quickly served lunchtime bar food includes pasties (65p), brown bread sandwiches (from 65p), soup (75p), ploughman's (£1.40), omelettes (from £1.50), good hotpot (£1.75), plaice (£1.95), chicken (£2.35), salads (from £2.60), scampi (£2.70), and perhaps a warmly recommended special such as rabbit pie. In the evening there's more concentration on meals, served in the restaurant, with soup (85p), several other starters (£1.50) and quite a wide choice of main dishes from pizza (£1.85) and chicken (£2.50) or local trout (£4.35) to sirloin steak (£4.95) – booking suggested. Readers' children have been offered a special menu and been well looked after. Dominoes, fruit machine, piped music; well kept Devenish and Cornish Best. There are benches on the sheltered front cobbled terrace, where barbecues are served in the summer. *(Recommended by P D Atkinson, Valerie and Tony Gibbons, D Griffin, Flt Lt A D Harkness, Patrick Young, Richard Cole, Richard Gibbs)*

Devenish · Licensee Colin Gilham · Real ale · Meals (lunchtime) and snacks Children in upstairs lounge · Open 11–2.30, 6.30–11 · Bedrooms tel St Agnes (087 255) 2375; £9/£15

MORWENSTOW SS2015 Map 1
Bush ★

Village signposted off A39 N of Kilkhampton

A ten-minute walk from Vicarage Cliff – one of the grandest parts of the Cornish coast, with 400-foot precipices – this delightful old-fashioned country pub is very welcoming. It has a strong claim to be one of the very oldest in Britain: it was once a monastic rest-house on a pilgrim route between Wales and Spain, and dates in part from just over 1,000 years ago (a Celtic piscina carved from serpentine stone is still set in one wall). The main bar is quite small, with ancient built-in settles, a big stone fireplace, and a snug side area with antique seats, a lovely old elm trestle table, and a wooden propeller from a 1930 De Havilland Gipsy. Good value home-made lunchtime food includes soup (50p), tasty pasties (60p), ham sandwiches (80p), toasted sandwiches (£1.10), stew or steak and kidney pie (£1.10). Evening dishes include cod (£1.40), chicken or scampi (£2), small mixed grills (£3), and local fresh fish and crab when available; you can have full evening meals in the separate dining-room (booking ahead only). Well kept Devenish Wessex on handpump, and St Austell BB (kept under a light CO_2 blanket) tapped from a wooden cask behind the wood-topped stone bar counter; pewter tankards line the beams above it. An upper bar, open at busy times, has built-in settles and is decorated with miners' lamps, casks, funnels, antique knife-grinding wheels and so forth. Darts, fruit machine. Seats outside are sheltered in the slightly sunken yard. *(Recommended by M N Bowman, BOB)*

Free house · Licensee J H Gregory · Real ale · Meals tel Morwenstow (028 883) 242; snacks · Children in dining-room · Open 10.30–2.30, 6–11

MULLION SW6719 Map 1
Old Inn

Near centre

The long lanternlit bar of this thatched village inn has a big inglenook fireplace with its original bread oven, comfortable seats on its wood-block floor, and crabbing photographs, together with coins and plates salvaged from local eighteenth-century shipwrecks, on the cream walls. Bar food includes sandwiches (from 70p, toasted 10p extra; local crab £1.50), soup (70p), well presented ploughman's

(£1.35), a choice of pizzas (from £1.90: half-size are half-price), home-made cottage pie (£2.25) and scampi (£2.50), with children's dishes such as fish fingers (£1.15). The small restaurant is popular with readers, offering main dishes such as lemon sole or whole baby chicken (£6), steaks (from £7) and fresh lobster (around £7); open summer evenings, Tuesday to Saturday. Well kept John Devenish and Cornish Best on handpump; sensibly placed darts, table skittles, shove-ha'penny, dominoes, cribbage and a fruit machine; piped music. The children's room has TV and a small aviary. You can sit outside. (*Recommended by D W Roberts, Prof A N Black, Miss P M Gammon, N Kirkby, S G Revill*)

Devenish · Licensee Jack Gayton · Real ale · Meals and snacks · Children in restaurant and children's room · Open 11–2.30, 6–11 · Bedrooms tel Mullion (0326) 240240; £11(£12B)/£20(£22B); also two self-catering cottages

nr MYLOR BRIDGE   SW8036   Map 1
Pandora ★   [*illustrated on page 116*]

Restronguet Passage: from A39 in Penryn, take turning signposted Mylor Church, Mylor Bridge, Flushing and go straight through Mylor Bridge following Restronguet Passage signs; or from A39 further N, at or near Perranarworthal, take turning signposted Mylor, Restronguet, then follow Restronguet Weir signs, but turn left down hill at Restronguet Passage sign

Since our last edition, this medieval thatched pub, marvellously placed on the waterfront (the star rating is largely for its position), has been taken over by a Cornish couple from a well known boat-building family. We inspected not long after, and found the interconnecting rooms of the rambling bar little changed: low wooden ceilings, some carpeting now joining the big flagstones and uneven red tiles, leatherette wall benches built around tables in cosy alcoves, a log fire in a high hearth (to protect it against tidal floods), and a highly polished kitchen range. Upstairs there is now a new oak buffet counter, but the food served is much as ever – quiche, crab, home-cooked joints and help-yourself salads (from £2.50), with good puddings; also pasties (£1), sandwiches and ploughman's. The room up here now functions as a restaurant in the evenings (main courses, especially fish, around £4–£7.50); we had scallops delicately cooked with purée potato soaked in cider, served with excellent lightly done interesting vegetables. St Austell BB, Tinners and HSD on handpump, and local farmhouse cider; the unmarked pump serves Bass. There are lots of picnic-table sets in front, by a long floating jetty. Dominoes, euchre; showers and launderette for visiting yachtsmen. (*Recommended by D J Milner, Mr and Mrs J W Gibson, Steve and Carolyn Harvey, Andy Jones and the P A Club, Elizabeth Haigh, Richard Cole, George Jonas, J P Berryman, G Joshua, Dr A K Clarke, D W Roberts*)

St Austell · Licensees Ralph and Vicky Mitchell · Real ale · Meals and snacks Children welcome · Impromptu singing and guitar usually Thurs · Open 11–2.30, 6–11

Please tell us if any Lucky Dips deserve to be upgraded to a main entry – and why. No stamp needed: write to *The Good Pub Guide*, FREEPOST, London SW10 0BR.

PELYNT   SX2055   Map 1
Jubilee

B3359 NW of Looe

Good value bar food in this comfortable inn – served quickly by neat and friendly waitresses – includes home-made soup (70p), big wholesome hot pasties (70p), a good choice of freshly cut sandwiches (from 80p, local crab £1.20), ploughman's, a hot dish of the day (£2.30), home-baked ham and eggs (£2.40), local plaice fillets (£2.60) and meat salads (from £3.20). There is also a restaurant. The friendly lounge bar has a cushioned seventeenth-century carved settle as well as Windsor armchairs around the circular oak tables, a winter log fire in a big stone fireplace, and attractively moulded oak beams in the front part. Behind is a cosy area decorated with mementos of Queen Victoria. A green carpet covers most of the handsome flagstones in here, but these are left bare in the public bar, which has pool, sensibly placed darts, dominoes, a juke box and a fruit machine. Well kept Flowers Original on handpump. There is a crazy-paved central courtyard, and barbecues are lit on most summer evenings.
(Recommended by J A and M R Catterall, C McDowall)

Free house · Licensee Frank Williams · Real ale · Meals and snacks Open 10.30–2.30, 6–11 · Bedrooms tel Lanreath (0503) 20312; £12.50 (£15B)/£25 (£30B)

PENDEEN   SW3834   Map 1
Radjel

This friendly and unpretentious granite village inn is close to the Cornish Coast Path, not far from Cornwall's stormy western tip, and handy for the excellent tin-mining museum at Geevor. Indeed, the traditionally furnished public bar is decorated with photographs of local tin mining, while there are those of local shipwrecks on the stripped stone walls of the lounge. Bar food includes sandwiches (from 70p, crab £1.40), ploughman's (£1.60), chicken (£1.90), fisherman's platter (£2.10) and scampi (£2.25), and when it's not too busy daily specials such as crab cooked in a cheese, wine and cream sauce. St Austell Tinners on handpump; also BB, HSD and XXXX Mild kept under light blanket pressure; darts, pool, dominoes, cribbage, juke box and a fruit machine. There are tables outside.
(Recommended by Annie Spencer, Patrick Young; more reports please)

St Austell · Licensee Antony Johnson · Real ale · Meals and snacks · Children in eating area · Three bedrooms tel Penzance (0736) 788446; £7.50/£15

PENDOGGETT   SX0279   Map 1
Cornish Arms

B3314

This slate-hung house is a good base for the north Cornish coast, with spotlessly comfortable bedrooms, and views down a valley to the sea (about a mile's walk). It has old-fashioned furniture in the two panelled rooms of the front bar, where high-backed built-in oak settles surround solid old wooden tables on the Delabole slate floor. Behind is a big, lively locals' bar, with more high-backed settles around stripped deal tables, a big woodburning stove, and darts, skittles, euchre, a fruit machine and maybe sports on the colour TV. The good lunchtime buffet includes home-made soup, a wide choice of salads with meat cut from home-cooked joints (£2.75), a hot dish of the day (around £2) and home-made fruit pies. In the evenings it's sandwiches (from 55p, crab £1.25) and pasties instead, in the bars, with ploughman's (£1.10, ham £1.40) and smoked mackerel (£1.40); a separate restaurant is open for meals then, too. Bass and a Special brewed for the pub on tap, with changing guest beers such as Cotleigh Tawny and Wadworths 6X, and Flowers Original on handpump. There are tables out on a corner terrace. *(Recommended by D A Lloyd, Paul A Smith, Elizabeth Haigh, Julia Hoyle)*

Free house · Licensees Nigel Pickstone, Alan and Margaret Wainwright · Real ale · Meals and snacks · Children lunchtime; restaurant only, evenings · Open 11–3, 5.30–11 · Bedrooms tel Port Isaac (020 888) 263; £23 (£25B)/£36 (£38B)

PENZANCE   SW4730   Map 1
Dolphin

Newlyn road; keep along waterfront; pub opposite harbour soon after swing bridge

Captain Hawkins used this harbourside inn as his HQ while he was down here to train fishermen for the navy that beat the Spanish Armada in 1588. It still has plenty of sailor customers, and the main bar makes a welcome change from many more touristy places, with its big windows looking over the road to the working harbour and the fishing boats, yachts and coasters. Extensive refurbishments since our last edition have made it much more comfortable, with beams and timbers splitting it into separate areas; nautical decorations include ships' equipment and sea photographs. There is now a choice of quickly served bar food, such as sandwiches (including steak), soups, sausages, scampi, omelettes and fish (all £1–£3.40); well kept St Austell BB, Tinners, HSD and XXXX Mild on handpump (under a light CO_2 blanket); darts and fruit machine, also a big separate pool-room with juke box, fruit machine and space game. *(Recommended by Pat and Malcolm Rudlin; more reports please)*

St Austell · Licensee Peter Hollis · Real ale · Meals and snacks · Children in room off main bar · Nearby parking can be difficult · Open 10.30–2.30, 5.30–11

Turks Head

At top of main street, by big domed building (Lloyds Bank), turn down Chapel Street

There has been a Turks Head here for over 700 years, and though most of the original one was burned down by a Spanish raiding party in the sixteenth century, the cellar room has been a bar for several hundred years. The main bar has lots of character, with old flat-irons, jugs and so forth hanging from the beams, and old pottery above the wood-effect panelling. Attractively priced and quickly served food includes a wide choice of seafood, such as prawn rolls (£1.40), white crabmeat sandwiches (£1.60), curried prawn baked potatoes (£1.65), fish pie (£1.80), garlic prawns (£1.95), local crab salad (from £2.50), scallop and prawn Mornay (£3.90), seafood platter (£3.95) and local lobster salad (from £5.60); there is also plenty of non-seafood fare (sandwiches lunchtime only), such as soups, ploughman's, salads, filled baked potatoes, giant sausages in French bread, pizzas, spaghetti Bolognese, and (at only £2.95) eight-ounce sirloin steaks. Well kept John Devenish and Cornish Best on handpump; fruit machine, space game, and a good juke box which attracts a lively young crowd in the evening. The sun-trap back garden has big urns of flowers. *(Recommended by Richard Cole, J P Berryman, Pat and Malcolm Rudlin, John Price)*

Devenish · Licensee William Morris · Real ale · Meals and snacks · Children in separate dining-room · Open 10.30–2.30, 6–11

PHILLEIGH   SW8639   Map 1

Roseland ★

The paved courtyard in front of this seventeenth-century pub has charming flowers among its attractive tables; the same care that has gone into choosing and looking after them shows inside, where it's clear that nothing is too much trouble for the licensee. It has lots of old sporting prints and other pictures under its low beams, a solemn old wall clock, old-fashioned seats around the sturdy tables on the flagstones, attractive bunches of fresh flowers, and a log fire. Excellent bar food, which changes from day to day, includes sandwiches (from 80p, rare beef £1, fresh crab £1.50), generous ploughman's, a choice of home-made pâtés (£1.60), and dishes such as crab or mixed seafood Mornay (£2) and well prepared fresh scallops (£3); winter stock-pot soup is popular. Well kept John Devenish and Cornish Best on handpump – the temperature-controlled cellars came into their own during the 1984 hot spell; dominoes, cribbage. The quiet lane leads on to the little half-hourly *King Harry* car ferry across a pretty wooded channel, with Trelissick Gardens on the far side. *(Recommended by Flt Lt A D Harkness, J P Berryman, Mrs A M Arnold, Richard Cole, George Jonas, John Price)*

Devenish · Licensee Desmond Sinnott · Real ale · Snacks (lunchtime only Sept–June, evenings too July–Aug; no food 25 Dec) · Children in lounge · Open 11–2.30, 6–11 (11–2.30, 7–10.30 in winter)

PILLATON   SX3664   Map 1

Weary Friar

Best reached from the good Callington–Landrake back road; OS Sheet 201 reference 365643

Comfortable bedrooms, each with its own bathroom, are at the moment our main reason for including this twelfth-century inn, by the church in a secluded village – this is because, as we went to press, new licensees had just moved in and were still working out what food they would be serving in the long and cosy carpeted bar. This is made up of four knocked-together rooms, with easy chairs around a little coal fire at one end, and a much grander old stone fireplace at the other (which has had hunting pictures under the beam-and-plank ceiling and leatherette seats around sturdy wooden tables). There's also a separate restaurant. Bass and St Austell Tinners on handpump, with St Austell HSD tapped from the cask. There are old-fashioned slatted teak seats outside, in the angle of the L-shaped black-shuttered building and across the quiet lane. *(Recommended by T P Lovesey; more reports please)*

Free house · Real ale · Meals and snacks (but see above) · Open 11–2.30, 6–11 Bedrooms tel St Dominick (0579) 50238; around £24B/£35B

POLKERRIS   SX0952   Map 1
Rashleigh

Readers rate this particularly highly for its setting – the big bay window of the bar, and tables outside by a figurehead on a flagstone terrace, look out over an isolated beach and attractively restored protecting jetty, to the far side of St Austell and Mevagissey Bays many miles away. But the food is popular too: it includes stock-pot soup (70p), open sandwiches such as beef, turkey or prawn (£2), filled pancakes such as ham and cheese or crab (£2.50), and cottage or steak pie (£3). People particularly like the extensive lunchtime cold buffet which might include sea trout and salmon as well as fresh local crab and at least five joints of meat (£3.50). There are summer barbecues out on the terrace. The bar has comfortably cushioned seats in its stripped-stone front part, and local photographs on the brown panelling of a more simply furnished back area. There is also a popular restaurant (dinner about £10). St Austell BB and Tinners on handpump; dominoes, euchre, fruit machine and piped music. This section of the Cornish Coast Path includes striking scenery, and there are safe moorings for small yachts in the cove. *(Recommended by D J Milner, Ian Meharg, Flt Lt A D Harkness)*

Free house · Licensee Kathryn Harrower · Real ale · Meals tel Polperro (0503) 72743; snacks · Children in eating area · Pianist most Sats · Open 11–2.30, 6–11

POLPERRO   SX2051   Map 1
Blue Peter ★

The Quay; on the right-hand side as you go round the harbour – a brisk 10-minute walk from the public car park

Very friendly and hospitable to strangers, this cosy pub is still a genuinely local focus for the life of the small working harbour which has survived the popularity of this picturesque village. The low-beamed L-shaped bar has a polished pew, a small winged settle and a seat cut from a big cask, as well as small dark blue leatherette

---

Pubs with particularly interesting histories, or in unusually interesting buildings, are listed at the back of the book.

armchairs. One window seat looks down on the harbour itself, another looks out past rocks to the sea; the nautical atmosphere is heightened by boat pictures, a big naval shell by the coal fire, and the gulls you hear screaming whenever the door is opened. Good value bar snacks include pasties (65p), sandwiches (especially local crab, £1.10) and ploughman's (£1.50); well kept Courage Best and St Austell Tinners and HSD on handpump, and local cider; darts, dominoes, sitting space game and a juke box or piped music, with an upstairs pool-room. There are slatted seats on the small V-shaped terrace, at the top of the flight of steps up to the door. *(Recommended by J Murray)*

Free house· Licensee Valerie Flood · Real ale · Snacks · Children in room upstairs, by pool-room · Open 11–2.30, 6–11

The Victory, St Mawes

nr PORT ISAAC   SW9980 Map 1

Port Gaverne Hotel ★

Port Gaverne signposted from Port Isaac, and from B3314 E of Pendoggett

This civilised early seventeenth-century inn has been kept by the same couple for nearly 20 years now. They've won a lot of support for the inn, and as people arrive to stay – most coming again and again over the years – they are greeted as old friends. The sandy cove a few yards away and the coast around are owned by the National Trust, and are splendidly unspoilt. The style of the bars fits in well: low beams, flagstones where there is no carpet, some exposed stone walls, big log fires, an enormous marine chronometer and a collection of antique cruets. In spring the lounge is filled with pictures from the local art society's annual exhibition, which over the years has raised more than £8,000 for the Royal National Lifeboat Institution. Bar food includes sandwiches (from 70p, local crab £1.50), good home-made soup (from £1, crab £1.35), cottage pie (£1.25), ploughman's (£1.35), excellent fish pie (£1.30), local plaice (£2.75), a good choice of salads such as sugar-baked gammon (£3), and a couple of main dishes such as home-made steak and kidney pie (£3). From the spring bank holiday until the end of September the food is served buffet-style in the dining-room at lunchtime, and there is the same arrangement for Sunday lunchtime (until 1.30 sharp) throughout the year; but otherwise it's served in the bar. In the evenings (unless dining in the restaurant), families should book a table in the Captain's Cabin: a little room where everything, except its antique admiral's hat, is shrunk to scale – old oak chest, model sailing ship, even the prints on the white stone walls. As well as well kept Flowers IPA and St Austell HSD on handpump, there is a very good choice of whiskies and other spirits such as ouzo, east Friesian schnapps, and akvavit; dominoes, cribbage, fruit machine. A raised terrace outside has a good sea view (the bar does not). A nice place to stay, and all rooms now have a private bath. *(Recommended by P T Young, John Pearson, Elizabeth Haigh, Martyn Quinn, Mrs J M Aston)*

Free house · Licensee Frederick Ross · Real ale · Meals and snacks · Children in cocktail bar at lunchtimes, and dining-room or Captain's Cabin · Open 10.30–2.30, 5.30–11; closed 15 Jan to 22 Feb · Bedrooms tel Bodmin (0208) 880244; £21.50B/£43B

PORTHLEVEN SW6225 Map 1

Ship

Colin Ridout, who made this well kept seaside pub such a friendly place, let us know as we went to press that he would be giving up the tenancy in autumn 1985. We've kept the pub in, even so, for its lovely position cut into the steep rocks over a working harbour, with good sea views, and hope the new licensee will keep the Courage Best (which has been available only in winter) as well as before. There's a simply furnished bar with a huge open fireplace, a lounge, and in summer a cellar bar with darts and a juke box. *(More reports please)*

Courage · Real ale in winter · Snacks · Parking can be difficult in summer Open 11–2.30, 6–11

PORTMELLON COVE   SX0144 Map 1
Rising Sun   [*illustrated on page 112*]

This sandy cove is much quieter than nearby Mevagissey, even in summer, and very peaceful indeed out of season. The sea – just over the road from the pub – is safe for swimming and boating, with an August regatta. Bar food includes sandwiches, basket meals, home-made lasagne and steak pie, with a choice of daily specials such as Tandoori chicken or whole local crab or lobster platter; in the evening there are also dishes such as Wiltshire ham in red wine and T-bone steaks (there's also a separate restaurant). The small front bar is crazy-paved, with a cool colour scheme, comfortable seats, and a winter log fire. A much larger summer bar with lots of tables has pool, a fruit machine, space game and a juke box, and big windows overlooking the sea, as does the good-sized family room which leads on to a terrace. The pub opens for home-made croissants and Danish pastries in the morning, and for cream teas in the afternoon. St Austell BB and HSD on handpump or tapped from a cask above the bar; cocktails include special ones for children. *(Recommended by D W Roberts, G Joshua)*

Free house · Licensee Jean Douglas · Real ale · Meals and snacks · Children in restaurant and family room · Live music about three times a fortnight · Open 11–2.30, 6–11; closed Oct–Mar (or week before Easter, if earlier)

POUGHILL   SS2207 Map 1
Preston Gate

Village signposted from A39 just N of Bude and Stratton; if you have to ask the way remember it's pronounced Poffle

Careful recent refurbishment has given this partly slate-hung sixteenth-century cottage an attractive bar: big dark flagstones with some carpeting, old photographs and paintings of the village, dining-room chairs and round red leatherette stools, and a nice alcove with pews along three specially made mahogany tables. Reasonably priced food, in generous helpings, includes sandwiches (from 80p), soup (85p), ploughman's (£1.50, with ham £1.75), giant sausage (£1.65), turkey pie with salad (£2.10), quiche (£2.50), scampi (£3.10), seafood platter (£3.50), trout stuffed with celery and walnuts (£5.50) and rump steak (£6); on our visit the daily special was a good beef curry (£2.50). Well kept Ushers Best and Founders on handpump; sensibly placed darts, dominoes, fruit machine; maybe piped music. There are picnic-table sets on a small tarmac terrace by the back car park. The nearby coast, north of Wrangle Point, is carefully preserved by the National Trust. *(Recommended by J A Price)*

Free house · Licensees Joyce and Ivor Measures · Real ale · Meals and snacks Children welcome · Open 11–2.30, 6–11

Stars after the name of a pub show that it has exceptional quality. One star means most people (after reading the report to see why the star has been awarded) would think a special trip worth while. Two stars mean that the pub is really outstanding – one of just a handful in its region. The very very few with three stars are the real aristrocrats – of their type, they could hardly be improved.

ST AGNES   SW7250   Map 1
Railway

Vicarage Road; from centre follow B3277 signs for Porthtowan and Truro

Part of an unassuming terrace, this friendly pub is full of interest. It
has a remarkable collection of shoes: minute or giant, made of
leather, wood, mother-of-pearl, fur, strange skins, or embroidered
with gold and silver; from Turkey, Persia, China or Japan; shaped
like fat pads or with all the toes distinct; from ordinary people or
famous men, and so on and so on. Besides some splendid brasswork,
there is also a notable collection of naval memorabilia from model
sailing ships and rope fancywork to interesting proclamations and
signals – such as that from Marshal Foch on the eleventh day of the
eleventh month of 1918 announcing the ceasefire which ended the
First World War. Well kept John Devenish and Cornish Best (served
from an unusually elaborate beer engine); generous helpings of good
value simple snacks; friendly service, with plenty of information
about the memorabilia; on our visit, piped pop music; sensibly placed
darts (with an antique telephone-dialling Bissett scoring machine).
(Recommended by Arnold Pearce, C J Winder, Valerie and Tony Gibbons)

*Devenish · Licensee Frederick John Williams · Real ale · Snacks · Open
11–2.30, 6–11 (7–10.30 in winter)*

ST DOMINICK   SX3967   Map 1
Who'd Have Thought It

Village signposted from A388 S of Callington; pub is beyond its S end

The decoration of this friendly country pub is a surprise for
Cornwall: tasselled blue plush stools, massively carved gothic tables
with dolphin feet on the Turkey carpet, high shelves of Staffordshire
pottery, gleaming copper jugs, lamps shining through neat ranks of
dimple Haig bottles, and some red flock wallpaper as well as bared
stone walls. Bar food includes soup (60p), sandwiches (from 90p,
fresh crab when available £1.35), basket meals (from £1.30), salads
(from £2.40, crab when available £3), seafood platter (£2.80), and in
the evenings steak cob (£3.25) and steaks (from £4.70) too; the
dining area has perhaps the best country views. Well kept Bass and
Courage Directors on handpump; the public bar has darts, a juke box
and a fruit machine. The endearing little Jack Russell terriers are
called Liz and Grimble. Well worth a visit is nearby Cotehele (see
Metherell entry) beside the Tamar estuary, which winds through this
peaceful countryside. (Recommended by Roger Bloye)

*Free house · Licensees Albert and Drew Potter · Real ale · Meals and snacks
Open 11–2.30, 7–11; closed 24 and 25 Dec evenings*

ST KEW   SX0276   Map 1
St Kew Inn

Village signposted from A39 NE of Wadebridge

Close to the church of this peaceful hamlet, the pub is much grander-
looking than you'd expect: quite a noble stone building, with parking

in what must have been a really imposing stable yard. In the bar you'll find a charming and warmly welcoming old-fashioned atmosphere: logs burnings in an open kitchen range under a high mantelpiece decorated with earthenware flagons, a Windsor armchair beside it, winged high-backed settles and varnished rustic tables on the lovely dark Delabole flagstones, a handsome window seat, and black wrought-iron rings for hanging lamps or hams from the high ceiling. Well kept St Austell Tinners and HSD tapped from wooden casks behind the counter (lots of tankards hang from the beams above it); fruit machine; talk of ferreting and hilarious poaching escapades – by customers of other pubs, of course. The local sirloin steaks, cooked in the evening, are highly recommended. Picnic-table sets shelter between the wings of the pub, by a pump with a stone trough on the front cobbles. *(Recommended by R C L, M W A Gover)*

St Austell · Licensee Harry Arkley · Real ale · Meals and snacks · Open 10.30–2.30, 5.30–11

ST MAWES   SW8537   Map 1
Rising Sun

The village is literally the end of the road, and the harbour serves little more than the hourly foot-ferry to Falmouth and the yachts moored in this charming bay. So the waterfront lane past this comfortable small hotel is normally very quiet – though one reader had the bad luck to be here when a variety of vans and trucks were turning, not to mention a stream of cars. People strolling gently by give an almost continental feel to its splendid crazy-paved terrace, which has sturdy stone tables and a low stone wall to sit on when those are full. Besides a back cocktail bar and an attractive and civilised easy-chair lounge, there's a friendly front bar with a big window seat overlooking the harbour. Quickly served bar food includes pasties (60p), sandwiches (from 85p, crab £1.75), West Country pie (£2), and a good range of seafood such as smoked mackerel salad (£1.80), grilled plaice or lemon sole (£2), scallops Mornay (£3) and when it's available lobster salad (£8); also a separate stylish restaurant. St Austell BB on handpump; darts, shove-ha'penny, fruit machine. A nice and very comfortable place to stay. *(Recommended by P D Atkinson, Col G D Stafford, St John Sandringham, Mrs A M Arnold, D A Lloyd)*

St Austell · Licensee Mrs Campbell Marshall · Real ale · Meals and snacks (lunchtime) · Children in cocktail bar or eating area · Open 11–2.30, 6–11 Bedrooms tel St Mawes (0326) 270233; £18.50 (£19B)/£37 (£45B)

Victory   [illustrated on page 124]

As we went to press we heard that the Roberts family had – after over 20 years here – just left this friendly little inn, taking with them their famous parrot. Their successors have opened a new salad bar, serving sandwiches (from 70p), pasties (70p), ploughman's (£1.40, with ham £1.70) and meat salads (£2.50). In the cosy bar, full of sailing and other sea photographs, the talk is mainly of the sea and boats. In the carpeted back part there are button-back banquettes, an antique settle and old prints of Cornish scenes. Benches outside in the alley, a few steep yards up from the harbour, give glimpses of the sea. Well kept John Devenish and Cornish Best on handpump; darts (used to be winter only) and a fruit machine. In this area the seaside churchyard at St Just is particularly worth visiting for its richly subtropical vegetation. *(Recommended by D A McLellan, S G Revill; up-to-date reports please)*

Devenish · Real ale · Snacks · Open 11–2.30, 6–11 · Bedrooms tel St Mawes (0326) 270324; no single rooms/£18

ST TEATH   SX0680   Map 1
White Hart

This companionable village pub serves good value simple food in generous helpings, such as pasties, pizzas and particularly tender rump steaks, with sandwiches (plain and toasted) and ploughman's at lunchtime too. The main bar, with a Delabole flagstone floor, is decorated with swords, a cutlass, and sailor hat-ribands and ships' pennants from all over the world; the ceiling over the serving counter (which has Inch's cider) is studded with coins, and there's a snug little high-backed settle between the counter and the coal fire. A carpeted room, mainly for eating, leads off, with modern chairs around neat tables, and brass and copper jugs on its stone mantelpiece; there is gentle piped music in here (in other rooms you will find not only a piano but also a venerable harmonium). The lively games bar has a good juke box, darts and a well lit pool-table. *(Recommended by J Edwards; more reports please)*

Free house · Licensee Mrs D Burton · Meals and lunchtime snacks · Occasional country music · Open 10.30–2.30, 5.30–11

TREBARWITH   SX0585   Map 1
Mill House Inn

Signposted from B3263 and B3314 SE of Tintagel

Idyllically placed in its own wooded combe running down to the sea, this well run seventeenth-century converted watermill was named Inn of the Year by the AA in 1985. A flagstoned terrace on several levels, attractively planted, makes the most of the sun. Inside, the big main bar has stripped pine settles, pews and handle-back chairs around oak tables on the Delabole stone floor; it's decorated with posies of fresh flowers, and on our visit had fairy lights strung among bunches of beech twigs in the ceiling. Bar food includes sandwiches (from 55p), home-made soup (85p), pâté (£1.30), ploughman's (cheese £1.25, gammon £1.75), a variety of basket meals from sausages (£1) to scampi (£2.20), plaice (£2), prawn platter (£3.25), pork chop (£3.90) and charcoal-grilled sirloin steak (£5.30). Well kept Flowers IPA and Original on handpump; friendly service. An airy communicating extension has pine tables in stable-stall-style booths, and pool, sitting space game and a fruit machine; also shove-ha'penny, dominoes and cribbage, with *boules* in summer. The separate evening restaurant is recommended by readers for good value seafood crêpes, trout and kebabs. A nice place to stay; the beach, a few minutes' walk away, is good for surfing. *(Recommended by H Paulinski)*

Free house · Licensees Angela and Harry Davy Thomas · Real ale · Meals and snacks · Children over 10 in restaurant and pool-room · Open 10–2.30, 6–11 (11–2.30, 7–10.30 in winter) · Bedrooms tel Camelford (0840) 770200; £19.10B/£38.20B

TREEN   SW3824   Map 1
Logan Rock

The low-beamed rambling bar of this cosy pub has in one of its alcoves a marvellous log fire in cool weather. This partly panelled room has old prints showing the story of the nearby Logan Rock (now, like the pub, owned by the National Trust). It's an 80-ton teetering boulder which someone once tipped from its clifftop fulcrum to show off his strength – then had to pay a small fortune to have it hauled up the cliff again. There's also a small snug with well made high-backed modern oak settles, and a carpeted family bar at the back where you go to order your food. This includes a wide choice of sandwiches (from 70p, local crab £1.50), big pasties (70p), basket meals such as plaice (£2.25) and salads (from £1.60, crab £4), with home-made dishes such as vegetarian quiche (£1.25), salmon and parsley flan or cheese, onion and potato pie (£1.75) and cottage pie (£2), and a popular fish and egg dish they call the Seafarer (£2.50). Except in high summer they do good charcoal-grilled steaks (rump £4.50, T-bone £5.75). They will heat baby foods on request. Well kept St Austell BB, XXXX Mild, Tinners and HSD on handpump; piped music, dominoes, cribbage and darts, and in the family room, a fruit machine and space game. A separate winter pool-room has table skittles. There are some tables in a small but attractive wall-sheltered garden, looking over fields. *(Recommended by FM, Prof David Brokensha, Steve Bacon, Charlie Salt)*

St Austell · Licensees Peter and Anita George · Real ale · Meals and snacks Children in family room · Open 10.30–2.30, 5.30–11 (10.30–2.30, 6–10.30 in winter)

TREWELLARD   SW3734   Map 1
Trewellard Hotel

Popular for its lively and cheerful atmosphere, this old-fashioned village inn has rambling and interestingly furnished rooms with a long and rather elaborately carved main serving counter, brightly coloured plates and mugs hanging from beams, and rugs on an elaborately tiled floor. A food bar serves a changing menu which might include soup (60p), sandwiches (from 60p, crab £1), cheese and onion pasties (60p), whitebait (£1.45), home-made Indian dishes such as curry or tandoori chicken (£2–2.25) with poppadums and pickles, shepherd's or steak and kidney pie, cod or plaice (£2.25), gammon and egg (£2.95) and rump steak (£4.25). A games room has two or three pin-tables, table football, darts, pool, shove-ha'penny, dominoes, cribbage, a fruit machine and several space games (and there's piped music when the juke box isn't on); separate children's room. Besides St Austell Tinners on handpump and Devenish and Cornish Best tapped from the cask, there is a wide range of bottled beers including more than 100 different lagers from all over the world. *(Recommended by FM, Patrick Stapley)*

Free house · Licensee J M Orriss · Real ale · Meals and snacks · Children welcome · Open 10.30–2.30, 5.30–11 (may very occasionally be closed lunchtime) · Bedrooms tel Penzance (0736) 788634; £7.50/£10

TRURO SW8244 Map 1
Market Inn
Lemon Quay, by central car park

Prices seem to be happily stuck in the past, in this friendly and simply furnished town pub; generous helpings of cheap home-made food include soup (45p), pasties (55p), pâté (65p), moussaka or jambalaya (90p) and shepherd's pie, lasagne or paella (95p), with a salad bar (from 90p). There are also sandwiches, which may include home-made brawn. Get there early to be sure of a seat and a good choice of food. Darts, shove-ha'penny, dominoes, cribbage, euchre, backgammon, a fruit machine and a juke box; there's a weekly quiz game, too. *(Recommended by Peter Dexter)*

Devenish · Licensee Bert Tucker · Meals (lunchtime, not Sun) and snacks (Mon–Sat lunchtime, Tues–Thurs evenings) · Parking sometimes difficult Country and western and golden oldies Sat · Open 11–2.30, 5–11

Lucky Dip

Besides the fully inspected pubs, you might like to try these Lucky Dips recommended and described by readers (if you do, please send us reports):

BODMIN [11 Honey St; SX0767], *Weavers*: good cold food in one-bar pub with beams, prints, old church pews, handpumped beer *(P T Young)*
BOLVENTOR [SX1876], *Jamaica Inn*: sixteenth-century coaching-inn in wild surroundings, with smuggling and highwaymen connections; basis of Daphne du Maurier's novel, very popular with tourists; bar food, restaurant; bedrooms *(Martyn Quinn)*
BUDE [SS2005], *Falcon*: big holiday pub by canal *(Bob Rendle)*
CANONS TOWN [SW5335], *Lamb & Flag*: Devenish; pleasant carpeted lounge, small tables, Windsor chairs, table skittles; big bar, fruit machines, juke box, fine flagstones; reasonably priced home-cooked bar snacks, friendly atmosphere *(Charlie Salt)*
CARBIS BAY [SW5239], *Cornish Arms*: friendly and very efficient staff, food excellent value lunchtime and evening, very clean with spotless WCs, nice yard; Devenish beer; children's room *(J S McCallum)*
nr CONSTANTINE [Nancenoy; SW731282], *Trengilly Wartha*: fairly remote family-run converted farmhouse on hillside with good buffet lunch and restaurant; well kept Devenish and other real ales including Bass, Flower and Wadworths 6X, also Spingo (from Blue Anchor, Helston – labelled Trengilly); recently redecorated bedrooms; live music Friday *(John Green, Patrick Young, Pat and Malcolm Rudlin)*
CRANTOCK [SW7960], *Old Albion*: new licensees in pleasantly placed thatched village pub with old-fashioned bar; smuggling background *(LYM, Colin Gooch)*

FALMOUTH [The Moor; SW8032], *Seven Stars*: warmly welcoming old-fashioned pub with well kept Bass, Flowers Original and St Austell HSD straight from the cask; simple snacks, tables on courtyard behind flower tubs; run as it has been for generations *(Jack Davey, BB)*; [Trevethan Hill; SW8032] *Sportsmans Arms*: exceptional harbour views and well kept Devenish beers in friendly local *(D A McLelland, LYM)*

FOWEY [Town Quay; SX1252], *King of Prussia*: harbour view from bow windows of upstairs bar with St Austell real ales, largely home-cooked food, juke box *(LYM)*

GUNNISLAKE [The Square; SX4371], *Cornish Inn*: welcoming owner in spacious and well laid out village inn with ample parking space, excellent bar food, bedrooms *(G Sandy)*

HALLWORTHY [A395; SX 1887], *Wilsey Down Inn*: old pub being restored by Norman Roberts, who until 1985 lovingly ran the Victory at St Mawes *(More reports please)*

HAYLE [SW5536], *Bird in Hand*: converted Victorian stables block in Bird Paradise; good choice of buffet food in summer, pasties winter; two beers brewed here and at least three guest beers on handpump *(Pat and Malcolm Rudlin)*

HELFORD PASSAGE [SW7627], *Ferry Boat*: spacious and friendly modern bar overlooking boating estuary *(LYM)*

HELSTON [nr Gunwalloe; SW7627], *Halzephron*: pleasant bar with good log fire and views over clifftop to sea and Mounts Bay; bedrooms *(LYM)*

KILKHAMPTON [SS2511], *London Inn*: free house with buffet bar lunchtime and evening (vegetables from own kitchen garden), excellent wines, very friendly owner, three cheap bedrooms *(G H Hughes)*

LANDRAKE [SX3760], *Bullers Arms*: popular food in central inn with bedrooms *(Anon)*

LANHYDROCK [SX0863], *Lanhydrock House*:good, well presented and reasonably priced simple food in pub attached to National Trust seventeenth-century mansion in well wooded surroundings *(D J Milner)*

LANNER [SW7240], *Coppice*: rambling old beamed pub with well kept real ales including Tetleys, young Lancashire licensee, reasonably priced bar food, family room and second bar recently refurbished in light pine; single bedroom, letting cottage *(John Green)*

LANREATH [SX1757], *Punchbowl*: flagstoned public bar, comfortable black-panelled lounge, Bass and bar food, restaurant, bedrooms *(T J Vernon, BB)*

LELANT SALTINGS [SW5437], *Old Quay House*: good value food, roomy lounge *(Sue Mutton, Anne Garton)*

LERRYN [SX1457], *Ship*: timbered and flagstoned bar with good Bass and Devenish, food in back room, in lovely position by estuary *(Steve and Carolyn Harvey)*

LISKEARD [SX2564], *Albion*: Watneys house, selling Bass *(Bob Rendle)*

LOOE [Barbican Road; SX2553], *Barbican*: food excellent value for money in pleasant surroundings; extremely friendly *(John Righton)*; [Fore St; SX2553] *Swan*: food, beer and wines good, in clean pub with courteous efficient service; children's room *(Mrs E Turner)*

LOSTWITHIEL [Duke St; SX1059], *Royal Oak*: old-fashioned bars with lots of real ales in thirteenth-century inn; popular food; bedrooms *(Anon)*

MARAZION [The Square; SW5231], *Cutty Sark*: main bar stone-walled, beamed, open coal fire; welcoming, with ships' wheels, bells and lights; extensive range of bar snacks and cooked meals, wide range of beers including real ales; good bedrooms *(D A Lloyd)*

MAWNAN SMITH [SW7728], *Red Lion*: good value simple food in friendly thatched village pub, with warm wood-burning stove in high-ceilinged lounge (pianist Friday), spacious public bar, well kept Devenish real ales; children in big family room *(Mr and Mrs K C Howard, BB)*

MOUSEHOLE [SW4726], *Ship*: friendly fishermen's local right by harbour in beautiful village; bar food, St Austell real ale *(Elizabeth Haigh, Andy Jones and the PA Club, LYM)*

NEWQUAY [Station Approach; SW8161], *Cavalier*: food very fresh (prepared to order), exceptionally tasty, surprising value; pleasant décor of painted walls and mock beams; comfortable, spacious and airy, with big tables in windows and tables on terrace *(Colin Gooch)*

PADSTOW [SW9175], *London Inn*: friendly and shipshape small inn with good choice of bar food, near attractive working harbour; bedrooms *(John Pearson, Elizabeth Haigh, Prof A N Black, LYM)*

PENRYN [SW7834], *Seven Stars*: cosy and popular Devenish pub with perhaps the biggest collection of brass in the country *(BB)*

PENZANCE [SW4730], *Admiral Benbow*: veritable maze of a place with extraordinary displays of ships' figureheads and other relics (some brought up by owner who is a diver); good plaice and omelettes, wide choice of beers; unusually good piped music *(Ian Meharg, Miss P M Gammon, C B M Gregory)*

PERRANARWORTHAL [SW7839], *Norway*: delicious Saturday night barbecues with generous salad, good bar service, good value, in flag-bedecked roadhouse with fancy-dress waitresses *(Anon)*

PHILLACK [SW5638], *Bucket of Blood*: cheerful pub with well kept St Austell beers and entertainingly gruesome ghost stories *(LYM)*

POLGOOTH [SW9950], *Polgooth*: lively if clannish rustic inn with own farmyard and horses drinking from tankards: well kept St Austell real ales; bedrooms *(Bob Rendle, LYM)*

POLMEAR [SX0853], *Ship*: good value food, cheerful helpful staff, spacious lounge, easy access for the disabled *(Sue Mutton, Anne Garton)*

POLPERRO [SX2051], *Crumplehorn Mill*: good terrace outside pretty pub with food ranging from sandwiches (inc. crab) to steak with lightly grilled lobster; real ales inc. St. Austell; back restaurant; bedrooms *(G G Strange, Martyn Quinn)*; *Ship*: very clean, good value for money, friendly *(John Righton)*

PORT ISAAC [SX0080], *Golden Lion*: old pub high over harbour in lovely steep village, nice view from the seat by the window; snacks, well kept St Austell Tinners *(Martin Jones, LYM)*

PORTHLEVEN [Peverell Terrace; SW6225], *Atlantic*: food lovely, friendly owners, very pleasant surroundings *(Anon)*

PORTSCATHO [SW8735], *Plume of Feathers*: friendly and rambling village pub with St Austell real ales and sensible bar food *(Mrs D Jasperson, LYM)*

ROCHE [SW9860], *Victoria*: useful A30 stop with popular food including excellent home-made pasties in softly lit character bar; well kept St Austell ales, panelled children's room, cheery service, restaurant *(Charlie Salt, LYM)*

ST COLUMB MAJOR [Market Square; SW9163], *Ring o' Bells*: several rooms going back from narrow frontage in friendly town pub with simple food and furnishings *(A A Worthington, BB)*

ST EWE [SW9746], *Crown*: good value wide choice of bar food and separate restaurant (must book) with quick service, in spotless white-painted seventeenth-century country pub in small pretty village; garden and children's room *(A A Worthington)*

ST ISSEY [SW9271], *Ring o' Bells*: cheerful and nicely modernised village inn with well kept Courage real ale and good value food; bedrooms *(Elizabeth Haigh, LYM)*

ST IVES [The Harbour; SW5441], *Sloop*: local photos on wall; three bars including cellar bar, pub meals; dates from 1312; sea views from window; can get crowded *(Martyn Quinn)*

ST JUST IN PENWITH [SW3631], *Star*: friendly local pub in centre of windswept town not far from Lands End *(LYM)*

ST MAWGAN [SW8765], *Falcon*: stone inn with good local real ales and nice garden, in attractive village, good food and service; bedrooms *(D J Milner, LYM)*

nr STITHIANS [Frogpool; SW7366], *Cornish Arms*: good value bar food and steak dinners in friendly village pub with well kept Devenish real ales; cheerful local atmosphere and comfortable sitting areas, maybe spontaneous entertainment *(BB, Margo and Peter Thomas)*

TRESILLIAN [SW8646], *Wheel*: smartly renovated thatched Devenish pub with good food and reasonable access for the disabled *(R F Davidson, Sue Mutton, Anne Garton, BB)*

TRURO [Kenwyn St, SW8244], *Royal Standard*: food good value, evenings as well as lunchtimes (rarity here), and very friendly cooperative landlord *(Pat and Malcolm Rudlin)*; *Wig & Pen*: food included garlic bread and ratatouille served by very friendly staff; old-fashioned, basic (but chic) interior, very good for lunches or early evening *(Flt Lt A D Harkness)*

TYWARDREATH [SX0854], *New*: well kept Bass and St Austells ales in friendly pub with nice village setting; bedrooms *(Bob Rendle, BB)*

WEST PENTIRE [SW7760], *Bowgie*: modernised inn with rolling lawns on magnificent headland; bedrooms *(LYM)*

ZENNOR [SW4538], *Tinners Arms*: well kept St Austells real ales in comfortable stripped-panelling pub near fine part of Cornish coast path; bar food *(John and Lucy Roots, Patrick Stapley, Prof David Brokensha, LYM)*

Cumbria

Three new entries jump straight in with stars this year: the Hare & Hounds in Talkin (the most welcoming little inn we've ever stayed at, with good value food and particularly well kept real ale), the Barbon Inn in Barbon (another splendid small inn, very friendly and civilised) and the Queens Head in Hawkshead (very good value simple food in a warm and lively atmosphere; the village is lovely). All three have comfortable bedrooms, as does the Queens Head in Askham – this entry was in previous editions, but has been promoted to a star rating this year for its all-round quality (even a splendid model railway). Among many pubs in particularly fine scenery we'd pick out the Old Dungeon Ghyll in Langdale and the Wasdale Head Inn for their superbly remote settings. Others surrounded by really attractive countryside include the Masons Arms on the side of Cartmel Fell (good food and a remarkable collection of bottled beers in splendidly traditional surroundings – the nicest pub we've found in the Lake District), the Pheasant by Bassenthwaite Lake (a lovely old inn below the wooded slopes of Sale Fell, nice to stay in), the old-fashioned Britannia by Elterwater (also nice to stay in), the Drunken Duck in the hills above Hawkshead (a lively country inn with good real ales), and the Burnmoor in Boot (in a quiet fell-foot hamlet, with comfortably renovated bedrooms and good simple food). Though in a village, the picturesque Kings Arms in Cartmel could scarcely have a finer setting. Other pubs where the food is good without being grand or pretentious include the Kings Arms in Stainton (a friendly village pub), stylish Punch Bowl in Askham, the Bridge at Buttermere (in National Trust countryside between

The Hare & Hounds, Levens

two lakes), unpretentious Hare & Hounds in Levens, the Blue Bell in Heversham and Pheasant in Casterton (both well run, with bedrooms), Shepherds Inn in Melmerby (extensively refurbished this year), Three Shires Inn in Little Langdale (a nice place to stay, in attractive surroundings), Kings Head in Ravenstonedale (welcoming, with bedrooms, in a pretty village), String of Horses at Faugh (very comfortable), cosy White Horse at Scales and – for its vast range of evening sandwiches – friendly Queens Arms in Warwick on Eden. The Glen Rothay Hotel in Rydal is a civilised place to stay, right in the centre of the Lakes. For sheer atmosphere, the Farmers Arms at Lowick Green stands out, while the Blackcock in Eaglesfield is a fine example of an unspoilt and homely village pub. With one or two high-priced exceptions such as the Punch Bowl at Askham, the Bridge at Buttermere, and Queen's Head in Troutbeck, drinks prices here tend to be among the lowest in Britain. Brewers from outside the area such as Matthew Brown, Marstons and Scottish & Newcastle seem to keep their prices down to the levels charged for the local Hartleys and Jennings beers. We found the Blackcock in Eaglesfield, the simple mountainside Swinside Inn near Keswick, the Shepherds at Melmerby and the White Horse at Scales particularly cheap.

ASKHAM   NY5123   Map 9
Punch Bowl

The rambling beamed main bar of this welcoming inn has Chippendale dining-chairs and rushwork ladderback seats around its sturdy wooden tables, an antique settle by an open log fire, and well cushioned window seats in the white-painted thick stone walls. A tribal rug hangs above the cushioned pews in one inner room, there's an old-fashioned wood-burning stove with a gleaming stainless-steel chimney in the big main fireplace, and little sprays of flowers decorate nooks in the wall. Tables out on a gravelled side terrace look over the village's attractive lower green, opposite the wall of the Lowther estate. Good home-cooked bar food includes hummus with pitta bread (90p), sandwiches, fisherman's pâté (£1.25), crêpes gruyère (£1.10), burgers (from £1.50), salads (from £2.50), chicken and leek pie (£2.75), haddock provençale (£2.85), goulash or lasagne (£2.95), and steak (from £4.85), with children's dishes (from 85p), home-made ice creams and other puddings (from £1). Readers like the Sunday lunch, and there is now a small separate restaurant. Whitbreads Castle Eden on handpump; dominoes, cribbage, backgammon, Trivial Pursuit, a fruit machine and piped music, and, in the separate public bar, darts, pool and juke box. The clean and comfortable bedrooms are good value. *(Recommended by Richard Franck, John Stamper, Kingsley Mills, Dinah Scott-Harden)*

The Good Pub Guide does not accept payment for inclusion, and there is no advertising or sponsorship.

Whitbreads · Licensee Aubrey Zalk · Meals and snacks · Children in eating area · Open 11–3, 6–10.30 (opens an hour later in winter) · Bedrooms tel Hackthorpe (093 12) 443; £11.50/£23

Queens Head ★

The efficient staff make people on holiday feel just as much at home here as the regular customers, who make sure that – even out of season – the two rooms of the main carpeted lounge are full of friendly bustle. They are comfortably furnished, with harness, horse brasses and old wooden blocks for printing calico arranged on the red flock wallpaper, and beams hung with gleaming copper and brass. Good waitress-served bar food includes soup (80p), well garnished sandwiches including meat cut off the bone (80p), cottage pie with red cabbage or fish pie (£2.25), a choice of ploughman's with cheese, beef, turkey or ham (£2.50) cheese and onion quiche (£2.50), prawn cheesecake (£3.50) and pork fillet with peppers, honey, pineapple, tomatoes and mushrooms (£3.75), with extra evening dishes such as Scotch salmon or nine-ounce sirloin steak (£6.50). A separate restaurant provides dinners at £12.50. Well kept Vaux Sunderland and Wards Sheffield Best on handpump. An elaborate model railway outside runs through an attractive miniature landscape of rocks and shrubs until quite late in the evening. There's a heated swimming pool next door and the pub is handy for the Lowther Wildlife Park. *(Recommended by PLC, Heather Sharland, Alan Franck, David Fearnley)*

Vaux · Licensees Anne and John Askew · Real ale · Meals and snacks · Children in side room · Open 11.30–3, 6.30–10.30 (opens half an hour later in winter) Bedrooms tel Hackthorpe (093 12) 225; £17.50/£32

BARBON   SD6385   Map 9
Barbon Inn ★

Village signposted off A683 Kirkby Lonsdale–Sedbergh; OS Sheet 97 reference 628826

A charming series of individually furnished and very comfortable small rooms open off the main bar – itself not large – of this friendly and relaxed family-run inn. There are attractively carved eighteenth-century oak settles, deep chintzy sofas and armchairs, open fires in cool weather (even in summer) and lots of fresh flowers; indeed, the sheltered garden here is a strong point, very attractively planted and well looked after, and floodlit at night. Home-made bar food includes soup (75p), sandwiches (from 75p), ploughman's or duck and chicken liver pâté (£1.95), Cumberland sausage (£2.50), steak and kidney pie (£2.95) and sirloin steak (£5.95) – there's also a cosy beamed dining-room (four-course dinner £10.25); well kept Theakstons Best and Old Peculier on handpump; dominoes. The old-fashioned bedrooms are clean and comfortable and very quiet. There is now a sun-bed room (£1 for half an hour). Tracks and paths lead up to the steep fells above the village; a nice place to stay. *(Recommended by Tim Halstead, Robert and Susan Phillips, Philip Asquith, Keith Myers, Paul West)*

Free house · Licensee Keith Whitlock · Real ale · Meals and snacks (no snacks Sat evening if restaurant very busy) · Children welcome · Open 12–3, 6–11 (closes 2 and 10.30 in winter) · Bedrooms tel Barbon (046 836) 233; £16/£28.50

BASSENTHWAITE LAKE   NY2228   Map 9
Pheasant ★

Follow Wythop Mill signpost at N end of dual carriageway stretch of A66 by Bassenthwaite Lake

The cosy bar of this charming old-fashioned inn has hunting prints and photographs on its smokily dark walls, with rush-seat chairs, library seats and cushioned settles all along the sides of its two rooms, linked by a fine wood-framed arch. Very friendly staff man the low serving counter, which has a hatch to the entry corridor through a traditional wood and glass partition. There are also attractively chintzy sitting-rooms with antique furniture, and a large and airy beamed lounge at the back (overlooking the garden, from which you can walk up into the beechwoods), with easy chairs on its polished parquet floor and a big log fire on cool days. Freshly made bar food served in here is inventive and enterprising, including soup (85p), savoury quiche (£1.40), ploughman's (£1.55), asparagus mayonnaise or pork, ham and egg pie (£1.60) and meat salads (£1.95); it's particularly strong on seafoods, such as smoked salmon mousse (£1.65), prawns with lobster sauce (£1.90), smoked trout (£2.15) and crab salad (£2.65); well kept Bass and Theakstons Best on handpump; also separate non-smoking dining-room. A nice place to stay, in lovely wooded surroundings below Sale Fell. *(Recommended by Margo and Peter Thomas, Tim Halstead, D A Angless, Philip Asquith, Mrs A M Arnold, Keith Myers, Heather Sharland, Paul West)*

Free house · Licensee W E Barrington Wilson · Real ale · Lunchtime snacks Open 11–3, 5.30–10.30; closed 25 Dec · Bedrooms tel Bassenthwaite Lake (059 681) 234; £22 (£23.50B)/£42.50 (£46B)

BOOT   NY1701   Map 9
Burnmoor

Village signposted just off the Wrynose/Hardknott Pass road, OS Sheet 89 reference 175010

In a pretty hamlet close to Dalegarth Station (the top terminus of the Ravenglass and Eskdale light steam railway), this simple inn has been comfortably refurbished since the Fosters took it over – it was run for many years by Mrs Foster's Austrian mother who in her last year there saw it into the first edition of the *Guide*. The surroundings, more peaceful than much of Lakeland even in high summer, are lovely, with the fells rising fairly gently at first towards Scafell, and lots of attractive tracks such as the one up along Whillan Beck to Burnmoor Tarn. The landlord, who shepherded for years on these hills, is expert at suggesting good walks. The beamed and carpeted bar, with red leatherette seats and an open fire, has good, quickly served food such as soup (50p), cheese and onion flan (£1.50), ploughman's (£1.60), breaded haddock (£1.90), beef or ham salad

(£2.20), local venison and pheasant pie cooked with fresh herbs, juniper berries, red wine and brandy (£3), wiener Schnitzel (£3.30) and sirloin steak (£4.30). There is also a separate evening restaurant. Well kept Jennings real ales; darts, dominoes, cribbage, a fruit machine, juke box, and pool-room. The newly done bedrooms are comfortable; there are seats outside. *(Recommended by Alan Cookson)*

Jennings · Licensees Tony and Heidi Foster · Real ale · Meals and snacks Children in eating area · Open 11–3, 6–11 · Bedrooms tel Eskdale (094 03) 224; £12 (£13B)/£24 (£26B)

BOWNESS-ON-WINDERMERE   SD4097   Map 9
Hole in t' Wall

There's a lot to take in (and in summer a lot of cheerful people doing just that) at this very friendly old stone tavern close to the centre of Bowness: slate floors, smith's giant bellows, old farm implements, ploughshares, a panelled upstairs room with handsome plasterwork in its coffered ceiling and on cool days a splendid log fire under a vast slate mantelbeam. The flagstoned front courtyard (where there are sheltered seats) has an ancient outside flight of stone steps to the upper floor. Good value lunchtime bar food, from sandwiches to hot dishes – some of them unusual; Hartleys XB on handpump in excellent condition; darts, pool, a fruit machine and juke box. A nineteenth-century innkeeper here, who was a champion Lakeland wrestler, demonstrated on Dickens the hold for which he coined the phrase 'bear hug': he 'has left his mark indelibly on our back, besides having compressed our ribs so that we cannot breathe right yet'. *(Recommended by Jane English, G Andrews; more reports please, particularly on food)*

Hartleys · Licensee Derek Alderson · Real ale · Meals (lunchtime, not weekends) and snacks (lunchtime) · Children in family room off tap-room Folk music Thurs evening, Sun lunchtime · Parking nearby can be difficult Open 11–3, 5.30–10.30

BUTTERMERE   NY1817   Map 9
Bridge Hotel

The welcoming carpeted lounge bar of this extended stone hotel is a comfortable place for stretching out when you come down off the fells. It has upholstered wall seats, and square stools around wooden or copper tables, and local photographs on the white walls, with a wrought-iron screen dividing it into two parts. A good choice of bar food includes soup (65p), clam fries (£1), ploughman's or home-made chicken liver or smoked mackerel pâté (£2), omelettes (£3), beef, lamb and black pudding hot-pot, Cumbrian beef stew or home-made Cumberland sausage (£3), trout (£3.50) and eight-ounce sirloin steak (£5.25); the choice may be different, and prices slightly higher, in the evening. Well kept Theakstons Best, Mild and Old Peculier on handpump, and very reasonably priced draught cider. There is a separate evening restaurant (dinner £9.50). A flagstoned terrace has

Pubs in outstandingly attractive surroundings are listed at the back of the book.

white tables by a rose-covered sheltering stone wall. The little village, full of walkers in fine weather, is surrounded by some of the best steep countryside in the county, with Crummock Water and Buttermere just a stroll away – both are owned by the National Trust and kept quite free from the power boats that plague other lakes (you can hire rowing boats). A comfortable place to stay. *(Recommended by George Jonas, Mrs K Clapp, Dr A K Clarke, John Ryden)*

Free house · Licensee Michael Dee · Real ale · Meals and lunchtime snacks Open 11–3, 6–10.30; closed Jan · Bedrooms tel Buttermere (059 685) 252; £20.50B/£41B

CARTMEL   SD3879 Map 9
Kings Arms

The Square

Though not large, this black and white pub at the head of Cartmel's lovely square has touches of stateliness in its picture-postcard looks outside, and in its rambling bar (the handsome heavy beams, for instance) – yet it is thoroughly friendly. A reader who knows his Lakeland pubs as well as anybody reckons this to be one of the most genuine. The bar has tankards hanging over the serving counter (with well kept Hartleys Bitter on handpump), a fox's mask and small antique prints on the walls, foreign banknotes on some beams, and a mixture of seats including old country chairs, and settles on the fitted carpet together with wall banquettes. Freshly made bar food includes soup (65p), sandwiches, salads (from £1.90, home-roast ham £2.90), burgers (£1.90), Cumberland sausage (£2), haddock (£2.30), roast chicken (£2.80), scampi (£2.85) and fillet steak (£6.50); the quiche salad, when it's available, and the puddings (95p) have been picked out by readers for particular praise. Darts, a fruit machine, space invaders, and unobtrusive piped music. This ancient village has a grand priory church, and close to the pub is a fine medieval stone gatehouse. *(Recommended by Dr M V Jones, MGBD)*

Hartleys/Whitbreads · Licensee Robert Skinner · Real ale · Meals and snacks (not Mon evening) · Children in family room off bar · Country music Tues Open 10.30–3, 6–11 all year

CARTMEL FELL   SD4288   Map 9
Masons Arms ★ ★

Strawberry Bank, a few miles S of Windermere between A592 and A5074; perhaps the simplest way of finding the pub is to go uphill W from Bowland Bridge (which is signposted off A5074) towards Newby Bridge and keep right then left at the staggered crossroads – it's then on your right, below Gummer's How; OS Sheet 97 reference 413895

Since our last edition, handpumps have been put in here, with Youngers IPA and a changing guest beer (often from far afield) to join the splendid and unusual range of some hundred bottled beers from all over the world. Many of these – particularly from Belgium – are imported by the licensees (who supply some other pubs); those that need it are properly chilled, while the rich Belgian bottle-conditioned beers are kept warm enough to go on developing. Readers strongly support last year's award of a second star, for the consistently friendly welcome, the good and imaginative home cooking (among the very best in Lakeland), and the sensitive restoration and preservation of the old-fashioned and interesting bars. The penalty of such exceptional quality, in such a popular tourist area, is that, increasingly, you may find the pub very busy indeed even at out-of-season weekend lunchtimes. The main bar has low black beams in its bowed ceiling, country chairs and plain wooden tables on polished flagstones, needlework samplers and country pictures, a big log fire, and by it a grandly Gothic seat with snarling dogs as its arms. A small lounge has oak tables and settles to match its fine Jacobean panelling. Food specially recommended by readers includes the soup (80p), sandwiches (from £1.20 – the beef one turned out to be a big bun full of thick-cut, tender, tasty pot-roast served with a plate of salad), barbecued spare ribs (£1.50 or £2.90), steak and kidney pie and chilli con carne (£2.90), beef casserole with shallots, chestnuts and mushrooms in a red wine sauce (£3.75), the salads such as thickly sliced ham, shrimp or crab (£3.90), vast helpings of home-made puddings such as jam roly-poly or sucre torte (£1), and the specials – several each day – such as kidneys Turbigo or tandoori chicken (usually around £2.75–£3.90). There is usually hummus, tsatsiki or taramasalata with pitta bread (£1.45–£1.75) and always a choice of vegetarian dishes such as celery and asparagus pancakes or lentil and vegetable casserole (£2.60). Service is excellent, even when the pub gets crowded. Darts and dominoes. Rustic benches and tables outside this remote white house face a grand view across the Winster Valley to the woods below Whitbarrow Scar, and this is shared by self-catering flats in an adjoining stone barn. (*Recommended by C McDowall, W A Rinaldi-Butcher, MGBD, Andrew Parffrey, Tim Halstead, Mr and Mrs E W Spink, N C Hodgson, D A Angless, Philip Asquith, Dennis Royles, Keith Myers, J A Catton, Paul West*)

Free house · Licensees Helen and Nigel Stevenson · Meals and snacks Children in area partly set aside for them · Open 11–3, 6–11 all year Self-catering flats tel Crosthwaite (044 88) 486

CASTERTON   SD6379 Map 9
Pheasant

A683 about a mile N of junction with A65, by Kirkby Lonsdale

A wide choice of popular bar food in this comfortably modernised village inn includes soup (90p), ploughman's (£1.85), salads (from £1.85), omelettes (£2), Cumberland sausage (£2), steak and kidney pie (£2.75), lamb chops (£4) and T-bone steak (£7), with other rarer dishes such as guinea-fowl and grapes. The two rooms of the beamed main bar have red plush stools and built-in button-back wall banquettes around the dimpled copper tables on the red carpet, and there's an open log fire in a nicely arched bare-stone fireplace. Well kept Youngers Scotch on handpump; piped music (on our visit, The Seekers). There's a pleasant separate no-smoking lounge, and a smart dining-room (praised by readers for its gargantuan helpings). Tables with cocktail parasols shelter in the front L of the white building, by the road. There are attractive pre-Raphaelite stained glass and paintings in the nearby church, built here for the girls' school of Brontë fame. *(Recommended by Robert and Susan Phillips, Mrs J N Bullough)*

Free house · Licensees David and Elizabeth Hesmondhalgh · Real ale Meals and snacks · Children welcome · Open 11–2.30, 6–11 all year; closed first two weeks Nov · Bedrooms tel Kirkby Lonsdale (0468) 71230; £14 (£19.50B)/£24 (£32B)

EAGLESFIELD   NY0928 Map 9
Blackcock
Village signposted from A5086

Well away from the main tourist bustle, this spick-and-span village pub keeps excellent, reasonably priced Jennings Bitter and Mild on handpump. The neatly kept bar, decorated with gleaming horse brasses on the black beams, is unpretentious, homely and pleasantly old-fashioned, with brass service bells for the wooden tables furthest from the counter. There's a good coal fire on cool days, and service is very friendly. Hooks in the shiny butter-coloured ceiling, once presumably used for storing hams, now serve as targets for a neck-cricking version of ring the bull. *(Recommended by H R McManus)*

Jennings · Real ale · Snacks · Open 11–3, 5.30–10.30

ELTERWATER   NY3305 Map 9
Britannia Inn ★
Off B5343

The little beamed bar at the back of this old-fashioned inn is a friendly place, traditionally furnished and without frills, which – unlike many Lakeland places – doesn't turn up its nose at walking boots. There is also a comfortable lounge, and a front bar (which may not always be open out of season) with oak benches, settles and Windsor chairs, and a couple of window seats looking across the pretty village green to glimpses of Elterwater itself, through the trees on the far side; coal fires in winter. The view is shared by seats in the garden above the front of the pub. Good home-cooked bar food includes tasty sausage soup (50p), steak and kidney pie (£2.10), rainbow trout (£3.10), various basket meals such as burger and chips (£1.15) and vegetarian dishes such as broccoli and cheese flan (£2.60), with a selection of salads (£2.60). At lunchtime there are also filled wholemeal baps (75p), bread and cheese (£1.20) and ploughman's (£1.70). Puddings include home-made brown Betty (70p). There is a separate restaurant. Well kept Bass, Tetleys Bitter and Mild, and Hartleys Best on handpump and several ciders; darts, shove-ha'penny, dominoes, cribbage. As the pub is so well placed for Langdale and the central lakes, with tracks over the fells to Grasmere and Easedale, it can get quite crowded in summer, but readers have

---

Children welcome means the pub says it lets children inside without any special restriction. If it allows them in, but to restricted areas such as an eating area or family room, we specify this.

found the service unruffled even when people flock here to watch Morris and Step and Garland Dancers on the green. *(Recommended by MGBD, A J Dobson, D A Angless, Stephen McNees, Mr and Mrs E W Spink, P J White, Mr and Mrs N G W Edwardes, Tim Halstead, Jenny Potter)*

Free house · Licensee David Fry · Real ale · Meals and snacks · Children welcome · Summer parking may be difficult · Open 11–3, 5.30–10.30 Bedrooms tel Langdale (096 67) 210 or 382; £15.75/£31.50

ESKDALE GREEN   NY1400 Map 9
Bower House

The sheltered lawn and garden, neatly kept and very pretty, is a most unusual bonus for the Lake District. It leads out directly behind the comfortable lounge bar, which is decorated with sporting prints and has cushioned settles and Windsor chairs in a spacious carpeted extension; this blends in well with the original beamed and alcoved nucleus around the serving counter. Bar food includes soup, sandwiches, smoked salmon pâté, open prawn sandwich, ploughman's, scampi, poussin, duck cooked with cherries, and venison casserole; well kept Hartleys XB and Youngers Scotch on handpump; darts, dominoes, cribbage; a warm welcome from the licensee – a Yorkshireman – and his family. There is also a separate restaurant, and a comfortable lounge with easy chairs and sofas. *(Recommended by Monica Darlington, R S Bailey, G V Simmons; more reports please)*

Free house · Licensee Cyril Smith · Real ale · Meals and snacks Children welcome · Open 11–3, 6–11 · Bedrooms tel Eskdale (094 03) 244; £19.50 (£21.50B)/£27 (£30B)

FAR SAWREY   SD3893 Map 9
Sawrey Hotel

B5285 towards Windermere ferry

A track up Claife Heights, which rise steeply behind the white hotel, leads straight to a splendid viewpoint over Lake Windermere, and seats by tables under cocktail parasols on the hotel's spacious front lawn look up to the lovely wooded Heights. On fine days readers enjoy bar lunches served out here. The food includes a wide choice of sandwiches (from egg and cress, 75p, to smoked salmon, £1.95), soup (60p), rollmop or ploughman's (£1.30), beef and tomato croquettes (£1.50), Cumberland sausage (£2), various meat salads (£2.40) and scampi (£2.60). The separate restaurant serves dinner in the evenings. The plushly comfortable lounges have well kept Theakstons Best and Old Peculier on handpump. Another quite separate bar, the Claife Crier, is done out as stables, with wooden stalls dividing the tables, and harness on its whitewashed stone walls. This has Jennings as well as the Theakstons, and shove-ha'penny, dominoes, cribbage, and sensibly placed darts, a fruit machine and a space game. The service is friendly. *(Recommended by Dennis Royles, M C Dickson)*

We say if we or readers have seen dogs or cats in a pub.

*Free house · Licensee David Brayshaw · Real ale · Meals and snacks
(lunchtime) · Children in eating area · Open 11–3, 5.30–10.30 · Bedrooms tel
Windermere (096 62) 3425; £11.95 (£13.90B)/£16.95 (£18.50B)*

FAUGH   NY5155 Map 9

String of Horses ★

From A69 in Warwick Bridge, turn off at Heads Nook, Castle Carrock
signpost, fork right at Heads Nook Station, Cumwhitton signpost, then follow
Faugh signs (if you have to ask the way, it's pronounced Faff)

The food is what readers enthuse about here: it includes sandwiches
(from 65p), a cold table with an excellent choice of home-cooked
cold meats (£3.85 – children under 10 free, one per adult) and
perhaps salmon or sea trout, hot dishes such as a wide choice of
curries (from £2.95), chicken in either a Chianti or a chilli sauce
(£3.25) and seafood platter (£3.25). The lunchtime choice is roughly
similar, though with ploughman's (£1.50), and quite a few grills from
Cumberland sausage (£2.25) to steaks (from £4.95), and dishes of the
day such as home-made steak and kidney or turkey, ham and
mushroom pie (£3.50). Evening bar food orders here are taken until
10.15 pm – unusually late for the area. Theakstons Best and Old
Peculier are kept under top pressure. This seventeenth-century inn is
pretty outside, with Dutch blinds and lanterns, and lots of lanterns
and neat wrought iron among the greenery of its sheltered terrace.
The open-plan bar has the cosy feel of several communicating rooms,
with fine old settles and elaborately carved Gothick seats and tables
among simpler Windsor and other chairs. It has some interesting
antique prints on its cream walls, the heavy beams are decorated with
brass pots and warming pans, and there are log fires in cool weather.
Piped music, dominoes, and a fruit machine set sensibly aside in a
lobby. The bedrooms are very comfortable, and residents have the
use of a jacuzzi, sauna, solarium and small outdoor heated pool.
(Recommended by Dr T B Brewin, C B M Gregory)

*Free house · Licensees Anne and Eric Tasker · Meals and snacks · Children
welcome · Open 11.30–3, 5.30–10.30 · Bedrooms tel Hayton (022 870) 297;
£37B/£46B*

GRASMERE   NY3406 Map 9

Swan

This low but substantial hotel has been plushly modernised inside,
but still has old prints and beams and one or two attractive settles in
its carpeted lounge. Good home-made food served in the small public
bar, which has leatherette seats and darts, includes sandwiches (from
80p, crab £1.50), soup (95p), large helpings of filled French bread
(£1.65–£2.45), cottage pie (£2.55), a vegetarian dish (£2.95),
fisherman's pie (£3.05) and steak and kidney pie (£3.25); the choice is
similar but more limited in the evening. There is of course a separate
restaurant. Readers have been finding this a comfortable place to
stay, with good breakfasts and friendly and courteous service. The
village is particularly popular for its connections with the
Wordsworths and Dove Cottage where they lived for nine years is

open (with a museum opposite). When Sir Walter Scott stayed with them, he used to slip along here for a secret morning drink. The truth came out when all of them called in to hire a pony for climbing the fells – which rise straight behind – to visit the spot on Helvellyn guarded by a dog for three months after his master had been killed in a blizzard there. *(Recommended by A J Dobson, L W Thomas, Mr and Mrs A Moore)*

Free house (THF) · Meals and snacks · Open 11–3, 6–10.30 · Bedrooms tel *Grasmere (096 65) 551; £35.25 (£41.25B)/£46 (£58B)*

HAWKSHEAD   SD3598   Map 9
Queens Head ★

Hugely popular, this friendly inn keeps up a remarkably high standard with its food in the bar and oak-panelled dining-room – and we marvel at the energy of the two chefs, maybe serving in the bar after producing 200 or so meals on a typical evening. Lunchtime bar food includes ploughman's with Stilton or Brie, smoked trout or Cumberland sausage (£2.50), open sandwiches such as seafood mayonnaise (£2.75) and scampi (£3.50), with concentration in the evening on main dishes such as pork chops with barbecue sauce or tagliatelle with a ham, cheese and mushroom sauce (£3.50) and eight-ounce rump steak (£5.25); dining-room prices are only slightly higher. Helpings are vast, ingredients good – if local ham is on the menu, jump for it: they've tracked down a smoker of fine-textured yet succulent hams to rival the great French ones from Bayonne or the Auvergne. The open-plan bar has red leatherette seats around heavy traditional tables, a shelf of blue and white plates between squared brown panelling and the heavy bowed black beams of the low ceiling, and a snug little room leading off. Well kept Hartleys Bitter and Mild on handpump, with Robinsons Old Tom tapped from the cask; piped music; splendidly welcoming atmosphere – the landlord has a fine knack of seeming to be in 20 places at once, yet always perfectly relaxed. The simple beamed bedrooms are comfortable, and the village is a charming and virtually car-free network of stone-paved alleys winding through huddles of whitewashed cottages. *(Recommended by RAB, J Field, Tim Halstead, Miss E R Bowmer, Philip Asquith, RCR, Keith Myers, George Jonas, Paul West, RAO)*

Hartleys · Licensee Allan Whitehead · Real ale · Meals and snacks · Children in room off bar · Open 11–3, 6–10.30 (opens 7 in winter; no food Christmas Day) · Bedrooms tel *Hawkshead (096 66) 271; £15 (£18B)/£25 (£30B)*

nr HAWKSHEAD   SD3598   Map 9
Drunken Duck

Barngates; hamlet signposted from B5286 Hawkshead–Ambleside, opposite the Outgate Inn; OS Sheet 90 reference 350013

Though the licensee has changed, the Bartons still own this remote pub, and on a recent visit we found little difference. Its three or four cosy beamed rooms have cushioned old settles, ladderback country chairs, blond pews and tapestried stools on fitted Turkey carpet, and are decorated with Cecil Aldin prints, lots of landscapes and a big longcase clock. Popular bar food includes big filled baps (from 90p), ploughman's (£2.30), chicken (£2.75), scampi (£3), duck (£3.50) and sirloin steak (£5.25). Imaginative home-made puddings (£1) include ones that do need work, such as charlotte russe. There may be service delays when the pub is busy. Well kept Jennings, Marstons Pedigree and Mild, Tetleys Bitter and Theakstons XB and Old Peculier on handpump, a good choice of whiskies (including a couple of Macallans) and good value house wines. Darts, dominoes; trout fishing in the inn's two private tarns. Seats under the bright hanging baskets on the front verandah have views of distant Lake Windermere, and to the side there are quite a few rustic wooden chairs and tables, sheltered by a stone wall with alpine plants along its top. (*Recommended by John DuBois, Tim Halstead, M C Dickson, N C Hodgson, Philip Asquith, Keith Myers, Paul West*)

Free house · Licensee David Dunlop · Real ale · Meals and snacks · Children in rooms without serving bar · Piano Weds · Open 11.30–3, 6–10.30 (opens half an hour later in winter); closed 25 Dec · Bedrooms tel Hawkshead (096 66) 347; £12.50/£25

HEVERSHAM   SD4983   Map 9
Blue Bell

A6 (now a relatively quiet road here)

The civilised bay-windowed lounge bar of this friendly and very well kept inn – once a vicarage – has comfortable cushioned Windsor armchairs, an antique carved settle and upholstered stools on its flowery carpet. Its partly panelled walls are decorated with small antique sporting prints, and pewter platters hang from one of the black beams. In cool weather there's an open fire. One big bay-windowed area has been divided off as a children's room, and the long public bar with a tiled floor has darts and dominoes. Good value bar food includes filled rolls (70p) and sandwiches (from 95p), home-made soup (75p, lunchtime only), locally baked steak and kidney pie (£1), home-made quiche (£1.10), home-made cottage pie (£1.20) and salads including fresh salmon (£3.50); well kept Hartleys XB on electric pump, with Tetleys, Youngers or Theakstons often kept too. The restaurant has a good value inclusive lunch. One reader who has been coming here for many years reckons that their standards never vary. (*Recommended by John Estdale, Dennis Royles*)

Free house · Licensee John Chew · Real ale · Meals and snacks · Children's room · Open 10.30–3, 6–11; closed 25 Dec · Bedrooms tel Milnthorpe (044 82) 3159; £19 (£24B)/£32 (£37B)

KESWICK   NY2624   Map 9
George

St Johns Street; off top end of Market Street

The open-plan main bar has old-fashioned cushioned settles under its Elizabethan beams, as well as banquettes upholstered to match the carpet (there are antique flooring-tiles in parts), and open fires in winter. Leading off is an attractive black-panelled room with a collection of old photographs and prints of the area. It is in here that the poet Southey used to wait for his friend Wordsworth to arrive from Grasmere. Bar food includes sandwiches (from 85p), broth (90p), home-made pâté (£1.25), ploughman's (£2), burgers (from £1.50), Cumberland sausage (£2.30) and scampi (£2.95); Theakstons Best and Youngers Scotch on handpump, Theakstons Old Peculier tapped from the cask, and maybe a bowl of punch; darts, dominoes. Comfortable bedrooms; there is a separate restaurant (meals £7.50), and trout fishing is available. *(Recommended by Tim Halstead; more reports please)*

Free house · Licensee Ken Burchill · Real ale · Meals and snacks (not Sun evening; and readers have reported no bar food some other evenings) Children welcome · Open 11–3, 5.30–10.30 · Bedrooms tel Keswick (0596) 72076; £14/£28

nr KESWICK   NY2624   Map 9
Swinside Inn

Newlands Valley: leaving Keswick on A66 to Cockermouth, turn left signposted Newlands Valley; follow signs to Stair (if you come to a hotel called Swinside Lodge you've taken a wrong fork – turn back, then take first left); at night keep your eyes skinned as the pub may not show front lights; OS Sheet 90 reference 242217

Looking over a quiet valley to the high crags and fells around Grisedale Pike, this friendly and unpretentious country inn has a comfortably modernised sixteenth-century lounge bar. There's also a long bright public bar with red plush banquettes against the cream-rendered walls; a central chimney with an open fire divides off the games area, which has darts, dominoes, pool, fruit machine, space games and jukebox or piped music. A modest range of bar food (mainly with chips) includes filled rolls (70p), a good selection of sandwiches (all 80p), generously garnished ploughman's (£1.90), omelettes (£2.50), Cumberland sausage with egg (£2.50), lasagne (£2.70), home-made steak pie (£2.70) or game pie (£3.50), local trout (£3.50) and rump steak (£5); Jennings on handpump (though not always available), and Jennings Mild on electric pump. The many seats outside, in the garden and on the upper and lower terraces, together with a largely glass-walled upstairs eating room, make the most of the marvellous hill views. *(Recommended by D W Roberts; more reports please)*

Jennings · Licensee James Dunn · Real ale · Meals and snacks · Children in eating area · Open 11–3, 6–10.30 · Bedrooms tel Braithwaite (059 682) 253; £11.50/£20

KIRKBY STEPHEN   NY7808   Map 10
King's Arms ★

Lunchtime bar food in this square-cut old market-town inn includes home-made soup (70p), sandwiches (from 65p, home-baked ham 80p, steak £2.50), macaroni cheese or ham and eggs (£1.60), ploughman's (£1.75), chicken and ham pie with salad (£2), seafood platter (£2.40) and meat salads (from £2.50); well kept Whitbreads Trophy on handpump. The snug oak-panelled lounge bar's solidly comfortable seats include bar stools with welcome backrests, and there's a good open fire in cool weather. It's civilised, with cut glass for shorts and maybe nuts and crisps on the serving counter. The small public bar has darts, dominoes and cribbage; also a separate restaurant. There is a garden behind the inn, and the town, with its robust defences against Scots raiders, is worth strolling through. It is set in relatively uncrowded but most attractive moorland, between Lakeland and the Pennines. *(Recommended by Tim Halstead, Philip Asquith, Keith Myers, Paul West; more reports please)*

Whitbreads · Licensee Keith Simpson · Real ale · Meals and snacks (lunchtime) Children in eating area · Entertainment planned monthly for 1986 in new functions room · Open 10.30–3, 6–10.30; closed 25 Dec · Bedrooms tel Kirkby Stephen (0930) 71378; £14 (£20B)/£27 (£32B)

LANGDALE   NY2906   Map 9
Old Dungeon Ghyll

B5343

They serve a choice of snuffs here – as well as well kept McEwans 70/–, 80/–, Theakstons Best, XB and Old Peculier and Youngers No 3 on handpump, and good value bar food such as home-made soup (75p), pies and pasties such as savoury beef and chicken with onion (50p), sandwiches (60p–75p), dishes of peas, quiche salad (£1.75) and Cumberland sausage (£1.85). Window seats cut into the enormously thick stone walls of the simply furnished walkers' bar have a grand view of the Pike of Blisco rising behind Kettle Crag. It can get really lively on a Saturday night, when there's a good deal of spontaneous music-making – though maybe with more *brio* than brilliance. Darts, shove-ha'penny, dominoes. This splendid spot is surrounded by towering fells, including Langdale Pikes and Harrison Stickle flanking Dungeon Ghyll Force waterfall (which inspired Wordsworth's poem 'The Idle Shepherd Boys'). *(Recommended by Patrick Stapley, Richard Gibbs, Tim Halstead, Philip Asquith, Keith Myers, Paul West; more reports please)*

Free house · Licensee N J Walmsley · Real ale · Meals and snacks (not Sun evening) · Children welcome · Open 11–3, 5.30–10.30 · Bedrooms tel Langdale (096 67) 272; £12.50 (£14.50B)/£25 (£29B)

LEVENS   SD4886   Map 9
Hare & Hounds   [*illustrated on page 135*]

Village signposted from A590 to A591; from centre follow signpost to Grange, past Methodist chapel

Good value simple food in this welcoming village pub includes soup (55p), home-cooked ham in open sandwiches (£1.40), Morecambe Bay shrimps (£1.60, full salad £2.75), plaice or haddock (£2.10), Cumberland sausage (£2.25) and sirloin steak (six-ounce £3.05, twelve-ounce £5.20). At lunchtime there are also sandwiches (from 65p), pâté or a generous ploughman's with good helpings of three

English cheeses (£1.40); well kept Vaux Sunderland on electric pump and Samson on handpump. The carpeted lounge bar, angled around the servery, has some low black beams, and on its sloping floor there is a wicker-backed Jacobean-style armchair and antique settle, as well as old-fashioned brown leatherette dining-seats and red-cushioned seats built into the partly panelled walls. The snug front public bar, with a shelf of gamebird plates above its serving counter, has darts, dominoes and fruit machine. A separate pool-room, down steps, has golden oldies on its juke box. All readers' reports mention the friendliness of the service, though there may be a longish wait for food when the pub fills up at weekends or in the evening. *(Recommended by D A Angless, MGBD, Frank Cummins, J A Blades)*

Vaux · Licensee James Stephenson · Real ale · Meals and snacks (perhaps not Mon evening) · Children in side area of lounge at lunchtime · Open 11–3, 6–10.30

LITTLE LANGDALE NY3204 Map 9
Three Shires

From A593 3 miles W of Ambleside take small road signposted The Langdales, Wrynose Pass, then bear left at first fork

Picked by the AA as its 1985 northern inn of the year, this stone-built house has pale plush armchairs and old-fashioned furniture (including a long-case clock) in the carpeted front cocktail bar/residents' lounge. Its big window has a lovely view out over the valley to the partly wooded hills below Tilberthwaite Fells; this view is shared by seats on the verandah, and on a neat lawn behind the car park, backed by a small oak wood. The neat and cosy back bar has antique carved oak settles and country kitchen chairs and stools around the cast-iron-framed tables on the big dark slate flagstones, with local photographs on the walls, and a coal fire in cool weather. Bar food includes sandwiches (from 75p), ploughman's or pâté (£2.10), local rainbow trout (£3.95), Barnsley chops (£4.25), butterfly pork chops in cider sauce (£4.50) and sirloin steak (£5.25); Websters Yorkshire and Wilsons Bitter on electric pump; darts, dominoes. There is also a separate restaurant. A friendly, comfortable place to stay. *(Recommended by MGBD, Jenny Potter)*

Free house · Licensee Neil Stephenson · Real ale · Meals and snacks · Children welcome · Open 11–3, 5.30–10.30 · Bedrooms tel Langdale (096 67) 215; £14.50 (£16B)/£29 (£32B)

LOWICK GREEN SD2985 Map 9
Farmers Arms ★

A595

The public bar of this rambling old hotel gives the impression of being little changed in centuries, with its massive wooden door, ancient heavy oak beams, old seats and settles on huge flagstones, and a handsome fireplace with a big open fire. The up-to-date touches are in side alcoves: interesting submariner photographs in one, table skittles, darts, a fruit machine and space game in another (there are also bar billiards, shove-ha'penny, dominoes and cribbage). Bar food includes home-made soup (60p), sandwiches (from 70p), ploughman's (£1.40), home-made pâté (£1.50), burgers (£1.60), sausages and fried egg (£1.70), haddock (£2.10), seafood platter (£2.30) and good scampi (£2.50); well kept McEwans 80/–, Youngers Scotch and No 3 on handpump, and a good choice of wines by the glass; maybe piped music. Across the courtyard, the hotel – which is attractively furnished, and has a well preserved spinning gallery – has its own plusher lounge bar and a separate restaurant. Coniston Water is not far away. *(Recommended by W A Rinaldi-Butcher, Dennis Royles, H D Leggatt, Tim Halstead, Patrick Stapley, Philip Asquith, Richard Gibbs, Keith Myers, Paul West)*

Scottish & Newcastle · Licensee Philip Broadley · Real ale · Snacks (lunchtime) and meals · Children in restaurant, family area and (lunchtime) lounge bar Open 10.30–3, 6–11 all year · Bedrooms tel Greenodd (022 986) 376; £14 (£20B)/£32B

MELMERBY   NY6237 Map 10
Shepherds

A686

A wide choice of good home-cooked food in this well run homely pub includes home-made pork pasties (50p), soup (90p), sandwiches (on special demand, if not too busy), ploughman's with home-baked rolls (£1.90), pork and port pâté (£2), Cumberland sausage hot-pot (£2.70), steak and kidney pie (£3.20), trout with lemon and mushroom stuffing (£3.40), steaks (from £4.90) and home-made puddings (£1). On Sundays there is a roast joint (£2.95). Very well kept Marstons Burton, Pedigree and Merrie Monk on handpump. At about the time this new edition is published, extensive renovations are planned to increase space for eating in the main area, which has cushioned wall seats, sunny window seats looking across the green of the unspoilt red sandstone village, an open fire and a good friendly atmosphere. There should also be more room in the light-panelled and cheerful games bar, which has darts, pool, shove-ha'penny, dominoes, fruit machine and juke box. In warm weather a barn extension, decorated with plants and ferns, is opened as an overflow. The Pennines climb immediately behind, and Hartside Nursery Garden, a noted alpine plant specialist, is just over the Hartside Pass. *(Recommended by G L Archer, George Wilson; more reports please)*

Marstons · Licensee Martin Baucutt · Real ale · Meals and snacks · Children in eating area · Open 11–3, 6–10.30; closed 25 Dec

NEAR SAWREY   SD3796 Map 9
Tower Bank Arms

B5285 towards the Windermere ferry

The main bar of this friendly country inn, owned by the National Trust, is traditionally furnished with high-backed settles on the rough

---

If we know a pub has an outdoor play area for children, we mention it.

slate floor, a big cooking range with a lovely log fire, a grandfather clock, and local hunting photographs under the low beams. It can get quite crowded with tourists in summer (it backs on to Beatrix Potter's farm), and is perhaps nicest out of season, when it has a much more local atmosphere. Bar food includes filled wholemeal rolls (from 80p), soup (80p), Cumberland sausage with apple sauce (£1.25), ploughman's (from £1.85), home-made quiche (£2.65), pie (£2.85), salads including home-cooked ham (£3.25) and Esthwaite trout (£3.75); at lunchtime the dining-room is used as a family room. Jennings Bitter and Matthew Brown Mild on handpump; darts, shove-ha'penny, dominoes and cribbage. Seats outside the quaint black and white cottage have a view of the wooded Claife Heights. *(Recommended by M C Dickson, John DuBois)*

Free house · Licensees David Holmes and Gordan Hall · Real ale · Snacks (lunchtime) and meals · Children in dining-room · Occasional live entertainment · Open 11–3, 5.30–10.30 · Bedrooms tel Hawkshead (096 66) 334; £13.50B/£23B

PENRITH   NY5130 Map 9
George
¾ mile from M6 junction 40: in town centre (Devonshire Street)

The old-fashioned lounge hall of this well run and substantial old hotel is a spacious place, with attractive oak panelling, an intricately tiled fireplace, a long-case clock, polished oak beams and handsome plasterwork ceiling mouldings. It has easy chairs and comfortable built-in high-backed winged oak settles (with matching nests of small tables) on a spread of tartan carpet – which presumably commemorates Bonnie Prince Charlie's stay here in 1745. Drinks are served from a small cocktail bar, and there is a lively back bar with soft red leatherette seats, stone fireplace, fruit machine and piped mainstream music. Lunchtime bar food includes sandwiches (80p), a help-yourself buffet (£3) and a hot dish of the day (£3.25); the restaurant lunches are very reasonably priced. Well kept Marstons Pedigree on handpump. The bedrooms have been simply but comfortably modernised, and are good value. The Steam Museum in Castlegate is worth visiting, with a working smithy and furnished Victorian cottage as well as the steam engines and models you'd expect. *(Recommended by Heather Sharland; more reports please)*

Free house · Licensee Tomas Niedt · Real ale · Meals (lunchtime, not Sun) and snacks · Children welcome · Open 10.30–3, 6.30–10.30 · Bedrooms tel Penrith (0768) 62696; £25B/£36B

RAVENSTONEDALE   NY7204 Map 9
Kings Head
Village and pub signposted off A685 W of Kirkby Stephen

Bar food is good value in this friendly black-beamed pub: portions are so big that, when one reader couldn't finish his vast helping of Yorkshire ham (£3 with egg, chips and peas), what was left was wrapped in foil for him and later made two lots of sandwiches for lunches. Other dishes include home-made soup (60p), sandwiches (from 70p), ploughman's (£1.75), haddock or plaice (£2), home-made shepherd's pie (£2.25), scampi or hot roasts (£2.50) and chicken (£2.80), with cold meats or seafood from a summer buffet (£3.50 – winter salads instead, £2.50). The restaurant has four-course dinners (£5.50, including steak and salmon in the choice). The two well kept rooms of the bar are divided by a sturdy stone chimney with good log fires; one side has built-in button-back banquettes and a couple of tables, the other has more tables with tapestried dining-chairs. The games room has sensibly placed darts, pool and fruit machine; also dominoes, cribbage and a juke box or piped music; well kept Tetleys Bitter and Mild on handpump. Tables outside include some across the quiet lane, beside Scandal Beck; the village is surrounded by attractive rolling moorland pasture. *(Recommended by Mrs R S Young, Frank Cummins)*

Free house · Licensees C and M Porter · Real ale · Meals and snacks · Open 12–3, 6.30–11 all year · Bedrooms tel Newbiggin-on-Lune (058 73) 284; £9/£18

RYDAL   NY3706   Map 9

Glen Rothay Hotel

A591 N of Ambleside

The Badger Bar of this pleasant small hotel has a stuffed pheasant, fox and badger as well as wild animal prints; it is furnished with tapestried built-in wall seats and stools around dimpled copper tables, with an elegant archway through to the serving area. Popular bar food includes home-made soup (85p), home-made pâté (£1.35), open sandwiches (£1.60), ploughman's (from £1.95), quiche, home-made steak and kidney pie and a vegetarian dish of the day (also £1.95), salads (from £1.95), plaice with prawns and scampi (£5.25) and 16-ounce T-bone steak (£6.95), with children's dishes such as fish fingers (90p). Bass and Hartleys XB on handpump; on our visit, piped pop music. The beamed hotel lounge bar, panelled in dark oak, has comfortable armchairs around its open fire, and there's a separate restaurant (five-course dinner £10.95). There are rustic seats on a pretty crazy-paved terrace and roadside lawn, where big rhododendrons cascade down among rocks from the woods above; the hotel has boats for residents on nearby Rydal Water. *(Recommended by John and Sue Tucknott, MGBD)*

Free house · Licensees Mrs Sandra Garside and Philip Prescott · Real ale Meals and snacks · Children welcome · Open 11.30–3, 6–10.30; closed 8–20 Dec 1985, 5–24 Jan and 8–19 Dec 1986 · Bedrooms tel Ambleside (096 63) 2524; £23B/£40B

SANDSIDE   SD4981   Map 9

Ship

This extensive modernised pub's special feature is its glorious view over the Kent estuary to the Lakeland hills. The water is about half a mile wide here, but dries to sand and a very narrow channel at low tide. The softly lit open-plan bar is well kept, with soft lighting, red button-back banquettes on the dark red carpet, recent dark wood panelling, piped mainstream music, and quite a lot of big stormy seascapes. An end section, bare-boarded, has bar billiards, darts and a juke box, and there are two fruit machines; well kept Youngers Scotch and No 3 on handpump. Bar food includes soup (50p), ploughman's (£1.35) and hot dishes such as chicken (£2.35), beef and onion pie or scampi (£2.45), sirloin steak (£4.95) and so forth; there is a quiet back dining-section (away from the views). In summer, barbecues are held outside every day during school holidays, but otherwise just at weekends. The big car park has a cluster of picnic-tables set under cocktail parasols, and since the last edition a children's play area has been opened with a slide and assault course. *(Recommended by Mr and Mrs B C Fletcher; more reports please)*

Scottish & Newcastle · Real ale · Meals and snacks · Children welcome · Open 11–3, 6–10.30 · Bedrooms tel Milnthorpe (044 82) 3113; £11/£21

SCALES   NY3427 Map 9
White Horse
A66 1½ miles E of Threlkeld

Local produce is used as much as possible in the cooking here – no chips or convenience foods. The results (good value) include home-made soup (85p, or £1 for a main-course-sized helping), and at lunchtime ploughman's with good fresh bread (£1.95), savoury flan (£1.95), cottage pie or a selection of open sandwiches (£2.25) and Cumberland ham and eggs (£3.50); a good choice of puddings (£1) includes home-made meringues with bilberries and cream. In the evenings (when booking is essential) there are cockles and mussels in a seafood dip (£1.95), local trout in white wine (£3.95), mixed grill or sirloin steak (£5.75) and so forth. The friendly bar has Windsor chairs on the red carpet, beams, local hunting cartoons and warm fires in winter, and there's a cosy little snug (in what used to be the dairy). Jennings on handpump, dominoes. From this isolated cluster of pub and farm buildings tracks lead up into the splendidly daunting and rocky fells around Blencathra, which have names like Foule Crag and Sharp Edge. *(Recommended by D W Roberts, Mrs M Branney; more reports please)*

Jennings · Licensees Laurence and Judith Slattery · Real ale · Snacks (lunchtime) and meals (not Mon evening) tel Threlkeld (059 683) 241 Children in eating area · Open 11–3, 6–10.30

STAINTON   NY4928 Map 9
Kings Arms
1¾ miles from M6 junction 40: village signposted from A66 towards Keswick, though quickest to fork left at A592 roundabout then turn first right

Generous helpings of simple freshly cooked food in this comfortably modernised old pub include sandwiches and toasties (from 55p, beef or tasty ham off the bone 65p), soup (50p), pâté (75p), beefburger roll (80p), ploughman's £1.10), beefburger and egg (£1.20), steak and kidney pie (£1.25), chicken (£1.90), scampi (£1.95), gammon or local trout (£2), sirloin steak (£3.80) and cold meat salads (£1.95); children's dishes with baked beans and good chips (95p). Service is friendly. The open-plan bar has leatherette wall banquettes, stools and armchairs, wood-effect tables, brasses on black beams, swirly cream walls; fairly quiet on weekday lunchtimes, it has a lively atmosphere in the evenings when it's full of local people and visitors. Sensibly placed darts, dominoes, fairly quiet juke box. There are tables outside on the side terrace and on a small lawn. *(Recommended by Keith and Rosemary Markham; more reports please)*

Whitbreads · Licensee Raymond Tweddle · Meals and snacks (not winter weekday evenings) · Children welcome to eat · Country and western Sun evening · Open 10.30–3, 6–10.30

TALKIN   NY5557 Map 10
Hare & Hounds ★
Village signposted from B6413 S of Brampton

The most warmly welcoming pub that we have ever stayed in, this small eighteenth-century village inn also has good value simple food, well kept real ales, and a friendly, lively atmosphere in the cosy main bar. This pair of knocked-through rooms, one black-beamed and timbered, the other with a shiny white plank ceiling, has red-cushioned country chairs, wicker armchairs and settles around its close-set dark elm rustic tables, big antique prints over its two open fires, a fine long-case clock (made in Brampton), and stained-glass municipal coats of arms over the serving counter. A quieter back room has stalls around rustic tables. Home-cooked food in big helpings includes soup (50p), baked potatoes with interesting fillings (from 55p), pizza (85p), burgers (95p), steak sandwich (£1.55), a range of main dishes such as plaice with ratatouille or poached trout (£2.60) and good local fillet steak (£4.75), cheap children's dishes, and lots of puddings (from 60p); well kept Hartleys XB (which on our visit you couldn't find anywhere else in the area) and Theakstons Best, XB and Old Peculier on handpump; darts, dominoes and connect 4, perhaps gentle piped music. The bedrooms are comfortable and cheerfully decorated; there are a few tables on a gravel side terrace, and you can walk straight from the small village into fine countryside (Talkin Tarn is a lovely spot for boating, fishing or just sitting, and there's a golf course virtually on the doorstep). *(Recommended by Roger Protz, Jack Lalor, BOB)*

Free house · Licensees Les and Joan Stewart · Real ale · Meals and snacks Children in back room· Open 12–2, 7–10.30, but closed weekday lunchtimes (except mid-July to Aug, Easter and Christmas); closed 25 Dec · Bedrooms tel Brampton (069 77) 3456; £11.50/£20

TIRRIL   NY5126 Map 9
Queen's Head
3½ miles from M6 junction 40; take A66 towards Brough, A6 towards Shap, then B5320 towards Ullswater

Coming in from the back entrance, we'd duck our heads (for the low beams) and walk right around the central servery of this old inn's bars to the furthest corner of the black-panelled front part, where old-fashioned high-backed settles and some armchairs and sofas nestle around a roomy inglenook fireplace (once a cupboard for smoking hams). Under the flowery carpet is raw rock which was quarried out as the inn's floor in the early eighteenth century. Bar food includes soup (70p), sandwiches (from 75p), smoked trout mousse (£1.65), open tuna sandwich (£1.85), scampi (£2.85), trout or spare ribs (£2.95) and eight-ounce sirloin steak (£4.95); also a separate restaurant. Matthew Brown Lion Bitter and Mild, Theakstons Bitter and Old Peculier on handpump, and a wide range of cocktails; darts, dominoes, fruit machine and juke box in the more modern back part – which quickly fills up at holiday times. *(Recommended by Jack Lalor; more reports please)*

Matthew Brown · Licensee Ian Sorrell · Meals and snacks · Children welcome Live music Thurs · Open 11–3, 6–10.30 · Bedrooms tel Penrith (0768) 63219; £12/£22

TROUTBECK   NY4103   Map 9

Queen's Head

A592 N of Windermere

A massive Elizabethan four-poster bed is the basis of this gabled seventeenth-century inn's serving counter, and readers with a taste for the unusual have enjoyed other oddities in the half-dozen knocked-together rooms of its bar. There is more fine antique carving, stuffed foxes and pheasants, cushioned antique settles, lots of alcoves, heavy beams, and two big open fires. Plenty of seats outside have a fine view over the Trout valley to Applethwaite moors. Bar food, which includes sandwiches, soup, basket meals and other dishes, is not cheap – £3 for a ploughman's for instance, or £5.50 for prawn salad; there's also a separate restaurant; darts, dominoes, pool, a space game and a juke box (the games are removed in summer); Wilsons Best and Mitchells ESB on handpump. Nearby Townend is a fine example of a seventeenth-century Lakeland farmhouse, and the church has an unexpected stained-glass window – done as a holiday project by Burne-Jones and pre-Raphaelite friends. *(Recommended by Dr A K Clarke, John DuBois, Tim Halstead, Patrick Stapley, Philip Asquith, Richard Gibbs, Keith Myers, Paul West)*

Free house · Licensee Mrs Marion Moffat · Real ale · Meals and snacks Children welcome · Open 11–3, 5.30–10.30 · Bedrooms tel Ambleside (0966) 32174; £12.50B/£25B

WARWICK ON EDEN   NY4657   Map 9

Queens Arms ★

2 miles from M6 junction 43: A69 towards Hexham, then village signposted

In the evenings there's a unique and delicious range of some 130 sandwiches here: from 50p to £1.75 for elaborate triple-deckers, and including things like Austrian smoked cheese with garlic sausage

(80p), crab with celery and pineapple (£1.25), chicken with scooped egg and stuffed prawns (£1.40) and Cumberland sausage with ham, chutney and tomato (£1.65), filled baked potates (from 70p), ploughman's (£1.45 with soup and coffee), Cumberland sausage (£1.45) and pizzas (from £1.75). There is a separate restaurant (in the evenings, except Saturdays, one child can eat free for each adult who has a meal). The lively traditional bar has seats and settles forming booths around tables in one room, and Windsor chairs, an old-fashioned settle and an open fire in another. It's decorated with big pictures of vintage motor-cycles and racing cars, yachts and steam locomotives. Well kept Tetleys on handpump, and a good range of bottled beers. The neat side garden, with roses, marigolds and other flowers, has rustic tables and seats, and a well equipped play area. *(Recommended by Roger Danes, Dr M V Jones, Jack Lalor, C B M Gregory)*

Free house · Licensee Lawrence Keen · Real ale · Meals and snacks · Children welcome · Open 11–3, 5.30–10.30; hotel areas open throughout the day; closed 25 Dec · Bedrooms tel Wetheral (0228) 60699; £22B/£29B

WASDALE HEAD   NY1808   Map 9
Wasdale Head Inn ★

This part of the Lake District is well away from the main tourist areas and quite unspoilt: the hotel is plumb in the very best part, with fells rising steeply all around, and Wastwater itself nearby – the most severely grand of all the lakes, surrounded by vertiginous screes. The main bar is a big slate-floored room with shiny panelling, cushioned settles, high ceilings, pool-table, and a masculine atmosphere that conjures up the days when this was a centre for the pioneer rock-climbers – there are fine George Abraham photographs of that period on the walls. This bar is named after the inn's first landlord, Will Ritson, who for his tall stories was reputed to be the world's biggest liar, and in his memory they still hold liar competitions here towards the end of November. There is also a panelled and comfortably old-fashioned residents' bar and lounge. Good home-made bar food includes sandwiches, soup (90p), filled baked potato (£1.10), cheese and onion quiche or fisherman's pie (£1.80), chicken liver pâté with French bread (£1.90), ploughman's with Alston cheese (£2.10), steak and kidney pie (£2.10), chicken and pepper casserole (£2.60) and mixed local smoked meat salad (£3.10). There is a good separate restaurant. Well kept Jennings, Hartleys and Theakstons Best and Old Peculier on handpump; dominoes, cribbage. The hotel is well run (with service both friendly and efficient), and is a comfortable place to stay; it also has a self-catering cottage and two flats in converted inn buildings nearby. *(Recommended by Monica Darlington, Philip Asquith, Mrs S B Q Leaney, J M Tansey)*

Free house · Licensee Mr Arthy · Real ale · Meals and snacks · Children in room off main bar area · Open 11–3, 5.30–11 all year · Bedrooms tel Wasdale (094 06) 229; £22B/£40B

WINTON NY7810 Map 10
Bay Horse
Just off A683 N of Kirkby Stephen

Just as this edition of the *Guide* goes to press new licensees tell us that they have only very recently taken over this friendly little moorland inn. We are keeping it in as a main entry as it is so usefully placed, and we gather that no major changes are planned for the two low-ceilinged rooms of the bar, simply but comfortably furnished, and decorated with Pennine photographs and examples of local fishing fly-tying. Bar food includes ploughman's or pâté (£1.25) and steaks such as sirloin (£4.30), with plans for shepherd's pie, steak and kidney pie and so forth as the new licensees find their feet. McEwans 80/– and Youngers Scotch on handpump; darts, pool, dominoes and a juke box. The garden behind the low white building (which is surrounded by farms and faces the village green) has tables looking up to Winton and Hartley fells. The bedrooms and bathrooms are being renovated. *(Up-to-date reports please)*

Free house · Real ale · Meals and snacks (see above) · Open 11–3, 6–10.30 Bedrooms tel Kirkby Stephen (0930) 71451; probably around £20B

Lucky Dip

Besides the fully inspected pubs, you might like to try these Lucky Dips recommended and described by readers (if you do, please send us reports):

AMBLESIDE [Smithy Brow; NY3804], *Golden Rule*: good food, excellent Hartleys beer in friendly pub just below Kirkstone Pass; children welcome *(Fred Holdsworth, Michael Quine)*
nr AMBLESIDE [A592 to Penrith; NY3804], *Kirkstone Pass*: remote mountain inn with wide choice of whiskies, lively amusements, all-day summer café, fine surrounding scenery, bedrooms *(Patrick Stapley, Tim Halstead, Richard Gibbs, Philip Asquith, Lesley Foote and Alan Carter, Keith Myers, Paul West, LYM)*
APPLEBY [Bongate; NY6921], *Royal Oak*: country-town coaching-inn with Youngers real ales, good bar lunches and service, bedrooms *(LYM, W A Rinaldi-Butcher)*
ARMATHWAITE [NY5146] *Red Lion*: fish from River Eden included in the good food in nice stable bar of early eighteenth-century inn with own fishing *(C B M Gregory)*
ASKHAM IN FURNESS [Duke Street; SD2177], *Vulcan*: good food at reasonable prices includes very reasonable buffet; clean pub with homely atmosphere *(L Foulkes)*
BAMPTON [NY5118], *St Patricks Well*: country village inn with good food and bedrooms *(Anon)*
BARROW-IN FURNESS [Holbeck Park Avenue, Roose; SD2069], *Crofters*: clean and friendly converted farmhouse with helpful uniformed staff, good food, barbecue park and children's facilities *(D J Boylan)*
BEETHAM [SD5079], *Wheatsheaf*: good food and pleasant lounge in genuine old inn with simple public bar and bedrooms *(MGBD)*
BOWNESS-ON-WINDERMERE [Queens Square; SD4096], *Albert Hotel*: a series of favourable reports often on photocopied report forms, or forms from one single source *(Mrs King, Mrs J Irvin, June Hargreaves, Mrs Thompson, Mrs D L, L J Steel, Mrs A Eastwood, Dr and Mrs M A Fitzgerald)*; [Lake Road] *Cabin*: unspoilt pub with no juke box or games; log fire, real ale, draught cider, live jazz or folk most nights in cellar *(MGBD)*; [Rayrigg Road] *John Peel*: cosy, quieter than some

around here; good beer; innards of watches as wall decorations *(Dr A K Clarke)*

BROMFIELD [NY1847], *Greyhound*: quaint and cottagey, with a minstrels' gallery *(C B M Gregory)*

BUTTERMERE [NY1817], *Fish*: simple ex-coaching-inn in lovely setting on National Trust land between Buttermere and Crummock Water, closed Dec-Feb; bedrooms *(HW)*

CARK IN CARTMEL [SD3776], *Engine*: friendly and comfortably modernised Bass pub with good range of whiskies, and tables out by the stream *(LYM)*

CARLETON [NY5329], *Cross Keys*: bar lunches good value in clean and welcoming pub with well kept beer, oak beams and brasses *(Clive Stephenson)*

CARLISLE [Devonshire Street; NY4056], *Friars Tavern*: chess upstairs; when Carlisle pubs were state-owned this was the only one with Bass *(C B M Gregory)*; [St Nicholas Street] *Theakston*: friendly, comfortably modernised pub with good value bar lunches, well kept Theakstons, darts, keen pool players *(Brian Whelan, Roger Danes)*; [Milburn Street] *Woolpack*: wide choice of good value bar meals in real ale pub popular with local CAMRA people; darts and dominoes *(Brian Whelan)*

COCKERMOUTH [Station Street; NY1231], *Tithebarn*: friendly old-fashioned local with well kept Jennings ales, good food, well reproduced pop music *(H R McManus, BB)*; [Main Street] *Trout*: solid old hotel with pleasant gardens by River Cocker and chintz red plush bar, good bar snacks, well kept Jennings, smart restaurant *(Patrick Stapley, Richard Gibbs, BB)*

CROOK [SD4695], *Sun*: friendly straightforward pub with sensible food, welcoming fire and well kept Vaux beers *(LYM, P J White)*

ESKDALE GREEN [NY1400], *King George IV*: food at lunchtime included excellent piping-hot scampi, generous helpings; seats outside *(Elaine and Gavin Walkingshaw)*

GRASMERE [NY3406], *Lamb*: good Cumberland sausage, steak, trout and other food in cheerful good value pub; children allowed *(Dr C D E Morris)*; *Travellers Rest*; home-made bar food, friendly staff, well kept Wilsons real ale, good value small bedrooms *(Mark Lyall)*

HAWKSHEAD [SD3598], *Red Lion*: comfortably modernised inn with old-fashioned touches, lively atmosphere, well kept Hartleys real ales, bedrooms *(Patrick Stapley, Richard Gibbs, LYM)*

HOWTOWN [NY4519], *Howtown Hotel*: modest countryman's pub by Ullswater, with flats and very good simple food *(David Fearnley)*

KENDAL [Market Place; SD5293], *Globe*: good genuine pub *(MGBD)*; *Duke of Cumberland*: well kept, friendly, not touristy *(MGBD)*

KESWICK [Lake Road; NY2624], *Dog & Gun*: solidly furnished two-room bar with lively town atmosphere, good log fire, friendly staff, good food, nice mountain photographs and Matthew Brown real ale *(Mrs K Clapp, LYM)*; [off Market Square] *Pack Horse*: small snug town tavern with low beams and good value Jennings real ales *(LYM)*

KIRKBY LONSDALE [SD6278], *Snooty Fox*: good home-made food, unusual soups, good atmosphere, no music (except in back bar) *(MGBD)*

LOW HESKET [NY4646], *Rose & Crown*: friendly all-round pub with good Marstons beer and food, pleasant inside, darts *(J S Bacon)*

MIDDLETON [SD6386], *Middleton Fells*: food includes good (but limited) snacks in quiet country inn with pleasant atmosphere *(MGBD)*

RAVENGLASS [SD0996], *Ratty Arms*: ex-railway bar with rustic furnishings, good games room, Jennings real ale; terminus for England's oldest narrow-gauge steam railway *(LYM)*

RAVENSTONEDALE [NY7204], *Black Swan*: large old inn in picturesque village, good bar food, no juke box, spacious restaurant, bedrooms *(G S Burrows)*

SEATOLLER [NY2414], *Yew Tree*: delicious food served in back bar behind good cottage restaurant, very good atmosphere *(S V Bishop)*

SEDBERGH [Finkle Street; SD6692], *Red Lion*: good food and drink in welcoming inn with nice bedrooms *(Mrs R S Young)*

nr SEDBERGH [7 miles N on A683; SD7299], *Fat Lamb*: well kept spacious moorland inn, good bar food and beer, restaurant, bedrooms *(G S Burrows)*

TEMPLE SOWERBY [MY6127], *Kings Arms*: comfortable hotelish lounge in handsome red sandstone inn with bedrooms *(LYM)*

TORVER [SD2894], *Church House*: quiet bar and lounge, not over-refurbished; good bar food *(MGBD)*

TROUTBECK [NY4103], *Mortal Man*: friendly staff and good, reasonably priced lunchtime bar food in seventeenth-century inn with evening restaurant *(MGBD, D C Turner)*

WINSTER [SD4293], *Brown Horse*: free house with good choice of beers. Very good menu from stew to gammon and specials (including lobster on our visit) *(G G Strange)*

WITHERSLACK [SD4384], *Derby Arms*: comfortable welcoming pub with good bar food, Wilsons ales, lots of brass, good wood-burning stove, games room, pop music (not too obtrusive) *(Frank Cummins)*

Derbyshire and Staffordshire

Rather unexpectedly, this area is strong on waterside pubs. Several are beside canals: the simple Boat at Cheddleton (close to a steam railway museum), the Star with its lockside terrace at Stone and above all the Black Lion at Consall – a real adventure to get to, in its remote wooded valley. The Worston Mill at Little Bridgeford is a handsomely converted watermill, close to Izaak Walton's cottage, and Walton no doubt fished in the river bordering the elegant old Peacock Hotel in Rowsley when he stayed there. The Marquis of Granby at Bamford is also by the River Derwent, and is unusual for its cocktail lounge decorated with materials from a luxury pre-war transatlantic liner. The John Thompson, near Melbourne, has attractive grounds running down to the River Trent, but is perhaps most notable for its beer, brewed on the spot by the man after whom it is named. Striking countryside surrounds many other pubs here: the Nags Head in Edale (a village in a sheltered valley at the start of the Pennine Way), the Little Mill at Rowarth (a good range of real ales in a delightful country setting), the Traveller's Rest at Flash (one of Britain's highest pubs, with a remarkable range of some 60 draught beers), the Barrel near Foolow (friendly and traditional, with

The Chequers, Ticknall

excellent views from its high ridge), and the Lathkil at Over Haddon (again, excellent views). Good pubs for food include the Sycamore in Birch Vale, the Jug & Glass near Hartington (which has a wide choice of well kept real ales), the Red Lion at Newborough, the Devonshire Arms in Beeley (on Chatsworth's doorstep), the White Swan in Melbourne, and particularly, the Holly Bush at Seighford and Red Lion in Litton. The George at Hathersage, Castle Hotel in Castleton and of course the Peacock are probably the most comfortable places to stay. Two splendidly unspoilt pubs here are the little Coopers Tavern opposite the Bass brewery in Burton on Trent, and the Three Stags Heads – a farm pub at Wardlow. The Whittington Inn at Kinver is a fine rambling old place, with good pub food and a civilised atmosphere, and at the immaculately kept Old Bulls Head in Little Hucklow you can see a good collection of old farm machinery. Two specially notable pubs are the Bull i' th' Thorn south of Buxton with its beautifully furnished fourteenth-century main bar, and the Yew Tree at Cauldon, crowded with such a remarkable collection of interesting things that we'd rate it as the most fascinating pub in Britain. Moreover, it sells the cheapest beer we have found here. In general, drinks and food prices tend to be low in the area.

ABBOTS BROMLEY (Staffs)   SK0724 Map 7

Crown

The carpeted and modern-panelled lounge bar of this simple well run inn has soft plush button-back banquettes, most friendly service and bar food such as sandwiches, ploughman's, pizza, salads, good plaice, home-cured gammon cooked with pineapple (£2.50), a good eight-ounce fillet or sirloin steak (£4 – cheaper than last year) and 20-ounce T-bone steak (£5.90). Well kept Bass on electric pump, maybe piped music. The lively and brightly lit public bar has darts, dominoes, cribbage and a fruit machine, and also a big painting showing the village's unusual horn dance, which in 1986 should be held on Monday 8 September. The antlers now used (which hang in the church) have been carbon-dated to about 1100, and the dance itself may be very much older – after all, these antlers may have replaced a long series of earlier sets. The bedrooms are comfortable and good value, and breakfasts are excellent. (Recommended by Roy McIsaac, J A Cox, Tony Gayfer)

Bass · Licensee Andrew Finch · Real ale · Meals and snacks · Children in eating area · Open 10.30–2.30, 5.30–10.30 · Bedrooms tel Burton upon Trent (0283) 840227; £8/£15

Meal times tend to vary from day to day and with season, depending on how busy the pub hopes to be. We don't specify them as our experience shows you can't rely on them. Avoid the disappointment of arriving just after the kitchen's closed by sticking to normal eating times for whatever area the pub is in.

ASHLEY (Staffs)   SJ7636 Map 7

Meynell Arms

Village signposted from A53 NE of Market Drayton

The lounge bar of this friendly village pub is deeply comfortable, with chintz-cushioned antique oak settles, rocking-chairs, sofas and blue plush bucket seats, warmed in winter by an old-fashioned cast-iron stove. One wall is stone-faced, others have oak timbers in butter-coloured plaster; the black beams are hung with plates, and a clock ticks sonorously. Well kept Bass on handpump, snacks such as sandwiches and a choice of filled baked potatoes (80p). There is a fruit machine. The carpeted public bar, which also has cushioned settles, has sensibly placed darts, bar billiards and table skittles; also dominoes, cribbage and a juke box. *(Recommended by William Meadon, Richard Steel)*

Bass · Licensees Alan and Hilda Armstrong · Real ale · Snacks (evening and Sun lunchtime) · Children welcome · Open 12–2.30, 6–11 all year; may be closed some quiet weekday lunchtimes: tel Ashley (063 087) 2343

BAMFORD (Derbys)   SK2083 Map 7

Marquis of Granby

A625 opposite junction with A6013

A spacious lawn, with old-fashioned slatted seats by neat gravel paths, runs down from this roadside hotel to the wooded River Derwent – but a more important connection here is with the sea. The cocktail bar has ornate carved panelling from the ss *Olympic*, the *Titanic*'s legendarily elegant sister-ship, and is furnished to match, with silvery plush brocaded seats, velvet curtains and fringed lamps. The more straightforward main outer bar has a good choice of sandwiches (from 60p, with popular club sandwiches such as prawn, crab or smoked salmon £1.50–£2.10), soup (60p), ploughman's (£1.40), home-made steak and kidney pie or mixed meat salad (£2.25), scampi (£2.50), game pie (£2.75), seafood platter (£3.50) and sirloin steak (£4.20), also children's dishes (£1.10). Stones on electric pump; darts, pool, dominoes, cribbage, a fruit machine and piped music. There is a separate evening restaurant (dinner £5.50; closed Sunday and Monday), and a 1950s disco on Sunday. *(Recommended by ILP; more reports please)*

Stones (Bass) · Licensee John Gabbard · Real ale · Meals and snacks (not Mon evening) · Children in room off main bar and reception area Piano Fri · Open 11.30–3, 5.30–11 all year · Bedrooms tel Hope Valley (0433) 51206; £16 (£17B)/£26 (£28B)

BEELEY (Derbys)   SK2667 Map 7

Devonshire Arms

This splendid old stone pub is handy for Chatsworth, and in summer the seats outside make the most of the attractive surroundings. In cool weather there are big open log fires – though a fireplace in the side cocktail bar has a grotto, waterfall and pool instead (coins thrown in go to charity). The black-beamed rooms have comfortably cushioned stone seats along their exposed stone walls as well as antique settles and simpler wooden chairs. Reasonably priced bar food includes soup, sandwiches, ploughman's (£1.55) and steak and kidney pie or country casserole (£2.20); darts, shove-ha'penny, dominoes, cribbage. Well kept Theakstons Best, XB and Old Peculier on handpump from the copper-topped bar counter. The separate restaurant is in a more modern extension. *(Recommended by Doug Kennedy, C P Price, Philip Whitney)*

Free house · Licensee Keith Reynolds · Real ale · Meals and snacks · Children in eating area and restaurant · Open 11–3, 6–11 all year

BIRCH VALE (Derbys)   SK0287   Map 7
Sycamore

From A6015 take Station Road towards Thornsett

In fine weather the do-it-yourself summer barbecues are a big draw here, on a high terrace with views across a small wooded valley. Dishes include a pair of four-ounce burgers (£1.50), mixed grilling meats (£2.50) and eight-ounce sirloin steak (£2.65). Down below there are good solid swings and so forth made out of tree-trunks and logs – and a splendid brightly painted hollow fantasy-tree – in grounds where the shrubs and saplings planted two or three years ago are beginning to look thoroughly at home. Indoors, a wide choice of popular food includes toasted sandwiches (from 75p, rump steak £1.95), open sandwiches (£1.35), ploughman's with a selection of cheeses (£1.65), home-made steak pie (£2.35), scampi (£3.15), Southern-fried chicken pieces or seafood platter (£3.45), home-butchered steaks (eight-ounce from £4.95, 16-ounce from £6.65) and good puddings (mostly £1.15). There's quite a variety of children's dishes (lunchtime only, £1.05–£1.95). Well kept Boddingtons and Marstons Pedigree on handpump, and Birch Vale ales brewed for the pub by Winkles. The four connecting carpeted rooms – which can get crowded, and always have a warm and friendly atmosphere – are furnished mainy with Windsor chairs, pews and red cushioned wall seats, with some high seats by eating-ledges along the walls. Tables can be booked (not weekends) in one room with handsome plush dining-chairs and settees. There is a sauna and sun-room. It is quite a steep climb from the main car park up to the pub. *(Recommended by Dennis Royles; more reports please)*

Free house · Licensees Malcolm and Christine Nash · Real ale · Meals and snacks · Children welcome up to 7.30 · Open 12–3, 5.30–11 all year Bedrooms tel New Mills (0663) 42715; £15.75B/£26.75B

BURTON ON TRENT (Staffs)   SK2423   Map 7
Coopers Tavern

Cross Street; off Station Street but a No Entry – heading N down High Street then Station Road from centre, pass Bass brewery and turn left into Milton Street (from which the pub has a back entrance)

'Space game' means any electronic game.

Opposite the vast and gleamingly modern metalwork of the Bass brewery, this welcoming little backstreet tavern has managed to preserve a marvellously old-fashioned and unspoilt atmosphere in its friendly back tap-room. Empty casks serve as the tables for settles built against its tall white walls (our favourite is the corner seat built up on a wooden platform), and you share the room with a row of five full casks from which well kept Bass is tapped – there's no bar counter. Good value really cheap snacks such as soup, filled cobs including corned beef or bacon, burgers, sandwiches and ploughman's with a pork pie – you can stuff yourself silly for about £1. In winter they do cottage pie and stew (£1.20). The simple carpeted front bar has darts, dominoes, cribbage and a piano. *(Recommended by MHG; more reports please)*

Bass Worthington · Licensee Peter Minns · Real ale · Meals (weekday lunchtimes in winter) and snacks (lunchtime, not Sun) · Children in front lounge up to 7.30 · Open 11–2.30, 5.30–10.30; opens 7 Sat

nr BUXTON (Derbys)   SK0673   Map 7

Bull i' th' Thorn ★

Ashbourne Road, Hurdlow Town; A515 a few miles S of Buxton; OS Sheet 119 reference 128665

Lots of people on this fast main road must swish straight past without a second look at what – at first glance – might be just another extended road-house. What a lot they're missing! Before you even go in, look at the vibrant Tudor carvings over the main entrance: the bull caught in the thorn-bush that gives the pub its name, an eagle with a freshly caught hare, and some spaniels after a rabbit. Inside, the well kept and welcoming main bar is a striking hall which has been entertaining travellers since 1472. It has old flagstones stepped shallowly down from the serving counter (with well kept Robinsons Best and Best Mild on handpump), masses of beams and joists, squared Tudor panelling with cushioned and panelled seats cut into the thick walls, some attractive settles, an elaborately carved hunting-chair, a long-case clock, lots of armour, swords, halberds, a blunderbuss and so forth, and a big open fire. Bar food includes soup (55p), sandwiches (from 50p), ploughman's (£1.20), cottage pie (£1.25), salads (from £1.50), chicken in the basket (£1.65), steak pie (£1.85), scampi (£1.90) and sirloin steak (£3.75), with children's meals such as beefburger and chips (80p), and Sunday roast beef lunch (£2.40); maybe piped mainstream music. An adjoining room has darts, pool, dominoes, a fruit machine and a juke box, and a family room opens on to a terrace and big lawn with swings. There are wicker chairs and tables in a sheltered angle outside at the front. A big functions room can be used for private parties (or coach groups). *(Recommended by BGD, R A Hutson, Dennis Royles, R K Whitehead, F T and A U Hargreaves and others)*

Robinsons · Licensees Bob and Judith Haywood · Real ale · Meals and snacks Children in family and games rooms · Open 11–3, 6–11 all year · Self-catering flat for four tel Longnor (029 883) 348; £75 a week

Places with gardens or terraces usually let children sit there – we note in the text the very very few exceptions that don't.

CASTLETON (Derbys)   SK1583 Map 7
Castle Hotel

In a popular village just below the ruins of Peveril Castle and close to
Derbyshire's most spectacular caves, this small hotel is quietly well
run. The bars have comfortable plush furnishings setting off the
stripped stone walls, finely carved early seventeenth-century beams
and, in one room, ancient flagstones. It's had good bar food, but just
as we went to press we heard of the owners' decision to move out in
November 1985 and concentrate their efforts on their other pub here,
the Olde Nags Head (see Lucky Dip). A comfortable place to stay,
which has some unusual tales to tell. The passage to the restaurant
(where readers have enjoyed good food) has been haunted by the
ghost of a bride who, instead of having her planned wedding
breakfast here, died broken-hearted when she was left at the altar.
Another woman is said to have been buried under the main
threshhold – a throwback to pagan rites designed to bring prosperity
to a new building. And there's another survival from pagan times in
the village's colourful band and horseback procession from pub to
pub on 29 May, which ends up with maypole dancing. Though this is
said to celebrate Charles II's escape, the custom is probably a good
deal older. (Recommended by A J Dobson, HKR; up-to-date reports please)

Bass · Licensee Graham Walker · Real ale · Meals and snacks · Children
in restaurant · Open 11–3, 6–11 all year · Bedrooms tel Hope Valley
(0433) 20578; £19B/£29B (four-poster £33B)

CAULDON (Staffs)   SK0749 Map 5
Yew Tree ★ ★ ★

Village signposted from A523 and A52 about 8 miles W of Ashbourne;
OS Sheet 119 reference 075493

The unique attraction here is Mr East's marvellous collection of
unusual antiques, spread haphazardly through several old-fashioned
rooms lit dimly by lamps hanging from the exposed beams. The real
highlight is what may be the best collection of Polyphons and
Symphonions in private hands. These, generally taller than a man, are
magnificent nineteenth-century developments of the much humbler
musical box, mimicking the sound of whole bands. All are in working
order, their great discs slowly swinging into action when you put in a
2p piece. There are also lots of eighteenth-century settles, old guns
and pistols, a couple of pennyfarthing cycles propped against the wall
as if they'd just been ridden here, a crowd of grandfather clocks, some
notable early Staffordshire pottery in an attractive marquetry cabinet,
several pianos and a pianola (which is played most evenings). More
modern piped music comes from a vintage valve wireless set,
underneath the crank-handle telephone. The atmosphere is friendly
and lively, and – quite remarkable when you consider that this is
perhaps the most interesting pub in Britain – prices for drinks and
snacks are among the lowest we've found anywhere. Well kept
Winkles Saxon Cross and Mild and Ind Coope Bitter on handpump,
Bass tapped from the cask; hot sausage rolls (17p), big pork pies
(32p), big salad-garnished ham (45p) and beef (50p) baps; darts,

shove-ha'penny, table skittles, dominoes and cribbage. The old brick pub, which does indeed hide behind a big yew tree, isn't far from Dovedale and the Manifold Valley. Closer by, a huge quarry and even more monstrous cement works are chewing their way towards the pub, from either side of Cauldon Low. *(Recommended by Pat Bromley, Lee Goulding, William Meadon, Richard Steel, Peter Hitchcock, John Price, RAB, Stuart Barker, D W Roberts, D A Haines, Stephen Locke, Janet Williams)*

Free house · Licensee Alan East · Real ale · Snacks · Children in Polyphon room Open 10–2.30, 6–10.30

CHEDDLETON (Staffs)   SJ9651   Map 7
Boat

Basford Bridge Lane; off A520

From the sunny front benches, or tables and seats under a Perspex roof, you can see (through the sheltering hedge) the brightly painted boats which crowd the little Caldon Canal below. A few hundred yards up the lane is the North Staffordshire Steam Railway Museum, and this is attractive countryside. So this cheerfully welcoming old bargees' pub is certainly well placed. Inside, it seems as long and thin as a narrow-boat itself, with low plank ceilings to match. It's simply furnished, with upholstered wall benches and wooden tables at one end, copper ones at the other – which is decorated with masses of local motor-cycling trophies. Well kept Marstons Burton and Pedigree on handpump; a juke box and a fruit machine. There are a couple of swings outside. *(Recommended by Simon Inger; more reports please)*

Marstons · Real ale · Snacks · Open 10.30–2.30, 6–10.30

CLIFTON CAMPVILLE (Staffs)   SK2510   Map 7
Green Man

Village signposted from A453 (and will be handy for M42)

The garden of this old-fashioned and welcoming fifteenth-century village pub has donkeys, rabbits, a fishpond and an aviary as well as a couple of swings, and there are space games and so forth in the children's room – so it's understandably popular with families. The spick-and-span public bar has brasses on its low black beams and sparkling brass platters on the walls, a fire in the inglenook, built-in leatherette-cushioned high settles and a big armchair. The plusher lounge is an airy room with big windows. Bar food includes soup, sandwiches and filled cottage cobs, ploughman's (£1.25), pizzas or burgers (£1.30), steak and kidney pie (£1.50), meat salads (£1.65), chicken (£1.75), beef curry, cottage pie or lasagne (£1.85) and gammon and egg (£2.20); well kept Ind Coope Bitter on handpump (and tea or coffee); sensibly placed darts, dominoes, cribbage, a fruit machine, maybe piped music. *(Recommended by Harry Blood; more reports please)*

If we know a pub has a no-smoking area, we say so.

*Ind Coope · Licensee John Allsop · Real ale · Meals (lunchtime) and snacks
Children in children's room · Open 10.30–2.30, 6–11 all year; closed evening
25 Dec*

CONSALL (Staffs)   SJ9748 Map 7
Black Lion

Consallforge; from A522 just S of Wetley Rocks (which is E of Stoke-on-Trent)
follow Consall turn-off through village. Just past the Old Hall a green footpath
signpost points to Consallforge. Park here and follow the signpost down over
the pastures – not towards the larches on your left, but towards the deciduous
copse on the right. In here, among mounds, pick up a good wide track down in
much the same direction, towards a wooded valley. In the wood, go down the
steps (there are 200 of them). About 20 minutes' walk altogether. The planned
Consall Nature Park, further along the same road, will eventually give closer
parking and more direct access; there is also a good but longer walk to the pub
along the Staffordshire Way (canal footpath) from Cheddleton. OS Sheets 118
and 119, reference 000491

A real find for the adventurous, this simple unspoilt pub is quite cut
off from the public roads, hidden deeply away beside the Caldon
Canal and the River Churnet in a rather wild wooded valley – quiet
on the benches outside except for the birdsong, the sound of the weir,
and perhaps a grumble from the pub's goat. No frills inside – just real
friendliness, café seats and Formica tables on the tiles, plain brick
walls, a good coal fire on cool days, simple bar food from sandwiches
to main dishes, and well kept Bass, Marstons Pedigree and Ruddles
County on handpump. Sensibly placed darts at one end, also table
skittles, dominoes, cribbage, maybe piped music. *(Recommended by
William Meadon, Richard Steel)*

*Free house · Licensee Mrs Ethel Morris · Real ale · Meals and snacks · Children
welcome · Open 10.30–2.30, 6–10.30*

EDALE (Derbys)   SK1285 Map 7
Nags Head

As you'd expect from its position at the start of the Pennine Way, this
rose-covered seventeenth-century stone pub's main customers are
walkers. They are well fed, with generous helpings of bar food such
as open salad sandwiches (60p–65p), and a choice between
convenience dishes such as sausages, pizzas, good pasties and faggots,
chicken, scampi and so forth (£1.10–£1.95) and home-made food
such as cottage pie or steak and kidney pie (£1.70). As well as the big
tiled hikers' bar there is a more comfortable clubby lounge for people
who have changed out of their boots. This has cushioned old settles,
red leatherette seats, a stag's head above the big stone fireplace, white
walls and a lofty pitched roof. Well kept Theakstons on handpump;
fairly loud and cheerful piped music, dominoes, cribbage and a fruit
machine. An airy back family room (with pool in winter, and a space
game) serves as an overflow for adults at busy times – this remote
village, almost cut off in its steep valley below the splendid hills of the
High Peak District, does attract a lot of visitors. *(Recommended by
Toby and Doreen Carrington, J Hilditch)*

Free house · Licensee Denis Liston · Real ale · Meals and snacks · Children in family room · Open 11–3, 6–11 (12–2.30, 7–11 in winter; also closed Weds in winter except Christmas and New Year)

FLASH (Staffs)   SK0267   Map 7

Traveller's Rest

A53 S of Buxton, near Quarnford

Isolated on the moors, this is Britain's third-highest pub, and has excellent views from the tables on the back terrace. But perhaps its main attraction is the extraordinary array of 60 or more beers on draught – the long serving counter bristles with pumps, taps and handpumps. The open-plan carpeted bar has tables and cushioned stools made from beer barrels, tartan ceilings and colourful wallpaper; darts, pool, dominoes, a loud juke box, and no shortage of fruit machines and space games. Bass, Marstons and Ruddles real ales; hot pies and toasted sandwiches. *(Recommended by William Meadon, Richard Steel)*

Free house · Licensee Jack Beswick · Real ale · Snacks · Open 11–2.30, 6–10.30

nr FOOLOW (Derbys)   SK1976   Map 7

Barrel

Bretton; signposted from Foolow which itself is signposted from A623 just E of junction with B6465 to Bakewell

As this friendly traditional pub perches right on the edge of a high ridge, it has marvellous views over the silvery-walled pastures below – especially from the front terrace. Inside, stubs of massive knocked-through stone walls divide the bar into several snug areas – we (and the pub's cats) particularly like the far end, with a leather-cushioned settle by an antique oak table in front of the open fire. Bar food includes sandwiches, ploughman's and salads; well kept Stones on electric pump. As one reader points out, John Wesley was teetotal – or he wouldn't have been able just to ride straight past this inviting pub two years running in the late 1770s. *(Recommended by A J Dobson, Dennis Royles, R K Whitehead)*

Bass · Licensee Edward Walsh · Real ale · Snacks · Open 11–3, 7–11 all year

nr HARTINGTON (Derbys)   SK1360   Map 7

Jug & Glass

Newhaven; on A515 about 1 mile N of junction with A5012; OS Sheet 119 reference 156614

By a lonely moorland road, this welcoming pub has some rare bottled beers as well as its good range of real ales on handpump – including Bass, Hardys & Hansons, Mansfield XXXX, Marstons Pedigree and Merrie Monk, Ruddles Rutland and County, Theakstons XB and occasional guest beers. The crowded little carpeted main bar is simply furnished and prettily decorated, with lots of flowery china hanging from the low beams, a cuckoo clock and a coal fire in winter (as well as central heating); piped pop music, darts, dominoes, cribbage, a fruit machine. Generous helpings of freshly cooked food include popular home-made broth, ploughman's with a choice of cheeses (£1.75), pasties (£1.80), chicken (£2.40), breaded haddock (£2.50), scampi (£2.75), gammon with egg and pineapple (£4.75), and eight-ounce steaks of local meat (sirloin £5.50, fillet £6); rolls and butter are served with every meal. There is a flock-wallpapered overflow bar (and a separate restaurant), and you can sit outside under cocktail parasols. *(Recommended by R A Hutson, MHG, C P Price)*

Free house · Licensee John Bryan · Real ale · Meals and snacks · Children welcome · Open 11–3, 6–11 all year (opens 7 in winter) · Bedrooms tel Hartington (029 884) 224; £7.50/£14

HATHERSAGE (Derbys)   SK2381   Map 7
George
Main road (A625)

The main bar of this inn is a spacious carpeted room, quiet and comfortable, with some of its stone walls stripped back to show elegant masonry. There are soft easy chairs and sofas in an inner lounge, which has free peanuts on the counter of its small cocktail bar. Lunchtime bar food includes a changing variety of sandwiches (from 75p) such as cheese, fresh beef or ham, and open prawn ones, home-made steak and kidney pie (£2.50), grilled plaice (£2.50) and a cold buffet (£3.50). The separate restaurant is open at lunchtime and in the evening every day. Fruit machine, background music. A neat flagstoned back terrace by a rose garden has white metal tables under cocktail parasols. The bedrooms are comfortable, and the staff take trouble over their customers. *(Recommended by ILP, Toby and Doreen Carrington, Peter Walker)*

Whitbreads · Licensees Sandro and Teresa Rossi · Meals and snacks (lunchtime, not Sun) · Children welcome · Open 11.30–3, 6.30–11 all year Bedrooms tel Hope Valley (0433) 50436; £35B/£43B

HOPE (Derbys)   SK1783   Map 7
Cheshire Cheese
Edale Road

As we go to press we hear that the licensees who in the last edition earned this sixteenth-century village pub a star for its good home cooking are to leave shortly. So we eagerly await reports on the food under the new régime. In the meantime, the pub keeps its main-entry status on the strength of its cosy layout. Its three small rooms, stepping down through thick stone walls, have red-cushioned seats around cast-iron tables, horse brasses on the oak beams, and lots of small pictures on the white walls; each room has a coal fire in cool weather. There has been a good choice of sherries, as well as well kept Wards Sheffield Best on handpump; darts. Parking can be a problem at busy times. Note that there is another Cheshire Cheese nearby, also selling Wards ales, on the main road in Castleton – not at all the

If we know a pub does summer barbecues, we say so.

same, though a comfortable and pleasantly lively young people's pub. *(More reports please)*

Free house · Real ale · Meals and snacks (not Sun evening) · Open 11–3, 5.30–11 all year (opens 6 on winter evenings)

KINVER (Staffs)   SO8483   Map 4
Whittington

A449

This fine old inn rambles about through sharp-angled passages into various areas with snug little alcoves, black panelling, old-fashioned leather seats and settles, and latticed windows. An airy big-windowed extension from the clubby main bar has green plush seats around the low elm or oak tables on its Turkey carpet, and some antique prints on its walls. Good food served in the back wine bar includes sandwiches (65p–£1), a cold buffet with a good collection of English cheeses as well as beef, turkey, ham, prawns, home-made quiches, turkey and cranberry pie and so forth (£2–£3), and home-cooked hot dishes such as fisherman's pie (£2.25) and beef stew or steak and kidney pie (£2.50). A separate restaurant is open Monday to Saturday evenings and Sunday lunchtimes. Well kept Bass, Courage Directors and Marstons Pedigree on handpump, and dishes of nuts on the bar counter. The neat lawned garden has sturdy wooden seats on a poolside terrace; pétanque played in summer, also barbecues on bank holidays. Dick Whittington lived here – or at least the present picturesquely timbered black and white Tudor building replaces an older hall built in 1310 by his grandfather. No motorcyclists. *(Recommended by N Worthington, Graham Andrews)*

Free house · Manageress Miss D J Pike · Real ale · Meals and snacks · Children in eating areas · Folk music Tues · Open 11–2.30, 6–10.30

LICHFIELD (Staffs)   SK1109   Map 4
Scales

Market Street; one of the central pedestrian-only streets

Visitors notice that even office-workers rushing in for a lunchtime drink seem to relax more – and more instantly – here than in other places, and the immaculate lounge bar does have that calming effect. Polished leatherette seats are built in to the dark oak panelling below a shelf of shiny blue and white Delftware, and the sparkling etched window glass has a satisfying feel if you run your fingers over it. Efficiently and charmingly served bar food includes soup (70p), beefburgers (75p), freshly cut sandwiches from brown or white bread, or rolls, plain or toasted (65p–£1.10), cottage or steak and kidney pie (£1.25), ploughman's (£1.40), lasagne (£1.65), a daily special such as beef Stroganoff and an attractive cold table with home-made coleslaws and Scotch eggs as well as the more usual meats and so forth (around £1.40–£1.75). Well kept Bass, Mitchells & Butlers Brew XI and Springfield on electric pump. The lively public bar has darts, shove-ha'penny, dominoes and an old piano, and is the home of an annual conkers competition. A fruit machine is sensibly segregated in a lobby, and there may be piped music. The black and white façade is very pretty, and an oak-beamed coach entry leads through to tables in an attractively planted back courtyard, a real sun-trap. *(Recommended by Michael and Alison Sandy, HKR)*

Mitchells & Butlers (Bass) · Licensee Michael Wilson Hawley · Real ale · Meals and snacks (lunchtime, not Sun) · Children welcome · Open 11–3, 5.30–11 all year

LITTLE BRIDGEFORD (Staffs)   SJ8727   Map 7
Worston Mill

2⅔ miles from M6 junction 14; signposted for Izaak Walton's cottage from A5013 to Eccleshall

Well run and very comfortably converted, this old watermill still has its vast iron gear-train at one end of the three communicating rooms that make up its long L-shaped bar. At the opposite end is a dresser filled with young house-plants for sale – the offspring of those which grow so exuberantly in a spacious quarry-tiled sun-room. Mainly, the beamed ceiling is quite low, but one higher area has a white spiral staircase up to a loft (with weekly folk music). Outside there are robust wooden seats and tables with neat miniature roofs on a gravel terrace by quite a big lawn, with swings, a slide and climbing frame, and white ducks on the old millpond and millstream; every so often electric trains swish by on the main railway line. Good value simple food includes sandwiches (from 70p), hot beef served with one or two roast potatoes (£1.50), filled baked potatoes (from £1), soup (90p), four-ounce burger (90p), ploughman's (£2.25), cottage pie, lasagne, curry, or steak pie (£2.50) and scampi (£3.50). Puddings (£1.30) come from the neat adjoining carvery, which has a choice of cold meat salads (£4.25) and hot roasts (£4.95), with weekday grills and so forth too. Booking is recommended for Sunday lunch. Well kept Ansells, Ind Coope Burton and Tetleys on handpump; on our visit, loudish piped pop music. Close to Izaak Walton's Cottage and museum. *(Recommended by Margo and Peter Thomas, Patricia Floyd)*

Free house · Licensee David Fernyhough · Real ale · Meals and snacks Children welcome · Folk music Tues · Open 11–3, 6–11 all year · Reservations tel Seighford (078 575) 710

LITTLE HUCKLOW (Derbys)   SK1678   Map 7
Old Bull's Head ★

Pub signposted from B6049

Year by year this meticulously kept pub tots up more awards, especially for its fine garden housing a growing collection of well restored and attractively painted old farm machinery. Out here, among the neatly kept flowerbeds and dry-stone walls, there's little sound except for the larks and sheep on the upland pastures around this quiet little village. Indoors, though, you're more likely to hear well reproduced Beethoven, Bach, Mozart, Chopin or Mahler. The two small rooms, one served from a hatch and the other over a polished bar counter, are traditionally furnished: there are old oak beams, thickly cushioned built-in settles, collections of locally mined semi-precious stones and of antique brass and iron household tools, and a coal fire in the neatly restored stone hearth. Well kept Winkles Saxon Cross and Ivanhoe on handpump; freshly cut sandwiches (65p) and ploughman's (£1.50); darts, dominoes, cribbage. (*Recommended by Mrs I E Holmes; more reports please*)

Free house · Licensee D G Hawketts · Real ale · Snacks · Open 12–3, 7–11 all year; closed weekday lunchtimes in winter

LITTON (Derbys)   SK1675 Map 7
Red Lion

This very popular village pub has Derbyshire landscapes on the partly panelled walls of its two small and low-ceilinged front rooms, which both have open fires in winter. It very much concentrates on food – though it has preserved much of the atmosphere of a cosy and friendly pub, as well as the small bar counter that serves well kept Stones and Ruddles County from handpump. It does serve snacks as well as full meals (which themselves come at unrestaurany prices). Certainly, what people enjoy most here is the food, which includes sandwiches or filled home-baked rolls, soup such as tomato and carrot (90p), pâté (£1.10), smoked mackerel and other salads (£1.40), cheese and spinach quiche (£3.50), filling steak and kidney pie (£3.80), rabbit stew (£4.20), baked cod with prawns (£4.25), roast lamb (£4.40), pork fillet in mushroom and curry sauce (£4.85) and poached salmon (£4.95). You should book a table if you want to eat. A bigger back room has pews around the gingham-covered tables on its stone floor, and big antique prints on the stripped stone walls. There may be soft piped music. Benches and tables outside face lime and sycamore trees on the village green. A caravan- and camp-site behind belongs to the pub. There are good walks nearby, especially to the south. (*Recommended by Elinor Goodman, Susanna Hillyard, Howard Gascoyne, Dennis Royles, R K Whitehead*)

Free house · Licensees Max and Pat Hodgson · Real ale · Meals and snacks (Tues to Sat evenings, weekend lunchtimes) · Children in back room · Folk music Tues evenings · Open 7–11 all year; closed weekday lunchtimes Reservations tel Tideswell (0298) 871458

nr MELBOURNE (Derbys)   SK3825 Map 7
John Thompson

Ingleby; village signposted from A514 at Swarkestone

Readers enjoy going out of their way to find this unique pub – unique for being named after the man who both owns it and brews its beer, on the spot. It's an attractive place too, set among beautifully kept flowerbeds and lawns running down to the rich watermeadows along the River Trent. Inside, button-back leather seats form bays around simple oak tables in the big carpeted lounge, which has some old oak settles at one end and is decorated with antique prints and paintings – some showing the building in its original guise as a thatched farmhouse. A couple of smaller cosier rooms off here. Bar food includes soup (55p), sandwiches, and a choice of salads such as beef, ham or tongue (£2.25), with roast beef and Yorkshire pudding in winter (£2.75) and various puddings (70p) or cheese and biscuits (from 50p); only sandwiches on Sunday and in the evenings; soup, sandwiches and puddings on Saturday lunchtime. Well kept Marstons Pedigree on handpump, as well as the house brew – really good value, considering its strength; maybe piped music. A partly covered outside terrace has its own summer serving bar, and there are lots of tables on the upper lawn. *(Recommended by Dave Butler and Les Storey, G L Archer, C P Price, J M Tansey, Stephan Carney)*

Own brew · Licensee John Thompson · Real ale · Meals (lunchtime, weekdays) and snacks · Children in eating area at lunchtime only, not Sun · Open 10.30–2.30, 7–11 all year

MELBOURNE (Derbys)   SK3825 Map 7
White Swan

Castle Square; from B587 in centre, turn down Potter Street at Industrial Estate signpost by Melbourne Hotel

This ancient pub has been strikingly restored to show the most interesting features of its structure: the sloping eaves in the back room, stonework and timbering where plaster has been carefully stripped away, massive low beams in the area by the serving counter. It's sympathetically furnished with cushioned antique settles, fat earthenware ginger-beer kegs and so forth on a high shelf, attractive early nineteenth-century prints (and some modern paintings of falcons), and a fine facsimile of a medieval swan above the big open fireplace. There's a popular separate restaurant, and readers praise bar food (sorry, no up-to-date prices from the pub) such as sandwiches, toasted sandwiches, salads, plaice, sole, salmon – the menu's been strong on seafood – and steaks. Marstons Pedigree on handpump. The narrow sheltered garden is well kept and attractive. *(Recommended by Michael and Alison Sandy, Stephan Carney; more reports please)*

Free house · Real ale · Meals and snacks · Open 10.30–2.30, 7–11 all year

MILLTHORPE (Derbys)   SK3276 Map 7
Royal Oak

B6051

The couple who run this seventeenth-century stone pub in such a friendly way serve good home-made food such as sandwiches and filled rolls (including strongly recommended black pudding and bacon toasted ones), cottage pie (£1.50), ploughman's (£1.75), lasagne (£1.75), seafood Mornay (£1.80), meat and potato pie (£1.95) and sirloin steak (£3.50), with game pie (£3) in the winter too. The main room is full of character, with robust traditional furniture under its old oak beams, bare stone walls and a warm winter fire. There's a smaller and more comfortably cushioned lounge (which may be quieter, too). Well kept Darleys Thorne and Wards Sheffield Best on handpump. There are picnic-table sets on a crazy-paved terrace, partly shaded by hawthorn, ash and other trees, and up on a side lawn. (*Recommended by Nick Barnes, Doug Kennedy*)

Free house · Licensees Harry and Elaine Wills · Real ale · Meals and snacks (sandwiches only Sun lunchtime, no food Thurs–Sun evenings) · Open 11.30–3, 5.30–11 all year

NEWBOROUGH (Staffs)   SK1325   Map 7
Red Lion

B5234

It's the simple but well cooked and attractively served food that brings readers to this comfortably modernised village inn. Prices are reasonable, too, and it's all home cooking: filled cobs (from 40p), sandwiches (from 60p, home-cooked gammon 75p), home-made soup (75p), ploughman's (from £1.50), quiche (£2.45), scampi (£2.55), steak and kidney pie (£2.85), meat salads (from £3.65, particularly good beef £3.95) and steaks (from £4.85), with a day's special such as lasagne (Tuesday to Friday, £2.80). Last summer they were experimenting with some Mexican recipes, for example using shrimps or prawns in a sauce for chicken. The carpeted lounge has dove-coloured plush banquettes and stools around copper-topped cast-iron tables, and a log fire in winter; well kept Marstons Pedigree on handpump; piped music and a fruit machine. There's also a cheerful lino-floored public bar, with darts, dominoes and another fruit machine. A couple of tables outside, sheltered by the front bays, face the church across a quiet square, and behind there are more tables on grass fenced off from the car park, and a swing. (*Recommended by Rachel Waterhouse, G K Sheppard*)

Marstons · Licensee John Norgrove · Real ale · Meals and snacks · Children in eating area · Open 10.30–2.30, 6.30–10.30 (opens 7 in winter) · Three bedrooms tel Hoar Cross (028 375) 259; £8.50/£17

OVER HADDON (Derbys)   SK2066   Map 7
Lathkil

Village and inn signposted from B5055 just SW of Bakewell

Big windows in the airy carpeted bar command a magnificent view over the wooded pastures of Lathkill Dale, and there's a friendly welcome, with warm winter fires in an attractively carved fireplace. This room has black beams, a high shelf of blue and white plates on one white wall, leatherette seats and old-fashioned settles; an adjoining more modern area has plenty of space for families at its tables. Bar food includes sandwiches (lunchtime only), soup (70p), excellent pies such as gamekeeper's, or steak and kidney to the proper recipe with oysters, elsewhere very rarely used (£2.35), cold meats with salads (£2.35) and six-ounce sirloin steak (£3.95); in the autumn of 1985 they opened a separate restaurant. Well kept Darleys Thorne and Wards Sheffield Best and Best Mild on handpump; piped jazz or classical music, dominoes, cribbage. You can sit on a long stone ledge or on the low wall at the front of the pub for an even better view. This inn is very popular with people out for walks – just nearby on the nature trail, say, or on the further moors. *(Recommended by BGD, Toby and Doreen Carrington, Susanna Hillyard, J M Tansey)*

Free house · Licensee Robert Grigor-Taylor · Real ale · Meals and snacks (not Sun evening) · Children in family room · Open 11–3, 6–11 all year · Bedrooms from autumn 1985 tel Bakewell (062 981) 2501; £17.50B/£35B

ROWARTH (Derbys)   SK0189   Map 7
Little Mill

Turn off A626 at Mellor signpost (in steep dip at Marple Bridge); fork left at Rowarth signpost, then follow Little Mill signpost

Tubs of flowers, roses and honeysuckle decorate the front terrace of this remote but popular stone-slated white house, which is open-plan inside. Stubs of walls and bare brick pillars keep it nicely divided, and comfortable little settees and not-quite-armchairs on the Turkey carpet combine with subdued lighting and unobtrusive pop music from the juke box to give a very relaxed friendly atmosphere. Largely home-made bar food includes soup (60p), sandwiches (from 80p), burgers (95p), good black pudding from Bury (£1.80), ploughman's (£1.85), salads (from £2.15), local trout (£2.20), steak and kidney pie (£2.70) and eight-ounce steaks (£4); the American carrot cake is a popular pudding. Sunday lunch is £4.60 (children £2.50). Well kept Boddingtons, Robinsons Bitter and Best Mild, Ruddles County and Winkles on handpump; darts, a fruit machine and two space games in one of several alcoves, also dominoes. This is a good area for walks, and the pub itself, in a steep dell by a millstream, is surrounded by various little lawns with ash trees, seats, swings, a climbing frame and even a 1932 Pullman railway dining car (how ever did they get it here?). As we went to press the owners were starting to fit this out with three Victorian railway-style bedrooms. *(Recommended by Dennis Royles)*

Free house · Licensees Chris and Vivien Barnes · Real ale · Meals and snacks Children welcome · Open 11.30–3, 5.30–11 all year (opens 7 in winter)

ROWSLEY (Derbys)   SK2566   Map 7
Peacock

A6 Bakewell–Matlock

Built in the seventeenth century as a dower house for Haddon Hall, this handsome house became an inn in 1828. It still has a nineteenth-century cockfighting chair (with one arm swollen into a little table) among the antique settles in its snug and gentlemanly bar, which is softly lit, with oak beams and stripped stone walls. By the copper-topped bar counter is an old-fashioned alcove seat for the red-coated lounge waiter – the lounge is quiet and spacious, with comfortable chairs as well as more antique settles and Windsor armchairs. Sandwiches (from £1.60) and seafood salad (£2.50) are served here from 9.30am to 5.30pm (not Sundays), and the restaurant offers light lunches (£4.75, not Sundays) as well as full meals. Well kept Ind Coope Burton on handpump. This attractively traditional small hotel is a nice place to stay, and it has a good stretch of fishing – no doubt tried by Izaak Walton himself when he visited here — on both Wye and Derwent (which runs alongside the gardens); it's close to Haddon Hall and Chatsworth. *(More reports please)*

Embassy Hotels (Ind Coope) · Licensee George Michael Gillson · Real ale Snacks · Open 11–3, 6–11 all year · Bedrooms tel Matlock (0629) 733518; £27.50 (£37.50B)/£43 (£54B) breakfast extra

SANDONBANK (Staffs)   SJ9428   Map 7
Seven Stars

4½ miles from M6 junction 14; A34 link road towards Stone but at first roundabout continue on A513 ring road, then turn left on to B5066; alternatively, from A51 in Sandon follow signpost B5066, Stafford

Waitress-served bar food in this popular and comfortably modernised pub includes ploughman's (£1.60), chicken chasseur, beef in red wine or beef Stroganoff (£3.20), turkey Cordon Bleu (£3.50), gammon and eggs (£3.75) and steaks (£6). There are plenty of blue plush stools and cushioned captain's chairs on the Turkey carpet, which sweeps even into the communicating restaurant and down the steps into a small lower lounge (used particularly for families). The open-plan bar has several cosy corners and good winter fires; there are little country prints on the swirly white plaster walls, lots of polished brass, and unobtrusive piped pop music. Well kept Burtonwood and Dark Mild on handpump. The pub does get busy at weekends. There is a swing on the grass behind, and some picnic-table sets in front of the shuttered white house. *(Recommended by William Meadon, Richard Steel, Andrew McKeand, L F Beattie)*

Burtonwood · Licensees Ron and Jill Roestenburg · Real ale · Meals and snacks Children welcome · Open 10.30–2.30, 6–11 all year

SEIGHFORD (Staffs)   SJ8725   Map 7
Holly Bush

3 miles from M6 junction 14: A5013 towards Eccleshall, left on to B5405 in Great Bridgeford, then first left signposted Seighford

Good bar food in this charming country pub includes sandwiches (from 55p), a choice of soups (from 75p), hot Brie in breadcrumbs (£1.35), hot mushrooms with Stilton and garlic (£1.55), ploughman's with pâté or cheese (£1.55), devilled whitebait (£1.65), kebabs (from £1.95), plaice (£2.25), home-made lasagne (£2.65), scampi (£2.95), chicken Kiev (£4.45), and steaks (from £5.45). There's also a seasonal three-course monthly menu (£6.50), usually interesting, served in both the bar and small restaurant. Otherwise main dishes in the restaurant tend to be around £6. The neat but spacious black-beamed bar is broken up into decently small areas, with wheelback chairs and comfortably modern but traditional-style settles around varnished rustic tables, mirrors studded with foreign coins and airy modern prints of poppies and landscapes on the white walls, and an attractively carved inglenook fireplace. Big windows look out on a neat back rose garden, where there are seats on a terrace, in a vine

Prices of main dishes usually include vegetables or a side salad.

arbour, and on the grass. Tetleys on handpump. *(Recommended by Miss K Woods and others; more reports please)*

Ansells (Ind Coope) · Licensee Mrs Louise Fowden · Real ale · Meals and snacks · Children in eating area and restaurant · Open 12–3, 7–11 all year; closed evening 25 Dec

STONE (Staffs)   SJ9034   Map 7
Star

Stafford Street; A520

This eighteenth-century canalside pub has a busily intimate little tiled public bar with simple furnishings, canal photographs and exposed joists; there's also a snug lounge and a family room. Outside, the narrow locks of the Trent and Mersey Canal, the soft sandstone cobbles and a neat garden opposite, make an attractive setting for the pub's terrace. Reasonably priced and well kept Bass and Mitchells & Butlers Springfield on handpump; quickly served sandwiches, cheese with oatcakes, pizza and fritters, and other hot dishes with chips, such as pasties, steak and kidney or chicken and mushroom pie, plaice and scampi – all under £2. *(Recommended by William Meadon and Richard Steel; more reports please)*

Bass · Licensee Maurice Hamer · Real ale · Snacks (lunchtime) · Children in eating area and family room · Open 11–3, 6–11 all year

TICKNALL (Derbys)   SK3423   Map 7
Chequers   *[illustrated on page 160]*

B5006 towards Ashby de la Zouch

This sixteenth-century pub's snug and heavy-beamed tartan-carpeted main bar has one of the biggest inglenook fireplaces that we've ever seen – with a couple of tables in it, as well as seats. There is also a pleasant window seat and a tiny traditional built-in settle by the bar, which serves well kept Ind Coope, Marstons Pedigree and Ruddles County on handpump or tapped from the cask, and some unusual spirits. Another room leads off. Good value bar food; dominoes, cribbage, fruit machine, maybe piped music. There is a fair-sized quiet garden behind the car park, separated by flowers and fruit-trees from a neat vegetable patch, with apple-trees around the lawn. *(Recommended by Stephan Carney; more reports please)*

Free house · Licensee Gladys Mather · Real ale · Snacks (lunchtime, not Sun or Mon) · Open 11–2.30, 6.30–10.30

WARDLOW (Derbys)   SK1875   Map 7
Three Stags Heads

Wardlow Mires; A623 by junction with B6465

Highly recommended to readers who like finding those really unspoilt pubs that take one right back in time, this friendly white-painted cottage is actually part of a farm, with open country beyond. Its charming little parlour bar has antique cushioned settles, high-backed

Windsor armchairs and simple oak tables on the lino, a double rack of willow pattern plates, a grandfather clock, and a gleaming copper kettle on the old cast-iron kitchen range which is still used for heating. An overflow room has plainer, more modern furnishings. Well kept Youngers Scotch on handpump. *(Recommended by R K Whitehead; more reports please)*

Free house · Licensees Mr and Mrs Fred Furness · Real ale · Open 11–3, 6–11 all year

WHITMORE (Staffs) SJ8141 Map 7

Mainwaring Arms ★

3 miles from M6 junction 15; follow signs for Market Drayton, Shrewsbury, on to A53

Named after the family that have owned most things around here – including the pub – for some 900 years, this charming old stone building faces a lovely village church. Its interconnecting rooms, which ramble up and down and in and out, are attractively furnished with some old-fashioned settles among comfortable more modern seats, reproduction memorial brasses on one of its cream walls, red velvet curtains on stout rails, and a big open fire in the lower room's large stone fireplace. Well kept Boddingtons, Davenports and Marstons Pedigree on handpump, under light top pressure; reasonably priced bar food includes sandwiches, a salad table with a choice of meats and pies, and hot dishes such as haddock créole, lamb goulash and steak pie (all £2) – one reader, enjoying the food, was surprised to find the menu quite free from cheese in any form; high marks for the friendly staff. There are seats outside. *(Recommended by Howard Winn, William Meadon, Richard Steel, Brian and Anna Marsden, D A Angless, M Buxton)*

Free house · Licensee Eric Chadwick · Real ale · Meals and snacks (lunchtime) Children in eating area · Open 11–2.30, 6–11 all year

Lucky Dip

Besides the fully inspected pubs, you might like to try these Lucky Dips recommended and described by readers (if you do, please send us reports):

ALREWAS [High Street; SK1714], *George & Dragon*: friendly local pub with attractive main bar decorated with commemorative cups; good food in side rooms, Marstons real ale, good value residents' supper, comfortable modern bedroom extension *(Colonel G D Stafford)*

ALSTONEFIELD [SK1355], *George*: sixteenth-century coaching-inn on village green in Peak District National Park. Good home-made food, real fire, comfortable chairs and settles, Burton real ale *(William Meadon, Richard Steel, Elinor Goodman, Norman and Ivy Battle)*

ALTON [SK0742], *Talbot*: good, reasonably priced bar food, excellent real ale; children welcome *(M F Waterhouse)*

AMINGTON [SK2304], *Gate*: old-fashioned canalside pub with moorings; well kept Marstons Pedigree, good bar food, garden *(Colin Gooch)*

ARMITAGE [SK0816], *Ash Tree*: canalside pub with popular carvery/restaurant, smart front lounge bar, good collection of cigarette cards *(Pat Bromley, LYM)*

ASHFORD IN THE WATER [SK1969], *Devonshire Arms*: stone pub in picturesque village with village cricket, and trout in stream nearby. Stones bitter *(Peter Walker, Wayne Rossiter, BB)*

BAMFORD [SK2083], *Anglers Rest*: food mostly home-made and good value; very pleasant surroundings *(Michael Main)*; *Olde Derwent*: food worth a detour – good and cheap, with Stones real ale *(M J Kelly)*

BIRCHOVER [SK2462], *Druids*: food well cooked and served, in wide and imaginative variety, in attractive village pub with nice terrace *(Peter Walker)*

BRADWELL [Smalldale; SK1781], *Bowling Green*: good views from terrace outside much-modernised village pub with lots of malt whiskies *(R K Whitehead, LYM)*

BROCKTON [SJ8131], *Chetwyn Arms*: food good and quickly served *(Anon)*

BURNHILL GREEN [SJ7900], *Dartmouth Arms*: licensees sent coordinated reports from over a dozen customers praising food, prices, service and beer; children welcome; reports from independent Pub-Guiders please!

BURSLEM [Newcastle Street; SJ8749], *Travellers Rest*: friendly pub with original cooking and well kept Ind Coope Mild, Bitter and Burton; over 60 malt whiskies *(A Wilson, W J Leese, M Peterson, William Meadon, Richard Steel)*

BUTTERTON [SK0756], *Black Lion*: folk music in one bar, excellent bar food, restaurant, helpful staff, relaxed atmosphere, and four cosy bedrooms in friendly old stone-built inn with lots of low beams, brass, plates and pictures; McEwans 70/– on draught; inn in pleasant village with lovely Peak District countryside, tables in garden *(G McHamish, John and Janet Street)*

CASTLE DONINGTON [SK4427], *Cross Keys*: very good food including some of the best pub soup ever, well kept real ales including Burton Bridge *(Dave Butler, Les Storey)*

CASTLETON [SK1583], *Olde Nags Head*: same ownership as Castle Hotel (see main entry); seventeenth-century inn with antique furnishings, public bar, lounge, comfortable bedrooms (one with antique four-poster) *(HKR)*; [How Lane] *Peak Hotel*: friendly and cheerful, sensibly priced good food, roomy bar, children welcome, upstairs summer family room, big vivid teenager-style Peakeasy room with darts, pop posters, juke box and pool table *(E Burke, Toby and Doreen Carrington)*

CHAPEL-EN-LE-FRITH [SK0681], *Kings Arms*: friendly welcoming inn with spacious comfortable lounge, bar food, dining-room, good bedrooms *(Hazel Morgan, E Burke, Toby and Doreen Carrington)*

CHELLASTON [Derby Road; SK3730], *Rose & Crown*: good beer; busy, very popular *(G Webberley)*

CHINLEY [SK0482], *Old Hall*: reasonably priced bar snacks and elegant restaurant, Thwaites and Marstons Pedigree, children welcome; sixteenth-century house in lovely spot *(Mrs Linda Gregory)*

nr DRAYCOTT IN THE CLAY [Dove Bank; SK1528], *Roebuck*: simple roadside Marstons pub with big inglenook and splendid landlady *(Pat Bromley, BB)*

EYAM [SK2276], *Miners Arms*: very comfortably modernised restaurant/pub with popular meals and cosy bedrooms *(W Marsland, LYM)*

FORTON [SJ7621], *Red Lion*: very popular and friendly basic little country pub, with well kept Banks's ales, open fire, beams, lots of local characters *(L Davies)*

FROGGATT EDGE [SK2477], *Chequers*: food good in oak-floored bar and restaurant of old Peak District inn, well kept Wards Sheffield Best; antique furniture; for pub location see OS Sheet 119 reference 761247 *(Howard N Kirkman, Nick Barnes)*

HARDWICK HALL [SK4663], *Hardwick*: golden stone lodge by park of Elizabethan hall; welcoming staff, well kept real ale, sturdy food, family room; handy for M1 junction 29 *(Toby and Doreen Carrington, Mrs M Lawrence, Stephan Carney, LYM and others)*

HATHERSAGE [SK2381], *Millstone*: food in bar excellent, reasonable prices, wide choice (but no evening meals); warm atmosphere, magnificent valley view; children welcome *(R J Hooton)*

nr HATHERSAGE [A625 towards Sheffield SK2381], *Fox House*: good value lunches and evening meals; supposed to be the White Cross Inn of *Jane Eyre* *(R Merrills)*

HAYFIELD [SK0387], *Pack Horse*: bar snacks, buttery meals and cosy restaurant with wide choice of good food in beautifully decorated sixteenth-century pub in attractive village *(Mrs Linda Gregory)*

HIGH OFFLEY [SJ7826], *Royal Oak*: food of high quality *(Anon)*

nr HOLMESFIELD [SK3277], *Robin Hood*: friendly bar staff and good choice of food in quaint converted farmhouse *(A J Dobson, M E Lindley)*

HOPE [SK1783], *Old Hall*: friendly with good food (choice of bar snacks and more expensive meals) and real ale *(R Merrills)*

HOPWAS [SK1704], *Chequers*: well kept open-plan pub near canal; frequent discos and live music *(Colin Gooch, LYM)*

HULME END [SK1059], *Manifold Valley*: popular for home-cooked food, well kept Wards real ale, local atmosphere *(Jane and Dave, E H Loudon, BB)*

KINGS BROMLEY [SK1216], *Royal Oak*: good food, jovial landlord, warm welcome *(Roger Duckworth)*

LEEK [SJ9856], *Jester*: food in friendly bar good, real ale including Winkles; historic watermill opposite; bedrooms *(Robert Aitken)*

LICHFIELD [SK1109], *Bald Buck*: smartly comfortable modern lounge with Banks's real ale *(Bob Rendle, BB)*

LITTLE LONGSTONE [SK1971], *Packhorse*: very small friendly pub, full of locals, well kept real ale; hikers welcome *(Kirsten Cubitt Hoffmann)*

LONGNOR [SK0965], *Olde Cheshire Cheese*: food in restaurant excellent and varied; olde-worlde atmosphere in comfortable lounge; unspoilt village *(Mrs J P Neuhofer)*

MARSTON [SJ8514], *Fox*: one of the best choices of real ales in the area *(N Worthington)*

MILFORD [A513; SJ9721], *Barley Mow*: friendly village pub with tasty bar food, fruit machine, juke box *(Colin Gooch)*

MONSAL HEAD [SK1871], *Monsal Head Hotel*: good value simple food, well kept real ales and marvellous views in friendly inn in fine walking area; bedrooms *(Kirsten Cubitt Hoffmann, Howard Gascoyne, Simon Inger, LYM)*

OLD BRAMPTON [SK3372], *Fox & Goose*: food good, including hot steak sandwiches; barbecue lunches in summer; friendly atmosphere in olde-worlde inn set in excellent scenery *(Richard Sullivan)*

ONECOTE [SK0555], *Jervis Arms*: riverside garden, lots of real ales, reasonably priced bar food (not weekday lunchtimes in winter); lovely moorland pastures above village *(William Meadon, Richard Steel, Mrs M Lawrence, LYM)*

PENKHULL [SJ8644], *Greyhound*: real fire and oak-panelled snug in friendly pub with well kept Burton *(William Meadon, Richard Steel)*

PILSLEY [SK2471], *Devonshire Arms*: food good in very old pub with open fires and so forth, in delightful village *(A J Dobson)*

RENISHAW [SK4578; handy for M1 junction 30], *Prince of Wales*: food good and service friendly in recently renovated pub, refreshingly furnished conservatory-style; Marstons Pedigree, Stones and Wards on handpump; restaurant *(Richard Thompson)*; *Sitwell Arms*: food in comfortable high-ceilinged bar, restaurant; comfortable hotel extension behind with good bedrooms *(C E Gay, LYM)*

RUSHTON SPENCER [Congleton Road; SJ9462], *Crown*: friendly simple local in attractive scenery, with busy front snug, bigger back lounge, games room, home-made food, Youngers real ales *(A J Melville, BB)*

SAWLEY [SK4731], *Steamboat*: food includes good bar snacks and excellent carvery restaurant in canalside pub full of sailing memorabilia; people messing about in boats outside *(William Meadon, Richard Steel)*

SHARDLOW [Aston Road; SK4330], *Dog & Duck*: good drop of Marstons, good bar food, useful family terrace; no Sunday food *(G Webberley)*; *Malt Shovel*: cheerful canalside ex-malt-house with good Marstons real ales; walls filled with mirrors, pictures and mugs; hard to find (from Wilne Lane off A6 turn left after crossing canal); food not always available [more details on timing please!] *(Stephan Carney, Hazel Morgan, LYM)*

SPARROWPIT [nr Chapel-en-le-Frith; SK0980], *Wanted Inn*: food from landlord's wife and well kept Robinsons in cosy friendly pub with open fires *(Dr B W Marsden)*

STAFFORD [central roundabout; SJ9223], *Malt & Hops*: lively rambling pub with good range of real ales and cheap food *(Bob Rendle, LYM)*; [Cannock Road] *Wild Wood*: modern open-plan pub with good value tasty food in well kept bar, friendly family atmosphere, video juke box, fruit machine *(Colin Gooch)*

STANDEFORD [SJ9107], *Harrows*: epitome of the neat Midlands pub *(Dr A K Clarke)*

STONE [SJ9034], *Mill*: converted old mill with Windsor chairs in very pleasant lounge; bar snacks, upstairs restaurant *(William Meadon, Richard Steel)*

nr STRETTON [SK3961], *Greyhound*: good pub, well made sandwiches *(I D G Mackie)*

TADDINGTON [SK1472], *Waterloo*: food very good in dining-room and bar, well kept Robinsons real ales, obliging landlord; near good walking in Miller's Dale; bedrooms *(A Webster)*

WEST HALLAM [SK4341], *Punch Bowl*: friendly warm atmosphere in bar and wine bar, good food (Thursday to Saturday) with barbecue in back garden *(John and Sue Tucknott)*

WETTON [SK1055], *Olde Royal Oak*: welcoming and genuinely unpretentious pub, out in the wilds, with bar food and real ales including Ruddles; open fires, fine landlord *(HKR)*

Devon

Over 20 *new Devon entries this year reflect a vigorous push
into the West Country – prompted by readers' reports
suggesting that this area needed thorough re-examination.
Certainly, thanks to readers, we've found some new gems.
We'd pick out particularly the Highwayman at Sourton,
where a great deal of ingenuity and money has been spent –
very successfully – on re-creating a piratical fantasy of low-
beamed hideaways. Other sparklers from the new batch
include the Turf Hotel near Exminster (gloriously placed at
the end of the ship canal from Exeter, under the same
ownership as the splendid Double Locks just outside that
city), the Grampus at Lee (beer kept just right, and a
wonderfully appealing atmosphere in a pub just a short stroll
from the sea) and the Kingsbridge Inn in Totnes (carefully
refurbished to bring out the best of its old-fashioned yet
thoroughly cheery atmosphere and style). Among the new
entries, we'd also pick out the Church House at Churchstow
(good food in an ancient low-beamed building), the Thatched
Barn at Croyde (a well run spacious inn close to a splendid
surfing beach), the Cherub in Dartmouth (the town's oldest
building, very pretty), the Palk Arms in Hennock (fishing chat
in a friendly inn with a lovely view out over the Dart valley,
and good food), the Hoops Inn at Horns Cross (four-poster
beds and carefully made new oak bar furniture), the Rising
Sun at Lynmouth (perhaps one of the most romantic early-
morning views from any West Country pub bedroom), the*

The Castle, Lydford

182

Who'd Have Thought It in the steeply sheltered little village of Miltoncombe (good food in very traditional surroundings), the Ferry at Salcombe (fine harbour views from bars on no less than three different levels), the Tradesmans Arms at Stokenham (an object-lesson in providing the best possible food by keeping the menu relatively short and searching out the very best fresh ingredients), the Passage at Topsham (waterside relaxation, with good seafood), the Old Smithy at Welcombe (with a charming country garden, beside a crafts pottery), the Westleigh Inn at Westleigh (lovely sea views from its garden) and the Rising Sun at Woodland (imagine finding a genuine full Greek meal miles from anywhere in the Devonshire countryside). From earlier editions, pubs still at the top of their form include the Masons Arms in Knowstone on the edge of Exmoor (good food, friendly welcome, lots of character and a pleasant place to stay), and – all in, or very close to, Exeter – the comfortable and stylish old White Hart in the city, the Bridge in Topsham (loads of well kept real ales, in very traditional surroundings), the friendly and well run Diggers Rest at Woodbury Salterton, the efficient but characterful Swans Nest in Exminster, and the excellent, idiosyncratic canalside Double Locks. On the other side of Dartmoor, the Elephant's Nest in Horndon has good simple food and is a fine pub; near it, the attractive Peter Tavy Inn has won a solid reputation for its good food, often vegetarian, accompanied by a fine range of real ales. Other pubs we'd recommend for food include the Cott in Dartington, the Two Mile Oak on the Totnes road from Newton Abbot, the Church House at Rattery (a marvellous pub with some claim to be among the very oldest in Britain), the medieval Mason's Arms in Branscombe (with spit-roasting in the bar some nights – awarded a star this year), the lively White Hart in Bratton Fleming (low prices for drinks as well as its simple food), the Anchor at Cockwood (seafood that even fishermen come for) and the Oxenham Arms at South Zeal – a magnificent old inn that has a built-in prehistoric monument. Besides pubs already mentioned, serious drinkers might head for the Nobody Inn at Doddiscombsleigh (a remarkable choice of wines, whiskies and real ales – again, upgraded to a star rating this year), Church House at Torbryan (an ancient place with over a dozen well kept real ales), and the Beer Engine at Newton St Cyres (brews its own, also cheap). On average, beer prices are higher than you might imagine – certainly markedly higher than in neighbouring Cornwall. The George at Hatherleigh (an attractive old inn to stay at), Old Inn in Kilmington, Half Moon in Sheepwash (again, nice to stay at, with good fishing) and Blue Ball in Sidford are relatively cheap, though. Besides pubs already mentioned, others really worth seeking out include the unspoilt Drewe Arms in Drewsteignton, White Hart in Moretonhampstead (a comfortable base for central Devon), Journey's End in Ringmore (nice to stay at) and Pilchard on Burgh Island (very romantic).

BANTHAM   SX6643   Map 1

Sloop

Good bar food in this cheerful old village inn includes pasties (60p), home-made turkey broth (70p), granary bread sandwiches (from 75p, fresh crab £1.40), ploughman's (from £1.35), home-made all-meat sausage with chips (£1.40), plaice (£1.90), locally smoked salmon with prawns (£2.40), generous salads from home-cooked turkey or roast ham (£2.85) to a mixture of several seafoods (£3.75), scampi or lamb chops (£3.20), grilled lemon sole (£3.45), and eight-ounce rump or sirloin steak (£4.55); well kept Bass and Ushers Best on handpump, and local Hill's cider; piped music, table skittles, darts, dominoes, a fruit machine and space games. The lively bar has country chairs and wooden tables on its polished flagstones, black beams and joists, and some panelling on its stone walls; there are easy chairs in a quieter room leading off, which has much more panelling of varnished marine ply, giving it quite a nautical atmosphere. There are seats around a wishing well in the yard behind – no doubt once used as a temporary cache by the wrecker and smuggler John Whiddon when he owned the inn. The Coast Path runs alongside, and the tidal creek which winds into the village is pretty; good sandy beaches are only a few minutes' walk over the dunes. The bedrooms are very comfortable. (*Recommended by Dr Nicola Hall, R K Whitehead and others*)

Free house · Licensee Neil Girling · Real ale · Meals and snacks Children in dining area and new family room · Open 11–2.30, 6–11 (opens 6.30–10.30 in winter) · Bedrooms tel Kingsbridge (0548) 560489; £11.50 (£12B)/£24 (£25B)

BICKLEIGH   SS9407   Map 1

Trout

A396, N of junction with A3072; don't let a map fool you into thinking this is close to M5, junction 28 – the roads are very narrow, steep and poorly signposted

The very efficient food counter is the dominant feature in this thatched white pub's comfortable and remarkably spacious lounge bar. Streamlined service dispenses a wide choice of food, from filled rolls (beef or ham £1.20), ploughman's, salads with a good variety of pâtés, quiche, prawn, trout baked in wine, turkey pie, pork, ham, roast beef and salmon, to hot dishes such as chicken basquaise, beef casserole or veal escalope, and some appetising puddings. Expect to spend around £3.50–£4 for a main dish, and don't try to get them to bend the rules by serving food after the kitchen is shut – even if you can see it on view. There are steaks in the evening; also a separate restaurant. Well kept Bass and Flowers Original on handpump. The lounge rambles comfortably around, with plenty of tables surrounded by cushioned Windsor chairs, modern settles and decorative button-back easy chairs. The atmosphere is relaxed, with gentle music, soft lighting and big vases of flowers. There are seats on a lawn hedged off from the road, prettily lined with laburnums and flowering shrubs. *(Recommended by Peter and Rose Flower, S Mason; more reports please)*

Free house · Licensees Sir Fred Pontin and Mrs Josie Hill · Real ale · Meals and snacks · Children in area partly set aside for them · Open 11–2.30, 7–10.30 Bedrooms tel Bickleigh (088 45) 339; £15/£25

nr BIGBURY   SX6544   Map 1
Pickwick
St Ann's Chapel; B3392

This traditionally furnished roadside inn's good, reasonably priced food changes from day to day, depending on the weather and on Mrs Gray's whim. It's generally sensibly straightforward, for example sandwiches (70p), pasties, home-made pâté or smoked mackerel (£1.30), ploughman's (£1.50), remarkably cheap oysters (£1.50 for half a dozen), curry, steak and kidney pie or lasagne (£1.95), scampi (£2), home-cooked ham with vegetables or salad (£3.50) and steaks (rump £4.30, 16-ounce T-bone £5.95); helpfully priced children's dishes. There are traditional high-backed settles as well as more modern upholstered seats in the friendly bar, and the décor is pleasantly unfussy. They have a choice of country wines such as dandelion and ginger with raisins, as well as farm cider and Bass, Flowers Original and IPA (though handpumps have now been installed they still tap some beers straight from the cask); in winter you may get mulled wine. Separate restaurant, and since last year's *Guide* a spacious new family room with access to a garden bar as well as the main one; pool, dominoes, cribbage, a fruit machine and a space game, maybe piped music. The garden is well sheltered from the road, and on the other side a track leads to St Ann's holy well. *(Recommended by Dr Nicola Hall, David Guthrie)*

Free house · Licensee Michael Gray · Real ale · Meals and snacks · Children in family room and restaurant · Live music monthly in winter · Open 11.30–2.30, 6–11 · Bedrooms tel Bigbury-on-Sea (054 881) 241; £9/£18

BRANSCOMBE   SY1988   Map 1
Mason's Arms ★
Village signposted S of A3052 Sidmouth–Lyme Regis

Readers' continued delight at the often unusual food now earns a star rating for this simple medieval inn. It includes good sandwiches, interesting fillings – such as home-made cream cheese mixed with anchovies and paprika – for French bread as well as the more usual ploughman's, whitebait, seafood platter and other fish dishes such as sardines grilled with herbs from the garden (£1.50), a wide choice of omelettes including crab, home-made steak and kidney pie and a

Tipping is not normal for bar meals, and not usually expected.

good range of summer salads. Reckon on around £2.50–£3.50 for main dishes. The rambling main bar is quaintly old-fashioned, with low beams, a grandfather clock, wooden settles, chairs and cushioned wall benches on its partly flagstoned floor, and a log fire in its massive central chimney. On Tuesday and Thursday evenings they roast joints on a spit here. Badger Best, John Devenish and Wessex Best on handpump are kept well: when one reader (in hot weather) pointed out that his Wessex Best was a bit cloudy they promptly changed the barrel – his replacement glass was perfect. Darts, shove-ha'penny, fruit machine; smart separate restaurant, where the food is also highly praised. The quiet flower-filled terrace in front of this creeper-covered inn has tables under thatched shades. Most bedrooms, in a newer back block, have a view of the little wooded hills around the village; the sea is half a mile down the lane. *(Recommended by Sue and Len Beattie, P D Atkinson, Col G D Stafford, R D Jolliff)*

Free house · Licensee Mrs J B Williams · Real ale · Meals and snacks · Children in restaurant · Open 11–2.30, 6–11 all year · Bedrooms tel Branscombe (029 780) 300; £16 (£23B)/£32 (£46B)

BRATTON FLEMING   SS6437 Map 1
White Hart

This lively and bustling village pub in the hills above the River Yeo serves attractively priced bar food such as sandwiches (50p), toasties (65p), burger, egg and chips (85p), home-cooked ham, egg and chips (£1.40), and salads such as ham, cheese or beef (£1.25). There is a useful take-away stall in the evenings. Drinks are cheap too, and include Flowers Original and Whitbreads on handpump, also draught cider from a big earthenware jug. The rambling bar has beams, flagstones and several cosy nooks and alcoves. It's traditionally furnished, with robust cushioned chairs and wooden stools, and a big stone inglenook fireplace. Darts, pool, fruit machine, space game and a juke box in one side section, also shove-ha'penny, dominoes and cribbage. There is a separate skittle alley, and a small flagstoned courtyard with seats. *(Recommended by Sara Price; more reports please)*

Free house · Licensees T and C E Nicholls · Real ale · Snacks · Children in dining area and room by entrance · Open 11–2.30, 5–11 all year

BROADHEMBURY   ST1004 Map 1
Drewe Arms

5 miles from M5 junction 28; A373 towards Honiton until village signposted left; pub is just on right of village crossroads

The charm of this fifteenth-century thatched inn is its unaffected simplicity: the quiet main bar has a big inglenook fireplace, neatly carved beams in its high ceiling, and handsome stone-mullioned windows, but it keeps an unspoilt village atmosphere. A family room opens off the main bar. Food includes sandwiches (from 55p), ploughman's (£1), basket meals (from £1.10), and plaice, scampi, gammon, or steak (£1.70 to £4.25); well kept Bass and a changing guest beer tapped straight from the cask; sensibly placed darts, shove-ha'penny, dominoes, cribbage, a fruit machine and a space game, maybe piped music. There is a skittle alley, and a flower-filled lawn sloping gently up towards the village church, which has a soporifically sweet-toned bell. This is an attractive village of cream-coloured thatched cottages. *(Recommended by R K Whitehead)*

Free house · Licensee Leslie Billings · Real ale · Meals (not Sun lunchtime or Mon) and snacks · Children in family room · Open 10.30–2.30, 6–11 all year Bedrooms tel Broadhembury (040 484) 267; £8/£16

BUCKLAND BREWER   SS4220 Map 1
Coach & Horses

Little rooms ramble around in this ancient pub that seems to have been designed for elves, so low are its heavy beams and so tiny the connecting doors. A wide choice of bar food includes sandwiches and big filled rolls (from 60p, toasted 10p extra), home-made soup (70p), baked potatoes (55p), pasties (65p), burgers (80p), ploughman's (from £1.20), quiche (£1.65), omelettes (from £1.70), salads (from £1.80), chicken (£1.85), cottage or steak and kidney pie (£1.95), scampi (£2.40) and steaks (£4.95), with roasts on Sundays; well kept Flowers IPA and Original on handpump; darts, dominoes, cribbage. Furnishings include antique settles as well as a variety of armchairs and tables, and you're likely to find logs burning even at midsummer in the big stone fireplaces. An attractive little back restaurant has main courses for around £5; piped music in here. There is a fruit machine and juke box in a side lobby. You can sit outside at wooden tables in the pretty little garden beside this long, low thatched house, and there's now a play area out here. *(Recommended by John Brundrett, Sara Price)*

Free house · Licensees R C Cessford and P Seward · Real ale · Meals and snacks Children in eating area and restaurant · Open 11–2.30, 5.30–11 all year

The Beer Engine, Newton St Cyres

BURGH ISLAND   SX6443   Map 1

Pilchard ★

Park in Bigbury-on-Sea and walk about 300 yards across the sands, which are covered for between six and eight hours of the twelve-hour tide; in summer use the Tractor, a unique bus-on-stilts that beats the tide with its eight-foot-high 'deck'

As we go to press there is a slight question mark over the future of this marvellously situated pub. Mrs Waugh ended her tenure in Autumn 1984, and the whole island was put up for sale. As a buyer had not been found the owners of the estate decided to take the pub under their own wing; they have kept it open and are taking a close interest in its management, so we are hopeful that all will be well for the future. It would be a tragedy if that turned out not to be the case, as this is one of Britain's pub treasures. The storm-shuttered ancient smugglers' look-out is perched well above the tidal sands, and its small L-shaped main bar has sea-view seats built into the thick window embrasures of the bared stone walls; there are also low chairs, settles edged with rope, and others with high backs forming snug booths, with lighting by big ship's lamps hanging from the beams of the plank ceiling, and in winter – when the atmosphere, without the holiday crowds, is even more evocative – a lively log fire. In summer, as readers say, it's very romantic to sit on the grass outside and watch the tide cutting you off from the mainland (knowing the Tractor will eventually rescue you). Another bar with white plastered walls is broadly similar, and has darts. In winter reasonably priced snacks have been confined to home-made soup and ploughman's; in summer a lunchtime salad bar serves home-baked ham, turkey, beef, pies and its speciality, garlic prawns, with crab and prawn sandwiches and filled baked potatoes in the evenings. A separate bistro then serves locally caught fish, local sausages, lamb cutlets and so forth. Well kept Palmers IPA and Best on handpump. *(Recommended by Stuart Barker, Doug Kennedy, Bob Rendle; more reports please)*

Free house · Manager Paddy Fortune · Real ale · Snacks · Children in area partly set aside for them · Open 11–2.30, 5.30–11 (mornings only in winter when tide is out)

BURLESCOMBE   ST0716   Map 1

Poachers Pocket

4 miles from M5 junction 27: A38 towards Wellington

Bar food in this simple, friendly and well kept inn includes sandwiches (60p–80p), soup (65p), chicken (£2.15), home-made cottage (£2.25) or steak and kidney pie (£2.45), home-cooked chicken or ham salad (from £2.25), scampi (£2.50), gammon and egg (£3.25) and rump steak (£4.25); there are children's dishes such as fish fingers (£1.25). The well modernised lounge bar is quietly comfortable, with horse-talk around the log fire, red leatherette button-back wall banquettes, stools and armed chairs on the Turkey carpet, and on our visit piped music. Well kept Ushers Best on handpump; darts, dominoes, cribbage, a fruit machine and a space game in the public bar. There is also a separate restaurant, and a skittle alley. *(Recommended by S V Bishop)*

Free house · Licensees John and Patricia Whitlock · Real ale · Meals and snacks Children welcome · Duos Sat · Open 11–2.30, 6–11 all year (opens 7 in winter) · Bedrooms tel Greenham (0823) 672286; £9/£18

CHAGFORD   SX7087   Map 1
Bullers Arms
Mill Street

The partly panelled walls of this pleasantly unpretentious pub are decorated with antique military hats, boots and medals; it has two log fires, and is traditionally furnished with settles and seats around heavy cast-iron-framed tables. Unusually for Devon, the ceilings are high and airy. Generously served bar food includes home-made pasties (55p) and pies (60p), sandwiches (from 65p), home-made soup (80p), bread and cheese (£1), ploughman's (£1.75), lamb cutlets (£1.95) and ham salad (£2.25). Well kept Bates (a fairly recent Devon beer, from Bovey Tracey), Devenish Wessex Best and Ushers Best on handpump; darts, pool, shove-ha'penny, dominoes and cribbage. There is an attractive and sheltered paved garden, and this little market village is on the edge of Dartmoor. *(Recommended by R H Inns, R P Setterington, E Dearing; more reports please)*

Free house · Licensee Peter Brown · Real ale · Meals (lunchtime, not Sun) and snacks (not Sun) · Open 11–2.30, 6–11 all year

CHERITON BISHOP   SX7793   Map 1
Old Thatch
Village signposted from A30

The wide choice of bar food in this old thatched inn is cooked to order – not instant food – and includes home-made soup (65p), sandwiches (from 70p, toasted from 90p), pâté or seafood scallop (95p), ploughman's with cheese, ham or rollmop mackerel (£1.50), plaice (£1.80), liver and bacon casserole (£1.95), steak and kidney pie (£2.20), scampi (£2.70), eight-ounce rump steak (£5.50) and daily specials such as braised lamb with bacon (£1.85). The open-plan bar has been comfortably modernised and rambles around a central fireplace; it's cheerful and relaxed, with gentle piped music. You can book tables in an annexe to the main bar. Ushers Best on handpump, and local cider; dominoes and cribbage. The inn has recently been added to the official Grade II list of buildings of historic or architectural interest. *(Recommended by P T Young, Julia Hoyle, N F Mackley, R K Whitehead)*

Free house · Licensee Brian Edmond · Real ale · Meals (not Sun evening, limited on Tues) and snacks · Open 12–2.30, 6–11 all year (opens 7 in winter) Bedrooms tel Cheriton Bishop (064 724) 204; £11/£21 (£22S)

Anyone claiming to arrange or prevent inclusion of a pub in the *Guide* is a fraud. Pubs are included only if recommended by genuine readers and if our own anonymous inspection confirms that they are suitable.

CHURCHSTOW   SX7145   Map 1

Church House

A379 NW of Kingsbridge

The good solid stonework of this pub, once a Benedictine hospice, has lasted over 700 years – note the fine rounded arch of the main door. Inside, the long Turkey-carpeted room has low and heavy black oak beams, a great stone fireplace with side bread oven, cushioned seats cut in to the deep window embrasures of the bare stone walls, an old curved high-backed settle, many red leatherette cushioned smaller settles by black tables, and a good lot of stools – each with its own brass coat-hook – by the long glossy black serving counter. One end is curtained off for the popular food, which includes sandwiches, trout (£3.10), fish pie made with wine and mushrooms, scampi, salads including crab when it's available, good rare rump and sirloin steaks (£5.95) and home-made puddings. Booking is recommended for the carvery: good helpings of rib of beef and another roast, on Wednesday to Saturday evenings (£4.25 including pudding) and Sunday lunchtime. Well kept Bass and Ushers Best and Founders on handpump; euchre, fruit machine. There are seats outside. (*Recommended by Lynda Brown, D P Evans*)

Free house · Licensee Nick Nicholson · Real ale · Meals and snacks; carvery bookings tel Kingsbridge (0548) 2237 · Children in eating area · Open 11–2.30, 6–11; closed evening 25 Dec (no food 25–26 Dec)

COCKWOOD   SX9780   Map 1

Anchor

Off, but visible from, A379 Exeter–Torbay

A new addition to the menu in this snug and traditionally furnished pub is the dish of clams, taken fresh from the River Exe just a couple of hundred yards away. Seafood is what they specialise in: prawns by the pint or – in generous helpings – cooked in garlic butter, outstanding fish soup, local crab, mussels, oysters, smoked mackerel, grilled red mullet and salmon. Lobster is usually available (from £9), and there are crusty bread sandwiches; the hot daily specials – all home-cooked by the manager's wife – concentrate on good value traditional English dishes such as beef stew with dumplings, steak and kidney pie, cottage pie and so forth (under £2). The bar has a string of communicating low-ceilinged black-panelled rooms, with sensibly large tables in its various alcoves, and it has a cheerful local atmosphere even at busy holiday times; one reader was glad to find the welcome extended to his large Airedale. There's also a small separate restaurant. Well kept Bass, Flowers IPA and Original and Huntsman Royal Oak on handpump, with quite a few wines by the glass; darts, shove-ha'penny, dominoes, cribbage, a fruit machine, maybe piped music. Tables on the sheltered verandah look over a quiet lane to yachts and crabbing boats in a landlocked harbour. (*Recommended by J Dobris, Timothy Hartley, W O Baldock, Elizabeth Haigh, Heather Sharland*)

Heavitree (who no longer brew) · Licensees M S Hernandez and P Reynolds Real ale · Meals and snacks · Open 10.30–2.30, 5–11 all year

CROYDE   SS4429   Map 1
Thatched Barn

B3231 NW of Braunton

Close to a fine surfing beach, this spacious thatched pub – known
locally as The Thatch – has a friendly rambling bar, with a mixture of
button-back plush chairs and older settles and banquettes, stripped
stone walls, and a blue and brown patterned carpet spreading around
the free-standing central fireplace (which has a log-effect gas fire).
The back part, with heavy low beams, is the snuggest. Popular bar
food includes home-made soup (95p), Exmoor pasties (95p),
sandwiches (from £1, local crab £1.75), home-made pâté (£1.75),
ploughman's with Cheddar, Stilton, Devon beef or home-cooked
ham (£1.95), quiche (£2.25), steak and kidney pie (£2.95), locally
caught lemon sole (£4.95) and 10- to 12-ounce sirloin steak (£5.95).
There is a good salad counter (from £2.95, mixed seafood £4.25);
shortly after our own visit, the Bass and Flowers IPA and Original on
handpump were changed to Courage Best and Directors, kept under
light top pressure; efficient service; darts, shove-ha'penny, a fruit
machine, a sitting space game and, on our visit, piped pop music,
with more space games in a separate lobby. There are wooden seats
on a sheltered front terrace, facing the village road. (Recommended by
M Hucks)

*Free house · Licensees Terry and Eddy Pickersgill · Real ale · Meals and snacks
Children in restaurant and part of bar · Open 11–2.30, 5–11 all year (morning
coffee from 10, restaurant extension to 3) · Bedrooms tel Croyde (0271)
890349; £10/£20*

CULLOMPTON   ST0107   Map 1
Manor House

½ mile from M5 junction 28: enter town and turn left at T-junction;
pub is on right

Only a couple of minutes from the motorway, this elegant inn has a
spacious and stately lounge bar. At one end of the L-shaped room a
food counter serves good value beef, ham and other salads; there are
also hot dishes and good puddings such as lemon meringue pie. Well
kept Whitbreads on handpump; friendly service. The room is neatly
furnished with small green plush seats around well spaced tables
under the moulded plaster ceiling, and a grandfather clock stands
against one of the attractively papered walls. There may be piped
music. There is a separate restaurant, and since the last edition
they've bought the next-door building, giving more room for the
public bar (which has darts, pool, dominoes, cribbage, a juke box and
a fruit machine) and for their functions suite. The bedrooms are well
equipped. (Recommended by W O Baldock; more reports please)

*Free house · Licensees Ronald and Eileen Peters · Meals and snacks (not Sun
evening) · Open 11–2.30, 5–11 all year · Bedrooms tel Cullompton (0884)
32281; £16.10B/£32.20B*

Though we don't usually mention it in the text, a number of pubs will now make
coffee – always worth asking. And some – particularly in the North – will serve
teas.

191

DARTINGTON SX7762 Map 1
Cott

In hamlet with the same name, signposted (insignificantly) off A385 W of Totnes opposite A384 turn-off

You can sit out on the big lawn beside this long, low, thatched fourteenth-century house, and there are good walks through the grounds of nearby Dartington Hall. The Totnes—Buckfastleigh steam railway is not far off, and Totnes itself is one of the prettiest towns in the West Country. But the reason why most people come here is the food. Its main feature is the attractively laid out buffet with its wide and interesting choice of cold dishes, such as freshly made Scotch eggs, good smoked mackerel (£3.75), a splendid pork pie (£4.35 with salads) and good home-cooked joints, and enterprising hot dishes such as salmon coulibiac (£4.95): in the evening or at weekends, get there early if you want the best choice. Rich puddings are served with lots of clotted cream. The communicating rooms of the heavily beamed bar have a civilised atmosphere, with large open fires and some flagstone flooring; they are furnished with sturdy high-backed settles, some elaborately carved. Well kept Bass on electric pump, Hill's cider, a good range of wines by the glass; darts, cribbage. There is a separate restaurant. (*Recommended by J A Glover, Mrs A M Arnold, N F Mackley, Mrs M Lawrence*)

Free house · Licensee Nigel Shortman · Meals and snacks · Children in dining area and restaurant · Open 11—2.30, 6—11 all year · Bedrooms tel Totnes (0803) 863777; £16/£32

DARTMOUTH SX8751 Map 1
Cherub

Higher Street

This quaintly charming little building – originally a fourteenth-century wool merchant's house, with each of its two heavily timbered upper floors jutting further out than the one below – is the oldest in the town, and one of the very few British pubs listed officially as a Grade I building. The small, cosy bar has tapestried seats under its creaky heavy beams, red-curtained latticed windows and an open stove in the big stone fireplace. Lunchtime bar food – which can also be taken to the upstairs dining-room – included on our visit sandwiches (from 85p, local crab £1.10, a special spiced toasted crab sandwich £1.25), home-made vegetable soup (95p), ploughman's (from £1.45), mince pie (£1.90), pâté (£2), rabbit and bacon casserole (£2.30) and seafood platter (£4). The dining-room changes its menus every month or so, concentrating on local ingredients such as creamed crab pâté (£2), fillets of brill (£6) and guinea-fowl from Blackawton (£7). Well kept Bass, Halls and Palmers IPA on handpump, and local elderflower wine; well reproduced classical music; friendly service. (*Recommended by Gordon and Daphne, Kate Morrison*)

Free house · Licensees Roy and Lois Thwaites · Real ale · Meals (lunchtime, not Sun) and snacks (not Sun lunchtime) · Children in dining-room · Open 10.30—2.30, 6—11 all year; closed Sun lunchtime in summer

DODDISCOMBSLEIGH SX8586 Map 1
Nobody Inn ★

This year the Nobody Inn wins a star for the continuing pleasure that it has been bringing readers, with its combination of attractive atmosphere, a splendidly well stocked bar, and rewarding home-cooked food. This includes sandwiches (from 80p), soup (80p), chicken liver pâté (90p), ploughman's (£1.90), hot stuffed pitta bread either vegetarian or ham (£1.90), lasagne (£2.20) and good dishes of the day such as a harvest pie with light wholemeal pastry, served with spinach, red peppers and green salad (around £2). The two low-beamed rooms of the lounge bar are attractively furnished with antique settles, some handsomely carved, Windsor chairs and Turkey carpet, and guns and hunting prints decorate a snug area by one of the big inglenook fireplaces. Drinks include a remarkable list of several hundred wines by the bottle (the wines by the glass are good value), an excellent choice of whiskies, well kept Bass, Bates from Bovey Tracey, Badger Best, Hancocks Best and sometimes Huntsman Royal Oak on handpump or tapped straight from the cask, and even properly mulled wine in winter. There is a separate restaurant, offering main courses at around £6. There are picnic-table sets in the most attractive garden, with views of the wooded hill pastures around the village (the stained glass in the church is well worth seeing). *(Recommended by Gwen and Peter Andrews, Mr and Mrs N G W Edwardes, Peter and Rose Flower, Richard Gibbs, R K Whitehead)*

Free house · Licensees Nicholas Borst-Smith and Philip Bolton · Real ale Meals and snacks · Open 11–2.30, 6–11 all year; closed evening 25 Dec Children in restaurant · Bedrooms tel Christow (0647) 52394; £10 (£15B)/£16 (£28B)

DREWSTEIGNTON SX7390 Map 1
Drewe Arms

All the recommendations of this thatched village alehouse are for its defiant simplicity – even its ordinariness. The unaffected friendliness that welcomes you, and the absolute informality, are eye-openers to people who've grown accustomed to the modern breed of pubs. This one's quite unspoilt: in the little public bar, villagers on simple built-in wooden benches face each other across bare tables on the herringbone-patterned Elizabethan brick floor, and the plain ochre walls have local team photographs and advertisements tacked to them. There's no serving counter – the landlady draws well kept Whitbread and draught cider in a back room. Though nearby Castle Drogo (open for visits) looks medieval, it was built earlier this century. *(Recommended by Trevor Williams, Richard Franck, Alan Franck, Stephan Carney)*

Free house · Real ale · Snacks · Open 10.30–2.30, 6–11 all year

---

Most of the big breweries now work through regional operating companies that have different names. If a pub is tied to one of these regional companies, we put the parent company's name in brackets in the details at the end of each main entry.

DUNSFORD   SX8189 Map 1
Royal Oak
Village signposted from B3212

The old-fashioned virtue of good value is what attracts readers to this simple village inn. Good home-made bar food includes sandwiches, pasties, cheese and bacon or other flans, soup (70p), ploughman's (£1.45), and hot dishes such as cottage pie (£1.70), lasagne (£1.80), trout from a nearby fish farm (£2.45), gammon and steaks (from £4.50); there is also a good choice of vegetarian food (70p–£1.50). The carpeted lounge bar is light and airy, with a big window-seat looking out over the thatched white cottages of this small hill village and beyond to the fringes of Dartmoor. There is a small separate restaurant, and a public bar with darts, bar billiards, dominoes and cribbage; well kept Ushers Best and Founders on handpump. There are tables outside in the sheltered back yard (barbecues each Friday in summer). The bedrooms are good for their price. (*Recommended by Mrs A W Macartney, Steve Bacon, Jack Davey; more reports please*)

Ushers · Licensee David Jevon · Real ale · Meals and snacks · Children in restaurant and side room · Occasional live music · Open 11–2.30, 6.30–11 all year · Bedrooms tel Christow (0647) 52256; £9.20/£18.40

EXETER   SX9292 Map 1
Double Locks ★
Canal Banks, Alphington; from A30 take main Exeter turn-off (A377/A396) then next right into Marsh Barton Industrial Estate and follow Refuse Incinerator signs; when road bends round in front of the factory-like incinerator, take narrow dead-end track over humpy bridge, cross narrow canal swing bridge and follow track along canal (much quicker than it sounds, and a very worthwhile diversion from the final M5 junction)

This ancient and remote canal lockhouse has a marvellously relaxed and easy-going atmosphere, and a splendid motley collection of nautical furnishings, including ship's lamps, model ships and a slatted steamer bench. Good value largely home-made snacks include sandwiches (from 50p, home-cooked turkey 65p, home-baked ham 75p), soups such as leek and potato or turkey-stock vegetable (50p), pasties (55p), filled baked potatoes (from 90p), mushrooms on toast, cottage or steak and kidney pie, leek and macaroni bake and vegetable or bacon quiche (£1), and ploughman's or salads (both from £1.20). There are home-made puddings (60p) such as brown-bread ice cream, carrot cake and chocolate-biscuit cake. Real ales in winter may include a choice of several strong ones as well as the regular range of Everards, Flowers Original, Golden Hill Exmoor, Huntsman Royal Oak and Marstons Pedigree, all tapped from the cask. Darts, shove-ha'penny, bagatelle, dominoes, cribbage, Scrabble and Trivial Pursuits in the main bar, bar billiards in another. There are picnic-table sets on the grass by the ship canal (built in 1546), and volley-ball may be played out here. (*Recommended by St John Sandringham, Alan Franck, Wayne Rossiter, Richard Gibbs, Stephan Carney*)

Free house · Licensee Jamie Stuart · Real ale · Snacks · Children welcome Occasional folk music or jazz (outside if warm) · Open 11–2.30, 5–11

Ship

St Martins Lane; off N side of Cathedral Close

Very handy for the cathedral, this striking fourteenth-century black and white timbered tavern has a handsomely carved upper storey jettied out over a very narrow alley. Inside there are heavy beams and some old stonework, but furnishings are modern with leatherette stools and seats on a red carpet. Food includes soup (50p), sandwiches (from 65p), pâté (95p), plaice or pork chop (£3.40), chicken (£3.65), Torbay sole and halibut (£4.50); a restaurant upstairs is open at lunchtime and in the evening (not Sundays or bank holidays). Well kept Bass, Flowers Original and Whitbreads on handpump; fruit machine, space game, piped music. This was already a tavern by Elizabethan times, and almost certainly used by Sir Francis Drake and his friends – they are known to have frequented Moll's coffee-house nearby. *(Recommended by Wayne Rossiter; more reports please)*

Whitbreads · Licensee R G A Barnes · Real ale · Meals and snacks (lunchtime, not Sun) · Children in restaurant · Open 11–2.30, 5–10.30; closed 25–26 Dec

White Hart ★

South Street; 4 rather slow miles from M5 junction 30; follow City Centre signs via A379, B3182; straight towards centre if you're coming from A377 Topsham Road

In May the main cobbled courtyard of this fourteenth-century inn is a cascade of wistaria. Leading off here, the Tap Bar is furnished sturdily after the style of an old-fashioned alehouse, and serves soup (70p), sandwiches (95p), good big sausages (£1), prawns (£1.30), ploughman's with a choice of cheeses (£1.30), cold turkey pie, beef or ham (£2.50), and charcoal-grilled steak (from £4.95), with daily hot specials (£2.75). A quiet sawdust-floored wine bar offers a rather wider choice of much the same food, including also toasted anchovy, sardine or Stilton fingers (£1.30) and good beef and oyster pie (£3.95). Opposite these, the main bar has long-barrelled rifles above the big fireplace, a glass cupboard of silver, moulded Tudor beams in

Who'd Have Thought It, Miltoncombe

the rich ochre ceiling, good sturdy oak tables and polished oak floorboards, and a set of splendid old brass beer engines in the bay window. Home-made pasties or filled rolls (75p) and a daily hot special are served here at lunchtime, but just ploughman's (£2) and salads (£2.75) on Sundays – when the other bars are closed; Bass tapped from the cask and Davy's Old Wallop, and a good range of 16 or more Davy's wines by the glass (big measures). Stairs take you up to a separate restaurant (also open for Sunday lunch), and to the old-fashioned bedrooms of the original building; leading off, there's also a very comfortable and well equipped modern bedroom block. Outdoor barbecues are held in good summer weather. A friendly and comfortable place to stay, and a good base for exploring the cathedral, splendid maritime museum, medieval guildhall, Rougemont gardens, and Exeter's attractive old buildings. *(Recommended by Stuart Barker, Stephan Carney, R K Whitehead and others)*

Free house · Licensee Brian Wilkinson · Real ale · Meals and snacks (not Sun evening) · Children in eating area (toys, high chairs, baby feeding and changing facilities) · Open 11–2.30, 5–11 · Bedrooms tel Exeter (0392) 79897; £20 (£26B)/£45B

EXMINSTER   SX9487 Map 1

Swans Nest ★

Pub signposted from A379 S of village

The spacious and rambling lounge bar of this country pub is attractively furnished with thoughtfully chosen high-backed winged settles (upholstered in buttoned green leather or flock red plush, and set out as booths around the tables), groups of sofas and armchairs, some heavily carved old-fashioned settles, lots of wheelback chairs, black beams, grandfather clocks, high shelves of willow-pattern platters and so on. There's a relaxed atmosphere, thanks to soft lighting, big vases of flowers and soothing piped music. An efficient food counter supplies good value sandwiches (from 95p, crab £1.40 – not Saturday evening or Sunday lunchtime), soup (95p), ploughman's (from £2.50), a good choice of salads (from £2.50 – prawn, crab and smoked salmon £5.25), and hot dishes such as cod (£2.95), scampi (£3.95) and several steaks (such as eight-ounce fillet at £6.50). There is a wide choice of rich ice creams and sundaes (from £1.25), and the food counter serves tea and coffee. Well kept Bass and Flowers Original, and a considerable range of cocktails. There is a vast neatly landscaped car park. *(Recommended by Sigrid and Peter Sobanski, Wayne Rossiter; more reports please)*

Free house · Licensees Pat and Clive Biddulph · Real ale · Meals and snacks Three-piece ballroom band Weds–Sat evening · Open 11–2.30, 6–11 all year

Turf ★

Continue past the Swans Nest (see previous entry) to end of track, by gates; park, and walk right along canal towpath for nearly a mile

This isolated seaside pub is under the same ownership as the Double Locks (see Exeter), and there's a marked family resemblance. The walk along the ship canal to its end by the pub is part of the pleasure: butterflies fluttering among the rushes, larks, swans and shelducks in the water-meadows on your right, and oyster-catchers piping out on the wide estuary beyond the canal on your left. The canal basin is full of sizeable boats, and to get to the pub you walk across the lock gates. If you're feeling really idle, the pub runs a 40-minute canal boat (bar on board; £1.50 return, charter for up to 56 people £60) from Countess Wear and back – and will quote for a full run from Exeter Maritime Museum. There are fine sea views from a connected series of airy high-ceilinged rooms with big bay windows; these have flagstones or broad bare floorboards, a wood-burning stove, fresh flowers on low varnished tables, canal photographs and big bright shore-bird prints by John Tennent on the white walls, above pale varnished plank panelling. Good value simple food includes lentil soup (50p), sandwiches (from 55p, toasted bacon 75p), unaccompanied steak and kidney pie (55p), pâté (90p), turkey pie (£1), ploughman's (from £1.10), steak roll (£1.30), ham and eggs (£1.70) and generous salads; well kept Flowers IPA and Huntsman Royal Oak on handpump, and Hill's cider; friendly service; darts, shove-ha'penny, dominoes, cribbage. A big lawn stretches to the shore under a couple of evergreen oaks, gaunt pines and an ash tree; at low tide the mudflats are full of gulls and waders. There are log seats and picnic-table sets, with a beached cabin boat for children to play in. Cook-it-yourself summer barbecues out here are very popular and good value, from burger with sausage in a bap (75p) to a full mixed grill (£3). *(Recommended by B E Petts)*

Free house · Licensee Kenneth William Stuart · Real ale · Meals and snacks Children in family room · Open 11–2.30, 6–11 all year · Bedrooms tel Exeter (0392) 833128; £10/£20

HATHERLEIGH SS5404 Map 1

George ★

Friendly and civilised, this thatched inn shows its age, of more than 500 years, to best advantage in its small and atmospheric front bar. Chiefly for residents, this has easy chairs, sofas and antique cushioned settles, an enormous fireplace, tremendous oak beams and stone walls two or three feet thick. The Jubilee Bar, its main one, is on the far side of a courtyard with rustic wooden seats and tables on its cobbles, and hanging baskets and window-boxes on its black and white timbered walls. This big, airy L-shaped room was built from the wreck of the inn's old brewhouse and coachmen's loft. It has antique settles around treadle sewing-machine tables, and steps down into a quieter extension with more modern furnishings. Good bar food includes sandwiches (from 75p), ploughman's (from £1.45), whitebait (£1.85), fry-ups (£2.45), salads (from £3.25) and grills including steaks and a mixed grill (£6.25). Well kept Courage Best and Directors on handpump; darts, cribbage, a fruit machine. There is a small separate restaurant. Outside by the car park (but well screened) is a small heated swimming pool, with a swing and white tables and chairs by a bank of shrubs. A friendly place to stay, with comfortable bedrooms – cheaper than in the last edition, and you can even stay without breakfast (deduct £3.75 a head from the prices below). *(Recommended by Dr R Wright, George Hughes, Mrs A M Arnold, David Gethyn-Jones)*

Free house · Licensees Nicola and Andrew Grubb · Real ale · Meals and snacks Children in area off Jubilee Bar · Open 10.30–2.30, 6–11 (Mon and Tues 8–4.30, 6–11) · Bedrooms tel Okehampton (0837) 810454; £15.25 (£22.25S)/£24 (£32B)

HAYTOR VALE   SX7677   Map 1

Rock

In a Dartmoor village, this civilised small inn is a friendly place to stay and has a charming lounge bar. Its two communicating rooms have chintz-cushioned high-backed settles, oak Windsor armchairs and easy chairs around polished antique tables, with good open fires in winter and flowers in summer. The walls are decorated with plates and small prints, and there's a fine Stuart iron fireback in the main fireplace. There's a jolly atmosphere, and a good range of drinks including well kept Bass, Huntsman Dorchester, Dorset and Royal Oak, and Devon cider. It does fill up quickly in summer, so get there early if you want to eat: waiter-served bar food includes sandwiches (from 69p), home-made soup (75p), ploughman's or filled baked potato (£1.65), omelettes (£2), quiche (£2.35), steak and kidney pie (£2.55), scampi (£2.75), Maryland chicken or trout (£3.99), and steaks (from £4.99). There's a small restaurant (dinner £8.35). The big garden is pretty and well kept, with good views of the surrounding moors. The nearby road from Bovey Tracey to Widecombe is much better than you'd expect from a map. The bedrooms are quiet, comfortable and well equipped. *(Recommended by A J Milman, Pat and Malcolm Rudlin, Stuart Barker, Elizabeth Haigh, Nick and Yvonne Mawby, Matthew Waterhouse, Alan Franck and others)*

Free house · Licensee Christopher Graves · Real ale · Meals and snacks Children welcome · Open 11–2.30, 6–11 all year · Bedrooms tel Haytor (036 46) 305; £12.50 (£16B)/£25 (£30B)

HENNOCK   SX8380   Map 1

Palk Arms

Village signposted from B3193; also a good road is the first right turn after leaving Chudleigh Knighton on B3344 for Bovey Tracey

A big picture window in the dining-lounge of this village inn gives lovely views over the Teign valley far below, and in the back bar there's likely to be talk of the state of the fishing in the River Teign – salmon flies for sale are on display on its butter-coloured walls. This friendly room has rugs on matting, cushioned built-in wall seats, small easy chairs and settees, a log fire in a bare stone fireplace, darts, dominoes, cribbage, a fruit machine and on our visit piped pop music. The dining-lounge, with comfortable seats around low rustic tables on its flowery red carpet, has an attractively set out buffet bar with over two dozen help-yourself salads (from £2.50). More good value food includes sandwiches (from 80p, toasted steak £1.95), a

good choice of ploughman's (from £1.40), steak and kidney pie
(£1.50), plaice (£2.50), gammon (£3.50) and rump steak (£6), with a
couple of daily specials such as vegetable quiche (£3) and several
puddings served with clotted cream (from 90p). Well kept Ushers
Best on handpump, farm cider. Picnic-table sets on the back lawn
look down over the valley. (Recommended by S V Bishop, Mrs Penny
Mendelsohn)

Free house · Licensees Brian and Geraldine Cook · Real ale · Meals and snacks
Children in dining-lounge · Open 11–3, 5.30–11 all year · Bedrooms tel
Bovey Tracey (0626) 833027; £8.50/£17

HOLNE   SX7069   Map 1
Church House

Perhaps the nicest way of getting to this medieval pub is the quarter-
hour walk from the Newbridge National Trust car park, and there
are many other attractive walks nearby, up on to Dartmoor as well as
along the wooded Dart valley. The carpeted lounge bar, which has
moorland views from its window seat, has civilised traditional
furnishings. The ancient heavy wooden wall-partition shows the age
of the inn, which – like so many others in Devon – got its name from
the fact that it grew up hand in glove with the church, originally
brewing church ale on feast days such as Whitsun. It has a quiet
friendly atmosphere, and serves well kept Badger Best, Blackawton
and Halls Harvest from handpump, Hill's farm cider, and a good
range of traditional country wines. Besides sandwiches and bar
snacks and meals there is a separate restaurant. The livelier public bar
has darts, bar billiards, dominoes, cribbage, a fruit machine and a
space game, and there is a family room. Charles Kingsley was born in
this village which is far enough off the beaten track to stay
surprisingly untouristy. (Several anonymous recommendations; more
reports please, particularly on food)

Free house · Licensees Mr and Mrs M J Angseesing · Real ale · Meals and
snacks · Children in family room · Open 11–2.30, 6–11 all year · Bedrooms
tel Poundsgate (036 43) 208; £9.50/£19 (£21B)

HORNDON   SX5280   Map 1
Elephant's Nest ★ ★

Pub signposted from A386 beside Mary Tavy Inn, then follow Horndon signs

White tables and chairs and picnic-table sets on the lawn outside this
isolated but warmly welcoming 400-year-old pub look over dry-stone
walls to the pastures of Dartmoor's lower slopes, and the rougher
moorland above. Inside there are captain's chairs on flagstones, big
rugs, cushioned stone seats built in to the windows and around the
walls, a good log fire on cool days and a beams-and-boards ceiling.
Popular bar food at lunchtime includes soup (75p), filled rolls (from
70p), pâté (£1.40), smoked mackerel salad (£1.55), chicken pie and
salad (£1.70), and hot home-made chilli con carne, stew and lasagne
(£1.55–£1.95). A giant ham ploughman's has come in for special
praise, as has the chicken tandoori (ordered 24 hours ahead). In the

evenings main meals only are served, including curry or scampi
(£2.95), local Tavy trout (£3.50) and steaks (from £4.95). Well kept
Palmers IPA, St Austell HSD and Tinners, Ushers Best and a guest
beer on handpump, and Countryman cider; sensibly placed darts,
and a fruit machine. Though you can walk from here straight on to
the moor or Black Down, a better start (army exercises permitting)
might be to drive past Wapsworthy to the end of the lane, at OS
reference 546805 on Sheet 191. *(Recommended by E M Watson,
R Sinclair Taylor, D R Kohler)*

*Free house · Licensees Owen and Dave Phillips · Real ale · Meals (evenings, not
Thurs) and snacks (lunchtime) · Children may be allowed into an area partly
set aside for them, at landlord's discretion, if it's wet · Open 11.30–2.30,
6.30–11*

HORNS CROSS   SS3823   Map 1
Hoops

A39 W of Bideford (and just W of village)

Stylishly solid modern leather-seated oak settles are a distinctive
feature of the well kept main bar in this extended and modernised
thatched inn, which dates back some 700 years and has log fires, oak
beams, parquet floor and clean white walls. Good bar food includes
home-made pasties (85p), sandwiches (from 90p, crab with home-
made mayonnaise £1.30), home-made soup (90p), home-made
burger (£1.35), pâté or ploughman's (from £1.50, maybe local goat's
cheese £1.60), curried chicken (£2.50), fried scampi and scallops
(£3), local crab salad (£3) and eight-ounce sirloin steak (£5.75);
there's also a restaurant. Flowers IPA and Original are tapped from
casks behind the bar; darts, a space game, maybe piped music. There
are picnic-table sets in a sheltered central courtyard. Comfortable
bedrooms include one with a four-poster, others with half-testers.
(Recommended by Steve and Carolyn Harvey)

*Free house · Licensee J E Malcolm · Real ale · Children in restaurant · Piano Sat
evening · Open 11.30–2.15, 6–11 all year · Bedrooms tel Horns Cross
(023 75) 222; £15 (£16.50)/£30 (£33)*

KILMINGTON   SY2797   Map 1
Old Inn

A35

The friendly and welcoming main bar of this white thatched pub has
cushioned benches built in to its partly panelled walls, cushioned
captain's chairs on its bare floorboards, and two high-backed
wooden armchairs by the open fire. At busier times they open the
lounge – larger but still cosy, with seats grouped around tables on its
carpet and a nice inglenook fireplace. Good value bar food includes
soup (70p), ploughman's (from £1.50), salads (from £2), cod (£2.20),
chicken (£2.45), fresh local trout (£3.25) and steaks (from £5.25);
there is a separate candlelit restaurant. Well kept Bass and Hancocks
on handpump; darts, shove-ha'penny, dominoes, cribbage, a fruit
machine, perhaps piped music; separate skittle alley. There are

picnic-table sets and a swing and climbing frame on the grass at the side, which is partly shielded by the car park from the noise of traffic on the fast trunk road. *(Recommended by David Grant; more reports please)*

Bass Charringtons · Licensee John Parish · Real ale · Meals and snacks Children in restaurant · Open 11–2.30, 6–11 all year

KING'S NYMPTON   SS6819   Map 1

Grove

Village signposted from B3226

This homely thatched village inn was taken over not long before this edition of the *Guide* went to press, and though the underlying theme of simplicity is to remain, the family now running it are making some useful changes: Sunday roast lunches can be booked, a Saturday night cold table has been started (from £2.25 for quiche, £3.25 for cold meats to £5.50 for steak, with as much salad as you can eat), cream teas are on offer in summer, and by now a small dining-room should have been opened. Normally, bar food includes soup (65p), home-made pasties (70p), toasted sandwiches (from 75p), ploughman's (from £1.35), home-made steak and kidney pie (£1.45), basket meals such as scampi (£1.95), chicken chasseur (£3.25) and rump steak (£4.95). Tuesday is a popular fish-and-chips only night. The bar is simply furnished with a long seat set in to its bare stone walls, dining-room chairs around rustic tables on the quarry-tiled floor, and in winter an open fire as well as the wood-burning stove. Well kept Ushers Best and Founders tapped from the cask (the handpump's now used for cider); darts, shove-ha'penny, dominoes, cribbage, maybe piped music; also pool, fruit machine, space game and a juke box in a separate carpeted area, and a skittle alley (which can be hired). This is attractive remote countryside, of humpy pasture and twisting wooded valleys. *(Recommended by N Lawson, Richard Merrills; more reports please)*

Free house · Licensees Stephen and Susan Paddon · Real ale · Meals and snacks Children in eating area, pool area and skittle alley · Open 11–2.30, 5.30–11 all year · Bedrooms tel Chulmleigh (0769) 80406; £7.50/£15

KINGSTON   SX6347   Map 1

Dolphin

This pretty yellow-shuttered sixteenth-century house, just below the imposing village church, is unusual in having its three bars separated by the quiet village lane. In the main bar a wide choice of food includes substantial rare roast beef sandwiches (95p), home-made pâté (£1.25), ploughman's (from £1.85), a half-pint of prawns (£1.95), home-made steak and kidney pie (£2.45), beef and Stilton casserole (£2.95) and home-made treacle tart with clotted cream (80p). This long and cheerful series of knocked-through rooms has rustic tables and cushioned seats and settles around the bared stone walls, beams (with visiting cards pinned to them), and piped music. The Tallet Bar serves a set-price buffet with more elaborate starters, cold food with good salads, and hot dishes; the third Stable Room serves charcoal-grilled steaks and seafood. Well kept Courage Best and Directors on handpump; euchre. Outside there are tables, swings, a children's summer snack bar, and summer barbecues. Half a dozen tracks lead down to the sea, and unspoilt Wonwell Beach, about a mile and a half away. *(Recommended by R K Whitehead; more reports please)*

Courage · Licensees Barry and Dee Fryer · Real ale · Meals and snacks Children in dining areas and restaurants · Occasional folk music · Open 11–2.30, 6–11

KNOWSTONE   SS8223   Map 1

Masons Arms ★ ★

This last year we have had more reports about this simple but very hospitable inn than any other in Devon. What strikes people above all is the charming friendliness of the owners (and of their bearded collie, Charlie, said by some to be the smartest dog around). Several people mention instances when the Todds have gone out of their way to be helpful to them, making this an inn which – as one reader told us – reminds you what the terms host and guest used to mean. Almost everyone picks out the good value food, all home cooked, for special mention. It includes filling and interesting soups (70p), usually a choice of pâtés (£1.05: both the chicken liver and the unusual combinations such as cheese and walnut have been singled out for special praise), ploughman's (from £1.15), salads, including a Greek one with Feta and olives (£1.50), a pie such as steak and kidney (£2.25), chicken curry (£2.25), scampi (£2.35), rump steak (£5.75) and various vegetarian dishes. Though they don't normally do sandwiches, they tend to offer them, with soup, to late arrivals if the kitchen is closed. There is also a separate restaurant offering good value three-course dinners (£6.50, if you're staying) and house wines. The small main bar has substantial rustic furniture on its stone floor, long narrow benches built in to the cream-painted stone walls (which are decorated with old farm tools), seats by a sunny window, lots of antique bottles hanging from its heavy medieval black beams, and a fine open fireplace with a side bread oven. A small lower sitting-room has cosy easy chairs, bar billiards and table skittles. Notably well kept Badger Best and Wadworths 6X tapped straight from the cask, also Hill's cider; several snuffs on the bar counter; darts, dominoes, shove-ha'penny, cribbage, shut-the-box, board games and jigsaws, and occasionally, if customers are in the mood for it, well reproduced music. A separate room has table skittles and bar billiards. Seats in front of the thatched stone inn look across the very quiet lane and part of the garden behind has recently been paved – tables out here have a view over the hilly pastures leading up to Exmoor; we gather that children sitting here are expected to have something to eat. *(Recommended by Flt Lt A D Harkness, Susan Grossman, H D Leggatt, Charles Lambert, Timothy Hartley, J S Evans, S G Revill, Brian Exley)*

Free house · Licensees David and Elizabeth Todd · Real ale · Meals and snacks Children in eating area and restaurant · Open 11–2.30, 5.30–11 (7–11 Mon–Thurs in winter); closed evening 25 Dec · Bedrooms tel Anstey Mills (039 84) 231; £12.50 (£15.50S)/£25 (£31S)

LANDSCOVE SX7766 Map 1
Live and Let Live

Woolston Green; Landscove is signposted from A38 as it passes Ashburton;
OS Sheet 202 reference 778661

The friendly new owners of this unassuming village pub are building
up a busy trade for their efficiently served bar food, including beef
and vegetable soup (95p), deep-fried corn on the cob (£1.30), liver
pâté or breaded mussels (£1.45), shepherd's pie (£2.25), pork chop in
cider (£2.75), steak and kidney hot-pot (£2.95) and spiced beef
(£3.75). They have their own range of country wines, as well as well
kept Courage Best and Flowers IPA on handpump, and Hill's cider.
Though the bar is open-plan, there's still a homely feel, with
wheelback chairs around black tables (candlelit at night) on the red
patterned carpet, a solid fuel stove in the stone fireplace, sporting
prints, and a sunny front area where red plush wall seats give an
attractive view over rolling hill pastures. Darts (with more games in
the back Stables Room); on our visit piped ballads. Across the lane
there are rustic benches and tables, and a swing, in a small orchard
between the car park and the fields. *(Recommended by Matthew
Waterhouse; more reports please)*

*Free house · Real ale · Meals and snacks · Children in Stables Room · Open
11–2.30, 6–11*

LEE SS4846 Map 1
Grampus ★

Old Farm; follow Lee signposts from B3231 W of Ilfracombe

Like so many West Country pubs this fourteenth-century house is at
its best out of season, with big logs crackling in the huge stone
fireplace, plenty of space, and that marvellously relaxing atmosphere
that comes from regular local customers who enjoy each other's
company but welcome strangers warmly too; even with summer
bustle it's still excellent. There are winged settles, wooden benches
covered with sheepskins, gin traps and scythe blades decorating the
beams and walls, and friendly efficient service. Good straightforward
bar food served from back quarters (which judging by the sounds are
staffed largely by boisterous budgerigars) includes sandwiches (from
75p, crab when it's available £1), wholesome pasties (80p), home-
made soup (80p), cheese and onion flan (90p), cheese or pâté
ploughman's with individual cottage loaves (£1.75) and steak and
kidney pie or chicken (£1.90); well kept Flowers Original on
handpump; on our visit, piped Country and Western and vintage
Louis Armstrong; darts, shove-ha'penny, dominoes, cribbage, sitting
space game and a fruit machine in an area behind the massive
chimney. There are picnic-table sets on a lawn below the steep
wooded valley, and a terrace by an aviary with golden pheasants
(which pipe eloquently as sunset comes); children's rocking machines

---

Most pubs in the *Guide* sell draught cider. We mention it specifically only if they
have unusual farm-produced scrumpy or specialise in it (as some pubs do in
Bristol, say).

are out here. Lee Bay is just a short stroll downhill. (*Recommended by Mrs M Allix, Mrs E Matthews, Mrs H Johnstone, Roger Protz, N B Pritchard*)

Free house · Licensee Mrs Rita Palmer · Real ale · Meals and snacks · Children welcome · Folk music Sun evening, morris dancing mid-week · Open 11–2.30, 6–11 (12–2.30, 7–11 in winter)

LYDFORD SX5184 Map 1
Castle ★ [*illustrated on page 182*]

Named after the nearby ruined Norman tower from which the grim Dartmoor tin-mining laws were administered (*First hang and draw, then hear the case by Lydford law*), this friendly Tudor inn has a comfortable and attractively furnished two-room bar. There are curved antique settles on the polished flagstones, sturdy Victorian tables, oak beams, winter log fires, and on the bare stone walls brightly coloured plates, stained glass, early butterfly cigarette cards, Victorian handbills advertising stud stallions owned by an ancestor of the landlord, and pictures of the inn in the old days. Good bar food includes home-made soup (90p), toasted sandwiches or ploughman's (95p), home-made pâté (£1.55), haddock (£1.55), excellent home-made steak and kidney pie (£1.60), local duck, and curries — a bowl at lunchtime (£1.85), full-scale in the evening. Well kept Bass and St Austell Tinners and HSD on handpump; darts. You can sit outside this pink-washed house, opposite a crafts barn. A nice place to stay, and the village, near Dartmoor, is beside a beautiful wooded river gorge owned by the National Trust. (*Recommended by Mrs A M Arnold, Gordon and Daphne, B R Shiner; more reports please*)

Free house · Licensee Stanley Bruce Reed · Real ale · Meals and snacks Children in dining area · Open 11–2.30, 6–11; closed 25 Dec · Bedrooms tel Lydford (082 282) 242; £12/£21

LYNMOUTH SS7249 Map 1
Rising Sun [*illustrated on page 219*]

Mars Hill; down by harbour

Perfectly placed on a quiet dead-end just above the little harbour, this fourteenth-century inn looks out past the boats to the sea, with the steep coast of Foreland Point in the distance. The rising sun really does stream into the bedrooms under the overhanging thatch, and this is a charming place to stay, with friendly and efficient service, appetising dinners (perhaps including reasonably priced freshly caught lobster) and good breakfasts in the small oak-panelled dining-room. The carpeted bar too is mainly panelled, with stripped stone at the fireplace end, black beams in its white ceiling, leatherette stools and cushioned built-in wall seats, and latticed windows facing the harbour (which dries to mud at low tide). Sandwiches and bar food from the same kitchen that serves the restaurant; on our visit, piped Bobby Womack. The inn is well placed for this fine stretch of coast, with a three-mile climb up to some of the best of Exmoor (parts of *Lorna Doone* were written here). (*Recommended by Martin Quinn, I H Agnew, BOB*)

Free house · Licensee Hugo Jeune · Meals and snacks · Open 11–2.30, 5.30–11 all year; closed Dec–mid Feb · Bedrooms tel Lynton (0598) 53223; £18.50/£37 (£48)

MEAVY   SX5467   Map 1
Royal Oak

This is almost unique, in that it's owned communally by the parish (the Plough in Horbling, Lincolnshire, is the only other example we know of). It's named after the nearby ancient oak tree under which villagers have danced since pre-Christian times – there's still an Oak Fair on the green in front of the pub, on the first Saturday in June. The L-shaped main bar has comfortable upholstered settles and stools around rustic tables, and a second simpler bar has oak beams and a fine open fireplace. Bar food includes pasties (50p), sandwiches (from 65p, good prawn and fresh crab £1.75p), ploughman's (from £1.10), pâté (£1.10), cottage pie (£1.10), home-made fish pie (£1.45), lasagne (£1.50) and daily specials such as curry or spaghetti bolognese (£1.35); Bass and Ushers Best on handpump, Inch's farm cider. The pub is close to a particularly attractive part of Dartmoor. *(Recommended by C McDowall, E M Watson; more reports please)*

Free house · Real ale · Meals and snacks · Open 11–2.30, 6–11 all year

MILTONCOMBE   SX4865   Map 1
Who'd Have Thought It ★ *[illustrated on page 195]*

Village signposted from A386 S of Tavistock

A wide choice of well kept real ales and of good value home-made food, together with the attractively old-fashioned main bar, win a star for this busy sixteenth-century pub in a little village at the bottom of a steep valley. Food includes home-made pasties (55p), good sandwiches in local granary bread (from 80p), minestrone (95p), generous ploughman's (from £1.60, lunchtimes only, not Sundays), cod (£2.10), chicken (£2.30), mixed seafood (£2.85), scampi (£2.90), salads (from £3), 10- to 12-ounce sirloin steak (£6.25) and various daily specials. Puddings include blackberry and apple crumble; Golden Hill Exmoor, Huntsman Royal Oak, Palmers IPA, Ushers Best and Wadworths 6X on handpump, with a choice of draught ciders. Some of the cushioned high-backed winged settles are grouped cosily around a wood-burning stove in the big stone fireplace, there are colourful plates on a big black dresser, and rapiers and other weapons hang on white walls above black panelling; two other rooms have seats made from barrels. Dominoes, a fruit machine. There are picnic-table sets on a small terrace by a swift little stream. Handy for the lovely gardens of the Garden House at Buckland Monachorum, Buckland Abbey, and for Dartmoor. *(Recommended by D A Lloyd, Pat and Malcolm Rudlin)*

Free house · Licensees Keith Yeo and Garry Rager · Real ale · Meals (restricted Sun and bank hols) and snacks · Sun evening folk club · Open 11.30–2.30, 6.30–11

If we know a pub does summer barbecues, we say so.

MORETONHAMPSTEAD   SX7585   Map 1

White Hart

Comfortable and well equipped bedrooms make this friendly and meticulously kept old inn, close to Dartmoor, a nice place to stay. The spacious Turkey-carpeted lounge bar is pleasantly furnished with wicker armchairs, plush seats and oak pews from the parish church; out in the hall is a splendidly large-scale 1827 map of Devon by Greenwood. The lively public bar has leatherette seats and settles under a white beam-and-plank ceiling. Bar food includes soup (95p), hot dishes such as quiche (£1.70), pork sausages (£1.70), home-made steak and kidney pie or chicken curry (£2.40), salads (£2.95) and scampi (£3). At lunchtime there are also sandwiches made from local cheese or home-cooked meat (95p) and a choice of ploughman's (£1.55), with pasty (95p) as an evening snack; several puddings include applecake or bread pudding with clotted cream (95p). No bar meals after 8pm; separate evening grill-room. They serve cream teas in the afternoon. Bass and Flowers IPA on handpump; darts, shove-ha'penny, dominoes, cribbage. You can sit on a pew in the small back courtyard. (More reports please)

Free house · Licensee Peter Morgan · Real ale · Meals and snacks Children in lounge · May have to park in the public car park, a short walk away · Open 10.30–2.30, 6–11 all year · Bedrooms tel Moretonhampstead (0647) 40406; £17.50 (£20B)/£30 (£35B)

nr NEWTON ABBOT   SX8671   Map 1

Two Mile Oak

A381 Newton Abbot–Totnes, 2 miles S of Newton Abbot

Readers warmly praise generous helpings of good food and welcoming service in this ochre-painted Tudor pub. The carpeted lounge is romantic at night, with candles on its dimpled copper tables, some seats in secluded alcoves, horse brasses on the beams, shelves of old china against the bared stone walls, and a handsome old settle as well as captain's chairs. The beams of the black-panelled and traditionally furnished public bar are decorated with old beer mats and lots of harness; on cool days it has a big log fire. The bar food here includes soup (60p), toasted sandwiches (80p), home-made pâtés (£1.30), ploughman's with warm wholemeal loaves (from £1.60; the cheeses are in fine form), chicken and ham pie (£2.60), locally smoked ham (£2.70) and rump steak (£5.20), with occasional specials such as seafood or hot-pot. In summer there are barbecues in the attractive back garden, which has seats on a terrace and a lawn which is sheltered and broken up by mature shrubs. Well kept Bass and Flowers IPA on handpump, with Huntsman Royal Oak tapped from the cask; darts, dominoes, cribbage, a fruit machine. (Recommended by Sue and Len Beattie, Mrs Stockwell, Mrs J Seller, D P Evans, Mary Joinson)

Heavitree (who no longer brew) · Licensee Helen Peers · Real ale · Meals and snacks · Children in lobby dining area by entrance · Folk music Thurs evening Open 11–2.30, 6–11 all year

NEWTON ST CYRES   SX8798 Map 1
Beer Engine [illustrated on page 187]

Sweetham; from Newton St Cyres on A377 follow St Cyres Station, Thorverton signpost

In the last year this friendly own-brew pub has added a hefty strong ale – appropriately called Sleeper – to its previous range, also punningly named, of Rail Ale and the well balanced rather stronger Piston. Downstairs, you can see the gleaming stainless brewhouse opened in 1983 by the enthusiastic young owner, who also sells local cider. Good value simple food includes pasties or filled baked potatoes (65p), ploughman's with local cheese (£1.40), a range of speciality sausages such as venison or piri-piri (£1.45), chilli con carne or fish pie (£1.75) and various salads such as quiche or turkey pie (from £2). The spacious and comfortable main bar, with partitioning alcoves, has Windsor chairs and some button-back banquettes round dark varnished tables on its red carpet. Darts, shove-ha'penny, dominoes, cribbage and a fruit machine; a space game in the downstairs lobby. You can sit out on a terrace, or on the little sheltered verandah. Occasionally a real ale/real train link-up has been arranged from Exeter. (Recommended by Chris Dawson, W Rossiter)

Own brew · Licensee Peter Hawksley · Real ale · Meals and snacks · Children in dining area · Jazz, blues and rock in cellar bar Weds, Fri and Sat · Open 11–2.30, 6–11 all year

NORTH BOVEY   SX7483 Map 1
Ring of Bells

Since last year's *Guide* the real ale strategy of this charming village inn has been refined, with the idea of including a spread of ales from each county west of Wiltshire and maybe one from Wales. They're all tapped straight from the cask, and typically might include Bass, Bates from Bovey Tracey, Flowers Original, Gibbs Mew Bishops Tipple, Golden Hill Exmoor, Huntsman Royal Oak, St Austell HSD and Wadworths 6X. In winter they add the awesome Crippledick, one of the most potent ales around. The popular lunchtime buffet counter serves sandwiches as well as a good choice of salads (around £2.50), and puddings with clotted cream. Evening bar food includes soup (70p), hot-pot (£2.50), rabbit casserole (£2.50) and venison casserole (£3), and there is a separate restaurant (three-course dinner £9.50, usually including roast game and local trout). The simply furnished carpeted bar is attractively lit to make the most of the shadowings of its white-painted stone walls; there are horse brasses on the beams. Darts, dominoes and, in winter, pool. The mossily thatched thirteenth-century inn is in a group of white cottages set back from the attractive village green (where there's a traditional fair on Saturday 19 July), with Dartmoor rising to Easden Down beyond. There are seats outside, on a terrace and small sheltered lawn, with a children's play garden closer to the green. As we went to press they were working on an outdoor floodlit swimming pool. Golf, fishing, shooting and pony-trekking can be arranged. (Recommended by J E F Rawlins, Matthew Waterhouse; more reports please)

Free house · Licensee George Batcock · Real ale · Meals (lunchtime salad counter only) and snacks · Children welcome (except in Snug Bar) · Open 10.30–2.30, 6–11 all year · Bedrooms tel Moretonhampstead (0647) 40375; £15.50B/£31B

PETER TAVY   SX5177   Map 1

Peter Tavy ★

On a frosty Monday lunchtime in February one reader was a little surprised to find this pub – miles from anywhere – quite full; only a little surprised, though, as he realised he could hardly be the only person to be lured great distances by the promise of a big log fire, unusually good food, an impressive range of well kept real ales, and a charming atmosphere. Food includes soup (often uncommon, such as fish chowder or carrot with orange, 85p), ploughman's, chilli con carne, beef casserole, thick slices of succulent ham (£1.10) or beef (£1.30), generous helpings of unusual salads, rump steak (£5.50) and above all vegetarian food good enough to tempt even confirmed carnivores. This includes creamy cashew nut fingers or nut loaf (99p), home-made wholemeal quiche, walnut and cheese burgers, appetising spinach pancakes (£2.12), and lentil lasagne or vegetable moussaka (£2.85). They use only fresh ingredients (which means they can't be cheap) and encourage you to come into the kitchen to pick and choose or even see your food being prepared. The range of ales, tapped from the cask and changed from time to time, might typically include Bass, Blackawton, Courage Best and Directors, Golden Hill Exmoor, Huntsman Royal Oak and Wadworths 6X; attractive music. The smallish low-beamed bar has high-backed settles on the

The Maltsters Arms, Tuckenhay

black flagstones by the imposing log-filled fireplace, smaller settles in the stone mullioned windows, and a snug little separate dining area. Picnic-table sets among fruit trees in a small raised garden have peaceful views of the moor rising above nearby pastures. A track opposite the church leads straight on to the moor, and another past the pub leads down to the River Tavy. *(Recommended by Pat and Malcolm Rudlin, Dr Nicola Hall, Elizabeth Haigh, R Sinclair Taylor and others)*

Free house · Licensees P J and J Hawkins · Real ale · Meals and snacks Children in dining area partly set aside · Open 11.30–2.30, 5.30–11 (7–10.30 in winter)

RATTERY SX7461 Map 1
Church House ★

Village signposted from A385 W of Totnes and from A38 S of Buckfastleigh

The original building here probably housed the craftsmen who built the Norman church, and may then have served as a hostel for passing monks. Parts of that ancient church house still survive in this fine old pub – notably, the flight of spiral stone steps on your left as you go in. They probably date from about 1030, making this one of the oldest pub buildings in Britain. The simple furnishings of the two bar rooms are quite in character: massive oak beams and standing timbers, large fireplaces, a grandfather clock and other antiques, Windsor armchairs, comfortable leather bucket seats and window seats, and prints on plain white walls. The good range of home-cooked food keeps the pub full throughout the year – and, for the reader who returns time after time for the generous fry-up, we have the happy news that its price has this year been cut to £2.80. Other food includes interestingly flavoured mainly vegetable soup (80p), wholemeal bread sandwiches (from £1; toasted with egg, bacon and mushroom £1–£1.40), ploughman's (from £1.40, rare beef £2.30), salads (from £2.25 – the crab is said to be especially good), and hot dishes such as good quiches including salmon, boiled bacon with parsley sauce, steak and kidney or cottage pie, beef in red wine, curries and grills (£2.45–£3). As well as spotted Dick or apricot crumble with custard, there's their own recipe ch'apple (Church House + apple = Chapel) pie made of shortcrust pastry, jam, apple, and softer pastry on top with ground almonds and cream (£1.20), and a remarkably successful concoction of ice cream, clotted cream, toasted almonds and butterscotch sauce. There is also a separate restaurant (Tuesday to Saturday evenings). Well kept Bass on handpump, and a wide range of malt whiskies; darts, dominoes, cribbage, maybe soft piped music. Outside, picnic-table sets on a hedged courtyard by the churchyard have peaceful views of the partly wooded surrounding hills. *(Recommended by D J Milner, Col G D Stafford, Mrs Stockwell, R Sinclair Taylor, J E F Rawlins, M Lawrence)*

Free house · Licensees William and Sylvia Kirk · Real ale · Meals and snacks Children in restaurant for bar meals lunchtime only by arrangement · Open 11–2.30, 6–11; closed evening 25 Dec

---

Prices of main dishes usually include vegetables or a side salad.

RINGMORE SX6545 Map 1

Journey's End

This partly medieval inn is friendly and old-fashioned, with
comfortably well equipped bedrooms, and just three-quarters of a
mile from the sea. The panelled lounge bar has settles, Windsor chairs
and built-in wall seats with rugs on its wooden floor, and another bar
has a drove of cask seats for the many summer visitors; darts, bar
billiards, dominoes, cribbage, a fruit machine, a space game and a
juke box in here. A wide choice of bar food includes good home-
made soups (from 75p), sandwiches (from 60p, local crab £1.95,
giant toasted double-deckers £2.25), a good range of ploughman's
(from £1.95), salads (from £2.50 – readers praise the crab) and
uitsmijter (a sort of open sandwich with ham, eggs and salad, from
£1.75) as well as pizzas (from £1.95) and more conventional pub hot
dishes such as shepherd's pie (around £1.65–£2.65) or sirloin steak
(£4.75). Home-made fruit pies are served with clotted cream (95p).
There is a separate restaurant open in the evenings. Service is good;
well kept Badger Best, Summerskills Bigbury, Golden Hill Exmoor,
Ushers Best and Wadworths 6X on handpump or tapped straight
from the cask. The charming flower garden at the back has rustic
seats. The inn is named after the anti-war play written here by
R C Sherriff. (Recommended by Mrs J M Aston, R Edmonds, Jane Pountney)

*Free house · Licensee Raymond Hollins · Real ale · Meals and snacks · Children
in room by main bar · Open 11–2.30, 6–11 (12–2.30, 7–10.30 in winter)
Bedrooms tel Bigbury (054 881) 205; £14.65 (£16.65B)/£29.30 (£33.30B)*

SALCOMBE SX7338 Map 1

Ferry

Inn signed down steps off Fore Street, by access to Portlemouth Ferry; park, if
there's room, in the public car park at the bottom of the street (by the old
water supply with its warning *Whoever is found cleaning fish or creating any
other nuisance at this watering place will be prosecuted according to law*), and
walk up

Bars on three levels follow the steep slope of the shore, and all look
out over the hill-sheltered anchorage. Our favourite bar is the middle
one, with a handsomely carved serving counter, a model three-
master, brass propeller and engine-room telegraph, long varnished
seat in the big picture window, cushioned varnished settles, small
dark casks serving as stools, black beams supporting creaking white
ceiling planks, and varnished panelling. Bar food is virtually all
home-made, using local ingredients. It includes sandwiches (from
75p, fresh crab £1.75), vegetarian or beef with Stilton pasties (90p),
soup (95p), ploughman's (£1.50), Salcombe mackerel smokies
(£1.55), steak sandwich (£2.25) and crab salad (£2.75), with daily
specials such as chilli con carne (£1.75). Well kept Palmers Bridport
and IPA on handpump. The comfortable upper bar has a fruit
machine, and the bottom one has a pool-table, juke box and a fruit
machine; it opens on to a sheltered flagstoned terrace with picnic-
table sets, just above the water. Very busy in summer. (Recommended
by William Meadon, Richard Steel; more reports please)

Palmers · Licensee Robert Holmes · Real ale · Open 10.30–2.30, 5.30–11

SAMPFORD PEVERELL ST0214 Map 1
Globe

1 mile from M5 junction 27; village signposted from Tiverton turn-off

Very handy for the motorway, this relaxing village pub has been
comfortably refurbished with green plush built-in settles and
wheelback chairs around heavy cast-iron tables on the fitted carpet;
there is a log fire and some stripped stone. Waitresses serve a wide
choice of good value food such as sandwiches (from 55p), soup (75p),
pâté (£1.10), ploughman's (£1.20), a big fry-up (£2), local trout
(£2.75), steaks (from eight-ounce sirloin at £3) and mixed grill
(£4.50), with daily specials (£1.75) and roast Devon beef and
Yorkshire pudding (£2.50) for Sunday lunch. Flowers IPA and
Original on electric pump; piped music (Country and Western on our
visit), sensibly placed darts, juke box and two fruit machines in the
public bar, pool-room with pin-table and two space games; also
dominoes, shove-ha'penny, cribbage, table skittles and a full skittle
alley. There are picnic-table sets in front by the road – very quiet now
the village has been bypassed. (Recommended by K R Harris)

*Whitbreads · Licensees D and A Trevelyan · Real ale · Meals and snacks
Children in eating area and family room · Open 11–2.30, 6–11 all year*

SHEBBEAR SS4409 Map 1
Devil's Stone

New licensees from Cornwall have taken over this friendly village
inn, named after the strange stone which shelters under an ancient
oak tree on the far side of the very quiet village square. The main bar
has cushioned chairs and built-in pews on the partly carpeted slate
floor, and lots of brasses on the walls and on the heavy black
chimney-beam above the wood-burning stove. Well kept Flowers
Original on handpump; darts, dominoes and a fruit machine; a
second darts board, a space game, pool and a juke box in a separate
double room. Besides bar snacks and meals (sorry, no prices yet from
the new owners) there is a separate restaurant. There are seats on the
grass at the side, and another seat in front of this low building –
attractively decorated with tubs, boxes and baskets of flowers. The
bedrooms are comfortable and well-appointed, and the breakfasts are
said by readers to be excellent and copious. (Recommended by
Mrs B Greenwood; more reports please)

*Free house · Licensees Dennis, Sylvia and Rod Botterell · Real ale · Meals and
snacks · Children in dining area · Open 11–2.30, 6–11 all year · Bedrooms tel
Shebbear (040 928) 210; £7.50 (£8.50S)/£15 (£16S)*

SHEEPWASH SS4806 Map 1
Half Moon

This civilised inn is smartly kept, with solid old furniture on the
Turkey carpet, a big log fire in cool weather (with bluish flagstones in
front of it), black beams, and mainly fishing pictures on its neat white
walls. Lunchtime bar snacks include home-made soup (60p), freshly
cut plain or toasted sandwiches such as cheese and pickle (60p) or

toasted home-cooked ham (80p), cheese or pâté ploughman's (£1.75), and salads (£2.25); there is also a separate restaurant. Bass and Courage Best (on handpump) are kept well in a temperature-controlled cellar, and there's a big earthenware keg of Amontillado sherry; darts, and a separate pool-room. The buff-painted inn takes up one whole side of the very colourful village square – blue, pink, white, cream and olive thatched or slate-roofed cottages. The unusually attractive inn sign (a curving salmon neatly interlocking with a crescent moon) hints at the establishment's fishing reputation: it can in fact arrange Torridge salmon or trout fishing for residents and non-residents. *(Recommended by N Lawson, Gordon and Daphne; more reports please)*

Free house · Licensees Benjamin and Charles Inniss · Real ale · Lunchtime snacks · Children in dining area · Open 10.30–2.30, 6–11 all year · Bedrooms tel Black Torrington (040 923) 376; £18B/£36B

SIDFORD   SY1390 Map 1
Blue Ball

A3052 just N of Sidmouth

Popular food in this thatched roadside inn, which has been run by the same family for over 70 years, includes good steaks (eight-ounce rump £4.75, 16-ounce T-bone £6.20), as well as freshly cut sandwiches (from 70p; home-cooked gammon 90p, good value local crab £1), home-made soup (60p), sausages and chips (£1), ploughman's (from £1.40), salads (from £1.75), savoury ham, cheese and egg flan (£2) and home-made steak and kidney pie (£2.40). The friendly lounge bar is partly panelled and has low heavy beams – the pub dates back some 600 years. It's furnished straightforwardly with Windsor chairs and upholstered wall benches around its tables, and on cool days has a big log fire in the stone hearth. John Devenish and Wessex Best, kept well in the temperature-controlled cellar, on handpump from the sensibly long serving counter; a plainer public bar has darts, dominoes and a fruit machine, and there's a family room. Tables on a side terrace look out over a pretty walled front flower garden, and there are more on a bigger lawn at the back where summer barbecues are held. *(More reports please)*

Devenish · Licensee Roger Newton · Real ale · Meals and snacks · Children in side room only · Open 10.30–2.30, 5.30–11 all year · Bedrooms tel Sidmouth (039 55) 4062; £15/£22

nr SIDMOUTH   SY1386 Map 1
Bowd

Junction of B3176 with A3052

After many years the Plowmans have retired from this thatched roadside pub which has been so popular for its wide choice of food. The new owners are running things much as before, with daily specials such as home-made chicken and ham pie (£2.50), émincés of liver in a sherry sauce (£2.75) or shrimp vol-au-vent (£2.80), as well as sandwiches (from 90p, fresh crab £1.30), ploughman's (from

£1.20), basket meals such as chicken (£2.40) or scampi (£2.90), and dishes such as steak and kidney pie (£2.40), salads (from £2.70), chicken forestière (£3.40) and steaks (from £4.90). Waitresses bring the food to tables in the cosy alcoves of the extensive carpeted and flowery-curtained lounge bar, whose heavy oak beams are liberally decorated with brass and copper. It has good window seats in its thick walls, warm winter log fires, and piped music. There is also an upstairs family dining-room. Devenish Wessex Best on handpump, served by neatly uniformed bar staff. Outside, there are two good-sized lawns, one particularly sheltered and attractively planted with shrubs. *(More reports please)*

Devenish · Licensees K L Hathaway and M T Place · Real ale · Meals and snacks · Children in dining-room · Open 11–2.30, 6.30–11

SOURTON   SX5390   Map 1
Highwayman ★ ★

A386 SW of Okehampton; also very well worth the short detour from the A30

This is the best embodiment of sheer fantasy in pub design that we have found anywhere. The owners have taken the twin themes of olde-worldiness and pirate haunts, and injected lots of unrestrained imagination as well as the undoubtedly enormous sum of money that must have been involved in securing meticulously detailed workmanship and first-class materials. The result far outclasses other 'theme pubs' and those places done up to look old-fashioned. We couldn't help gasping with pleased astonishment when we went in – and judging from what we heard from other customers, that's the typical reaction. You go in through a porch like the inside of a nobleman's carriage, to find the main bar a warren of up-and-down alcoves burrowing cavernously through gleaming stripped stonework. Red plush seats are discreetly cut into the higgledy-piggledy walls, and other seats on the flagstones include fantastical pews, a leather porter's chair, Jacobean-style wicker chairs and seats in the quaintly bulging small-paned bow windows. Tables have been converted beautifully from antique spinning wheels, cider presses, little dog carts, blacksmith's bellows and so forth, and in the mysterious lighting it's quite hard to tell the real cat from the stuffed sleepy-looking badgers. Even better is Rita Jones' Locker: a perfect Disneyesque vision of the inside of a galleon, full of elaborately carved woodwork and splendid timber baulks, with red-check tables in the embrasures that might have held cannons. The bar counter is beautifully made from Dartmoor bog oak, and one end rears up in a natural dragon shape. The landlord has if anything even more character than his pub, and his wife almost bubbles over with welcoming charm. Though beers are keg, you can buy local farm cider by the bottle (£1) to take away; on our visit, there was 1930s piped music. By the tables outside, playthings for children echo the style of the inn itself, with little black and white roundabouts like those in a Victorian fairground; there's a good-sized fairy-tale pumpkin house and an old-lady-who-lived-in-the-shoe house. *(Recommended by Gordon and Daphne)*

*Free house · Licensees John and Rita Jones · Meals and snacks · Open 10–2,
6–10.30 · Bedrooms tel Bridestowe (083 786) 243; £9/£20*

SOUTH POOL   SX7740   Map 1

Millbrook

The enterprising can find their way here by water – it's 45 minutes by
hired boat from Salcombe, then just a few moments' stroll from
Southpool Creek. The cosy back bar is extremely welcoming, and
warmly comfortable. There's an easy chair as well as handsome
Windsor chairs, with drawings, watercolours and a chart on the
cream walls, fresh flowers in summer and perhaps a Burmese cat on
the rug in front of the small but efficient coal fire in winter. Summer
bar food consists of excellent value large sandwiches including crab
(£1.50), soup (70p), hot pasties (70p), ploughman's (from £1.75) and
salads such as ham or beef (£2.95); in winter they do hot dishes such
as cottage pie. Well kept Bass on tap, Worthington on handpump and
Hill's cider; helpful and unflappable service. The small public bar,
with colourful cushions on its old-fashioned settle, has darts. You can
sit by the flowers in front of this pretty village house, and there's a
narrow back terrace by a lively little brook. *(Recommended by Lynda
Brown, Dr Nicola Hall, D P Evans)*

*Free house · Licensees Geoffrey and Patricia Gibson · Real ale · Snacks
Children in one bar · Open 10.30–2.30, 6–11 (11–2.30, 6.30–10.30 in
winter)*

SOUTH ZEAL   SX6593   Map 1

Oxenham Arms ★

Village signposted from A30

You can tell from the handsome polished granite entrance and the
stately mullioned windows that this is no ordinary pub, and inside
this comfortable and distinguished old inn there are touches of
grandeur such as antique tables and Stuart fireplaces. The building,
mentioned in Kingsley's *Westward Ho!*, incorporates the remains of a
Norman monastery, and – even more imposing – an awesome
prehistoric standing stone, taller than a man, built in to the wall of
the TV family room behind the bar. But there's a thoroughly warm
and unassuming welcome here, too, and good bar food includes
sandwiches (excellent roast beef 95p), home-made meat and fish
pâtés (£1.40), a generous ploughman's with both Cheddar and
Stilton (£1.50), eggs florentine (£1.95), steak and kidney pie or
carbonnade of beef (£1.95), good prawns provençale (£2.75) and
beef or chicken salad (£2.75). The dish of the day might be mixed
shellfish pot pie or Devonshire squab (pigeon) pie and salmon in
season. The beamed and partly panelled bar has Windsor armchairs
around low oak tables, Everards Tiger, Flowers Original and local
cider on tap, and shove-ha'penny, dominoes and cribbage; there may
be piped music. Outside, stately curved stone monastery steps lead up
to the garden with its spreading sloping lawn. A nice place to stay.
*(Recommended by R G Bentley, P T Young, R and S Bentley, R H Inns and
Stephan Carney)*

*Free house· Licensee James Henry · Real ale · Meals and snacks · Children in
room behind bar · Open 11–2.30, 6–11 all year · Bedrooms tel Okehampton
(0837) 840244; £20 (£25.50B)/£28 (£35.50B)*

STICKLEPATH   SX6494   Map 1

Devonshire Inn

As the A30 bypass is completed, this sixteenth-century thatched
village inn will recover the tranquillity that suits its beamed and
carpeted main bar, which is attractively furnished with Windsor
armchairs around its tables and in front of the big log fire. There's
also a cosy sitting-room with easy chairs, on the way through to the
small restaurant – where readers have found the food excellent
(sorry, no up-to-date price details; nor for the bar food, which does
include sandwiches). The landlord is friendly and welcoming; well
kept Courage Best and Ushers Best on handpump; darts, shove-
ha'penny, dominoes, cribbage, a fruit machine, space game and a
juke box in the separate public bar. Next door is the interesting Finch
Foundry Museum, comprising a mill factory and a forge restored as a
crafts museum using water power from the millstream behind the
inn; the River Taw is just a short walk away. *(Recommended by
C J Winder)*

*Free house · Licensee V F Chell · Real ale · Meals and snacks · Children in
eating area · Occasional live music · Open 10.30–2.30, 6–11 all year
Bedrooms tel Okehampton (0837) 840626; £11.50B/£23B*

STOKENHAM   SX8042   Map 1

Tradesmans Arms

Just off A379 Dartmouth–Kingsbridge

As many tables as possible – sturdy antiques, surrounded by neat
little Windsor chairs – have been worked in to the carpeted bar of this
attractive thatched cottage, with seats more in the style of booths up a
step or two at the back. They're all needed: the food is very popular
for its imaginative good value. It includes a ploughman's (from
£1.40), excellent home-made chicken liver, cheese and avocado,
prawn and salmon pâtés (£1.30–£1.50), carefully chosen fish direct
from Plymouth – sea bass, say, as well as halibut, plaice or lemon sole
– madeira-flavoured roast gammon (£3.25), local rump steak (£4.25)
and a special vindaloo Madras curry on Sunday (£4.25 – they suggest
booking). The cheesecake and apple pie are popular. There is a solid-
fuel stove in the big fireplace, black beams nicely set off by the white
ceiling and walls, red leatherette window seats, and in the entry
passage a couple of old-fashioned settles for the overflow. Well kept
Bass and Ushers Best on handpump, over 100 malt whiskies; maybe
piped classical music. Picnic-table sets outside, flanked by some
carefully chosen shrubs, look across a field to the village church.
(Recommended by TPA, David Stranack)

*Free house · Licensee A L Matthew · Real ale · Meals, tel Kingsbridge (0548)
580313, and snacks · Children in dining-room · Open 11–2.30, 6–11; closed
evenings Mon–Thurs Jan–Mar*

TOPSHAM   SX9688   Map 1

Bridge

2¼ miles from M5 junction 30; Topsham signposted from exit roundabout; in Topsham follow signpost (A376) Exmouth

The most favoured regulars find their way into the little tap-room parlour of this friendly sixteenth-century pub. It's from here that up to 15 well kept real ales are drawn straight from the cask, including local favourites such as Blackawton and Golden Hill Exmoor, besides ones from further away such as Fullers London Pride, Marstons Owd Rodger and Theakstons Old Peculier. One visitor who's been coming for 25 years says that the atmosphere and décor of the rambling little rooms in this ex-maltings haven't changed: the best room is probably the dimly lit and partly panelled lounge, with its curved high-backed settle and other old seats, sonorous grandfather clock, guns and swords as well as country pictures on the walls, mugs hanging from the beams, and small serving hatch. The pasties are excellent.

(Recommended by Greg Parston, Ann Casebeer, P W J Gove, Wayne Rossiter, B G Steele-Perkins, Stephan Carney, R K Whitehead)

Free house · Licensee Mrs Phyllis Chaffers · Real ale · Snacks · Children in room away from servery · Open 12–2, 6–10.30

Passage

2 miles from M5 junction 30: Topsham signposted from exit roundabout; in Topsham, turn right into Follett Road just before centre, then turn left into Ferry Road

This busy waterfront pub has been modernised carefully, so as not to lose its snug old-fashioned feel: electrified oil lamps hanging from big black oak beams in the ochre ceiling, some plank panelling, leatherette pews and bar stools, and windows looking out to the estuary. Good value bar food includes soup (75p), sandwiches (from 85p, crab £1.65, four-ounce steak £1.95), pâté or burger (95p), ploughman's (from £1.10), quiche (£1.45), a half-pint of prawns (£1.85), steak and kidney pie (£1.95), ham and eggs (£2.50), salads (from £2.75), trout (£3.50), langoustines (£3.85), fresh scallops (£4.85), eight-ounce rump steak (£4.99) and Exe salmon (£5.50). You can book tables in the cheerful timber and brick dining area. Well kept Bass, Flowers IPA and Original on handpump; sensibly placed darts and fruit machine in the public bar (crazy-paving flagstones, plank panelling, beams). There are benches and tables in a front courtyard, and more seats on a terrace right by the water, across the quiet lane and beyond the small car park. *(Recommended by Barry Steele-Perkins)*

Heavitree (who no longer brew) · Licensee Robert Evans · Real ale · Meals and snacks; reservations tel Topsham (039 287) 3653 · Open 11–2.30, 5–10.30

Steam Packet

2 miles from M5 junction 30: Topsham signposted from exit roundabout; in Topsham keep on until you reach the sea

The two communicating rooms of this attractively renovated pub are partly panelled, partly stripped stonework or timbered bare brick. There are captain's chairs or small high-backed pews around highly polished treadle sewing tables on the flagstones and scrubbed boards, and sea pictures on the walls. Food includes home-made soup, filled rolls, jacket potato, ploughman's (from £1.25) and quite a range of main dishes (around £2.25–£2.50) and salads; well kept Bass, Flowers Original and Whitbreads on handpump, a fruit machine tucked away at the back. The pub opens on to a boat-builder's quay, and there's a hint of a sea view from its windows. *(Recommended by Andrew McKeand, B G Steele-Perkins; more reports please)*

Free house · Real ale · Meals and snacks · Open 11–2, 5–10.30

TORBRYAN SX8266 Map 1
Old Church House

Most easily reached from A381 Newton Abbot–Totnes via Ipplepen

The range of well kept real ales served in this pretty white thatched pub has gone on swelling, and on a recent sampling comprised (in price order, starting with the cheaper ones) Golden Hill Exmoor, Janners, Cotleigh Tawny, Badger Best, Wadworths 6X, Bates, Summerskills Bigbury, their own Church House, Marstons Pedigree and Merrie Monk, Old Buzzard, Janners Old Original, Gibbs Mew Bishops Tipple, Whistlebelly Vengeance (a new one on us – but with a name like that we didn't dare try it) and Marstons Owd Rodger. Generous helpings of bar food include soup (75p), sandwiches (from 95p, toasted £1.25, steak £1.95), ploughman's (£1.40), curried sausage pie, chicken pie or steak and kidney pie (£2.45), curries (from £2.75), trout (£3.45) and various salads (from £1.95). The bar on your right as you go in has benches built in to Tudor panelling, a red plush cushioned high-backed settle, leather-backed small seats, bare stone walls that may date back some 800 years, and a big log fire in winter. A series of comfortable and discreetly lit lounges leads off, one with a marvellously deep inglenook fireplace with a side bread oven. The separate restaurant serves a wide choice of reasonably priced food (salads from £2.80, seafood platter £4.25, steaks from eight-ounce rump £4.95). There's a hillock of lawn between the pub and the church. *(Recommended by Sue and Len Beattie, R H Inns, Gordon and Daphne)*

Free house · Licensees Christine and Eric Pimm · Real ale · Meals and snacks Children in restaurant and family room · Open 11–2, 5.30–11 all year (opens 7 in winter)

TOTNES SX8060 Map 1
Kingsbridge ★

Leechwell Street; going up the old town's main one-way street, bear left into Leechwell Street approaching the top

New licensees in this old pub have been winning firm friends for their good value food. It includes deliciously filled home-baked rolls (from 70p, local crab £1.20), home-made meat and vegetable soup (85p), filled baked potatoes (from 95p), ploughman's (from £1.30), garlic mushrooms (£1.50), steak and kidney pie, devilled kidneys, lamb in stout or cider-baked pork (£2.50–£2.75), various salads, maybe turkey cooked with water chestnuts (£3) or fresh Dart salmon (£4.50). The small rambling rooms have been attractively refurbished over the last year. By the entrance there's an area with broad stripped plank panelling; then you go through, under low heavy beams in the deep-ochre ceiling, to rooms with bare stone or black and white timbered walls, and comfortable peach plush seats around rustic tables on the dark carpet. There's an elaborately carved bench in one alcove, secret as a confessional, an antique water-pump and log-effect gas fire. Well kept Flowers IPA and Original on handpump; cheerful and welcoming atmosphere. (Recommended by Gordon and Daphne, JH)

Free house · Licensees Richard and Joyce Steward · Real ale · Meals and snacks
Children in area down a couple of steps from bar · Open 11.30–2.30, 5.30–11 all year

TUCKENHAY SX8156 Map 1
Maltsters Arms [illustrated on page 208]

On a rather narrow road along W side of Dart estuary, 4 miles S of Totnes

In the week we went to press the Culverhouses left this pub that they've won so many friends for, with their honest food and friendly atmosphere. However, though we don't yet know what sort of food the new licensees will offer, or whether they'll keep up the tradition of serving four or five well kept real ales, we are keeping the pub in as a main entry on the strength of its marvellous waterside position. Picture windows in the neatly modernised and extended Turkey-carpeted lounge bar give its snug built-in settles and Windsor armchairs a lovely view of the wooded creek below, and tables outside look down on it too. There's a separate family dining-room. (Recommended by Stuart Barker, RK Whitehead; more reports please)

Free house · Meals and snacks · Open 11–2.30, 6–11

UGBOROUGH SX6755 Map 1
Anchor

On B3210; village signposted from Ivybridge (just off A38 E of Plymouth)

The traditional public bar of this friendly and well kept village pub has brown leatherette wall settles and seats around the wooden tables on its polished woodblock floor, a log fire in its stone fireplace, and old oak beams. Well kept Bass and Wadworths 6X are tapped from casks behind the corner serving counter; darts, dominoes, euchre, a fruit machine, and maybe piped music. The comfortable carpeted lounge has Windsor armchairs. Readers praise the food – especially the changing hot dish of the day, say steak and kidney pie (£2). Other food includes sandwiches (toasted bacon and mushroom £1.35), pâté (95p), ploughman's (£1.30), basket meals such as chicken (£1.65) or scampi (£2.25), gammon (£2.60), salads (from £2.75), seafood

---

Soup prices usually include a roll and butter.

platter (£2.75) and steaks (from sirloin at £5). The village is attractive, and unusual for its spacious central square. *(Recommended by A A Worthington, D P Evans)*

Free house · Licensee Mrs Monica Baker · Real ale · Meals and snacks · Open 11–2.30, 5.30–11

WELCOMBE SS2218 Map 1
Old Smithy

Village signposted from A39 S of Hartland; pub signposted left at fork

The pretty, sheltered garden of this thatched country pub has rustic seats and picnic-table sets on several levels – noise is confined mainly to goats, chaffinches and horses' hooves. In cool weather there are log fires at both ends of the open-plan carpeted bar, which has button-back red leatherette banquettes and wheelback chairs around its shinily varnished tables, and little snug windows in the butter-coloured walls. Food includes pasties and burgers (75p), sandwiches (80p), soup (90p), ploughman's or pâté (£1.45), plaice (£2.20) and sirloin steak (£5.75); well kept John Devenish and Wessex Best on handpump; sensibly placed darts, juke box and bustling fruit machine, also shove-ha'penny, dominoes, cribbage; pool in the more simply furnished Forge Bar. The neighbouring building is a crafts pottery. The lane past the pub leads eventually to parking down by Welcombe Mouth – an attractive rocky cove. *(Recommended by Mr and Mrs S Crossingham; more reports please)*

Free house · Licensees Mr and Mrs C E Stanton · Real ale · Meals and snacks Children in Forge Bar (which may not be heated in cold weather) · Open 11–2.30, 6–11 all year · Bedrooms tel Morwenstow (028 883) 305; £12.50B/ £25B

Rising Sun, Lynmouth

WESTLEIGH   SS4628   Map 1

Westleigh Inn

Village and pub signposted from A39 NE of Bideford

Seats on the lawn face the evening sun, with a lovely view over the Torridge estuary and Appledore, not to mention the tight hillside huddle of this village. There are swings and so forth for children out here. Inside the pub is cosy, with modern seats carefully matched to the older chairs and settles on the patterned carpet, a couple of coach horns hanging from the dark joists, and a log fire. Freshly prepared and wholesome simple food includes hot pasties (50p), sandwiches (55p), burgers (75p), a choice of ploughman's (from £1.20), smoked mackerel (£1.40) and curry, fish pie or chilli con carne (£1.50); well kept Ushers Best and Founders on handpump, and mulled wine in cool weather; friendly service. Popular with local people – we noticed the distinguished biographer Leslie Frewin. The separate Cricketers Bar has darts, table skittles, shove-ha'penny, dominoes, cribbage, pool, a fruit machine and a space game. (Recommended by K R Harris)

Ushers · Licensee Kevin Starr · Real ale · Meals and snacks · Children welcome
Open 11–2.30, 6–11 all year

WINKLEIGH   SS6308   Map 1

Kings Arms

Off B3220, in village centre

The flagstoned main bar, with a pleasantly pubby atmosphere, a big log fire in winter and flowers in summer, has a longer section on one side where tables are ranged neatly almost as a series of booths, under fringed red-shaded lamps. The home-made soup (90p) is picked out by most readers as excellent, as are the puddings (95p), which may include an excellent brown bread ice cream. Other home-made bar food includes Scotch eggs (60p), pies, flans and quiches (90p), pâtés and terrines (£1.50), cold meats (£3), with as much salad as you want (80p). Lunchtime daily specials might include savoury meat loaf, liver and bacon or steak and kidney pie (about £3 including soup and coffee). There is a three-course Sunday roast lunch (£5.50 – you must book). Evening main dishes are restricted to the cold buffet and (early evening only) chicken or scampi and chips, but a separate restaurant serves full dinners (Tuesday to Saturday, booking necessary). Ushers Best on handpump, maybe piped music. There are a couple of picnic-table sets under cocktail parasols in a small front courtyard by the village square, sheltered by large shrubs. (Recommended by Mr and Mrs J A Laws, J S Evans, G C Coe, Mr and Mrs A Peace)

Free house · Licensees Dennis Hawkes and Roy Falkner · Meals and snacks (not Mon, no hot dishes after 7.45, limited Sun) · Children in eating area (not Fri or Sat evening) · Serviced holiday flat sleeps four, tel Winkleigh (083 783) 384; £105 a week · Open 10.30–2.30, 6–11 all year; closed Mon (except bank hols), three weeks end Nov, two weeks end Feb

---

Please tell us if the décor, atmosphere, food or drink at a pub is different from our description. We rely on readers' reports to keep us up to date. No stamp needed: The Good Pub Guide, FREEPOST, London SW10 0BR.

WOODBURY SALTERTON   SY0189   Map 1

Digger's Rest ★

3½ miles from M5 junction 30; A3052 towards Sidmouth, village signposted on right about ½ mile after Clyst St Mary; also signposted from B3179 SE of Exeter

Named after a former landlord, this friendly thatched Tudor pub has both a big open fire and an ornate solid-fuel stove in its bar, partly carpeted and partly flagstones. There are heavy black oak beams, plates on the walls, comfortable old-fashioned country chairs and settles around polished antique tables, a grandfather clock, and a dark Jacobean oak screen dividing off a small area used as a family room. Reasonably priced food includes excellent home-made soup, generously garnished sandwiches (95p, fresh crab £1), ploughman's (from £1.50), salads with home-cooked ham, beef, chicken or (£3.55) fresh crab, changing home-made specials such as steak and kidney pie or lasagne (£2.45), seafood vol-au-vent (£2.50) and scampi or seafood platter (£2.95). Well kept Bass, Blackawton and Flowers pulled by ancient and unusual handpumps, and farmhouse cider. Sensibly placed darts in the small public bar (which has stripped brick walls), and an enthusiastically used skittle alley. The terrace garden has views of the countryside. *(Recommended by Mr and Mrs F W Sturch, Greg Parston, Ann Casebeer, D A Lloyd, N G Langdon, R K Whitehead)*

Free house · Licensee Sally Pratt · Real ale · Meals and snacks · Children if quiet in family room · Open 11–2.30, 6–11

WOODLAND   SX7968   Map 1

Rising Sun

Leaving Ashburton on A38 towards Exeter, turn right at Woodland, Denbury signpost; OS Sheet 202 reference 790697

Greek-owned and run, this isolated country pub is well kept and comfortable, with wheelback chairs around wooden tables on the Turkey carpet that sweeps through the open-plan bar. Lots of ancient keys hang from its decidedly rustic beams, there's a good winter log fire, and the walls are either stripped bare or painted without plaster so as to show the texture of the stonework. A busy efficient kitchen serves bar food including sandwiches (from 70p, crab £1.60, hefty French bread open ones from £1.70), filled baked potatoes (from £1.10), ploughman's (from £1.30), basket meals such as chicken (£2.05), and salads (from £2.20); well kept Blackawton and Courage Best and Directors on handpump; juke box, dominoes, and a carpeted verandah, with some seats, has a fruit machine and sitting space game; there may be piped music. The separate restaurant's unusual speciality, which must be booked 24 hours ahead, is meze, a Greek meal of several small dishes; £18 for two people. There are picnic-table sets on a crazy-paved terrace by a lawn under a grove of Monterey cypresses. *(Recommended by Mr and Mrs K Oliver, H Paulinski)*

Free house · Licensees A and S Distras · Real ale · Meals and snacks; reservations tel Ashburton (0364) 52544 · Children in verandah · Country music Thurs · Open 11–2.30, 6–11 all year, with supper licence extension

Lucky Dip

Besides the fully inspected pubs, you might like to try these Lucky Dips recommended and described by readers (if you do, please send us reports):

ASHBURTON [West Street; SX7569], *Exeter*: mainly seventeenth-century, parts much older; bar snacks, dinner at night, Badger, Blackawton and Ushers real ales; friendly, with character *(F A Goodall)*

ASHILL [ST0811], *Ashill Inn*: clean and relaxed village pub with good sun lounge, log fire in carpeted bar, good simple food reasonably priced, well kept Whitbreads and draught cider *(Peter and Rose Flower)*

ASHPRINGTON [SX8156], *Durant Arms*: unpretentious free house, in delightful village; good bar food, warm welcome *(L W Norcott, BB)*;*Watermans Arms*: good food and drink in comfortable lounge or flagstoned front bar with high-backed settles; tables outside by river across lane *(R H G Michelmore, LYM)*

AXMOUTH [SY2591], *Ship*: attractive garden (a sort of convalescent home for owls and other birds from Newbury Wildlife Hospital), Devenish real ales, bar meals, evening buttery bar concentrating on fish *(M Lawrence, LYM)*

BISHOPS TAWTON [SS5630], *Chichester Arms*: nice old pub, very well run, with good food *(J B Earle)*

BLACK DOG [SS8009], *Black Dog*; one room, unusual atmosphere, tales of black magic; for pub location see OS Sheet 191 reference 805098 *(Richard Gibbs)*

BLACKAWTON [SX8050], *Normandy Arms*: welcoming bars, good value interesting food, well kept Blackawton real ale; interesting wartime memorabilia of area; some bedrooms *(Brian and Dill Hughes)*

BRANSCOMBE [SY1988], *Fountainhead*: real old-fashioned free house; lounge was village forge; Badger and Devenish on handpump, cider, snacks *(Anon)*

BRIXHAM [SX9255], *Churston Court*: big manor-house converted into hotel with restaurant, big garden, two or three bars with panelling, plush seating and prints of old coasters; bedrooms; for pub location see OS Sheet 202 reference 904564 *(Sue and Len Beattie)*; [Fore Street] *Globe*: friendly, cosy, good selection of bar snacks, Courage beers, separate restaurant *(Sue and Len Beattie)*; [Drew Street; SX9255] *Old Town Arms*: food includes terrific value dish of the day and children's dishes *(Mrs O Morgan)*

BUCKLAND MONACHORUM [SX4868], *Drakes Manor*: food good in old inn associated with Drake *(D P Evans)*

CHITTLEHAMHOLT [SS6521], *Exeter*: imaginative food in sixteenth-century thatched country inn decorated with bank notes and exotic matchboxes; local ales and cider, comfortable bedrooms *(Robert Mitchell)*

CHUDLEIGH [SX8697], *Coaching Inn*: food good in well run old pub *(D P Evans)*; *Highwaymans Haunt*: food includes excellent carvery service at very reasonable prices in very nice clean thatched pub; good choice of beers *(T C Bowen)*

CHUDLEIGH KNIGHTON [SX8477], *Claycutters Arms*: good value bar food and separate restaurant, good atmosphere, real ale *(Mrs H J C Taylor)*

CLEARBROOK [SX5265], *Skylark*: food and service good, fire in winter *(D P Evans)*

COMBEINTEIGNHEAD [SX9071], *Coombe Cellars*: big holiday pub with lots of activities; included for its river views *(LYM)*

COUNTISBURY [SS7449], *Blue Ball*: quiet and friendly Exmoor-edge pub with good home-made food, all sorts of board games; good walking country *(Elinor Goodman)*

DARTMOUTH [11 The Quay; SX8751], *Royal Castle Hotel*: sixteenth-century hotel with attractive big bars overlooking River Dart, very popular with locals; bedrooms *(Heather Sharland)*; [Smith Street] *Seven Stars*: food in restaurant good; welcoming service, lively public bar *(Anon)*

DAWLISH [SX9676], *Anchor*: food good and competitively priced, delightful atmosphere; quite the nicest pub we've been in for some time *(P and E Nightingale)*; *Castle*: though near resort, frequented mainly by locals; pleasant country pub with small beer garden, children's room *(Wayne Rossiter)*;

Smugglers: popular with summer visitors and locals; smuggling history, very good sea view *(Wayne Rossiter)*

DEVONPORT [6 Cornwall Street; SX4555], *Swan*: biggest choice of well kept beers in Plymouth, getting very popular *(Bob Rendle)*

nr DREWSTEIGNTON [Fingle Bridge; SX7390], *Anglers Rest*: sprucely renovated pub in remote wooded waterside beauty spot, lots of tourist souvenirs, well kept John Smiths and Wadworths 6X, good pub food, restaurant; very busy in summer *(Doug Kennedy, H J B Wilson, Patrick Young, LYM)*

EAST BUDLEIGH [SY0684], *Sir Walter Raleigh*: super welcome; excellent good value food, friendly atmosphere *(B G Steele-Perkins)*

EAST PRAWLE [SX7836], *Pigs Nose*: friendly atmosphere; well kept Ushers, good choice of hot and cold foods; on village green *(Neil F Doherty)*

EXETER [Topsham Road; SX9292], *Buckerell Lodge*: rather smart hotel, saloon bar has a nice feel to it and is in no way pretentious *(Dr A K Clarke)*; [North Bridge Road] *Crown & Sceptre*: pleasant upstairs bar serves good food; cellar-like atmosphere and piano player in downstairs bar and adjacent room; often crowded weekend evenings *(Alan Franck)*; [Exe Street] *Papermakers Arms*: cosy city pub with cheap pub meals, Whitbreads real ale, darts, juke box, fruit machine, space game; clean and tidy *(Charlie Salt)*; [Main Street] *Turks Head*: Flowers ale well kept, main bar done up to emphasise Dickens connection; tasty beef and ale pie, good value ploughman's; piped music in WCs! *(Mrs J Seller)*

nr EXMOUTH [SY0080], *Knappe Cross House*: food and service excellent, reasonable prices, environment imposing and graceful; grounds overlook Exe estuary *(Ernest Hart-Thomas)*

GOODLEIGH [SS6034], *New Inn*: well kept much modernised village local on edge of Exmoor, good Ushers real ale, generous helpings of food which may include laver *(J B Campbell)*

GREAT TORRINGTON [The Square; SS4919], *Newmarket Hotel*: old inn with welcoming lounge, low-priced food; pictures show licensees' Navy association *(F I Britton)*

HARBERTON [SX7758], *Church House*: ancient pub in attractive steep village – used to have antique furnishings and medieval panelling, but no reports since change of ownership *(LYM)*

HATHERLEIGH [SS5404], *Tally Ho*: reasonably priced good food under friendly new owners *(Mrs R Simons)*

HIGHWEEK [SX8471], *Highweek Inn*: food good in very quiet, clean, exceptionally welcoming pub; terrace *(Len Beattie)*

HOLBETON [SX6150], *Dartmoor Union*: free house with well kept Bass and good food in bar and restaurant; busy but untouristy all year *(Howard Allum)*

HONITON [Ferry Bridges; ST1500] *Palomino Bay*: Bass, Wadworths and other real ales, good choice of bar meals *(G G Strange)*

HOPE COVE [SX6640], *Hope & Anchor*: good value friendly family-run inn with real local atmosphere, very close to attractive cove; simple bedrooms *(RAB, LYM and others)*

HORSEBRIDGE [SX3975], *Royal*: good food well presented in charming and comfortable little fifteenth-century pub next to magnificent bridge; real ales include one brewed on the spot *(J E F Rawlins)*

IDE [High Street; SX8990], *Huntsman*: good food includes double-decker sandwiches, real ale; small garden, nice setting by ford; unusually long pub sign *(Matthew Waterhouse)*

KENN [SX9285], *Ley Arms*: family-owned thatched inn dating from thirteenth century; good cold table, warm and friendly atmosphere, old oak beams *(Colin Watson)*

KINGSBRIDGE [Fore Street; SX7344], *Kings Arms*: oak-beamed inn with comfortable bar, restaurant, four-poster bedrooms, heated indoor swimming pool *(more reports please)*

KINGSKERSWELL [SX8767], *Birds Nest*: free house with restaurant, run by Margaret and Stephen Winter and their family – who ran the Church House at

Holne when it was a popular main entry in the *Guide* (*up-to-date reports please*)

KINGSTEIGNTON [SX8773], *Old Rydon*: food superb and imaginative in friendly family-owned pub with log fires and original roof beams; good beers (*Dr S P K Linter*)

LIFTON [SX3885], *Arundel Arms Hotel*: good cold table, especially ploughman's and home-made pâté; a Best Western hotel (*Mr and Mrs J W Gibson*)

LITTLEHAM [SS4323], *Crealock Arms*: good value food and well kept real ale in friendly and simply renovated farmhouse inn (*F I Britton, Mrs M Allix, BB*)

LITTLEHEMPSTON [SX8162], *Pig and Whistle*: good choice of food such as steak with prawns, Dart salmon and daily specials such as lamb hot-pot; real ales including Wadworths 6X (*G G Strange*)

LUSTLEIGH [SX7881], *Cleave Arms*: good value food in well run and well furnished sixteenth-century pub (*D P Evans*)

nr LUTON [Haldon Moor; SX9076], *Elizabethan*: fine freehouse with bar food on outskirts of National Trust land (*Wayne Rossiter*)

LUTTON [SX5959], *Mountain*: log fires and window seat overlooking Dartmoor foothills in village pub with simple bar food (*LYM*)

LYDFORD [SX5184], *Dartmoor Inn*: very good food – especially Sunday lunch buffet – and cheerful service (*CRB*)

LYNMOUTH [SS7249], *Barque*: friendly smuggling-theme pub with nautical pictures and memorabilia; bar food (*Martyn Quinn*)

LYNTON [North Walk; SS7149], *Lynton Cottage*: food in bar (or served on terrace) excellent value, in beautiful building (more hotel than pub) with breathtaking views (*Mr and Mrs L Armitage*)

MARY TAVY [SX5079], *Mary Tavy*: extremely good atmosphere and home-cooked food (*Mr and Mrs Brabants*)

MODBURY [SX6551], *Exeter*: food good in old pub (*D P Evans*)

MONKTON [*nr* Honiton; ST1803], *Monkton Court Inn*: excellent range of substantial bar snacks and meals, good atmosphere, good value bedrooms (*Mr and Mrs J W Gibson*)

MORTEHOE [SS4545], *Kingsley*: friendly welcome from helpful staff, open fire, Courage real ale, good home cooking; lovely clifftop village (*MJ*)

MUDDIFORD [SS5638], *Muddiford Inn*: small communicating rooms with nice atmosphere in friendly and attractive old inn; good bar food, Ushers real ale, nice garden for children in pleasant valley (*N Lawson*)

NEWTON ABBOT [Courtney Street; SK8671], *Globe*: excellent bar food served in attractive panelled room, good local beer, comfortable bedrooms (*JH*)

NEWTON TRACEY [SS5226], *Hunters*: delightful ancient village pub with enthusiastic young licensees, good bar food in attractive lounge with nice fireplace, big separate games bar, small garden (*F I Britton*)

NORTH TAWTON [SS6601], *Copper Key*: good value omelettes and trout, well kept beer (*W Burton*)

NOSS MAYO [SX5447], *Old Ship*: food good in well placed harbourside pub (*D P Evans*)

PAIGNTON [Blagdon Road; SX8960], *Barton Pines*: wide range of good food, mainly home cooked, in friendly recently refurbished Elizabethan manor in lovely pinewood gardens overlooking Torbay; good choice of well kept beers and wine; live music at weekends, darts, pool, lots of children's facilities (*C B Thornton*)

PARKHAM [SS3821], *Bell*: comfortably refurbished thatched village pub with good freshly cooked food and a choice of real ales (*F I Britton, LYM*)

PLYMOUTH [Torridge Way, Efford; SX4755], *Royal Marine*: popular and roomy estate pub with well kept Courage Heavy and Best (*Bob Rendle*); [50 Eastlake Street; SX4755] *Unity*: fresh and unusual home-cooked food, reasonably priced; good range of beers, well chosen wines, fresh orange juice; good friendly service (*Mrs S A Carroll*)

PLYMPTON [SX5356], *Lyneham*: well kept main road Courage pub with congenial atmosphere, food, children's playground (*A Woods*)

POSTBRIDGE [SX6579], *East Dart*: cheerful family bar in roadside central

Dartmoor hotel with some 30 miles of fishing; bedrooms *(LYM)*

nr POSTBRIDGE [B3212 1¾ miles NE; SX6579], *Warren House*: quite alone on Dartmoor, open to 3pm, well kept Ushers, traditional furnishings, bar food, fire burning since 1845; friendly welcoming atmosphere *(Martin Quinn, Richard Franck, Peter and Rose Flower, LYM)*

PRIXFORD [SS5436], *New Ring o' Bells*: generous helpings of food including excellent Sunday lunches; nice setting in small country village with a gentle sweep to the pub *(Flt Lt A D Harkness)*

RACKENFORD [SS8518], *Stag*: ancient thick-walled pub with friendly atmosphere and good bar food; recently changed hands *(Sara Price, BB; up-to-date reports please)*

SAMPFORD COURTENAY [SS6301], *New Inn*: attractive sixteenth-century building, small cosy bars, good food, well kept Flowers IPA and draught cider, pleasant tables outside; welcoming and cheerfully run *(N Lawson, Prof A N Black)*

SCORRITON [SX7068], *Tradesmans Arms*: small village pub, children's room said to have fine view of the gentle slopes of S Dartmoor *(more reports please)*

SHALDON [Ringmore Road; SX9372], *Shipwrights Arms*: friendly village local with good beer and very moreish crab sandwiches; November 1984 landlord raffled Beaujolais Nouveau on condition winners poured it down the sink! *(S V Bishop, LYM)*

SLAPTON [SX8244], *Tower*: fourteenth-century village inn which has been popular for cosy bars and wide choice of real ales; bedrooms; now under new ownership *(LYM, Mick and Yvonne Mawby; up-to-date reports please)*

STAVERTON [SX7964], *Sea Trout*: comfortably renovated lounge with well kept real ale and good bar food; also restaurant and bedrooms *(G G Strange, BB)*

STOCKLAND [ST2404], *King's Arms*: good atmosphere, amiable and helpful staff, well kept Bass, wide choice of good food; skittle alley, outdoor terrace *(Nigel Clegg)*

TEDBURN ST MARY [SX8193], *Kings Arms*: well kept Whitbreads and other real ales, wide choice of good value bar food, in cosy and friendly traditional old pub with character; outstandingly good WCS *(B G Steele-Perkins, Linda and Alex Christison)*

TEIGNMOUTH [SX9463], *Blue Anchor*: used to have lots of budgerigars *(Bob Rendle)*

THURLESTONE [SX6743], *Village Inn*: good food in old inn *(D P Evans)*

TIPTON ST JOHN [SY0991], *Golden Lion*: food in this very attractive pub includes excellent dish of the day, good crab soup and better than average ploughman's *(Mrs Joan Harris)*

TOPSHAM [Fore Street; SX9688], *Globe*: popular seventeenth-century hotel with bar food and restaurant; well kept Bass and Hancocks *(Peter Gove)*; (Shoreside), *Lighter*: spacious and well kept comfortably refurbished pub with red plush seats, efficient food bar and good Badger real ales, by waterside; good choice of board games; bedrooms *(B E Petts, BB)*

TORQUAY [Fore Street, St Marychurch; SX9264], *Snooty Fox*: new family-owned free house, very friendly atmosphere, luxuriously fitted out *(John Allen)*

TORCROSS [SX8241], *Start Bay*: food speciality is fish (often caught by landlord that day), in delightful, thatched sea-front pub several hundred years old; extensive well organised children's facilities *(David Stranack)*

TYTHERLEIGH [ST3103], *Tytherleigh Arms*: attractive reasonably priced bar meals and good restaurant in very friendly pub *(Ian and Julie Taylor)*

WIDECOMBE [SX7176], *Olde Inn*: well run refurbished stone pub in famously beautiful (if commercialised) Dartmoor village *(LYM)*

YELVERTON [SX5267], *Rock*: former hotel now converted to self-catering flats, but bars and kitchens still open: splendid ploughman's and other bar food, Bass and Ushers on handpump, friendly efficient staff, open fire in big comfortable lounge; small locals' bar, games room, family room *(Pat and Malcolm Rudlin)*

Dorset

More than a quarter of the pubs here are new entries this year. These include the Ilchester Arms in Abbotsbury (rambling old-fashioned charm, with a sight of the sea from its back bedrooms), the George at Bridport (a town pub that takes great trouble over even the simplest snacks and drinks – their fresh orange juice is fit for a king), the Barley Mow at Colehill (decent country pubs within striking distance of Bournemouth are always at a premium), the Greyhound in Corfe Castle (a handsome and welcoming pub in a fine position), the Volunteer in Lyme Regis (run by the town crier – a good value, lively pub just up the road from the sea), the Marquis of Lorne at Nettlecombe and the Three Horseshoes at Powerstock (neighbouring villages in lovely remote countryside: both pubs have good food), the New Inn at Stoke Abbott (with a charming garden, in a peaceful village, and popular for its food) and the Square & Compass at Worth Matravers (an unspoilt traditional pub overlooking the sea). Carried over from last year, particularly attractive country or village pubs with good food include the Spyway at Askerswell (a very welcoming place to stay, with plenty of atmosphere), the Royal Oak at Cerne Abbas (with a skilful ex-merchant navy chef–landlord), the Hambro Arms in Milton Abbas (a nice simple place to stay, in a delightful thatched village), the Shave Cross Inn (with a lovely garden, a charming atmosphere, and an excellent ploughman's), the Anchor near Chideock (for good crab sandwiches in a splendid seaside

The Smith's Arms, Godmanstone

setting), the Bottle in Marshwood (simple but good value), the Fox at Corscombe (freshly cooked food in a neat thatched pub by the village stream), the Elm Tree at Langton Herring (often adventurous food, with a good range of changing specials, in very comfortable surroundings), and the Fox at Ansty (a very popular cold table, and remarkable decorations including one of the largest collections of toby jugs in the country). The Winyard's Gap near Chedington is notable for its magnificent view, described in a long poem by Thomas Hardy. Nice places to stay include the friendly Fleur-de-Lys in Cranborne (connections with Rupert Brooke as well as Hardy) and the thatched Castle, quite close to the sea at West Lulworth. The lively and well run Bakers Arms at Lytchett Minster has a remarkable series of collections, with all sorts of things from holograms to working bees. In the last year or two drinks prices in the area have been creeping up towards the national average, but the Three Horseshoes at Powerstock and, particularly, the Spyway at Askerswell are cheap (which cannot be said for the entries near Christchurch and in Kingston, Langton Herring, Lyme Regis and Tarrant Monkton). Dorset pubs are often notable for the way that they have preserved traditional values and an old-fashioned charm. Many of those listed here have a wider range than usual of real pub games, lots have full-scale skittle alleys, and in several the Purbeck longboard – a king-size mahogany shove-ha'penny board often worn to a glassily brilliant polish by decades of play – is still the centre of attraction.

ABBOTSBURY   SY5785   Map 2

Ilchester Arms

B3157

In a lovely golden stone village, this handsome old inn has cosy bars with lots of character, connected by rambling corridors. The main bar has a medley of mainly old seats and chairs, harness and horse brasses hanging from its high beams, and pictures of the swans that since time immemorial have nested in hundreds at the nearby swannery (which is closed for visits during the nesting season). There are swans painted on the serving counter, too, which has handpumps to dispense well kept John Devenish and Wessex Best from under a thatched canopy. The friendly and welcoming staff make sure of a relaxed atmosphere. Bar food includes soup (75p), ploughman's (from £1.30), home-made cottage or steak and kidney pie (£2), plaice or haddock (£2.50), scampi (£2.50), seafood platter (£3) and a daily special (£2.25), and readers have enjoyed restaurant dinners here; maybe piped music. You can see the sea from the windows of the back bedrooms, which are pretty and comfortable, and lanes lead from behind the pub into the countryside – the nearby abbey and its subtropical gardens are well worth visiting. (Recommended by A L Furreddu, Gerald Newman, David Whitelock)

Devenish · Licensee Peter Bowring · Real ale · Meals and snacks · Children in eating area · Open 10.30–2.30, 6–11 all year · Bedrooms tel Dorchester (0305) 871243; £20B/£32B

ANSTY ST7603 Map 2
Fox ★

Village well signposted in the maze of narrow lanes NW of Milton Abbas; pub signposted locally

A star this year for the extensive cold table that readers like so much here: a dozen or more meats that might include game and duck as well as excellent turkey and rare beef, and a wide choice of salads – help yourself to as much as you like (£4.50). There's also a 'potato bar' serving baked potatoes with various fillings (from 90p), soup, ploughman's, smoked mackerel, and so forth, and a charcoal bar serving steaks, kebabs, chops and so on (£4.50). There is a choice of good home-made puddings in generous helpings (£1.10). The high-ceilinged front bar has lots of brightly decorated plates covering its walls, and a fireplace that's like a slate grotto. A more spacious and brightly lit side bar (where the potatoes come from) is decorated with more than 600 toby jugs: in a separate part of this second bar there are darts, shove-ha'penny, dominoes, cribbage, a juke box, fruit machine and space game, and there may be piped music. There is also a candlelit restaurant (the Lair – the décor matches its name). The children's Vixen Bar in a separate side building has a rocking horse as well as bar billiards, space game and other amusements, and the pub also has a full-scale skittle alley and pool table. Badger Best, Hector's and Tanglefoot on handpump. Though the service is efficient, the pub does get packed sometimes, especially at holiday periods – you may be lucky to get a table even arriving at noon. Plenty of room outside, on the grass under the trees. This is excellent walking country, with some fine views; riding can be arranged. They've got an outdoor swimming pool and a sauna. *(Recommended by Mr and Mrs B E Witcher, Pat and Malcolm Rudlin, Mark Stocker, A F and M T Walker, P J White and others)*

Free house · Licensees Peter and Wendy Amey · Real ale · Meals and snacks Children welcome · Open 11–2.30, 6.30–11 all year · Bedrooms tel Milton Abbas (0258) 880328; £12 (£15B)/£20 (£24B)

ASKERSWELL SY5292 Map 2
Spyway ★ ★

Village signposted N of A35 Bridport–Dorchester; inn signposted locally; OS reference 529933

Readers are as enthusiastic as ever about the continuing good value and good quality of this pub's home-cooked food: generous helpings and prompt lunchtime service in comfortable and friendly surroundings. The food is unpretentious, including sandwiches, a choice of ploughman's (from £1, Stilton £1.10, home-cooked ham

---

Food details, prices, timing and so on refer to bar food, not to a separate restaurant if there is one.

£1.20), three-egg omelettes (£1.20), seafood platter, generous Barnsley chop (£2.75), popular sweet-and-sour duckettes, gammon and egg (£3), and steaks (from £4.10 for eight-ounce rump); there are good puddings such as blackcurrant cheesecake. Well kept Ushers PA and Best and Poole Dolphin Best on handpump; darts, shove-ha'penny, table skittles, dominoes and cribbage. One of the small carpeted bars has old-fashioned high-backed settles, a grandfather clock, and old printed notices and local bills on its ochre walls; another has cushioned seats built in to its walls, a nice window seat and ceiling beams, with harness and a milkmaid's yoke for decoration. There's also a comfortable family room, with pine furnishings. The bedrooms are good value. The quiet and neatly kept garden, with a small duck pool and pets' corner, looks across to Askerswell Down (the story is that this used to be a smugglers' lookout), and the lane past the pub opens on to many paths and bridleways (not to mention badger tracks), and leads on up to Eggardon Hill, which has splendid views. *(Recommended by Mr and Mrs F W Sturch, Richard Cole, Mr and Mrs Rudlin, Peter and Rose Flower, John Dimmock, R D Jolliff, Sue White, Tim Kinning, A J Milman, Gordon and Daphne, Mr and Mrs W Gregory, Elena Rawlins, Mr and Mrs P G Bardswell, Mr and Mrs B E Witcher)*

Free house · Licensees Don and Jackie Roderick · Real ale · Meals and snacks Children in family room · Open 10–2, 6–11 all year · Bedrooms tel Powerstock (030 885) 250; £22 (£24B)

BRIDPORT SY4692 Map 1

George

South Street

This friendly old-fashioned town local does a marvellous orange juice – a big glass of fresh crushed orange, with a slight added tang of fresh limes, for little more than the price of a half of bitter. Bar food is good value, too, and you can watch them preparing it: home-made soup (70p), sandwiches (from 75p, toasted bacon and mushroom £1.20), quiche (80p), crudités, pâté or croque monsieur (£1.30), a choice of omelettes (£1.40), kipper (£1.75), home-made shepherd's pie (£2), sauté kidneys (£2.50), Finnan haddock (£4) or entrecôte steak (£4.75). Seats upholstered in knobby green cloth are built against the walls, which are papered in green and gold; there are also country seats and wheelback chairs around the sturdy wooden tables on the flowery carpet, with more tables through in the dining-room. Well kept Palmers Bridport and IPA on handpump; a log fire in winter; an ancient pre-fruit machine ball game; maybe piped music. *(Recommended by Nigel Clegg, J W L Ludeman)*

Palmers · Licensee John Mander · Real ale · Meals and snacks (not Sun lunchtime) · Children in dining-room · Open 10–2.30, 6–11 all year; also open for Continental breakfast 8.30–11.30; closed evening 25 Dec · Bedrooms tel Bridport (0308) 23187; £12.50/£25

In next year's edition we hope to pick out pubs that are specially nice to stay at, alongside the star ratings. Please tell us if you think any pub – in the *Guide* or not – deserves a 'Stay Award'. No stamp needed: *The Good Pub Guide*, FREEPOST, London SW10 0BR.

CERNE ABBAS ST6601 Map 2

New Inn

Though called new, this well kept inn must date back at least 300 years: the comfortable L-shaped lounge bar has oak beams in its high ceiling, and seats in mullioned windows overlooking the main street of this attractive village. Bar food brought to your table includes sandwiches (80p for cheese), quite a few starters (from 70p), ploughman's, a wide choice of salads from the buffet bar, pizzas, fish, daily specials, puddings (from 70p), and steaks including steak chasseur (£6.25) – unfortunately we can't give more precise prices as the pub tells us its menus are too expensively printed for it to send us one. Well kept Huntsman Dorchester, Dorset and Royal Oak on handpump; there may be piped music. There is a sheltered back lawn past the old coachyard (which still has its pump and mounting block); a good track leads up on to the hills above the village, where the prehistoric (and rather rude) Cerne Giant is cut into the chalk. The bedrooms are comfortable. (Recommended by J B Lawrence, D A Angless)

Huntsman · Licensees Brian and Maria Chatham · Real ale · Meals and snacks Children in eating area and family room · Open 11–2.30, 6–11 all year Bedrooms tel Cerne Abbas (030 03) 274; £14.37/£28.75

Royal Oak ★

Long Street

New to last year's Guide, this sturdy and welcoming Tudor inn earns a star rating this year for the unvarying quality of its atmosphere and home-cooked food – several readers use the word 'delightful'. The food is cooked by the landlord, an ex-merchant seaman, and includes soups, sandwiches including chopped steak and onion, hot sausage or home-cooked beef (80p–£1), ploughman's with Cheddar, Stilton or Austrian smoked cheese (£1.25), pâté with a hot roll and salad, perhaps savoury mince with courgettes, a wide choice of omelettes (£1.80–£2.25), excellent home-made quiche, steak and kidney pie (£2.25), good scampi (£3), gammon (£4.25) and sirloin steak (£5), with daily specials such as excellent turkey curry or chilli con carne (£2.25) and lasagne (£2.75); puddings include gateaux and cheesecake (£1). It's worth booking if you want to be sure of a table, though service is good even at peak times. The bar is made up of three attractive communicating rooms – old oak beams or wood-panelled ceilings, farm tools and old photographs of the village on the partly panelled bare stone walls, good log fires in winter, and flagstones along the long serving counter. Last Christmas, readers really enjoyed the decorations here. John Devenish and Wessex Best on electric pump; maybe discreet piped music. (Recommended by S V Bishop, Prof M A Epstein, Sue White, David Regan, D G T H, B M Atkinson, Ian Cobbold, J E F Rawlins)

Devenish · Licensee B J Holmes · Meals (not Sun lunchtime) and snacks (limited Sun lunchtime) tel Cerne Abbas (030 03) 270 · Open 11–2.30, 6–11 all year

CHEDINGTON   ST4805   Map 2

Winyard's Gap   [*illustrated on page 238*]

A356 Dorchester–Crewkerne

The comfortably furnished and carpeted rooms of this old inn –
Thomas Hardy described the view from here in his long poem *At
Winyard's Gap* – have been knocked through and extended, and
include a dining-room and a spacious skittle alley. Freshly made and
generously served bar food includes sandwiches, soups, chilli or
chicken curry, steak and kidney or chicken and mushroom pie, trout,
braised topside of beef and charcoal-grilled steaks (£5); well kept
Bass, Huntsman Dorset and Dorchester on handpump – and good
value morning coffee. Darts, dominoes, cribbage, fruit machine and
piped music. Seats by the windows have a glorious view from this
National Trust hillside over the little rolling fields far below, as do
old-fashioned seats at tables on a small crazy-paved terrace outside.
There are many more tables across the side lane, on a big stretch of
grass with a climbing-frame and slides. Good paths lead off the lanes
on either side of the main road (beware of too many heavy lorries
squeezing slowly through its steep narrows). (*Recommended by Andrew
Hares; more reports please*)

*Free house · Licensee John Hancock · Real ale · Meals and snacks · Children in
skittle alley and dining-room · Open 10.30–2.30, 6–11 all year (opens 7 in
winter)*

nr CHIDEOCK   SY4292   Map 2

Anchor ★

Seatown; signposted off A35 from Chideock

This is a friendly pub, and its two snug bars have comfortable seats
and neat tables, with some sailing pictures under the low white-
planked ceilings. But what marks it out is its position – quite alone by
a seaside cove and virtually straddling the Dorset Coast Path. Tables
by the small windows, and on the front terraces outside, look across a
brown pebble beach to the sea, and across a stream to seaside sheep
pasture rising by cliffs towards Doghouse Hill and Thorncombe
Beacon. Food includes good crab sandwiches (£1.30), ploughman's
(£1.40), pork and brandy pâté – enough for a full meal (£1.60) –
smoked mackerel (£1.80), plaice or ham and egg (£2.20), crab salad
(£3.70) and (evenings only) seafood platter (£4.20) and eight-ounce
rump steak (£4.95); Palmers Bridport, IPA and Tally Ho on handpump. (*Recommended by J L Matthews and others; more reports please*)

*Palmers · Licensee Arthur Banwell · Real ale · Meals and snacks · Children in
family room · Open 11–2.30, 6–11 all year · Adjacent self-catering cottage*

CHILD OKEFORD   ST8312   Map 2

Union Arms

On lane entering village from A357 Sturminster Newton–Blandford Forum

New licensees have bought the freehold of this unspoilt village pub –
we're glad to say that they plan to leave it quite unchanged, and to tell

you that the pub (which under its previous ownership was one of our favourites) is in good hands. The licensees used to run the Nags Head in Northend (Buckinghamshire), which was recommended as a full entry in previous editions of the *Guide*. The Union Arms is quietly welcoming and beautifully preserved, with high-backed wooden settles huddled snugly around the big open fireplace. Bar food now includes freshly cut sandwiches (70p–90p), home-made soup (75p, winter), ploughman's (£1–£1.20), and home-made cottage pies, casseroles, and so forth. At the moment they are serving Badger Best and Hectors from handpump, but now that the pub is no longer tied to the brewery they may sell other real ales, depending on demand. If you turn right at the road at the top, the walk up Hambledon Hill takes you to fine views (and prehistoric remains). *(Recommended by Steve and Carolyn Harvey, G H Windsor; more reports please)*

Free house · Licensee John Corby · Snacks (not Weds evening) · Parking may be difficult · Open 11–2.30, 6.30–11

nr CHRISTCHURCH SZ1593 Map 2
Fisherman's Haunt

Winkton; on B3347 Ringwood road nearly 3 miles N of Christchurch

Fairy lights outside this extensively modernised hotel reflect something of the atmosphere in its series of interconnected bars, which have piped music, a fruit machine and a couple of space games in one area, fancy wallpaper in another, some copper, brass and plates, and of course the fishing pictures and stuffed fish that you'd expect from the location – kept company in one room by oryx and reindeer heads. Big windows look out on the neat front roadside garden. Bar food includes soup (85p), sandwiches (from £1, toasted £1.25, fresh crab £1.45), ploughman's (from £1.40) and home-made chicken and ham or turkey and ham pie (around £1.65), with fried fish at lunchtime (from £2.40), chicken and chips (£2.30) and scampi or seafood platter (£2.85) in the evening; Bass and Ringwood Best on handpump; the separate restaurant is open throughout the week. You can sit outside this creeper-covered hotel close to weirs on the River Avon – perhaps the nicest place is the back lawn among shrubs, roses and other flowers, with a swing. The bedrooms are comfortable and well equipped. *(Recommended by Miss J P Field, Mark Stocker, F W Weir, A J Milman)*

Free house · Licensee James Bochan · Real ale · Meals (not Sat evening or Sun lunchtime) and snacks · Children in eating area and restaurant · Open 10–2.30, 6–11; closed evening 25 Dec · Bedrooms tel Christchurch (0202) 484071; £15 (£17.50B)/£29 (£32B)

CHURCH KNOWLE SY9481 Map 2
ISLE OF PURBECK
New Inn

One of the area's smarter pubs, this has comfortable button-back red leather seats and Windsor chairs on its parquet floor, unusually high raftered ceilings, and stripped stone walls decorated with miniature gipsy caravans alongside urns and china. Popular bar food includes home-made soup (70p), sandwiches and Danish open sandwiches (90p, fresh local crab £1.30), a wide choice of ploughman's (from £1.30 to £4.75 for king prawns), salads (from £2.60), and hot dishes such as chicken (£1.90) and scampi (£2.70), and several daily specials. They serve breakfasts from 8.30 to 11 and sell picnics to take away. The separate restaurant (the Purbeck Nugget; telephone Corfe Castle (0929) 480357) rather concentrates on fish (around £5 for a main course). Devenish and Wessex Best are kept under light blanket pressure, and they hope to stock real ales soon. Darts, shove-ha'penny, alley skittles, cribbage, fruit machine, space game and juke box. (Recommended by David Sarjant, Sue White, Tim Kinning, G G Strange)

Devenish · Licensee I H Williams · Meals and snacks · Children in eating area, restaurant and children's bar · Open 10.30–2.30, 6–11 (7–10.30 in winter)

COLEHILL   SU0201 Map 2
Barley Mow

Village signposted from A31 E of Wimborne Minster, and also from Wimborne Minster itself; in village take Colehill Lane opposite big church among pine trees; OS Sheet 195 reference 032024

One of the better country pubs within easy reach of Bournemouth, this does get so busy at weekends that you have to be prepared for a wait for service. The main bar is comfortably carpeted and furnished, with old beams, some nicely moulded oak panelling and, in winter, a fire in the huge brick fireplace. There are tables among the tubs of flowers in front of this thatched house, and on the back grass (sheltered by oak trees). Bar food includes soup, sandwiches, filled baked potatoes, ploughman's, home-made cottage pie, steak and kidney pie or faggots, and salads; Badger Best, Hectors and Tanglefoot on handpump; darts, fruit machine, maybe piped music. (Recommended by W H B Murdoch)

Badger · Licensee David John Parker · Real ale · Snacks · Children in eating area · Open 11–2.30, 6–11

CORFE CASTLE   SY9681 Map 2
ISLE OF PURBECK
Fox

West Street, off A351; from town centre, follow dead-end Car Park sign behind church

For centuries the Company of Marblers and Stone-Cutters has met here on Shrove Tuesday (when the pub cooks special savoury pancakes) to present the Lord of the Manor with a pound of peppercorns, and, more important, to show that they can run across the road without spilling their brimming pints. It is the unspoilt character and interesting traditions which make readers like this old tavern, which has been in the same family for some 50 years. It's so small that the front bar, lit by one old-fashioned lamp, scarcely has

---

Bedroom prices normally include full English breakfast, VAT and any inclusive service charge that we know of.

room for its single heavy oak table and the cushioned wall benches that surround it. Among other pictures above the ochre panelling is a good old engraving of the ruined Castle (which you can see very well from the narrow garden behind the pub). This room's served by a hatch, though in the usual Purbeck style many people just stand in the panelled corridor by the servery to get their Whitbreads Strong Country or Pompey Royal tapped from the cask. A back lounge is more comfortable, though less atmospheric. Bar food includes sandwiches (from 80p, crab £1.10), ploughman's (£1.50 for cheese with an apple to £1.60 for pâté) and salads (from £2.40, crab £3.50); ham or cheese savoury pancakes when available (£2.40) and a seasonal crab quiche (£1.90); there are home-made fruit pies and a bread pudding served with gravy. (Recommended by D A Angless)

Whitbreads · Licensee Annette Brown · Real ale · Meals and snacks (lunchtime) Open 11–2.30, 6–11; closed 25 Dec

Greyhound

A351

Well placed just below the Castle, this old-fashioned place has a charmingly relaxed dignity – a porticoed entrance, then mellowed oak panelling in its snug low-ceilinged bars (which are decorated with old photographs of the town). Good value simple bar food includes large cob rolls (from 60p, fresh Swanage Bay crab or prawns £1), ploughman's (from £1.40), a good choice of filled baked potatoes (from £1.20), steak and kidney pie (£2), home-cooked beef or turkey salad (£2.50), and lots of seafood such as fresh cockles from Poole (£1.20), crab claws or a half-pint of prawns (£2.20), crab salad (£4) and mixed seafood platter (£5). Well kept Whitbreads real ales; darts sensibly placed in the back room. (Recommended by David Sarjant)

Whitbreads · Real ale · Meals and snacks · Open 11–2.30, 6–11

CORSCOMBE   ST5105   Map 2

Fox

One small room of this neat thatched pub has traditional black built-in high-backed settles on its dark flagstones, a big fireplace, and antlers and whips for decoration. A second, similarly old-fashioned room has a high-backed elm settle by the fire, lower ones under the beams, and some china on the white walls, which have been stripped back in one place to show the old stone. Lunchtime food, freshly cooked to order (don't expect instant fast food here), includes Stilton and walnut soup (85p), ploughman's (from £1.40 for local farmhouse Cheddar to £1.75 for home-made pâté), omelettes (from £1.25 for one with fresh garden herbs), beef and Guinness pie (£2.25) and crab and mushroom Mornay (£2.45); they serve locally baked granary bread with all dishes. In the evening they concentrate more on main courses such as mixed grill (£3), trout stuffed with prawns and mushrooms (£3.40) and pork steak with brandy and mushroom sauce (£4). Home-made puddings include treacle tart. They can also cater for vegetarians and people on diets. John Devenish and Huntsman IPA on handpump; darts, dominoes, cribbage. You can sit across the quiet village lane on a lawn by the little stream that just down the road serves an unusual moated farmhouse. *(More reports please)*

Free house · Licensee Stephen Marlow · Real ale · Meals and snacks (not Mon lunchtime) · Open 11.30–2.30, 7–11 all year; closed Mon lunchtime except bank hols

CRANBORNE   SU0513   Map 2
Fleur-de-Lys

B3078 N of Wimborne Minster

During the winter of 1984–5 this friendly and welcoming family-run inn extensively refurbished its seven bedrooms (and they now use cotton sheets). The oak-panelled lounge bar still has the 'fine hoppy ale and red firelight' that Rupert Brooke praised in a poem wryly cataloguing its virtues, though the ale is now Badger Best, Hector's or Tanglefoot well kept on handpump. Food is served at one end of the attractively modernised lounge and includes home-made soup with French bread (85p), ploughman's (Cheddar £1.45, Stilton £1.55), pâté and toast (£1.50), whitebait (£1.80), various salads (from £2.50), home-made steak pie (£2.35), lemon sole (£3.35) and eight-ounce rump steak (£4.95). In the separate restaurant there is an extensive à la carte menu and a three-course fixed price menu (£6.95); it's closed on Saturday nights. There is also a small room off the bar which is useful for families. The simply furnished beamed public bar has darts, shove-ha'penny, dominoes, cribbage, a fruit machine and juke box. There are swings and a slide on the lawn behind the car park. The attractive rolling farmland around the village marks its closeness to the New Forest with occasional ancient oaks and yews. Thomas Hardy stayed in the inn for part of the time that he was writing *Tess of the d'Urbervilles*, and if you fork left past the church you can follow the downland track that Hardy must have visualised Tess taking home to 'Trentridge' (actually Pentridge) after dancing here. *(Recommended by Roy McIsaac, A J Milman, D A Angless and several others)*

Badger · Licensee Charles Hancock · Real ale · Meals and snacks · Children in eating end of lounge and in restaurant · Live guitar and mouth organ Thurs Open 10.30–2.30, 6–11 · Bedrooms tel Cranborne (072 54) 282; £12 (£16B)/£19 (£28B)

EVERSHOT   ST5704   Map 2
Acorn

Village signposted from A37 8 miles S of Yeovil

This friendly village inn, which in winter has a good log fire in its lively flagstoned public bar, is popular with local young people for its sensibly placed darts, pool, shove-ha'penny, table skittles, dominoes, cribbage, pin-table, fruit machine, space game and juke box. There is a fine adjoining skittle alley. Copies of the inn's deeds dating from the seventeenth century are hung on the partly hessian-covered bare

---

Pubs close to motorway junctions are listed at the back of the book.

stone walls in the comfortable lounge bar, which also has a log fire.
Bar food includes a daily home-made soup (90p), sandwiches (80p–
£1.10 for prawn), ploughman's (£1.50 for Cheddar to £2.15 for
home-cooked ham), daily specials such as home-made lasagne, chilli
con carne or prawn crêpes (£2.50), home-made steak and kidney pie
(£2.75), pork spare ribs (£2.95) and steaks (£5.50) with sauces, such
as mushroom. Children's meals are available (99p). The separate
restaurant's full menu can be served in the lounge too; a wide range
of ales includes Bass, Devenish Wessex, Huntsman IPA and Royal
Oak and Wadworths 6X (some are kept under light blanket
pressure); maybe piped music. A nice village to stay in, 600 feet up in
real Hardy country – the inn was the model for Evershead's Sow and
Acorn in *Tess of the d'Urbervilles*. There are good walks here, though
not all local farmers respect rights of way as they should.
(Recommended by BOB; more reports please)

*Free house · Licensees Messrs Baker and Morley · Real ale · Meals and snacks
Children welcome · Open 11.30–2.30, 6–11 all year; opens 7 in winter
Bedrooms tel Evershot (093 583) 228; £9.50 (£13.50S)/£19 (£27S)*

GODMANSTONE SY6697 Map 2
Smith's Arms   *[illustrated on page 226]*
A352 N of Dorchester

This cosy and friendly little one-roomed pub was originally a smithy,
and it has been billed as 'England's smallest inn'. Well kept John
Devenish and Wessex Best tapped from casks behind the bar; darts,
shove-ha'penny, table skittles, dominoes, cribbage and maybe piped
music. Food includes sandwiches, country cottage pie (£1.45),
lasagne bolognese (£1.55), cod and prawn pie (£1.80) and bread
pudding and cream (60p). Pictures of Mandarin, the 1962
Cheltenham Gold Cup winner, and other National Hunt racing
pictures hang above the antique waxed and polished small pews
around its walls, there's one elegant little high-backed settle, and the
high leather bar stools have comfortable backrests. You can sit on a
crazy-paved terrace outside the pretty thatched flint building, or on a
grassy mound by the narrow River Cerne – and from here you can
walk over Cowdon Hill to the River Piddle, one of the rivers the devil
is supposed to have pissed around Dorchester. *(Recommended by
Gordon and Daphne; more reports please)*

*Devenish · Licensee John Foster · Real ale · Meals and snacks · Open 10–2.30,
6–11 all year (opens half-hour later in winter)*

KINGSTON SY9579 Map 2
ISLE OF PURBECK
Scott Arms
B3069

Since last year a new bar has been built (among other refurbishments)
overlooking the garden and fine views of Corfe Castle, the Purbeck
Hills and even distant Poole Harbour. This creeper-clad stone house,

Waterside pubs are listed at the back of the book.

with its family food bar, is furnished with button-back leatherette wall benches below old-fashioned pictures, long tables, and on cool days logs burning in the big stone fireplace. Typically, food might include home-made soup (75p), smoked fish platter or home-cooked ham with salad (£1.90), and steak and kidney pudding (£2.50). Popular puddings include treacle tart, Dorset applecake or upside-down pudding (65p). There are several other varied rooms that include one with melodramatic antique prints, old panelling and stripped stone walls; a snug decorated with scenes from local location filming; and an upstairs pool-room with sensibly placed darts. One is a family room. John Devenish and Wessex Best on handpump, several draught ciders and a row of country wines dispensed from an unusual array of wall taps; shove-ha'penny, cribbage, fruit machine, space game and maybe piped music. *(Recommended by Dave Butler and Leslie Storey, Mrs Rosemary Wilmot, Tim Bracey, Mr and Mrs Walker, Tony Coleman)*

Devenish · Licensee Gerald Lomax · Real ale · Meals and snacks · Children in food bar and family room · Open 10.30–2.30, 6–11.30 all year · Bedrooms tel Corfe Castle (0929) 480270; £10/£20

LANGTON HERRING   SY6182 Map 2
Elm Tree
Village signposted off B3157

The food and the efficient service (now with some help from Mrs Ross's parents, the Plowmans, who used to run the Bowd Inn near Sidmouth) are what draw so many people to this attractive pub with its creeper-hung front terrace and tables set in the pretty little sunken garden (in which one reader found wasps a problem). The reasonably priced menu includes home-made soup of the day (45p), sandwiches and a choice of ploughman's (Cheddar £1.30, Stilton £1.35), various hors d'oeuvre including whitebait (£1.40), egg and prawn mayonnaise (£1.85), Dorset or smoked mackerel pâté (£1.20–£1.25), basket meals (from £1.10, £2 for scampi), platters (from £1.50, £2.50 for silverside of beef) and fish dishes such as king prawns (£3.85) and crispy clam fries (£2.75). The blackboard specials change daily and might include dishes like avocado pear with crab, seafood pancakes or home-made quiche as well as puddings. The two main rooms are smartly furnished, with beams festooned with copper and brass, cushioned window seats, red leatherette stools, Windsor chairs and plenty of tables on the patterned carpet; maybe piped music. There is a central circular modern fireplace in one room, an older inglenook (and some old-fashioned settles) in the other. Devenish Wessex Best on handpump kept under light top pressure, and a good choice of cocktails listed sensibly, with succinct descriptions. A track leads down to the Dorset Coast Path, which here skirts the eight-mile lagoon enclosed by Chesil Beach.
(Recommended by Richard Cole, Mr and Mrs N Hawkins, MHG, Miss J Pratt, A J Holland, S J E Woosnam)

Devenish · Licensee D Ross · Real ale · Meals and snacks · Open 10.30–2.30, 6–11

Pubs in outstandingly attractive surroundings are listed at the back of the book.

DORSET

LANGTON MATRAVERS   SY9978 Map 2
ISLE OF PURBECK
King's Arms
B3069

The traditionally furnished and partly panelled beamed main bar has
a fine fireplace cut from local marble by the masons who gave the pub
its original name, and communicates with a small flagstone-floored
room where the servery dispenses good Whitbreads Strong Country
on handpump. The centre of attraction in this typically friendly
Purbeck local is often the antique longboard – the local type of shove-
ha'penny board, made of deeply polished mahogany and far longer
than usual. Snacks include filled salad rolls (70p) and ploughman's
(£1.20). Pool in a separate room; also sensibly placed darts,
dominoes, cribbage, fruit machine and space game. You can sit
outside behind this white-painted stone village house, which is
decorated with attractive window boxes in summer.

Whitbreads · Licensee Darrell Elford · Real ale · Snacks (lunchtime)
Children's room · Open 10.30–2.30, 6.30–11

LYME REGIS   SY3492 Map 2
Pilot Boat
Bridge Street

The snug front bar has a lively nautical décor, with lobster-pot lamps,
porbeagle sharks' heads, sailors' hat ribands, navy ship and
helicopter photographs and many local pictures. The long and
narrow lounge bar at the back, overlooking the little River Lym, has
an interesting collection of local fossils. The seafood is still very
popular and includes prawn sandwiches (£1.20), fresh crab
sandwiches (£1.40), cod, plaice or delicious fresh dab (£2.80), a daily

Winyard's Gap, Chedington

238

shellfish special such as locally caught scallops au gratin (£2.80), scampi (£2.90), seafood platter (£3.10), crab salad (£3.70), and a seafood special with crab, whole prawns, cockles and mussels (£3.75). Other food includes sandwiches (from 60p), baked potatoes with various fillings (from £1), ploughman's (£1.40), pasty (£1.50), steak and kidney pie (£2.20) and daily dishes such as lasagne (£1.60). Palmers beers under top pressure; darts, dominoes, cribbage, maybe piped music. The Lassie story was probably inspired by the pub's dog which, in the First World War, lay by the body of a sailor from HMS *Formidable* – believed drowned, until the dog's warmth was found to have kept him alive. *(Recommended by E St Leger Moore, Mrs D Jasperson, S J E Woosnam)*

Palmers · Licensee Andrew Nimmo · Meals and snacks · Children in area partly set aside for them · Open 11–2.30, 7–11 all year

Volunteer

Top of Broad Street (A3052 towards Exeter)

In July you may find the ebullient landlord in his town crier's regalia – he's been world champion twice, and at competition time town criers from even Bermuda, Canada and the United States turn up here for a drink. The part-panelled main bar is a cosy place, with a cushioned high-backed settle, cushioned window seats and wheelback chairs around the shiny rustic wooden tables, and dozens of chamber-pots, copper pots, flasks and glass net floats hanging from the low plank ceiling. Good value simple food includes home-made soup (80p), sandwiches (from 95p, local crab £1.50), burgers (£1.40), ploughman's (£1.50), home-made steak and kidney pie or turkey and ham kebab (£2.25), breaded plaice with prawn and mushroom filling (£2.75), salads (from £2.95) and eight-ounce rump steak (£4.95); well kept Hancocks HB tapped from the cask; on our visit, piped Radio 2. *(Recommended by Peter Barnard)*

Bass · Licensee Richard Fox · Real ale · Meals and snacks · Traditional piano Sat evenings, and Weds in summer · Open 10.30–2.30, 6–11

LYTCHETT MINSTER   SY9593   Map 2

Bakers Arms

Dorchester Road

Babycham's Pub of the Year 1984, this is a delight for people with the magpie instinct. There is a good collection of English stamps, watches, cigarette cards, antique Dorset buttons, models, army and police badges, bayonets and horse bits, together with a run of annual statistics on some 60 items from 1900 onwards; also birds' eggs (shown with pictures of the birds), butterflies, and even a glass beehive with working bees. The walls show a complete set of £5, £1 and 10/- English notes and of English silver and copper coins minted since 1837. There are plenty of comfortable seats and tables on the Turkey carpet in the roomy open-plan bar, and video displays indicate when you can collect your order from the efficient food

---

Pubs open all day (alas, all in Scotland) are listed at the back of the book.

counter: basket meals (from £1.75), steak and kidney pie (£3.25), a range of help-yourself salads (£4.25), and a carvery (£4.25–£4.95) in the evenings and all day at weekends. The swarms of customers are served efficiently along the big, curved bar counter. Well kept Flowers Original. There's a fruit machine and a communicating skittle alley, and behind the thatched pub with tables beside it is an adventure playground. *(Recommended by Jamie Allen, Rex Haigh; more reports please)*

Free house (part tied to Whitbreads) · Licensees Tom Porter and Pat Howell Real ale · Meals and snacks · Children in eating area · Open 10.30–2.30, 6–11

MARNHULL   ST7718   Map 2

Crown

B3092, N of Sturminster Newton

This oak-beamed public bar seems like something out of one of Thomas Hardy's novels, and indeed this was 'The Pure Drop' at 'Marlott' in *Tess of the d'Urbervilles*. There are window seats cut into thick stone walls, logs burning in a big stone hearth, and antique settles and elm tables on the unusually large flagstones. A few dining-tables lead off the small and comfortable lounge bar. Bar food includes sandwiches (from 40p, toasted bacon and mushroom 95p, fresh crab or prawn £1), ploughman's (£1.20), a choice of home-cooked pâtés and taramasalata (£1.50), generous omelettes (from £3) and a dish of the day that could be tagliatelle, roast pork or steak and kidney pie (£1.95–£2.10), scampi (£3.30), gammon (£3.80) and rump steak (£5.10). There is a separate restaurant. Badger Best on handpump – appropriately enough, a stuffed badger lurks half way up the stairs to the bedrooms. Darts, fruit machine and a skittle alley. You can sit at picnic-table sets on the lawn (where there's a swing), or by the rose-covered lichened walls of the thatched inn, looking across to the church.

Badger · Licensee Thomas O'Toole · Real ale · Meals and snacks · Children in eating area and restaurant · Open 10–2.30, 6–11 · Bedrooms tel Marnhull (0258) 820224; £12/£24

MARSHWOOD   SY3799   Map 2

Bottle

Set in pretty walking country near Lambert's Castle (a National Trust hill fort), this quaint country pub has a friendly local atmosphere and simple furnishings: cushioned benches, one high-backed settle, an inglenook fireplace with a big log fire in winter, and a bare composition floor. Bar food uses locally produced cheese and ham, and includes sandwiches (from 55p, fresh crab £1.20), home-made soup (65p), home-cooked pasty (60p), ploughman's (£1.25 for local Cheddar to £2.25 for local ham), plus specials at weekends – chicken and mushroom pie, beef casserole in wine, cottage pie, steak and kidney pie (£1.65–£1.85); home-made quiche, veal and ham pie and other salads (£1.40–£2.40), local plaice (£1.95). There is a separate restaurant, and they also sell free-range eggs and other local produce. Well kept Axe Vale Best, Ushers Best and Founders on handpump, and local farmhouse cider; darts (they are keen players here) and a fruit machine in a smaller side room, which also has shove-ha'penny, table skittles, dominoes and cribbage; the skittle alley is used most keenly by the ladies' teams. There is a bench by the smallish car park in front of the thatched white Elizabethan building, and a good big back garden, with beyond it a paddock where tents can be pitched (and caravans parked by members of the Caravan Club). *(Recommended by S J Edwards; more reports please)*

Free house · Licensee Michael Brookes · Real ale · Meals and snacks · Children in eating area and restaurant · Country and western or folk music usually Thurs, occasional morris men · Open 10.30–2.30, 6–11 · Caravan parking tel Hawkchurch (029 77) 254; £2.50 a night

MILTON ABBAS   ST8001   Map 2

Hambro Arms

The lane which winds gently uphill through the village and between the surrounding woods is lined by lawns and cream-coloured thatched cottages – a 1770s exercise in landscape art – and this simple inn, with not-so-simple food, is one of them. A maze of stone corridors opens on to its beamed front lounge bar, with a bow window seat looking down over the village, captain's chairs and round tables on the flowery carpet, a gently ticking wall clock, and in winter an excellent log fire. Food in the bar is home made, changes daily and includes soup (85p), prawn cocktail (£1.75), and good value dishes such as herb sausage, or bubble and squeak, sausage and beans (both £1.50), fish and seafood pie or parson's pork and apple pie (£2.25), lasagne or chilli (£2.50), steak and mushroom pie (£2.75), lamb chops in madeira sauce (£3.25), and sweet-and-sour pork tenderloin (£4.25). During the summer, food is served buffet-style at lunchtimes, and on Sunday there is a special three-course buffet lunch with a choice of six starters and four main courses, including two roasts, and a choice of puddings (£6.50): bookings only. A separate candlelit restaurant is open on Saturday evenings; otherwise this is used as a family room. The breakfasts are said to be magnificent, and the two bedrooms are comfortable (one now has a four-poster bed). Well kept Devenish Wessex Best tapped from casks racked behind the bar; darts, juke box and fruit machine in the cosy back public bar. *(Recommended by Elizabeth Meara, Pat and Malcolm Rudlin, Dr M K Paffard)*

Devenish · Licensee John Dance · Real ale · Meals and snacks (not Sun evening) Open 10.30–2.30, 6–11 (11–2.30, 7–10.30 in winter); closed evenings 25 and 26 Dec · Children in restaurant · Bedrooms tel Milton Abbas (0258) 880233; £13 (£15S)/£20 (£24S)

NETTLECOMBE   SY5195   Map 2

Marquis of Lorne

Close to Powerstock: follow directions under next entry

In a very quiet hamlet on an almost unused back road through peaceful countryside, this small inn has been carefully restored by the young couple who took it over two years ago. They have quickly won a reputation for good value food, such as home-cooked beef or ham sandwiches (85p), home-cooked soup (£1.10), ploughman's (£1.50), smoked salmon mousse (£1.85) and daily specials such as fillets of plaice (£1.85), steak and kidney pie (£2.75), chicken in barbecue sauce (£2.55), scampi (£2.95), fresh lobster salad (£5.95), a wide range of puddings including an excellent raspberry sorbet (£1–£1.20), and a very good Sunday lunch (£5.25). The main bar has a frieze of rosettes won by local prize cattle decorating its varnished panelling, with green plush button-back small settles and round green stools by highly varnished tables on a flowery blue carpet; a similar side room decorated in shades of brown opens off it. Well kept Palmers Bridport and IPA on handpump, on our visit faint piped pop music and a log fire. The big garden has masses of swings, climbing-frames and so forth among the picnic table sets under its apple trees. On winter weekdays bed and breakfast for two in a double room is only £10 if both people have the £8.95 restaurant dinner – and there's a wide choice on the menu. *(Recommended by Gordon and Daphne, Mr and Mrs F W Sturch, B H Pinsent, Iain Maclean)*

Free house · Licensees Bob and Philippa Bone · Real ale · Meals and snacks Open 11–2.30, 6–11 · Bedrooms tel Powerstock (030 885) 236; £12 (£13B)/£24 (£26B)

POWERSTOCK   SY5196   Map 2
Three Horseshoes

Take Askerswell exit off A35 then keep uphill past the Spyway Inn, bearing left all the way around Eggardon Hill – a lovely drive, but roads are steep and narrow; a better road is signposted West Milton off A3066 Beaminster–Bridport, then take Powerstock road

There are charming views from well spaced picnic-table sets on the neat lawn perched steeply above this isolated stone-and-thatch village, and in summer the friendly landlord runs barbecues out here (40p for sausages, £3 for sirloin steak). Bar food (and the separate dining-room) concentrates on fresh local fish, such as grilled sardines in garlic butter (£1.70), a pint of prawns or moules marinière (£2.50), cod in batter (£2.60), grilled plaice or wing of skate poached in a court bouillon (£3.25), scallops in white wine (£4.95) and grilled Dover sole (£6.75); there are also sandwiches (from 70p, fresh crab £1.10), French country soup (75p), a good choice of ploughman's (from £1.60), mixed grill (£5.50), steaks (from £5.60, £7.50 for steak au poivre) and home-made puddings (£1.25). The comfortable L-shaped bar has country-style chairs around the polished tables, and on our visit pictures on the stripped panelling were being sold in aid of the Royal National Lifeboat Institution; well kept Palmers IPA and Coates farm cider on handpump; swings and a climbing-frame outside. *(Recommended by A R Spence, John and Lyn Spencely)*

Palmers · Licensee P W Ferguson · Real ale · Meals and snacks (not Sun evenings Apr to Oct · Children in eating area of bar and separate restaurant Open 10.30–2.30, 6–11 all year · Bedrooms tel Powerstock (030 885) 328; £12.50/£20

Post Office codings confusingly give the impression that some pubs are in Dorset, when they're really in Somerset – which is where we list them.

Ship

Bleke Street; you pass pub on main entrance to town from N

This seventeeth-century pub is friendly and unpretentious, with
traditional seats built in to the snug black-panelled alcove facing the
bar counter (which has a striking old oak staircase climbing up
behind it), and another traditionally furnished and panelled room on
the left. Down on the right a more modern room has pool and darts.
Well kept Badger Best and Tanglefoot on handpump; dominoes,
cribbage, fruit machine and juke box. Bar food includes soup (70p),
sandwiches (from 75p, toasties from 85p), filled baked potatoes (£1),
ploughman's (from £1.20), chicken or haddock (£2.25), Wiltshire
ham (£2.25), eight-ounce fillet steak (£5.95) and home-made
puddings (from 75p, speciality ice-cream in a bottle 95p). There's a
small beer garden outside this handsome stone building. An
innovation this year is that they are letting bedrooms in a bungalow
three minutes' walk away. *(Recommended by Martyn Quinn, S V Bishop,
Gordon and Daphne)*

*Badger · Licensees Bob and Anne May · Real ale · Meals and snacks · Children
in eating area · Open 10.30–2.30, 6.30–11 · Bedrooms tel Shaftesbury
(0747) 3219; £10/£20*

The Ilchester Arms, Symondsbury

SHAVE CROSS SY4198 Map 2
Shave Cross Inn ★

On back lane Bridport–Marshwood, signposted locally; OS Sheet 193 reference 415980

This remote but friendly and civilised country pub has several very strong attractions, besides its beautiful Marshwood Vale position. The flagstoned and timbered bar has one big table in the middle, a smaller one by the window seat, a row of chintz-cushioned Windsor chairs, and an enormous inglenook fireplace with plates hanging from the chimney-breast – a lovely room. The ploughman's is first class: plenty of good cheese and fresh bread, with a generous helping of local butter – no sticky-finger foil wrappings here – and a little fresh salad (95p, remarkably, as they've kept the price at what it was in the very first edition of the *Guide*). Other bar food includes burgers (95p), Dorset pâté (£1.25), sausages made specially for the pub (£1.45), fresh crab salad (£2.95) and in summer fresh lobster salad and local strawberries with clotted cream. Well kept Badger Best, Bass, Devenish Wessex Best and Huntsman Royal Oak on handpump, besides the house special cocktail – a 'Slade', which is an elaborated Martini; darts, dominoes and cribbage. At busier times there's extra seating inside in the carpeted side lounge, which has modern rustic light-coloured seats making booths around the tables, and cottagey touches like the dresser at one end set with plates. Another major plus point is the garden, sheltered by the thatched, partly fourteenth-century pub and its long skittle alley, and prettily planted with lots of flowers; it has a thatched wishing-well and a goldfish pool. (*Recommended by Mr and Mrs F W Sturch, J E F Rawlins, Gordon and Daphne*)

Free house · Licensees Bill and Ruth Slade · Real ale · Snacks (not Mon, except bank hols) · Children in family room · Open 11–2.30, 7–11 all year; closed Mon (except bank hols)

STOKE ABBOTT ST4500 Map 1
New Inn ★

Village signposted from B3162 and B3163 W of Beaminster

The garden has soporific views of sheep grazing on the sides of the valley in which the inn nestles with the rest of this peaceful backwater village. The garden – very well kept, like the inn itself – shelters behind a golden stone wall which merges into an attractively planted rockery; there are swings and long gnarled silvery logs to sit on as well as wooden benches by the tables. Inside, the black-beamed carpeted bar has wheelback chairs and cushioned built-in settles around its simple wooden tables, with one settle built in to a snug stripped-stone alcove beside the big log fireplace. There's a good matchbox collection behind the bar, with old coins framed on the walls. A wide choice of good food includes ploughman's (from £1.50), cheese and onion quiche or home-made pizza (£1.95), home-made curries (from £2.65), home-made steak and kidney pie (£2.75), duck with orange (£5.50), ten- to twelve-ounce rump or sirloin steak (£5.95) and mixed grill (£5.95), though grills are available evenings

only; well kept Palmers Bridport and IPA on handpump; table
skittles; friendly service. On our visit a couple of budgerigars were
twittering a disrespectful accompaniment to the romantic piped
music – they have an enormous choice of tapes. *(Recommended by
John and Lucy Roots, John and Lyn Spencely, Dr A K Clarke)*

*Palmers · Licensee David Livingstone · Real ale · Meals and snacks · Children
in restaurant · Open 11–2.30, 7–11 all year · Bedrooms tel Broadwindsor
(0308) 68333; £10/£20*

SYMONDSBURY   SY4493   Map 2
Ilchester Arms   [illustrated on page 243]

Village signposted from A35 just W of Bridport

The food in this little village pub continues to draw favourable
comments from our readers. The open-plan bar has a high-backed
settle built in to the bar counter next to the big inglenook fireplace
and there are rustic benches and tables, as well as seats in the
mullioned windows. When the cheerful local regulars are there, the
atmosphere is lively and friendly. The menu is extensive and
everything is home made. The food includes soup (75p), ploughman's
(a variety of cheeses, beef or gammon £1.55), pâté (£1.75), quiche
and salad (£1.75), pies such as ham, cider and mushroom, steak and
kidney in ale, and rabbit (£2), vegetarian dishes such as chestnut and
mushroom pie, parsnip and tomato bake and peanut roast (£2),
lasagne, beef curry or goulash (£2.50), scampi, cod or chicken
(£2.60), fish dishes including Bretonne fish flan or Mr Pickwick's fish
pie (£2.45), salads (£3.25), steaks with a brandy, cream and
mushroom sauce (from £5.25), and puddings such as fresh apricots in
Grand Marnier, fresh cherries in cherry brandy sauce, apple and
cinnamon pie and Dorset apple cake (£1). Daily specials might
include pigeon casserole or local whiting (£2.75), venison in red wine
(£3.50) and poached salmon (£6.95). Sandwiches are not listed, but
they will make them for you. Well kept John Devenish and Wessex
Best on handpump; darts, shove-ha'penny, table skittles, dominoes
and cribbage. There is a separate skittle alley with more tables, and
tables outside in a quiet back garden by a stream. The high-hedged
lanes which twist deeply through the sandstone behind this village of
pretty stone houses lead to good walks through the wooded low hills
above the Marshwood Vale. *(Recommended by M A Taylor, David
Whitelock, A J Milman)*

*Devenish · Licensees Bill and Caroline Wiscombe · Real ale · Meals and snacks
Children in eating area and skittle alley · Open 10.30–2.30, 6–11; opens
7 in winter · Bedrooms tel Bridport (0308) 22600; £10/£15*

TARRANT MONKTON   ST9408   Map 2
Langton Arms

Village signposted from A354, then head for church

The cheerful and lively main bar of this pretty thatched pub has
settles built to form a couple of secluded booths around tables at the
carpeted end, window seats and another table or two at the serving

end where the floor's tiled. The food is popular, so to be sure of a table get there early (though one reader who did so and ordered by 7.15 didn't get served until 8.30). There's a choice of mulligatawny, minestrone or lentil and onion soup (50p), corn on the cob (90p), pâté or salmon mousse (£1.20), ploughman's (from £1.25), hot steak sandwich (£1.20), moussaka, shepherd's pie, chilli con carne, chicken and vegetable curry, steak and kidney pudding and fish and mushroom pie (£1.90), and in the evenings grills such as gammon or plaice fillet (£3.50) and rump steak (£4.50), with puddings such as gooseberry fool or pancakes (80p). They also have ethnic evenings – on Tuesdays and Fridays there are home-made pizzas, on Wednesdays a curry, and Thursdays Chinese food. A separate restaurant serves a good value set-price dinner. The public bar, with a big inglenook fireplace, has darts, pool, shove-ha'penny, dominoes, cribbage and a juke box, while a skittle alley with its own bar and more tables has a space game and fruit machine. Well kept Bass and Hancocks HB on handpump or tapped straight from the cask, with Butcombe, Gales BBB and HSB, Hook Norton Best and other guest beers. The pretty garden has a barbecue which is used at lunchtime on Sundays in summer. To get to the pub – by the village church – you drive through a shallow ford, and the surrounding countryside is attractive, with tracks leading up to Crichel Down above the village. Badbury Rings, a hill fort by the B3082 just south of here, is very striking. *(Recommended by Anthony Fernau, Sue White, Tim Kinning, A L Humphrey)*

Free house · Licensees Chris and Diane Goodinge · Real ale · Meals and snacks Children welcome · Open 11.30–2.30, 6–11 · Bedrooms tel Tarrant Hinton (025 889) 225; £7.50/£15

WAREHAM   SY9287 Map 2
Kings Arms
41 North Street; A351, N end of town

Small Windsor chairs are set around modern oak tables in front of an inglenook fireplace, there is a cushioned window seat and an antique high-backed settle in the main bar of this friendly tavern – one of only four thatched houses in Wareham. The old-fashioned flagstoned corridor leads to a back counter serving Whitbreads Strong Country and Pompey Royal, well kept on handpump. A smaller room on the right has copper-topped tables on its carpet. Reasonably priced bar food includes sandwiches (70p–£1 for toasties), soup (60p), jumbo sausage with French bread (90p), ploughman's (from £1.20), pizzas (£1.10), baked potatoes with various fillings (£1.40), quiche (£1.80), fresh trout (£1.80), good steak and kidney pie (£1.85), and scampi (£2.50); dominoes, fruit machine. You can sit out in a back garden. The Tank Museum, nearby at Bovington Camp, is the world's biggest, with over 140 armoured vehicles going back to 1915. *(Recommended by Mrs O Morgan, Tony Coleman; more reports please)*

Whitbreads · Licensee Howard Leatham · Real ale · Meals and snacks (not Fri to Sun evenings) · Children in eating area · Singer every other Fri · Open 10.30–2.30 (Thurs 3.30), 6.30–11 all year

WEST LULWORTH   SY8280   Map 2
Castle

B3070

This attractive little thatched inn is very popular for its quickly served and reasonably priced bar snacks, including generous filled rolls and sandwiches, home-made pies, a wide choice of fish and other hot dishes, and cold meat salads on display at the food counter (there is also a separate candlelit restaurant). Comfortable button-back leatherette seats form a maze of booths around the tables on the polished flagstones in this lively public bar, which has well kept Devenish and Wessex Best on handpump; darts, shove-ha'penny, table skittles, dominoes, cribbage, and a juke box (maybe piped music instead). A smaller lounge bar is more snugly furnished with comfortable blue banquettes under the countryside prints on the walls, and pewter tankards hanging from one beam. During the winter they do speciality weekends like painting, fishing and a rough shoot. There is a large barbecue area in the garden on the lawn above steeply terraced rose beds behind the thatched white house. Best to walk down to Lulworth Cove from here, as the car park at the bottom is expensive; there are lots of fine walks in the area, usually with splendid views. A nice place to stay. (*Recommended by Hugh Calvey, A F and M T Walker, Susie Boulton, D A Angless*)

Devenish · Licensee Graham Halliday · Real ale · Meals and snacks · Children in eating area and restaurant · Occasional live music · Open 11–2.30, 7–11 Bedrooms tel West Lulworth (092 941) 311; £11 (£15B)/£22 (£25B)

WORTH MATRAVERS   SY9777   Map 2
ISLE OF PURBECK
Square & Compass

At fork of both roads signposted to village from B3069

A personal favourite of several readers who write to us regularly, this defiantly traditional pub makes no concessions to stylised comfort – if you go there expecting carpets, plus banquettes, smart microwaved cuisine, fruit machines or piped music you'll be disappointed. People looking instead for unruffled relaxation, regular local customers letting their hair down, and well kept beer in old-fashioned surroundings love it. There are wall benches around the elbow-polished old tables on the flagstones of the main bar, which has interesting local pictures under its low ceilings. Whitbreads Strong Country is tapped from a row of casks behind a couple of hatches in the flagstoned corridor (local fossils back here, and various curios inside the servery), which leads to a more conventional summer bar. Darts, shove-ha'penny, dominoes, cribbage, bar snacks such as pasties, filled rolls and ploughman's. Seats outside the low white building look down over the village rooftops to the sea showing between the East Man and West Man (hills that guard the sea approach); on summer evenings you can watch the sun set beyond Portland Bill. (*Recommended by Pat and Malcolm Rudlin, Dave Butler, Lesley Storey, Steve and Carolyn Harvey, Jon and Ros MacKenzie*)

Whitbreads · Real ale · Snacks · Children in eating area and small children's room · Open 10–3, 6–11 (10–2.30, 6–10.30 in winter)

Lucky Dip

Besides the fully inspected pubs, you might like to try these Lucky Dips recommended and described by readers (if you do, please send us reports):

ALMER [SY9199], *Worlds End*: friendly welcome, Badger ale from the wood, good home-made lunchtime food in thatched pub with old red-brick floor *(Howard Winn)*

BEAMINSTER [ST4701], *Red Lion*: has good bar food, pleasant service *(C Rollo)*

BISHOP'S CAUNDLE [ST6913], *White Hart*: good food (including award-winning ploughman's in variety), skittle alley, children's play area in beer garden; may be very busy *(John and Betty Rhoades-Brown)*

BOURNEMOUTH [Holdenhurst Road; SZ0991], *Gander on the Green*: friendly pub with nice atmosphere and good beer *(Miss D A Ridings)*

BOURTON [ST7430], *White Lion*: friendly staff make you very welcome in attractive village pub with excellent value home-cooked food and welcoming landlord, lovely atmosphere *(Simon Riggall, Mr and Mrs B E Witcher)*

BRANKSOME [Pinewood Road; SZ0590], *Inn in the Park*: food good, real ale very well kept and log fire, warm friendly atmosphere, good children's area *(Michael Pateman)*

BROADMAYNE [SY7286], *Black Dog*: friendly staff and superb choice of reasonably priced good food, with some unusual dishes such as brill with walnuts; well kept Devenish beers *(G Jones, D P Cartwright)*

CATTISTOCK [SY5999], *Fox & Hounds*: friendly and unspoilt village pub *(Cassandra Kent, LYM)*

CHESIL [SY6873], *Cove House*: reasonably priced food and well kept Devenish in old pub on edge of Chesil Beach where main attraction is marvellous sea views; bar decorated with pictures of local shipwrecks *(H Graves, W H B Murdoch)*

CHIDEOCK [SY4292], *Clock*: good value buffet and separate restaurant in simple thatched inn with biggish aquarium in pool-room and public bar; bedrooms *(B R Shiner)*; *George*: food in single bar or dining-room excellent lunchtime and evening, at modest prices; small 300-year-old thatched country pub, pleasant garden, games room; taped music in bar doesn't intrude; children welcome *(R C R B)*

CHRISTCHURCH [Church Street; SZ1593], *Castle*: family-run pub with very good Bass, Ringwood Best, Forty-niner and Old Thumper; good reasonably priced food; on Castle moat, and a Norman wall forms part of the kitchen *(G S Crockett)*; *Olde Starre*: smartly renovated pub with popular lunchtime food, lively young evening crowd *(LYM)*; *Roast Inn*: modern, well furnished pub in pleasant riverside setting, busy but lively; efficient staff; good outside seating by river *(David Sarjant)*

CORFE MULLEN [SY9798], *Coventry Arms*: food and beer good in very welcoming pub with interesting odds and ends; very much a country atmosphere *(Steve and Carolyn Harvey)*

DORCHESTER [High East Street; SY6890], *Kings Arms*: food includes excellent pâté with hot toast, served efficiently and quickly; good cider, Devenish real ales; smart and comfortable old hotel *(John and Lyn Spencely, LYM)*; *Ship*: food good value in nice simple relaxing pub decorated with ship theme *(Martyn Quinn)*

GILLINGHAM [ST8026], *Buffalo*: well done restoration of small back-street pub, lively clientele *(Dr A K Clarke)*

HOLYWELL [ST5904], *Strangways Arms*: food and wine excellent, at reasonable prices, in most friendly and welcoming inn; bedrooms *(Anon)*

LANGTON MATRAVERS [SY9978], *Ship*: robust and friendly locals' pub with Purbeck longboard shove-ha'penny, cheap bedrooms *(LYM)*

LONGHAM [Ringwood Road; SZ0698], *Bridge House*: spotless, well furnished riverside pub, open-air balconies in summer and an island with children's play area; extensive menu including carvery, real ales *(G W Simpson)*

LYME REGIS [Bridport Road; SY3412], *London Inn*: reasonable prices in comfortable pub, good-sized garden with splendid view, children welcome in big games/family room *(Mrs G Palmer); Mariners*: smashing meal: 'gumbo' fish soup, sugared ham, turbot *(Steve King);* [Broad Street] *Royal Lion*: old fashioned many-roomed bar with food, games room, restaurant, bedrooms *(LYM); Village Idiot*: very enjoyable place to finish the evening, enjoying a joke with local customers *(Steve King)*

MANSTON [ST8115], *Plough*: food-orientated pub popular for family lunches, with unusual decorative plasterwork *(LYM)*

MARNHULL [Burton Street; ST7718], *Blackmoor Vale*: friendly and welcoming young licensees, log fires, good bar food, in pleasantly furnished pub (Rollivers at Marlott in *Tess of the d'Urbervilles*) *(Angela Evans)*

MUDEFORD VILLAGE [SZ1892], *Ship in Distress*: genuine village pub; interesting side saloon has varnished woodwork and nautical flavour; good Pompey Royal and Best on handpump *(J E Temple)*

PIMPERNE [ST9009], *Anvil*: excellent food and open fires in beamed and thatched pub; comfortable, very quiet, well equipped bedrooms *(Dr M K Paffard)*

POOLE [Quayside; SZ0190], *Poole Arms*: simple waterfront tavern with splendid green-tiled façade and friendly atmosphere; by Poole Aquarium *(LYM)*

PLUSH [ST7102], *Brace of Pheasants*: charmingly placed thatched pub with home-cooked food, good real ales and whiskies, comfortable character, beamed bars, nice garden, with a welcome for children; previous owner whose food was so popular handed over a couple of years ago – up-to-date reports please *(David Regan, LYM)*

SHAFTESBURY [High Street; ST8622], *Mitre*: small inn with lovely view from cosy lounge bar, generous helpings of food, comfortable bedrooms *(EAM, LYM)*

STURMINSTER NEWTON [ST7814], *Crown*: good pub, well worth a visit *(E Wilson)*

SUTTON POYNTZ [SY7083], *Springhead*: good food in newly refurbished village pub with well kept Devenish on handpump – good example of a food pub *(W H B Murdoch)*

SWANAGE [The Square; SZ0278], *Ship*: central hotel with comfortable and spacious maritime-theme modern bar; well kept real ales, quite near sea; bedrooms *(LYM)*

WAREHAM [South Street; SY9287], *Black Bear*: good value food in bar, also restaurant; small well stocked bar with Huntsman ales, log fire *(K Cooper)*

WEST BEXINGTON [SY5387], *Manor*: food of excellent quality and variety in pleasing cellar bar; bedrooms *(E Howard)*

WEST STAFFORD [SY7289], *Wise Man*: well kept Devenish bitter and Wessex and excellent snacks (especially double-deckers) in cosy bar *(T Drake)*

WEYMOUTH [High Street; SY6778], *Boot*: ancient small-roomed pub with lively young customers and a ghost *(LYM);* [Barrack Road] *Nothe Tavern*: large and lively locals' pub with harbour and sea views from back lawn *(W A Hall, LYM);* [Customhouse Quay] *Ship*: spacious waterfront pub with modern open-plan bar *(LYM)*

WIMBORNE MINSTER [The Square; SZ0199], *Kings Head*: pleasant atmosphere in lounge bar of THF hotel; real ales and lunchtime bar food including very good ploughman's *(David Potter);* [East Street] *Rising Sun*: comfortably refurbished and attractive open-plan pub, Badger beers, pleasant atmosphere; balconied terrace overlooking little River Allen, flowers and weeping willow along bank *(W H B Murdoch, BB)*

WINTON [Ensbury Park; SZ0993], *Ensbury Park*: food good in this very good pub with small bars; darts and football teams *(E Wilson)*

YETMINSTER [ST5910], *White Hart*: traditional comfortable Dorset pub, popular with locals (get there early to get a table!); excellent food in pleasant lounge; separate saloon with darts, pool, and so on; friendly staff *(S W Riggall)*

Durham and Northumberland (including Cleveland and Tyne & Wear)

More than half the pubs we include in this area have been added to the Guide as new entries in the last couple of years. In particular, we have this year made some determined Tyneside forays. People who live there won't need its virtues extolled, but we can report to others that in the evenings even city-centre traffic is surprisingly light in Newcastle, and parking is then easy. So it's well worth penetrating, perhaps to try out some of the Lucky Dips here, and certainly to visit the main entries, all in the centre. These are the Bridge Hotel (a stylish Victorian pub, with fine Tyne views from its terrace and a notable folk club), the Baltic Tavern (an interesting and

The Lord Crewe Arms, Blanchland

successful exercise in brewery-sponsored refurbishment) and the Cooperage (lots of real ales, in one of the city's most ancient buildings). Even Tynesiders might like to be reminded of the useful fact that North Shields pubs are open for half an hour later in the evening than central Newcastle ones. Out here, two exceptional new entries are the Tynemouth Lodge (excellent beer – the owner is a former leading light of the Campaign for Real Ale) and the Wooden Doll (such a nice, unspoilt atmosphere that it goes straight into our star ratings – and it has splendid views down over the harbour, as well as good food and drink). Other good seaside pubs include the Jolly Fisherman at Craster (with excellent cheap crab sandwiches), the marvellously nautical Olde Ship at Seahouses (a nice place to stay, and a wider choice of food this year) and the Ship at Saltburn-by-the-Sea (right on the beach where the fishing boats are hauled up); the Lord Crewe Arms below Bamburgh Castle (a comfortable place to stay) is only a stroll away. This year we recognise the continued great pleasure that readers have had in the Linden Pub at Longhorsley (a splendid newly converted place in the attractive grounds of a country house hotel, with good food, lots of games facilities for children and so forth) by awarding it a star. Good places to stay – and of course just to visit – in attractive countryside include the remarkable Lord Crewe Arms in Blanchland (with a crypt bar going back 700 years), the Rose and Crown in Romaldkirk (a welcoming and traditional Teesdale inn), and the George at Chollerford (a smart hotel with lovely gardens by the upper Tyne); the Bay Horse in West Woodburn has horses to hack by the hour, day or week. Several other pubs are notable for their fine surroundings: the welcoming and pleasantly refurbished High Force Hotel alone in the forests near England's highest waterfall, the Jolly Sailor (with good value food, and a new restaurant this year) on the moors by Moorsholm, the neat thatched Black Bull (with a quoits pitch outside, close to the ruined castle at Etal), the Carts Bog Inn on the moors road south of Langley, and the Blue Bell with its grassy slope running down to the River Tees at Egglescliffe. Drivers on the A1 have a useful choice of food stops between the spacious and relaxed Ridley Arms at Stannington, the stylish Blue Bell at Belford (a comfortable place to stay) and the much simpler Cook and Barker Arms in Newton-on-the-Moor. Other places for food include the Three Tuns in Eggleston (an attractive village), which uses a lot of local produce, Granby at Longframlington, Heart of All England in Hexham, Forge in Ulgham and Fox & Hounds in Cotherstone; the snacks are good value at the Feathers in Hedley on the Hill, though it's the real ale that attracts most customers to this friendly village *pub. Not many more than half the pubs listed here keep real ale – a far lower proportion than usual in England – but in those that do it's generally fairly cheap and well kept.*

BAMBURGH (Northumberland)   NU1835   Map 10
Lord Crewe Arms

The magnificent Norman castle in Bamburgh – still lived in – commands a splendid stretch of coast, with a good beach of tidal sand nearby and plenty of bracing walks. The inn, on the village green, is well placed for all this, and a comfortable place to stay (with colour TV in all bedrooms). Its intriguingly decorated back cocktail bar is an entertaining place for a drink, too – its beams are festooned with swordfish swords, armadillo skins, miners' lamps, lobster pots, fishing nets and lots more, and its bar counter is inlaid with thousands of pre-decimal polished copper coins. There are comfortably upholstered banquettes, Windsor armchairs and the like around cast-iron traditional pub tables, and a winter log fire. The side bar is more modern, with big hunting pictures. Bar food includes toasted sandwiches (65p), the grill-room has, for example, local kippers, and two separate restaurants offer three-course dinners (£8.50). Dominoes, juke box. The castle, which has a splendid collection of arms and armour, is open on summer afternoons, and the Grace Darling Museum commemorates the local heroine of an 1838 shipwreck rescue. *(Recommended by Roy McIsaac, S V Bishop, W T Aird, Patrick Stapley, Richard Gibbs)*

Free house · Licensees Brian and Kathleen Holland · Meals and snacks Children in side bar · Open 11–3, 6–11 · Bedrooms tel Bamburgh (066 84) 243; £18.50/£31 (£36B); hotel closed Nov–Mar, one bar still serving meals then (reduced hours)

BELFORD (Northumberland)   NU1134   Map 10
Blue Bell

Market Place

In an area where there are few really comfortable pubs, this well kept and even luxurious place makes a relaxing escape from the A1 (which bypasses the village): the lounge bar has quality gold-tinted flowery wallpaper, matching fabric for the comfortable seats, thick carpet and Audubon bird prints, and is very neat and clean. Bar food includes soup (55p), sandwiches (70p), omelettes (£1.80), and a few other main dishes such as grilled cod (£1.80) and lamb cutlets or pork chop (£2), with cold meat salad (£2.50) and home-made apple pie (75p); children's helpings on request. In the evenings there is a dish of the day, scampi (£3.50) and steaks (£4.50). Sunday roast lunch (£5.50) in the separate dining-room, which may serve fruit and vegetables from the hotel's attractive and spacious garden – the sort of place children like running around and exploring. Darts, fruit machine. *(Recommended by G L Archer, Ian Clay)*

Vaux (a Swallow hotel) · Licensee Allan Black · Meals and snacks (not Sun lunchtime, maybe not bank hols) · Children in bar lounge · Open 11–3, 6–11 · Bedrooms tel Belford (066 83) 543; £22 (£28B)/£38 (£40B)

BLANCHLAND (Northumberland)   NY9750   Map 10

Lord Crewe Arms ★   [*illustrated on page 250*]

This ancient stone inn was built originally in 1235 as part of the
guest-house of a Premonstratensian monastery. There are remains of
the cloister in the neatly terraced gardens, and one bar is down in a
crypt – simply furnished, with pews against massive stone walls
under a barrel-vaulted ceiling. The Hilyard Bar (once the kitchen,
now a family room with rocking-chairs) has a priest's hole which you
can still see by the great twelfth-century fireplace – not used for fires,
but impressive architecturally. One of the family who owned the
house, the Jacobite Tom Forster, is said to have hid in the priest hole
after escaping from prison in London, on his way to exile in France.
People say that the ghost of his sister Dorothy – who never saw him
again, after arranging his escape – still asks visitors to take a message
to him there. Opening on to the garden, the Derwent Room has old
settles, low beams and sepia photographs on its walls. Good bar food
consists of freshly made sandwiches and cold meats and salads, with
hot dishes such as pies, roasts and casseroles added in cold weather; a
separate restaurant also overlooks the gardens. Vaux Sunderland and
Samson on electric pump; darts, dominoes, cribbage. Service is
friendly, and the comfortable bedrooms have quite a bit of character.
The inn and its matching village – robust enough to resist most
Scottish raiding parties, though it was sacked by them more than
once – is surrounded by grand moorland with the Derwent Reservoir
nearby. (*Recommended by Susan Campbell, L W Thomas, Gordon and
Daphne*)

*Vaux · Licensee Ermes Oretti · Real ale · Meals and snacks (lunchtime)
Children welcome · Open 11–3, 6.30–10.30 · Bedrooms tel Blanchland
(043 475) 251; £30B/£45B*

CHOLLERFORD (Northumberland)   NY9372   Map 10

George

B6318, just W of junction with A6079 N of Hexham

Its beautiful setting, with immaculate gardens running down to the
upper Tyne by a fine eighteenth-century stone bridge, singles out this
luxurious and spacious hotel. There is a pub part: the Fishermans Bar
in the original stone inn has three cosy communicating rooms, with
blue-cloth settles on their Turkey carpet, cream hessian walls, pool-
table, darts, dominoes, juke box and a fruit machine; closed winter
mornings. The cocktail bar in the more modern main hotel block has
a better view over the gardens and river, and has deep brown plush
seats spread well out, with a big mountain painting over the fireplace.
It opens on to a prettily planted terrace with white tables and chairs
under cocktail parasols. Bar food includes sandwiches, soup and a
three-course cold summer buffet (any two courses £3). Residents
have the use of a leisure area with indoor swimming pool, jacuzzi and
so forth, opening on to another sheltered sun terrace. Well placed for
Hadrian's Wall, which crossed the Tyne nearby at Cilurnum Fort and
Chesters: the B road which follows the wall almost from Newcastle

Pubs with outstanding views are listed at the back of the book.

to Carlisle is exceptionally long-legged. *(Recommended by W T Aird, D G Bland)*

Free house · Licensee Anthony Eley · Meals and snacks (lunchtime) · Open 11.30–3, 7–11 all year · Bedrooms tel Humshaugh (043 481) 205; £34B/£50B

COTHERSTONE (Durham)   NZ0119 Map 10

Fox & Hounds

B6277

It's the helpful service and home-cooked food which bring readers to the relaxing L-shaped lounge bar of this neatly kept village pub. They've recently introduced a popular Sunday roast (£3.45), and on other days the food – meals rather than snacks – includes soup (65p), mussel salad (£1.30), home-made pâté (£1.45), deep-fried chicken, or curry (£2.60), scampi (£2.85), steak and kidney pie (£2.95), chicken chasseur (£3.10) and salads such as chicken and ham pie (£2.75), honey-roast ham (£2.80), beef (£3.10) or prawns (£3.20), with home-made fruit pies (90p). In summer they have salmon from Whitby. The comfortable bar has thickly cushioned wall seats in its various alcoves, beams in the ceiling, brasses, a few country pictures on the walls, an open fire in winter and simple wooden chairs around the many neatly ordered tables. The old white-painted stone house looks over a little saucer of village green. *(More reports please)*

Free house · Licensee Peter Cockill · Meals (not Mon) · Children in eating area Self-catering holiday cottage tel Teesdale (0833) 50241 · Open 12–2, 7–10.30; closed Mon (except bank hols)

CRASTER (Northumberland)   NU2620 Map 10

Jolly Fisherman ★

Off B1339 NE of Alnwick

Lovely sea views, superb local crab sandwiches (only 70p), well kept Drybroughs Pentland on handpump, and the welcoming landlady lift this unpretentious local right out of the ordinary. One reader with a good knowledge of pubs in the north-east rates it as the best north of the Tyne. Opposite a kippering shed, it's just above the working harbour, and a big picture window in the airy extension looks down over the short turf to the sea. Other food includes hot pies, pasties, toasted sandwiches and beefburgers (50p), home-made pizzas (60p) and good local salmon sandwiches (85p); darts, shove-ha'penny, dominoes, cribbage, juke box, fruit machine and a space game. From here there is a splendid clifftop walk to Dunstanburgh Castle. *(Recommended by Eileen Broadbent, Ian Clay, Jon Dewhirst, Roy McIsaac, G L Archer, Gordon and Daphne, Eirlys Roberts)*

Drybroughs (Watneys) · Licensee A George · Real ale · Snacks · Children welcome · Open 11–3, 6–11 all year

---

If you have to cancel a reservation for a bedroom or restaurant, please telephone or write to warn them. A small place – and its customers – will suffer if you don't.

DURHAM   NZ2743   Map 10

Dun Cow

Old Elvet; turn off A177 by Royal County Hotel,
away from centre

Good value cheap snacks in this unpretentious local include
sandwiches such as cheese and onion, tomato or pickle, corned beef
and beetroot (both 30p), and ham with cheese (35p–45p), pork or
ham and egg pie, and steak pie with mushy peas (50p). The friendly
and welcoming carpeted back lounge is simply but comfortably
furnished, with an attractively moulded low ceiling; the snug little
front public bar has pictures on its cream-painted vertical panel
boards. Well kept Whitbreads Castle Eden and Trophy on
handpump; shove-ha'penny, dominoes and a fruit machine. This is a
pretty black and white timbered cottage (dwarfed by the surrounding
buildings), just a stroll from the centre of this fine hilltop city – largely
pedestrianised and an easily manageable size, with a number of things
to visit including the cathedral, castle and Gulbenkian eastern art
museum. *(Recommended by Mr and Mrs Michael Parrott, D W Roberts)*

Whitbreads · Licensee Thomas Wilson · Real ale · Snacks · Children welcome
Open 11–3, 5.30–10.30

EGGLESCLIFFE (Cleveland)   NZ4213   Map 10

Blue Bell

663 Yarm Road; A67

This friendly pub is included for its fine position at the top of a goat-
cropped grassy slope giving a commanding view of the broad River
Tees. The big windows of the comfortable and spacious main bar,
and the outside terrace, both make the most of this, and of the
splendid sight of the 1849 railway viaduct, nearly half a mile long
with 43 arches. Bar food includes sandwiches, soup (55p), salads
(from £1.60), burgers (from £1.40), ploughman's (£1.70), home-
made shepherd's or steak and kidney pie (£2) and scampi (£2), with
up to four or five daily specials, and children's dishes such as fish
fingers or bangers and beans (£1, including ice-cream cornet or lolly);
darts, dominoes, fruit machine, maybe piped music. There is also a
separate restaurant. *(More reports please)*

Scottish & Newcastle · Licensees Liam and Susan Sweetman · Meals and
snacks (lunchtime, not Sun) · Children welcome · Open 11–3, 5.30–10.30

EGGLESTON (Durham)   NY9924   Map 10

Three Tuns

Set above a broad village green, this neat stone pub serves generous
helpings of wholesome home-made food such as soup (65p), filled
rolls (70p–80p), cheese or pâté ploughman's (£1.55), cottage pie
(£1.75), giant sausage or beefburger with egg and chips (£1.95 – the
eggs they use are their own free-range ones), scampi (£2.95), duck
(£3.65), eight-ounce sirloin steak (£4.85) and puddings (95p); there is
also a separate restaurant (bookings only). The roomy open-plan

beamed bar has a pleasantly relaxed atmosphere, three old oak settles on its carpet, one with amusingly horrific Gothick carving, as well as Windsor armchairs and the like, and a log fire; dominoes. A newer back buttery bar has big windows for the good country view, shared by the back terrace and garden. The B6282, B6278 and B6279 are fine moorland roads. *(Recommended by C Rollo, J H Tate; more reports please)*

Whitbreads · Licensees James and Christine Dykes · Meals and snacks (not Mon, not Sun evening); restaurant bookings tel Teesdale (0833) 50289 Children in eating area and restaurant · Open 11.30–2.30, 7–10.30; closed Mon (except bank hols) and 25 Dec

ETAL (Northumberland)   NT9339   Map 10
Black Bull
Off B6354, SW from Berwick

There's a quoits pitch in front of this pretty thatched country pub, which is only a stroll through the neat village from a ruined castle on the banks of the River Till – Heatherslow working watermill is not far away. Inside, the friendly and smartly modernised carpeted lounge bar has glossy beams, black Windsor chairs and a good range of bar food including ham or cheese sandwiches (from 50p), sausage and chips (£1), fish (£1.60), scampi (£2.20) and salads such as ham (£2.20) or Tweed salmon (£3.10). Well kept Lorimers Scotch on handpump; darts, dominoes, cribbage, fruit machine, maybe piped music. *(Recommended by F J Bastock; more reports please)*

Vaux · Licensee T Halls · Real ale · Meals and snacks · Children in eating area Open 12–3, 7–11; closed Mon lunchtimes in winter

HEDLEY ON THE HILL (Northumberland)   NZ0859   Map 10
Feathers
Village signposted from New Ridley, which is signposted from B6309 N of Consett; OS Sheet 88 reference 078592

Though there's too little trade on weekday lunchtimes here for them to open at all then, this solid little stone pub pulls in people from all over the place in the evenings and at weekends, so you may find it really buzzing. The atmosphere is easy-going, without any frills, and the furniture is good sturdy country stuff: robust old brown leatherette settles in the beamed and Turkey-carpeted bar, country pictures on the walls (which are partly stripped back to the bare stone), and wood-burning stoves. A side lounge is broadly similar, with a flowery carpet. Apart from the atmosphere, the well kept Matthew Browns and Theakstons Bitter and XB on handpump are what people come here for; bar food includes reasonably priced sandwiches and salad rolls (from 50p, prawn or steak only 65p), home-made pâté and ploughman's; darts, shove-ha'penny, table skittles, dominoes (handicap last Thursday each month), and a space game in the games room. *(Recommended by Jon Dewhirst, Hugh and Jayne Welch)*

Free house · Licensees Marina and Colin Atkinson · Real ale · Snacks (evenings and weekends) · *Children in games room* · *Open 11–3, 6–11; closed weekday lunchtimes*

HEXHAM (Northumberland)   NY9464 Map 10
Heart of All England

5 Market Street; off central market place

The quickly served bar food in this town pub's comfortably modernised lounge bar is good value. It includes stottie-cake sandwiches (60p), various snacks, such as quiche Lorraine, with coleslaw or pickles (75p), and huge helpings of five changing hot dishes such as chicken or beef curry (£1.80), mince with dumplings (£1.80) and home-made steak and kidney pie (£1.90). McEwans 80/– and Youngers Scotch on handpump are well kept and served, and there is a very good range of whiskies. There are red plush seats and banquettes under hunting prints on dark panelled walls; maybe piped pop music. This is an attractive town, and the ancient abbey church has a beautiful Celtic cross, the stone seat which St Wilfrid used 1,300 years ago, and marvellous medieval carvings in the choir stalls. *(Recommended by Jon Dewhirst, Anthony Rota)*

Scottish & Newcastle · *Licensee David Graham* · *Real ale* · *Meals and snacks (not Sun or Mon evenings)* · *Car parks a short walk away* · *Open 11–3, 6–11 all year*

HIGH FORCE (Durham)   NY8728 Map 10
High Force Hotel

B6277 about 4 miles NW of Middleton-in-Teesdale

This remote but warmly welcoming and now very well run hotel is surrounded by pinewoods, and tracks from it lead straight up to the high moors – the pub serves as a mountain rescue post. England's biggest waterfall (which gives the place its name) is within earshot and just a short stroll away on the other side of the road. The snug and cheerful public bar has robustly simple furniture on its woodblock floor, piped music, darts and dominoes, and the other public rooms – including a comfortable hotel lounge – have had some pleasant refurbishments. Quickly served bar food includes sandwiches and toasted sandwiches (from 45p), half a baked potato filled with cheese or ham and onion (60p), soup (65p), ploughman's (£1.50), casserole or curry (£1.60), cold meat salads (£2.50), home-made steak and kidney pie (£2.50, lunchtime only), scampi (£3) and steaks (from £4.75); also a separate restaurant. There's quite a good choice of malt whiskies. *(Recommended by Eileen Broadbent; more reports please)*

Free house · *Licensees Barrie and Lilian Hutchinson* · *Meals and snacks Children welcome at lunchtime, eating areas only at other times* · *Open 11–3, 6–10.30 (opens 7 in winter)* · *Bedrooms tel Teesdale (0833) 22222; £10/£18*

Pubs shown as closing at 11 do so in the summer, but close earlier – normally 10.30 – in winter unless we specify 'all year'. Often, country pubs don't open as early as we say at quiet times of the year.

nr LANGLEY ON TYNE (Northumberland)   NY8361 Map 10

Carts Bog Inn

A686 S of town

People travelling along this lonely moorland road find this friendly pub rewarding for its quickly served bar food such as burgers (from 50p), open sandwiches (from £1), sausage (£1.25), haddock (£1.50), home-made steak and kidney pie (£2) and scampi (£2.50), and for the well kept Tetleys and Theakstons Best on handpump. Its cosy main beamed bar, still used by local people as well as the many summer tourists, has Windsor chairs, upholstered seats built against white walls, copper-topped tables, and a stone fireplace (with good open fires in winter). A separate lounge, with more wall banquettes, has pool, darts, dominoes, cribbage, a fruit machine, space game and a juke box. There are summer barbecues (£1.50), and you can play quoits as well as sit outside, looking out over the dry-stone-walled high sheep pastures. (*Recommended by Philip Rutherford; more reports please*)

Free house · Licensee D J Wright · Real ale · Meals and snacks (not Mon evening) · Children in back lounge · Open 12–2, 7–11

LONGFRAMLINGTON (Northumberland)   NU1301 Map 10

Granby

A697

Expect a mammoth breakfast if you stay in one of the comfortable bedrooms in this clean and tidily modernised small inn. Good bar food includes soup (70p, lunchtime only), garnished sandwiches such as ham, beef, turkey, gammon or steak (£1.50–£1.65), ploughman's (£2.30), cod or plaice (£2.65), home-made steak and kidney pie (£2.65), smoked salmon (£3), salads (from £3.25), roast chicken (£3.85), saddle of lamb (£4.15) and steaks (from £5.15) – there's also a separate restaurant. There are comfortable red leatherette ex-barrel seats and upholstered wall banquettes around the many glass-topped copper tables in the two flowery-carpeted rooms of the black-beamed bar; piped music. You can sit outside in summer. (*Recommended by A J Dobson, G L Archer*)

Bass · Licensee Gilbert Hall · Meals and snacks · Children in restaurant and, if over eight, in lounge (lunchtime only) · Open 11–3, 6–10.30 · Bedrooms tel Longframlington (066 570) 228; £15 (£16.50B)/£30 (£33B)

LONGHORSLEY (Northumberland)   NZ1597 Map 10

Linden Pub ★

Part of Linden Hall Hotel; long drive off A697 full of 'sleeping policemen'

Everything about this smartly restored country-house hotel (of which the pub is just one small part) is very carefully done. The pub building itself is a two-floor conversion of the stone granary behind the main house. Food served from an efficient side counter is consistently good. The menu changes from day to day, but might typically include a couple of soups (75p), sandwiches (£1.25), ploughman's (£2.10), salads with a choice of pâté or four meats (£2.40), and nine or ten hot dishes such as steak and kidney pie, pork chop, sausage with liver and onions, chicken à la king and game pie (mostly £2.95). There are lots of puddings (from 90p). The pub is very clean and well run: airy, comfortable and relaxed, with lots of woodwork and bare stone, light-coloured wooden seats, a log-effect gas fire in a large round central hearth, and a remarkable number of carefully collected enamel advertising signs. It's very popular with families at weekends. Well kept Marstons Pedigree on handpump; darts, pool (both sensibly placed), shove-ha'penny, dominoes, cribbage, piped music. You can sit in the flagstoned yard, where some tables shelter under a Perspex roof, and there are barbecues in good weather. Boules, quoits and garden draughts are played out here, and there is a good outdoor games area in the attractively planted grounds of the hotel as well as the play area by the pub. *(Recommended by Ian Clay, G L Archer)*

Free house · Licensee Alan Blenkinsopp · Real ale · Meals and snacks · Children on first floor · Folk night second Tues of month · Open 11–3, 5.30–10.30 Bedrooms and restaurant in separate hotel tel Morpeth (0670) 56611, telex 538224

MOORSHOLM (Cleveland)   NZ6914 Map 10
Jolly Sailor
A171 nearly a mile E of Moorsholm village turn-off

Since the last edition, the friendly and enthusiastic young owners have added a small new restaurant to this attractive moorland stone-built pub. The old restaurant has been turned into a lounge, adding to the seating space of the beamed main bar – a long cheery room with lots of booths upholstered in a greenish brown flowery print around its heavy black tables, and some heavy-horse harness on the walls. Popular bar food includes home-made vegetable soup (65p), home-made pâté (£1.30), ploughman's (£1.95), Cumberland sausage (£2.20), scampi (£2.85), home-made steak and kidney pie (£3), ham salad (£3.25), gammon and pineapple or eight-ounce burger topped with prawns (£3.50), and sirloin steak (£5.95). The choice for Sunday lunch includes roast goose. Fruit machine, space game and a good juke box. You can sit outside (there are some children's playthings out here); the pub stands quite alone on moorland pasture, with heather and bracken on the rising ground behind. *(Recommended by E R Suckling; more reports please)*

Free house · Licensees Elaine and Andy Ford · Meals and snacks (not Mon lunchtime except bank hols) · Children welcome · Open 11–2.30, 7–11 all year; closed weekday lunchtimes Oct–Feb, Mon lunchtime all year except bank hols

NEWCASTLE UPON TYNE (Tyne & Wear)   NZ2266 Map 10
Baltic Tavern
Broad Chare; just off Quayside E of the bridges; some parking daytime, easy in the evening

The brewery has made an excellent job of converting this old shipping warehouse, in a largely derelict area, into a spacious and comfortable pub: nicely stripped and lit brick walls and pillars make a warren of separate areas, with some bare floorboards, some flagstones, some Turkey carpet, coal-effect gas fire, plush seats, black beam-and-plank ceilings at varying heights and angles, tables like sturdy octagonal rope winches, and big ship construction drawings. Good bar food includes filled baps (from 50p, hot pork 85p, hot beef or mussels in garlic mayonnaise 95p), a generous version of ploughman's served on a wooden platter (£1.50), salads (from £1.50), chilli con carne (£1.75), daily specials such as mince with baked dumplings (£2.25) or steak and kidney pie with black pudding (£2.50), and roast leg of pork (£2.50) and topside of beef (£2.75); well kept Whitbreads Castle Eden and Durham on handpump; sensibly segregated pool-table, darts, good juke box and fruit machines. (Recommended by John Pepper, David Gristwood, Martin Murrish)

Whitbreads · Real ale · Meals and snacks · Open 11–3, 6–10.30

Bridge Hotel

Castle Garth; just by start of High Level Bridge; only a few parking meters nearby, evening parking easy

The imposing Victorian lounge needs its lofty ceiling to fit in the remarkably grand mahogany fireplace – complete with its mirror at just about the right height for a giant to shave in. The bar counter is also a massive piece of craftsmanship, and has unusual pull-down wooden slatted snob screens. The neatly kept room has green plush banquettes and elegant small chairs on its brown carpet, and a decorous clientele. The public bar, interesting for its cheerful turn-of-the-century stained glass, has a good juke box, pool, darts, dominoes, and a fruit machine (there's another in the lounge lobby). Well kept Sam Smiths OB on handpump, either Newcastle Exhibition or Youngers No 3, and a guest beer (Felinfoel on our visit); bar snacks such as toasted sandwiches (50p) and stottie cakes with meat and salad (55p). The folk club here is one of the country's oldest. A few picnic-table sets on the flagstoned back terrace by the remains of the city wall have a fine view down over the Tyne and the bridges (unfortunately a sycamore sapling largely blocks this view from inside the lounge – it badly needs cutting back). (Recommended by John Pepper, David Gristwood, Martin Murrish, Jon Dewhirst)

Free house · Licensee Dave Shipley · Real ale · Snacks · Newcastle Folksong and Ballad Club Thurs · Open 11–3, 6–10.30; closed 25 Dec, 1 Jan

Cooperage

The Close, Quayside; immediately below and just to the W of High Level Bridge; parking across road limited at lunchtime, easy in the evening

One of the city's oldest buildings, this wonky timbered Tudor house (where, as its name implies, casks were indeed once made) creates a fine contrast to the cluster of bridges which stride over it so loftily. Inside tends to be crowded, but service is busily efficient; there are heavy oak beams, exposed stonework, leatherette-cushioned seats and green plush stools around the black tables. Since construction of a new cellar (and – coincidentally, but very useful – closer lavatories than the old ones), there are usually half a dozen real ales (most on handpump, the real blockbusters tapped from the cask). Their favourites tend to be Ansells Bitter and Mild, Arrolls 70/–, Big Lamp Old Genie and ESB (brewed in the city), Drybroughs Pentland, Halls Harvest, Ind Coope Burton, Marstons Pedigree and Owd Rodger, Tetleys and Theakstons Old Peculier. The 'reserve team' includes Adnams, Fullers ESB, Gales HSB, Greene King Abbot, Hartleys XB, Ruddles County, Shepherd Neame Bitter and Invicta, and Theakstons XB, and if there's a demand they will put on any other beer they can get; they keep Coates farm cider. Bar food includes cod chunks (95p), steak sandwich (£1.10), four-ounce charcoal-grilled burgers (from £1.30), scampi (£1.80) and six-ounce charcoal-grilled rump steak (£2.40). Pool-room, with darts, pin-table, also a fruit machine and juke box; upstairs restaurant (three-course Sunday lunch £2.25). *(Recommended by Peter Neate)*

Free house · Licensee Michael Westwell · Real ale · Meals (lunchtime) and snacks · Children in restaurant · Live music Thurs · Open 11–3, 5.30–10.30; closed 25 Dec

NEWTON-ON-THE-MOOR (Northumberland)
NU1605 Map 10
Cook and Barker Arms

Village signposted from A1 Alnwick–Felton

The simple bar food is good value in this well kept and friendly locals' pub – very handy for the A1, yet a world away from its roaring bustle. It consists of a wide choice of rolls and sandwiches (from 55p, toasted 5p extra), burgers (from 55p), home-made soup (60p), and at lunchtime a generous ploughman's (£1.65). The long bar is straightforwardly furnished with green leatherette seats built in to the partly panelled walls and plastic-topped tables; it has a coal fire at each end, and black beams in the high ceiling. Well kept McEwans 80/– and Youngers No 3 on handpump; darts, dominoes, fruit machine, juke box; pool in a separate carpeted room along the corridor. *(Recommended by G L Archer; more reports please)*

Scottish & Newcastle · Licensee Mrs Maureen Williamson · Real ale · Snacks Children welcome (lunchtime only) · Open 11–3, 6–11

NORTH SHIELDS (Tyne & Wear)   NZ3468 Map 10
Tynemouth Lodge

Tynemouth Road (A193); a few minutes' walk from the Tynemouth Metro station

Included for the superb condition of its real ales – readers' reports praise it effusively and unanimously – this small and otherwise unassuming pub has a relaxed, buoyant and masculine atmosphere. There's a coal fire in winter in its neat Victorian tiled fireplace, and copper-topped cast-iron tables and button-back green leatherette seats built against the walls, which are papered in rather an oriental bird-of-paradise design. Bar food includes stottie sandwiches (55p, even for crab and cucumber) and pot meals such as chilli con carne with pitta bread or lamb hot-pot (£1.45). But it's really the ales you'd come here for. The pub's owner used to edit the local Campaign for Real Ale newsletter *Canny Bevvy*. On our visit the ales, in fine fettle, were Belhaven 80/–, Drybroughs Pentland, Greenmantle, Jennings, Marstons Pedigree and Sam Smiths OB, served on handpump; there was also Bland's farm cider. *(Recommended by D G Turner, J Skiner, J Bloxsom and others)*

Free house · Licensee Hugh Price · Real ale · Meals and snacks (lunchtime, not Sun) · Open 11.30–3, 5.30–11

Wooden Doll ★

103 Hudson Street; from Tyne Tunnel, follow A187 into town centre; keep straight ahead (when A187 turns off left) until, approaching the sea, you see pub in Hudson Street on right

The views, good value food, good choice of well kept real ales, but above all the friendly, relaxed atmosphere earn a star for this decidedly unassuming pub in what is perhaps not the most elegant area of Tyneside. It's not been changed much since it was built (in 1794): from the Sitting Room – down a long corridor – big windows look over a meccano landscape of harbour derricks and gantries, the bustling boats and warehouses of the Shields Fish Quay immediately below, and the outer harbour with its long piers, headlands, and low Black Middens rocks. On our visit the panelling-effect walls were decorated with 1870s Tyneside photographs by Edgar Lee (with a glorious use of light and shade), but there may be paintings by local artists instead, for sale. Well kept Matthew Browns Lion Bitter, Mild and John Peel, Newcastle Exhibition, Theakstons Best and XB, and Youngers No 3 on handpump, Old Peculier tapped from the cask, and farm cider; food includes filled rolls, soup (75p), pâté (£1.10), moules marinière (£1.30), hot beef sandwich (£1.50), ploughman's (£1.75), fish pie or chilli con carne (£1.95 – both good), salads (from £1.95, crab £2.20) and, on our visit, a half-dozen oysters (£3.50). Sitting space game, shove-ha'penny, dominoes, cribbage, backgammon, chess and Connect 4 in this simply furnished room (brown and green leatherette chairs, a brown plush long settle, Formica-topped cast-iron tables, coal fire); on our visit, piped soul music; TV and fruit machine in the other bar. *(Recommended by Jon Dewhirst, Neil Doherty, J Skiner, J Bloxsom)*

Free house · Licensee Pat Jones · Real ale · Meals (not Sun lunchtime) and snacks (not Sun) · Children in eating area · Folk music Weds, classical quartet Sun evening · Open 11–3, 6–10.30; closed evening 25 Dec

ROMALDKIRK (Durham)   NY9922 Map 10
Rose and Crown ★

Just off B6277

In some ways – particularly bearing in mind the very good value special winter rates – it may be nicest to stay out of season in this comfortable old coaching-inn facing the green of a lovely Teesdale village. It gets very busy at weekends and in summer, and it's at quieter times that the atmosphere is more in tune with the days when it was the local of Richard Watson the Teesdale poet, and when bedrooms in the main building give a lovely view of the late dawn coming up behind the bare-branched rookery over the green. (There are also comfortable newly converted rooms leading off the back courtyard.) The snug front bar has old-fashioned seats facing its warm fire, lots of gin-traps, some old farm tools and a large chiming clock on its cream walls, and Camerons, Theakstons Best and Old Peculier and Tetleys on handpump; darts, shove-ha'penny, dominoes, maybe piped music. At lunchtime, a larger area has a trestle table with a cauldron of home-made soup, cold ham and good rare beef with help-yourself salads, and puddings (£3.50 including coffee – a nice touch is the 55p reduction for pensioners). Other bar food then includes sandwiches (from 85p), ploughman's (£1.50), trout (£3.95). In the evenings there is soup (80p) and other starters, with main dishes ranging from noodles with bolognese sauce (£2.35) to 10-ounce sirloin steak (£6.50). There is an attractive panelled restaurant. *(Recommended by Jon Dewhirst, C Rollo, J H Tate, Annie Taylor; more reports please)*

Free house · Licensees David and Jill Jackson · Real ale · Meals and snacks Children in eating area · Open 11–3, 6–10.30 · Bedrooms tel Teesdale (0833) 50213; £18.50 (£24B)/£33 (£38B)

SALTBURN-BY-THE-SEA (Cleveland)   NZ6722   Map 10

Ship

A174 towards Whitby

This old pub is included chiefly for its marvellous views out to sea, and, from teak seats on the terrace by a low sea wall, of the spectacular gaunt red Huntscliff along the coast. It stands right on the beach, where inshore fishermen pull their boats up on its small boulders. The original bars have a pleasantly nautical feel: small brick tiles or larger black and red ones on the floor, some ply panelling, big brass lanterns hanging from the black beams, traditional leatherette wall seats and heavy rustic tables in one room, plush stools and seats in the other. An extensive summer overflow dining-lounge is comfortably furnished with wheelback chairs around the dark rustic tables on its red patterned carpet. Good value bar food includes sandwiches, savoury pie (£1.40), lasagne (£1.60), steak and kidney pie (£1.95), chicken supreme or Spanish-style (£2), and salads from ham or turkey (£2) and local crab (£2.70) to fresh salmon (£3); children's dishes such as fish fingers, sausage and chips (90p) or beef (£1.10). The restaurant menu runs from local cod (£1.85) and scampi (£2.70) to 16-ounce T-bone steak (£6.50). Drybroughs Pentland and 80/– from the Scottish style of air pressure tall dispensing fount, kept good and cool even in the warmest weather; darts, dominoes, fruit machine and juke box. *(Recommended by Dr and Mrs R Wright; more reports please)*

Pubs with attractive or unusually big gardens are listed at the back of the book.

Drybroughs · Licensees Bill and Elizabeth Jack · Real ale · Meals and snacks (sandwiches only Sun evening) · Children in eating area, restaurant and children's room · Open 11–3, 6–10.30 (restaurant supper extension to 11.30)

SEAHOUSES (Northumberland)   NU2232   Map 10
Olde Ship ★ ★
B1340 coast road

Readers are increasingly enthusiastic about the good value home cooking and small but comfortable bedrooms of this seaside inn, but what makes it stand out is its nautical atmosphere and superb position. The one clear window of the welcoming saloon bar looks out over the harbour to the Farne Islands (the rest have stained-glass sea pictures). If it's too murky to see the fishing boats coming in, you can watch them on radar (good early warning for the bar staff, too – readers like the way that local people from the harbour still congregate here). The floor is scrubbed ship's decking, and the walls are loaded with more and more finely polished brass and other ship's equipment given up by local mariners, as well as old lifeboat oars, knotted rope fancywork and sea photographs. There is another low beamed snug bar, and a back room with stuffed seabirds; throughout, teak and mahogany woodwork, shiny brass fittings and small rooms give the inn something of the character of a beached ship. This last year, bar food has continued to develop, and now includes home-made soup (60p), more rolls and sandwiches than before (from 60p – local fresh crab at 70p is still the favourite), ploughman's (£1.10), a range of salads (from £1.50) and filled baked potatoes (from 55p). The hotel dining-room now does a summer lunchtime hot and cold buffet (£3–£3.50) and Sunday roast lunch (£3.50), and four-course evening meals (£6.50) in summer. They have added some uncommon bottled beers to their collection of unusual blended whiskies; pool, dominoes, a fruit machine. There are pews around barrel tables in the back courtyard, and a battlemented side terrace with a sun-lounge looks out on the harbour. The boat trip to the Farne Islands is well worth while (you may see seals and puffins), and there's a bracing hour's walk along the coast to Bamburgh Castle. *(Recommended by G F Scott, Roy McIsaac, A J Dobson, Ian Clay, Dr R F Fletcher, M E Lawrence, Gordon and Daphne)*

Free house · Licensees Mr and Mrs Alan Glen · Meals (lunchtime) and snacks (evenings sandwiches only) · Children in sun-lounge · Open 11–3, 6–11 Bedrooms tel Seahouses (0665) 720200; £13.50 (£15B)/£27 (£30B)

STANNINGTON (Northumberland)   NZ2279   Map 10
Ridley Arms
A1; both turn-offs on E side lead to pub – great care needed if you are heading N, especially rejoining A1

The two spacious open-plan serving bars and food bar of this well run pub are a relaxing escape from the A1. Inside has been carefully divided up into cosy areas with plush built-in button-back banquettes and small armchairs on the carpet. There are some biggish coaching prints on the white-painted or stripped stone walls, and a coal-effect gas fire in the central stone chimney. Good ready-filled rolls such as ham with pease pudding (40p), with a choice of wholemeal or white bread, are sold from the drinks counters, which have well kept Whitbreads Castle Eden on handpump. An efficient separate food counter supplies good dishes such as home-made steak pie, liver casserole, Cumberland sausage with black pudding, fresh cooked haddock, scampi, home-made quiche and beef olives (all around £2.25), as well as rump steaks and puddings (90p). There is also a communicating restaurant. Darts, fruit machine, piped music. *(Recommended by G L Archer; more reports please)*

Whitbreads · Licensee Alan Bone · Real ale · Meals and snacks · Children in front lounge eating areas · Open 11–3, 6–10.30; closed 25 Dec

ULGHAM (Northumberland)   NZ2392 Map 10
Forge
B1337

As this edition of the *Guide* went to press the airy and comfortable lounge and the cheery public bar were being refurbished. Since last year the range of bar food has been extended, and includes generously presented sandwiches with a side salad (ham or chicken (£1.20, steak £1.70), filled jacket potatoes (£1.50), ploughman's (£2.10), spaghetti or chilli con carne (£2.80), steak and kidney pie (£2.90) and scampi (£3.10), with specials served every day now, such as lasagne (£2), chicken chasseur (£2.80) and roast duck (£2.90). There is a separate evening restaurant. The lounge opens on to a terrace and a sheltered neat lawn, which has swings, a climbing frame, croquet and quoits. The high-ceilinged public bar is also carpeted, decorated with horse shoes (this was a smithy once), has an open fire, darts, dominoes, cribbage and juke box. There may be piped music. *(Recommended by Hugh and Jayne Welch; more reports please)*

Free house · Licensee David Craigs · Meals and snacks (not Mon, not Sun evening) · Children in eating area · Open 11–3, 6–11 (7–10.30 in winter)

WEST WOODBURN (Northumberland)   NY8987 Map 10
Bay Horse
A68

This small and friendly old coaching-inn runs five-day (or longer) riding holidays for adults (and children with them) over the fine fells above the village, and along the Rede valley – the river runs past here. The horses are Irish hunters, which provide real riding for experienced horsemen rather than pony-trekking. The horses can be taken by the hour (£3.50) or day (£15, including packed lunch). The low-ceilinged carpeted lounge bar is welcoming, with armchairs in front of a good open fire in one part, and another part trimly done out in stripped pine – including seats built in to one enormous old stone fireplace. There are small country pictures on the white walls. Good value bar food includes nice home-made soup, wholemeal stottie-cake sandwiches, filled jacket potatoes, pizzas, home-made steak and kidney pie, chicken, gammon, trout, duck and steak (which can also be served in a separate dining-room); darts, pool, dominoes, fruit machine and a juke box.*(Recommended by PLC and others; more reports please)*

Free house · Licensee Hilda Wright · Meals and snacks · Children in eating area and dining-room · Open 11–3, 6–11 · Bedrooms tel Bellingham (0660) 60218; £13/£23

Lucky Dip

Besides the fully inspected pubs, you might like to try these Lucky Dips recommended and described by readers (if you do, please send us reports):

ALLENDALE [NY8456], *Golden Lion*: good bar meal; restaurant looks promising with several regional dishes *(Henry Partridge)*

ALNWICK [NU1913], *Oddfellows Arms*: comfortable lounge bar with real fire, good Vaux Samson, food (not sampled) *(G L Archer)*; [Narrowgate] *Oddfellows Arms*: friendly town pub near castle entrance; good freshly made bar food, restaurant, Vaux real ales, very friendly atmosphere, tourists made to feel genuinely welcome; bedrooms *(C M Harnor)*; *Tanners Arms*: friendly lively atmosphere, well kept real ale, lunchtime food in little young people's pub *(Sgt Lord)*

AMBLE [Coquetside; NU2704], *Harbour*: stone built, facing harbour, small cosy bar. Big room for kids at the side, machines and so on. Main bar has fishing talk: once a week (usually Thursday) is relaxing folk or sing-along music, sometimes with free food. Early evening is happy hour several nights a week. Friendly management, real ales *(C M Harnor)*

BARNARD CASTLE [NZ0617]. *White Swan*: dramatic setting on rocks above River Tees, opposite castle ruins; straightforward inside *(LYM)*

BEAMISH [NZ2254], *(Open Air Museum)*: Sun Inn rescued from Bishop Auckland and newly reconstructed/reopened here as old-style pub, with stables for retired dray horses. Also here: mining village, steam railway, nineteenth-century farms, and tramway *(reports please)*; *Shepherd & Shepherdess*: good generous lunchtime bar food, pub very clean *(Ronnie and Daffy Carr)*

BELFORD [NU1134], *Black Swan*: friendly atmosphere and landlord; good food *(Arthur Brough)*; *Salmon*: cheerful basic local with Lorimers real ale and lively pool-room *(LYM)*

BELLINGHAM [NY8483], *Cheviot*: inexpensive pub meals, also evening and Sunday lunchtime restaurant specialising in game; five bedrooms *(Anon)*

BELSAY [NZ1079], *Highlander*: free house with well kept beers and good salads and hot dishes; a Henderson Inn, with separate restaurant; handy for Newcastle airport *(J M Ragg, David Regan)*

BIRTLEY [NY8878], *Tone*: bar meals in simple pub on A68; may be closed winter weekday lunchtimes *(LYM)*

BISHOP AUCKLAND [Market Place; NZ2130], *Kings Arms*: popular free house, brews own bitter; nicely restored restaurant with late-night licence in old coaching-stables *(Anon)*

BOWES [NY9914], *Ancient Unicorn*: comfortably modernised open-plan bar, good bedrooms in well converted stables block, in coaching-inn with *Nicholas Nickleby* connections *(LYM)*

CASTLE EDEN [NZ4338], *Castle Eden*: nice well kept pub, good beer from brewery opposite, reasonable food, comfortable *(G L Archer)*

CORBRIDGE [NY9964], *Black Bull*: food excellent in small restaurant, courteous service; no piped music, good atmosphere and service in bar *(Peter Robinson)*

nr CORBRIDGE [NY9964; about 3 miles N], *Errington Arms*: food above average and very friendly welcome in pleasant setting *(Dr S G Bauer)*

DURHAM [NZ2743], *Cock o' the North*: food includes excellent reasonably priced carvery and bar meals, good beer, large well kept pub with plenty of car parking *(G L Archer)*; [Claypath] *Travellers Rest*: attractively timbered low-beamed free house with good value lunchtime food, cosy downstairs, recent upstairs extension, real ale *(John Pepper, Anne Johnson, David Gristwood, Martin Murrish)*

EGGLESCLIFFE [NZ4214], *Pot & Glass*: friendly local atmosphere, interesting carved bars, seats in back garden, lunchtime food; pretty village *(Ian Taylor)*

EMBLETON [NU2323], *Dunstanburgh Castle*: food in nicely furnished dining-room fresh and good; beautifully placed near magnificent coast *(Eileen Broadbent, W T Aird)*

GREAT WHITTINGTON [NZ0171], *Queens Head*: friendly bar staff and home-cooked food in fine old Northumberland village pub with open fires and old murals *(Dr S P K Linter)*

GRETA BRIDGE [NZ0813], *Morritt Arms*: beams and log fire in biggish Georgian inn with Dickens connections; two-acre garden, good bar food, real ale, separate restaurant *(Anon)*

GUISBOROUGH [NZ6016], *Black Swan*: good value home-made food, good traditional atmosphere *(H M Witzer)*; [Bow Street] *Fox*: comfortable open-plan bar in modernised coaching-inn, good value quickly served bar food *(LYM)*

HALTWHISTLE [Main Street; NY7164], *Manor House Hotel*: food and beer good value in relaxed and friendly bar *(C Rollo)*; [Rowfoot, Featherstone Park] *Wallace Arms*: used to be attractive country inn, but no recent knowledge *(BB)*

HAMSTERLEY [NZ1231], *Cross Keys*: food very good and efficiently served (even when busy), in friendly village pub *(W A Rinaldi-Butcher)*

HART [NZ4735], *Raby Arms*: good friendly pub, well run *(Sue White, Tim Kinning)*

HARTLEPOOL [Durham Street; NZ5133], *New Inn*: busy bar and lounge and best Camerons in town; oasis in a pub desert *(Jon Dewhirst)*

HAYDON BRIDGE [NY8464], *General Havelock*: remarkably good steaks and more imaginative food in clean and quiet little restaurant behind pub, overlooking Tyne (restaurant closed Sunday lunch, Monday and Tuesday); pleasant service *(Anon)*

HEIGHINGTON [NZ2522], *Bay Horse*: seventeenth-century pub by green of attractive village *(Anon)*

HOLMSIDE [NZ2249], *Wardles Bridge*: remarkable collection of whiskies in friendly country pub *(LYM)*

HOLYSTONE [NY9503], *Salmon*: comfortably furnished local with good value simple food and lively pool room, in attractive Coquet Valley countryside close to Holy Well *(LYM)*

HUTTON MAGNA [NZ1312], *Oak Tree*: good simple food including generous sandwiches in neatly kept pub with lots of decorations *(Anon)*

JESMOND [Osborne Terrace; NZ2567], *Carriage*: imaginative snacks in old converted station which includes as part of pub a pre-war rail coach; lots of old LNER equipment; beer not cheap *(Robert Wade)*

LOWICK [NY0239], *Black Bull*: recently renovated village pub with snacks, Pentland and McEwans real ale *(G L Archer)*

MARSDEN [NZ4164], *Grotto*: pub used to be approached by lift from clifftop, with seaside 'smugglers' cave'; no recent knowledge *(BB)*

MARSKE BY THE SEA [NZ6423], *Mermaid*: plush and spaciously comfortable modern Bass Charrington estate pub with good bar food, friendly *(H M Witzer, BB)*

MICKLETON [NY9724], *Rose & Crown*: very friendly place to stay, bar meals and dining-room, Sunderland real ale, Pennine views from garden *(D L Greengrass)*

NETHERTON [NT9908], *Star*: for aficionados of the unspoilt spartan rural pubs of yesteryear, very popular with north-east real ale drinkers *(Jon Dewhirst)*

NEWCASTLE UPON TYNE [Cloth Market; NZ2266], *Balmbra's*: includes music hall mentioned in *Blaydon Races (Anon)*; *City Vaults*: good value lunchtime food includes steaming sides of beef and ham salad *(J Skiner)*; [The Side, by Dean

Street] *Crown Pasada*: largely unchanged turn-of-the-century pub near dockside; long narrow room with small snug, often crowded; Bass real ale *(Jon Dewhirst, Patrick Stapley, Richard Gibbs)*; [Pink Lane] *Forth*: traditional Tyneside pub: very cosy and friendly atmosphere in lounge and bar; Tetleys on handpump, juke box, darts *(F S Bastock)*; [Grey Street] *Royal Buffet*: two small Victorian-screened rooms, well kept real ale, old posters from adjoining Theatre Royal; real character *(Jon Dewhirst)*

OTTERBURN [NY8992], *Tower*: castellated hotel with big garden, plush main bar and lively Stables Bar (which has good pop music) *(LYM; up-to-date reports please)*

PIERCEBRIDGE [NZ2116], *George*: comfortably modernised and friendly old stone inn with riverside garden; bedrooms *(LYM)*

ROTHBURY [NU0602], *County*: used to be a lovely place for trout fishing on the Coquet *(W T Aird)*

SEATON SLUICE [NZ3477], *Waterford Arms*: fish superb, good Vaux Samson real ale and nice seafront position *(G L Archer)*

SEDGEFIELD [West End; NZ3629], *Nags Head*: food in bar and restaurant good, especially French onion soup, home-made bread, Mexican fried ice cream; nice atmosphere *(J Nevard)*

SHOTTON [First left after southernmost Peterlee exit from A19; NZ4140], *Black Bull*: attractive and well kept pub, good atmosphere *(Sue White, Tim Kinning)*

SUMMERHOUSE [NZ2019], *Raby Hunt*: beautifully modernised and comfortable free house with well kept Camerons Strongarm and Theakstons on handpump, big open fire, good lunchtime bar meals (not Sunday), swift courteous service *(Stephanie Sowerby)*

SUNDERLAND [NZ4057], *Saltgrass*: old-fashioned nautical interior in friendly riverside pub. Excellent Vaux real ale *(John Pepper, David Gristwood, Martin Murrish)*

THROPTON [NU0302], *Cross Keys*: traditional three-bar village pub, handy for Seaton Delaval Hall and Cragside *(LYM)*

UPSALL [NR5616], *Cross Keys*: home-cooked food, changing daily, usually interesting; salads and steak and kidney pie good; get there early *(Jean Hellier)*

WARENFORD [NU1429], *Warenford Lodge*: food in bar outstanding *(G L Archer)*

WARKWORTH [Castle Street; NU2506] *Hermitage*: friendly and comfortable, bar food and small restaurant *(K L Dixon, Peter Robinson, Stephanie Miles, BB)*; [Castle Terrace] *Sun*: food reasonably priced and interesting with a good choice, real ale, rambling place with several rooms; opposite castle; bedrooms – a nice place to stay *(C M Harnor)*

WHITLEY BAY [The Front; NZ3672], *Ark Royal Bar*: lots of ex-aircraft-carrier equipment, brassware, radar, punishment cell bed; real ales; restaurant, disco; bedrooms *(Robert Wade)*

WINSTON [A67; NZ1417], *Bridgewater Arms*: good value food, friendly atmosphere, good service, pleasant surroundings *(S Wooler)*

WITTON GILBERT [NZ2346], *Travellers Rest*: charming inside, very friendly, several well kept real ales, good food, live honky-tonk piano Sunday and Wednesday, garden and boules lawn *(Mugs Vernon)*

WITTON LE WEAR [NZ1531], *Victoria*: food very good value, pleasant atmosphere; beer garden with magnificent view over Weardale; Vaux Samson beer *(Frank and Irene Berner)*

WOLVISTON [NZ4526], *Wellington*: pleasant comfortably redecorated pub, busy but uncrowded, friendly service, good Bass on electric pump; no food *(Jon Dewhirst)*

WOOLER [High Street; NZ9928], *Red Lion*: food excellent in friendly, roomy, comfortable open-plan pub with huge stone fireplaces and walls, and plenty of wooden settles and small tables; pool, darts and unobtrusive TV at one end *(Roy McIsaac, F J Bastock)*; *Tankerville Arms*: food in comfortable bar good, wide range (albeit not cheap); well kept McEwans 80/– on handpump; separate restaurant *(Roy McIsaac, Roger Hemingway)*

YARM [NZ4213], *George & Dragon*: where Stockton & Darlington Railway Co first met; modernised comfort, good value lunchtime food, prompt service *(C Rollo, LYM)*

Essex

This year the attractive old Bell at Woodham Walter, Wooden Fender at Ardleigh and homely and welcoming Dolphin at Stisted have all made advances in the food line, and are now particularly worth drawing attention to for that. Perhaps the best pub food in the county is to be had in the comfortable Marlborough Head in Constable's Dedham (costly refurbishments this last year have unobtrusively made the most of its fine Tudor features), in the strikingly timbered Eight Bells in Saffron Walden (particularly its fresh seafood) and at the fine Tudor Woolpack in Coggeshall. Others to mention specially for food are the most attractively furnished Axe & Compasses in Arkesden (a different theme each night), neatly kept old Bell in Horndon-on-the-Hill (so long as you don't start on their extraordinary collection of fossilised hot-cross buns), friendly Generals Arms in Little Baddow (good simple stuff), unspoilt Green Man, Little Braxted (excellent ploughman's and variations), thatched Half Moon, Belchamp St Paul (splendid sandwiches), and White Harte at Burnham on Crouch (also excellent sandwiches as well as good restaurant meals; it's a nice place to stay for its splendid waterfront position). On fine days there are some good pubs for outdoor drinking: particularly the waterside Swan near Great Henny, Compasses in the countryside near Coggeshall, Cats at Woodham Walter, and the Bell not far from the castle in Castle Hedingham. At Purleigh, the Bell on its hill has a

The Wooden Fender, Ardleigh

remarkably fine view for what is generally such a flat area, as well as a really good welcoming atmosphere. Beer prices are often rather low in pubs tied to Ridleys (based here) or Greene King; the Pheasant at Gestingthorpe – with a new pianist licensee this year – brews its own beer. Among the Lucky Dip entries at the end of the chapter, we'd particularly pick out for your attention the Swan at Chappel (good food), the Parsons Barn in North Shoebury (an interesting converted barn), the Swan at Thaxted (an atmospheric inn, cooking some of its food on the Aga behind the bar), the Duck at Newney Green (interesting decorations, large attractive garden), the Green Man in Toot Hill (good food, lovely views and some excellent reasonably priced wines) and the Fleur de Lys in Widdington (recently taken over by the landlord who in earlier editions made the Nags Head at Little Hadham so popular with readers); do let us know what you think of these, and whether you feel they deserve inspection as potential main entries.

ARDLEIGH   TM0529   Map 5

Wooden Fender   [*illustrated on page 269*]

Harwich Road; A137

The open-plan beamed bar of this friendly roadside pub has comfortable red leatherette seats on its red carpet, and is decorated with horse prints and brasses. Lunchtime bar food includes sandwiches (from 65p), a choice of ploughman's (£1.20), home-made steak and kidney pie, home-cooked roast beef with Yorkshire pudding, or vegetarian cauliflower and mushroom lasagne (£2) and seafood pasta (£2.25). On weekday evenings they now do ham and cheese macaroni, whitebait, gammon, scampi or moussaka (£1.75– £2.40), and on Friday or Saturday evenings a three-course meal with steak, seafood pancake or mixed grill as a main course (£7.50; booking advisable). Well kept Adnams, Greene King IPA and Abbot, and guest bitters; maybe piped music. The pub is very old: it's where Matthew Hopkins the 'Witchfinder General' stayed when he was in the area to hunt down and burn witches. They still have ring the bull, a pub game from his days or earlier. The back garden has a pool and swings (including a tiny tots' one). *(Recommended by Aubrey Saunders; more reports please)*

Free house · Licensees G Harling and C Munn · Real ale · Meals (not Sun evening) and snacks (lunchtime only, not Sun); meal bookings tel Manningtree (0206) 230466 · Children in dining area · Open 11.30–2.30, 6–11 all year

ARKESDEN   TL4834   Map 5

Axe & Compasses ★

Food is the strong point in this well run and interesting old thatched country pub. At lunchtime it is straightforward but good value: typically, home-made soup (60p), half a dozen hot dishes such as sausages (£2), plaice, gammon, home-made turkey pie, a fresh roast

(£2.75) and rump steak (£3.75), and salads (£2.95). Each evening, there's a different choice: on Tuesday fresh fish and scampi from Lowestoft (£2.75–£3.50); Wednesday a £6 meal with steak or plaice as the main course, incuding a glass of wine or pint of bitter; on Thursday traditional English cooking – bangers, cottage pie, steak and kidney pie or lamb cutlets (£2–£2.75); Friday and Saturday a grander range of full meals (£10) as well as bar snacks from bangers to steaks; and on Sunday, roast lunches (£6). You can eat in either the restaurant or the carpeted saloon bar, which rambles comfortably up and down, with old wooden tables, cushioned oak and elm seats, and quite a few easy chairs. There are sensibly placed darts, shove-ha'penny, cribbage and a fruit machine in the smaller public bar, which has snug built-in settles. Well kept Greene King Light Mild and Abbot, and Rayments BBA (from nearby Furneaux Pelham). There are seats outside, on a side terrace. *(Recommended by Dennis Royles, Aubrey Saunders, Howard Gascoyne; more reports please)*

Rayments (Greene King) · Licensee Jerry Roberts · Real ale · Meals and snacks (not Sun or Mon evenings); restaurant bookings tel Clavering (079 985) 272 Children in dining-room · Open 11–2.30, 6–10.30

BELCHAMP ST PAUL   TL7942   Map 5
Half Moon

The Belchamps are quite well signposted within the
Sudbury–Clare–Sible Hedingham triangle

The sandwiches in this pretty Elizabethan thatched white pub are excellent, with thick-cut fresh local bread (from 65p, with egg and bacon £1.10); other bar food includes ploughman's (£1.20), beefburger and chips (£1.35), salads (around £1.80), chilli con carne (£2), scampi (£2.10), eight-ounce sirloin steak (£5) and 16-ounce T-bone steak (£6.50). The neat lounge bar has beams in its cream ceiling (steeply sloping under the low eaves), cushioned built-in wall benches and Windsor chairs on the dark red carpet, a glass-fronted solid-fuel stove, and a cosy cubby by the serving counter. Its big bow window looks out over the broad green of the quiet village. Well kept Adnams, Greene King IPA and Mauldons on handpump; juke box and a fruit machine. The lively locals' bar has darts, dominoes, and shove-ha'penny. In summer, a Stable Bar in the back beer garden serves soft drinks, sweets and so forth. *(More reports please)*

Free house · Licensees John and Janis Goss · Real ale · Meals and snacks (not Tues evening) · Children in eating area · Open 11–2.30, 6–11 all year

BURNHAM-ON-CROUCH   TQ9596   Map 5
White Harte

The Quay

This old inn is a nice place to stay, with bedrooms overlooking the broad estuary of the River Crouch and at night the sound of ropes and sheets slapping idly against the metal masts of yachts moored out there. There are views too from the good window seat in the front bar, where yachtsmen sink into other comfortably cushioned old-

271

fashioned seats around oak tables on the polished parquet floor. Other high-ceilinged rooms open off, also traditionally furnished, their panelled or stripped brick walls decorated with sea pictures. Attractively priced bar snacks consist of a very good choice of sandwiches or filled rolls (from 50p, toasted bacon 80p, smoked salmon 95p, steak £1.95, giant steak £3.50) and ploughman's (65p); three-course meals are served in the dining-room (lunch £4.50, dinner £5 – one of the very few eating-places in the area open on bank holidays). Well kept Adnams and Tolly on handpump; dominoes. There are seats on the inn's private jetty, overhanging the water. *(Recommended by Hazel Morgan; more reports please)*

Free house · Licensee Granville Lewis · Snacks · Children in dining area Open 10–2.30, 6–11 all year · Bedrooms tel Maldon (0621) 782106; £12.75 (£17B)/£21.50 (£25B)

CASTLE HEDINGHAM   TL7835   Map 5
Bell

B1058 towards Sudbury

The beamed and timbered bar of this friendly pub is furnished with Jacobean-style seats and Windsor chairs around oak tables; beyond standing timbers left from a knocked-through wall, there are steps up to a little gallery. Bar food includes home-made soup (90p), Welsh rarebit, sausages or burgers (£1–£1.30), ploughman's (£1.30), shepherd's pie (£1.50), mussels or mushrooms in garlic butter (£1.60), home-made pâté (£1.60), pizzas (£1.60) and sirloin steak (£4.40); well kept Greene King IPA and Abbot tapped from the cask; maybe piped music. A games room behind the traditionally furnished public bar has darts, dominoes, cribbage, a fruit machine and a space game. Besides seats on a small terrace in the car park, there's a fine big walled garden – an acre or so, with grass, trees and shrubs. The twelfth-century castle keep is very striking. *(More reports please)*

Grays (who no longer brew) · Licensee Mrs Sandra Ferguson · Real ale · Meals and snacks (not Mon evening, unless a bank hol) · Children welcome (not in public bar) · Open 11–2.30, 6–11 all year

COGGESHALL   TL8522   Map 5
Fleece

West Street, towards Braintree

Fine carved beams and a grand fireplace distinguish the comfortably refurbished lounge bar of this handsome Elizabethan pub, which, since our last edition, has been taken over by a new licensee. Bar food includes sandwiches, ploughman's, salads, hot dishes such as beef casseroles, curries, home-made steak and kidney pie and sirloin steak; as we went to press prices had not been finalised, but they've been reasonable here in the past. Well kept Greene King IPA and Abbot on handpump; maybe piped music, and in a separate area darts, bar billiards, table skittles, dominoes, and a fruit machine. The garden behind is spacious and well protected, with a children's play area. Paycocke's – one of England's most lovely timber-framed houses, and just next door – is open on Wednesday, Thursday and Sunday afternoons in summer. This town figures in one of those senseless seventeenth-century jingles:

> *Braintree for the pure*
> *and Bocking for the poor.*
> *Cogshall for the jeering town*
> *and Kelvedon for the whore.*

(Recommended by Dave Hoy; more reports on the new regime please)

Greene King · Licensee Alan Potter · Real ale · Meals and snacks · Open 10.30–2.30, 6–11 all year

Woolpack

91 Church Street; B1024 towards Earls Colne

Good freshly cooked bar food in this striking timber-framed Tudor inn relies as much as possible on local produce, and includes vegetable soup with garlic bread (95p), pâté or taramosalata (£1.50), chilli con carne or seafood quiche (£2.50), home-cooked ham salad (£2.95), beef and venison pie (£3.50) and several daily specials, perhaps Dover sole (£3.50), with home-made puddings such as bread and butter pudding (95p). The lounge bar is attractive, with handsomely carved heavy beams, ancient timbered walls (decorated with a somewhat surprising mixture of good prints and off-the-shelf pictures and stickers), a fine open fireplace (with a good log fire in winter), snugly low-ceilinged alcoves and old-fashioned furnishings; but perhaps the strongest impression you have is of the friendliness of the staff – one reader, arriving late after a long drive, was served with what had been intended for the landlord's own supper. Well kept Benskins, Ind Coope and Taylor Walker on handpump, and decent wines by the glass. A separate dining-room is open in the evenings (on crowded weekend lunchtimes, readers have wished it might be open then too). The public bar has darts, dominoes, cribbage, and a fruit machine. Tables out on the grass, with flowers around them, look across to the graceful neighbouring church; the Woolpack was first turned into an inn by the grandson of a vicar who'd bought it for his home after being ejected from his living in 1665 for being a Puritan.
(Recommended by Jeff Cousins, Miss A Findlay, Dave Butler, Les Storey)

Ind Coope · Licensees Bill and Judith Hutchinson · Real ale · Meals and snacks (not Sun evening) · Open 11.30–2.30, 6.30–11 all year · Bedrooms tel Coggeshall (0376) 61235; £16/£28

nr COGGESHALL   TL8522 Map 5
Compasses

Pattiswick; signposted from A120 about 2 miles W of Coggeshall; OS Sheet 168 reference 820247

Charming in summer, this secluded country pub is surrounded by lawns, orchard, and a children's play area, with quiet farmland beyond. Good bar food includes sandwiches (from 65p), home-made soup (85p), ploughman's (£1.20), sprats or soft roes on toast (£1.50), mussels in season (£1.90), cottage pie (£1.95), home-made steak and kidney pie (£2.20), gammon or scampi (£2.25), open steak sandwich (£2.50) and sirloin steak (from £4.50). There is a separate restaurant (Sunday lunch £5.50; booking recommended at weekends). The open-plan lounge is rather elegant, with a suspended slat ceiling, green and gold wallpaper, soft banquettes and gentle piped music, and even the more simply furnished public bar has touches of elegance to go with its traditional wooden seats, bared brick walls and floor-tiles; darts, shove-ha'penny, dominoes in here, a fruit machine in the lounge. Well kept Greene King IPA and Abbot and Steward & Patteson on handpump. *(Recommended by Miss A Findlay)*

Free house · Licensee F G Johnson · Real ale · Meals and snacks; restaurant bookings tel Coggeshall (0376) 61322 · Children in dining area and restaurant Open 10.30–3, 6–11 all year

COLCHESTER   TM0025   Map 5
Rose & Crown

East Street; leaving centre for Ipswich, Manningtree and Harwich, close to A1231/A137 junction

When you see it for the first time, this handsome Tudor building (curved to fit the road, with its upper floor overhanging the pavement) almost tugs you inside – it's been a favourite with some readers for about 40 years. Though of course there has been substantial modernisation, the forest of old woodwork, beams and standing timbers, leather armed seats, plush-cushioned small pews and old prints on the walls of the rambling bar are very evocative, as is the buttery bar – visibly made up from parts of a prison which was one of the earlier buildings standing here. Food served here includes soup (55p), sandwiches (75p), ploughman's (£1.25), salads from a buffet table (£2.50) and a hot dish of the day (£2.95); there is also a separate restaurant. Well kept Tolly tapped from the cask.
(Recommended by John Kemp; more reports please)

Free house · Licensee J De Andrade · Real ale · Meals and snacks (lunchtime, not Sun) · Children welcome · Open 10.30–2.30, 6–11 all year · Bedrooms tel Colchester (0206) 866677; £22.50 (£27.50B)/£27.50 (£36.50B)

DEDHAM   TM0533   Map 5
Marlborough Head

The reasonably priced food served in this handsome inn – since our last edition, refurbished at a cost of £60,000 to make the most of its medieval features – is unusually good. The wide choice includes sandwiches (from 85p, home-boiled bacon £1, cream cheese with asparagus £1.30), excellent soup (85p), filled baked potato (85p), a bowl of cockles (£1.25), ploughman's (£1.35), pâté or taramosalata (£1.95), filling mussel chowder (£2), spinach flan or bacon, mushroom and tomato quiche (£2.50), crab thermidor (£2.75), Tibetan vegetarian roast (£3), steak and kidney pie (£3.35), poached cod in prawn and anchovy sauce (£3.50), Aga-roasted back bacon with peaches or chicken breast with bananas and pineapple (£4) and fillet steak (£6.75). Vegetables are just right and the puddings are popular. There is Ind Coope on handpump. Perhaps the most interesting room is the central lounge with a wealth of finely carved woodwork, though the newly refurbished beamed and timbered Constable Bar – with many tables in wooden alcoves around its plum-coloured carpet – is more sensible for eating. There are seats in the garden behind. Constable went to school just across the road, and his peaceful countryside surrounds the village. *(Recommended by Jeff Cousins, Brigid Avison, Miss A Findlay, Cdr and Mrs E St Leger Moore, J and M Sergeant, D J Oldrenshaw, Gwen and Peter Andrews)*

Ind Coope · Licensee Brian Wills · Real ale · Meals and snacks · Children in family area adjoining bars · Open 11–2.30, 6–11 all year · Bedrooms tel Colchester (0206) 323250; £15/£25

EASTHORPE   TL9121 Map 5
House Without A Name

Village signposted from A12

Unusually for the area, there's a good choice of real ales here – Adnams, Greene King IPA and Abbot, and Mauldons (from Sudbury) on handpump, with regular guest beers (as well as hot toddies in cold weather). Low Tudor beams and heavy standing timbers, the winter log fire and the dark colour scheme of the soft plush button-back banquettes and little cask seats, make for a snug and old-fashioned atmosphere in the roomy bar. Bar food includes soup (75p), a good range of sandwiches (from 70p, hot salt beef £1, smoked salmon £1.50), sausage in French bread (£1), a choice of ploughman's (£1.50), home-made salmon pâté (£1.50), cottage pie (£1.50), whole avocado with prawns (£1.75), lasagne (£2), salads (from £2) and steaks (from £5); darts, a fruit machine, gentle piped music. A small sheltered lawn behind the pink-washed and weatherboarded house has tables under walnut and apple trees. *(Recommended by Jeff Cousins, Miss A Findlay, J Gargan, A Saunders)*

Free house · Licensee Barry Medcalf · Real ale · Meals and snacks (limited on Sun) · Children in dining area · Country and western music first Weds of month Open 10.30–2.30, 6–11 all year

GESTINGTHORPE   TL8138 Map 5
Pheasant

Village signposted from B1058; pub at Audley End end

The Harwoods who have just taken over from Mr and Mrs Ruth plan to keep everything here much as before – including the pub's own rich dark golden Pheasant bitter, brewed each fortnight in the cellar. It certainly is the sort of pub you want to be preserved unchanged. The little lounge bar has a big pheasant-print cushioned bow-window seat looking out over the quiet lane to gently rising fields, a raised log fire, and old-fashioned furnishings: a grandfather clock, arts-and-crafts oak settle, and a pew. The red-walled public bar, with more orthodox pub furniture, has another log fire in winter, and sensibly placed darts; also dominoes and a fruit machine. Food includes sandwiches (from 75p), pâté or ploughman's (£1.20), chilli con carne

(£1.50), smoked trout (£2), steak and kidney pie (£3), rainbow trout (£3.50) and beef in red wine (£4). Besides the Pheasant Bitter, the Greene King IPA and Abbot and Wethereds on handpump are kept well. Mr Harwood has been a professional pub, club and cruise-liner pianist for many years; he's sticking to impromptu entertainment for the moment but hopes to arrange some good musical evenings and sing-alongs in future. There are two picnic-table sets out by a back rockery. *(Recommended by A Saunders; up-to-date reports on the new regime please)*

Own brew · Licensees Mike and Jeanne Harwood · Real ale · Meals and snacks Children in eating area · Open 11–2.30, 6–11 all year · One bedroom tel Halstead (0787) 61196; £7.50/£13

nr GREAT HENNY   TL8738   Map 5
Swan

Henny Street; The Hennys signposted from A131 S of Sudbury; OS Sheet 155 reference 879384

It's the delightful lawn by a weir on the River Stour, with rustic benches among the willows, that draws people to this country pub, once a barge house. Inside there's a pleasantly old-fashioned atmosphere, with a big fireplace, and military prints on the timbered walls. Bar food includes good sandwiches (from 65p), soup (65p), sausage with peas and chips (£1.30), home-made steak and kidney pie and scampi (£2); well kept Greene King IPA and Abbot on handpump; darts, dominoes and cribbage, maybe piped music. The little separate restaurant does full meals (from £6.50 for three courses, booking essential). There is a flower-edged terrace with a summer house. Fishing permits are available (50p a day). *(Recommended by Heather Sharland; more reports please)*

Greene King · Licensee Brian May · Real ale · Meals and snacks (not Sun or Mon evenings); restaurant bookings tel Twinstead (078 729) 238 · Children in eating area and restaurant · Open 11–2.30, 6–11 all year

GREAT SALING   TL7025   Map 5
White Hart

Village signposted from A120

The attractive timbered lounge bar of this flower-decked Tudor pub has stairs up to an unusual little gallery with roughly timbered walls and easy chairs on its wide oak floorboards; this looks down to the main area, which has Windsor chairs on its antique tiles and guns hanging behind the bar. The generous giant huffer sandwiches which have been a long-standing speciality here (£1.20) are very popular with readers, and there are also rollmops, home-made pâté and more conventional sandwiches. Well kept Ridleys PA on handpump; darts, dominoes and a fruit machine in the public bar. You can sit outside, either on the bench built right round the trunk of a fine lime-tree, or at picnic-table sets. *(Recommended by J Madley; more reports please)*

Ridleys · Licensee Michael Clapton · Real ale · Snacks · Open 11–3, 6–11 all year

HIGH EASTER   TL6214   Map 5
Cock & Bell

The Easters are signposted from the Rodings, on B184/A1060

This heavily timbered black and white medieval house is very much the focal point of the village, but though it has a pleasantly lively local atmosphere the staff go out of their way to welcome strangers (and their small children). There are comfortably cushioned Windsor chairs and easy chairs in the carpeted lounge bar, where massive oak beams contrast with little vases of fresh flowers. There are steps up to the dining area; bar food includes sandwiches (from 80p, steak sandwich £3) and soup (85p), with grills such as scampi (£3.50), cutlets (£3.75), liver (£4), sirloin steak (£4.50) and mixed grill (£4.75) on Mondays to Thursdays; for the rest of the week they do rather more elaborate dishes, such as fresh plaice (£4), lemon sole or trout (£4.25), lamb with rosemary (£4.95), chicken Kiev (£5.10) and beef Wellington (£5.95), and it might then be wise to book. Well kept Trumans on handpump; piped music. The cheerful public bar has darts, dominoes, a fruit machine and a juke box. *(Recommended by Celia Kemp; more reports please)*

Trumans (Watneys) · Licensee A G F Deeks · Real ale · Meals and snacks; meal bookings tel Good Easter (024 531) 296 · Children in dining area · Open 11–2.30, 6–11 all year

HORNDON-ON-THE-HILL   TQ6683   Map 3
Bell

Good bar food in this well kept partly medieval pub includes a changing variety of freshly made dishes such as chicken liver pâté (£1.65), rabbit and hazelnut terrine (£1.95), home-made cannelloni (£2.95), steak and Guinness pie (£3.10), game pie or coq au vin (£3.50) and pigeon cooked in burgundy (£5.60); there's also a separate restaurant (booking advisable). The fossilised objects hanging from the bar ceiling are hot-cross buns – collected, one a year, since 1900. This is a pleasant open-plan room, with timbering and panelling, flagstones or highly polished oak floorboards, and – besides some more modern seating – some antique high-backed settles, and seats in a bow window at the back. There's a view over fields from here and from picnic-table sets in the sheltered back yard. Bass and Charrington IPA on handpump. There is a well-attended pub fun run once a month in summer (on the strength of this training, the Bell has won the pub section of *The Sunday Times* Hyde Park runs for four consecutive years), and on the last weekend in June the High Road outside is closed (by Royal Charter) for period-costume festivities and a crafts fair; the pub holds a feast then. *(Recommended by Miss H R Morgan, Jeff Cousins, J L Thompson, Nick Dowson, Alison Hayward, D J Bridge)*

Charringtons · Licensee John Vereker · Real ale · Meals and snacks (not Sun lunchtime, nor 25–30 Dec); restaurant bookings tel Stanford-le-Hope (0375) 673154 · Children in eating area and restaurant · Open 10–2.30, 6–10.30

We say if we know a pub has piped music.

LITTLE BADDOW TL7807 Map 5
Generals Arms

The Ridge; minor road Hatfield Peverel–Danbury

The friendly welcome and relaxed, chatty atmosphere is as attractive as ever here, like the good value simple food. This includes pork pie salad (85p), asparagus quiche (£1.50), turkey and ham pie (£1.80) and generously filled interesting baked potatoes (£1.60); at lunchtimes there are also good big filled rolls (from 65p, crab or spare rib £1), giant sausage in French bread, with chips too, or pâté (£1), ham and egg or chicken (£1.80) and smoked haddock pie (£2); in the evenings there are some other salads. The left-hand bar, with tables set for food at lunchtime, is packed with antique military tunics, while the central snug, with red plush button-back wall banquettes and dimpled copper tables, has a very big collection of sailor hat ribands. Well kept Charringtons IPA and Springfield on handpump; darts, dominoes, cribbage and a fruit machine, with a sensibly placed pool-table. There are picnic-table sets on the big lawn at the side, among neatly kept rosebeds and three fine old holly trees. *(Recommended by Jeff Cousins, Gwen and Peter Andrews, Andrew Barnett)*

Charringtons · Licensee Shirley Kingham · Real ale · Meals (lunchtime, not Sun) and snacks · Open 11.30–2.30, 6–11 all year

LITTLE BRAXTED TL8314 Map 5
Green Man

Kelvedon Road; village signposted off B1389 by NE end of A12 Witham bypass – keep on patiently

In cool weather there's a warm log-and-coal fire in the cosy little traditional lounge of this pretty country pub, which is decorated with harness, horse brasses, and mugs hanging from one beam. In good weather, the picnic-table sets in the sheltered back garden – where you may find hens poking around on weekdays – are an attraction. Good value snacks include sandwiches, excellent ploughman's, hot locally baked French bread filled with ham off the bone, sardines, liver sausage, chicken, turkey, beef or even haggis brought from Scotland, salads and winter soups, with a hot dish such as shepherd's pie, fish pie or lasagne. Well kept Ridleys is dispensed from handpumps in the form of 50-millimetre brass cannon shells. The tiled public bar leads to a games room with sensibly placed darts, shove-ha'penny, dominoes, cribbage, a fruit machine and space game. *(Recommended by Jeff Cousins, Miss A Findlay, J Gargan)*

Ridleys · Licensee Eion MacGregor · Real ale · Snacks · Open 10.30–2.30, 6–11 all year

PURLEIGH TL8401 Map 5
Bell

This fine pub is warmly welcoming, friendly and relaxed – qualities which regularly win it awards (most recently, as the area Campaign for Real Ale group's pub of the year). The landlord's mother makes good simple food such as sandwiches (60p, toasted 70p), giant sausage in bread (70p), ploughman's (from £1.20), large pizza (£1.20, chips 40p extra), ham and egg (£1.70), salads (from £1.70), plaice (£2) and scampi (£2.50). The rambling main bar has heavy black beams and timbers in butter-coloured plaster, a huge log-filled fireplace, cushioned wall banquettes and Windsor chairs on the carpet. One of the nicest places to sit is in the front bow window, which makes the most of the marvellous view over hedged flatlands to the Blackwater estuary – the pub is set on the only hill for miles (with New Hall Vineyard just below). Well kept Ind Coope on handpump; dominoes, cribbage, a fruit machine. There's the same view from picnic-table sets on the side grass, which merges into the yard of the neighbouring church. George Washington's great-great-grandfather was rector here until, in 1642, he was turned out for spending too much time in taverns. *(Recommended by Aubrey Saunders, R Ellis)*

Ind Coope · Licensee Robert Cooke · Real ale · Meals (not Sun, nor Fri–Sat evenings) and snacks · Open 10–2.30, 6–11 all year

SAFFRON WALDEN   TL5438 Map 5
Eight Bells
Bridge Street; B184 towards Cambridge

This handsomely timbered black and white Tudor pub's neatly kept and busy open-plan bar has modern oak settles forming small booths around its tables, and is divided up by the old timbers of a knocked-through wall. Readers' reports repeatedly praise the seafood, mostly fresh from Lowestoft, such as taramosalata (£1.85), mussels provençale (£1.95), prawns (£2.35), grilled plaice (£3.25), scampi (£3.45), devilled crab or prawns in a white wine and cheese sauce served with garlic bread (£3.75), and skate (£4.25). Other dishes include omelettes (from £2.15), home-made lasagne (£2.90), home-made steak and kidney pie (£3.25), mixed grill (£3.95) and charcoal-grilled steaks (from £5.95); there's a popular summer cold buffet, and at lunchtime a choice of good ploughman's (£1.75). Children have a good selection of dishes (85p to £1.45, at lunchtime and in the evening up to 7.30, including a drink), and quite a few things on the main menu are served in half portions; the tiled-floor tap-room has recently been remodelled as a family room. Benskins and Ind Coope Burton on handpump; fruit machine. A separate restaurant in a splendidly timbered hall with lofty rafters has high-backed settles forming booths, and a very long refectory table. There are seats in the garden behind. Nearby Audley End makes a good family outing. *(Recommended by G H Theaker, D A Angless, Dennis Royles, A Saunders)*

Benskins (Ind Coope) · Licensees Robin and Heather Moore · Real ale · Meals and snacks; restaurant bookings tel Saffron Walden (0799) 22790 · Children in family room · Open 11–2.30, 6–10.30; closed 25–26 Dec

STISTED   TL7924 Map 5
Dolphin
A120 E of Braintree

Good value bar food in this useful roadside pub now includes sandwiches (from 60p, steak 95p), home-made soup (75p), ploughman's (£1.05), steak and kidney pie (£1.60), macaroni cheese (£1.75), Jamaican vegetarian bean pot or lasagne (£1.95), scampi (£2), lamb with apricot (£2.10) and steaks (£4.25). There are comfortable banquettes on the black wooden floor of one heavily timbered and beamed room, which has soft lighting, an open fire, piped music and a pleasantly homely atmosphere; the other room has a collection of chamber-pots. Darts, dominoes, cribbage and a fruit machine. Well kept Ridleys PA and XXX Mild are tapped from wooden casks behind the bar. There are tables outside, where an aviary has rabbits as well as cockatiels. (*Recommended by Miss A Findlay, M E Sumner*)

Ridleys · Licensee Leslie Brown · Real ale · Meals and snacks · Children in dining area · Open 11–3, 6–11 all year

WOODHAM WALTER   TL8006 Map 5
Bell

As the licensees who took over a couple of years ago have settled in, readers who know this pub well have found its atmosphere, which was always welcoming, become even more friendly, and have been pleased with a greater concentration on home cooking. Bar food now includes toasted sandwiches (from 70p, cheese with bacon £1, steak £1.65), good soup (£1), giant sausage in French bread or cheeseburger (£1), ploughman's (from £1.20), salads (from £2.65), scampi (£3.50, or £1.85 as a starter) and daily specials such as good home-cured ham (£2.25), liver and onion (£2.50) and steak and kidney pie (£2.75), with rump steak at £5.25. The cosy lounge bar has comfortable seats and some snug alcoves, and there is a prettily decorated dining-room in a partly panelled gallery up steps from the main bar (full evening meals here). Ind Coope Burton on handpump. The tiled and timbered Elizabethan building is a really striking sight as you drop down into this quiet village. (*Recommended by Gwen and Peter Andrews, Aubrey Saunders, Heather Sharland*)

Ind Coope · Licensee David Roblin · Real ale · Meals (not Sun lunchtime) and snacks; restaurant bookings tel Danbury (024 541) 3437 · Children in dining area · Open 10.30–2.30, 6–11 all year

Cats
On back road to Curling Tye and Maldon, from N end of village

This is one of the few pubs in the area where you still find local people talking about crops and livestock in the rambling traditional bar, with its button-back red leatherette seats, bow windows, black beams and timbering set off well by neat white paintwork. The food is very simple and straightforward, the welcome a warm one, and the Adnams and Greene King IPA and Abbot on handpump particularly well kept. Since our last edition they've added another real ale, brewed specially for them and so far untried by us or our readers – it's called Cats Piss. The pretty and well kept garden, looking out over quiet fields, makes this black and white timbered cottage – its roof decorated with prowling stone cats – an attractive place in summer. *(Recommended by Gwen and Peter Andrews)*

Free house · Snacks · Real ale · Open 10.30–2, 6.30–10.30

Lucky Dip

Besides the fully inspected pubs, you might like to try these Lucky Dips recommended and described by readers (if you do, please send us reports):

ABRIDGE [TQ4696], *Blue Boar*: well run dining area with good value carvery and home cooking (one of Whitbreads' Roast Inns), separate lively bar *(Anne Wilks)*; *Maltsters Arms*: good choice of real ales in clean old-world pub with lunchtime food, garden *(Mr and Mrs C A Welsby)*·

nr ALTHORNE [TQ9199], *Huntsman and Hounds*: attractive country pub previously popular – and a main entry – for its unspoilt atmosphere, nice garden and well kept Greene King ales, but recently revamped *(C H Cole; up-to-date reports please)*

AYTHORPE RODING [TL5815], *Axe & Compasses*: used to be a favourite sandwich lunch stop for the Editor some years ago, but no recent knowledge *(BB)*

BATTLESBRIDGE [Hawk Hill; TQ7894], *Barge*: Ind Coope pub by river; favoured by Thames TV outside broadcast team *(Anon)*

BEAZLEY END [TL7428], *Cock*: neatly refurbished pub with two bars, well kept Fremlins (not common around here), decorated with corn dollies and whisky-advertising jugs *(Gwen and Peter Andrews)*

BLACKMORE [TL6001], *Bull*: comfortable, quiet timber-framed Tudor pub with wide choice of freshly made food and Ind Coope real ales *(Aubrey Saunders)*

BOCKING [TL7524], *Old Court*: comfortable pubby bar with well kept Greene King ales, some unusual dishes, evening carvery, friendly landlord, in sixteenth-century hotel with attractive garden *(Gwen and Peter Andrews)*

BRADWELL [TL8022], *White Swan*: free house with well kept Greene King on handpump and good bar snacks; skilfully modernised old road-house *(P N Goodwin)*

BRADWELL-ON- SEA [Waterside; TM0006], *Green Man*: interestingly furnished flagstoned fifteenth-century pub with games room and garden; close to sea *(LYM)*; *Kings Head*: cosy old pub with consistently good bar food *(G H Theaker)*

BRAINTREE [Bocking End; TL7622], *White Hart*: good sandwiches, salads and at least one hot dish from buffet counter next to bar in beamed Tudor Room; Greene King IPA and Abbot, atmosphere smilingly brisk; children in Yeomen Room; bedrooms *(Gwen and Peter Andrews)*

BRIGHTLINGSEA [TM0816], *Cherry Tree*: food excellent value, in pleasant atmosphere; well kept Greene King beer *(J F Pettitt)*

BROXTED [TL5726], *Prince of Wales*: food very good value for money in clean pub with nice atmosphere and welcoming landlord *(T Imlach)*

CHAPPEL [TL8927], *Swan*: particularly good snacks and full meals – ingredients fresh from London markets – in fourteenth-century riverside pub with lots of plants in relaxed timbered bars, new dining extension and busy games bar; continental sun-trap courtyard bright with flowers and parasols; cheerful service, well kept Greene King real ales; nineteenth-century viaduct high overhead carries Colne Valley line (steam HQ nearby); children welcome *(Gwen and Peter Andrews, R B H Baker, Miss A Findlay)*

CHELMSFORD [Moulsham Street; TL7006], *Anchor*: good friendly welcome and atmosphere in nice pleasant surroundings *(K J Williams)*; [Howe Street] *Green Man*: good food includes carvery, lasagne and home-made strawberry cheesecake; good value bar wines; friendly relaxed atmosphere in spacious lounge and public bar *(Gwen and Peter Andrews)*; [Roxwell Road] *Horse & Groom*: friendly staff in popular and attractively furnished mock-Tudor pub with busy but relaxed atmosphere; good reasonably priced salads and hot dishes (not Sun); benches outside; Trumans real ale *(David Sarjant, Debbie and Ian Trotman)*; [4 Duke Street] *Wine Cellar*: food above average, good wine list and house wines in a pleasant atmosphere with excellent service *(B G Kemp)*

nr CHELMSFORD [Cooksmill Green; TL7006], *Fox & Goose*: spaciously extended and well kept pub with lively evening atmosphere, good Trumans beer, sandwiches and other food *(Doug and Betty Adams, LYM)*

CHIGNALL ST JAMES [TL6609], *Three Elms*: quiet pub, pleasant for sitting outside on a summer's evening; Trumans *(Jeff Cousins)*

CLAVERING [TL4731], *Fox & Hounds*: friendly local village pub *(Trevor Vincent)*

COGGESHALL [West Street; TL8522], *Cricketers*: good value food and very friendly staff in small, quiet and attractive pub with homely log fire *(Miss A Findlay)*; *White Hart*: very old inn, more a restaurant and hotel (with a ghost) than a pub; good food (wide choice of bar dishes at lunchtime), Adnams real ale, nice courtyard with flowers and tubs; good comfortable bedrooms *(Heather Sharland)*

DEDHAM [TM0533], *Sun*: comfortably refurbished Tudor inn with quick-service food counter and attractive back lawn; bedrooms *(LYM)*

DUNMOW [TL6221], *Star*: good service and food (ingredients brought daily from London markets); primarily a restaurant rather than a pub *(Laura Blond)*

EPPING FOREST [TQ4197], *Owl*: busy, popular pub with plenty of tables out on the grass under mature trees with forest views; Metropolitan Police firing practice and helicopter training opposite; OS Sheet 166 reference 396970 *(Anne Wilks)*

nr FRYERNING [Mill Green; TL6400], *Viper*: quiet and simple Trumans pub with fresh lunchtime snacks, lovely garden, cricket-loving landlord; in the middle of some woods – just the place to drop in to when walking the dog *(Jeff Cousins, Gwen and Peter Andrews)*

GREAT BADDOW [TL7204], *White Horse*: food and service good, great atmosphere *(Donald Honsberger)*

GREAT WALTHAM [TL6913], *Windmill*: plush bars in well kept civilised pub with good snacks and range of beers *(Gwen and Peter Andrews)*

HATFIELD HEATH [TL5215], *White Horse*: charmingly situated sixteenth-century pub with old ship's timbers; three bars to suit all tastes: Greene King on handpump, lunchtime meals, evening cold buffet, friendly staff, no piped music *(Jon Simons)*

HEMPSTEAD [TL6337], *Rose & Crown*: comfortably modernised low-beamed pub with good choice of real ales and bar food; Dick Turpin was brought up here as his father was the landlord *(LYM)*

HIGH RODING [TL6017], *Black Lion*: interesting bar food and separate restaurant, Ridleys real ales and log fires in fifteenth-century beamed and timber-framed building *(Aubrey Saunders)*

INGATESTONE [TQ6499], *Bell*: old pub with genuine beams and inglenook fires; Bass *(Jeff Cousins)*

KIRBY LE SOKEN [TM2221], *Red Lion*: food excellent in beamed pub with good beer, pleasant staff and atmosphere; very busy *(M W Withycombe)*

LITTLE BROMLEY [Shop Road; TM0928], *Wheatsheaf*: friendly and genuinely unspoilt old village pub, of a type fast disappearing: pleasant garden with quoits, well kept Adnams and Greene King, reasonably priced bar meals, quiet background music, no machines; children if well behaved *(Bill Godden)*

LITTLE THURROCK [Docks Road; TQ6377], *Bull*: old oak-beamed building with character, friendly and lively atmosphere, friendly staff, winter fire and big garden *(S A Berry)*

LITTLE WALDEN [TL5441], *Crown*: good lunchtime food and choice of beers with friendly staff, in quiet village surroundings *(J M Buxton)*

LOUGHTON [Pump Hill; TQ4296], *Gardeners Arms*: good home-cooked food, Ruddles real ale *(Sue Leggate)*

MALDON [High Street; TL8506], *Kings Head*: new licensees are warmly welcoming in Tudor timbered inn with good bar snacks, carvery, and dining-room with steaks and so forth; Trumans real ale; billiard-table annexe; jazz, children in family room; bedrooms *(Gwen and Peter Andrews)*

MUCH HADHAM [TL4319], *Bull*: good friendly pub (already licensed by 1727) with bar food; mini-zoo in big garden, children welcome *(Anon)*

NEWNEY GREEN [TL6507], *Duck*: interesting free house with efficient food service (when ordering you are given a large wooden duck with the order number), well kept Adnams, Greene King and Crouch Vale real ales; old beams, unusual decorations including antique farm and garden tools, even wind-up gramophone with pre-war record of Wolf *Lieder*; large garden with ponds *(Jeff Cousins, Gwen and Peter Andrews)*

NORTH SHOEBURY [Frobisher Way; TQ9485 – easiest to use ASDA car park, just off A13], *Parsons Barn*: wide range of food, well kept beers (including foreign bottled ones), in spacious gas-lit eighteenth-century barn, well restored and attractively converted; children in family room *(D G Ball, Aubrey Saunders)*

NOUNSLEY [TL7910], *Sportsmans Arms*: delightful country pub with good choice of freshly made bar food and well kept Ind Coope beer; warmly welcoming new Welsh landlord; climbing-frame in big garden *(Gwen and Peter Andrews)*

PAGLESHAM [TQ9293], *Plough & Sail*: wide choice of food and well kept Manns IPA and Websters Yorkshire in friendly and attractively decorated timbered seventeenth-century pub; big garden with aviary; nice nearby riverside walk *(Gwen and Peter Andrews)*; [East End] *Punchbowl*: food good and lovely atmosphere in immaculate bar with open fire, copper and brass; tall weatherboarded building stands out in flat countryside near church; interesting landlord; weekday happy hours *(Jenny Newman, David Surridge)*

PERRY GREEN [TL8021], *Hoops*: good bar food in pretty building; big garden *(David Surridge)*

PELDON [TL9916], *Rose*: dark-beamed seventeenth-century pub with small communicating flagstoned rooms, cheerfully served food and Adnams; tables in courtyard and big peaceful willow-screened gardens, swing and see-saw *(Gwen and Peter Andrews)*

PLESHEY [TL6614], *White Horse*: free house with old beams and bar and restaurant food, in interesting old village with many pargeted and thatched cottages; single women made to feel welcome *(Jeff Cousins, Gwen and Peter Andrews)*

RAMSDEN HEATH [TQ7195], *White Horse*: old character; Watneys *(Jeff Cousins)*

RAMSEY [TM2130], *Castle*: good meals and snacks in welcoming well kept pub *(Mr and Mrs F R Wilkinson)*

RAYLEIGH [The Chase; TQ8190], *Rayleigh Lodge*: Trumans and Ridleys on handpump, bar snacks, separate carvery; said to be haunted *(Tony Gayfer)*

ROCHFORD [Howe Green; TQ8790], *Cock*: friendly atmosphere, good food, wide choice of beers *(A King)*

SAFFRON WALDEN [High Street; TL5438], *Saffron*: food very good in restaurant and bar, well kept Greene King and Ruddles County beer; bedrooms *(D A Angless)*

STANSTED MOUNTFICHET [Pines Hill; TL5124], *Old Bell*: good food in bar and restaurant, excellent service *(Mr and Mrs J Goodhew)*

STEEPLE [TL9302], *Star*: friendly family pub with roomy L-shaped bar, log fire, much food from owner's own farm, Adnams real ales; also children's room, pool bar and garden *(Gwen and Peter Andrews)*

THAXTED [Bullring; TL6130], *Swan*: excellent food cooked on Aga behind bar, also soups, and other hot dishes, good puddings; cheerful atmosphere and service, Greene King and Rayments real ales; bedrooms *(Roger Doughty, N and J D Bailey)*

THEYDON BOIS [TQ4599], *Bull*: food cheerfully served at reasonable prices, with a good choice, in friendly and comfortable local with well kept Ind Coope real ale; can get crowded at weekends *(J R Main and others)*

TOOT HILL [TL5102], *Green Man*: good food and well kept Websters

Yorkshire – not to mention good wines and at least 10 champagnes – in friendly pub with chintzy lounge bar, restaurant, and fine views from tables in flowery garden *(D A Williams, Gwen and Peter Andrews)*

WEST BERGHOLT [TL9627], *White Hart*: cheap pub lunch, friendly hosts; was three farm cottages, converted about 100 years ago; garden *(M D Ripley)*

WEST HANNINGFIELD [TQ7399], *Three Compasses*: quiet pub with some beams and a good log fire; Trumans *(Jeff Cousins)*

WICKHAM BISHOPS [TL8412], *Mitre*: food good, friendly atmosphere; Ridleys real ale *(Jeff Cousins)*

WIDDINGTON [High Street; TL5331], *Fleur-de-Lys*: former tenant of Nags Head, Little Hadham (which in his hands was a main entry in previous *Guide* editions); good bar food and real ales, fine atmosphere, old-fashioned décor, friendly staff *(David Surridge)*

WILLINGALE [TL5907], *Bell*: old pub with real ale and much character, nooks and crannies; opposite two Norman churches unique for sharing the same churchyard *(Jeff Cousins)*

WITHAM [TL8214], *Green Man*: bar food and good beer, delightful setting *(Dave Butler, Les Storey)*; *White Hart*: friendly cheerful service, nice atmosphere, good reasonably priced food and drink *(W J Wonham)*

WIVENHOE [Black Buoy Hill; TM0321], *Black Buoy*: attractive welcoming pub with full range of Tolly beers; river views from dining-room *(Annie Taylor)*; *Rose & Crown*: good river views (with coasters passing windows at high tide) from friendly waterside pub with jovial landlord who has now installed well kept Ind Coope real ales *(Howard Gascoyne)*

WOODHAM MORTIMER [TL8104], *Hurdlemarkers Arms*: old pub with character and real ales including Greene King; usually well decorated at Christmas with real holly and ivy *(Jeff Cousins)*

Gloucestershire

Three pubs here gain a star award this year — the Kings Head in Bledington for its careful refurbishments (including pretty bedrooms) and good food, the Green Dragon near Cowley (again, good food, in an attractively simple and old-fashioned pub) and the New Inn at North Nibley (a surprising range of real ales, good food, and lovely surroundings). We can also report that the food at the friendly Crown in Blockley (imaginative daily specials) and at the elegant Hunters Hall at Kingscote has this year earned an even firmer claim to attention, while the new menu at the riverside Yew Tree at Chaceley Stock is warmly praised by readers. Among newcomers to this edition the Old Lodge in its fine position on Minchinhampton Common (good value home cooking and a range of real ales), the traditional stone-built Swan at Southrop (interesting recipes, daily changes of menu) and the well run old Royal Oak in the pretty little town of Painswick (highly rated daily specials) all have good food; among the older stagers we'd still pick out for their food the civilised Village Pub in Barnsley, the carefully renovated Wyndham Arms in Clearwell (near the Forest of Dean), the cheerfully traditional Plough at Ford and the Fossebridge Inn (with a terrace by the Coln and lakeside lawns); sandwich-lovers should head for the old Hobnails at Little Washbourne with its outstanding range of filled baps. Another newcomer this year, the Crown of Crucis at Ampney Crucis, scores for its

The Snowshill Arms, Snowshill

cheapness (both food and drinks). Places to stay, generally in attractive surroundings, include the Crown in Blockley, the stylish old Noel Arms in Chipping Campden, the Fossebridge Inn, the Lamb in Great Rissington (lovely views, particularly from its garden), the friendly Bathurst Arms in North Cerney, the rambling Mill Inn at Withington, the New Inn in Coln St Aldwyns, the elegantly old-fashioned Wild Duck at Ewen and the George by the ruined castle in St Briavels above the Wye; these last three are new to this edition. Several of the pubs already mentioned stand by rivers, and others whose waterside position is an attraction include the Fox at Great Barrington (a simple inn by the little Windrush), the Trout near Lechlade (with a big lawn by the upper Thames), and the Boat at Redbrook (steep gardens tumbling down to the Wye — and a good collection of real ales). A few of the Lucky Dips at the end of the chapter look as if they deserve a particularly thorough scrutiny of the small print: the Fox in the attractive village of Broadwell, the Crown at Frampton Mansell (particularly for its buffet), the Glasshouse in the village of that name (an unpretentious pub in lovely surroundings), the Mount at Stanton (for its views and its friendly old-fashioned atmosphere) and the Duke of York in Stroud (new owners concentrating on both real ale and real food). Prices are generally now relatively low in the area — and the local Donnington beer stands out as good value.

AMPNEY CRUCIS   SP0602   Map 4
Crown of Crucis
A417 E of Cirencester

On our visit this village pub was humming with the chat of older people out for lunch. It has been stripped back to bare stone and oak beams (sloping down low over the stripy cloth banquettes at the back), and its open-plan main room has plenty of leatherette seats around practical Formica-topped round tables. There are bright brass wall lamps in here, and modern pictures on the hessian walls of a side room serving food; this has a help-yourself lunchtime cold table (£2.75), and other lunchtime dishes include home-made soup (60p), a dish of the day (£1.60–£1.80) and a choice of ploughman's (£1.20). Other bar food includes sandwiches (from 65p, toasted from 80p, steak £2.10), basket meals such as sausages (£1.05) or scampi (£1.65), plaice (£1.40), filled baked potatoes (from £1.60), American-style burger (£2.10), vegetarian pancakes (£2.25), chicken stuffed with mushrooms and cream cheese (£2.75), steaks (from £4.75) and evening salads (from £2.10), with children's dishes (from 60p). A restaurant is open in the evening. Unusually low-priced Archers Village and Marstons Pedigree on handpump. There are lots of tables on the grass at the back, by a stream with ducks and maybe swans. *(Recommended by Sigrid and Peter Sobanski, CEP)*

Free house · Licensee R K Mills · Real ale · Meals and snacks · Children welcome · Open 10.30–2.30, 6–11 all year

BARNSLEY   SP0705   Map 4
Village Pub

A433 Cirencester–Burford

The low-ceilinged communicating rooms of this friendly and civilised pub's lounge are comfortably furnished with country-house-style chairs on a patterned brown carpet. Each room has its own log fire in winter, and some walls are stripped back to the bare stone. At one end a candlelit buttery bar, with table service, has more the atmosphere of a restaurant – the food is good and reasonably priced. It includes home-made soup (90p), sandwiches (from 95p, good prawn sandwiches £1.50), ploughman's (from £1.30), pâté (£1.50), pizza (£2), big Gloucester sausages (£3.25), plaice (£3.50), ham or beef salad (£3.50), roast chicken (£3.50), scampi (£4.50), good pink Bibury trout (£4.50) and sirloin steak (£5.25), with home-made apple pie (90p) and other puddings. Flowers IPA and Wadworths 6X on handpump, and a range of country wines; maybe piped music; dominoes, cribbage, backgammon. Tables on a small back terrace are sheltered by the house from the traffic which speeds down the village street. *(Recommended by Hope Chenhalls, Martin, Jane, Simon and Laura Bailey, Peter Baker, Tim Bracey, C Rollo)*

Free house · Licensee Derek Blakeley · Real ale · Meals and snacks · Children welcome · Open 11.30–2.30, 7–11 all year; closed 25 Dec

BLEDINGTON   SP2422   Map 4
Kings Head ★

B4450

The Smiths – quite new to pub-keeping until they took this one over a couple of years ago – have quickly found many friends among readers of the *Guide*, and this year win a star for their attractive Cotswolds pub. The changes they have made here have all been good, especially their careful refurbishments, and as we were going to press they heard that they were among the finalists in a Publican of the Year competition. The flagstone-floored bar now has high-backed settles and gateleg or pedestal tables, and there's a log fire in the inglenook fireplace; a new garden room leads off. The modernised kitchen is now producing good bar food, much of it home made, such as soup (95p), ploughman's (from £1.50), chicken curry (£2.25), pancake stuffed with prawns and mushrooms, grilled ham and egg, or leek and ham in cheese sauce (£2.75), rabbit pie (£3.95) and steak and wine pie (£4.95), with good crunchy summer salads (maybe ham off the bone) and puddings such as treacle tart or walnut and toffee tart. The restaurant does main courses such as Bibury trout stuffed with prawns and herbs and poached in wine (£5.25). A good choice of malt whiskies and country wines from the barrel, as well as well kept Hook Norton Best and Wadworths Devizes and 6X, on handpump from the antique bar counter; maybe piped music. The public bar has darts, pool – the Smiths have a remarkable collection of billiards and snooker antiques – Aunt Sally, dominoes, cribbage, shove-ha'penny, a fruit machine and a juke box. The three comfortable bedrooms are pretty and well equipped. There are tables among flowers in the garden behind the sixteenth-century house (which has a new terrace), with more on the front terrace, looking over the attractive village green with its ducks and stream. *(Recommended by Heather Sharland, B S Bourne, Virginia Jones, G H Theaker, S V Bishop)*

Free house · Licensees Graham and Rita Smith · Real ale · Meals and snacks Children in restaurant · Open 10–2.30, 6–11 all year · Bedrooms tel Kingham (060 871) 365; £29B

BLOCKLEY SP1634 Map 4
Crown ★

High Street

Readers pick out the daily specials for particular praise in this friendly and unpretentious Elizabethan inn, set in a golden-stone Cotswold village. Recently, they've included stewed eel, tripe espagnole with garlic bread (£2.25), chicken pizzaiola (£2.55), bacon pudding, lamb stew with caper sauce, cider casserole and mixed seafood bake (all £2.95). From the regular menu (which runs up to a 12-ounce rump steak at £5.99), favourites are the ploughman's (from Cheddar to smoked salmon pâté), home-baked ham and egg (£2.75), the local pink trout (£4.35), and the puddings, such as a light Bakewell tart. Soup is worth having when it's on the menu, and with a day's notice they'll do vegetarian dishes (and indeed, if they can, any other special fancy you might have). The Sunday roast lunch (£5.25, booking advised) has the same vast helpings as their weekday food. Well kept Butcombe, Cirencester Cellar (a fairly new local bitter), Hook Norton Best and a changing guest beer on handpump, also draught cider and in winter good mulled wine; maybe piped music. The snug little lounge bar has been recarpeted this year, and fitted out with traditional cast-iron-framed tables and extra Windsor chairs; it also has a pleasant window seat and a good log fire in winter, and steps lead up to the small dining-room. The old-fashioned settle has been moved through to the lively public bar, which has sensibly placed darts, shove-ha'penny, dominoes, cribbage and a fruit machine. There are white metal tables and chairs in the steep terraced coach-yard – or you can sit in front and have your drinks handed down from the window by the bar counter. The skittle alley has its own bar and is available for parties, skittle evenings, and so forth. Batsford Park Arboretum, with a beautiful collection of rare trees and shrubs, is nearby. A nice place to stay, and a good centre for walking. *(Recommended by S V Bishop, Frank Cummins, E M Burr, Tim Bracey, Jean Lockey)*

Free house · Licensee Ron Coomber · Real ale · Meals (not Sun evening) and snacks (not Sun) · Children welcome · Open 11–2.30, 7–11 · Bedrooms and meals tel Blockley (0386) 700245; £13.50/£22.50 (new rooms with own bathrooms planned by summer 1986), also an attractive adjacent self-catering cottage

Waterside pubs are listed at the back of the book.

CHACELEY STOCK   SO8530   Map 4
Yew Tree

Chaceley signposted from B4211 – follow road straight through village to river; or from B4213 turn N just W of Mythe Bridge (Haw Bridge), then right in Chaceley

The new à la carte menu in the spacious and pleasant river-view dining-room of this beautifully situated remote pub is good value, with regular main dishes including plaice (£2.75), trout (£3, or with their own special stuffing £4.95), scampi (£3.85) and steaks (from eight-ounce sirloin £5.20), daily specials such as duck in gooseberry and apple (£5.95), a good choice of children's dishes (from 65p), and a carvery – hot or cold. They also do Sunday roast lunches. There are bar snacks such as steak sandwich (85p), ploughman's (£1.15) and basket meals (£1.40–£2.35). From the original sixteenth-century core (low beams, soft lighting, comfortable seats, bared brick and stone walls), the bar area extends into a flagstoned room done up as a log cabin, with juke box and fruit machine; and a skittle alley with three pool- or full-size snooker-tables, sensibly placed darts, dominoes and cribbage. Uley Bitter (a new local brew), Wadworths 6X and Youngers No 3 on handpump. Attractive lawns with white tables and chairs by willow trees run down to a very quiet stretch of the River Severn, where the pub has its own floating moorings, and fishing rights here and from the meadows nearby (75p a day). No motor-cyclists or leathers; no dogs. *(Recommended by Aubrey Saunders, Mr and Mrs P May)*

Free house · Licensee Alan John Barlow · Real ale · Meals and snacks Children in dining-room · Open 11–2.30, 6–11

CHIPPING CAMPDEN   SP1539   Map 4
Noel Arms

The bar of this ancient stone inn has some attractive old tables, seats and settles among the Windsor chairs, a log fire, casks hanging from its beams, and bared stone walls decorated with farm tools, horseshoes and gin traps. Bar food includes freshly cut sandwiches (85p), pâté (£1.45), ploughman's (from £1.65), a variety of salads from pork pie or cheese and mushroom quiche to cold meats (£1.45– £2.50), steak sandwich (£3.95) and a changing choice of hot dishes such as mixed seafood savoury (£2.25) or steak and kidney pie (£2.50); Bass and Flowers Original on handpump. Beyond the hall, with Jacobean oak chairs and a wall hung with armour, there are comfortable and traditionally furnished lounges and a panelled restaurant. The inn is said to have been licensed since 1360, and Charles II is reputed to have stayed here on his flight after the Battle of Worcester. You can sit outside in the coach-yard. A nice place to stay, in a lovely village. *(More reports please)*

Free house · Licensee R P Sargent · Real ale · Meals and snacks (lunchtime) Children in lounges · Open 10.30–2.30, 6–11 all year · Bedrooms tel Evesham (0386) 840317; £22.50(£25.50B)/£30.50 (£39.50B)

Real ale to us means beer which has matured naturally in its cask – it is not pressurised and has not been filtered.

CLEARWELL SO5708 Map 4

Wyndham Arms

B4231; signposted from A466 S of Monmouth towards Lydney

The carefully renovated beamed bar of this well kept country inn has red plush seats and red velvet curtains, a collection of flat-irons by the log-effect gas fire in its spacious stone fireplace, and two big unusual patchwork pictures on the bared stone walls. Good bar food includes home-made soup (90p), sandwiches (from £1.15, fresh or smoked salmon £2.15), a choice of ploughman's (£1.95), egg and prawn mayonnaise (£2.35), spaghetti bolognese (£2.50), grilled local trout or sardines (£2.75), prawn curry (£2.75) and in season fresh salmon salad (£4.50). There is also a separate restaurant. Flowers Original and Whitbreads West Country on handpump, and free olives and gherkins on the brass-fringed bar counter. There are seats out on the well kept stone-terraced lawns (they won't serve food outside), and the village is in attractive countryside close to both the Wye Valley and the Forest of Dean. *(Recommended by RN, Graham Simpson, Dr and Mrs R Neville; more reports please)*

Free house · Licensees John and Rosemary Stanford · Real ale · Meals and snacks · Children welcome · Open 11–2.30, 5.30–11 all year; closed Christmas holiday · Bedrooms tel Dean (0594) 33666; £19/£38

COLN ST ALDWYNS SP1405 Map 4

New Inn

On good back road between Bibury and Fairford

This sixteenth-century stone inn, in a peaceful Cotswold village, is a pleasant place to stay. There's a friendly and informal atmosphere in the snug series of traditionally decorated knocked-through rooms which make up its bar, with lots of beams, antique high-backed settles, comfortable easy chairs (some by a big inglenook fireplace), Windsor armchairs, and some flagstones – though it's mainly carpeted. Bar food includes sandwiches, home-made soup (95p), home-made pâté (£1.30), asparagus and cheese flan (£1.50), steak and kidney pie (£2.50) and pink trout from the next village (£2.75); well kept Morlands (they still use the ancient arched-roof malt-house cellars) on handpump; darts, dominoes, cribbage. The separate restaurant serves evening meals from around £9. There are seats among tubs of flowers in front, and on a side lawn. *(Recommended by C F Walling)*

Free house · Licensee Bob Warren · Real ale · Meals and snacks · Children welcome (except in bar serving-room) · Open 11.30–2.30, 6–11 all year Bedrooms tel Coln St Aldwyns (028 575) 202; £17B/£34B

nr COWLEY SO8319 Map 4

Green Dragon ★

Cockleford; pub signposted from A435 about 1½ miles S of junction with A436; OS Sheet 163 reference 969142

The food has quickly established this charmingly renovated and welcoming country pub as a favourite with readers, and now that its new owners are well settled in we are awarding it a star. The menu changes weekly, with around seven hot dishes a day – over the year, they don't repeat any. The choice might include smoked haddock pâté or bread and Cheddar (£1.20), chilled almond soup or courgette and egg bake (£1.50), ploughman's (£1.60), first-class home-cured ham with salad (£1.70), vegetarian quiches (£1.75), rare beef salad (£1.90), asparagus and prawn mousse (£2), trout in ginger and butter sauce, lamb with fennel, squid in red wine, spiced beef in red cabbage, beef casserole with walnuts (all £2.95), and good puddings such as hazelnut meringue (£1.20). During the last year the dining-room has begun to function, and there's an attractive traditional bar, with big flagstones as well as some red carpet, logs burning – all year – in a spacious stone fireplace, beams, hunting prints on the cream walls, and steps down to a lower side area. Well kept Hook Norton Best on handpump, and Butcombe, Marstons, Ruddles and Theakstons Best tapped from the cask. There are seats outside by the car park, and by the honeysuckle climbing up the pub's stone front. *(Recommended by J H, Nigel Williamson, Herbert and Mary Gutfreund, J G Heath, N P Gibney)*

Free house · Licensee C J Phillips · Real ale · Meals and snacks · Children may be allowed in at licensee's discretion · Traditional jazz Mon · Open 11–3, 6–11 all year

nr ELKSTONE   SO9612   Map 4

Highwayman

Beechpike; A417 6 miles N of Cirencester

The softly lit bar of this attractive roadside pub rambles about under low beams and past old stripped stone walls, with cushioned antique settles as well as wheelbacks and Windsor armchairs around the tables, and logs burning in big fireboxes. Bar food includes soup (8op), cheese and ham toastie (£1), ploughman's (£2), substantial open sandwiches (£2), home-made liver pâté (£2), home-made pizzas (from £2.50), avocado pear with prawns, tuna or Stilton (£2.50), chicken or scampi in a basket (£2.95), sirloin steaks (from six-ounce £4.50) and home-made daily specials (£2.95), with summer salads such as quiche, prawn, beef and home-baked ham (from £2.50), and in winter filled baked potatoes (from £1.50), chilli con carne (£2.95) and home-made steak and mushroom pie (£3.25); there are children's dishes like fish fingers (£1.75), and puddings such as home-made fruit crumble (80p) or treacle tart (£1). A separate restaurant does duck, steaks and so forth. Well kept John Arkells, BBB and Kingsdown on handpump; a space game and a fruit machine in a back carpeted room (with a water buffalo head on the wall), and maybe piped pop music. There are picnic-table sets behind the pub on a neat sheltered rose lawn, and a good climber, slide and swings among a veritable forest of young conifers for children to chase around in. *(Recommended by Sigrid and Peter Sobanski)*

Arkells · Licensees David and Heather Bucher · Real ale · Meals and snacks Children in two family rooms · Open 11–2.30, 6–11 (10.30 Mon–Weds in winter)

Pubs brewing their own beers are listed at the back of the book.

EWEN   SU0097 Map 4

Wild Duck

Village signposted from A429 S of Cirencester

Quietly placed on the edge of a peaceful village yet handy for
Cirencester, this well kept and old-fashioned inn has a civilised bar
with candle-style lamps set on big wooden wheels hanging from its
high beams, old guns, swords, horse brasses and duck pictures on the
walls, a long-case clock, and attractive seats and tables among the red
rugs on its parquet floor. In winter there's an open fire in the
handsome stone fireplace. Bar food includes soup, sandwiches (from
£1.25 – the steak sandwich is very good), home-made chicken liver
pâté (£1.50), ploughman's (£2), cottage pie (£2.25) and scampi
(£3.25); Archers Village and Wadworths 6X on handpump, gentle
piped music. Full meals are served in two pretty and cosy dining-
rooms at the back, and there are teak tables and chairs in the
sheltered and well kept garden. The bedrooms are very comfortable.
*(Recommended by Sigrid and Peter Sobanski, Roger Cossham, Mr and Mrs D
Dodd, F A Noble)*

*Free house · Licensee Martin Pulley · Real ale · Meals and snacks · Open
10.30–2.30, 6.30–11 all year · Bedrooms tel Kemble (028 577) 310;
£32.50B/£45B*

FORD   SP0829 Map 4

Plough ★

B4077

Readers continue to enthuse about the generous ploughman's here –
Cheddar or Stilton with a big salad including maybe pear, grapes and
fresh pineapple (£1.75). In May (and later if supplies allow) there are
asparagus feasts (£6), and other popular dishes have included soup
(85p), avocado pear with Stilton (£2), steak and kidney pie (£2.50),
duck pie (£4), home-cured bacon or scampi (£4.50) and fresh crab or
lobster (£6.50). The friendly and lively rambling bar has beams, bare
stone walls, log fires, and old settles and benches on its flagstones.
Every evening the scrubbed deal tables in one snug carpeted alcove
are set with candles and tablecloths. The old sign outside says *Step in
and quaff my nut-brown ale* – Donnington BB, SBA and XXX Mild
on handpump; darts, shove-ha'penny, dominoes, cribbage and a fruit
machine. There are benches in front of this pretty stone roadside
house, and rustic tables and chairs on grass by white lilacs and fairy
lights, shielded from the road by a stone wall. *(Recommended by
B S Bourne, Doug Kennedy, PLC, Tim Bracey, Gordon and Daphne,
Anthony Blond)*

*Donnington · Licensee Leslie Carter · Real ale · Meals and snacks · Children
welcome · Pianist most nights, band Sat · Open 10.30–2.30, 5.30–11 all year
Bedrooms tel Stanton (Glos) (038 673) 215; £20*

Prices of main dishes usually include vegetables or a side salad.

Post Office address codings confusingly give the impression that some pubs are
in Gloucestershire, when they're really in the Midlands – which is where we list
them.

Fossebridge

A429 Cirencester—Stow-on-the-Wold

This handsome Georgian inn has a lakeside lawn and a terrace by the little River Coln, and, in summer, tables set out here deservedly draw the crowds; but all year round its bar food – served in an older Tudor area – is an attraction. It includes sandwiches (from £1, beef or crab £1.50), ploughman's with a choice of cheeses (£1.50), home-made soup (£1.50), home-made fish terrine (£2.50), omelettes, grilled avocado with crab stuffing or cottage pie (£2.90), home-made steak and kidney pie (£4.25), trout served in several ways (from £4.50), steaks (from £6.80) and perhaps salads with meats carved off the bone, or fresh salmon in season. The two rooms of this bar area, linked by arches in a thick bare stone wall, have oriental rugs on the flagstones, a carpeted dining area with plush seats and prints on the walls, and a heartening log fire on those wet and windy days which seem the rule for readers' walks here. Well kept Ushers Best and Founders and Theakstons Best on handpump, and a useful choice of good malt whiskies and reasonably priced wines; sensibly placed darts and a fruit machine. Close to Denfurlong Farm Trail, and not far from the Chedworth Roman villa (you can walk all the way from the inn, along the pretty river valley). *(Recommended by Robert Anderson, S V Bishop, William Meadon, Richard Steel, Herbert and Mary Gutfreund, A Saunders, Tim Bracey)*

Free house · Licensee Alan Prior · Real ale · Meals and snacks · Children in eating area and restaurant · Open 11–2.30, 6–11 all year; closed 25 Dec Bedrooms (no children under 10) tel Fossebridge (028 572) 310; £18.80 (£24B)/£25 (£32B)

The Dog at Over, nr Gloucester

nr GLOUCESTER   SO8019 Map 4

Dog at Over   [*illustrated on page 293*]

A40, just W of city

Since our last edition this handy roadside pub has been redecorated and refurbished in keeping with its age – and it is much older than you might expect from outside. Through the door you can see heavily timbered walls (covered with pictures and cigarette cards of all sorts of different breeds of dog), low beams at the front, and flagstones sloping up towards the back, where there are quite high black rafters. Bar food includes sandwiches and ready-filled rolls, soup (85p), ploughman's, pizza, toad-in-the-hole or giant sausage (£1.55), cheese and onion flan (£1.60), cottage pie (£1.65), curry (£1.85), turkey pie (£1.95), scampi (£2.15) and roast beef (£2.65); gentle piped music, friendly service, and a fruit machine. In the evening the restaurant has had good value special-offer suppers with a choice from half a dozen main courses, including a drink. There are tables under cocktail parasols on a side lawn. (*Recommended by F I Britton; more reports please*)

Bass · Licensee Ronald Sills · Meals and snacks · Children in eating area Occasional live music · Open 10.30–2.30, 6–10.30

GREAT BARRINGTON   SP2013 Map 4

Fox

Village signposted from A40 Burford–Northleach; pub between Little and Great Barrington

There's a warm welcome in the low-ceilinged bar of this simple Cotswold inn, which has rustic wooden chairs, tables and window seats, bare stone walls, warm winter fires, and a satisfying absence of frills and pretensions. Bar food includes 'home-brewed' soup (65p), toasted sandwiches (80p–90p), ploughman's (£1.40), pâté (£1.50), salads, and hot dishes such as chicken, fish, scampi and pies served with salad or chips and peas (£1.40–£2.50); well kept Donnington BB, SBA and XXX Mild on handpump; sensibly placed darts, dominoes, cribbage, and a fruit machine. There is a skittle alley out beyond the sheltered yard, which has seats by the little River Windrush: it was from here that stone, quarried nearby, was ferried downstream for the building of St Paul's Cathedral. (*Recommended by G H Theaker, Heather Sharland*)

Donnington · Licensee F W Mayer · Real ale · Meals (not Sun) and snacks Open 11–2.30, 6.30–11 all year · Bedrooms tel Windrush (045 14) 385; £10/£20

GREAT RISSINGTON   SP1917 Map 4

Lamb

The comfortable lounge bar of this friendly, partly seventeenth-century Cotswold inn has wheelback chairs grouped around polished tables on the carpet, plates and lots of small pictures decorating the cream walls, a good range of often unusual real ales, and normally winter log fires in its stone fireplace. In summer readers have found the pub coming into its own, with its pretty little garden sheltered by the way it's set into the hillside, and by its neat stone walls and stone pergola. There is a play area and an aviary, and it has a charming view across the rest of the valley and village to the hills beyond. Bar food includes home-made soup (85p), home-made chicken liver pâté (£1.40), home-made shepherd's pie (£2.45), smoked mackerel salad (£2.75), chicken (£2.95), scampi (£3.45), home-made steak and kidney pie (£3.65), grilled lamb steak or local trout (£4.85), sirloin steak (£6.45) and puddings such as raspberry and redcurrant pie (95p); they will do sandwiches. There is a separate dining-room. Well kept Boddingtons, Burton Bridge XL, Flowers Original, Hancocks HB and Wadworths 6X on handpump; maybe piped music. The bedrooms are attractively furnished. *(Recommended by J H, Leith Stuart, Jamie Allan; more reports please)*

Free house · Licensees Richard and Kate Cleverly · Real ale · Meals and snacks Children in eating area, dining-room and area partly set aside for them · Open 11.30–2.30, 6.30–11 all year · Bedrooms tel Cotswold (0451) 20388; £12.50/£21

KINGSCOTE   ST8196   Map 4

Hunters Hall ★

A4135 Dursley–Tetbury

Now well settled in to this fine Tudor pub, Mr Barnett-Roberts has firmly established the food as a major attraction. Served with friendly efficiency in a pleasant buffet bar which looks out over the big garden, this includes sandwiches, avocado and prawns (£1.50), turkey and ham pie (£2) or quiche (£2.20) with salad, home-made steak and kidney pie or seafood pancakes (£2.75), king prawns with garlic bread or local trout with almonds (£3.25), rare roast beef salad (£3.50), charcoal-grilled steaks (from £5 for eight-ounce rump) and duckling in honey and chestnut sauce (£5.25). The several high-ceilinged connecting rooms have comfortable easy chairs and sofas and one fine old box settle, velvet curtains, elegant beams, exposed stone walls and a winter log fire; Bass and Fussells Best on handpump. The low-ceilinged public bar has sturdy settles and oak tables on the flagstones in front of another big log fire; shove-ha'penny, dominoes, sensibly placed darts, pool in a separate games area (which has a juke box), and a fruit machine in the entry lobby. In fine summer weather they have weekend barbecues, and throughout the year a good separate restaurant is open on Tuesday to Saturday evenings. *(Recommended by David Surridge, Col D G Stafford, Miss H F Kavanagh)*

Free house · Licensee David Barnett-Roberts · Real ale · Meals and snacks Children in buffet bar · Open 11–2.30, 7–11 all year; closed 25 Dec

nr LECHLADE   SU2199   Map 4

Trout

St John's Bridge; 1 mile E of Lechlade on A417

The extensive riverside lawn makes this a charming spot in summer: tables by a venerable walnut-tree look over a broad, still stretch of the upper Thames where, under an ancient royal charter, the pub has two miles of coarse fishing rights. There is a summer bar and family marquee out here, with barbecues on fine Sunday lunchtimes. Inside, the low-beamed and partly panelled bar, decorated with stuffed pike and trout, has Windsor chairs on polished flagstones, with leatherette bucket seats around copper-topped tables in a carpeted area beyond a wrought-iron room divider. A wide choice of good value home-made bar food includes soup (£1), ploughman's, home-made macaroni cheese with roll and butter (£1.75), various basket meals, scallops in a prawn and mushroom white wine sauce (£2.50), pizza (£2.95), chicken and mushroom pie (£3.95) and steaks, with daily specials, several puddings and children's dishes; in summer there are salads (from £4.50), including good crab. Though they don't normally do sandwiches, they may be able to if it's really quiet. Courage Best, Simonds and Directors on handpump; dominoes, cribbage. There's a small separate evening dining-room (prices 10 per cent higher). (Recommended by S V Bishop)

Courage · Licensee Ronald Turnbull · Real ale · Meals and snacks; dining-room bookings tel Faringdon (0367) 52313 · Children in eating area and (at lunchtime, or if it's not being used) in dining-room · Occasional live music Open 10.30–2.30, 6–11 all year

LITTLE WASHBOURNE   SO9933   Map 4
Hobnails

A438 Tewkesbury–Stow-on-the-Wold

This mossy-tiled white pub, partly fifteenth-century, has a charming little front bar with old wall benches by a couple of tables on its quarry-tiled floor and pewter tankards hanging from its low sagging beams. A bigger carpeted back bar is more modern, with comfortable orange button-back leatherette banquettes, and there is a little panelled dining-room (must book) with old-fashioned touches. The most unusual aspect of its bar food is the marvellous range of over 50 different filled baps (from 75p, liver and onion £1, liver and mushroom or gammon and pineapple £1.25, steak with egg and mushroom £2.10). There are also home-made soups such as oxtail with sherry (85p) and puddings such as chocolate gateau with cream or banana rum pudding (90p). On Tuesday to Saturday evenings a full menu includes gammon, scampi, steaks and so forth (around £4–£6.50). Flowers IPA and Original and Whitbreads West Country PA on handpump and electric pump; darts, shove-ha'penny and a fruit machine. A separate skittle alley (for hire Monday to Friday evenings) has more tables. A terrace beyond the car park has good tables by a small lawn and flowerbed. (Recommended by William Meadon, Richard Steel, Rachel Waterhouse, Phyllis Deane, A Nicol)

Flowers (Whitbreads) · Licensee Stephen Farbrother · Real ale · Meals (evenings, not Sun or Mon) and snacks; dining-room bookings tel Alderton (024 262) 237 · Children in skittle alley (lunchtimes, and evenings if not booked) and dining-room · Open 10.30–2.30, 6–11 all year; closed 25–26 Dec

LOWER SWELL   SP1725   Map 4

Golden Ball

B4068 W of Stow-on-the-Wold (sometimes still called A436 on maps)

By the little village stream, the quiet back garden belonging to this friendly seventeenth-century inn is a pleasant place to sit in summer, and in the winter there's a log fire – and lots of local atmosphere – in the simply furnished stripped-stone-wall bar. Bar food includes soup (65p, cold weather only), sandwiches (from 65p), ploughman's (from £1.45), steak and onion pie (£1.75), steak and kidney pie (£1.80), stovies or turkey and ham pie (£1.85) and chicken Cordon Bleu, seafood platter or scampi (£2.50); the well kept Donnington BB, SBA and XXX Mild on handpump comes from little more than a mile away. Behind the fireplace a games area has sensibly placed darts and a fruit machine. *(Recommended by Tim and Ann Bracey, C F Walling)*

Donnington · Licensee John Roe · Real ale · Meals and snacks · Accordion sing-alongs some Fri nights · Bedrooms tel Stow-on-the-Wold (0451) 30247; £9/£18

MINCHINHAMPTON   SO8600   Map 4

Old Lodge

Minchinhampton Common; from centre of common take Box turn-off then fork right at pub's signpost

Based on a sixteenth-century royal hunting lodge that's reputed still to be haunted by a lady in grey, this pub is beautifully placed on the high plateau of a National Trust common, surrounded by neatly grazed grass and Iron Age earthworks. Good home-made food includes filled rolls and sandwiches (from 50p, toasted 10p extra, particularly good value steak 75p), soup (65p), ploughman's (from £1.10), giant sausage (£1.30), salads (from £1.50), four-ounce hamburger or scampi (£1.75), liver and bacon (£2.25), lamb chops (£3.25) and eight-ounce rump steak (£4.50), with at least eight freshly made specials each day, such as cannelloni (£1.30), Breton pie (like shepherd's but topped with cauliflower cheese, £1.75), steak and kidney pie (£2.25 – they make their own pastry, too), stuffed peppers (£2.75), pork chops in cider or lamb noisettes (£2.95) and local trout (£3.25). There is a children's menu (from 65p), a choice of delicious puddings (mostly 80p), and a good value Sunday roast lunch (two courses £3.25, children's £2.75). Service is friendly and helpful. The simply furnished blue-carpeted central bar – serving Fullers London Pride, Hook Norton Best, Mitchells, Smiles and Theakstons – is small and snug, opening into a pleasant bared brick family room and an airy stripped stone dining area; maybe piped music. There's also a lively separate public bar, with darts, pool, juke box and a fruit machine. Tables on a neat lawn by an attractive herbaceous border look over grey stone walls to the common and beyond. The common has pony-trekking and a golf course. *(Recommended by A Close, Jane Alexander)*

Free house · Licensees Mr and Mrs Michael Peacock, Mrs S Kempton · Real ale Meals and snacks · Children in eating area and family room · Open 11.30– 2.30, 6.30–11 (12–2.30, 7–11 in winter)

NORTH CERNEY SP0208 Map 4
Bathurst Arms

A435 Cirencester—Cheltenham

Good value as a place to stay, this friendly and relaxed old inn has high-backed antique settles and nice window seats, with Windsor chairs on the Turkey carpet of its beamed and black-panelled bar. There's a splendid stone fireplace in here, with good winter log fires, and pewter tankards hang above the bar counter, which has well kept Archers Best, Flowers Original and a changing guest beer on handpump. A similar communicating area behind has tables set for the bar food (which includes sandwiches), and at weekends a separate restaurant is open, with a full menu running to lamb cutlets, steaks and so forth. The simply furnished public bar has darts and a fruit machine, and there is a quite separate Stables Bar with a lively young atmosphere: red lighting in a loosebox décor, an array of space games and a good loud juke box or piped pop music. There are tables outside on a pretty front lawn by the little River Churn, with summer barbecues. (*Recommended by Michael Main, Miss R Edmunds, R A B, D A Gatward, David Varney, Patrick Stapley*)

Free house · Licensees Norma Judd and Chris Kite · Real ale · Meals and snacks Children in eating area · Open 11–2.30, 6–11 all year · Bedrooms tel North Cerney (028 583) 281; £19B/£25B

NORTH NIBLEY ST7496 Map 4
New Inn ★

Waterley Bottom; inn signposted from lanes around village; one route is from A4135 S of Dursley, via lane with red sign saying Steep Hill, 1 in 5 (just SE of Stinchcombe Golf Course turn-off), turning right when you get to the bottom; OS sheet 162 reference 758963

Readers' continuing surprise at finding just how very good this pub is (especially bearing in mind its remote position) prompts us this year to award it a star – in the hope of giving people a better idea of how much they can expect. It scores in several ways: an exceptionally welcoming landlady, the remarkable range of well kept real ales, good value home-made bar food including sandwiches, ploughman's, salads, farmhouse pâté (£1.20), lasagne or chilli con carne (£1.60), meat and onion pie (£1.90) and puddings such as apricot and rhubarb crumble (75p), and lovely views. There are usually more than half a dozen real ales in stock, a changing range that often includes Cotleigh Tawny, Smiles Best and Exhibition and Theakstons Old Peculier, as well as WB (a bitter brewed for the pub by Cotleigh). There are also quite a lot of unusual bottled beers, as well as Inch's and other even less common ciders. A fine collection of antique handpump beer engines includes the ones actually in use. Cushioned Windsor chairs and varnished high-backed settles against the partly bared stone walls of the cosy carpeted lounge bar (which has piped music) give a view through picture windows of a beautifully kept rose terrace, the garden beyond, and then a bowl of quiet pastures, rising to a fringe of woods. The simply furnished public bar has sensibly placed darts, dominoes played every night, shove-ha'penny, cribbage, chess, backgammon and a fruit machine. At the far end of the garden are swings and slides in a small orchard. A comfortable place to stay, in pleasant walking country; you have to book a long way ahead. *(Recommended by Miss E R Bowmer, Alan Franck, Prof H Gutfreund, P A Woolley)*

Free house · Licensee Ruby Sainty · Real ale · Meals and snacks · Open 11–2.30, 6–11 all year (opens 1 hour later in winter) · Two bedrooms tel Dursley (0435) 3659; £9.50/£19

PAINSWICK   SO8609   Map 4
Royal Oak

St Mary's Street

In the centre of a charming small stroll-about hillside town of old stone buildings, narrow alleys and antique shops, this pub has a convivial lounge bar, with seats and copper-topped tables made from barrels, an elegant oak settle (and lovely panelled oak door), some walls stripped back to silvery stone, and an open fire in the massive chimney which divides the room into two parts. There's a second bar on the left, and a small sun-lounge in a sheltered sun-trap courtyard with wistaria and colourful pots of geraniums and calceolaria. Sandwiches or large filled rolls (from 70p), home-made soup (80p), ploughman's (from £1), home-made chicken liver pâté (£1.30), salads (from £2.40) and a good range of hot dishes, changing every day (£1.85–£5); well kept Flowers Original and Whitbreads PA on handpump; quick, efficient service. *(Recommended by Peter Wigens, Capt F A Bland)*

Flowers (Whitbreads) · Licensee David Morris · Real ale · Meals and snacks (not Sun) · Open 11–2.30, 6–11 all year

REDBROOK   SO5410   Map 4
Boat

Pub's car park in village on A466 Chepstow–Monmouth; from here 100-yard footbridge crosses Wye (pub actually in Penallt in Wales – but much easier to find this way)

A steep terraced garden behind the pub has tables among little waterfalls, a pond cut into the rocks with ducks, and splendid views of the river. Inside, the chief charm is the changing choice of real ales, tapped straight from casks behind the long curved bar counter, such as Butcombe, Flowers IPA or Original, Hook Norton Best and Theakstons Old Peculier. Good value food includes ploughman's with a generous choice of cheeses (£1.65), quiche, chilli con carne or vegetarian lasagne with salad (£2.25) and roast chicken or turkey Cordon Bleu (£3.25). The simply furnished two-roomed bar has some of its walls stripped back to bare stone; darts, dominoes, cribbage, a fruit machine and a space game. *(Recommended by Pamela and Merlyn Horswell, Roger Entwistle, Anne Morris, Jenny Woolf, Monica Darlington; more reports please)*

Free house · Real ale · Meals and snacks · Children in snug adjoining bar · Has had folk music Tues, traditional jazz Thurs · Open 11–3, 6–11 all year

ST BRIAVELS SO5605 Map 4

George

The flagstoned terrace behind this old village inn – becoming very popular under its new owners Mr and Mrs Day – has an outdoor chess board, and tables among roses, herbaceous plants and a pear tree; it looks over a grassy 'moat' to the massive silvery stone wall of the largely ruined thirteenth-century castle. There's a lively local atmosphere in the three main areas of the rambling black-beamed bar, which is partly divided by a thick stone wall, with green-cushioned small settles, old-fashioned built-in wall seats, some booth seating, and a big wood-burning stove. Home-made bar food includes sandwiches, soup (90p), good chicken liver pâté, cauliflower cheese or chilli con carne (£1.80), salads (from £2), shepherd's pie or good celery and ham Mornay (£2.50) and fresh trout or steak and kidney pie (£3.50); well kept Marstons Pedigree and Wadworths IPA and 6X on handpump; a fruit machine and a juke box. *(Recommended by Mr and Mrs Roy Wales; more reports please)*

Free house · Licensee Maurice Edward Day · Real ale · Meals (not Sun lunchtime or Mon evening) and snacks · Open 11–2.30, 6–11 all year Bedrooms tel Dean (0594) 530228; £12/£18

SNOWSHILL SP0934 Map 4

Snowshill Arms [*illustrated on page 285*]

Lots of old photographs of this pretty honey-coloured Cotswold village (and its bygone cricketers) decorate the partly panelled and stripped stone walls of this friendly pub's open-plan beamed bar. From the back there are fine country views, and seats in the front bow windows look up to steep pastures rising behind the attractive church on the other side of the small green. Simple furnishings include comfortable sturdy leatherette benches and seats on a sea-green patterned carpet. Good value food is served such as sandwiches, creamy home-made soup, generous ploughman's, lasagne and sweet chicken curry; well kept Donnington BB and SBA on handpump; sensibly placed darts, dominoes, sitting space game, fruit machine and a skittle alley. There are lots of swings and a slide and climber in the garden behind, with a Tannoy out here to announce when food is ready. The neighbouring manor is open in summer (not Monday or Tuesday) and at weekends in April and October. *(Recommended by Frank Cummins, L N Goulding, P L C, Fl Lt F H Goodacre)*

Donnington · Licensee Hans Schad · Real ale · Meals and snacks · Children in eating area · Open 10.30–2.30, 6–11 all year (opens 6.30 in winter)

SOUTHROP SP1903 Map 4

Swan

Village signposted from A417 and A361, near Lechlade

Quiet at lunchtime, this welcoming village pub fills up in the evenings for its good home-made food, which changes from day to day but might typically include soup (£1.20), pâtés (£1.60), deep-fried

Camembert with cranberry and mint sauce (£1.60), smoked prawns, or scampi and prawns in pastry (£1.90), buckwheat pancakes filled with chicken and bacon or salmon and asparagus (£4.55), fruity pork fillet cooked in cider (£4.75), seafood in puff pastry (£4.95), tandoori poussin (£5) and charcoal-grilled sirloin steak (£5.35). Some of each day's evening dishes are sold, more cheaply, at lunchtime: on our visit, chilled cucumber soup, avocado and curd cheese pâté (£1.50), taramosalata (£1.90), moussaka or grilled sardines (£2.20) and seafood in puff pastry (£2.50); also sandwiches then. The small low-ceilinged front lounge bar feels cottagey, with studded leatherette chairs and rugs on a parquet floor, and winter log fires. A much more roomy stripped stone back skittle alley, nicely modernised and carpeted, with plenty of well spaced tables, has steps down to its bar counter (with a juke box and a fruit machine), and there are tables in the sheltered garden behind this creeper-covered stone-tiled pub. Well kept Morlands PA and Hook Norton Best on handpump; darts, cribbage. (Recommended by R Wilson, Mr and Mrs R Kemp)

Free house · Licensee Patrick Keen · Real ale · Meals and lunchtime snacks Children in skittle alley · Open 12–2.30, 6.30–11 all year (opens 7 in winter)

nr STOW-ON-THE-WOLD SP1925 Map 4
Coach & Horses

Ganborough; A424 2½ miles N of Stow; OS Sheet 163 reference 172292

Good home cooking and friendly, attentive service make this a welcome stop. The main bar area has leatherette wall benches, stools and Windsor chairs on a flagstone floor, with steps up to a carpeted part which has high-backed settles around the tables, and coach horns on the ceiling joists, and at the other end (beyond a central chimney with a winter log fire) a games area with bar billiards and sensibly placed darts – popular with visiting firemen from the nearby fire college. The walls are decorated with good lively photographs of customers and other wildlife. Food includes game soup (85p), sandwiches (85p), toasties such as Stilton and celery (£1), macaroni cheese (95p), cottage pie (£1.20), prawns (£1.40), ploughman's (from £1.50), home-made lasagne (£1.60), omelettes (£2.30), lemon sole (£2.40), scampi (£2.90), steak and kidney pie (£3), good local pink trout (£3.20) and sirloin steak (£5.95); particularly well kept Donnington BB and SBA from the nearby brewery on handpump. There are seats outside on a terrace and a narrow lawn. (Recommended by Angela and Colin Underwood, Dr A K Clarke, Michael Sandy, Eirlys Roberts)

Donnington · Licensees Dave and Joy Langdon · Real ale · Meals and snacks (not Sun evening, perhaps not Tues evening) · Open 10.30–2.30, 6–11 all year

WITHINGTON SP0315 Map 4
Mill Inn ★

Village signposted from A436 and from A40; from village centre follow sign towards Roman villa (but don't be tempted astray by villa signs *before* you reach the village!)

The rambling carpeted bar of this mossy-roofed old stone inn is full of nice little nooks and corners, with antique high-backed settles and big cut-away barrel seats under its beams, an attractive bay window seat, log fires on cool days, and a high shelf of old china and pewter. The inn and the old mill opposite are virtually alone in a little valley surrounded by beech and chestnut trees and a rookery, and its neatly kept gardens include a pretty series of islets in the little River Coln which winds through them (and on down to the Roman villa – a goodish walk from the pub). Food includes sandwiches, ploughman's, salads, basket meals such as chicken (£2.45) or scampi (£2.60) and steak and kidney pie (£2.45); Bass on handpump; pleasant management. The quarry-tiled public bar has darts, shove-ha'penny, fruit machine and a space game. Don't expect to have the place to yourself on fine weekends, even in winter. A nice place to stay, with plenty of walks nearby. *(Recommended by N F Mackley, Robert Aitken, D A Gatward, Heather and Roy Sharland)*

Free house · Licensee M G P Stourton · Real ale · Meals and snacks · Children in eating area · Open 11.30–2.30, 6.30–10.30 · Bedrooms tel Withington (024 289) 204; £17/£32

Lucky Dip

Besides the fully inspected pubs, you might like to try these Lucky Dips recommended and described by readers (if you do, please send us reports):

ALDERTON [SP0033], *Gardeners Arms*: cosy thatched Tudor pub with old-fashioned atmosphere, civilised food and décor, Whitbreads real ales and sheltered terrace *(LYM)*

ANDOVERSFORD [SP0219], *Royal Oak*: friendly family pub, good reasonably priced food, Flowers and guest real ales, log fires, pub games; upstairs restaurant *(Gwyn Jones)*

APPERLEY [SO8628], *Farmers Arms*: friendly atmosphere, efficiently run pub with interesting range of bar snacks and good value separate restaurant; Flowers and West Country on handpump *(A Saunders)*

ARLINGHAM [SO7111]. *Old Passage*: comfortably modernised pub alone on banks of River Severn, well kept Wadworths real ales *(LYM)*

BERKELEY ROAD [SO7200], *Prince of Wales*: convenient for Berkeley Castle and Slimbridge; short detour from junctions 13 and 14 of M5 *(S V Bishop)*

BROAD CAMPDEN [SP1637], *Bakers Arms*: imaginative food and Whitbreads real ales in welcoming Cotswold stone pub; seats outside, children welcome *(Anon)*

BROADWELL [SP2027], *Fox*: cosy pub on green of attractive Cotswold village, good food (none Tuesday or Sunday), particularly friendly service, draught cider and well kept Donnington ales; fine collection old beer and cider mugs, winter log fires, large garden; close to Joe Elliott's famous alpine plants nursery *(S A Lovett, J G Heath, Mr and Mrs M J Burchnall, D Wynne, Prof A N Black, Dr A K Clarke)*

BROCKWEIR [SO5401], *Brockweir*: well kept choice of real ales and straightforward bar food in simple bare-stone-wall Wye Valley village inn, well placed for walks *(J A Johnson, Doug Kennedy, LYM)*

CHEDWORTH [SP0511], *Seven Tuns*: good simple home cooking, friendly service, cosy little lounge with inglenook, attractive surroundings *(P J Brooks)*

CHELTENHAM [Alma Road; SO9422], *Bass House*: food and beer (including Hook Norton) good with friendly, efficient service; large welcoming modern estate pub *(JH)*; [Portland Street] *Cotswold*: pleasant comfortable town pub with well kept Wadworths IPA and 6X *(David Symes)*; [North Place] *Dog & Pheasant* (was *Fountain*): remarkably good pizzas in friendly, roomy, comfortable Regency pub with helpful staff; good range of real ales including Robinsons; handy for western end of main shopping area *(Michael and Alison Sandy, David Symes)*; [St Georges Road] *Lodge Bar*: good lunchtime food and drinks in pleasantly furnished place on borderline between pub, wine bar and restaurant *(Mrs Jenny Blake)*; [High Street] *Restoration*: food very good, excellent choice of ales, unusual décor *(Linda Thomas)*

CHIPPING CAMPDEN [SP1539], *Kings Arms*: has been very popular with readers for unusual food and stylish accommodation, but under new management since late 1984; more reports please *(S V Bishop, B W Williams, JH, LYM)*; *Lygon Arms*: the place for a good big snack at a reasonable price *(Anon)*

CIRENCESTER [SP0201], *Crown*: good bistro-style food in newly opened pub decorated like a wine bar with lots of stripped pine, oriental rugs and second-hand books; Courage Directors, Wadworths and wine *(L R Hickish)*

COATES [SO9700], *Tunnel House*: good cheap food in lively, friendly pub with warm cosy rooms; well kept Flowers Original, Wadworths 6X, nostalgic juke box; popular with Royal Agricultural College students; under same ownership as *Bathurst Arms*, North Cerney (see main entry) *(L R Hickish, BB)*

COLESBOURNE [SO9913], *Colesbourne*: food good in comfortable lounge *(Sigrid and Peter Sobanski)*

CRANHAM [SO8912], *Royal William*: pleasantly placed in Cranham Woods; bar food *(K Mills)*

DURSLEY [Kingshill; ST7598], *Kingshill*: friendly, clean pub with 1920s décor; good range of unusual and reasonably priced home-cooked dishes; Whitbreads beers *(K R Harris)*

EBLEY [Westward Road; SO8205], *Old Crown*: home-made food with big helpings, in friendly and homely pub with choice of ales *(J B Tippett)*

EDGE [SO8509], *Edgemoor*: nicely refurbished old village pub with log fires, good atmosphere, beer and food – especially 18-ounce T-bone steak *(AM)*

FOREST OF DEAN [SO6212], *Speech House*: food in bar – especially salads – good, with wide choice and ample helpings; nice garden; THF hotel, alone in forest *(W J Wonham, John Milroy)*

FRAMPTON MANSELL [SO9102], *Crown*: well kept Wadworths 6X; generous helpings of good meat with salads from buffet in dining-room can be eaten in comfortably old-fashioned lounge; friendly service *(Frank Cummins, CEP)*

GLASSHOUSE [SO7122], *Glasshouse*: good simple bar snacks and several well kept beers in gem of an unpretentious pub, at idyllic spot near National Trust May Hill *(Alan Cookson)*

GLOUCESTER [SO8318], *County Arms*: notable for its large range of cheap ciders *(Anon)*; [Barton Street] *Crown & Thistle*: pleasant no-frills town pub with good choice of well kept real ales *(David Symes)*

nr GLOUCESTER [A46; SO8318], *Greenways*: good food and drink in country-house setting *(R Squire; can any reader give us more precise directions?)*

GUITING POWER [SP0924], *Farmers Arms*: simple stone village inn with good value Donnington real ales and skittle alley; close to Cotswold Farm Park; bedrooms *(LYM)*; *New Inn*: good home cooking (best chips for miles) in two small, friendly bars with open fires *(P J Brooks)*

nr HORSLEY [Nailsworth; ST8397], *Tipputs Inn*: pleasant well renovated pub with good range of real ales *(P A Woolley)*

LANGFORD [SP2402], *Bell*: friendly and inviting pub with good beer and excellent bar snacks *(R Wilson)*

LECHLADE [SU2199], *Red Lion*: well renovated after recent fire; good food in bar and restaurant, friendly staff, Wadworths real ales *(G H Theaker)*; *Two Horseshoes*: friendly unobtrusive service, good choice of beer, good value food, cosy fire *(Ian Meharg)*

LONGHOPE [Ross Road; SO6919], *Nags Head*: tasty food, pleasant service *(Miss M Salter, J G Duncan)*

MICKLETON [Chapel Lane; SP1543], *Three Ways*: good bar food and well kept Hook Norton real ales, comfortable neat bar and restaurant; bedrooms *(Frank Cummins)*

MINSTERWORTH [SO7716], *Appletree*: friendly service and good value food and drinks in pleasant, clean surroundings *(R Squire)*

MISERDEN [SE9308], *Carpenters Arms*: food good in nice village pub *(Sigrid and Peter Sobanski)*

nr NEWNHAM [Broadoak; SO6912], *White Hart*: good food (even on Sundays) in beamed bar, with glassed-over well, Severn views and riverside terrace; also restaurant *(N M Williamson, Joan Olivier)*

NORTH NIBLEY [ST7496], *Black Horse*: good ploughman's in busy beamed inn (being refurbished) with attentive landlord; restaurant, bedrooms *(Miss E R Bowmer)*

ODDINGTON [Upper Oddington; SP2225], *Horse & Groom*: friendly landlord and staff in attractive Cotswold stone inn with real ale and home-cooked bar food; quiet spot; bedrooms *(J W Strother)*

PAINSWICK [SO8608], *Falcon*: generous helping of good lunchtime food in popular central pub *(Miss E R Bowmer)*

PERROTTS BROOK [A435; SP0105], *Bear*: very helpful service, reasonably priced food, children welcome to eat *(Mrs S Braisted)*

SAPPERTON [SO9403], *Bell*: friendly village pub, heavily timbered inside; good beer and bar food, darts, bar billiards *(Pat Bromley)*; *Daneway*: refurbished isolated pub by derelict canal; remarkable mahogany fireplace, good Wadworths real ale, quiet garden *(Patrick Stapley, Richard Gibbs, LYM)*

SHIPTON MOYNE [ST8989], *Cat & Custard Pot*: terraced stone village pub, quite unspoilt and local, with well kept real ale, plain public bar and small smoke room; named after the pub where the hunt met in Surtees' *Handley Cross (Richard Gibbs)*

SOUTH CERNEY [SU0497], *Horse & Groom*: full range of drinks and very nicely cooked food in excellent pub, very efficiently run *(Capt F A Bland)*

STANTON [SP0634], *Mount*: snug with varnished wood tables and barrel seats, log fire, hatch service; newer extension with wall settles and chairs, tall windows with lovely views down valley towards Bredon Hill; well kept Donnington ales, good value food, friendly service, seats outside; pub perched at top of beautiful village *(Frank Cummins, L N Goulding, D Wynne)*

STONEHOUSE [High Street; SJ5070], *Globe*: friendly and homely pub with good selection of home-made food in big helpings and choice of ales *(J B Tippett)*

STOW-ON-THE-WOLD [The Square; SP1925], *Queens Head*: good choice of lunchtime food and well kept Donnington ales in smart stone Cotswold pub *(Tim Bracey, Dr A K Clarke)*; [The Square] *White Hart*: friendly inn with good choice of well cooked bar meals and range of beers served in pleasant surroundings; restaurant; bedrooms *(G H Theaker)*

STROUD [Clarence Street; SO8504], *Duke of York*: real food and wide choice of real ales in cosy one-bar pub, comfortable and welcoming *(D A Lloyd)*

TETBURY [Market Place; ST8893], *Crown*: nice friendly pub with a hunting motif *(Dr A K Clarke)*

TEWKESBURY [High Street; SO8932], *Black Bear*: rambling heavy-beamed old pub, recently largely refurbished, with bar food, real ales; riverside lawn *(LYM)*; *Swan*: good lunchtime bar food in two roomy and comfortable bars with friendly atmosphere *(P J Taylor)*

TWYNING [SO8936], *Village Inn*: good value home cooking and well kept beer in welcoming and genuine country pub facing village green; skittle alley, small pleasant garden *(BL)*

nr UPPER LYDBROOK [Joyford; SO6116], *Dog & Muffler*: small, cosy, cottagey; real ale, bar meals, welcoming licensees; nice gardens *(Gordon and Daphne)*

WINCHCOMBE [High Street; SP0228], *George*: old but much modernised inn with striking ancient timbered courtyard; bedrooms *(LYM)*

WOODCHESTER [SO8302], *Ram*: good food and real ale in interesting bar with plenty of nooks and crannies *(Roger Entwistle)*; *Royal Oak*: good food and real ale in pleasant, friendly village pub *(Roger Entwistle)*

Hampshire

Several new entries here include the Milbury's at Beauworth, with a remarkable donkey-wheel well in the bar (and a nice pub all round), the Ship at Owslebury (well kept real ales and good value straightforward food in a friendly village pub) and the Pig & Whistle near Privett (a much-extended pastiche of old England, brewing its own beer). And we'd particularly like to direct attention to some of the Lucky Dip entries, which sound promising as candidates for future main entry status: the Cedars at Binsted (good food in a simple country pub), the Red Lion at Boldre (beamy and atmospheric, with lots of old farm tools and good simple food), the Fox & Hounds in Crawley (enterprising food, friendly licensees), the Bridge at Shawford (a nice summer pub), the Frog & Frigate in Southampton (enjoyable re-creation of sawdust-and-spittoon days, brewing its own ales), the Bear & Ragged Staff at Timsbury (cheerful and old-fashioned, with a garden), the Woolpack at Totford (home cooking in an attractive little beamed pub with enthusiastic new owners), the Hoddington Arms in Upton Grey (a wide range of toasted sandwiches in a relaxed village pub), the Rising Sun in Warsash (sea views from a comfortable revamped pub), the Weyhill Fair in Weyhill (an interesting free house), the Mayfly near Wherwell (an outstanding position by the River Test) and the Wykeham Arms in Winchester (very civilised small hotel with good food and enterprising new owners). Among the main entries, the White Horse near Petersfield is one of the best pubs in Britain, with an excellent choice of real ales and country wines in surroundings which have pleased a great many readers. The Bush at Ovington, a really relaxed country pub, has been winning even wider support than before for its food, and food

The Boot, nr Vernham Dean

is also a strong point at the Passfield Oak near Liphook (backing on to National Trust walks, with a special welcome for families), at the Harrow in Steep (the epitome of a timeless village pub, with good snacks), the Three Lions in Stuckton (perhaps the best pub in the county for food), the New Inn in Heckfield, the Crown in Kingsclere, the Red Lion in Mortimer West End, the Rose & Thistle in Rockbourne (particularly the seafood) and the Chequers in Well (French food and wines in a very English old pub). Waterside pubs include the Jolly Sailor in Bursledon with its garden running down to a colourful yachting basin, another Jolly Sailor near Fawley looking out to the Southampton shipping lanes, the Olde Whyte Harte in Hamble (one of the south coast's best yachting villages), the Royal Oak in Langstone where you can sit feeding the swans as you think back to its smuggling days, and the Still & West right on the narrow entrance to Portsmouth harbour. In the New Forest there is the unspoilt and basic Royal Oak in Fritham, the well run and spacious High Corner near Linwood and the atmospheric old Queens Head in Burley. In less touristy but decidedly attractive countryside, the ancient Red Lion in Chalton is handy for the Iron Age farming settlement reconstruction in the Queen Elizabeth Country Park, the Cricketers at Tangley has an MP landlord and its own flock of sheep, the determinedly traditional George at Vernham Dean keeps its real ale particularly well, and the Boot near the same village is cheerfully cottagey. The Fox & Hounds in Bursledon (with the best range of cheeses for ploughman's that we found in the area) and Crown and Cushion at Minley both have splendid pastiches of medieval feasting halls, while the Red Lion in Southampton has a surprisingly genuine one; the Red House in Whitchurch still has the atmosphere to go with its highwayman past; and the Eclipse close to Winchester Cathedral is a striking timbered building some 600 years old. Though bar food in the area is often cheap, Hampshire beer prices are now rather high – in general, you should head away from the main tourist areas to find the lowest prices. Gales, who brew in Horndean, produce two or three dozen traditional country wines stocked by many pubs in the vicinity. Summer opening until 11pm is now much more common than it was.

ALRESFORD   SU5832   Map 2

Horse & Groom

Broad Street; on corner of A31

This carefully renovated rambling open-plan bar has black beams, some walls stripped back to show attractive timbered brickwork, decorated with old photographs of the town, shelves of earthenware jugs and bottles, and one huge fireplace converted to take a table and several chairs – there's a good open fire in another. There are neat modern settles, Windsor chairs and round stools on the flowery carpet, and tables snugly fitted into three bow windows that give a pleasant view of the passers-by in this wide street. An efficient back food bar serves good value sandwiches, winter soup, a choice of ploughman's (from £1.50), pâté (£1.70), burger (£2.10), home-made pies such as steak and kidney (£2.60), fish (£2.65) or good venison in red wine (£3.10), gammon and egg (£3.85), trout stuffed with prawns and mushrooms or mixed grill (£3.95) and steaks (from £4.75), with daily specials such as macaroni cheese (£1.85), and summer salads such as avocado, ham and mushroom or asparagus and Stilton quiche (£2.65); well kept Flowers Original and Whitbreads Strong Country on handpump from the central servery; a fruit machine and maybe piped music. *(Recommended by Mr and Mrs G D Amos, Gordon and Daphne)*

Whitbreads · Licensee Peter Clements · Real ale · Meals and snacks · Open 10.30–2.30, 6–11 · Daytime parking nearby may be rather difficult

BEAUWORTH   SU5726 Map 2
Milbury's

Turn off A272 Winchester–Petersfield at signpost saying Beauworth ¾, Bishops Waltham 6, then continue straight on past village

The remarkable feature of this recently nicely restored old pub is the well in the side room. Probably dug 600 years ago, it is cut nearly 300 feet into the chalk and carefully spot-lit so that in its narrow depths you see the twinkle of water reflections. If you drop an ice cube through the safety grid, you can count off nearly five seconds before the reflections shatter. This was the pub's only water supply until well into the 1940s, and the room-high wooden treadwheel that used to wind up the original 18-gallon water cask is still in place. In the war, when the landlord had to give up the donkey he'd used to wind the wheel, he found it took him 678 paces to pull up his water. Now, getting liquid here is the much simpler business of having your well kept Flowers Original, Gales BBB or HSB, Wethereds or Sam Whitbreads pulled by handpump (there are also masses of liqueurs and several dozen whiskies). Bar food includes sandwiches (from 95p, steak £2.60), home-made soup (95p), ploughman's (£1.75), home-made pâté (£2.50), salads (from £2.50), fried chicken (£2.60), chilli con carne (£2.65), scampi (£3.95) and daily specials such as mussels in garlic (£3.15), beef curry (£3.75) and 10-ounce rump steak (£6.50), with children's dishes (£1.50), a good choice of puddings (from 95p) and Sunday roasts. There are broad flagstones, sturdy beams, gnarled rustic tables with good cushioned seats built in to the stripped brick walls, massive open fireplaces (one with a deep bread oven), and up steps a wooden gallery overlooking the well room. Rather muffled piped music; separate restaurant. There are weekend summer barbecues out in the garden, where rustic seats have quite a view. *(Recommended by GSS, Gordon and Daphne)*

Free house · Licensees Greg and Jackie Gregory · Real ale · Meals and snacks Children in well room · Open 10.30–2.30, 6–11 · Bedrooms tel Brandean (096 279) 248; £18 (£20B)/£28 (£35B)

BUCKLERS HARD   SU4000   Map 2
Master Builders House

The two bars here are an attractively done rendition of old-world pubbiness, with partly carpeted quarry tiles, beams, timbering and a vast fireplace in which massive logs look as if they'd take all winter to smoulder away. The name comes from the building in which the bars have been made: it used to be the home of the shipbuilding Adams family, who launched Nelson's favourite the 64-gun *Agamemnon* among dozens of other men-o'-war here. The Yachtsman's bar – busy at weekends and in summer, and the warmer of the two bars in winter – has lots of good photographs, ancient and modern, of yachts, and the lower buffet bar serves soup (usually good), hot dishes such as shepherd's pie, and salads with real mayonnaise such as smoked mackerel (£2.30) and ham or turkey (£2.90). Halls Harvest and Ind Coope Burton on handpump; darts. There is a spacious separate restaurant (the pub is part of quite a substantial hotel and conference centre), and you can sit in the garden. The waterside village is attractive, with a maritime museum; it's part of the Beaulieu estate. *(Recommended by Patrick Young, Peter Barrett; more reports please)*

Free house · Licensee R C Dinnage · Real ale · Meals and snacks · Children in buffet bar · Country and western music Thurs · Open 11–2.30, 6–10.30 Bedrooms tel Bucklers Hard (059 063) 253; £15 (£30B)/£49B

BURLEY   SU2003   Map 2
Queens Head

On back road between Ringwood and Lymington

This rambling New Forest pub – largely Tudor behind its tile-hung façade – is decorated to recall its smuggling days, with flagstones, low beams, panelling and timbering, an old-fashioned wood-burning stove, lots of horse brasses and harness, daggers, knives and pictures of olde England. There's a good pub atmosphere, with well kept Whitbreads Strong Country and Samuel Whitbread on handpump; maybe piped music; darts, shove-ha'penny, dominoes, cribbage and a fruit machine, and a possibility of bar billiards this winter. A self-service food bar has reasonably priced sandwiches, home-made soup, a choice of ploughman's, basket meals such as burger or chicken, salads, home-made steak and kidney pie, gammon and steaks, with children's dishes such as fish fingers or burgers. One of the three bars is named after Peter Warne, the most famous local smuggler who used it; another has a surprisingly elegant high ceiling with elaborate rococo plasterwork. Both village and pub are packed in summer – so it might be best to come here out of season. There is a gift and souvenir shop in the courtyard. *(Recommended by Anthony Lewis Furreddu; more reports please)*

Whitbreads · Licensees Peter and Shirley Reeve · Real ale · Meals and snacks (not Sun evening) · Children in food bar and family room · Live music Sat evenings in winter · Open 10.30–2.30, 6.30–11 (11–2.30, 7–10.30 in winter)

BURSLEDON   SU4809   Map 2
Fox & Hounds ★

Hungerford Bottom; from A27 follow Old Bursledon signpost into Long Lane, turn right into School Road then first left into Hungerford

The Lone Barn is the name under which many readers know this pub – the fine vaulted barn at the back looks and is ancient (the stone foundations are thought to be some 1,200 years old) but surprisingly it hasn't been here for long. It used to stand on a lonely down above Winchester, and was carefully dismantled and then rebuilt here. It's used as part of the pub now, and has a splendid friendly atmosphere, but room to move. A very long table hewn from an oak trunk stretches down the centre, and along the walls – which are decorated with masses of antique farm tools – there are lantern-lit stalls with upholstered bench seats around trestle tables. A food bar, quick at lunchtime (there may be longish waits in the evening), has a good choice of cold food, including sandwiches, ploughman's with a remarkable selection of some 18 cheeses (£1.40), quiche, salads, and home-made hot dishes such as chicken or steak and kidney pie, lasagne, liver and onions or braised steak (£2.40). In the evenings there are basket meals and steaks, and on Sundays roast joints (£2.80). Well kept Gales HSB, Ushers Best and Websters Yorkshire on handpump, and quite a few country wines; maybe loud piped music. There are picnic-table sets outside on a sheltered flagstone courtyard between the barn and the original pub – old enough itself, with a fine collection of tankards and shaving-mugs hanging from its beams, but mainly modern furniture on the flagstone floor; the public bar has darts, pool, shove-ha'penny, cribbage, a fruit machine and a juke box. *(Recommended by J Smith, R J D, Glyn Edmunds; more reports please)*

Watneys · Licensee Terence McEvoy · Real ale · Meals and snacks · Children in Lone Barn · Open 11–2.30, 6–11; closed evening 25 Dec

Jolly Sailor

From A27 follow Bursledon Station signpost, keeping left

So many pubs in this smartly popular yachting area have been given expensive and elaborate face-lifts that it's a real pleasure to discover the friendly, old-fashioned and unaffected charm of this one – right on the waterfront. Bow windows in the light and airy front bar look out over the water, packed with yachts (as do tables in a new functions room, where meals can be served). This room has ship pictures on its walls, shells in the net strung from its ceiling, and Windsor chairs and settles on the oak stripped floor; maybe piped music. An older flagstoned back bar has a very large fireplace, and beams above its pews and settles; dominoes, cribbage, and a space game. Bar food includes ploughman's, salads, basket meals, ham or sausage and egg, and home-cooked daily specials such as steak and kidney pie, fisherman's pie or quiche Lorraine (around £2.20); well kept Badger Best, Courage Directors and Wadworths 6X on handpump, with Old Timer in winter. There are old-fashioned wooden seats and tables under a big yew beside the pretty brick house, and a group of picnic-table sets on its wooden jetty. There's a children's bar out here at busy times. Note that it's a steep walk down to the pub – and back up. (Recommended by Gordon and Daphne, David Symes, B R Shiner)

Free house · Licensee Jack Mellan · Real ale · Meals and snacks
Children in functions/dining-room · If parking in the lane is full you have to
use the station car park · Open 11–2.30, 6–11

CHALTON   SU7315   Map 2
Red Lion
Village signposted E of A3 Petersfield–Horndean

The county's oldest pub, it was licensed in 1503 and may date partly from 1150, when a workshop on the site was involved in the rebuilding of the Norman church opposite. It's a pretty thatched building, timbered and jettied. Inside is cosy and welcoming, with high-backed settles, bentwood armchairs, elm tables, heavy beams, panelled walls and a fine inglenook fireplace with a frieze of burnished threepenny bits set into its mantelbeam. Good value low-priced bar food includes soup, sandwiches, ploughman's (from 80p, beef or ham £1.50), sausage and egg (£1.50), ham and egg (£1.75), scampi (£2.50), seafood platter (£2.85), steaks, and in winter home-made cottage, meat and potato or steak and kidney pies. Well kept Gales BBB, HSB and XXX Mild on handpump, with XXXXX in winter, draught cider and three dozen different country wines; maybe piped music. You can sit outside in summer. This quiet downland hamlet is fairly close to the extensive Queen Elizabeth Country Park, which includes a working reconstruction of an Iron Age farming settlement. (Recommended by G P Hewitt, Glyn Edmunds)

Gales · Licensee Ron Stirzaker · Real ale · Meals (lunchtime; only cold food
Sun lunchtime) and snacks · Open 10.30–2.30, 6–11

nr FAWLEY   SU4503   Map 2
Jolly Sailor
Ashlett Creek; from A326 turn left into School Road, signposted Fawley ½; at Falcon pub crossroads take Calshot road, then fork left almost at once

Included for its splendid waterside position, this comfortably renovated pub has picnic-table sets on a long side lawn looking out over a dinghy park to the tidal saltings where curlews and sandpipers strut at low water, and beyond to the distant bustle of Southampton Water. The rough plaster and dark oak walls of the carpeted and wood-ceilinged bar are decorated with photographs of liners that have used Southampton, and of the creek itself at the turn of the century. This room has soft banquettes, a central open fire, and red velvet curtains, and opens into a restaurant section (three-course meals around £6.50) which looks out towards the shipping-channel and is hung with sailing prints. Reasonably priced bar food includes sandwiches and filled rolls (at lunchtime – including hot fillings and steak), soup, ploughman's, basket meals such as scampi (these are the only dishes served on Sunday evenings), home-made steak and kidney pie and daily specials such as lasagne or curry; Flowers Original and Whitbreads Strong Country on handpump; fruit machine, maybe piped music. Not far from the magnificent Rothschild rhododendron gardens at Exbury. *(More reports please)*

Whitbreads · Licensee Ron Burnett · Real ale · Meals and snacks (limited Sun evening) · Open 11–2.30, 6.30–11 (7–10.30 in winter)

FRITHAM   SU2314   Map 2
Royal Oak

4 miles from M271 junction 1; village signposted off B3028 Cadnam–Downton: follow dead end lane through village

Deep in the New Forest, this thatched pub must make the brewers itch to turn it into some vast food-and-drinks machine. As it's in such a popular tourist area, it's a real surprise that it has managed to stay so basic and unspoilt. Its two small rooms are simply furnished and utilitarian rather than cosy, with kitchen chairs, a plain deal table, and a couple of high-backed settles, and in one corner stairs up to the licensee's own quarters. Well kept Whitbreads Strong Country and Pompey Royal tapped from the barrel; sensibly placed darts, and a fruit machine. There are seats outside. *(Recommended by Gordon and Daphne, David Symes and others)*

Whitbreads · Licensee A Taylor · Real ale · Children in back room · Open 10–2.30, 6–11

FROYLE   SU7542   Map 2
Hen and Chicken

A31 Alton–Farnham

Just as we went to press we heard that new licensees were moving in to this old favourite: we await readers' verdicts on whether the food still comes up to the high and generous standards that have been set here over the last year or so. In any event, there's plenty of character to enjoy here. The main bar, dating back some 400 years though partly rebuilt in the eighteenth century, has creaky old settles and oak tables on the carpet in front of the huge fireplace, which still has the rack used for messages in coaching days – there are several antique coaching prints, too. There is a separate panelled restaurant, in addition to the bar food and buffet counter; maybe changing guest beers as well as Badger Best and Tanglefoot, Bass, Brakspears SB (and Old in winter) and Gales HSB on handpump, and a good choice of ciders; dominoes. There are seats on a terrace facing the road, and more in a beer garden behind. *(Recommended by Hazel Morgan, Mr and Mrs K Virgin, Glyn Edmunds; up-to-date reports on the new regime please)*

Free house · Real ale · Meals and snacks · Children in buttery bar and restaurant · Open 10.30–2.30, 6–11

HAMBLE   SU4806   Map 2
Olde Whyte Harte

3 miles from M27 junction 8; on B3397 (High Street)

This genuine and welcoming yachtsmen's pub, listed officially as having special architectural interest, has settles and Windsor chairs on its Tudor flagstones, low beams decorated with mugs and rope fancywork, white panelling, and some copper pans. Good value bar food includes sandwiches and toasties (45p–75p), shepherd's pie (80p), ploughman's (90p), chilli con carne or curry (£1), salads (from £1.35), fish and chips (£1.60) and scampi; Gales BBB and HSB and XXX Mild on handpump, with XXXXX in winter; dominoes, cribbage, a fruit machine, and maybe piped music. Besides barrel seats on the small front terrace, there is a back terrace by the lawn and sheltered garden, which has a big fig-tree trying to climb over its wall. *(Recommended by Ray Kerswell; more reports please)*

Gales · Licensee Colin Partridge · Real ale · Meals (lunchtime, not Sun) and snacks · Children in snug bar · Open 10.45–2.30, 6–11

HAVANT   SU7106   Map 2
Old House At Home

South Street; entering town on main street from A27, turn right at church

Since our last edition the main bar of this comfortably modernised Tudor pub – which used to be the vicarage – has been extended to give more room, which is useful for the many people who crowd in at lunchtime for a wide range of reasonably priced home-made food. This includes sandwiches, toasted sandwiches, filled rolls, chicken and ham fries, basket meals and four or five piping hot daily specials including curries, beef bourguignonne or roast beef, with more concentration since last year on savoury dishes such as Hungarian pork or curried crab, tuna and prawns (nothing more than £2.20). It's a fine black and white timbered building with an overhanging upper storey, and, inside, the main Tudor bar has big beams in its ochre ceiling, with button-back red plush seats on the patterned carpet, a winter log fire, subdued lighting and piped music. The saloon bar is similar, with brocade instead of plush. Well kept Gales BBB and HSB on handpump; friendly and attentive service, particularly from the landlord's father who is in charge on Tuesdays; darts, a fruit machine. *(Recommended by A J V Baker, Glyn Edmunds; more reports please)*

Gales · Licensee B L Worth · Real ale · Meals and snacks (lunchtime, not Sun) Parking difficult · Open 10.30–2.30, 6–11

HECKFIELD   SU7260   Map 2
New Inn

B3349 Hook–Reading (still called A32 on many maps)

We used sometimes to play the organ in the village church across the fields from here. The pub has changed vastly since those days – greatly extended from its original low-beamed heart, it has lots of well spaced tables with cushioned wheelback chairs and round stools in its various carpeted bays, alcoves and extensions, with a couple of good log fires and some more traditional furniture including an attractively carved early eighteenth-century settle. It's very popular now for its wide choice of good value simple food, including sandwiches and toasties (from 90p, crab, smoked salmon or steak £2.50), ploughman's (from £1.40), home-made pâté (£1.55), whitebait (£1.70), three sausages with eggs (£2.25), eight-ounce burgers (from £2.90), lasagne (£2.50), salads (from £2.50 – a good choice), pizza (£2.60), lemon sole (£2.80), scampi (£3.90), mixed grill (£4.30), steaks (from eight-ounce rump £5.40) and a wide range of puddings (90p). Service is friendly and efficient (with announcements when food is ready). Well kept Bass, Badger Best and Youngs Special on handpump; fruit machine and unobtrusive piped music. Lots of picnic-table sets on the grass away from the big car park. *(Recommended by J A C Edwards; more reports please)*

Free house · Licensee Basil Francis · Real ale · Meals and snacks Open 10.30–2.30, 6–10.30

HURSTBOURNE TARRANT   SU3853   Map 2
George & Dragon

A343 Andover–Newbury

Attractive for its cosy old-fashioned layout, this is the last survivor of several old coaching-inns which used to compete fiercely when this was a major coaching-route. The low-beamed little lounge bar's fireplace, with big logs burning in cool weather, still has a coaching-era message rack above it, and there are steps up to a partly panelled section where the ostlers, sitting by the red-curtained windows, used to keep an eye out for trade. As we went to press a change of tenancy was planned, so we hope for readers' reports on whether the food is up to the standard set by the previous tenants, both in the bar and – beyond a dividing line of old oak timbers – the separate restaurant; a good point in any event is that the nearby butcher used by the pub has a fine local reputation (we hope they'll keep his sausages, among other things, on the menu). There's been well kept Courage Best and Directors on handpump. The public bar has darts, bar billiards, shove-ha'penny and a fruit machine. *(Up-to-date reports on the new regime please)*

Courage · Real ale · Meals (not Mon evening) and snacks · Children in eating area and restaurant · Open 10.30–2.30, 6–11 · Bedrooms tel Hurstbourne Tarrant (026 476) 277; £12/£20

IBSLEY   SU1509   Map 2
Old Beams

A338 Ringwood–Salisbury

In this pretty and efficiently run thatched pub, most of the well kept and spaciously airy extended back bar is taken up by tables set for the food, which includes sandwiches (from £1.15), a choice of ploughman's, hot dishes such as lasagne, chicken, trout or curry (£2.95), a daily roast, and a tasty buffet of cold meats and salads (£3.95), with steaks in the evening. But there's also a good range of real ales on handpump from the long bar counter in here, generally including Courage Directors, Gibbs Mew Bishops Tipple, Huntsman Royal Oak, Ringwood and Wadworths Farmers Glory and 6X. There's a snug little front bar with beams and latticed windows, and a partly tree-shaded back garden has picnic-table sets. *(Recommended by Frank Cummins, F W Weir, A J Milman; more reports please)*

Free house · Licensee R Wilson · Real ale · Meals and snacks · Children welcome · Open 10.30–2.30, 6–11

KINGSCLERE   SU5258   Map 2
Crown ★

A339 Newbury–Basingstoke

This pub's long and comfortably furnished lounge is a popular place to eat. Its partly panelled walls are decorated with old posters for penny-dreadful novels, pictures of steam engines, and a high shelf of china; there's a central log fire, and maybe piped music. The food includes soups such as Stilton and watercress, mushroom and walnut or tomato and ham (95p), a good range of toasted sandwiches such as banana with bacon, cheddar and sweetcorn and buttered shrimps with cucumber (£1.80–£2.25), smoked mackerel pâté or prawn and salmon terrine (£1.65), ploughman's (£1.95), home-made lasagne or local Bratwurst (£2.50) and daily specials such as steak and mushroom pie (£2.75), spicy Thai chicken (£3.25), chicken, apricot and brandy pie (£3.50), or six-ounce rump steak (£3.95). Salads are good, and home-made puddings include rum and brandy mousse, chocolate and almond cheesecake and treacle tart with cream (£1.35–£1.50). Well kept Courage Simonds, Best and Directors on handpump. The simpler public bar, quiet at weekday lunchtimes but lively in the evenings and at weekends, has darts, dominoes, cribbage, shove-ha'penny, and a fruit machine. There is a terrace outside. *(Recommended by E U Broadbent, Nigel Williamson, D A Angless, Glyn Edmunds)*

Courage · Licensee Gregory Worrall · Real ale · Meals and snacks (not Sun, except ploughman's lunches) · Children in family room · Open 11–2.30, 6–11; opens 7 Sat; closed evenings 25, 26 Dec

LANGSTONE   SU7105   Map 2
Royal Oak ★

High Street; last turn left off A3023 (confusingly called A324 on some signs) before Hayling Island bridge

The fine waterside position earns this pub its high rating. Seats in the bow windows, and waterside benches in front, look out on the landlocked natural harbour where the Langstone Gang used to land their smuggled brandy in the eighteenth century, floating it in on submerged rafts to avoid *The Griper*, the Excise brig which patrolled the harbour. The rafts had a candle burning below the water in an air tube, which eventually – they hoped when the coast was clear – lit a fuse and set a bright lamp alight, so the brandy kegs could be located. Of course, it sometimes lit too soon: in 1833 a sudden flare of light right under the excisemen's noses gave away a float of 63 brandy kegs. The pub's cream walls are decorated with old and informatively labelled prints of seabirds and fish, and some stuffed gulls and oyster-catchers (at low tide the saltings between here and Hayling Island fill with wading birds), and it has rugs on the wooden parquet and worn flagstones, and Windsor chairs around its old tables. Bar food served from the counter (they call your number when it's ready) includes sandwiches, salads, chilli con carne, lasagne or moussaka, a daily special such as steak and kidney pie and steaks, with good rare beef from a lunchtime carvery; Flowers Original, Wethereds, Whitbreads Strong Country and Pompey Royal on handpump; a space game and a fruit machine. There are more seats outside on a back lawn, with roses and a swing. *(Recommended by A J Milman, Glyn Edmunds; more reports please)*

Whitbreads · Licensee Christopher Handscomb · Real ale · Meals and snacks Children in eating area · Parking at all close may be very difficult · Open 11–2.30, 6–11

LINWOOD   SU1810 Map 2
High Corner ★

Linwood signposted via Moyles Court from A338; follow road straight up on to heath and eventually pub signposted left down a gravelled track; OS Sheet 195 reference 196107

Remote in the New Forest, this pub has a fine big woodside lawn with well spaced picnic-table sets and summer cook-it-yourself barbecues (from £3, 16-ounce T-bone steak £5.90). Its rather dimly lit rambling rooms include a comfortable low-ceilinged inner bar (where there's an aquarium), another bar with rustic tables and chairs up some steps in a beamed extension, a family room between with darts, dominoes, chess, Othello, cards and a pin-table (the pub also has a fruit machine), and a sun-lounge. A separate stable bar – with the barbecue area – may be open during the summer, and can be booked at any time of the year for private parties. The wide choice of bar food includes home-made soup (60p), freshly cut sandwiches (from 75p), toasted sandwiches (from 90p), ploughman's (from £1.35, good Stilton £1.65), home-made liver pâté (£1.50), omelettes (from £1.70), curries, basket scampi or fresh Avon trout with masses of almonds (£2.95), home-made steak and kidney pie (£3.25), lamb chops (£3.85), a very generous mixed grill (£5.75), plenty of puddings such as home-made bread pudding (£1), and children's basket meals (95p). Well kept Bass and Whitbreads Strong Country on handpump; maybe piped music. There is a squash court, and also a separate restaurant. *(Recommended by George Hughes, Frank Cummins, H G and C J McCafferty, Sue White, Tim Kinning, A J Milman, John, Tim, Andrew and Sue Kemp, Glyn Edmunds, T G W Carrington)*

It is illegal for bar staff to smoke while handling drinks.

Free house · Licensee Roger Kernan · Real ale · Meals and snacks · Children in family room and sun-lounge · Open 10.30–2.30, 6–11 (10.30–2.30, 7–10.30 in winter) · Stable bar bookings tel Ringwood (042 54) 3973

nr LIPHOOK   SU8331   Map 2
Passfield Oak

Passfield; B3004 towards Alton

With a particular welcome for families, this well kept and spaciously comfortable pub has an unusual range of real ales and does good reasonably priced bar food, including sandwiches (from 70p), ploughman's with a mixture of cheeses and ham (from £1.30), home-made eight-ounce burgers (£1.60), and daily hot specials such as farmhouse pie with home-made coleslaw, spaghetti bolognese, pork and pineapple curry, lamb and pepper goulash, steak and kidney pie, garlic prawns and a choice of salads (around £2.25). The family room doubles as a bistro-style restaurant from Thursdays to Saturdays, with a very wide choice of starters such as herby mushrooms flamed in brandy and port (£1.50) or langoustines in garlic butter (£2.50), main courses such as chicken cooked with calvados (£3.50), and enterprising steaks (booking recommended). In fine weather there are Sunday lunchtime barbecues. Besides well kept Ballards Best, Flowers Original, Gales HSB, Marstons Pedigree and Wethereds on handpump, with Ballards Wassail tapped from the cask, they do adult milk-shakes with liqueurs, ice cream and cream; dominoes, cribbage, chess, Scrabble and other games, and a fruit machine. Tables on the front lawn look across to the village green, and behind the big and securely fenced back garden is a wooded common owned by the National Trust (beyond that is Army territory). They are opening a functions room in their renovated seventeenth-century barn. *(Recommended by R M R Parker, Simon Bleach)*

Free house · Licensees Tony and Jenny Strickland · Real ale · Meals – tel Passfield (042 877) 205 – and snacks · Children in eating area and family room Occasional folk nights and specials, such as Burns Night · Open 11–2.30, 6–11

LONGPARISH   SU4344   Map 2
Plough

With a large and attractively planted garden, this well kept village pub has some comfortable easy chairs as well as the simpler wooden ones in the various alcoves of its rambling open-plan lounge bar. Food includes pies such as fish with prawns and wine, squab, and steak and kidney (around £5) (there is also a separate restaurant); well kept Flowers Original and Whitbreads Strong Country on handpump; fruit machine. It's usefully placed on good B roads that, depending on where you're heading, could be a relaxed alternative to either the A34 or the A30. *(Recommended by Prof A N Black, Andy Jones)*

Whitbreads · Licensee Trevor Colgate · Real ale · Meals and snacks (not Mon evening) · Open 10.30–2.30, 6–11 (11–2.30, 7–11 in winter)

Sunday opening is 12–2 and 7–10.30 throughout England.

MINLEY   SU8357   Map 2

Crown and Cushion ★

From A30 take B3013 towards Fleet, then first left turn signposted Minley, Cove, Farnborough

The special attraction of this pub is its separate candlelit and raftered 'Meade Hall', a great timbered tiled barn full of scythes, pitchforks and so forth, a colossal open fire, two very long communal tables stretching down its flagstone floor, and smaller more intimate ones in side stalls – not unlike the Lone Barn at the same brewery's Fox & Hounds in Bursledon. A quick-service food counter offers a wide choice of home-cooked meats and good fresh salads (from £1.80), ploughman's (£1.10) and a home-made lunchtime hot dish such as steak and kidney pie or lasagne (around £2), with a wider choice of evening hot dishes such as gammon, plaice and basket meals (around £2–£3). Gales HSB, Tamplins, Ushers, Websters Yorkshire and Watneys Stag on handpump (kept under light blanket pressure), with a couple of draught ciders and a choice of country wines – and mead of course; maybe piped music. The pub itself has Windsor chairs and leatherette wall banquettes under its low sixteenth-century beams, and serves sandwiches; darts, cribbage, a fruit machine and a space game. Outside, picnic-table sets look over a woodside cricket pitch. The pub's name commemorates the closest that anyone has come to stealing the crown jewels – Colonel Blood from nearby Minley Warren was caught here in 1671 with the jewels in his saddlebags, after a subtle raid on the Tower of London. (Recommended by Tim and Ann Bracey, Glyn Edmunds)

Phoenix (Watneys) · Licensee Leonard Brown · Real ale · Lunchtime meals (not Sun) and snacks · Open 10.30–2.30, 5.30–11

MORTIMER WEST END   SU6363   Map 2

Red Lion

From Mortimer–Aldermaston road take turn signposted Silchester 1¾

New owners are serving very much the same sort of food in this attractively restored country pub as was previously popular with readers. It includes home-made soup (85p), home-made pies from cottage (£1.30) to seafood, chicken, duck, steak and kidney and venison (£4–£5.25), ploughman's (from £1.85), cod (£3.25), scampi (£4), charcoal-grilled sirloin steak (£5.50), and home-made puddings, ice cream or sorbet (85p). A public address system calls your number when your food is ready. The big carpeted main room has stripped ceiling beams, some walls showing bare brick above the stripped panelling and others with photographs of the pub in the old days, upholstered stools around the many tables and a good winter log fire. There is farmhouse cider as well as well kept Badger Best, Huntsman Dorset and Royal Oak, Wadworths IPA and 6X on handpump; piped music (middle-of-the-road in taste since the change of ownership). The separate restaurant (closed Monday evening and Sunday) has £8.50 lunches and evening main courses for around £6. Old-fashioned teak seats outside are sheltered by the wings of the attractive brick house. *(Recommended by Mr and Mrs J Bushby, Gordon and Daphne; up-to-date reports on the new regime please)*

Free house · Licensee Peter Neal · Real ale · Meals and snacks; restaurant bookings tel Mortimer (0734) 700169 · Open 11–2.30, 6–11

OVINGTON SU5531 Map 2
Bush ★

Village signposted from A31 on Winchester side of Alresford

Readers' reports all enthuse about the home cooking in this charming country pub. Bar food includes home-made country soups such as spicy duck (£1.15), generously filled wholemeal baps (from £1.20), ploughman's (from £1.60), pâté (£1.85), taramosalata (£1.95), vegetable curry (£2.75), salads (from £2.85, with an excellent platter of smoked salmon, oysters, prawns, cockles, mussels, lumpfish roe and smoked mackerel for £5.25), chicken (£2.80), barbecued pork strips (£2.95), two or three daily specials such as home-made steak and kidney or chicken and mushroom pie with very good pastry (around £3), natural-tasting puddings, and a Sunday roast lunch (when the choice of other dishes may be more limited). The dimly lit main bar has cushioned high-backed settles, pews and kitchen chairs, elm tables, copper pans above the open fire at one end, an old solid-fuel stove at the other, crowds of prints on the deep green walls, and lots of plants in the windows. Readers like thoughtful touches such as fresh flowers in the ladies' lavatory. There is a much better choice than usual of wines by the glass, and a monthly guest beer such as Wadworths Farmers Glory alongside well kept Flowers Original, Wadworths 6X, Wethereds SPA and Whitbreads Strong Country on handpump. The intimate low-ceilinged separate restaurant serves wine-bar-style lunches and, from 8pm, full meals with main courses for around £8; since the last edition it has had a summer pergola terrace added, with white wrought-iron seats and tables by the big pool and fountain. Outside is very leafy and peaceful, with fairy lights at night and by day quiet except for birdsong. *(Recommended by G S S, W A Gardiner, Gwen and Peter Andrews, C J A Davis, A Saunders, J H DuBois, Comus Elliott, Gordon and Daphne)*

Free house · Licensees Mr and Mrs Geoffrey Draper · Real ale · Meals and snacks; restaurant bookings tel Alresford (096 273) 2764 · Children in eating area lunchtime only · Open 11–2.30, 6–11

OWSLEBURY SU5124 Map 2
Ship

In a high downland village, this friendly local has well kept Marstons Burton, Pedigree and Mercian Mild on handpump in its simply furnished but comfortable main bar — built-in cushioned wall seats and wheelback chairs around shiny wooden tables (decorated with little vases of fresh carnations on our visit), varnished black beams and oak props, a winter fire in the big central hearth, and modern ship prints (such as Lord Mountbatten's HMS *Kelly* off the Norway coast in 1940). Generous helpings of popular food: from sandwiches (75p) through avocado and prawns (£1.40), seafood platter (£3.50), to eight-ounce sirloin steak (£5.95); darts and a fruit machine. The Mess Deck is a snug and pleasant family eating room. There are picnic-table sets on neat side grass, by a flower bed, with more behind in a spacious area with swings, climber and a slide, overlooking the fields. *(Recommended by David Preston, Gordon and Daphne)*

Marstons · Licensee Robert O'Neill · Real ale · Meals and snacks · Children in Mess Deck · Open 11–2.30, 6–11

nr PETERSFIELD   SU7423   Map 2

White Horse ★ ★ ★

In Priors Dean – but don't follow Priors Dean signposts: simplest route is from Petersfield, leaving centre on A272 towards Winchester, take right turn at roundabout after level crossing, towards Steep, and up on the downs – passing pub and garage on your right – turn right towards East Tisted at crossroads signposted East Tisted/Privett, then almost at once turn right on to second gravel track (the first just goes into a field); OS Sheet 186 or 197 reference 715290; alternatively, from A32 5 miles S of Alton, take road by bus lay-by signposted Petersfield 6, then, after 1¾ miles, turn off as above at East Tisted/ Privett crossroads

Evidently visited by more readers than any other pub in the book, this remote country pub appeals enormously to an overwhelming majority of them. But as two or three readers have been surprised at the rating we'll take this opportunity – as we did in the last edition – of stressing that our star ratings have nothing to do with luxury facilities or a specially exotic range of food. They depend mainly on atmosphere and character. In this particular case, that means a pub which has decided to stay as it is instead of expanding into a much less interesting complex of extra bars, and it therefore can't be expected to cope with demands that go beyond the limits which it sets itself. So, for example, when it is time for the cook to have her own lunch (say, at half past one on a Sunday – otherwise food service is from 11.30–2, 7–10) then you won't get food, even if you've come all the way from London. And there are times (not always predictable) when it does get packed: five minutes after a February Sunday opening time an American reader (after cycling 30 miles on icy lanes) couldn't get a seat, though we found plenty of room, and absolute peace, on our most recent visit, on a Saturday towards the end of July. There's no doubt that the Pub With No Name (as most of its regulars know it – there's no inn sign) really comes into its own when it is quiet, and can settle back into something closer to the peace that inspired the first poem published by Edward Thomas, the poet who was killed in the First World War. It's just a couple of simple individually furnished parlours, with rugs on the floor, antique oak settles, drop-leaf tables and chairs (some of which have seen better days), a long-case clock, old pictures, stuffed antelope heads, farm tools on the walls, maybe dogs wandering around, and a winter log fire. For us, that makes a perfect setting for the remarkable range of real ales, on handpump or tapped straight from the cask, which includes their own very strong White Horse No Name, as well as Ballards Bitter (brewed just the other side of Petersfield), Bass, Bishops Best (from Somerset), Gales HSB, Huntsman Dorset IPA and

Royal Oak, Marstons Burton, Pedigree and Merrie Monk, Ringwood Fortyniner and Wadworths 6X, Farmers Glory and Old Timer. There's also a splendid choice of country wines such as parsnip and peach, tapped from small china kegs. Food is limited to an excellent weekday country soup, sandwiches (from 50p), toasties (from 55p), ploughman's (from £1) and salads (from £1.90) – sandwiches alone in the evenings and on Sunday; shove-ha'penny. You may be able to buy local cream or even pheasants. In summer you can sit outside on rustic seats or chunks of tree-trunk; the view over this high rolling downland is clearest in winter, when the surrounding trees are not in leaf. (Recommended by Paul Edwards, John Hill, P T Young, Frank Cummins, Steve and Carolyn Harvey, James Ryan, Fod Barnes, H G and C J McCafferty, W A Gardiner, J Madley, Mrs A M Arnold, Annie Taylor, Patrick Stapley, Tim Halstead, Prof A N Black, Alan Franck, Stuart Barker, Glyn Edmunds, A V Chute, Peter Barrett, L Kirkpatrick, Simon Bleach and others)

Free house · Licensees Jack Eddleston and B L Reed · Real ale · Snacks · Open 11–2.30, 6–11

PORTSMOUTH   SZ6501 Map 2
Still & West   [illustrated on page 322]

Bath Square; follow A3 and Isle of Wight Ferry signs to Old Portsmouth water's edge

This pub wins its entry on the strength of its marvellous waterside position. It's right on the mouth of Portsmouth harbour – so narrow here that passing ships and boats seem almost within touching distance. The best views are from upstairs or on the terrace. The bars are comfortably decorated in nautical style, with ship models, an early brass submarine periscope and so forth. There's a plainly furnished side family room, with space games. Coffee here is so good as to be preferred by some to the Gales BBB and HSB on electric pump; straightforward pub food; fruit machine. Quite near HMS Victory. (Recommended by Andy Jones and the PA Club, Howard Gascoyne)

Gales · Licensee K H W Becker · Real ale · Meals and snacks (lunchtime, not Sun) · Children in family room · Open 10–2.30, 6–11

nr PRIVETT   SU6726 Map 2
Pig & Whistle

A32, 2 miles N of junction with A272, between Privett and West Tisted; OS Sheet 185 reference 672286

Generously extended to include a Hungry Traveller eatery at one side, this roomy roadside pub has a cheerful open-plan bar full of stripped brick and panelling, beams and so forth; on our visit a coach party of pensioners, spread out among the rather worn chintz armchairs and sofas, were enjoying themselves hugely to the sound of loud piped country-dance music. Its special feature is the old-fashioned brewery behind glass at one end, which brews the pub's own Joshua Privetts English Ale; they also keep Ballards Best and Wassail, Flowers Original, Ringwood Best and Fortyniner and Wadworths 6X on handpump. Bar food includes home-made soup

(85p), sandwiches (from 85p), burgers (from £1.25), ploughman's (£1.55), omelettes (from £1.75), spaghetti bolognese or lasagne (£2.25), salads (from £2.45) and scampi (£2.95). There is a good children's play area in the back garden. *(Recommended by G E Bennett)*

Own brew · Real ale · Meals and snacks · Children welcome
Open 11–2.30, 6–11

ROCKBOURNE   SU1118 Map 2
Rose & Thistle

Signposted from B3078

This neatly run and comfortable thatched village pub specialises in seafood: taramosalata or prawns (£1.95), home-made fish pie (£2.30), and king prawns, fresh or smoked salmon, Dorset crab or lobster salads (£5.50–£8.50 or more), with daily fresh fish such as moules marinière (£2.80) and Dover sole (£5.50). Good sandwiches include home-cooked ham (90p), rare beef (£1.10) and fresh salmon (£1.35), and there are home-made non-fish dishes such as pea and ham soup (80p), chicken liver pâté (£1.50) and steak and kidney pie (£3.50). The carpeted and curtained lounge bar has prettily upholstered stools and small settles, a shiny white plank ceiling, old engravings on the walls, quite a lot of polished brass, and in winter a good log fire. The public bar is rather plainer, with seating more in the style of booths. Well kept Whitbreads Strong Country and Pompey Royal on handpump; faint piped music. There are tables in the neat front garden, beside a thatched dovecot. This charming village has the excavated remains of a Roman villa. *(Recommended by A Larman; more reports please)*

Whitbreads · Licensees Peter and Pam Read · Real ale · Meals and snacks
Open 10.30–2.30, 7 – 10.30; closed 25 Dec

SELBORNE   SU7433 Map 2
Queen's

B3006 Alton–Petersfield

You can take the walk from the village into the National Trust woodland around Selbourne Hanger, besides many other downland walks particularly evocative for readers of Gilbert White. As this was his village, the pictures of birds, butterflies and plants decorating the lounge bar of this small and homely white inn are appropriate. It is comfortably furnished with small leatherette armchairs, a brocaded corner wall bench and high-backed seats. Food from a buttery bar includes ploughman's, Welsh rarebit, home-made steak and kidney pie or boiled ham with parsley sauce (£1.80) and roast beef with Yorkshire pudding (£1.90); open from 9am to 9pm, this serves teas in the afternoon. Courage Best and Directors on handpump; the bigger public bar has darts, shove-ha'penny, dominoes, cribbage, a juke box and a fruit machine. Chawton, where Jane Austen lived from 1809 to 1816, is three miles away. *(Recommended by Mr and Mrs P A Pritchard, A J Milman, Tim Halstead, Glyn Edmunds)*

Soup prices usually include a roll and butter.

Courage · Licensee Bernard B Paton · Real ale · Meals (not Sun) and snacks
Children in restaurant and buttery · Bars open 10–2.30, 6–11 · Bedrooms tel
Selborne (042 050) 272; £13 (£16B)/£23 (£26B)

SHERFIELD-ON-LODDON   SU6857   Map 2
White Hart

Village signposted from A33

The lounge of this comfortably modernised and well kept ex-
coaching-inn has a very attractive bow window seat in what was
originally the coachmen's separate roadside room. Hunting mugs
hang from beams in the red ceiling, and there is a dumpy wood-
burning stove in the big inglenook fireplace, though apart from a
splendidly fat barrel seat the furnishings are straightforward. Bar
food includes soup (60p), individual sausages (25p), cheese and
biscuits (from 85p), a wide range of plain or toasted sandwiches
(from 75p, bacon and Stilton £1.30), ploughman's (£1), ravioli
(£1.40), and hot main dishes such as steak and kidney pie, gammon,
grilled fish, casseroles and steaks (£3–£8); well kept Courage Best
and Directors on handpump; a fruit machine, maybe piped music;
separate restaurant. *(Recommended by Gordon and Daphne; more
reports please)*

Courage · Licensee Ronald Brown · Real ale · Meals (not Sun, Mon evening or
Sat lunchtime) and snacks (not Sun or Mon evenings) · Children in eating area
and restaurant · Open 10.30–2.30, 6–11

The Still & West, Portsmouth

SOUTHAMPTON   SU4212 Map 2
Red Lion

55 High Street; turning off inner ring road, in S of city

Though you'd never guess it from outside in the busy city street, the main bar is a remarkable medieval hall, with a creaky upper gallery running around the timbered walls below steeply pitched rafters. Above dark Tudor panelling hang arms, suits of armour, and a flag reputed to have been presented to Southampton by Elizabeth I in 1585. Though the building alone deserves a visit, the straightforward food served in the lower-ceilinged back bar has recently been an additional pleasure – sandwiches or filled rolls, ploughman's (£1), cod (£2.10), steak and kidney pie (£2.20), scampi (£2.95) and rump or sirloin steak (£4.95); Gales, Ushers and Websters Yorkshire on handpump; a fruit machine, maybe piped music. Though there's no concrete evidence to support the story, the building is of the right age and stature to fit in with the tradition that it was here that Henry V, before sailing for Agincourt, sentenced to death Lord Scrope and his own cousin Richard, Earl of Cambridge, for plotting against him. (*Recommended by David Potter, C J McCafferty*)

Watneys · Licensee I J Williams · Real ale · Meals and snacks · Children in dining-room · Duo Tues evenings · Daytime parking nearby difficult · Open 10–2.30, 6–11

STEEP   SU7425 Map 2
Harrow ★

Village signposted from A325 and A3 NE of Petersfield; then watch for pub sign

On weekdays the little public bar of this peaceful village local is at its most charming, with flowers on the scrubbed deal tables, built-in wall seats, maybe a fat cocker spaniel asleep on the black and red tiles in front of the big inglenook fireplace, and people from the village dropping in to buy eggs, borrow books, play dominoes, or just chat over a pint of the well kept Flowers Original, Whitbreads Strong Country or Samuel Whitbreads tapped from the casks behind the counter, or perhaps some country wine or traditional cider. Nourishing home-made food includes Scotch eggs (60p), sandwiches (from 73p), excellent soup (£1.10), ploughman's (£1.50), lasagne (£2.50) and salads with meat loaf (£2.60) or home-cooked ham (£3.85). There are seats in the big flower-filled garden, or at tables in front, by the quiet lane. As we've said before, it would be kind not to descend on this carefully preserved old village tavern at weekends or other busy holiday times, as it's really too small to cope with droves of outsiders. (*Recommended by Gordon and Daphne, Mrs A M Arnold, C H Cole, Glyn Edmunds, Annie Taylor, Chris Lamb*)

Whitbreads · Licensee E C McCutcheon · Real ale · Snacks Open 10–2.30, 6–11

In next year's edition we hope to pick out pubs where the food is specially good, alongside the star ratings. Please tell us if you think any pub – in the *Guide* or not – deserves a 'Food Award'. No stamp needed: *The Good Pub Guide*, FREEPOST, London SW10 0BR.

STUCKTON   SU1613   Map 2

Three Lions

Village signposted from B3078 turn-off towards Cadnam, from A338 just
S of Fordingbridge

Though this plain but comfortable red-brick house is certainly a pub
rather than a restaurant, its meals, cooked with care by the landlord,
are of good restaurant quality, and, as you'd reasonably expect, the
prices (particularly in the evening) reflect that. The wide and
changing choice includes for lunch a dozen or more dishes such as
game soup (£1.75), chicken liver pâté (£1.90), spiced herring fillets
with chives or soufflée beignet Aida or sweet-cured herring (£1.95),
home-made burger (£2.40), interesting pasta (from £2.50),
Sauerkraut with Cumberland sausage (£2.60), baked mushrooms
with seafood (£3.30), curries (£4.50), pork cutlet (£4.60), Avon trout
(£4.75), and steak and kidney pie, fresh plaice, dab or brill (£4.95).
The lighter of these dishes serve as evening starters, too, when main
courses might include veal cutlet with sorrel and tarragon sauce,
stuffed woodpigeons (£6.30), local calf's liver with Dorset bacon or
medaillons of roebuck (£6.80) and roast guinea-fowl (£6.90). Since
our last edition they've started charging separately (£1.30) for a
choice of vegetables or salad to avoid them going to waste. There is
always a good range of puddings. An excellent choice of wines,
particularly by the bottle and half-bottle, as well as Huntsman
Dorset, Dorchester and Royal Oak on handpump (kept under light
blanket pressure); cushioned Windsor chairs on the dark red carpet
of the communicating rooms, lots of flowers and plants, and in winter
two warm coal fires. Service is briskly friendly. Beware that last
lunchtime food orders are taken by 1.30pm, supper by 9pm, that
tables must be booked in the evenings, and that there's no food at the
start of the week. (Recommended by W H B Murdoch, Nicci Carey, Simon
Swift, G S Crockett)

Huntsman · Licensee Karl-Hermann Wadsack · Meals (not Sun evening, Mon
or Tues lunchtime)–tel Fordingbridge (0425) 52489–and snacks (lunchtime,
not Mon or Tues) · Open 11–2.30, 6–11 (7–10.30 winter evenings); closed
Mon, also Feb, Easter week, two weeks July/Aug, last week Oct, Christmas
to New Year

TANGLEY   SU3252   Map 2

Cricketers Arms

Tangley Bottom, towards the Chutes from village centre; OS Sheet 185
reference 326528

The sort of place where you drop in for a quick drink and stay all
evening, this pretty little white tiled pub has a warmly friendly
atmosphere. There are lots of cricketing prints on the clean cream walls
of the stylishly simple bar, a big fireplace (which still has its bread oven
and a splendid iron fireback, as well as a good winter log fire), and
plain light-coloured wheelback chairs around wooden tables. Well
kept Whitbreads Strong Country on handpump; ploughman's,
sandwiches and toasties; darts (there's a massive collection of darts
cups), shove-ha'penny, dominoes, cribbage; maybe cabbage, lettuce or

other plants for sale (proceeds to charity). There are rustic seats and a big wooden climbing-frame on the grass beyond the car park – and beyond that, on the edge of this remote downland hamlet, the pub's own flock of sheep. The Etonian landlord is Conservative MP for Romsey. (*Recommended by Gordon and Daphne; more reports please*)

Free house · Licensees Mrs Mary Perry and Michael Colvin · Real ale · Snacks Well behaved children allowed at licensees' discretion · Open 11–2.30, 6.30–11; closed Tues

VERNHAM DEAN   SU3456 Map 2
George

Since our last edition they've stopped doing food, which was anyway never much more than a footnote to this old-fashioned downland village pub with its cosy, rambling bars. The smooth curve of the tiles over the first-floor windows gives the old timbered brick and flint building a raised-eyebrows look. Inside, it's welcoming and relaxed, with easy chairs and a grandfather clock by the bar billiards-table in one side room, maybe a couple of cats dozing by the log fire in the main room's big inglenook fireplace, beams, old polished elm tables and comfortably cushioned captain's chairs and built-in wall benches. Well kept Marstons Burton, Pedigree and sometimes Mercian Mild on handpump, and occasional wine bargains; darts (the regulars are keen and good), shove-ha'penny, cribbage and dominoes; maybe up-to-date piped pop music. (*Recommended by Gordon and Daphne; more reports please*)

Marstons · Licensee Mike Beere · Real ale · Meals and snacks · Occasional folk or traditional jazz · Open 12–2.30, 7–11; closed Tues lunchtime

nr VERNHAM DEAN   SU3456 Map 2
Boot [*illustrated on page 305*]

Littledown; follow village signs from Vernham Dean

This isolated but friendly downland flint cottage has an appropriately splendid collection of model boots and shoes in its low-beamed white-panelled bar. This cottagey room has just had its fireplace knocked out into the original inglenook shape, and has been extended since our last edition to include more tables, some of which are set aside for meals in the evening. There's also a cosy side room (which can be booked for parties of eight to twelve and is then almost filled by a big old-fashioned dining-table). Good bar food includes sandwiches (from 60p), ploughman's (£1.25), ham and egg (£1.85), half-pint prawns (£1.90), salads (£2.50), gammon (£2.70), scampi (£2.75), chicken Kiev (£4.50) and steaks (from £5.75). Badger Best, Marstons Burton and Pedigree tapped from the cask, and a growing collection of malt whiskies. There is a darts board in a conservatory (which is not really suitable for use in the winter); they also keep dominoes. Since the last edition they've built a terrace, leading into the garden – where the climbing-frame and horse-drawn caravan should appeal to children. (*Recommended by Prof A N Black, Glyn Edmunds; more reports please*)

Free house · Licensee David Catherine · Real ale · Meals (not Sun evening or Mon) and snacks (not Mon); dinner and party bookings tel Linkenholt (026 487) 213 · Children in conservatory · Open 12–2.30, 6–11; closed Mon except bank hols

WELL SU7646 Map 2

Chequers ★

Back lane, W of Farnham

The surprise in this so-English pub, with its antique settles, comfortable country seats and stools, warm winter log fire, and rustic tools and brasses in the intimate alcoves of its snug and civilised low-beamed bar, is that the cooking (and indeed the landlord) is French. The wide range of bar food includes good Brie or pâté as well as Cheddar or Stilton for the ploughman's (£2.20), cold meats with attractive salads (£2.85), coq au vin or beef bourguignonne (£3.15), king prawns in mayonnaise (£3.20) and freshly cooked crab mayonnaise (£3.85), with good puddings. There are a couple of dozen French wines, as well as Badger Best on handpump. The separate restaurant (closed Sunday evening, all day Monday) has a surprisingly grand moulded plaster ceiling (this was once quite an important coaching-stop, though the old highway has now become a quiet country lane). Outside, there are rustic seats and tables in a front arbour, strung with coloured lights at night. The pub, well known in the area, does get busy. *(Recommended by Evan Davies, Richard Franck, Peter Barrett)*

Free house · Licensee Maurice Bernard · Real ale · Meals and snacks (not Sun evening or Mon) · Children in restaurant · Open 11–2.30, 6–11; closed Mon lunchtime

WHITCHURCH SU4648 Map 2

Red House

London Street; B3400 Andover–Basingstoke, on Basingstoke side of town centre

The nicest spot in this attractive steeply tiled old pub is under the heavy beams by the inglenook fireplace at the serving end of the main bar, where seats on the ancient flagstones are warmed by a solid-fuel stove. Bar food includes filled baked potatoes (60p), good toasted sandwiches (from 65p) or rolls, ploughman's made with home-baked bread (£1.50) and home-made cottage pie or chicken curry (£1.80); well kept Halls Harvest and Ind Coope Burton on handpump. The friendly saloon bar has darts, pool, a fruit machine, space game and a juke box. There are picnic-table sets on the wall-sheltered lawn. *(Recommended by Andy Jones and the P A Club, Ray Kerswell; more reports please)*

Halls (Ind Coope) · Licensee Stuart Fee · Real ale · Meals and snacks (not Sun evening) · Children in eating area or saloon bar · Open 10–2.30, 6–11

Cribbage is a card game using a block of wood with holes for matchsticks or special pins with which to keep the score; regulars in cribbage pubs are usually happy to teach strangers how to play.

WINCHESTER SU4829 Map 2

Black Boy

Wharf Hill; from bottom of High Street follow road round to right signposted Southampton, Portsmouth, then take first right turn

Since the *Guide*'s last edition the range of food in this interestingly furnished and well run pub – with its good choice of real ales – has been extended to include sandwiches (from 60p), toasties (from 65p), a wide variety of ploughman's (from £1), filled baked potatoes (from £1), open sandwiches (from £1.20), and the straightforward hot dishes such as burgers and chicken (£1.40), charcoal-grilled hamburger (£1.30), scampi, and charcoal-grilled steaks, with a wide and changing choice of other hot dishes such as cottage pie, steak and kidney pie, Boston beans with bacon, creamed haddock with prawns, seafood platter, dressed crab or turkey and bacon with chestnuts. The comfortable L-shaped bar has button-back red leatherette seats forming bays below the high shelves of old china jars and house plants, a flowery carpet and red velvet curtains. The real ales change weekly, and on a typical visit might include Courage Best, Fullers ESB, Gales HSB, Simpkiss and Wadworths IPA and 6X, all on handpump. There may be piped music, and in the evening, with a lively young crowd, the good juke box comes into its own; also fruit machine and a space game. There are seats on the front terrace and in a sheltered beer garden overlooking the old mill house, and an attractively refurbished old barn has now been turned into a parties and functions room. From here you can walk along the Itchen towpath, or through the water-meadows to the ancient hospice at St Cross. *(Recommended by G P Bird and John, Tim, Andrew and Sue Kemp)*

Free house · Licensee Ciff Cederberg · Real ale · Meals and snacks (lunchtime, not Sun) · Live music Mon, occasionally Sat · Open 11–2.30, 6–11

Eclipse

The Square; between High Street and cathedral

Very handily placed for visiting the cathedral, this friendly and attractive pub (mainly sixteenth-century, but dating back partly to the fourteenth) was originally the rectory for the little church of St Lawrence. Inside there are heavy beams with lots of mugs hanging from them, oak settles and country prints, and since our last edition a wall has been knocked through to expose some more sixteenth-century timber work. Food includes good value sandwiches (from 70p), ploughman's (from £1.20), macaroni or ravioli snacks (£1.10), pâté (£1.20), home-baked ham and egg (£1.60), plaice (£1.95), salads (£2.25), scampi (£2.75) and sirloin steak (£3.95); Whitbreads Strong Country and Pompey Royal are kept under light blanket pressure; darts in a smaller back room, dominoes, cribbage. There are pavement benches under the hanging baskets which decorate the striking black and white timbered façade; in 1685 Lady Lisle was led out from an upstairs window to the scaffold on which she was beheaded for allegedly supporting the Duke of Monmouth's rebellion; but after her death a Parliamentary inquiry found her innocent. *(Recommended by A J V Baker; more reports please)*

Whitbreads · Licensees Trevor and Jan Marpole · Meals (weekday lunchtimes) and snacks · Children in eating area · Daytime parking nearby may be difficult Open 10–2.30, 6–11

Lucky Dip

Besides the fully inspected pubs, you might like to try these Lucky Dips recommended and described by readers (if you do, please send us reports):

ALRESFORD [West Street; SU5832], *Bell*: Georgian coaching-inn with bar food and bedrooms *(Anon)*; [Broad Street] *Globe*: good pub on the edge of the Roman-built Alresford pond, with seats outside – though you sometimes share the space with the ducks! *(GSS)*; [West Street] *Swan*: good value simple food in restored coaching-inn; bedrooms *(Anon)*

ALTON [The Butts; SU7139], *French Horn*: friendly service and good food in pleasant building with skittle alley and wonderful cat *(Julian Dean)*

AMPFIELD [SU4023], *Potters Heron*: nice watermill-style bar with comfortable well spaced tables, good buffet bar, well kept Flowers Original and other real ales *(A N Black)*

BASING [SU6653], *Bolton Arms*: attractive inside and out: long cheerful bar with open fires at each end, beams, pleasant pictures on walls; colourful window boxes *(Gordon and Daphne)*

BENTLEY [SU7844], *Bull*: friendly welcome, good food (and separate dining area), pleasant service and interesting choice of drinks *(Ian Meharg)*

BENTWORTH [SU6640], *Sun*: good food and drink *(Glyn Edmunds)*

BIGHTON [SU6134], *Three Horseshoes*: unusual collection of mostly stringed musical instruments in popular traditional country pub with Gales real ale (for pub location see OS Sheet 185 reference 615344) *(Mike Hallett)*

BINSTED [SU7741], *Cedars*: food excellent and freshly prepared (may take half an hour but worth it), especially home-cooked ham, in simple, cheerful country pub with no music *(Julian Dean, W A Gardiner)*

BISHOPS SUTTON [SU6031], *Ship*: cosy main road pub, bar food *(LYM)*

BLACKNEST [SU7941], *Jolly Farmer*: good food in bar and restaurant, well kept Adnams, Badger, Huntsman; garden, skittle alley, spotless WCs; unobtrusive piped music (for pub location see OS Sheet 186 reference 798416) *(W A Gardiner)*

BOLDRE [SZ3298], *Red Lion*: good hot and cold food in very popular beamy pub with old farm tools, mugs, glasses, bottles and so forth; welcoming owners, good service; Huntsman real ales *(P T Young and others)*

BRAISHFIELD [Newport Lane; SU3725], *Newport*: food good and cheap, including generous ploughman's, with well kept Gales ale in small secluded local with 1950s-style lounge and pleasant shaded garden *(B R Wood, Richard Bone)*

BRAMDEAN [SU6128], *Fox*: fairly quiet charmingly old pub with comfortable lounges, good hot or cold food and efficient service *(G S Burrows)*

BRIMPTON [Brimpton Common; SU5564], *Pineapple*: food good in thatched beamed pub with stone and tiled floors, rustic furniture, tree-trunks, open fire, bar billiards, darts, fruit machine; Wethereds real ales *(Jane English)*

BROCKENHURST [SU2902], *Jugged Hare*: good food with help-yourself salads in modern atmospheric pub with cosy open fire in winter *(H G and C J McCafferty)*; *Rose & Crown*: food wholesome and generous in large pub with weekend restaurant; log fires, pool, skittle alley, children's room, big garden; good atmosphere – landlord from Prospect of Whitby in East London *(T G W Carrington)*; *Snakecatcher*: one long bar with plenty of space; malt whiskies, Huntsman ales *(Martyn Quinn)*

BROUGHTON [High Street; SU3033], *Greyhound*: good value basket meals in nineteenth-century pub with Cunard liner theme; well kept Marstons *(Richard Bone)*

BUCKS HORN OAK [SU8041], *Halfway House*: good food and friendly service in clean well kept pub with warm welcome and popular restaurant *(Nicholas Rolfe)*

BURGATE [SU1415], *Tudor Rose*: friendly old thatched cottagey building, warm, with beams and antiques; good restaurant *(Martyn Quinn)*

BURSLEDON [Oak Hill; SU4809], *Crows Nest*: pleasant atmosphere, good bar food, well kept Courage ales; excellent garden for children *(R W Garnett)*; [School Lane] *Vine*: warmly welcoming local close to River Hamble with good bar food and well kept Marstons *(B R Shiner)*

CADNAM [SU2913], *Sir John Barleycorn*: good value food and friendly atmosphere in attractive thatched and beamed twelfth-century pub with log fire, selection of ales and extensive choice of cigars; barbecues in garden *(V Guy)*

CHANDLERS FORD [Winchester Road; SU4320], *Mount*: good modernised pub with bar and restaurant; seats outside *(B R Shiner)*

CHERITON [SU5828], *Flowerpots*: unspoilt and genuine country village local with friendly landlady and customers; beer from barrels in lobby *(Gordon and Daphne)*

CHILWORTH [SU4018], *Clump*: good 'cocktail bar' pub with well run single bar, interesting mixed clientele, garden *(Anon)*

CHIMBOLTON [SU3939], *Abbots Mitre*: good lunchtime meals, very friendly welcoming clubby atmosphere, good landlord *(Hugh Butterworth)*

CRAWLEY [SU4234], *Fox & Hounds*: big helpings of good value freshly made food (not Sunday or Monday) and well kept Flowers Original, Whitbreads Strong Country and Wadworths 6X in homely red-brick pub with friendly licensees and unusual Bavarian-style wood façade; attractive village *(P L Fullick, W H B Murdoch, Gordon and Daphne, BB)*

nr DENMEAD [SU6611], *Chairmakers Arms*: wide choice of bar food and well kept Gales ales in knocked-together rooms of popular pub surrounded by paddocks and farmland; no music *(Gwen and Peter Andrews, Glyn Edmunds, LYM)*

DROXFORD [SU6018], *White Horse*: the owners who earned this rambling old inn high praise in previous editions left last year *(LYM; up-to-date reports on the new regime please)*

DUNDRIDGE [SU5718], *Hampshire Bowman*: simple isolated downland pub with good Gales ales, straightforward food, friendly welcome; big lawn (for pub location see OS Sheet 185 reference 579185) *(LYM)*

EAST END [SZ3697], *East End Arms*: food good in two-bar pub with well kept Whitbreads real ales *(Patrick Young)*

EMSWORTH [SU7406], *Ship*: good value simple food and well kept Bass in plain but comfortable well kept pub *(Glyn Edmunds, LYM)*

EVERSLEY CROSS [SU7861], *Chequers*: comfortably modernised partly fourteenth-century Watneys pub with quickly served bar food *(LYM)*

EWSHOT [SU8149], *Queens Arms*: attractive woodland pub, clean and well run with willing staff, good snacks and back restaurant *(C A Foden, G Atkinson)*

FORDINGBRIDGE [High Street; SU1414], *George*: friendly welcome, warm atmosphere, good value food and choice of real ales in delightfully placed pub with large riverside terrace *(W H B Murdoch)*

FROYLE [Lower Froyle; SU7542], *Prince of Wales*: good food and drink *(Glyn Edmunds)*

GOSPORT [Crescent Road; SZ6199], *Anglesey Hotel*: genuine Regency pub with good bar food and restaurant *(W Counsell)*

HAMBLE [High Street; SU4806], *Bugle*: yachtsmen's pub with river views from restaurant, real ales, bar food; in previous editions as a main entry, but as we went to press they told us of plans for an unspecified complete change of direction *(LYM; up-to-date reports on the new set-up please)*; [High Street] *King & Queen*: good local atmosphere in well kept pub *(Ray Kerswell)*

HAMBLEDON [SU6414], *Bat & Ball*: good food, well kept Ind Coope real ales, relaxing atmosphere, interesting china and long cricketing history – in previous editions as a main entry but now more of a restaurant than a pub *(Steve and Carolyn Harvey, M V Fereday, Glyn Edmunds, LYM)*

HAMMER VALE [SU8832], *Prince of Wales*: straightforward local that won a main entry in previous editions for its exceptionally good management giving fine atmosphere and well kept real ales; but new tenants since summer 1985

329

(LYM; up-to-date reports on the new regime please)

HAWKLEY [SU7429], *Hawkley*: good value bar snacks and well kept Marstons Pedigree and Badger Best in efficiently run isolated pub with basic wooden furniture and stripped pine bar, Delft tiles and plates; unusual terrace *(Steve and Carolyn Harvey)*

HEDGE END [Shamblehurst Lane; SU4812], *Shamblehurst Barn*: friendly landlady and good food in refurbished 400-year-old bar with plenty of charm and character including big wood-burning stove and lots of exposed timber; bar snacks, restaurant *(L Davies)*

HINTON ADMIRAL [SZ2196], *Cat & Fiddle*: long low thatched building with beams, brasses, antiques, open fire; modernised somewhat but has kept atmosphere; restaurant *(Martyn Quinn)*

KINGS SOMBORNE [SU3631], *Crown*: attractive old thatched village pub with cosy fireplace in split-level lounge; lively local public bar, garden *(Gordon and Daphne)*

KINGS WORTHY [SU4933], *Cart & Horses*: rambling trendily old-fashioned public bar and spacious lounge, serving Marstons ales and bar food *(S Egle, LYM)*

LANGSTONE [SU7105], *Ship*: wide range of sandwiches, salads and other good bar food, and Gales ales, in simple pub with superb waterside position and lots of sitting space along quay; no motor-cyclists *(W Counsell, A J V Baker)*

LASHAM [SU6742], *Royal Oak*: good food and real ale, excellent atmosphere *(G V Prater)*

LONGSTOCK [SU3536], *Peat Spade*: friendly locals' bar in straightforward Test Valley inn *(Ray Kerswell, LYM)*

LYMINGTON [SZ3295], *Angel*: welcoming much-modernised hotel bar with adjoining well run food bar; bedrooms *(A J Milman, LYM)*; [Ridgeway Lane] *Chequers*: food includes superb mussels in roomy and welcoming single-bar pub with wooden chairs and bare floorboards *(H G and C J McCafferty)*; [Silver Street] *Three Bells*: good value food in much extended pub with new décor *(Anon)*

LYNDHURST [SU2908], *Fox & Hounds*: food good in pleasant pub with very helpful staff; nice family room *(Mrs G Palmer)*; [Swan Green] *Swan*: friendly welcome and good cheap bar food; exceptional efforts made for disabled customers *(Nigel Hill)*

MARCHWOOD [SU3810], *Pilgrim*: immaculately sprightly décor in smart thatched pub with Huntsman beers and lunchtime snacks; neat garden *(A K Hardy, LYM)*

MATTINGLEY [SU7358], *Leather Bottle*: busy, popular open-plan pub with good simple snacks *(W T Aird)*

NETHER WALLOP [SU3036], *Five Bells*: homely and welcoming old country pub near downland village church *(Ray Kerswell, Andy Jones and the PA Club, LYM)*

NETLEY [Victoria Road; SU4508], *Prince Consort*: recently revamped in Victorian style with well kept real ales, good bar food (especially seafood), separate restaurant, pleasant young licensees *(Ian Jackson, S Egle)*

NORTH GORLEY [SU1611], *Royal Oak*: good food in pleasant pub with back garden fenced in from ponies, cows and donkeys; ducks on front stream *(Mrs P Kemp)*

NORTH WARNBOROUGH [SU7351], *Anchor*: friendly and welcoming pub with well kept Courage beers and good plain food at reasonable prices – excellent ham sandwiches *(H J P Chetwynd-Talbot)*; *Jolly Miller*: food very good value for money *(A M Stratton)*

NORTHAM [Shamrock Quay; SU4212], *Waterfront Café Bar*: near water and boats with waterside tables; good food, children in eating area *(B R Shiner)*

ODIHAM [SU7450], *Bell*: charming unspoilt pub with delicious seafood *(Mr and Mrs P Lewis-Jones)*; *George*: well kept Courage real ales and food in old-fashioned bar; bedrooms *(W T Aird, LYM)*

PETERSFIELD [College Street; SU7423], *Good Intent*: quiet old pub, comfortable, convivial and welcoming, with good Ballards real ales, log fires, bar food and restaurant *(G E Judd, Steve and Carolyn Harvey, J Dean)*

PORTSMOUTH [Bath Square; SU6501], *Coal Exchange*: first-floor harbour views in pleasant and atmospheric pub with efficient staff *(H G and C J McCafferty)*; [High Street] *Dolphin*: pleasant atmosphere and welcome; good hot and cold buffet *(M V Fereday)*; [High Street] *Sallyport*: food in bar good, and real ales including Gales HSB and Ushers; sombrely nautical décor *(Aubrey Saunders)*

PRESTON CANDOVER [Axford; SU6041], *Candover Crown*: friendly and attractive little family-run pub on hillside; well kept Marstons Pedigree and Wadworths 6X, some bar food; garden *(Gordon Mair)*

RINGWOOD [Hightown; SU1505], *Elm Tree*: home cooking in cosy thatched pub with log fires, Flowers Original and Wadworths 6X, restaurant; some live music in Barn Bar, children welcome; parking for 200 *(Mrs P Kemp, Hugh Butterworth)*; *Fish*: comfortably modernised Whitbreads pub with lawn by River Avon *(LYM)*

ROCKFORD [SU1608], *Alice Lisle*: open-plan bar with Bass and Ringwood real ales, good food including charcoal-grilled steaks, evening restaurant; Wendy house with games in garden; on New Forest green *(BB, A J Milman)*

ROMSEY [SU3521], *Old House At Home*: congenial little low-ceilinged pub with Gales real ales *(David Symes)*

ROPLEY [SU6431], *Chequers*: pleasant and comfortable pub with friendly staff, Courage ales and good food *(C J A Davis)*

SELBORNE [SU7433], *Selborne Arms*: pleasant atmosphere in simple and friendly pub with good food and beer garden for children *(Mrs A M Arnold, AB)*

SETLEY [SU3000], *Filly*: quite well done New Forest roadside pub *(Dr A K Clarke)*

SHAWFORD [SU4624], *Bridge*: quickly served bar food, good choice of real ales, obliging staff, attractive riverside garden with swings and cook-it-yourself barbecues; special events such as custom-car rallies *(Prof A N Black, B R Shiner)*

SOBERTON [SU6116], *White Lion*: good value food and real ales including Friary Meux, Gales HSB, Huntsman Royal Oak, Ushers Best and Ringwood; friendly atmosphere, log fires, restaurant *(AS)*

SOUTHAMPTON [Padwell Road; SU4212], *Avenue*: quick and friendly service in clean and roomy pub with photos of old Southampton; very busy *(SE)*; [Carlton Place] *Cricketers Arms*: quick friendly service in clean nicely decorated single bar which can get crowded – but plenty of seats *(SE)*; [Canute Road] *Frog & Frigate*: purpose-built replica of old-fashioned pub with 10 real ales including ones brewed on premises; happy atmosphere, with Saturday evening sing-alongs *(G E Bennett, David Potter)*; [Freemantle] *Wellington Arms*: good comfortable pub with lots of brass, well kept Wadworths, Ringwood and other real ales *(David Symes)*

SOUTHSEA [Eldon Street; SZ6498], *Eldon Arms*: good food in bar and restaurant, excellent atmosphere, Huntsman Royal Oak *(P J Wooding)*

SPARSHOLT [SU4331], *Plough*: well run with excellent local reputation, particular welcome for children *(GSS)*

ST MARY BOURNE [SU4250], *Coronation Arms*: friendly village local with welcoming landlord and well kept Marstons real ale *(Ray Kerswell)*

STOCKBRIDGE [High Street; SU3535], *Vine*: has been very popular with readers and star-rated for its imaginative food, but the family who have run it so well for many years are leaving; reports on the new regime please! *(LYM)*; *White Hart*: recently refurbished old inn with efficient bar service; some furniture made from chain-sawn logs; bedrooms good value *(Pat and Malcolm Rudlin)*

SWANMORE [Hill Grove; SU5716], *Hunters*: fantastic children's play area and good bar food (for pub location see OS Sheet 185 reference 582161) *Mike Hallett, Glyn Edmunds)*; [Chapel Road] *New*: good value and interesting home-cooked food, friendly atmosphere and well kept Marstons real ales under its new tenants *(F N Clay)*

TICHBORNE [SU5630], *Tichborne Arms*: well kept Courage, Marstons and Wadworths 6X, good range of bar food, friendly atmosphere, log fires and two comfortable lounges in old pub with big garden and covered back terrace; lovely village *(Marian and Ron Marriner, David Phelips, JKW)*

TIMSBURY [SU3424], *Bear & Ragged Staff*: good hot food, Flowers Original and Whitbreads Strong Country; log fire in inglenook, cheerful atmosphere; play area in flower garden *(Patrick Young, BMI, Andy Jones and the PA Club, Michael Samuel)*

TITCHFIELD [SU5305], *Wheatsheaf*: good value food and well kept ales including Gales and Ushers; large lounge, small public bar, friendly family atmosphere; restaurant, pretty garden *(P C Biles, Mr and Mrs T M Dwyer)*

TOTFORD [SU5738], *Woolpack*: home cooking in small seventeenth-century alehouse with log fire, exposed brick and beams, and well kept Gales, Marstons and Websters Yorkshire; garden, skittle alley *(Gordon Mair, GSS)*

UPTON [SU3555], *Crown*: spick-and-span comfortable country pub with flock wallpaper, dolls and china collection, home-cooked bar food and well kept Gibbs Mew ales; piped music *(Gordon and Daphne, BB)*

UPTON GREY [SU6948], *Hoddington Arms*: very wide choice of toasted sandwiches among other home-cooked food in contented village pub with Courage real ales, farm cider, children's room and garden *(David Guthrie, H J P Chetwynd-Talbot)*

WARNFORD [SU6223], *George & Falcon*: good value food in pleasant bar with well kept beer; restaurant *(Mrs S Cowherd)*

WARSASH [Fleet End Road; SU4906], *Jolly Farmer*: good food and welcoming atmosphere; collection of farm tools, Whitbreads beers, garden (for pub location see OS Sheet 196 reference 509062) *(Mike Hallett)*; *Rising Sun*: fabulous views towards Southampton Water from upstairs picture windows of revamped pub overlooking the Hamble; good open sandwiches *(H G and C J McCafferty)*

WEYHILL [SU3146], *Weyhill Fair*: interestingly refurbished ex-Whitbreads free house, serving Morrells, usually Bourne Valley, and guest real ale, also good value bar food; children in family room *(Andy Jones and the PA Club)*

nr WHERWELL [Testcombe, A3057 Andover–Stockbridge; SU3941], *Mayfly*: outstanding riverside position and very popular buffet lunches, good cheeses *(G H Windsor, GSS, B R Beswick, LYM)*

WHITSBURY [SU1219], *Cartwheel*: friendly and welcoming pub with good range of beers and ciders, nice home-cooked food, efficient informal service, children welcome *(M R Lane)*

WINCHESTER [High Street; SU4829], *Bakers Arms*: little pub in inconspicuous alleyway, that wins prizes for flowers around open-air overspill area; good food and drink *(GSS)*; [Northern outskirts] *Jolly Farmer*: pleasant and spacious pub with highwayman associations; tables outside *(GSS)*; [The Square] *Old Market*: food and drink good and promptly served in pleasant Whitbreads corner pub; soft piped music; handy for cathedral *(GSS, BB)*; [Little Great Minster Street] *Old Vyne*: good lunchtime food, well kept Courage real ale, cheerful prompt service, no music; near cathedral *(Roger Doughty, GSS)*; [Royal Oak Passage] *Royal Oak*: a tradition that the stone-floored cellar with wooden tables and old farm tools is the oldest bar in England; good value food in popular ground-floor bar areas *(Martyn Quinn, GSS, BB)*; [Wales Street] *Ship*: popular for home-cooked food and beer; garden *(Keith Chuck, R H J Newman, A Hibberd)*; [Kingsgate Street] *Wykeham Arms*: friendly atmosphere, log fires, good food and drink, including well kept Huntsman real ales, in bar and bistro-style restaurant; bedrooms; efficiently run by new owners *(GSS)*

WOLVERTON [Towns End; SU5558], *George & Dragon*: friendly and relaxing with welcoming licensees, open brick fire and standing timbers from knocked-through wall *(Gordon and Daphne)*

Hereford and Worcester

Perhaps the most important news here is that the new licensees at the Fleece in Bretforton have proved to be just what this marvellous old antiques-laden pub needed: it now has our highest rating as one of Britain's most interesting pubs. Our congratulations too this year go to the welcoming and ancient Rhydspence at Whitney on Wye, where we had our most memorable meal of the year and which has the best pub food in the area. Two pubs here have been celebrating important anniversaries in 1985: the pretty little Cottage of Content at Carey is now five hundred years old, and the lively and friendly Pandy at Dorstone (a new entry this year, with wholesome simple food and excellent drinks) has been celebrating its eight-hundredth birthday — it's the county's oldest pub. After an absence from our pages, the Lough Pool at Sellack is back in with a bang under its capable new licensees with a star award for its tasty food and fine country atmosphere. And another important piece of news is that licensing hours in the area have been changing, with more pubs open until 11pm (but rather more tending to stay closed later in the morning, too). Besides pubs already mentioned, good value food is to be had at the Green Dragon in Bishops

The Cottage of Content, Carey

Frome (quick service and an interesting choice of real ales in cheerfully traditional surroundings), the Coach & Horses at Weatheroak Hill (again, simple cooking, also an excellent range of real ales), the idiosyncratic Kings Arms and the more sober Crown & Sandys Arms (both in Ombersley), the aptly named and civilised Swan in Upton upon Severn, the Butchers Arms in Woolhope (an out-of-the-way inn, well worth finding) and at the Farriers Arms close to Worcester Cathedral (with a wider choice than before of vegetarian food among other enterprising dishes). Two charming places to stay are the lovely black and white timbered Red Lion in Weobley (probably the area's prettiest village), and the very stylish old Lygon Arms in Broadway. Though the pleasantly basic Mug House virtually in the village churchyard at Claines is reasonable, perhaps the cheapest drinks are to be had at the friendly Olde Anchor in Upton upon Severn — especially the good beer it brews on the premises. In the long Lucky Dip section at the end of the chapter, pubs we'd pick out as specially promising are the Round o' Gras at Badsey (particularly if you like asparagus), the Firs by the canal at Dunhampstead (home cooking in an attractive pub), the Camp House at Grimley (for its garden crowded with animals and fowls from tiny chicks to peacocks), the friendly fourteenth-century Talbot at Knightwick, the Old Talbot in Ledbury (a charming sixteenth-century timbered inn with a poltergeist), the Royal Oak in Leominster (friendly efficient service with good bar snacks and comfortable bedrooms), the Bell at Pensax (recently improved, with a chatty parrot), the Hope & Anchor on a nice bend of the river at Ross-on-Wye (good food and real ale) and the friendly Sun at Winforton (original food). The Broad Oak near Garway — which we have checked out — would certainly be a main entry for its excellent food and attractive atmosphere, but is disqualified by the fact that, though pleasantly pubby, it's really a restaurant; you can't just drop in for a drink.

BELBROUGHTON   SO9277   Map 4
Bell

2 miles from M5 junction 4; A491 towards Stourbridge, beside right turn signposted Romsley

This handsome old building stands well above and away from the dual carriageway, and its smart lounge bar has green plush stools and modern settles on its Turkey carpet, a striking stone inglenook fireplace, and lots of copper jugs and ladles hanging from its heavy beams; in the separate Belfry Bar the walls have been stripped back to the ancient neat brickwork. Bar food includes sandwiches (from 65p), soup (80p), ploughman's (£1.40), home-made pâté (£1.70) and chicken (£2.60), fish pie, steak and onion pie, chicken and mushroom pie, and scampi (all £2.80). There may be piped music. The lounge/restaurant in a big split-level barn of a room at the back, with a central log fire and red wine stored in the dark wood rafters, has been praised for its fish. You can sit outside. *(Recommended by C J Castledine; more reports please)*

Mitchells & Butlers (Bass) · Licensee John Narbett · Meals and snacks (lunchtime, not Sun) · Children in eating area · Open 12–2.30, 5.30–11

BISHOPS FROME   SO6648   Map 4

Green Dragon ★

The wide choice of simple bar food is good value in this traditionally furnished and uncommonly cheerful old pub – and what's more, the enthusiastic licensees keep an excellent range of real ales, such as Baileys, Hook Norton Best, Robinsons Best and Old Tom, Timothy Taylors Landlord and Woods, with Symonds' Scrumpy Jack, Westons Country and local Compton Oaks farmhouse ciders. The food, quickly served, includes sandwiches (from 65p, steak £2.25), egg mayonnaise (75p), corn on the cob (90p), soup (95p), cheese baked potatoes with salad (£1.25), ploughman's (from £1.55), shepherd's pie or bacon and tomato quiche (£2.50), salads (from £2.50), steak and kidney pie (£2.90), cider chicken or beef carbonnade (£2.95), scampi (£3.20), trout (£3.70) and steaks (from eight-ounce rump at £5.45, to 16-ounce T-bone at £7.45), with quite a few savoury dishes, lots of puddings (mostly 75p) and a wide choice of children's dishes (£1.15). The cosy bar has old pews and settles on its polished flagstones and red tiles, heavy beams just about managing to support the yellow plaster ceiling, and logs burning in a big stone fireplace, and there's a separate dining-room. There are a few tables by the paeonies and fruit-trees on a small raised lawn. *(Recommended by PLC, Jane English, T A Pritchard, J L Phillips, R J Slawson)*

Free house · Licensees Norman, James and Hannelore Bristow · Real ale Meals and snacks · Open 12ish–2.30, 6.30–10.30

BISHOPSTONE   SO4142   Map 6

Lord Nelson

Bridge Sollers; A438 about 6 miles W of Hereford

Since our last edition, this relaxing and neatly kept pub – to keep up with the demand for its popular food – has opened a second restaurant; the Captain's Table is small and cosy, the larger Trafalgar Room doubles as a parties and functions room. Bar food includes soup, sandwiches, ploughman's (£1.65), often a dish of the day such as home-made steak and kidney pie (from £2.35), salads (from £2.35), plaice, chicken, curry or scampi (£2.50) and steaks (rump £5.95, fillet £6.50). On Saturday evenings the restaurant takes precedence (though if things are fairly quiet there may be bar snacks later on), and at lunchtime on Sundays there's a roast lunch (or at peak periods such as bank holiday weekends) and a help-yourself salad table. The lounge bar has red plush seats on its gold and red

---

The Good Pub Guide does not accept payment for inclusion, and there is no advertising or sponsorship.

flowery carpet, with polished antique parquet flooring by the serving counter, and a log-effect gas fire in the big stone fireplace. In this area the original low ceiling has been taken out (leaving the old timbers) so that you see clear through to the pitched rafters of the roof. They've now got milk on draught, as well as Symonds' farm cider; gentle piped music; an end area has darts, dominoes and a fruit machine. Outside, there are lots of tables by a biggish flower-fringed side lawn. *(Recommended by Cdr D H Jones; more reports please)*

Free house · Licensees Mr and Mrs Roy Edwards · Meals and snacks (see above for Sat evening and Sun lunchtime limitations) · Children welcome if supervised, not encouraged after 8 · Live music Sun (not Jan—Feb) and Thurs Open 11.30—2.30, 7—11 (12—2, 7.30—11 in winter); closed Tues lunchtime Nov—Feb, maybe 10 days Jan: to check ring Bridge Sollars (098 122) 208

BRETFORTON SP0943 Map 4

Fleece ★ ★ ★

B4035 E of Evesham: turn S off this road into village; pub is in centre square by church

The great majority of recent reports from readers suggests that its new licensees have preserved the qualities of this exceptional medieval pub so well that we can in this edition restore its third star. We must stress from the start that what earns such a high rating here is the intrinsic quality of the building itself and its furnishings. There are massive beams and exposed timbers, worn flagstones (scored with marks to keep out demons), many antique seats including the curved high-backed settle facing the big log fire of the main room, another inglenook fireplace with a deeply polished chimney beam and a rack of heavy pointed iron shafts that are sometimes thought to have been hefty precursors of darts (but look to us better suited to spit-roasting), handsome grandfather clocks, polished oak and elm tables, ancient dressers filled with antique plates or a remarkable 48-piece set of Stuart pewter trenchers. A farm from Tudor or even earlier times, it was run as a pub by the same family from 1848 until 1977 when Lola Taplin, the great-granddaughter of the original licensee, left it to the National Trust, who have preserved it just as it had been for the previous century or so. Outside is most attractive, too, with seats on the grass which spreads around a splendid timbered barn (and may have a goat tethered), as well as at the front by a stone pump trough. In summer there are barbecues out here (two kebabs £1.90, eight-ounce steak £3). Simple quickly served bar food includes sandwiches (from 65p), ploughman's (from £1.40), good home-cured ham (£1.80), Gloucester sausage (£1.90), plaice (£2), scampi (£2.20), chicken and mushroom or steak and kidney pie (£2.40), gammon (£2.80) and eight-ounce sirloin steak (£3.75); Ind Coope Burton, Hook Norton Best, Mitchells & Butlers Brew XI, Highgate Mild and a guest beer such as Marstons Pedigree on handpump, with mulled wine or hot toddy in winter; darts, dominoes, shove-ha'penny. *(Recommended by L N Goulding, John and Mary, William Meadon, Richard Steel, Mr and Mrs Michael Parrott, Joan Olivier, A Royle, P D Atkinson, G L Archer, John Milroy, Tim Halstead, P L C, F Walling, Tim Bracey, Chris and Tony Cox, Stuart Barker, Dr and Mrs R Neville, Gordon and Daphne, J M Tansey, Stephan Carney, David and Ruth Hollands)*

Free house · Licensees Dan and Nora Davies · Real ale · Meals and snacks
Children in room with pewter · Open 10.30–2.30, 6–11 all year

BROADWAY   SP0937   Map 4
Lygon Arms
A44

This remarkably handsome hotel is a stately and civilised building
dating largely from 1620, though parts may have been a fourteenth-
century manor house. It has been sensitively restored and extended,
and furnished very sympathetically. The well kept cocktail bar is
simple but stylish, with handsome oak panelling and partly bared
stone walls, a collection of antique drinking glasses and wine jugs,
backgammon and chess on hand, and of course the main attraction –
the well mixed cocktails. You can wander from here into other
grander or more comfortable rooms, including a cosy beamed lounge
with easy chairs in front of the massive inglenook fireplace where the
inn's cooking used to be done, and (besides the hotel's fine restaurant)
an adjoining wine bar, Goblets, serves imaginative food at lunchtime
and in the evening: sandwiches, starters such as anchovy and Stilton
stuffed eggs or smoked trout, main courses such as garlic bread
stuffed with turkey, pineapple and pasta or steak and Guinness flaky-
pastry pie, and puddings such as chocolate and strawberry Pavlova in
raspberry liqueur. In summer you can sit in the courtyard,
surrounded by trees and shrubs, and the neatly kept hotel gardens are
very attractive. A beautiful though expensive place to stay.
(Recommended by P L C; more reports please)

Free house · Licensees D J Barrington OBE and K Ritchie · Children welcome
Open 10.30–2, 6–10.30 · Bedrooms tel Broadway (0386) 852255;
£50B/£86B

CAREY   SO5631   Map 4
Cottage of Content ★   [*illustrated on page 333*]
Village, and for most of the way the pub itself, signposted from good road
through Hoarwithy

This last year, 1985, has seen the five-hundredth anniversary of this
out-of-the-way and very pretty little medieval inn, which is aptly
named. The cosy and cottagey lounge bar has plain wooden benches
built in to the timbered and partly panelled walls, dark beams, worn
rugs on the wooden floor, and comfy leather seats. The broadly
similar public bar, with sensibly placed darts, dominoes, cribbage and
a fruit machine, has a winged high-backed settle in one snug corner,
as well as simple wooden chairs; there is another antique settle in an
alcove on the way through, and maybe unobtrusive piped music. Two
small rooms in the pub itself are normally used as dining-rooms at
lunchtime, and an adjoining converted barn comes into service at
busier times. Good bar food, largely home made, includes soup (75p),
sandwiches, a good ploughman's (£1.35), and a selection of dishes
such as vegetable hot-pot or beef in beer (£2), crab Mornay, seafood
platter, free-range chicken or fish quenelles (£2.50), home-cured ham
(£3.50) and chicken curry or rabbit casserole (£4.50). Well kept

Flowers Original and Hook Norton Best, Old Hookey and Mild on handpump, with other guest bitters. Tables on a back terrace look up to a steep expanse of lawn beyond a rock wall, and there are a couple more on the flower-filled front terrace, facing the very quiet village lane. The bedrooms are comfortable though not plush – good value, especially the two-day breaks (from £34 a person, including dinner). (Recommended by John Milroy, Prof G M and Dr G S Stephenson, Tim and Ann Bracey, J A Cox, E O F Stocker, T P A, Gordon and Daphne)

Free house · Licensee Peter Nash · Real ale · Meals and snacks · Children welcome · Open 11.30–2.30, 6.30–11 all year · Bedrooms tel Carey (043 270) 242; £17/£24

CLAINES   SO8558 Map 4
Mug House

3 miles from M5 junction 6; A449 towards Ombersley; leave dual carriageway after nearly 3 miles at second exit point for Worcester; village signposted from here, and pub in Cornmeadow Lane

Having watched the crops rotate from cereals to pasture and more recently sugar beet in the field one walks around to reach the tavern's side entrance, we reckon that this year it'll be barley or maybe winter wheat – at least when it isn't grass it's easier to see where the fields stop and the pub's sizeable garden starts. On the other side it merges into the village churchyard – and these rustic surroundings certainly suit the ancient timbered pub itself, quite unspoilt and basic, with Windsor chairs and a few plain tables on the woodblock floor of its cheerful old-fashioned public bar, and a fire on cold days. There's a carpeted but similarly straightforward lounge. Well kept Banks's Bitter and Mild, both on electric pump and on handpump – very unusual to have the choice; good value cheap sausage rolls, rolls filled with cheese, ham, beef, pork or corned beef, and cold pork pies. (Recommended by Jane English, Derrick Turner, Gordon and Daphne)

Banks's · Licensee G F Connolly · Real ale · Snacks (not Sun) · Children in snug away from servery · Open 11–2.30, 6–11

DORSTONE   SO3141 Map 6
Pandy

Pub signposted off B4348 E of Hay-on-Wye

Herefordshire's oldest inn, this fine half-timbered pub has in 1985 been celebrating its eight-hundredth anniversary – it was originally used for Richard de Brico's workers while they were building the church here, in atonement for his part in the murder of Thomas à Becket. Inside, there's nothing fusty in spite of its great age: the atmosphere is really friendly, lively and warm. The main room, on the right as you go in, has wheelback chairs on its worn flagstones, small pictures on the timbered walls, a yellowing ceiling and a massive open fireplace; the carpeted games room on the left, with stripped stone walls and a big wood-burning stove, has pool, darts, dominoes, cribbage, a quoits board, juke box and fruit machine.

Good simple bar food includes home-made soup (85p), sandwiches, a generous ploughman's with three cheeses and ham (£1.75), lasagne (£2.25), beef curry (£2.50), gammon (£2.95) and Wye salmon or steak – sometimes massive pieces (£4.95). Besides particularly well kept Bass, Springfield and maybe a guest beer on handpump, they keep a good range of spirits such as Jack Daniels, calvados, 100-degree Navy rum and several Irish whiskies, with a malt on optic (and Plymouth gin instead of London). There are picnic-table sets on the neat grass of the side garden, looking out to the lush partly wooded hills which surround the quiet village. (Recommended by P J Taylor, D A Lloyd, P and HB)

Free house · Licensees Chris and Margaret Burtonwood · Real ale · Meals and snacks (not Weds) · Children welcome · Occasional piano sing-songs or folk nights · Open 12–2.30, 7–11 all year; closed Weds lunchtime except summer hols

ELMLEY CASTLE SO9841 Map 4
Old Mill

Mill Lane; village signposted from A44 and A435, W or S of Evesham; lane leaves main street beside Plough

The French windows of this well kept pub's spacious L-shaped lounge open on to its lawn, which borders the village cricket pitch and looks up to Bredon Hill. At lunchtime the comfortable leather chairs quickly fill up with people who've driven over for the waitress-served bar food which includes sandwiches, fresh cod (£1.95), a home-made daily special (£2.15), home-cooked ham or sirloin salad (£3.25), eight-ounce fillet steak (£6.50) or smoked salmon salad (£6.75); there is also a separate restaurant. Well kept Flowers IPA and Wadworths 6X on handpump, and a range of cocktails; darts, shove-ha'penny, dominoes, cribbage, a fruit machine and maybe piped music. The pub has a separate private snooker club. This old brick building was originally a millhouse, and in front still has the large millpond – usually with some pochard or other ducks on it. (Recommended by William Meadon, Richard Steel, Mr and Mrs R Houghton)

Free house · Licensees Doug and Evelyn Gerrard · Real ale · Meals and snacks (not Tues or Sun evenings) · Children in eating area · Open 11–2.30, 7–11 all year; closed evening 25 Dec

nr EWYAS HAROLD SO3929 Map 6
Trout ★

Dulas; Ewyas Harold is signposted from A465 at Pontrilas – go straight through and past Dulas Court

Locally known as the Found Out, this delightfully simple and old-fashioned pub has easy chairs in the left-hand parlour, with a high shelf of plates and a horn gramophone; the flagstoned bar has darts, shove-ha'penny, table skittles, table quoits and dominoes. Bar food includes sandwiches, toasted sandwiches (from 65p), home-made soup (85p), ploughman's (£1.75), curries (from £1.95), spaghetti bolognese (£2.75) and sirloin steak (£5.75); at lunchtime main dishes are cooked only if ordered in advance (May to October only). They will also do full meals to order, in the separate dining-room (from £5). The beers are as out-of-the-way as the pub itself: well kept Baileys Superbrew and Woods Special on handpump, and changing guest bitters. The heavy stone slabs of the front terrace are brightened by marigolds, columbines, pinks, geraniums and less common plants: out here, you look across the quiet lane to what is a cricket pitch in summer (the pub has a team) but is really a sheep pasture at other times. There are more seats — and more flowers — on the lawn behind the house, beside a gently splashing stream, and the little valley is surrounded by steeply wooded pastures. *(Recommended by John Milroy, Annie Taylor, Jenny Woolf; more reports please)*

Free house · Licensee Mrs Pauline Smith · Real ale · Meals (evening) and snacks Children may be allowed in if well behaved and pub not too busy Open 11–2.30, 6–11 all year

FINSTALL   SO9869   Map 4
Cross

34 Alcester Road; village signposted from A448 on Redditch side of Bromsgrove

Popular lunchtime food in this friendly pub includes sandwiches (from 70p), ploughman's (from £1.40), home-baked ham (£1.70), scampi (£2.40) and seafood platter or gammon (£2.95), with a good choice of around eight daily specials such as steak bap (£1.25), lamb's liver or various pizzas (£2.05), fresh cod or steak and kidney pie (£2.25), cheese, bacon and potato pie (£2.85), and winter casseroles (from £2.05). The neatly kept and friendly lounge bar has comfortable wheelback chairs around traditional cast-iron-framed tables on the carpet, and an open fire (the stone chimney-breast is decorated with crossed swords). The pub is perched well above the steep village road, giving an airy feel that's accentuated by big windows and light-coloured panelling. Well kept Flowers IPA and Original on handpump; juke box and a fruit machine. There are seats among flowers on the back lawn, which is sheltered by trees behind. *(Recommended by Rex Johnson; more reports please)*

Flowers (Whitbreads) · Real ale · Meals and snacks (lunchtime, not Sun) Children at landlord's discretion (lunchtime only) · Live music Mon · Open 12–2.30, 7–10.30; closed evening 25 Dec

FOWNHOPE   SO5834   Map 4
Green Man

B4224

The licensees who took over this striking fifteenth-century timber-framed inn last year have impressed readers with the welcoming atmosphere they've produced, and good value food including home-made soup (80p), sandwiches (from 60p, toasted from 95p), home-made pâté (£1.40), ploughman's (from £1.45), local chicken (£1.99), steak sandwich (£2.25 – named after Tom Spring, the 1823 champion pugilist who was born in the village), home-cooked ham or beef with salad (£2.25), lasagne (£2.45), trout with almonds (£2.95) and rump steak (£4.95). On Sundays there is a hot roast and informal carvery buffet. The lounge bar is quite stately, with high beams, comfortable armchairs, tall latticed windows with bench seats set into them, and timbered ochre walls; a second bar is smaller but similar, with darts, dominoes, cribbage and quoits, and there are two separate dining-rooms. At weekends the pub can get quite crowded. Well kept Hook Norton Best, Marstons Pedigree and Sam Smiths Tadcaster and OB on handpump. The garden behind has robust benches and slatted wood tables and seats on a big lawn, among trees and flowerbeds – quiet, except for the chattering of the swallows that swoop across it. The well equipped bedrooms have four-posters. *(Recommended by Lawrence and Nan Payne, John Milroy, Paul and Inge Sweetman, Richard Balkwill, Anne Morris, Gordon and Daphne)*

Free house · Licensee Arthur Williams · Real ale · Meals and snacks · Children in eating areas · Open 10.30–2.30, 6–11 all year · Bedrooms tel Fownhope (0432 77) 243; £15B/£25B

LEDBURY   SO7138   Map 4
Feathers
High Street; A417

The marvellous black and white timbering of this hotel dates mainly from 1521, though the top floor – you can see the differences if you look closely – was added later in Jacobean times. Inside is old-fashioned, with heavily timbered walls, quiet alcoves leading off the main open-plan lounge bar, Spy cartoons on the panelling, a high shelf of plates, old local legal documents, and plushly cushioned armchairs and wall seats. Bar food includes soup (75p), large club sandwiches (£1.50), a slimmer's salad roll with celery, apple, nuts and raisins (£1.75), asparagus, spinach, cheese and ham quiche (£2.10), salads (£2.75), spicy sausage and cider pie (£2.65), steak and kidney pie (£2.95) and venison pie (£3.15); Bass and Mitchells & Butlers Brew XI on electric pump. There is a separate restaurant which does Sunday lunches too. *(Recommended by John Milroy, William Hill, John Price, G L Archer)*

Mitchells & Butlers (Bass) · Licensees David Elliston and Michael Hester Real ale · Meals and snacks (lunchtime, not Sun) · Children in lounge · Open 10.30–2.30, 6–11 · Bedrooms tel Ledbury (0531) 5266; £32B/£45B

OMBERSLEY   SO8463   Map 4
Crown & Sandys Arms
Good value bar food in the Georgian lounge here includes home-made soup (75p), dressed crab sandwiches (£1.15), a dish of the day such as jugged hare (£2.25–£2.50), 10-ounce rump or sirloin steak (£5.10) and a good choice of cold meats and seafood with up to 10 help-yourself salads from a buffet counter (from £2.45). The black-beamed and timbered room has old prints and maps on its walls, and a carpet over its dark flagstones; a snug corner by the inglenook fireplace (with the royal arms on its hefty iron fireback) has a high-backed settle and two easy chairs, and elsewhere there are brocade-

cushioned Windsor armchairs and settles and plush built-in wall seats. Well kept Bass, Hook Norton Best and Old Hookey and Marstons Burton on handpump; dominoes, cribbage. There is a separate restaurant. The garden beside this Dutch-gabled white house has picnic-table sets looking up to the gentle sheep-pasture hills behind. There is an antique shop in the back stables, open on Tuesday, Friday and Saturday. *(Recommended by A Royle, M S Everett)*

Free house · Licensee R E Ransome · Real ale · Meals and snacks (not Sun evening Jan–Apr) · Children (not toddlers) if well mannered · Open 11–2.30, 6–11 all year; closed 25 Dec

Kings Arms

Runner-up in the 1984 trade journal competition, Pub Caterer of the Year, this charming rambling pub is very popular indeed for its changing home-made food, which might typically include soup (85p), sandwiches (lunchtime only), chicken liver or smoked mackerel pâté (£1.75), button mushrooms in garlic butter (£2.25), spinach and mushroom cannelloni (£2.95), and dishes served with chips and peas or salad such as steak and kidney pie (£3.25), cheese and spinach flan (£3.50), pork chop (£3.50), a plate of cold beef, turkey and ham (£3.75) and sirloin steak (£5.25), with good puddings (85p). The friendly bars have a profusion of black oak Tudor beams and timbers, hung with pots and yokes. A squirrel and a pygmy owl peep out of crannies by the polished brick inglenook fireplace, and other stuffed creatures include a raven and a Canada goose. One room has seventeenth-century royal arms moulded into a decorated plaster ceiling (this is reputed to have been Charles II's first stop on his flight after the Battle of Worcester in 1651). Bass and Springfield on handpump; darts. There are tables under cocktail parasols in an attractive courtyard behind the black and white timbered building, sheltered by yew, laurel and ash-trees. *(Recommended by David Gethyn-Jones; more reports please)*

Mitchells & Butlers (Bass) · Licensees Chris and Judy Blundell · Real ale Meals and snacks (not Sun) · Children over 6 if eating, up to 8pm · Open 11–2.30, 6–11 all year

SELLACK SO5727 Map 4

Lough Pool ★

Back road Hoarwithy–Ross-on-Wye; OS Sheet 162 reference 578268

The licensees who took over this beautifully placed country pub a couple of years ago have made it very welcoming, and do good meals including home-made soup (85p), pâté (£1.40), peach halves stuffed with cottage cheese (£1.55), deep-fried Brie (£1.65), sausage and chips (£1.75), scampi (£2.50), moussaka or vegetarian risotto (£2.95), garlic-fried chicken (£3.75), home-cooked beef salad (£3.75), lamb in cherry sauce (£4.15) and trout grilled with prawns and lemon butter (£4.45); there's a separate restaurant. They've got rid of the plastic flowers, electronic machines and piped light music that we remember from a few years ago; there are now comfortable and thoroughly appropriate traditional furnishings, beams and flagstones, and big open fires in winter. Bass, Hereford, Springfield and Wadworths 6X are kept under light blanket pressure. There are plenty of tables on the well kept lawn in front of this attractive tiled, black and white cottage. (*Recommended by John Milroy, Mr and Mrs Malcolm Skinner*)

Free house · Licensees Paul and Karen Whitford · Meals · Children in restaurant · Open 12–2.30, 6.30–11 all year (opens 7 in winter)

UPTON UPON SEVERN   SO8540 Map 4

Olde Anchor

High Street

The beer that they started brewing a couple of years ago at this lively and friendly sixteenth-century pub is both good and cheap. But quite apart from that it's a nice place to visit. The friendly U-shaped carpeted bar has timber-framed windows looking out on the street, old black timbers propping its low ceiling, old-fashioned settles and Windsor chairs around oak tables, and quite a lot of copper and brass including an unusual copper mantelpiece. Efficiently served and reasonably priced bar food, from £1.50 to £5.75 (for a 16-ounce T-bone steak), includes ploughman's, hot dishes such as chicken, lasagne, chilli con carne, burgers, gammon, scampi and salads (also fresh crab when they can get it); besides the house beers, guest beers such as Courage Directors, Flowers Original and Hook Norton Best are on handpump, and Old Hookey is tapped straight from the cask; maybe nostalgic 1970s pop music. The separate garden bar overlooks seats on the back terrace outside. This Severn-side village is a charming one, and the black and white timbered pub, with its upper floor jettied out over the pavement, is one of its most attractive buildings. (*Recommended by G L Archer, William Meadon, Richard Steel, Mr and Mrs Michael Parrott, A Royle, Gordon and Daphne, C G*)

Own brew · Licensees Chris and Janet Callaghan · Real ale · Meals and snacks Children in family room · Live music weekends · Open 11–2.30, 6.30–11 all year

Swan

Riverside

Recommended for those who like their comforts, this attractively restored Severn-side pub has river views from its civilised lounge bar. There are antique settles and comfortable easy chairs with the Windsor chairs under the beams, and a warm open fire at one end; good lunchtime food served here and in the adjacent food bar includes smoked haddock in a cream and cheese sauce (£2.35), home-made steak and kidney pie (£2.95), seafood gratinés or veal sweetbreads with a cream sauce in puff pastry (£3.25) and baked Wye salmon (£4.50). Well kept Butcombe and Wadworths 6X on handpump, and a reasonably wide wine list; maybe piped music. A

Post Office address codings confusingly give the impression that some pubs are in Hereford and Worcester, when they're really in the Midlands, Shropshire, Gloucestershire and even Wales — which is where we list them.

back bistro is open for full evening meals (Tuesday to Saturday). There are tables outside (with waitress service), and the pub has its own moorings by a lawn across the quiet lane. *(Recommended by William Meadon, Richard Steel, Tim and Ann Bracey, Dr D B Fox)*

Free house · Licensees Peter and Sue Davies · Real ale · Meals and snacks (not Sun evening or Mon); bistro bookings tel Upton upon Severn (068 46) 2601 Open 11.30–2.30, 6.30–11 all year; closed Mon lunchtime except bank hols

WEATHEROAK HILL SP0674 Map 4
Coach & Horses ★

Between Alvechurch and Wythall; coming S on A435 from Wythall roundabout, filter off dual carriageway so as to turn right about a mile S, then in Weatheroak Hill village turn left towards Alvechurch

This relaxed and leisurely country pub keeps an excellent range of reasonably priced real ales such as Banks's, Bass, Courage Directors, Davenports, Everards Old Original and Tiger, Holdens, Robinsons, Sam Smiths OB, Wadworths 6X and Woods Special, with Banks's and Holdens Milds. They reckon to have not less than eight on the go at a time, and as people do come a long way for them the turnover is brisk enough to ensure that they are in good condition. Good value home-cooked simple food includes filled rolls (34p–50p), soup (40p), lots of pizzas (from 85p), ploughman's (£1.20), gammon, egg and chips (£1.45–£2.45, depending on size), steak and kidney, chicken and mushroom or cottage pies (£1.90), chicken, quiche or ham off the bone with help-yourself salads (from £1.90), lasagne (£2.10) and eight-ounce sirloin steak (£3.95). The quiet two-level brown-carpeted lounge is simply furnished with plush seats below the big windows; maybe piped music. The livelier public bar, with red and black flooring tiles, has sensibly placed darts, dominoes, cribbage and a fruit machine (there's another in the lounge). There's an assortment of elderly seats on the grass of the big peaceful garden, with newer ones on a terrace. *(Recommended by John McLaughlin; more reports please)*

Free house · Licensee Philip Gough Meads · Real ale · Meals (not Sun, not Sat evening, and no service after 8.30) and snacks · Children in eating area · Open 11.30–2.30, 6–10.30

WEOBLEY SO4052 Map 6
Red Lion

Village signposted from A4112 SW of Leominster and A480 Hereford–Kington

On our most recent visit the village bowls team were playing a leisurely summer-evening match on the beautiful green between this striking fourteenth-century black and white timbered and jettied inn and the graceful church. The quiet village is really lovely, and this small hotel is perhaps its finest building – the heavily timber-framed back cottage is thought to be one of the county's oldest. The friendly old-fashioned lounge bar has easy chairs and sofas as well as high-backed winged settles, antique prints of apples and pears on its heavily timbered butter-coloured walls, and charming service. An extensive cold carvery provides sandwiches (90p), ploughman's (£1.80) and full salads or a freshly cooked hot dish (£3.50). A plainer back bar with a flagstoned and tiled floor has low built-in wooden wall seats; darts, dominoes, cribbage, and a fruit machine. Besides Flowers Original on handpump they keep a good range of spirits including Macallans whisky. There is a separate restaurant (main courses around £6), and the good value Sunday roast lunch (£6) is so popular that it really needs booking. Behind the building is a little sheltered terrace, and there are tables on the neat grass at the side, edged with a mass of oriental poppies (there are sometimes summer barbecues out here). The tea shop across the road doubles as a worthwhile art gallery. A nice place to stay, with comfortable and well equipped old-fashioned bedrooms. (*Recommended by P L C, John Price, J A Martin, Sigrid and Peter Sobanski*)

Free house · Licensees E Townley-Berry and M D Grover · Real ale · Meals and snacks (not Sat evening or Sun lunchtime) · Children welcome · Open 10.30–2.30, 6–11 · Bedrooms and restaurant tel Weobley (0544) 318220; £26B/£38B

WHITNEY ON WYE   SO2747 Map 6

Rhydspence ★ ★

Signposted from A438 S of Whitney

We had our most memorable pub meal of the year in this fine old black and white timbered inn. Their new, but simply furnished old-fashioned dining-room has huge pulley switches for its antique brass and etched-glass lamps. When we sat down at the place we'd booked – a very high-backed winged settle at a scrubbed oak table – we found an unexpected couple of quail's eggs in a pretty little salad nest waiting for us, under the big bowl of honeysuckle and marguerites. We had tender succulent smoked goose breast delicately interspersed with slivers of peach (£3), then pink rack of lamb, served with baked baby beetroots in an oven-crusted cheese-and-cream parsley sauce, then a gorgeous unblemished peach, perfectly peeled and cooked in brandy with burnt almonds, served with a separate dish of Chantilly cream. Besides a good choice of daily specials such as these (which, like the regular main dishes, are served at the same price in both bars and dining-room), bar food includes stock-pot soup (£1.25), ploughman's (from £1.60 – the choice of some 20 British cheeses in summer, fewer in winter, is exceptional), good home-made pâté (£2.25), whopping ham sandwiches (£2.30), landlord's favourites (concoctions of chopped ham and egg or smoked haddock and mushroom in spicy sauce, under grilled cheese and breadcrumbs – £2.25–£2.75, depending on size), an interesting choice of Devon farm sausages (£3.25), vegetarian food such as mushrooms gratinés (£3.50) or vegetable curry (£5), home-baked ham with salad and home-made pickles (£4.50), steak and kidney pie (£5), lemon sole (£5.50), 10-ounce local rump steaks (£7), spit-roasted duck (from £7.50) and bistecca alla fiorentina (massive chunks of rib-steak grilled to a crust outside, but rare inside, from £5.80). Both these last need at least two people ordering them, and given 24 hours' notice Mr Wallington will spit-roast suckling-pig and serve it with gooseberry sauce (£7.50). Though prices have gone up quite a bit, the bustle of customers – many of them return visitors – confirms our view that they are quite fair. The central bar has a big stone hearth, cushioned benches built in to the heavily timbered walls, old library chairs, and among other smaller ones a large round table spread with magazines and newspapers; other similar rooms lead off, with low beams and stuffed fish, and there's a very relaxed atmosphere. Well kept Hook Norton Best and Robinsons Best on handpump. Dunkerton's farm cider, and a notable range of uncommon and reasonably priced Italian wines; an excellently friendly atmosphere; darts, dominoes, table quoits. Tables on the terraces outside and on the sloping lawn have a fine view of the Wye valley and the hills beyond. A nice place to stay; readers praise the substantial breakfasts. *(Recommended by John Milroy, B S Bourne, Jon Dewhirst, P L C, Pamela and Merlyn Horswell, Monika Regan, Mrs E S Sharp, John Price, P J Taylor, Gordon and Daphne)*

Free house · Licensees David and Florence Wallington · Real ale · Meals and snacks (not Mon) · Children in eating area · Open 12–2.30, 7–11 all year; closed Sun evening, Mon, and in winter Tues · Two bedrooms tel Clifford (049 73) 262; £16 (£29B)/£32S (£32B)

WOOLHOPE   SO6136 Map 4

Butchers Arms ★

Signposted from B4224 in Fownhope; carry straight on past village

Tucked away down a country lane through a gentle wood-rimmed valley, this remote fourteenth-century inn has welcoming twin bars with low beams, log fires in winter, old monochrome engravings (including ones of the pub), large sombrely ticking clocks, and built-in wall benches and Windsor chairs on the Berber carpets. Good home-cooked bar food includes wholemeal sandwiches such as smoked ham with soft cheese (£1.05, lunchtime only), ploughman's with home-made apple chutney and pickles (£1.45), brandied chicken liver pâté (£1.55), a half-pint of prawns (£1.85), vegetarian dishes such as cheese and herb quiche or mushroom biriani with lentil dhal (£2.15), rabbit and bacon pie cooked with local dry cider or steak and kidney pie (£2.55) and prawns in mayonnaise salad (£3.15); also a separate restaurant (Wednesday to Saturday evenings). Well kept Hook Norton Best and Old Hookey and Marstons Pedigree on handpump, also Westons cider; a fruit machine and a juke box. Sliding windows open on to a charming terrace with wooden seats, roses, casks of geraniums and a rockery built around a millstone, separated from the fields by a tiny stream under willows, ash-trees and poplars. A nice place to stay; breakfasts are said to be particularly substantial. *(Recommended by John Milroy, Dr Richard Taylor, G R Evans, D Stone, I Clark, Mrs E S Sharp)*

Free house · Licensees Mary Bailey and Bill Griffiths · Real ale · Meals and snacks · Children in bar (lunchtime only) and restaurant · Open 11.30–2.30, 6–11 all year (opens 7 in winter) · Bedrooms tel Fownhope (0432 77) 281; £12.50/£25

Please let us know what you think of a pub's bedrooms. No stamp needed: write to *The Good Pub Guide*, FREEPOST, London SW10 0BR.

WORCESTER   SO8555   Map 4

Farriers Arms

Fish Street; off pedestrian High Street, just N of cathedral

Enterprising food in this attractively furnished seventeenth-century town pub has since our last edition added quite a few more vegetarian dishes, such as baked stuffed aubergine, cheese and leek pasties (75p), tomato, cheese and onion bake and mushroom and cheese vol-au-vent; other dishes include soup (65p), toasted sandwiches (from 60p), hummus (95p) or taramosalata (£1.20) with pitta bread, ploughman's (£1.20), chilli con carne or lasagne (£1.60), quiche, turkey and ham pie or beef and mushroom pie to their own recipe (£1.85), a couple of daily specials such as beef and mushroom cobbler or seafood paella (£1.40), and good puddings (from 70p). Everything is cooked by Nona Pettersen and her mother. The snug black-beamed lounge bar, decorated with locally made jewellery (for sale), has some attractive old seats among the copper-topped tables, and a grandfather clock carved with writhing lizards; the simpler rambling public bar has sensibly placed darts, shove-ha'penny, dominoes, cribbage, passe-temps, an old penny arcade machine (which works with 2p pieces), a fruit machine and a juke box. Well kept Courage Directors on handpump, and possibly Courage Best. The pub has some seats and tables outside, and is very handy for the cathedral. (*Recommended by William Meadon, Richard Steel, Tim Halstead, A Royle*)

Courage · Licensee Nona Pettersen · Real ale · Meals and snacks · Open 10.30–2.15, 5.30–11 all year

---

Lucky Dip

Besides the fully inspected pubs, you might like to try these Lucky Dips recommended and described by readers (if you do, please send us reports):

ASTON CREWS [SO6723], *White Hart*: food good with intelligent use of garlic; welcoming atmosphere (*John Milroy*)

BADSEY [SP0743], *Round o'Gras*: as the name implies this pub is all about asparagus, grown around here in quantity; good food such as steak and kidney pie or home-baked ham (*A F F, Joan Olivier*)

BELBROUGHTON [SO9277], *Talbot*: good food and Hansons beer; helpful staff (*D S Braisted*); *Queens*: good Marstons and pleasant homely atmosphere; can get crowded (*Graham Andrews*)

BERROW [SO7934], *Duke of York*: happy and courteous, always ready to meet individual needs, wide choice of bar food served quickly (*V Hunter, P Collins*)

BEWDLEY [SO7875], *Black Boy*: unspoilt: part of cottage row in old area of village; Banks's Mild and Bitter on electric pump (*John McLaughlin*)

BIRTSMORTON [SO7935], *Farmers Arms*: fine beamed sixteenth-century country pub with good bar food and real ale; garden safe for children, with skittles (*D Stone, P J Taylor*)

BISHOPS FROME [SO6648], *Chase*: free house with good home-made food and ales; garden, terrace, children welcome; bedrooms (*P L C*)

BOURNE HEATH [Dodford Road; SO9474], *Gate*: attractively decorated pub with nice garden for children; well kept Flowers and Whitbreads (*D S Braisted, G Andrews*)

BREDON [Church Street; SO9236], *Fox & Hounds*: good value hot and cold food in comfortable oak-beamed lounge; well kept Whitbreads; restaurant, garden *(M E Sumner)*

BRIMFIELD [SO5368], *Roebuck*: warm and cosy traditional country village pub with expensive home-cooked food, using only fresh vegetables, in bar and recently opened small restaurant *(John Pearson, P A Roughton)*

BROUGHTON HACKETT [SO9254], *March Hare*: comfortable and neat, with well in lounge bar *(C B M Gregory)*

CLEEVE PRIOR [Main Street; SP0849], *Kings Arms*: a series of reports received at much the same time praise the food and atmosphere; views from regular reporters particularly welcomed

DODFORD [SO9372], *Dodford Inn*: well kept Davenports ale, food, gardens and nice views *(Graham Andrews)*

DRAYTON [SO9076], *Robin Hood*: food appetising and beer good in well kept pub *(A Royle)*

DROITWICH [Celvestune Way; SO8861], *Pillar of Salt*: well kept beer and good value home cooking in fairly new estate pub, with cheerful service *(A Royle)*

DUNHAMPSTEAD [SO9161], *Firs*: good choice of home-cooked food; children welcome; attractive inside with warm fires; nice position alongside railway and canal (OS Sheet 150 reference 888610) *(D J Braisted, A Royle)*

EARDISLAND [SO4258], *Cross*: friendly family-run simple old inn with straightforward food *(Glyn Edmunds, LYM)*; *White Swan*: beamed pub with big open fire in cosy back bar; efficient service and good value food in separate dining area; Marstons real ale; garden *(Anne Morris)*

ECKINGTON [SO9241], *Anchor*: attractive spick-and-span canalside pub in pretty village; well kept Wadworths; big log fire *(Mr and Mrs J E Holmes)*

ELMLEY CASTLE [SO9841], *Queen Elizabeth*: ancient pub with attractive old-fashioned tap-room offering well kept Marstons real ale, in pretty village below Bredon Hill *(LYM)*

FLYFORD FLAVELL [SO9754], *Red Lion*: big pub with basket meals, and plenty of atmosphere *(C B M Gregory)*

GARWAY [SO4522], *Broad Oak*: charming seventeenth-century pub/restaurant – you do have to eat here, not just have a drink – with entertaining landlord, very good food, well kept Flowers; children welcomed; big garden *(Gregory Parston, Roger Clive-Powell, BB)*

GRIMLEY [SO8360], *Camp House*: good value straightforward food in riverside pub with quaint little lounge bar and garden with goats, pheasants, and all kinds of fowl (the chicks are popular with children); a pair of peacocks crow from the roof in summer *(Timothy Powell)*; *Wagon Wheel*: spotlessly comfortable Severn-side pub with well kept Marstons Pedigree, and good chateaubriand steaks and so forth in pleasant restaurant; attentive landlord *(C P Davies, C B M Gregory)*

HADLEY [SO8663], *Hadley Bowling Green*: pleasantly placed by bowling green said to be England's oldest *(William Meadon, Richard Steel)*

INKBERROW [SP0157], *Old Bull*: interesting timbered pub, model for the Archers' Bull in Ambridge; well kept Flowers Original, and bar snacks with cheerful service *(Frank Cummins, LYM)*

KINGTON [The Bourne; SO9855], *Red Hart*: friendly atmosphere, log fires, good choice of bar food, restaurant and garden; children and dogs welcome *(P J Brooks)*

KNIGHTWICK [SO7355], *Talbot*: fourteenth-century inn with open fires in big comfortable sporting-print lounge; well kept Bass and Flowers real ales, good bar food (also restaurant), served by friendly young staff; games bar, tables outside; bedrooms *(Frank Cummins)*

LEDBURY [New Street; SO7138], *Old Talbot*: ancient half-timbered building, charming inside, chatty atmosphere and entertaining landlord; three well kept real ales, good food in bar and restaurant; bedrooms *(John Milroy, Tim Halstead, D W Ball)*

LEOMINSTER [West Street; SO4959], *Black Swan*: food and beer good, with pleasant lounge and customers; bedrooms *(J B Hull)*; [Etnam Street] *Chequers*: friendly efficient staff serving good food and beer; handy car park *(J B Hull)*; [South Street] *Royal Oak*: friendly welcoming manager offering choice of real ales and good house wines, with tasty bar food including excellent rare beef sandwiches; comfortable lounge bar, also cellar bar and restaurant; good bedrooms *(Brig A F Freeman, J B Hull, I D G Mackie)*; [West Street] *Talbot*: food and beer recommended; has the ring of a bygone age, ideal for the older traveller; bedrooms *(J B Hull)*

LYONSHALL [SO3355], *Royal George*: original food at reasonable prices; warm welcome and nice cosy atmosphere in spotless lounge *(G R Evans)*

MALVERN WELLS [SO7742], *Railway*: food good, and Marstons Burton and Pedigree well kept, in comfortable and nicely appointed pub with pleasant atmosphere, charming management and no juke box (for pub location see OS Sheet 150 reference 772438) *(JCLC)*

MARDEN [SO5147], *Volunteer*: welcoming new licensees in Whitbreads pub serving outsize ploughman's and other snacks; pleasant bright lounge *(Gwen and Peter Andrews)*

NEWLAND [SO7948], *Swan*: good food (fish on Fridays) in renovated old pub with separate lunchtime restaurant; seats outside *(Anon)*

NEWTOWN CROSS [SO6245], *Newtown*: food served in big helpings, well kept beer; very welcoming and comfortable *(John Milroy)*

ORLETON [SO4967], *Boot*: nicely furnished country pub with comfortable atmosphere, good food, Flowers Original, and garden *(G R Evans)*

PEMBRIDGE [SO3958], *New*: ancient timbered inn – once a jail – with heavy beams, and wistaria-draped back courtyard; bedrooms *(Brian Green, LYM and others)*

PENALT [SO5729], *Bush*: food includes free haggis on New Year's Eve and Burns Night; nice friendly pub *(M Lewis)*

PENSAX [SO7269], *Bell*: good value food and excellent range of well kept real ales; open fires in winter, friendly bar staff and talkative parrot; recent improvements *(Paul Denham)*

ROMSLEY [SO9679], *Sun*: good Hansons beer in nicely decorated pub, popular with all ages *(G Andrews)*

ROSS-ON-WYE [SO6024], *Hope & Anchor*: small traditional pub on the river with good range of real ales and tasty home-cooked food *(A C S M, W L Congreve)*

nr ROSS-ON-WYE [at Lea; SO6024], *Farmers Boy*: real ale, food, nice setting *(Hilary Evans)*

SHRAWLEY [SO8164], *New*: small village pub with friendly landlord, good value food, well kept ales including Simpkiss, and lovely garden *(G R Andrews)*

STOURBRIDGE [The Cross, Lye; SO8984], *Gate*: food in bar cheap and sustaining; well kept Banks's Bitter and Mild *(HFJ)*

STOURPORT-ON-SEVERN [Severnside; SO8172], *Angel*: good bar snacks and well kept Banks's real ales; attractive riverside position *(H F Johnson)*; [Gilgal] *Steps House*: cheerful pub built in to town wall *(Anon)*; [York Street] *York House*: fine old Georgian house overlooking canal boat marina, with comfortable friendly lounge and good range of bar snacks; wine bar below and carvery above; Manns on handpump *(F A Goodall)*

UPTON SNODBURY [SO9454], *March Hare*: good food and wide choice of beers in superb atmosphere; nice garden *(A King)*

UPTON UPON SEVERN [SO8540], *White Lion*: good food in popular hotel lounge with lively and warm atmosphere, comfortable sofas, stag's head and old prints; bedrooms *(BB)*

WHITNEY ON WYE [SO2747], *Boat*: friendly inn with big windows looking over Wye and garden; bedrooms *(Jenny Woolf)*

WHITTINGTON [SO8752], *Swan*: well kept Banks's real ale and good choice of food (hot lunchtime only) in comfortable lounge; garden *(S Mason, M E Sumner)*

WINFORTON [SO2947], *Sun*: nicely furnished clean and friendly country pub with big open fire, well kept real ales, original food and attractive garden *(G R Evans, Dr Richard Taylor)*

WOOLHOPE [SO6136], *Crown*: neat country pub with good home cooking and well kept Smiles and Theakstons *(P and H B)*

WORCESTER [London Road; SO8555], *Mount Pleasant*: friendly yet stylish, conservatory-style back bar, with big helpings of food served by good-natured staff; occasional live entertainment, otherwise not too obtrusive piped rock music; beware sloping floor if pixilated *(Timothy Powell)*

nr WORCESTER [A44, 3 miles E of M5 junction 7; SO8555], *Bird in Hand*: impressive range of salads (as much as you want) with any main dish, in unusual purpose-built premises *(Timothy Powell)*

WYRE PIDDLE [SO9647], *Anchor*: 400-year-old pub with pleasant gardens terraced steeply to River Avon (own moorings); good bar food (not Sunday evening) and restaurant; children welcome *(J A C Edwards, Nick and Yvonne Mawby)*

Hertfordshire

Changes to note since the last edition of the Guide include
extensive refurbishments at the attractively placed canalside
Fishery in Boxmoor (which appropriately enough is now
concentrating more on fish dishes), the rejigging of the very
popular Wicked Lady near Wheathampstead, giving more
room for the people who flock there for the good range of real
ales and unusual food, the ever-widening range of traditional
games at the cheerful Fox and Hounds in Barley (which brews
its own good beer, including a new one – Nat's P, and has
reasonably priced robust food), and the new licensees who are
bringing a spot of colour into the popular salads at the Three
Horseshoes, tucked away on the common just outside
Harpenden. Though the Guide has had to drop several entries
in the county this year, it's nice to welcome back the Fighting
Cocks in St Albans – well kept real ale in a beautifully placed
building with a long history. The St Albans area (the
headquarters of the Campaign for Real Ale) stands out for its
variety of pubs, with a friendly atmosphere and wide choice of
real ales at the Goat, good food and nice touches like roasting
your own chestnuts at the Rose and Crown, old-fashioned
civilised comfort in the White Hart (where you can stay), and
– just outside at Tyttenhanger Green – an enormous range of
reasonably priced real ales, and country barbecues, at the
Barley Mow. The Lucky Dip section at the end of the chapter
has a number of entries for the town, too, including
particularly the Adelaide Wine House useful for very late

The Crooked Billet, Colney Heath

closing in an otherwise early-to-bed county, the Irish-orientated Abbey, the Lower Red Lion (a rare outlet for Youngs ales) and the Peahen (a rambling inn owned by McMullens). Among main entries elsewhere, we'd particularly pick out the Two Brewers facing the green in Chipperfield (unpretentiously civilised, with tasty bar food and comfortable bedrooms – one of the nicest THF country inns we've come across), the rustic Bricklayers Arms and the well run Green Dragon (where you can 'phone in your food orders ahead if you're in a hurry), both in Flaunden, the lively Alford Arms (which brews its own beer) on the edge of National Trust woods at Frithsden, the Elephant & Castle at Amwell (big garden, lots of character), the Brocket Arms at Ayot St Lawrence (one of the county's most atmospheric old pubs, close to a romantic ruined church and in one of the most attractive parts of Hertfordshire), the Garden Gate at Chorleywood (for its buttery bar which stays open throughout the day, and good walks nearby), and the Boot (facing Sarratt's pretty green). All these are in or very close to attractive countryside. The friendly American-run but ever-so-English Eagle on the A41 north of Kings Langley has a good garden for children, as well as jazz nights and summer barbecues; the Crooked Billet on the edge of open country at Colney Heath has a pets' corner which children specially like, and a good range of well kept real ales. We particularly enjoy the friendly country atmosphere in the unspoilt Moon & Stars at Rushden, which has one of the nicest pub dogs we've met. The county on the whole does very well for real ale drinkers, with most pubs we've listed keeping it, several stocking a wide or unusual range, even tied houses often stocking guest beers from other breweries, and two pubs (mentioned above) brewing their own. Beer prices are in general hardly higher than the national average, which is better than most of the Home Counties. Among the Lucky Dip entries at the end of the chapter, we'd say that particular ones to watch are the Valiant Trooper on Aldbury Common (good value food, wide choice of real ales), the interestingly decorated Boot at Chipperfield, the Plough at Dane End (with a real theatre organ), the Three Horseshoes at Letchmore Heath (very popular for its food and village atmosphere), the King William IV – the Willie – at Sawbridgeworth for good food and atmosphere, the White Horse at Shenley (in the same hands as the well kept Green Man, a main entry at London Colney), the Plume of Feathers at Tewin for its traditional bars and steak restaurant, the picturesque old Bull at Watton-at-Stone (good food) and the Tin Pot near Wheathampstead (beams-and-inglenook atmosphere and good real ale).

Pubs open all day (alas, all in Scotland) are listed at the back of the book.

AMWELL   TL1613 Map 5

Elephant & Castle ★

Village signposted SW from Wheathampstead

This attractively restored and friendly country pub houses a well-shaft 200 feet deep in the main bar, as well as an inglenook fireplace, low beams, some panelling, other walls stripped to the timbered brick, high-backed bucket seats and low leatherette-cushioned stalls on its red and black tiled floor. Lunchtime bar food includes sandwiches and ploughman's, individual home-made dishes such as cottage pie, macaroni cheese or chilli con carne (£1.35), steak and kidney pie (£1.75), fillet of cod or plaice (£1.95), salads (from £1.95), scampi (£2.25) and gammon steak (£2.50); in the evening you can have three-course meals in the small dining-room, priced by the main course (curried beef £6.50, lemon sole stuffed with prawns £7.50 and sirloin steak £8.65). Well kept Benskins, Ind Coope and Burton on handpump, or tapped from casks behind the bar counter. Seats outside are spaced well apart among fruit-trees and a weeping willow on the sweeping front lawn, which is floodlit at night and where barbecues are held on fine summer evenings from Friday to Sunday, and at Sunday lunchtime. A neat and secluded back garden is kept free from dogs and children. (*Recommended by M G McKenzie, Wayne Rossiter, Paula Beever*)

Benskins (Ind Coope) · Licensee John Taylor · Real ale · Meals and snacks (not Mon evening or Sun, not summer evenings) · Children in eating area · Open 10.30–2.30, 5.30–10.30

AYOT ST LAWRENCE   TL1916 Map 5

Brocket Arms ★

The two old-fashioned snug rooms in this sixteenth-century tiled house have a cosy and relaxed atmosphere; there's a big inglenook fireplace (though in early spring this last year, several readers wished for more warmth), orange lanterns hanging from the sturdy oak beams, a long settle built against the walls of one parquet-floored room and a wide choice of piped music from Bach to pop. Apart from ploughman's (from £1.85) and the summer lunchtime buffet (from £1.85 including salads), bar food changes frequently and might include soup, filled jacket potato, pâté, smoked mackerel, beefburger, steak and kidney pie, with a choice of home-made puddings. In the evenings full meals are served in the restaurant for £11 or £12.75, booking advised. On winter Sundays there is a traditional roast lunch. Well kept Greene King IPA and Abbot, Hook Norton Best and Wadworths 6X; darts. There are tables on the big lawn behind the white-painted brick house and just over the road is the romantic ivy-covered ruin of a medieval church. George Bernard Shaw's home is nearby. (*Recommended by Nicolas Dowson, J H DuBois, D L Johnson, S J Barker, J Madley; more reports please*)

Free house · Licensee C T Wingfield Digby · Real ale · Meals and snacks (not Sun or Mon evenings); restaurant bookings tel Stevenage (0438) 820250 Children in restaurant · Open 11–2.30, 6–10.30 all year

353

BARLEY   TL3938   Map 5
Fox and Hounds ★

This fifteenth-century white house, which was originally called the Waggon & Horses, became an inn in 1797. The low-ceilinged rambling rooms have been thoughtfully furnished by the lively and enthusiastic licensees – one of the stripped wood tables has a brightly painted cast-iron base which used to be a wringer. There are substantial log fires on both sides of a massive central chimney and an assortment of simple but comfortable furniture in the various alcoves. A big bonus is the fact that they brew their own beer: Nat's P and Hogshead (plus three guest beers). A cheery dining area opens off the main bar; food includes sandwiches, ploughman's (£1.40), lobster and brandy pâté (£1.25), taramosalata (£1.50), veal cutlets or beefburgers (£1.95), big helpings of lasagne, moussaka and chicken (£2.25, vegetarian lasagne £1.95), steak and kidney pie or liver and bacon casserole (£2.45), and steaks (£4.50); there is quite a range of seafoods such as fisherman's pie or plaice (£2.25), scampi, trout or fresh prawns (all £3.25), and seafood platter (£3.65). They also do an all-day breakfast (£2.25). An excellent range of games includes darts (two league darts teams), bar billiards, shove-ha'penny, table skittles, dominoes (two schools), cribbage, fruit machine, and the juke box has a nostalgic repertoire. The pub also has a league football team. There are swings, a slide and climbing-frame as well as picnic-table sets on grass around the car park. *(Recommended by Wayne Rossiter; more reports please)*

Own brew · Licensee Rita Nicholson · Real ale · Meals and snacks · Children in eating area · Open 11.30–2.30, 6.30–10.30 (opens 7 in winter)

BOXMOOR   TL0306   Map 5
Fishery

3½ miles from M1 junction 8; straight through Hemel Hempstead on dual carriageway, right on to A41, then first right turn (you can see the pub from the main road)

As we went to press, this early nineteenth-century canal inn had been undergoing some changes. The main upstairs bar area overlooking the canal is now open-plan, and there is an additional downstairs bar with a canalside terrace and bench seats. The bar food is concentrating on fish, with prices ranging from £1.20 to £4 – they've stopped doing sandwiches. Well kept Ind Coope and Burton on handpump; darts, dominoes, cribbage, a fruit machine and piped music. There are picnic-table sets in the garden by the brightly painted canal boats. The A41 – a field away – carries heavy traffic. *(Recommended by John Estdale; up-to-date reports please)*

Ind Coope · Licensee George Spencer · Real ale · Meals and snacks · Open 10.30–2.30, 5.30–11 all year

---

Soup prices usually include a roll and butter.

Post Office address codings confusingly give the impression that some pubs are in Hertfordshire, when they're really in Bedfordshire or Cambridgeshire – which is where we list them.

CHIPPERFIELD   TL0401   Map 5
Two Brewers

Facing the pretty tree-flanked village cricket green, this low white tiled inn serves good lunchtime bar food in its comfortable bow-windowed lounge: home-made soup (95p), a good choice of ploughman's including duck liver pâté, hot sausage and mackerel (£1.95), a daily hot dish of the day, local baked ham and savoury bacon quiche (£2.35) and Hertfordshire tea-cup trifle (75p). Tables in this room are spread with linen cloths at lunchtime and there are easy chairs and sofas. The black-beamed bar beside it has cushioned antique settles and a friendly, relaxed atmosphere with a mixture of local villagers and smarter folk; it too looks over the green. The early nineteenth-century prints of bare-knuckled pugilists on its walls are a reminder that Jem Mace, Bob Fitzsimmons and others trained in its back club room. Well kept Bass, Greene King IPA and Abbot and Marstons Pedigree on handpump. There is a separate restaurant, and the comfortable bedrooms are in unobtrusive modern extensions behind. *(Recommended by Tim and Ann Bracey, T N de Bray, Mark Stocker)*

Free house (THF) · Real ale · Meals and snacks (lunchtime, not Sun) · Children in lounge and restaurant · Open 10.30–2.30, 5.30–11 all year · Bedrooms tel Kings Langley (092 77) 65266; £42.95B/£57.90B

CHIPPING   TL3532   Map 5
Countryman

A10

This seventeenth-century roadside pub, friendly and well kept, is often a-bustle with people tucking in to the popular bar food, which includes soup, sandwiches (£1), ploughman's (£1.75), home-made burgers (£1.75), fresh cod (£2.25), lasagne and moussaka (£2.50), pizzas (£2.75), trout (£3.50), plaice (£3.75), pheasant (£6) and steaks (from £6); there is a separate restaurant. The busy beamed bar, with a cosy fire, has comfortable traditional-style settles under the gin traps, ancient sickles, billhooks and a high frieze of gundog and horse plates on its timbered walls; piped music. Well kept Benskins Bitter, Ruddles County and, brewed for the pub, Yokel Ale on handpump from the attractively carved bar counter. Quite a big lawn, walled off from the car park, has chickens and a hutch of rabbits, and behind a post and rails fence is a friendly donkey (available for summer rides). *(Recommended by Alan Neale, Wayne Rossiter; more reports please)*

Free house · Licensees Geoff and Ann Neaum · Real ale · Meals and snacks Children in dining-room at lunchtime · Occasional live music · Open 11–2.30, 5.30–11; closed 25 Dec · Camping in garden free

CHORLEYWOOD   TQ0295   Map 5
Garden Gate

A404 just over ½ mile W of A405

This friendly pub would suit walkers on the well wooded common nearby, as it's open for food from noon to 9.30 pm. The red-tiled buttery bar is comfortably modernised with horsy plates on the walls. It serves French onion or seafood soup (£1.20), hot garlic mushrooms with Stilton (£1.90), deep-fried Brie in batter (£2.20), salad cocktails (such as mussels and celery, £2.60, or lychee and prawns £3.20), quick steaks (from £3.90) and larger ones (for example six-ounce sirloin £4.90, eight-ounce fillet £6.90), and house specialities like aubergine au gratin (£2.40) or seafood Bargemon – a bowl of massive prawns in dry wine, tomato, cream and pepper (£7.20); there are blackboard dishes daily and a children's menu with egg and chips (£1.30) and burgers (£1.90). The lounge is plushly comfortable, with well kept Benskins and Ind Coope Burton on handpump. There are tables on the pretty back lawn and on a fairy-lit verandah under honeysuckle and clematis. *(Recommended by M H G; more reports please)*

Benskins (Ind Coope) · Licensee Robert Leighton · Real ale · Meals (not Sun evening) and snacks (not Sun) · Children welcome · Open for drinks 11–3, 6–11 (and see above)

COLNEY HEATH   TL2005 Map 5
Crooked Billet   *[illustrated on page 351]*
B6426 between A6 and B556

For many people the great attraction here is the collection of well kept real ales. They always have one or two quickly changing guest beers as well as their regular Adnams, Badger, Greene King Abbot, Marstons Pedigree and Whethereds, with Adnams Old in winter, and strong ales around Christmas. They also keep lots of bottled beers including some unusual ones for serious collectors – not to mention draught cider, and even milk on draught, and milk cocktails. The traditional tiled public bar has a free book exchange, and there are comfortable modern seats in the carpeted lounge; both rooms are cosy and quite small. At lunchtime the bar food includes sandwiches or filled rolls, ploughman's or Stilton with biscuits (£1.20), beefburgers, French bread pizza, big pasties, a selection of salads, and various pies – such as steak and kidney (80p) or chicken and mushroom with fresh vegetables (£1.80); the evening menu has hot dishes such as lasagne, spaghetti or beef curry (£1.50). Shove-ha'penny, fruit machine and a juke box. The garden around this white weatherboarded village pub, backed by open fields, has a pets' corner with rabbits, quail, uncommon breeds of hens and bantams (which poke around the grass, too), geese, goats, and ponies in the stables – children can ride them in summer, when there are Saturday evening barbecues. The barbecue can be booked for groups or parties on other evenings too – and is then open for use by anyone. The roofed-over terrace has plenty of room for families. Motor-cyclists now have a special parking area and are welcome. *(Recommended by John Paul Davey, S J Grundell, Paula Beever)*

Free house · Licensee David Hughes · Real ale · Meals and snacks Occasionally folk groups or morris dancers · Open 10.30–2.30, 5.30–10.30 all year; closed evening 25 Dec

---

Children welcome means the pub says it lets children inside without any special restrictions.

nr DATCHWORTH · TL2717 Map 5

Horns

Bramfield Road, Bull's Green; back road between Datchworth and Bramfield

This tiled and weatherboarded Tudor house, facing a little village green, has an interestingly decorated bar with a friendly and welcoming atmosphere. One end has a high-raftered ceiling, with tables and attractive rugs on a patterned brickwork floor, and the other has a big inglenook fireplace under the low beams and a part of the wall carefully stripped back to show the way the internal studs and laths were laid 500 years ago. Bar food includes fresh sardines (£1), cheese and mushroom flan (£1.40), steak and kidney pie (£1.40), ploughman's with pâté or Stilton (£1.40), braised steak or chicken casserole (£2), a good choice of salads (£2.20–£2.80), and basket meals (weekday lunchtimes, and the only evening food on Monday, Friday and Saturday) such as scallops, scampi or chicken (£2.75). There is fresh seafood at lunchtimes (not Sunday) and Tuesday to Thursday evenings, such as king prawns (£3.50), dressed whole crab (£4.25) and a selection of mixed seafoods (£2.75), with sandwiches on Saturday lunchtime (70p–£1.50). They say it's wise to book a table at lunchtime. Well kept Flowers Original and Wethereds on handpump, and a range of cocktails; dominoes. On a warm summer's day or evening, the seats outside on the crazy-paved terrace, among the roses, are very pleasant. *(Recommended by S J Barker; more reports please)*

Whitbreads · Licensee Jack Francis · Real ale · Meals – table reservations tel Bulls Green (043 879) 367 – and snacks (not Sun) · Piano Sat evening · Open 11.30–2.30, 5.30–10.30 all year

FLAUNDEN   TL0100 Map 5

Bricklayers Arms

Hogpits Bottom; from village centre follow Boxmoor, Bovingdon road and turn right at Belsize, Watford signpost

This low brick and tiled pub, covered with Virginia creeper, looks almost cottage-like, and inside the beamed bar there's a warm welcome from the cheery licensees. Stubs of the knocked-through oak-timbered walls give the snug feeling of its three original rooms, with dark brown painted traditional wooden wall seats and buff leatherette armchairs on the bright carpet, and open fires in winter; Adnams, Arkells, Everards and Ind Coope Bitter on handpump. It's a peaceful spot in summer, with picnic-table sets and older tables and chairs under big apple-trees on a lawn surrounded by foxgloves along its sheltering hawthorn and ivy hedges. Just up the Belsize road there's a path on the left, through woods, to more Forestry Commission woods around Hollow Hedge. *(Recommended by Wayne Rossiter, Anthony Hooper, Marsha Tedeschi)*

Free house · Licensee Ken Keen · Real ale · Snacks · Open 11–2.30, 5.30–10.30

Planning a day in the country? At the back of the book is a list of pubs in really attractive scenery.

Green Dragon

This attractively restored Georgian village pub has a warm and friendly atmosphere, thanks to Mrs Green (who used to sing on the West End stage). It's beautifully neat and very cosy with traditional flooring-tiles – old and worn in the public bar (which has darts, shove-ha'penny, dominoes and cribbage) and more recent red and black ones in the main bar with its fresh half-panelling, comfortable pews and snug carpeted alcove. If you are in a hurry they will take your food orders over the phone before you arrive: good value sandwiches (from 70p), ploughman's or pâté (£1.30), main dishes (from £2) and a choice of salads (£2.50–£3). Well kept Ind Coope and Marstons Pedigree on handpump; piped music. Outside, the neat side lawn has tables and a summer house, with canaries and budgerigars in aviaries alongside. *(Recommended by A Saunders, Dave Butler and Lesley Storey, Anthony Hooper, T N de Bray, Stephan Carney)*

Free house · Licensee Mrs Barbara Green · Real ale · Meals (lunchtime, not Sun) and snacks · Open 11.30–2.30, 6–11 all year

FRITHSDEN   TL0110   Map 5
Alford Arms

Furnishings are simple in this country pub that faces an old cherry orchard and National Trust woods: lots of pictures from Taddy cigarette cards and steam engine photographs to rustic cherry-picking scenes on the embossed Anaglypta above the brown-stained half-panelling with wheelback chairs and russet plush stools. The bar – very busy, with mainly young people – angles around a central servery, with steps down to a small stripped-brick eating area. The good value and popular bar food at lunchtime includes sandwiches (from 50p), ploughman's (£1), plaice (£1.40), steak and kidney pie (£1.60), scampi or seafood platter (£1.65), lasagne (£1.75) and gammon and egg (£1.80); in the evening there are giant sausages in French bread (90p), beefburgers (£1.30), four crispy cod rolls (£1.40) and chicken (£1.50). The pub has been successful in brewing its own beers on the premises: the main one is Cherry Pickers (the others are Pickled Squirrel and Rudolphs Revenge), though they also serve well kept Brakspears PA, Flowers Original and Wethereds on handpump, with Ruddles by the pint bottle. There are picnic-table sets on the front terrace by the quiet lane, sensibly placed darts, a fruit machine and piped music. *(Recommended by Tim and Ann Bracey, Wayne Rossiter)*

Own brew/Wethereds (Whitbreads) · Licensees Martin and Maggie Winship Real ale · Meals and snacks (lunchtime, not Sun) · Open 10.30–2.30, 5.30–10.30

nr HARPENDEN   TL1314   Map 5
Three Horseshoes

East Common; from A1081 about 600 yards S of the S edge of Harpenden, follow sign towards Ayres End, Amwell, then turn left at Harpenden Common sign; OS Sheet 166 reference 144120

In the last few years this attractively placed pub has had several changes of licensees, and new ones moved in not long before this edition of the *Guide* went to press. Mrs Shaw tells us that she is fond of colour in the presentation of her food, and the huge salads that accompany most dishes contain three types of peppers, flower-cut tomatoes and so forth; everything is home made and includes baked potatoes with various fillings (50p–90p), sandwiches with several types of bread (70p–95p, 10p extra for toasties), mackerel pâté (£1.30), ploughman's (£1.30 for cheese, £2 for prawn), jumbo Cornish pasty (£1.50), and several daily specials like lasagne, steak and kidney pie or onion flan (£2.30), scampi, plaice or a huge quiche (£2.50). Well kept Wethereds on handpump. The comfortable and open-plan modernised bar has some snug alcoves, inglenook fireplaces with open fires in winter, cushioned rustic-style seats and stools around the many dark wood tables, and horse brasses on the timbers and beams of a partly knocked-through wall which helps to divide the space. Sensibly placed darts; maybe gentle piped music. Tables on the side lawn and the terrace in front of this old white-painted tiled house (which has a newer brick front wing) are surrounded by a quiet common, with tracks running through it and a right of way over the golf course that's on the other side of the lane. (*Reports on the new regime, please*)

Whitbreads · Licensees Mr and Mrs R Shaw · Real ale · Meals and snacks (lunchtime, not Sun) · Open 11–2.30, 6–10.30

HITCHIN TL1929 Map 5
Red Hart

Bucklersbury; off Market Square

This sixteenth-century pub may be Hitchin's oldest building, though the rambling high-beamed front lounge (which may be candlelit at night) has been comfortably modernised. There's a pretty little courtyard with baskets of flowers suspended from the overhanging upper floors of its two black and white timbered wings. The town's last public hanging took place here, and the apparition of an old man is said to have been seen from time to time. The cheerful back public bar has pool, darts, a space game and a fruit machine, with evening discos. Bar food includes sandwiches, ploughman's and hot dishes such as shepherd's or steak and kidney pie; well kept Greene King IPA and Abbot on handpump; loud well reproduced pop music. (*More reports please*)

Greene King · Licensee F Whitney-Watson · Real ale · Meals and snacks (lunchtime, not Sun) · Nearby parking difficult · Open 11–2.30, 5.30–10.30

nr KINGS LANGLEY TL0702 Map 5
Eagle

A41 just N of town

This well run former coaching-inn has a thoroughly English feel – it's one of the few pubs with a licensee from America (though Mrs Webster has been in charge here for over five years now). The friendly lounge bar is simply furnished, with button-back wall banquettes and red leatherette seats on the carpet, brasses and lots of prints from coaching scenes to L S Lowry among the wall timbers; there's also a narrow low-beamed panelled alcove running down along the bar counter, which has a row of high stools set cosily against it. Bar food includes sandwiches, a choice of ploughman's (from £1.30), several hot dishes such as trawlerman's pie, moussaka, lasagne, Welsh hot-pot and steak and kidney pie (£2.25) and a cold meat platter or selection of pies with salads (£2.50). In summer there are occasional barbecues. Well kept Benskins and Taylor-Walker on handpump; piped music. Outside on the neatly kept lawn rustic seats are screened from traffic noise by the brick building itself. A second lawn spreading away to the side has a good children's play area with slides, climber, seesaw, swings and so forth. (Recommended by D L Johnson, Gordon Leighton; more reports please)

Benskins (Ind Coope) · Licensee Sue Webster · Real ale · Meals and snacks (lunchtime, not Sun) · Children in eating area · Jazz Tues and Thurs · Open 10.30–2.30, 6–11; closed 25 Dec · Bedrooms tel Kings Langley (092 77) 62563; £17.25/£23

LONDON COLNEY   TL1704 Map 5
Green Dragon
Waterside; just off main street by bridge at S end

This wistaria-covered old tiled house is immaculately kept, with lots of black beams and timbers, cushioned wall benches and country chairs below the profusion of horse brasses and harness on the walls. You can buy sandwiches, toasties such as prawn and cheese or ham, asparagus and cheese (£1.10) and ploughman's with mixed cheeses or meats (including rare beef) from the salad bar (£1.20). Well kept Benskins on handpump. Tables face young weeping willows and chestnut trees on a quiet green by the River Colne. Nearby Salisbury Hall (off the A6 towards London) is a good family outing: a moated Stuart mansion with a collection of de Havilland aeroplanes. (Recommended by J Cunningham; more reports please)

Benskins (Ind Coope) · Licensee John Johnson · Real ale · Meals (lunchtime, not Sat or Sun) and snacks (lunchtime, not Sun) · Open 11–2.30, 5.30–11

NEWGATE STREET   TL3005 Map 5
Coach & Horses
1 mile N of Cuffley

The friendly licensee of this civilised old country pub has created a cheerful atmosphere in the open-plan bar; surviving wall ends have cosy built-in settles, around a mellow mix of carpet and large flagstones, with good fires in winter at either end, subdued lighting and perhaps piped music. Bar food includes a wide range of sandwiches (75p) and heavy-duty toasted sandwiches such as Reg's Special (cheese, salami, onion, tomato and more, £1.50), as well as ploughman's (£2). Well kept Ind Coope and Burton on handpump; dominoes, cribbage, and (decently segregated) silenced space game and a fruit machine. There are tables on a lawn with high trees

around it, and more on the forecourt of the densely ivy-covered tiled
house. You can walk in nearby rolling fields (there are lots of paths)
or in vast woods such as the Great Wood country park (from the
Northaw road, take the B157 towards Brookmans Park).
(Recommended by A F; more reports please)

*Benskins (Ind Coope) · Licensee Reg Newcombe · Real ale · Snacks (lunchtime,
only rolls on Sun) · Children in family room or club room · Open 11–2.30,
5.30–10.30*

PUCKERIDGE   TL3823 Map 5
Crown & Falcon

Pepys, who stayed here in 1662, might still recognise the high
Elizabethan beams, timbered walls and open fires in this old inn, with
its distinctively steep tiled roof above the partly overhanging upper
storey. The carpeted lounge bar has comfortable modern seats
around its low tables, and salads such as cheese (£2), prawn, ham or
beef (£3.25) are served from its cold table. Other bar food includes
sandwiches (from 75p),home-made soup (75p), ploughman's
(£1.35), basket meals (from £1.60), beefburgers (£1.95), home-made
steak and kidney pie (£2.75), venison or guinea-fowl in red wine, or
pork in cider and apple sauce (£4.75) and sirloin steak (£5.75); well
kept Ind Coope and Burton on handpump. There is also a separate
beamed and timbered restaurant. The public bar has darts, dominoes,
cribbage, a fruit machine and a juke box. *(More reports please)*

*Benskins (Ind Coope) · Licensee Gordon Payne · Real ale · Meals and snacks
Children in eating area and restaurant · Open 10.30–2.30, 6–11 all year;
closed 25 Dec · Bedrooms tel Ware (0920) 821561; £12.65/£25.30*

REED   TL3636 Map 5
Cabinet

High Street; village signposted from A10

Friendly and relaxed, this tiled and weatherboarded village house has
been a pub for centuries. The small main bar is cosy, with a couple of
old-fashioned settles by the inglenook fireplace, studded leatherette
stools around traditional cast-iron tables, and a low buttery-cream
ceiling; there are darts (sensibly segregated in a side alley), shove-
ha'penny, table skittles, dominoes, and cribbage; maybe piped music.
On the other side of the servery is the recently refurbished sitting-
room with comfortable wheelback chairs and some dining-tables.
The good range of real ales, tapped from casks behind the bar,
includes Adnams, Bass, Flowers, Gibbs Mew Bishops Tipple, Greene
King IPA and Abbot and Sam Smiths. Reasonably priced bar food
includes soup (60p), sandwiches (from 55p, toasties from 60p),
baked potato (60p), pâté or turkey and ham pie (£1.10), ploughman's
(£1.20), a good range of salads (from £1.80; £2.80 for smoked
salmon), and hot dishes such as lasagne (£1.40), scampi (£2.35) and
six-ounce rump steak (£4). There are a couple of tables by lavender
bushes and roses facing the quiet lane in front, and behind is a big
lawn with old teak seats and tables among fruit-trees, and a children's

summer bar when it's busy enough. *(Recommended by Wayne Rossiter; more reports please)*

Free house · Licensees Andrew Johnson and Mrs June Johnson · Real ale Meals and snacks (not Mon or Tues evenings) · Children in special area Open 10.30–2.30, 5.30–11

RUSHDEN   TL3031   Map 5
Moon & Stars

Village signposted from A507 Baldock–Buntingford, about a mile W of Cottered

It's a shame that most of the people who find their way to this friendly out-of-the-way pub do so by accident when looking for the other better-known Rushden in Northamptonshire. This pretty, tiled white country pub really is worth heading for. It still has an unspoilt and cottagey feel, with heavy beams in the low ceiling, a big white-panelled inglenook fireplace, Windsor chairs around a long stripped wooden table, and a bustling little dog called Sheba. Bar food includes sandwiches and toasties (from 50p), and hot dishes such as sausage and/or ham with eggs and chips (from 95p), home-made pasty (£1.50), several seafood dishes such as scallops, seafood platter or scampi (£1.95) and stuffed plaice with prawns and garlic (£2.25). Greene King IPA, Abbot and KK Mild kept under pressure; darts, dominoes, cribbage and a fruit machine, maybe piped music. There is a garden behind, with tables, a climbing-frame and swings; also benches by the hanging baskets in front. *(More reports please)*

Greene King · Licensees Betty and Bob Pitcher · Meals and snacks (not Sun lunchtime, only sandwiches Sun evening) · Open 11–2.30, 6–11 all year

ST ALBANS   TL1507   Map 5
Fighting Cocks

Off George Street, through abbey gateway (you can drive down, though signs suggest you can't)

Under a quaintly conical tiled roof, this has a comfortably modernised bar, more or less circular; after it was first opened as an alehouse in 1600 it was known as The Round House for nearly 300 years. There's a good log fire in the inglenook fireplace, heavy beams in the low ceiling, and some pleasant window alcoves and other nooks and corners (one, down steps, used to be part of a Stuart cock-fighting pit). There are good helpings of straightforward bar food, reasonably priced (only sandwiches in the evening), and well kept Benskins, Friary Meux and Ind Coope Burton on handpump. The surroundings are very attractive: seats in the garden, then beyond that lots of ducks on the River Ver, a lakeside park, and the Roman remains of Verulamium. Traditions of great age are associated with the pub – a building on the site may have been used as a boat-house or fishing-lodge by the abbey (the pub was called the Fisherman in the nineteenth century), or alternatively may have housed a silk mill and, before that, a flour mill. Certainly there was some sort of building here virtually from the Abbey's foundation in 795, and by Norman times served as a battlemented gatehouse (the upper fortifications were demolished in 1300). *(Recommended by Stuart Barker, Roger Protz, Gareth Morrell, Simon Rees)*

Benskins (Ind Coope) · Real ale · Meals (lunchtime) and snacks · Children in eating area · Open 11.30–2.30, 5.30–10.30

Goat ★

Sopwell Lane; a No Entry beside Crispins on Holywell Hill, the main southwards exit from town – by car, take the next lane down and go around the block

One of the main attractions of this friendly and popular old pub is the good range of real ales, which doesn't neglect the mild ales and strong bitters. A regular core includes Hook Norton Best and Old Hookey, Marstons Pedigree and Mercian Mild, Morrells Light Mild, Wadworths 6X and Charlie Wells Bombadier, as well as changing guest beers. They are served from handpump in the front bar, but tapped from the cask at the back; also farmhouse cider on handpump, and mulled wine in winter. The stylish but simple furniture in the network of linked rooms includes old-fashioned benches by the windows, pews, polished elm tables, and stalls around tables in a quieter room. Bar food is waitress-served: home-made soup (65p), filled French bread or granary bread (sausage 85p, Stilton £1.30), various ploughman's with a choice of relish (£1.20–£1.75), summer treats like Danish-style open sandwiches on granary or black rye bread (rollmop herrings £1.45, vegetarian nut salad £1.95, shredded chicken with curried mayonnaise £2.45 and many more), and daily specials such as the minute steak in French bread (£1.55), goatherder's pie (£1.95), or barbecued spare ribs (£2.75); in winter there is a good choice of filled baked potatoes (or deep-fried baked potato skins with a garlic cheese dip, all from £1.30). A children's menu is available with food such as small burgers or ravioli (99p) and a three-course lunch drawn from the main choice (£3.55); dominoes and a fruit machine. Tables on the neat lawn-and-gravel back yard are sheltered by what, 200 years ago, used to be the most extensive stables of any inn here. *(Recommended by Stanley Faulkner, Tim and Ann Bracey, M Quine, John Pepper, David Gristwood, Martin Murrish, J Cunningham)*

Free house · Licensees Peter and Anthea Ransome · Real ale · Meals (not Sun) and snacks (lunchtime, not Sun) · Children in back functions room · Jazz Sun lunchtime · Nearby parking may be rather difficult · Open 11.30–2.30, 5.30–10.30 (opens 6 Fri and Sat evenings); closed 25 Dec · Plans for bedrooms mid-1986 tel St Albans (0727) 60881

Rose and Crown

St Michael's Street; from town centre follow George Street down past Abbey towards Roman town

This civilised old pub – hidden behind its elegant Georgian façade – has unevenly timbered walls, old-fashioned wall benches, a pile of old *Country Life* magazines, and black cauldrons in the deep fireplace. The friendly licensees continue to add distinctive touches: help-yourself apple baskets in summer (any money goes towards guide dogs), roast-your-own chestnuts in the autumn, punch and mulled wines in winter, and a range of snuffs. Bar food includes sandwiches to order, home-made soups (in winter), ploughman's and several home-made dishes, sometimes to old English recipes: cheese, potato and onion pie (75p), cottage pie, rustler's pot (corned beef and onions topped with potato and melted cheese), fidgit pie and ham, apple, leek and potato pie (all 95p); casseroles in winter. Benskins, Friary Meux and Ind Coope Burton on handpump (in good condition); darts (placed sensibly to one side), dominoes, cribbage, fruit machine and a juke box. *(Recommended by Michael and Alison Sandy; more reports please)*

Benskins (Ind Coope) · Licensees John and Paula Milligan · Real ale · Snacks Folk music Thurs · Open 11–2.30, 5.30–10.30

White Hart

Holywell Hill

This lofty-ceilinged old inn's bars and dining-room include original eighteenth-century oak panelling, gateleg oak tables (many of them antique), and recently opened-up fireplaces. These go well with the character of the comfortable and friendly bars that loop around a well run central servery; the building dates partly back to one called the Harts Horn, let as an inn by the abbey in 1535. Two hundred years ago Lord Grosvenor's butler, here to keep an eye on her ladyship, smelled a rat when a familiar-looking country farmer walked in. The clothes were plain, but the face was the Duke of Cumberland's. That night, the butler bored two holes through the lady's bedroom door to spy through, then burst in, and claimed that on the pillow was the distinct impression of Cumberland's head. In an extraordinary case heard before the House of Lords, the whole matter depended on whether this was the truth, or whether – as the inn's landlady said – there was no impression on the pillow. In the end, the Lords believed What The Butler Said He Saw, and the duke had to pay Lord Grosvenor £10,000 damages for that one adulterous night (equivalent in today's terms to about a million pounds). There is one large menu for bar food and à la carte meals, but both are now eaten in the dining-room; sandwiches on request (from 80p), soup (85p), ploughman's (£1.45), cold meats and salads (from £2.10) and several dishes that you can eat as a starter or main course: French bread, diced chicken, peppers and garlic (£1.45), mushrooms with cider, thyme and cheese (£2.25) or emperor crab claws flamed in brandy and served on an orange slice (£3.95); White Hart grill or gammon rolled and filled with peaches, cinnamon and covered with puff pastry (£2.75), scampi (£3.25), steak and kidney pie (£3.75), a pub special – fillet steak cooked in mushrooms and Guinness sauce (£5.25), roast fore-rib of beef (£5.50) and poached salmon (£6.50); puddings such as lemon and ginger syllabub, Scotch trifle and speciality ices (all £1.25). Children's menus are £1.25–£1.65. Benskins and Ind Coope Burton on handpump; shove-ha'penny, dominoes, shut-the-box, devil among the tailors. *(Recommended by Stanley Faulkner, Michael and Alison Sandy, M H G)*

Benskins (Ind Coope) · Licensee Peter Lloyd · Real ale · Meals and snacks
Children in dining-room · Open 11–2.30, 6–10.30 · Bedrooms tel St Albans
(0727) 53624; £38B/£50B

nr ST ALBANS   TL1507   Map 5
Barley Mow

Tyttenhanger Green; from A405 just under 2 miles E of A6/A1081
roundabout, take B6426 signposted St Albans, then first left turn

Hidden down a narrow country lane, this lively pub stocks a
remarkable collection of some 15 real ales on handpump, though the
evening and weekend crowds make sure the casks are depleted far too
quickly for them to go off. They're reasonably priced and well kept,
and include Adnams, Brakspears SB, Courage Directors, Everards
Tiger, Fullers London Pride and ESB, Gibbs Mew Bishops Tipple,
Greene King IPA and Abbot, Marstons Pedigree and Owd Rodger,
Ruddles County, Sam Smiths OB, Wadworths 6X and Youngs
Special. The main bar, with its sensibly long serving counter, is
comfortable and cheerful – airy by day, with sunny window alcoves,
and softly lit by carriage-lamps at night; shove-ha'penny, dominoes,
cribbage, a fruit machine, space game, and maybe piped music. There
is a small separate panelled room. Bar food includes well filled French
bread rolls (65p), steak and kidney pie (£1.10), gypsy stik (marinated
pork and onion with chilli relish £1.20), Cornish pie or pasty (£1.25),
gammon and egg (£1.50) and scampi (£1.80). In summer there is a
barbecue outside, where there are plenty of picnic-table sets and
rustic seats, with swings, wandering St Bernards, and ponies in one of
the adjacent fields. *(Recommended by Dave Butler and Lesley Storey,
J Cunningham; more reports please)*

*Free house · Licensees Mr and Mrs John Blackwell · Real ale · Meals and
snacks (lunchtime, not Sun) · Children in small room weekend lunchtimes only
Open 10.30–2.30, 5.30–10.30*

SARRATT   TQ0499   Map 5
Boot

The Green

There are cosy rambling rooms in this attractive, early eighteenth-
century tiled house facing the village green: comfortable cushioned
benches along the part-panelled walls with carpet or dark flooring-
tiles, a fine early eighteenth-century inglenook fireplace with a good
winter log fire, and a friendly welcome from the licensee (who used to
sing professionally). Bar food includes sandwiches, ploughman's and
various home-made dishes such as Aunty Leala's piggy pie, chicken
curry and cottage pie (£1.60) and steak and kidney pie (£1.80);
puddings (fruit pie and cream 60p). Well kept Benskins and Ind
Coope Burton on handpump; sensibly segregated darts, cribbage,
fruit machine, space game and piped music. It has an old-fashioned
black wrought-iron bench under a pair of pollarded lime-trees in
front, and more seats on a pretty, sheltered lawn with roses, fruit-
trees and a weeping willow. *(More reports please)*

We say if we or readers have seen dogs or cats in a pub.

Benskins (Ind Coope) · Licensee Allan Grant · Real ale · Meals and snacks (lunchtime) · Open 11–3, 5.30–11 all year

WALKERN TL2826 Map 5
White Lion

B1037

This comfortable and welcoming old pub, with cosy beamed alcoves, is popular for its good bar food: sandwiches, ploughman's, steak and kidney pie, chicken curry or fresh fish and chips (all £2.75), tandoori chicken, beef in beer and kidneys with mushrooms (£3.25), smoked salmon (£3.75) and peppered steak (£5.95); there is also a small separate restaurant. The open-plan bar (with very low beams where its individual rooms have been knocked together) has an inglenook fireplace with a good fire in winter, comfortable leatherette banquettes and lots of tables, ticking clocks, and gentle piped music. The Greene King beers have been kept under pressure; darts, shove-ha'penny, dominoes, cribbage. The outside of the seventeenth-century brick building has been sensitively restored, and there are tables in a pretty little terrace arbour, and more on the neat lawn behind. In 1711 when it was the Rose & Crown, the pub housed the judges who were the last in this country to condemn a woman to death for witchcraft; her sentence was later commuted to life imprisonment. *(Recommended by D A Angless; more reports please)*

Greene King · Licensee Michael Windebank · Meals and snacks (not Sun or Mon evenings) · Children in eating area · Open 10.30–2.30, 7–10.30

WESTMILL TL3626 Map 5
Sword in Hand

Village signposted W of A10, about 1 mile S of Buntingford

On weekday lunchtimes, this half-timbered and colour-washed pub, in a most attractive village, is very peaceful: there are comfortably cushioned seats on the Turkey carpet or parquet floor, murmured conversations in quiet corners, a cat snoozing by the log fire, and country prints on the black and white timbered walls. The pub takes its name from the crest of a local landowner – the first licensee, a blacksmith, used to make tools for his Caribbean sugar plantations. Bar food ranges from sandwiches, soup and ploughman's to lasagne, steaks and so forth, and there is a separate restaurant; well kept Benskins and Ind Coope Burton on handpump; darts, a fruit machine. There are tables on a partly crazy-paved sheltered side garden. *(More reports please)*

Benskins (Ind Coope) · Licensee Ian Johnson · Real ale · Meals (not Sun, not Sat lunchtime) and snacks (not Sun lunchtime) · Children in restaurant · Open 11–2.30, 5.30–10.30

nr WHEATHAMPSTEAD TL1713 Map 5
Wicked Lady ★

Nomansland Common; B651 ½ mile S of village

Since the *Guide*'s last edition, this popular pub has been altered to give far more room – the whole ground floor is now the bar area, and a new bar has been added in a timber-clad old barn with York flagstones and church pews. However, what is particularly special about this friendly country pub is its wide range of food and drink. Besides a better range of packeted snacks than many pubs have, the bar food, all home cooked, includes onion or vegetable soup (60p), burger (75p), giant sausage in a granary loaf (£1.10), ploughman's with Cheddar, Stilton, ham or beef (£1.25–£1.30), vegetable or ham and asparagus quiche (£1.80), fresh mussels (£1.80), various salads (£1.80) and daily specials that might include Gaelic beef (pieces of beef marinated in Guinness and brown sugar) or ham, turkey and tarragon pie (£1.85). The regular ales, tapped from casks in a back alcove and priced fairly, are Burts Bitter (from the Isle of Wight – this is the only mainland pub we've found stocking it), Fullers London Pride, Gales HSB, Greene King IPA and Abbot, Marstons Pedigree and Owd Rodger, Robinsons and Wadworths 6X, with guest beers changing each week, several draught ciders and quite an interesting choice of wines (all the drinks are also sold to take away). There is a covered terrace in the large garden. The rolling countryside around here, and the wooded common itself, are good for walks.
(Recommended by Michael and Alison Sandy, Gareth Morrell, D G, Wayne Rossiter, Paula Beever)

Free house · Licensee Michael Delaney · Real ale · Meals and snacks · Children in eating area and restaurant · Open 10.30–2.30, 5.30–10.30

Lucky Dip

Besides the fully inspected pubs, you might like to try these Lucky Dips recommended and described by readers (if you do, please send us reports):

ALDBURY [Aldbury Common; SP9612], *Valiant Trooper*: nice clean free house with big range of real ales and good value food *(Wayne Rossiter, Mrs R Horridge)*
ALDENHAM [TQ1398], *Game Bird*: new fun-pub popular with youngsters but appealing to all age groups; full of bric-à-brac and hanging signs; good value bar snacks, real ale *(MHG)*
ARDELEY [TL3027], *Jolly Waggoner*: welcoming two-bar pub with log fire, home-cooked snacks, Greene King Abbot, IPA and (at Christmas) Winter Ale on tap; popular with locals and walkers *(Mr and Mrs P G Bardswell)*
ASHWELL [TL2639], *Bushel & Strike*: tasty food in bar and restaurant, including Sunday lunch; relaxed, comfortable atmosphere, pleasant garden, in pretty village *(Chris Waldron)*
BALLINGER [SP9103], *Pheasant*: good small pub with real ale including Marstons Pedigree *(Wayne Rossiter)*
BARKWAY [TL3835], *Chaise & Pair*: plushly modernised small pub with bar food from sandwiches to steaks and real ale; restaurant *(W R Rossiter, LYM)*
BATFORD [Marquis Lane; TL1415], *Marquis of Granby*: good value food in friendly and welcoming tastefully renovated pub with big open fires – chestnuts in winter for roasting; well kept Ruddles County and Websters Yorkshire on handpump *(M G McKenzie)*
BISHOPS STORTFORD [TL4820], *Black Lion*: good home-cooked food and helpful staff in town pub done up in old style; Benskins real ale, juke box, space game, pool, fruit machine; garden *(Charlie Salt)*; [Rye Street] *Wheatsheaf*: tiny crowded pub with amazing collection of hot-water bottles and chamber-pots; good hot dishes, well kept Rayments beer *(Jack Davey)*

BOURNE END [TL0206], *White Horse*: friendly atmosphere, good snacks, and wide choice of well kept real ales *(G T Huxtable)*

BRENT PELHAM [TL4330], *Black Horse*: real ales only, no music, no fruit machines in homely pub with good sandwiches and bar snacks; big garden with play area *(Hugh Murchie)*

BUSHEY [Main Street; TQ1395], *Royal Oak*: wide range of beers including Boddingtons (rare down here) *(Wayne Rossiter)*; [Park Road] *Swan*: homely atmosphere in rare surviving example of single-room terraced pub (reminiscent of 1920s) *(Stephan Carney, LYM)*

CHANDLERS CROSS [TQ0698], *Clarendon Arms*: well kept beers including Youngs Special, Ruddles County, Sam Smiths *(Wayne Rossiter)*

CHARLTON [TL1727], *Windmill*: friendly and efficient staff in modernised and comfortably busy old pub with nice clientele; excellent reasonably priced food; no juke box, spotless WCs; ample seats by own duck pond *(R Heeks)*

CHESHUNT [Windmill Lane; TL3502], *Red Cow*: quiet and pleasant well run Charringtons pub, with terrific collection of hats above saloon bar; open fire, machines in public bar *(Martin Patrick Egan)*

CHIPPERFIELD [Tower Hill; TL0401], *Boot*: friendly snug pub with lunchtime snacks, well kept Benskins and Ind Coope Burton, open fires and splendid collections of military hats, china washing sets, beer-barrel taps, brasses, old prints and photographs; dogs allowed on leads *(John and Denise Keable, Tim and Ann Bracey)*

CHORLEYWOOD [TQ0295], *White Horse*: good Greene King pub with well kept beer *(Wayne Rossiter)*

CODICOTE [TL2118], *Goat*: plushly renovated rambling old Benskins pub with full meals and smartly uniformed bar staff *(Stuart Barker, LYM)*

COLEMAN GREEN [TL1812], *John Bunyan*: friendly staff in pleasant surroundings, serving reasonably priced food, good McMullens beer; lots of jugs and mugs *(M G McKenzie)*

COTTERED [TL3129], *Bell*: spick-and-span pub with Benskins, Ind Coope Burton, also coffee; dining area; warmly friendly licensees *(Gwen and Peter Andrews)*; *Bull*: good food and very well kept Greene King ales in clean, comfortable, warm and welcoming pub *(WRW)*

DANE END [TL3321], *Plough*: friendly, relaxed atmosphere and reasonably priced food, with genuine theatre organ, played regularly *(Simon Clark)*

DATCHWORTH GREEN [TL2718], *Inn on the Green*: well kept and popular free house *(Wayne Rossiter)*; *Plough*: simple and friendly pub with well kept Greene King real ales *(Diane Phillips, LYM)*

GREAT OFFLEY [TL1427], *Green Man*: comfortable country pub with good food in bar and restaurant, very popular at lunchtime *(R Pearson)*

HARPENDEN [St Johns Road; TL1314], *Engineer*: cosy and welcoming free house with well kept Ruddles County, terrace with trellis and hanging ivy *(M G McKenzie)*; [High Street] *Old Cock*: very comfortable series of knocked-through rooms with smartened-up old beams; cheerful landlord offering good food especially evenings, well kept Trumans and Sampson; jazz Sunday lunchtime *(Michael Sandy)*; *Silver Cup*: wide range of bar food in comfortably refurbished Charles Wells pub with cosy open fire *(J Cunningham)*

HATFIELD [TL2309], *Eight Bells*: seventeenth-century, with highwayman connections; said to be the place Dickens had in mind for Bill Sikes' refuge after he'd murdered Nancy *(John Powell)*; *Green Man*: welcoming pub *(John Powell)*; [Old Great North Road] *Red Lion*: very nice lounge bar with well served McMullens beer; very clean *(Stanley Faulkner)*; [Old Great North Road] *Wrestlers*: food hot and tasty at lunchtime in old beamed pub with horse brasses and inglenook log fire; well kept Ind Coope beer; happy staff and landlord *(Stanley Faulkner, John Powell)*

nr HATFIELD [Sleapshyde; TL2309], *Plough*: well kept pub with good food (for pub location see OS Sheet 166 reference 202070) *(John Powell)*

HERTFORD [The Folly; TL3213], *Old Barge*: comfortably renovated canalside pub with well kept Benskins beer *(LYM)*; [High Street] *Salisbury Arms*: food at lunchtime in restaurant is mainly Chinese – this sound country town pub is run by Chinese who keep McMullens beer well; bar snacks/sandwiches with cuts off large joints *(Rev Ian Watson)*

HINXWORTH [Main Street; TL2340], *Three Horseshoes*: cosy and homely old thatched village pub, with open fire in winter; darts, dominoes, friendly relaxed atmosphere; good Greene King IPA on handpump, and unusual range of cocktails *(Steve Lawrence)*

HODDESDON [High Street; TL3709], *Golden Lion*: genuinely old (1532), with friendly service, good Ind Coope beer in excellent public bar *(Martin Patrick Egan)*

ICKLEFORD [TL1831], *Old George*: rambling heavy-beamed Tudor pub by churchyard, serving good value bar food and Greene King beers *(LYM)*

LEMSFORD [TL2111], *Sun*: cheerful Courage pub close to River Lea with lots of beams and timbers; serves good filled rolls; where Joseph Arch's pioneer Agricultural Labourers Union used to meet *(LYM)*

nr LEMSFORD [TL2111], *Crooked Chimney*: roomy and smartly refurbished open-plan bar around central chimney; sandwiches and hot bar meals, Ind Coope real ales; garden by fields *(LYM)*

LETCHMORE HEATH [TQ1597], *Three Horseshoes*: tasty home-made food and Benskins real ale in small and very popular – and therefore maybe crowded – village pub with smart but informal décor; some tables bookable, remarkable mix of customers, attractive bar staff; garden, pleasant setting opposite pond *(MHG, D L Johnson)*

LILLEY [TL1126], *Silver Lion*: good food, well kept Greene King ales, warm friendly people *(P W Whittingham)*

LITTLE GADDESDEN [SP9913], *Bridgewater Inn*: Georgian inn surrounded by National Trust property; own range of food and beer *(Wayne Rossiter)*

LITTLE HADHAM [TL4422], *Nags Head*: well kept Rayments real ales in simple sixteenth-century pub *(W R Rossiter, LYM)*

LITTLE WYMONDLEY [TL2127], *Bucks Head*: handy for A1(M), chintzy and friendly with well kept Wethereds beer; attractive garden *(LYM)*

MARKYATE [TL0616], *Sun*: low-beamed old Benskins pub with log fire in inglenook; garden *(LYM)*

NUTHAMPSTEAD [TL4034], *Woodman*: friendly country pub, Adnams and Greene King *(Dennis Royles)*

PETERS GREEN [TL1419], *Bright Star*: friendly regulars and landlord in cosy lounge bar with fairly priced food and well kept McMullens real ale *(M G McKenzie)*

PIRTON [TL1431], *Cat & Fiddle*: homely pub facing village green; well kept Charles Wells real ales, bar food; swing on back lawn *(LYM)*

POTTERS BAR [Warrengate Road; TL2501], *Old Maypole*: quiet and secluded pub with family room *(Joslin Lewis)*

PUCKERIDGE [TL3823], *White Hart*: good food, especially fish, and well kept McMullens in rambling bars; useful tables outside *(D L Johnson, Richard Gibbs, RAB, LYM)*

RIDGE [Crossoaks Lane; TL2100], *Old Guinea*: friendly little local, its one bar decorated with seafaring memorabilia and nick-nacks; good steaks and other food, and well kept Ind Coope Burton and bitter *(T M Bracey)*

nr HEMEL HEMPSTEAD [Briden's Camp; TL0506], *Crown & Sceptre*: old-fashioned country pub, highly rated in previous editions for its welcoming atmosphere and wide choice of well kept real ales, but recently changing management (for pub location see OS Sheet 166 reference 044111) *LYM; up-to-date reports please)*; [Picotts End, N of town] *Marchmont Arms*: lovely food, reasonably priced, in unpretentious old pub with peaceful atmosphere and nice garden *(Michael and Alison Sandy)*

ST ALBANS [Holywell Hill; TL1507], *Abbey*: food and sandwiches in bar, and good Ind Coope real ale; live entertainment by Irish show bands and singers – landlord also plays and sings; big functions room *(L A Monaghan)*; [Adelaide Street] *Adelaide Wine House*: notable for staying open till the small hours on Fridays and Saturdays, this three-floor pub has a simply furnished upstairs bar with lunchtime food and real ale, downstairs wine bar and restaurant, and top-floor discos and live bands (J Cunningham, LYM); [Hatfield Road] Cock: comfortably modernised town pub with interesting history – it once had a floor of human bones (probably from second Battle of St Albans, 1461) (LYM); [French Row] Fleur de Lys: historic medieval building, comfortably modernised (Paula Beever, LYM); [Fishpool Street] Lower Red Lion: attractive old pub with exposed beams, log fire, Youngs real ale, snacks, and friendly regulars (Tim Bracey, Wayne Rossiter); [London Road] Peahen: large rambling hotel and bar owned by McMullens, with good value well kept Country Bitter (Roger Protz); [St Michaels] Six Bells: comfortable, neat low-beamed Benskins pub with wide choice of bar food and good real ales (LYM)

SARRATT [Church Lane; TQ0499], Cock: country pub included in previous editions for its unusual traditional two-room layout, inglenook fireplace and so forth; recent restaurant expansion (Stephan Carney, LYM; up-to-date reports please); Plough: food and Benskins Bitter good in cosy country pub with quiet, comfortable atmosphere (at lunchtime anyway) and small but peaceful garden (C F Walling)

SAWBRIDGEWORTH [Vantorts Road, Far Green; TL4814], King William IV: friendly local, atmosphere and food not stereotyped; small and traditional with good real ale, and no coin machines or loud music; sometimes a bit crowded (G A Wright, Rev John Quill)

SHENLEY [London Road; TL1800], White Horse: nice food and well kept drinks in clean, bright and friendly pub; recently remodelled on similar lines to main entry Green Dragon at London Colney (same licensee); two big log fires, newly extended large garden (D N Fenn, A G Gray)

TEWIN [Upper Green Road; TL2714], Plume of Feathers: good beer, in friendly, warm and comfortable pub with sturdy old furniture; tasty food in bars and steak restaurant (Michael Woodley, Michael and Alison Sandy)

TRING [SP9211], Kings Arms: friendly landlords and good real ales in characterful building well decorated with old church pews, and dinosaurs on tiles in gents; good value food, especially hot beef sandwiches (Alan Eardley)

WALTHAM CROSS [TL3600], Queens Head: tastefully refurbished genuinely ancient pub in the old centre, Charringtons (Martin Patrick Egan)

WARE [High Street; TL3614], Brewery Tap: folk and jazz nights every week; local personality John Creasey provides lively atmosphere with good value food and well kept Greene King Abbot (Colin Higgins); [Church Street] French Horn: wholesome help-yourself salad lunches, baked potatoes, pies and other food, with well kept McMullens real ales, in neat lounge bar; tables outside (Charlie Salt)

WATFORD HEATH [Pinner Road; TQ1196], Load of Hay: Benskins and food from pizzas to steak in country-style pub with jovial staff; back terrace (Charlie Salt)

WATTON-AT-STONE [High Street; TL3019], Bull: picturesque coaching-inn with interesting food in pleasant restaurant; tasty bar snacks such as prawns in spicy sauce, prawn sandwiches and dish of the day; lots of daily newspapers for customers; antique furnishings (Rev Ian Watson, Michael and Alison Sandy)

WELL END [Rowley Lane; TQ2098], Mops & Brooms: name commemorates battle between gypsies and townsfolk; light and airy extension; fountain in garden (John Estdale)

nr WHEATHAMPSTEAD [Gustard Wood; TL1713], Cross Keys: Benskins real ales and simple bar food in open-plan pub alone in rolling wooded countryside (LYM); [Gustard Wood] Tin Pot: old-world friendly pub with low beams, inglenook fireplace, weekday food, well kept Benskins and Ind Coope Burton; very well thought of locally (D W Sanders, D Lewis)

WHITWELL [TL1820], Maidens Head: friendly welcome and atmosphere in cosy carpeted lounge with open fires, good value snacks and well kept McMullens ales; darts in public bar (D Lewis, D L Johnson)

WILLIAN [TL2230], Three Horseshoes: good food and well kept Greene King real ales in warmly welcoming pub very handy for A1(M) – left after Letchworth turn-off (LYM)

Humberside

A good point about this area is that pub food tends to be generally cheap, and sometimes very good, as at the civilised old St Vincent Arms at Sutton upon Derwent (which also has a fine range of wines and real ales). This year we've had warmer praise than before for the food at the well run Plough in Allerthorpe and the piratical Royal Dog & Duck in Flamborough; it's also good value in three pubs which are newcomers to the Guide this year – the Black Horse in Ellerker (surprisingly cottagey for the area), the spacious Dacre Arms in Brandesburton and the elegant Londesborough Arms in Market Weighton (which has bedrooms). There's a remarkable range of opening times in the county – yet another new entry, the friendly Gate at Millington, doesn't open until 7.30 pm, but then stays open until very late at night. In Hull (with its imaginatively restored waterside and largely pedestrianised centre) the Olde White Harte is a very attractive and civilised tavern with interesting furnishings to go with its long history, as well as a friendly atmosphere and good value food; the George there has a bustling Victorian bar with popular lunchtime food. A wide choice of Lucky Dip pubs in the city includes several that sound specially promising, such as the traditional Black Boy,

The Altisidora, Bishop Burton

the King Edward VI (for its unusual range of real ales) and the pierside Minerva (which brews its own beer – named after the Humber pilots who patronise the pub). Another town pub among the main entries, the homely gas-lit White Horse in Beverley, is interesting for the way that it conjures up an unretouched Victorian atmosphere. Country pubs include the friendly Tiger on the village green in North Newbald, the Triton by the walls of Sledmere House (a hospitable eighteenth-century inn), and the refurbished Green Dragon at Welton (where Dick Turpin was finally caught – an attractive village in a popular walking area). The Lucky Dip section includes other interesting possibilities, such as the Duke of Cumberland in Cottingham (with books in its comfortable lounge), Light Dragoon at Etton (a pleasant family pub), Queens Head at Kirkburn (good home cooking in the granary dining-room of a former farm), waterside Star in North Dalton (comfortably refurbished by new owners), Pipe & Glass at South Dalton (tasty food in a rambling pub with an attractive garden), the traditionally furnished old Gold Cup in Low Catton and Three Cups at Stamford Bridge, and the Ferguson Fawsitt Arms in Walkington (popular food).

ALLERTHORPE   SE7847 Map 7

Plough

Off A1079 nr Pocklington

Good home-made bar food in this friendly village pub is priced attractively, and includes daily specials such as chilli con carne (£2.40) and pork Stroganoff or (in season) game pie (£2.50), with open sandwiches (from 75p), Yorkshire puddings with onion gravy (80p), soup (90p), ploughman's with meat and pâté as well as cheese (£1.40), spare ribs (£1.50), lasagne (£1.75), salads (from £1.80), roast chicken (£2.20) and steaks (from £4). There are children's dishes (from £1; there's a family room away from the bar), roasts on Sunday, and a separate lunchtime restaurant. The two communicating rooms of the main carpeted bar are comfortably furnished with cushioned settles and stools, and have open fires, snug alcoves, hunting prints and mementoes of squadrons 102 (RAF) and 405 (RCAF) which in the war flew Halifaxes, Liberators and Wellingtons from here. Well kept Theakstons Best, XB and Old Peculier on handpump; maybe piped music. The public side has pool, dominoes, shove-ha'penny, cribbage, a fruit machine and a space game. There are tables on the gravel outside this pretty white house, which is handy for Burnby Hall (stuffed sporting trophies and attractive lily-pond gardens). *(Recommended by Tim Halstead, Philip Asquith, Keith Myers, Paul West, L N Goulding)*

Free house · Licensee David Banks · Real ale · Meals and snacks · Children welcome · Open 11–3, 7–11

Please let us know what you think of a pub's bedrooms. No stamp needed: write to *The Good Pub Guide*, FREEPOST, London SW10 0BR.

BEVERLEY   TA0340   Map 8
White Horse ('Nellies')
Hengate; runs off North Bar Within

Close to the minster, this pub is included for its carefully preserved
décor. This, you feel, is what Victorian pubs were *really* like, before
foam-filled cushions and vacuum cleaners were invented. Its small
rooms have bare floorboards, antique cartoons and sentimental
engravings on the walls, a deeply reverberating chiming clock, a gas-
lit pulley-controlled chandelier, brown leatherette seats (with high-
backed settles in one little snug), and open fires – one with an
attractively tiled fireplace. Well kept Sam Smiths on handpump; good
value well filled baps or sandwiches (75p), home-made chicken and
mushroom or steak and kidney pie (£1) or scampi (£1.75); darts.
*(Recommended by G L Archer, Jane English, Jon Dewhirst, Tim Halstead,
Philip Asquith, Keith Myers, Paul West)*

*Sam Smiths · Real ale · Meals and snacks (lunchtime, not Sun) · Children
welcome · Open 11.30–2.30, 6–10.30*

BISHOP BURTON   SE9939   Map 8
Altisidora   [*illustrated on page 371*]
A1079 Beverley–York

This friendly and well kept old village pub, comfortably modernised,
has cushioned benches and higher settles fitted neatly into the corners
and alcoves of its lounge, which rambles about, and up and down
steps, under very low beams. Reliable and good value bar food
includes soup (60p), burgers (75p), sandwiches (from 90p),
ploughman's or Welsh rarebit (£1.25), home-made steak and kidney
pie, fish pie or cottage pie (£2), salads and omelettes (£2) and quick
dishes such as scampi (£2) or lasagne (£2.15). Fruit machine; the
saloon bar has another fruit machine, also pool, bar billiards and
dominoes. The pub is beautifully placed on the edge of a pretty village
green, and you can sit outside in summer on the side terrace or under
the tiled roof of a little loggia. Children like the flocks of ducks and
geese on the pond almost opposite. Over the years, the pub has
cantered down a string of horsy names, from the Horse & Jockey and
Evander to the present one – winner of the 1813 St Leger for its local
owner. *(Recommended by Roger Bellingham, G L Archer, KM, Tim
Halstead, Philip Asquith, Keith Myers, Paul West)*

*North Country · Licensee P R Anfield · Meals and snacks · Children in upper
part of bar · Open 11–3, 6–10.30*

BRANDESBURTON   TA1247   Map 8
Dacre Arms
Village signposted from A165 N of Beverley and Hornsea turn-offs

Good value simple bar food in this comfortable and spacious village
pub includes soup (65p), home-made chicken liver pâté (£1.35, with
garlic bread £1.75), ploughman's (Wensleydale £1.35, Stilton £1.55),
basket meals (from sausages at £1.35 to scampi at £2.30), salads

(from £1.60, home-cooked ham or turkey around £2.30), lasagne (£2.05), chicken curry or steak and kidney pie (£2.80), gammon and eggs (£3.15) and eight-ounce sirloin steak (£4.35). There are purple plush bucket seats on a purple patterned carpet, also beams and swirly white plaster; the right-hand area is quite snug, the left roomier, and there's a separate restaurant. Well kept Tetleys Bitter and Mild and Youngers IPA and Scotch on handpump (with Theakstons Old Peculier kept under pressure); fruit machines, maybe piped music. *(Recommended by C H Kenington, Lee Goulding)*

Free house · Licensee B C Jefferson · Real ale · Meals and snacks · Children welcome lunchtime and early evening · Open 11–2.30, 6.30–11 all year

ELLERKER SE9229 Map 8
Black Horse
Village signposted from A63 at junction with A1034

A pleasant surprise for the area, this cottagey village pub has a cosy and low-beamed main bar, candlelit at night, with softly cushioned seats cut in to the thick stone walls, as well as red leatherette wheelback chairs, velvet curtains to match the green carpet, a long-case clock, log-effect gas fire in the big stone fireplace, and on our visit nostalgic piped music. The new owners now do soup (65p), sandwiches such as home-cooked ham (70p) or rare beef (75p), Bratwurst with coleslaw (£1.75), chilli con carne (£2.30), home-made burgers (£1.60), steak and kidney pie (£2.30), large scampi (£3.60), sirloin steak (£4.20) and home-made puddings such as cheesecake or apple pie (from 65p). A £10 bargain for two people is sirloin steak with a bottle of wine included – book ahead. Well kept Pennine and Websters Yorkshire on handpump; darts in the bar on the right; sun-lounge with cheery red seats and red check curtains. There are some tables by the car park, and beyond is the village green with a children's play area. *(Recommended by M T Swallow)*

Free house · Licensees Mike and Marjorie Kingston · Real ale · Meals – tel North Cave (043 02) 3270 – and snacks · Open 12–3, 7–10.30

ELLERTON SE7039 Map 7
Boot & Shoe [*illustrated on page 378*]
Village signposted from B1228

After at last tracking down this attractive village pub, we heard just as we went to press that it was coming up for sale. Nevertheless, we are including it as a main entry in the hope that readers will give us early news of any changes – it is after all an appetising place. It's a low tiled cottagey house sheltering under a spreading tree, and its comfortable and friendly bar has wheelback chairs and dove-grey plush wall seats around dimpled copper tables, a nice bow window seat, low black beams in its butter-coloured ceiling, and an open fire in cool weather. It's had well kept Timothy Taylors, Tetleys and Youngers Scotch on handpump, and good value food in the bar and the small side dining-room. *(Recommended by M T Swallow; up-to-date reports on the new regime please)*

Free house · Real ale · Meals and snacks · Open 11–3, 6–10.30 (may be closed weekday lunchtimes)

FLAMBOROUGH   TA2270   Map 8
Royal Dog & Duck ★
Dog & Duck Square; junction of B1255 and B1229

The original snug back bar of this 300-year-old inn is full of nautical nick-nacks, pirate pictures and grimacing toby jugs – the friendly landlord (who serves mulled wine in winter) looks as if he'd be thoroughly at home if Long John Silver strolled in. Several other rooms ramble around its partly covered courtyard (where there are tables in summer), one of them a good value food bar serving home-made soup (60p), sandwiches (from 50p, crab when it's available 75p), ploughman's (£1), plaice (£1.80), scampi (£2), seafood platter (£2.50) and three or four daily specials such as chicken and mushroom pie (£1.50), fresh plaice (£2.25) and mixed seafood salad (£3), with Sunday roasts (£2.50). They prefer you to order evening meals ahead (at least at busy times of year), with main dishes in the separate restaurant ranging from lasagne (£1.50) to locally caught salmon poached in champagne (£5.50), grilled king prawns (£6) and a variety of steaks (from £6), also ham and eggs (£1.75) and fisherman's platter (£2.25). In the main building there are shove-ha'penny, dominoes, cribbage, a fruit machine, a juke box (or piped music) and a space game. The pub is close to the open country above the cliffs of Flamborough Head. *(Recommended by Lee Goulding; more reports please)*

Bass · Licensee Barrie Crosby · Meals and snacks (not Sun–Thurs evenings in winter, not Sun or Mon evenings in summer) · Children in food bar · Bedrooms and meals tel Bridlington (0262) 850206; £15/£15

HULL   TA0927   Map 8
George
Land of Green Ginger; park just outside town centre and walk in: Land of Green Ginger is a lane at far end of pedestrians-only Whitefriargate, which leads out of centre opposite City Hall

On a weekday lunchtime the long bar of this well run Victorian pub bustles with people here for the good value filled rolls and sandwiches (from 55p), burgers (from 70p), ploughman's or home-made pâté with garlic bread (£1.50), and hot dishes such as lasagne, spaghetti bolognese, chilli con carne (£1.50), with salads such as home-cooked beef or ham (£1.60) and traditional light snacks such as pork pies (45p) or home-made Scotch eggs (55p). The high bar stools along the long copper and mahogany counter have sensible little backrests, and there's squared oak panelling, high beams, old latticed windows, and well kept Bass and Mild on handpump. Down at the quieter far end there are more seats around tables, and upstairs is a plush traditionally furnished dining-room. On your way into this old shuttered coaching-inn, look out for the narrow slit window just to the left of the coach entry, where wary ostlers investigated late-night arrivals in case they were highwaymen. The pub is handy for the excellent Docks Museum. *(More reports please)*

Bass · Licensee P E Cattaneo · Real ale · Meals (lunchtime, not Sun) and snacks (not Sun) · Children in eating area · No nearby parking · Open 11–3, 5.30–10.30 (no weekend extension to 11)

Olde White Harte ★

Off Silver Street, a continuation of Whitefriargate (see previous entry); pub is up narrow passage beside the jewellers' Barnby and Rust, and should not be confused with the much more modern White Hart nearby

Since our last edition this fine pub has had a fortnight's close-down for refurbishment, but it's hard to spot any changes – better to think of it as more of a spring-clean (with a nice new inn sign) for this excellently preserved period piece. Its heavy carved ceiling beams support black ceiling boards, there are attractive stained-glass windows over the bow window seat, fancy polished flooring-tiles, and brocaded Jacobean-style chairs in the inglenook by a fireplace decorated with Delft tiles. The curved copper-topped bar counter serves well kept Youngers IPA and No 3, and good value bar food includes sandwiches (hot roast beef £1), Scotch egg or quiche with a side salad (60p), ploughman's (£1.10), chicken salad (£1.50) and generous helpings of home-cooked hot dishes such as home-made steak and kidney pie (£1.50) – the service is pleasant and efficient. A handsome old staircase zigzags up past a grandfather clock to a heavily panelled room where on St George's Day 1642 Sir John Hotham, the town's governor, decided to lock the gate at the far end of Whitefriargate against King Charles: a crucial start to the Civil War, depriving the king of the town's arsenal. The restaurant (open on Sunday lunchtimes, as well as the bar food times below) serves meals with robust main courses such as farmhouse grill (£2.75) at lunchtime, and more elaborate ones – including old English dishes such as lamb and apple pie to an eighteenth-century recipe (£3.75) – in the evening. There are seats in the courtyard outside, with plans to extend it. All in all, a fine place for eating Hull cheese (an eighteenth-century euphemism for enjoying a great deal to drink – the town was known then for its very strong ales). *(Recommended by ILP, L N Goulding, Tim Halstead, Philip Asquith, Keith Myers, Paul West)*

Youngers · Licensee Derrick Graeme Sykes · Real ale · Meals and snacks (not Sun, not Fri or Sat evenings) · Children in eating area and restaurant · No nearby parking · Open 11–3.30, 5.30–10.30 (no weekend extension to 11)

MARKET WEIGHTON   SE8742   Map 8
Londesborough Arms

A1079

The elegant high-ceilinged Regency lounge bar, the Devonshire Room, has an attractively set out cold buffet with pork pie, pâté, good rare beef or honey-baked ham (£2.40–£2.75), fresh salads and maybe a salmon; other good value bar food includes home-made soup (65p), sandwiches (from 65p), ploughman's (£1.65) and hot dishes such as four-egg omelettes (£1.75), haddock or steak and kidney pie (£1.95), winter stews such as navarin of lamb (£1.85–£2) and six-ounce sirloin steak (£2.85 – a week later, and a good deal further south, we found pubs charging £5.15 for precisely this). There are comfortable pink plush chairs on the dark red flowery carpet, tall luxuriously curtained windows looking out over the grassy churchyard, the 1901 Bluemarket Races series of Cecil Aldin prints, and little bunches of flowers on the tables. Well kept North Country Bitter, Original and Mild on handpump, piped background music, friendly service. A smaller more local back bar is named after William Bradley the town's eighteenth-century giant, 7 feet 8 inches tall when he was 19, and there's a small cocktail bar and separate restaurant. *(Recommended by G L Archer)*

North Country · Licensee David Peter Cuckston · Real ale · Meals and snacks Children in Devonshire Room · Open 11–3, 6–11 · Bedrooms tel Market Weighton (0696) 72214; £21B/£32B (with four-poster bed)

MILLINGTON   SE8352   Map 7
Gate
Village signposted from Pocklington

A welcoming and unaffected village pub, with good Wolds walks and remarkable East Riding views from just up the hill. Besides altogether more modern simple furnishings, an antique high-backed winged settle snuggles up to the log fire in the big stone fireplace of the main room, which has black beams supporting the ochre planks of its ceiling, and horse brasses and bits above the serving counter (which also serves a back room which has darts and a pool-table). Plates decorate the beam over an opening through to a rather parlourish second front room, which has a set of antlers above its log fire. Well kept Theakstons Black Bull on handpump and Old Peculier tapped from the cask; good cheap food such as sandwiches (from 65p), basket meals (from £1 for sausages), steak and kidney pie (£1.75, weekends only), gammon (£2.50) and steak (£4.50); if you ring them the day before, for a party of six or more they'll do a roast. Dominoes, fruit machine, space game, may be piped music. *(Recommended by Dorian Lowell, Tim Halstead, Philip Asquith, Jane English, Keith Myers, Paul West)*

Free house · Licensee Alan Moore · Real ale · Meals – tel Pocklington (075 92) 2045 – and snacks · Children welcome · Open 12–2, 7.30–12 all year

NORTH NEWBALD   SE9136   Map 8
Tiger
Village signposted off A1034

This friendly village pub faces a quiet green (it's off the main road) and gently rolling countryside beyond; there are tables by tubs of rhododendrons and geraniums in front. Good bar food includes soup (45p), rolls or sandwiches (from 55p), burgers (from £1.15), savoury pancake rolls (£1.45), grilled sardines (£1.80), salads (from £2.25), stuffed turkey (£2.80) and fillet steak (£4.35). There are popular puddings such as fresh local raspberries or apple pie and cream (50p); also a separate restaurant (with a late supper licence), open Tuesday to Sunday evenings. Keg beers and some good malt whiskies. The main beamed bar has sturdy armed leatherette settles and stools on its

377

carpet, with a fruit machine in a partly panelled communicating area, and easy chairs in another cosy room; maybe gentle piped music; darts and dominoes. *(Recommended by Mrs J P Pearce; more reports please)*

John Smiths (Courage) · Licensee Mrs P M Castle · Meals (not Sun lunchtime or Mon evening) and snacks (not Mon evening) · Children in eating area or restaurant · Open 11–3, 6.30–10.30

SLEDMERE   SE9365   Map 8

Triton

Junction of B1252 and B1253 NW of Great Driffield

This sturdy eighteenth-century inn by the walls of Sledmere House, on an old posting road that strides over fine open rolling country, is a friendly place, with stately high-backed cushioned settles by a blazing winter fire in the attractive traditional lounge bar. Well kept Youngers Scotch on handpump, and bar food such as freshly cut sandwiches (from 60p), sausage (£1.25), pizza or burger (£1.75), cod or steak and kidney pie (£2), chicken (£2.50) and scampi (£2.75). A separate restaurant, simple but comfortable, serves a traditional Sunday lunch (£4.75, children £3). The public bar has darts, dominoes, a fruit machine and a juke box; maybe piped music. *(Recommended by Jon Dewhirst; more reports please)*

Free house · Licensee John Regan · Real ale · Meals and snacks · Children welcome · Live music Fri–Sun · Open 11–2.30, 7–11 all year · Bedrooms tel Driffield (0377) 86644; £10.50/£21

Boot & Shoe, Ellerton

SUTTON UPON DERWENT   SE7047   Map 7

St Vincent Arms ★

B1228 SE of York

In the evenings there's more the feeling of a restaurant than of a pub in the cosy, almost parlourish, panelled front bar of this old-fashioned and civilised place. There's certainly no bias against people just dropping in for a drink – they have a particularly good range of well kept real ales, with a more or less weekly guest beer as well as Theakstons Best and Old Peculier, Tetleys and Youngers IPA and Scotch, on handpump. It's simply that people enjoy the food here so much. This includes sandwiches (from 65p), home-made soup (70p), cockles or mussels (90p), hot smoked mackerel (£1), ploughman's (from £1.20), avocado with prawns (£1.40), ham, beef or prawn salad (from £2.50), eight-ounce burger (£2.90), good home-made steak and kidney pie (£3.10) and eight-ounce sirloin steak (£5.35); they're happy to do plain boiled potatoes instead of the chips that so dominate this part of England, and the choice of wines by the bottle is unusually good for the area. There are traditional high-backed settles and a cushioned seat in the bow window as well as Windsor chairs, brass, copper and a shelf of plates just under the high ceiling, a coal fire and a massive old wireless set; another lounge and separate restaurant open off here, and a games room has pool, a juke box, space game and a fruit machine (there are also darts and dominoes). It's worth booking a table if you want a full meal, especially at weekends. For summer, there are seats in an attractive garden. (*Recommended by Tim Halstead, Roger Bellingham, Philip Asquith, ILP, Keith Myers, Jane English, PLC, Paul West*)

Free house · Licensee Richard Frederick Tyson · Real ale · Meals (restricted Sun lunchtime) and snacks; restaurant tel Elvington (090 485) 349 · Children in eating area · Open 12–2.30, 7–11; closed evening 25 Dec

WELTON   SE9627   Map 8

Green Dragon

Village signposted from A63 just W of Hull outskirts

Comfortably refurbished and extended, this old pub has attractive outside tables, well kept North Country Riding or perhaps Ruddles County real ale, and reasonably priced bar food. A quick service counter offers four or five daily hot specials or cold dishes – including quite a lot of shellfish – with salads, and to order there are sandwiches, soup, ploughman's, children's dishes (£1.50), burgers, scampi, kebabs, steaks and so forth. A separate restaurant (evenings, not Sunday or Monday; supper licence to 11.30) does full meals with main dishes for around £4.50. Fruit machines, maybe piped music; dominoes in the public bar. It's in an attractive area, usefully placed for walkers. And it has a powerful claim on our imagination. Some 250 years ago a man called John Palmer was arrested here for brawling with other customers who didn't like the way he used the hens and ducks on the village green for target practice. It then emerged that he'd stolen a blind old mare and her foal from a local farmer, and while he was in jail he wrote to his brother in Essex asking for help. But the postman there (also the village schoolmaster) recognised the handwriting and as a result 'John Palmer' was unmasked as Dick Turpin, who was eventually hanged in York (primarily, and unglamorously, for sheep-stealing). *(Recommended by Jon Dewhirst, L N Goulding; more reports please)*

North Country · Licensee Frederick Turner · Real ale · Meals and snacks Children in restaurant and top part of lounge · Open 11–3, 6–10.30

Lucky Dip

Besides the fully inspected pubs, you might like to try these Lucky Dips recommended and described by readers (if you do, please send us reports):

BARTON-UPON-HUMBER [TA0322], *Humber Bridge*: fire in pleasant lounge, wide choice of beers, good food in bar and restaurant; conservatory and pleasant garden; bedrooms *(K Mills)*

BEEFORD [TA1354], *Black Swan*: good value food and Tetleys real ale in big pleasant roadside pub with friendly atmosphere; separate games room with pool, space games and pin-ball *(Lee Goulding)*

BEVERLEY [Butcher Row; TA0340], *Angel*: food-orientated pub close to minster, with two smart rooms (back one best when crowded); well kept Bass on handpump; popular with young people *(Lee Goulding)*; [North Bar Within] *Beverley Arms*: comfortable and very well kept THF hotel with choice of several places to eat and good bedrooms, in attractive country town *(G L Archer, Roger Bellingham, ILP, LYM)*; [North Bar Without] *Rose & Crown*: good food in relaxing lounge of spacious pub; bigger back bar with games caters for younger people; good Woods and Darleys beers; convenient for racecourse *(Lee Goulding)*; *Woolpack*: small, cosy and very welcoming pub serving real ale *(Jane English)*

BRANTINGHAM [SE9429], *Triton*: spacious and comfortable modernised pub with well kept Websters real ales, popular buffet in roomy and airy sun-lounge, also restaurant and games bar; sheltered garden with children's play area; near wooded dale *(Lee Goulding, BB)*

BRIDLINGTON [Flamborough Road; TA1867], *Beaconsfield Arms*: Bass pub with comfortable lounge and airy, lively public bar, near promenade *(S B Wrigley, LYM)*; [Fortyfoot] *Seabirds*: good bar food and Sunday lunches in dining-room with friendly service; well kept Camerons Lion and Strongarm *(Andrew Armstrong)*; [Windsor Crescent] *Windsor*: good value bar food and well kept Camerons beers in friendly inn near harbour, with nautical atmosphere and games room; bedrooms *(Lee Goulding)*

BRIGG [TA0007], *King William IV*: neat and friendly homely local with well kept Darleys; welcoming landlord a keen competitor in horse shows *(Jon Dewhirst)*

BROUGHTON [SE9608], *Thatched Cottage*: lovely garden; cosy inside with welcoming landlord; bar food *(KM)*

BURTON AGNES [TA1063], *Blue Bell*: food good, at reasonable prices, in nice comfortable bar *(GMA)*

COTTINGHAM [King Street; TA0633], *Duke of Cumberland*: impressive white pub in big village square, with books in comfortable L-shaped lounge, popular with mainly younger people; Ruddles County; seats outside *(Lee Goulding)*

EPWORTH [Mowbray Street; TA7804] *Mowbray Arms:*, good home-made food in country pub opposite the old rectory (the Wesleys' home), in attractive village *(James Alan Sleight)*

ETTON [SE9843], *Light Dragoon*: wide range of bar food including generous sandwiches, also well kept Youngers real ales, in two roomy comfortable bars with inglenook fireplace; garden with children's play area *(LYM and others)*

FRIDAYTHORPE [SE8759], *Cross Keys*: taken over in 1984 as free house, being renovated by hospitable new owners *(G R Brown)*

HULL [High Street; TA0928], *Black Boy*: small traditional friendly pub with fine panelled downstairs bar, old maps and documents on walls, also bedpan, crossbow and so on; good Tetleys, small upstairs bar; can get crowded *(Lee Goulding)*; [Carr Lane] *King Edward VI*: reasonably priced choice of real ales, usually Darleys, Wards and guest beers; nice upstairs bar *(Lee Goulding)*; [Pier] *Minerva*: well renovated in nautical style, has jovial atmosphere and open fire; brews own good beer; near attractive marina with good views of Humber bridge *(Lee Goulding)*; [Alfred Gelder Street] *White Hart*: food at lunchtime good in civilised and attractively decorated central pub with lots of pictures and friendly bustle; serves North Country Riding and Ruddles County real ales *(Lee Goulding)*

KIRKBURN [SE9855], *Queens Head*: ex-farmhouse with small bar, attractive dining-room with minstrels' gallery in granary, and tasty home-made food *(Dr D E and Mrs E Webster)*

LITTLE DRIFFIELD [TA0158], *Downe Arms*: well kept Camerons real ale; open fire and warm atmosphere *(Andrew Armstrong)*

LOW CATTON [SE7053], *Gold Cup*: good value bar food, also restaurant; cosy atmosphere with high-backed settles and antiques; well kept Tetleys and John Smiths; garden; children welcome *(Lee Goulding)*

NORTH DALTON [SE9352], *Star*: smartly refurbished pub with Tetleys real ales and home-cooked food; charming setting by attractive village pond *(Reports on new management please)*

NORTH NEWBALD [SE9136], *Gnu*: food pleasant and good choice of beer in pub by village green with cheerful local feel *(Doug Kennedy)*

PAULL [Main Street; TA1626], *Humber Tavern*: fine Humber views from welcoming riverside local with well kept Bass, Bass Mild and Stones; good juke box, space games *(Lee Goulding)*; [Main Street] *Royal Oak Hotel*: small, friendly and comfortable pub with interesting local shipping photographs and good river views from terrace; well kept Darleys *(Lee Goulding)*

POCKLINGTON [SE8049], *Feathers*: comfortable and popular open-plan lounge with bar meals and Youngers real ales; children welcome; comfortable motel-style bedrooms *(Lee Goulding, LYM)*

REDBOURNE [Main Street; SK9799], *Red Lion*: popular Bass pub, opposite village green with preserved 1831 fire station, bar food, games bar with pool; bedrooms *(KM)*

SOUTH DALTON [SE9645], *Pipe & Glass*: low rambling old pub with well kept bars and dining-rooms, serving interesting food including home-made duck pie; attractive and spacious lawn *(ILP)*

STAMFORD BRIDGE [SE7155], *Three Cups*: beamed and panelled pub with stained glass; well kept Bass, friendly welcome (pub actually just over river, therefore in Yorkshire)

WALKINGTON [SE9937], *Ferguson Fawsitt Arms*: well run pleasantly mock-Tudor pub with good choice of hot and cold food in airy flagstoned buffet bar, open fires; pool in games bar *(Mr and Mrs N Bailey, LYM)*; *Dog & Duck*: comfortable and friendly village pub with pretty back garden, cheerful local atmosphere, food and well kept Ruddles County *(Lee Goulding)*

Isle of Wight

The Isle of Wight's brewery, Burts, produces very cheap good beer (virtually unobtainable on the mainland – but see our Wheathampstead entry under Hertfordshire), and the island also benefits from sensible licensing hours with frequent late extensions (it's always worth asking about these). Most important, considering its size, it has an unusual number of good pubs to enjoy these things in – and the great majority caters for families. The cheerful and old-fashioned New Inn at Shalfleet stands out for its good seafood: its landlord is an ex-fisherman who still uses his own boat to catch much of it. Other particularly good pubs include the lively Wight Mouse (part of the Clarendon Hotel at Chale – a nice place to stay), which has not-too-obtrusive live music every night, good real ales, reasonably priced bar food, a new family room (and terrace) overlooking the sea, and a splendid collection of malt whiskies; the thatched Fisherman's Cottage, right on the beach under steep Shanklin Chine, which this year has become a proper pub rather than a private club; the Buddle at Niton, especially for its lawn giving marvellous views out over the cliffs of St Catherine's Head; the well run White Lion at Arreton, near the Elizabethan manor which houses the National Wireless Museum; the old thatched Crab in Shanklin, fun inside, with quite a range of straightforward food (including crab, of course); and the friendly Chequers at Rookley, with good value simple food. The no-frills Hole in

Buddle Inn, Niton

the Wall in Ventnor is outstandingly cheap. Among Lucky Dips at the end of the chapter, the Seaview Hotel at Seaview (good seafood in well run small hotel), the picturesque low-beamed Sun at Hulverstone, the White Horse in Whitwell (with a splendid garden), the thatched white Hare & Hounds in Downend and the Sportsmans Rest in the village of Porchfield (simple home cooking; surrounded by National Trust land) all look promising – we'd be specially grateful for reports on these.

ARRETON SZ5486 Map 2
White Lion

A3056 Newport–Sandown

This attractive old white house has a family Cabin Bar – full of old farm tools – in its beer garden, and you can also sit out in front by the tubs of flowers. Inside, the lounge is roomy and relaxed, with brass, horse-harness and some guns on the beams or partly panelled walls of the communicating rooms, and cushioned Windsor chairs on the brown carpet. The smaller, plainer public bar has dominoes, a fruit machine and, in winter, darts. The home-made food includes sandwiches (some with hot fillings such as bacon or sausage), soup, various pâtés, quiche, pies and pasties, chicken and salads and shellfish dishes – prices from around 75p to £3; Whitbreads Strong Country and Flowers Original on tap; piped music. It's close to Elizabethan Arreton Manor (which houses the National Wireless Museum) and the twelfth-century village church. *(Recommended by Steve and Carolyn Harvey, Comus Elliott)*

Whitbreads · Licensees David and Maureen James · Real ale · Snacks · Children in separate room and Cabin Bar · Open 10.30–3, 6–11 (11–3, 7–11 in winter)

BONCHURCH SZ5778 Map 2
Bonchurch Inn

Bonchurch Shute; from A3055 E of Ventnor turn down to Old Bonchurch opposite Leconfield Hotel

Cut partly in to the steep rocks of the Shute, this simple old stone inn – once stables for the nearby manor house – has a relaxed atmosphere. The high-ceilinged and friendly public bar conjures up an image of salvaged shipwrecks: its floor is of narrow-planked ship's decking, and there are folding chairs of the sort that old-fashioned steamers used to have and a solid-fuel stove in one corner. Darts, bar billiards and dominoes in here; there's also a smaller saloon. Bar food consists of sandwiches (75p–95p for crab: toasties 10p extra), home-made minestrone soup in winter (85p), beefburger and pizza (£1.50), ploughman's with a choice of Cheddar or pâté (£1.50), antipasto with meats, prawns and pâté (£1.80), seafood risotto or lasagne (£2.30), scampi (£2.50), chicken stuffed with cream cheese and mushrooms (£2.95) and a wide choice of salads such as cheese, home-cooked meats or crab; there's also a separate restaurant (closed Sunday and Monday). Flowers Original and Whitbreads Strong Country tapped from the cask. Across the cobbled courtyard another converted stable, with a splendid arched entrance, is now a café. *(Recommended by Steve and Carolyn Harvey; more reports please)*

Whitbreads · Licensee Ulisse Besozzi · Real ale · Meals and snacks · Children in room partly set aside for them · Piano Weds, winter only · Open 11–2.30, 7–11 all year · Bedrooms tel Ventnor (0938) 852611; £11/£22

CHALE   SZ4877 Map 2

Clarendon/Wight Mouse ★

In village; B3399, off A3055

The attractive and well run small Clarendon Hotel has a lively, separate bar, the Wight Mouse; this has live music on every night of the year except Christmas night: Country and Western on Tuesday and Saturday (and Sunday lunchtime), jazz trio with guest musicians, often impromptu (Sunday, Monday and Thursday), and singer-guitarists (Wednesday and Friday). The licensees are keen that the music is soft-pedalled to the extent that it doesn't interfere with talking. A new family room and second beer garden have just been completed, both overlooking the sea. The bar has two main areas connected by a narrower part along the serving counter, and is simply but comfortably furnished. The food is home cooked and locally produced and comes in generous helpings: sandwiches (from 70p, hot bacon 90p, fresh crab £1.45 and a giant Clarendon salad sandwich with meat £1.50), soup (95p), ploughman's (from £1.25), salads (from £1.90), ham and eggs (£1.95), burgers (four-ounce from £1.90, eight-ounce from £2.40), chicken (£2.10), pizzas (from £2.30), wiener Schnitzel (£2.85), scampi (£2.75), crab, prawns, cockles, mussels and clams with salad (£3.95), mixed grill (£4.15) and steaks (from eight-ounce rump, £5.50). An excellent collection of around 150 malt whiskies is backed up by uncommon brandies, madeiras and country wines, and well kept Burts VPA, Flowers Original and Whitbreads Strong Country on handpump. Darts at one end, fruit machine, piped music; an adjoining games room has pool, shove-ha'penny, a space game and a juke box. Booking is recommended for the separate hotel restaurant, attractively decorated with pleasing watercolours. Picnic-table sets on a side lawn, with many more on the big back lawn looking over the fields to the sea. *(Recommended by Steve and Carolyn Harvey, Comus Elliott)*

Free house · Licensees John and Jean Bradshaw · Real ale · Meals and snacks Children welcome · Live music every night and Sun lunchtime · Open 11–3, 6–11 all year – Bedrooms and restaurant tel Niton (0983) 730431; £16/£32 (£36B)

NITON   SZ5076 Map 2

Buddle   *[illustrated on page 382]*

From A3055 in extreme S of island, take village road towards coast

This old smugglers' house has an attractive garden with tables spread over the sloping lawn and more on stone terraces which look over the cliffs and St Catherine's lighthouse: at night you can watch its beam sweeping round the sea far below you. Closer at hand, there's a model of the lighthouse in the middle of the garden, with a great fortress made partly of clipped dwarf juniper. Inside, there are flagstones, beams, stripped deal panelling and two log fires. Bar food includes sandwiches (80p–£1.50, fresh crab £1.40), ploughman's (£1.40), an unusual seafood pâté (£1.50), various dishes with chips (around £2.50–£3); and at lunchtime home-made steak and kidney pie or pudding (£3), fresh roasts (from £3) and various desserts (75p). Along one side of the lawn, and helping to shelter it, is a Smugglers' Barn cafeteria. A fruit machine, juke box, space game, and sometimes piped music. *(Recommended by Roy McIsaac, Steve and Carolyn Harvey, Comus Elliott)*

Whitbreads · Licensee Gilbert Bailey · Meals and snacks · Children in Smugglers' Barn and eating area · Open 10.30–2.30, 6–11 all year (opens 7 in winter)

ROOKLEY   SZ5084   Map 2
Chequers
Niton Road; signposted S of village

There's a useful choice here between the lively flagstoned public bar with its good juke box, sensibly placed darts, bar billiards, dominoes, cribbage and space game, and the friendly carpeted lounge which is unusually comfortable, with a group of easy chairs and settees down at one end by the glowing winter log fire, as well as more usual furniture, and is decorated with cottagey ornaments; there is also a fruit machine. It is popular with young people, and as it's quite out of the way it tends on summer evenings to have a more villagey atmosphere than many of the island's pubs. Bar food includes sandwiches cut to order (from 60p), ploughman's (from £1.20), giant sausage (£1.55), salads (from £1.60), baked potatoes with a choice of fillings and served with salads (from £1.65), plaice or scampi (£2.40), honey-roast ham and egg (£2.75), seafood specials (£3.75), steaks (from £5.25) and daily hot specials; Whitbreads Strong Country and Pompey Royal on handpump. There is a small separate olde-worlde restaurant. The garden has picnic-table sets, with a swing ball, badminton, swings and a playhut for children. *(Recommended by Comus Elliott; more reports please)*

Whitbreads · Licensee Keith Garnham · Real ale · Meals and snacks · Children in restaurant or area partly set aside for them · Open 11–3, 7–11 all year (with midnight supper licence)

SHALFLEET   SZ4189   Map 2
New Inn ★
A3054 Newport–Yarmouth

The good beer and food, especially fish and seafood, continue to entice readers across from the mainland to this cheerful and friendly old pub. The landlord was a working fisherman before he took over here, and still uses his own small trawler and lobster boat to supply much of his food, which – depending on what's been caught locally – might include prawns (£1 a half-pint), moules marinière (£2), prawn curry (£2.95), poacher's pie (£3.50), Dover sole, cod, plaice, bass and fresh crab and lobster when available; in winter there are live mussels and oysters. The food's not all fish, of course, and as well as a daily changing blackboard menu (the soups, particularly the mushroom, are very popular) there are sandwiches to order (from 60p), five different ploughman's (from £1.20), lasagne or chilli con carne (£2.50) and a large selection of fresh salads. The public bar has partly panelled walls and boarded ceiling, scrubbed deal tables on the flagstones, Windsor chairs and a cushioned built-in settle, and on cold days a roaring log fire in the big stone hearth, which has guns and an aleyard hanging above it. In winter the beamed lounge bar, with its stone walls, Windsor chairs and wall banquettes around small tables, becomes a fish restaurant. Well kept Flowers Original and Whitbreads Strong Country and Pompey Royal tapped from the cask, also guest bitters and traditional cider. There are rustic tables outside by the road. *(Recommended by Aileen Hall, Steve and Carolyn Harvey, B R Shiner and others)*

Whitbreads · Licensees Brenda and Nigel Simpson · Real ale · Meals – tel Calbourne (098 378) 314 – and snacks · Children in eating area · Open 11–3, 6–11 all year

SHANKLIN   SZ5881 Map 2
Crab

High Street, Old Town; on A3055 leaving centre for Ventnor

There are tables on a sunny terrace in front of this pretty, old thatched pub, and inside quite a good range of food such as sandwiches (from 65p, fresh crab £1.30), ploughman's (from £1.10), basket meals such as three sausages with chips (£1.15), home-made cottage pie (£1.30), fisherman's pie (£1.50), crab Mornay (£2.30) and hot daily specials, and salads (from £2.50, fresh crab £3.50). In summer a shellfish bar sells cockles, mussels, prawns and so forth. Well kept Whitbreads Strong Country and Pompey Royal are served. The rambling low-beamed bar, partly panelled, is softly lit, with an aquarium, yachting pictures and lots of heraldic shields; there are steps up to an area like part of a sailing ship, with curved wooden sides and a skylight hold-hatch in its deck-planked ceiling. Darts, pool, dominoes, cribbage, a fruit machine, space game, and a juke box or piped music. *(Recommended by Roy McIsaac, Lesley Foote, Alan Carter)*

Whitbreads · Licensee George William Moore · Real ale · Meals and snacks Children in games room and (to 8.30) cocktail bar · Open 10.30–3, 6–11 all year

Fisherman's Cottage

At bottom of Shanklin Chine

This marvellously placed thatched cottage was squeezed into earlier editions of the *Guide* as a bit of a cheat – it was hardly eligible as it was a club. But now our conscience is clear, as it has re-opened as a genuine pub. Its position is almost irresistible – alone on a pebbly beach, with a precipitous path zigzagging down the picturesque Chine (but you can also drive down). The new owners have added another bar, and the low-beamed rooms, with flagstone floors and stripped stone walls, are now prettily decorated with fresh flowers. Food comprises sandwiches (70p–£1 for crab), burgers (90p), ploughman's (from £1.10), sausages (£1.15), kipper pâté (£1.25), Malaysian chicken (£1.50), fresh plaice (£1.65) and a range of salads (from £2.50). Real ales include John Smiths and Courage Best; cocktails too. You can sit outside on a terrace which runs straight into the beach. *(More reports please)*

Free house · Licensee Miss A P P Macpherson · Meals and snacks · Open 11–3, 7–12 all year

VENTNOR SZ5677 Map 2
Hole in the Wall

Market Street; opposite main central car park

This quaintly squint-walled old pub's two bars serve one of the cheapest pints in Britain – the local Burts VPA, kept under top pressure. Food is good value too: filled rolls (from 35p, a Hole special 50p), toasted sandwiches (from 50p), ploughman's (£1) and a range of hot dishes such as pizza (50p), steak and kidney pie (65p), egg and chips (£1, with a sausage as well £1.30), shepherd's pie (£1.10), chicken or cod (£1.60) and scampi (£2.10); salads (from £1.10). There are plain settles and chairs on the lino floor in the partly panelled split-level public bar with sloping ochre ceiling boards. It has darts, pool, cribbage, a fruit machine, a space game, a juke box and maybe piped music. The small saloon bar is more comfortable, and by the courtyard garden (where there are tables) they keep their Barn Bar family room open throughout the year. *(Recommended by Steve and Carolyn Harvey, Comus Elliott, Bryan Shiner, Alan Carter, Lesley Foote)*

Burts · Licensees Ted and Gayle Parsons · Snacks and meals (lunchtime) Children in Barn Bar family room · Open 11–3, 6–11 all year

Mill Bay

Esplanade

Big bay windows look over the shore road straight out to sea and the pier, and the light and airy décor and comfortable leatherette armchairs around the small tables make this a pleasant place to enjoy the well kept Burts Best or Mild, on handpump at attractive prices. Sandwiches; sensibly placed darts, fruit machine and space game in a side room. The pub has a pretty fairy-lit upper balcony. *(Recommended by Comus Elliott; more reports please)*

Burts · Real ale · Snacks · Open 11–2.30, 7–11 all year

YARMOUTH SZ3589 Map 2
Bugle

St James' Square

The street façade of this seventeenth-century hotel is very striking, and the abundant woodwork throughout gives a nautical feeling that's thoroughly appropriate to this yachting town – particularly in the comfortable and aptly named Galleon Bar. The serving counter looks like the stern of a galleon, and there are captain's chairs, black plank walls and ceiling with a few burgees hung below it, pictures of ship and marine designs and a giant photograph of the harbour making up an entire side wall. Bar food includes filled rolls, fresh vegetable soup (80p), sandwiches (90p–£1.25 for crab), ploughman's (from £1.25), half a pint of prawns (£1.35), plaice in fresh breadcrumbs (£1.90), pan-fried trout or home-made moussaka (£1.95) and a Sunday roast loin of pork (£2.75); home-made puddings such as apple crumble or chocolate pudding (65p). Whitbreads Strong Country on handpump; fruit machine, maybe piped music, and in winter a Sunday evening pub quiz league. There is a separate restaurant, and a sizeable garden. The hotel is close to the pier and the Tudor castle. (Recommended by Comus Elliott; more reports please)

Whitbreads · Licensees Horst Gritsch and Paul McKillop · Real ale · Snacks (lunchtime) · Children in restaurant · Open 10.30–2.30, 6–11 all year Bedrooms tel Isle of Wight (0983) 760272; £16.50 (£18B)/£33 (£36B)

Lucky Dip

Besides the fully inspected pubs, you might like to try these Lucky Dips recommended and described by readers (if you do, please send us reports):

CHALE GREEN [SZ4879], *Star*: cheerful flagstoned village pub with darts, pool-room, fruit machine and piped music *(Steve and Carolyn Harvey, BB)*

COWES [Folly Lane, East Cowes; SZ4896], *Folly*: big windows overlooking water in comfortably modernised pub popular with local businessmen; tables on waterside terrace *(Peter Barrett, LYM)*

DOWNEND [SZ5387], *Hare & Hounds*: whitewashed thatched pub of some character, with Burts beer *(Steve and Carolyn Harvey)*

FRESHWATER BAY [SZ3484], *Starkes*: spacious comfortable lounge and bistro in old stone pub *(BB)*

HULVERSTONE [SZ4083],*Sun*: picturesque, with low beams, and Whitbreads straight from the cask; busy in high season, quiet and friendly out of season *(C M Harnor)*

NITON [SZ5076], *White Lion*: cheerful village atmosphere in well run local with good beer; entertainment, children's room *(Comus Elliott)*

PORCHFIELD [SZ4491], *Sportsmans Rest*: modest but interesting choice of food, well kept Flowers and Whitbreads real ales, hunting theme; games bar, terrace, children's room opening on to play area *(Steve and Carolyn Harvey)*

SEAVIEW [SZ6291], *Seaview Hotel*: small well run hotel with nautical lounge bar, more rustic back bar, Burts and other beers, extensive choice of food – especially seafood including good value lobster; bedrooms *(Steve and Carolyn Harvey, PJS)*

SHANKLIN [SZ5881], *Chine*: quiet old-fashioned pub with good cheap Burts beer in lovely spot – a bit of a climb *(Comus Elliott)*

SHOREWELL [SZ4582], *Crown*: fine pub with good food and garden; has been undergoing internal alterations *(Comus Elliott)*

VENTNOR [SZ5677], *Walmer Castle*: friendly one-roomed backstreet local with very cheap Burts beer *(Comus Elliott)*

WHITWELL [SZ5277], *White Horse*: well kept and friendly thatched village pub

with good children's room, goats in garden and attractive surroundings
(Dr A K Clarke, Comus Elliott)
WOOTTON BRIDGE [SZ5492], *Sloop*: fine position overlooking boats; good food and atmosphere *(Comus Elliott)*
WROXALL [SZ5579], *Star*: very cheap Burts real ale and bar food (not winter evenings Sunday to Tuesday) in simple lounge and bar; rebuilt in 1981 after fire *(W B Goldring, Steve and Carolyn Harvey)*

Kent

Changes here since last year's edition include new licensees at several pubs: the aptly named Little Gem in Aylesford (they're keeping its extensive range of real ales), the handsome old Rose & Crown in Brenchley (refurbished bedrooms now; a wide choice of real ales, and concentration on home cooking); the beautifully placed White Horse in Chilham; and the Tickled Trout in Wye (lovely riverside lawn, now popular for reliable straightforward food and service). The idyllic Dove in Dargate, carefully refurbished, gains a star award this year for its garden, reliable simple food, and warm welcome. For food, places that stand out include the snug little King William IV in Benenden, the rambling Three Chimneys near Biddenden (the county's nicest pub, with a smashing garden), the Gate at Hildenborough (more praise than ever this year for its seafood), the stately and ancient George & Dragon at Speldhurst (owned by the father of the Gate's licensee), and the Carpenters Arms in Eastling — all these are really nice pubs. On a simpler level, the food served by the Cock at Ide

The White Horse, Chilham

Hill and the interesting Black Pig at Staple have been gaining ground in readers' affections, and quite a lot of pubs here now do summer barbecues. Pubs in Kent often stand out for their character – unusual old buildings, sometimes interestingly furnished: the Wheatsheaf at Bough Beech (a high-raftered medieval hunting-lodge); fifteenth-century pilgrims' inns such as the Flying Horse on the cricket green at Boughton Lees or the friendly Bull at Wrotham; the recently refurbished Leather Bottle at Cobham (much as it was when Dickens admired it – they now play bat and trap here, as they do, under the critical eye of an outspoken parrot, at the Stanhope Arms in Brasted); the Ship at Conyer Quay (a jolly, nautical pub with quizzes, lots of traditional games, and secondhand paperbacks on sale for charity); the Mounted Rifleman in the orchards at Luddenham (an unspoilt throwback to some 50 years ago); the Bell near Smarden (a delightful small-roomed country inn with a fine atmosphere); and the charmingly idiosyncratic Compasses up on the Downs at Sole Street. Most of these are in attractive surroundings, and other particularly well placed pubs are the civilised old Castle in the National Trust village of Chiddingstone, the Spotted Dog with its marvellous views over Penshurst and far beyond, and the Golding Hop with its steep sun-trap lawn near Plaxtol. Drinks prices are in general slightly on the high side of the national average; we found them rather low for the county at the King William IV in Benenden and Mounted Rifleman in Luddenham. Among Lucky Dip entries at the end of the chapter, ones that look specially promising include the Woolpack at Brookland (a lovely old Romney Marsh pub), Toastmasters in Burham (interesting, with lots of real ales), two pubs in Elham – the Palm Tree (choice of real ales, goats and other animals in its big garden) and Rose & Crown (food, also character), Shipwrights Arms on its isolated creek near Faversham, Gun & Spitroast in Horsmonden (daily spit-roasts and other appetising food), Plough near Ivy Hatch (old-fashioned with good food and beer), homely Black Bull in Newchurch (food and drink recommended), Leicester Arms in Penshurst (tasty food in a fine old building), isolated unspoilt Ringlestone Inn, Coastguard at St Margarets Bay (lovely sea views), George at Trottiscliffe (home cooking), La Galoche Bar in Tunbridge Wells (fine wine and food), ancient Yew Tree in Westbere and Three Post Boys in Wrotham (delightful seventeenth-century inn).

ALDINGTON TR0736 Map 3
Walnut Tree

This old smugglers' pub, dating back some 650 years, is included for the charm of its back 'kitchen bar'; there's a wood-burning stove and the original side bread oven, a brick floor and above this what must have been a very cosy cupboard bedroom reached by ladder. The public bar is popular with locals, with sensibly placed darts, shove-ha'penny, dominoes, cribbage and a fruit machine, and a comfortable saloon bar; maybe piped music. Home-made food includes sandwiches, ploughman's and hot dishes from cottage pie through mussels or prawns in garlic butter to scampi and steaks; summer barbecues also, and a separate restaurant. Shepherd Neame Bitter, Best and Mild on handpump, and in winter Stock Ale. There are tables in a sheltered garden, with a pool. *(Recommended by Duncan Hallows; more reports please)*

Shepherd Neame · Licensee Ray Brewer · Real ale · Meals and snacks Children in eating area of bar · Open 10–2.30, 6–11 all year

AYLESFORD   TQ7359   Map 3
Little Gem   [*illustrated on page 409*]

3 miles from M2 junction 3; A229 towards Maidstone, then first right turn, following signposts to village. Also 1¾ miles from M20 junction 6; A229 towards Maidstone, then follow Aylesford signpost; 19 High Street

The chief attraction at this quaint little pub dating back nearly 900 years is its good choice of real ales, on handpump or tapped from the cask: Bass, Everards Old Original, Goachers, Greene King Abbot, Marstons Owd Rodger, Ruddles County, Sam Smiths, Theakstons Old Peculier, Wadworths 6X, Youngs special and one guest each week. Since our last edition new licensees have taken over this tiny place, but happily they want to keep things as they are. Dimly lit and heavily timbered, it has a friendly and cosy atmosphere, especially in winter when there's a big open fire. It has an unusual high pitched ceiling following the line of the roof, but there's much less headroom at the back by the bar counter because of the very low beams supporting a small gallery overhead: it seems rather appropriate that the stools on the Turkey carpet down here are unusually low, with gnarled and twisted legs. Bar food includes various pasties, sausage rolls and Scotch eggs (40p–70p), sandwiches (65p), steak and kidney and other pies (65p), soup (70p), ploughman's (Cheddar 90p, Stilton £1.05), pâté (£1), a piece of sausage and hot bread (£1), and their special plate of mixed meats (£1.60). *Recommended by Carol Turney, Ian Simister, Peter Hitchcock; up-to-date reports on the new regime please)*

Free house · Licensee Robin Brenchley · Real ale · Snacks · Open 10–2.30, 6–11 all year

BENENDEN   TQ8033   Map 3
King William IV

B2086

The food in this low-ceilinged village tavern is warmly praised: although it changes day by day you can find dishes like crab croquettes with garlic mayonnaise, or stuffed tomatoes provençale (£1.65), French onion tart served with salad and new potatoes

(£2.25), queen scallops gratinées, pasta Mediterranean and beef Stroganoff (all £2.95) or red wine casserole and Raffles lamb and mango curry (£3.45). The fresh and herby duck liver pâté is delicious; note that when they mention garlic they really mean it. Even simpler snacks like toasted cheese and ham sandwiches are well made, and fresh warm bread is served with good-sized lumps of butter with the ploughman's; well kept Shepherd Neame and Mild, and an English wine from Queen Court by the glass as well as some decent French and German ones. You can buy free-range eggs cheaply here. The furnishings are carefully unsophisticated – an open fire in the restored inglenook fireplace, cushioned shiny pews, kitchen chairs and half a dozen plain oak and elm tables with flowers on them (at the weekend you have to get there early if you want a place). The public bar has sensibly placed darts, dominoes, a juke box and a fruit machine. You can sit out on the small but sheltered side lawn. (*Recommended by Philip Denison, Rita Davies, Margaret Sargent, B O B*)

Shepherd Neame · Licensee Nigel Douglas · Real ale · Meals and snacks (not Sun, or Mon and Tues evenings) · Open 11.30–2.30, 6–11 all year; closed 25 Dec

BENOVER TQ7048 Map 3
Woolpack

B2162

There's a rustic feel to this pretty tile-hung building, with black ceiling beams and simple panelling, brick floor under the carpets, an old fireplace, and farm tools hanging over the upholstered wall benches. Food includes sandwiches (from 70p), ploughman's (£1.20), hot dishes such as pizza (£1.20), cottage pie (£2), chilli con carne (£2.25), basket meals (£2.30) or rump steak (£4.20). There's a big lawn behind, with barbecues on Wednesday and Saturday evenings in summer. Well-kept Shepherd Neame Bitter, and Mild on handpump, with Stock Ale in the winter; piped music. The public bar at the back has darts, pool, cribbage and, like the front bar, an open fire in winter. (*More reports please*)

Shepherd Neame · Licensee L H Orton · Real ale · Meals (evening) and snacks (not Mon evening) · Children in family room or pool-room · Open 11–2.30, 6–11 all year

nr BIDDENDEN TQ8538 Map 3
Three Chimneys ★ ★

A262, 1 mile W of village

This beautiful and well kept country pub serves good food in the series of very small and traditionally furnished rooms, partly candlelit at night, which radiate from its central bar counter. There are good fires in winter. The food, often using original recipes, changes all the time and includes a choice of at least four starters, four main courses and four puddings. The starters might include leek and potato or mushroom soup (£1.10), Stilton quiche (£1.30), courgettes au gratin (£1.40), cucumber and prawn mousse (£1.55) and hot crab or salmon and egg (£1.65); for main courses a choice of quiches such as tuna and mushroom, prawn and mushroom, Lorraine or asparagus (£2.75), celery and ham Mornay (£3.30), stuffed green peppers, home-baked ham or savoury meat pie (£3.45), sherried kidneys (£3.50), beef or lamb casserole (£3.65), Chimneys fish dish (£3.75) and game pie or chicken breast in wine and mushroom sauce (£3.95); puddings might be almost anything, such as date and walnut pudding, pineapple soufflé or Bakewell tart (£1.10), fresh orange cheesecake, sherry trifle or lemon and ginger flan (£1.20) and chocolate crunch, fresh fruit Pavlovas and hazelnut meringues (£1.25). A very interesting range of real ales is tapped from casks behind the bar counter: Adnams Best, Fremlins, Goachers (from Maidstone), Godsons Black Horse, Harveys Best and Marstons Pedigree; in winter Harveys Old Ale. The simple, more spacious public bar has darts, shove-ha'penny, dominoes and cribbage. Besides the main bars, which can get very full, there is a useful overspill Garden Room, popular for families, where you can book tables; as this part isn't licensed you have to carry your drinks in from the main bar. There is a charming garden, with tables well spread out along the lawn among herbaceous borders, shrubs and shrub roses. It is just down the road from Sissinghurst. *(Recommended by Gordon and Daphne, Stephen Hayes, A L Crowland, Alan Franck, Mr and Mrs G Turner, Philip Denison, Mrs Heather Sharland, Peter Hitchcock, S J Barker, Peter Holmes, Patrick Stapley, Richard Gibbs)*

Free house · Licensees C F W Sayers and G A Sheepwash · Real ale · Meals and snacks; Garden Room reservations tel Biddenden (0580) 291472 · Children in Garden Room · Open 11–2.30, 6–11; closed 25–26 Dec

BOUGH BEECH   TQ4846   Map 3

Wheatsheaf   [*illustrated on page 403*]

B2027, S of reservoir

This handsome old pub, part tile-hung and part clad with weatherboarding and roses, has a pretty sheltered lawn with flowerbeds, fruit-trees, roses and flowering shrubs. The smart main bar, thought to have been a fifteenth-century royal hunting lodge, is unusually high-ceilinged with lofty timbers and a massive stone fireplace. A couple of lower rooms lead off, furnished attractively with Windsor chairs and older seats, and decorated with various curios such as swordfish spears, buffalo horns and stuffed armadillos. Bar food includes freshly cut sandwiches (from 60p, toasties 5p extra), soup (75p), home-made pâté (85p), jumbo sausage (£1.10), omelettes (from £1.15), ploughman's (from £1.35), home-cooked ham with egg and chips (£2), salads with home-cooked meats (£2.25), deep-fried seafood platter (£2.45) and steaks (£5.25); also home-made puddings and ice creams (from 60p). Well kept Fremlins and Flowers on handpump; sensibly placed darts, shove-ha'penny, dominoes, cribbage, a fruit machine, and maybe piped music. *(More reports please)*

Fremlins (Whitbreads) · Licensees Ron and Barbara Smith · Real ale · Meals (lunchtime, not Sun) and snacks (not Weds or Sun evenings) · Children in eating area · Open 10–2.30, 6–11

BOUGHTON LEES   TR0247   Map 3

Flying Horse

This fifteenth-century village inn, facing a broad cricket green, is on
the ancient Pilgrims' Way to Canterbury and was probably built for
the 'pilgrim traffic'. There's lots of standing space by the neat lines of
upholstered modern wall benches and tables in the friendly and
comfortable open-plan bar; there may be piped music. Further inside,
its age shows handsomely in the shiny old black panelling, as it does
in the attractively arched windows. Food ranges from sandwiches,
plain or toasted (65p to £1.60), to salads, pizzas and home-made
pies, puddings or roasts (£2.50); weekend barbecues are popular with
families. Courage Best and Directors on handpump. You can sit in
the rose garden, and the clean and comfortable bedrooms are good
value. *(Recommended by Robert Anderson; more reports please)*

*Courage · Licensee Leonard Nolan · Real ale · Meals and snacks · Children in
unused restaurant · Open 11–2.30, 6–11 · Bedrooms tel Ashford
(0233) 20914; £10 (£15S)/£17 (£20S)*

BRASTED   TQ4654   Map 3

Stanhope Arms

Church Road; turn off A25 beside the Bull

This unpretentious village pub has three big bay windows
overlooking its small secluded lawn where there are picnic-table sets
among the roses and lilacs; here, the pub's Red-fronted Amazon
parrot sits in state on one of the tables beside the bat and trap pitch.
Inside it's friendly and simply furnished, with darts, shove-ha'penny,
dominoes, cribbage, a fruit machine, space game and juke box or
piped music. Bar food includes sandwiches (from 65p, £1.20 for
prawn), soup (75p), ploughman's (£1.10), home-made dishes such as
quiche, lasagne and steak and kidney pie (£1.50–£2.50), and steaks ·
(£3.50–£5.50); well kept Friary Meux on handpump. *(Recommended
by Julie Lewis; more reports please)*

*Friary Meux (Ind Coope) · Licensee Robert Vaughan · Real ale · Meals and
snacks (not Sun, not Mon evening) · Children in eating area · Open 11–2.30,
6–10.30*

BRENCHLEY   TQ6741   Map 3

Rose & Crown

Already an inn 300 years ago, this pretty tiled building has sturdy
timbers adorned with elaborate wrought iron and sparkling brass.
The new licensees have refurbished the bedrooms, and the well kept
lounge bar, with its comfortably upholstered seats and neatly
polished rustic tables, is as good as ever. Home-made bar food
includes soup (80p), pasty (75p), freshly cut sandwiches,
ploughman's with Cheddar, Stilton or pâté (£1.50), salads – the ham
is home cooked – (from £1.95), home-made pies (£2.45), scampi
(£2.65), and a choice of puddings (£1.25); there is also a separate
restaurant with a six-course meal on Wednesday to Saturday

evenings (£9.95). Well kept Badger Best, Bass, Charringtons IPA, Fremlins, Harveys and Shepherd Neame Bitter on handpump; background music; a separate room has shove-ha'penny, dominoes, cribbage and a space game. There are tables on a paved side terrace, with a play area for children. In one of the bedrooms there is a four-poster, where you can have a champagne breakfast *(Up-to-date reports on the new regime please)*

Free house · Licensees Michael Watson and Peter Selig · Real ale · Meals (not Sun or Mon evenings) and snacks · Children in restaurant and cellar area (nicer than it sounds) · Open 11–2, 6–11 all year · Bedrooms tel Brenchley (089 272) 2107; £24B/£32B

CHIDDINGSTONE   TQ4944   Map 3
Castle

This tile-hung building, some 600 years old, has been an inn since 1730 and, like the rest of this beautiful village of timbered buildings, is owned by the National Trust. The beamed bar has been neatly modernised, with well made settles forming booths around the tables on its partly carpeted oak floor, cushioned sturdy wall benches, latticed windows, and an attractive mullioned window seat in one small alcove. Popular bar food includes home-made soup (90p), baked potatoes with various fillings (95p, and sometimes special fillings such as seafood £1.50), sandwiches (beef or ham £1.35, smoked salmon £2.05), local sausages with a baked potato (£1.60), submarines (huge chunks of French bread stuffed with meats or cheese and salads £1.65), ploughman's (from £1.65), home-made pâté (£1.85), beef and vegetable curry or chilli con carne (£2.35), hot king prawns with garlic mayonnaise (£2.75) and salads such as prawn, beef or ham (£3.45) and smoked salmon (£3.95); there is also a separate restaurant. Throughout the summer there are barbecue grills in a back building: giant sausages, beefburgers, chicken and kebabs (£3.50–£12.25 for beef fillet fondue for two, with starters such as corn on the cob, melon or smoked mackerel included in the prices). Well kept King & Barnes, Shepherd Neame Bitter and Best and Youngs Special on handpump, with quite a number of wines by the bottle; the public bar has darts, shove-ha'penny, dominoes and cribbage. The garden behind is pretty, with a small pool and fountain set in a rockery, and tables on a back brick terrace and the neat lawn surrounded by shrubs. There's a legend that a sandstone block behind the schoolhouse was the 'Chiding Stone' to which scolding wives were tied, though it is no longer thought that that is how the village got its name. *(Recommended by Hazel Morgan, Simon Small, A G Thompson, Patrick Stapley, RAB)*

Free house · Licensees Joseph and Nigel Lucas · Real ale · Meals and snacks Children in eating area · Open 10–2.30, 6–11

CHILHAM   TR0753   Map 3
White Horse   [illustrated on page 390]

This pub's very special feature is its position in the prettiest village square in Kent: a couple of white tables out on the corner give a perfect view of the timber-framed Tudor houses. Inside, the comfortably modernised open-plan lounge bar which spreads around the neat central servery has a massive fireplace with the Lancastrian rose carved at the end of its mantelbeam – a relic of the Wars of the Roses, uncovered only in 1966 during refurbishments. The handsomely carved ceiling beams are as old, and there's a theory that two skeletons found under the floor were victims of a skirmish in the fourteenth-century Peasants' Revolt. Bar food includes sandwiches (90p–£1.20 for prawn), ploughman's (Cheddar £1.50, Stilton or pâté £1.60) and daily dishes such as cottage pie, moussaka or home-style potatoes and sausage (from £1.85); the new licensees here have started doing weekend specials such as gammon, kebabs or local trout stuffed with prawn sauce (from £3.25). Fremlins on handpump; sensibly placed darts, and dominoes, cribbage, and a space game; there may be piped music. The grand park of nearby Chilham Castle makes a good outing, particularly on one of its special days (jousting, falconry and so on). *(Recommended by Susan Grossman; up-to-date reports on the new regime please)*

Whitbreads · Licensees Malcolm and Lesley Buck · Real ale · Meals and snacks Open 10.30–2.30, 6–11

CHIPSTEAD   TQ4956   Map 3
George & Dragon

39 High Street

The furnishings in this attractive old painted brick house, though modern, do tone in with the heavy black beams (some of them nicely

The Cock, Ide Hill

carved), the Windsor chairs and oak tables on the flowery carpet and the black upright timbers which prop the brown ceiling of this friendly open-plan bar. Food includes sandwiches (60p for egg and cress to £1.20 for prawn), salads (£1.70–£2.90) and at lunchtime soup (55p), pâté (90p), sausage and chips (95p), quiche (£1.10), ploughman's (from £1.20), Cornish pasty with chips and peas (£1.50), seafood platter (£1.90), plaice (£2.25), gammon steak (£3) and steaks (from £5.50); in the evening, pizzas (75p–£1.35), beefburgers (from £1), and golden turkey fillets (£1.90) are added, but no steaks then. Well kept Courage Best and Directors on handpump, and wines on tap; dominoes, cribbage, maybe piped music. There are tables on neatly kept grass, beside roses and tall trees, behind the car park. (Recommended by Mrs S Brooks, D P Stevens; more reports please)

Courage · Licensee David Gerring · Real ale · Meals and snacks (not Sun) Open 10–2.30, 6–10.30

COBHAM   TQ6768   Map 3
Leather Bottle
2½ miles from M2 junction 1; village signposted from A2 (towards London) on B2009

The Dickens connection is very strong in this ancient half-timbered house, as he often used to end up here after strolling through the splendid park of Cobham Hall and mentions it fondly in *Pickwick Papers* as 'clean and commodious'. The staff wear period costume to match what you see in the interesting and extensive collection of prints of Dickens' characters, including early postcards and teacards. The spacious open-plan bar of this inn, dating from 1650, serves food that includes sandwiches (beef or cheese £1), ploughman's (£2), Scotch egg (£2), quiche Lorraine (£2.25), scampi or beef, kidney and mushroom pie (£3.50) and other daily dishes; Trumans Bitter, Best and Sampson, and Websters Yorkshire. There's a separate restaurant in the older front part, with its timbered walls crowded with old Dickensian prints. Bedrooms include honeymoon suites with four-posters. Tables, and a bat and trap pitch, are laid out on a sizeable back lawn, and in the orchard at the bottom there's an outdoor summer tuck-shop; afternoon teas served, too. Besides Cobham Park, the village itself is pretty, with medieval almshouses, and outstanding brasses in the church. (Recommended by Tim Halstead, Capt S E Watson, Capt P Watson)

Trumans (Watneys) · Licensee R J R Bailey · Real ale · Meals and snacks (not Mon, Tues, Sat or Sun evenings) · Children in eating area or restaurant · Open 11–2.30, 6–11 all year · Bedrooms tel Meopham (0474) 814327; £16/£26 (£36B)

CONYER QUAY   TQ9665   Map 3
Ship ★
This snug, small-roomed pub on the edge of a creek packed with small boats has a relaxed nautical atmosphere and décor to match: wall boards, a planked ceiling, and bare boards under the rugs with

various nautical nick-nacks and a notice-board with boating advertisements. Bar food includes a good choice of sandwiches (from 50p), filled baps or long rolls (from 70p) and toasted sandwiches (from 90p), with hot pies (from 85p), burgers (from £1), filled double baked potatoes (from £1.60), triple decker sandwiches (ham £1.55, steak £1.65) and ploughman's (£1.65). There is also a wide choice from the separate restaurant, including soup (65p), shepherd's pie (£1.65), giant Cornish pasty (£1.95), salads (from £2.40), lasagne (£2.20), duckettes (£2.85), curries (£3.60) and sirloin steak (£5.95). Well kept Flowers and Fremlins on handpump, with prices cut by 10p a pint between 6 and 7 o'clock (7 and 8 on Sundays), when wine and spirits are served in doubles for the price of singles. Bar billiards, shove-ha'penny, bar skittles, dominoes, cribbage, Scrabble, dice, backgammon, chess and other board games, and a general knowledge and musical quiz each Tuesday; also a fruit machine, and maybe piped music. Used paperbacks are sold and exchanged; proceeds go to charity. Tables on a narrow gravel terrace face the waterfront. *(Recommended by J G C, Miss H R Morgan, Dr W I Jenkins, Mrs D E Woollett, Capt S E Watson, Capt P Watson, P I Witts)*

Fremlins (Whitbreads) · Licensee Alec Heard · Real ale · Meals and snacks; restaurant bookings tel Teynham (0795) 521404 · Open 10.30–3, 6–11 all year

The Golding Hop, nr Plaxtol

DARGATE   TR0761 Map 3
Dove ★
Village signposted from A299

This honeysuckle-clad brick house is very pretty: picnic-table sets
under pear-trees, with roses, lilac, paeonies and many other flowers,
besides a dovecot with white doves, and a swing. In summer you may
find tortoises and baby black rabbits out here, not to mention house
martins nesting under the eaves, and bluetits in the nesting box on the
handy outdoor privy. Carefully refurbished since our last edition, the
pub is notable for its friendly atmosphere and its generous helpings of
good simple food, much of which is home made: sandwiches (50p–
£1.75 for prawn), soup (95p), pâté (£1.05), ploughman's (from
£1.75), salads (from £1.80), locally made burgers and daily specials
such as chicken pie or quiche Lorraine (£2.50), local gammon steak
(£2.95) and steaks (from £4.25). Well kept Shepherd Neame Bitter,
Invicta and Mild on handpump, served in three- or four-pint
stoneware jugs (to keep it cool) for garden drinkers; dominoes,
cribbage, maybe piped music. They do litre bottles of pop with plenty
of paper cups – a good way of keeping children quiet. There is a good
log fire in winter. The peaceful hamlet is surrounded by strawberry
fields and orchards, and a bridlepath leads up into Blean Wood.
(Recommended by Bob and Val Collman, Anne Wilks, L E Ayris,
Michael Pearce)

*Shepherd Neame · Licensee John Evans · Real ale · Meals and snacks · Children
in eating area · Open 10.30–3, 6–11 all year*

EASTLING   TQ9656 Map 3
Carpenters Arms ★

In summer you can sit by an outbuilding covered with jasmine,
clematis and roses; this is sheltered by the steep roof, the half-
timbered brickwork and white clapboarding of the old village inn.
The beamed front rooms have a quietly relaxed and welcoming feel,
with a big inglenook fireplace, and easy chairs or pews around
simple, candlelit wooden tables on the carpet. Two small back rooms
have a vast fireplace with well-restored bread ovens, rough-hewn oak
beams, rugs on their brick floors, and kitchen chairs, pews and oak
tables with candles in bottles. Bar food includes sandwiches, home-
made pâté or a Cheddar and giant sausage ploughman's with good
warm bread (both £1.95), crab quiche (£2.25), and generously
garnished main dishes such as chicken in red wine (£4.25), beef in ale
(£4.50), and a selection of game in season and year-round wild rabbit
dishes (about £3.75 – maybe cooked in wine with chestnuts, and
served with beetroot, cabbage and baked potato). Steak and kidney
pie (£4.75) is cooked in true Edwardian style – the recipe includes
oysters. There is also a separate restaurant. Well-kept Shepherd
Neame Bitter, Invicta and Mild on handpump, with Stock Ale in
winter. A side room has darts, bar billiards, shove-ha'penny,
dominoes, cribbage and a fruit machine; there may be piped music.
(Recommended by C H Cole, Dr W I Jenkins; more reports please)

Shepherd Neame · Licensee Mrs Maureen Wright · Real ale · Meals (not Sun) and snacks · Children in eating area and restaurant · Open 11–3, 7–11 all year

GOUDHURST TQ7238 Map 3
Star & Eagle [*illustrated on page 405*]

This medieval inn with wood balconies and timbered gables was, together with the neighbouring church, the scene of a remarkable gun battle in which George Kingsmill and his bloodthirsty Hawkhurst smuggling gang were defeated by law-and-order villagers. The spacious open-plan bar is now a very peaceable and civilised place, with old latticed windows, and settles and Jacobean-style seats under its heavy beams; cocktails are served, as well as handpumped Fremlins and Wethereds. The buttery bar, which has a fine seventeenth-century refectory table among plainer modern ones, serves snacks such as sandwiches, generous ploughman's (£1.30), pâté and salad or steak and kidney pie (£2.75), scampi (£2.90), a help-yourself cold buffet (£3.50), quiche (£3.70) and steak platter (£6.75); in the evening, bar food is limited to basket snacks, but there's a separate restaurant. Three or four white tables out under an old pear-tree at the back have a fine view of the hop fields rolling away to the south. Bedgebury Pinetum, the national collection of conifers, is a couple of miles down the B2079, and the splendid gardens around the moated ruins of Scotney Castle are not much further. A nice place to stay. (*Recommended by J S Evans, John Wright, E U Broadbent, Eileen Broadbent*)

Fremlins (Whitbreads) · Licensee Christopher John Satchell · Real ale · Meals and snacks · Children in restaurant and area away from serving bar · Open 10.30–2.30, 6–11 (opens 11 in winter) · Bedrooms tel Goudhurst (0580) 211512; £24.50B/£30 (£34B)

nr HADLOW TQ6349 Map 3
Artichoke

Hamptons; from Hadlow–Plaxtol road turn right (signposted West Peckham – the pub too is discreetly signposted, on an oak-tree); OS Sheet 188 reference 623523

This pretty old cottage, partly tile-hung and shuttered, is quiet during the day and on many evenings, but very popular with young people on weekend evenings. There are two small low-ceilinged rooms with little pews and wooden farmhouse-kitchen chairs on its Turkey carpet, lots of country pictures – mainly hunting scenes – on the walls, and an open fire in winter. Bar food includes sandwiches, ploughman's (£1.50), home-made chicken and mushroom or steak and kidney pie (£2.50), mixed grill (£2.95) and steaks (£2.95–£7.25); they do a roast beef Sunday lunch (£3.95). There's a tiny separate restaurant. Everards Tiger and Youngs Special on handpump, with a good range of spirits. There are seats on a fairy-lit covered terrace in front, and more built around a tall lime-tree across the lane. (*Recommended by Hugh Calvey, Patrick Stapley; more reports please*)

It's against the law for bar staff to smoke while handling food or drink.

Free house · Licensees Barbara and Terry Simmonds · Real ale · Meals and snacks · Children welcome · Open 11.30–2.30, 6.30–11 all year (opens 7 in winter)

HILDENBOROUGH TQ5648 Map 3
Gate ★

From B245 take Noble Tree Road by war memorial at N end of village, then turn left at Watts Cross Road, signposted Hildenborough Station

This friendly Victorian pub has won unanimous and warm approval for its food – almost exclusively fish and shellfish. Moreover, the attractive period decorations, with original printed wallpaper, stripped woodwork, gas lamps and furnishings to match, add a great deal to the pleasure of eating here. The menu changes daily, depending on what the landlord has been able to buy fresh or even live that morning, and might include the pub's own home-potted shrimps (£1.75), Cornish clams with garlic (£2.50), Scotch scallops poached in wine with bacon (£2.75), a mixed shellfish marinière (£3), Helston oysters (£5.50), palourdes (rather like clams – eaten raw, £4.50 for six), with crawfish chowder (£6), Scotch salmon en croûte or Dover sole (£6.60), dressed crab (£8.50) and Cornish lobster or spiny lobster (from £12). There are one or two light non-fish dishes too, and plenty of puddings, and they do ploughman's (£1.75) and a hot dish such as steak and kidney pudding at lunchtime. Booking is now essential for the separate restaurant. Well-kept Flowers, Fremlins and Wethereds on handpump, and a sensible choice of wines; fast, cheerful service in spite of the crowds. Get there early to be sure of a table. In summer the side garden has a salad bar and a children's play area. (*Recommended by R F Warner, Philip Denison, Stephen Hayes, G H G Harris, J S Lomax, Patrick Stapley and R A B, M A Jones and others*)

Fremlins (Whitbreads) · Licensee Guy Sankey · Real ale · Meals and snacks (not Sun or bank hols); restaurant bookings tel Hildenborough (0732) 832103 Children in eating area · Open 11–2.30, 6–11 all year; closed 25–26 Dec, Suns and bank hols

IDE HILL TQ4851 Map 3
Cock [*illustrated on page 397*]

The inside of this pretty, partly tile-hung house has been comfortably modernised, with cushioned settles and Windsor chairs on the polished floorboards and red carpet, and a big hearth with an elaborate iron fireback. Good bar food, served by cheerful staff, includes freshly cut sandwiches (and toasties), home-made soup (90p), hot salt beef in French bread (£1.50), whitebait (£2), burgers (from £2.40), fresh cod or prawns (£2.70), fresh Dover sole (when available, £4.50) and sirloin steak (£5.50). Well kept Friary Meux and Ind Coope Burton on handpump; shove-ha'penny, dominoes, a fruit machine and piped music. The pub is on a quiet village road, close to National Trust woodland, and behind it you can get through to a public playing-field with swings, see-saw and slide, overlooking

Pubs in outstandingly attractive surroundings are listed at the back of the book.

the woods and rolling fields. There are seats outside in front.
(Recommended by E G Parrish, Patrick Stapley)

Friary Meux (Ind Coope) · Licensee Robert Arnett · Real ale · Meals (not Sun)
and snacks (not Sun evening) · Open 11–2.30, 6–11 all year

LUDDENHAM   TQ9862 Map 3
Mounted Rifleman

3½ miles from M2 junction 6; follow Faversham signpost to A2, turn left on
to A2 then follow Dare, Luddenham signpost; take first left turn (signposted
Buckland, Luddenham), then turn right just before railway crossing); OS Sheet
178 reference 981627 – hamlet marked as Elverton

This old brick house, remote in a quiet orchard setting, has an
unspoilt simplicity and truly old-fashioned standard of welcoming
hospitality; its two communicating rooms have bare benches, kitchen
chairs and the like on their lino floors, and some hunting prints on the
ochre walls. The well-kept Fremlins is tapped in the cellar and
brought up on a tray; sandwiches on request; darts, dominoes and
cribbage. There are a couple of tables out behind, by the roses on the
way to the vegetable patch. *(More reports please)*

Whitbreads · Licensee Bob Jarrett · Real ale · Snacks (lunchtime, not Sun)
Open 10–3, 6–11

The Wheatsheaf, Bough Beech

LUDDESDOWN   TQ6766   Map 3

Golden Lion

3 miles from M2 junction 2; A228 towards Snodland, first turn right towards Meopham

This friendly and simple pub is surrounded by beautiful valley farmland and woods, criss-crossed with footpaths and officially classified as an Area of Outstanding Natural Beauty and a Special Landscape Area. The open-plan bar has a big solid-fuel stove in one fireplace and a log fire opposite, a brown plank ceiling and comfortable modern seats. Filled rolls (35p), and well kept Trumans Bitter, Best and Dark Mild on handpump. There are a few tables on the grass beyond the car park. Popular with walkers. (*Recommended by M Wilkes, J Philpott*)

Trumans · Licensee Denis Bennett · Real ale · Open 11.30–2.30, 6–11.30 all year (opens 7 in winter)

PENSHURST   TQ5243   Map 3

Spotted Dog

Smart's Hill; going S from village centre on B2188, fork right up hill at telephone box: in just under ½ mile the pub is on your left

Perhaps the best thing about this quaint tiled and white weatherboarded house is its position, which gives idyllic summer views: 20 miles of countryside, with the lush Medway valley curling round towards medieval Penshurst Place and looking marvellous from the rustic tables and benches on the split-level terrace, which is partly floodlit at night. The bar, licensed since 1520, has a fine brick inglenook fireplace decorated with copper pans, one elegantly panelled alcove and some antique settles as well as the wheelback chairs on its rugs and tiles, together with heavy beams and timbers; on weekend evenings there is quite a crowd of young regulars. An attractive olde-worlde restaurant has a good value £10.95 set menu on Monday to Thursday evenings, and bar food includes freshly cut sandwiches (70p–£1.75 for smoked salmon), soup (£1), various ploughman's (from £1.50), Penshurst sausage (£1.50), hot potted shrimps on toast (£1.75), locally smoked trout, home-made quiche or fillet steak sandwich (£2.25), fresh seafood platter (£4), fresh Dorset crab salad (£4.50) and steaks (from £5.50). Fremlins on handpump. (*Recommended by Philip Denison, Simon Small, L V Nutton, Lissa Halliday, Richard Gibbs*)

Free house · Licensees Peter and Valerie Jones · Real ale · Meals and snacks (not Sun evening); restaurant bookings tel Penshurst (0892) 870253 · Children in eating area and restaurant · Jazz Weds evenings · Open 11–2.30, 6–11

nr PLAXTOL   TQ6053   Map 3

Golding Hop   [*illustrated on page 399*]

Sheet Hill; from Plaxtol, follow Tree Lane from war memorial and church, then keep straight on through Yopps Green; from A227, nearly 1 mile S of Ightham, turn off down unmarked lane beside lonely white cottage named

Bewley Bar, then turn right at oast house, signposted Plaxtol

This tiled white pub, surrounded by orchards, is popular with young people. It's in a very secluded spot, and across the lane has a big south-facing lawn, so sheltered and warm that it's nicknamed Alice Springs. It slopes down to a little stream stocked with trout (no fishing). Inside, the main room has simple country furniture under its shiny plank ceiling, and there are more densely placed tables up steps in a half-timbered extension; cosy wood-burning stoves in each bar in winter. Simple bar food includes toasted sandwiches, beefburgers, pizzas, home-made steak and kidney pie and basket meals. Everards Tiger on handpump, Youngs Special tapped from the cask, and a choice of ciders which sometimes includes one made here; fruit machine, sit-down space game, piped music. *(Recommended by Patrick Stapley; more reports please)*

Free house · Licensee E Mortimer · Real ale · Meals and snacks (not Mon evening) · Open 10–2.30, 6–11 all year

ROCHESTER TQ7467 Map 3
Royal Victoria and Bull

16 High Street

Dickens used this substantial hotel as the model for the Blue Boar in *Great Expectations*, and also worked it into *Sketches by Boz* and the *Pickwick Papers*. The coach entry takes you through to quite a complex of modernised bars and restaurants, including a Great

The Star & Eagle, Goudhurst

Expectations bar at the back, done up with theatrical playbills and postcards of actors and actresses, old press cuttings, cut-glass advertising mirrors over red plush button-back banquettes, a flowery red carpet and stuffed birds. At the front there's a real ale bar with Courage Best and Directors, Fremlins, Websters Yorkshire and Youngs Special on handpump. A wide choice of reasonably priced and cheerfully served bar snacks ranges from sandwiches (55p), pies, pasties, and ploughman's to salads, lasagne and chilli con carne (top price £1.75), and there is a separate restaurant. Fruit machine, piped music. *(More reports please)*

Free house · Licensee J P Rabaiotti · Real ale · Meals and snacks · Children welcome · Jazz Sun lunchtime; pop music Tues, Weds and Thurs evenings Open 10.30–2.30, 6–11 all year · Bedrooms tel Medway (0634) 46266; £20.90 (£23.10B)/£31.90 (£34.10B)

ST MARGARET'S AT CLIFFE   TR3644   Map 3
Cliffe Tavern Hotel

High Street

Comfortable well equipped bedrooms and home-made bar food make this inn – close to the coast – worth knowing. The bar (with a striking picture of a World War II aerial dogfight above the village) and the larger open-plan lounge are comfortable, and food served in them includes sandwiches (from 80p, fresh crab £1.30), smoked haddock chowder (£1.35), a range of curries and individual pies such as fish or steak (all £1.85), plaice (£1.90), chicken fillets or seafood platter (£2.65), salads (from £2.50), 10-ounce burger (£2.90), grilled halibut (£3.70) and 10-ounce rump steak (£5.10), with a choice of puddings (from 95p); there is a separate restaurant. Well kept Courage Directors, Fremlins and Shepherd Neame on handpump; two fruit machines. There are tables on the quiet back lawn, sheltered by sycamores and a rose-covered flint wall. Most of the bedrooms are in two little cottages across the yard from the main building. The inn is in the high part of the little town, set back from the National Trust coastal cliffs. *(Recommended by Gordon Leighton; more reports please)*

Free house · Licensees Frank and Christopher Waring Westby · Real ale · Meals and snacks · Children in restaurant · Bedrooms tel Dover (0304) 852749 or 852400; £18.70B/£28.60B

SANDWICH   TR3358   Map 3
King's Arms

Strand Street; A257

This friendly and unpretentious inn has some striking Elizabethan carving inside and out, and the furnishings are pleasantly simple. Bar food includes sandwiches, soup, ploughman's, Welsh rarebit, grilled cheese with apple and bacon, mushrooms and bacon on toast, sausage and mash, cottage pie, a good choice of omelettes and chicken pie or scampi; there is also a restaurant. Well kept Fremlins on handpump. The public bar has darts, pool, shove-ha'penny, dominoes and cribbage. *(Recommended by Gordon Leighton)*

Fremlins (Whitbreads) · Licensee Mrs A M Bliss · Real ale · Meals and snacks (not Sun) · Children in restaurant · Open 10–2.30, 6–11 all year · Bedrooms tel Sandwich (0304) 617330; £13.75/£27.50

nr SMARDEN   TQ8842   Map 3
Bell ★

From Smarden follow lane between church and The Chequers, then turn left at T-junction; or from A274 take unsignposted turn E a mile N of B2077 to Smarden

This old country inn has a fine range of real ales on handpump: Flowers, Fremlins, Fullers London Pride, Shepherd Neame, Theakstons Best and Old Peculier and Youngs Special; also Biddenden cider, Murphy's Milk Stout, and when the weather calls for it mulled wine. The back rooms are small and cosy, with low beams, bare brick or ochre plastered walls, brick or flagstone floors, an inglenook fireplace, and pews and the like around the simple candlelit tables. Bar food includes sandwiches (from 70p), ploughman's, pizzas (£1.25), salads, chicken, scampi, or plaice, home-made daily specials, and steak (£5.40). The lively and friendly front bar is more popular with the locals, with darts, bar billiards, shove-ha'penny, dominoes, cribbage, a fruit machine and a juke box; part of it is set aside for families with children. You can sit out at the side, among fruit-trees and shrubs, admiring the pub, which is hung with fancy tiles and covered with roses. A good value place to stay. *(Recommended by Gordon and Daphne, Peter Hitchcock, Sheila Keene, Peter Holmes)*

Free house · Licensee Ian Turner · Real ale · Meals (not Sun lunch) and snacks Children in family area · Open 11.30–2.30, 6–11; closed 25 Dec · Bedrooms tel Smarden (023 377) 283; £10/£20

SOLE STREET   TQ6567   Map 3
Compasses ★

On back lane betwen Godmersham (A28) and Petham (B2068); OS Sheet 189 reference 095493

The front bar of this ancient and well preserved country tavern, standing almost alone on its quiet lane over the North Downs, is a long, narrow room with beams in the shiny ochre ceiling, rows of salvaged theatre seats along some walls, simple antique tables on its polished bare boards, and a log fire in winter. At the back of the pub is an atmospheric room with a carefully restored massive brick bread oven, narrow wooden wall benches round the big kitchen table on the polished flagstone floor, and enamelled advertisement placards on the walls; also a Cresset Auto Machine, an entertaining and far more skill-demanding forerunner of the fruit machine. Good bar food includes filled rolls baked on the premises (60p), home-made soup (80p), ploughman's, also using home-made bread (£1.40), sausages (made by the local butcher), egg and chips (£2), fresh fish (£2.10), omelettes (£2.40–£2.60), home-made pies such as steak and kidney or, in winter, game (£2.40), salads with home-cured ham (£2.80) and eight-ounce rump steak (£5); service is friendly. Canterbury,

Fremlins, Fullers London Pride, Shepherd Neame and Youngs Special on tap, also local cider; bar billiards; fairly frequent festivities such as summer jazz barbecues. You can sit out among the fruit-trees behind this remote brick cottage, alongside the donkeys, geese and rabbits. The area is good for walking, and cobwebbed with footpaths. *(Recommended by Duncan Hallows, Peter Hitchcock, J Madley, Mrs N Sharland)*

Free house · Real ale · Meals and snacks (not Weds and Sun evenings) Children welcome · Open 11–2.30, 6–11 all year

SPELDHURST TQ5541 Map 3
George & Dragon

This distinguished old pub is based on a manorial great hall dating from 1212, and has antique cushioned settles, Windsor chairs, panelling, snug alcoves, a massive stone fireplace, heavy beams (installed during 'modernisation' in 1589 – until then the room went up to the roof), and some of the biggest flagstones you can find anywhere – it is said that Kentish archers returning from their victory at Agincourt rested on them in 1415. Bar food changes daily and typically might include sandwiches (from 85p, freshly cut Scotch smoked salmon £1.85), home-made soup (£1), ploughman's with generous chunks of Cheddar, Stilton or Brie (£1.50), salads (from £2, freshly dressed Cornish crab £3.50), Speldhurst sausage and mash with savoury beans (£2), roast chicken (£2.50) and poached salmon (£4.25). Well kept Fremlins, Harveys, King & Barnes and Shepherd Neame on handpump; darts, dominoes, cribbage. During the week, at least at lunchtime, it's fairly quiet, but it gets very busy at weekends, especially in the evenings. The striking first-floor restaurant under the original massive roof timbers has good but expensive food and is served by a truly splendid wine cellar – a place for special occasions. There are white tables and chairs on the neat little lawn, ringed with flowers, in front of this very handsome timbered house. *(Recommended by D J Penny, Philip Denison, W J Wonham, Patrick Stapley and R A B)*

Free house · Licensee Richard Sankey · Real ale · Meals and snacks · Children in eating area and restaurant · Open 10–2.30, 6–11 all year

STAPLE TR2756 Map 3
Black Pig

Barnsole; pub signposted from Wingham–Sandwich back road through Staple on Sandwich side of village

One of the rare places within easy reach of Canterbury that combines an interesting atmosphere with good food (even on a Sunday), this largely unspoilt old village pub has a heavy beam-and-plank ceiling in its rambling main bar, an unusual fireplace with a sort of semi-inglenook which may originally have been a smoking cabinet in its massive central chimney, and comfortable chairs on the carpet; decorations include a couple of stuffed ermine and a turtle. Bar food consists of sandwiches, ploughman's, cottage pie, beef casserole and a good range of seafood, reasonably priced, and there's a separate steak bar and a larger restaurant (with a dance floor). Well kept Bass and Ind Coope Burton on handpump; darts, snooker, juke box and piped music; a genuinely friendly welcome. There are seats outside the half-timbered pub, including some under an old yew, by the quiet village lane. (*Recommended by Jack Taylor; more reports please*)

Free house · Licensee Phillip Aunger · Real ale · Meals and snacks · Children in eating areas · Open 11–2.30, 6–11 all year

WEST FARLEIGH   TQ7152 Map 3
Chequers
B2010 towards Yalding

The decorations in this friendly village pub are on the riotous side of flamboyance: the lounge bar ceiling is festooned with sailors' hat ribands, pennants, matchboxes, tankards, a Lancaster bomber and a giant bone, and its walls are packed with old advertisements, playbills, postcards, paintings, masks and a drum from New Guinea. The room looks crowded even when it isn't, as the bentwood chairs have such a mob of colourful cushions. A display of the Second World War desert campaign reflects the landlord's time as a Gurkha officer there. Even the plainer public bar, with its mainly young customers, has a host of playbills, pin-up calendars, naughty

The Little Gem, Aylesford

postcards, locally painted cartoons, and beer mats: in here are darts, pool, a fruit machine, space game and a juke box. In key with the general atmosphere, time being called is quite a performance, involving bells, cymbals, hooters, whistle and a glockenspiel. Bar food includes freshly cut sandwiches (plain from 55p, toasties from 60p), pasties (60p), pizzas (from 80p), quiche (£1), ploughman's with a choice of cheeses and pâté (£1.10–£1.20), and king rib – French bread with pork rib (£1.20). Well kept Fremlins on handpump; maybe subdued piped music. Wooden seats out in front face the village road; there are more in the side garden. *(Recommended by Pat Bromley; more reports please)*

Fremlins (Whitbreads) · Licensees Len and Joan Platts · Real ale · Snacks (lunchtime) · Piano most Sat evenings · Open 11–2.30, 6–11 all year (opens 6.30 in winter)

WROTHAM TQ6159 Map 3
Bull

1¾ miles from M20 junction 2: follow Wrotham and then Bull Hotel signposts

This small hotel dates from a fourteenth-century hospice on the Pilgrims' Way; there's a big Victorian pilgrimage print, and part of the ceiling is decorated with a stylised modern relief of pilgrims – though what has caught readers' attention most has been the Battle of Britain pilots' signatures on another part of the ceiling. The bar has two rooms divided by a wooden arch, and is comfortably furnished with upholstered wall benches, leatherette seats and one fine long bare wooden table among other smaller ones, curly brass chandeliers, hunting prints, mounted antelope heads, and in winter a log fire at each end. A handsome veteran five-handpump beer engine dispenses well kept Bass, Canterbury, Greene King, Springfield and Youngs Special; bar food includes home-made soup (£1), sandwiches (£1.50), sausage and chips (£1.60), ploughman's (£1.50), cottage pie (£1.75), lasagne and chilli con carne (£1.95), risotto or steak sandwiches (£2.20) and scampi and chips (£2.30); the separate restaurant does a good value Sunday lunch (£6.50). Shove-ha'penny, table skittles, piped music and a fruit machine. There are tables on a small sheltered terrace backed by the church, and a climbing-frame on side grass, by a goat pen. *(Recommended by Eileen Broadbent, Dave Butler, Lesley Storey, Gillian Watson, J M Cooley, H M Beer)*

Free house · Licensees J M and E Dunnell and S V Taylor · Real ale · Meals and snacks · Open 11–2.30, 6–11 all year · Bedrooms tel Borough Green (0732) 883092; £16/£28 (£35B – four-poster suite)

WYE TR0546 Map 3
Tickled Trout

Food and service have made this renovated riverside pub – under new management this last year – popular with readers. It's open-plan inside, with comfortable wall banquettes around dimpled copper tables under the heavy timbers that have been added to its stripped brickwork; at least in summer the nicest place to sit is outside on the lawn which runs down under ash trees to the clear, shallow waters of the Great Stour, here swirling under a graceful ancient bridge (with unsympathetic modern reinforcements), and a playground for fluffy little ducklings. Bar food – none of it fried – includes sandwiches (from 75p), filled baked potatoes (from 75p), ploughman's (1.40), salads (from £2, fresh crab £4.25), lasagne or spaghetti (£2.25), chicken curry (£3.25), local trout (£3.95), steaks (from rump, £4.75) and daily specials such as king prawns (£1.95) or kebabs (£2.25); Fremlins and Tusker on handpump. The Downs on the far side of the village have beautiful walks. *(Recommended by B Prosser; more reports please)*

Fremlins (Whitbreads) · Licensees Mike and Clare Burton · Real ale · Meals and snacks · Open 10–2.30, 6–10.30

Lucky Dip

Besides the fully inspected pubs, you might like to try these Lucky Dips recommended and described by readers (if you do, please send us reports):

ADDINGTON [TQ6559], *Angel*: old country pub overlooking village green, with varied bar food; very popular *(C D Bond)*

AYLESFORD [TQ7359], *Bush*: good lunchtime food, attractive décor, friendly service, and Courage ales *(M W Withycombe)*

BIDDENDEN [TQ8538], *Castletons Oak*: welcoming atmosphere, varied menu, pleasant licensees; very clean *(B & B McKenzie)*; *Red Lion*: nice old pub with lots of beams in attractive split-level bar, serving well kept Fremlins real ales and bar meals; lovely village *(Gordon and Daphne)*

BLEAN [Tile Kiln Hill; TR1260], *Hare & Hounds*: welcoming locals and staff in dark brown pub with home cooking *(Anne Wilks)*

BRASTED [TQ4654], *White Hart*: quiet, friendly well kept hotel, with food, sun-lounge and pleasant garden; children welcome; bedrooms *(Mrs S Brooks, BB)*

BRIDGE [TR1854], *Plough & Harrow*: clean and pleasant, with friendly atmosphere, well kept beer, and first class WCS *(A Beasley)*

BROOKLAND [TQ9825], *Woolpack*: fifteenth-century pub built from even older ships' timbers; inglenook fire; well kept Shepherd Neame ales, good food, friendly atmosphere; lovely Romney Marsh setting, and stream at bottom of garden *(Simon Evans, Stuart Barker)*

BURHAM [Church Street; TQ7361], *Toastmasters*: friendly and interesting, with a good range of well kept real ales *(Dave Butler, Lesley Storey)*

CANTERBURY [Palace Street; TR1557], *Bell & Crown*: very good value food in unspoilt pub with humorous décor (and landlord) *(C Wise)*; [Mill Lane] *Millers Arms*: crowded studenty pub, unpretentiously comfortable with open fire, serving Canterbury Ales brewed here; converted in eighteenth century from three millers' cottages *(M Wilkes, J Philpott)*; [Orange Street] *Seven Stars*: warm and friendly atmosphere, interestingly decorated spacious dining-room with good value food; well kept Flowers and Fremlins *(O Richardson)*

CASTLE HILL [TQ6942], *Castle*: wide choice of reasonably priced and often interesting food; well kept Fremlins, Harveys and Wethereds on handpump *(P A Edwardes)*

COOPERS CORNER [TQ4849], *Frog & Bucket*: local jazz bands two or three times a week; interesting mix of young and old customers; outdoor barbecues in summer; upstairs restaurant *(T J Powell)*

DARTFORD [Lonfield Street; TQ5373], *Two Brewers*: Ind Coope beers in comfortable homely pub with friendly staff; bar food, small terrace *(Annette Summerskill)*

DEAL [Marine Parade; TR3752], *Forester*: good bar food with freshly cut sandwiches, quick cheerful service in clean pub; back beer garden *(Gordon Leighton)*

DETLING [TQ7958], *Cock Horse*: nice little restored pub with warm atmosphere and good beer *(Dr A K Clarke)*

DOVER [Snaregate Street; TR3141], *Arlington*: tiny cosy pub, handy for Hoverport, with good food, real ale and friendly licensee *(Alexander Schouvaloff)*; [Chapel Place] *New Mogul*: anachronistically and attractively sparse décor; restaurant *(Stephan Carney)*

DUNTON GREEN [London Road; TQ5157], *Dukes Head*: modernised pub, comfortable, with friendly landlord, bar food, garden; Saturday pianist *(D P Stevens, BB)*

EAST SUTTON [TQ8349], *Shant Hotel*: tastefully converted 300-year-old pub (previously Prince of Wales) with good food; children welcome; bedrooms *(Anon)*

EDENBRIDGE [TQ4446], *Old Crown*: cheerful Tudor smugglers' pub, not over-modernised, popular for simple bar food; has 'gallows' inn-sign spanning street – one of just a handful left in Britain *(LYM)*

ELHAM [TR1743], *Palm Tree*: lots of real ales in country pub with goats, sheep, donkey and chickens in garden; simple bar food *(Anon)*; *Rose & Crown*: fresh moules marinière a speciality when in season, and other interesting dishes (some Portuguese) in old village pub of great character, once a court house; ancient smoke-blackened beams, open fires, warm welcoming atmosphere, well kept beer; two bedrooms *(KGM)*

EYNSFORD [TQ5365], *Malt Shovel*: busy pub with young customers in attractive village *(Dr A K Clarke)*

FARNINGHAM [London Road; TQ5466], *Farningham Hotel*: classic roadside pub with lots going on, good beer and friendly staff *(Dr A K Clarke)*

FAVERSHAM [Abbey Street; TR0161], *Phoenix*: good food and willing service in well kept friendly pub, a pretty street *(D M Jarrett, Anne Wilks)*; [West Street] *Rising Sun*: old Shepherd Neame pub in conservation area; good fire in winter, and friendly customers *(Peter Hitchcock)*

nr FAVERSHAM [Hollow Shore; TR0161], *Shipwrights Arms*: isolated creek-side pub close to passenger ferry to the Ferry Inn at Harty on Sheppey (this runs erratically in summer); smuggling atmosphere *(Hugh Calvey)*

FORDWICH [TR1759], *Fordwich Arms*: well kept pub with good atmosphere in attractive village *(Peter Hitchcock)*

GOATHURST COMMON [TQ4952], *Woodman*: good food in bar and restaurant, reasonably priced; nice cosy atmosphere in split-level bar with open fires, recently modernised; willing service and interesting choice of wines *(W J Wonham)*

GOODNESTONE [TR2554], *Fitzwalter Arms*: unspoilt seventeenth-century pub with cheerful atmosphere, owned by manor (for pub location see OS Sheet 179 reference 255546) *(David Holloway)*

GOUDHURST [A262; just E; TQ7238], *Green Cross*: fine old inn with good food, interesting choice of real ales, and friendly atmosphere; six bedrooms *(John Wright)*

GRAVESEND [South Town Pier; TQ6473], *Pier Hotel*: busy town pub; brews own beer – cellar visits *(Dr A K Clarke)*

GROOMBRIDGE [TQ5337], *Crown*: attractive old inn in nice spot with plenty of seats outside; real ales, good value restaurant; bedrooms *(Alison Graham, Gwen and Peter Andrews, LYM)*

HARVEL [TQ6563], *Amazon & Tiger*: strange name for nice little pub with lively clientele and well kept beer *(Dr A K Clarke)*

HAWKHURST [Rye Road; TQ7630], *Oak & Ivy*: old Wealden house with particularly well kept Fremlins; summer weekend barbecues on pleasant lawn *(P L Young)*

HEADCORN [TQ8344], *Bell*: wide choice of traditional pub food, large attractive garden, well kept Fremlins and Youngs; popular with parachute jumpers (club nearby); good access for disabled people *(Lesley Foote)*

HEVER [TQ4744], *Henry VIII*: country pub with pondside lawn and Boleyn connections, bought when Lord Astor's estate split up and refurbished to cater for people visiting Hever Castle (Philip Denison, LYM)

HILDENBOROUGH [TQ5648], *Flying Dutchman*: clean pub nicely furnished, with pleasant staff, wholesome food, and unobtrusive piped music – you really feel at home here (Mr and Mrs C S Carter)

HORSMONDEN [TQ7040], *Gun & Spitroast*: daily spit-roasting and consistently good home-made snacks and sandwiches; cheerful atmosphere, cosy and attractive bar, terrace, restaurant; lovely setting in hop country (Gillian Walton, H R P, Eileen Broadbent)

IDE HILL [TQ4851], *Frog & Bucket*: fine sing-alongs, froggy plant-pots, pictures and ornaments everywhere, in newly extended pub with restaurant and good bar food; surrounding countryside attractive (B A Brown)

IDEN GREEN [TQ8032], *Royal Oak*: has good food (Anon); *Woodcock*: attractive little pub, well run (C F W S)

IGHTAM [The Street; TQ5956], *George & Dragon*: well preserved middle-sized pub in delightful village, worth a visit (Dr A K Clarke)

IGHTAM COMMON [TQ5755], *Harrow Inn*: separate restaurant with good food in friendly pub with local atmosphere (SAB)

nr IVY HATCH [Stone Street; TQ5754], *Plough*: home-made food and well kept Batemans, Ind Coope and Ruddles in charming old pub with friendly owner; fine old wooden furniture, real fires, no fruit machines or juke boxes (Simon Evans); *Rose & Crown*: spacious garden with Friday evening summer barbecues behind straightforward pub in attractive countryside; children's room in barn (LYM)

KILNDOWN [TQ7035], *Globe & Rainbow*: pleasant country pub, one part with darts, the other more comfortably furnished with small restaurant leading off (where children are allowed); exposed beams, good choice of bar snacks, Fremlins and Youngs on handpump; big garden behind with goat (for pub location see OS Sheet 188 reference 700353) (Howard Gascoyne)

KINGSDOWN [TR3748], *Zetland Arms*: good beer in very old pub on edge of beach overlooking Channel; snacks (B Prosser)

LAMBERHURST [TQ6735], *Horse & Groom*: real ales and bar food in well kept small Shepherd Neame pub; small restaurant (Harry Blood); [Lamberhurst Down] *Swan*: wide range of reasonably priced freshly cooked bar food in clean, cosy and attractive country inn overlooking village green; old-fashioned décor (C D Bond, M A North Lewis)

nr LAMBERHURST [Hook Green; TQ6535], *Elephants Head*: ancient country pub near Bayham Abbey and Owl House; was particularly popular for enterprising choice of real ales and friendly atmosphere, but now under new owners – more reports please (Simon Small, LYM)

LANGTON GREEN [TQ5538], *Greyhound*: pleasant atmosphere in well run pub with really hot food; children welcome in ex-coffee-room (Mrs M Cooter)

LEEDS [TQ8253], *George*: tasty food in busy village pub (Sigrid and Peter Sobanski)

LITTLE CHART [TQ9446], *Swan*: well kept and comfortable pub (Peter Hitchcock)

LITTLEBOURNE [TR2057], *King William IV*: good food and attractive and comfortable furnishings in hospitable inn; comfortable bedrooms (H L McDougall)

LOWER HARDRES [TR1552], *Three Horseshoes*: old-fashioned furnishings in country pub with Papas prints of Canterbury, choice of real ales, and bar food including wide selection of cheeses for ploughman's (LYM)

MARGATE [Victoria Road; TR3571], *Spread Eagle*: wide choice of real ales in pretty back-street pub with good food (Anon)

NEW ASH GREEN [The Centre; TQ6065], *Badger*: very lively young person's pub with lots of games – a real oasis in this urban desert (Dr A K Clarke)

NEWCHURCH [TR0531], *Black Bull*: quiet and friendly pub with armchairs, homely lighting, maps, pictures and some polished brass on walls, warmly welcoming staff, well kept Shepherd Neame Mild and Bitter, most generous beef sandwich imaginable, and cat and dog dozing by fire (Peter Hart)

NEWENDEN [TQ8227], *White Hart*: good food, especially fish and chips, obliging staff, decent wine and friendly atmosphere (J R Dow)

NORTHBOURNE [TR3352], *Hare & Hounds*: clean free house, tasty food in combined bar/restaurant – gets booked up for dinner in high season *(Gordon Leighton)*

PEGWELL BAY [TR3563], *Sportsman*: appetising food and friendly atmosphere in pleasant pub with good licensee *(B Prosser)*

PENENDEN HEATH [TQ7656], *Bull*: well run suburban pub with lots of games including outdoor ones such as boules; bar food, restaurant, summer barbecues *(S J Tilyard, BB)*

PENSHURST [TQ5243], *Bottle House*: friendly and relaxed atmosphere in pleasant oak-beamed pub *(Philip Denison)*; *Leicester Arms*: good bar food in comfortable old ivy-clad pub; beamed ceiling in bar, splendid corner grandfather clock; restaurant behind recommended *(MHG, M H Lawson)*

PETT BOTTOM [TR1552], *Duck*: bar and restaurant food reliable under new owners; well kept Shepherd Neame and Marstons from the cask; two cosy bars with log fires, 1930s big band music; garden in lovely valley *(JLH)*

PLUCKLEY [TQ9245], *Black Horse*: old village pub with superb fireplace, friendly local customers and visitors, bar food *(Peter Hitchcock)*; [Station Approach] *Dering Arms*: varied food (menu changes daily) and interesting range of ales in atmospheric ex-hunting-lodge; bedrooms *(Malcolm Lee)*

RAMSGATE [Ashburnham Road; TR3865], *Australian Arms*: recently renovated pub with good food, service and beer *(B Prosser)*; [King Street] *Red Lion*: wide choice of bar snacks, well kept Trumans, modern atmosphere; pool, darts, space game *(P Woodward)*; [Harbour Parade] *Royal Oak*: food and service reliably good *(B Prosser)*; [The Paragon] *Van Gogh*: efficient service in spacious London-style pub with fine sea views; loud juke box *(P Woodward)*

RHODES MINNIS [TR1542], *Gate*: typical Kent country pub with well kept Fremlins, simple inexpensive food, and nice garden with geese and pond *(P L Young)*

RINGLESTONE [TQ8755], *Ringlestone*: remote North Downs country pub – unspoilt and cosy, with brick-and-timber walls, candles on tables and mirrored wall sconces, lovely old furnishings, lots of atmosphere; also good home cooking *(D M Jarrett, Gordon and Daphne and others)*

ROCHESTER [High Street; TQ7467], *North Foreland*: unexpected wooden interior, with superb carving above fireplace; interesting Naval items; pleasant beer and nice simple food *(Dave Butler, Les Storey)*

ST MARGARETS BAY [TR3844], *Coastguard*: marvellous views from modernised pub by sea below National Trust cliff; tasty straightforward food, good choice of beers, tables outside *(B Prosser, Anne Wilks, LYM)*; *Granville*: on National Trust ground looking down on sea; daintily served bar meals, hotel very clean, with friendly service; ample seats on terrace *(E G Parish)*

SANDGATE [Brewers Lane; TR2035], *Clarendon*: excellent moules marinière; delightfully friendly landlady *(Susan Corker)*

SEASALTER [Joy Lane; TR0965], *Rose in Bloom*: well renovated by new licensee; bar food; outstanding view from garden over sea or mudflats, depending on tide, to Sheppey and beyond to Essex; swings and seesaw *(Anne Wilks)*

SHEERNESS [Victory Street; TQ9174], *True Briton*: fairly priced snacks in olde worlde town pub with very friendly village atmosphere; local beers from the wood *(CLW)*

SMARTS HILL [TQ5241], *Bottle House*: friendly olde worlde oak-beamed pub *(AA)*

SOUTHBOROUGH [Main Street; TQ5842], *Weavers*: big timbered building with smart furnishings, popular for functions *(Joan Olivier)*

nr STURRY [TR1760], *Fox & Hounds*: good meals in restaurant-like buffet; well kept Shepherd Neame ales; a lot of effort being put into getting everything right *(Mrs M Cooter, Peter Hitchcock)*

TENTERDEN [High Street; TQ8833], *White Lion*: good food and welcoming landlord and staff in attractive and well kept inn; efficient restaurant service; bedrooms *(Canon P E Keightley, Simon Small)*

TILMANSTONE [TR3051], *Plough & Harrow*: varied range of snacks and meals;

cheerful traditional atmosphere and genial landlord; wide choice of real ales
(J F Stackhouse)

TONBRIDGE [High Street; TQ5946], *Castle*: small riverside terrace outside
friendly town hotel; bedrooms *(D A Ingram, BB)*; [Shipbourne Road] *George &
Dragon*: friendly pub with food and sensibly planned internal layout
(D A Ingram)

TROTTISCLIFFE [TQ6460], *George*: tasty home-cooked food and Whitbreads
ales in lovely village pub with super log fire; always very busy; children's room
with machines *(M Boniface, Annette Summerskill)*

TUNBRIDGE WELLS [Mount Ephraim; TQ5839], *Beau Nash*: wide choice of
food in quaint little pub with interesting range of real ales; large terrace
(W H B Murdoch); [Spa Hotel] *Equestrian Bar*: long, light and comfortable room
with steeplechasing pictures and unusual equestrian floor-tile painting; wicker
and velveteen furnishings, friendly uniformed staff, good lunch snacks, well
kept Fremlins and King & Barnes on handpump *(BB)*; [Mount Edgecumbe
Hotel] *La Galoche Bar*: carved out of rocks under hotel; popular meeting
place for wine buffs, excellent cellar kept, also good value food *(KGM, Patrick
Stapley, RAB)*; [off Nevill Street] *Sussex Arms*: pub has been main entry in
previous editions for collections of chamberpots, traditional furnishings, and
well kept Harveys ales; up-to-date reports please *(LYM)*

nr UPSTREET [Marshside; TR2263], *Gate*: in pleasant spot, with garden;
friendly and obliging staff, log fire, well kept Shepherd Neame, good bar food,
local photos *(Prof G M and Dr G S Stephenson)*

WAREHORNE [TQ9832], *Woolpack*: fine food and wines in bar and restaurant
of historic pub *(H S Allen)*

WARREN STREET [TQ9253], *Harrow*: good home-cooked food, choice of real
ales, in recently rebuilt isolated inn – local farmers' haunt; no machines, quiet
background music; bedrooms *(Peter Neate)*

WESTBERE [TR1862], *Yew Tree*: well restored twelfth-century building in sleepy
village with several local characters; good garden with views over lake (and
railway); under new ownership *(Peter Hitchcock, C Leach)*

WHITSTABLE [Seafront; TR1166], *Neptune*: good down-to-earth alehouse
(Derek Cooper); *Pearsons Arms*: excellent for oysters, crabs and smoked fish;
well kept *(Derek Cooper)*

WINGHAM [TR2457], *Red Lion*: civilised bar in handsome and comfortable inn,
originally part of fourteenth-century college founded by Archbishop of
Canterbury – in previous editions as main entry, but now under new licensees;
attractive small courtyard, restaurant, bedrooms *(LYM; up-to-date reports on the new
regime please)*

WINGHAM WELL [TR2356], *Eight Bells*: comfortable rambling beamed pub
near 4,000-year-old cave dwelling, ghostly footsteps close by *(BB)*

WITTERSHAM [TQ9027], *Ewe & Lamb*: friendly atmosphere in Romney Marsh
pub with satisfying food, well kept beer and good local cider *(A Beasley)*

WROTHAM [High Street; TQ6159], *Rose & Crown*: attractive, lively good-
natured local with welcoming licensees; inexpensive bedrooms *(John Curtis)*;
[The Square] *Three Post Boys*: charmingly renovated seventeenth-century
village inn with good value bar food, big inglenook fireplace; new licensees last
year *(C D Bond, Dr A K Clarke)*

YALDING [TQ7050], *Walnut Tree*: tasty home cooking in bar and restaurant of
beamed pub with inglenook *(Anon)*

Lancashire (including Greater Manchester and Merseyside)

One of the cheapest parts of Britain for good beer and generous helpings of bar food, this has some fine pubs, usually in attractive surroundings – and almost always with a notably welcoming atmosphere. Among many newcomers to this edition, there are the White House on Blackstone Edge (a warm and comfortable moorland pub, right on the Pennine Way), Coal Clough House in Burnley (good value food in a handsome house, standing in attractive grounds), Old Rosins up on the moors above Darwen (friendly, with fairly priced food), the Tandle Hill Tavern (a simple farm pub in unspoilt country near Middleton), the Crown at Standish (good all

Coal Clough House, Burnley

round with its own bowling green) and the Black Bull near Tockholes (popular for its straightforward food). The best food of all in the area is probably to be had at the White Bull in Ribchester, a civilised inn, incorporating some Roman remains in its building. There's also inviting food at the Inn at Whitewell (not cheap, but a charming inn in a lovely position by the River Hodder), the Hark to Bounty in the attractive village of Slaidburn (another comfortable place to stay in the Forest of Bowland), the Romper near Marple (very comfortable and handy for the Goyt Valley), and in the well kept Old Sparrow Hawk at Wheatley Lane (especially its roasts, hot or cold). Two Manchester pubs stand out for their remarkable choice of cheeses: the smart waterside Mark Addy in Salford (an unusual and interesting pub), and the friendly Royal Oak in Didsbury. The Yew Tree near Rochdale has tables in an intimate Pullman dining-car, and the Railway near Chorley has good value simple food, and is attractively placed in the recently formed North West Pennine Recreational Park. Other pubs in fine surroundings include the spacious Moorcock alone on the moors at Blacko (new licensees this year), the cosy and traditional Horse & Jockey near Delph (with a good range of real ales), the Bulls Head up at Grains Bar above Oldham (its theatre-organist landlord plays nostalgic favourites), two neighbouring pubs above Uppermill, the comfortable Church and the lively and interesting Cross Keys, the Hodder Bridge Hotel near Clitheroe (with terraces just above the pretty River Hodder), the Golden Ball at Heaton with Oxcliffe (an atmospheric old pub, alone by the broad River Lune), the interesting Water Witch by the canal in Lancaster (taken over this year by Yates Wine Lodges), and Th'Owd Tithebarn in Garstang (an imaginatively furnished waterside barn). Among city-centre pubs, the Philharmonic in Liverpool is notable for its magnificently opulent Victorian décor, and the idiosyncratic Tommy Ducks in Manchester has been moving up in readers' esteem. The long Lucky Dip section at the end of the chapter includes some particularly promising possibilities, such as the canalside Gannow Wharfe and welcoming Kettledrum in Burnley (we should add that Lucky Dip selections in and around Burnley are the result of a very exhaustive screening process by most assiduous correspondents there, to whom we are particularly grateful), the Dog & Partridge in Chipping (tasty bar food and smart restaurant), several around Fence (pubs in the shadow of Pendle Hill often seem specially good, for some reason), the picturesque canalside Saracens Head at Halsall, the well kept thatched Wheatsheaf at Raby (good food and beer) the farmhouse-type Same Yet in Simister, the smart canal-boat-style Narrow Boat in Swinton, the Swan in

*Whalley (good value bar food) and lots in Manchester —
especially the own-brew back-to-basics Lass o' Gowrie, the
traditional Old Wellington (close to our main entry Sinclairs
Oyster Bar), and the interesting Why Not. Of all the Lucky
Dips, the isolated and charming Strawbury Duck in Entwistle
is perhaps the strongest candidate for main entry status.*

nr BALDERSTONE (Lancs)   SD6332   Map 7

Myerscough Hotel

2 miles from M6 junction 31; A59 towards Skipton

Handy for the motorway and this busy trunk road, the spacious bar is
softly lit and full of alcoves. The leaded-light windows are packed
with geraniums, begonias and house plants, and decorations include
a herd of black Ceylon elephants on a high shelf above the oak
panelling, a Welsh dresser filled with dainty china, lots of brass and
copper, and big bunches of flowers. There are well made matching
oak settles around dimpled copper or heavy cast-iron-framed tables
on a dark red carpet. Quickly served bar food includes home-made
soup (85p), sandwiches and toasties (from 90p, prawn or crab
£1.85), filled baked potatoes (£1.35), ploughman's (£1.85), home-
made lasagne or steak and kidney pie (£2.45), salads (from £3.35), a
choice of omelettes (£3.35) and sirloin steak (£3.95); there are plans
for a small separate dining-room. Robinsons Best and Mild on
handpump, from a serving counter with a fine padded elbow-rest; on
our visit, piped theatre-organ favourites and Greek music. If the old
oak beams creak a bit, it's probably the miniature poodle chasing the
standard poodle around upstairs. They, with Tiger the grey tabby, are
normally kept out of the bar — as of course is Pearl, the pub's white
goat. *(Recommended by Mrs Joyce Thorpe; more reports please)*

*Robinsons · Licensee Robert Griffiths · Real ale · Meals and snacks (not Mon
evening) · Children in small side room · Open 11.30–3, 6–11 all year*

BLACKO (Lancs)   SD8541   Map 7

Moorcock

A682; N of village towards Gisburn

High on the moors, with superb views and surrounded by good
walks, this inn is surprising for its spaciously comfortable décor —
modern green cloth seats, big picture windows for the view, high
cream walls hung with brass ornaments, rather than the small low-
beamed rooms you tend to expect in this sort of position. There's a
separate dining-room, which has been closed on Monday and at
lunchtime on Sunday. Thwaites Bitter and Best Mild is kept under
light blanket pressure; juke box, fruit machine. The back garden,
busy of course at weekends, is peaceful during the week — silent
except for the noise of curlews and sheep. The Brandstatters, who
have made this pub additionally popular with readers for their
garlicky Austrian and middle-European dishes, will be leaving at
around the time this edition of the *Guide* is published; we don't know
what sort of food their successors plan. *(Recommended by Sue and Len*

Beattie, Do and Ken Hummer, D A Angless; up-to-date reports on the new regime, please)

Thwaites · Meals and snacks · Children welcome · Open 11–3, 7–12 (supper licence) all year · Bedrooms tel Nelson (0282) 64186; £13S/£22S

BLACKSTONE EDGE (Greater Manchester)   SD9716 Map 7

White House

A58 Ripponden–Littleborough, just W of B6138

The mist on this high moors road was so thick that we almost missed this isolated refuge, which was relaxed and welcoming inside. Past the long enclosed porch (for walkers to leave their muddy boots), the beamed and Turkey-carpeted main serving area has a good coal fire under a large-scale map of the district. Off to the left is a spacious room with comfortable seats around its tables, a map of the world with coloured pins to show where foreign visitors have come from, and a big horseshoe window looking out over the moors. To the right, the snug Pennine Room has small soft settees with brightly coloured antimacassars. Bar food includes home-made vegetable soup (75p), sandwiches (from 70p, steak 85p), ploughman's (£1.50), Cumberland sausage with egg (£1.60), quiche Lorraine (£1.65), lasagne or moussaka (£1.80), salads (from £1.95), steak and kidney pie (£2.25) and eight-ounce sirloin steak (£4), with daily specials such as seafood mousse (80p), mushrooms au gratin (£1.25) and mince and onion pie (£1.80). Booking needed for gourmet Saturday-night restaurant dinners (£9); at other times, even breakfast, the restaurant can be booked for private parties. Well kept Thwaites Bitter and Mild on handpump. Walkers are welcome here, and there are lovely moorland paths from the pub, on both sides of the road – actually part of the long-distance Pennine Way. *(Recommended by Ian Clay; more reports please)*

Thwaites · Licensees Neville and Toni Marney · Real ale · Meals and snacks; restaurant bookings tel Littleborough (0706) 78456 · Children welcome Open 11.30–3, 7–11 all year (opens 6 Fri and Sat)

nr BROUGHTON (Lancs)   SD5235 Map 7

Plough at Eaves

4½ miles from M6 junction 32; take M55 turn-off, then A6 N, then about 1 mile N of Broughton traffic lights first left into Station Lane; after 1½ miles on this road bear left at fork; OS Sheet 102 reference 495374

This warmly welcoming and spotlessly clean country pub has generous helpings of good value food such as home-made soup (65p), giant sausages (95p), well garnished triple-decker sandwiches (from £1.50 – so big and so full, that you can't really get your hands around them satisfactorily and so need a knife and fork), burgers (from £1.50), ploughman's with three cheeses (£1.95), gammon and egg or home-made steak pie (£1.95), Friday fish pie (£1.95) and scampi (£2.50). Little latticed windows, very low dark beams, open fires, rush-seated chairs around the dark wooden tripod tables, an antique oak linen chest and corner cupboard, a row of Royal Doulton

figurines above one fireplace, and a complete absence of machines
and music make for a pleasantly old-fashioned atmosphere. Well kept
Thwaites Bitter and Mild on handpump; darts. There are curly metal
and wood-slat seats and cast-iron-framed tables in front, by the quiet
lane, and at the back there's a good children's play area.
(Recommended by Sue and Len Beattie, Anthony Rota, M C Dickson)

*Thwaites · Licensee Peter Cartwright · Real ale · Meals and snacks (not Mon,
not Sun – Tues evenings) · Children welcome · Folk night Thurs · Open 11–3,
7–11 all year*

BURNLEY (Lancs)   SD8332   Map 7
Coal Clough House ★   [*illustrated on page 416*]

Coal Clough Lane; between Burnham Gate (B6239) and A646; OS Sheet 103
reference 830818

A handsome late Victorian house with a seventeenth-century core,
standing in secluded and peaceful grounds, this has been carefully
developed into an elegant yet thoroughly friendly pub. The spacious
lounge has antique prints on its oak panelling, a lovely carved
mantelpiece around the big open fireplace, and an elaborately
moulded high plaster ceiling. There are button-back brown
leatherette seats and wall banquettes, some in big leaded-light bay
windows, others in a snug adjoining room. Good value quickly
served bar food includes home-made soup (50p), sandwiches (75p),
ploughman's (£1.50), a couple of dishes of the day (£1.75), home-
made steak and kidney pie (£2.20), salads (from £2.25) and gammon
and egg (£2.60) – excellent chips; there is also a popular restaurant
(closed Saturday lunchtime, Sunday evening, Monday); a fruit
machine, maybe piped music. A sunny flagstoned terrace has tables
by the wistaria, and there are more on the lawn, beside roses and trees
such as a weeping ash and a monkey-puzzle. *(Recommended by Sue and
Len Beattie, Mrs B Greenwood)*

*Greenalls · Licensee Adelmo Fidanza · Meals and snacks (not Sun evening)
Children in restaurant and conservatory · Open 11–3, 6.30–11 all year*

nr CHORLEY (Lancs)   SD5817   Map 7
Railway

2 miles from M61 junction 8; A674 towards Blackburn, then about 1 mile
from motorway turn right at Heapey, White Coppice 1½ signpost

This clean, friendly and comfortably refurbished pub has honest
home cooking, and is attractively placed in the North West Pennine
Recreational Park: from down the lane you can follow various nature
trails or take lots of walks – up the side of Anglezarke Moor, say. The
food includes soup in winter (40p), plain and toasted sandwiches
(from 70p, rump steak barm cake £1.25, big open Danish ones
£1.95), cod (£1.50), trout (£1.60), chilli con carne, curry or tandoori
chicken (£1.75), Sunday roasts (£2.20) and puddings such as fruit pie
(60p) or trifle (75p). Well kept Matthew Browns Bitter and Mild on
handpump; darts, a juke box and (in a separate room) pool. The pub
has an excellent collection of cigarette cards, mostly pre-war, and

outside has a big garden, with swings, climbing-frame and so forth. The railway from which the pub gets its name has been dismantled, and the neighbouring station has become a combined blacksmith's forge, livery stables and boarding kennels. Down the lane past it there is good coarse fishing (day tickets available), and the pub holds a clay pigeon shoot each Sunday morning. *(Recommended by Sue and Len Beattie, Dennis Royles, Andrew Kemp and Odile Roudot)*

Matthew Browns · Licensee Philip Barry · Real ale · Meals and snacks Children in family room · Open 11.30–3, 6–10.30

nr CLITHEROE (Lancs)　SD7441　Map 7
Hodder Bridge Hotel

At Higher Hodder Bridge, near Chaigley, on the old Clitheroe–Longridge high road that parallels the B6243; OS Sheet 103 reference 699412

Alone on a country lane, this simple inn is included for its position, handy for walks along the pretty River Hodder. There are new terraces looking down on the wooded river (with a salmon pool below, by the bridge), and barbecues are held out here in fine weather. The spacious dining-room has picture windows looking out on this same view, and on Sundays serves high teas all day, as well as a popular carvery from noon to 5pm, then (with live organ music) 7 to 9.30; eat as much as you can (£4.45, children £2.95); there's the same sort of thing, with a disco, on Saturday night until 2 am (£5.95). There's also an L-shaped panelled back lounge with a coal fire; bar food includes home-made soup (50p), sandwiches (from 75p), ploughman's (£1.25), salads (from £1.90), plaice, mixed grill or home-made steak and kidney pie (£1.95) and sirloin steak (£3.75), with various children's dishes such as fish fingers (90p). A games bar has darts, pool, dominoes and a space game; also fruit machine and piped music; Tetleys on handpump. *(Recommended by M T Shuff; more reports please)*

Free house · Licensee Val Bolger · Meals and snacks · Children in family room and dining-room · Open 11–3, 6–11 all year · Organ and drums Sun evening Bedrooms tel Stonyhurst (025 486) 216; £12(£15B)/£15(£30B)

COWAN BRIDGE (Lancs)　SD6477　Map 7
Whoop Hall

Burrow-by-Burrow; A65 between Cowan Bridge and Kirkby Lonsdale

Good simple bar food in this cheerful sixteenth-century pub includes soup (70p), sandwiches (from 75p), ploughman's (£1.95), salads (from £1.95), haddock or chicken (£2.95), home-made steak and kidney pie (£3.75) and daily specials such as cottage pie or lasagne (£2.95). The bar is old-fashioned and homely, with its antique open-back oak settles as well as more modern seats, copper-topped tables and bar counter, pots of flowers on window shelves in the thick walls, carpeted stairs up to the family's living quarters, and open fires at each end. There is also a separate restaurant. Well kept Tetleys and Youngers Scotch and No 3 on handpump; piped music. There are swings and slides outside by the car park, and tables under cocktail parasols on a neat small lawn with roses and oak-and ash-trees beside it. *(Recommended by K W Lomas; more reports please)*

Free house · Licensee Mrs Shirley Russell Backhouse · Real ale · Meals and snacks (not Mon or Tues evenings) · Children welcome · Open 11–3, 6–11 all year

nr DARWEN (Lancs)   SD6922 Map 7

Old Rosins

Pickup Bank, Hoddlesden; from B6232 Haslingden–Belthorn, turn off towards Edgeworth opposite the Grey Mare – pub then signposed off to the right; OS Sheet 103 reference 722227

This friendly country pub's big picture windows, filled with house plants, look over the moors and down to a mill in a wooded valley. Lots of mugs, whisky-water jugs and so forth hang from the high joists of the big open-plan lounge, which has comfortable red plush built-in button-back banquettes, stools and small wooden chairs around its dark cast-iron-framed tables, and is decorated with little prints, plates and old farm tools. Bar food, virtually all home made, includes generous helpings of soup (60p), sandwiches (from 75p), ploughman's (£1.50), home-made meat pie (£1.70), a choice of salads (£1.75), a dish of the day such as sweet and sour pork (£1.75), steak and kidney pie (£2.25), beef in Theakstons Old Peculier (£2.50) and eight-ounce sirloin steak or mixed grill (£3.95); the chips are good here. A separate upstairs restaurant is open in the evenings (not Monday) and for Sunday lunch. Matthew Brown and Theakstons beers are kept under pressure; a log fire in winter; darts, dominoes, a fruit machine and a juke box, with a disco on Friday evenings. There are picnic-table sets on a spacious crazy-paved terrace, with see-saws, swings and a climber on the lawn; summer barbecues out here on Friday evenings and Sunday lunchtimes. *(Recommended by Sue and Len Beattie)*

Free house · Licensee Bryan Hankinson · Meals and snacks · Children in eating area · Open 11–3, 6–11 all year (opens 7 in winter)

nr DELPH (Greater Manchester)   SD9808 Map 7

Horse & Jockey

Junction of A62 and A670

With lovely views over the high moors, this welcoming pub has a good range of well kept real ales, with usually three changing guest beers as well as Marstons Pedigree, Timothy Taylors Landlord and Wards Best on handpump. The two rooms, one panelled and served from a high hatch, are comfortably furnished with some settees and easy chairs as well as Windsor chairs on the carpet, and have soft lighting and (except in really warm weather) log fires. Bracing moorland walks from the pub include one down to the site of a Roman fort by Castleshaw reservoir. *(Recommended by Andrew Kemp and Odile Roudot; more reports please)*

Free house · Licensee David Kershaw · Real ale · Open 7–11 all year; closed weekday lunchtimes

DENSHAW (Greater Manchester)   SD9710   Map 7
Rams Head

2 miles from M62 junction 22; A672 towards Oldham – pub N of village

With fine views over the moors and down the Tame valley, this comfortable pub, backing on to the farm of which it is a part, has traditional settles and benches built in to the panelling of its thick-walled small rooms, beam and plank ceilings, and log fires. Well kept Youngers Scotch, IPA and No 3 on handpump, and Theakstons Old Peculier tapped straight from the barrel; unobtrusive piped music, friendly landlord and customers. It can get crowded on weekend evenings; on Sunday, when it's open at lunchtime, it's well placed for walks – up towards Brushes Clough reservoir, say. *(Recommended by Nigel Thomson, L N Goulding, William Meadon, Richard Steel, T J Vernon)*

Free house · Licensee Geoffrey Haigh · Real ale · Open 6.30–11 all year; closed Mon–Sat lunchtimes, 25 Dec

GARSTANG (Lancs)   SD4845   Map 7
Th'Owd Tithebarn ★

Church Street; coming N on B6340 slip road from A6, street is first left as you enter one-way system

The White Bull, Ribchester

This pretty creeper-covered barn has been splendidly converted, with pews and shiny varnished tables on the flagstones under its high rafters, masses of antique farm tools and stuffed animals and birds, and upstairs the Lancaster Canal Museum and Information Centre. It's spacious, and very jolly (the efficient waitresses wear period costume with mob-caps). One end, under a lower beamed ceiling, is snugger, with an old kitchen range and prints of agricultural equipment on the walls. Reasonably priced home-cooked food includes soup (65p), ploughman's (£1.40), prawns (£1.65), hot-pot (£2.20), steak and kidney pie (£2.75), salads (from £2.85), a choice of roast meats (£3) and ham and eggs (£3.50), with a good children's menu made up of small helpings of the main dishes as well as burgers, sausages, baked potatoes and so forth (from £1.10). On Tuesdays to Fridays there is a barbecue (from burger at (£1.60 to eight-ounce sirloin steak at £4.75). In winter they have bar billiards (there's really no room for them in summer!). There are rustic tables outside on a big stone terrace by the duck-filled canal basin, where lots of boats are moored. *(Recommended by J Young, Dennis Royles, N W Acton)*

Free house · Licensee Roger Barker · Meals and snacks · Children in restaurant Open 11–3, 7–11 (opens 6 Sat) all year; closed Sun evening, Mon

HEATON WITH OXCLIFFE (Lancs)   SD4460 Map 7
Golden Ball, *known as* Snatchems ★

Lancaster Road; coming from Lancaster on B5273, turn left by sandy wasteland where sign warns road liable to be under water at high tide (should also be signposted Oxcliffe, Heaton, but sign may be removed by vandals)

From this friendly and old-fashioned pub's little flowery-curtained windows, and from the teak seats on the raised front terrace, there are views out over the broad River Lune and its waterski boats. Well kept Mitchells Bitter and Mild, on handpump, are served from a hatch in a little low-beamed room with an old high-armed carved chair and built-in benches around cask tables. Other snug rooms lead off, with more beams, warm open fires in winter, cushioned antique settles, old-fashioned upright chairs, pictures of the tall ships which used to tie up outside and a high shelf of china. There are darts, dominoes and a fruit machine in one side room, and a space game upstairs in the long, neat family room; maybe piped music. Bar food includes steaming hot home-made soup (35p), baked potatoes (30p), cheese and onion flan (50p), sandwiches (from 55p, with home roast beef or ham 70p, and when it's available fresh salmon from the Lune £1), steak or meat and potato pies with mushy peas (80p), steak sandwich (95p), curry or bacon ribs (£1.20) and ploughman's (£1.30). As you might expect from its superb position, the pub can get crowded in summer. The Snatchems name comes from the days when the press-gangs used to swoop on the pub, snatching customers too drunk to get away for service as sailors. *(Recommended by Mr and Mrs Michael Parrott, J Young, Mr and Mrs D G Shipton, Mr and Mrs L R Gill)*

Mitchells · Licensee Fred and Lesley Jackson · Real ale · Meals and snacks Children upstairs · Open 11–3, 6–11 all year (opens 12 and 6.30 in winter)

Howe Ghyll

Green Lane; heading N on A6, last turning on right leaving speed restriction

In summer, children happily keep well out of the way here, with a spreading wood-fringed lawn to play on besides swinging ropes and other adventure playthings. By the side of the house (this was just a large private residence until recently) there are tables on a neat terrace, prettily lined by a rockery, a pool, and some attractive plants. Indoors a series of spacious rooms have been carefully knocked together to make up the lounge bar: pillars and fine plasterwork, and plush russet seats and banquettes to match – even the bar counter is carpeted. A family dining area opening off has lots of tables and a quick and efficient lunchtime food counter serving soup (50p), a bowl of chips (45p, with gravy 50p), sandwiches (from 85p, steak 95p), filled baked potatoes (from 90p), burgers (from 95p), ploughman's (£1.50), plaice (£1.95), salads (from £2.25), scampi (£2.95) and grills (from gammon or pork chop £3, to eight-ounce sirloin steak £4.75 – not Sundays); there are daily specials such as steak and kidney pie, moussaka or hot-pot (£1.95), a children's menu (95p), and roast Sunday lunches. Evening food for big parties is available by arrangement. Well kept Mitchells Bitter, Mild and Extra Special on handpump at attractive prices (it's brewed locally); usually piped music. The public bar, with an enormous gleaming copper brew kettle in the centre, has a juke box, pool, darts, dominoes, cribbage and a fruit machine and space game. *(Recommended by Mr and Mrs D H Shipton; more reports please)*

Mitchells · Licensee Bill Bland · Real ale · Meals (lunchtime) and snacks (not Mon evening) · Children in family room · Open 11–3, 6–11 all year

Stonewell Tavern

Lower Church Street; in central one-way system look out for public car parking sign, off Stonewell, and park there

This city-centre pub is popular with local business people at lunchtime for its home-made bar food, which includes soup (50p), sandwiches or filled buns (75p), salads from the buffet counter (£1.50), hot dishes such as hot-pot, cottage pie, chicken and ham pie or steak and onion pie (£1.50), and daily roasts (£1.80). Well kept Thwaites on electric pump (now that Thwaites have taken over and closed down the local Yates & Jacksons brewery to which the pub used to be tied). Though it's old enough to have tales about a secret tunnel to the castle, the pub has a comfortably modern atmosphere inside, with big windows, a very high ceiling at the front (but much lower and snugger at the back – there's an eating area above there), up half a dozen steps, dimpled copper tables and russet wall banquettes on the grey tiled floor. In the evening well reproduced pop music, and a good juke box attract younger customers; darts, dominoes, fruit machine. *(Recommended by Mr and Mrs D G Shipton; more reports please)*

Thwaites · Licensees Phil and Krys Peel · Real ale · Meals and snacks (lunchtime, not Sun) · Children in eating area · Open 11–3.30, 7–11 all year

Water Witch

Canal Side; entering city on A6 from S, pass Royal Lancaster Infirmary on your left, take next left turn into Aldcliffe Road, and park; you have to walk 200 yards, over the canal bridge

Taken over since our last edition by Yates Wine Lodges, this interesting canalside pub has lost its charcoal grill but otherwise still does much the same sort of reasonably priced food such as sandwiches, children's burgers and other dishes (£1.10), ratatouille (£1.60), steak canadien or home-made steak and kidney pie (£1.90), chilli pancake (£2.20), seafood pancake (£2.75), beef, lamb and pork kebab (£3.50) and eight-ounce sirloin steak (£4.25); there are puddings such as pancakes with cream (99p). Moreover, Yates have a fine reputation for leaving old-fashioned premises unspoilt, and there is every sign that this simply furnished place will continue much as before. Built against the vast sloping stone canal embankment, it used to be stabling for the tow-horses and has bare stone walls and a flagstone floor – expect a warm and friendly atmosphere in unusual surroundings, rather than luxury. At one end, beyond the main bar, there's a high-raftered area with a wine-bar atmosphere and an attractive tiled stove; at the other is a small games room with darts, pool, dominoes, cribbage and a fruit machine; there's also a juke box. Well kept Tetleys, Thwaites and Youngers No 3 on handpump, a good value range of wines and ports, and tea, coffee, hot chocolate or Horlicks and rum. There are tables built from hefty timber baulks outside by the canal. (Recommended by Michael Hyde, Mr and Mrs Russell Allen, S A Maddison, G L Archer, Mr and Mrs D G Shipton; up-to-date reports on the new regime please)

Free house · Licensee Ken Barwise · Real ale · Meals and snacks · Children welcome · Piano Sun lunchtime · Open 10.45–3, 5.45–11 all year

LIVERPOOL (Merseyside)   SJ4395   Map 7

Philharmonic ★

36 Hope Street; corner of Hardman Street

Handsomely restored, this sombrely ornate and spacious pub gives a good idea of the opulent gin palaces that adorned Liverpool in its heyday at the end of the nineteenth century. The mosaic-faced central serving counter, now with well kept Ind Coope Burton as well as Tetley-Walkers Bitter and Mild on handpump, is the hub, and heavily carved and polished mahogany partitions radiating from it divide areas that vary in size from cosy little cubicles to a vast mosaic-floored hall with richly decorated panelling, stained glass including contemporary portraits of Boer War heroes, and an intricate plasterwork high ceiling. If you ask, the licensees are happy to point out some of the most interesting features. Home-made bar food including sandwiches, soup and main dishes such as quiche, chilli con carne and steak pie (£1.85) is served in a handsomely Grecian room with half-naked art nouveau plaster goddesses reclining high above the squared panelling, and there are two plushly comfortable sitting-rooms; fruit machine, juke box. Even the gents – all marble and mosaic – is a period piece. There is an upstairs functions and parties room. (R A Hutson; more reports please)

Tetley-Walkers (Ind Coope) · Licensees Mr and Mrs E Smithwick · Real ale Meals (lunchtime, not Sat or Sun) and snacks (lunchtime, not Sun) · Children in eating area · Jazz Mon–Tues, bands Weds · Metered parking nearby · Open 11.30–3, 5–10.30 (no late extension Fri or Sat)

MANCHESTER   SJ8284   Map 7
Crown & Kettle

Oldham Road, junction with Great Ancoats Street; junction A62/A665

The unusual décor of this most ornate yet very friendly Victorian pub includes a giant caricature model of Churchill, and is notable too for its original elaborate finish, with tall arched windows fitted carefully into the almost mosque-like design of intricate Gothick internal arching. It is furnished in character, with lots of mahogany, mirrors and red plush. Well kept Wilsons on handpump; sandwiches, including steak sandwiches, and pies, with extras at lunchtimes such as home-made steak and kidney pie or chilli con carne; fruit machine. *(Recommended by Howard Gascoyne, L N Goulding, Dr A K Clarke)*

Wilsons (Watneys) · Real ales · Meals (lunchtime, not Sun) and snacks Open 11–3, 5.30–10.30

Mark Addy

Stanley Street, Salford, Manchester 3; look out not for a pub but for what looks like a smoked-glass modernist subway entrance

This waterside pub has the feel of breaking new ground, with its elegant furnishings, attractive service and smartly dressed customers; it has russet or dove plush seats, and upholstered stalls around side tables in a tastefully converted series of barrel-vaulted brick bays that were originally waiting-rooms for river-boat passengers, and later a boat club. The photographs with which it is decorated give a vivid impression of what the area used to be like in its less salubrious past, and lightly smoked glass from floor to ceiling provides a view over the narrow flagstone tow-path to the River Irwell from which the eponymous Mark Addy saved over 50 drowning people in the last century, when it was a foetid open sewer rather than the calm stream that it is now. A biggish sheltered canalside courtyard, also flagstoned, has tables among flowers. Bar food consists of a vast range of cheeses – up to 50 at a time – from England, Scotland, Wales and several European countries, served in remarkably generous helpings, and a choice of Belgian pâtés (with granary bread, dill cucumbers and sliced onions, £1.50); so few people can finish their helpings that you should accept it as a compliment if they don't automatically give you a bag to take away your likely leavings. They'll also do sandwiches, on request. Well kept Boddingtons on handpump, and quite a few wines; piped music. *(Recommended by Howard Gascoyne, L N Goulding, Roger Berrisford, R A Hutson, Mrs M C Jones)*

Free house · Licensee David Ashford · Real ale · Snacks · Open 11.30–3, 5.30–10:30

If we know a pub sells sandwiches we always say so; if they're not mentioned, you'll have to assume you can't get one.

Royal Oak

729 Wilmslow Road, Didsbury, Manchester 20

This friendly high-street suburban pub has a quite remarkable choice of cheeses and pâtés, at lunchtime spread out over much of the central island serving counter – probably the best range you can find anywhere in the country. For £1.60 they heap your plate up with phenomenal helpings, more than many people can get through, with take-away bags for what's left over. As you might expect this fills the pub to bursting with satisfied lunchers, but it's really busy in the evenings too, with a cheerful local atmosphere and efficient, attractive service: simple seats around the tables (which have old-fashioned brass anti-spill rims), theatrical handbills under the high shelves of china, and a quieter snug bar. Well kept Marstons Burton and Pedigree on handpump. There are some seats outside. (*Recommended by L N Goulding, Howard Gascoyne, Elaine Lloyd Davis*)

Marstons · Licensee Arthur Gosling · Real ale · Snacks (lunchtime, not Sat or Sun) · Open 11–3, 5.30–10.30

Sinclairs Oyster Bar

Shambles Square, Manchester 3; in Arndale Centre between Deansgate and Corporation Street, opposite Exchange Street

A surprise to find in the middle of such a modern shopping complex, this ancient pub, which dates from the end of the eighteenth century and was carefully restored when the complex was built in 1971 – part of the process involved lifting it bodily by nearly five feet. The alcovey ground floor has a low ochre ceiling and squared oak panelling, with high small-backed stools among the tall marble-topped eating-bar: food, with prices unchanged since last year, includes cheese and onion or steak and kidney pies (£2), salads (from £2), home-roasted beef or turkey (£2.50), poached salmon (£2.50), seafood platter or good beef and oyster pie (£3) and oysters (£3.15 the half-dozen); well kept Sam Smiths OB on handpump, a fruit machine and maybe piped music. A quieter and quite genteel upper bar with neatly uniformed barmaids has low old-fashioned wall settles, a scrolly old leather settee, and pictures of old Manchester; at lunchtime there's also a food servery up here (with filled cut rolls and side salads), and there's a separate restaurant. Outside, there are picnic-table sets in a pedestrians-only square. (*Recommended by Lee Goulding, Sue and Len Beattie, Brian and Anna Marsden, Howard Gascoyne*)

Sam Smiths · Licensee Peter Wild · Real ale · Meals (lunchtime, not Sun) and snacks · Children in restaurant · Nearby parking difficult · Open 11–3, 5.30–10.30

Tommy Ducks

East Street, Manchester 2

There's a fine atmosphere in this black and white Victorian pub which so strikingly survives in this sea of construction work and tall modern buildings. The new landlord has restarted the famous collection of knickers, given by customers, that hang from its red ceiling in such exuberant profusion. The pub's communicating rooms have been done up in Victorian style, with gold-fringed plush button-back banquettes, heavy swagged red curtains, and a large old-fashioned black cooking range. The mirrored walls are covered with antique theatrical posters, photographs and music hall cards – the pub featured prominently in last summer's TV film on lost theatres. Bar food includes sandwiches (from 50p), ploughman's, steak and kidney pie (£1.65), and lasagne, scampi, chicken curry, country beef pie or roast beef salad (£1.85); since last year, Greenalls Local and Original on handpump; juke box. Quiet and relaxed on most evenings, it can be very busy at lunchtime. (*Recommended by Sue and Len Beattie, L N Goulding, Howard Gascoyne*)

Greenalls · Licensee Clive Vickerstaff · Meals (lunchtime, not Sun) and snacks (not Sat–Weds evenings) · Panama Jazz Band Sun evening · Open 11–3, 5.30–10.30

MARPLE (Greater Manchester)   SJ9588 Map 7
Romper

Ridge End; from A626 Stockport Road in Marple, coming in from Manchester side, look out for Church Lane on your right (third turning after railway bridge and just after a garage); once in Church Lane, follow The Ridge signposts

Since our last edition the owner of this comfortable and well kept country pub – always popular for its mostly home-cooked food – has decided to devote his own time wholly to preparing the food. His menu has also been neatly computerised (the nicest-looking computer menu we've yet seen): an encouragement to experiment with new dishes. Typically, the wide choice includes soup (85p), devilled kidneys in a baked potato (£1.40), ploughman's (from £1.95), Cumberland sausage (£2.30), prawns in their shells (£1.95) or in hot garlic butter or paprika sauce (£2.35), open sandwiches (from meats, £2.15, to Scotch smoked salmon, £2.75), salads such as dressed crab (£2.95), steak sandwich (£3.20), seafood casserole, chicken Italian-style or curried, or steak and kidney pie (£3.50) and eight-ounce rump steak (£4.95); well kept Ruddles County, Timothy Taylors Landlord and another bitter carrying the pub's own name, on handpump; efficient, charming service by uniformed waitresses. A little waterfall grotto of flowers and ferns behind a wrought-iron grill decorates one of the knocked-through oak-beamed rooms, which are gently lit and comfortably furnished with soft blue corduroy seats and some antique settles around the many tables. This was originally a row of hatters' cottages, and there are some pretty door arches linking them. The pub stands alone on the steep side of the Goyt Valley with good views along it; you can walk down towards the Peak Forest Canal from a car park attractively set in a hilly common, 100 yards along the Marple Road. (*Recommended by L N Goulding, A P Marriott, Dennis Royles, T J Vernon*)

Free house · Licensee Michael Musgrave · Real ale · Meals and snacks Children welcome (lunchtime only) · Open 12–3, 6–10.30; closed 25 Dec

---

Stars after the name of a pub show that it has exceptional quality. One star means most people (after reading the report to see why the star has been awarded) would think a special trip worth while. Two stars mean that the pub is really outstanding – one of just a handful in its region. The very very few with three stars are the real aristrocrats – of their type, they could hardly be improved.

MIDDLETON (Greater Manchester)   SD8606   Map 7

Tandle Hill Tavern

Thornham Lane; this, with Thornham Old Road, is a largely unmade track between A664 and A671 just S of (but not quickly accessible from) M62 junction 20; OS Sheet 109 reference 899090

A real curiosity, this: firmly in the Manchester built-up area, but in fact a farm pub reached by nearly a mile of rough track, with paths leading off into open country on all sides (including the Tandle Hill Country Park). Surrounded by ducks, ponies and ageing tractors, it has two snug rooms, spindleback chairs around dimpled copper tables, lots of brass candlesticks on the mantelpiece above the coal fire, and some benches outside. Traditional ales on handpump; sandwiches and hot pies (mainly 40p–50p); darts, dominoes, cribbage. The landlord is a wrestler. (*Recommended by J R Glover; more reports please*)

Free house · Licensee Peter Lawler · Real ale · Snacks · Children in tap-room Open 12–2.30, 5–10.30

NETHER BURROW (Lancs)   SD6275   Map 7

Highwayman

A683

Since our last edition, this comfortably furnished pub has made its good value food available at the same prices in both the bar and the restaurant (in which you can book tables). Served in generous helpings, it includes home-made soup (75p), sandwiches, egg with mushrooms and onions in a light cheese sauce (£1.20), pâté (£1.50), Cumberland sausage (£1.95), spaghetti bolognese or with ham and cheese (£2.20), lasagne (£2.50), salads (from £2.50), grilled haddock or home-made steak and kidney pie (£2.75), curries (£2.95), trout (£3.25), chicken in red wine (£3.50) and steaks from £5.75). The spacious bar has brown plush button-back banquettes built against the cream walls; a stripped stone arch encloses snug seats by the open fire, and there are steps down to a lower beamed part. Well kept Tetleys, Theakstons and Youngers Scotch on handpump, some unusual lagers, cocktails, liqueur coffees; darts, dominoes, a fruit machine and a juke box or piped music. Service is friendly and welcoming. French windows open on to a terrace outside the substantial old stone house, and there is a swing and climbing-frame beyond the big gravel car park. (*Recommended by David Morphy; more reports please*)

Free house · Licensee John Parr · Real ale · Meals and snacks; restaurant bookings tel Tunstall (046 834) 249 · Children in eating area and restaurant Country and western music Tues · Open 11–3, 6–11 all year

nr OLDHAM (Greater Manchester)   SD9608   Map 7

Bulls Head

Grains Bar; out of town on A672 towards Halifax at junction with B6197

If we know a pub has an outdoor play area for children, we mention it.

Most nights Mr Wilson – who used to be a theatre organist – puts on his velvet jacket, sits down at this village pub's own organ, and launches into lively renderings of nostalgic favourites. So the comfortably cushioned seats of the two snug communicating rooms are usually pretty full. Lots of gleaming brass and copper jugs, funnels and ornaments hang from the black oak beams and above the gas fires, and cut-glass windows give views out over the surrounding moors. Sandwiches (55p) are always available, and at lunchtime soup, a choice of main dishes, and pudding costs £2.95; well kept Bass and Cask Bitter (Brew Ten) on handpump. *(More reports please)*

Bass · Licensee William Wilson · Real ale · Meals and snacks (weekday lunchtimes) and snacks (lunchtime) · Organ nightly · Open 11.30–3, 5–11 all year

RIBCHESTER (Lancs)   SD6435   Map 7
White Bull ★ *[illustrated on page 423]*
Church Street; turn off B6245 at sharp corner by Black Bull

The unusual food here – the most interesting of any pub in the county – is what earns this pub its high rating. It changes to some extent day by day, depending partly on what herbs and vegetables are ready in the licensees' own garden, and besides soup (75p), ploughman's with cheese or ham (£1.75), and several familiar dishes such as steak and kidney pie, the wide choice might include taramosalata with hot pitta bread (95p), freshly made kibbeh filled with meat or mushrooms and cheese and served with tabbouleh (£1.45), chicken legs braised in mustard and thyme sauce, tarragon-flavoured rabbit pie or Chinese-style roast pork (£2.25), stifad (Greek beef stew with wine and herbs) or lamb chops cooked Greek-style with lemon and spices (£2.75), and sirloin pieces cooked with a spicy sauce to an old north-of-England recipe (£3.25). There are puddings such as whimberry pie, gooseberry pie or rum and hazelnut vacherin (85p), and you can eat either in the bar or in a separate dining-room; if they're not too busy they may do sandwiches. There are occasional barbecues on the back terrace (where there are tables), and either the barbecue or the dining-room can be booked for parties, with a menu worked out to suit what you want to pay. The spacious and well kept main bar has comfortable old settles, and is decorated with Victorian advertisements and prints of Preston pubs, pencil drawings and Lowry prints. Well kept Chesters Best on handpump; pleasant piped music, mainly classical and not too loud; darts and dominoes. The pillars of the porch are Tuscan, and have stood here or nearby for nearly 2,000 years; the remains of a Roman bath house are just behind the pub, and some of the Roman pottery which has been dug up in the garden is on show in the bar. There's a small explanatory museum close by. *(Recommended by ABC, Sue and Len Beattie, Janet Brooks, D C Turner, Dr C M King)*

Whitbreads · Licensee David Best · Real ale · Meals and snacks (not Mon evening) · Children in dining-room and snug bar · Occasional English or Irish folk music · Open 12–3, 7–11 all year

---

Though we don't usually mention it in the text, a number of pubs will now make coffee – always worth asking. And some – particularly in the North – will serve teas.

nr ROCHDALE (Greater Manchester)   SD8913 Map 7

Yew Tree

3 miles from M62 junction 20: follow motorway spur towards Rochdale, but
keep right at exit roundabout to join A664 ring road; turn right on A671 at
traffic lights; pub in Oldham Road, Thornham, on A671 just S of where it
underpasses M62

Carefully prepared good value food in this well run and plushly open-
plan pub includes soup (55p), sandwiches (from 70p, hot salt beef in
crispy French bread £1), a serve-yourself-with-as-much-as-you-like
cold table with seafood salad, ham, beef and other meats (£2.50), and
three or four hot dishes such as chicken curry, scampi, lasagne and
steak and kidney pie (£2.50, including plenty of vegetables). On
Sundays there's a carvery (lamb £2.75, beef £3); but perhaps the most
interesting thing in the food line here is the splendid Pullman dining-
car stationed alongside, with some of the tables having intimate
compartments to themselves: bookings essential from Thursday to
Sunday evenings. Sam Smiths on handpump; dominoes, a fruit
machine, and piped music. There are picnic tables under cocktail
parasols, facing the front car park. *(Recommended by T J Vernon; more
reports please)*

*Sam Smiths · Licensee Paul Richardson · Meals (lunchtime) and snacks;
Pullman dining-car reservations tel Rochdale (0706) 49742 · Children in
eating area and restaurant · Open 11.30–3, 6–10.30 (plus one hour restaurant
extension evenings)*

SLAIDBURN (Lancs)   SD7152 Map 7

Hark to Bounty ★

Quite off the beaten track in a peaceful old Forest of Bowland village,
this delightfully welcoming and very well kept inn is good value as a
place to stay (all its comfortable bedrooms have their own
bathroom). Bar food includes home-made soup (75p), well filled
sandwiches (from 80p, hot steak muffin £1.15, fresh salmon £1.45),
ploughman's (£2.20), sausages made locally for them (£2.35), scampi
(£2.50), steak and kidney pie (£2.60), pork chop (£2.70) and salads
from home-made quiche (£2.35) to salmon (£3.60). The spacious
lounge bar has one or two easy chairs, a Victorian settle and an
antique settee on its muted brown carpet, an open fire, and local
photographs, big Victorian engravings and a few Victorian fashion
plates on the plain cream walls. Moorhouses Premier and Pendle
Witches Brew and Thwaites Bitter and Best Mild on handpump are
well kept; dominoes. The restaurant serves dishes such as halibut
with prawn sauce and home-made turkey and mushroom or venison
pie, with traditional Sunday lunches. There are high fells beyond the
gently rolling wooded hills around here, and fly fishing can be
arranged on the River Hodder and the nearby Stocks Reservoir.
*(Recommended by C Rollo, Sue and Len Beattie, J A Catton, Andrew and John
Kemp; more reports please)*

*Free house · Licensee Mrs Jean Turner · Real ale · Meals and snacks · Children
welcome · Open 11–3, 6–11 all year · Bedrooms tel Slaidburn (020 06) 246;
£15.50B/£31B*

STALYBRIDGE (Greater Manchester)   SJ9698 Map 7
Stalybridge Station Buffet

A rarity, this: run privately, and lovingly, it's quite unlike any other
station buffet, and as Victorian in style as a stove-pipe hat, with barge
and railway pictures set in to the red bar counter, and more railway
pictures and some old station signs on the high walls. There's a
homely welcome, well kept Robinsons Best and Ruddles on
handpump, tea (made fresh by the pot) and cheap snacks such as
black-eyed peas or chilli beans as well as sandwiches and hot or cold
pies. Proceeds from a paperback library on the piano beside the black
coal stove go to a guide dog charity. *(Recommended by Sandy Parkinson,
Steve Suttill)*

*Free house · Licensee Mrs Dorothy Redfern · Real ale · Snacks · Open during
station hours*

STANDISH (Greater Manchester)   SD5610 Map 7
Crown

4 miles from M6 junction 27; straight through Standish on B5239, at T-
junction turn left into Worthington – pub signposted left, into Platt Lane

Strongly recommended to us by a reader who has been to 11,000
different pubs, this well run and friendly place hides away behind an
unpromising façade not only a remarkably comfortable lounge bar
but also a bowling green. Carefully refurbished in 1984, the various
knocked-together rooms have attractively upholstered Chesterfields
and armchairs, bunches of flowers, ship prints, coal fire, sky-blue
ceiling, and on our visit soft piped radio. Well kept Bass, Hammonds,
Marstons Pedigree and usually other real ales are dispensed from
handsome brass-mounted handpumps on a good solid counter with
brass elbow rest and kicking ledge, and panelling to match the walls.
Good value bar food includes home-made soup (60p), sandwiches
(from 75p), ploughman's (£1.30), cheeseburgers (£1.35), bacon and
egg (£1.50), spaghetti or chilli con carne (£1.65), plaice (£1.85),
home-made steak and kidney pie (£1.85), scampi (£2) and a choice of
hot daily specials such as cheese and onion pie (£1.65) and liver and
onion (£1.75). In summer there may be barbecues out by the bowling
green, which is up steps from a small back courtyard. *(Recommended
by Comus Elliott)*

*Free house · Licensee Kathlean Scott · Real ale · Meals and snacks · Open
11.30–3.30, 5.30–10.30*

STOCKPORT (Greater Manchester)   SJ8991 Map 7
Red Bull

14 Middle Hillgate; turn off A6 beside town hall following fingerpost towards
Marple and Hyde into Edward Street; turn left at traffic lights – pub almost
immediately on your left

Particularly well kept Robinsons Best on handpump and good value
food, all home made, make this welcoming old-fashioned pub really
worth knowing. Its snug rooms opening off the central island serving

counter are traditionally furnished with substantial settles and seats built in to the partly panelled walls. There are open fires, beams, some flagstones, and for decoration lots of brassware, sketches and paintings. The food, which varies daily, includes soup (80p), a choice of cheeses (£1.30), open sandwiches (from £1.40), pies such as chicken and mushroom, pork and ham or steak and kidney pie (£2.65) and a full roast beef lunch (£3.70); dominoes, cribbage, piped music; friendly efficient service. (Recommended by L N Goulding)

Robinsons · Licensee Brian Lawrence · Real ale · Meals (lunchtime, not Sun) and snacks (lunchtime, not Sun, and early weekday evenings) · Open 11–3, 5.30–10.30

TOCKHOLES (Lancs)   SD6623 Map 7
Victoria

Village signposted from A6062 on S edge of Blackburn; though not signposted, a good route is on pretty moorland road about 1½ miles N of Belmont, just past AA telephone box (on opposite side)

Cosy and friendly, this comfortably modernised moorland village pub is popular for its wide choice of entirely home-made bar food which includes soup (50p), black pudding salad (70p), sandwiches (from 60p, steak 65p, open prawn on granary bread with egg and salad or steak on French bread with chips (£1.50), ploughman's (£1.25), cheese and onion pie or steak pudding (£1.25), salads (from £1.25), chicken curry (£1.50), steak and kidney pie (£1.75) and scampi or mixed grill (£2.25). The walls, attractively stripped back to bare stone in parts, are decorated with hanging plates, and the stub ends of knocked-through walls provide snug alcoves for tables, which have comfortably cushioned banquettes and Windsor chairs around them. Fruit machine, piped music. There is a separate restaurant, and a popular parties and functions room. (Recommended by Sue and Len Beattie)

Free house · Licensee Jack Threlfall · Meals and snacks · Children in restaurant and area partly set aside · Occasional live music Weds · Open 11.30–3, 6.30–11 all year

nr TOCKHOLES (Lancs)   SD6623 Map 7
Black Bull

Brokenstones Road, Livesey; between Tockholes and Blackburn, OS Sheet 103 reference 665247

Big windows look out over Blackburn, far below the high pastures surrounding this popular and comfortably modernised pub. The open-plan lounge, divided into alcoves by wooden pillars, has sturdy brown button-back wall banquettes on its red patterned carpet, big pictures and horse brasses on its cream walls, and friendly attentive service. Food includes soup (40p), sandwiches (from 70p), basket snacks such as steak muffin (70p), salads (from £1.30), ploughman's with ham as well as cheese (£1.45), steak and kidney pie (£1.75) and pizzas (£2.25); well kept Thwaites Bitter and Mild on handpump; on our visit, piped Frank Sinatra. There's a fine old slate-bed snooker-table in the separate games bar; some seats outside. *(Recommended by Sue and Len Beattie)*

Thwaites · Licensee Henry George Richards · Real ale · Meals and snacks Children in small room off lounge · Open 11.45–3, 7–11 all year

UPPERMILL (Greater Manchester)   SD9905 Map 7
Church

Church Road; from A670 in Uppermill turn into New Road, by a zebra crossing close to the chapel; this is the most practical-looking of the lanes towards the high moors and leads directly into Church Road

Its setting by an isolated church on a steep slope of the moors – giving fine valley views from outside, and from the smallish window by the bar counter – makes this old pub worth visiting. It also has good freshly made filled rolls or steak sandwiches, and at lunchtime ploughman's, steak and kidney pie, mixed grill, salads and so forth, quickly served (as we can't get up-to-date price details out of the pub itself we'd be very grateful for news of these from readers); well kept Matthew Browns John Peel and Youngers IPA and No 3 on handpump. Comfortable furnishings include captain's chairs and some old-fashioned settles, and the walls – some stripped back to bare stone – are decorated with horseshoes, sporting trophies, the bellringers' practice handbell set, and the horsecollar worn by the winner of the pub's annual gurning championship; piped classical music. You can sit outside, listening to the geese up the hill.
(Recommended by Roy Gawne, Tim Halstead, J Baker, E M Lees; more reports please)

Free house · Real ale · Meals (lunchtime) and snacks · Open 11.30–3, 6.30–11 all year

Cross Keys ★

Runninghill Gate; from previous entry go further up hill

Particularly popular with walkers, this low-beamed hill pub is the headquarters of the Oldham mountain rescue team and various outdoor sports clubs: tracks from it lead straight up towards Broadstone Hill and Dick Hill. It's very cheery and lively, and it sponsors road running or fell races in the first week in June and on the last Saturday in August (there are lots of colourful photographs of these among the older prints on the walls). An attractive flagstoned terrace behind, with bright flowers sheltered by a dry-stone wall, has good views, and there are swings, a slide and a climbing-frame out here. Inside, several connecting rooms ramble about, with pews, settles, some low beams and flagstones, and the original cooking range. A wide choice of bar food includes sandwiches, and at lunchtime lasagne, lemon sole, cod Mornay, seafood platter, scampi, beef stew with dumplings and steak and kidney pie; well kept Lees Bitter and Mild on handpump; darts, dominoes, cribbage, a bridge school on Monday and Thursday, and a fruit machine. The Saddleworth Clog and Garland Girls treat this as their HQ.

'Space game' means any electronic game, even a thoroughly earth-bound one.

(Recommended by Tim Halstead, Philip Asquith, Keith Myers, Paul West, John and Andrew Kemp)

Lees · Licensee Philip Kay · Real ale · Meals (lunchtime) and snacks · Children in side room and room with kitchen range · Clog dancing Mon, folk music Weds · Open 11.30–3, 6–11 all year (opens 6.30 in winter)

WHEATLEY LANE (Lancs) SD8338 Map 7
Old Sparrow Hawk

Towards E end of village road which runs N of and parallel to A6068; one way of reaching it is to follow Fence, Newchurch 1¾ signpost, then turn off at Barrowford ¾ signpost

Always welcoming and busy, this spacious and attractively modernised pub serves reliable food including home-made soup (60p), a good range of sandwiches (from 50p, toasted cheese and ham £1, steak or bacon and turkey £1.70), ploughmans (£1.25), and lots of salads from the efficiently manned cold counter, including Grosvenor pie, prawn, roast meats, smoked ham or mackerel and smoked salmon (£2.50–£3.25). Upstairs there's a pleasant mock-Tudor hot carvery with good roasts (lunch, not Saturday, £6.45; dinner £6.95). There are some pleasantly snug quiet corners in the communicating rooms of the open-plan lounge, which has some studded leather seats, long button-back banquettes, dark oak panelling (some of the wall has been stripped back to show the old masonry), gleaming copper hoods over the log-effect gas fires, a stained-glass dome, and three stuffed sparrowhawks. Well kept Bass, Cask Bitter (Brew Ten), and Jennings (from Cumbria) on handpump. Tables on a fair-sized terrace give a view over to the moors behind Nelson and Colne, and Pendle Hill rises behind the pub.
(Recommended by Do and Kenneth Hummer, Sue and Len Beattie, J A Catton)

Bass · Licensee Don Butterworth · Real ale · Meals and snacks · Children upstairs and in small snug · Open 11.30–3, 5.30–11 all year

WHITEWELL (Lancs) SD6546 Map 7
Inn at Whitewell ★★

Most easily reached by B6246 from Whalley; road through Dunsop Bridge from B6478 is also good

Alone by a church in the Forest of Bowland, this mellow and substantial stone inn has lawns running down to the River Hodder. Its lovely setting, the friendly and pleasantly old-fashioned standards of service, and comfortable traditional furnishings earn it its high rating, and it serves good bar good including home-made soup with granary bread (85p), sandwiches (from 85p), pâté (£2), ploughman's (£2.60), spicy Cumberland sausage, steak and kidney pie or creamy haddock pie (£2.95), seafood pancake (£3.60) and locally smoked Lune salmon (£4.85), with a choice of salads such as home-baked ham in cider (around £3), and excellent puddings (around £1); there is also a separate restaurant, overlooking the river. The bars have antique settles and oak gateleg tables, old cricketing and sporting prints, heavy curtains on sturdy wooden rails, log fires (the lounge has a particularly attractive stone fireplace), and sonorous clocks; Moorhouses (from Burnley) on handpump is well kept, and the staff service the small bar counter very efficiently, even on summer weekends when it can be crowded. The public bar has darts, pool, shove-ha'penny, dominoes, space game and a juke box, with a 1920s game-of-skill slot machine, and a piano is conspicuously available for anyone who wants to play. Seats outside in front catch the afternoon sun. The inn has eight miles of trout, salmon and sea trout fishing on the Hodder, and a mile on the Ribble. It can also (with notice) arrange shooting. The countryside around – quite off the usual tourist track – consists of well wooded rolling hills set off against higher moors. A nice place to stay. *(Recommended by D C Turner, Sue and Len Beattie, Tim Halstead, Philip Asquith, Keith Myers, Paul West, Carol Pearson, J A Catton, J A and M R Catterall)*

Free house · Licensee Richard Bowman · Real ale · Meals and snacks (not Sat evening) · Children welcome · Open 11–3, 6–11 all year · Bedrooms tel Dunsop Bridge (020 08) 222; £25 (£29B)/£35 (£39B)

Lucky Dip

Besides the fully inspected pubs, you might like to try these Lucky Dips recommended and described by readers (if you do, please send us reports):

ACCRINGTON [SD7528], *Greyhound*:useful lunchtime stop, with sandwiches and other bar food, and Websters Yorkshire real ale *(David Regan)*
AFFETSIDE [Watling Street; SD7513], *Pack Horse*: food good, and Hydes beer well kept, in partly fifteenth-century remote country pub with skull of Lord Derby's Civil War executioner *(J S Bacon)*
BELMONT [SD6716], *Black Dog*: moorland village pub with traditional communicating rooms, warm open fires, friendly atmosphere and cheap Holts real ales; has been a main entry, previously very popular with readers, but new licensee *(LYM; up-to-date reports on the new regime please)*
BILLINGE [Crank Road; SD5300], *Holts Arms*: good local with small rooms, coal fires, handpump Burtonwood ales, bowling green, and welcoming licencees; snacks only *(J A Ball)*
BELTHORN [SD7224], *Dog*: friendly old-world Whitbreads pub with lots of brass, wolfhound's head over fireplace, fine views; very much concentrating on the good restaurant, and very busy *(Anon)*
BIRKENHEAD [Chester Street; SJ3289], *Woodside Hotel*: fine big modern bar overlooking ferry; bedrooms *(W T Aird)*
BLACKPOOL [Topping Street; SD3035], *Criterion*: busy efficient town pub with good atmosphere (at least out of season) *(Dr A K Clarke)*
BOLTON BY BOWLAND [SD7849], *Coach & Horses*: in attractive spot below church on smaller of two village greens with stocks and whipping post *(Anon)*
BROOKHOUSE [SD5464], *Black Bull*: simple bar meals and well kept Thwaites real ales in comfortably modernised stone pub just below moors *(Mr and Mrs D G Shipton, LYM)*
BURNLEY [Gannow Lane; SD8332], *Gannow Wharfe*: friendly atmosphere in recently refurbished Bass canalside pub near M65; good food, big rooms, including games room (for pub location see OS Sheet 103 reference 821327) *(L F Beattie)*; [Red Lees Road] *Kettledrum*: friendly cosy small pub named after local Derby winner, decorated with collections of ships' clocks, bayonets, boomerangs and brass; good quick bar snacks, and separate restaurant (for pub location see OS Sheet 103 reference 873305) *(Sue and Len Beattie)*; [Glen View Road] *Scarecrow*: farm tools, stuffed birds decorating ceiling, and plastic ivy in stables-like décor, for new pub built in old style with stone roof and

floors; good food, Thwaites ales (for pub location see OS Sheet 103 reference 837309) *(L F Beattie)*

nr BURNLEY [High Halstead; SD8833], *Roggerham Gate*: in hills by Swinden reservoirs, with restaurant and real ale (for pub location see OS Sheet 103 reference 884337) *(Anon)*

BURY [The Wylde; SD8010], *Two Tubs*: friendly staff, imaginative snacks and good Thwaites real ale in small old-fashioned vault; also restaurant *(Colin McLaren)*

nr BURY [Ellbutt Lane, Birtle; SD8010], *Pack Horse*: cosy friendly country pub on hills with views; Lees beers (for pub location see OS Sheet 109 reference 836125) *(Brian and Anna Marsden)*

CHIPPING [Hesketh Lane Village; SD6243], *Dog & Partridge*: partly sixteenth-century pub on edge of Forest of Bowland with good traditional bar food, excellent smart evening restaurant for reasonably priced six-course meals, and good value Sunday roast lunches *(Mr and Mrs J J Kennedy)*; [Windy Street] *Sun*: in attractive village; real ale pub with stream running under cellar, said to be haunted *(Anon)*

CHURCHTOWN [SD3618 – the one near Southport], *Hesketh Arms*: food and beer good in spaciously renovated yet warmly unspoilt Victorian pub *(James Roberts)*

nr COLNE [SD8839], *Herders*: substantial helpings of good value food, and well kept Youngers Scotch and Tetleys, served by welcoming staff *(D C Turner)*

CRAWSHAWBOOTH [Burnley Road; SD8125], *Jester*: food and beer good in friendly unpretentious pub, recently modernised; lovely views from bay window (for pub location see OS Sheet 103 reference 812255) *(Len Beattie)*

DIGGLE [Sam Road, Saddleworth; SE0008], *Diggle*: clean and friendly, efficiently run pub, built in 1840s by entrance to Standedge canal/railway tunnel, serves appetising food, and well kept Timothy Taylors Landlord; children allowed in small snug *(Warwick Peirson)*

ECCLES [Church Street; SJ7798], *Duke of York*: big friendly straightforward pub with good range of well kept real ales, cheerful atmosphere and quiet no-smoking room; regular live music *(Brian and Anna Marsden)*

EDGWORTH [SD7416], *White Horse*: good food and beer, interesting lacquered panelling, log fires; busy at weekends (for pub location see OS Sheet 109 reference 742168) *(Sue and Len Beattie)*

ENTWISTLE [SD7217], *Strawbury Duck*: fine old remote pub in country park, with good choice of well kept beers and snacks, very friendly and obliging service, beams and interesting furnishings including wooden settles, cheese-press table, and good atmosphere. (Though everyone calls it the Strawberry Duck, as we did in the last edition of the *Guide*, the above spelling is the right one!) (For pub location see OS Sheet 109 reference 726177) *(M N Bowman, Gareth Ratcliffe, Brian and Anna Marsden, Sue and Len Beattie)*

FAILSWORTH [SD9002], ten tied houses from ten different breweries in a one-mile stretch of the main road here – a superb pub crawl! *(Barrie Pepper)*

FENCE [Wheatley Lane Road; SD8237], *Bay Horse*: food good in lively, long low pub with a few nooks, and Matthew Browns ales *(Len Beattie)*; [Harpers Lane] *Harpers*: very good bar snacks in lively, recently refurbished neat and clean open-plan pub (for pub location see OS Sheet 103 reference 828376) *(Len Beattie)*; [Wheatley Lane Road] *White Swan*: about a dozen different real ales on handpump, including excellent Timothy Taylors Landlord, in open-plan rooms with paintings of horses and racing silks, table-tops formed from sawn logs, lively atmosphere and friendly welcome *(Sue and Len Beattie)*

FORTON [SD4851], *New Holly Hotel*: warm welcome and good value bedrooms (for pub location see OS Sheet 102 reference 492505) *(PLC)*

FRECKLETON [SD4228], *Ship*: wide variety of food with at least 30 dishes at once-round-the-table help-yourself lunchtime buffet, in quite large pub, well kept and charmingly modernised; beautiful situation overlooking River Ribble *(G S Burrows)*

GARSTANG [SD4845], *Farmers Arms*: good value food, friendly helpful staff, well kept Tetleys *(Dennis Royles)*

nr GARSTANG [Churchtown; SD4845], *Horns*: food good value for money *(DL)*

GREASBY [SJ2587], *Greave Dunning*: Boddingtons, Ind Coope and Tetleys real ale in fairly recently opened long building with three or four well-planned bars *(R L Wilson)*

GREAT MITTON [SD7139], *Aspinall Arms*: food, beer and welcome good in village pub close to River Ribble; separate lounge where you can take children; jazz Monday and Thursday (for pub location see OS Sheet 103 reference 716377) *(Sue & Len Beattie)*

HALSALL [just off A567; SD3710], *Saracens Head*: good food and real ale in picturesque canalside pub, cosy and warm in winter, genuinely friendly licensees; can get crowded at weekends *(James Roberts, G S Burrows)*

HASLINGDEN [Manchester Road; SD7823], *Woolpack*: good beer in free house which used to be Clive Lloyd's digs, opposite Haslingden Cricket Club *(Bryan Shiner)*

HAWK GREEN [SU9687], *Crown*: reasonably priced food and Robinsons real ales with attentive service in well kept friendly pub on village green *(C R Carey, Mrs G Fish)*

HESWALL [Telegraph Road; SJ2782], *Drift Inn*: was in 1984 Which? Wine Guide as Basil's; now under new management, still does food and is more of a pub specialising in real ale *(Anon)*

HEYWOOD [Pilsworth Road; SD8612], *Three Arrows*: friendly staff serving snacks and Lees beers; garden *(Colin McLaren)*

HIGHTOWN [SD2903], *Pheasant*: recently extended old pub, sympathetically modernised and spacious, with appetising lunchtime food; quiet open country *(G S Burrows)*

HORNBY [SD5869], *Royal Oak*: cheerful pub with friendly welcome and open fire, also good range of reasonably priced food *(Richard Taylor)*

HYDE [Manchester Road; SJ9494], *Cheshire Ring*: big friendly many-roomed pub (was Navigation Inn), with lots of real ales, two pool-tables and good juke box *(Lee Goulding)*

LANCASTER [Morecambe Road; SD4862], *Lancastrian*: tasty food and well kept Boddingtons in nice pub with medieval décor *(H R Hackson)*

nr LANESHAW BRIDGE [SD9240], *Hargreaves Arms*: small clean open-plan pub with collection of plates, friendly landlord, well kept Websters Yorkshire, and good food (for pub location see OS Sheet 103 reference 933412) *(Sue and Len Beattie)*

LIVERPOOL [Wapping; SJ4395], *Baltic Fleet*: old dockside pub reopened as lively free house with several real ales; live music *(Anon)*; [Renshaw Street] *Grapes*: lively Irish pub with well kept Tetley-Walkers beers, popular with university students *(Alan Carter, Lesley Foote)*; [Cumberland Street] *Poste House*: good lunchtime food in small, busy, but neat, two-floor Higsons pub *(J A C Edwards)*; [Dale Street] *Saddle*: tasty lunchtime food in busy well kept central pub *(J A C Edwards)*; [Wood Street] *Swan*: attractive wall decorations and juke box, well kept real ale, often crowded *(P A Woolley)*

LONGTON [Marsh Lane; SD4726], *Dolphin*: real ale pub near marshes, may be closed at lunchtime (for pub location see OS Sheet 102 reference 457254) *(Anon)*

MANCHESTER [Great Bridgewater Street; SJ8398], *Britons Protection*: quite plush Victorian décor, haunted; well kept Tetleys real ales *(Dr A K Clarke)*; [Oldham Street] *Castle*: archetypal 'Rovers Return' pub with friendly atmosphere and bar staff; wooden panels, tiled mural, lots of paintings, lit by oil lamps; well kept Robinsons and Old Tom, pool, TV; quiet relief from nearby city-centre pubs *(L N Goulding, A P Marriott)*; [Portland Street] *Circus Tavern*: tiny cosy pub with warm atmosphere *(Dr A K Clarke)*; [Brunswick] *Falcon*: new Banks's pub in open space near university, with lively, warm welcome, good food and well kept beer *(Dr A K Clarke)*; [Northenden] *Jolly Carter*: modern pub with character *(Bob Rendle)*; [Charles Street] *Lass o' Gowrie*: Whitbreads own-brew pub, ornately tiled outside, but with bare floorboards and stripped walls, gas lamps, hop sacks and so forth inside; food counter, windows into brewery; small traditionally furnished side parlour *(Howard Gascoyne)*; [Rochdale Road] *Marble Arch*: renovated Victorian pub (tiled ceiling shows alcoholic delights), bustling and friendly, with wide range of real ales including guest beers from all over the country *(Brian and Anna Marsden)*; [Shambles Square] *Old Wellington*: flagstones and gnarled oak timbers, good bar snacks, well kept Bass, oak-panelled bar and small second-floor restaurant; can get very busy *(Lee Goulding, Colin McLaren, BB)*; [St Annes Square] *Royal Exchange Theatre*: coffee bar open to non-patrons 10 am – 9.30 pm, drinks during licensing hours; good for a theatre bar, somewhat trendy *(Colin McLaren)*; [Errwood Road, Burnage; SJ8591] *Sun in September*: cheap Sam Smiths beers and popular good value lunchtime food in comfortable Spanish-style building with varied piped music and lots of house plants *(Lee Goulding)*; [Ashton New Road, Bradford; SJ8591] *Why Not*: good beer in enterprising free house wallpapered with wartime newspapers and full of interesting objects – hat collections, old wireless sets, clocking-on machines, theatrical pictures and so forth (reminiscent of Yew Tree, Cauldon, on a smaller scale); games room, superb prawn barm cakes *(Lee Goulding)*

MAWDESLEY [Hall Lane; SD4915], *Mawdesley Eating House*: country pub in pleasant surroundings with friendly and cheerful young staff serving good food at reasonable prices; tends to get crowded (especially Saturday evenings) *(Wendy Hillary, Keith Huyton)*

MIDDLETON [Market Place; SD8606], *Jacques*: reasonably priced bar food and separate restaurant, in converted police station (some cell bars left), with recreated old shop fronts down side alley; beer garden; evening pianist *(Richard Glover)*

MOSSLEY [Manchester Road; SD9802], *Roaches Lock*: big open rooms, comfortable seating, clean, good service; original stone walls and attractive, unusual décor *(Miss B Charlton)*

NEWTON [Frankby Road; SD4431], *Ridger*: good lunchtime food at reasonable prices with wide choice; pleasant décor and nice atmosphere; very popular *(J A Blades)*

NEWTON-LE-WILLOWS [Southworth Road; SJ5896], *Bulls Head*: friendly and cheerful customers and staff, good real ale, good value food; bedrooms *(K M Crook)*

PARBOLD [Alder Lane; SD4911], *Stocks Tavern*: well kept Tetleys, and wide choice of wines and whiskies; also good value food *(P Leatherbarrow)*

PENDLETON [SD7539], *Swan With Two Necks*: friendly welcome, well kept beer, and good value homely food in attractive village below Pendle Hill *(Dennis Royles)*

PLEASINGTON [Victorian Road; SD6426], *Butlers Arms*: warm atmosphere in well kept comfortably modernised pub serving good Matthew Browns; bowling green outside *(Sue and Len Beattie)*

PRESTON [Church Street; SD5330], *Grey Horse*: food good and reasonably priced in refurbished Yates Wine Lodge (but definitely a pub) with unusual design; Theakstons and Thwaites, and excellent range of wines and ports; lively, friendly young person's pub *(M C Dickson)*

RABY [The Green; SJ3180], *Wheatsheaf*: comfortable early seventeenth-century thatched pub with coal fires, charming furnishings, choice of real ales, and wide range of lunchtime food *(Mr and Mrs J H Adam, W H Harrison)*

ROCHDALE [Toad Lane; SD8913], *Baum*: good food in small cosy upstairs restaurant, in listed building; conservatory behind bar; well kept Wilsons and Boddingtons *(P H Drabble)*

nr ROCHDALE [Ashworth Moor, A680; SD8913], *Owd Betts*: low-beamed moorland pub with lots of bric-à-brac, wooden settles and good atmosphere (for pub location see OS Sheet 109 reference 831161) *(Sue and Len Beattie)*

SIMISTER [Simister Lane; SD8305], *Same Yet*: two-roomed farmhouse-style pub in rural setting with pleasant atmosphere, old bric-à-brac, darts and dominoes, open fires, and pianist some nights *(J R Glover)*

SWINTON [East Lancs Road; SD7701], *Narrow Boat*: a barge you can sit in along one wall with mock lock gates and water, stained-glass entrance doors, good service and atmosphere with smart staff; well kept Greenalls *(Michele Butterworth)*

THORNTON HOUGH [SJ3081], *Seven Stars*: friendly and attractive country village pub, small and spotless with tasty bar meals at reasonable prices *(Mrs M C Andrews)*

TIMPERLEY [SJ7988], *Hare & Hounds*: good bar food and smart restaurant; summer terrace *(ACH)*

TOCKHOLES [SD6623], *Royal Arms*: stuffed animals, big game pictures, guns in many small rooms of pub opposite nature trail; Thwaites real ale, large open fires *(Gareth Ratcliffe, BB)*

TUNSTALL [SD6173], *Lunesdale Arms*: good food (especially lasagne) and drink *(Mrs R S Young)*

TWO MILLS [SJ3474], *Tudor Rose*: upstairs pub restaurant is comfortable with good food and service *(W T Aird)*

WENNINGTON [SD6270], *Bridge*: genuine country pub with good value bar meals, hidden away on road outside village – quite a find *(MGBD)*

WESTHOUGHTON [Chorley Road; SD6505], *Brinsop Arms*: well kept Bass, Boddingtons, Hammonds and Hartleys, lunchtime bar food Monday to Saturday, and cold table; bedrooms planned *(Jack Lalor)*

WEST KIRBY [SJ2187], *Dee Arms*: roomy chatty local with cheerful atmosphere *(W T Aird)*; *Moby Dick*: friendly and efficient, with older clientele; separate restaurant, and varied choice of lunchtime food in comfortable lounge *(W T Aird)*

WHALLEY [SD7336], *Swan*: wide choice of beers, bar food includes excellent sandwiches, new manager trying hard; plenty of tables *(Dr H B Cardwell)*

WHEELTON [SD6021], *Top Lock*: food good, service excellent *(Jenny Betts)*

WIGAN [Standish Lower Ground; SD5805], *Royal Oak*: wide choice of bar food, very popular especially at weekends; children admitted early evening *(Neil Davenport, Jo Cook)*

WOODLEY [Hyde Road; SJ9392], *Lowes Arms*: friendly pub, nice and clean, with lovely meals; big helpings of homely cooking at reasonable prices; children allowed if eating (specially priced small helpings) *(John Beswick)*

WOOLTON [SJ4187], *Elephant*: attractive with cheerful atmosphere, and well kept beer *(Alan Carter and Lesley Foote)*

WYCOLLAR [SD9339], *Herders*: good beer and simple food in very pleasant pub on high road overlooking Wycollar Country Park; wooden settles and Victorian chaise longue; coal-burning stoves, friendly cat; juke box not too loud *(Sue and Len Beattie)*

Leicestershire, Lincolnshire and Nottinghamshire

There have been quite a few recent changes worth noting here. Most importantly, the charmingly old-fashioned Crown in Old Dalby has reinforced its reputation for good food in a fine relaxed atmosphere so strongly that we have this year awarded it a second star, and now rate it as the nicest pub in the area. The Bell at East Langton, under its friendly French licensee, has also consolidated its reputation for fine food, and the French Horn at Upton, without doing anything fancy, has this last year won a national competition for the quality of its food and drink. The Noel Arms in Langham (no longer a Ruddles tied house) and the Bull in Market Deeping, both in very different ways good pubs, are under new management now; and there have been quite a lot of less striking but

The Angel & Royal, Grantham

important changes in opening times (still very varied in this county), internal layout and the sort of food and drink that's sold, in many of the other pubs we mention. One thing, though, hasn't changed – and that's this area's remarkable reputation for value for money. It has some of the best value cheap snacks in Britain, its more elaborate pub food is usually attractively priced, and among drinks prices (which are on average rather low) there are one or two outstanding bargains – the friendly and extraordinarily old-fashioned Cap & Stocking in Kegworth and the neo-classical New Market Hotel in Nottingham are among the very cheapest places in Britain. Though it isn't cheap, we'd put the George in Stamford among the best places here for food, though its greatest appeal, very strong indeed, is for its fascination as a marvellous old building; it's a fine place to stay. Among many pubs offering straightforward food at sensible prices we'd pick out the Griff Inn in Drakeholes (very neatly kept bars and garden, with attractive views), the comfortable and relaxed Five Bells in Edenham, the Fox & Hounds at Exton (a handsome old coaching-inn), the Beehive in Grantham (for its ploughman's and other cheap snacks – and its remarkable old live beehive inn-sign), Bewicke Arms in Hallaton (particularly for its daily specials), the Old Kings Arms in Newark (which has expanded its evening meals since our last edition), the unusually decorated Red Lion in Newton (for its remarkable cold table), the warmly welcoming Jackson Stops in Stretton, the comfortable Bulls Head in Wilson (another excellent cold table) and the homely Kings Arms in Wing. The interesting old Wig & Mitre in Lincoln usefully stays open all day for food, from breakfast-time onwards. For something unusual, you might try the winter spit-roasts at the Angel & Royal in Grantham – an inn with a pedigree going back many centuries to the Knights Templar. We've got a soft spot for the well filled cobs and home-pickled eggs at the altogether humbler Woodlark in Lambley, and the daily lunchtime summer barbecues at the lively Three Wheatsheaves in Nottingham are highly recommended. The Olde Trip to Jerusalem in the same town is well worth visiting for its uniquely cavernous bars cut out of the castle rock; the venerable Saracen's Head in Southwell still has some of the atmosphere that it would have done when it was the scene of Charles I's last night of freedom; the Hercules in Sutton Cheney has a good collection of real ales in old-fashioned surroundings. After two years in which we more than doubled the number of main entries included for this area, we have this last year added no new full entries: we have as it were left the Lucky Dips fallow, to give a chance for information from readers to build up and produce a really good crop of candidates for inspection for a future *edition. As we go to press with this one, several of the Lucky Dips, besides quite a number in Leicester, Lincoln and Nottingham, are looking particularly promising: the Brookside at Barkby (remarkable collection of toby jugs), Old Plough at Braunston (good food in a country pub), Cross Keys at Castle Donington (tasty food in a pub run by former Campaign for Real Ale leading lights), canalside Lime Kilns at Hinckley, civilised George at Leadenham, old-fashioned King William by the river at Scaftworth, and – especially – the interesting Fox & Goose at Illston and (for good food and beer in charming comfort) Crown at Tur Langton.*

BARHOLM (Lincs)   TF0810 Map 8

Five Horseshoes

Particularly well kept Adnams, Batemans XXXB (from Wainfleet All Saints, near Skegness) and guest beers, on handpump, and the welcoming easy-going atmosphere are what bring so many people to this comfortable and almost homely village pub. Its purple-carpeted lounge bar, which still preserves the shapes of separate knocked-together rooms, has well cushioned sturdy seats by spick-and-span copper tables. One of the beams is decorated with lots of race and horse-show members' tickets. Darts, fruit machine, a space game and maybe piped music. The lawn behind this attractive stone village house has tables by the flowerbeds, backed by paddocks. *(Recommended by John Armstrong)*

Free house · Licensee A Lilley · Real ale · Open 10.30–2, 5.30–11 all year; closed Mon lunchtime except bank hols

BARROW ON SOAR (Leics)   SK5717 Map 7

Riverside Inn

The attraction here is the waterside position, with a floodlit lawn by the slow wide river. Inside, the main lounge area, looking out to the river, has comfortable banquettes around copper-topped tables. Bar food is served, such as sandwiches, ploughman's with salad niçoise, lasagne, basket meals and a dish of the day which might be home-made pie (£2.25). A distinct, but communicating area, with curly red plush button-back wall banquettes and younger customers, has a good juke box, darts and a space game; there are also bar billiards, dominoes and a fruit machine. A separate restaurant is open fully at weekends, with lower children's prices. *(More reports please)*

Free house · Licensee Ashley Denis Moore · Children in end lounge (lunchtime only) and restaurant · Live music dinner-dance Sat · Open 11–2.30, 6–10.30 all year

There are report forms at the back of the book.

In next year's edition we hope to pick out pubs that are specially nice to stay at, alongside the star ratings. Please tell us if you think any pub – in the *Guide* or not – deserves a 'Stay Award'. No stamp needed: *The Good Pub Guide*, FREEPOST, London SW10 0BR.

BLYTH (Notts)   SK6287   Map 7

Angel

The first of the great inns built here 250 years ago, when the Great North Road coaching traffic started to build up, this is now a welcoming and cheerful pub. The clean and spacious modernised lounge has comfortable red plush seats and banquettes, coal fires in winter, and is decorated with horse brasses, pictures and colourful ornaments. Bar food includes soup (60p), sandwiches (from 60p), a basket of chips (70p), a pint of prawns (£1.80), salads (from £2.30), scampi in a basket (£2.50), seafood platter (£3.30), grilled gammon (£3.50) and steak (£4.30), with daily specials such as plaice stuffed with slightly garlicky prawns (£3.20); well kept Hardys & Hansons Best and Best Mild on electric pump; juke box or background music, and a fruit machine in a separate lobby outside the public bar, which has dominoes, cribbage and a pool-room. *(Recommended by D A Angless, Tony Gayfer, Tim Halstead, Philip Asquith, Keith Myers, Paul West)*

Hardys & Hansons · Licensee Peter Wragg · Real ale · Meals and snacks Children welcome · Open 11–3, 6–10.30 · Bedrooms tel Blyth (090 976) 213; £12/£24

DRAKEHOLES (Notts)   SK7090   Map 7

Griff Inn

Village signposted from A631 in Everton, between Bawtry and Gainsborough

This part of the world isn't exactly noted for its splendid views, but the little bluff on which this civilised and well run pub stands counts almost as a mountain here, and one reason why people like the pub is that it does give peaceful views out over a basin of the old Chesterfield Canal and the flat valley of the River Idle – a charming prospect, even when it's misty. The well kept lounge bar has small grey or dusky pink plush seats around its neat tables, and little landscape prints on the silky-papered walls. Its bar food includes sandwiches (from 80p), soup, home-made steak and kidney or ham and chicken pie, gammon or freshly battered haddock (£2.75), scampi (£3) and seafood platter or steak (£3.50); Bass and Websters Yorkshire kept under light pressure; friendly service, piped music. Besides the comfortable separate restaurant (with a cosy cocktail bar), there's a continental-style summer room with a fountain (mainly catering for weddings), and a functions room. There are tables outside in the neatly landscaped gardens. *(Recommended by Flt Lt A Darroch Harkness, ILP)*

Free house · Licensee John Griffiths · Meals and snacks (not Mon, or Sun evening in winter) · Children welcome · Open 12–3, 7–11 all year; closed Mon lunchtime in summer, all day Mon and Tues lunchtime in winter

EAST LANGTON (Leics)   SP7292   Map 4

Bell

The Langtons signposted from A6 N of Market Harborough; East Langton signposted from B6047

The food has now become so popular at this pretty white pub that virtually all the space is devoted to people eating, and the French landlord's stylish cooking concentrates on meals rather than snacks. At lunch, for example, three courses (£6.95) might include as starters watercress soup, smoked trout, chicken in turmeric rolled in bacon and then deep-fried in a beer-moistened batter, or avocado baked with Stilton and celery in cream and cider; then grilled lemon sole, lamb's kidneys and liver, lamb leg steak, trout or swordfish; followed by Barbados cream, chocolate roulade, bread and butter pudding or treacle tart. Though they no longer reckon to make pub snacks, they will still do sandwiches on request. Many of the tables can be booked, and there are more made of stripped oak, in a properly pubby area, with comfortable brown banquettes against the bare stone walls, and black beams in the white ceiling. On a weekday when it's quiet and peaceful you can still have a civilised drink here, perhaps chatting to the friendly *chef/patron*; Manns and Watneys Stag on handpump, kept under light blanket pressure; a fruit machine decently tucked away by the door, maybe piped music. The attractive village is set in peaceful countryside. *(Recommended by D and J W Michael Cooke, Lee Goulding, Cdr Patrick Tailyour)*

Manns · Licensee Pascall Trystram · Meals – tel East Langton (085 884) 567 – *and snacks (not Sun; no food first fortnight Aug) · Children welcome · Open 12–3, 6.30–12 all year*

EDENHAM (Lincs)   TF0621   Map 8
Five Bells

A151

The comfortably modernised open-plan lounge bar of this popular old stone pub is softly lit and relaxing, with seats built in to separate bays around the wood-effect tables, a good winter fire, and unobtrusive piped music. Friendly waitresses serve a wide choice of good value bar food such as sandwiches (from 60p), vegetable soup (70p), whitebait (£1.35), deep-fried mushrooms stuffed with home-made chicken liver pâté (£1.65), ploughman's (£1.95), plaice, lasagne or steak and kidney pie (£2.25), salads (from £2.25), fisherman's platter (£3.50), generous hors d'oeuvres (£3.75), and eight-ounce fillet or 16-ounce rump steak (£5.75), with roast beef on Sunday (£2.25). A children's menu includes beefburgers, fish fingers and so forth, with beans and chips (85p). Well kept Sam Smiths OB on handpump; dominoes, cribbage, fruit machine. The separate restaurant has a Saturday disco dinner-dance. There are seats by oak-trees in the garden, which has a fairy-tale tree playhouse. Just up the road the village churchyard with its spreading cedars is attractive. *(Recommended by John Armstrong; more reports please)*

Melbourns (no longer brews but has kept its tied houses) · Licensee Paul Stark Real ale · Meals and snacks · Children welcome · Open 11–2, 7–11 all year

---

Bedroom prices normally include full English breakfast, VAT and any inclusive service charge that we know of. Prices before the '/' are for single rooms, after for two people in double or twin; B denotes private bath, S a private shower. If there is no '/', the prices are only for twin or double rooms (as far as we know there are no singles).

EXTON (Leics)   SK9211   Map 8

Fox & Hounds

Remarkably imposing for a country inn, this strikingly tall stone building owes its grandeur largely to the fact that the quiet back road running along the unusual wooded village green was once the main Oakham coach route. Large helpings of good value freshly made bar food include sandwiches and ploughman's, chicken and leek soup (90p), pâté (£1.25), quiche (£1.75), smoked fish pie (£1.90), casseroles such as liver and tomato (£1.95) and lamb cutlets (£2.50) at lunchtime, with scampi (£3.90), poached chicken (£4.15), trout (£4.20), gammon (£4.95) and steak (£6.75) in the evening. On Sundays at lunchtime there's a choice between ploughman's and a traditional roast lunch. Food is brought by waitresses to an elegant high-ceilinged lounge bar, where two communicating rooms have some dark red plush easy chairs as well as wheelback seats around plenty of dark tables, hunting and striking military prints on the walls, and a winter log fire in a big stone fireplace; there is also a separate restaurant. Well kept Sam Smiths OB on handpump, unobtrusive piped music. The lively and quite separate public bar has darts, pool, dominoes, a juke box and a fruit machine. There are seats among large rosebeds on the well kept back lawn, overlooking paddocks. Rutland Water is about two miles away. *(Recommended by Alan Franck; more reports please)*

Melbourns (who no longer brew) · Licensee David Hillier · Real ale · Meals and snacks (not Mon) · Children welcome · Open 11–2.30, 6.30–11 all year Bedrooms tel Oakham (0572) 812403; £13.50B/£22B

GRANTHAM (Lincs)   SK9135   Map 8

Angel & Royal   *[illustrated on page 442]*

High Street

On the left of this striking old stone inn's coach entry, in the plush hotel bar, you can sit in an elegantly restored oriel window and think that this might have been the very spot where Richard III sat on 19 October 1483, when he ordered the death of the treacherous Duke of Buckingham. This is one of the country's very oldest inns, and on its elaborately carved façade you can still make out the heads of King Edward III and his queen on either side of the central angel, carved over 600 yeas ago to commemorate their visit when this was still a Commandery and Hospice of the Knights Templar. The popular bar on the opposide side of the entry has high beams, tapestry hangings, and a massive inglenook fireplace where, from November to March, whole pigs, venison or barons of beef are spit-roasted once a month or so – details of timings from the inn. Other bar food includes sandwiches, mushroom and Stilton fritters (£1.20), filled French bread (£1.50), daily hot specials (£2) and a lunchtime cold fish buffet in summer; well kept Bass, Batemans XXX and Ind Coope Burton on handpump in the right-hand bar, and they mix non-alcoholic and children's cocktails and serve morning coffee and afternoon teas. There is a separate restaurant. In general, the furnishings (like the buildings of the hotel itself, extended behind) are modern.

(Recommended by T Mansell, Howard Gascoyne, Stephan Carney)

Free house (THF) · Licensee Peter Willcock · Real ale · Meals and snacks Children in lounge · Open 11–3, 6–11 all year · Bedrooms tel Grantham (0476) 5816; £31 (£36B)/£45 (£51B)

Beehive

Castlegate; from main street turn down Finkin Street opposite George Hotel

The inn-sign here is quite unique, and not to be missed by people with a taste for pub curiosities. It's an old-fashioned beehive with live bees, mounted in the lime-tree outside, and has been the pub's sign since certainly 1830, and probably the eighteenth century. An old rhyme mentions it:

> *Grantham, now two rarities are thine:*
> *A lofty steeple and a living sign.*

(The steeple, 272 feet high, is that of the fourteenth-century St Wulfram's church.) Mr Bull, who has to use a ladder to tend to his bees, practically invented the ploughman's lunch some 25 years ago, and besides very cheap full-size ones, with chicken or ham as well as cheese (from 70p) he does small ones (only 37p), a wide choice of freshly cut sandwiches (from 40p), home-made soup (48p), cottage pie or macaroni cheese (98p) and home-baked ham salad with jacket potato (£1.20). The bar, completely refurbished since our last edition, is comfortable, with a fruit machine, space game and good juke box.

Free house · Licensee Sidney Bull · Meals (lunchtime) and snacks (not Sun) Open 11–3, 6.30–11 all year

HALLATON (Leics)   SP7896   Map 4

Bewicke Arms

On good fast back road across open rolling countryside between Uppingham and Kibworth

In the evening and at weekends, the popular bar food quickly fills the two small rooms of this cheerful thatched village pub's beamed main bar. It includes sandwiches (from 90p, with salad), ploughman's (from £1.35), salads (from £2.45), scampi (£2.95), gammon and egg (£3.30) and eight-ounce sirloin steak (£5.40), with several changing home-made daily specials such as mussels in white wine sauce or egg and prawn mayonnaise (£1.90), lasagne (£3), beef and wine casserole or Cromer crab salad (£3.60) and seafood casserole or steak and pheasant pie (£4.05); this is also served at lunchtime (when it's much quieter), and in a separate restaurant with bookable tables. The bar is cosy, with old-fashioned furniture and four gleaming copper kettles over the log fire in its stone hearth, and the landlord is sociable. Well kept Marstons Pedigree, Ruddles Bitter and County and Theakstons on handpump; darts, bar billiards and dominoes in the public bar, a fruit machine in the side corridor, and maybe piped music. Picnic-table sets on a crazy-paved back terrace look over the ex-stableyard car park to the hills behind. This attractive village has a traditional Easter Monday 'bottle-kicking' race (actually miniature barrels). *(Recommended by Michael Cooke, Lee Goulding, S E Hammond, Cdr Patrick Tailyour, Hugh Calvey)*

Free house · Licensee Neil Alan Spiers · Real ale · Meals (limited Sun lunchtime) and snacks; restaurant tel Hallaton (085 889) 217 · Children welcome · Open 12–2.30, 7–11

HORBLING (Lincs)   TF1135 Map 8
Plough

Spring Lane; off B1177

This creeper-covered village inn is almost unique in being owned by the parish council (the Royal Oak in Meavy – see Devon main entries – is the only other one we know of). Its lounge bar, which includes a nice old-fashioned high-backed settle in one corner, has a friendly local atmosphere, and serves bar food such as sandwiches or filled rolls (from 35p), hamburgers (65p), ploughman's (£1.10), curried chicken or steak and kidney pie (£2.15), gammon (£2.95) and rump

The Wig & Mitre, Lincoln

steak (£4.45); well kept Batemans XXXB on handpump; piped music. The lively public bar has pool, dominoes and sensibly placed darts. *(More reports please)*

Free house · Licensee Fred Andrew · Meals and snacks · Open 11–2, 7–11 all year · Bedrooms tel Sleaford (0529) 240263; £8/£16

HOSE (Leics)   SK7329   Map 7
Rose and Crown
Bolton Lane

This welcoming old village pub has popular bar food, and a good range of well kept real ales on handpump or tapped from the cask – usually half a dozen or more, such as Adnams, Hook Norton Best and Old Hookey, Hoskins, Marstons Pedigree and Theakstons Best, XB and Old Peculier, with other guest bitters such as Batemans, Greene King Abbot, Wadworths 6X or Woodfordes (from Norfolk). The well kept beamed lounge bar has been neatly modernised, and separated into two areas by three broad carpeted steps. It has comfortable green plush seats around dimpled copper tables, flickering electric candles, and lots of plates and some prints of Old Master paintings on its cream walls. An attractive cold counter has a good range of salads (from £3.10), and other bar food includes sandwiches or filled baps (from 55p), home-made meat and vegetable soup (60p), pâté (£1.10), ploughman's (from £1.25, local Stilton £1.50), pizza or plaice (£1.75), chicken (£1.95), ham or beef with chips (£2.20), scampi (£2.25), a wide choice of steaks (from six-ounce rump, £3.25) and winter daily specials such as steak and kidney pie or liver and bacon (£2–£2.50); there's also a small separate dining-room. The simpler public bar has darts, pool, a fruit machine, space game and juke box. There are tables on a fairy-lit terrace, sheltered behind the building and extended since our last edition. *(Recommended by Tony Field; more reports please)*

Free house · Licensee Carl Routh · Meals and snacks · Children in eating area and restaurant · Open 11.30–2.30, 6.30–11 all year (opens 7 in winter)

KEGWORTH (Leics)   SK4826   Map 7
Cap & Stocking

Under a mile from M1 junction 24; follow A6 towards Loughborough; in village, turn left down one-way High Street, then left and left again into Borough Street

Well worth finding, this splendidly unspoilt pub gives you the sensation of travelling back in time – many readers have been surprised that such a place can still survive. Good Bass, Springfield or Mitchells & Butlers Mild at wonderfully low prices, is brought up in foaming jugs from the cellar to a corner servery, where it's poured at a hatch by the extremely friendly licensee. You can stand in the central corridor, sit on the traditional leatherette wall benches of the popular tap-room on the right (where the walls are decorated with locally caught stuffed fish and a vast case of stuffed birds and animals, and there's lots of etched glass), or you can ply the ancient juke box with sixpences in the smoke room on the left. There are light bar snacks at lunchtime; shove-ha'penny, skittles, dominoes, and a fruit machine. *(Recommended by Lee Goulding, Michael Cooke, Philip Denison, H P Moss, Stephan Carney)*

Bass · Licensee Arthur Large · Real ale · Snacks (lunchtime, not Sun) · Open 11–2, 6–10.30

LAMBLEY (Notts)   SK6245   Map 7
Woodlark
Church Street

The lively and simply furnished vaults bar of this well preserved mining-village pub, decorated with lots of sailor hat ribands on its beams and a model battleship, serves good value simple snacks such as home-pickled eggs (15p), a wide choice of well filled fresh cobs (from 35p), small jars of cockles or mussels (39p) and ploughman's (from 85p). Well kept Home Bitter on electric pump; darts, dominoes and cribbage, maybe unobtrusive piped music. An upstairs bar has pool, a juke box, space game and another darts board; there is a separate skittle alley (also table skittles); a small annexe has a fruit machine; and there's a comfortably plush little snug lounge. You can sit out on a small terrace, well below road level but pleasantly airy: on the way out, notice the pub's unusual arched side windows. *(Recommended by E H Loudon; more reports please)*

Home · Licensee John Verney · Real ale · Snacks · Children in skittle alley and annexe · Open 10.30–2.30, 6–10.30

LANGHAM (Leics)   SK8411   Map 8
Noel Arms

Since our last edition this civilised pub has severed its connection with Ivo Vannocci's small chain of Poste Hotels and with Ruddles – it had been that brewery's only tied house. But they still keep Ruddles Bitter and County on handpump – in fine condition, what with the village brewery being just around the corner – and have added Marstons Pedigree and Youngers Scotch. The handsome low-ceilinged main lounge is still furnished much as before, too, with old settles and comfortable brown settees and chairs around shiny tables, horsy prints on buff hessian walls, and a free-standing log fire. Another inner room, with plush sofas and seats and woodland wallpaper, is quieter, and in summer you can sit on a stylish covered terrace surrounded by flowers. Bar food includes filled French bread (from 65p), ploughman's (around £1.65), stuffed mushrooms, omelettes, home-made steak and kidney pudding and turkey curry, and there is an extensive spread of help-yourself salads with home-made pâté, home-baked ham, rare beef, turkey, smoked salmon and so forth on a fine old oak farmhouse table. The separate restaurant has been newly decorated. Darts, dominoes. *(Recommended by L N Goulding, Capt F A Bland; up-to-date reports on the new regime please)*

Tipping is not normal for bar meals, and not usually expected.

Free house · Licensee Alan Eacott · Real ale · Meals and snacks · Children welcome · Open 11–2.30, 6–11 all year

LEICESTER   SK5804   Map 4

Globe

43 Silver Street

The old-fashioned layout of this city pub includes a little black-partitioned Turkey-carpeted snug on the right of the tiled entry bar, then a serving bar with elaborate black woodwork, and beyond that a big lounge with a gas fire, and hunting prints above its red leatherette wall banquettes. How well the pub's period features could be brought out by a really sympathetic restoration! Lunchtime main dishes are served in an upstairs lounge, and bar snacks include filled cobs (from 40p, bacon 50p), sandwiches (from 60p), ploughman's, prawn omelette (£1.75), home-made rabbit or steak and kidney pie (£1.95), scampi (£2.50) and sirloin steak (£2.60); well kept Everards Bitter, Tiger, Old Original and a guest beer on handpump or electric pump. A games room has sensibly placed darts, bar billiards, shove-ha'penny, dominoes, cribbage, a juke box, two fruit machines and a space game. *(Recommended by Lee Goulding, M V Cooke, Wayne Rossiter, T Mansell)*

Everards · Licensee Robb Cross · Real ale · Meals (lunchtime, not weekends) and snacks (lunchtime, not Sun) · Children upstairs · Open 10.30–2.30, 5.30–11 all year

LINCOLN   SK9872   Map 8

Wig & Mitre ★   [*illustrated on page 449*]

29 Steep Hill; just below cathedral towards centre

The most unusual feature of this attractively restored and decorated fourteenth-century pub is the way that it serves a full range of food throughout the day, from 8am until midnight (we show licensed hours for drinks service below; the restaurant has a midnight supper licence). Tables can be booked upstairs in a raftered room with Victorian armchairs, settees and elegant small settles, ancient and modern pictures of lawyers and churchmen, and a relaxed, almost clubby atmosphere. The cheerful downstairs bar is tiled, with a collection of Players cigarette cards, pews and other more straightforward furniture. Food choice changes frequently, and typically includes plain or toasted sandwiches (from 70p), ploughman's with a selection of cheeses or several home-made pâtés (from £1.45), salads (from £2.45) and a wide choice of hot dishes such as carrot and orange or vegetable soup (85p), melon and honey cocktail (£1.25), cauliflower portugaise with garlic toast (£1.50), avocado and mackerel bake (£1.60), rice croquettes in tomato sauce or vegetarian stuffed cabbage (£1.75), salmon dumplings in prawn sauce (£1.95), pork and lime casserole (£2.50), red mullet in herb and tomato sauce (£3.25), kidney and bacon kebabs or chicken cooked with Stilton and cream (£4.25), and steaks (from £5.45). We've had one or two reports from people who know the pub well (and remain firm supporters) suggesting that value for money has not always been quite what it was before, though the great majority remain well pleased. A very wide choice of wines by the glass (perhaps a better choice here than the Sam Smiths OB and Museum on handpump), and freshly squeezed orange juice. There are seats on a sheltered back terrace, with a small pool and fountain. The pub is on a steep and picturesque alley not far below the cathedral. (*Recommended by Dr L J C Easton, T Mansell, R A Hutson, the Bailey family, I L P, John Price, Sally Terry; more reports please*)

Sam Smiths · Licensees Michael and Valerie Hope · Real ale · Meals – tel Lincoln (0522) 35190 – and snacks · Children upstairs and front part of lower bar · Open 11–3, 5.30–11 all year; closed 25 Dec

MAPLEBECK (Notts)   SK7160 Map 7
Beehive

Village signposted from A616 and A617

Seats on the terrace in front of this friendly little white pub face a sleepy grassy hollow surrounded by old trees, and there are swings over in the side grass. The snug beamed bar has traditional built-in cushioned wall benches, and serves well kept Shipstones from the copper-topped bar counter. A side room has a workmanlike gun hanging above the fire, as well as some harness and other horse trappings. Darts, dominoes, and a juke box – this is the only pub we know where you never have to put any money in (the music doesn't include any punk rock, or anything wild). The pub is on a very quiet lane through countryside teeming with partridges, pheasants and hares. (*Recommended by John and Andrew Kemp*)

Free house · Licensee David Eyre · Real ale · Open 11–2.30, 6–10.30

MARKET DEEPING (Lincs)   TF1310 Map 8
Bull

Market Place

A change of management since our last edition seems to have altered nothing significant at this early Georgian stone-built inn: it still has a splendidly friendly and lively atmosphere in its network of simply furnished and traditional low-ceilinged rooms. Well kept Everards Tiger, Old Original and Burton Mild on handpump, with the casks kept down in the Dugout Bar – a long, cellar-like narrow room down a few steps, with heavy black beams and roughly plastered walls made from enormous blocks of ancient stone. You can sit out in the pretty back coachyard. (*Recommended by John Armstrong, Steve Coley*)

Everards · Real ale · Snacks (lunchtime) · Nearby daytime parking may be difficult · Open 11–2, 6–11 all year · Bedrooms tel Market Deeping (0778) 343320; £15B/£28B

NEWARK (Notts)   SK8054 Map 7
Old Kings Arms

19 Kirkgate; follow To The Market Place signpost opposite Maltby agricultural engineers on A46

This welcoming traditional pub serves good value bar food such as sandwiches (from 45p), ploughman's with a choice of Cheddar, Brie or Stilton (from 80p), chilli con carne or curry (£1.10 or £1.65, depending on size of helping), and three daily specials which might be tuna and peanut risotto or curry (£1.30 or £1.95, again depending on how much you want), sausage and mash or cottage pie (£1), casseroles such as braised liver or pork (£1.60), roast meats (£1.60), or steak and kidney pie (£1.70); there's always something for vegetarians. In the evenings there are also full meals including several starters and extra main dishes, for example steaks (from £5.70). The bar has cushioned wall benches and other traditional seats around stripped deal tables, and a vaulted ceiling; dominoes, cribbage, a fruit machine, and a juke box. Upstairs there's a simply furnished dining-room. As you'd expect with a licensee who is a former chairman of the Campaign for Real Ale, the Marstons Burton, Pedigree, Merrie Monk and Owd Rodger on handpump is well kept. The coat of arms outside is unusually handsome, and the castle ruins are just a stroll away. *(Recommended by Mrs H M Beer; more reports please)*

Marstons · Licensee Christopher Holmes · Real ale · Meals (not Sun or Mon evenings) and snacks · Children upstairs · Contemporary music Sun evening, jazz Mon · Restricted nearby parking · Open 11–2.30, 6–10.30

NEWTON (Lincs)   TF0436 Map 8
Red Lion

Village signposted from A52; at village road turn right towards Haceby and Braceby

This civilised and interestingly furnished village pub has a very sensible pricing policy for its excellent and attractively displayed cold carvery, serving prawns and cuts from a whole fresh salmon as well as pies and roasts: choosing as much as you like of the salads, with four different types of fish or meat, costs £4.25; rein in your appetite a little, and it's 50p cheaper; and children up to 10 are charged only £1. Other bar food includes some Lincolnshire specialities such as stuffed chine and spicy local sausages, as well as sandwiches, filled rolls, winter soups, and home-made puddings such as lemon meringue pie. The communicating rooms have old-fashioned oak and elm seats, one Gothick carved settle, and cushioned benches built in to the cream-rendered or bare stone walls, which are profusely decorated with farm tools, maltsters' wooden shovels, a stuffed fox, stag's head and green woodpecker, pictures made from pressed flowers, a dresser full of china, old advertisements, hunting and coaching prints, and even a penny-farthing cycle. Well kept Batemans XB on handpump; a fruit machine, and during the day squash courts run by the pub can be used by non-members. The well sheltered and very neat back garden has tables under cocktail parasols on the grass and on a terrace, as well as a swing. *(Recommended by Dave Butler, Lesley Storey)*

Free house · Licensee John William Power · Real ale · Meals and snacks (not Sun evening or Mon) · Children welcome · Open 10.30–2.30, 6–11 all year

Note that there is no 11pm weekend extension in this city – pubs close at 10.30 then too

New Market Hotel

Lower Parliament Street, at junction with Broad Street; inner ring road passes the pub – severely neo-classical, it looks more like a bank

This friendly pub has drinks prices which are among the half-dozen cheapest in this book, with a spirits double costing barely more than a single measure down in London. At those prices, you can't expect frills and furbelows – but in fact the back lounge is comfortable, with curvy button-back banquettes and pretty wallpaper. Bar food includes samosas (25p), a good choice of filled rolls (35p–45p), baked potatoes with cheese and pickles (60p), home-made cottage pie or steak and kidney pie with mushy peas (80p) and fresh fish (£1.30); hot dishes only in winter (unless ordered ahead). Well kept Home Bitter and Mild (brewed in Daybrook in the north of the city) on electric pump and on handpump; maybe piped music. The high-ceilinged public bar is plainly furnished, and has railway lamps, notices and engine numberplates on its walls; darts, shove-ha'penny, table skittles, dominoes, cribbage and any other legal card games, backgammon, chess, draughts and a fruit machine. There are seats on a terrace. One of the few pubs in the city to allow dogs. *(Recommended by T Mansell, Bob Rendle)*

Home · Licensee Bill Green · Real ale · Meals (lunchtime, not Sun) and snacks Children in back lounge · Open 10.30–2.30, 5.30–10.30

Olde Trip to Jerusalem ★

Brewhouse Yard; from inner ring road follow The North, A6005 Long Eaton signpost until you are in Castle Boulevard then almost at once turn right into Castle Road; pub is up on the left

This quaint white mainly seventeenth-century house earns its star award for its unique upstairs bar: it's cut into sandstone rock below the castle, and the walls, panelled at the bottom, soar steeply up into remote and shadowy heights, with cosy and simply furnished hollowed-out side alcoves. (This room may be closed at lunchtime if for example it's sunny enough for everyone to want to sit out on the terrace.) The downstairs bar is also mainly carved from the rock, with leatherette cushioned settles built in to the dark panelling, barrel tables on the tiles or flagstones, more low-ceilinged alcoves, and the friendly atmosphere of a genuine local rather than the tourist attraction which it might so easily have become. These caverns may have served as cellerage for an early medieval castle brewhouse which stood here, and they still keep the pub's wide range of real ales: Bass, Everards Old Original, Marstons Pedigree and Owd Rodger, Ruddles County and Sam Smiths OB or the like, on handpump. Fruit machine, ring the bull. *(Recommended by T Mansell, William Meadon, Richard Steel, Martyn Quinn, MHG, ILP, Stephan Carney, Dr A K Clarke)*

Free house · Licensees Janet Marshall and Charles Heard-Ward · Real ale Snacks (lunchtime) · Open 10.30–2.30, 5.30–10.30

Three Wheatsheaves

402 Derby Road, Lenton; A6200 (A52)

This rambling old pub has several rooms, mostly with flagstone floors, swirly butter-coloured plaster above low dark panelling, and simple traditional furnishings; a carpeted back room has inglenook seats by a big round wood-burning stove. Bar food includes pasties and filled rolls (50p), sandwiches to order, barbecued hot dogs or belly pork (60p), bacon steaks (85p), ploughman's (£1.50), and salads from a buffet counter (£1.60), with hot winter dishes such as lasagne and stew with dumplings (£1.50); well kept Shipstones on handpump; darts, dominoes, a fruit machine (in a back lobby), a space game, and a juke box. There is a surprisingly big raised lawn at the back, with standard roses and young silver birches, as well as a covered alley; daily summer lunchtime barbecues out here, and occasional garden parties. *(Recommended by Mrs E Matthews, Mrs H Johnstone; more reports please)*

Shipstones · Licensee Mick Sisson · Real ale · Meals and snacks (lunchtime) Open 10.30–2.30, 5.30–10.30

Vernon Arms

Waverley Street, junction with Forest Road

Good value bar food in this well kept and comfortable Italian-run suburban pub includes chip butties (45p), plain or toasted sandwiches (from 50p), soup (50p), cannelloni or spaghetti bolognese (95p), ploughman's with Cheddar or Stilton (£1.20), pizza (£1.25), basket meals such as chicken (£1.45) or scampi (£1.65) and sirloin steak (£3.60). The airy lounge is a spacious double room, comfortably furnished with grey leatherette button-back banquettes on the Turkey carpet, and gilt flock wallpaper below a dark green ceiling. Its big windows overlook the park which drops down to Forest Recreation Ground; a fruit machine, piped music. A separate restaurant serves full meals with main courses such as coq au vin or contre-filet of beef niçoise. There are tables on a sizeable side terrace, raised above the road. *(Recommended by Cdr Patrick Tailyour)*

Mansfield · Licensee Dario Tortore · Meals (not Sun evening, limited Mon evening) and lunchtime snacks (not Sun) · Open 11–2.30, 5.30–10.30

OAKHAM (Leics)   SK8508   Map 8

George

Market Place

The comfortable oak-beamed lounge bar of this friendly old stone coaching-inn, in the centre of Rutland's capital, has hunting prints, oak panelling and chintzy curtains, and unobtrusive piped music. It opens into an inner Market Bar whose banquettes make cosy booths around tables where you can eat sandwiches, home-made soup, ploughman's, freshly made salads, steak and kidney pie, lasagne and

---

The details at the end of each main entry start by stating whether the pub is a free house or if it's tied to a brewery (which we name).

the like; well kept Ruddles Bitter and John Smiths on handpump. There is also a separate restaurant (booking recommended). There is a fruit machine in the lively public bar. *(More reports please)*

Free house · Licensee I Watt · Real ale · Meals and snacks · Children in eating area and restaurant · Open 10.30–2, 6–11 all year · Bedrooms tel Oakham (0572) 56971; £25(£34.50B)/£30(£39.50B)

OLD DALBY (Leics)   SK6723   Map 7

Crown ★ ★

By school in village centre turn into Longcliff Hill then left into Debdale Hill

Under the young owners who took it over two or three years ago this hidden-away converted farmhouse has gone from strength to strength. It has become a personal favourite of several readers who have visited many dozens of other pubs included in the *Guide*, and – awarding it a second star this year – we reckon that it has become the nicest pub in this part of England, ideal for long, relaxing lunches (the food is unusually good) or idyllic evenings (the choice of real ales could hardly be bettered). It's furnished almost like a private house, with easy chairs, one or two antique oak settles and Windsor

The Noel Arms, Whitwell

armchairs in three or four small rooms, Cecil Aldin and Victor Venner hunting prints on the white walls, and snug open fires (one fireplace is covered in summer by an embroidered bird-of-paradise firescreen). The attractive garden has rustic seats on a terrace and a big, sheltered lawn sloping down among roses and fruit-trees; you can play boules or croquet here. The nicely prepared food includes sandwiches (from 65p, steak £1.95), soup (95p), a good choice of ploughman's (£2.50), melted Stilton dip with crudités (£1.95), baked avocado with prawns and crabmeat in cheese sauce or pasta spindles with seafood, onions, eggs, cream and Parmesan cheese (£3.50), fried chicken strips with a garlic and lemon yoghurt dip or pork loin in an egg, parsley and cheese sauce (£3.95) and noisettes of lamb in puff pastry with duxelles and madeira sauce (£4.95). A small separate restaurant serves more elaborate food. An excellent choice of ales (Adnams, Charles Wells Bombardier, Greene King Abbot, Hardys & Hansons Bitter and Mild, Hook Norton Best, Liddingtons Litchborough and Tudor, Marstons Burton, Pedigree, Owd Rodger and Merrie Monk, Ruddles County and Theakstons XB) is tapped from casks behind a hatch by the back door; with so many available, they use a very light blanket of carbon dioxide to keep them in good condition. One room has darts, dominoes, cribbage and table skittles. *(Recommended by Dave Butler, Lesley Storey, Lee Goulding, Michael Craig, Michael Cooke, H P Moss, Stephan Carney)*

Free house · Licensees Lynne Bryan and Salvatore Inguanta · Meals and snacks (not Mon or Sun evenings) · Children welcome · Open 10–2.30, 6–11 all year

RATBY (Leics)   SK5105   Map 4
Plough
Boroughs Road; turn off main street at Bulls Head

On weekend evenings there's a memorably cheerful atmosphere in this unpretentious village pub. Its two snug little front rooms have beams, cast-iron tables, café chairs and a coal fire; one is red tiled, the other – down a step – carpeted. A bigger lounge has lots of wheelback chairs around its tables, and red flock wallpaper. Lunchtime bar food includes fresh filled cobs (from 30p), sandwiches (from 80p), salads (from £1) and changing hot dishes (from £1.10); well kept Marstons Burton and Pedigree on handpump; darts, dominoes, cribbage, maybe piped music. Seats out on a terrace and in the big back garden (which has an enclosed play area with swings and so forth). The quiet lane opens on to a recreation ground, and there are woodland and other walks. *(Recommended by G Webberley; more reports please)*

Marstons · Licensee Ray Vanstone · Real ale · Meals (lunchtime, not weekends) and snacks (lunchtime, not Sun) · Children in club room · Friday piano sing-alongs · Open 11–2.30, 5.30–11 all year

RAVENSHEAD (Notts)   SK5956   Map 7
Little John
Main Road (B6020)

The big, airy lounge of this well organised modern pub has been redecorated and recarpeted since our last edition, and there's new, comfortable seating around its low tables; the walls are enlivened by large Little John and Robin Hood pictures and a big, bubbling aquarium. Bar food includes filled cobs, soup (70p), egg mayonnaise or garlic mushrooms (95p), home-made pâté (£1.55), ploughman's (£1.65), king prawns (half-pint £1.55, pint £2.55), home-made pizza (from £1.75), half a chicken (£2.30), salads (£2.75) and rump steak (£4.50), with extra hot dishes such as home-made steak and kidney pie (£2) at lunchtime, and chicken tikka (£3.25) in the evening. The public bar has darts, pool, dominoes, cribbage, juke box, fruit machine and a space game, and there is another fruit machine in the lounge, which may have piped music. The separate restaurant is popular for business lunches and Sunday lunch (£6.25, children £4.25), and there's a functions room (with barbecues and skittles available) in a recently converted barn. There are seats outside. *(Recommended by C E Gay; more reports please)*

Mansfield · Licensee Clive Wisdom · Meals and snacks (not Sun lunchtime) Children welcome · Open 11–3, 6–10.30

SHEEPY MAGNA (Leics)   SK3201   Map 4
Black Horse

B4116

The knocked-through lounge of this well modernised village pub is comfortably furnished, with Windsor chairs around copper-topped tables and little plush armchairs in one bay window. It has an unusual broad stone archway sweeping over a central brick hearth with a polished copper free-standing chimney. Well kept Bass, Liddingtons Litchborough and Mitchells & Butlers Brew XI on handpump; darts and a fruit machine in the lively and roomy public side, which has black leatherette seats around the tables on its carpet. *(Recommended by Alain Skelding, John Gilhooley; more reports please)*

Free house · Licensee Rodger Frost · Real ale · Open 11.30–2.30, 6.30–11 all year

SOUTH LUFFENHAM (Leics)   SK9402   Map 4
Boot & Shoe

10 The Street; turn off A6121 at the Halfway House, then first right

This attractive stone inn, on a quiet lane behind the pretty village church, has a welcoming landlord and a snug carpeted lounge rambling through several areas where stripped stone walls have been knocked through. This has chintzy easy chairs by the log fire (or an electric fire on cold summer evenings), red plush stools and armed wooden seats, some red and gold flock wallpaper, and varnished beams. Bar food includes soup, sandwiches, ploughman's (from £1), sausage and eggs (£1.30), good home-made steak and kidney pie (£1.60), cottage pie and seafood pancakes (£2), scampi (£2.20) and good gammon or four-ounce sirloin steak (£2.50); there's also a separate restaurant. Well kept Sam Smiths OB on handpump; darts, fruit machine, space game and a juke box. There are old-fashioned seats on the quiet lawn of the neatly kept small garden, and more on a sunny back terrace by the car park. *(Recommended by Rachel Waterhouse, John Higgins – no connection with the landlord, D F Cameron)*

Melbourns (who no longer brew) · Licensee Gordon Higgins · Real ale · Meals and snacks · Children in dining area · Open 11.30–2.30, 6–11 all year Bedrooms tel Stamford (0780) 720177; £9/£18

SOUTHWELL (Notts)   SK6953 Map 7
Saracen's Head

The largely modernised L-shaped beamed bar of this handsome half-timbered Tudor inn has nice leather seats on its Turkey carpet, and friendly and attentive service; since our last edition they've put in John Smiths real ale on electric pump. It leads through to a quietly old-fashioned inner hall, with antique settles and comfortable easy chairs under its oak beams – some of these may have been salvaged from an eleventh-century or twelfth-century inn which stood here before the present one was rebuilt 600 years ago. Bar food includes home-made soup (75p), baked potato filled with Cheddar or Stilton (90p), sausage and chips (£1.10), ploughman's or pâté (£1.20), home-made steak and kidney pie (£1.80) and home-made lasagne (£1.85), with quiche and other salads from a buffet table (from £1.30); there's also a panelled restaurant (not Saturday lunchtime). The bedrooms are in a more modern block, off the attractive cobbled and half-timbered coachyard; it's a comfortable place to stay. *(Recommended by Howard Gascoyne; more reports please)*

John Smiths (Courage) · Licensee Richard Howdle · Snacks (lunchtime, not Sun) · Children in eating area or restaurant · Jazz night monthly (Fri) Bedrooms tel Southwell (0636) 812701; £38.50B/£48.50B

STAMFORD (Lincs)   TF0207 Map 8
Bull & Swan

High Street, St Martins; B1081 leaving town southwards

The lounge bar of this comfortably refurbished low stone inn has sturdy red plush seats, a wood-burning stove set in to the stripped stone wall, and heavy beams hung with lots of highly polished copper kettles and so forth by the bar counter, which has well kept Sam Smiths OB on handpump. Bar food includes soup (80p), ploughman's (£1.60), steak sandwich (£2.25), lasagne or sweet-and-sour spare ribs (£2.35), trout or seafood platter (£2.60), scampi (£2.90), mixed grill (£3.30) and steaks (from £3.90), with winter dishes such as steak and kidney pie (£2.50). The restaurant serves some Portuguese food such as pork Braga, salmon transmontana or scampi and smoked bacon kebab. Fruit machine, space game and piped music; friendly service. *(Recommended by William Meadon, Richard Steel, T Mansell)*

Melbourns (who no longer brew) · Licensee William Morgado · Real ale Meals and snacks · Children welcome · Open 11–2.30, 6–11 all year Bedrooms tel Stamford (0780) 63558; £18/£24

All main entries have been inspected anonymously by the Editor. We accept no payment for inclusion, no advertising, and no sponsorship from the drinks industry – or from anyone else.

George ★ ★

71 St Martins

Readers agree with the *Guide*'s view that the nicest place to eat in this beautifully preserved ancient inn – decidedly something more than just a pub – is its imaginative Garden Lounge, with well spaced white cast-iron furniture around a tropical grove of flowers, ferns, banana trees, rubber plants and creepers. It has an attractively displayed spread of salads and cold meats including glazed salmon, succulent ham, tempting game pie, and good beef (£5.95 for as much as you like). Other food served here or in the bars includes minestrone soup (£1.85), open sandwiches (from £2.65), chicken liver pâté (£2.95), vegetable fritto misto (£2.95), turkey and mushroom pie (£3.35), stir-fried beef with beansprouts and oyster sauce (£4.25) and a plate of Parma ham, salami, smoked meats and crudités (£4.95); puddings include good apple and blackberry tart. No smoking in here; there's also a separate panelled restaurant. The best drinks are the Italian wines, many of which are good value (the handpump ale is kept under pressure). The front bar, the panelled York Room, is one of a pair of rooms still named after the destinations of the coaches – twenty a day each way – which changed horses here in the eighteenth and nineteenth centuries. Opposite it, the quietly ornate London Room has tall shuttered windows, plush chairs around neat mahogany tables, and carved panelling. The inn was built in 1597 for Lord Burghley (whose splendid Elizabethan house nearby is well worth visiting). It includes parts of a much older Norman pilgrims' hospice, and a crypt under the present cocktail bar – which has attractive old wicker furniture and a fine locally made grandfather clock – may be more like 1,000 years old. A comfortable and spacious lounge has a magnificent and cunningly lit arched stone fireplace and lots of exposed stonework, and the building is full of heavy beams, sturdy timbers and broad flagstones. There are unusually comfortable seats around cloth-covered tables in the charming cobbled courtyard, made attractive with tubs of plants, and in one area it has a glass canopy decorated with bright hanging flower baskets. In summer there are frequent barbecues out here. The well kept walled garden has an ancient mulberry tree, and a sunken lawn where croquet is often played. This is the headquarters of Ivo Vannocci's small but illustrious empire of well run Poste Hotels, and is a comfortable place to stay. *(Recommended by Aileen Hall, T Mansell, William Meadon, Richard Steel, P Marsh, Rita Horridge, Dr H B Cardwell, Alan Franck, N F Mackley, G L Archer, Patrick Stapley, Richard Gibbs, D A Angless, J A Catton, Heather Sharland, Stephan Carney and others)*

Free house · Licensees Ivo Vannocci and Jolyon Gough · Meals and snacks Children welcome · Open 11–2.30, 6–11 all year · Bedrooms tel Stamford (0780) 55171; £42.50B/£58B

STRETTON (Leics)   SK9416   Map 8

Jackson Stops ★

From A1 follow village signposts

Good value home-made bar food in this unspoilt pub – warmly

friendly to strangers, combining with the regulars' contentment to make a fine atmosphere – includes soup (75p), sandwiches (from 80p), pâté (£1.10), local sausages (£1.30 with bread, £1.80 with egg and chips), ploughman's or bread and very well kept Stilton (£1.30), quiche (£1.90), salads (from £1.95), smoked chicken (£2.40), changing home-made pies (£2.60), grilled lamb cutlets (£3.60), mixed grill (£4.95) and sirloin steak (£6.50). The small snug room by the door and a bigger Barn room have old-fashioned high-backed settles, armchairs, country tables and chairs, rugs and so forth – and the bigger room is decorated with yokes, antlers and stuffed animal heads. Well kept Ruddles and County are tapped from casks behind the bar; darts, shove-ha'penny, dominoes, cribbage and nurdles (not a game we're well up in ourselves, but they tell us it's been on TV recently). There's a small separate dining-room, and private rooms for parties and so forth. The pub, as you might guess from the picture on its inn-sign, used to be called the White Horse, but got its present name from the estate agent's sign that it carried some years ago, when it was up for sale for quite a time. *(Recommended by Steve Coley, S E Hammond, Dr H B Cardwell, G L Archer, J Dewhirst, C P Price, Annie Taylor, Susie Boulton, Stephan Carney)*

Free house · Licensees Frank and Sue Piguillem · Real ale · Meals and snacks Children in eating area and restaurant · Open 10.30–2.30, 6–11 all year

SUTTON CHENEY (Leics)   SK4100   Map 4
Hercules

This easy-going, attractive eighteenth-century stone pub – once quite an important coaching-inn, but long ago left in a relative backwater – has an old-fashioned long bar with a mainly flagstoned floor, traditional high-backed settles, an open log fire, and copper bedwarmers and willow pattern plates on its butter-coloured walls. Well kept Cotleigh Tawny, Courage Directors, Everards Old Original, Shipstones Mild and a beer brewed for the pub on handpump or tapped straight from the cask, and a mystery guest bitter – you receive an appropriate prize if you guess its name; sensibly placed darts, dominoes, fruit machine and space game, and piped music (sometimes loud). Bar food includes sandwiches (50p, mushroom and sausage special £1.20), cod (£1.70), scampi (£1.90), ploughman's (£2), roast beef salad (£2.30), home-made steak and kidney pie (£2.50), gammon (£2.95) and lots of steaks (from eight-ounce rump £3.25), with cheaper children's helpings. There's also a restaurant, which has been flirting with the idea of turning itself into a comfortable lounge. Handy for Bosworth Battlefield. *(Recommended by Keith Myers, Robert Aitken, S E Hammond; more reports please)*

Free house · Licensee K Rolfe · Real ale · Meals and snacks (not Mon or Tues evenings) · Children welcome · Open 11–2.30, 6.30–11 all year

SWITHLAND (Leics)   SK5413   Map 4
Griffin

Village signposted from A6

This civilised country pub, in an attractive village, serves well kept Everards Bitter, Tiger, Old and Mild from handpump, and good fresh bar snacks, though perhaps its greatest appeal is the friendliness of the licensee. Its three communicating rooms have carpet and parquet flooring, hunting prints, some modern panelling, beams, brocaded wall seats by dimpled copper tables, and easy chairs near the fire in the quieter end room; darts, and a skittle alley in the quite separate back Stable Bar. A small stream runs along the grass behind the big car park. *(Recommended by Lee Goulding, Dave Butler, Les Storey)*

Everards · Licensee Norman Jefferson · Real ale · Snacks · Open 11–2, 6–10.30

UPTON (Notts)   SK7354   Map 7
French Horn
A612

The good food in this well kept pub won its licensees the title of Pub Caterers of 1985, in a national competition organised by the trade journal *Pub Caterer*. It includes chip butties (50p), sandwiches or filled rolls (from 65p), home-made soup (70p), home-made chicken liver and brandy pâté (£1.50), deep-fried clams (£2.25), home-made beef and Guinness casserole (£2.30), meat salads (from £2.50), large burgers (£2.50), steak and kidney pie (£2.75), scampi (£3.25), chicken Kiev (£4.95) and sirloin steak (£5.20), with vegetarian dishes such as curry (£2.70). There is a separate restaurant (closed on Sunday). The friendly open-plan bar has frequent shows of local artists' work on its partly panelled walls, and is comfortably furnished with cushioned captain's chairs and wall banquettes around glossy tables. Outside, there are picnic-table sets on a big sloping back paddock, which looks out on farmland. A very nice pub – we're surprised we haven't had more reports. *(Recommended by ILP)*

John Smiths (Courage) · Licensees Graham and Linda Mills · Meals and snacks Children in eating area or restaurant · Open 11–2.30, 6.30–10.30

WEST LEAKE (Notts)   SK5226   Map 7
Star
Village signposted from A6006

The beamed and tiled-floor public bar of this village pub is traditionally furnished with heavy settles and plain oak tables, with whips, harness and foxes' masks on its ochre walls. Its set of cockfighting prints recalls the reason why it's still known as the Pit House – the cats that have the run of the place now wouldn't have dared come near the fighting cocks it was famous for in the past. A smarter Turkey-carpeted lounge, partly panelled, has a good log fire and comfortable armed chairs. Food includes salads with cold meats, pies, cheese and smoked mackerel, and daily hot dishes, or a three-course weekday lunch; well kept Bass and Springfield on handpump. There are picnic-table sets in front of the old house, which stands on a quiet village lane. *(Recommended by Stephan Carney, J P C Burgess; more reports please)*

Bass · *Licensee Frank Whatnall* · *Real ale* · *Meals and snacks (lunchtime, not Sat or Sun)* · *Open 10.30–2.30, 6–10.30*

WHITWELL (Leics)   SK9208   Map 8
Noel Arms   [*illustrated on page 457*]

Handy for Rutland Water, this snug thatched cottage of a pub now has an airy and spacious back dining-lounge, with tables well spread around its Turkey carpet. Popular waitress-served bar food includes sandwiches (from 65p), home-made soup (85p), ploughman's (£1.65), a cold table with home-made quiche or crab (£2.95) and three meats (£3.50), and usually four daily specials such as lasagne (£2.95), chicken and ham or steak and kidney pie (£3.25), goujons of cod (£3.25) or mixed grill (£3.95), with Friday curries. Down in the original front part there are two snug little rooms with cosy armed leather seats and pews, harness, brass scales and country prints on the walls, and a cheerful local atmosphere. Well kept Ind Coope Bitter, Marstons Pedigree and Ruddles County on handpump; fruit machine. There is also a separate restaurant, doing full evening meals. The sun-trap back terrace which slopes up behind is sometimes used for summer barbecues. Beware that the narrow entrance to the car park can be rather trying. (*Recommended by Michael Cooke, T Mansell, Stephan Carney*)

Free house · *Licensee Michael Healey* · *Real ale* · *Meals and snacks* · *Children in dining areas* · *Open 11–2.30, 6–11 all year*

WILSON (Leics)   SK4024   Map 7
Bulls Head

This comfortable beamed pub – carefully modernised to keep an attractive variety of quiet little alcoves – serves generous helpings of good value food. The most popular (so much so, indeed, that to be sure of a seat you should get here early) is the wide range of cold dishes, served efficiently from the buffet counter, such as smoked mackerel or rollmop (£2.75), home-made pâté or home-cooked chicken (£2.85), beef, ham or tongue (£2.95), smoked trout (£3), seafood platter (£3.10), and dressed crab, cold fresh salmon or freshly cut smoked salmon (when available, £3.50–£3.85). There are also sandwiches (from 85p), soup (65p), ploughman's with Cheddar (£1.20) or Stilton (£1.35), hot roast beef (£3.75) and one daily hot special (£2.50). Well kept Ind Coope on handpump; dominoes. The main bar has a friendly atmosphere, with maroon plush seats around black tables on its Turkey carpet. One of its alcoves has some fine modern prints of immensely magnified insects, another interesting old sepia racing car photographs. (*Recommended by J A Cox, Tony Field; more reports please*)

Ind Coope · *Licensee Michael Johnson* · *Real ale* · *Meals and snacks (not Sun or Mon evenings)* · *Children in eating area* · *Open 10.30–2.30, 6–10.30*

People named as recommenders after the main entries have told us that they feel the pub should be included. But they have not written the report – we have, after anonymous on-the-spot inspections.

WING (Leics)   SK8903   Map 4

Kings Arms

Top Street

The lounge of this friendly early seventeenth-century stone inn has an unusual central open fireplace under a gleaming copper chimney-funnel, and its well spaced furnishings include an antique settle, an attractive window seat and a handsome old elbow-polished table among more conventional wheelback chairs. Good value home-cooked food includes sandwiches, soup (75p), pâté (£1.15), ploughman's with a choice of Cheddar or Stilton (£1.35), whitebait (£1.55), shepherd's pie, fish or sausage, egg and chips (£1.75), vegetables in cheese sauce, steak and kidney or chicken and sweetcorn pies (£1.95), gammon and egg or chicken (£2.10), trout from Rutland Water (£3.25), venison casserole (£3.75) and steak (£4.20); well kept Greene King IPA and Ruddles Bitter and County on handpump. Darts, dominoes and cribbage in the public bar. There are wooden seats in the sunny yard, with a separate restaurant on the other side. A medieval turf maze some 17 yards across is just up the road. (Recommended by C P Price; more reports please)

Free house · Licensee Norman Attenborough · Real ale · Meals and snacks (not Sun evening) · Children in family room behind main bar · Open 10.30–2, 6–11 all year · Five-person flat tel Manton (057 285) 315; £45 a week

---

Lucky Dip

Besides the fully inspected pubs, you might like to try these Lucky Dips recommended and described by readers (if you do, please send us reports):

ASHBY FOLVILLE [SK7011], Carrington Arms: good food (not Friday or Saturday) in popular and attractive pub; doesn't serve motor-cyclists (LP)
BARKBY [SK6309], Brookside: attractive décor includes some 300 toby jugs, in waterside pub in pretty village (Michael Cooke)
BARNBY MOOR [SK6684], White Horse: freshly made food good value in cosy pub with willing service and well kept beer; evening restaurant (M J Connor)
BEESTON [SK5872], Jolly Anglers: good beer and friendly service in well designed estate pub (Dr A K Clarke)
BINBROOK [TF2193], Chicken: remote renovated pub with good value bar snacks (R K Whitehead)
BOURNE [TF0920], Nags Head: attractive unspoilt lounge, helpful staff and Burton real ale; quiet traditional front room with tiled floor; juke box in back room for younger customers (John Armstrong)
BRAUNSTON [SK8306], Old Plough: good food and cheerful service in delightful country pub set in tranquil village (Capt F A Bland, Bryan Stafford)
CASTLE DONINGTON [Bondgate; SK4427], Cross Keys: reasonably priced food – especially excellent soup – and well kept Everards Tiger and Old Original, Bass and Burton Bridge on handpump, in simply furnished but cosy pub with warm log fire and bar billiards (J L Thompson, Dave Butler, Lesley Storey)
nr CASTLE DONINGTON [Kings Mills; SK4427], Priest House: unusual drinks including good real ales, hearty snacks and grills in rambling beamed bars of inn with medieval tower by River Trent, popular with young people; bedrooms (Simon Porter, William Meadon, Richard Steel, LYM)
CLIPSHAM [SK9616], Olive Branch: friendly staff and good food and drink in comfortable inn; restaurant, garden, well modernised bedrooms (D J Milner)
COLEBY [SK9760], Bell: good carvery, wide choice of salads and hot dishes, in

pleasant bars with open fires *(NMO)*

COSBY [SP5495], *Huntsman*: good value food, roomy lounge, with cheerful and helpful staff; easy access for the disabled *(Sue Mutton, Anne Garton)*

COTES [SK5520], *Cotes Mill*: lively atmosphere and wide range of well kept real ales in large converted watermill, attractively placed; a continuing favourite of several readers but given a rest from the main entries this year – more reports please, particularly on standards of service *(C P Price, J P C Burgess, L N Goulding, Michael Cooke, G Pomfrett, LYM)*

COTTESMORE [Main Street; SK9013], *Sun*: traditional seventeenth-century stone pub; popular food may include pheasant sandwiches *(Anon)*

CROPSTON [SK5510], *Bradgate Arms*: good value old-fashioned village pub with hatch service, and wide range of well kept real ales; biggish garden; rather clubby atmosphere *(J M Tansey, LYM)*

DYKE [TF1022], *Wishing Well*: family-run stone pub with beams and inglenook; wide choice of beers, and tasty reasonably priced food in bar and restaurant, nicely served *(GCS)*

EARL SHILTON [Keats Lane; SP4597], *Dog & Gun*: friendly pub with locals' bar, cosy snug and quiet lounge *(J M Tansey)*

EASTGATE [TF1019], *Waggon & Horses*: well kept Bass in tastefully modernised pub with separate restaurant *(David Wilkin)*

FOXTON [SP7090], *Bridge 61*: attractive white pub with canalside garden (ducks and geese); quiet during the week (when not open at all until 8pm); well kept Everards Old Original, heavily modernised inside *(Michael Cooke)*

FRISBY ON THE WREAKE [Main Street; SK6917], *Bell*: food good, with wide choice, in refurbished old-world pub with pleasant staff *(G F Hollingworth)*

FRISKNEY [Main Road; TF4555], *Barley Mow*: good value food in restaurant, friendly smart lounge, and willing service; darts, fruit machine, juke box in public bar; bedrooms good value *(B Ray)*

GAINSBOROUGH [SK8189], *Elm Cottage*: friendly local with strong sporting connections; good value lunches; no juke box or space games; Bass Brew X and Mild on handpump *(David Wilkin, Bob Rendle)*

HALLATON [North End; SP7896], *Fox*: friendly local with good cheap meals and Burton on draught *(Dennis Edensor)*

HARBY [SK7331], *Nags Head*: food good in old-world pub with warm welcome *(G F Hollingworth)*

HINCKLEY [Watling Street; SP4294], *Lime Kilns*: unself-consciously preserved small pub by Ashby Canal: tap-room, panelled public bar, plenty of character but quiet; well kept Marstons real ales *(David Perrott, Dr and Mrs C D E Morris)*

HOTON [SK5722], *Packe Arms*: spacious and comfortable Bird Bar and recently refurbished original older front part in welcoming pub *(Oliver Tame, BB)*

HOUGHTON ON THE HILL [SK6703], *Rose & Crown*: Italian-owned pub includes Italian dishes among good bar snacks and salads; cocktails *(Cdr Patrick Tailyour)*

HUNCOTE [SP5197], *Red Lion*: attractive, neat clean pub with several bars *(Dr A K Clarke)*

ILLSTON ON THE HILL [SP7099], *Fox & Goose*: very interestingly decorated cottage-style village inn with sofas in peaceful front lounge like farmhouse sitting-room; well kept Everards Tiger and Old Original, piped classical music, conscientious landlord *(Lee Goulding, Michael Cooke)*

KILBY BRIDGE [SP6097], *Navigation*: old pub on Grand Union Canal with probably Leicestershire's smallest public bar, crammed with nautical and canal memorabilia, and fish in tanks; popular with anglers *(M V Cooke)*

LEADENHAM [High Street; SK9552], *George*: friendly welcome in roomy well furnished inn with open fire and children's game vestibule; excellent range of ales, more than 300 whiskies, wines imported directly from Herr Walter Peril of Boppard-am-Rhein; good bar food, and pleasant restaurant; bedrooms *(Victor Peskett)*

LEICESTER [Oxford Street; SK5804], *Angel*: high-ceilinged two-roomed pub with good lunchtime food *(J M Tansey)*; [Aylestone Road] *Freemans*: looks very much like a London pub from the outside; interesting for large bottle collection, old books, and unusual back courtyard *(Michael Cooke)*; [between Market and St Martins shopping precinct] *Jetty*: period flavour in Yates Wine Lodge with well kept Marstons Owd Rodger *(Michael Cooke)*; [London Road] *Old Horse*: pleasant atmosphere, well kept Everards Old Original *(Wayne Rossiter)*; [Beaumanor Road] *Tom Hoskins*: an 1895 brewery bought from Hoskins family two or three years ago and now run as working museum; this tap-room has traditional furnishings, and brewery memorabilia *(Anon)*

LEIRE [SP5290], *White Horse*: friendly, with local atmosphere *(Bob Rendle)*

LINCOLN [High Street; SK9872], *Blandings*: good choice of nicely cooked reasonably priced food, and well kept ales, in attractive bar and small dining-room *(Mrs Dorothy Johnson)*; [Alfred Street] *City Vaults*: small friendly side-street pub with good Wards real ale served from central hatch *(Bob Rendle)*; [Skellingthorpe Road] *Monson Arms*: modern pub with cheapest beer in area (Home real ales) and good service; near Hartsholme Country Park *(David Wilkin)*; [Greerwell Gate] *Morning Star*: welcoming pub near cathedral, run by same family for 60 years; well kept Manns *(David Wilkin)*; [High Street] *Roebuck*: friendly town tavern with well kept Shipstones real ales *(Bob Rendle)*; [Bailgate] *White Hart*: Orangery Bar (part of this THF hotel) is unusual single-roomed bar with astrodome roof and tree in centre, serving good range of food and beer; own entrance in Eastgate; bedrooms *(T Mansell)*

LITTLE CAWTHORPE [TF3583], *Royal Oak*: good value food (especially inclusive three-course meal) and fine service; known locally as 'The Splash' *(Mrs J M Danning)*

LYDDINGTON [SP8797], *Marquess of Exeter*: comfortable pub adjoining three-star hotel (when bar is full you can eat good food at bar prices in hotel dining-room); attractive village; bedrooms *(Capt F A Bland)*

MARKET BOSWORTH [SK4003], *Red Lion*: small-roomed beamed pub, now partly knocked through, with unfussy atmosphere and well kept Hoskins real ales, in attractive village *(Mick Walker, J M Tansey, Keith Myers, LYM)*

MARKET HARBOROUGH [SP7388], *Three Swans*: food very good, with friendly service *(E B Beck)*

MARSTON [SK8943], *Thorold Arms*: food and Batemans real ale good, at moderate prices; friendly landlord, restaurant; next to Marston Hall *(C J Dowling, Tony Gayfer)*

MEDBOURNE [SP7993], *Neville Arms*: food good value, and wide range of beers in interesting old pub, in attractive setting *(Miss J P Field)*

MELTON MOWBRAY [High Street; SK7518], *George*: smartly refurbished seventeenth-century inn; bedrooms *(Anon)*; [Nottingham Street] *Half Moon*: friendly, small and clean, good restaurant-style food, well kept Bass; room for children in yard *(G F Hollingworth, T Mansell)*; [Burton Street] *Harboro Hotel*: big friendly hotel, well kept, moderately priced; bedrooms *(G F Hollingworth)*

NEWARK [Market Place; SK8054], *Clinton Arms*: spacious and smoothly modernised lounge bar, with Home real ales and restaurant, in Georgian inn (previously a base of highwayman John 'Swift Nicks' Nevison); bedrooms *(LYM)*

NEWINGTON [Newington Road; SK6794], *Ship*: unpretentious and friendly roadside pub with well kept Home ales and lively public bar *(S Gee, LYM)*

NORTH COTES [TA3500], *Fleece*: spacious, attractive and comfortable, good real ale and snacks; a favourite out of this regular correspondent's many recommendations *(R K Whitehead)*

NOTTINGHAM [18 Angel Row; SK5640], *Bell*: quaint fifteenth-century central pub, with busy downstairs bar with Tudor theme, and somewhat quieter heavily panelled upstairs bar and restaurant; wide range of real ales, simple bar food, jazz Monday and Wednesday *(William Meadon, Richard Steel, S E Hammond, T Mansell, BB)*; *Castle*: well run with good atmosphere *(William Meadon, Richard Steel)*; [North Sherwood Street] *Hole in the Wall*: recently opened free house with hi-tech Habitat-style interior, serving good bar food and well kept real ales (good value happy hour until 7pm); landlord local rugby football captain *(S E Hammond)*; [Sneinton] *Lord Nelson*: tasty roast beef at lunchtime, friendly atmosphere and well kept real ale; clean and comfortable, open fires, intricate décor with lots of little nick-nacks (Monika Regan, Dr A K Clarke, Jane Marshall); [Canalside] *Morton Clayton & Fellows*: magnificent hot beef sandwiches in studiously scruffy canalside development with brewery (visible) attached: own-brewed beer good (Dave Butler, T Mansell); [Maid Marion Way] *Salutation*: ancient back part with flagstones and heavy beams, and plush open-plan front part with Wethereds and Castle Eden ales; good juke box and pool upstairs, popular with young people (Martyn Quinn, William Meadon, Richard Steele, BB); [Nuthall Road, Aspley] *Whitemoor*: friendly atmosphere in popular pub just outside centre, with nice landlord and landlady and good value food from salads to curries and roasts (John Roe)

OLD SOMERBY [SK9633], *Fox & Hounds*: good real ale and food in bar and dining-room (C J Dowling)

PRESTON [SK8602], *Kingfisher*: real ales, good food, friendly licensees; pleasant lounge, pool-room, garden (Bryan Stafford)

RADCLIFFE ON TRENT [High Street; SK6439], *Oak*: small, friendly clean pub, attractively old-fashioned with two beamed bars; snacks (PF)

RUDDINGTON [Easthorpe Street; SK5733], *Red Heart*: good town local with landlord who's been on the Generation Game; well kept Shipstone beer, parrot called Fred (Dr A K Clarke)

SCAFTWORTH [SK6692], *King William*: generous helpings of well presented home-made food including locally famous pies; cosy old-fashioned settles, coal fires, friendly staff, huge riverside lawn (A Darroch Harkness)

SCOTTER [SE8801], *White Swan*: big cheerful two-level done-up village pub opposite green, with decent food and respectable customers; tables outside, music weekly (K Mills, ILP)

SHEARSBY [SP6290], *Chandlers Arms*: well kept Adnams (not common here), cosy family atmosphere and good garden for children (Mick Walker)

SIBSON [SK3500], *Old Cock*: good food in bar and restaurant, interesting choice of beers, in friendly old-fashioned pub dating from thirteenth century (R Lewis)

STAMFORD [High Street, St Martins; TF0207], *Anchor*: good food in ancient pub modernised inside, by river; bedrooms (R S Varney); [Broad Street] *Lord Burghley*: renovated town pub worth a visit for its unusual range of real ales, popular with young people; back terrace (John Armstrong)

nr STAMFORD [Barnack; TF0605], *Millstone*: conscientious new landlord, serving well kept beer and good value food; in picturesque village (Steve Coley)

STOKE GOLDING [SP3997], *Three Horseshoes*: food available in bar and restaurant, also good choice of well kept real ales in old canalside pub; bit of a garden (Dr and Mrs C D E Morris)

nr STONEY STANTON [SP4894], *Mill on the Soar*: attractive recently opened roomy riverside pub with mill wheel; good food, upstairs restaurant (PEG)

SUTTON BONINGTON [SK5025], *Old Plough*: good value bar food and well kept Shipstone real ales in roomy well run modern pub (C A Price, LYM)

SUTTON IN ASHFIELD [Newark Road, Sutton Junction; SK5059], *Cardinal*: good value food, Mansfield ales, friendly local customers (Richard Bastow)

SWINFORD [SP5779], *Cave Inn*: well kept real ale, good atmosphere (MD)

TATTERSHALL THORPE [TF2259], *Blue Bell*: old-fashioned low-beamed pub with bar food and friendly, efficient licensees (J A Stuart)

TETFORD [TF3374], *White Hart*: food appetising, pleasant welcome and considerate service – wholesome in every respect and a delightful surprise to find in this lovely Wolds country! (Bill Packer); *White Hart*: friendly sixteenth-century inn with well kept Ind Coope beers, attractive bars, good restaurant; bedrooms (Anon); *Black Horse*: friendly small old pub with excellent food; attractive little village (Hugh Calvey)

TUGBY [SK7600], *Fox & Hounds*: wide choice of real ales including guest beers, and good food from large filled cobs to main dishes; open fire, bar billiards, helpful landlord (S E Hammond)

TUR LANGTON [SP7194], *Crown*: long, comfortable rambling pub with antique furnishings, interesting decorations, good food in bar and restaurant, well kept Marstons Pedigree and Ruddles; friendly atmosphere, kind to children;

beautiful back terrace with hanging baskets *(L N Goulding, Michael Craig, C P Price, LP)*

UPPER HAMBLETON [SK9007], *Finches Arms*: simple village pub in charming location on hill above Rutland Water; friendly farming landlord, good ham baps *(Michael Cooke, PH, BB)*

UPPINGHAM [High Street West; SP8699], *White Hart*: food good in comfortable lounge; friendly atmosphere *(B Stafford)*

WADDINGHAM [High Street; SK9896], *Marquis of Granby*: popular and friendly country local with well kept Wards real ales *(Bob Rendle)*

WALKERINGHAM [SK7792], *Brickmakers Arms*: food good, beers well kept; this out-of-the-way pub is worth finding *(M J Connor)*

WALTHAM ON THE WOLDS [SK8024], *Royal Horseshoes*: charmingly presented buffet with wide choice of salads in solidly furnished Wolds village inn with comfortable new bedrooms *(Dr H B Cardwell, J S Taylor, LYM)*

WOLLATON [SK5139], *Admiral Rodney*: friendly country pub with tasty bar food – can get full, especially at lunchtime *(Carolyn West, Martyn Quinn)*; *Hemlockstone*: food at lunchtime popular with business people and students from Nottingham University (nearby) *(John Roe)*

WOODHALL SPA [Tattershall Road; TF1963], *Abbey Lodge*: nice home-cooked bar food, cheerful atmosphere, John Smiths real ale *(J Stuart)*

WOODHOUSE EAVES [The Brand; SK5214], *Wheatsheaf*: lively country pub with good beer and friendly service; open fire, beer garden *(HPM)*

WRAGBY [TF1378], *Turnor Arms*: good value food and Home ales; 1960s décor in Victorian pub; young licensees trying hard *(Michael Main)*

Lincolnshire *see* Leicestershire

Midlands
(Northamptonshire,
Warwickshire and West
Midlands)

*Some important changes here include fine new extensions to
the Butchers Arms in Farnborough (very popular for its food
and country-style atmosphere) and the Red Lion in Long
Compton (an exuberant inn with interesting old decorations
and good value food). One of the area's most interesting pubs,
the Old Swan at Netherton (known as Ma Pardoe's), came up
for sale in 1985, and a company has been formed with lots of
ordinary pub-going shareholders to 'rescue' it and to preserve
it as the marvellous traditional own-brew pub it's been. Good
value food is often a mark of Midlands pubs, and (besides the
Butchers Arms and Red Lion already mentioned) is to be
found at the Old Coach House in Ashby St Ledgers (lots of
character in its rambling rooms), the Black Horse in
Nassington (well kept and particularly civilised), and, less
ambitiously, at the picturesque Kings Head in Aston Cantlow,
friendly Windmill at Badby (Sunday spit-roasts), comfortable*

The Bear, Berkswell

471

old Bear in Berkswell (winner of a local award for its food), fine old Dun Cow in Dunchurch, rambling early medieval Holly Bush in Priors Marston, Bell in the attractive village of Tanworth-in-Arden (interesting specials), spacious Wheatsheaf in Titchmarsh, Old Friar at Twywell (especially its steaks), Narrow Boat in Weedon (with a big canalside garden) and exuberantly stylish Crossroads, also in Weedon (well worth a visit for its atmosphere, and a comfortable place to stay). Many pubs in the area stand out for character and interest: the Barton Arms in Birmingham (an outstanding Edwardian palace of a pub, with a good value traditional seafood stall), the Castle, a battlemented folly built where King Charles raised his battle standard on Edge Hill (ghostly cavalrymen still gallop past), the Glynne Arms in Kingswinford (extraordinarily lopsided after subsidence, with good cheap beer and home-made snacks), the Marston Inn in Marston St Lawrence (a quite unspoilt village pub), the Old Washford Mill at Studley (a converted mill with attractive waterside gardens, which not only brews its own beer but also serves wine from its own vineyards), the squint-walled fourteenth-century Old Mint in Southam (with a collection of antique arms and armour), the Old Boat Inn (run by the same family for over a century) opposite the waterways museum on the canal at Stoke Bruerne, and the Saracen's Head in Towcester (with its kitchen bar where Dickens' Pickwick Papers characters couldn't be stopped from fighting until they were stuffed into sacks; bedrooms here). A good choice in Stratford ranges from the sawdust-floored Garrick and the famous actors' pub, the Dirty Duck (alias Black Swan), to the luxurious Shakespeare, which has a very cheery real ale bar. The Durham Ox at Shrewley is notable for its spacious garden (with lots of birds from doves to peacocks) — and welcome low prices. After a couple of years in which we virtually doubled the number of main entries in this area, we've given it a bit of a rest from inspections this year, so that we can get enough readers' reports on new possibilities to indicate clearly which of them are worth inspecting as candidates for upgrading to main entries — obviously, the more reports we get on a particular pub, the clearer a picture we'll get of it (so do help by reporting too). As we go to press, there already seem to be some really interesting prospects among the Lucky Dips, such as the stylishly converted Old Mill in Baginton, the lively Atkinson Bar of the Birmingham Midland Hotel, the Falcon in Fotheringhay (good food), the friendly Fox & Hounds in Great Wolford (some readers love it — it's been a main entry in previous editions), the attractive stone-built Crown in Harbury (home cooking), the well kept Saracens Head in Little Brington, the old-world Butchers Arms in

Priors Hardwick (good food), the Old Crab Mill in Preston Bagot (doing well under its new licensees, who ran the Black Bear in Tewkesbury when it was a main entry), the cheerful Boat in Newbold-on-Avon (cheap quick food), the White Bear in Shipston-on-Stour (rave reports from readers – and from several other guide books), the Vane in Sudborough (good food), the Bell in the pretty riverside village of Welford-on-Avon, the stylish Palms in Wellingborough, the White Horse in Welton (good value food), the Masons Arms in Wilmcote (good food in a friendly old pub), the Pheasant in Withybrook (sounds a real find for the area) and the canalside Navigation in Wooton Wawen.

ASHBY ST LEDGERS (Northants) SP5768 Map 4

Old Coach House ★

4 miles from M1 junction 18, A5 S to Kilsby, then A361 S towards Daventry; village signposted left

Readers are enthusiastic about the imaginative food and good selection of beer in this friendly stone house: giant prawns or slices of local pork pie (75p each), ploughman's with local cheese or home-made pâté (£1), a good range of salads including locally smoked trout, seafood quiche, home-baked ham or rare roast beef (from £1.75), garlicky mince hot-pot with sweet corn, peas and tomatoes (£1.75), Danish-style fresh mussels, herrings in madeira sauce, smoked mackerel or lumpfish roe and poached salmon (all around £2.25); they are also doing vegetarian dishes such as garlicky mushrooms baked in an individual wholemeal cottage loaf. There is a pretty little rustic dining-room up steps at the back. Besides well kept Marstons Burton and Pedigree, and Sam Smiths OB, there may be guest beers such as Theakstons XB and Liddingtons Litchborough on handpump. There is quite a grand collection of wines by the bottle, and hot toddy in winter. A series of small, cosy rooms makes up the well kept lounge bar: high-backed winged settles and old kitchen tables on the polished black and red tiles, hunting pictures (often of the Pytchley, which sometimes meets outside), harness on a few standing timbers, fresh flowers, a big log fire in winter. One front room has darts, and there are table skittles, pool, dominoes and piped classical music. In summer barbecues are held outside, or in the conservatory, and there are seats among fruit trees and under a fairy-lit arbour, with a climbing-frame, slide and swings. The village has thatched stone houses, with wide grass verges running down to the lane. *(Recommended by Kurt Wilkinson, David Surridge, CEP, Sue White, C F Walling, Robert Aitken, Evan Davies, J A Blades, MD)*

Free house · Licensees Douglas and Frederika Jarvis · Real ale · Meals and snacks (not Sun evening) · Children in three snug areas · Open 11.30–2.30, 7–11 all year · Bedrooms planned for 1986 tel Rugby (0788) 890349

Post Office address codings confusingly give the impression that some pubs are in the Midlands, when they're really in the Derbyshire, Leicestershire or Shropshire areas that we list them under.

ASTON CANTLOW (War)   SP1359 Map 4

Kings Head

This beautifully timbered pub is lovely in early summer, when it's decorated with colourful hanging baskets and the wistaria rambling along the warm red-tiled roof is still in flower. It was probably built a little too late to support the local tradition that John Shakespeare and Mary Arden held their wedding feast here in 1557 – her house in nearby Wilmcote is worth visiting in spite of the crowds. Under new licensees who moved in a couple of years ago, it's become locally popular for its bar food, which includes home-made soup (£1), ploughman's (from £1.30), home-made pork and duck liver pâté (£1.40), cottage pie (£2), vegetarian dishes such as asparagus wholemeal quiche (£2.40) or vegetable and cheese pie (£2.80), tagliatelle or fisherman's pie (£2.50), duck and pepper curry or scampi (£3) and steaks, from eight-ounce fillet to sixteen-ounce T-bone (all £5.90). There are children's helpings of some dishes. The right-hand flagstoned bar has been carefully refurbished, with wooden settles and an old-fashioned snug around its massive central fireplace; the carpeted main bar has attractive window seats and Windsor chairs around its oak tables. Well kept Flowers IPA on handpump; darts, cribbage, fruit machine. There are tables outside in the back garden. *(Recommended by S V Bishop; more reports please)*

Flowers (Whitbreads) · Licensee Joe Saunders · Real ale · Meals and snacks (not Mon evening) · Children in area partly set aside · Open 11.30–2.30, 6–11.30 all year (opens 6.30 in winter)

BADBY (Northants)   SP5559 Map 4

Windmill

Village signposted off A361

Half the space in the snug L-shaped bar of this lively and cheerful stone village inn is taken up by an enormous inglenook fireplace. This simply furnished room, with beams and a tiled floor, has a fruit machine, dominoes and cribbage; also darts. Leading off is a little family lobby up some steps, then a pool-room. At the back there's a high-raftered dining-room with scrubbed deal tables, a good juke box and a solid-fuel stove in yet another vast hearth. Beyond the gravelled yard is a quite separate games room with a juke box, and up beyond the car park is a field with a children's play area (you can camp in the field). The popular bar food includes sandwiches, bread pizza or chilli, home-made soup with crusty or garlic bread, black pudding with horseradish sauce, ploughman's, salads or omelettes, smoked ham and egg, plaice and chicken curry (prices from £1.50); puddings include treacle tart with cream; there's a children's menu, and on Sunday lunchtimes the big event is barbecue spit-roasting of maybe a whole pig or lamb or a large joint. There is a separate restaurant. Well kept Everards Tiger and Old Original and Hook Norton Best on handpump; there may be piped music. *(Recommended by R Sinclair-Taylor, A J Silvester; more reports please)*

Free house · Licensee Gavin Baxter · Real ale · Meals and snacks · Children in

eating area of bar and in restaurant · Open 10.30–2.30, 6–11 all year
Bedrooms tel Daventry (032 72) 2363; £11.50/£19

BERKSWELL (W Midlands)   SP2479   Map 4

Bear   [*illustrated on page 471*]

Spencer Lane; village signposted from A452

The upstairs bar of this heavily timbered old building is set in to the
timbered eaves of the sloping roof and is unabashedly comfortable.
There's a roomy partly panelled downstairs bar with armchairs as
well as more upright seats, and some military prints and relics such as
a guardsman's bearskin head-dress. The bar food won the licensees a
regional newspaper's award in 1985: soup, sandwiches and filled
rolls, ploughman's, chicken and chips (£1.95), pizzas, quiche
Lorraine and assorted salads, scampi (£2.30) and a hot dish of the
day such as a casserole or steak and kidney pie (£1.95); Manns on
handpump. A separate restaurant serves four-course dinners. There
are tables and chairs out on the tree-sheltered back lawn. The cannon
in front of this picturesque building is a veteran of the Crimean War
and blasted nearby buildings when it was fired with blank
ammunition during local festivities some years ago. In the village, the
church, in a very pretty setting, is well worth a visit. (*Recommended by*
Nick Dowson, Alison Hayward; more reports please)

Manns (Watneys) · Licensee Peter Withall · Real ale · Meals and snacks
Children welcome · Open 11–2.30, 6–11 all year

BIRMINGHAM (W Midlands)   SP0786   Map 4

Bartons Arms ★ ★

Birmingham 6; 2 miles from M6 junction 6; leave junction on A38(M) towards
city centre but take first exit, going right at exit roundabout into Victoria
Road, and left at next big roundabout into Aston High Street (A34 towards
city centre); pub on next corner at Park Lane (B4144), so turn left into Park
Lane and immediately right to find a parking space behind the pub (may be
difficult); pub also an unmissable landmark on A34 going N from town centre

This splendid pub is a fine combination of magnificent Edwardian
opulence with a really lively up-to-date atmosphere. It is very
spacious, and has various well kept rooms from cosy snugs to palatial
salons with sparkling cut-glass mirrors and stained glass, elaborate
richly coloured and painted tilework (perhaps its most striking
feature), highly polished mahogany and rosewood, rich curtains,
plush seating, heavy brass hanging lamps, and around its central bar
counter a full set of painted cut-glass snob screens – little swivelling
panels that you open when you want a drink, and shut when you
want privacy. A lunchtime cold table has reasonably priced salads,
and there are hot dishes such as casseroles, a good lasagne and home-
cooked pies such as steak and Guinness (£2.25). A traditional
seafood bar sells shellfish, jellied eel and seafood salads (£2.50). Well
kept Springfield and Mild on handpump; fruit machine, piped music.
(*Recommended by J M Fox; more reports please*)

Mitchells & Butlers (Bass) · Licensee Terry Long · Real ale · Meals (lunchtime, not Sat or Sun) and snacks (lunchtime) · Children in eating area · Pianist Mon and Weds, folk music Thurs and Sun, jazz club Fri · Open 11–2.30, 5.30–10.30

Old Contemptibles

176 Edmund Street, Birmingham 3

This spacious Edwardian pub in the city centre has rather a dual personality, popular with local business people at lunchtime for its good value cold table, and full of younger people in the evening, when the main bar has good loud pop music (though even then there's a more sedate atmosphere in a side bar, and a quite separate upstairs double bar to escape to). The main room is unusually high-ceilinged, with button-back banquettes around its walls. The cold table includes a wide choice of salads from jumbo sausages (£1.30), home-made quiche or smoked mackerel (£1.45) through fidget pie or poacher's pie (£1.65) to honey-baked ham (£1.95) or roast beef (£2.25), and there are toasties or filled rolls (75p), taramosalata with pitta bread (£1.25), ploughman's (£1.45) and baked potatoes with various fillings (£1.65). Well kept Bass and Springfield on handpump; also double measures of spirits for the price of singles (weekdays from 5.30 to 6.30 – when parking nearby is usually easy); fruit machine, maybe piped music. *(Recommended by Martyn Quinn, Richard Gibbs; more reports please)*

Mitchells & Butlers (Bass) · Licensee Francis McLiddy · Real ale · Meals (lunchtime, not Sun) and snacks (not Sat evening or Sun) · Nearby parking metered · Open 11–2.30, 5.30–10.30

DUNCHURCH (War)   SP4871   Map 4

Dun Cow

1⅓ miles from M45 junction 1, on junction of A45 and A426

Though this inn – which inspired Longfellow's *Village Blacksmith* – was largely rebuilt in the late eighteenth century, much of it, like the L-shaped main bar, is a couple of hundred years older. In recent years it's been handsomely refurbished, with a liberal introduction of antique settles, old prints and so forth: it's very much a comfortable hotel now (and indeed even feels rather above being included in this *Guide*). But that certainly shouldn't put you off – you'll find a warm welcome in its civilised and pleasantly old-fashioned main bar, which has comfortable traditional furnishings, a very large inglenook fireplace, and gleaming copper jugs and pewter tankards hanging from the high and heavy beams. Bar food includes filled rolls and sandwiches (from 80p), ploughman's with Cheddar, Stilton or pâté, quiche Lorraine, faggots, baked York ham and steak and kidney pie. There's also a smart and attractive separate restaurant (with main courses including jugged hare and well hung steaks), and a small panelled cocktail bar. Outside there are tables in the pretty coachyard (quite enclosed by the inn buildings) and on a sheltered side lawn. The bedrooms are comfortable and well equipped. *(Recommended by C E Gay; more reports please)*

Bass · Licensee Richard Ryan · Meals and snacks · Children welcome · Open 11–2.30, 6–10.30 · Bedrooms tel Rugby (0788) 810233; £28 (£33B)/£38 (£48B)

EDGE HILL (War)   SP3747   Map 4
Castle

This battlemented octagon was built as a hilltop folly in 1749 to mark the spot where Charles I raised his standard at the start of the Battle of Edge Hill. There are arched doorways, the walls of the lounge bar have the same eight sides as the rest of the main tower, and the lavatories have a separate battlemented tower all to themselves. Photographs of filmed versions of the battle and some swords, pistols and guns hang on the high walls of this friendly lounge – it's said that after closing time you can hear ghostly sounds of the battle here, and there's even been the apparition of a cavalry officer galloping through with a bloodily severed wrist. Good value bar food includes sandwiches (50p), ploughman's £1.20, sausage and chips (£1.20), chicken curry (£1.40) and salads; Hook Norton Best and Old Hookey on handpump are kept under very light carbon dioxide; darts, and the plainer public bar has pool, dominoes, cribbage, a fruit machine, space game and juke box. An attractive side lawn, with a children's bar at weekends in summer and occasional barbecues, gives glimpses of the Warwickshire plains through its sheltering screen of beech and ash trees. Upton House is nearby on the A422, and Compton Wynyates, one of the most beautiful houses in this part of England, is not far beyond. *(Recommended by Robert Aitken; more reports please)*

Hook Norton · Licensees Roger and Mo Figures · Meals and snacks · Children welcome · Live folk or pop music Fri and Sat · Open 10.30–2.30, 6.30–11 all year

FARNBOROUGH (War)   SP4349   Map 4
Butchers Arms ★

The room that readers now head for in this friendly and welcoming pub is the barn-like extension; there are huge timbers, a flagstone floor, Laura Ashley fabrics and lots of plants, and the walls are decorated with brass, copper and bric-à-brac; at one end French windows overlook a colourful rockery. Interesting and popular bar food includes filled rolls (65p–95p), home-made soup (90p), four-ounce steak in a bap (95p), pâté (from £1.25, game or vegetarian £1.50), beefburgers (£1.40), herby Lincolnshire sausages (£1.55), ploughman's (Stilton, Cheddar, maybe their own goats' cheese £1.95), basket meals such as scampi (£2.45), honey-glazed roast leg of duck (£2.50), seafood basket and chicken (£2.55), a changing selection of help-yourself salads with Cotswolds ham, home-roast beef, anchovy, onion and olive flan, rustlers pie or smoked mackerel (all £3.95) or Norwegian prawns, Chinese-style spare ribs, lasagne, spring vegetables in Stilton and cream sauce, fisherman's pie and butterbean au gratin (all £4.50); there is a daily hot dish such as casserole of hare with chestnuts (£5.25) and home-made pies with

477

good flaky pastry – steak and kidney, game, seafood or chicken and mushroom; puddings include honeycomb cream (freshly whipped cream, honey and crushed Crunchie bars), fruit pies and Dutch, Hungarian and Greek dishes; vegan puddings on request. If you are coming any distance and depending on a meal, it might be wise to ring first (Farnborough (029 589) 615). There is a children's menu (from 85p) and a separate restaurant. Well kept Bass, Hook Norton Best and Old Hookey on handpump, and cocktails. The main lounge bar (which opens into this newer extension) is a farmhouse-style room with simple well made stout deal tables and stripped deal pews on the carpet. Since the last edition of the *Guide* the front public bar has been enlarged and carpeted in a deep plum colour; darts, pool, hood skittles, fruit machine and a juke box. The safely fenced-in front lawn is equipped with playthings such as climb-in toadstools, a sandpit, a sputnik with slide and so forth; there are often goats down here. There are tables and swings by a yew tree on another flower-edged lawn which slopes up behind the creeper-covered stone house (which, with its matching stable block opposite, is set well back from the village road). Farnborough Hall is open on Wednesday to Sunday afternoons in summer and has a lake in its park. Nearby Burton Dassett Hills Country Park (via Avon Dassett) is excellent for walks and views. (*Recommended by M S Hancock, P G Evans, J H DuBois, Frank Cummins, Mr and Mrs Michael de Cort, Mr and Mrs P May*)

Free house · Licensees Jim and Sue Hilton · Real ale · Meals and snacks Children welcome (not in public bar) · Open 11–2.30, 6–11 all year

GAYTON (Northants)   SP7054   Map 4

Queen Victoria

The cold carvery in this village pub has been popular, and other bar food includes sandwiches such as turkey, pork or ham cut off the bone (75p), home-made soup (80p), ploughman's or Brixworth pâté (£1.50), basket meals (fish £1.50; £1.95 for seafood platter), home-made steak and kidney pie (£2.50), golden duckettes (£2.95) and a daily special (£2.25); a smart separate restaurant serves Sunday lunches as well as other meals. The comfortable back lounge bar has old hunting prints on the walls, and wheelback chairs arranged neatly around dark tables. The simply furnished front public bar is a lively place, with darts, hood skittles, a fruit machine and piped music (there is also a pool-room); Fullers ESB, Hook Norton Best and Marstons Pedigree on handpump, and a beer brewed specially for the pub. The grass behind the car park has picnic-table sets and a toddler's toadstool playhouse. (*Recommended by J W Strother; more reports please*)

Free house · Licensee John Harding · Real ale · Meals and snacks · Children in eating area · Open 11–2.30, 7–11 all year; midnight supper licence

KINGSWINFORD (W Midlands)   SO8889   Map 4

Glynne Arms ★   [*illustrated on page 479*]

Signposted as The Crooked House from B4176 Gornalwood–Himley

This unusual pub is set in surprisingly peaceful and remote-seeming countryside in spite of being so close to dense industrialisation. It is, literally, staggering: as the result of mining subsidence, the pub has tilted wildly with very steeply sloping walls and floors – even getting the doors open is an uphill struggle. Because nothing is level, you feel quite tipsy without a single drop of their well kept cheap Banks's Bitter or Mild (on electric pump): it's all so disorientating that if you put a bottle on its side on one sloping table it actually rolls 'upwards' against the apparent direction of the slope. Bar food includes sandwiches, small rolls (30p) and jumbo salad rolls (60p); there are barbecues most Saturdays, weather permitting; dominoes, cribbage. There are tables out on a terrace. *(Recommended by G R Andrews, Gordon and Daphne, Stephan Carney, Richard Gibbs)*

Banks's · Licensee Gary Ensor · Real ale · Snacks · Children welcome · Open 11–2.30, 6–10.30

LONG BUCKBY (Northants)   SP6267   Map 4
Buckby Lion

A428, just S of junction with B5385

This comfortably refurbished and friendly pub – a useful main-road stop – has a broad sweep of picture windows overlooking steeply rolling countryside and strips of woodlands. The plush lounge bar has gilt tables and wallpaper, a log-effect gas fire in a central hearth, a fruit machine and on our visit jolly piped music. Lunchtime bar snacks include sandwiches (cheese 60p, beef or ham £1) and cannelloni (£1.25), and there is a separate restaurant (not Sunday evening). Bass and Manns on handpump. *(Recommended by Charles Gay; more reports please)*

Free house · Real ale · Meals (not Sun evening) and snacks (lunchtime) Children in restaurant · Open 11–2.30, 6–11 all year

The Glynne Arms, Kingswinford

479

LONG COMPTON (War) SP2832 Map 4

Red Lion

A34

This friendly eighteenth-century roadside inn has been handsomely extended into its carefully converted back buildings since the last edition. In the original part, the lounge has a congregation of 80 toby jugs, old-fashioned built-in settles, a stuffed little owl, a collection of ties, copper kettles, jugs, high brown panelling, flagstones, beams and bare stone. There is a log fire here and another in the adjoining area decorated with farm tools. Further on is a brewing-history area with an old mash tun and a collection of beer bottles from all over the world. Bar food includes soup (95p), home-made pâté (£1.25), bread and cheese (£1.40), lamb casserole or vegetarian pie (£1.60), several pies such as fidgit (£1.65), fisherman's (£1.75) or steak with Stilton and red wine (£1.80), gammon salad or home-made quiche and salad (£2.50). A new restaurant has been built on; it includes a three-course menu on Friday and Saturday evenings (£8.40–£8.80). Besides well kept Bass and Mitchells & Butlers Brew XI on handpump, there are several ports and madeiras by the glass, as well as Cona coffee; darts, dominoes, cribbage and piped music. There is a thatched gazebo in the garden (where boules is played). *(Recommended by Brian and Anita Randall, Philip Wray, Jack and Laura Strohalm; more reports please)*

Mitchells & Butlers (Bass) · Licensees Ray and Jo Hoare · Real ale · Meals and snacks · Children in eating area and restaurant · Open 10.30–2.30, 5.30–11 (11–2.30, 6–10.30 in winter) · Bedrooms tel Long Compton (060 884) 221; £12.50/£25

MARSTON ST LAWRENCE (Northants) SP5342 Map 4

Marston Inn

You have to look twice to see that this is a pub. The tall stone house, part of a terrace, has vegetables growing in front, and ducks and geese in the car park – the back garden is a peaceful place to sit in summer, with interesting foreign birds in its aviary. Inside, it's a fine example of a quite unspoilt village pub. There's no bar counter: well kept Hook Norton Best, splendidly cheap here, is drawn from a cask in the back room, and you can drink it either in the plain room by the serving hatch (darts here, and a fire in winter), or in a purple-carpeted sitting-room (TV and antique hunting prints). It is nicely placed near Sulgrave Manor, with its George Washington connections; rolling countryside surrounds the village. *(Recommended by T M Bracey; more reports please)*

Hook Norton · Licensee Frank Gillett · Real ale · Open 11–2.30, 7–11 all year

NASSINGTON (Northants) TL0696 Map 5

Black Horse

This seventeenth-century village inn has a relaxed and friendly atmosphere in which to enjoy a comfortable meal; a beamed ceiling, easy chairs, small settees and a bar counter that has panelling from

Rufford Abbey links two civilised separate eating areas. Here, dishes of the day include pork curry, chilli con carne, steak and kidney pie and braised steak (£3.50–£3.75), and there's a wide choice of fish, from whitebait (£2.25) to scallops Mornay or fourteen-ounce Dover sole (£7.95). Other dishes include soup (95p), pâté (£1.95), prawns with brandy sauce (£2.65), baked aubergine slices with Mozzarella cheese and tomatoes (from £2.25), toasted steak sandwich (£2.95), seafood pancakes (£3.65), turkey breast with Mozzarella cheese (£5.85) and stir-fried chicken with shrimps, mushrooms and cucumber (£5.95). A four-course Sunday lunch is £6.75 (young children £4.75). They will normally do sandwiches, ploughman's or omelettes on request. Well kept Adnams and Greene King IPA and Abbot on handpump. The pub was completely modernised a few years ago, which uncovered the lounge's splendid big stone fireplace, probably brought from Fotheringhay Castle (which had been destroyed some time earlier) when the pub was built. You can sit outside on the neatly kept and attractive sheltered lawn. *(Recommended by D R Crafts, T Mansell, Mr and Mrs W J Weed)*

Free house · Licensee Tom Guy · Real ale · Meals and snacks · Children in eating areas · Open 10.30–2.30, 6.30–11 all year

NETHERTON (W Midlands)   SO9387   Map 5
Old Swan [★]

Halesowen Road; A459 towards Halesowen just S of Netherton centre

As we went to press a new company was being formed – with backing from the Campaign for Real Ale and many of its individual branches and members – to take over and preserve this remarkable and unspoilt Victorian pub known as Ma Pardoe's, which the owners had decided to sell. It's been famous for years for brewing its own fresh and fragrant beer which it manages to sell at remarkably low prices (the brewmaster is likely to stay on). The small, cheerful bar has a splendidly warm atmosphere. Though there are no frills, it does have some notable features such as the enamelled swan picture set in to its ceiling, the swan design engraved in the mirrors behind the bar, and the old-fashioned cylinder stove with its stove-pipe angling away to the wall. We hope that the new arrangements will keep all this intact – the star award which the pub has had for its exceptional unspoilt atmosphere and very good value beer goes into brackets until we see how things turn out. *(Recommended by J A Cox, Rachel Waterhouse, J M Tansey, Richard Gibbs and others; up-to-date reports please)*

Own brew · Licensee Sidney Allport · Real ale · Snacks (not Sun) · Nearby daytime parking may be difficult · Open 11–2.30, 6–10.30

nr NORTHAMPTON   SP7560   Map 4
Britannia

3¾ miles from M1 junction 15; A508 towards Northampton, following ring road, then take A428 towards Bedford; shortly, pub is to the left on Bedford Road

This heavily beamed and flagstoned riverside pub has one side room

481

which is a converted eighteenth-century kitchen, with its cast-iron cooking range and washing copper still intact. The open-plan bar rambles around several roomy alcoves, with stripped pine chairs and pews, kitchen tables, cupboards and shelves of plates and books, dim coloured lanterns and Victorian prints and enamelled advertising placards on its stripped vertical plank panelling. The pub has a good juke box, two fruit machines and space game, and a disco on Monday, Thursday and Sunday; it's very popular mainly with young people. Reasonably priced bar food includes ploughman's, quiche and summer salads, or hot dishes in winter such as home-made pork curry, steak pie and so forth. Well kept Manns IPA, Ushers Founders and Wilsons Original on handpump. The flagstoned terrace by the River Nene is partly Perspex-roofed, and has a children's rocking machine as well as picnic-table sets; in good weather they sometimes stage energetic games which may involve people getting ducked. (More reports please)

Manns (Watneys) · Licensee Robert Cox · Real ale · Meals and snacks
Children in eating area · Open 10.30–2.30, 5.30–11 all year

PRIORS MARSTON (War)   SP4857 Map 4
Holly Bush

From village centre follow Shuckburgh signpost, but still in village take first right turn, not signposted

This thirteenth-century pub is a friendly and quaint place, with rambling small rooms, beams and some bare floorboards (though it's largely carpeted), and some stripped stone walls, old-fashioned pub seats with massive curly arms, black built-in settles, pegged wooden benches, and a good log fire, and is partly candlelit at night. Bar food includes filled rolls (75p–95p), burgers (75p–£1.45), home-made soup (95p), toasted sandwiches (95p), home-made pâté (£1.65), and home-made dishes such as cottage pie (£2.25), chicken crumble (£2.45) or steak and kidney pie (£2.65), and (at £4.85) grills such as gammon, trout, scampi, or ten-ounce Angus sirloin steak (£6.85), with a roast Sunday lunch (£5.85). Well kept Bass, Flowers Original and Marstons Pedigree and Burton and Theakstons are served from handpumps on the copper-topped bar counter. There are monthly guest beers, and on April Fool's Day they have a yard of ale drinking contest. Darts, dominoes, table skittles, a fruit machine and space game. The peaceful lawn beside this golden stone house has hitching posts for customers on horseback; an adventure playground is being built. The village has some most attractive stone houses.
(Recommended by Mike Douglass; more reports please)

Free house · Licensees Kathryn and Ian Robinson · Real ale · Meals and snacks
Children welcome · Open 11–2.30, 7–11 all year

ROWINGTON (War)   SP2069 Map 4
Tom o' the Wood

Finwood Road; from B4439 at N end of Rowington follow Lowsonford signpost

Close to a humpy bridge over the Grand Union Canal, this well kept and comfortably modernised pub is quiet on weekdays at lunchtime, but very popular in the evenings and at weekends. Windsor chairs and cushioned rustic seats are set around the dark varnished tables on the carpet of its communicating rooms, and there are log-effect gas fires. Bar food includes sandwiches (from 70p), toasties, a choice of ploughman's (up to £1.85), lasagne (£2.25), scampi (£3.15), gammon and egg or pineapple (£3.25) and steaks (from £5.25), with lunchtime additions such as sausage or bacon with egg and chips (£1.45), cod (£2.25) and plaice (£2.45). There is also a separate restaurant. Well kept Flowers IPA and Original on handpump; fruit machine, maybe piped music. There are picnic-table sets on a neat side lawn, with more on a terrace by the big car park. Grinning Jenny and Bouncing Bess were other local windmills beside the one after which this pub was renamed in 1975. (Recommended by R Sinclair-Taylor; more reports please)

Flowers (Whitbreads) · Licensees Peter and Christine Scoltock · Real ale Meals and snacks · Children in restaurant and in area set aside for them · Open 11.30–2.30, 6.30–11 all year

SAMBOURNE (War)   SP0561   Map 4
Green Dragon

This well run and friendly pub, facing the village green, looks very pretty with roses climbing against its shuttered and timbered façade. Several oak-beamed and comfortably modernised rooms run into one another; they have little armed seats and more upright ones, small settles, big colour prints of Second World War aeroplanes, and one of Prince Charles in flying kit. Reasonably priced bar food, served by helpful and cheery staff, includes sandwiches, plain or toasted (such as sausage or egg with smoked bacon), pizza, steak baps, omelettes, good steak and kidney pie and home-made curry, Loch Fyne kippers, grilled lemon sole and other fresh fish, and ten-ounce sirloin steak; well kept Bass and Springfield on handpump. There is a separate dining-room. It has picnic-table sets and teak seats among flowering cherries on a side courtyard by the car park. (Recommended by S V Bishop, Fl Lt F H Goodacre)

Bass · Licensee Joseph Kimber · Real ale · Meals and snacks (not Sun, not Mon evening) · Children welcome · Open 10.30–2.30, 6–11 all year

SHREWLEY (War)   SP2167   Map 4
Durham Ox

From B4439 follow Shrewley (not Little Shrewley) signpost towards Claverdon

Though the pub dates from 1762, the special attraction here is the enormous lawn – a vast spread, with fine cocks strutting around, pens of peacocks and guinea-fowl along one side and a flight of pigeons which live in several beer-barrel dovecotes perched here and there on telegraph poles. The two black-beamed lounges have been comfortably furnished with Windsor chairs around low oak tables on a patterned carpet, a set of cobblers' lasts in one fireplace, and a carved gothick settle. Good value simple bar snacks include sandwiches (from 35p) and steak and kidney or chicken and mushroom pies (40p), and the well kept Mitchells & Butlers Brew XI and Mild is very cheap. The spacious tiled-floor public bar has darts, dominoes, cribbage, a fruit machine and space game. *(More reports please)*

Free house · Licensee Ron Reeves · Real ale · Snacks (not Sun) · Open 10.30–2.30, 5.30–11 all year

SOUTHAM (War)   SP4161 Map 4
Old Mint

Coventry Street; A423 towards Coventry

This quaint rather squint-walled fourteenth-century stone building was originally a monks' hospice, though it was named after the fact that in the Civil Wars it was used to melt down commandeered silver for coin to pay King Charles' troops before the Battle of Edge Hill. It's a quiet and casual place; the two rooms of the interestingly shaped bar have one or two snug little alcoves, sturdy old seats and settles, a handsome grandfather clock, and masses of toby jugs behind the serving counter. Under the heavy beams the walls are peppered with antique guns, powder flasks, rapiers, sabres, cutlasses and pikes. The new licensees have a good value bar menu which includes freshly made sandwiches, soup (50p), beefburger or filled baked potato (60p), good mushroom and garlic dip (£1), pâté or ploughman's (£1.20), pizza (£1.25), quiche (£1.40), several salads (from £1.20, home-cooked meats £1.80, prawn £2.20) and specials such as steak and kidney pie or pork ragout (£2.50); grills and steaks are available in the Buttery Bar (ten-ounce rump £5.25). Well kept Adnams, Hook Norton Bitter, Litchborough, Sam Smiths OB, Theakstons XB and changing guest beers on handpump. Through the medieval arch of the back door (which also leads to the outside lavatories) there are tables and chairs on a small raised lawn and on the cobbles and laid bricks of a sheltered yard, which has clematis on a side wall and is fairylit at night. *(Recommended by Frank Cummins, P J Taylor, Dr N A Hedger, Dennis Royles)*

Free house · Licensees Kenneth Sawyer and Ivan Currie · Real ale · Meals and snacks · Children in restaurant · Open 11.30–2.30, 6–11 all year

STOKE BRUERNE (Northants)   SP7450 Map 4
Boat ★ *[illustrated on page 487]*

3½ miles from M1 junction 15; A508 towards Stony Stratford, then Stoke Bruerne signposted on right

This friendly old canalside pub, owned and run by the same family for over a century, is particularly popular in summer. The small windows of its cosy bar and tap-room look out onto the neatly painted double locks of the Grand Union Canal, the colourful narrow-boats on the canal itself, and on the other side a handsome row of eighteenth-century warehouses and houses (where an interesting canal museum has been set up). These lively and old-fashioned rooms have low ceilings, simple and brightly coloured vignettes of barges and barge life painted on the walls, worn tiled floors, built-in wall benches and a separate alley for the vigorous local game of hood skittles. They open on to the canalside where there are tables outside the thatched stone pub (be prepared for engine fumes if the lock is busy). Behind the pub (and away from the canal) is a much smarter lounge bar extension, with stripped stone walls and a stylish high timber ceiling. Served throughout the busy pub, a wide range of food includes soup (60p), pasties (50p), sandwiches (from 70p, toasties 85p), ploughman's (from £1.10), hamburgers (£1.10), basket meals (£1.10–£3.20 for seafood platter), home-made beef loaf (£2.25), light mixed grill (£2.75), salads (£2.35–£2.75), and chicken Kiev or eight-ounce sirloin steak (£4.50), with puddings such as home-made apple pie and cream (80p). Everards Old Original, Marstons Pedigree, Ruddles County and Sam Smiths are well kept on handpump; a range of English country wines, and cocktails; dominoes, cribbage, a fruit machine and space game; maybe piped music. A big-windowed upstairs separate restaurant, again with much bare stone and timber, has good canal views, and the bar food is served throughout the day in tea-rooms by the towpath (March to October). So far as we know uniquely, the pub is 'twinned' with a restaurant in the United States, much as towns in different countries are. (*Recommended by Sue White, Tim Kinning, Dr A K Clarke, Tim Halstead, Philip Asquith, Keith Myers, Paul West, J Dobris, Howard Gascoyne*)

Free house · Licensee John Woodward · Real ale · Meals and snacks · Children welcome · Live entertainment by arrangement for large parties · Parking may be difficult at peak holiday times · Open 11–2.30, 6–11 all year

STRATFORD-UPON-AVON (War)   SP2055 Map 4
Black Swan
Waterside

This seventeenth-century pub, known as the Dirty Duck by actors from the Royal Shakespeare Company, has a side bar full of signed photographs of them, and you are quite likely to see familiar faces in here. It's only five minutes' walk from the Memorial Theatre, and caters for theatre-goers with its restaurant serving both before-theatre and after-theatre meals. There are built-in wooden wall benches and winged settles in the side bar, and an antique settle and oak panelling but otherwise mainly modern furnishings in the main area. Bar food includes filled rolls (40p), macaroni cheese (40p), pies, pasties and shepherd's pie (70p), ploughman's (85p) and apple pie (65p); well kept Flowers IPA and Whitbreads Traditional on handpump (the Flower family, whose brewery was sited in the town until Whitbreads took it over and closed it, were prominent in getting the Memorial Theatre going – so Flowers is certainly the appropriate drink here). An attractive crazy-paved front terrace raised above the quiet road looks over the riverside gardens, and has a gnarled and ancient mulberry sprouting from the stone walls of the pub. (*Recommended by Martyn Quinn*)

Flowers (Whitbreads) · Licensee Pamela Harris · Real ale · Meals and snacks
Children in restaurant · Parking nearby may be difficult · Open 11–2.30,
5.30–11 all year; closed evening 25 Dec

Garrick

High Street; close to Town Hall

This elaborately timbered pub has small and often irregularly shaped
rooms which have been engagingly stripped back to basics, with high
ceiling beams and heavy wall timbers, sawdust on the wooden floor,
some walls stripped back to bare stone, others heavily plastered with
posters. In the evenings it has a lively young atmosphere. On
Mondays they do only sandwiches, but during the rest of the week
the bar food includes filled rolls (from 46p), filled baked potatoes
(from 65p), ploughman's with a choice of cheeses (from £1.50) and at
lunchtime steak and kidney pie (£1.70), a cold buffet of quiche
(£1.80), and pies such as fidgit (spiced ham and apple, £2.20) or
lasagne (£2.40); well kept Flowers IPA and Original on handpump as
well as guest beers; a fruit machine, maybe piped music. The
adjoining house – like this, a striking elaborately timbered building –
was the family home of Katherine Harvard whose son founded
America's best known university. *(More reports plese)*

Flowers (Whitbreads) · Licensee Nicholas Eborall · Real ale · Meals
(lunchtime, not Sun or Mon) and snacks · Children in eating area · Nearby
daytime parking difficult · Open 10.30–2.30, 5.30–11 all year; closed 25 Dec

Shakespeare

Chapel Street; close to Town Hall

Originally several merchants' houses put together, this handsome and
lavishly modernised early Tudor building was rebuilt for Sir Hugh
Clopton using oaks from the Forest of Arden. It has the cocktail bar
and stylish restaurants that you'd expect from such a hotel, and also a
friendly Froth & Elbow Bar, decorated with Spy and Ape caricatures
on suede walls the colour of blood oranges, and comfortably
furnished with old-fashioned settles, wooden armchairs, and well-
polished captain's chairs on a thick royal blue carpet. Well kept Bass,
Courage Directors and Hook Norton Best on handpump in here, and
bar food including soup (95p), home-made pâté (£1.65),
ploughman's with Cheddar or a choice of cold meats (£1.95–£2.65),
turkey and ham pie (£2.10), salads (from £2.75), with steak and
kidney pie (£2.75) and one other varying hot dish (£2.95); bar
billiards, shove-ha'penny, table skittles and cribbage. Sandwiches can
be had in the main lounge. There are white tables under cocktail
parasols in a paving-and-lawn back courtyard. A good place to stay,
close to the theatre and all the things you'd want to see. *(More reports*
please)

Free house (THF) · Licensee Tim Ireson · Real ale · Meals and snacks
(lunchtime) · Children in eating area and restaurant · Pianist in lounge area
Tues–Sat · Open 11–2.30, 6–11 all year · Bedrooms tel Stratford-upon-Avon
(0789) 294771; £47.50B/£67.50B

White Swan

Rother Street; leads into A34

This old-fashioned and heavily beamed bar, under new
ownership, is long and quiet with handsomely carved ancient oak
settles as well as heavily cushioned leather armchairs, plush smaller
seats and a nice window seat; one fireplace has a handsomely carved
chimney-piece, another smaller one an attractive marquetry
surround. In 1927, during renovations, a 1560 wall painting of
Tobias and the Angel with the miraculous fish was discovered, hidden
until then by the highly polished Jacobean oak panelling which covers
much of the rest of the room. A cheerfully staffed food counter
outside serves soup, filled French bread (ham, beef or prawn from
£1.35), home-cooked beef or ham with salads (£2.95) and hot dishes
with rice or salad (from £2.95). Well kept Marstons Pedigree,
Ruddles County and Wadworths 6X on handpump. There is a
separate hotel restaurant. This was the Kings Head in Shakespeare's
day, and a popular enough inn then for him to have almost certainly
drunk here. *(Recommended by David Lewis; more reports please)*

*Free house (THF) · Licensee Christopher Jackson · Real ale · Meals and snacks
(lunchtime only) · Children in eating area of bar · Open 10.30–2.30, 5.30–11
all year · Bedrooms tel Stratford-upon-Avon (0789) 297022; £29.95
(£35.95B)/£45.90 (£51.90B)*

The Boat, Stoke Bruerne

STUDLEY (War)   SP0673   Map 4
Old Washford Mill

Icknield Street Drive; heading N on A435, this is first real left turn
after B4093 roundabout

This is the only pub we know of which, besides serving beer it brews
itself (Studley and Old Glory), produces its own wine — it has two
vineyards. It's a converted watermill with pretty waterside flower
gardens, and ducks, geese and swans on the river, picnic-table sets on
the grass and older teak seats under a creeper-covered pergola, and
for children two red boats on the grass, a boot house and a slide.
Inside, extensive carpeted bars ramble around and up and down
steps, with beams, black wood, wheelback chairs, and several quiet
alcoves. The old iron millwheel turns slowly behind glass. This main
bar serves home-made soup (from 60p), sausage (£1.25) or chicken
(£2.50) in a basket, quite a wide range of pizzas (from £1.65) and a
choice of cold pies, quiches and meats with salads (from £2.50); they
also do specials such as lasagne, moussaka, chilli and a range of
chicken (coq au vin) and pork (sweet-and-sour) dishes (£2.50).
Courage Directors and Marstons Pedigree tapped from the cask;
piped pop music, fruit machine and space games. There's a
communicating wine bar and a separate upstairs restaurant.
(Recommended by E D Hurford; more reports please)

*Own brew · Licensee John Knox · Real ale · Meals and snacks · Children in
eating areas and children's room · Open 11–2.30, 6–11 all year*

TANWORTH-IN-ARDEN (War)   SP1170   Map 4
Bell

The windows in the long, spacious wallpapered lounge of this old
pub overlook the small, peaceful village green and beautiful early
fourteenth-century church (which is well worth looking inside).
There are armchairs, seats and stools around wooden tables on its
patterned carpet, and panelling around the fireplace at one end. It's
well kept and has a relaxed, local atmosphere. Reasonably priced bar
food served by waitresses includes sandwiches, pâté (75p),
ploughman's (£1.20), and home-made specials such as Yemeni
chicken (£2) and fried trout with thyme (£2.25); there's also a small
separate dining-room. Well kept Flowers Original and IPA on
handpump; darts, dominoes, cribbage, fruit machine and space game
in the cosy public bar. *(Recommended by G T Peters; more reports please)*

*Whitbreads · Licensee Peter Moist · Real ale · Meals and snacks (not Mon
evening or Sun) · Children in eating area and restaurant · Open 10–2.30, 6–11
all year*

TITCHMARSH (Northants)   TL0279   Map 4
Wheatsheaf

Village signposted from A604 and A605

The home-made food is the attraction in this extended stone village
pub and includes French onion soup, pâté, steak and mushroom pie

(£2.40), kebabs (£2.75), gammon (£2.75), steak (£3) and a more elaborate choice in the neat little restaurant. There are comfortable little plush bucket seats and a sweep of button-back banquettes around tables in one spacious area, as well as Windsor rocking chairs in its smaller original beamed lounge. There is a pool-table in a separate room, with darts and a fruit machine, and picnic-table sets out on the grass, among flowers, by the car park. *(Recommended by J M Haddon; more reports please)*

Free house · Licensee James Andrew Wells · Meals and snacks (not Mon or Tues–Thurs lunchtimes) · Open 10.30–2.30, 7–11 all year

TOWCESTER (Northants)   SP6948   Map 4
Saracen's Head
Watling Street; A5

'Beds here, sir . . . everything clean and comfortable. Very good little dinner, sir, they can get ready in half an hour – pair of fowls, sir, and a weal cutlet; French beans, 'taters, tart and tidiness.' So promised Sam Weller of this inn in the *Pickwick Papers*; there have been changes, of course, but the service is still friendly and obliging and they will bring you good rare beef or fresh salmon sandwiches and crisp fresh salads, as well as hot dishes like bacon and eggs, chicken and chips or steak and kidney pie (£1.80), and the day's casserole; there's also a separate restaurant. The most interesting bar is on the left of the coach entrance as you face the big brick building. It used to be this seventeenth-century coaching-inn's kitchen, and the cavernous fireplace held the cooking range beside which a quiet after-dinner smoke turned into that memorable brawl between the rival editors Slurk and Pott in the *Pickwick Papers*. The room has such a high ceiling that there's space above the comfortable leatherette wall banquettes for several rows of hunting prints, then above those a shelf of willow pattern china. Well kept Charles Wells Eagle IPA and Bombardier on handpump. *(More reports please)*

Charles Wells · Licensee John Smith · Real ale · Meals and snacks · Children in eating area and restaurant · Open 10.30–2.30, 5.30–11 all year · Bedrooms tel Towcester (0327) 50414; £18/£28

TWYWELL (Northants)   SP9478   Map 4
Old Friar
Village signposted from A604 about 2 miles W of Thrapston

Readers say the steaks here (£4.25) are among the best in the area, and on Sunday there's roast beef (£3.10); other bar food ranges from sandwiches upwards. The lounge of this stone pub is extended into the neighbouring thatched cottage: neat and glossy tables on the carpet, log-effect electric fires in bare stone fireplaces, dark beams in the low butter-coloured swirly plaster ceiling, pot plants in the windows, and piped music. Darts, dominoes, cribbage and a fruit machine; back skittles room. Well kept Manns Bitter and IPA and Ushers on handpump; maybe fresh farm eggs for sale. *(Recommended by J M Haddon; more reports please)*

Manns (Watneys) · Licensee David Crisp · Real ale · Meals and snacks Children welcome · Open 11–2, 6ish–11 all year

WEEDON (Northants)   SP6259   Map 4

Crossroads ★

3 Miles from M1 junction 16; A45 towards Daventry – hotel at junction with A5 (look out for its striking clock tower)

The main bar of this well run hotel is cosy and cheerful, and the decoration, like the rest of the hotel, is interesting, even exuberant, and reflects what has clearly been a great deal of personal interest on the part of the owners. The serving counters are made from the elaborate mahogany fittings of an antique apothecary's shop, and there are various cosy alcoves, walls papered with either soft yellow hessian or flamboyant bird of paradise wallpaper, softly cushioned old settles and bucket seats on the pastel-toned carpet, shelves of plates and sets of copper jugs; antique clocks are a recurring theme. A snug parlourish room leading off has soft easy chairs. Smartly served and good value bar food includes ploughman's with a selection of cheeses (from £1.85), smoked mackerel, prawns, cold meats and salads (around £2.40), beefburger, scampi and a hot dish of the day such as steak and kidney pie (£2.95). The luxuriously decorated dining-room (where the wheels of a penny-farthing suspended from the rafters cycle ghostily) serves dishes such as charcoal-grilled steaks (from nine-ounce rump, £6.95). Well kept Adnams, Bass and Ushers on handpump, and freshly squeezed orange juice; piped music, shove-ha'penny. Breakfast or coffee is served to non-residents from 7.15 (9 on Sundays); the airy and pleasant coffee shop, open when the bars are not, overlooks the garden. *(Recommended by Mr and Mrs G Norfolk, Mrs R Horridge, Bryan Shiner, J Gargan, C P Price, C E Gay)*

Free house · Licensee Richard Amos · Real ale · Meals and snacks (also see above) · Children in restaurant and area off main bar · Open 10.30–2.30, 5.30–11 all year; closed 25–26 Dec · Bedrooms tel Weedon (0327) 40354; £34.50B/£44.50B

Narrow Boat

Stowe Hill; A5 just S of Weedon

This friendly canalside pub has a spacious terrace with tables and a large garden that runs down to the Grand Union Canal. Besides peacocks and pheasants on the big lawn, you're likely to find a macaw in the U-shaped lounge bar, and a huge and aloofly friendly English mastiff. There are good canal photographs by Ron Griffin in this main bar, which has leatherette banquettes on its carpet; darts, piped music, and a fruit machine. Leading off is an older high-raftered kitchen converted into a family room, with an old-fashioned solid-fuel stove and a blackboard to scribble on. Bar food, all home made, includes sandwiches (steak sandwich £1.30), ploughman's with mature Cheddar, Stilton or pâté in big specially baked crusty rolls, fresh fish and chips, maybe kedgeree, or various curries (£2.25), and steak and kidney pie (£2.50); there are barbecues in the summer, and a separate restaurant does oriental specialities. Well kept Charles

Wells Eagle on handpump. *(Recommended by Prudence Peskett; more reports please)*

Charles Wells · Licensee John Ketley · Real ale · Meals and snacks · Children in restaurant and family room · Open 11–2.30, 6–11 all year

Lucky Dip

Besides the fully inspected pubs, you might like to try these Lucky Dips recommended and described by readers (if you do, please send us reports):

ALCESTER [SP0857], *Stag*: now has chef who earned good reputation at his previous pub – the Blue Boar at Temple Grafton *(S V Bishop)*

ANSTY [SP3983], *Crown*: small, cosy, simple pub with low beams, open fire, miniature bottle collection, pottery for sale, well kept Mitchells & Butlers Brew XI, food, warm welcome, kind to children *(Dr and Mrs C D E Morris, Martyn Quinn)*

ASHTON [SP7850], *Old Crown*: food good with warm friendly welcome and interest in customers; old pub recently decorated *(Guy S Bartlett)*

BAGINTON [SP3474] *Old Mill*: stylishly converted watermill with original millwheel, well kept, good food in bar and restaurant; also cocktail bar, riverside garden *(C E Gay, Robert Aitken and others)*

BARFORD [SP2760], *Granville Arms*: good food in pleasant, friendly pub; children welcome *(Angela Crowton)*

BARNWELL [TL0484], *Montagu Arms*: old stone pub in conservation village, good bar snacks, Adnams and Ansells ales *(G H Theaker)*

BEDWORTH [SP3587], *Navigation*: canalside pub with three real ales, bar food, garden; children welcome *(Dr and Mrs C D E Morris)*

BILSTON [High Street; SO9495], *Royal Exchange*: well kept Holdens ales, good service, interesting décor, character, live jazz most nights and Sunday lunchtime; known as the Trumpet *(E P Booth)*

BIRMINGHAM [Stephenson Street; SP0786], *Atkinson Bar*: five well kept real ales in interesting and busy bar of plush Midland Hotel (Best Western), popular with university staff and students; bedrooms *(Mike Wood, T Mansell, Graham Andrews)*

BODYMOOR HEATH [SP2096], *Dog & Doublet*: comfortably renovated lockside canal pub, beams and brass, snacks served quickly on good paper plates, well kept Mitchells & Butlers ales, waterside garden with doves; fruit machines popular with young people *(Allan J Hill, Colin Gooch)*

BRAUNSTON [SP5466], *Boatman*: canalside inn with well kept Manns IPA, Watneys Stag and Wilsons, bar food, restaurant, swings in garden, bedrooms *(Dr and Mrs C D E Morris)*

BROOM [High Street; SP0853], *Broom Tavern*: good food in bar and restaurant of attractive brick and timbered pub in Shakespeare country, warm and pleasant *(Gordon and Daphne)*

BUBBENHALL [SP3672], *Three Horseshoes*: good food, especially lunchtime buffet, in village local with well kept bass *(Brian and Anita Randall)*

BUCKBY WHARF [SP6065], *New Inn*: simple food and Marstons real ale in several rooms radiating from central servery, hood skittles and other games, canalside terrace (OS Sheet 152 reference 607654) *(LYM)*

CHADWICK END [SP2073], *Orange Tree*: spacious pub with good value food, Flowers Original, large garden with adventure playground and evening barbecues *(N B Pritchard)*

CHURCHOVER [SP5180], *Haywaggon*: carefully modernised old pub on edge of village, functioning on weekday lunchtimes solely as a restaurant (the reason it isn't a main entry) serving good food, also dinners Thursday to Saturday evenings; well kept Hook Norton Best and Ruddles County, friendly and quite pubby atmosphere *(B E Myers, BB)*

CLIPSTON [The Green; SP7181], *Old Red Lion*: good value food, well kept

Charles Wells, obliging licensees, garden with barbecue, playground, duck pond, aviary *(Michael Chapman)*

COLLYWESTON [Main Street; SK9902], *Cavalier*: stone-built inn with pleasant atmosphere, bar food, real ales, restaurant Tuesday to Saturday evenings bedrooms *(KC)*

COVENTRY [Short Street; SP3379], *Admiral Lord Rodney*: popular real ale pub which has now started good home cooking *(Robert Aitken)*; [Spon Street] *Old Windmill (Ma Browns)*: good simple food and friendly helpful staff in medieval timber-framed building with tiny rooms, open fires and remains of brewhouse *(Robert Aitken)*; [Bond Street] *Town Wall*: food at lunchtime good in cosy Victorian pub with real fire, award-winning garden and lovely locals *(Sandy Parkinson and Steve Suttill)*

CURDWORTH [SP1792], *Beehive*: food well cooked (especially at Sunday lunchtime), with excellent choice; pleasant atmosphere and good service *(Mr and Mrs Norman Smith)*

DARLASTON [Walsall Road; SO9796], *Prince of Wales*: food at lunchtime imaginative and cheap, well kept Holdens Mild, Bitter and Special, in unpretentious pub welcoming children *(Dr and Mrs C D E Morris)*

DENTON [SP8358], *Red Lion*: small unpretentious pub in sleepy hollow of thatched stone houses, family atmosphere, fairylit shelves of 1950s china animals and so forth, canaries in outside aviary *(BB)*

EAST HADDON [High Street; SP6668], *Red Lion*: smart pub/restaurant with quality furnishings: as cosy and comfortable as a living-room at home, yet big enough to take a crowd *(David Surridge)*

ETTINGTON [SP2749], *Chequers*: good food in extended lounge, well kept Bass, Mitchells & Butlers and Everards Old Original *(S V Bishop, Hugh Butterworth)*

EYDON [Lime Avenue; SP5450], *Royal Oak*: food and range of beers and malt whiskies good in welcoming attractive old village pub; children welcome *(Brian Wood, J L Thompson)*

FOTHERINGHAY [TL0593], *Falcon*: particularly good food at moderate prices (not Monday), interesting real ales and excellent service in popular small pub with links to Mary Queen of Scots; attractive village, especially church *(CEP, Dave Butler, Lesley Storey)*

FRANKTON [SP4270], *Friendly Inn*: old ceilings, wooden settles, tables made from treadle sewing machines, coal fire, good value lunchtime food in friendly old pub *(Jill and Ted George)*

GREAT HOUGHTON [SP7958], *Old Cherry Tree*: good beer with pleasant staff and customers in nice village pub with cosy lounge and good facilities *(Keith Garley)*

GREAT WOLFORD [SP2434], *Fox & Hounds*: cosy low-beamed old-fashioned bar in easy-going Cotswold stone pub with well kept real ale and popular bar meals; bedrooms comfortable in nicely converted stable block *(Keith Marchant, Brigid Avison, N M Williamson, Gordon and Daphne, KL, LYM)*

HAMPTON IN ARDEN [SP2081], *White Lion*: attractive old pub only a few minutes from National Exhibition Centre *(Anon)*

HARBURY [Crown Street; SP3759], *Crown*: good Whitbreads/Flowers on handpump, good home-cooked food in bar and restaurant, big fires in comfortable lounge, games and juke box in public bar, friendly service, attractive stone-built pub *(A N Harrison, MSH)*; [Chapel Street] *Gamecock*: good cheap lunchtime home cooking in simple one-bar village pub with friendly service *(MSH)*

HARTWELL [Oxford Road; SP7850], *Bugle Horn*: reasonably priced bar food and restaurant (not Sunday evening), well kept Benskins and friendly atmosphere in ex-farmhouse with conservatory and big garden *(Joan Olivier, MHG)*

HAWKESBURY [Blackhorse Road; SP3684], *Boat*: old-fashioned basic pub with well kept Ansells, roaring coal fires, darts, dominoes, cribbage, garden; children allowed in snug *(Dr and Mrs C D E Morris)*

KENILWORTH [High Street; SP2871], *Virgins & Castle*: old pub with lots of rooms to suit lots of tastes, locals and visitors alike, with well kept Davenports ales, bedrooms *(Kevin Lyne, Tony Lewis, Anne Dabbadie, Sue White, Tim Kinning)*; [Warwick Road] *White Lion*: good value lunchtime buffet and well kept Ansells Mild and Bitter and Ind Coope Burton in small cosy comfortable pub *(S V Bishop)*; *Woodcock*: no-smoking lounge *(Bob Rendle)*

KINETON [Bridge Street; SP3351], *Red Lion*: old coaching-inn with refurbished lounge, snug and basic public bar; welcoming landlord, bar snacks; children welcome *(Brian Wood)*

KINGS NORTON [SP0479], *Bulls Head*: consistently good Mitchells & Butlers, very pleasant atmosphere *(J P G Vernon)*

LIGHTHORNE [SP3355], *Antelope*: good value home cooking and Flowers IPA in large but cosy flagstoned bar with two open fires, small lounge; children welcome *(M E Sumner)*

LITTLE BRINGTON [SP6663], *Saracens Head*: charming well kept village pub with hood skittles, bar food, Manns real ale, piano some evenings; quite near M1 junction 16 *(F S Golder, Jill and Ted George, BB)*

LITTLE COMPTON [SP2630], *Red Lion*: simple but civilised Cotswold-stone inn with good value bar food, open fire, well kept Donnington ales, games in public bar, safe play area in garden, cheap bedrooms *(David Wynne, LYM)*

LOWSONFORD [SP1868], *Fleur de Lys*: cosy canalside pub, fires in winter, good beer, god bar food (especially Gloucestershire sausages) but not served outside *(Ronald Easterby)*

MEER END [SP2474], *Tipperary*: friendly and comfortable pub with Davenports real ale, bar snacks enormous goldfish in ex-piano aquarium, guinea-fowl pen in garden *(S Mason, LYM)*

NAPTON [SP4661], *Crown*: games room, varied menu, good Manns real ale, friendly atmosphere; attractive village *(M Parkes)*

NASSINGTON [Station Road; TL0696], *Queens Head*: good food and Greene King ales in single-bar pub with stuffed fish on walls, Rugby rosettes, riverside garden; HQ of the Nassington Band *(T Mansell)*

NEWBOLD-ON-AVON [SP4777], *Boat*: food cheap and quick, well kept Davenports and cheerful staff in popular old pub with garden, children welcome *(Dr and Mrs C D E Morris)*

nr NUNEATON [Sibson; SP3592], *Cock*: full of atmosphere and historical interest, very clean, good food in bar and restaurant, well kept Bass *(Harry Blood)*

OVER WHITACRE [SP2590], *White Swan*: good lunchtime food in timbered pub with welcoming licensees *(R J Herd)*

OXHILL [SP3247], *Pheasant*: old beamed pub with original inglenook, good licensee, good food in bar and small restaurant; neat village *(S V Bishop)*

POTTERSPURY [A5; SP7543], *Old Talbot*: relaxing lounge bar, Manns and other Watneys group real ales, bar food and small restaurant, traditional games in public bar, bedrooms; main entry in previous editions but licensee leaving late 1985 *(LYM)*

PRESTON BAGOT [SP1765], *Old Crab Mill*: attractive beamed pub with five log fires in winter, five well kept real ales and good home-cooked food in bar and small restaurant *(Mrs C K Hudson, P H Drabble)*

PRINCETHORPE [SP4070], *Three Horseshoes*: friendly old pub with good bar food, real ale and atmosphere, popular with horsemen *(Fergus Bastock, Martyn Quinn)*; *Woodhouse*: good food in bar and restaurant of extensive converted house with several rooms and spacious gardens *(Charles Gay)*

PRIORS HARDWICK [SP4756], *Butchers Arms*: old-fashioned atmosphere in medieval beamed and flagstoned pub with log fire, good lunchtime bar food and restaurant, attractive garden *(Anon)*

PYTCHLEY [SP8574], *Overstone Arms*: good food in well kept interesting pub *(Douglas Jarvis)*

ROCKINGHAM [SP8691], *Sondes Arms*: well placed on beautiful village street curving up to the castle which commanded the Rockingham Forest *(W T Aird)*

RUGBY [Chapel Street; SP5075], *Black Swan*: ancient town pub known as the

Duck, with panelled bar, excellent lounge and snug; well kept Adnams and Hook Norton, lots of local characters *(Richard Fowler)*

SELLY OAK [Bristol Road; SP0382], *Gun Barrels*: friendly meal in pleasant Toby Inn steak restaurant with good service; modern pub with Mitchells & Butlers real ale *(Graham Andrews)*

SHIPSTON-ON-STOUR [High Street; SP2540], *George*: good food in recently well refurbished inn with Donnington real ales; bedrooms *(S V Bishop)*; [High Street] *White Bear*: bustling village inn with good home-cooked food in bar and restaurant, Bass Brew XI; comfortable bedrooms; rated 1985 best Midlands inn by AA *(S V Bishop, Sigrid and Peter Sobanski)*

SHOTTERY [Hathaway Lane; SP1755], *Bell*: pleasantly placed in nicest part of Old Shottery near Anne Hathaway's cottage; comfortable lounge, snug, public bar, covered-in area where children can sit, very friendly atmosphere *(S V Bishop)*

SHUSTOKE [SP2290], *Griffin*: fine spacious old pub like ex-farmhouse, friendly staff, well kept Marstons Pedigree Mitchells & Butlers Mild and Theakstons Old Peculier *(John McLaughlin)*

SIBBERTOFT [SP6782], *Red Lion*: good food in bar and restaurant, pleasant décor and atmosphere, welcoming, Ruddles real ale, skittles *(C J Strudwick)*

SMETHWICK [Waterloo Road; A457/A4136/A4092; SP0288], *Waterloo*: simple but splendidly tiled Victorian public bar with cheap Mitchells & Butlers and Springfield ales, more orthodox comfortable lounge, grandly decorated basement grill-room *(Rachel Waterhouse, LYM)*

STRATFORD-UPON-AVON [Shipston Road; SP2055], *Old Tramway*: Davenports real ale, lunchtime bar meals, large outdoor drinking area, children's playground *(J A C Edwards)*; *Punt & Cushion*: good food and beer in clean pub with quick service, good view by river; allows children and dogs *(Mrs Terri Burman)*; *Windmill*: fine food bar (until 8pm); diabetics' paradise with range of allowable drinks including dry cider, English Ale, etc. – genuine good value *(Don Sutton)*

STRETTON-ON-DUNSMORE [SP4172], *Oak and Black Dog*: old pub in pleasant village *(Martyn Quinn)*

SUDBOROUGH [SP9682], *Vane*: good home cooking with imaginative touches for old favourites (like spicy chicken drumstick dippers with tarragon sauce), good value, well run *(Cdr Patrick Tailyour)*

SULGRAVE [Manor Road; SP5545], *Star*: old pub close to George Washington's ancestral home *(Anon)*

SUTTON COLDFIELD [SP1296], *Station*: friendly atmosphere and good beer *(K Mitchell)*; [Birmingham Road] *Wylde Green*: good bar snacks, real ale, garden with tables under cocktail parasols, adjoining steak bar *(Mrs E Fenwick)*

TOWCESTER [Watling Street; SP6948], *Plough*: wide choice of good bar food including chicken and prawn curry specialities *(E M Burr)*

ULLENHALL [SP1267], *Winged Spur*: Flowers ale well kept, excellent clean and airy décor, friendly staff, good bar food served in garden too *(Jean and Theodore Rowland-Entwistle, G Andrews)*

UPPER BRAILES [SP3039], *Gate*: friendly staff in village local with caricatures of ex-jockey landlord, darts in public bar, newly renovated lounge, generous helpings of simple food, well kept Hook Norton ales *(Dr and Mrs G J Sutton)*

WADENHOE [TL0083], *Kings Head*: seventeenth-century inn with garden by River Nene *(Anon)*

WALSALL [Broadway; SP0198], *Fullbrook*: food good in lounge furnished as railway carriage *(R J Herd)*

WARWICK [Birmingham Road; SP2865], *Black Horse*: wide choice of well kept real ales, good carvery and home-made puddings in welcoming and well run town pub *(Miss L Gadd)*; [Guy's Cliffe] *Old Saxon Mill*: old building over weir: turning millwheel can be seen through window in one bar, water rushing below thick glass floor panel *(Joan Olivier)*; [Church Street] *Zetland Arms*: good value simple food and well kept Davenports beer in lively inn with charmingly kept sheltered back garden; bedrooms *(J M Tansey, LYM)*

WELFORD-ON-AVON [High Street/Binton Road; SP1452], *Bell*: good value simple food in comfortable low-beamed lounge with lots of tables, well kept Flowers ales, pool-room off flagstoned public bar, neat garden; in attractive riverside village *(M E Sumner, C F Walling, S Mason, LYM)*; [High Street] *Four Alls*: food, surroundings and service good in Whitbreads pub *(S V Bishop)*; [Maypole] *Shakespeare*: well kept Flowers, bar snacks, unusual character and atmosphere *(S V Bishop, A N Harrison)*

WELLESBOURNE [SP2755], *Kings Head*: old-fashioned high-ceilinged bar of inn handy for Stratford, Mitchells & Butlers Brew XI on electric pump, lively separate public bar, lunchtime buffet from dining-room and hot dishes; bedrooms; licensees who earned it a full entry, and wide praise from readers, for friendly atmosphere and good food left early in 1985 *(I W Bell, Frank Cummins, LYM; up-to-date comments on new regime please)*

WELLINGBOROUGH [SP8969], *Palms*: friendly atmosphere in rather sophisticated bar selling cocktails and other drinks, wine club and extensive wine list; live music nearly every night *(Mrs B Fedigan)*

WELTON [SP5866], *White Horse*: good cheap food in bar and restaurant and well kept Wilsons in friendly and nicely modernised old pub; children welcome *(Dr and Mrs C D E Morris)*

WEST BROMWICH [A41, next to The Hawthorns; SP0091], *Woodman*: unpretentious good cheap bar food in cheery busy pub *(C Rollo)*

WHATCOTE [SP2944], *Royal Oak*: food good in cosy and welcoming old pub with inglenooks, good choice of wines and beers including Fremlins *(AFF, S V Bishop)*

WILMCOTE [Aston Cantlow Road; SP1657], *Masons Arms*: good varied food, often unusual, Flowers Original and Whitbreads on handpump, in old village pub with beams, flagstones and small cosy rooms; friendly staff and landlord, who runs village cricket team *(S V Bishop, Dr and Mrs G J Sutton)*; *Swan House*: good substantial food and good value duck suppers, well kept Everards Tiger and Old Original, close to Mary Arden's house *(S V Bishop)*

WITHYBROOK [SP4384], *Pheasant*: unusually varied food for the area, in bar and restaurant, Everards Original, attractive old beamed building crowded with small tables, huge open fire, courteous service, pleasant atmosphere, streamside garden; often crowded *(Sue White, Tim Kinning, Robert Aitken)*

WOLLASTON [SO8984], *Foresters Arms*: friendly pub with good food, well kept real ale, welcoming staff and customers *(J A Cashmore)*

WOLSTON [SP4175], *Half Moon*: charming bar with armchairs, sofa, open fires, pictures, good food, hood skittles in wood-floored public bar *(Robert Aitken)*

WOOTTON WAWEN [SP1563], *Bulls Head*: attractive sixteenth-century pub with good bar snacks, friendly service, small pretty garden *(Mrs C K Hudson)*; *Navigation*: friendly service, good beer and wholesome food in good country pub; old-fashioned inside – bar in room like early 1950s private lounge, second slate-floored room overlooks canal *(C M Long)*

YARDLEY [Coventry Road; SP1285], *Swan*: good value quick lunchtime food in busy spacious pub, real ales, large wine list, cocktails *(Angela Crowton)*

Norfolk

Four of the pubs here — the handsome and friendly Feathers near Dersingham, the rambling many-faceted Ferry Boat in Norwich, the Ferry House at Surlingham (where there's still a rowing-boat ferry over the Yare) and the civilised Green Man near Wroxham, with its well kept bowling green — have had new licensees since we last reported on them. All have already made useful improvements, particularly at the Ferry House where early reports on the new regime have been enthusiastic about the atmosphere and range of food. Food is a strong point at a good many Norfolk pubs, particularly the Buckinghamshire Arms at Blickling (civilised and handsome, in attractive surroundings, with nice bedrooms), the interesting and old-fashioned Jolly Sailors at Brancaster Staithe (close to extensive National Trust reserves around the natural harbour), the handsomely restored Greyhound in Diss, the friendly Bluebell at Hunworth, the Kings Head at Hethersett and the other at Letheringsett (almost like a family country house, with lawn and park outside), the quaint and attractive Adam & Eve in Norwich (our oldest pub here), the elegant old Scole Inn (one of the most striking buildings in this Guide), the atmospheric Lifeboat at Thornham (with cheerful old oil-lit rooms looking out over the salt marshes, and with bedrooms) and in the friendly old Fishermans Return at

The Fishermans Return, Winterton-on-Sea

Winterton-on-Sea (another place with bedrooms). We've also had good news of the food at several Lucky Dip entries that we haven't yet been able to inspect ourselves, notably the Old Red Lion in Aldborough (a restaurant rather than a pub now, but good), the pretty White Horse near the harbour in Blakeney, the riverside Ship at Brandon Creek, the Hare Arms in Stow Bardolph and (a special favourite of several readers) at the well kept old Rose & Crown in Snettisham. The number of Lucky Dip entries on or close to the water has been greatly increased this year, thanks to the efforts of some enthusiastic boating readers; there have been several particularly warm reports on the Bell at St Olaves (near Great Yarmouth) and comfortable Swan in Horning, but one of the Lucky Dips that sounds most intriguing has only a tenuous link, through its namesake, with the water – the unspoilt Admiral Nelson at Burnham Thorpe.

BLAKENEY   TG0243   Map 8
Kings Arms

West Gate Street

The pub isn't far from the harbour, so, as you might expect, it can get packed at busy times. Its three low-ceilinged knocked-together rooms aren't smart but have a pleasantly relaxed and friendly feel: framed reprints of old Schweppes advertisements, a banquette facing the bar counter, and slat-backed seats around traditional cast-iron tables. The regulars favour the red-tiled end room, where the flint walls have been exposed above low panelling. Bar food includes sandwiches (from 55p, local crab 95p), home-made soup (95p), a wide choice of ploughman's, with locally smoked ham, home-cooked silverside or rollmops (£1.60–£2.95), and extra hot dishes in the evening such as roast chicken, gammon, cod, seafood platter and steaks. Steward & Patteson and Websters Yorkshire on handpump are kept under light blanket pressure; darts, dominoes, fruit machine and unobtrusive piped music. There are picnic-table sets on grass and gravel outside this pretty white cottage, which has the date 1760 picked out in black tiles on its red roof. (Recommended by Martyn Quinn; more reports please)

Norwich (Watneys) · Licensees Howard and Marjorie Davies · Meals and snacks · Children welcome · Open 10.30–2.30, 6–11 all year

BLICKLING   TG1728   Map 8
Buckinghamshire Arms ★

Readers unanimously enjoy the civilised and relaxed atmosphere of this handsome buff-washed Jacobean inn. The small, snug front bar is simply furnished, with fabric-cushioned banquettes, some brass tack above the open fire and an antique seed-sowing machine in an alcove. A bigger lounge bar has neatly built-in pews and stripped deal tables, with landscapes and cockfighting prints on its walls. Generous helpings of good home-made simple bar food include soup (95p), sandwiches (from 95p, in French, brown or white bread), Cheddar or Stilton ploughman's (£1.95), meat, fish or vegetarian hors d'oeuvres (from £2), home-made pâté (£2.30), steak in French bread with dill pickle and mayonnaise (£3.25), salads (from £2.30), fresh Cromer crab when available (£3.50), daily changing specials such as cottage pie, baked ham Mornay or steak and kidney pie (around £3.75), and a good choice of puddings. It's served efficiently, indoors or out on picnic-table sets under cocktail parasols, on a peacefully secluded lawn and a wide stretch of neatly raked gravel between the inn and a splendid Dutch-gabled stable block; there is a climbing-frame, slide and swing out here. The separate restaurant is open every evening, and for a £5.95 Sunday roast lunch. Well kept Adnams, Ind Coope Burton and Greene King IPA and Abbot on handpump. A nice place to stay: it was built to match stately Blickling Hall, and two of its three bedrooms overlook it – you can walk through the park of the National Trust hall at any time, though the seventeenth-century mansion itself is open only from April to mid-October (and has been closed on Fridays). (Recommended by Max Rutherston, MHG, Richard Page, Tony Gayfer, Stephen Brough, Peter Hitchcock, Sandy Roberton)

Free house · Licensee Nigel Elliott · Real ale · Meals and snacks · Children in restaurant · Open 10.30–2.30, 6–11 all year · Bedrooms tel Aylsham (0263) 732133; £28 (£28B)/£36 (£36B)

BRANCASTER STAITHE   TF7743 Map 8
Jolly Sailors ★

The three gently restored bar rooms of this friendly and pleasantly informal country pub have white-painted rough stone or bare brick walls, antique high-backed settles as well as more modern seats, unusually big old flooring-tiles, shorebird pictures, and three stuffed albino birds. The log fire has one of those old-fashioned sturdy guards you can sit on. Home-made bar food includes soup (85p), sandwiches, liver pâté (£1.80), ploughman's with Cheddar or Stilton (£2.10), taramosalata with pitta bread (£2.40), rabbit casserole (£2.50), seafood stuffed pancake (£2.60), scallops with Stilton and cream (£2.90) and lasagne or beef curry (£3), perhaps excellent crab salad, and in winter very local mussels baked with garlic butter or white wine and cream (£2). There is also a popular separate restaurant, which for example might serve stuffed quail in puff pastry or roast local pheasant and has a good wine list. Well kept Greene King IPA on handpump; sensibly placed darts in one room, also shove-ha'penny, table skittles, dominoes and warri. There are seats by flowering shrubs on a sheltered lawn, or on a canopied side terrace, and the pub is on the edge of thousands of acres of National Trust dunes, salt flats and Scolt Head Island nature reserve, surrounding the Brancaster natural harbour. (Recommended by K G Brown, Dr J L Innes, Roger Wain-Heapy)

Free house · Licensee Alister Borthwick · Real ale · Meals and snacks; restaurant bookings tel Brancaster (0485) 210314 · Children in darts room or restaurant · Open 11–2.30, 5.30–11 all year (opens 7 on weekdays in winter); closed evening 25 Dec (no food that lunchtime)

There are report forms at the back of the book.

COLTISHALL   TG2719 Map 8

Rising Sun

B1354 towards Wroxham, at end of village

This well kept and comfortably modernised pub's great appeal is its position on a pretty curve of the River Bure (it has good free moorings for its customers – up to 24 hours). Its spacious L-shaped bar is divided into areas by bare brick stub walls, with black button-back leatherette banquettes and Windsor chairs on the carpet, net curtains and a cheerful atmosphere. Bar food is good value for the area, and includes soup (45p), sandwiches (from 65p, Cromer crab when it's available £1.20), toasties (from 70p, steak bap £1.20), ploughman's (£1.70), salads (from £1.75, crab £2.80, roast beef or pork £3.50), basket-type meals such as chicken or scampi (£2.25), and grills such as gammon or rainbow trout (£3.50) and steaks (£5.60), with children's dishes (from 85p). As you might expect from the pub's position, there can be fair delays on summer weekends. Well kept Steward & Patteson, Ruddles County and Websters Yorkshire on handpump; fruit machine, space games, piped music. The separate Granary Bar functions room can be used as a family room. There are tables on the grass down by the staithe, and more on a terrace by the pub. *(Recommended by A V Chute; more reports please)*

Norwich (Watneys) · Licensees Arthur and Jeannie Butcher · Real ale · Meals and snacks · Children in Granary Bar · Open 10.30–2.30, 5.30–11 all year

DERSINGHAM   TF6830 Map 8

Feathers

Manor Road; B1440 towards Sandringham

New tenants have been working hard to please customers in this handsome, dark sandstone seventeenth-century inn, and there's now a friendly and relaxed atmosphere in the two separate bars. Here, the food, good value for the area, includes sandwiches (from 50p, good rare beef 70p), soup (55p), pâté with French bread (95p), generously served ploughman's with Cheddar or Stilton (£1.10), basket meals such as chicken (£1.90) or scampi (£2.60) and salads (from £2.60). The comfortable carpeted bars have wall settles, carved wooden chairs, soft plush seats, brass warming-pans, and dark panelling and carving (one fireplace is dominated by the Prince of Wales' feathers – this was a favourite retreat from Sandringham for Edward VII when Prince of Wales). One of the bars opens on to a small terrace overlooking the neatly landscaped garden, which now includes a play area with swings, slide, sand-pit and so forth. Well kept Adnams, Bass and Springfield on handpump; dominoes, cribbage, fruit machine, maybe piped music. The restaurant, serving à la carte meals with main courses such as eight-ounce rump or sirloin steak (£5.40), or three-course meals with a good choice that might include a roast and steak and kidney pie (£5), gets very busy at the weekend. Comfortable bedrooms, with a good breakfast. *(Recommended by Frank Cummins, J H DuBois, Frank and Daphne Hodgson, D P Cartwright, John Kemp)*

Pubs in outstandingly attractive surroundings are listed at the back of the book.

*Charringtons · Licensee Anthony Paul Martin · Real ale · Meals and snacks
Children welcome · Open 10.30–2.30, 5.30–11 all year · Bedrooms tel
Dersingham (0485) 40207; £15/£25*

DISS   TM1179 Map 5
Greyhound

St Nicholas Street

Attractively restored by the brewery in 1982, this quite stately house
– by the grandly pillared Corn Hall – has handsomely moulded
Tudor oak beams in the high ceiling of its comfortable bar. This is a
friendly room, a meeting place for farmers from the surrounding
countryside, and in cool weather has a hearty log fire blazing in the
unusually large brick fireplace, under a replica of one of a pair of
James II coats of arms moulded in the upstairs plasterwork. Low
modern settles are upholstered to match the beige flowery carpet, and
there are small armchairs and stools; the hand-pushed harrow
hanging from the ceiling looks hard work. Readers particularly rate
the steaks and gammon here for tenderness and there are dishes of the
day such as sausage and onion casserole with crusty French bread
(£1.75). Well kept Steward & Patteson Best and Websters Yorkshire
on handpump, soft piped music, and a garden at the back.
(Recommended by Don Sutton; more reports please)

*Norwich (Watneys) · Real ale · Meals and snacks · Open 10–2.30, 6–11
all year*

HETHERSETT   TG1505 Map 5
Kings Head

The comfortable Turkey-carpeted lounge of this deep pink colour-
washed pub has a long and sturdy old red leatherette settle as well as
little Windsor chairs, and fat logs burn in its big fireplace. Bar food
includes home-made soup in winter (60p), sandwiches (from 50p),
toasted sandwiches (from 55p), pâté or cheese ploughman's (£1.30),
three or four daily specials such as hotpot, meat pudding, braised
liver and pork or lamb casserole (£1.95) and – though they try to
tempt people away from chips – chicken, fish or scampi (£1.85). Well
kept Steward and Patteson and Websters Yorkshire on handpump;
fruit machine, maybe unobtrusive piped pop music. A cosy public bar
has darts, dominoes and cribbage. As the village has been bypassed,
the big neatly kept back lawn is attractively quiet on sunny days.
(Recommended by Mrs Taylor; more reports please)

*Norwich (Watneys) · Licensee Robert Ross · Real ale · Meals and snacks (not
Mon evening) · Children in dining area only · Open 11–2.30, 5.30–11 all year*

HEYDON   TG1127 Map 8
Earle Arms   [*illustrated on page 501*]

Village signposted from B1149

Popping up in period films from time to time as the archetypal basic
village inn, this, like the green it faces, seems hardly to have been

updated since it was built 300 years ago. A hatch serves the flagstoned lobby, which opens into the main bare-boarded bar on the right, where well kept Adnams and one other real ale are tapped straight from the cask. It still has stabling behind, and on its front wall what looks like a figurehead from a wrecked ship – perhaps a trophy brought back from the Dutch Wars by a customer, left there as if he had just hung it up last weekend. Late into the evenings this is a lively place, with darts, pool, a juke box and a fruit machine, and is recommended to lovers of the unpolished and unspoiled.
(Recommended by D B Pascall, Sandy Roberton)

Free house · Licensee Paul Easton · Real ale · Snacks · Simple bedroom accommodation tel Saxthorpe (026 387) 376; £8.50/£17

HUNWORTH TG0635 Map 8
Bluebell

Village signposted off B roads S of Holt

The cosy L-shaped bar of this welcoming and well run country village pub has comfortable settees – some of them grouped around the log fire – as well as Windsor chairs around dark wooden tables. There are Norfolk watercolours above the low panelling. In good weather there's bar service to the tables under cocktail parasols on the back lawn. Generous helpings of briskly served bar food include filled French bread, good fresh salads such as beef, ham or crab, giant sausages, chicken and chips, and a changing dish of the day; there is a good choice of well kept real ales such as Adnams, Everards Tiger and (from Norwich) Woodfordes Wherry; sensibly placed darts.
(Recommended by D B Pascall, Tony Gayfer, Sandy Roberton)

Free house · Real ale · Meals and snacks · Children welcome · Occasional live music · Open 10.30–2.30, 6–11 all year

The Earle Arms, Heydon

LETHERINGSETT   TG0538 Map 8
King's Head
A148

The atmosphere here is almost that of a friendly family house, and
even the decorations of the main bar have a personal feel – lots of
Battle of Britain pictures especially involving East Anglia, picturesque
advertisements, a panoramic view of Edward VII's first opening of
Parliament, a signed John Betjeman poem, jokey French pictures of
naughty dogs. Good value bar food includes soup (70p), freshly cut
sandwiches (from 65p, crab £1), toasted sandwiches (85p, evening
only), ploughman's (£1.25), four-ounce burgers (£1.60), home-made
pasties (£1.85), chicken in a basket (£2.20), home-cooked steak and
kidney pie or ham (£2.25), salads (from £1.95, Cromer crab £2.50
when available), and eight-ounce rump or sirloin steaks (£5.10,
evening only); they will do cheaper children's helpings. They have
been hoping to open a smallish restaurant here too. Well kept Greene
King IPA and Abbot, Ind Coope Burton and Tolly Original on
handpump; maybe piped music. A separate games room has darts,
pool, dominoes, cribbage, fruit machines and a space game, and there
is a small plush lounge bar. The pub, rather like a small country
house, is surrounded by a spacious lawn with lots of picnic-table sets;
park and paddock slope up beyond a post-and-rails fence. The church
over the road has an unusual round tower. *(Recommended by Sally
Terry, Martyn Quinn, the Bailey family, Sandy Roberton)*

*Free house · Licensee Thomas King · Real ale · Meals and snacks · Children
welcome · Country and folk evening Mon · Open 10.30–2.30, 6–11 all year*

NORWICH   TG2308 Map 8
Adam & Eve
Bishopgate; follow Palace Street from Tombland N of cathedral

Norwich's oldest pub, this certainly looks the part – a very pretty
Dutch-gabled brick and flint house, with clematis and baskets of
flowers by the quiet terrace. Inside is furnished traditionally, with
snug bars upstairs and downstairs (this lower part may be some 700
years old): old-fashioned high-backed settles, one handsomely
carved, cushioned benches built in to the partly panelled walls, tiling
or parquet floors. Lunchtime tends to be busy, with people walking
here from the city centre for home-made bar food such as sandwiches
(from 55p), chip buttie (60p), filled long rolls (from 70p),
ploughman's (from £1.10), chicken and mushroom vol-au-vent
(£1.20), shepherd's pie or whitebait (£1.50), salads (from £1.50),
mussels and king prawns (£1.75), good cheesy scallops (£1.80), and
dishes of the day that might include seafood crumble (£1.75), hot-pot
(£1.80) or steak and kidney pie (£1.95). Ruddles County, Steward &
Patteson and Websters Yorkshire on handpump. *(Recommended by
N F Mackley, Martyn Quinn, Richard Gibbs)*

*Norwich (Watneys) · Licensee Richard Gray · Real ale · Meals and snacks
(lunchtime) · Children in side room · Open 10.30–2.30, 5.30–11 all year*

Waterside pubs are listed at the back of the book.

Ferryboat

King Street: close to end furthest from centre, where it meets ring road between station and A146

Behind the handsomely carved timbered façade, this rambling place has an interesting variety of different areas. A beamed top part by the street has a comfortably old-fashioned atmosphere, with traditional furnishings, a big fireplace and a grandfather clock. Further down, other areas include a long, lively room with pews and a juke box, and also a spacious high-raftered place with pews built in to booths, sturdy settles, café-style chairs, stuffed birds, harness and nets draped around, a grand piano and an ancient Wurlitzer, and mainly flagstone or bare-board flooring on several different levels. It's likely that in 1986 there'll be some changes down in this part – there are plans for an airy garden-style restaurant. Already the new licensee has moved firmly down the line towards widening the range of food, which now includes a choice of daily specials (£1.50–£2.50) as well as sandwiches and other bar snacks, with a selection of three Sunday roasts (£2.50) and various children's dishes. Well kept Greene King IPA and Abbot on handpump; fruit machine, piped music. The River Wensum flows past the garden (small at the moment – they plan to enlarge it, adding a children's play area), which has tables under a huge plane-tree, and maybe summer barbecues. (*Recommended by T Mansell, H G Pope; up-to-date reports on the new regime please*)

Free house · Licensee David Audley · Real ale · Meals and snacks · Children in bottom room · Jazz Thurs, piano Wed and Sat, some live music most other evenings · Open 10.30–2.30, 5.30–11 all year

SCOLE   TM1576 Map 5
Scole Inn ★

The high-beamed lounge bar of this stately and well run inn has antique settles and leather-cushioned seats and benches around oak refectory tables on its Turkey carpets, a log fire in a big fireplace with a coat-of-arms iron fireback and handsomely carved oak mantelbeam, and a seventeenth-century iron-studded oak door. A busy, bustling place, it has a fine relaxed atmosphere. Waitress-served bar food is all freshly made (nothing frozen) and includes home-made soup, sandwiches (mainly 80p, crab £1.10), ploughman's (from 95p), home-made pâtés – liver, smoked mackerel (£1.20), or Stilton, celery and port (£1.30), garlic mushrooms (£1.20), smoked haddock in cheese sauce (£1.50) and salads (from £1.80, meats £2.30, crab £3.10), with daily hot specials such as steak and kidney pie (£2.40); well kept Adnams, Charrington IPA and Greene King Abbot on handpump; maybe unobtrusive piped music. The bare-boarded public bar has stripped high-backed settles and kitchen chairs around oak tables, and another good open fire; darts, shove-ha'penny, dominoes, cribbage and a fruit machine. There is a civilised separate restaurant, with main courses such as duck and lamb pie (£5.20) or charcoal-grilled steaks (from £5.10). A comfortable place to stay; some of the bedrooms are in the recently converted early nineteenth-century coaching stables, where a handsome figure of a white hart discloses the inn's older name. It is a remarkable building to look at, with Grade I preservation listing – a Dutch-gabled brick mansion built for a rich Norwich merchant in the seventeenth century. It used to be famous for its enormous round bed that could sleep 30 people at a time (feet to the middle) and for its elaborately carved and sculptured giant 'gallows' sign spanning the road. It still has many points of interest, such as the gate half-way up the great oak stairs to stop people riding their horses up and down (as John Belcher the highwayman is said to have done; you can certainly see horseshoe marks). *(Recommended by Dr A K Clarke, Mrs I Stickland, John Kemp, Susie Boulton, G L Archer)*

Free house · Licensee Bob Nylk · Real ale · Meals and snacks · Children welcome · Open 10.30–2.30, 6–11 all year · Bedrooms tel Diss (0379) 740481; £21 (£24B)/£31 (£36B)

SURLINGHAM   TG3206   Map 5
Ferry House

From village head N; pub is along a track (beware of potholes) which both the back village roads fork into

This pub was built for the old chain ferry when the lane was the main road between Beccles and Wroxham, and there's still a rowing-boat to take you across. It's in a fine position, alone on an attractive reach of the River Yare. The spacious and softly lit modernised bar has comfortable banquettes and tables all along the walls, and looks out on the river; a cheery place indeed, with its new licensees generating a fine atmosphere. A wide range of bar food now includes sandwiches and snacks as well as main dishes such as trout (£4.65), Dover Sole (£4.85) and mixed grill or 10-ounce rump steak (£5.65). Given advance notice, they'll cook you almost anything you want; there's a separate restaurant. Well kept Steward & Patteson and Websters Yorkshire on handpump; darts, dominoes, cribbage, table skittles, fruit machine, maybe piped music. There are good moorings here (free for 24 hours). *(Recommended by P Wayne Brindle, P E Peskett)*

Norwich (Watneys) · Licensees Mike and Jan Morley-Clarke · Real ale · Meals and snacks · Children in eating area and restaurant · Live music Sat · Open 11–2.30, 6–11 all year (opens 7 in winter)

SUTTON STAITHE   TG3823   Map 5
Sutton Staithe

Signposted from A149

Tucked away on a quiet branch of the River Ant which winds through the woody marshes of silted Sutton Broad (with improved moorings now), this has two bars, one with a cushioned antique settle and built-in alcove seat as well as Windsor chairs, the other opening on to a front terrace where there are three or four tables among roses and small trees. Bar food includes filled rolls or sandwiches (55p), home-made pâté (£1.75), ploughman's with cheese or locally smoked gammon (£1.95), and (in a big modern restaurant extension behind) home-made soup (90p), moules marinière (£1.25), shepherd's pie (£2.10), pie made with locally caught fish (£2.10) or game pie (£2.35); they've recently opened a much smaller more traditional restaurant in which used to be the farmhouse kitchen. Well kept

Adnams Best, tapped from the cask; fruit machine, space game, piped music. The bedrooms are comfortable, and we've heard that they do traditional breakfasts. In July 1985 they held the first annual steam rally – land and water – here. *(Recommended by Victor Peskett, R Aitken, M Davis, Dr B D Wheeler, Dr F I Macadam; more reports please)*

Free house · Licensee Norman Ashton · Real ale · Meals and snacks · Children in eating area or restaurant · Country music Sun evening, occasional music other nights · Open 11–2.30, 6–11 all year (opens 7 in winter) · Bedrooms tel Stalham (0692) 80244; £13.50 (£19.50S)/£22.50 (£29.50S)

THORNHAM TF7343 Map 8
Lifeboat ★

Turn off A149 by Kings Head, then take first left

The main bar of this welcoming old country pub, on the edge of remote coastal salt flats, is at night lit largely by antique oil lamps, and the furnishings of its small and cosy rooms are romantic: carved oak tables and panelling, pews, low settles and window seats, shelves of china, rugs on the tiled floor. The heavy beams are hung with guns, black metal mattocks, reed-slashers and other antique farm tools, and in winter there are no less than five open fires. Popular home-made bar food includes soup (95p), a good choice of sandwiches (from 95p) and of ploughman's (£1.95), children's dishes (from 95p), cod (£2.50), half a dozen local oysters (£3.35), baked potato filled with prawn and cheese, with salad (£3.50), beef pie (£3.65), eight-ounce rump steak (£5.95), and daily specials such as fresh whitebait with lime (£1.95), hot cockles in garlic butter (£2.50) and fish bake (£3.50). There are usually mussels cooked in wine and cream (£2.50), but out of season these are replaced by lamb kebab with pitta bread (£2.95); tempting puddings include home-made ice creams. The quaint and pretty little restaurant does a good value Saturday evening set menu (£8.50), and at other times has main courses running up to an elaborate fish pie (£8.25); booking recommended. Adnams, Greene King IPA and Abbot and Tolly on handpump, and changing guest beers; shove-ha'penny, dominoes, cribbage and an antique penny-in-the-hole bench. Behind, there's a cockatiel's cage under a big vine in a glazed terrace which opens into a sheltered courtyard with old-fashioned seats among small trees; there's sometimes a summer barbecue out here. *(Recommended by Susan Campbell, the Bailey family, Frank Cummins, Max Rutherston, Susie Boulton, Martyn Quinn, Howard Gascoyne)*

Free house · Licensee Nicholas Handley · Real ale · Meals and snacks Children welcome · Guitarist Sat and Sun · Open 10.30–2.30, 6–11 all year · Bedrooms tel Thornham (048 526) 236; £16/£26

WINTERTON-ON-SEA TG4919 Map 8
Fishermans Return [*illustrated on page 496*]

From B1159 turn into village at church on bend, then right into The Lane

Not far from a sandy beach, this picturesque old brick inn is friendly and snug, with neat brass-studded red leatherette seats in its small white-painted panelled lounge bar; the low-ceilinged public bar is panelled too – and glossy varnish adds to its nautical feel. Good value bar food includes sandwiches, charcoal-grilled burgers (from £1.25), pâté or ploughman's with a choice of cheeses (£1.50), smoked salmon pâté or cottage pie (£1.75), pizza (£2), a substantial omelette with bacon, onion, mushroom and cheese (£2.75), salads with, for instance, local prawns and crab (from £2.50), charcoal-grilled steaks (from eight-ounce sirloin £6) and children's dishes such as beefburger or fish fingers (£1); well kept Steward & Patteson, Websters Yorkshire and Ruddles County on handpump; darts, dominoes, cribbage, with a fruit machine and juke box in the public bar. A back bar (with its own serving counter) opens on to a terrace and sheltered garden, and more seats face the quiet village lane. *(Recommended by R E Jarman; more reports please)*

Norwich (Watneys) · Licensee John Findlay · Real ale · Meals and snacks Children in dining-room off lounge · Open 10.30–2.30, 6–11 all year (opens 11 and 7 in winter) · Bedrooms tel Winterton-on-Sea (049 376) 305; £12.50/£24

nr WROXHAM   TG2917 Map 8
Green Man
Rackheath; A1151 towards Norwich

This pleasant and well kept roadside pub's popular bar food includes French bread sandwiches (from 65p), home-made soup served with croûtons, a choice of ploughman's (£1.10), good steak and kidney pie (£1.70) and roast beef (£2.85). The open-plan beamed and timbered bar has easy chairs, green plush button-back banquettes and wheelback chairs on its Turkey carpet, log fires, and, up five steps, a quieter dark green area with substantial armed seats. Well kept Steward & Patteson and Websters Yorkshire on handpump; a fruit machine and perhaps piped music. The pub has a beautifully kept bowling green beyond its back terrace. *(Recommended by Prof A N Black; more reports please)*

Norwich (Watneys) · Licensee A G Hodgson · Real ale · Meals and snacks Children in dining area · Open 11–2.30, 6–11 all year

---

Lucky Dip

Besides the fully inspected pubs, you might like to try these Lucky Dips recommended and described by readers (if you do, please send us reports):

ACLE [TG3910], *Bridge*: right by the River Bure (where most boat users break their journey); Granary Bar with unusual circular thatched high pitched roof *(Robert Aitken)*
ALDBOROUGH [TG1834], *Old Red Lion*: a restaurant now, so not eligible for a full entry but included for its ambitious food, attractive and homely dining-room, and pretty position on huge village green *(BB)*
BLAKENEY [TG0243], *White Horse*: close to harbour, picturesque, good choice of food (ham sandwiches and crab salads strongly recommended), and interesting selection of beers; attractive lounge, restaurant *(D B Pascall, Robert Aitken)*
BRANDON CREEK [TL6091], *Ship*: friendly and well appointed riverside pub

with good value bar food (especially crab salad), and Websters Yorkshire *(Ronald Easterby, PEG, E E G Frost, JGW)*

BRESSINGHAM [Thetford Road; TM0781], *Garden House*: pleasant service, atmosphere and surroundings; well kept real ale, and tasty food in bar and restaurant *(David Regan)*

BURNHAM THORPE [TF8541], *Admiral Nelson*: completely rustic and unspoilt: no bar, but proprietor roams around and takes orders (a real character and expert on Nelson); full of Nelson memorabilia, on green of pretty village where he was born; real ale, folk music *(A R Spence)*

COLTISHALL [TG2719], *Red Lion*: good value bar food (especially steaks); bedrooms *(Dr F I Macadam)*

CROMER [Tucker Street; TG2142], *Old Red Lion*: clifftop Victorian hotel with real ale *(Anon)*

DENVER SLUICE [TF6101], *Jenyns Arms*: peacocks on lawns by River Ouse, children's rides, popular food *(Anon)*

EAST BARSHAM [TF9133], *White Horse*: friendly service and good selection of hot and cold snacks in medieval pub of character, with separate dining-room; Tolly Cobbold beer *(G Neighbour)*

FRAMINGHAM EARL [TG2702], *Railway Tavern*: good value home-cooked food, well kept Steward & Patteson, Ruddles and Websters Yorkshire, with friendly efficient service *(Mr and Mrs C A Welsby)*

GAYTON [TF7219], *Crown*: elegant old Greene King pub with unusual features *(LYM)*

GELDESTON [TM3991], *Locks*: several real ales, home-made wine, usually bar food, summer evening barbecues, live Sunday rock band in remote riverside pub with big new extension for summer crowds; closed winter weekdays *(T P Abraham, LYM)*; *Wherry*: good food and beer in friendly clean pub *(P Gillbe)*

nr GREAT YARMOUTH [St Olaves; TG5207], *Bell*: welcoming old beamed and timbered Whitbreads pub with comfortably modernised open-plan bar, open fire, real ale, bar food and restaurant; garden by River Waveney with play area and summer barbecues; near priory windpump *(David Perrott, Mr and Mrs J Goodhew, BB)*

HAPPISBURGH [TG3830], *Old Hill House*: good bar food in old oak-beamed village inn with pictures, brasses, open fire, board games, and pool-room; good value bedrooms *(R A Edwards)*

HEMPTON [TF9129], *Bell*: reasonably priced home cooking; pleasant quiet lounge, busy public bar *(D B Pascall)*

HICKLING [TG4123], *Pleasure Boat*: good cold buffet and real ale in waterside pub with own moorings and big garden; restaurant (welcoming children), shop, morning coffee and afternoon teas; water nature trail boat starts here *(Robert Aitken)*

HOLKHAM [TF8943], *Victoria Hotel*: several simply but comfortably furnished hotelish bar rooms in pleasantly informal coastal inn by entry to Holkham Hall, with bar food from sandwiches to sirloin steak, and Tolly real ale; children welcome; bedrooms *(Howard Gascoyne, BB)*

HORNING [TG3417], *Swan*: good food in bar and restaurant, Websters real ale, super position on bend of River Bure – views, riverside garden and moorings; paddle steamer based here; Austrian owner; good value comfortable bedrooms *(Robert Aitken and others)*

HORSEY [TG4522], *Nelsons Head*: isolated and unspoilt simple Whitbreads pub, near coast and actually below sea level (Horsey Gap down the lane a weak part of the sea defences) *(BB)*

NORWICH [St Benedicts; TG2308], *Ten Bells*: unusual and wide range of real ales, good simple snacks and sandwiches, in small friendly pub – very popular *(Russell Fox, Martyn Quinn)*; [St George Street] *Wild Man*: friendly and comfortable central Tolly pub, serving good choice of lunchtime food with generous helpings *(K R Harris)*

ORMESBY ST MICHAEL [TG4614], *Eels Foot*: beautifully sited Whitbreads Broads pub with spacious waterside lawn, but found closed last year – up-to-date news please *(LYM)*

RANWORTH [TG3514], *Maltsters*: simply furnished pub with rather boat-like bar, real ale and good food; just over road from Malthouse Broad and handy for nearby wildlife conservation area *(Robert Aitken, LYM)*

REEDHAM [TG4101], *Ferry*: good bar food and real ale in popular pub by the last Broads chain-operated car ferry; fine old rooms, stone floor *(Robert Aitken)*

REEPHAM [Market Square; TG0922], *Old Brewery House*: unusual tasty food in bar and two restaurants, children welcome (with half-price full-helping food), courteous service; bedrooms *(David Banks)*

RINGSTEAD [TF7040], *Gintrap*: good bar food, Adnams and Woodfordes real ale, in comfortable pub with pleasant service and sheltered garden *(Frank Cummins)*

SALHOUSE [Vicarage Road; TG3014], *Lodge*: spacious well converted Georgian vicarage with good lunchtime cold buffet, attractive five-acre garden with children's play area, lots of malt whiskies and real ales *(Robert Aitken)*

SCOLE [TM1579], *Crossways*: bar food, restaurant and lunchtime carvery in sixteenth-century inn with children's room, big garden, and well equipped bedrooms *(Anon)*

SNETTISHAM [Old Church Lane; TF6834], *Rose & Crown*: well presented bar food in civilised and nicely kept fourteenth-century low-beamed pub with happy helpful staff, log fires, winter mulled wine, neat garden and summer barbecues *(Michael de Boehmler, Frank and Daphne Hodgson, Susan Campbell, Martyn Quinn, D B Pascall)*

STOKE FERRY [TL7099], *Blue Bell*: good value food in welcoming village pub with Steward & Patteson and Websters Yorkshire *(Rodney Collins)*

STOW BARDOLPH [TF6205], *Hare Arms*: good home-made bar food (Stilton and bacon soup specially recommended) and friendly atmosphere in roomy and popular country pub with winter log fires and restaurant *(Sara Price, Mrs Edwards)*

STRADSETT [TF6604], *Foldgate*: quickly served food in well placed pub *(Bill Packer)*

THETFORD [King Street; TL8783], *Bell*: attractive timbered and beamed Priory Bar with Adnams and Greene King real ales in THF inn with spacious and comfortable modern hotel block *(BB)*; [White Hart Street] *Thomas Paine*: good Adnams and Tolly Original in friendly and comfortable hotel lounge bar with bar food; children welcome; bedrooms *(Hugh Paget, N and J D Bailey, LYM)*

THORNHAM [High Street; TF7343], *Kings Head*: welcoming new licensees since late 1984, offering freshly cooked food in bar and restaurant; seats outside; bedrooms *(Eleanor Chandler)*

THURNE [TG4015], *Lion*: good food and Wethereds real ale in friendly pub at end of Thurne Dyke – moorings and showers (a welcoming haven for cold wet yachtsmen) *(Robert Aitken)*

TITCHWELL [TF7543], *Manor*: reasonably priced bar meals in Best Western hotel; bedrooms *(Michael Keene)*

WALSINGHAM [Shire Hall Plain; TF9236], *Bull*: good value food in unspoilt village pub with Websters Yorkshire real ale *(Russell Fox)*

WELLS-NEXT-THE-SEA [TF9143], *Crown*: appetising food in bar and restaurant of nice friendly small inn with Marstons real ale; fairly priced bedrooms *(John Townsend)*

WEST SOMERTON [TG4619], *Lion*: good value food, well kept Greene King ales and friendly service in airy and cheery roadside pub with children's room *(Robert Aitken, Mr and Mrs K Oliver)*

Oxfordshire

This county is unusually rich in good pubs – particularly ones serving good value food. For food, we'd pick out the White Hart in Adderbury (with cosy, attractively furnished little rooms), the marvellously old-fashioned and well kept Lamb in Burford (a nice place to stay), the neat Bell in Charlbury (again, comfortable bedrooms), the extraordinarily stylish Sir Charles Napier in the Chilterns just above Chinnor, the Red Lion opposite the churchyard in Cropredy, the well kept and attractively furnished Bear & Ragged Staff in Cumnor, both our attractive ex-coaching-inn entries in Faringdon, the Bell and the Crown, the Merry Mouth in Fifield (a fine friendly atmosphere and home cooking using fresh or local ingredients), the remarkable medieval White Hart in Fyfield (a wide range of real ales here, too), perhaps the Olde Leatherne Bottle in its unspoilt riverside setting near Goring, the traditional Falkland Arms in Great Tew (one of the country's most attractive pubs, in a lovely village setting), the Five Horseshoes in Maidensgrove (delicious steaks), the spick-and-span Nut Tree in Murcott (its landlord is a master butcher), the Carpenters Arms in its very peaceful wooded enclave just outside Nettlebed, the stylish old Thames-side Rose Revived at Newbridge, the friendly Plough at Noke (with a nice

The Swan, Great Bourton

garden), the beautifully placed Crown at Pishill, the determinedly old-world Beehive not far away from it at Russell's Water, both the contrasting Shipton-under-Wychwood entries, the highly polished little Lamb and the interesting and graceful Shaven Crown (both are pleasant places to stay), the civilised Mason Arms in South Leigh (good fresh ingredients), the lively Harcourt Arms in Stanton Harcourt (comfortable bedrooms), the civilised little Red Lion in Steeple Aston (both these last two have particularly appetising food), and the White Hart in Wytham (an old-fashioned pub with an excellent cold table). Other pubs in the area score high marks for their character and charm: the Red Lion in Blewbury (snug, with beams and bare bricks), the Woodman at Fernham (a rambling old place with clay pipes to smoke), the King William IV up in the Chilterns at Hailey (warmly welcoming, with an excellent collection of old farm tools and machinery inside and out), the Sparrow at Lecombe Regis (a simple, friendly place, looking up to prehistoric Segsbury Camp), the Old Swan at Minster Lovell (a dignified old inn, with a long history), the Turf at Oxford (a remarkable, ancient survivor), the Lamb at Satwell (an unpretentious and old-fashioned local country pub), the Crooked Billet at Stoke Row (a quite unspoilt Chilterns pub with no bar counter − drinks are brought to you, and the North Star at Steventon (with an old-fashioned snug, and a good value ploughman's). Quite a few riverside pubs in the area are fully listed in the Special Interest lists at the back of the book, but among them we'd pick out the venerable Barley Mow at Clifton Hampden, and the Maybush at Newbridge (remarkably good value for the area). The county is quite peppered with Lucky Dip entries, with food again a prominent feature. For food, we'd pick out as among the most promising the Rose and Crown at Ashbury, the Chequers in Churchill (a typical Cotswold pub), the Peacock just below the Chilterns at Henton, the Spindleberry in Leafield, the Golden Ball in Lower Assendon (with a nice garden), the Bull in Nettlebed, the Baskerville Arms in Shiplake (which also does summer barbecues), and, particularly, the White Horse in Duns Tew, the cosy, thatched Lamb in Little Milton, White Hart in Shiplake Row and the fine old beamed Chequers in Watlington. Other specially promising Lucky Dips, in the running for future elevation to main entry status, are the Fox at Bix, the well modernised Chequers at Burcot, the Bull in Burford, the Eight Bells at Eaton, the unusual Pound at Goosey, the John Barleycorn at Goring, the waterside Angel and traditional Old White Hart, both in Henley, the old Gate Hangs High near Hook Norton, the unspoilt traditional Dun Cow at Northmoor, the Gardeners Arms in Oxford, the

Flowing Spring, near Shiplake, for its streamside garden, the Star at Stanton St John, the Hare & Hounds in Watlington (an old-fashioned coaching-inn, full of character), and the cosy, thatched North Arms in its charming setting at Wroxton. Reports on these from readers will help us to sift out the strongest contenders for future inspection.

ADDERBURY SP4635 Map 4
White Hart

Tanners Lane: off Thornhill Road (signposted to Bloxham) towards W end of village

Good value food in this cosy little pub includes soup (85p), ploughman's (£1.10), salmon or asparagus mousse (£1.50), a popular pâté with crunchy granary bread (£1.50), steak sandwich (£1.75), spaghetti bolognese (£1.95), moussaka or lasagne (£2.50), a casserole (£3) and cold meat salads (£3.50), with a three-course Sunday roast lunch (£5.50) served in a little dining-room (it's otherwise available for private parties; telephone Banbury (0295) 810406). The tiny heavy-beamed and red-carpeted bar and two rooms leading off, one of them a very snug little cubby-hole, have been attractively furnished with eighteenth-century seats and other old-fashioned settles and armchairs, and decorations include a model sailing clipper, paintings, antique prints and a pair of signed old racing-car photographs. Manns and Marstons Pedigree on handpump; shove-ha'penny. *(Recommended by J W Gibson, Trevor White)*

Free house · Licensee Jane Purcell · Real ale · Meals and snacks · Children in eating area · Not much parking space nearby · Open 10.30–2.30, 6.30–11 all year

BARFORD ST MICHAEL SP4332 Map 4
George

Lower Street, at N end of village; coming from Bloxham, take first right turn

This rambling thatched pub looks most attractive from outside in the quiet village back lane, with its golden stone and mullioned windows. Inside is modernised, with cushioned rustic seats and captain's chairs around the dark wooden tables on the flowery brown carpet of the knocked-through lounge, where food includes triple sandwiches (from 60p), toasties (from 70p), filled baked potatoes (from 85p), ploughman's or pâté (£1.30), scampi (£1.95), home-cooked ham and egg (£2.25) and seven-ounce rump steak (£3.95); the licensee and his French wife have been planning to open a restaurant. Well kept Bass and Wadworths 6X on handpump; the public bar has pool, dominoes, cribbage, a fruit machine, space game and juke box, and there may be piped music. Seats on the grass behind look out over fields. *(Recommended by Nicholas Swan; more reports please)*

Free house · Licensees Michael and Daniele Harvey-Smith · Real ale · Meals and snacks (not Mon lunchtime) · Children in eating area · Open 12–2.30, 7–11 all year; closed Mon lunchtime (except bank hols)

Pubs open all day (alas, all in Scotland) are listed at the back of the book.

BLEWBURY SU5385 Map 2
Red Lion

Chapel Lane, off Nottingham Fee; narrow turning northwards from A417

Interesting decorations in the beamed bar of this friendly and well run old village pub include brewing tools, cupboards and miniature cabinets filled with ornaments, a steadily ticking station clock, foreign banknotes and a stuffed partly albino pochard. It is furnished with upholstered wall benches and armed seats on its scrubbed quarry tiles, and in winter has a big coal fire. Freshly made bar food includes sandwiches and notably good fry-ups (there is also a tiny dining-room open in the evening which is popular for steaks and so forth); well kept Brakspears PA, SB and Old on handpump; shove-ha'penny, dominoes. There are tables on the back lawn. *(Recommended by Gordon and Daphne; more reports please)*

Brakspears · Licensee Patricia Shaw · Real ale · Meals (Weds–Sat evenings) and snacks (lunchtime, not Sun) · Open 11–2.30, 6.30–11 all year

BLOXHAM SP4235 Map 4
Elephant & Castle [*illustrated on page 528*]

Humber Street; off A361

Bar food is very reasonably priced in this old stone inn: crusty bread sandwiches (from 50p), ploughman's with Cheddar (75p), Stilton or ham (85p), haddock (£1.65), scampi (£1.95) or rump steak (£4), say. It's also an interesting building. Its coach entry is a very steep climb up through the arch from the village street, so that although it's on the same level as the coachyard the airy public bar, with a splendid seventeenth-century stone fireplace and a strip-wood floor, is perched high above the street. The comfortable lounge has a massive fireplace in the very thick wall which divides it into two rooms. They play Aunt Sally in the yard, which has a sun-trap lawn by the back wall edged by lots of flowers. Indoor games include sensibly placed darts, dominoes, a fruit machine, a shove-ha'penny – the board is over a century old. Very reasonably priced Hook Norton Best and Old Hookey on handpump. *(More reports please)*

Hook Norton · Licensee Chas Finch · Real ale · Meals and snacks (lunchtime, not Sun) · Children in eating area · Open 10.30–2.30, 6–11 all year

BURFORD SP2512 Map 4
Lamb ★ ★

Sheep Street

This old Cotswold stone inn has delightfully old-fashioned bars, charmingly friendly atmosphere and service, a sheltered and pretty garden, and good food. Changing day by day, might include sandwiches, turkey and beetroot soup (85p), filled baked potato (£1.45), ploughman's (from £1.50), open prawn sandwich (£1.95), salads (from £1.95), steak sandwich (£2), and four or five hot dishes, such as tagliatelle or chicken and mushroom pancake (£2.25) and steak and oyster pie (£2.50). The restaurant's full meals include main dishes such as veal done with Pernod, and cream and duck with black cherries (around £10), and a good value Sunday lunch; helpings are particularly generous. Both the public and the lounge bar are served from a glassed-in cubicle, with an antique handpump beer engine pulling well kept Wadworths IPA. The public bar has high-backed settles and characterful old chairs on flagstones. The more spacious, partly panelled beamed lounge has oriental rugs on its broad flagstones and polished oak floorboards, bunches of flowers on polished oak and elm tables, attractive pictures, rather distinguished old seats including a chintzily upholstered high winged settle, ancient cushioned wooden armchairs, easy chairs and seats built into its stone-mullioned windows, a grandfather clock, shelves of plates and other antique decorations, a writing desk, a good log fire in winter under the elegant mantlepiece, and a comfortable residents' TV room opening off the far end. Altogether, a very pleasant place to take a Burford bait (in the eighteenth-century this was a polite way of describing having a lot to drink, as people baiting – or breaking their coach journey – in Burford had so many inns in which to drink). The rest of the building is furnished to match, with simple but comfortable old-fashioned chintzy bedrooms where they still bring you morning tea. The garden has a pretty terrace leading down to small neatly kept lawns surrounded by flowers, flowering shrubs and small trees – quite a sun-trap, as it is totally enclosed by the inn's stone buildings. A nice place to stay. (*Recommended by Tim and Ann Bracey, Steve and Carolyn Harvey, S V Bishop, M E A Horler, Martyn Quinn, C Rollo, Alan Crawford, John Thirlwell, G H Theaker, Will Peskett, Joel Dobris, Heather Sharland*)

Free house · Licensees R M de Wolf and K R Scott-Lee · Real ale · Meals and snacks (lunchtime, not Sun) · Children welcome · Open 11–2.30, 6–11 all year Bedrooms tel Burford (099 382) 3155;£17.50/£35(£41B)

CHARLBURY   SP3519   Map 4
Bell

Church Street

Good bar food in this civilised inn includes home made mushroom soup (65p), French bread open sandwiches (from £1; they'll do you a ploughman's if you ask), occasional freshly made crab bisque, scampi (£2.35), game and venison pies (£2.50), and daily specials such as spaghetti bolognese, calamari alla romana, lasagne and steak and kidney pie (£1.80–£2.30). The quiet bar has broad flagstones, walls stripped back to the warm, almost orange-coloured stone, brass chandeliers and lots of pink Venetian glass and bells. By an enormous fireplace (almost as big as the room itself), a seat built into the big bow window looks over roses to the steep stone-slab village rooftops. Even at weekends this is a quiet room with more the atmosphere of an inn or small hotel (which of course this is) than a pub. Wadworths IPA and 6X on handpump, and friendly service. There are seats on the little back terrace – a real sun-trap, sheltered by the long stable wing (where there are comfortably equipped bedrooms). There is a popular separate restaurant. (*Recommended by D J Milner, the Bailey family*)

Free house · Licensees Carlos and Dorothy Da Cruz · Real ale · Meals (lunchtime, not Sun) and snacks (not Sun) · Children welcome · Open 10.30–2.30, 6–11 all year · Bedrooms tel Charlbury (0608) 810278; £27.50(£31B)/£39.50(£43B)

nr CHINNOR   SP7500   Map 4
Sir Charles Napier

Spriggs Alley; from B4009 follow Bledlow Ridge sign from Chinnor; then, up beech wood hill, fork right (signposted Radnage and Spriggs Alley); OS Sheet 165 reference 763983

Though virtually everyone using the small front bar of this pub is on their way to the restaurant (a remarkably smart one), and customers are really expected to be here for the food, readers enjoy the unique atmosphere here so much that we've no doubt about its place in the *Guide*. It really is fun to find what remains essentially a little brick-built Chilterns tavern serving champagne on draught, with people dropping in for lunch by helicopter. Especially at lunchtime during the week (when it's easier to find a seat) there is still a pubby character – even if, as we said in the last edition, it's a bit like Noël Coward acting the part of a country yokel. The bar has highly polished tables (with fresh flowers) on the wood-block or tiled floor, bare boards in the low ceiling, and gleaming copper pipes running from the back boiler behind the log fire. On weekdays they serve bar lunches which might typically include leek and potato soup (£1), avocado and prawn salad, or eggs florentine (all £1.25), good cold beef salad or pasta carbonara (£2.50), seafood coquille or roast lamb with rosemary (£3) and calves' liver and bacon (£4), with more or less similar food as a three-course evening bar meal (£8.75). (Sunday lunches, by the way – perhaps the most fashionable meal of the week here – are now à la carte, and could cost a party of four around £100.) Besides the champagne (by the glass or half-litre) there are well chosen wines by the bottle, well kept Wadworths IPA and 6X on handpump, and freshly squeezed orange juice; huge loudspeakers reproduce good music unusually faithfully. In summer they serve lunch in a charming crazy-paved back courtyard with rustic tables by an arbour of vines, honeysuckle and wistaria, and there are peaceful views over the croquet lawn and the paddocks by the beech woods which drop steeply away down this edge of the Chilterns.
(Recommended by David Surridge, HKR, Doug Kennedy, V and F Irish, BOB, Ianthe Brownrigg)

Free house · Licensee Mrs Julie Griffiths · Real ale · Bar meals (lunchtime, not Sun or Mon) · Children welcome at lunchtime (and, over 8; in restaurant in the evening) · Open 11.30–4, 6.30–1am; closed Sun evening and Mon

CHIPPING NORTON   SP3127   Map 4
Crown & Cushion

High Street

This comfortably modernised sixteenth-century coaching-inn has warm-coloured ancient flagstones by its attractively old-fashioned bar counter, and some of its partly knocked-through walls are stripped to bare stone. The atmosphere in the mainly carpeted beamed bar is relaxed and cosy, especially in winter with a log fire, and there are cloth-upholstered seats, some with high backs, around the wooden tables, some of which are in a snug low-ceilinged side alcove. Windows look out on the narrow brick-paved creeper-hung coach entry, which leads to tables on a sun-trap terrace. Bar food, using fresh ingredients, includes ploughman's (£1.50), double-decker sandwiches (from 50p), pâté (£1.75), cod or haddock (£1.95), grilled rainbow trout (£2.75) and local sirloin steak (£4.75); well kept Hook Norton Best, Wadworths Devizes and 6X, and changing guest beers on handpump; and there may be piped music. A separate cosy restaurant does full meals. *(Recommended by Doug Kennedy, S V Bishop)*

Free house · Licensees Jim and Margaret Fraser · Real ale · Meals and snacks Children in TV lounge by bar · Open 10.30–2.30, 6–11 all year · Bedrooms tel Chipping Norton (0608) 2533;£15B/£29B

CLIFTON HAMPDEN   SU5495   Map 4
Barley Mow ★

Back road S of A415 towards Long Wittenham

This low, thatched cream-painted inn earns its star for its pictureque old-fashioned interior. Built 700 years ago, it uses ship's timbers for its end wall, and has a rambling very low-beamed lounge bar, with dark antique high-backed settles and engravings on the walls – still (in spite of a fire some years ago, and careful rebuilding) very 'once-upon-a-timeyfied', as Jerome K Jerome put it in *Three Men in a Boat*; he reckoned it to be the quaintest and most old-world inn on the Thames. The black-flagstoned public bar is broadly similar, with a collection of foreign banknotes pinned to its beams; a side room has Windsor chairs around its handsome squared oak panelled walls. Bar food includes soup, ploughman's, a good value selection of meats, pies and salads from a buffet table (£1.95), lamb pepperoni, chilli con carne or casseroles (£2.30), beef and mussel or steak and kidney pie (£2.60) and a hot roast carvery (£3); Ushers PA, Best and Founders on handpump; shove-ha'penny, dominoes cribbage, maybe piped music. There's also a separate restaurant. There are rustic seats among the flowers on a well kept sheltered lawn, and the Thames bridge is a short stroll away. *(Recommended by Joan Olivier, MHG, Martyn Quinn; more reports please)*

Ushers (Watneys) · Licensee Paul Turner · Real ale · Meals and snacks (not Sun evening) · Children in panelled room · Open 11–2.30, 6–11 all year Bedrooms tel Clifton Hampden (086 730) 7847;£13.50/£25

CROPREDY   SP4646   Map 4
Red Lion

Off A423 4 miles N of Banbury

Over the lane from a sleepy churchyard where sheep may be safely grazing, this old thatched stone pub is cosy and welcoming inside, and simply furnished in traditional style, with high-backed settles under its beams and brasses on the walls. Good value bar food includes sandwiches, ploughman's (from £1.25), good home made pizzas (from £1.75), burgers (from £1.75), salads (from £1.95), home made lasagne (£1.95), scampi (£2.95), trout (£3.25), steak and kidney pie (£3.95) and rump steak (£4.75). Well kept Liddingtons Litchborough and Tudor and Watneys Stag on handpump; darts, shove-ha'penny, dominoes, cribbage, a fruit machine, space game and juke box. The restaurant does Friday and Saturday three-course bargain meals that could include rump steak as a main course (£5.95). There are seats in the back garden. Just a few yards away there's a narrow lock on the Oxford Canal. *(Recommended by C F Walling; more reports please)*

Manns (Watneys) · Licensee R E Fletcher · Real ale · Meals and snacks (not Sun evening) · Children in restaurant · Open 11–2.30, 6.30–11 all year

CUMNOR SP4603 Map 4
Bear & Ragged Staff ★

Village signposted from A420: follow one-way system into village, bear left into High Street then left again into Appleton Road – signposted Eaton, Appleton

Originally a sixteenth-century farmhouse, this comfortable pub has several rooms knocked together: Turkey carpet here, polished black flagstones there, soft reddish lighting, and easy chairs and sofas as well as more orthodox cushioned seats and wall banquettes. A three-foot model of the Warwick heraldic bear from which the pub gets its name stands by a big log fire. It's popular for meals out from Oxford, with quite elaborate bar food including a fine cold table, in summer, with lots of salads, ploughman's (£1.65), pâté, and hot dishes such as ham and asparagus quiche or spicy sausage flan (around £3), and chicken and ham parcels in mushroom sauce, grilled salmon with caper butter, breaded sweetbreads in tartare sauce, beef and apricot pie, beef Stroganoff and sirloin steak provençale (all around £4). Well kept Morrells and Varsity on handpump; quick, courteous service. There's a big smartish restaurant (closed Sunday evening, all day Monday). There is a swing and climbing frame on the grass by the back car park. The pub can get crowded at weekends, but is otherwise roomy. *(Recommended by Martyn Quinn, M A Skelon, Dr D A Pendleton, Dorian Lowell)*

Morrells · Licensee Howard Hill-Lines · Real ale · Meals and snacks · Children in eating area and restaurant · Open 10.30–2.30, 6–11

CUXHAM SU4588 Map 4
Half Moon

4 miles from M40, junction 6; B480

Spotlessly kept, this friendly thatched village pub has country-style seats and tables in its low-beamed bars, glistening horse brasses on leather harnesses, and hundreds of polished copper coins embedded in the brickwork above its open fire. Apart from filled rolls (40p) they've stopped doing bar food now, but there's well kept Brakspears PA, SB and Old on handpump; darts, bar billiards. There are seats sheltered by an oak tree on the back lawn, and across the road a stream runs through this quiet village. *(Recommended by Gordon and Daphne, Martyn Quinn; more reports please)*

Brakspears · Licensee P Healy-Yorke · Real ale · Snacks · Children welcome Open 11–2.30, 7–11 all year

EAST HENDRED SU4588 Map 2
Wheatsheaf

Chapel Square; village signposted from A417

This attractive black and white timbered village pub serves a wide choice of food in generous helpings, including home made soup (80p), freshly cut sandwiches (from 60p, toasted 5p extra), hot dogs, pizzas and burgers, filled baked potatoes (from £1.60), salads (from £2.20), home-cooked ham and egg (£2.30), home-made hot dishes such as curry or lasagne (around £3) and eight-ounce rump steak (£5.95), with a children's menu and several puddings of the day. The main area has high-backed settles and stools around tables on quarry tiles by an open fire, and up some steps is a cork-wall-tiled and carpeted section where low stripped deal settles form booths around tables. Well kept Morlands Mild, Bitter and Best on handpump; a good, lively atmosphere; darts, shove-ha'penny, maybe piped pop music. There are wood and curly metal seats on the back lawn among roses and other flowers, conifers and silver birches, with a swing, climbing-frame and budgerigar aviary. The village, just below the Downs, is attractive. *(More reports please)*

Morlands · Licensees Paula and Jackie Clarke · Real ale · Meals and snacks Open 11–2.30, 6–11 all year

FARINGDON SU2895 Map 2
Bell

Market Place

Carefully modernised to preserve its old features, this well run coaching-inn still has in its bar the antique glazed screen through which customers would have watched coaches trundling through the alley to the back coach yard – now the hallway. It also has some unusual fragments of ancient wall painting, a seventeenth-century carved oak chimney-piece over its splendid inglenook fireplace, and is attractively furnished with buttoned-red leather settles below Cecil Aldin hunting prints. A side room has an attractive modern panoramic mural by Anthony Baynes. Consistently good bar food includes egg mayonnaise, ham or beef French bread sandwiches (95p–£1.25), ploughman's (£1.55), lasagne, cottage pie, gammon in parsley sauce, hot-pot (all £1.95) and crab or prawn pancakes (£2.55), and there's a popular restaurant. Well kept Wadworths Farmers Glory and 6X on handpump, with Old Timer in winter; dominoes, shut-the-box, maybe piped music. The cobbled and paved yard, warmly sheltered by the back wings of the inn, has wooden seats and tables among tubs of flowers. The pink façade, with its steep stone-slab roof and enormous bell, is very pretty, and the old-fashioned bedrooms are cosy. *(Recommended by Doug Kennedy, William Meadon, Richard Steel, S V Bishop)*

Wadworths · Licensee William Dreyer · Real ale · Meals and snacks · Children in restaurant and lounge · Open 10.30–2.30, 5.30–11 all year · Bedrooms tel Faringdon (0367) 20534; £23.75 (£31.75B)/£32.75 (£38.75B)

Crown ★

Market Place

Good home-made bar food in this old inn includes fine daily specials such as herby beef casserole, fluffy turkey pie and West African groundnut stew (around £2–£3), as well as sandwiches (from 55p), attractively filled baked potatoes (around £1.20), ham and egg (£1.70), scampi (£2.35) and an excellent lunchtime cold table (£1.80–£2.30, not Sunday). The massively beamed front bar, with its stone-mullioned windows, panelling and big log fire, is furnished to match, and the Stuart Bar by the cobbled inner courtyard is named to commemorate the inn's loyalist Civil War connections (there's said to have been a tunnel between the inn and nearby pro-Stuart Faringdon House). Well kept Courage Directors, Flowers Original, Hook Norton Best, Morlands Best and Ruddles County on handpump. There is a separate restaurant. The courtyard is most attractive, with lots of shrubs and trees, hanging baskets decorating the creeper-covered stone walls of the inn buildings, and white fantail pigeons strutting along the steep stone-slab roofs. *(Recommended by S V Bishop; more reports please)*

Free house · Licensees R H and A M Deane · Meals and snacks · Children in restaurant · Guitarist, singer and traditional jazz on 1st and 3rd Sun of month Open 11–2.30, 6–11 all year · Bedrooms tel Faringdon (0367) 20196; £16 (£18B)/£22 (£25B)

FARNBOROUGH, near Banbury

This village is actually in Warwickshire, and therefore included in our Midlands chapter. We mention this particularly here because the Butchers Arms is a special favourite of many readers who are misled by the Post Office's addressing conventions into thinking that it's in Oxfordshire – and wonder why they can't find it in the Guide

FERNHAM   SU2992   Map 2

Woodman ★

Odd touches in this heavily beamed, rambling seventeenth-century village pub may include a hot-pot simmering over the big central log fire in winter, hot saké, and even clay pipes, ready-filled for smoking. There are tables made simply from old casks, pews and Windsor chairs, as well as cushioned benches built into the rough plaster walls, which are decorated with a miscellany of boomerangs, milkmaids' yokes, leather tack, coach horns, an old screw press, good black and white photographs of horses, and so forth. Lighting – partly by candles – is subdued. There's an excellent atmosphere, even when it gets crowded. Morlands PA and BB, Theakstons Old Peculier and

Gibbs Mew Bishops Tipple – not cheap, but particularly well kept – tapped from the casks behind the bar (where the regulars gather in force). Bar food includes home-made soup (80p), filled hot crusty rolls (from £1), ploughman's or home-made pâté (from £1.35), spaghetti (£2), lasagne or curry (£2.40), and moussaka or steak and kidney pie (£2.50), served with fresh vegetables in winter and salads in summer. A restaurant in a raftered barn serves dinners (main courses such as beef bourguignonne £4.50, steak £5.50), and can be booked by large groups – 30 to 40 people – for colourful medieval banquets at £16.50 each; telephone Uffington (036 782) 643. *(Recommended by Stuart Barker, Mrs V Morgan, Gordon and Daphne, Martyn Quinn; more reports please)*

Free house · Licensee John Lane · Real ale · Meals and snacks · Children in eating area · Guitarist Fri and Sat · Open 11–2.30, 6–11 all year

FIFIELD SP2318 Map 4
Merry Mouth

A424 4 miles N of Burford

Good value bar food in this isolated but warm and friendly old stone pub is all home made and includes soup (80p), sandwiches (from 70p; not made if they're desperately busy), macaroni cheese, fish and cheese hot-pot, chicken provençale or courgettes and prawns in cheese sauce (£2.50), steak and Guinness pie (£2.75), ham off the bone with egg and chips (£3.50), fresh local trout (£4.95) and eight-ounce sirloin steaks (£5.50), with some basket meals such as chicken or scampi (around £2.85) and, if the landlord's been successful with his gun, pigeon pie or winter game pie. The pub dates back in part some 700 years, and the Domesday Book mentions an inn on this site. The simple but comfortably furnished L-shaped bar has nice bay-window seats; horse brasses and antique bottles hang from the beams; some walls are stripped back to the old masonry; and there is an open fire in winter. There's also a nicely set out restaurant. Well kept Donnington BB and SBA on handpump; darts, dominoes, and a fruit machine. The bedrooms are warm and quaint. There are seats under three cocktail parasols beyond the car park (a little noise from fast traffic on the road). *(Recommended by F T and A K Hargreaves, Richard Coles, D Angless, Martyn Quinn)*

Donnington · Licensee Philip Waller · Real ale · Meals and snacks · Children in restaurant and children's room · Open 11–2.30, 6–11 all year · Bedrooms tel Shipton-under-Wychwood (0993) 830759; £10/£20

FYFIELD SU4298 Map 2
White Hart ★

In village, off A420 8 miles SW of Oxford

The main room of this striking and unusual medieval pub has soaring eaves and huge stone-flanked window embrasures, with an attractive carpeted upper gallery looking down into it. A low-ceilinged side bar has an inglenook fireplace with a huge black urn hanging over the grate. The impressive range of real ales, which changes from time to time, might typically consist of Flowers Original, Gibbs Mew Bishops Tipple, Morlands, Ruddles County, Theakstons XB and Old Peculier and Wadworths 6X and Farmers Glory, and there is a choice of draught ciders. Besides sandwiches and ploughman's, good bar food includes soup (80p), ploughman's or venison or duck pâté (£1.25), sardines or squid (£1.95), plaice or moussaka (£2.15), chicken and ham, game or steak and kidney pies (£2.65), braised pigeon, hare or venison casserole (£2.95) and rump steak (£5.75); the puddings are good, and service is friendly and efficient. In summer the rambling and sheltered back lawn is popular. For its first hundred years this was a chantry house for priests whose duty was to pray for the soul of its builder, Sir John Golafre. When they were thrown out during the Reformation the building was bought by St John's College, Oxford, and for the 400 years since then has been run as a pub under their ownership. The priest's room is now a restaurant, as is the barrel-vaulted cellar. Not far from the delightful gardens of Pusey House. *(Recommended by B H and N R Robinson, Mr and Mrs G D Amos, William Meadon, Richard Steel, Jane English, J H DuBois, R J McLeod, N M Pickford, Stuart Barker, MHG, Joel Dobris, Mrs I E Holmes, Martyn Quinn)*

Free house · Licensee Edward Howard · Real ale · Meals and snacks · Children welcome · Open 10.30–2.30, 6–11 all year

GODSTOW SP4708 Map 2
Trout

Follow Wytham signpost from roundabout at N end of Woodstock Road

Included for its delightful setting this pretty, creeper-covered medieval pub has an attractive cobbled riverside terrace that is almost legendary, with sturdy old tables right by a stone-channelled stream where greedy trout flick about lazily in the clear water, waiting for crumbs. The beamed main bar has cushioned old settles on the flagstones and bare floorboards, old Oxford views and sporting prints on the walls, and a weight-driven spit in front of its big stone fireplace. There is a separate beamed restaurant with a wide choice of good salads, and during the busier times a more modern extension bar is open for snacks such as sandwiches, pies and quiche. The present building replaced one destroyed by Cromwell in 1646 which had been set up in 1138 as a hospice for the nearby nunnery, where Henry II's mistress, Fair Rosamund, was forced to drink poison by his wife, Queen Eleanor. *(Recommended by Martyn Quinn, MHG, Jonathan Mindell, Guy Atkins, Gordon and Daphne, Lorna Mackinnon)*

Charringtons · Snacks (see above) · Children in restaurant, and at lunchtime (weekends only in winter) in extension sandwich bar · Open 11–2.30, 6–11 all year

nr GORING SU5080 Map 2
Old Leatherne Bottle

Cleeve; off B4009, about a mile towards Wallingford

Unusual among Thames-side pubs for its unpretentious atmosphere and unspoilt setting, this welcoming and friendly pub serves sandwiches (from 75p), toasties (for 80p), home-made soup (90p), a good choice of ploughman's (£1.50, or £3 for specially generous ones), home-made pizza, barbecue chicken fillets or home-baked ham off the bone (from £2.50), a couple of daily specials such as hot-pot, lasagne, shellfish (mussels, crab or prawns) and chicken and mushroom or steak and kidney pie (£3–£4), and sirloin steaks (£6.50). There are lots of window seats in the three take-them-as-you-find-them connecting rooms of the bar and dining-room; they look over a terrace with a black gondola to a quiet reach of the river, where nothing much ripples the calm except for ducks, swans, and maybe a few sailing dinghies. There is some very old stone masonry and an assortment of interesting decorations, from stuffed fish to drinking horns and wooden caryatids – with a colourful lifesize effigy of a drunken seaman outside. Well kept Brakspears PA, SB and Mild; bar billiards, and a fruit machine. The ground which rises sharply behind the pub gives it a particularly attractive hidden-away feeling; nice on a summer's evening. *(Recommended by Brian and Rosemary Wilmot, S J Tims, Gordon and Daphne)*

Brakspears · Real ale · Meals and snacks · Open 10.30–2.30, 6–11 all year

GREAT BOURTON   SP4545 Map 4
Swan   [*illustrated on page 510*]

Just off A423, 3 miles N of Banbury

Extended since our last edition, the bar of this thatched village pub has comfortable seats on the carpet in front of its huge inglenook fireplace. Well kept Wadworths Devizes, Farmers Glory and 6X on handpump, with Old Timer in winter; darts, shove-ha'penny, dominoes, cribbage, tip-it, dubbers, and maybe piped music. Bar food includes sandwiches and toasties, filled baked potatoes in winter (from 75p), soup (80p), pâtés, ploughman's (from £1), a salad bar at lunchtime (£2.25), and various hot dishes (around £3–£4); there's a separate dining-room. Aunt Sally can be played in the well kept back garden, where they now hold summer barbecues on fine Friday and Saturday evenings. *(Recommended by Martyn Quinn, J L Thompson, Barry Stainton; more reports please)*

Wadworths · Licensee Mrs Gill Crosby · Real ale · Meals and snacks · Children in eating area and dining-room · Open 11–2.30, 6–11 all year (opens 11.30 in winter) · Bedrooms tel Cropredy (029 575) 8181; £8.50/£17

GREAT TEW   SP3929 Map 2
Falkland Arms ★ ★

Off B4022 about 5 miles E of Chipping Norton

Everything about this pub is splendidly traditional. Its partly panelled bar has high-backed settles around plain stripped tables on flagstones and bare boards, dim converted oil-lamps hang from the latticed windows, and the bar is decorated with antique Doulton jugs, mugs and tobacco jars. You can buy clay pipes filled ready to smoke (70p), choose from some 50 different snuffs, and play darts, shove-ha'penny, dominoes or cribbage. There are always several reasonably

priced and well kept guest beers – more in summer, when extra
customers mean less risk of casks lingering on beyond their peak – as
well as regular Donnington, Hook Norton Best, McMullens and
Wadworths 6X (in a year, they reckon to get through over 200
different beers). They also keep country wines and draught and farm
ciders, and do mulled wine in winter. Lunchtime bar food includes
tomato soup, ploughman's (£1.20) and two or three home-made
stews or pies such as steak and Guinness, pork in cider or rabbit
(£1.85). Service is friendly and cheerful, and the pub is well used by
local people as well as visitors. In summer, sit on the wooden seats
among the roses on the front patio, with doves cooing among the
lumpy cushions of moss on the heavy stone roof-slabs, and look over
to what must be one of the prettiest village schools in the world. This
whole village was largely created in the early nineteenth century as an
experiment in artificial landscaping by pioneer planner J C Loudon,
and is now an outstanding conservation area of golden stone
thatched cottages and quiet wooded slopes. (Recommended by Martyn
Quinn, Dave Butler, Lesley Storey, R H Inns, William Meadon, Richard Steel,
Aubrey Saunders, Brigid Avison, MHG, C F Walling, Heather Sharland)

Free house · Licensee John Milligan · Real ale · Snacks (lunchtime, not Sun or
Mon) · Folk music Sun evening · Open 11–2.30, 6–11 (11.30–2.30, 6–10.30
in winter); closed Mon lunchtime · Three bedrooms tel Great Tew
(060 883) 653; £10/£19

HAILEY   SU6485 Map 2
King William IV ★

Signposted, with Ipsden, from A4074 S of Wallingford; can also be reached
from A423; OS Sheet 175 reference 641859

Readers' reports show that we are not alone in finding this simple pub
addictive: of the great many pubs we see, this is one that we always
try to find an excuse to come back to again – and again. A remote but
welcoming white house on the edge of a Chilterns village, it's
charming and quietly cosy in winter, popular on summer evenings
(but, surprisingly, not too busy on Saturday mornings). It's been
turned into something of a rural museum by its splendid bearded
landlord (who drives a shire horse and dray): the beams in the glossy
ruby-smoked ceiling and the timbered bare brick walls are festooned
with well restored farm tools – forks, ratchets, shovels, crooks,
grabbers, man-traps, wicker sieves and so on, with bigger equipment,
such as smartly painted veteran cattle-cake-breakers and chaff
cutters, on the lawn behind. There's good sturdy furniture on the tiled
floor in front of the big log fire in winter, and this main room opens
into two broadly similar carpeted areas. Well kept Brakspears PA, SB,
XXXX Old and Mild tapped from casks behind the bar, and pies,
pasties or good filled rolls such as ham, cheese and pickle, corned beef

The Post Office makes it virtually impossible for people to come to grips with
British geography by using a system of post towns that are often across the
county boundary from the places they serve. So the postal address of a pub often
puts it in the wrong county. We use the correct county – the one the pub is
actually in. Lots of pubs which the Post Office alleges are in Oxfordshire are
actually in Berkshire, Buckinghamshire, Gloucestershire or the Midlands. Some
pubs are in Norfolk when they're really in Suffolk – which is where we list them.

(35p), and a range of ploughman's with home-made soup in winter.
Seats outside look down over a fine rolling stretch of wood-fringed
Chilterns pasture, and a stroll up the lane opens up vast views over
the Thames valley and beyond. *(Recommended by Jane English, Brian and
Rosemary Wilmot, T N de Bray, Gordon and Daphne, Dr D A Pendleton,
BOB)*

*Brakspears · Licensee B E E Penney · Real ale · Snacks · Open 10–2.30, 6–11
all year*

HENLEY SU7882 Map 2

*Besides the two pubs described below, you might like the Little Angel in
Remenham, Buckinghamshire – another county, but in fact just a stroll across
the bridge*

Argyll

Market Place

As far as we know the only pub here selling Morlands beer (Mild,
Bitter and Best on handpump, well kept), this has a long neatly-kept
tartan-carpeted lounge, its ply panelling decorated with Highland
regimental dress prints and battle scenes. It's popular at lunchtime for
its buffet – sandwiches, ploughman's (£1.10), and as much salad as
you want with quiche (£1.95), prawn vol-au-vent or home-roasted
glazed gammon (£3), with hot dishes such as curry or pork and cider
casserole (£2.40), steak and kidney pudding (£2.50) and roast beef
(£4.50), all served with limitless fresh vegetables. There are puddings
such as treacle tart (70p), and on Sundays they do traditional roasts.
There are white cast-iron-look tables on a back terrace by a small car
park – which in turn backs on to the big municipal one. *(Recommended
by W T Aird, MHG; more reports please)*

*Morlands · Licensees Ray and Veronica Boswell · Real ale · Meals (lunchtime)
and snacks (lunchtime, not Sun) · Children in eating area · Open 10–2.30,
6–11 all year*

Three Tuns

5 Market Place

The two small rooms of this cosy and unpretentious pub open off a
long tiled and panelled corridor (which leads to a small back terrace).
The panelled front public bar has darts, shove-ha'penny, dominoes,
cribbage and a fruit machine; then, beyond the old-fashioned central
servery, is a snug, heavily beamed buttery, with a central chimney and
log-effect gas fire dividing off its back part. Food – served throughout
the afternoon in the buttery, as well as during normal opening hours
– includes sandwiches (from 47p; bacon, lettuce and tomato £1.05),
soup (48p), Cornish pasty (75p), ratatouille (£1.08), home-made
chicken liver pâté (£1.11), ploughman's (from £1.35), egg, bacon,
sausage and chips (£1.74), savoury chicken (£2.10), scampi (£2.88)
and an interesting hot dish'of the day such as egg, spinach, onion and
green pepper herby pie in wholemeal pastry (£1.98). Besides chips,
they do croquettes, chunky fritters and baby baked potatoes. Well
kept Brakspears PA, SB and XXXX Old on handpump, and in winter

hot cider punch and hot chocolate as well as coffee and tea; piped music. *(Recommended by Martyn Quinn, Maurice Southon, W T Aird, MHG)*

Brakspears · Licensee Jack Knowles · Real ale · Meals and snacks · Children in back part of buttery · Open 10–2.30, 6–11 all year (and see above)

LETCOMBE REGIS   SU3784   Map 2

Sparrow

Follow Village Only sign as far as possible

This unspoilt and friendly village pub looks up the slope of the Downs to the prehistoric Segsbury hill fort – the best view from inside is from the big table in the front window. Simple, good value food includes sandwiches (from 45p), combination toasties, home-made soup, ploughman's (£1.15), salads (from £1.35), home made pasties (£1.40) or quiche (£1.50) and a variety of popular fry-ups and omelettes (around £1.65). Well kept Morlands Mild and Bitter on handpump; darts, pin-table, dominoes, cribbage, a fruit machine and piped music. The small L-shaped bar is partly quarry-tiled, with a few dark beams in its low ceiling, and has a pleasant, relaxed atmosphere. Outside the pretty little tiled white cottage a stretch of safely fenced grass has swings and a climbing frame as well as scaffold-and-wood tables and benches. *(Recommended by Jane English, Gordon and Daphne)*

Morlands · Licensee I J Shaw · Real ale · Meals and snacks (lunchtime, not Sun) Open 10.30–2.30, 7–11 all year

MAIDENSGROVE   SU7288   Map 4

Five Horseshoes

W of village, which is signposted from B480 and B481; OS Sheet 175 reference 711890

Steak-lovers in pilgrimage mood thread their way through the beech woods to the lovely common high in the Chilterns where this remote, low-ceilinged, rambling pub serves some of the best Scotch meat you can find anywhere. Besides the sirloin, fillet and T-bone steaks (£6.50–£8), they do other good home-made food, including toasted sandwiches, ploughman's (from £1.50), starters such as soup (£1), garlic mushrooms and a range of pâtés (around £1.50 – readers specially like the creamed avocado and the smoked trout), and main dishes (from £2.80) such as stuffed savoury pancakes, steak and mushroom pie, beef fillet in green peppercorn sauce, and halibut with prawn sauce and nutty pork. In summer there are salads with dishes such as crab and prawn quiche, prawns with avocado ice-cream, and country meat pie, and in winter there are stuffed baked potatoes. They always have at least one vegetarian dish such as nut burgers and ratatouille, and a good choice of popular puddings including home made sorbets (with or without liqueur flavourings) and treacle and walnut pie. Well kept Brakspears PA and SB are tapped from casks behind the bar, which has lots of foreign banknotes overhead. Though furnishings are mainly modern – wheel-back chairs around shiny dark wooden tables – there are some attractive old seats and a sturdy baluster-leg table, as well as a good log fire in winter. Get there early to be sure of a table. An obvious pub for walkers: the separate bar in which boots are welcome is quite comfy (darts in here), and there are picnic-tables on the grass and under a fairylit Perspex arbour outside this pretty little brick house. *(Recommended by Gordon and Daphne, Doug Kennedy, John and Lucy Roots, T Folwell and others)*

Brakspears · Licensee Colin Funnell · Real ale · Meals (not Mon lunchtime or Sun) and snacks (not Sun evening) · Open 11–2.30, 6–11 all year

MINSTER LOVELL   SP3111   Map 4
Old Swan ★

Just N of B4047; follow Old Minster signs

This smartly modernised and well run ancient inn is beautifully placed in a picturesque village. Three or four quiet and attractive rooms open off its small central bar, with log fires in huge fireplaces, low beams, easy chairs with Liberty-print loose covers and an antique box settle, china in corner cupboards and Turkey carpets on the polished flagstones. Lunchtime bar snacks include sandwiches, creamed garlic mushrooms or sausage ploughman's (£2), and prawns in a spicy dip (£2.50); there is a substantial restaurant in what used to be the brewhouse. Well kept Halls Harvest and Ind Coope Burton on handpump, and a good choice of wines. The neatly kept lawn has a lily pond, flowers and shrubs, and some shade from chestnut and scyamore trees. The nearby bridge over the pretty River Windrush is remarkably narrow – to help the toll collector count the sheep being herded from Wales to market in London. In the other direction, past the village, are the romantic riverside ruins of the Hall. *(Recommended by William Meadon, Richard Steel, Martyn Quinn, G H Windsor, Heather Sharland, D J Milner, MHG, Andrew Cox, P J Darby, H E Emson)*

Halls (Ind Coope) · Licensee Timothy Turner · Real ale · Snacks (lunchtime, not Sun) · Children in eating area · Open 10.30–2.30, 6–11 all year Bedrooms tel Witney (0993) 75614; £29.50B/£44.50B

MOULSFORD   SU5983   Map 2
Beetle & Wedge

Ferry Lane; off A329, 1½ miles N of Streatley

This friendly old-fashioned Thames-side hotel has big river-view windows in its airy lounge bar, as well as armchairs, sofas, an antique oak settle and Windsor chairs. Bar food includes soup (95p), ploughman's (from £1.20), pâté (£1.35), home made six-ounce burger (£1.75), smoked mackerel or half-pint of prawns (£1.80), spaghetti bolognese (£2.20), curried prawns (£2.45), steak and kidney or chicken and game pie (£2.60), sirloin steak (£5.50) and a choice of cold meats and salads from a buffet counter (£3.50); well kept Bass and Charringtons IPA on handpump. There is a fruit machine, space game, and there may be piped music. There is a separate smart restaurant. The garden has lots of white cast-iron-style tables and chairs on lawns by rose beds, and geese and ducks may be padding around; beyond the inn's own moorings and jetty is a wide reach of the river with reeds, willows and, opposite, open pastures roamed by white horses. There are summer weekend barbecues when it's fine. *(Recommended by Michael Sandy, H G and C J McCafferty; more reports please)*

Free house · Licensees Mr and Mrs D Tiller · Real ale · Meals and snacks Children welcome · Open 10.30–2.30, 6–11 all year · Bedrooms tel Cholsey (0491) 651381; £26B/£45B

MURCOTT   SP5815   Map 4
Nut Tree

Very pretty behind its neat duckpond and tidy lawns, this smartly painted white thatched house is just as well kept inside, with fresh flowers on the tables of the beamed lounge which is stylishly decorated in shades of red and has plenty of tables set for food. There's a log fire in winter, and a quiet friendly atmosphere during weekday lunchtimes – it's busier in the evenings and, as it's handy for walks through the boggy Otmoor wilderness, at weekends. The landlord, a master butcher, is particularly proud of his Scotch steaks (from £6.50), and other bar food includes giant sausages, home made soup (80p), sandwiches, home-made five-ounce burgers (£1 in a bun, more with chips), ploughman's with a choice of cheeses (£1.65), seafood platter (£4.75), gammon (£4.95), good cold meat salads (around £4) and daily specials such as fresh fish or beef provençale. Well kept Halls Harvest and Wadworths 6X on handpump (plus, in winter, a cask of Old Timer on the bar counter). Darts, shove-ha'penny (both on Sundays only), and dominoes. Besides the ducks, there are usually plenty of animals to see outside. *(Recommended by Annie Taylor, G G Riddick, Miss J I Olivier, Martyn Quinn)*

Free house · Licensees Gordon and Diane Evans · Real ale · Meals and snacks (not Sun) · Open 10.30–2.30, 6.30–11 all year

NETTLEBED   SU6986   Map 2
White Hart

A423, in centre

There are cosy leather easy chairs, other old-fashioned seats and settles, and a pleasantly calm and civilised atmosphere in the beamed lounge bar of this big brick and flint former coaching-inn. It's been knocked through into an extensive series of sitting areas, with shallow steps between: there's a highly polished grand piano in one snug side area, another has a good log fire in winter, and there's a big Act of Parliament wall clock. Brakspears BB and SBA on handpump; reasonably priced bar food from sandwiches to fried plaice, grills, and a salad counter (there's also a separate restaurant, which does a good value Sunday lunch); shove-ha'penny. *(Recommended by Martyn Quinn, MHG, H G and C J McCafferty]*

Brakspears · Licensee Neil Cooper · Real ale · Meals and snacks · Children in eating area and restaurant · Open 10.30–2.30, 6–11 all year · Bedrooms tel Nettlebed (0491) 641245; £14/£28

There are report forms at the back of the book.

nr NETTLEBED   SU6986   Map 2

Carpenters Arms

Crocker End; hamlet signposted from A423 on W edge of Nettlebed

In a quiet enclave of houses surrounded by woodland, this relaxed and well kept cottagey pub does good food, including home-made soup (85p), ploughman's (from £1.50), salads with French bread, such as cockles (£1.30), smoked mackerel or hummus (£1.75) to honey-roast ham (£2.20), spit-roasted chicken (£3.95), pork or lamb (£4.50), and a dish of the day such as navarin of lamb, shepherd's pie, chicken and broccoli lasagne or Old Ale casserole (£2.50). There are country pictures on the cream walls of the carpeted main room which has wheel-back chairs and flowery-cushioned dark small pews. Comfortable seats in a partly panelled side salon bar, with old prints on the walls, include a small settee. In summer there are white tables and seats on the sunny front terrace, by cotoneaster and a lovely New Dawn rose, with little sound but the swallows and woodpigeons; in winter there are no fewer than three log fires indoors. Well kept Brakspears PA and SB on handpump, with Old Ale in winter; maybe piped music. *(Recommended by W T Aird)*

Brakspears · Licensees Jo and Dave Oakley · Real ale · Meals and snacks Children in saloon · Open 10.30–2.30, 6–11 all year

NEWBRIDGE   SP4101   Map 4

Maybush

A415 7 miles S of Witney

By one of the prettiest bridges on the Thames, this honeysuckle-covered tiled and shuttered stone pub has tables on its back riverside terrace, and on the grass beyond. Inside, a good choice of reasonably priced lunchtime bar food includes toasted sandwiches (from 75p),

The Elephant & Castle, Bloxham

ploughman's (£1.20), plaice or haddock (£1.55), chicken Cordon Bleu (£2.30), and freshly made daily specials, such as smoked haddock and Stilton quiche or steak and kidney casserole (£1.45), avocado pear and crab with salad, or pork chop in cider (£1.60); in the evening they do dishes like basket scampi or chicken kebabs (£2.60) and gammon with pineapple (£2.95). The low-beamed bar has a warm and relaxed atmosphere, with comfortable red leatherette seats around its copper-topped tables. Well kept and – for the location – attractively priced Morlands Bitter, Best and Mild on handpump (if, in the depths of winter, say, the beer is hanging around too long for its own good, they sensibly may keep it under a very light carbon dixoide blanket); dominoes, cribbage, and a fruit machine. *(Recommended by S D Lovett, W Warre)*

Morlands · Licensee J S S Phillips · Real ale · Meals (lunchtime) and snacks (not Mon evening) · Open 10.30–2.30, 6–11 all year

Rose Revived ★

A415 7 miles S of Witney

It's not so long since evening closing time was half an hour earlier at the Maybush across the river; when time was called there people would pop over the bridge for a reviver at this civilised old stone inn – hence the name, and the inn sign of the wilting rose in a pint of Morlands. The lovely garden stretches along a quiet stretch of the upper Thames with a long lawn, crazy-paved paths, weeping willows and, in spring, crowds of daffodils and scillas, with a colourful herbaceous border in summer, in front of a sheltering shrubbery. Inside there are cushioned antique settles on polished flagstones, deep ochre ceilings, lots of pictures, and (especially out of season) a quietly intimate atmosphere, with maybe Honey – the friendly labrador – dozing in front of a log fire. The oldest part is probably the inner bistro, with its candles in bottles, pianist, handsome sixteenth-century stone fireplace with an oak lintel, and polished tile floor (three-course evening meals in here from £4.25). Fairly priced and freshly made bar food served in a buttery includes sandwiches, soup (80p), ploughman's (from £1.75), filled baked potatoes (£1.20), salads (around £2), and generously served home made pies such as mutton and turnip or steak and kidney (£2.75); well kept Morlands PA, SB and Mild on handpump; maybe piped music. An airy à la carte restaurant looks out to the river. *(Recommended by Gordon Mair, Joan Olivier, Hope Chenhalls, Mrs A M Arnold)*

Morlands · Licensee Alan Jefferson · Real ale · Meals and snacks · Children welcome · Jazz Sun evening · Open 10.30–2.30, 6–11 all year · Bedrooms tel Standlake (086 731) 221; £18 (£18B)/£32 (£32B)

NOKE   SP5413   Map 2
Plough ★

Village signposted from B4027, NE of Oxford

The three knocked-together rooms of this unusually welcoming pub have close-spaced seats, including comfortable wicker easy chairs, and there are bright pictorial plates on some of the dark beams. It's perhaps in summer that the place comes into its own, with plenty of seats out in the pretty garden (which backs on to farmland), and good walking nearby in the unusual Otmoor wilderness. But at any time of year there's good value food including filled rolls (36p), burgers (45p), soup (55p), sandwiches (55p), toasties (from 65p, egg and bacon £1), spring roll (85p), ploughman's with cheese or ham (95p), basket meals (from sausages at £1 to scampi at £2.15), cod stuffed with prawns (£1.75), a popular egg, sausage and bacon fry-up (£1.75), home-made steak and kidney pie (£2), lamb chops or chicken (£2.25), mixed grill (£3.95), and puddings such as apple pie (55p). Well kept Courage Best and Directors on handpump; a space game and well chosen piped music. *(Recommended by Joan Olivier, Rex Haigh, Dave Green)*

Courage · Licensee Peter Broadbent · Real ale · Meals (not Weds evening) and snacks · Country music Sun and Tues · Open 12–2.30, 7–11 all year

OXFORD SP5106 Map 4
Bear

Alfred Street

In its coaching hey-day this used to stretch the whole way down the street, and parts of the surviving structure date back 700 years. Even the handpumps – serving well kept Halls Harvest and Ind Coope Burton – are over a century old, and the four low-ceilinged and partly panelled rooms have a genuinely old-fashioned feeling, with their traditional built-in benches and plain tables. In term-time there may be a throng of students from Christchurch and Oriel colleges. Beware of wearing a really uncommon club tie here – they still keep their scissors ready to add specimens to what may be the country's best collection of chopped-off club ties. Home-made pâté (£1.50), quiche (£1.55), and chicken or steak and kidney pie (£1.75). There are tables on a side terrace. *(Martyn Quinn, MHG, Heather Sharland)*

Halls (Ind Coope) · Licensee Michael Lindsay Rusling · Real ale · Meals and snacks · Nearby parking very limited · Open 10.30–2.30, 5.30–11 all year

Perch

Binsey; leaving Oxford on A420, keep your eyes skinned for narrow Binsey Lane on right – it's just before Bishops' furniture depository

Considering it's within the boundaries of a busy city, this spacious thatched pub preserves a remarkably secluded country atmosphere – thanks to the riverside meadows which surround it. It rambles about comfortably, with wooden dividers between stone pillars, high-backed built-in settles (as well as cushioned wheel-backs), some flagstoned areas, high shelves of plates, and a couple of log fires in winter. The bare stone walls have quite a few pictures (especially of perches – including the us Submarine *Perch* sunk in 1942). Bar food has changed with new licensees, and now includes ploughman's (from £1.20), a good choice of salads (£1.65–£2.95), and home-made hot dishes such as lasagne, cannelloni (£1.95) and steak and

kidney pie (£2.25); Halls Harvest and Ind Coope Burton on
handpump; fruit machines, piped music. There's now a kiddies' ride
out by the picnic-table sets, beside a weeping willow on the edge of
the meadows. *(Recommended by Mrs D O Cassie, Martyn Quinn, Gordon
and Daphne, MHG; up-to-date reports on the new regime please)*

*Halls (Ind Coope) · Licensee A J Little · Real ale · Meals and snacks · Children
in eating area · Singer Sun lunchtime · Open 10.30–2.30, 5.30–11 all year*

Turf ★

Bath Place; via St Helen's Passage, between Holywell Street and
New College Lane

A low-ceilinged tavern up a court, this small-roomed dark-beamed
medieval stone inn is still much as Hardy described it when Jude the
Obscure discovered that Arabella the barmaid was the wife who'd
left him years before. It buzzes with life in term-time, but is always
fun, and even in winter (thanks to the warmth of a brazier) crowds
can overflow into the flagstoned or gravel courtyards which surround
it, cut off from the modern bustle of the city by the high stone walls of
some of its oldest buildings, including part of the ancient city wall.
The extensive cold buffet (out of doors in summer) has cold meats
priced by the thick slice, quiche, and pasties and salads priced by the
spoon. Hot dishes include a choice of filled baked potatoes from a
special serving bar (£1.50), chilli con carne (£2.25), shepherd's pie
(£2.50), and individual home-made hot pies such as fish with mussels
and prawns, chicken and ham, beef with wine and mushroom, and
venison and blackcurrant (all around £3). There are home-made
puddings such as cherry tart with cream, and the breakfasts – if you
stay here – are good. Hook Norton Best and Old Hookey, Wethereds
SPA and Youngs Special on handpump, with a guest beer changing
every ten days or so; they bring in mulled wine or a hot rum punch in
winter, and have a Pimms fruit punch in summer, besides a range of
country wines and farm cider. Fruit machine. *(Recommended by John
Hill, Jane English, Mrs A M Arnold, M S Hancock, Rita Davis, MHG, F T and
A K Hargreaves, William Meadon, Richard Steel, David Varney, Martyn
Quinn, Andrew Barnett, HKR, Robert Anderson, Mrs N Sharland, Heather
Sharland (no relation))*

*Free house · Licensee Wally Ellse · Real ale · Meals and snacks · Children in
eating area · Folk music weekend evenings · No nearby parking · Open
10.30–2.30, 5.30–11 all year; closed 25 Dec · Comfortable bedrooms in
separate cottages tel Oxford (0865) 243235; £16/£26*

PISHILL   SU7389   Map 2

Crown

B480 N of Henley

There are records of a monastic building on this site in the eleventh
century, and the thatched barn they use for parties and functions is
some 500 years old. There are picnic-tables on the side lawn – an
attractive spot, with wistaria covering the pub, and the quiet and
pretty valley surrounding it. Inside, the latticed-window bar stretches

back from a front area with old photographs on its partly panelled walls, through a red-and-gold carpeted part with black beams, little blocky country chairs and stools around wooden tables, and an elegant corner cabinet of decorated plates, to a quiet back part with knocked-through standing oak timbers. Good bar food includes sandwiches, ploughman's or home-made pâté (£1.50), spaghetti bolognese (£1.95), lasagne or chilli con carne (£2.25), chicken and mushroom vol-au-vent (£2.50), scampi or steak and kidney pie (£2.25), meat salads (£3.25), a roast (£4.95) and sirloin steak (£5.25); a comfortable, communicating restaurant has a fine big brick fireplace. Well kept Arkells BBB, Brakspears PA and Huntsman Dorset and Royal Oak on handpump; faint piped music. *(Recommended by Mrs Rosemary Wilmot, H G and C J McCafferty)*

Free house · Licensee Jeremy Capon · Real ale · Meals and snacks (not Sun or Mon evenings) · Children in restaurant · Jazz Sun evening · Open 11.30–2.30, 6–11 all year

RADCOT SU2899 Map 4
Swan
Radcot Bridge; A4095 2½ miles N of Faringdon

The lawn outside this homely and friendly old inn overlooks the Thames and its oldest bridge (built in 1174 – there has been an inn of some sort here ever since), and is nice in summer – though at holiday times it can get crowded. The bar has button-back leatherette seats on the flagstones, log fires, stuffed fish and some flock wallpaper on the walls, and a William Morris oak chair – his home, Kelmscott Manor, is nearby. Reasonably priced bar food includes freshly cut plain or toasted sandwiches, pâté, ploughman's with Cheddar or Stilton, hot dishes (with chips or boiled potatoes) such as sausages, burgers, egg, chicken, plus cold ham off the bone, or scampi (around £1.25– £2.85). There are children's dishes such as sausages and fish fingers and, in winter, home-made soup and shepherd's pie. Well kept Morlands Bitter, Best and Mild on handpump; darts, shove-ha'penny, dominoes, cribbage, a fruit machine and a juke box. In summer there are riverboat trips from the pub's camping ground on the opposite bank. *(More reports please)*

Morlands · Licensee Peter Williams · Real ale · Meals and snacks · Open 11–2.30, 6–11 all year; closed evening 25 Dec · Bedrooms tel Clanfield (036 781) 220; £10/£18

RUSSELL'S WATER SU7089 Map 2
Beehive
Up a short rough track past duck-pond from centre of village, which is signposted from B481 S of junction with B480

Good value bar food in this elaborately olde-worlde, secluded Chilterns pub includes sandwiches, a choice of Cheddar, Stilton, ham or pâté ploughman's, and home-made hot dishes such as garlic mushrooms with garlic bread (£1.95), lasagne (£3), lamb curry, moussaka with Greek salad or steak and kidney pie (£3.50), scampi (£3.85) and steaks (from £5.50 for an eight-ounce sirloin); there is a lunchtime cold buffet on Sundays in summer, with hot snacks in winter. You can eat either in a separate dining-room behind a wrought iron divider, or in the main bar, which has high wrought-iron bar stools with slung leather seats, a bar counter of copper-bound barrel staves, armed Windsor chairs, some old-fashioned settles including one elaborately carved in Jacobean style, a big wood-burning stove and subdued red lighting. Service is friendly (so is the pub Alsatian, and the cat); well kept Brakspears PA, Morlands Best, Ruddles County and Wadworths 6X on handpump; unobtrusive piped music; darts, pool and bar billiards in the quite separate public bar. There are tables outside in front on a rose-fringed terrace or under a fairylit arbour. *(Recommended by Jane English, Geoffrey Raymont, H L McDougall and others)*

Free house · Licensees Pat and Arthur Bennett · Real ale · Meals and snacks Children in dining-room · Open 11–2.30, 6–11 (11–2.30, 6.30–10.30 in winter)

SATWELL   SU7083 Map 2
Lamb

Just off B481 2 miles S of Nettlebed; follow Shepherds Green signpost

Included for lovers of the utterly unspoilt, this country cottage has a couple of small tiled-floor rooms, low black beams, simple red leatherette seats around rustic tables, and logs shoved end-on into its big brick fireplace (to save sawing). Bar food includes toasted sandwiches (from 55p, bacon 85p, steak £1.25), home-made pizzas (from 65p), ploughman's (£1.25), ham and egg (£1.45), and chicken and mushroom bake (£1.50); Brakspears PA and SB tapped from the cask; darts, bar billiards. There are tables on a sheltered terrace and on neat back grass, with a set of stocks (and tall trees behind); there's a farmyard beside it. *(Recommended by Gordon and Daphne, R B Entwistle, Jane English)*

Brakspears · Real ale · Snacks · Open 11–2.30, 6–11 all year

SHIPTON-UNDER-WYCHWOOD   SP2717 Map 2
Lamb

Just off A361 to Burford

Popular bar food in this cleanly modernised Cotswold village pub may include Welsh rarebit (85p), soup (90p), duck and orange pâté (£1.35), ploughman's (£1.50), local pink trout (£2.95), steak and kidney pie or Cotswold pie (£3.25) and roast garlic lamb (£3.50). The beamed bar is pretty, comfortable and quite spotless; there are long pews and a fine oak-panelled settle on the good wood-block floor, flowery curtains in the small windows of the old, partly bared stone walls, and a well made modern oak bar counter which serves well kept Hook Norton Best and perhaps Old Hookey from handpump. In summer, when bar lunches revolve around the buffet table, hot dishes such as those listed above are served in the evenings. The separate restaurant is particularly popular for its good value Sunday roast lunch. There are tables among roses behind this quiet village house, which is a comfortable place to stay – it was among half a dozen finalists in Egon Ronay's 1985 pub of the year competition. (*Recommended by John Paton, Heather Sharland, D A Angless, S V Bishop; more reports please*)

Free house · Licensees Hugh and Lynne Wainwright · Real ale · Meals and snacks · Open 11.30–2.30, 6–11 · Bedrooms tel Shipton-under-Wychwood (0993) 830465; £20B/£30B

Shaven Crown

On a grander scale than our other entry in this village, this ancient inn has a loftily-beamed front cocktail bar, comfortable and stylishly old-fashioned, with a double stairway sweeping down. This part of the building is mainly Tudor, and is said to have been used as a hunting lodge by Elizabeth I, but parts of it were a fourteenth-century hospice for the monastery of Bruern. Bar food is served in a separate, lower-beamed and rather humbler bar at the back of the courtyard, which has seats forming little stalls around the tables and upholstered benches built in to the walls. It includes soup (95p), sandwiches, a choice of ploughman's (from £1.35), fried potato skins (£1.70), whitebait (£1.75), mushroom and walnut pancake (£2.15), spinach and bacon lasagne (£2.50), steak sandwich (£2.75), steak and kidney pie (£2.95), lightly curried prawns on saffron rice (£3.15) and sirloin steak (£3.75), with a choice of puddings and home made ice-creams; Flowers Original and Hook Norton Best on handpump. There is a proper restaurant, too. In summer pehaps the most pleasant place is the courtyard garden, entirely enclosed by the heavily stone-roofed buildings, with a lily pool, roses, and old-fashioned seats set out on the stone cobbles and crazy paving. The inn, which faces the spreading village green, has its own bowling green. (*Recommended by Mrs A M Arnold, S V Bishop, William Meadon, Richard Steel, W J Wonham, H Emson*)

Free house · Licensee Trevor Brookes · Real ale · Meals and snacks · Children in eating area · Open 11–2.30, 6–11 all year · Bedrooms tel Shipton-under-Wychwood (0993) 830330; £18/£36 (£44B)

SOUTH LEIGH   SP3908   Map 4

Mason Arms

Village signposted from A40 Witney–Eynsham

The food in both the bar and restaurant of this handsomely rethatched sixteenth-century former farmhouse is good, benefiting from the landlord's thirty-year background in the wholesale fruit and vegetable business and his forays into the London markets for fresh ingredients: besides the fresh fruit and vegetables you'd expect, the steaks and other meat dishes are also praised by readers (there are soups, sandwiches, and ploughman's with a choice of Cheddar, Camembert or Stilton, too). The attractive lounge has built-in cushioned settles curving around the corners: there are rugs on the flagstoned floor, a heavily ticking wall clock, a real fire in the stone hearth at one end and a log-effect gas fire at the other – the two halves of this quiet cosy room are separated by a wrought-iron divider. Well kept Glenny Eagle, from nearby Witney. There are peacocks in the big garden, where a small grove of what look like Balearic box trees shelter picnic-table sets. *(Recommended by Mervyn Harris, Trevor Boswell, T M Bracey, Martyn Quinn, MHG)*

Free house · Licensees David and Doreen Theobald · Real ale · Meals and snacks (not Mon, not Sun evening) · Children in eating area and restaurant Organist and singer or guitarist Sun evening · Open 11.30–2.30, 6.30–11 all year; closed Mon (but open 12–3 bank hol Mons)

SOUTH STOKE   SU5983   Map 2
Perch & Pike

Off B4009 2 miles N of Goring

This friendly pub is just a field away from the Thames, and its brick-floored and low-beamed public bar has stuffed perch and pike on its shiny orange walls, and a collection of plates painted with fish. In summer there are benches by tubs of flowers and honeysuckle outside the flint building, and further back from the quiet lane, past a black wooden barn, is a spacious flower-edged lawn with a slide, seesaw and swings – boules is played here in summer. Bar food includes home-made soup (mostly in winter, 55p–60p), freshly cut sandwiches, plain or toasted (55p–65p), and ploughman's (£1); well kept Brakspears PA, SB and Mild on electric pump, or tapped from the cask; bar billiards, shove-ha'penny, dominoes, cribbage, a fruit machine and juke box in the saloon. The pub sells fishing tickets (50p a day). *(More reports please)*

Brakspears · Licensee Reginald Harper · Real ale · Snacks · Open 10.30–2.30, 6–11 all year

STANTON HARCOURT   SP4105   Map 4
Harcourt Arms

B4449 S of Eynsham

In the evening the candlelit small rooms of this friendly inn bustle and hum with life – the good food served here makes it a very popular outing from Oxford. In the three carpeted rooms that open off the quarry-tiled stand-up bar area the tables are all set for diners though they make a point of serving their simplest snacks as readily as a full meal. The bar food, all home made and served in big helpings, includes soup (£1.50), ploughman's (from £2), garlic mushrooms with garlic bread (£2.25), deep-fried squid, steak sandwich (£2.95), chilli con carne (£3.95), grilled prawns, and ten-ounce rump steak (£7.25). There's also a three-course evening menu (£10.75) with a wide choice, and any dish off this can be had on its own – on our visit, the choice included chicken liver pâté, terrine, small kebabs in good satay sauce, grilled Dover sole, all sorts of steaks, grilled liver and bacon, chicken breast in apricot and cream sauce, lotte with béarnaise sauce (an unusual but satisfying combination), lobster and lots of puddings such as creme brûlée, home made cassis sorbet, fresh fruit with cream and a good raspberry, strawberry and apple pie. The steaks are often done on a gridiron over the log fire in one of the room's massive stone fireplaces. Well kept Morrells Best and Varsity on handpump. The dining-areas – simply furnished with spindle-back chairs around wooden tables – are attractively decorated (on our visit, with bunches of fresh sweet peas from their own garden), service is charming, and the bedrooms, in a separate new building, are comfortable, quiet and well equipped. There are tables on a neat side lawn. *(Recommended by J A Douglas, M T Buller, Mrs N W Briggs, David Regan)*

Morrells · Licensees George and Cargie Daley · Real ale · Meals and snacks Children in dining-rooms · Open 10.30–2.30, 6–11 all year · Bedrooms tel Oxford (0865) 882192; £24.50B/£35B

STEEPLE ASTON   SP4725   Map 4
Red Lion

Off A423 12 miles N of Oxford

Good lunchtime bar food in this calm and civilised pub includes imaginative soups such as celery with almond (60p), sandwiches such as thickly cut rare beef, Cheddar ploughman's with local crusty bread (£1.40), home made pâté or taramosalata (£1.50) and, in winter, varying hot-pots such as bouillabaisse, mussels in white wine, or game (from £1.75), with salads in summer instead (from £2.50, fresh crab or salmon £3.75). On Tuesday to Saturday evening there are full meals in the small dining-room (£11), with main courses such as guinea-fowl cooked with crushed juniper berries or salmon with béarnaise sauce. The beamed bar has dark hessian above its panelling, an antique settle – among other good furniture – a collection of rather crossword-oriented books, and a relaxed, even soothing, atmosphere. Well kept Hook Norton Best on handpump, a good choice of malt whiskies, and good wines in the restaurant. There is a real sun-trap of a terrace outside the stone house. *(Recommended by Dr and Mrs R P R Dawber, MHG, T G Brierly, G A Wright and others)*

Free house · Licensee Colin Mead · Real ale · Snacks (lunchtime) · Open 11–2.30, 6–11 all year

STEVENTON   SU4691   Map 2
North Star

The Causeway; central westward turn off main road through village, which is signposted from A34

Named after an 1837 steam locomotive, this simple and friendly pub is a delight for connoisseurs of the unspoilt: once through a low-ceilinged, tiled entrance passage you find a main bar with a traditional snug formed by high, cream-painted settles around a couple of elm tables by an electric bar fire. It's decorated with veteran steam engine pictures and interesting local horse brasses, and there's a small, parlourish lounge with an open fire, and a very simply furnished dining-room. Well kept Morlands Mild, Bitter and Best is tapped in a side room (there's no bar counter); cribbage. Cheap bar food includes a celebrated so-called mini ploughman's – two rolls, a thick slice of wholemeal bread, chunks of Cheddar, blue cheese and a soft plain cheese, a big slice of pressed beef, fresh tomato, cucumber, onion, spring onion, lettuce and chutney, all for £1.10. A few large old-fashioned benches stand out on the side grass, by roses and cabbages; there was a time when the gateway to this pub was cut through a living tree. *(Recommended by Gordon and Daphne; more reports please)*

Morlands · Licensee R Cox · Real ale · Meals and snacks (weekday lunchtimes only) · Open 10.30–2.30, 6.45–11 all year

STOKE ROW   SU6784   Map 2
Crooked Billet

Newlands Lane

There's no bar counter here: if you go into the parlour on the right you'll find a big table taking up most of the space by the solid fuel stove, under a single lamp hanging from the one bowed beam in the ochre ceiling. When you've sat down, one of the other people sitting around it (talking to his friends, or maybe just immersed in a newspaper) looks up and asks what you'd like to drink – that's when you discover he's the landlord. He'll bring you well kept Brakspears PA, SB, Mild and XXXX Old, tapped from casks in a back room, and if it's quiet cut you a good fresh ham or cheese roll – readers who've known the pub for over twenty-five years say that the way it's run has hardly changed at all in that time. The public bar hasn't changed much, either – a couple of scrubbed deal tables in front of a vast open hearth. From the pub, where there are benches in front by the very quiet lane (the only noise is from the geese and bantams in the back yard), you can walk straight in to Chilterns beech woods. *(Recommended by Tim Bracey, Gordon and Daphne)*

Brakspears · Licensee Nobby Harris · Real ale · Snacks · Open 10.30–2.30, 6–11 all year

SWINBROOK   SP2712   Map 4
Swan

Back road 1 mile N of A40, 2 miles E of Burford

The idyllic surroundings are the makings of this simple, seventeenth-century stone inn. Smothered in wistaria, with old-fashioned benches in front by a low stone wall and a fuchsia hedge, it's close to the River Windrush. Inside is friendly and unpretentious, with country benches and, in winter, a huge log fire in the simple flagstone-floored public bar, and Windsor chairs in the plain carpeted lounge. Bar food includes sandwiches (from 50p), pâté, ploughman's (£1), giant sausage (£1.10) and scampi (£1.75); well kept Morlands Bitter and Wadworths 6X on handpump; darts, shove-ha'penny, dominoes, cribbage. *(Recommended by Will Peskett, MHG)*

Free house · Licensee Geraldine Archer · Real ale · Snacks (lunchtime) · Open 11–2.30, 6–11 (11.30–2.30, 6.30–10.30 in winter) · One bedroom tel Burford (099 382) 2165; £20B

WANTAGE   SU4087 Map 2
Lamb
Mill Street; A417 towards Faringdon

Snugly comfortable, this pretty pub has horse brasses on the low beams of its mainly carpeted bar, which is divided into several separate snug areas: there are a couple of green plush easy chairs as well as the plush stools and comfortable wall banquettes around the two or three tables in one part by a log-effect gas fire, for example, big Windsor armchairs in another part, and olde-worlde prints on the timbered white wall of a third area (most of the walls are red hessian). At lunchtime it's busy with local regulars tucking into ploughman's (from £1.45), filled, oven-baked (not microwaved) potatoes (from £1.50), pasties (£1.50), prawns (£1.95), and nicely presented salads such as salmon pâté or Stilton, port and cream pâté (£1.80), farmhouse pie or home-baked ham (£1.80), butterfly prawns (£2.20) and, in summer, fresh crab and lobster. The salads are freshly made, and all dressings and mayonnaise are home made too. Well kept Morlands Mild and Bitter on handpump; juke box, fruit machine. There are scaffolding and wood tables and benches on the grass behind, with swings, climbing-frame and seesaw, and in summer this area is attractively decorated with flowers and hanging baskets. *(Recommended by Martyn Quinn; more reports please)*

Morlands · Licensee John Forbes · Real ale · Meals and snacks (not Sun) · Open 10.30–2.30, 6–11 all year

WYTHAM   SP4708 Map 4
White Hart
Village signposted from A34 ring road W of Oxford

The big self-service cold table (around £1.85–£2.35) neatly laid out in one room of this tall, creeper-covered seventeenth-century stone pub – with some fourteen salads and a good choice of cold meats and home made pies – is particularly good value (from £1.95). At lunchtime in winter there is home-made soup (60p) and one hot dish such as a casserole or hot pie (around £2). In the evenings there are hot dishes throughout the year, from gammon (£3.05) through chicken Kiev (£3.45), to steaks (seven-ounce rump £3.50, ten-ounce sirloin £4.50). The main room, flagstone-floored, has wheel-back chairs and high-backed black settles built almost the whole way round its cream walls, with a shelf of blue and white plates above them, and has a fine relief of a hart on the iron fireback. Well kept Halls Harvest and Ind Coope Burton on handpump, and a good choice of malt whiskies; the atmosphere is cosy and relaxed, but get there early if you want a table. The concrete back yard has a Perspex roof over its picnic-table sets, and even a heater in cold weather, and there are more seats outside in the garden. *(Recommended by Martyn Quinn, I Hollis, Gordon and Daphne; more reports please)*

Halls (Ind Coope) · Licensee Richard Godden · Real ale · Meals · Children in dining-room and yard room · Open 11–2.30, 6–11 all year

---

Pubs close to motorway junctions are listed at the back of the book.

Lucky Dip

Besides the fully inspected pubs, you might like to try these Lucky Dips recommended and described by readers (if you do, please send us reports):

APPLETON [SP4401], *Three Horseshoes*: nice, cheap meals in friendly village pub with games area and fire; walls and ceiling covered in farm tools – free drinks if you can tell what each was used for *(Marina Christopher)*

ASHBURY [SU2585], *Rose & Crown*: friendly staff, interesting food in bar and restaurant of comfortable inn with sofas, etc., relaxed, near Ridgeway; bedrooms *(Ian Meharg, Michael and Alison Sandy)*

ASTHALL [SP2811], *Windmill*: good food in bar and restaurant (which has fine views) in interesting conversion from an old barn; Mitford family associations *(T A V Meikle)*

BAMPTON [SP3103], *Talbot*: food good and quickly served; pleasant surroundings; warm welcome from new licensees; comfortable bedrooms *(Mrs M M Affleck-Graves)*

BANBURY [Parsons Street; SP4540], *Reindeer*: good value bar food including sandwiches, pastas and grills in much-refurbished Hook Norton pub with long history and interesting gallows sign across street *(LYM)*

BEGBROKE [SP4613], *Royal Sun*: small but popular seventeenth-century pub, friendly, attractively decorated; bar meals, real ale, small garden *(Joan Olivier, Martyn Quinn)*

BICESTER [Church Street; SP5822], *Six Bells*: friendly, big garden with children's play area, bar food, pub games *(Anon)*

BINFIELD HEATH [SU7478], *Bottle & Glass*: good food and beer, friendly service, old scrubbed tables with flagstone floor *(R B Entwistle)*

BIX [SU7285], *Fox*: friendly atmosphere in clean pub with well kept Brakspears, warm fire and traditional cooking (no chips), especially good curries; garden recently extended, lovely surroundings *(JML, W T Aird)*

BLOXHAM [SP4235], *Joiners Arms*: Scottish décor in friendly stone pub which includes some remains of an ancient monastery *(LYM)*

BRIGHTWELL BALDWIN [SU6595], *Lord Nelson*: good home cooking and beer in small and convivial seventeenth-century pub in village off the beaten track; busy at lunchtime, cheerful service *(B W Williams, Joan Olivier)*

BURCOT [SU5695], *Chequers*: carefully modernised with reasonably priced good original food, busy but quiet *(Dr Richard Taylor)*

BURFORD [High Street; SP2512], *Bull*: good range of bar meals and restaurant in inn recently rebuilt, well refurbished in comfortable antique panelled style of the original (destroyed by fire in 1982), Wadworths real ales, friendly staff, bedrooms *(Martyn Quinn, G H Theaker, Gordon and Daphne, LYM)*

CAULCOTT [SP5024], *Horse & Groom*: good value food with massive pizzas and good real ales including Ind Coope Burton and Wadworths 6X – very friendly to USAF men from Upper Heyford *(Brian Larson, Sue Howell)*

CHARLTON ON OTMOOR [High Street; SP5615], *George & Dragon*: one of the few real cider pubs in Oxfordshire: friendly service in split-level pub with bar snacks and real fire *(Dave and Dob Lewis)*

CHIPPING NORTON [SP3127], *Blue Boar*: stone-built pub with good value bar food and traditionally furnished high-raftered restaurant – under same ownership as the main entries for Woburn (see Cambridgeshire) and Ampney Crucis (Gloucestershire) *(Anon)*; *Fox*: ancient stone pub, rambling lounge comfortably furnished with antique oak settles, open fire, Halls Harvest, bar snacks and restaurant *(LYM)*

CHRISTMAS COMMON [SU7193], *Fox*: low-ceilinged small rooms, log fire, no piped music, publican like a College servant; splendid Chilterns escarpment walks all around *(Oliver Knox)*

CHURCHILL [SP2824], *Chequers*: typical Cotswold stone village pub, nicely carpeted rather small dark saloon, stone walls, open fire, welcoming efficient service, good bar food *(Mr and Mrs J P Garrick, W H Lightbown)*

CLANFIELD [SU6916], *Clanfield Tavern*: miscellany of furniture in beamed

539

flagstoned bar, choice of real ales, interesting bar food, small restaurant, friendly atmosphere, garden, skittle alley, bedrooms *(John Paton, LYM)*; *Plough*: substantial old stone inn with lovely Elizabethan façade, attractive gardens and civilised atmosphere; has been a main entry in previous editions but reported to be more of a hotel/restaurant now; bedrooms *(LYM)*

CLIFTON HAMPDEN [SU5495], *Plough*: simple, friendly thatched country pub with Ushers real ale, two bedrooms *(Martyn Quinn, BB)*

CULHAM [SU5095], *Coach & Horses*: food includes good cold buffet with wide choice of salads and several hot dishes; cheerful, bustling, tables outside *(Mrs D O Cassie)*

DEDDINGTON [Oxford Road; SP4631], *Holcombe*: good meals, friendly service and Hook Norton and Wadworths beers on handpump in comfortable stone-built bar; bedrooms *(J L Thompson)*; *Kings Arms*: good meals and good beer in attractively refurbished pub with quiet, relaxed atmosphere in pretty village *(Dr A K Clarke)*

DORCHESTER [SU5794], *George*: comfortable bar with leather chairs, open fire, good bar food, well kept Brakspears, helpful staff, restaurant; bedrooms *(Sheila Keene, LYM)*; *White Hart*: smartly modernised attractive old coaching-inn, friendly, comfortable bar restaurant, bedrooms *(Martyn Quinn)*

DUNS TEW [SP4528], *White Horse*: welcoming sixteenth-century thick-walled stone pub with well kept John Smiths, good food – especially Sunday roast lunches; children welcome *(S V Bishop)*

EAST HENDRED [SU4588], *Plough*: good village pub in attractive surroundings *(BOB)*

EATON [SP4403], *Eight Bells*: well run unspoilt village pub by lane leading to Thames ferry, good value simple food, real ale, friendly atmosphere, attractive garden around yew tree *(W Warre)*

ENSLOW [SU4818], *Rock of Gibraltar*: two bars and restaurant in friendly pub with antiques and brasses, near Oxford Canal; meals, garden *(Martyn Quinn)*

ENSTONE [SP3724], *Harrow*: good food, especially cold buffet, and well kept Morrells in handsome sixteenth-century pub with big garden *(Graham Turner)*

nr EYNSHAM [Swinford Bridge; SP4309], *Talbot*: food includes wide choice of filled baked potatoes and other good snacks, in attractive old house with log fires and Halls real ale; close to Thames *(JRM)*

nr FARINGDON [Coxwell; SU2895], *Plough*: good varied food, big helpings, in roomy pub with real ales including Bass, Charringtons IPA; children's room *(S V Bishop)*

FULBROOK [SP2513], *Masons Arms*: free house with changing beers near Burford: straightforward but friendly local with cosy atmosphere, real fire in old fireplace separating the two bars; good value food *(MHG)*

GOOSEY [SU3591], *Pound*: good value food in out-of-this-world variety (beware of the deathburgers!); real ale, big open fire, friendly and humorous landlord who (along with variety of dogs and cats) creates marvellous atmosphere – Irish wolfhound called Boot is part of the furniture, another dog will buy a Milky Way at the bar *(Jane English)*

GORING [Manor Road; SU6080], *John Barleycorn*: Brakspears, old beams, pleasant atmosphere, good food in bar and restaurant *(Roger Wain-Heapy, Gordon and Daphne)*

GORING HEATH [SP6579], *Pack Saddle*: good Gales beers in friendly country pub with bayonet-practice rifles on beams, good ploughman's, pretty garden *(Gordon and Daphne, S J Tims)*

GREAT MILTON [SP6202], *Bull*: good food and service in well kept sixteenth-century pub *(F C White)*

HENLEY [SU7882], *Angel*: famous waterside pub with landing stage slap in middle of Henley; simple but good food, well kept Brakspears, very popular with visitors *(Hugh Calvey)*; *Little White Hart*: nice restaurant, spacious bar snacks, garden; nice clean place, friendly service *(Martyn Quinn)*; *Old White Hart*: warm and friendly, oak-beamed ancient pub with lovely old furnishings, bar food, good restaurant *(Sigrid and Peter Sobanski, Martyn Quinn)*

HENTON [SP7602], *Peacock*: good food in bar and restaurant, good choice of real ales, lots of room in two connected bar areas, log fire in winter, friendly helpful staff *(T A V Meikle)*

HETHE [SP5929], *Whitmore Arms*: pleasant village local, bright and cheerful lounge bar with flowers on tables, friendly bar staff *(Gordon and Daphne)*

HOOK NORTON [SP3533], *Pear Tree*: well kept beer, pleasant traditional atmosphere, children welcome *(David Wynne)*

nr HOOK NORTON [SP3533], *Gate Hangs High*: friendly and snug pub with inglenook, home-grown ingredients in good value home-cooked meals and salads, well kept Hook Norton real ales, country garden; isolated, quite near Rollright Stones; small Caravan Club site *(David Gittins, LYM)*

HOPCROFTS HOLT [SP4625], *Hopcrofts Holt*: modernised fifteenth-century pub once used by highwayman Claude Duval, real ales including Wadworths 6X, malt whiskies, old photographs on wall; restaurant *(Martyn Quinn)*

IFFLEY [Church Road; SP5203], *Prince of Wales*: uncommonly good choice of real ales in longish main bar, good value food, charming staff, tables in garden *(John Green)*

ISLIP [SP5214], *Swan*: pretty country village pub, attractively refurbished *(BB)*

KIDMORE END [SU6979], *New*: friendly low-ceilinged old pub, nice garden with goat, good steak sandwiches *(Mr and Mrs J Bushby)*

KINGSTON BLOUNT [SU7399], *Shoulder of Mutton*: recently improved Brakspears pub with country character, welcoming atmosphere, larger-than-life landlord *(Gordon and Daphne)*

LEAFIELD [Lone End; SP3115], *Spindleberry*: good food including vegetarian dishes in attractive restaurant, also – more limited choice – in comfortable lounge bar of Cotswold stone village inn, wide choice of real ales including Devenish Wessex, Liddingtons, Morlands Best and Wadworths 6X, lots of whiskies, welcoming hosts *(D A Lloyd)*

LITTLE MILTON [SP6100], *Lamb*: consistently good reasonably priced food with warm bread, fresh salad, good simple puddings, in well kept, friendly, cosy and comfortably renovated thatched pub with good Halls Harvest, pleasant service and garden *(A Sheard, Michael and Alison Sandy, Joan Olivier, LYM)*

LONG HANBOROUGH [SP4214], *Bell*: good value food, especially lunchtime buffet, in comfortable L-shaped pub quite near Blenheim; children welcome *(M J F Waterhouse)*; *George & Dragon*: friendly fifteenth-century country pub with burger-style bar food, Halls real ale, restaurant, garden *(Miss J Olivier)*

LONGWORTH [SU3899], *Blue Boar*: friendly and warm village local with games room, lounge and bar, meals *(Marina Christopher)*

LOWER ASSENDON [SU7484], *Golden Ball*: wider choice of good food under new licensees, especially hot pies made with brown flour in pottery dishes; good Brakspears, log fire, pleasant garden *(BHP, W T Aird)*

NETTLEBED [High Street; SU6986], *Bull*: well renovated and congenial old coaching-inn with good value home-cooked food, including restaurant's Sunday roasts, big garden *(Martyn Quinn, David Regan)*

NORTH NEWINGTON [SP4139], *Roebuck*: good food in lounge and small dining-room of pleasant village pub *(John Thompson)*

NORTHMOOR [SP4202], *Dun Cow*: small basic rural local, landlord brings Morlands beer from back tap-room, friendly and relaxing atmosphere, traditional pub games *(MHG)*

OXFORD [Merton Street; SP5106], *Eastgate*: interesting updated pub part in hotel with good bedrooms *(Dr A K Clarke)*; [Plantation Road] *Gardeners Arms*: good food and Morrells real ale in quiet and relaxed pub with several side rooms, separate dining-room, big garden; not touristy, no juke box *(Andrew Barnett, Peter Bently)*; [Iffley Lock] *Isis*: included for its Thames-side position and good range of bar games – dominoes, darts, cribbage, shove-ha'penny (with real ½d pieces), bar billiards (30p for about 15 minutes); coal fire in winter, riverside garden, sandwiches *(Garry Rowlands)*; [Hythe Bridge Street] *Nags Head*: good fresh lunchtime sandwiches with generous fillings, friendly bar staff, reasonably priced beer, good atmosphere *(Garry Rowlands)*; [Headington] *White Hart*: filling meals and friendly staff, two bars, games area; popular with local hospital staff *(Martyn Quinn)*; [London Road, Headington] *White Horse*: good choice of food and friendly staff in spacious Morrells pub with some secluded corners, popular with students from Oxford Poly, seats in front *(Joan Olivier, Martyn Quinn)*

POSTCOMBE [SU7099], *Pig & Whistle*: food good value *(Bob Rendle)*

PYRTON [SU6896], *Plough*: unusual pub with interesting layout, home cooking including good grills and filled baked potatoes, Adnams, Badger Best and Halls Harvest on handpump; don't take your dog *(John Hyde, Bruce King)*

ROKE [SU6293], *Home Sweet Home*: friendly, good atmosphere, wide range of good food including some home-grown vegetables, fresh pasta, good wines and beer *(RJL)* [Rokemarsh] *Horse & Harrow*: small, old locals' pub, big inglenook in lounge, jolly public bar, good value food, well kept Brakspears; fine licensees *(Gordon and Daphne)*

SALFORD HILL [SP2628], *Cross Hands*: lots of tankards on beams of friendly and comfortable lounge, good choice of bar food from ploughman's to steaks *(Eirlys Roberts, LYM)*

SANDFORD ON THAMES [SP5301], *Catherine Wheel*: good filled baked potatoes, interesting cigarette card collection, friendly and efficient staff *(Peter Cattell)*; [Church Road] *Kings Arms*: modernised fifteenth-century riverside pub, smart food counter doing generous helpings, log-effect gas fire, piped music; by Sandford Lock with narrow terrace overlooking Thames (OS Sheet 164 reference 531013) *(Joan Olivier)*

SHENINGTON [SP3742], *Bell*: very small and cosy, in nice surrounding village *(Sigrid and Peter Sobanski)*

SHEPHERDS GREEN [SU7183], *Green Tree*: enjoyable to sit out in nice secluded garden of friendly local on a summer evening *(Gordon and Daphne)*

SHILLINGFORD BRIDGE [SU5992], *Shillingford Bridge*: Thames-side hotel with comfortable bar, peaceful riverside lawn and outdoor swimming-pool; bedrooms *(Bob Rendle, BB)*

SHIPLAKE [SU7578], *Baskerville Arms*: good hot and cold food, especially ham off bone and cold beef, fresh sandwiches; well kept Wethereds, summer barbecues in big garden, spotless roomy modern pub; the hound is a little Yorkshire terrier called Sadie; near good river walks *(GHW, W T Aird)*

nr SHIPLAKE [SU7476], *Flowing Spring*: unusual as the bar is on the top floor – go up stairs on outside of building; main attraction is nice gardens down to stream; friendly landlord and bar staff, Fullers beers, darts (OS Sheet 175 reference 746768) *(Jane English, H G and C J McCafferty)*

SHIPLAKE ROW [SU7578], *White Hart*: carefully open-planned pub with attractive dining end (children can eat there), well kept Brakspears, good food including grills and about three daily specials; lovely garden, country views *(Mrs M W Hancock, W T Aird)*

SOUTH WESTON [SU7098], *Salisbury Arms*: pretty, cottagey, small cosy bars, not overplush, friendly, Brakspears, extensive menu *(Gordon and Daphne)*

STANTON ST JOHN [SP5709], *Star*: interesting public bar with weaponry such as swords, daggers, bayonets on walls (moustachioed landlord is ex-Grenadier RSM, a great character); Wadworths beers, bar food *(Gordon and Daphne, C Elliott)*

STEVENTON [SU4691], *Cherry Tree*: well kept pub with good food and seven real ales *(J Stone)*

STOKE LYNE [SP5628], *Peyton Arms*: small Hook Norton pub which until recently used to include the village shop, still pleasantly basic *(Gordon and Daphne)*

STONOR [SU7388], *Stonor Arms*: good food and excellent service at the right price; wide choice of real ales *(P G Woodward)*

SYDENHAM [SP7201], *Crown*: charming décor and atmosphere, excellent beer *(Anon)* *Sun*: real village local, welcoming cheerful landlord, up steps to games area with bar billiards, shove-ha'penny, space game, juke box *(Gordon and Daphne)*

THAME [SP7005], *Bird Cage*: reasonably priced lunchtime food and Courage real ales in quaint black and white timbered pub once a medieval jail *(LYM)*; *Black Horse*: old-fashioned calm in panelled and chintzy back lounge, little sheltered courtyard, bar meals and restaurant; bedrooms *(LYM)*

THRUPP [SP4815], *Boat*: friendly pub handy for Oxford Canal *(Anon)*

TOWERSEY [Chinnor Road; SP7304], *Three Horseshoes*: old-fashioned flagstone-floored country pub with roomy garden; licensee praised for previous enterprising food left early in 1985 *(LYM; up-to-date reports on the new regime please)*

UFFINGTON [SU3089], *Fox & Hounds*: open fire in lovely and friendly old pub with well kept Morrells, generous food, small garden with view of White Horse Hill *(John Paton)*

WALLINGFORD [SU6809], *George*: much done-up series of bars and places to eat in hotel with spacious and attractive sycamore-shaded courtyard; bedrooms *(LYM)*

WANTAGE [Market Place; SU4087], *Bear*: wide choice of food from home-made soup through sandwiches and baked potatoes to ham and eggs, meat salads and curries; well kept Ushers real ales, in big bustling bar with chintzy easy chairs and sofas; restaurant; bedrooms *(BB)*

WARBOROUGH [SU5993], *Cricketers*: good well presented snacks and meals, reasonably priced, Morlands on handpump, in comfortably modernised stone pub; very pleasant new licensees *(T A V Meikle)*; *Six Bells*: well kept and recently refurbished low-ceilinged thatched pub facing cricket green with seats in small back orchard, well kept beer; main entry in previous editions *(MHG, LYM; up-to-date reports on the new regime please)*

WATLINGTON [Love Lane; SU6894], *Chequers*: food with lots of good specials – no chips – and well kept Brakspears beer in nice old beamed and timbered pub, attractive bar staff *(HKR, Gordon and Daphne, John Hyde)*; [Town Square] *Hare & Hounds*: delightful lounge bar with easy chairs, high-backed old settles, big open fire, comfortable public bar, relaxed atmosphere, good range of beers including Brakspears, separate darts room, in unspoilt ex-coaching-inn *(MHG, Gordon and Daphne)*; [High Street] *Royal Oak*: big open fire, good smiling service, bistro meals and Sunday roasts, Hook Norton, Theakstons, Ruddles *(David Regan)*

WESTON ON THE GREEN [SP5318], *Chequers*: sixteenth-century thatched ex-coaching-stop: one bar in ex-stables serves meals, also dining-room in ex-forge *(Martyn Quinn)*

WITNEY [Newland; SP3510], *Carpenters Arms*: food choice good – excellent chips – good log fire in attractive lounge *(David Regan)*; [Corn Street] *Eagle*: small homely pub with well kept Hook Norton and Morlands on handpump, basic but comfortable seating and welcoming open fire in winter *(Steve Keen)*; [West End] *House of Windsor*: straightforward pub with warm welcome and friendly atmosphere; varying well kept guest real ales *(Steve Keen)*; [High Street] *Plough*: old, with lively atmosphere, warm welcome, Courage Best on handpump, and pleasant garden behind backing on to River Windrush *(Steve Keen)*; [High Street] *Royal Oak*: small, friendly pub with interesting odds and ends, well kept Hook Norton, Morlands and Wadworths 6X, lunchtime food *(Steve Keen)*

WOLVERCOTE [SP5009], *Trout*: see main entry under Godstow

WOODSTOCK [Park Street; SP4416], *Bear*: plush and atmospheric ancient coaching-inn; bedrooms *(Anon)*; *Black Prince*: atmospheric with suit of armour, collection of military hats, antiques, swords and axes, open fire; also games room, music room, restaurant *(Martyn Quinn)*; *Kings Head*: good value cheap and filling meals in very popular two-bar pub with warm fire and garden; children welcome *(Martyn Quinn)*

nr WOODSTOCK [two miles N on A34; SP4416], *Duke of Marlborough*: friendly attentive service, good choice of food, separate restaurant, Sunday special menu, garden; well kept pub *(Ian Brindley)*

WOOTTON [SP4702], *Bystander*: modern Morlands pub with friendly new licensees, reasonably priced home cooking, big garden, pool in public bar, family lounge bar – don't confuse with village of same name near Woodstock *(Joan Olivier)*

WROXTON [SP4142], *North Arms*: good food in cosy and friendly thatched

Hornton stone pub with good Manns Bitter, IPA and Watneys Stag and milk shakes, lovely garden overlooking Wroxton Abbey *(S V Bishop, E W Bell)*

YARNTON [Woodstock Road; SP4712], *Grapes*: friendly seventeenth-century beamed pub with log-effect gas fire, reasonably priced hot and cold bar food, recently extended restaurant with Italian cooking, Halls Harvest *(Miss Joan Olivier)*

Shropshire

We find this part of England peculiarly tantalising. There is now a respectable number of main entries here, one or two of which are outstanding. And the number of Lucky Dip entries has more than doubled since last year. Yet the total of pubs that we can recommend here is still far lower than in most other counties of the same size. Is it really that there aren't that many good pubs here? Whenever we are in the county it seems so promising, with all the ingredients that elsewhere usually nourish a good crop of attractive pubs: lovely countryside, pretty villages, good walks to get a thirst up, and those elements of very early small-scale industrialisation that elsewhere so often have gone hand in hand with charming little taverns. Given all that, we'd really expect Shropshire, like its neighbouring English counties, to be overflowing with many more marvellous little pubs and inns. But where are they? If you know, please tell us! Meanwhile, read on: there's plenty to be going on with – and a specially good point is that at least in the country areas prices for food, drink and accommodation here tend to be low. The friendly and charmingly furnished Crown at Hopton Wafers would stand out as exceptional anywhere, with its wide choice of good value and often imaginative home-cooked food. In their quite different ways, three are most attractive buildings: the timbered medieval Horseshoe at Llanyblodwel with its warren of small rooms beside the pretty River Tanat (where

The Horseshoe, Llanyblodwel

the inn has trout fishing); the Feathers of Ludlow with its remarkably intricate timbered façade and civilised old-fashioned comfort – handsomely rearranged inside this year; and the Lion in Shrewsbury, a stately hotel with a distinguished coaching history. The Railwaymans Arms in Bridgnorth stands out for its surroundings – a nostalgic steam railway station – and also has an unusual range of attractively priced real ales. The Three Tuns at Bishop's Castle, recently refurbished, has just achieved official Grade I listing as a building of outstanding interest, for the unique Victorian tower brewhouse where its own beer is brewed. The unpretentious Royal Oak at Cardington deserves special mention for its out-of-the-way country friendliness, and if you stay there you will enjoy massive breakfasts. Another place for good breakfasts is the civilised Red Lion at Llanfair Waterdine. The very English Ragleth in the charming village of Little Stretton surprisingly turns out to have a landlord from Vermont. Among the Lucky Dips, there are several each in Ludlow, Much Wenlock and Shrewsbury.

BISHOP'S CASTLE   SO3289   Map 6
Three Tuns

Salop Street

This family-run pub has recently been renovated and officially classified as a Grade I listed building. The reason for visiting it is the many-storeyed Victorian brick brewhouse across the yard in which its own beers are brewed – XXX Bitter, Mild, and an old-fashioned dark somewhat stoutish ale called Steamer. The brewhouse is unique among pub breweries for its traditional tower layout, with the various stages of the brewing process descending floor by floor; brewery tours can be arranged. Home-made bar food includes sandwiches, ploughman's with Cheddar, Stilton or Shropshire blue (£1.50–£1.85), hot beef and ham in French bread (£1.50), cottage pie (£1.75), salads from quiche (£1.75) to beef, ham or turkey (£2), ratatouille and cheese (£1.95), chilli con carne and pitta bread (£2), lasagne (£2.50), trout with ham and garlic (£5.25) and steaks (from £5.95). Darts, dominoes, cribbage and quoits in the public bar. (*Recommended by K McQueen, Dennis Royles*)

Own brew · Licensees Jack and Robert Wood · Real ale · Meals and snacks Children welcome · Occasional live music · Open 11.30–2.30, 6.30–11 all year

BRIDGNORTH   SO7293   Map 4
Railwaymans Arms

A458; part of station, opposite Holyhead Inn, on E side of centre

The Severn Valley steam railway terminus surrounds this cheerful and bustling platform-side bar, and its two rooms are furnished much as you'd expect in old-fashioned station style. There are engine numbers and some old nameplates on the flowery papered walls, and an ancient twin-bell wall telephone to reach the stations down the line. Even if you're not interested in the trains, you might be attracted by the good, changing choice of well kept real ales, all on handpump and mostly uncommon. There should be around half a dozen at a time, probably including Bathams, Courage Directors, Davenports and Timothy Taylors Landlord. They also have draught cider, and good value hot pies and pasties (45p), with sandwiches at the weekends; darts, shove-ha'penny, dominoes. The car park costs 40p, refundable either against your train ticket or what you spend in the pub. (Recommended by John and Mary, Sue and Len Beattie, Mike Wood)

Free house · Licensee Peter Williamson · Real ale · Snacks · Children welcome (lunchtime) · Parking may be difficult at peak holiday times · Open 11–2.30, 7–11

CARDINGTON SO5095 Map 4
Royal Oak

Signposted up narrow lanes from A49; perhaps more easily reached from B4371

This remote mossy-tiled white stone house is plainly very old indeed: it has been licensed as a pub for longer than any other in Shropshire. The more or less open-plan, low-beamed room still has the old standing timbers of a knocked-through wall; there's an easy chair in front of the vast inglenook fireplace, with its roaring winter log fire, cauldron, black kettle and pewter jugs. Rambling corners have comfortable settees, and high-backed settles face each other in one alcove by a window. Good value lunchtime bar food includes sandwiches, toasted sandwiches (95p), ploughman's (£1.40) and at least seven dishes such as macaroni cheese (£1.30), cauliflower cheese (£1.40), chicken cobbler (£1.60), lasagne (£1.65), and cottage pie (£1.75) or steak and kidney pie (£1.80), served on their own. The choice in the evening (no orders after 8.30) is generally similar and always includes trout (£2.85), gammon (£3.20), rump steak (£4.25) and evening specials such as poacher's roll or pasty (£2.20). Well kept Ruddles County on handpump, with Bass and Springfield, also on handpump, kept under light blanket pressure. Besides darts, dominoes and cribbage in the main bar, a brightly lit upstairs room has pool, a fruit machine, space game and juke box. Tables besides roses in the front court look over to hilly fields, and a mile or so away, from the track past Willstone (ask for directions at the pub), you can walk up Caer Caradoc Hill which has magnificent views. A nice place to stay. (Recommended by Miss L Gardner, A Royle, Dennis Royles, J M Fox, A Ash)

Free house · Licensee John Seymour · Real ale · Meals and snacks · Children welcome (lunchtime) · Open 12.30–2.30, 7–11; closed Mon lunchtime Nov–March except school hols · Self-contained double bedroom tel Longville (069 43) 266; £20

In next year's edition we hope to include a few really interesting, attractive, unusual or just plain odd bars abroad. If you know any, please tell us about them as evocatively as possible. No stamp needed if posted in the UK to *The Good Pub Guide*, FREEPOST, London SW10 0BR.

CLAVERLEY SO7993 Map 4
Crown
High Street

In one of Shropshire's prettiest villages, this picturesque timbered pub is close to a fine red sandstone church notable for its set of Norman paintings above the nave. The cosy lower bar, built in 1580, is an unspoilt and friendly room served from a hatch, with fabric-cushioned wall seats, an old-fashioned settle and a coal fire in winter. The heavily beamed upper lounge, which also has an open fire, is comfortable and neatly kept, with red plush cushioned seats around the wooden tables on its patterned carpet. Yet another hatch serves a little lobby by the garden entrance. The home-made bar food is good value, including sandwiches (from 40p), ploughman's or pâté (£1.50), steak and kidney pie, cottage pie or curry (£1.95), home-cured ham, beef, pork or prawn salads (£1.95), chicken (£2.25), grilled gammon or goujons of plaice (£2.45) and eight-ounce sirloin steaks (£3.50); half-price small helpings for children. Well kept Hansons Best and Mild on electric pump; pleasant, efficient service; darts, dominoes, cribbage, maybe unobtrusive piped music. There are tables by a waterpump and tubs of flowers, roses and clematis on a fairy-lit back terrace (some noise here from a cooler); beyond an arch through the old stables block is an extensive lawn sheltered by trees and shrubs, with more tables and a children's play area. Back here, a children's shop sells sweets, ices and so forth on fine weekends and evenings. *(Recommended by Frank Cummins, Gordon and Daphne)*

Hansons · Licensee Leslie Stewart · Real ale · Meals (lunchtime, not Sun) and snacks (rolls only Sun lunchtime) · Children in area partly set aside, lunchtime Open 12–2.30, 7–11 all year

CLUN SO3081 Map 6
Sun
High Street; B4368 towards Clunton

This small Tudor inn has a relaxed and friendly lounge bar with built-in cushioned wall benches, a carved antique oak armchair, one or two high-backed winged settles and some attractive old tables. It's quietly decorated, with foxhunting pictures, a coaching horn, mugs hanging from the beams, and a collection of big brass plaques from safes among its very sturdy wall timbers; it opens on to a sheltered back terrace, with tables among pots of geraniums and other flowers. The L-shaped public bar has traditional settles on its flagstones, an enormous open fire, and darts, dominoes, cribbage and a fruit machine. There may be piped music. Reasonably priced bar food includes sandwiches (at lunchtime only, from 60p), home-made soup (70p), home-made pâté (£1.15), ploughman's (£1.20–£1.40), local sausage and egg (£1.30), salads (from £1.60), home-made quiche (£1.65), scampi (£2.15), seafood platter (£2.75), and steaks (from £4.15); also daily specials such as double lamb chops (£3.75), escalope of pork (£3.50) or fresh poached salmon (£5.25). Well kept Springfield and Woods Parish (brewed a few miles away at the Plough in Wistanstow) on handpump, and Basque wine imported direct by the inn. There is a separate restaurant. The Sun runs a vegetable competition on the first Sunday after mid-September. This quiet village is surrounded by wooded hills. *(Recommended by A Royle, P and M Horswell; more reports please)*

Free house · Licensee Rodney Marsden · Real ale · Snacks (lunchtime) and meals · Children in eating area · Open 11–2.30, 6–11 all year · Bedrooms tel Clun (058 84) 559 or 277; £10(£15B)/£20(£26B)

HOPTON WAFERS   SO6476   Map 4

Crown ★ ★

A4117

Readers continue to enthuse about the friendliness and wide range of imaginative food in this charming creeper-covered stone pub. It's all home made, brought to your table, and includes sandwiches (from 70p on white or brown bread, granary 20p extra), a choice of soups (tomato, vegetable or cream of Stilton 85p), ploughman's (from £1.40), good pâté (£1.70), three-egg omelettes (from £2), salads (£2.50–£2.90), excellent filled pancakes such as spinach, cheese and mushroom or salmon, egg and cheese (£2.40), saffron prawns or seafood special (mussels, cockles, scallops, prawns, mushrooms and egg in a cheese and wine sauce £2.50), smoked salmon and sour cream blinis made with wholewheat and rye flour, steak and kidney pie, lasagne or chilli con carne (all £2.75), grilled baby chicken (£3.20) and steaks (from £5.50). There are several children's dishes (£1), and a really generous plate of good chips (65p). The choice of home-made puddings is enormous: baked syrup sponge or chocolate hazelnut charlotte with Grand Marnier (90p), chocolate roulade or black cherry Pavlova (95p) or hot fudged bananas with cream and brandy (£1.10). The wide range of ice creams and sorbets includes some unusual ones such as Strega or damson (85p), and their Hopton Wafers (banana and praline ice cream topped with whipped cream and sliced fresh fruit, with continental wafers) is said to be unbelievably delicious. On top of the general menu, there are usually specials of the day – sea trout, say, and nectarine Melba. With so much fresh cooking going on, don't expect instant service. There is also a good separate (and very low-beamed) restaurant. The bar spreads from a snug part by the serving counter into a bigger room where you may be greeted by the friendly black labrador, and a lot of thought has clearly gone into decorating it: oil paintings, flowery cushions on the black settles, silver band instruments hanging from the beams, and small open fires in both rooms. There's a fruit machine by the bar counter, and the further room has pool; also dominoes, maybe piped music. Well kept Hook Norton and Marstons Burton and Pedigree on handpump. Outside the substantial and attractive stone building there are tables under cocktail parasols on the terraces with plenty of tubs of bright flowers. *(Recommended by PLC, Philip Denison, C W E Redman, J A Cashmore, Paul Denham, Jane English, Frank Cummins, D S Braisted, Richard Balkwill, Sue and Len Beattie, Patrick Wrigley, Mrs J Robertson)*

Free house · Licensees Julian and Virginia Harrison · Real ale · Meals and snacks (not Mon, except bank hols) · Children welcome · Open 11–2.30, 6.30–11 all year (opens 7 in winter); closed Mon except bank hols

LITTLE STRETTON   SO4392   Map 6

Ragleth

Ludlow Road; village well signposted from A49

This attractive pub – unusual for its American landlord, who runs the pub with his Shropshire wife and her parents – has recently had its dining-room extended. In here they serve full evening meals with main courses such as marinated lamb kebab (£4.50) or salmon poached in white wine (£5.95), and will on request do them at lunchtime too. Home-cooked bar food includes sandwiches (from 55p), soup (75p), filled baked potatoes (from £1.35), ploughman's (from £1.50), cottage pie with pickled red cabbage (£1.65), herby home-made chicken liver pâté (£1.75), daily hot specials such as steak and mushroom pie, and six-ounce charcoal-grilled steak (£3.85). The bay-windowed lounge bar, which has one unusual curved corner (possibly to do with its sixteenth-century days as a ropeworks), has comfortable seats built around it, a good fire in winter, and maybe piped music. There's a huge inglenook fireplace in the brick and tiled floor public bar (which has darts, dominoes, fruit machine, space game and a juke box). Well kept Bass on handpump. Tables on the lawn look across to an ancient-seeming thatched and timbered church (actually built in this century). Long Mynd, above the village, is a spacious heather-and-bracken plateau owned by the National Trust with fine views. (*Recommended by A Royle, Eirlys Roberts; more reports please*)

Free house · Licensee David Graziano · Real ale · Meals – tel *Church Stretton (0694) 722711 – and snacks · Children in eating area and restaurant · Open 11–2.30, 6–11 all year*

LLANFAIR WATERDINE   SO2476   Map 6

Red Lion

Village signposted from B4355; turn left after crossing bridge

This peaceful old white-painted stone inn has seats on the grass at the back looking down over the River Teme. Inside, the small black-beamed tap-room has a wood-burning stove, plain wooden chairs on its polished brick floor, and table skittles, dominoes, cribbage and sensibly placed darts. The rambling lounge bar, with cosy alcoves, has little polished wooden seats on its Turkey carpet, earthenware jugs hanging from the beams, easy chairs and some long, low settles as well as a big open fire. Bar food includes quiche with salad (£1.50), basket meals such as sausage, chicken and fish (£1.75–£2), steaks – when available – (£4.85) and a choice of puddings (from 75p); there's a separate restaurant (dinner is £9, bookings only). There are more seats on flagstones among roses by the quiet lane in front of the pub; the track off this lane, before you get to the main road, leads to a good stretch of Offa's Dyke and the long-distance walkway there. Though the bedrooms aren't big, they're clean and comfortable, and the breakfasts could hardly be bettered. (*Recommended by Lt Col C C G Ross, Brian Green; more reports please*)

By law, pubs must display a list of their drinks prices. Let us know if you are inconvenienced by any breach of this law.

Free house · Licensee James Rhodes · Meals and snacks · Open 10.30–2.30, 7–11 all year · Bedrooms tel Knighton (0547) 528214; £18(£22B)/ £30(£32.50B)

SHROPSHIRE

LLANYBLODWEL   SJ2423   Map 6

Horseshoe ★   [*illustrated on page 545*]

Village and pub signposted from B4396

This black and white timbered medieval inn is right by the River Tanat which rushes around the boulders under a little red stone bridge; the inn has a mile of fly-fishing for trout or grayling here – free for residents, or £2.50 a day. The low-beamed rooms have a fine, friendly local atmosphere. There are traditional black built-in settles alongside more modern chairs around oak tables in the front inglenook bar, which has a collection of china and bottles on a high beam, brass buttons and other brass, and the beginnings of a collection of key fobs. Good value bar food includes sandwiches (summer only), ploughman's (£1.10), home-made chilli con carne (£1.25), home-made curry (£1.80), plaice (£2.40) and sirloin steak (£4.50). In the various rooms leading off you will find darts, pool, shove-ha'penny, dominoes, cribbage and a space game. There are picnic-table sets in front of the pub, with a good view of the river. (*Recommended by B S Bourne; more reports please*)

Marstons (now that they've bought and closed Border to whom this pub used to be tied) · Licensee Philip Hindley · Meals and snacks (not Tues evening in winter) · Children in eating area of bar · Open 11–2.30, 6–11 all year (opens 7 in winter) · Bedrooms tel Llansantffraid (069 181) 227; £10/£16

LUDLOW   SO5175   Map 4

Feathers

Bull Ring

The beautifully proportioned timbering of this balconied and gabled inn, with creatures and figures worked into its intricately carved tracery, is more handsome than any other we have seen. Inside is friendly and busy. There's been quite a bit of internal reorganisation since our last edition, with one room redesigned specifically to improve bar snacks service, and another comfortably set aside for families. Throughout, there's an attractively old-fashioned flavour, with high beams, some Jacobean panelling and plasterwork, seventeenth-century carved oak armchairs and massive antique settles, antique prints and open fires (one with a handsome Jacobean carved chimney-piece). The bar food includes soup in winter, sandwiches with white or brown bread or baps (turkey £1, beef with horse-radish £1.25, smoked salmon £1.50; toasted 5p extra), ploughman's or quiche (£1.50) and pâté (£1.50–£1.65); the panelled and high-raftered restaurant has a good value lunchtime buffet (three courses £5.25) as well as full meals, and for a wider choice of bar food the nearby Angel (see our Lucky Dip entries at the end of the chapter) is under the same management and has a buttery bar. Flowers IPA and Original on electric pump. A nice, comfortable place

Tipping is not normal for bar meals, and not usually expected.

551

to stay. Ludlow is a pretty town, full of things to see. *(More reports please)*

Free house · Licensee Peter Nash · Real ale · Snacks (not Sun) · Children in Tanners Room · Open 10.30–2.30, 6–11 · Bedrooms tel Ludlow (0584) 5261; £35B/£54B

SHREWSBURY   SJ4912   Map 6

Lion

Wyle Cop; follow City Centre signposts across the English Bridge

Since our last edition, handsome redecoration has continued at this grand old inn. A stately series of spacious high-ceilinged rooms with silver-golden plush armchairs and sofas, one with a huge stone fireplace, sweep around the snug oak-panelled bar, which has stylish red leather chairs, good Bass on handpump (kept under a very light blanket of CO_2), an attentive barman, and dominoes and cribbage. Waitress-served bar food includes freshly cut sandwiches (from 80p), home-made soup (85p), pâté (£1.50), Cheddar or Stilton ploughman's (£1.60) and seafood platter (£3.75), and there is a separate restaurant. Paganini once played in the lofty and well restored pillared Adam ballroom, but below all the Georgian splendour is a maze of Tudor cellars which were used as secret Roman Catholic chapels during the Reformation. The bedrooms are very comfortable. *(Recommended by Pamela and Merlyn Horswell; more reports please)*

Free house (THF) · Licensee Matthew Solomonson · Meals and snacks Children welcome · Open 10.30–3, 6–11 all year · Bedrooms tel Shrewsbury (0743) 53107; £36B/£53B

Lucky Dip

Besides the fully inspected pubs, you might like to try these Lucky Dips recommended and described by readers (if you do, please send us reports):

BINGS [SJ5418], *Dog in the Lane*: bar food includes snacks and sandwiches in well kept pub with red and gold furnishings, varnished tables, eighteenth-century pictures, polished brass and beams; family area and machines area *(Frank Cummins)*

BRIDGNORTH [Ludlow Road; SO7293], *Down*: under new management; good value food *(R F Usmar)*

BROCKTON [SO5894], *Feathers*: bar food and well kept real ales in country pub with large collection of little china houses; pretty covered back terrace *(Philip Denison, LYM)*

LEEBOTWOOD [SO4898], *Pound*: friendly welcome and convivial atmosphere; good lunchtime cold buffet *(C F Walling)*

LLYNCLYS [SJ2824], *White Lion*: friendly and comfortable main-road pub with sandwiches, freshly fried chicken, gammon, pies and so on *(BB)*

LOPPINGTON [SJ4229], *Blacksmiths Arms*: refurbished country tavern with inglenook public bar and fairy-lit country garden with play area; German-speaking licensees are MG enthusiasts *(Jon Dewhirst, LYM)*

LUDLOW [Broad Street; SO5175], *Angel*: Flowers real ale well kept, lunchtime bar snacks good in comfortable lounge with efficient service; bedrooms *(Pamela and Merlyn Horswell)*; [Corve Street] *Bull*: good beer and reasonably priced bar food in historic half-timbered pub *(Pat Bromley)*; *Church*: good food and atmosphere, friendly service and wide range of real ales including Fullers *(M F Pearson)*

MUCH WENLOCK [SJ6200], *Gaskell Arms*: friendly reception, warm and cheery public rooms, and good range of bar meals *(F A Noble)*; *George & Dragon*: sixteenth-century pub with well kept Simpkiss real ale and home-cooked food including vegetarian meals; folk night Sunday, jazz and blues Monday *(Anon)*; *Talbot*: nice food and pleasant service, always very welcoming *(DM)*

NORBURY [SO3693], *Junction*: good value food includes locally made game pies served by friendly staff in clean lounge; well kept Banks's real ales; children welcome; at canal junction *(Roger Danes)*

SHREWSBURY [Port Hill Road; SJ4912], *Boat House*: quiet lounge bar and sheltered terrace by River Severn; Whitbreads real ale and bar food; change of management since last year – up-to-date reports please *(LYM)*; [Abbey Foregate] *Dun Cow*: bar food from baked potatoes to steaks in comfortable open-plan pub with almost life-size cow effigy on porch; near Norman abbey church *(LYM)*; [Mardol] *Kings Head*: quaint heavily timbered pub with unusual construction (upstairs windows just part of the timbering, for instance, without separate frames) has choice of real ales, friendly modern atmosphere and good juke box in low-beamed bar *(LYM)*; [Wenlock Road] *Peacock*: good summer cold buffet, well kept beer, warm and friendly atmosphere *(J Nicholson)*

TILSTOCK [SJ5438], *Horseshoes*: licensee (from Blacksmiths Arms, Loppington) has transformed this Wem pub; excellent atmosphere *(A M Rossell)*

TONG [SJ7907], *Bell*: good lunchtime food, especially cold table, in welcoming pub with well kept Banks's *(P J Taylor)*

Somerset and Avon

*Pubs that stand out for good value food in this area — so
unusually rich in inviting pubs — include the Ashcott Inn
(friendly and old-fashioned), the Square & Compass near
Ashill (enterprising young licensees who have quickly made
this simple but comfortable country pub a firm favourite with
many readers), the traditional Albion in Bristol
(straightforward lunches in splendidly generous helpings), the
civilised Rose & Crown at East Lyng, the Three Horseshoes
at Langley Marsh (often very interesting food, also good real
ales), the attractive old Queens Head in Milborne Port (a nice
place to stay), the Notley Arms in Monksilver (again, often
uncommon food — this is one of a dozen Somerset pubs which
weren't in our last edition), the handsome and comfortable
King's Arms in Montacute (especially for its buffet lunch), the
Anchor at Oldbury-on-Severn, the firmly traditional
Greyhound at Staple Fitzpaine (preliminary reports on its new
owners suggest that the interesting food here is at least as
good as in the past), the well run Rest & Be Thankful at
Wheddon Cross, the Royal Oak in Withypool on Exmoor (a*

The White Horse, Stogumber

lovely place to stay) and the Red Lion at Woolverton (most enjoyable even when it's really busy). Some pubs here, by contrast, stand out for their utter simplicity: the Globe at Appley, Cotham Porter Stores in Bristol, Tucker's Grave at Faulkland (the new owners seem to be keeping it that way), Rose & Crown (Eli's) at Huish Episcopi, and Seven Stars in Timsbury. Several of these keep a good farm cider, or indeed quite a number of them do, and pubs here in general are a particular delight for cider lovers. Other interesting pubs and inns include the Ship at Porlock Weir (an ancient and civilised thatched inn in a lovely position between the sea and Exmoor), its near neighbour the friendly Ship just under Porlock Hill (its chimney is as fat as a lighthouse), the George & Pilgrims in Glastonbury (with its marvellous ancient carved stone façade), the George at Norton St Philip (among the country's very oldest pubs, with a charming, partly Norman, cobbled courtyard), the White Horse in the unspoilt village of Stogumber, the Exmoor Forest Hotel in Simonsbath on Exmoor itself (a civilised inn with one of the country's best collections of whiskies), the Cottage Inn at Nether Stowey (superficially nothing special, but splendidly relaxing and well worth finding), and the Fleece & Firkin in Bristol (a splendid conversion of an elegant stone wool-hall, brewing its own beers). There's a very large number of Lucky Dip suggestions at the end of the chapter, on which we'd particularly like to have readers' views; among them, some especially interesting ones seem to be the homely Bowl in Almondsbury, the Lamb in Axbridge (attractive all round), the Wheatsheaf at Combe Hay (for its lovely position), the Waldegrave Arms in East Harptree (good food, lots of nooks and crannies), the nicely old-fashioned Stag at Hinton Charterhouse, the unspoilt fifteenth-century Pack Horse at South Stoke and, particularly, the cosy and charming Hop Pole in Limpley Stoke.

APPLEY (Somerset)   ST0621 Map 1

Globe

Hamlet signposted from the network of back roads between A361 and A38, W of B3187 and W of Milverton and Wellington; OS Sheet 181 reference 072215

This cheerful and unspoilt country tavern, situated in a maze of little twisting lanes, has an entry corridor leading to a serving hatch where Ushers PA and a range of ciders are tapped from their casks. A simple beamed front room has bare wooden tables, benches and a settle built in to its part-panelling, with rugs on its brick floor, while the back room has a pool-table under its tongue-and-groove ceiling, and a big Victorian chromolithograph of 'The Meet of the Four-in-Hand Club' on its white-panelled wall. Bar snacks include filled rolls (35p), sandwiches (50p) and ploughman's (£1). The surrounding hilly pastures are very pretty and there are seats outside in the garden; the path opposite leads eventually to the River Tone. *(More reports please)*

Free house · Licensee Timothy Enticott · Real ale · Snacks · Open 11–2.30, 6 30–11 all year

ASHCOTT (Somerset)   ST4337   Map 1
Ashcott Inn
A39

This friendly old wayside pub is especially popular for its wide choice of good food: sandwiches such as rare and tender beef (85p), or ploughman's with Cheddar, Brie, Stilton or ham (£1.25), served at virtually any time during licensed hours; and at mealtimes dishes include soups (from 70p), Somerset smokie (smoked haddock in a wine and cheese sauce £1.25), ratatouille with rice and cheese or garlic bread (£1.10), home-made pâté (£1.15), baked garlic mussels (from 1.35 for six), spaghetti bolognese (£1.85), salads (from £1.50), chicken (£1.50), ham and eggs (£1.95), moussaka (£2.50), celery hearts and ham baked in cheese sauce (£2.35), fisherman's platter (£2.95), chicken pieces in a wine and cider sauce with peppers, aubergines, mushrooms and tomatoes (£3.25) and charcoal-grilled steaks (from £4.55), with lots of puddings (from 65p); there are also daily specials such as cauliflower cheese with grilled bacon (£2.35) and pork spare ribs in cider and cream (£3). On most days you'll have to book for the cosy little communicating dining-room. A sturdy central chimney with a fine royal coat-of-arms fireback for its log-effect gas fire divides the two rooms of the Turkey-carpeted bar: mugs and tankards hang from beams (most attractively restored in the inner room), a chaise longue and a curved high-backed settle are among other more conventional seats, old-fashioned pictures on stripped stone walls, a chiming clock, and good oak and elm tables. Well kept Butcombe, Flowers Original and Huntsman Dorchester on handpump; darts sensibly placed in an alcove, shove-ha'penny, a fruit machine, alley skittles and piped radio music. There are swings and a slide by the seats on the lawn behind this pub, among shrubs and well kept peat-beds. *(Recommended by R H Inns, R F Davidson, Brig W S Mullin)*

Free house · Licensee Peter Milne · Meals – tel Ashcott (0458) 210282 – and snacks (not Sun lunchtime) · Children in dining-room · Open 10.30–2.30, 6–11 all year; closed Sun lunchtime

nr ASHILL (Somerset)   ST3217   Map 1
Square & Compass
Windmill Hill; turn off A358 at Stewley Cross Garage

Readers continue to praise the food in this friendly and simply furnished country pub. Most is home made and freshly prepared by the friendly young licensees: sandwiches or filled rolls (from 85p), soup (75p, especially recommended is the unusual beef soup), hot beef in French bread (£1.25), ploughman's or pâté (£1.30), savoury pancake, chilli con carne or lasagne (£1.60), venison sausages (£1.95) and salads such as ham (£2.10) or home-cooked beef (£2.95), steak and kidney pie or scampi (£2.95), steaks (from £3.95), chicken chasseur (£4.25) and pork and Stilton (£4.50); children's menus (99p) and vegetarian dishes. Puddings include pancakes (65p) and special ice creams (95p). There is also a small separate restaurant (Sunday roast lunch here costs £2.85). Well kept Golden Hill Exmoor on handpump; piped music. The cosy bar has upholstered window seats (which overlook the rolling pastures around Neroche Forest) and brown leatherette armchairs on the brown carpet, and in winter has a good little open fire; darts. There are picnic-table sets on the grass outside, with a swing, climbing-frame and bright blue hay-wagon; in summer there are Shetland ponies for children to ride, and a cook-it-yourself barbecue for steaks, sausages, hamburgers, chicken and fish. A two-acre caravan and camp site includes holiday caravans to let (from £50 a week). *(Recommended by JSW, Evan Davies, J E F Rawlins, JH, Mrs M J E Middleton, Peter Mason, Ian Williams, Mary Joinson)*

Free house · Licensees Tony and Caroline Shepherd · Real ale · Children in restaurant and play caravan · Open 11.30–2.30, 6–11 all year; closed Tues Caravans tel Hatch Beauchamp (0823) 480467

BATH (Avon)   ST7565   Map 2
Bladud Arms
Gloucester Road, Lower Swainswick (A46)

This friendly and simple pub is especially popular for its lively range of games. Upstairs or downstairs you can play darts, pool, dominoes, cribbage, space games and a fruit machine, and outside there's a full-scale skittle alley. At lunchtime good value food includes sandwiches, giant hot dog (60p), and – with chips and peas – ham and egg (£1.50), plaice (£1.70), home-made steak and kidney or chicken and mushroom pie (£1.75) and mixed grill (£1.90). Well kept and reasonably priced Archers, Bass, Butcombe, Marstons Pedigree, Wadworths 6X and Whitbreads West Country PA on handpump. Furnishings and décor are sensibly simple, including a couple of nice old high-backed settles. You can sit outside in summer. *(Recommended by Dr A K Clarke)*

Free house · Licensee Donald Meylan · Real ale · Meals and snacks (lunchtime, not Sun) · Open 11–2.30, 6–10.30 all year

Crystal Palace
Abbey Green; via Church Street, opposite end from abbey

This comfortably modernised pub, in a quiet Georgian square with a tree-shaded green, has a sheltered courtyard decorated with hanging baskets and tubs of flowers; there are plenty of tables both here and in the well furnished heated conservatory. Inside, one black-panelled and beamed bar has comfortable soft seating, and another leading off has button-back seats and traditional cast-iron tables below a series of religious admonitions and exhortations. The new licensees are continuing with home-made, good value food: sandwiches (from 80p, toasties 10p extra), filled baked potatoes (95p), cottage pie (£1.45), a choice of ploughman's (from £1.60), chilli con carne (£1.75), quiche with salad (£1.80) and steak and kidney pie (£2).

Huntsman Dorchester, Dorset and Royal Oak on handpump; a couple of fruit machines. *(Recommended by David Symes, Mark Stocker, Dr A K Clarke; up-to-date reports please)*

Huntsman · Real ale · Meals and snacks · Children in heated conservatory Nearby parking may be difficult, metered · Open 10.30–2.30, 6–10.30

BRADLEY GREEN (Somerset)   SS0434 Map 1
Malt Shovel

Pub signposted from A39 W of Bridgwater, near Cannington

The main bar of this out-of-the-way inn has robust modern winged high-backed settles around wooden tables, some nice modern elm country chairs, cushioned window seats and little cushioned casks. A black kettle stands on a giant fossil by the wood-burning stove. A restaurant leads off a little red hessian-walled snug. Bar food includes sandwiches (from 45p), soup (85p), ploughman's (£1.50), steak and kidney or fisherman's pie (£2.30) and sirloin steak (£4.25); well kept Butcombe and Wadworths 6X on handpump, all served by friendly young staff. On our visit faint Radio 1; separate skittle alley. There are picnic-table sets on the grass behind (an adjoining field may be used by touring caravans). West of the pub, Blackmore Farm is a striking medieval building. *(Recommended by C Elliott)*

Free house · Licensees Robert and Frances Beverley · Real ale · Meals and snacks · Open 11.30–2.30, 6–11 (opens half an hour later in winter) Bedrooms tel Spaxton (027 867) 332; £12/£20

BRISTOL (Avon)   ST5872 Map 2
Albion

Off Boyce's Avenue, Clifton

The lunchtime hot dishes at this friendly and unpretentious pub are excellent value: besides roast meats (around £2.10), there are two or three a day such as liver and bacon casserole (£1.80), lamb kebab (£1.80), steak and kidney pie (£2.10) and chicken or beef cooked in red wine (£2.20), and they're served with a choice of roast, boiled, baked or chip potatoes with four vegetables, or salad or rice. The flagstoned front courtyard looking down this quiet cobbled lane is the only one of its age left in the city, and inside there's a relaxed and old-fashioned feeling in the traditionally furnished L-shaped public bar. Beyond a lobby with hatch service – which supplies well kept Bass and Courage Best from hand pump, and Directors tapped straight from the cask – there's a more comfortable lounge. Shove-ha'penny, dominoes, a fruit machine, and maybe piped music. *(Recommended by D C Turner)*

Imperial Inns (Courage) · Licensee Gerald Garth Gilling · Real ale · Meals and snacks (lunchtime, not Sun) · Open 12–2.30, 5.30–10.30

Coronation Tap

Between Sion Place and Portland Street, Clifton

This cheerful and bustling low-ceilinged little tavern, at the end of a

quiet cul-de-sac, sells only ciders and beers, including well kept
Courage Best and Directors on handpump; rows of big cider-barrels
dominate its otherwise warmly red décor. Bar food includes
sandwiches and rolls (50p), casseroles (85p), ploughman's (90p), and
liver and onion or cottage pie (£1.20); there are daily specials
Monday to Saturday (£1.20–£1.50); dominoes and cribbage are
played here. A stroll away from Clifton suspension bridge.
(Recommended by D C Turner, Dr A K Clarke, Deborah Mattinson)

Courage · Licensee B W Wood · Real ale · Meals (lunchtime, not Sun) and
snacks (lunchtimes and Mon–Fri evenings) · Open 11–2.30, 5.30–10.30
(7–11 Fri and Sat evenings)

Cotham Porter Stores

15 Cotham Road South

Long benches built in to the panelling serve a line of close-set tables
down the narrow bar of this lively cider pub – for every two feet of
space, reckon on at least three arguments about politics, sport, or just
life. When the arguments get too heated, the juke box is turned up to
drown them, but in contrast it's switched right off when any of the
singers and musicians, who use this as their local, feel swayed by
inspiration – plentiful here, in the form of well kept Courage Bitter
and Best on tap at attractive prices, as well as the ciders. Cheap
snacks include filled rolls (40p), cheese toasties (40p) and home-made
individual cottage pies (45p); sensibly placed darts, dominoes,
cribbage. *(Recommended by Richard Gibbs; more reports please)*

Courage · Licensee James McGreene · Real ale · Snacks (lunchtime, not Sun)
Open 10.30–2.30, 5.30–10.30

Fleece & Firkin

St Thomas Lane; pub visible from Victoria Street, which leads into the
main A4 to Bath

This handsome eighteenth-century three-storey building was
originally a wool-hall; it has been stripped spaciously back to its
original flagstones inside, with a 15-foot ceiling supported by stout
iron pillars, scrubbed butcher's tables, and the frightful puns that
mark David Bruce's other home-brew pubs (in London) jostling with
some antique wool-merchant shopfittings. Interestingly, this pub,
unlike his others, is managed for him by Halls (Ind Coope) and tied to
them. Besides the pub's own brews – Bootlace, Bristol Best, Coal
Porter and Dogbolter – they keep guest beers for a month, serving
four at a time: Archers Headbanger, Boddingtons, Camerons
Strongarm, Fullers London Pride, Gibbs Mew Bishops Tipple, Greene
King Abbot, Halls Bristol Pride, Hartleys XB, Tetleys, Theakstons
Old Peculier and Timothy Taylors Landlord are kept under a very
light blanket of CO_2. Soft piped pop music, live music Monday to
Saturday evenings, and a mainly studentish-looking crowd of
customers then; it gets packed on Saturday evenings. Bar food
includes sandwiches, large filled baps (£1), baked potatoes with

Sunday opening is 12–2 and 7–10.30 throughout England.

various fillings (80p–£1.10), omelettes (£1 or £1.75), salads, lasagne or shepherd's pie (£1.65) and steak and kidney pie (£1.75). *(Recommended by Mark Spurlock, David Symes)*

Own brew · Licensee Thomas Balls · Real ale · Meals (lunchtime, not Sun) and snacks (lunchtime and Mon–Thurs evenings) · Open 10.30–2.30, 5.30–10.30

Pump House

Merchants Road; by Cumberland Basin

Outside this imposing towered building there's an unusually big dockside terrace with cast-iron-look tables and chairs, which have good views not only of the dock but of the nearby swing bridge when it goes into action. Inside it has smart tiling, new charcoal-grey brickwork, and old engravings on the remarkably high partly panelled walls. Well kept Eldridge Pope Royal Oak and Bass on handpump; a food counter as well as a separate restaurant; darts, a fruit machine, space invaders and a juke box. *(Recommended by Mary Roddick, D A Lloyd; more reports please)*

Free house · Licensee M B McGowan · Real ale · Meals and snacks (lunchtime) Metered parking, not very close · Open 10.30–2.30, 5.30–10.30

CHISELBOROUGH (Somerset)   ST4614 Map 1
Cat Head

Village signposted off B3165 between A3088 and A30 W of Yeovil

The main bar of this rather smart old pub has a traditional atmosphere and furniture to match: stripped high-backed old settles, a flagstone floor, seats in the honey-coloured Ham-stone mullioned windows, and a big solid-fuel stove. Much of the bar food is home made and includes sandwiches, filled rolls (75p–90p), a very good onion soup (85p), pâté (95p), ploughman's (£1.30 for Cheddar, £1.40 for Stilton), half-pint of prawns, lasagne (£1.95), chicken curry (£2.10), ham and egg (£2.25), seafood pancake (£2.50), crab salad (£3.25), beef Stroganoff (£4.95) and 10-ounce rump steak (£5.25); they also do vegetarian dishes (£1.75–£1.95). There's a popular separate restaurant and it's best to book. Ushers PA, Best and Founders on handpump; sensibly placed darts, dominoes, cribbage, a fruit machine and a juke box, maybe piped music. There is a separate skittle alley, and you can sit outside in an attractive garden looking up to the lumpy surrounding hills. *(Recommended by Patrick Young, Alan and Audrey Chatting)*

Ushers · Licensees Martin and Linda McMahon · Real ale · Meals and snacks (not Mon lunchtime or Sun evening) · Children in restaurant · Occasional live music Sun evenings · Open 11.30–2.30, 6.30–11 all year; closed Mon lunchtime · Bedroom and restaurant bookings tel Chiselborough (093 588) 231; £8/£14

EAST LYNG (Somerset)   ST3328 Map 1
Rose & Crown

A361 about 4 miles W of Othery

The very prettily planted back garden, largely hedged off from the car park, with picnic-table sets, a big children's playground and a pony paddock behind – and a full skittle alley – is a pleasant summer complement to the relaxing charm of the big open-plan beamed lounge bar. Besides some modern sturdy black tables, it has traditional furnishings such as a dresser of plates, a corner cabinet of glass, china and silver, a winter log fire in a modernised fine old stone fireplace, and stacks of old issues of *Country Life* on a bow window seat by an oak drop-leaf table. Sandwiches (75p), ploughman's (£1.80), and a wide choice of main dishes from sausages and chips (£1.75) or ham and egg (£2.10), omelettes, salads or plaice (all around £2.50), and trout or gammon (£3.25) to duck with orange and honey or sirloin steak (£4.25 – other steaks up to £6.40); barbecues in summer. There is also a separate dining-room. Well kept Butcombe, Devenish Wessex Best and Huntsman Royal Oak on handpump; piped music. *(Recommended by A D Collins; more reports please)*

Free house · Licensee P J Thyer · Real ale · Meals (not Sun lunchtime) and snacks · Children in eating area · Open 11–2.30, 6.30–11 all year

FARMBOROUGH (Avon)   ST6660   Map 2
Conways

A39, just N of village

This smart and very neatly kept mock-Tudor road-house is known to our readers as the New Inn – the name it has had for ages. The licensee who recently rechristened it after his own name has just left, so we have hopes that it will in due course revert to its proper name. But a more material change is that a separate bar is now planned, where the new licensee hopes to do a wider range of bar food and snacks. The popular restaurant opens from the bar and keeps an elegantly informal atmosphere by echoing the style of the bar itself: bevelled cut glass, comfortable red plush seats on the flowery carpet and a high ceiling – in the bar, its joists are hung with copper funnels, lamps, curly brass motor-horns, cooking-pots and so forth. Well kept Flowers Original, Halls Harvest and Ruddles County on handpump. You can eat or drink in the garden in summer. *(Recommended by Commander A R C Rowe, Dr A K Clarke; up-to-date reports on the new regime please)*

Free house · Licensee Michael Naylor · Real ale · Meals and snacks · Open 11–2.30, 7–11 all year

FAULKLAND (Somerset)   ST7354   Map 2
Tucker's Grave

A366 E of Village

This farm-cottage pub has a tiny room where two old cream-painted high-backed settles face each other across a single table, with casks of well kept Bass and Whitbreads in an alcove on the left; also Cheddar Valley cider. This, the smallest pub in the *Guide*, has recently been taken over by new licensees, who we understand hope to preserve its unspoilt simplicity. We certainly hope they succeed. Shove-ha'penny in a side room. There are seats outside. *(Recommended by Dr A K Clarke, Gordon and Daphne, Annie Spencer; up-to-date reports on the new regime please)*

Free house · Licensees Ivan Gerald and Glenda Swift · Real ale · Open 11–2.30, 6.30–11 all year; closed 25 Dec

GLASTONBURY (Somerset)   ST5039   Map 2

George & Pilgrims

High Street

Originally a hospice attached to the abbey, this medieval inn has a remarkable carved stone façade, recently very handsomely restored by the brewery. Inside the lounge bar, the nicest place to sit is probably in the great fourteenth-century traceried bay window; it's a comfortably modernised room, with sporting prints, a log-effect gas fire and so forth, as well as some traditional oak seats, and bar food includes soup (45p for a small bowl, 60p larger, home-made bread and farm butter 35p), sandwiches (from 70p, with home-made bread 20p extra), quiche Lorraine (£1.10), ploughman's (from £1.20), cod (£1.65), salads (from £1.80) and scampi (£2.25). As we went to press they were planning to keep one of their two separate restaurants open for 14 hours a day, and this will mean a wider choice of bar food. Well kept Bass on handpump. *(Recommended by P J Taylor, Dr A K Clarke)*

Bass (part tie only) · Licensee Jack Richardson · Real ale · Meals and snacks Children in restaurants · Open 10.30–2.30, 6–11 all year · Bedrooms tel Glastonbury (0458) 31146; £28B/£44B

Rifleman's Arms ★

4 Chilkwell Street; A361, SE of town centre

The welcoming main bar in this cheery and unconventional pub has an unusually wide variety of pictures, often interesting, on the stripped stone walls under its low ceilings; there is a high-backed settle, several smaller ones, cushioned seats in the Tudor mullioned windows, and a row of stools along the bar counter. There's a family room with space games and so forth, bright and sunny, with doors on to the terrace, where tables look down to the River Brue and South Moor. Bar food concentrates largely on big filled ham or cheese salad rolls (70p); there is also ploughman's (£1), and from the back family bar home-made soups (75p), sausage, egg and chips (£1.25), pasty or pie with vegetables (£1.45) and a daily vegetable bake or hot-pot (£1.30). Well kept Butcombe, Farmers and Ushers Best and Founders on handpump, and Wilkins' farm cider tapped from the cask. The back room has sensibly placed darts, shove-ha'penny, dominoes, cribbage, a fruit machine and a juke box, as does the side pool-room, but the special game of the house is Tor tennis. The Tor is just a stroll away, as is the Holy Well. *(Recommended by MHG; more reports please)*

Food details, prices, timing and so on refer to bar food, not to a separate restaurant if there is one.

Free house · Licensee Josephine Spooner · Real ale · Meals and snacks (not Sun lunchtime, not after 8pm) · Children in back family bar · Open 12–2.30, 6–11 all year

HUISH CHAMPFLOWER (Somerset)   ST0429 Map 1
Castle

The picnic-table sets on the neatly kept grass a little above this friendly little village pub look out to a patchwork of hill pastures above the church tower, and are serenaded by enthusiastic thrushes, blackbirds and wrens. Inside it's comfortable, with a wood-burning stove in the big white fireplace, and polished brass platters on red and gold wallpaper above the shinily painted panelling. Well kept Golden Hill Exmoor on handpump; simple and fairly priced bar food includes toasted sandwiches, sausage and chips, scampi and chips, and rump steak – there's also a separate restaurant. A communicating back room has darts, pool, a fruit machine, juke box and space game, and there is a skittle alley. *(Recommended by Elizabeth Haigh, A P Smith; more reports please)*

Free house · Licensee R Hodge · Real ale · Meals and snacks (not Mon) Children welcome · Occasional live music · Open 11–2.30, 6–11 all year

HUISH EPISCOPI (Somerset)   ST4326 Map 1
Rose & Crown

A372 E of Langport; note that this is some 25 miles from the previous entry

This unspoilt and cheerful country pub is known to its regulars as Eli's, after the present licensee's father – it has been in the same family for 120 years or more, and when she retires her own family will carry on the tradition; as you can see from the Sturgeon print in one front room, the pub hasn't changed much over the years. Its heart is the flagstoned central still-room which is the only thoroughfare between three cosy and somewhite untidy parlours with unusual pointed-arch windows, old rugs on stone floors, and basic well used seats. It's this room where you go for your well kept Bass or Badger Best to be drawn from the cask, or for the wide choice of Somerset farm ciders which stand on ranks of shelves around it (drinks here are very cheap). Food is also cheap, but simple: sandwiches (from 40p), pies and pasties, toasted sandwiches (from 43p–50p), beans on toast (60p), ploughman's (65p), various seasonable snacks, and at weekends assorted filled rolls (30p). There's a fruit machine in one of the front rooms, and shove-ha'penny, dominoes and cribbage are available. A much more orthodox family room in the big back extension has darts, pool, table skittles, pin-table, space game, juke box and a small children's roundabout. Hens – now ruled by a dignified Rhode Island Red rooster – scrape around in the back yard by the picnic-table set. *(Recommended by John and Mary, Andy Jones, Gordon and Daphne)*

Free house · Licensee Mrs Eileen Pittard · Real ale · Snacks · Children in family room · Open 11–2.30, 6–11 all year

Pubs with outstanding views are listed at the back of the book.

KILVE (Somerset)   ST1442 Map 1

Hood Arms

A39 E of Williton

The carpeted main bar of this well run village inn has brown leatherette seats around its wooden tables, a wood-burning stove in the stone fireplace (decorated with horse brasses on their original leathers), old local photographs on the walls, and dark beams and joists in its cream ceiling. It leads through to a little cosy lounge with red plush button-back seats. Popular home-made lunchtime bar food includes sandwiches (from 65p), soup (75p), pâté or ploughman's (from £1.45 for local Cheddar), salads (from £2.25), and fried chicken or steak and kidney pie (£2.50); they also do daily specials such as chicken and mushroom pie, gammon, vegetarian shepherd's pie or chilli con carne; there is an evening grill-room (closed Monday and Tuesday). Well kept Flowers IPA and Original on handpump; on our visit, gentle piped music. A sheltered back terrace, by an award-winning garden with a prettily planted old wall behind, has white metal and plastic seats and tables. Spacious and comfortable bedrooms lead off a cobbled courtyard. *(Recommended by B St C Matthews; more reports please)*

Free house · Licensees Robbie Rutt and Neville White · Real ale · Meals and snacks · Open 10.30–2.30, 6–11 all year · Bedrooms tel Holford (027 874) 210; £13 (£15B)/£22 (£25B)

LANGLEY MARSH (Somerset)   ST0729 Map 1

Three Horseshoes

Village signposted off A361 from Wiveliscombe

There's a good range of real ales and interesting, good-value food in this friendly red sandstone pub. In summer there's an average of 30 dishes to choose from, in winter around 20: those always available include sandwiches, home-made soup (75p), home-made pâté (£1), ploughman's (£1.20), piquant prawns (£1.35 as a starter, £1.60 as a main course), fisherman's platter (£1.65) and several vegetarian dishes such as black-eyed bean pâté or hummus (£1), lentil and spinach casserole or spaghetti with aubergine (£1.50); other dishes include moussaka, cider-soused herring or mussels in a cream and curry sauce (£1.50), home-cooked ham or tongue salad (£1.75), rabbit and mushroom pie (£1.85), falafel baps or quail with garlic purée (£1.90), beef with prunes and walnuts (£2.15), lemony chicken with fresh coriander or stargazy pasty (£2.25), and steak baps (£2.40). Puddings range from very good home-made cider ice cream (65p) to bread and butter pudding suprême (85p). There's also a simple restaurant. The well kept real ales include Cotleigh Tawny and Golden Hill Exmoor, both brewed down the road in Wiveliscombe and tapped from the cask, Badger Best, Devenish Wessex, Gibbs Mew Salisbury and Palmers IPA on handpump. There's also a wide range of bottled beers, and several ciders including Perry's farm cider. The two rooms give a choice between comfort at the back (low modern settles on the carpet, dark red wallpaper) and the lively front room with sensibly placed darts, table skittles, shove-ha'penny, dominoes, cribbage and a fruit machine; there may be piped music. A special plea: if you do take children inside the pub, please keep them under quiet control. There are rustic seats on the verandah or you can sit in the sloping back garden, with a climbing-frame, swing and slide, maybe the pub's dog, a St Bernard, and a view of farmland.

(Recommended by Jacqueline Hill, Mr and Mrs G Amos, George Jonas, Dr and Mrs Richard Neville)

Free house · Licensee John Marsden · Real ale · Meals and snacks · Children in eating area if well behaved · Open 12–2.30, 6–11 all year

MILBORNE PORT (Somerset) ST6718 Map 2
Queens Head

A30 E of Sherborne

There's a warm and friendly atmosphere in the beamed lounge bar of this golden stone old coaching-inn, with pews and solid country chairs on its brown carpet, fresh flowers, and walls that are partly salmon-pink hessian and partly stripped back to the original stone

The Ship, Porlock

and decorated with photographs. It's divided into two parts by a big central chimney, knocked through so that the log fire warms both sides. The public bar is broadly similar, with some stripped panelling: it has darts, table skittles, dominoes, cribbage and a fruit machine. Good and popular lunchtime bar food includes sandwiches (from 65p, toasties 5p extra, toasted bacon £1), home-made soup (95p), home-made chicken liver pâté (95p), a choice of children's dishes (£1.15), filled French bread (from £1.25), ploughman's (£1.30), smoked haddock in cheese and cider sauce (£1.40), steak sandwich (£1.55), hot quiche (£1.55) and lasagne (£1.80); evening food is more or less the same but includes grills such as gammon (£4.95) and rump steak (£5.95), and there's a separate restaurant. Changing guest beers join the well kept regular Hook Norton Bitter and Best, Smiles Best and Wadworths 6X, and there are two farm ciders. The three bedrooms are clean and comfortable. The old-fashioned garden, with hops and vines growing over the golden stone walls, also has a children's play area with a thatched hollow-tree house. There are more tables in a sheltered flagstoned courtyard, prettily decorated with hanging baskets and troughs of flowers. (Recommended by Pamela and Merlyn Horswell, Pat and Malcolm Rudlin, E St Leger Moore, L D Callaghan)

Free house · Licensee Nicholas Turner · Real ale · Meals and snacks · Children welcome except in bars · Open 11.30–2.30, 6.30–11 all year · Bedrooms tel Milborne Port (0963) 250314; £12.50/£19.50

MONKSILVER (Somerset)   ST0737   Map 1
Notley Arms
B3188

The charming cottage garden behind this quiet village inn runs down to a swift clear stream. In the L-shaped beamed bar, the emphasis is on good home-made food: cream of cauliflower soup, say, imaginative snacks such as their shepherd's purse (wholemeal pitta bread generously filled with garlicky lamb and salad, £1.50) as well as ploughman's (£1.40), rich coarse pâté (£1.55), freshly made pasta with ham (£1.75), lasagne (£2.25), steak and kidney pie with light puff pastry (£2.60), salads (from £2.95) and puddings such as treacle tart or lemon meringue pie with clotted cream (£1). There are kitchen chairs and small settles around the plain country wooden tables, Old Master and other prints on the black-timbered white walls, and a couple of very businesslike wood-burning stoves. Well kept Ushers Best on handpump, well reproduced classical music, notably cheerful and friendly service (even under pressure from summer crowds) and a bright little family room with a space game. (Recommended by Elinor Goodman, Katherine Currie, Phyllis Deane, W E S Bond, Mary Cross)

Ushers · Licensee Alistair Cade · Real ale · Meals and snacks · Children in family room · Open 11–2.30, 6–11 · Bedrooms tel Stogumber (098 46) 317; £10/£20

In next year's edition we hope to pick out pubs that are specially nice to stay at, alongside the star ratings. Please tell us if you think any pub – in the Guide or not – deserves a 'Stay Award'. No stamp needed: The Good Pub Guide, FREEPOST, London SW10 0BR.

MONTACUTE (Somerset)   ST4951 Map 2

King's Arms

The new landlords of this early Georgian inn with its handsome golden stone façade are keen to keep on the nicely prepared lunchtime buffet that has proved so popular. A selection from this costs £3.45 or £3.95, depending on how much you want; starters and the good puddings are £1.50. Other bar food includes home-made soup (90p), Dorset pâté or quiche (£2.50) with salad, several freshly cooked daily specials, prawn salad (£3.95) and scampi or an eight-ounce beefburger (£5.50) including pudding and coffee. There is also a separate restaurant in the evening. The loung bar is very comfortable with soft armchairs, grey-gold plush seats, chintz sofas, a high curved settle, and – towards the front, where the walls have recently been stripped back to the handsome masonry – plush seats around tables. Bass and Gibbs Mew Salisbury on handpump. The village includes the stately Elizabethan mansion of the same name, and behind the hotel wooded St Michael's Hill is owned by the National Trust. (Recommended by J E F Rawlins, A C S McFarlane, Mr and Mrs F W Sturch)

Free house · Licensees Roger and Joan Skipper · Real ale · Meals and snacks (not Sun evening) · Children in restaurant and eating areas · Open 11–2.30, 6–11 all year · Bedrooms tel Martock (0935) 822513; £30B/£40B

NETHER STOWEY (Somerset)   ST1939 Map 1

Cottage Inn

Keenthorne; A39 E of village

Relaxing and well run, this tiled pink-washed roadside pub serves big helpings of good value simple food such as sandwiches (from 60p), ploughman's (£1.20), three sausages (£1.20), plaice (£1.50) or roast beef (£1.95); the Youngers Scotch on handpump, not that common around here, is very well kept, and there is Somerset farm cider. The friendly oak-beamed lounge bar has comfortable red plush winged easy chairs (some grouped around the wood-burning stove in one end wall), red plush window seats and stools, and bunches of flowers. There's a quieter further room with with a good matchbox collection, and the other end opens into a spacious carpeted games room with two pool-tables, juke box and a fruit machine; skittle alley. There are a few picnic-table sets on grass by the car park. (Recommended by N B Pritchard; more reports please)

Free house · Licensees David and A M Morgan · Real ale · Meals and snacks Open 11–2.30, 6–11 all year

NORTON ST PHILIP (Somerset)   ST7755 Map 2

George ★ [illustrated on page 573]

A366

This ancient pub, already an inn by 1397, earns its star for the character of its massive stone-walled building and its charming half-timbered and galleried back courtyard with an external Norman stone stair-turret. It was originally built to accommodate merchants buying wool and cloth from the rich sheep-farming Hinton Priory at the great August cloth market. The main bar has high mullioned windows, lofty beams hung with harness and copper preserving pans, wide bare floorboards, and is simply furnished with plain old tables, leather seats and square-panelled wooden settles. A long, stout table serves well kept Bass, Wadworths Devizes and 6X from handpump, and bar food includes sandwiches, ploughman's, baked potatoes, salads, lasagne, moussaka, casseroles, scampi and steaks. Beside it a panelled lounge is furnished with antique settles and tables, and there is a separate restaurant. Off the courtyard is the cellar Dungeon Bar, named to recall the men imprisoned there after the rebel Duke of Monmouth had been defeated. When a sympathetic customer held the courtyard gate open for them as they were led out to their execution, he was bundled along with them and executed too. The duke had stayed here before the battle of Sedgemoor, and after a skirmish nearby his Colonel Holmes used one of the inn's carving knives to finish amputating his own arm. Just up the road towards Trowbridge is Oldfield Nurseries, with an unusual and attractively priced range of plants, and a stroll over the meadow behind the pub leads to a pleasant churchyard around the medieval church whose bells struck Pepys (dining here on 12 June 1668) as 'mighty tuneable'. (*Recommended by James Forbes, A Saunders, Ann Fleming, Annie Taylor, CG*)

Wadworths · Licensee M F Moore · Real ale · Meals and snacks · Children in area away from serving bar · Open 10–2.30, 6–11 all year

OLDBURY-ON-SEVERN (Avon)   ST6292   Map 2
Anchor

Village signposted from B4061

The good value food in this old stone village pub is served quickly by friendly staff, despite weekend crowds: steak and kidney pie (£1.45), lasagne (£1.50), savoury mince (£1.65), chicken with cheese sauce (£1.85), prawn and mussel chowder or seafood Italian style (£1.95), leg of lamb (£2), fresh salmon salad (£2.95) or sirloin steak (£3.95). Well kept Bass, Butcombe, Marstons Pedigree, Robinsons and Theakstons Best on handpump, or tapped straight from the cask. The beamed lounge is comfortably furnished with cushioned window seats, easy chairs, a curved high-backed settle facing an attractive oval oak gateleg table, winged seats against the wall and a big log fire in winter. The public bar has darts, shove-ha'penny, dominoes and cribbage. You can sit outside in the garden in summer. St Arilda's church nearby is interesting, on its odd little knoll with wild flowers among the gravestones, and there are lots of paths over the meadows to the sea dyke or warth which overlooks the tidal flats. (*Recommended by Sue and Nick Cowan; more reports please*)

Free house · Licensee Michael Dowdeswell · Real ale · Meals and snacks Open 11.30–2.30, 6.30–11

Sunday opening is 12–2 and 7–10.30 in all Welsh pubs allowed to open on that day (we mention in the text the few that aren't).

PORLOCK (Somerset)   SS8846 Map 1
Ship ★ [illustrated on page 565]

A39

The low-beamed front bar in this thatched white village cottage has a
huge inglenook fireplace, traditional old benches on its tiled and
flagstoned floor, and hunting prints on its walls. Bar food includes
sandwiches (from 55p), soup (65p), ploughman's (£1.10), home-
made steak and kidney pie (£1.10), pizza (£1.45), plaice (£1.50), ham
and egg (£1.70) and daily specials such as chilli con carne (£1.80) or
trout with salad (£2.20); puddings (from 80p) are served with clotted
cream. There is a separate restaurant. Courage Best and Flowers
Original on handpump, also Perry's farm cider. The carpeted back
lounge has a Gothick settle and plush red banquettes; shove-
ha'penny, dominoes, cribbage and a fruit machine, a separate pool-
room (which has sensibly placed darts, too, in winter), and a full
skittle alley. You can sit in the garden behind the pub, with its
enormous chimney – needed to make the fire draw even in the tricky
down-draughts off Porlock Hill, which from here climbs over 600
feet to the Exmoor plateau in little more than half a mile.
(Recommended by Bill Roberts, Prof David Brokensha, Richard Gibbs)

Free house · Licensee K M Bickerstaff · Real ale · Meals and snacks · Children
in eating area · Open 10.30–2.30, 5.30–11 all year · Bedrooms tel Porlock
(0643) 862507; £13.03(£14.42B)/£26.06(£28.84B)

PORLOCK WEIR (Somerset)   SS8547 Map 1
Ship

This little thatched inn, a larger neighbouring hotel, and a few old
stone houses around a small tidal harbour are quite alone down here,
in a lovely spot between the steeply wooded slope of Exmoor and a
long pebble and boulder beach. The original Ship Bar at the back is
our favourite: a smallish, atmospheric room with a stone floor,
hanging-straps from its beams, an attractively panelled bar counter
serving well kept Bass and Ushers Founders, and red leatherette wall
benches; also darts, dominoes, cribbage and in winter table skittles.
This could be the room where Jan Ridd's father had his last drink, on
his way home from Porlock market, before the Doones ambushed
and killed him just past the top of Porlock Hill. Except at the busiest
periods this bar may be closed on some weekday evenings from May
to September, though the licensees assure us that it should always be
open in winter. The lively Mariners Bar in a modern front extension
is neatly furnished with red gingham tablecloths, Windsor chairs on a
swirly red carpet, with pool and two space games in a separate family
room leading off. Bar food includes sandwiches (85p), ploughman's
(£1.45), quiche (£2.25), steak and kidney pie (£2.25), with more
expensive main dishes such as game pie or curry (£5.75) and steak
(£8.55) served as well in the evenings from the attractive separate
dining-room. Some of the inn's comfortably creaky old-fashioned
bedrooms, popular with the poet Southey, look across a big car park
to the sea (and even, on a clear night, the lights of towns in Wales). So
do most of the white tables and chairs among roses in the front

courtyard; there are more outside seats, including an antique settle, in a sheltered inner corner. A nice place to stay; if you do want to book here, make clear that it's the Ship you want rather than the (perfectly good) Anchor Hotel, with which it is run in tandem. *(Recommended by Roy McIsaac, Derrick Turner, Prof P M Deane, Richard Gibbs, James Cane, Lissa Halliday, S E Boulton, RAB)*

Free house · Licensees Pandy Sechiari and D H Wade · Real ale · Meals and snacks · Children in separate room · Open 11–2.30, 6–10.30 · Bedrooms tel Porlock (0643) 862753; £19.50(£22.50B)/£39(£45B)

nr PRIDDY (Somerset)   ST5251   Map 2
Hunters Lodge

Unclassified but good road from Priddy E to A39; leaving Wells on A39, pass long hill with TV mast on left then take next left turn: OS Sheet 183 reference 549502

You're sure of a warm welcome in this isolated old inn not far from Wells and Wookey Hole, and surrounded by high rolling country; it's an area popular with walkers and potholers and is dotted with prehistoric circles and barrows. The main bar has a friendly atmosphere, flagstone floor, old pictures above the benches built against its dark walls and a log fire; there is also a straightforwardly comfortable lounge and a big summer extension bar. They keep a good range of well kept real ales, tapped from casks behind the counter: Badger Best, Bass, Butcombe, Cotleigh and Farmers. Bar food includes filled rolls (40p), pasties (50p), faggot and peas (90p), bread, cheese and pickles (90p), and cottage pie or curry (£1); shove-ha'penny, dominoes, cribbage and a fruit machine. A nice place to stay – good value too. *(Recommended by Michael and Alison Sandy, Dr B W Marsden, Robert Mitchell, David Symes)*

Free house · Licensee Roger Dors · Real ale · Snacks · Open 11–2.30, 6.30–11 all year · Bedrooms tel Wells (0749) 72275; £7S/£15S

SIMONSBATH (Somerset)   SS7739   Map 1
Exmoor Forest Hotel

B3223/B3358

This friendly and civilised inn in the middle of Exmoor has around 300 different whiskies in stock, one of the biggest collections in the country. The two bars have log fires on cool days, and high walls decorated with attractive pictures of Exmoor and country life. The lounge has chintzy sofas and easy chairs on its carpet, while the public bar – crowded with local customers on some evenings – has pool, shove-ha'penny, table skittles, dominoes, and a fruit machine, space game and a juke box. There is a separate skittle alley. Bar food includes sandwiches, home-made pasties, ploughman's, pizza (£1.50), chilli con carne (£2), home-made steak and kidney pie (£2.30), chicken cooked in wine or chicken and ham pie (£2.50). There is also a separate restaurant. Well kept Flowers IPA, and a beer brewed for the pub, Simonsbath Bitter, on handpump or tapped straight from the cask. You can sit outside in summer. A nice place to stay, with well equipped bedrooms and nine miles of trout fishing free to residents. *(Recommended by Richard Gibbs; more reports please)*

Free house · Licensee T G Woodward · Real ale · Meals and snacks · Children welcome · Open 10.30–2.30, 5.30–11 all year · Bedrooms tel Exford (064 383) 341; £12.65/£25.30

STAPLE FITZPAINE (Somerset)   ST2618   Map 1
Greyhound [★]

Village signposted from A358 Taunton–Ilminster at Hatch Beauchamp; or (better road) from Shoreditch on B3170, just after crossing M5 S of Taunton

This attractively old-fashioned little country inn has a new landlord, and as we went to press it was undergoing major alterations including inside lavatories, a new kitchen, extensions to the bar and restaurant areas, and the addition of a small conference room; by 1986 all the bedrooms should have private facilities. The landlord is anxious to make sure that the atmosphere which readers have previously enjoyed so much will not be lost; the flagstone floors and log fires will stay, as will antique furnishings and vases of wild flowers. Preliminary reports from readers suggest that the food remains as good as ever, both in the choice of dishes and size of helpings, but we have put the pub's star award in brackets until we have firmer news – we look forward to getting up-to-date reports. Depending on what fresh ingredients are available, prices range roughly between around £1.75 (for charcoal-grilled sardines) and £5.75 (pork fillet stuffed with fresh ginger and pineapple): ploughman's with farmhouse Cheddar and home-made chutney (£1.75), spring lamb and vegetable pie or hedgerow pie (£3.25) and chicken and vegetable kebab on saffron rice with a spicy yoghurt sauce (£3.75). Other dishes readers have enjoyed include a Stilton and celery soup, fresh trout and stuffed pork fillet, fish and meat and vegetable pies (especially Pigley pie – pork in cider with apple, onion and lemon), salads with real mayonnaise, mussels cooked with saffron, spinach, cream and wine, rabbit cooked with pigeon breasts, and beef in beer. There are always several vegetarian dishes and children's portions. They keep many country wines (several readers have liked the dry nettle wine) and a fair number of whiskies, as well as well kept Golden Hill Exmoor, Wessex Bitter and a beer brewed specially for the pub on handpump. A separate dining-room has tables on flagstones polished so richly that they're almost like rough marble, with food such as prawn and quail's eggs thermidor (£3.65), fresh crab and mango with tarragon (£3.75) and fillet of lamb with fresh tomato and basil sauce (£6.95). There is a no-smoking area. In front of this creeper-covered Georgian house there are some seats among troughs of flowers, with more in the gravelled stable-yard behind – where there is a skittle alley. Just to the south you can walk in the hillside woods of Neroche Forest, which has a signposted nature trail. *(Recommended by J H Dubois, John Milroy, G F Scott, Alan Franck, Mr and Mrs R French, PLC, Patrick Young, P L Crosland, Peter and Rose Flower, J Murray, P T Young, Julia Hoyle; up-to-date reports on the new regime please)*

Free house · Licensee Martin Tarr · Real ale · Meals and snacks · Children welcome · Open 11–2.30, 5.30–11 all year; closed 25 Dec · Bedrooms tel Hatch Beauchamp (0823) 480227; £25B/£35B

STOGUMBER (Somerset)   ST0937   Map 1
White Horse [*illustrated on page 554*]

Seats in front face the red stone church of this closely huddled village, and the garden behind is quiet except for rooks and lambs in the surrounding low hills. Inside there's a long room with cushioned captain's chairs and settles around the heavy rustic tables on the patterned carpet, a coal fire in cool weather, and old-fashioned built-in settles at one end with a red tiled floor. They have local farm cider as well as well kept Cotleigh Tawny and Golden Hill Exmoor together with a guest beer on handpump, and home-cooked food includes sandwiches (from 55p, a hot bacon roll 60p), soup (65p), giant sausage in French bread (65p), maybe filled baked potatoes (from 65p), ploughman's (from £1.10), fried haddock (£1.40), salads (from £1.50), liver and bacon casserole (£1.60), trout with almonds (£2.70) and steak (from £4.40 – for an eight-ounce sirloin); also a separate restaurant (three courses £6.50). A side room has sensibly placed darts and a fruit machine; piped music – soothing piano and strings on our visit; a separate skittle alley. (*Recommended by H E A Lewis; more reports please*)

Free house · Licensee Peter Williamson · Real ale · Meals and snacks · Open 11–2.30, 6–11 all year · Bedrooms tel Stogumber (098 46) 277; £19B

TIMSBURY (Avon)   ST6658   Map 2
Seven Stars

North Road; B3115

This friendly and unspoilt local has two simply furnished rooms that open off the little bar, one brightly lit, with a big wood-burning stove, darts, shove-ha'penny, cribbage, a fruit machine and two space games; the other with a couple of small leather-seated settles against its old white panelling. Beyond this is a sitting-room with easy chairs and cushioned pews built against the walls; there's also a pool-room. The music from the juke box is well reproduced in all rooms. Well kept Courage Best and Directors on handpump, attractively priced; there's a swing and climber on the grass behind, by the small car park. (*Recommended by Dr A K Clarke*)

Courage · Licensee Victor Shobbrook · Real ale · Open 10.30–2.30, 6–10.30

TINTINHULL (Somerset)   ST4919   Map 2
Crown & Victoria

Farm Street; from village, which is signposted off A303, follow signs to Tintinhull House

This mellow stone village pub, close to Tintinhull House with its beautiful gardens, is warm and welcoming. The open-plan carpeted bar has a couple of easy chairs by the big winter log fire in one bared stone wall, as well as comfortable low modern settles, Windsor chairs, and some with more old-fashioned higher backs. Food includes sandwiches (70p–£1.10 for prawn), ploughman's (£1.30–£1.65), lasagne (£1.75), fried trout (£2.25) and steaks (from £5), with a daily special such as steak and kidney pudding, pork chop in ginger beer or chicken in wine (£2.25). There are half portions for children, and beefburger or sausages and chips (75p). At lunchtime on Sundays there is a cheeseboard on the bar counter. Bass and Huntsman Royal Oak on handpump, and Wadworths 6X and a guest beer tapped from the cask, kept under light blanket pressure; darts, pool, shove-ha'penny, dominoes, cribbage, a fruit machine and juke box, with a skittle alley. The big lawn behind the pub is attractive and peaceful in summer, when there are occasional barbecues; it has white chairs, cocktail parasols, swings and a goldfish pool set in a rockery – and a friendly goat. *(Recommended by St John Sandringham, M E J Cathrine, Mr and Mrs D Dalligan, Clive Wyatt-Ingram)*

Free house · Licensee Richard Knight · Meals (not Sun) and snacks · Children in eating area and skittle alley · Open 10.30–2.30, 6–11 all year

TORMARTON (Avon) ST7678 Map 2

Compass

Under 1 mile from M4 junction 18; A46 towards Stroud, then first right

Handy for the M4, this much-extended inn has an understandably busy atmosphere. It has a series of separate serving bars with various

The George, Norton St Philip

rooms radiating off them; the nicest is probably the conservatory which is light and spacious with flowers and a few orange- and fig-trees dotted around the tables; you can also sit here at night when it's attractively lit, and in winter when the heating is switched on. Bar food is all home made and includes sandwiches, turkey and mushroom pie (£2.75), steak and kidney pie, chicken Mediterranean and fisherman's pie (£2.85) and several puddings such as freshly made ice creams; Archers Village, Bass and Wadworths 6X on handpump, with maybe mulled wine in winter. There's a separate restaurant. Outside, the crazy-paved terrace has bright flowers and some stone tables. Close to Badminton and Dodington. (*Recommended by PLC, Pamela and Merlyn Horswell, Dr A K Clarke, D A Lloyd*)

Free house · Licensees the Monyard family · Real ale · Meals and snacks Children in eating areas (lunchtime only) · Open 10.30–2.30, 5.30–10.30; closed evenings 25 and 26 Dec · Bedrooms telBadminton (045 421) 242/577; £23.50 (£29.95B)/£33.95 (£42.95B)

UPTON (Somerset)   SS9928   Map 1

Lowtrow Cross

B3190 about 7 miles N of Bampton; OS Sheet 181 reference 006293

Alone in attractive countryside near the Clatworthy and Wimbleball reservoirs, this friendly inn has a welcoming local atmosphere: low beams support a shiny white plank ceiling, and there's a fat wood-burning stove in the enormous stone inglenook fireplace. The regulars snuggle into a little alcove almost behind the bar, with sporting prints on its panelled walls, but the main area — partly woodblock, partly red carpet — has captain's chairs and wooden stools around well spaced tables. Food includes sandwiches (from 50p), pâté (£1.20), quiche, pizza or salads (from £1.50), ploughman's (from £1.50), steak and kidney pie (£1.60), ham and egg (£1.95), scampi (£2.25) and children's dishes such as baked beans on toast (50p); in the evening they also do trout with almonds (£4.25), mixed grill (£4.95) and 10-ounce sirloin steak (£4.95). Well kept Cotleigh Tawny on handpump; on our visit rather fuzzy Radio 1. There are swings and a climbing-net on the neat side lawn, and seats on a front terrace by the roadside car park; to one side a field has space for touring caravans. (*Recommended by P Pope*)

Free house · Licensee P R Willis · Real ale · Meals and snacks · Open 11–2.30, 6–11 all year

WHEDDON CROSS (Somerset)   SS9238   Map 1

Rest & Be Thankful

Junction of A396 and B3224, S of Minehead

This friendly and well run roadside pub under Dunkery Beacon dates from the seventeenth century. The comfortable lounge is divided into two communicating brown-carpeted rooms by its central chimney (with log fires in cool weather); it has tapestried built-in banquettes and chairs around modern wood tables, a white plank ceiling, and graceful goldfish in a big aquarium. Bar food includes sandwiches (from 70p – not Sunday lunchtime), home-made soup (75p), pasty or steak and kidney pie (80p), three sausages (£1.40), home-made pâté (£1.60), ploughman's (from £1.65), salads such as home-cooked ham, beef or turkey (£2.60), pork cooked with Stilton (£4.15), coq au vin (£4.50) and eight-ounce rump steak (£4.95). Well kept Ushers Best on handpump; on our visit gentle piped music. A communicating games area has pool, darts, a juke box and a space game, and there is a skittle alley. *(Recommended by Miss A C Rogers, Joan Olivier)*

Free house · Licensees Michael and Christine Weaver · Real ale · Meals and snacks · Children in buffet bar and games/skittle alley · Open 10.30–2.30, 6–11 (12–2, 7–10.30 in winter)

WINSFORD (Somerset) SS9034 Map 1
Royal Oak

Village signposted from A396 about 10 miles S of Dunster

This thatched Exmoor inn, considerably extended behind as a hotel, dates back some 700 years in parts, and in the seventeenth century its customers were regularly plundered by the Exmoor highwayman Tom Faggus on his strawberry roan, in exploits which R D Blackmore, a frequent visitor, worked into *Lorna Doone*. From a cushioned big bay-window seat in the partly panelled and cosy lounge bar you can look across the road towards the village green and the foot and packhorse bridges over the River Winn, which joins the Exe here. There are other comfortably cushioned seats on the red carpet, and in winter logs burn in the big stone fireplace, which has a magnificent iron fireback. Horse brasses and pewter tankards hang from the beam above the attractively panelled bar counter, from which well kept Flowers IPA and Original are served by handpump. Another similarly old-fashioned bar has darts and shove-ha'penny. Home-made bar food includes soup (95p), sandwiches (75p, toasted steak sandwich £2.25), Stilton croquettes (£1.15), pâté (£1.30), ploughman's (£2.50), savoury mince pasty (£2.80), steak and kidney pie or a daily special (£3.50), beef bourguignonne (£4.50) and sirloin steak (£4.75); home-made puddings (£1); there is also a separate restaurant with daily three-course, good value menus (£10). In the 1880s Ernest Bevin's mother worked in the kitchen of this inn until she died, leaving him an eight-year-old orphan. Plenty of nearby walks, for example up Winsford Hill for magnificent views, or over to Exford. A nice place to stay. *(Recommended by Don Mather, David and Ruth Hollands; more reports please)*

Free house · Licensees Charles and Sheila Steven · Real ale · Meals and snacks Children in eating area of bar and in restaurant · Open 11–2.30, 6–11 all year Bedrooms tel Winsford (064 385) 232; £30B/£45B

WITHYPOOL (Somerset) SS8435 Map 1
Royal Oak

Village signposted off B4233

The village is tucked down below some of the most attractive parts of Exmoor – there are grand views from Winsford Hill just up the road, tracks lead up among the ponies into the heather past Withypool Hill, and the River Barle runs through the village itself, with pretty bridleways following it through a wooded combe further upstream. The cosy beamed lounge bar has a log fire in a raised stone fireplace, comfortable button-back brown seats and slat-backed chairs, and a stag's head and several fox masks on its walls, and another quite spacious bar is similarly decorated. Readers have enjoyed a good range of home-made bar snacks, particularly praising the soup (75p) and pâté (£1.95); other food includes Somerset pasty (from £1.80), Danish open sandwiches (from £2), home-cooked gammon (from £2.50), two large sausages (a choice of pork and garlic, pork and herb or venison and bacon, £3), smoked salmon salad (£4.50) and sirloin steak (£5.50); five-course dining-room evening meals (£12.50); well kept Ushers Best on handpump. There are white metal and plastic chairs and tables under cocktail parasols on the front terrace, by the very quiet village lane. A comfortable place to stay. *(Recommended by Mr and Mrs R C E French, Mrs K Sadler)*

Free house · Licensee Michael John Bradley · Real ale · Meals and snacks Open 11–2.30, 6–11 all year · Bedrooms tel Exford (064 383) 236; £18 (£25B)/£32 (£40B)

WOOLVERTON (Somerset)   ST7954 Map 2
Red Lion
A39, at N end of village on W side of road

This popular and attractively extended pub was a farm 300 years ago: there's an inner core of flagstones, cushioned farmhouse chairs, old panelling, beams, and a winged high-backed settle by the big stone hearth. The main lounge has an expanse of parquet flooring with oriental-style rugs and lots of comfortably cushioned seats around decent elm tables, with cream walls and ceiling and flowery curtains. It's busy – crowded at weekends – but friendly, with a good relaxed atmosphere, and serves huge helpings of popular food. In summer, besides sandwiches (95p–£1.10), ploughman's (£1.40) and home-made pâté (£1.55), they stick to cold foods: salad bowls such as garlic croûtons, smoked bacon and cheese (£2.30) and tuna, prawns, avocado, pineapple, sweetcorn and Caribbean dressing (£3.05), chicken with curry-flavoured mayonnaise, orange and nuts (£2.60) seafood platter (£4.80) and a selection of cold continental meats and sausages (£4.90). In the winter they do hot dishes as well as some from the cold menu. Well kept Bass and Wadworths IPA and 6X on handpump. You can eat outside under the trees. *(Recommended by Dr Nicola Hall, Sue White and Tim Kinning, Dr A K Clarke, GGR, PLC)*

Wadworths · Licensee Barry Lander · Real ale · Meals and snacks · Children welcome · Open 11–2.30, 6–11 all year

---

Lucky Dip

Besides the fully inspected pubs, you might like to try these Lucky Dips recommended and described by readers (if you do, please send us reports):

ALMONDSBURY [ST6084], *Bowl*: good food in delightful homely atmosphere, and interesting drinks including foreign bottled beers *(Roger Entwistle, Dr A K Clarke, R Lander)*

AUST [ST5789], *Boars Head*: food good, well kept Courage Directors, in old pub with welcoming winter log fire; village itself now rather isolated by motorway; children welcome *(Steve and Carolyn Harvey, Mr and Mrs G D Amos)*

AXBRIDGE [The Square; ST4255], *Lamb*: tasty food and good choice of well kept real ales in very attractive pub with friendly efficient staff; interesting artefacts, traditional pub games, skittle alley, and garden *(Jack Rayfield, Graham Stone, Alison Cull)*

BARROW GURNEY [Bridgwater Road; ST5268], *Fox & Goose*: wide choice of good value food, with efficient service in pleasant pub, all clean and bright *(Roger Cossham, S E Reeves)*; [Link Road] *Princes Motto*: good range of real ales including Bass, Butcombe, Courage, Jacobs and Wadworths 6X, in quaint welcoming country pub with high-backed settles and solid rustic furnishings – also winter log fire; filled rolls; nice garden *(Stephen and Carolyn Harvey)*

BATH [Belvedere, Lansdown Road; ST7565], *Beehive*: local petitioners prevented closure of basic two-room terraced pub where Taunton cider is the favourite drink *(A K Hardy)*; [Walcott Street] *Bell*: lively, with well kept real ale and good cheap bar snacks; frequent live jazz *(Dr A K Clarke, Nick Dowson, Alison Hayward)*; [Northumberland Place] *Coeur de Lion*: tiny central tavern in pretty flagstoned alley *(Dr A K Clarke, LYM)*; [St John's Place] *Garrick's Head*: strong theatrical flavour with signed production photos on walls; simple lunchtime snacks (has gay rights noticeboard) *(Flt Lt A D Harkness, Dr A K Clarke)*; [Bathampton] *George*: good somewhat pricey food from sandwiches to hot food, with pleasant service and friendly atmosphere, in old canalside pub with spacious terrace, popular for business lunches *(John Rathband, Paul A Smith)*; [Lansdown Hill] *Hare & Hounds*: good bar food – especially Camembert fritters – and well kept beer in pub with fantastic Bath city views from beautiful gardens *(Paul and Jane Davis)*; [Lansdown Road] *Olde Farmhouse*: wide range of beers in an atmosphere dedicated to appreciating them; no frills in small pub with some live jazz *(Dr A K Clarke, David Symes)*

BISHOP SUTTON [ST5859], *Red Lion*: true country pub with good beer, cider and some food; quiet and welcoming; fair-sized garden *(Mark Spurlock)*

BISHOPS LYDEARD [ST1629], *Rose Cottage*: cosy small-roomed pub/restaurant with good home-made food including unusual ice creams; closed Sunday and Monday; open for coffee from 10.30am *(TPA, PLC, BB)*

BISHOPS WOOD [ST2512], *Candlelight*: friendly, warm pub with wide choice of real ales and good value meals in oak-beamed dining-room *(Anon)*

BITTON [ST6869], *White Hart*: friendly atmosphere in large, neat comfortable old village pub with well kept Courage Directors, good food in bar and restaurant and efficient service *(M Wilcox, G Mellins, K R Harris)*

BLACKFORD [ST4147], *Sexeys Arms*: old-fashioned welcoming pub with good bar food, imaginative meals in dining-room and substantial Sunday lunch; children welcome *(Jon Collinson)*

BLAGDON [ST2118], *Live & Let Live*: small and cosy village pub, friendly, generous helpings of good food, well kept beer *(Stanford Cole)*

BRENDON HILLS [SS0434], *Ralegh's Cross*: isolated high inn with views to Wales on clear days; roomy bar, open fires, well kept Golden Hill Exmoor real ale; family room, bar food and restaurant with good service; spacious lawns; bedrooms *(Phyllis Deane, Derrick Turner)*

BREWHAM [ST7136], *Bull*: wide choice of quickly served food *(S V Bishop)*

BRIDGE YATE [ST6873], *Griffin*: interesting wall decorations and well kept beer in big open-plan pub *(Dr A K Clarke)*

BRISTOL [Stapleton Road; ST5872], *Armoury*: good lunchtime food, well kept real ale, and service with a smile, in interesting bar with suit of armour and low beams *(K J Alderman)*; [Henbury Road] *Blaise*: handy for the picturesque cottages of Blaise hamlet designed by Nash and Repton, and for the parkland of Blaise estate; Courage beers *(LYM, Mark Spurlock)*; [Prince Street] *Bristol Clipper*: good food and real ale in friendly old-world Berni Inn with interesting seafaring atmosphere and old oak furniture *(KC, Mark Spurlock)*; [Pembroke

Road] *Channings Hotel*: fair-sized hotel with two good bars and friendly staff; nice spacious lawn with fishpond; bedrooms *(Mark Spurlock)*; [Baltic Wharf, Cumberland Road] *Cottage*: recently excellently refurbished; good range of hot and cold food, Wadworths 6X; tables on wharf *(Aubrey Saunders)*; [Cotham Hill] *Crockers*: lively redecorated lower bar with soothing lighting, comfy seats, good juke box, food, Courage real ales; nice quiet upstairs bar *(Mark Spurlock)*; [Longwell Green] *Crown*: comfortably refurbished, nice atmosphere *(Dr A K Clarke)*; [Pill Road] *George*: warm and welcoming, great for Sunday lunchtime *(Mark Spurlock)*; [Clifton] *Greyhound*: food good and landlord friendly in small, dark old pub *(Richard Franck, Richard Gibbs)*; [King Street] *Jolly Cobblers*: good choice of beer including Theakstons Best *(Mark Spurlock)*; [Kingsdown Parade] *Kingsdown Vaults*: friendly pub with well kept beer and nice range of lunchtime rolls; attractively furnished *(Mark Spurlock)*; [off King Street/Welsh Back] *Llandoger Trow*: very old pub (now Berni Inn) by canal, with maritime connections: R L Stevenson based the *Treasure Island* Spyglass on it, and Defoe met Selkirk (model for Crusoe) here; brasses, photos and pictures; several bars and eating areas, real ales *(Martyn Quinn)*; [Broad Street] *Malt & Hops*: one of the city's most popular real ale pubs, serving a good choice of beer including Wadworths 6X *(David Symes, D A Lloyd)*; [Lower Guinea Street] *Ostrich*: friendly Courage pub with bar food and dockside terrace where round-the-harbour ferry stops *(Richard Gibbs, LYM)*; [Park Place, Clifton; ST5773], *Quinton House*: food at lunchtime good in this small pub *(Dr A K Clarke)*; [Whiteladies Road, Clifton] *Vittoria*: architecturally interesting, lively and unpretentious, with warmly welcoming and friendly licensees serving well kept beer, and good winter specials *(Dr A K Clarke, David Surridge)*; [next to coach station] *White Hart*: historic (dates from 1672) and friendly, with one bar and different rooms, piped music, meals *(Martyn Quinn)*

BRUTON [High Street; ST6834], *Castle*: excellent ploughman's and steaming stew, wide range of real ales served by knowledgeable efficient barman, pleasant décor, well behaved Alsatian in cosy pub run by former Tiller Girl *(Anne Morris, Dr A K Clarke)*

CATCOTT [ST3939], *King William*: popular old free house with Wadworths and draught cider, and good range of food *(C Elliott)*

CHIPPING SODBURY [High Street; ST7282], *Grapes*: delightful architecturally interesting pub with good beer and friendly staff *(Dr A K Clarke)*

CHURCHILL [Skinners Lane; ST4560], *Crown*: simple food in quaint cottagey pub with excellent choice of real ales under new licensees *(A C Reed, Steve and Carolyn Harvey)*

CLAPTON-IN-GORDANO [ST4773], *Black Horse*: friendly and unspoilt flagstoned country house serving Courage beers and range of mainly cold snacks; horse brasses, various agricultural nick-nacks, settles and solid old benches and tables; separate games/children's room; nice views (for pub location see OS Sheet 172 reference 473739) *(J G Dapling, Steve and Carolyn Harvey)*

CLUTTON [ST6259], *Warwick Arms*: nice, upgraded roadside pub with extensive lunch bar *(Dr A K Clarke)*

COMBE FLOREY [ST1531], *Farmers Arms*: well kept country pub in tiny cluster of houses; being rebuilt after thatch fire in early 1985 *(Donald Mather, BB)*

COMBE HAY [ST7359], *Wheatsheaf*: good food and well kept Courage Directors served by friendly staff in pleasant village pub; big garden in delightful hillside position *(A G Neale, Jon Collinson, Nick Dowson, Alison Hayward)*

COMPTON MARTIN [ST5457], *Ring o' Bells*: fairly large roadside pub with big garden; good beer *(Dr A K Clarke)*

CONGRESBURY [Wrington Road; ST4363], *White Hart & Inwood*: friendly service, family facilities and good food *(Duncan Collins)*

CREECH HEATHFIELD [ST2827], *Crown*: attractive seventeenth-century thatched pub with pleasant atmosphere; food, Ushers beers, restaurant, skittle alley, children's play area *(John Poole)*

CROSCOMBE [ST5844], *Bull Terrier*: village pub recommended for enterprising choice of real ales and good lunches *(David Symes)*

nr DOULTING [Chelynch; ST6443], *Poacher's Pocket*: generous helpings of home-cooked food in charming country pub, with well kept real ales; closed Monday lunchtime *(PC)*

DOYNTON [ST7173], *Cross House*: pleasant garden; good food and excellent service *(JER)*

DUNSTER [SS9943], *Luttrell Arms*: comfortable THF hotel in interesting and historic stone building with attractive timbered back bar, and friendly staff serving good value food and well kept Devenish Wessex or Golden Hill Exmoor; sheltered flagstone courtyard, good restaurant dinners; comfortable bedrooms *(David and Ruth Hollands, W A Rinaldi-Butcher, LYM)*

EAST HARPTREE [ST5655], *Waldegrave Arms*: generous home-cooked food, outstanding, good value wine, in well kept pub full of little nooks and crannies; family room *(Commander A R C Rowe, Dr A K Clarke)*

EAST LAMBROOK [ST4318], *Rose & Crown*: well kept beer in friendly, cheerful pub *(J Edwards)*

EVERCREECH [Evercreech Junction; ST6438], *Natterjack*: good value food in bar and restaurant of comfortable and friendly country pub *(Tony Cullen)*; *Pecking Mill*: low-ceilinged stone-walled pub with ornate solid-fuel stove, long-barrelled rifles and harness decorating walls; Flowers real ale, and food in bar and restaurant; seats outside *(BB)*

EXFORD [SS8538], *Crown*: good food, local beers and cider in nice bar with pine furniture and log fire; separate from hotel (which has bedrooms) *(Heather Sharland)*; *White Horse*: three-storey Exmoor village hotel with well kept Courage real ales and log fire in traditional tiled-floor partly panelled public bar; bedrooms *(BB)*

FALFIELD [ST6893], *Huntsman House*: quiet pub with pleasant shaded garden, play area, and food; near petrol station useful for M5 refuelling *(Margo and Peter Thomas)*

FROME [Market Place; ST7747], *Angel*: small town pub with friendly landlord, lively clientele, and well kept beer; architecturally quite interesting *(Dr A K Clarke)*

HANHAM [High Street; ST6472], *Blue Bowl*: old pub with Civil War connections, well refurbished; real ale tapped from the cask by friendly staff *(Dr A K Clarke)*; [Hanham Mill] *Chequers*: pleasant and popular, by river; Websters Yorkshire and other real ales, and good value food *(Graham Andrews)*; [High Street] *Jolly Sailor*: well kept town pub with good beer and friendly atmosphere *(Dr A K Clarke)*

HARDINGTON MANDEVILLE [ST5111], *Mandeville Arms*: local beer (used to be brewed on the premises) and bar food in friendly, comfortable country pub *(Roy McIsaac, LYM, Mr and Mrs F W Sturch)*

HARDWAY [ST7134], *Bull*: impressive choice of bar food, Wadworths 6X and farm cider; restaurant open Wednesday/Saturday evenings and Sunday lunchtime *(S V Bishop)*

HATCH BEAUCHAMP [ST3220], *Hatch*: polished carpeted lounge bar with lots of copper and brass, nice seats in bow window; Bass and a choice of ciders; pool-room behind yard *(S G Palmer, BB)*

HILLESLEY [ST7689], *Fleece*: food good, and fair choice of real ales, in pleasant comfortable country pub with many interesting photos and collection of taps *(Steve and Carolyn Harvey, J A Johnson)*

HINTON BLEWITT [ST5957], *Ring o' Bells*: well kept Wadworths Farmers Glory, 6X and (in winter) Old Timer in welcoming little pub with log fire, good value food and separate restaurant; small terrace *(Steve and Carolyn Harvey, Dr A K Clarke)*

HINTON CHARTERHOUSE [ST7758], *Stag*: attactively furnished ancient pub with good range of well kept real ales, often enterprising freshly cooked food, and warm open fire *(Herbert and Mary Gutfreund, Wyndham Westerdale, LYM)*

HINTON DYRHAM [ST7376], *Bull*: pleasantly modernised stone-and-beams pub, with open fire in winter; Wadworths real ale, good value food; nice village atmosphere *(Stephen Best, Dr A K Clarke)*

HINTON ST GEORGE [ST4212], *Poulet Arms*: good bar food in friendly, roomy and comfortable pub with efficient service; handy for Scotts of Merriott nurseries *(Mrs R Wilson)*

ILMINSTER [ST3614], *Shrubbery*: comfortable hotel with real ale and good bar food; bedrooms *(J P Berryman)*

IRON ACTON [ST6884], *Lamb*: simple old seventeenth-century pub, with Whitbreads real ales; has had occasional folk nights *(Steve and Carolyn Harvey)*; *White Hart*: food recommended for specialities cooked in wood-fired clay oven; well kept Courage Best and Directors *(Tony Gayfer)*

KEINTON MANDEVILLE [ST5430], *Quarry*: biggish village pub tastefully refurbished, with pleasant garden; skittle alley *(Dr A K Clarke)*

KEYNSHAM [Bitton Road; ST6568], *Lock Keeper*: welcoming landlord, good value bar food, well kept Courage Best and Directors, small upstairs restaurant; attractive big riverside garden, children's playroom *(M J R Woodyer)*; [Temple Street] *Ship*: friendly pub with remarkably nice public bar – better than many saloon bars – and well kept beer *(Dr A K Clarke)*

KILMERSDON [ST6952], *Jolliffe Arms*: fine old pub with antique furnishings in sixteenth-century bar, with old court room above; well kept Benskins, Manns and Ushers, and careful home cooking; skittle alley, bedrooms *(R S Varney)*

KNAPP [ST2925], *Rising Sun*: good value traditional Sunday lunch, especially for families; well kept real ale and reasonably priced wine *(G F Scott)*

LEIGH-ON-MENDIP [ST6847], *Bell*: choice of bar food in free house with two log fires in bar; restaurant, skittle alley *(Jack Rayfield)*; *Lamb*: food good and nice atmosphere in attractive pub, helpful with children; quiet village with nice church *(Dr N Hall)*

LIMPLEY STOKE [Woods Hill; ST7860], *Hop Pole*: interesting old pub with warm and cosy panelling, small cheerful beamed public bar, elegant sedate lounge, cheerful service, good value food; garden *(Dr A K Clarke, Gordon and Daphne, Brian Barefoot, F A Noble)*; *Limpley Stoke Hotel*: grand-style hotel with huge bar and wonderful views over Avon valley; bedrooms *(Dr A K Clarke)*

LITTLETON-ON-SEVERNY[ST5990], *White Hart*: large sixteenth-century ex-farm with good food, interesting choice of real ales, open fire, and pleasant atmosphere; restaurant, tables outside *(G G Strange, S K Best)*

LITTON [ST5954], *Olde Kings Arms*: friendly welcome and good choice of real ales, tasty food, in extended old pub with garden; can get crowded *(Dr A K Clarke, Paul A Smith, G G Strange)*

LYDFORD ON FOSSE [ST5531], *Cross Keys*: friendly landlord who understands real ale, in interesting pub *(Dr A K Clarke)*

MARK [ST3747], *White Horse*: clean and friendly pub with good value straightforward bar food (especially home-made soup) and well kept Flowers Original *(Iain C Baillie, W F Coghill)*

MARSHFIELD [ST7773], *Crown*: quaint updated pub with seats outside in nice little courtyard *(Dr A K Clarke)*; *Lord Nelson*: good beer and service, with friendly, cosy atmosphere *(JER)*

MARTOCK [Church Street; ST4619], *George*: good value food, pleasant lounge, and helpful staff; easy access for the disabled *(Sue Mutton, Anne Garton)*

MELLS [ST7249], *Talbot*: friendly atmosphere, good food and real ale in delightful coaching-inn *(R H Inns)*

MONKTON COMBE [ST7762], *Wheelwrights Arms*: very old inn with pretty hanging baskets; good value comfortable small bedrooms with enjoyable breakfast *(Mrs J Fordham)*

MONTACUTE [ST4916], *Phelips Arms*: decent choice of real ales in simple and friendly pub with attractive secluded back garden *(BB)*

NORTH BREWHAM [ST7236], *Old Red Lion*: good food in simple flagstoned pub (shut Monday) *(Anon)*

NORTH PERROTT [ST4709], *Manor Arms*: welcoming landlord creates lots of atmosphere, also good value snacks, in old village pub *(David Gaunt)*

NORTH PETHERTON [ST2932], *Walnut Tree*: good value bar food and Wadworths 6X, also restaurant and motel bedrooms; handy for M5 junction 24 *(K R Harris)*

NUNNEY [ST7345], *George*: appetising food in old inn opposite moated ruins in picturesque village; bedrooms *(Anon)*

OLD DOWN [ST6187], *Fox*: homely free house with log fires and nice watercolours of pub and local buildings; Bass, Davenports and Flowers real ales, filled rolls, darts – probably two cottages knocked into one *(Steve and Carolyn Harvey)*

OLD SODBURY [ST7581], *Cross Hands*: comfortably done-up inn where The Queen took refuge from the 1981 blizzard; real ales, two restaurants, handy for M4 junction 18; bedrooms *(LYM)*

OLDBURY-ON-SEVERN [ST6292], *Ship*: friendly Turkey-carpeted long bar with two open fires, well kept Courage ales and bar food; piped music, skittle alley, children's play area *(Jenny Woolf, BB)*

OLVESTON [ST6088], *White Hart*: sandwiches, ploughman's and other food in carefully modernised and cleanly kept old pub with stripped stone walls, beams and skittle alley *(BB)*

PANBOROUGH [ST4745], *Panborough Inn*: comfortably refurbished pub with well kept Wadworths IPA, Devizes, 6X and Old Timer *(David Symes)*

PILNING [ST5585], *Plough*: cosy and comfortable in pleasant countryside, with Wadworths real ales including Old Timer, and reasonably priced bar food *(Stephen Best)*

PRIDDY [ST5251], *Queen Victoria*: unfussy without being spartan and cosy without being plush; good range of real ales *(David Symes)*

RADSTOCK [Frome Road; ST6954], *Fromeway*: enjoyable free house incorporating a butcher's shop; well kept beer, friendly staff, interesting old local photos, cosy brown lounge *(Dr A K Clarke)*

RIDGEHILL [ST5462], *Crown*: good food in bar and restaurant; log fires, picture window overlooking countryside, well kept Wadworths real ales; small back garden *(Steve and Carolyn Harvey)*

SEAVINGTON ST MICHAEL [ST4015], *Volunteer*: warm welcome in sixteenth-century posting-inn/cider house with Badger and Websters Yorkshire, also lots of scrumpy; home-cooked food using local produce *(Gwen and Peter Andrews)*

SHEPTON MALLET [Leg Square; ST6243], *Kings Arms*: food, nice beer and lots of games in this low-ceilinged multi-roomed pub near the prison *(Dr A K Clarke)*

SHEPTON MONTAGUE [ST6731], *Montague*: remarkably friendly refurbished pub; books for sale *(Dr A K Clarke)*

SOMERTON [ST4828], *Globe*: friendly atmosphere in attractive building with wide range of food; well kept Bass and Taunton traditional cider *(William Plowden)*

SOUTH STOKE [ST7461], *Pack Horse*: very traditional and unspoilt fifteenth-century farmers' pub with choice of farm ciders; cheap well kept Courage ales, rolls, pies and ploughman's; shove-ha'penny, nice back garden; a real bit of heritage *(Nick Dowson, Alison Hayward, Dr J Livesey)*

STANTON DREW [ST5963], *Druids Arms*: very friendly, in interesting village – gets its name from stone circles here *(Dr A K Clarke, Mark Spurlock)*

STANTON WICK [ST6162], *Carpenters Arms*: serve-yourself food and excellent restaurant are the main attractions in this picturesque pub, which can be crowded at weekends *(Commander A R C Rowe, Dr A K Clarke, Paul A Smith)*

STOCK [Common Road; ST4562], *Bakers Arms*: good value bar food and separate restaurant in popular single-bar timbered pub with warmly welcoming service, and well kept Trumans; pleasant garden *(Peter Andrews)*

TOCKINGTON [ST6186], *Swan*: food good in big pub with open fire and pleasant atmosphere; Courage real ales; tables outside *(S K Best)*

TOLLDOWN [ST7577], *Crown*: well kept Wadworths real ale and lunchtime bar food in heavy-beamed bar with old-fashioned furnishings and log fire; stone-built pub, handy for M4 junction 18 *(Dr A K Clarke, LYM)*

TYTHERINGTON [ST6688], *Swan*: clean, warm and comfortable with pleasant service, wholesome, inexpensive food, and real ale *(J A Johnson)*

WEDMORE [ST4347], *George*: traditional furnishings in stripped-stone bar of rambling coaching-inn with real ale and bar food; lively bar popular with local young farmers; sheltered lawn; helpful with children; bedrooms *(Nick and Yvonne Mawby, LYM)*

WELLINGTON [High Street; ST1320], *Eight Bells*: range of home-cooked food,

Ushers real ales, friendly service; near M5 *(K R Harris)*

WELLOW [ST7458], *Fox & Badger*: tables outside in pleasant courtyard – surrounding village is pretty; flagstoned lounge with open fire; was full entry in previous edition for charming décor and atmosphere, but now under new management *(Up-to-date reports please)*

WELLS [St Stevens Street; ST5545], *Fountain*: wide choice of nice bar food, with local cider and well kept Courage Directors; pleasant atmosphere, lots of tourists and locals; shove-ha'penny popular *(Ian Blackwell)*; [High Street] *King Charles*: small hotel bar, usually quite quiet; well kept Royal Oak, Butcombe and Wadworths 6X *(David Symes)*; [High Street] *Star*: small quiet and comfortable back bar in sixteenth-century coaching-inn, with well kept Wadworths 6X, IPA, Devizes and Old Timer; good lunches *(David Symes)*

WEST COKER [ST5113], *Castle*: friendly licensees, real home cooking, good range of cheap food *(Jack Rayfield)*

WEST HUNTSPILL [ST3044], *Crossways*: seventeenth-century free house with choice of well kept real ales and cheap uncomplicated home-made food – especially main courses; friendly and unpretentious, large garden; bedrooms *(David Regan, W F Coghill)*

WEST PENNARD [ST5438], *Apple Tree*: good food, clean and cosy; quick cheerful service even when busy *(A J Lloyd)*

WESTPORT [ST3819], *Barn Owl*: food generally good and generous, with well kept Devenish Wessex, in well run transformed pub (used to be the Clarence) *(J E F Rawlins, PLC)*

WIDCOME [ST2216], *Holman Clavel*: comfortably modernised Whitbreads pub named after its holly chimney-beam; bar food and restaurant; handy for Blackdown Hills and Widcome Bird Garden (for pub location see OS Sheet 193 reference 222160) *(BB)*

WINFORD [High Street; ST5365], *Prince of Waterloo*: straightforward pub with log fire and flagstones, cosier lounge beyond wooden partition; Courage ale, sandwiches; darts and fruit machine *(Stephen and Carolyn Harvey)*

WOOKEY [ST5145], *Burcott*: attractive and comfortable fresh-feeling pub, can be quite busy; bar food, blazing winter fire, well kept real ales including Butcombe *(Dr A K Clarke, David Symes)*

WRANTAGE [ST3022], *Wheelwrights Arms*: choice of food with excellent sandwiches, helpful landlord; good fires, nice atmosphere and plenty of room even when busy *(P H Wainman)*

WRINGTON [High Street; ST4662], *Plough*: pleasant service and wide choice of bar food (much home made) in comfortable Courage pub with separate restaurant *(Steve and Carolyn Harvey)*; *White Hart*: fair choice of real ales and lots of farm tools in pub with quite separate food bar and big garden *(Steve and Carolyn Harvey)*

YEOVIL [Wine Street; ST5516], *Hole in the Wall*: friendly town pub with exceptional landlady *(Dr A K Clarke)*; *Wine Vaults*: popular neat town pub with well kept Bass and rather winebar-like décor *(K P Doyle, LYM)*

Staffordshire *see* Derbyshire

Suffolk

This county's best pubs are often in fine surroundings, such as the White Horse at Badingham (with its own bowling green), the unfussy Eels Foot at Eastbridge (in splendid walking country near the Minsmere bird reserve – good simple food), the neatly kept old Red Lion at Icklingham (close to a nature reserve and country park), the Bull in Long Melford (a distinguished Tudor inn with good food, in a lovely village), the Volunteer within sight of the pretty windmill at Saxtead Green (good value food), and the stylish and very civilised old timbered Swan – itself one of the most attractive buildings in the historic village of Lavenham, and awarded a special merit star this year. Waterside pubs include the Butt & Oyster at the old Pin Mill barge quay near Chelmondiston, the Ferry Boat at Felixstowe Ferry, the small-roomed Jolly Sailor, a smugglers' inn at Orford, the Ramsholt Arms in its lovely isolated position on the River Deben at Ramsholt, and the Harbour, a fisherman's haunt in Southwold. The distinguished old White Hart looking down on the waterside marshes at Blythburgh has good food, the old-fashioned Ship (under new owners who are making the most of its garden) is

The Swan, Hoxne

*just a short stroll from the sea in the curious sinking village of
Dunwich, as is the low-ceilinged Cross Keys in Aldeburgh,
and the bedrooms in the cosy old Bell at Walberswick
overlook the water. Pubs of considerable character include
particularly the Kings Head at Laxfield, with old fashioned
table service, traditional furnishings, and its own bowling
green, the unspoilt Ship in Blaxhall, the Tudor Crown looking
down the market place in Framlingham (a pleasant place to
stay), the Elizabethan Swan at Hoxne, the White Horse at
Sibton (an old-fashioned bar with a minstrels' gallery), the
carefully refurbished Crown in Great Glemham and the
creaky-bedroomed Kings Head in Orford – all these have
good food, though it's often simple. The Golden Key at Snape
is perhaps the best pub for food in the county, and other pubs
combining good food with friendly service include the Fleece
at Boxford (Italian cooking in a very English old pub), the
elegantly restored Peacock in Chelsworth (winter weekend
spit-roasts – a nice place to stay), the Crown at Great
Glemham (friendly new owners, another nice place to stay),
the Seafarer at Clare (for seafood), and the simple Plough at
Sutton (especially good curry; pleasantly redecorated this
year). Particularly promising Lucky Dips at the end of the
chapter include the White Horse at Easton (for food), the
White Hart in Newmarket (under good new management),
the Red Lion in Southwold (good all round), the stylish
Crown at Stoke-by-Nayland (excellent food, especially in its
restaurant), the Brook at Washbrook (good food in attractive
surroundings) and the Bell at Kersey (it's been compared to
the Peacock at Chelsworth). The Crown at Westleton has
been one of the most admired pubs in the area, but just as we
went to press we heard from the licensee (who made its food
so popular with his fishing expeditions in his own boat) that
he plans to leave it and return to the sea. Prices in the area are
in general rather low.*

ALDEBURGH   TM4656   Map 5
Cross Keys

Crabbe Street

By tradition this sixteenth-century pub used to stay open whenever
the lifeboat was out, and the back gravel courtyard, with wooden
seats and tables, opens directly on to the promenade and shingle
beach, with the lifeboat station close by. Inside, nineteenth-century
sailing prints decorate the walls of the two communicating rooms,
which are divided by a sturdy central chimney – a log fire on one side,
solid-fuel stove on the other. There's a pleasant local atmosphere,
even when summer visitors are crowding out other pubs in the town,
and furnishings include some settles as well as Windsor chairs and
traditional wall benches. Bar food changes daily and might typically

include ploughman's with Cheddar (£1.40) or Stilton (£1.75), avocado pear with prawns (£1.50), home-made pâté (£1.90), honey-roast gammon (£3), king prawns with garlic mayonnaise (£3.25) and local crab salad (£3.75). Well kept Adnams on handpump, with Old Ale in winter; darts, shove-ha'penny, dominoes, cribbage and a fruit machine. *(Recommended by Tony Gayfer, George Hughes, Heather and Roy Sharland)*

Adnams · Licensees Peter and Jenny Cresdee · Real ale · Meals and snacks (not Sun evening) · Open 11–2.30, 6.30–11 all year

BADINGHAM TM3068 Map 5
White Horse

A1120

This old-fashioned and well run pub has its own bowling green. The main bar has cushioned settles as well as rustic tables and stools, copper brewing equipment hanging over the big fireplace, and a snug little alcove by the serving bar with an aquarium and a grandfather clock. The friendly Kitchen Bar, furnished with high-backed curved settles and a little window seat, has darts, shove-ha'penny, dominoes, nine men's morris and indoor quoits. Bar food includes home-made soup (50p), sandwiches (from 60p, toasties from 70p), giant sausages with chips, lasagne, cannelloni, scampi and pizzas (under £2), a lunchtime cold buffet in summer and daily specials such as moussaka, goujons of salmon and goulash (£2), and (in winter) steak and kidney pie (£2.25); vegetarian dishes (£2.25) and a children's menu (50p–£1); also a separate restaurant. Well kept Adnams on handpump; maybe piped music. There are tables on a terrace by the vines trained up the front of the house, and more on a roadside green. There are seats also in the rambling garden beyond the bowling green with swings and a climbing-frame among its trees. *(Recommended by Eric Walmsley; more reports please)*

Adnams · Licensee Ian Robertson-Peek · Real ale · Meals and snacks · Children in restaurant · Open 11–2.30, 7–11 all year

BLAXHALL TM3657 Map 5
Ship

This is George Ewart Evans' village, and in the public bar of this early eighteenth-century house you can listen to the old men who've lived round here all their lives singing old traditional Suffolk songs. There are low beams, antique high-backed settles on its red tiles, a log fire, local notices on the cream walls and plenty of local regulars; darts, pool, shove-ha'penny, dominoes, cribbage and parlour quoits. Generously served bar food includes soup or cheese sandwiches (40p), beefburgers (from 50p), sausage, egg and chips (£1), basket meals (£1.50–£1.75) and steaks from £5.25; well kept Tolly Bitter and Mild on handpump. The cosy wallpapered lounge has spindleback chairs around the neat tables on its carpet. There are seats on the front terrace, and a caravan used as a children's playroom in the back garden. *(Recommended by Eric Walmsley)*

Tolly · Licensees Jim and Sue Grubbs · Real ale · Meals and snacks (not Mon)
Traditional folk music every bank hol Mon lunchtime · Open 11–3, 6–11 all
year (opens 7 in winter); closed evening 25 Dec · Two bedrooms tel Snape
(072 888) 316; £10/£20, also a tent campsite

BLYFORD   TM4277   Map 6
Queen's Head
B1123

There are seats on the grass outside this popular and friendly
fifteenth-century house, opposite the small village church. The bar
has low oak beams, heavy wooden tables and stools, some antique
settles as well as the benches built in to its cream walls, and a huge
fireplace with attractive brickwork. The new landlord does home-
made bar food which includes sandwiches, scampi (£2.50), chicken
(£2.65), salads (£2.95–£3.95), gammon (£3.25), rump steak (£4.95)
and dishes of the day such as beef Stroganoff, paella, pies, moussaka
and chilli con carne, with winter stews (£2.50–£3.20). Well kept
Adnams on handpump; dominoes, maybe piped music. *(Recommended*
by Jamie Allan; more reports please)

Adnams · Licensee John Hales · Real ale · Snacks and meals · Children's room
Open 10.30–2.30, 6–11 all year (opens 7 in winter)

BLYTHBURGH   TM4575   Map 5
White Hart
A12

There has been a building on this spot above the marshes for over 800
years, originally an ecclesiastical courthouse for the priory here, but
an inn since at least 1548 (serving the drovers bringing sheep to
auction outside). There's a fine Stuart staircase and Elizabethan
woodwork as well as some lovely carved oak beams. The open-plan
L-shaped bar has log fires at either end and cushioned benches
around its dark oak tables. Bar food includes tasty home-made pies,
ploughman's, a good salad buffet (£2–£3.50) with a choice of several
cold meats, a hot bar lunch, including steaks (from £4). Much the
same sort of thing is also served in the evening, when you can also
have a three-course dinner in the separate restaurant, with game, fish
and so forth, from £7. The Adnams Bitter and Mild on handpump,
and in winter Old Ale too, are well kept. If you want a table in
summer, turn up early. The spacious lawn behind has an aviary with
canaries and oriental pheasants; ducks and fowls run free and there is
a dovecot as well. The marshy flats beyond stretch along the River
Blyth; there's a right of way from the pub along the drily earthed-up
river bank. The church down the lane on the other side of the main
road is one of East Anglia's grandest. *(Recommended by John Townsend,*
Eric Walmsley; more reports please)

Adnams · Licensee Peter Wickham · Real ale · Meals and snacks · Children in
restaurant · Open 10.30–2.30, 6–11 all year

All *Guide* inspections are anonymous. Anyone claiming to be a *Good Pub Guide*
inspector is a fraud, and should be reported to us with a name and description.

BOXFORD   TL9640 Map 5
Fleece

Broad Street

This welcoming pub is especially popular for its imaginative Italian home cooking. As well as sandwiches and pâté (£1.50), food includes spaghetti or tagliatelle bolognese (from £2), fish soup or tagliatelle with mushroom sauce (£2.25) and lasagne (£2.50), both highly praised, filled pancake (£2.75), fresh sardines alla nizzarda (£3), haddock San Remo or escalope of chicken milanese (£3.80), scallops al peperoni (£6) and sirloin steak (£6.25); puddings include Italian ice creams and sorbets (80p). Main dishes are served in a partly partitioned-off dining area; booking is advisable for Friday or Saturday evening. Tolly Original tapped from the cask. The main bar is an attractive and old-fashioned room with regulars' polished tankards hanging above the bar counter, small flowery-cushioned easy chairs by traditional pub tables, a big solid-fuel stove, and game bird pictures on the ochre walls. The smaller Corders' Bar has some handsome panelling that came from the village church (which has a tablet to the memory of a woman whose death in 1746 was brought on by a fall – at the age of 113). Darts, piped music. *(Recommended by A Saunders, Melvin D Buckner)*

Tolly Cobbold · Licensees Franco and Jane Crocco · Real ale · Meals—tel Boxford (0787) 210247—and snacks · Children in eating area · Open 12—2.30, 7—11 all year; closed evening 25 Dec

BRANDESTON   TM2460 Map 5
Queens Head

Towards Earl Soham

This friendly and well run country pub has a spacious open-plan bar divided into separate alcoves by the stubs of surviving walls; old pews, panelled walls and brown leather banquettes are built around them. Bar food is home made and good value: sandwiches, prawns (£1), cottage pie or cheesy banger (£1.40), various quiches (£1.65), lasagne (£1.70), curry (£1.80), barbecue chicken (£2) and salads (from £2.20). Well kept Adnams Bitter tapped from the cask; darts, shove-ha'penny, dominoes, cribbage, a fruit machine, faint piped music, and (in a separate family room) pool and table skittles. There's a big garden with tables on neatly kept grass among roses, and there is a climbing-frame and slide. The inn has a campsite behind. There is a nine-hole golf course a couple of miles away, and you can visit a nearby vineyard. *(Recommended by Aubrey Saunders, Eric Walmsley, Dave Hoy, Ron Salmon, J C Kemp)*

Adnams · Licensees Ray and Myra Bumstead · Real ale · Meals and snacks Children in family room · Open 11—2, 5.30—11 all year · Bedrooms tel Earl Soham (072 882) 307; £8.50/£17

Children welcome means the pub says it lets children inside without any special restriction. If it allows them in, but to restricted areas such as an eating area or family room, we specify this. Places with separate restaurants usually let children use them, and hotels usually let them into public areas such as lounges.

nr CHELMONDISTON   TM2037 Map 5

Butt & Oyster   [*illustrated on page 600*]

There's a fine view of the big ships coming down the river from
Ipswich from the seats in the big bay window of the main bar (and in
the separate dining-room), and it's interesting to see the long lines of
retired black barges moored outside this old bargemen's pub. There
are high-backed and other old-fashioned settles on the tiled floor in
this half-panelled room which is decorated with model sailing ships.
Bar food is good and generously served and includes sandwiches,
ploughman's with a choice of granary or crusty white bread (£1.20),
a selection of salads (£2.20), home-made pies and quiches (£2.45),
changing home-made hot dishes such as casseroles (even jugged hare)
or steak and kidney pie (£2.75), giant prawns in garlic butter (£2.85),
and chicken fillets, turkey kebabs, plaice, seafood platter and so
forth; Tolly Bitter, Original and Mild are tapped from casks behind
the serving counter; shove-ha'penny, table skittles, dominoes and
cribbage. A small smoke-room has an interesting carving over its
mantelpiece of a man and a woman. (*Recommended by Commander and
Mrs E St Leger Moore, G A Wright, George Hughes*)

*Tolly Cobbold · Licensees Dick and Brenda Mainwaring · Real ale · Meals and
snacks · Children in dining area and smoke-room · Open 11–2.30, 5–11 all
year (opens 6.30 in winter)*

The Bell, Clare

CHELSWORTH TL9848 Map 5

Peacock ★

The Street; B1115

This fine old village inn, elegantly restored, has a big log fire in winter, when a rib of beef is spit-roasted on Saturday evenings and eaten at Sunday lunchtime. The large beamed bar is divided into several areas by a partly open timbered partition and its splendid stone inglenook fireplace. Other bar food includes home-made soup (90p), sandwiches (from 80p), beefburger (90p), a choice of cheese, ham or pâté ploughman's (£1.45), chicken or chicken curry (£2.75), salads (from £2.75), scallops (£3.10), steaks (from £5.35) and a good cold buffet in summer as well as daily specials such as home-made pies or lasagne (they also do afternoon teas). Some apparently Tudor brickwork has been exposed in the cosy inner lounge and the walls are decorated with local paintings for sale (there is a craft shop behind the garden). Well kept Adnams, Greene King IPA and Abbot and Mauldons on handpump; darts, cribbage and well reproduced rock music. The bedrooms have been praised for their old-fashioned comfort; a nice place to stay, with the rich parkland of Chelsworth Hall just over the bridge. (Recommended by D A Angless, Gwen and Peter Andrews)

Free house · Licensees Lorna and Tony Marsh · Real ale · Meals and snacks Children in eating area · Piano player on Fri and Sun evenings · Open 11–2.30, 6–11 all year · Bedrooms tel Bildeston (0449) 740758; £13.50/£27

CLARE TL7645 Map 5

Bell [illustrated on page 589]

This small hotel in the market place is an attractive timbered building, and the friendly lounge bar rambles around under splendidly carved black beams; small dark green leatherette armchairs sit on its red carpet, and there's panelling and woodwork around the open fire and local notices on the hessian walls. Another room leads off, and to eat you go through to a tiled-floor room with masses of prints, mainly foxhunting, on its walls: food here includes soup (60p), sandwiches (from 70p), ploughman's (from £1.50), good clam fries (£1.50), home-cooked ham and eggs. (£1.95), salads (from £1.95), fresh haddock or home-made steak and kidney pie (both £2.25), chicken or home-made game pie (£2.50), scampi (£3.95) and steaks (from £3.50). Well kept Adnams, Greene King IPA, and Mauldons on handpump; dominoes and a fruit machine. There are some tables on a back terrace by the small, sheltered lawn; several other striking buildings in the village include the remains of the priory and the castle. (Recommended by J Mackay, W T Aird; more reports please)

Free house · Licensee Hugh Jones · Real ale · Meals and snacks · Children in eating room · Open 11–2.30, 5–11 all year · Bedrooms tel Clare (0787) 277430; £18 (£25B)/£26 (£38B)

Please tell us if the décor, atmosphere, food or drink at a pub is different from our description. We rely on readers' reports to keep us up to date. No stamp needed: The Good Pub Guide, FREEPOST, London SW10 0BR.

Seafarer

Nethergate Street; A1092, W end of town

Readers are as enthusiastic as ever about the seafood here: goujons of salmon (£1.90), crab claws or seafood chowder (£2), prawns (£2.50), tuna and sweetcorn pancake (£2.80), seafood salad (£4) and a mixed seafood bake (£5); other bar food includes sandwiches (from 50p), home-made soup (80p), ploughman's (£1.20), enchiladas (£2.20), lamb or chicken curry (£3) and steaks (£4.50). The neatly set tables and high-ceilinged airiness give the comfortable Fo'c's'le Bar something of a restaurant atmosphere, but darts in the spacious communicating side area – not to mention the well kept Adnams Bitter and Mild on handpump, dominoes, cribbage and a fruit machine – remind you that it's a proper pub. There is a side garden. *(Recommended by Melvin D Buckner)*

Free house · Licensee Ian Blanshard · Real ale · Meals and snacks · Children welcome · Open 11–2.30, 6.30–11 all year

CRETINGHAM   TM2260   Map 5
New Bell

The comfortably modernised lounge bar of this fifteenth-century pub still has the standing timbers of a knocked-through wall, exposed beams and a large old fireplace; there are some long pews, leatherette rustic seats and stools on the burnt-orange carpet. Bar food is good and reliable and includes plain or toasted sandwiches (from 55p, fillet steak sandwich £1.40), home-made soup (70p), home-made pâté (from 95p), ploughman's (£1.10), Suffolk sausages and chips (£1.35), Danish open sandwich (£1.75), scampi (£1.95), salmon goujons (£2.10) and seafood platter (£2.85). Beyond is a restaurant (open Wednesday to Saturday evenings, and for Sunday roast lunch). Adnams on handpump. The quarry-tiled public bar has darts, shove-ha'penny, dominoes and cribbage. There are rustic tables and seats on the grass in front, which is sheltered by the buff-washed tiled building, with more on another lawn by rose bushes and a fine old oak-tree on the corner. The local harriers meet here each New Year's Day. *(Recommended by Eric Walmsley)*

Free house · Licensees David Hooper and Charles Lingard · Real ale · Meals (lunchtime only) and snacks · Children in eating areas · Jazz Tues evening Open 10.30–2.30, 6.30–11 all year

DALHAM   TL7251   Map 5
Affleck Arms

B1085 E of Newmarket

Thatched, like many other houses here, this pink pub is set back from the road, behind a little stream where they have a few tables sheltered by a chestnut-tree. On the left is a cosy and low-beamed locals' bar with a good winter log fire; a very workmanlike flintlock gun adorns the handsome brick chimneypiece. Other rooms, with tables spaced well out on the red flowery carpet, ramble off to the right; popular –

with USAF airmen among others – as a comfortable and relaxing place to eat. Bar food includes soup (85p), ploughman's (£1.50), pizza (£1.80), salads (from £2.30), a range of omelettes (£2.50), pork chop (£3.20) and six-ounce sirloin steak or mixed grill (£5.15), with a choice of children's dishes (£1); a fruit machine, piped pop music. There is a candlelit restaurant. *(Recommended by Frank W Gadbois)*

Greene King · Licensee B W Hollis · Meals and snacks · Open 11.30–2.30, 6.30–11 all year

DUNWICH   TM4770 Map 5
Ship

This small and old-fashioned inn is relaxed and quiet at night when the day trippers have left this famous village, which for hundreds of years has been slowly slipping into the sea. The L-shaped bar has cushioned wall benches, pews and captain's chairs on its antique tiled floor, fire irons by the open fire in its brick hearth, and harness and scales on the walls below the dusky ochre ceiling. Well kept Adnams Bitter and Mild and Greene King Abbot on handpump at the handsomely panelled bar counter, with Old Ale in winter. Bar food, all home made, includes soup (60p), pâté or quiche (75p), ploughman's with Cheddar (£1.35) or Stilton (£1.55), salad platter (£1.50) and fresh local fish and chips (£2.30) at lunchtime, with home-cooked ham (£3.50), local fish fillets (£4), dressed crab and prawn salad (£5) and steak (£5.50) added in the evening, and puddings such as apple pie (75p); there is a separate restaurant. The public bar area has darts, dominoes, cribbage, a fruit machine, space game and piped music. New owners have taken the garden in hand and you can sit in the conservatory with its vine and jasmine-covered walls or outside on the back terrace, facing the tangle of honeysuckle by the path and an enormous fig-tree. *(Recommended by D and J W, Eric Walmsley)*

Free house · Licensees Stephen and Ann Marshlain · Real ale · Meals and snacks · Children in restaurant and special room · Open 11–2.30, 6.30–11 all year · Bedrooms tel Westleton (072 873) 219; £12/£24

EASTBRIDGE   TM4566 Map 5
Eels Foot

Off B1122; the narrow lanes E between Theberton and Leiston Abbey which lead here are now signposted

This friendly village pub gets its name indirectly from the tradition that the village priest managed to tie the devil up in his boot and fling it out to sea – as the original crude painting of this episode on the inn sign faded, people came to see it instead as a booted eel. It's a popular place for lunch and you can order your food from a stable-door hatch outside the kitchen and eat it on the quiet front terrace. It includes pizza and chips (£1.20), beefburger, sausage or salmon fishcakes (£1.40), meat pie (£1.65), plaice (£1.70), salads (from £1.70) and scampi with salad (£2.15), with sandwiches if there isn't a rush on; evening meals from Whitsun to end of September only. Well kept

Adnams on handpump, or a cheap cup of tea (they do coffee too). The upper part of the bar has a couple of handsome built-in antique arched cupboards and crisply varnished red leatherette seats on its bright carpet; down a step there are simpler wooden seats on lino; darts, dominoes, cribbage and a fruit machine. The pub is close to the Minsmere bird reserve and there is a good walk on the very long shingly beach towards Sizewell. *(Recommended by Dave Butler and Les Storey, Stephen Brough)*

Adnams · Licensee John Badger · Real ale · Meals and snacks (not Thurs evening) · Children in eating area · Open 10.30–2.30, 6–11 all year (opens 7 in winter); closed evening 25 Dec

FELIXSTOWE FERRY   TM3337 Map 5
Ferry Boat

This old pub, named after the Bawdsey ferry across the River Deben, is only a few moments' walk from the sand dunes and harbour; high sea defences shelter it (as well as a place selling fresh-landed fish cheaply). The big tiled public bar has low black beams, wooden wall benches well polished by years of use, and spotlessly attractive old wooden tables; the carpeted lounge, a step up, has more padded seats, and outside picnic-table sets are sheltered by a glass verandah. Bar food includes soup (70p), sandwiches (from 55p), cod's roe or smoked eel on toast (£1.40), ploughman's (from £1.40), salads (from £2.20 – crab £3.50) and a hot dish of the day (£2.20); well kept Tolly Bitter, Original and in winter Old Strong Ale tapped from casks behind the counter; darts, dominoes, cribbage. *(Recommended by Howard Gascoyne, Jeff Cousins)*

Tolly · Licensee Christopher Chambers · Real ale · Meals and snacks (lunchtime, not Sun) · Open 11–2.30, 6–11 all year

FRAMLINGHAM   TM2863 Map 5
Crown

Market Hill

What is now the comfortable lounge hall of this small black and white timbered Tudor inn once had coaches clattering through into a flagstoned courtyard – now very prettily planted. The cosy bar, opening off the hall, has an antique carved settle, dark green plush armed seats, a log fire, high heavy beams, and a window overlooking the unusual sloping triangular market place (market day is Saturday, when nearby parking may be difficult). Bar food includes a generous ploughman's; Adnams and Greene King Abbot on handpump. There is a separate restaurant. A friendly place to stay. *(Recommended by D S Marshall; more reports please)*

Free house (THF) · Licensees Mr and Mrs Robert Steen · Meals and snacks Children in lounge areas · Open 10.30–2, 5.30–11 all year · Bedrooms tel Framlingham (0728) 723521; £32 (£35B)/£42 (£52B)

Post Office address codings confusingly give the impression that some pubs are in Suffolk when they're really in Norfolk or Cambridgeshire – which is where we list them.

GREAT GLEMHAM   TM3361 Map 5

Crown

This old brick house has a friendly and relaxed atmosphere in its open-plan lounge, helped by the enormous double fireplace in the middle with logs blazing on one side in winter, and a black wood-burning stove on the other; ceiling beams, local paintings and drawings on the white walls, red cord button-back wall banquettes and captain's chairs around stripped and waxed kitchen tables and one or two big casks. A side eating room has flowers and pot plants. Though the pub is under new ownership the bar food remains much the same; soup (from 70p), sandwiches (from 70p, toasted from 75p), ploughman's (£1.20), various omelettes (£1.40), home-made chilli con carne (£1.75), salads (from £1.75) and fisherman's platter (£2.50); there is also a separate restaurant (game soup 90p, steaks around £6.50, Sunday roast beef lunch £5). Well kept Adnams, Greene King IPA and Abbot and Mauldons on handpump; darts, shove-ha'penny, dominoes, cribbage, a fruit machine, and piped music. There are seats outside on a neat lawn, flower-fringed and raised above the corner of the quiet village lane by a retaining wall. A nice place to stay with comfortable bedrooms and good breakfasts. *(Recommended by D and J W, John Townsend, Heather and Roy Sharland, Eric Walmsley)*

Free house · Licensee Mike Berry · Real ale · Meals (not Mon evening) and snacks · Children in restaurant · Open 11–2.30, 6.30–11 all year · Bedrooms tel Rendham (072 878) 693; £13.50S/£22.50B

HOXNE   TM1777 Map 5

Swan [*illustrated on page 584*]

This timbered Elizabethan inn is close to the site of King Edmund's martyrdom on 20 November 870. The lounge bar rambles about among standing timbers, and is comfortably furnished with flowery easy chairs, a sofa, an old-fashioned settle and plush bucket seats. The simpler public bar has darts, shove-ha'penny and a fruit machine (and some linenfold panelling around its fireplace). Bar food includes sandwiches (from 65p), home-made soup (65p), ploughman's with cheese or pâté (£1.70), chilli con carne with pitta bread or chicken curry (£1.75), grilled trout (£2.75), gammon steak (£3.50) and sirloin steak (£6.50), daily specials such as steak and kidney pie or liver and onions (£1.65), fruit pie and cream (75p), and there is a separate restaurant (supper Thursday to Saturday, and Sunday roast lunch); well kept Steward & Patteson and Websters Yorkshire on handpump; maybe piped music. The lawn behind this most attractive herringbone brick and timbered pub used to be a bowling green; a nice place to sit in summer, sheltered by a willow and other trees and its shrub-covered wall. *(Recommended by Eric Walmsley; more reports please)*

Free house · Licensees Chris and John O'Brien · Real ale · Meals and snacks Children in eating area and restaurant · Open 11–2.30, 6.30–11 all year Bedrooms tel Hoxne (037 975) 275; £10/£20

ICKLINGHAM TL7772 Map 5
Red Lion

This white thatched pub, close to West Stow Country Park and the Anglo-Saxon village, has a softly lit and well kept lounge with a neatly restored inglenook fireplace with a huge iron fireback, elegant little green leatherette bucket seats around its black tables, heavy beams in its yellowing and sloping ceiling, red and gilt flock wallpaper, and a restaurant section beyond a wrought-iron divider. Bar food includes sandwiches (from 60p), ploughman's (from £1.25), shepherd's pie and a choice of quiches (£1.65), dressed crab or a choice of raised pies (£2), bacon chop (£2.15), salads (from £2.25) and scampi (£2.40); Greene King ales kept under blanket pressure; piped music. The big public bar has darts, dominoes, cribbage and a fruit machine. Picnic-table sets on a raised back terrace face the fields – including an acre of the pub's running down to the River Lark, with Cavenham Heath nature reserve beyond. In front (the pub is well set back from the road) old-fashioned white seats overlook the car park and a flower lawn. *(Recommended by David Regan; more reports please)*

Greene King · Licensee Douglas King · Meals (not Sun evening) and snacks Children in restaurant only · Open 11–2.30, 7–11 all year

LAVENHAM TL9149 Map 5
Swan ★

This carefully modernised Elizabethan inn, one of several fine timbered buildings in this once prosperous wool town, is by no means cheap – but so many readers have been enjoying its uncommon architectural charm and its friendly and comfortable housekeeping that this year we are awarding it a star. Its extensive and comfortable lounge areas ramble around among the beams and timbers; its heart is a small and friendly tiled-floor bar, the local for the us 48th Bomber Group in the Second World War, with leather chairs, a set of handbells that were used for practice by the church bellringers, and well kept Adnams Bitter and Greene King IPA and Abbot on handpump. Overlooking the neat and sheltered courtyard garden is an airy garden bar, where a buffet counter serves freshly made sandwiches (£1.25 for tuna and cress to £3.25 for smoked salmon), a trio of pâté, seafood platter or smoked meat platter (£3.25); morning coffee and afternoon tea. There is also a lavishly timbered restaurant (with a minstrels' gallery). The photogenic inn is close to Shilling Street where Jane Taylor wrote 'Twinkle Twinkle Little Star', and the Tudor guildhall has a folk museum. A nice place to stay, understandably very popular with foreign visitors; over two nights, dinner, bed and breakfast is £35.50 a head each night. *(Recommended by R B W Bolland, David Potter, Brian and Rosemary Wilmot, J S Evans, Jeff Cousins, Heather Sharland)*

Free house (THF) · Licensee P J Manby · Real ale · Snacks (not Sun) · Children welcome · Live music in restaurant Sat evening · Open 11–2.30, 6–11 all year Bedrooms tel Lavenham (0787) 247477; £40.95B/£57.90B

Pubs with attractive or unusually big gardens are listed at the back of the book.

LAXFIELD   TM2972 Map 5

Kings Head ★

Behind church, off road towards Banyards Green

This unspoilt Tudor pub has preserved an old-fashioned atmosphere and traditions, with the barman serving you at your table. The open fire in the tiled-floor front room is cosily surrounded by a high-backed built-in settle, and a couple of other rooms have pews, old seats, scrubbed deal tables, and a quietly ticking clock. Well kept Adnams (and Old Ale in winter), Greene King Abbot, Mauldons Special or James White's farmhouse cider — mulled, if you want — are tapped from casks in a back room; darts, dominoes, cribbage. The new stable bar has a pool-table and piped music. Bar food includes toasted sandwiches, oak-smoked kippers (£1), ploughman's with cheese or pâté and home-baked granary bread (£1), smoked Suffolk sausages (£1.20) and home-made pies such as chicken, ham and apricot or venison and juniper (£1.90). Going out past the casks in the back serving room, you find benches and a trestle table in a small yard. From the yard, a honeysuckle arch leads into a sheltered little garden with vegetables at the far end, and to the pub's own well kept and secluded bowling green. This year (1986) the pub will have its fourth annual traditional village fair. *(Recommended by Will Peskett, Stephen Brough, Bridget Boulting, Douglas Free)*

Free house · Licensee Mrs Janet Parsons · Real ale · snacks · Children in eating area · Occasional live music · Open 10.30–2.30, 6–11 all year

LEVINGTON   TM2339 Map 5

Ship

Gun Hill; village signposted from A45, then follow Stratton Hall sign

Three snug and friendly little rooms have beams, ship prints and photographs of sailing barges, and benches built in to the wall, and upholstered small settles (some of them grouped around tables, as booths). The middle room has a big black round stove, an energetic green parrot and the serving counter with a marine compass set in to it, and casks of well kept Tolly Bitter and Original behind. Benches out in front look over the quiet lane to the distant water. Food has sometimes included good home-cooked ham, in sandwiches or salads. *(Recommended by Aubrey Saunders, Howard Gascoyne; more reports please)*

Tolly · Real ale · Snacks (lunchtime, limited Sun) · Open 11.30–2.30, 7–11 all year

LONG MELFORD   TL8645 Map 5

Bull

A134

This splendid black and white timbered building, originally a medieval manorial great hall, has been an inn under its present name since 1580, and the high beams in the lounge include one with a woodwose — the wild man of the woods that figures in Suffolk folk-tales – carved at one end. This comfortable room has an antique settle, wing chairs on its carpet, a big open fireplace, a grandfather clock, and paintings of horses and country scenes. A more spacious back bar has a good selection of cold meats and salads (£4.35), and also serves sandwiches, soup (£1), ploughman's (£2.15) and steak and kidney pie or scampi (£3.55); there is also a separate restaurant. Bass, Greene King IPA and Abbot and Mauldons on handpump. There are tables in the paved central courtyard. In 1648 a local man, arguing about Civil War politics, was murdered in a brawl just inside the front door (and buried in the yard of the magnificent church – look for the memorial to Richard Evered). Either he or his hanged killer haunted the hotel until recently, throwing things around, moving furniture, and casting a ghastly chill around the dining-room door. The Elizabethan Melford Hall and moated Tudor Kentwell Hall are both fine buildings in attractive grounds. A bargain weekend rate includes dinner, bed and breakfast for £32.50 a head. *(Recommended by E St Leger Moore; more reports please)*

Free house (THF) · Licensees M Di Sora and P E Evans · Meals and snacks (lunchtime, not Sun) · Children welcome · Open 11–2.30, 6–11 all year Bedrooms tel Sudbury (0787) 78494; £39.95B/£57.40B

MARTLESHAM   TM2547 Map 5
Black Tiles

A12; W side of village, on N side of road

This spacious and well kept road-house has a high ceiling, button-back upholstery and muted carpets. The bar food is reasonably good value, served quickly, and includes home-made soup (70p), lots of sandwiches (from 60p, tuna with egg, onion, apple, celery and mayonnaise 90p), hamburger (£1.10), a choice of ploughman's (£1.35), tacos (from £1.60), salads (£2.95), home-made steak and kidney pie or chilli con carne (£1.70), roast chicken (£1.95) and steaks (from £3.95). There is also a separate restaurant. Well kept Adnams on handpump; sensibly placed darts, fruit machine and piped music. The grass outside, floodlit at night, has picnic-table sets and a fish pond and fountain in front. *(Recommended by Eric Walmsley; more reports please)*

Adnams · Licensee Don Williamson · Real ale · Meals and snacks · Children in restaurant only · Open 11–3, 5.30–11 all year (opens 6 in winter)

MENDHAM   TM2782 Map 5
Sir Alfred Munnings

The new landlords of this cream-painted tiled hotel building (which in part dates from the sixteenth century) have plans to refurbish much of it. The main open-plan bar is comfortable with tapestry banquettes and stools around wood-effect tables. There is a cheerful and relaxed atmosphere, with well kept Adnams and Courage Directors on handpump (and quite a range of vermouths and whiskies on the dispensing optics), and darts, pool (in a sensibly separate area opening off the main room), a fruit machine and piped music. Bar food includes sandwiches (from 45p), home-made soup (80p), ploughman's or pâté (£1.50), pasties (from £1.75), lasagne, chilli con carne, curries and scampi (£2), steak and kidney pie (£3.50) and trout or sole (from £4.50). Wrought-iron gates lead through to the separate restaurant. The inn is well placed for the lovely water-meadows along the nearby River Waveney. There's a heated swimming pool for residents. *(Recommended by Gwen and Peter Andrews, P E Peskett; more reports please)*

Free house · Real ale · Meals and snacks · Children welcome · Open 11–2.30, 6–11 all year · Bedrooms tel Harleston (0379) 852358; £18.50 (£20B)/ £25 (£28.50B)

ORFORD   TM4250 Map 5
Jolly Sailor ★

This waterside smugglers' inn stands by a busy little quay on the River Ore, opposite the great gravel bank of Orford Ness (which grows year by year, and has gradually taken the open sea several miles away from this previously important port), and close to marshy Havergate Island where avocets breed. The pub was built mainly from wrecked ships' timbers in the seventeenth century, and the floor of one room is made of flagstones that in the days before tarmac were part of the street. Several cheerful rooms are served from counters and hatches in an old-fashioned central cubicle, which has well kept Adnams and Mild on handpump. One main room, straightforwardly comfortable, is warmed in winter by a good solid-fuel stove, and has an uncommon spiral staircase in one corner. Often, seats are pews: one small room is popular with the dominoes and shove-ha'penny players, another has pool and a fruit machine. The pub has some curious stuffed 'Chinese muff dogs', about half the size of a chihuahua – said to be Tudor, though no one's sure. Orford has always specialised in the odd: in the twelfth century fishermen netted the Wild Man of Orford – a strange half-human bald-headed hairy thing that later escaped back to the sea. Bar food includes sandwiches, ploughman's (£1.10), smoked mackerel (£1.55), scampi, chicken, plaice or giant sausages (all with chips and salad, £2.20) and sirloin steak (£5.35). Salads include local crab when it's available (£2.20). *(Recommended by AVC, D A Angless, Heather and Roy Sharland, GW, Patrick Stapley, Richard Gibbs, Susie Boulton)*

Adnams · Licensee Patrick Buckner · Real ale · Snacks · Children in pool-room Live entertainment most Sats · Open 11–2, 6–11 all year · Bedrooms tel Orford (039 45) 243; £12.50/£19.50

Kings Head
Front Street

The friendly and welcoming main bar of this predominantly Tudor inn – with parts dating back 700 years – has carved black oak beams, an open fire and one or two fine old wooden chairs, as well as comfortable blue leatherette seats and cushioned wall benches grouped around the low tables on its carpet. Lunchtime bar food includes home-made soup (£1.10), ploughman's (£1.70), home-made pâté (£1.90), local plaice (£2.10), prawns with a Stilton dip (£3), scallops in sherry and cheese sauce (£4), king-size prawns in garlic (£4.50) and summer salads. The separate evening restaurant specialises in tasty fish dishes, and the good breakfasts often include grilled plaice or poached whiting. Well kept Adnams on handpump; fruit machine. It's a nice place to stay, with simple creaky-floored bedrooms leading off the uncommonly low-ceilinged corridor. There are views of the well restored keep of the nearby twelfth-century castle. (Recommended by Eric Walmsley, Heather Sharland)

Adnams · Licensee Mrs Phyl Shaw · Real ale · Meals and snacks (lunchtime) Children in dining-room · Open 11–2.30, 6–11 all year · Bedrooms tel Orford (039 45) 271; £12.50/£25

RAMSHOLT   TM3141 Map 5
Ramsholt Arms
Village signposted from B1083; then take turning after the one to Ramsholt Church

Included for its beautiful setting, this pub is quite isolated by an old barge quay on the River Deben which winds shinily past to the sea. It's surrounded by quiet pine woods, and is silent but for the distant noise of gulls, curlews and waders. On summer weekends expect a lot of boating activity. The pub is furnished with attractive simplicity: red tiles or parquet flooring, red leatherette or green upholstered seats, a big picture window, some neatly nautical woodwork, tide tables and charts. There are tables outside on crazy paving. Well kept Adnams and Tolly on handpump; home-baked rolls, a choice of ploughman's (£1.45), seafood platter (£2.35), steak and kidney or chicken and ham pies (£2.35), with evening hot meals including steaks; sensibly placed darts. (Recommended by LAU, Howard Gascoyne; more reports please)

Free house · Real ale · Meals and snacks · Occasional live music · Steep longish walk down from car park · Open 11.30–2.30, 6.30–11 all year (opens 7 in winter)

RISBY   TL7966 Map 5
White Horse
Village signposted from A45 W of Bury St Edmunds; pub on service road (old A45) W of village

Reliable, good value, simple food, served quickly in generous helpings, fills all the tables in this comfortable pub, popular with travellers passing regularly and with businessmen from Bury. It includes a good choice of sandwiches, plain or toasted (from 80p), several pizzas (£1.20), omelettes (from £1.80), salads (from £1.90) and a good dish of the day such as braised lamb chops (£2.20); readers particularly praise the sirloin steaks (£5.75). There are tables in a big bow window, others, with wheelback chairs and red plush wall banquettes, down the length of the carpeted main room, which has black joists in its ochre ceiling and country prints and some harness on the walls. A smaller, partly panelled side room has more tables, and there is a smartly furnished restaurant. Well kept Courage

Best and Directors on handpump; fruit machine; on our visit, soft and nostalgic piped pop music; friendly, considerate service. Wise to book unless you get there early. *(Recommended by Alan Bayes, MJH)*

Free house · Licensee James O'Neill · Real ale · Meals – tel Bury St Edmunds (0284) 810686 – and snacks · Open 11–2.30, 6–11 all year; closed 25 and 26 Dec

SAXTEAD GREEN   TM2665 Map 5
Volunteer

B1119

Unfortunately the local council has weighed in and forced the removal of the tables that used to be such a nice feature on the grass in front of this tiled pink-washed house, with their view of the striking white windmill up the road, and in summer the house-martins which nest here keeping up a continuous fly-past. But there are still some by a small rockery pool on a pretty little back terrace. Inside, the light and airy lounge bar has cream walls decorated with little pictures and comfortable dark russet plush furniture on its green carpet. There's an open fire in winter. Popular bar food includes home-made pasties (90p), plain or toasted sandwiches (from 80p), ploughman's (£1.30), ham and crusty bread (£1.50), sausage and chips (£1.65), plaice (£1.90), a choice of salads (from £2.75), and a dish of the day such as lasagne, meat loaf, Mexican pork, a roast, harvest pie, savoury lamb chops, toad-in-the-hole or beef olives (£2.15–£2.60). They make their own ice cream. Tolly and Original, drawn from handpumps on a remarkably solid bar counter, are well kept. The public bar has shove-ha'penny, dominoes, cribbage, a fruit machine and juke box. *(Recommended by Roberta Coe, Eric Walmsley)*

Tolly Cobbold · Licensee J E Appleby · Real ale · Meals and snacks · Children in corner bar · Occasional live music · Open 10.30–2.30, 6–11 all year

The Butt & Oyster, nr Chelmondiston

SIBTON   TM3669 Map 5

White Horse ★

Halesworth Road; village – and in Peasenhall even pub – signposted
from A1120

Friendly and well kept, this sixteenth-century inn is attractively
furnished in an old-fashioned style: little red plush armchairs by a
wood-burning stove, cushioned settles, a big rug on the black and red
tiled floor, and lots of tack, horse brasses and plates on the yellowing
walls. Five steps take you up past an ancient, partly knocked-
through, timbered wall into a carpeted area with comfortable armed
seats around rustic tables. Good bar food includes soup (50p), a wide
choice of toasted sandwiches (from 60p), ploughman's (£1.55),
sausage and egg (£1.90), lasagne (£2.10), smoked trout (£2.10),
delicious home-baked ham (£2.25), and a specially good value full
meal with a choice of starters, then rump steak or the ham, and a
glass of wine or a pint of bitter (£4.75). The separate restaurant does
main dishes such as beef and chicken curries or seafood platter
(£3.50) and sirloin steak (£5.95). Well kept Adnams and Mauldons
on handpump; piped music sometimes. There are tables under
cocktail parasols out on the gravel and cobblestone courtyard, by
some pretty window-boxes. (Recommended by AVC, Eric Walmsley; more
reports please)

Free house · Licensees John and Evelyn Mumford · Real ale · Meals and snacks
Children in dining area · Open 11–2.30, 6–11 all year (opens 7 in winter)
Bedrooms tel Peasenhall (072 879) 337; £12.50B/£21B

SNAPE   TM3959 Map 5

Golden Key ★

Priory Lane

Readers are drawn to this quietly elegant, yet friendly and
unpretentious pub by its good and plentiful food. All home made, it
includes soup (95p), cockles and mussels (£1.25 as a starter, £2.25 as
a main course), ploughman's with Cheddar, Stilton, Brie or ham, pâté
with salad and French bread (£1.75–£2.50), spinach and mushroom
or smoked haddock quiche (£2.95), sausage, egg and onion pie
(£2.95), locally caught crab with salad (£2.95), eight-ounce sirloin
steak (£5.95), lobster (from £5.25) and daily specials such as roast
beef, cottage pie or steak and kidney pie (£2.25–£3.50); a choice of
puddings such as fruit pies or lemon cake (95p–£1.10). The low-
beamed lounge bar is attractively furnished with stripped modern
settles around heavy Habitat-style wooden tables on a Turkey carpet,
a solid-fuel stove in its big fireplace, and nice pictures on the cream
walls – pencil sketches of customers, a Henry Wilkinson spaniel and
so forth. The serving end, where there's a tiled floor and an open log
fire in winter, has an old-fashioned settle curving around a couple of
venerable stripped tables, and there are sofas and more tables in a
brick-floored side room. Well kept Adnams and Mild tapped from
cooled casks, with Old Ale in winter, and James White's cider. There
are tables on the gravel in the small, sheltered front garden – a lovely
mass of flowers in summer. (Recommended by Gwen and Peter Andrews,

Dave Hoy, SLH, Heather Sharland, Christopher and Jean Cowan, Stephen Brough, Eric Walmsley)

Adnams · Licensees Max and Susie Kissick-Jones · Real ale · Meals and snacks Open 10.30–2.30, 5.30–11 all year, with afternoon and evening extensions during Aldeburgh Festival

SOUTHWOLD   TM5076   Map 5

Harbour

Blackshore Quay; entering Southwold on A1095, turn right at Kings Head and go past golf course and water tower

This quaint and friendly old waterside pub stands among the fishermen's small black huts (where you can buy fresh fish) and the dinghies and yachts beached by the River Blyth, and, as you can see from markers on the wall, is submerged by sea floods every few years. It still is, as it has always been, a sort of unofficial clubhouse for the fishermen, and has a ship-to-shore radio as well as a wind speed indicator. The front bar is tiled and panelled with low beams and antique settles, and is served from a hatch high in the wall. Up some steps there's more stripped panelling, with a lot of local ship and boat photographs. It specialises in good fish and chips served in newspaper (£1.20 – an extra 3p if you want a fork), and also serves sausage or beefburger (£1.10), chicken (£1.25) and scampi (£1.75), all with chips. At lunchtime on Sundays there is only a ploughman's (£1.20). Well kept Adnams Best and Mild on handpump, attractively priced; a fruit machine and a space game. There is often locally smoked eel for sale for your freezer. A couple of picnic-table sets behind have rather a fine view of the town beyond the shore grasslands, below its striking white lighthouse, and there are more in front facing the jumbly waterside bustle. *(Recommended by Howard Gascoyne; more reports please)*

Adnams · Licensees Ron and Nan Westwood · Real ale · Meals (not Sun lunchtime, not Tues or Thurs evenings) and snacks (Sun lunchtime) Apr–Oct Open 10.30–2.30, 6–11 all year

Sole Bay

7 East Green; entering Southwold on A1095, fork left following Methodist Church signpost

Named after the 1672 victory over the Dutch fleet, which supplied many older pubs than this with good sturdy purloined ships' timbers for building, this square-cut Victorian pub huddles under the big white lighthouse and is only a stroll from the sea. It has well kept Adnams and Mild on handpump – and so it should, with the brewery over the road. Bar snacks include sandwiches (from 55p), hot pasty or giant sausage in French bread (70p), ploughman's (£1.25) and salads (good value local crab £2.50). It has simple traditional furnishings, sensibly placed darts, shove-ha'penny, dominoes, cribbage and a fruit machine, and there are seats outside. *(Recommended by Russell Fox, A Saunders, Bridget Boulting)*

Adnams · Real ale · Snacks (lunchtimes, not Sun) · Nearby parking may be difficult at peak holiday times · Open 10.30–2.30, 6–11 all year

SUTTON   TM3046 Map 5
Plough

B1083

There are picnic-table sets in front and by the fruit-trees behind this
tiled white house which is surrounded by Sutton Common. Inside, an
extra dining-room has been opened and the pub has been completely
redecorated since our last edition. A small and cosy front room has
snug button-back wall banquettes, and there's a more spacious room
round the side. Good value bar food includes rich home-made soup
(80p), sandwiches (from 65p), ploughman's (from £1.20),
hamburgers (from £1.45) and hot dishes from sausages and chips
(£1.50) to fillet steak (£6.10). In the evening a rather grander choice
concentrates particularly on fish, from fried squid rings (£2.25) or
scallops (£2.45) as starters to Dover sole (£6.45), and on steaks
(mostly around £6) – but readers rate the chicken curry (Tuesday and
Thursday evenings only, £3) as the dish worth coming miles for.
Norwich Bitter and Mild and Steward & Patteson on handpump;
sensibly placed darts and a fruit machine. (Recommended by LAU,
Eric Walmsley)

*Norwich (Watneys) · Licensees Michael and Anne Lomas · Real ale · Meals
(not Mon) and snacks (lunchtimes only) · Children in eating area · Open 11–
2.30, 6.30–11 all year*

TOSTOCK   TL9563 Map 5
Gardeners Arms

Village signposted from A45 and A1088

A sheltered lawn beside this pretty deep pink house has picnic-table
sets among roses and other flowers, and a steel quoits pitch (readers
say it's idyllic here on a summer evening when a match is on). The
friendly lounge bar has lots of what used to be called carving-chairs
(dining-chairs with arms) around the black tables under its low and
heavy black beams; hefty standing timbers and a curtain divide off a
restaurant (bookings only). The new licensees have introduced a
larger and more varied bar menu: sandwiches (from 60p),
ploughman's (£1), beefburger (£1.10), home-made quiche (£1.50),
prawns with home-made granary bread (£1.60), home-made savoury
stuffed pancakes (£1.80), home-cooked beef or ham salad (£2.50)
and a range of daily specials such as steak and kidney pie or
moussaka (£2); home-made puddings (85p). The lively tiled-floor
public bar has darts, pool, shove-ha'penny, dominoes, cribbage, a
juke box and a fruit machine. Greene King ales from cash-register
handpumps, though real ones – doing away with the light blanket
pressure – are to be fitted soon. (Recommended by Howard Gascoyne;
more reports please)

*Greene King · Licensee R E Ransome · Meals and snacks (not Tues evening or
Sun lunchtime); restaurant bookings tel Beyton (0359) 70460 · Children in
eating area · Open 11–2.30, 7–11 all year*

Most pubs in this book sell wine by the glass. We mention wines only if they are a
cut above the average.

WALBERSWICK   TM4974 Map 5
Bell ★
Just off B1387

This quiet inn has a sizeable lawn with seats and tables among roses
and other flowers, sheltered by a hedge from the worst of the sea
winds – but you can still hear and smell the sea, which is only a short
stroll away, and the bedrooms all look over the sea or the river.
Inside, the oak-beamed bar rambles around very attractively with
curved high-backed settles on well worn flagstones, tiles and flooring-
bricks that were here when this sleepy village was a flourishing port
600 years ago. There is a wood-burning stove in the big fireplace, and
tankards hang from oars above the bar counter, which serves well
kept Adnams and Mild from handpump; to one side there is a
smarter and more conventionally comfortable area decorated with
local photographs. Bar food includes sandwiches (70p, toasted 80p),
ploughman's (£1.50, ham £1.75), fish (£2.25), with a good choice of
summer salads such as smoked mackerel or home-made quiche
(£2.25), scampi (£2.50) and prawns or crab (£2.90); in winter there
are more hot dishes. There's a separate restaurant (evenings only).
Shove-ha'penny, cribbage, a fruit machine and space game.
(Recommended by Mrs R Wilmot, John Townsend, Jenny Potter)

Adnams · Licensee Mark Stansall · Real ale · Meals and snacks (lunchtime)
Children in small room off bar · Open 11–2.30, 6.30–11 all year; closed 25
Dec · Bedrooms tel Southwold (0502) 723109; £14/£28

WENHASTON   TM4276 Map 5
Star

The small lounge of this simple village local is gloriously sunny on
fine days, with a bow window seat overlooking the tables on the
spacious lawn beyond a herbaceous border, by the quiet lane. This
room has leatherette seats around three rustic tables on its green
carpet; the lino-floored public bar has darts and a fruit machine. Well
kept Adnams Bitter and Mild drawn from casks built in to lockers
behind the bar; the new licensee has enlarged the bar menu to include
sandwiches, beefburger (£1.05), fish and chips (£1.20), fish or cottage
pie, curry or lasagne (£1.90) and rump steak (£2.95); darts, shove-
ha'penny, dominoes, cribbage, a fruit machine and piped music.
(Recommended by D S Marshall; more reports please)

Adnams · Licensee F M Bryant · Real ale · Snacks · Children in eating area
Open 11–2.30, 6.30–11 all year (opens 7 in winter) · Bedrooms tel
Blythburgh (050 270) 240; £7.50/£15

WETHERDEN   TM0062 Map 5
Maypole
Village signposted from A45

The main bar of this village pub is open-plan, with high trussed
ceilings at the back (low beams and timbering at the front, where
children are allowed if they're eating a meal), copper pots hanging

from the rafters, guns on its cream walls, and a well among the
Windsor chairs. Bar food includes sandwiches, ploughman's (from
£1.50), salads (from £2.20), scampi (£2.35), trout (£4.95) and sirloin
steak (£5.95); well kept Adnams and Wethereds on handpump;
darts, dominoes, cribbage, a fruit machine, space game and juke box.
(Recommended by Mr and Mrs A D Clayton; more reports please)

*Adnams · Licensee Barry Conner · Real ale · Meals and snacks · Children in
front bar if eating · Rock and country and western music Fri and Sat; disco
Wed and Sun · Open 11–2.30, 6–11 all year*

WOOLPIT   TL9762   Map 5
Swan
The handsome black beams of this neatly kept inn date from the
sixteenth century, though the substantial side extension (now the
brewery's regional headquarters) was built in the Georgian coaching
boom, when the rest of the inn was refaced in brick. The spacious
bay-windowed bar is partly panelled, with a big antique hunting
print, red leatherette seats and low settles and open fires in winter.
Lunchtime bar food includes sandwiches or toasties (45p–75p), soup
(50p), pies (£1.20), omelettes (£1.50) and individual-dish meals
(£1.75); in the evenings sausages (£1.80), ham salad (£2.25),
gammon (£2.50), chicken (£3) and rump steak (£4.75). Well kept
Websters Yorkshire on handpump; darts, dominoes, cribbage, a fruit
machine, maybe piped music. There is also a separate dining-room
mainly for residents. The village, bypassed by the A45, is very quiet
now; the bedrooms are comfortably well equipped. *(Recommended by
D A Angless, Sue Leggate)*

*Norwich (Watneys) · Licensee Joseph Thompson · Real ale · Meals (Mon–
Weds and Sun evenings) and snacks (lunchtime) · Children in lobby or dining-
room, if eating · Open 11–2, 5.45–11 all year · Bedrooms tel Elmswell
(0359) 40482; £11.50/£21 (£24B)*

Lucky Dip

Besides the fully inspected pubs, you might like to try these Lucky Dips
recommended and described by readers (if you do, please send us reports):

ALDEBURGH [TM4656], *Mill*: good *(Gordon Treadway)*
ALDRINGHAM [TM4461], *Parrot & Punchbowl*: good food in cosy
unpretentious surroundings with warm hospitality – even though we were on
motor-bikes! *(GW)*
BARDWELL [TL9473], *Six Bells*: food recommended (especially steaks); well
kept beer and lively atmosphere in nicely refurbished old village pub; log fires
in winter *(AM)*
BLUNDESTON [TM5197], *Plough*: handy for Jacobean Somerleyton Hall –
smartly modernised Watneys pub which was the home of Barkis the carrier in
David Copperfield (LYM)
BOXFORD [TL9640], *White Hart*: good value three-course lunch with generous
helpings; pleasant staff and cosy surroundings *(Mrs B J Brookes)*
BRAMFIELD [TM4073], *Queens Head*: home-made food in clean and friendly
pub with Adnams real ale, charmingly decorated in Stuart style by friendly
licensees; children's room *(A V Chute and others)*
BRANTHAM [TM1033], *Bucks Horns*: varied, well cooked and interesting bar

food, Adnams real ale and reasonably priced wine *(Helen Cooper)*

BROMESWELL [TM3050], *Cherry Tree*: generous helpings of bar food in comfortably modernised beamed lounge with open fire and velvet curtains; seats outside; charming inn-sign *(Eric Walmsley, BB)*

BURY ST EDMUNDS [Crown Street; TL8564], *Dog & Partridge*: friendly bar in unusual and very old building with roomy comfortable seating, well kept Greene King ale from nearby brewery, and a wide choice of bar food with some unusual snacks *(Trevor Williams)*

CLARE [High Street; TL7645], *Swan*: friendly and comfortable local with reliable and often innovative bar food; well kept real ale *(Melvin D Buckner, BB)*

CODDENHAM [TM1354], *Dukes Head*: well kept Tolly ales in friendly, modernised village pub, with simple bar food; steps to lawn above *(Howard Gascoyne, LYM)*

DARSHAM [Darsham Station; TM4169], *Stradbroke Arms*: cheery high-ceilinged pub by level crossing with good value bar food, Adnams real ale, high-backed settles, darts and bar billiards, pretty garden with primroses and bluebells under ash-trees *(Eric Walmsley, BB and others)*

DEBENHAM [TM1763], *Red Lion*: fine sixteenth-century plaster ceiling in nicely furnished lounge; Tolly beers *(BB)*

DENNINGTON [TM2867], *Queens Head*: stylishly simplified Tudor pub with good range of real ales; garden by village church *(Susie Boulton, LYM)*

EAST BERGHOLT [TM0734], *Kings Head*: good value cheap food, nice log fire, welcoming landlord, quite cosy in beautiful area; folk group Sunday evenings *(Mrs R Wilmot)*

EASTON [TM2858], *White Horse*: imaginative bar food with very generous vegetables and small restaurant with unusual Sunday lunches (Stilton fritters, baked partridge, then chocolate roulade) *(Christopher and Jean Cowan)*

EXNING [Oxford Street; TL6165], *White Swan*: food at lunchtime good and largely home cooked in charming old country pub with five beers; garden *(Alan Bayes)*

EYE [TM1473], *White Lion*: Elizabethan beamed public bar, panelled lounge and small Georgian ballroom in unpretentious inn with well kept Adnams and Websters Yorkshire; bedrooms *(LYM)*

nr HADLEIGH [TM0343], *Brewers Arms*: Greene King IPA, excellent food; good garden for kids with a few rides *(R L Wilson)*

HAUGHLEY [TM0262], *Kings Head*: food good quality and good value in old beamed village pub *(Anon)*

HOLBROOK [Ipswich Road; TM1636], *Compasses*: fresh hot bar food is good value in clean pub with friendly, informal atmosphere and willing service; old store refurbished as Thursday to Saturday night and Sunday lunchtime restaurant *(Colin Craven-Sands)*

HOLLESLEY [TM3544], *Fox*: food well cooked and well presented in nicely furnished and comfortable pub with good beers; warm in winter *(LAU)*

HOLTON [TM4077], *Cherry Tree*: good food in pub well run by two young couples *(Mr and Mrs Burr)*

IXWORTH THORPE [TL9173], *Oak*: cheerful simply furnished country pub with popular food, sensibly placed darts and pool-table; quite near Bardwell working windmill *(Alan Chitty, BB)*

KELSALE [TM3865], *Eight Bells*: food includes good value lunchtime snacks, in large village inn with Adnams real ale in good condition *(Russell Fox)*

KENTFORD [TL7066], *Bull*: simple but comfortable furnishings; dining-room with good up-market food *(W T Aird)*

KERSEY [TL9944], *Bell*: good value food and well kept beer in fine old timbered pub; spotless; willing service; charming village *(Dr F Peters, M Haydon)*

LAVENHAM [TL9149], *Angel*: good food in well kept pub, lovely medieval village *(T G Brierly)*

LAXFIELD [TM2972], *Royal Oak*: food includes excellent puddings, and service is obliging; clean *(Eric Walmsley)*

MARTLESHAM [TM2547], *Douglas Bader*: reasonably priced food with some interesting dishes, in big cheerful L-shaped bar *(Eric Walmsley)*; *Red Lion*: good value Barnaby's restaurant, and cheaper food in bars *(Eric Walmsley)*

NAYLAND [TL9734], *Bear*: comfortable hotel with good food and cheerful friendly service; pleasantly furnished bedrooms *(Anon)*

NEEDHAM MARKET [TM0855], *Swan*: nice cheap food with willing service *(E Walmsley)*

NEWMARKET [High Street; TL6463], *White Hart*: under new management; spacious lounge has good food and service, and well kept Tolly beer; nice clean bedrooms *(Graham and Charmaigne Allman, W T Aird)*

POLSTEAD [TL9938], *Brewers Arms*: good value food in bar or restaurant; well kept Adnams and Greene King IPA in lively free house, with entertaining landlord and parrot; quick service *(David Stevenson)*

RATTLESDEN [TL9758], *Brewers Arms*: friendly and unpretentious village pub with lively public bar (pool, darts and so forth) *(Sue Thomas, Sue Leggate, LYM)*

REDE [TL8055], *Plough*: good food in attractive pub with pleasant licensees *(Bruce Shepherd)*

SHOTLEY GATE [TM2434], *Bristol Arms*: big bay windows give good views over the Stour estuary, Harwich and Felixstowe harbours; comfortable; bar food, Tolly real ales *(Howard Gascoyne)*

SNAPE [TM3959], *Crown*: front room supposed to be the model for the Boar in Britten's *Peter Grimes*, in comfortable much done-up pub with well equipped bedrooms; Adnams *(Dave Hoy, Michael Sandy, LYM)*

SOUTHWOLD [TM5076], *Lord Nelson*: attractive pub close to sea, with lively local atmosphere in single bar; useful food, no music, Adnams beer *(Anon)*; [South Green] *Red Lion*: good food especially salads in summer buffet room (snacks in winter), well kept Adnams, family room, winter log fire, nice atmosphere and cheery welcoming service; juke box, tables outside *(LAU, Hope Chenhalls)*; [Market Place] *Swan*: good value food, comfortable friendly atmosphere; bedrooms *(W J Wonham)*

SPEXHALL [Stone Road; TM3780], *Huntsman & Hounds*: food good in small, friendly, clean two-bar free house with Adnams and Mauldons *(Anon)*

STOKE-BY-NAYLAND [TL9836], *Crown*: spacious series of comfortably modernised rooms in lounge bar with reliable bar food; very good restaurant, and Tolly on handpump *(D B Pascall, TBR, Cmdr and Mrs E St Leger Moore, LYM)*

STRATFORD ST MARY [TM0434], *Swan*: good lunchtime cold table in Ind Coope pub with garden by River Stour, in pleasant bypassed village *(Gwen and Peter Andrews)*

SUDBURY [Friars Street; TL8741], *Ship & Star*: choice of food, friendly host and hostess, unusually wide selection of real ales, in interesting conversion of very old building *(David Stevenson)*

TUNSTALL [TM3555], *Green Man*: good value food in comfortable and airily modern village inn *(Eric Walmsley, BB)*

WALDRINGFIELD [TM2844], *Maybush*: tastefully renovated pub in idyllic setting on River Deben, with Giles' originals on walls; well kept Tolly Cobbold and bar snacks *(P N Goodwin)*

WASHBROOK [TM1042], *Brook*: wide choice of well presented food and Tolly real ales at pleasant civilised pub in quiet village *(Eric Walmsley, Tony Gayfer)*

WESTLETON [TM4469], *Crown*: pleasant village inn with simple bedrooms in attractive area; highly rated in previous editions for its food – much caught by its local fisherman-landlord, who now plans to return to the sea *(Up-to-date reports on the new regime please)*; *White Horse*: friendly and attractive village pub with well kept beer *(Dave Butler, Lesley Storey)*

WHERSTEAD [Bourne End; TM1540], *Ostrich*: good food in welcoming surroundings with charming managers *(Graham and Charmaigne Allman)*

WINGFIELD [TM2277], *Village Pub*: reasonably priced food in small village pub with log fires and warm welcome *(MMMB)*

YOXFORD [TM3968], *Kings Head*: good value food including tender steaks *(Eric Walmsley)*

Surrey

It sometimes seems a surprise to find absolutely unspoilt and simple pubs in this area – so close to London and after all relatively wealthy. Yet they are there: places like the Dolphin at Betchworth (tied to Youngs now, but still quite unpretentious with its flagstone floor and gas lighting); the Skimmington Castle just outside Reigate (up a lonely track, old-fashioned furnishings in its small rooms); the Scarlett Arms at Walliswood (full of fresh flowers and friendliness); and even on the outskirts of London itself, the small-roomed low-beamed White Lion in Warlingham. Often the surroundings are lovely here, too: as at the traditional old Abinger Hatch on Abinger Common (surrounded by magnificent woodland), the Cricketers opposite the green near Cobham, the White Horse in the lovely village of Shere (itself a fascinating ancient pub), the Parrot on the green at Forest Green (great sandwiches, good real ales); also, the Well House

The King's Head, Shepperton

at Chipstead (for its pretty garden, in a peaceful valley), the very smart Withies outside Compton (again, a very attractive garden), the Surrey Oaks at Newdigate (quite a menagerie in its extensive grounds), the Bell at Outwood (with a good range of real ales, just a stroll from a working windmill), and the grand old Crown facing the equally ancient church at Chiddingfold. But perhaps food is the strongest point here: as in the Plough at Blackbrook (unusual specials, and good real ale, in a flower-filled pub), the William IV just outside Bletchingley (cheap and hearty food, and a nice garden), the Plough near Cobham (always popular for its good value food, with a new carvery), the Harrow at Compton (civilised, with tasty specialities such as paella or a two-person seafood platter), the Queen's Head in East Clandon (home cooking that includes some antique recipes), the many-roomed Glyn Arms in Ewell (a place that for once is right to be proud of its hamburgers), the Windmill near Ewhurst (fine food while you look out over a spectacular view), the Three Horseshoes at Laleham (particularly for its good range of sandwiches), the Wattenden Arms in Kenley (honest lunchtime value in a very friendly pub), the Punch Bowl near Ockley (simple and traditional), the Jolly Farmer at Runfold (good lunches in a big well run pub with a good children's play area and frequent barbecues), the Red Lion at Shamley Green (unusual food in large helpings), the charmingly civilised old Three Horseshoes at Thursley (excellent sandwiches, dinners on Friday and Saturday), the bustling, friendly Chequers in Walton on the Hill (some readers regularly drive across London for lunch there), the Jolly Farmer at Worplesdon (good choice of real ales, too) and the Wotton Hatch in Wotton (good value changing dishes in its friendly bars and smart and comfortable dining-room). The Lucky Dip section at the end of the chapter includes so many pubs that, wherever you are, you'll be close to one worth trying. A few that seem particularly promising – and, depending on the reports we get from you, firmly in the running for elevation to main entries – are the quaint old country Blue Bell at Batts Corner, the Red Barn at Blindley Heath (history, old books), the nice old Dog and Pheasant at Brook, the Swan at Chiddingfold (for its food), the old-world Plough at Effingham, the Donkey near Elstead (lots of character), the Ram at Farncombe (no less than 16 ciders), the Seven Stars at Leigh (a pretty and comfortable country pub) and the handsomely restored Lincoln Arms in Weybridge. Prices for both food and drinks – with some very honourable exceptions which we pick out in the text – are on the whole higher in this county than anywhere except London itself.

ABINGER COMMON   TQ1145 Map 3

Abinger Hatch

Off A25 W of Dorking, follow Abinger signpost, then turn right towards Abinger Hammer

In a clearing in the marvellous mixed woodland that covers these rolling hills, this pub faces the church across a village green. It has wistaria tumbling over its tiled roof, and picnic-table sets under fir-trees on a neat stretch of side grass sheltered by beech- and rose-hedges; a big fig-tree grows in front. Inside, the main area has flagstones, beams, a log fire, and easy chairs and other armed seats as well as brown plush button-back banquettes; up a step, a side carpeted part has pews forming booths around oak tables and another big square log-filled fireplace. Bar food includes sandwiches (from 70p), soup (95p), ploughman's (from £1.20), whitebait (£1.50), filled baked potatoes (from £1.50), pork chop or steak and kidney pie (£2.50) and fillet steak (£6), with dishes of the day such as turkey, bacon and chestnut casserole or chicken filled with Stilton and leek (£3); there's also a separate dining-room with a small adjoining bar. Well kept Flowers Original, Badger Best, King & Barnes and Whitbreads Pompey Royal on handpump. Very quiet on a weekday lunchtime, it gets packed on weekends and sunny summer evenings. (Recommended by Robert L Scott, Doug Kennedy, Mrs N E Ibbott, Margaret Whitby, Colin Harry, M P Kerschbaum, D J Penny)

Free house · Real ale · Meals and snacks · Open 10.30–2.30, 5.30–11

ADDLESTONE   TQ0464 Map 2

White Hart

New Haw Road; corner of A318 and B385

This cheerful pub is included chiefly for its waterside garden, fairy-lit at night, with tables among lots of flowers on the neat little lawn, and greedy white ducks on the stream (there's a bit of traffic noise, to remind you how lucky you were to find that nearby parking slot). The well kept bars are decorated with caricatures of some of its lively young customers, who find the good value simple food a particular attraction: rolls and sandwiches (from 40p), steak and kidney pie, cottage pie, liver and bacon and so forth (from £1.40), and various meals with chips, for example cod (£1.65), ham and egg (£1.70) or gammon (£2.15). Courage Best and Directors on handpump; darts, bar billiards, dominoes, cribbage, a fruit machine and a juke box. (More reports please)

Courage · Licensee Tim Gill · Real ale · Meals and snacks (lunchtime, not Sun) Pianist Sat · Open 11–2.30, 5.30–11

BETCHWORTH   TQ2049 Map 3

Dolphin ★

The Street

Since our last edition this fine old traditional pub has become tied to Youngs, so no longer stocks the interesting range of other real ales that it was previously well known for. But we're pleased to report that Mr Johnson is staying on, and that it's as attractive as ever in other ways, with kitchen chairs and plain tables in its flagstone-floored front bar, a gas lamp by the big open fireplace, and a warm and unpretentious welcome. The black-panelled saloon bar at the back is carpeted, with robust old-fashioned oak or elm tables, and has a sonorous long-case clock (built in Molesey), and as we went to press we heard of plans for a buttery bar or restaurant. Well kept Youngs Bitter and Special on handpump; a wide choice of well made sandwiches (from 80p), Cheddar or Stilton ploughman's (£1.50), good home-made shepherd's pie (£2) and some other hot dishes (£2.50). There are some seats in the small laurel-shaded front courtyard, and more beyond the car park opposite the church (by this coming summer they may have extended the garden). No leather jackets allowed. *(Recommended by D J Penny, Donald Mather, NAW, C H Cole, K W Potter)*

Youngs · Licensee Bob Johnson · Real ale · Meals (not Sun or Mon evenings) and snacks (not Sun evening) · Open 10.30–2.30, 5.30–11

BLACKBROOK   TQ1846 Map 3
Plough

On byroad E of A24, parallel to it, between Dorking and Newdigate, just N of the turn E to Leigh

The saloon bar, with bunches of fresh flowers on its copper-topped trestle tables, is a pleasantly light and airy place in which to concentrate on this pub's good value and often interesting food: specials might include goulash soup (95p), guacamole (basically chopped avocado) with tortilla chips (£1.55), Mozzarella and tomatoes with Italian dressing (£1.95), prawns with a herby garlic mayonnaise (£2.25), liver and bacon hot-pot (£2.75), tacos with spicy salad (£2.95), seafood hot-pot (£3.25), prawn and bacon kebabs with satay mayonnaise (£4.45) or duck with blackcurrant sauce (£5.95), besides a wide choice of regular dishes such as substantial ploughman's with Cheddar, Stilton, Camembert or hot smoked mackerel fillet with fresh granary bread (£1.45), lasagne or chicken curry (£2.95), scampi in a basket (£3.10) and Scotch sirloin steaks (from eight-ounce, £5.75); good carrot pudding. Friendly service, and well kept King & Barnes Sussex, Festive, Mild and in winter Old Ale on handpump; the pub regularly wins its brewery's annual best-kept cellar competition. There may be piped music. The public bar, down some steps and given smart new upholstered seats since our last edition, has quite a formidable collection of ties, and darts, shove-ha'penny, dominoes, cribbage and a fruit machine. You can sit outside at the front, or more quietly on the grass or a small terrace at the back, which in summer is full of flowers. Just south is a good stretch of attractive oak wood with plenty of paths and a big pond. *(Recommended by Jill Cox, S D Lovett, Richard Balkwill)*

King & Barnes · Licensees Robin and Chris Squire · Real ale · Meals and snacks (not Mon evening) · Open 11–2.30, 6–10.30 (Thurs–Sat 6–11); closed 25 Dec, evenings 26 Dec and 1 Jan

BLETCHINGLEY   TQ3250   Map 3

Whyte Harte

2½ miles from M25 junction 6; A22 towards East Grinstead then
A25 towards Redhill

Comfortable bedrooms with hearty breakfasts make this old inn –
not that far from Gatwick – a pleasant place to stay. It dates partly
from the thirteenth century, and though probably not licensed as an
inn until the coaching era, has been in business for nearly three
centuries. The mainly open-plan bars have comfortable old plush-
covered settles and stools, rugs on the neat woodblock floor, an
inglenook fireplace with a heavily sagging chimney-beam, low and
dark ceiling beams, and old-fashioned prints on the walls. Bar food
includes sandwiches, ploughman's, pâté, salads, a dish of the day
(£1.90), generous helpings of whitebait, curry or scampi (£2.20) and
steak (£4.30). Well kept Friary Meux and Ind Coope Burton on
handpump, also a fair range of wines. There's bow-tie service in the
separate restaurant. You can sit out in front, sharing the cobbles with
tubs of flowers, looking across the wide, sloping village street to the
church. There are more tables on a strip of lawn behind, sheltered by
an old stone wall and the backs of two of the Tudor cottages that are
a feature of this pretty village. *(Recommended by MHG, D R Mather,
P T Young)*

*Friary Meux · Licensee Derek King · Real ale · Meals and snacks · Children in
entrance hall and restaurant · Open 10–2.30, 6–11 all year · Bedrooms tel
Godstone (0883) 843231; £16.45 (£18.35B)/£30.35 (£34.15B)*

William IV

3 miles from M25 junction 6; A22 towards East Grinstead, A25 towards
Redhill; turn up lane N of A25 on Redhill side of village, close to Red Lion

This cosy and friendly country pub is popular for its good value
lunchtime bar food: besides a weekday special such as leek and ham
Mornay or steak and mushroom pie (£1.85), there are eight ounces of
chips (50p), cheese on toast, eggs and chips or crispy bacon sandwich
(£1), gammon steak with chilli sauce in French bread (£1.30),
ploughman's (from £1.30), toasties or fat club sandwiches (£1.50),
salads (from £1.80), ham, egg and chips (£2), gammon and pineapple
(£2.75), half a pound of scampi (£2.85), mixed grill (£4) and eight-
ounce rump steak (£4.50). Good news is that – subject to planning
permission for general refurbishments – they may during 1986 be
able to serve this in the evenings, too. Well kept Bass and Charrington
IPA on handpump. The back bar has darts sensibly placed down at
one end, dominoes, cribbage and a fruit machine. The pretty tile-
hung and weatherboarded house has lots of flowerbeds, roses, a
rockery, a swing for children, and plenty of tables in the garden – in
summer there are barbecues out here on Saturday evening and
Sunday lunchtime, with burgers, sausages, kebabs, steaks and so
forth. *(Recommended by B H Pinsent; more reports please)*

*Charringtons · Licensee Ian Young · Real ale · Meals and snacks (lunchtime,
not Sun–but see above) · Open 10.30–2.30, 6–11*

CHIDDINGFOLD   SU9635 Map 2
Crown

This splendid old timbered building – an inn for 600 years – is a fine place to take foreign visitors. There are massive chimneys, oak beams more than two feet thick, handsome oak panelling, lovely oak mullioned windows, a magnificently carved inglenook fireplace, and a cabinet of coins going back some 400 years found here during renovations. It is based on a thirteenth-century hospice for Winchester monks on the pilgrimage to Canterbury. A bistro bar serves Stilton and walnut pâté, fresh salads, cold meats, and hot dishes such as home-cooked pies and lasagne, with puddings such as home-made cheesecake; it's also open for breakfast and tea. Further through is a luxurious little cocktail bar, creaky-boarded and old-fashioned, and a panelled and tapestry-hung restaurant. Well kept Youngs Special. In early summer the building's a marvellous sight, with lots of wistaria, laburnum and lilac, and seats looking across the village green to the church, which is much the same age. There are also tables in a sheltered central courtyard, where there are weekend barbecues. On 5 November there is a fireworks party on the village green. A nice place to stay. *(Recommended by Mrs Heather Sharland, Doug Kennedy, C A Foden, G Atkinson)*

Free house · Licensee Kenneth Playter · Real ale · Meals and snacks · Children welcome · Open 10.30–2.30, 6–11 · Bedrooms tel Wormley (042 879) 2255; £38B/£51B

The Punch Bowl, nr Ockley

CHIPSTEAD   TQ2757 Map 3

Well House

3 miles from M25 junction 8; A217 towards Banstead, turn right at second roundabout following Mugswell, Chipstead signpost into Chipstead Lane

Quite alone in a country valley, this cottagey-looking pub does indeed have a well – a wishing well (proceeds to charity) on the sheltered back terrace. The garden is attractive in summer: steep, with neat small flowerbeds, an old yew-tree, coppice then taller trees behind, and masses of birdsong. Inside there are low and heavy fourteenth-century oak beams, a central room with mainly standing space and a few tables and wheelback chairs around the edge, and red Turkey carpet sweeping through from here into a quieter room with many more tables and comfortable tapestried seats. A side room has darts and a fruit machine; also dominoes and cribbage. Well kept Bass and Charrington IPA on handpump, and food ranging from sandwiches to full main dishes. *(Recommended by Marilynne Blyth, Donald Mather)*

Bass Charringtons · Licensee W G Hummerston · Real ale · Meals and snacks (lunchtime, not Sun) · Children in eating area · Open 10.30–2.30, 5.30–10.30

COBHAM   TQ1060 Map 3

Cricketers

Downside Common; from A245 on Byfleet side of Cobham follow Downside signpost into Downside Bridge Road, follow road into its right fork (away from Cobham Park) at second turn after bridge, then take next left turn into the pub's own lane

With beams so low that it has crash-pads on them, this snug and rambling country pub has simple and traditional furnishings, horse brasses and big brass platters on the walls, some ancient time-bowed standing timbers, a good winter log fire, and in places you can see the wide oak ceiling-boards and ancient plastering laths. A neat and charming garden with standard roses, dahlias and other bedding plants, urns and hanging baskets, overlooks the broad green. Bar food includes sandwiches (80p), ploughman's (from £1.25), and hot dishes such as lasagne, moussaka, fisherman's pie and steak and kidney pie (£2.25), and readers have enjoyed the neat separate restaurant. Well kept Combes, Ruddles County, Watneys Stag and Websters Yorkshire on handpump. *(Recommended by Robin Leggett, Doug Kennedy; more reports please)*

Watneys · Licensee B J W Luxford · Real ale · Meals (not Sun evening) and snacks · Children in restaurant and area partly set aside · Open 11–2.30, 6–11 all year

Plough

Plough Lane; from A245 take Downside Bridge Road, signposted Downside, then first right turn

This last autumn they've opened a new carvery here, with a wide choice of hot and cold home-cooked meats (from £2.15 for gammon), and other popular freshly cooked food in this cheerful, lively pub includes a good choice of sandwiches (from 55p, toasties from 65p, hot sausage 75p, eight-ounce steak £2.75), a range of filled baked potatoes, ploughman's (£1.10), lunchtime daily specials such as shepherd's pie or steak and kidney pie (£1.85), basket meals such as scampi or seafood platter (£2.25), and grills from pork chop (£2.75) to eight-ounce sirloin steak (£5). The long red-carpeted lounge bar has red-shaded lamps just under the low black joists, and modern tables, Windsor chairs and tapestried stools and benches around the walls; well kept Courage Best and Directors and John Smiths on handpump. You can sit outside the pretty black-shuttered brick house – which is thought to date back some 500 years – either on a long bench outside the snug little bare-boarded bar the real locals use, or at the picnic-table sets on the terrace and grass behind the car park, near flowers against a high brick garden wall. Darts, shove-ha'penny, dominoes, cribbage, maybe piped music. *(Recommended by Capt F A Bland, RJF, Jack Taylor)*

Courage · Licensee John Huetson · Real ale · Meals (lunchtime) and snacks Children in eating area · Open 10.30–2.30, 5.30–11 all year

COMPTON   SU9546 Map 2
Harrow
B3000

Popular for its straightforward good value food, this comfortably modernised country pub serves sandwiches, including crab and smoked salmon, and toasties garnished with chips and salad (85p–£2.20), home-made winter soups such as leek and potato (£1) and goulash or seafood (£1.50), ploughman's (from £1.80), baked potatoes with an interesting filling of the day (£1.95–£2.95), scampi or quiche (£3.25), and half a dozen changing hot dishes – one of which is always vegetarian – such as spare ribs, paella, sweet and sour pork, steak and kidney pie, moussaka, chicken with tomatoes, mushrooms and wine or lasagne (£2.50–£3.50); sometimes they do a hefty seafood platter for two (£8.50). The main bar has some interesting racing pictures below the ancient ceiling, mostly portraits of horses such as Nijinsky, jockey caricatures and signed race-finish photographs. Other beamed rooms with latched rustic doors open off, and there's an attractively relaxed atmosphere. Friary Meux and Ind Coope Burton on handpump; charming service; piped music, a fruit machine. You can sit outside in summer, round by the car park but looking out to gentle slopes of pasture. In the pretty village the art nouveau Watts Chapel and Gallery are interesting, and the church itself is attractive. *(Recommended by MHG, Aubrey Saunders)*

Friary Meux · Licensees Roger and Susan Seaman · Real ale · Meals (lunchtime) and snacks · Children in eating area · Open 10.30–2.30, 6–11

The Withies
Withies Lane; pub signposted from B3000

This smart country pub is now mainly a good restaurant (closed Sunday evening – readers haven't been keen on a bookings system for two-session dinners) but still preserves a very small but civilised and genuinely pubby bar, with settles (one rather splendidly art nouveau), beams, a big inglenook fireplace, and some attractive panels of seventeenth-century carving between the small windows. Lunchtime bar snacks (they refuse to give us up-to-date prices) such as ploughman's, pâté and granary bread, and smoked salmon or prawn and mayonnaise sandwiches. Besides pricey Friary Meux on handpump, you can get buck's fizz by the bottle, a well made Pimms, and a wide choice of wines by the bottle. The garden is very pretty, with tables under an arbour of creeper-hung trellises, more on a crazy-paved terrace, and yet more under old apple-trees; the neat lawn in front of the steeply tiled white house is bordered by masses of flowers. *(Recommended by Peter Barrett; more reports please)*

Free house · Licensee Claudio Bono · Real ale · Lunchtime snacks · Children in restaurant · Open 10.30–2.30, 6–11

DORKING   TQ1649 Map 3
Cricketers

81 South Street; from centre follow signs to Horsham (A2003)

Cheerful and well kept, this attractive town pub has an enthusiastic local following, some of whose members have for some time been trying to persuade us to include it as a main entry. We confess that the evidence of collusion between them did originally put us off (it's our normal policy not to inspect pubs at all if we suspect that recommendations have been a put-up job, or if recommenders have 'conspired' together). But as we were in the area recently, and as the collaborators had been so clearly good-natured and well intentioned, we did pay a visit – and well worthwhile it was, too. The spick-and-span carpeted and modernised bar dog-legs around a central servery, which has a big modern etched-glass mirror with cricketers, and is comfortably furnished with well cushioned sturdy settles and library chairs around cast-iron-framed tables. Its clean stripped-and-sealed brick walls are decorated with Spy cricketer caricatures and other cricketing pictures, and on our visit it had above its log-effect gas fire a huge bowl of fresh sweet peas (from a customer who had just won nine firsts at the local flower show). Up steps at the back there's a very pretty little sheltered terrace, interestingly planted with roses, a good red honeysuckle, uncommon shrubs and herbaceous plants, and gently floodlit at night. Bar food at lunchtime (when it's very much quieter than in the evenings) includes ploughman's (£1), liver and mushroom pâté (£1.40), smoked mackerel (£1.60), fish or sausages and chips (£1.85) and scampi (£2), with daily specials such as savoury quiche (£1.80), grilled bacon chop with broad beans and parsley sauce (£1.90) or lamb fillet (£1.95), and they keep a variety of well filled big baps. Really well kept Fullers Chiswick, ESB and London Pride on handpump, and a fine, friendly atmosphere; darts (the board is decorated with an appropriate gift from a Staffordshire pub's tug-o'-war team which this pub has competed against). *(Recommended by NAW – and Peter Barnard and others)*

Fullers · Licensee Bill Bower · Real ale · Meals (weekday lunchtimes) and snacks (not Sat evening or Sun) · Children may be allowed in if it's raining Nearby daytime parking difficult · Open 11–2.30, 5.30–11

EAST CLANDON   TQ0651 Map 3

Queens Head

This civilised and traditionally furnished half-timbered village pub
has a big inglenook fireplace, a fine elm bar counter, and a faded but
interesting Victorian foxhunting embroidery, with comfortable but
more usual upholstered chairs, little beer-keg seats, brasses and
copper. It can get crowded in the evening. The wide choice of home-
cooked food (in winter you can sometimes smell the cooking)
includes old-fashioned dishes such as Mrs Beeton's good family soup
(95p), steak pie with mango and spices (£3.85), Victorian game pie
(£4.30) and Eliza Acton's puddings (around £1), tipsy-cake, as well
as sandwiches (lunchtime only), fresh prawns from Selsey (£2.20),
fish and cider pie (£3.25), steak and kidney pie (£3.85), rabbit pie
(£3.95) and steaks (from eight-ounce sirloin, £5.25); on bank
holidays prices may be higher. Friary Meux and Ind Coope Burton on
handpump. You can sit on roadside benches in front, or by the
flowers around a tree-sheltered side lawn. The car park backs on to
an orchard behind the pub, where children can run wild. Nearby, off
the road south to Shere, you can walk through splendid beech woods.
(Recommended by Roger Doughty, Jack Taylor, J S Evans)

*Friary Meux · Licensees Frank and Cynthia Allchin · Real ale · Snacks
(lunchtime) and meals · Open 11.30–2.30, 6.30–11*

EWELL   TQ2262 Map 3

Glyn Arms

45 Cheam Road (A232)

Since our last edition, a change of nationality for both licensees and
dogs in this handsome Georgian pub: they're British, not New
Zealanders, and their dogs are Alsatians not Airedales. But the
atmosphere is as pleasant as ever, in this well kept and popular series
of separate rooms (one very small and snug, the others more
spacious) rambling into one another, connected by lobbies and
passages. A separate Barn Bar which overlooks the neatly kept beer
garden is larger, with a lofty pitched ceiling, and tables set for the
home-cooked food – the burgers (from £2.35) are particularly good,
and other food includes sandwiches, bacon and egg (£2.45), chicken
(£2.65), fish or scampi (£2.95), and charcoal-grilled mixed grill (£5)
or eight-ounce rump steak (£5.75). Well kept Bass and Charrington
IPA on handpump; a fruit machine, open fires in winter, maybe piped
music. *(Recommended by John Townsend, Marilynne Blyth, 'Arry Hart
and others)*

*Charringtons · Licensees J Hawkins and T Wick · Real ale · Meals and snacks
(not Sun) · Open 10.30–2.30, 5.30–11 all year*

nr EWHURST   TQ0940 Map 3

Windmill ★

Ewhurst–Shere back road; follow Shere signposts from E end of Ewhurst main
street, or ask for Pitch Hill

This friendly woodside pub has spectacular views, and is a great

favourite with readers for its good home-made food, including soups
(50p), sandwiches such as rare beef (from £1.25), ploughman's (from
£1.10), chicken liver (£1.35) or smoked salmon (£1.50) pâtés,
sausages and mash (£1.35, children's helping 75p), curry (from £2),
salads (from £2.50), chicken casseroled in red wine (£3.75) and
sirloin steak (£5.95 evenings only), with changing seasonal dishes
such as pheasant casserole and other game or seafood chowder
(£3.50) in winter, and in summer fresh prawns, crabs and lobster.
The main bar, with easy chairs and a patterned carpet, has picture
windows which look out over terraced lawns that drop steeply away
below, and on a clear day you can see right across to the south coast –
useful at the time when this pub was a smugglers' look-out. Service is
friendly and helpful, though it can get crowded at weekends, even in
winter. A sparser back bar, without the view, has darts, dominoes,
cribbage, shut the box, a fruit machine and a space game. Well kept
King & Barnes Sussex and Youngs Special on handpump. There are
plenty of seats out on the beautifully kept lawns among flowers and
shrubs, and the nearby woods are marvellous for walks.
(Recommended by Jack Taylor, Miss P M Gammon, Gwen and Peter
Andrews, Doug Kennedy, A G Thompson, Pamela Bishop)

Free house · Licensee C B B Holland · Real ale · Meals and snacks · Children in
back bar or two furnished porches · Possible parking difficulties on sunny
summer weekends · Open 10.30–2.30, 6–11

FOREST GREEN   TQ1240 Map 3
Parrot ★
Off B2126/B2127

Hoping to visit the Parrot just before this edition of the Guide went to
press we found it closed and looking dead, with signs of building
work in one corner – and were unable to get through on the
telephone or receive any reply to letters. We trust that there's nothing
amiss, as this quaint and warmly welcoming pub is so handy for the
lovely woodland walks in the hills around Abinger. Moreover, one
reader reckons it serves the best prawn sandwiches in Surrey (other
food includes salads, fish or scampi, mixed grills and daily specials,
and there's a separate restaurant), and they keep a changing range of
good beers which might typically consist of Badger Best, Flowers
Original, King & Barnes Sussex and Old, Youngs Bitter and Special,
and Whitbreads Pompey Royal. The rambling bars are full of parrot
designs, ingeniously worked in to some of the most unlikely
materials. There is a comfortable carpeted area by the old central
fireplace with its massive beams (and blazing logs in winter), and a
plainer section with walls of partly bared stonework and partly
cream-painted brick. Round here, the brick floor has been worn to a
fine lustre. Darts, a fruit machine, maybe piped music. There is plenty
of room outside: on one side of this heavily tile-hung house, which
overlooks the village cricket field, there's a good-sized terrace by a
lawn with apple-trees and rosebeds, and on another side a bigger
stretch of grass has some swings. (Recommended by Jack Taylor,
C H Cole; up-to-date reports please)

Free house · Real ale · Meals and snacks (not Sun evening) · Children welcome
Open 10.30–2.30, 6–11

GUILDFORD   SU9949   Map 2
Bull's Head
123 High Street

Carefully restored after the last war, when its massive sixteenth-century timbers were so rotten and bulging that it was almost condemned as unsafe, this reborn town pub has a busy, welcoming and comfortably refurbished downstairs bar, long and narrow, with heavy beams, neat fancy brickwork, and a sturdy old-fashioned footrail along the bar counter. Lunchtime bar food includes filled rolls and sandwiches, filled baked potatoes (from £1.40), ploughman's (from £1.45), chicken and mushroom pie and tandoori chicken (£2), with just the baked potatoes and pizzas in the evening and on Sundays. A more expensive dark-timbered upstairs salad bar, decorated with dried flowers, also has a good selection of carefully made salads (though there's no choice of dressings). Well kept Bass, Flowers Original, Marstons Pedigree, Shepherd Neame, Wethereds and SPA on handpump, with different guest beers each month. *(Recommended by Gabriele Berneck, David Symes)*

Free house · Licensees David Riley and Tom Brown · Real ale · Meals (lunchtime, not Sun) and snacks (not Sun lunchtime, not Fri or Sat evenings) Daytime parking some way away · Open 10.30–2.30, 5.30–11 all year

HORLEY   TQ2842   Map 3
Olde Six Bells

3 miles from M23 junction 9: from Gatwick turn-off follow A23 towards Reigate and London, then Horley signpost at roundabout; after 600 yards pub signposted by sharp left turn into Church Road, which is first real left turn

The busy and cheerful rambling bar of this striking old building, with its roof of heavy Horsham stone slabs, is open-plan, with a tiled floor, heavy beams, butter-coloured plaster walls and ceiling, and some copper measuring dippers for decoration. Upstairs is quieter, carpeted, with high rafters and heavy wall timbering: you can book tables up here for the popular home-made food, such as sandwiches, soup (90p), a choice of ploughman's (from £1.45), salads including quiche or chicken (£2.95), turkey, ham, pork or beef (around £3.50), and goulash, hot-pot, beef in ale or pork in cider (£4.40), with a good choice of puddings. At lunchtime on Sundays they may hand out free hot herb bread. Well kept Bass and Charrington IPA on handpump; maybe piped music; darts, shove-ha'penny, dominoes, a fruit machine. Close by the attractive church, this was in the fourteenth century a hospice for the Dorking monastery. From the bar, steps down into a carpeted saloon area take you into what is thought to have been a chapel, with memorial niches in the wall on the right. Beyond a sheltered back flagstone terrace with jasmine on the wall is a sizeable garden beside the little River Mole. *(Recommended by Marilynne Blyth, 'Arry Hart, Mrs N E Ibbott)*

Charringtons · Licensees G A and P A Noble · Real ale · Meals – tel Horley (029 34) 2209 – and snacks (not Sun lunchtime – but see above) · Children welcome · Music alternate Thurs · Open 10.30–2.30, 5.30–10.30

KENLEY   TQ3259   Map 3

Wattenden Arms

Old Lodge Lane; turn left (coming from London) off A23 beside Reedham
Station; persevere up narrow lane

Repeatedly a finalist in the *Evening Standard*'s London pub of the
year competition, the 'Watt' is a welcome country escape from the
nearby London suburbs. Good value home-made bar food includes
soup (80p), sandwiches, dressed crab or baked crab with Stilton
(£1.60), casseroles such as rabbit and bacon or beef and walnut (£3),
river trout in white wine (£3), braised duck with Southern Comfort
sauce or roast beef with Yorkshire pudding (£4) and sirloin steak
(£5). The snug and cheerful bar has dark panelling, and booths
formed by small settles around the tables on the red patterned carpet;
well kept Bass and Charrington IPA on handpump, maybe piped
music. In the evenings the atmosphere changes to much more of a
lively local, when it could be difficult to find a table to eat at (though
food is still then available). Outside, seats on its little side lawn look
across to a tangly copse. (*Recommended by Mike Muston, E G Parish,
Mrs G Milford-Scott*)

*Charringtons · Licensee Ron Coulston · Real ale · Meals (not Sun) and snacks
Open 11–3, 5.30–11 all year*

LALEHAM   TQ0568   Map 3

Three Horseshoes

B377

There's been an inn here since the thirteenth century, and when
Edward VII as Prince of Wales, Sir Arthur Sullivan, Marie Lloyd and
the like used to come out here it was just an old stone-flagged country
tavern. The façade is still almost hidden by wistaria, hanging baskets
and cartwheels, but inside it's comfortably modernised now, with
padded leather-look seats on the red carpet of the open-plan bar,
cock-fighting prints on the red walls, and clouds of big copper pans
hanging from beams. One small alcove still has high-backed settles,
and the main fireplace is hung with blacksmith's tools – the pub is
named after the old village forge next door. Bar food ranges from an
excellent choice of sandwiches (from 60p), pâté (from 75p) and
ploughman's (£1.50) to grills such as steaks (£5.25), with a wide
selection of salads; there is also a separate restaurant. Combes,
Ruddles County, Watneys Stag and Websters Yorkshire on
handpump. The garden has plenty of tables, some under a cleverly
rainproofed 'arbour' of creepers, as well as a few statues, and the lane
almost opposite leads down to a stretch of the Thames that is popular
for picnics and sunbathing. (*More reports please*)

*Watneys · Licensee Roland Thanisch · Real ale · Meals and snacks (not Sun)
Open 11–2.30, 6–11 all year*

'Space game' means any electronic game, even a thoroughly earth-bound one.

If you enjoy your visit to a pub please tell the publican. They work
extraordinarily long hours, and when people show their appreciation it makes it
all seem worthwhile.

NEWDIGATE   TQ2042 Map 3
Surrey Oaks

Parkgate Road

Since our last edition the spacious garden of this friendly and cheerful country pub has been extended to include a new rockery with illuminated pools, fountains and a waterfall, and on our most recent visit there was a flock of pure white doves on the lawn – they also have sheep, a calf, and an aviary of budgerigars, and all sorts of fowls. They sell their own free-range hens', duck and goose eggs from the bar, too. The main lounge has tapestried seats in little partly curtained booths, with rustic tables lit by lanterns hanging low from beams decorated with fairy-lights. A much older part on the right has a little snug beamed room by a coal-effect gas fire, then a real open fire in a room with extraordinarily large flagstones. Bar food – all with help-yourself salad – includes sandwiches (95p–£1.30), ploughman's with two sausages, Cheddar, Stilton, ham or pâté, with home-baked bread (£1.85), moussaka, cannelloni, lasagne or chilli con carne (£2.30) and a good choice of vegetarian dishes such as mung bean and mushroom biriani or Bulgar wheat and walnut casserole (£2.50); they've found these extremely popular. On Friday and Saturday evenings they do a carvery. Well kept Friary Meux and Ind Coope Bitter and Burton on handpump. A separate games room has a well lit pool-table, darts, shove-ha'penny, dominoes, cribbage, a fruit machine, space game and a juke box. A little way down the lane there is a bridlepath through Reffolds Copse, the oak wood behind the pub. (*Recommended by Jenny Woolf; more reports please*)

Friary Meux (Ind Coope) · Licensees Colin and Janet Haydon · Real ale · Meals and snacks (not Sun evening) · Children in eating area · Middle-of-the-road live music Sun evening · Open 11–2.30, 6–11

OCKLEY   TQ1439 Map 3
Cricketers Arms

A29

With flagstones on the floor, an inglenook fireplace, pewter tankards hanging from the low beams, and shinily varnished rustic seats, this friendly seventeenth-century pub is handy for the wooded walks and marvellous views around Leith Hill. There are seats on a sunny terrace, full of lavender, roses and other flowers – a nice setting in front of the old stone pub with its imposing roof of huge, mossy old stone slabs and colourful window-boxes in the latticed windows. Simple food includes home-made soup, giant sausage with hot French bread, steak and kidney pie, steak and so forth. Well kept Badger Best, Fullers ESB, King & Barnes Sussex and Youngs Special on handpump; a fruit machine, darts to one side, maybe piped music. Leith Hill Place, just outside the village, is sometimes open in summer. (*Recommended by Dave Butler, Les Storey; more reports please*)

Free house · Licensees C H and B W Pegram · Real ale · Meals (lunchtime, not Sun, and Sun evening) and snacks · Open 11–2.30, 5.30–11

If we know a pub has a no-smoking area, we say so.

nr OCKLEY   TQ1439   Map 3

Punch Bowl ★   [*illustrated on page 613*]

Oakwoodhill (some maps and signposts spell it Okewoodhill); village
signposted off A29 S of Ockley

Pleasantly traditional, this country pub has a relaxing atmosphere,
with huge logs smouldering gently on the vast round hearth of the
inglenook fireplace, many beams and some timbering, an antique
settle among simpler country seats on the deeply polished big dark
flagstones, and scrubbed deal tables. Good value food includes a
regularly changing range of home-cooked specials as well as home-
made soup (95p), sandwiches, ploughman's (£1.50) and pâté (£1.75).
Well kept Badger Best and Tanglefoot, Charrington IPA, King &
Barnes Sussex and Youngs Special on handpump; a good choice of
whiskies. Another plainer bar has sensibly placed darts, a juke box
and a fruit machine, and there's a simple separate dining-room. You
can sit outside the fine old house, partly tile-hung with a heavy slab
roof, at tables on several different birdsong-serenaded terraces, and
fields with oak-trees and woods stretch away on all sides.
(*Recommended by D R Mather, R G Britten, R Wilson, L V Nutton;
more reports please*)

*Free house · Licensee Robert Chambers · Real ale · Meals and snacks (not Sun
and Mon evenings) · Children in room above inglenook bar · Duo Thurs night
Open 10.30–2.30, 530–11*

OUTWOOD   TQ3245   Map 3

Bell ★

The peaceful and well managed garden behind and to the side of this
traditional country pub is a lovely spot on a nice day, with its tables
on a lawn among flowers and shrubs, sheltered by a belt of pine-trees,
having a fine view over rolling fields dotted with oak-trees and
woods. There's a barbecue available every day in summer. Just up the
lane, there's a fine white working windmill on the broad village green.
Inside, the long carpeted front bar has elm and oak tables and chairs,
some in Jacobean style, under its low beams, and the more simply
furnished public bar has a vast stone inglenook fireplace. There's
another lounge bar at the back. Bar food includes fried potato skins
(90p), pâté (£1.75), scampi (£2.95), steak and kidney pie (£3.65) and
charcoal grills such as Barnsley chop with rosemary and tarragon
(£4.10) and steaks (from £6.85), with half a dozen or so daily specials
such as turkey and ham pie (£2.95), sausages and mash (£3.25) and
grilled swordfish steak (£4.50). They will do sandwiches or filled baps
and ploughman's (more likely at lunchtime), and on Sundays there's a
roast lunch (or ploughman's) instead. Since our last edition they've
started doing afternoon teas, as well as morning coffee. Well kept
Bass, Charrington IPA, Felinfoel Double Dragon, Everards Old
Original, Fremlins and King & Barnes Sussex and Festive on
handpump. (*Recommended by E G Parish, C H Cole, Roy and Shirley
Bentley, Dave Butler, Les Storey*)

*Free house · Licensee Harry Pam · Real ale · Meals and some snacks · Open
11–2.30, 6–11*

PYRFORD LOCK   TQ0458 Map 3
Anchor

Lock Lane; service road off A3 signposted to RHS Wisley Gardens – continue past them towards Pyrford

Included for its position, this spacious pub alone in the country has masses of tables under cocktail parasols on a big pink and white terrace by a canal lock, quite busy with narrow-boats which then have to edge their way gingerly through a steep hump-backed bridge. The comfortably modern open-plan bar has big picture windows for the view. Courage Best and Directors on handpump, quickly served salads, basket meals and specials such as steak and kidney pie – get there early to be sure of a table. The Royal Horticultural Society's nearby gardens are open every day (members only on Sunday mornings). *(Recommended by P G Rossington, Robin Leggett)*

Courage · Real ale · Meals and snacks (lunchtime and early evening, not Mon) · Open 11–2.30, 6–11

REIGATE HEATH   TQ2349 Map 3
Skimmington Castle ★

3 miles from M25 junction 8: A25 through Reigate, then on W edge of Reigate District turn S into hamlet of Reigate Heath; after about ½ mile turn left into Bonny's Road (unmade, very bumpy track); after crossing golf course fork right up hill

This cottagey pub, at the end of an unmade dead-end track, has old-fashioned settles and Windsor chairs in its snug, partly panelled back rooms, one of which has a big brick fireplace with its bread oven still beside it. The main front bar, with bigger windows looking down the hill, has more of the homely furniture, and the old game of ring the bull. The small but efficiently run central serving counter, framed in simple dark panelling, has a collection of oddly shaped pipes dangling over it. Bar snacks include hot sausages (25p), Cornish pasties (60p) and – if they're not too busy – things like cheese with warm French bread (£1.15) or toasted sandwiches (from 75p). At lunchtime there are also salads (from £2.50), with hot specials in winter, such as steak, kidney and mushroom pie or potato-packed Lancashire hot-pot (£2.20). Handpumped Friary Meux and Ind Coope Bitter and Burton. A small room down steps from the back tap-room has a space game, and there are darts, shove-ha'penny, dominoes and cribbage. This little tiled white house perches on a low hill, with a few other houses down the track past the parked cars. You can sit outside on the crazy-paved front terrace or on the grass by lilac bushes, and from here paths wind into the surrounding wooded countryside. *(Recommended by MHG, Alan Franck, Annie Taylor, Peter Hitchcock, Stephan Carney)*

Friary Meux · Licensee Andrew Fisher · Real ale · Meals (lunchtime, not Sun) and snacks · Children in games room · Open 10.30–2.30, 5.30–11

In next year's edition we hope to pick out pubs where the food is specially good, alongside the star ratings. Please tell us if you think any pub – in the *Guide* or not – deserves a 'Food Award'. No stamp needed: *The Good Pub Guide*, FREEPOST, London SW10 0BR.

RUNFOLD   SU8747   Map 2
Jolly Farmer

A31 just E of Farnham

Very well run, this big open-plan roadside pub has good value lunchtime food such as soup, sandwiches (60p), ploughman's (£1.30), pâté (£1.40), plaice (£2.40), roast beef (£3.95) and a daily special such as boiled beef with almond dumplings (£3.50). The evening menu tends to be considerably more ambitious (there's a separate restaurant). It's well furnished, friendly and busy, with some massive rough-cut elm tables and chairs as well as more conventionally comfortable seats, and has an unusual painted vine-leaf dado around its cornices. At one end big windows look out on the back garden and terrace, where there are plenty of tables among some flowers and shrubs, and a good adventure playground; they have fine-weather summer barbecues out here on Wednesday, Friday and Saturday evenings, and at Sunday lunchtime. Darts, shove-ha'penny, dominoes, a fruit machine and unobtrusive piped music; well kept Courage Best and Directors on handpump, also children's cocktails (and adult ones). The pub is a regular winner of the local newspaper's pub of the year competition. (*Recommended by Col D A Cash, MRP*)

Courage · Licensee Laurie Richardson · Real ale · Meals and snacks · Children in eating area and restaurant · Open 10.30–2.30, 5.30–11

SHAMLEY GREEN   TQ0343   Map 3
Red Lion

B2128 S of Guildford

Very popular for its food, this pub fills up quickly at lunchtime – and if you want their traditional Sunday lunch (£4.75) you have to book. On weekdays, the wide choice – with very big helpings quickly served – includes good soups such as ham and lentil or chicken and sweetcorn, with croûtons (£1.20), toasted sandwiches (from £1.65), sandwiches such as good rare beef with home-baked wholemeal bread (£1.80), ploughman's (from £1.85, Brie with peppers or mushrooms £1.95), sausage and eggs (£2.45), home-baked ham and eggs (£2.55), barbecued spare ribs, curried cottage pie, vegetarian lasagne, borghal wheat casserole or mung bean bran (all £2.95), prawn and cheese omelette (£3.85), good pies with nice pastry such as smoked haddock with courgettes or steak and kidney (£4.25) and eight-ounce rump steak (£6.65). A good mixture of furniture includes a handsome panel-back armed settle, red-brocaded high-backed modern settles forming booths around tables, some kitchen chairs, a couple of antique clocks, and old photographs on the cream walls – some of cricket played on the opposite green. There's a dining-room area on the left, and everywhere a pleasant murmur of conversation – it's a place where local ladies meet for lunch. Ind Coope Bitter, Best and Burton tapped from casks behind the bar; a fruit machine in a brick-floored side lobby. The licensee takes obvious care to make sure customers here are happy. (*Recommended by Anthony Stephenson*)

Free house · Licensee C C Ross · Real ale · Meals – tel Guildford (0483) 892202 – and snacks · Open 10.30–2.30, 5.30–11

SHEPPERTON   TQ0867   Map 3

King's Head   [*illustrated on page 608*]

Church Square; E side of B375

Since our last edition the licensee has laid oak parquet flooring in the lounge, to match the floor in its other small rooms, and in redecorating it has uncovered and restored an inglenook fireplace. Parts of this building date from the fourteenth century, and it has dark panelling, oak beams, and some bottle glass in its thick-framed old windows. Courage Best and Directors on handpump; bar food includes sandwiches, soup, ploughman's, salads and hot dishes such as lasagne, steak and kidney pie or steaks; darts and a juke box in the public bar. With its window-boxes and black shutters, it's a pretty place to sit outside in summer, looking across the village square to the brick and flint church. There are also tables under cocktail parasols on a back terrace sheltered by high walls covered with honeysuckle, climbing roses, Russian vine and hanging baskets of flowers. (*More reports please*)

Courage · Licensee David Longhurst · Real ale · Meals and snacks (not Sun) Children in eating area · Open 10.30–2.30, 5.30–11

SHERE   TQ0747   Map 3

White Horse ★ ★

Carefully restored and modernised, this fine old pub is comfortable and friendly inside, and for summer has seats charmingly placed among prettily planted troughs of flowers and bright hanging baskets on a sunny cobbled courtyard. The open-plan main lounge bar has interesting, genuinely ancient features including antique oak wall seats, massive beams, a huge inglenook fireplace (with warm log fires in winter), old manuscripts on the walls, and elegant Tudor stonework in a second inglenook fireplace through in the Pilgrim's Bar. The floors are uneven – no foundations here, just salvaged ships' timbers plunged into the ground some 600 years ago. The food, all cooked to order, includes a wide range of sandwiches, various ploughman's, salads (around £2–£3), plaice or barbecued chicken (£2.50), home-made steak and kidney pie (£2.80), chicken and mushroom pie (£2.90), poached local rainbow trout (£3.25), poussin (£3.40) and steaks (from eight-ounce sirloin £4.95); helpings are usually generous – so much so in one case that our correspondents had to roar with laughter, and found it hard to prise themselves out of their seats afterwards. Well kept Combes, Ruddles County, and Websters Yorkshire on handpump. This is such a pretty village that sometimes at weekends the ancient half-timbered pub (after all one of its finest features) is remarkably crowded; though most readers have found the friendly staff cope very well even under those circumstances, one or two have felt occasional strain. There is good walking in the beech woods on the road north towards East Clandon. (*Recommended by Brian and Rosemary Wilmot, D R Mather, Miss P M Gammon, Tim Halstead, E G Parish, W J Wonham, Stuart Barker, H Graves, Jack Lalor*)

Watneys · Licensee Barry Whitaker · Real ale · Meals and snacks (not Sun evening) · Children in Pilgrim's Bar · Open 11–2.30, 6–11

STAINES TQ0471 Map 3

Swan

The Hythe; south bank of the Thames, over Staines Bridge

It's the Thames-side setting that brings readers to this sensitively restored old inn. There's a charming sycamore-shaded terrace by the tow-path, with some tables protected by an overhanging upper balcony, and both main bars have good river views. They're well run and pleasantly furnished with armchairs, tapestried settles and leatherette seats, and the original fireplaces have been carefully exposed. Bar food includes sandwiches (from 85p, toasted 15p extra), filled baked potatoes (from £1.10), home-made soup (£1.20), French bread generously filled with beef (£1.90), ploughman's (from £1.55), home-made pâté (£1.65), lasagne (£2.50), basket meals such as scampi (£3), salads (from £2.25), and home-made dishes of the day such as cottage pie or steak and kidney pie (from £2.25); well kept Fullers ESB and London Pride from electric pumps (most unusual down here); a fruit machine, maybe piped music. The upstairs restaurant, nicely redecorated in a heavily old-fashioned style, includes a big bay window overlooking the river. (Recommended by David Regan, C Elliott, D S Smith)

Fullers · Licensees K J G Kothe and A Curtis · Real ale · Meals and snacks Children in large lounge without serving bar · Open 11–2.30, 5.30–11 Bedrooms tel Staines (0784) 52494; £19.50/£27.50

THURSLEY SU9039 Map 2

Three Horseshoes ★

We enjoy the dark and cosy bar of this civilised old tile-hung stone pub very much indeed, with its fine country furniture, including lovingly polished elm tables and a handsome set of brass and porcelain beer engines for the well kept Gales ales. Its decorations include original Brockbank cartoons (he lived here) and three horseshoes from the 1952 Olympic three-day event winner Jubal (a Christmas present from the trainer). There is a good choice of excellent sandwiches, and hot dishes are carefully home cooked – you can have your meals served in a simply furnished small back dining-room. On Friday and Saturday evenings the dinners are well worth booking; there's just bread and cheese on Sundays. A good range of less common spirits and drinks like Pimms or buck's fizz are available. For us, part of the pub's very considerable charm is the way that it firmly reflects the personality of its licensee – the pub is very clearly his, and you'll enjoy it most if you put yourself in the frame of mind of being a guest in the home of someone you don't yet know well. There are tables outside on a big roundel of grass under pine-trees at the front, and in summer there's a garden bar. (Recommended by C J McCafferty, Annie Taylor, Peter Barrett; more reports please)

Gales · Licensee Valentine de Burgh · Real ale · Meals (not Sun lunchtime, not Mon–Thurs evenings) and snacks (lunchtime, also Sun evening); dining-room bookings tel Elstead (0252) 703268 · Children in dining-room (lunchtime only) · Open 11–2.30, 6–10.30

WALLISWOOD   TQ1138   Map 3
Scarlett Arms

Village signposted from Ewhurst—Rowhook back road; or follow
Oakwoodhill signpost from A29 S of Ockley, then follow Walliswood signpost
into Walliswood Green Road

A surprise for this part of the Home Counties: delightfully unspoilt,
welcoming you straight back into altogether more relaxed days. This
neat red-tiled white building used to be a pair of labourers' cottages,
and still preserves the old small-roomed layout: two communicating
rooms with heavy black oak beams in the low brown ceiling,
sparkling clean red lino and deeply polished flagstones, a little winter
fire by the bar counter and a vast heap of logs smouldering in the
other room (or big bunches of flowers instead in the summer),
country prints and a couple of photographs of old Shell oil tankers,
and simple but perfectly comfortable benches, high bar stools with
backrests, and trestle tables. Food is limited to sandwiches (50p),
home-made soup (60p) and ploughman's (£1); well kept King &
Barnes Bitter, Festive and Old Ale tapped in a back room; darts and
shove-ha'penny in a small room at the end. There are old-fashioned
seats and tables in the garden. *(Recommended by Paul Dudley,
C M Harnor)*

*King & Barnes · Licensee Mrs Booie Thompson · Real ale · Open 11–2.30,
6–11*

WALTON ON THE HILL   TQ2255   Map 3
Chequers

Chequers Lane (B2220, S of centre)

You might easily swish straight past this big mock-Tudor suburban-
looking pub, if you hadn't heard what was inside: good value food,
well kept Youngs Bitter and Special, and a first-class atmosphere –
friendly staff even when they're busy, and welcoming customers. The
front part is thoroughly old-fashioned, with a string of snug little
interconnecting carpeted rooms, cosy leatherette seats around their
walls, low beams, open fire, and attractive décor (for instance a good
set of 1936 Gallahers jockey cigarette cards). Darts, a fruit machine.
Round the back is an airy and spacious new tiled room, with youthful
customers spread around the well spaced tables and a more familiar
Youngs cream and brown décor; big windows look out on the terrace
and neat garden – where there are summer barbecues at lunchtime
and in the evening with reasonably priced burgers, trout, steaks and
so forth. Throughout the year an efficient food bar in this back room
serves honest fare such as sandwiches, sausages, ham salad, filled
baked potatoes, and fresh hot dishes such as cottage pie, chilli con
carne or chicken curry. The adjoining restaurant is very popular
(booking advised; closed Sunday evening, Monday). In the last
moments before we went to press we heard that the Koppanys might
be moving back into London – please keep us posted about any
changes. *(Recommended by Donald Mather, Lesley Foote, Jean and
Theodore Rowland-Entwistle, Alan Carter, R B Entwistle, A Darroch
Harkness)*

*Youngs · Licensees Chris and Rachel Koppany · Real ale · Meals (lunchtime)
and snacks; restaurant bookings tel Tadworth (073 781) 2364 · Children in
restaurant · Traditional jazz Thurs · Open 10.30–2.30, 5.30–10.30*

WARLINGHAM TQ3658 Map 3
White Lion

B269

A real surprise for these outer fringes of London, this is the most
interesting pub for miles around. It has a friendly warren of dimly lit
black-panelled rooms, with extremely low beams, deeply aged
plasterwork, and woodblock floors. Its snug heart is a fine Tudor
fireplace, more or less enclosed by high-backed settles. Food includes
sandwiches, a choice of pâtés, salads and hot dishes such as steak and
kidney pie; Bass and Charrington IPA on handpump. A room with
some amusing early nineteenth-century cartoons has darts, a fruit
machine and a space game. There are good sturdy wooden seats on
the immaculate back lawn, surrounded by a herbaceous border, with
a goldfish pond; in summer the garden has its own bar. *(Recommended
by Mike Muston, St John Sandringham; more reports please)*

*Charringtons · Licensees Anthony Brand and William Delea · Real ale · Meals
and snacks (lunchtime, not Sun) · Open 10.30–2.30, 6–10.30*

WITLEY SU9439 Map 2
White Hart ★

Petworth Road

This pretty tile-hung house is largely a Tudor reconstruction of an inn
first mentioned 700 years ago, and some of its customers have been a
rum bunch – like Captain Luke Angell, discovered in the late
eighteenth century slicing open a barmaid's blouse with the tip of his
sword, or Martin Lofts, who in 1544 broke both legs jumping out of
an upstairs window because he thought the king's men were after him
– in fact they were searching out the parson to take him to the Tower
for his 'lewd and naughty' behaviour. George Eliot, retreating here
from the labours of writing *Daniel Deronda*, used to sit in the
inglenook seat just on the bar side of the fireplace; this room has good
oak furniture on its woodblock floor, and pewter tankards hanging
from the beams. The other bar, Ron's Bar, once used to be stables –
the notches in the very low beams held the uprights for the stalls. Bar
food includes sandwiches (from 60p, smoked salmon or prawn
£1.50), toasties (from 80p), burger in a home-made roll (60p),
ploughman's (£1), home-made shepherd's pie (£2), scampi (£2.75),
three-egg omelettes (£3), gammon (£4.25), trout (£4.75) and steak
(£5.50), with children's dishes such as fish fingers (£1.50); there is
also a separate restaurant, and they do three-course Sunday lunches
(£4.50). Watneys Stag on handpump; sensibly placed darts, also
dominoes and shove-ha'penny; maybe unobtrusive piped music. You
can sit on the front terrace outside the pub, which is almost dwarfed
by its steeply pitched roof; sunny and quite sheltered, though it's by
the road. There's also a children's playground. The inn-sign is a copy

of a much older one, which was touched up in the last century by Birkett Foster and is now in the Victoria and Albert Museum. This is an attractive village: some of its half-timbered cottages are as old as the pub, parts of the church are much older. You can stroll on the wooded common. *(More reports please)*

Phoenix (Watneys) · Licensee Mrs Daphne Terry · Real ale · Meals and snacks Children in restaurant · Open 10.30–2.30, 5.30–11

WORPLESDON   SU9753   Map 2
Jolly Farmer

Burdenshott Road; from Guildford take A320 towards Woking, and turn left at Worplesdon Station signpost (NB not the Worplesdon turning itself)

There's a fine range of well kept real ales on handpump in this popular country pub, changing from time to time but including ones like Badger Best, Fullers ESB, Gales HSB, Gibbs Mew Bishops Tipple, Sam Smiths OB, and Wethereds Bitter and SPA. The prices tend to keep the simply furnished L-shaped bar more civilised (though not always less crowded) than it might be in other pubs serving so many real ales; there's also a wide choice of spirits and cocktails. Good bar food includes hot soup (90p), gazpacho (£1.10), sandwiches (from £1.25), filled baked potatoes (from £1.45), pâté (£1.95 – may be the cheapest thing served on Sundays), home-made pizza (£2.20), gammon and other salads (from £3.75), and daily specials such as lasagne (£3.75); they rather specialise in generously filled savoury pancakes (from £4.75). There's also a separate olde-world restaurant, with a midnight supper licence extension. Dominoes, piped music (unobtrusive on quiet weekday lunchtimes, may be loud at other times). There are picnic-table sets under cocktail parasols on a big, sheltered lawn, with fruit-trees and some flowers. *(Recommended by David Symes, N J Roberts, M J Hale; more reports please)*

Free house · Licensee David Rowley · Real ale · Meals and snacks (not Mon evening) · Children in restaurant · Open 10.30–2.30, 5.30–11 all year

WOTTON   TQ1247   Map 3
Wotton Hatch

A25 Dorking–Guildford; coming from Dorking, start slowing as soon as you see the Wotton village sign – the pub's round the first bend

Comfortable and well kept, this seventeenth-century pub has good food in both bars and restaurant. The low-ceilinged front bar has cushioned wheelback chairs around copper-topped tables on its patterned carpet, and bar food, changing daily, might typically include ploughman's (£1.60), pâté (£1.70), fried chicken (£1.80), pizza or cheese and onion flan (£1.85), pork pie salad (£1.90), beef hash (£1.95) and plaice with ham and cauliflower cheese sauce (£2); they will normally cut sandwiches. Well kept Fullers Chiswick, London Pride and ESB on handpump; on our visit, local eggs for sale, and Radio 1. An adjacent tiled-floor public bar has darts, dominoes, cribbage and a fruit machine. Off to one side a handsome cocktail bar, with gentle piped music and medieval-style seats ranked around its panelled walls under a high frieze of plates and Victorian pilgrim's-progress wallpaper, leads into an attractive and spacious panelled dining-room. This has some tables in a conservatory extension, looking out over a white pergola on a neat lawn. The menu here, changing fortnightly, might typically include Mexican beef stew or pork chops as lunchtime main courses (three courses (£9.85), with pan-fried salmon for dinner (three courses £14). Outside, beyond a screen of roses and sweet peas, there are picnic-table sets on a second lawn by a pavilion. *(Recommended by D S Smith, MHG, H G and C J McCafferty)*

Fullers · Licensee R Bagnall · Real ale · Meals (not Sun, not Mon evening) and snacks (not Sun evening); restaurant bookings tel Dorking (0306) 885665 Children in restaurant · Open 10.30–2.30, 5.30–11

Lucky Dip

Besides the fully inspected pubs, you might like to try these Lucky Dips recommended and described by readers (if you do, please send us reports):

ABINGER HAMMER [Dorking Road; TQ0947], *Abinger Arms*: friendly (very) and reasonably priced, with good beers and good food *(Timothy George Foss)*

ADDLESTONE [High Street; TQ0464], *Holly Tree*: good value food, pleasant atmosphere *(N J Searle)*

ALBURY HEATH [Little London; TQ0646], *William IV*: friendly, small pub in heart of countryside; lunchtime menu recommended *(Miss P M Gammon)*

ALFOLD [TQ0334], *Crown*: cheerful pub with home-made bar food; several rooms; well kept garden, in quiet village *(LYM)*; [Dunsfold Road] *Three Compasses*: remote country inn on quiet back lane with inglenook in public bar and an airy saloon *(LYM)*

ASH [Shawfield Road; SU8950], *Cricketers*: small, cosy and attractive, with wide range of good bar food and friendly service; big garden *(Ian and Julie Taylor)*

ASHTEAD [The Street; TQ1858], *Leg of Mutton & Cauliflower*: old friendly and roomy Charringtons pub *(Marilynne Blythe)*

BATTS CORNER [SU8240], *Blue Bell*: good bar snacks and range of real ales from cask in quaint and welcoming old free house by Alice Holt Forest; big garden – tables, swings, apple-trees, tree house; no music (for pub location see OS Sheet 186 reference 820410) *(W A Gardiner, R M R Parker)*

BEARE GREEN [TQ1842], *Dukes Head*: characterful public bar in pretty roadside Ind Coope pub with well kept real ales and pleasant garden *(A J Milman, LYM)*

BISHOPSGATE [SU9871], *Fox and Hounds*: Monday evening live jazz, pleasant green with tables on front terrace; by an entrance to Windsor Park *(S J Tims)*

BLINDLEY HEATH [Tandridge Lane; TQ3645], *Red Barn*: single big library bar full of books; big open fireplace, warm welcome, always busy, wide range of beers including Pilgrim (from Woldingham) *(T J Powell, Michael Kerschbaum)*

BRAMLEY [High Street; TQ0044], *Jolly Farmer*: cheerful and lively front bar in Watneys pub with good value simple food; bedrooms *(LYM)*

BROOK [SU9337], *Dog and Pheasant*: welcoming old pub with wide choice of good value food, friendly service, real ale; opposite village cricket field in pretty scenery (for pub location see OS Sheet 186 reference 930380) *(Theresa Lister, B S Matthews)*

CHARLESHILL [SU8944], *Donkey*: comfortable pub with brass in polished bars, good atmosphere, and well kept Courage Directors; playground for children, and donkey *(Keith and Ruth Brothwell)*

CHARLWOOD [Church Road; TQ2441], *Half Moon*: plainly modernised old Friary Meux pub with good local atmosphere, and freshly made sandwiches;

bar billiards, shove-ha'penny, space game, darts and a fruit machine *(Stuart Barker, Simon Evans, BB)*

CHERTSEY [London Street; TQ0466], *Crown*: smartly restored old Youngs pub, with warm atmosphere *(Lesley Foote and Alan Carter)*; [High Street] *George*: friendly old pub said to be haunted and mentioned in H G Wells' *The War of the Worlds*; reasonably priced bar food *(LYM)*

CHIDDINGFOLD [SU9635], *Swan*: lively three-room Ind Coope village pub with back buttery bar (children welcome here) and big helpings of good value freshly cooked appetising food *(Ian Meharg, Mrs K Ware, BB)*

CHOBHAM [High Street; SU9761], *Sun*: low-beamed lounge bar in quiet timbered Courage pub, handy for M3 *(LYM)*

DUNSFOLD [TQ0036], *Sun*: elegantly symmetrical eighteenth-century pub overlooking cricket green; bar food and separate cottage dining-room, Ind Coope real ales *(LYM)*

EAST MOLESEY [TQ1267], *Albion*: good atmosphere, pleasantly furnished; restaurant *(Marilynne Blyth)*

EFFINGHAM [Bell Lane; TQ1253], *Plough*: friendly atmosphere and service in old-fashioned pub, with good value home-made food and well kept beer; outside seats *(Robin Leggett, J S Evans)*

EGHAM [Egham Hill; TQ0171], *Eclipse*: good food and well kept Courage real ales in neat inn; bedrooms *(J P Berryman)*

ELLENS GREEN [TQ1035], *Wheatsheaf*: clean and well run, modernish, has good service and tasty bar food *(R Wilson)*

nr ELSTEAD [SU9143], *Donkey*: well kept highly polished bars full of brass and flowers, carved wooden chairs and settles, wooden farm tools and old clocks; friendly landlord, well kept beer; neat garden and children's playground *(Maureen Guthrie)*

ESHER [High Street; TQ1464], *Albert Arms*: good range of real ales and sensibly priced French regional wines in lively Victorian pub/bistro with popular bar food *(LYM)*; *Cricketers*: good choice of hot and cold food, reasonably priced; pleasant, friendly, quiet music; Trumans *(Nigel Williamson)*

FARNCOMBE [SU9844], *Ram*: lovely garden, good lunchtime food at weekends and very friendly staff in pub specialising in ciders *(David Manners)*

FARNHAM [Long Garden Walk; SU8446], *Hop Blossom*: straightforward real ale pub with wide choice; by major construction project *(David Symes)*; [The Borough] *Queens Head*: pleasant, quiet and comfortable town centre pub, with well kept Gales ales and country wines *(David Symes, W A Gardiner)*; [Bridge Square] *William Cobbett*: Cobbett's picturesque birthplace, now a lively young people's pub with cheap food and lots of amusements – good fun, but over 30s are geriatrics *(LYM)*

FETCHAM [Bell Lane; TQ1456], *Bell*: food at lunchtime recommended; evening snacks, and special dinners and barbecues; good Courage beer, darts, pool; witty, charming landlord; garden *(RJF, Mr and Mrs Jeff Bohm)*

GODALMING [SU9743], *Kings Arms & Royal*: warren of partitioned rooms and rather splendid Tsar's Lounge in substantial and busy eighteenth-century coaching-inn; good cheap home-made lunches *(Mr and Mrs K Virgin, BB)*

GODSTONE [TQ3551], *White Hart*: interesting old inn now converted into Beefeater steak house (Whitbreads); food and service good *(Noel Giffard, LYM)*

GOMSHALL [Dorking Road; TQ0847], *Black Horse*: friendly Youngs pub with large lounge and public bar, open fires, well kept real ale, restaurant; popular with sports car clubs; helpful staff; bedrooms *(Timothy George Foss, Keith and Ruth Brothwell)*

GRAFFHAM [Smithbrook; TQ0241], *Leathern Bottle*: well kept main road pub with open fire, antique guns and wooden tables in saloon bar, games in public bar; well kept King & Barnes, good food, friendly service; tables outside *(C Rosling)*

GUILDFORD [Portsmouth Road; TQ0049], *Cannon*: pleasant, good lunches and Friary Meux; pool-table *(David Symes)*; [Rydes Hill] *Cricketers*: pleasant bar and terrace with seats and tables on lawn, and big two-storey wooden Wendy house for children; well kept beer, bar food served *(Jack Lalor)*; *Jolly Farmer*:

generous helpings of good value food; nice riverside setting near theatre *(Robin Leggett)*

HASCOMBE [TQ0039], *White Horse*: French café-restaurant atmosphere (and good food) in attractive rose-draped English country pub, handy for Winkworth Arboretum *(P J Darby, LYM)*

HASLEMERE [SU9032], *Crown & Cushion*: popular food pub with good vegetarian dishes as well as wide choice on blackboard; well kept Friary Meux and Ind Coope Burton; not cheap *(Doug Kennedy, LYM)*; [High Street] *Swan*: genuinely old Watneys pub given mock-medieval face-lift, with reasonably priced bar food *(LYM)*

HOLMBURY ST MARY [TQ1144], *Kings Head*: very friendly to walkers, lots of atmosphere, log fires, good bar food (also separate restaurant) and real ale *(Jack Taylor, M D Hampson)*

HORLEY [Victoria Road; TQ2842], *Foresters Arms*: unspoilt old-fashioned pub with high bar hatch to tiny back rooms – a charming anachronism in this modern town centre *(LYM)*

LEIGH [TQ2246], *Seven Stars*: cosily cushioned carpeted lounge with interesting early eighteenth-century wall inscriptions, good food, and well kept King & Barnes; garden overlooking green *(C M Harnor, Simon Evans, Stuart Barker, LYM)*; *Seven Stars*: friendly, with good food (even on Sunday) and beer; pretty and comfortable *(Simon Evans)*

MICKLEHAM [TQ1753], *Running Horses*: good food in bar and restaurant of delightful pub with well kept Friary Meux; peaceful village setting *(Capt F A Bland)*

NEW CHAPEL [TQ3642], *Blacksmiths Head*: friendly and warm atmosphere, with good bar snacks *(AA)*

NORTHCHAPEL [SU9529], *Half Moon*: food good and pub restaurant always well booked; friendly, large open fire in winter; country 'souvenirs' on walls *(Nicholas Rolfe)*

OCKHAM [TQ0756], *Hautboy*: spectacular red stone building like Gothick thriller film-set, with unusually good range of real ales in darkly panelled high-raftered upstairs bar; good value food: parrots flying free in minstrels' gallery; lots of seats outside *(MHG, LYM)*

OCKLEY [TQ1439], *Red Lion*: decent choice of real ales, also bar food and restaurant in smartly modernised pub with quiet décor of old beams and some panelling *(BB)*; *School House*: well kept King & Barnes on handpump, good bar food and restaurant, in gleamingly tidy pub with pleasant licensees *(D R Mather)*

OUTWOOD [TQ3245], *Dog & Duck*: food value for money with high standards of service, yet intimate and friendly atmosphere; good mix of beers including Badger and Youngs, wide variety of food, well run *(M E Coomber)*

OXSHOTT [Leatherhead Road; TQ1460], *Victoria*: good food, well stocked bars and attractive layout, popular with old and young; occasional happy hours *(Capt F A Bland)*

PIRBRIGHT [SU9455], *Royal Oak*: good lunchtime food – especially ploughman's and unusually interesting range of well kept real ales in smart up-market main road pub *(M C Ryan, David Symes)*

REDHILL [TQ2650], *Red Lion*: popular at lunchtime for reasonably priced plain food *(LYM)*

REIGATE [Reigate Hill Road; TQ2550], *Yew Tree*: small attractive main road pub with Courage ales, good snacks, nice atmosphere – relaxing break only ½ mile from M25 junction 8 *(W A Gardiner)*

RIPLEY [High Street; TQ0556], *Anchor*: old-fashioned connecting rooms in Tudor inn with lunchtime bar food, games in public bar, and Ind Coope real ales; tables in coachyard *(LYM)*; [High Street] *Talbot*: old village-centre pub with two bars and salad and steak bar; very friendly, low beams, well kept Bass *(Julian Grundy)*

ROWLEDGE [Cherry Tree Road; SU8243], *Cherry Tree*: good choice of reasonably priced lunchtime food, also evening meals; friendly service in attractive pub in village setting *(Mr and Mrs K Virgin)*

SHEPPERTON [Feltham Road; TQ0867], *Harrow*: choice of beers, good bar food including some unusual dishes *(David Regan)*

STAINES [The Hythe; TQ0471], *Jolly Farmer*: real local, small but busy, with reliably well kept Courage ales including mild *(S J Tims, R A Corbett)*; [The Causeway] *Ship*: warm, friendly, obliging service, with good value freshly cooked food in smaller dining-room off bar; well kept beers and wines *(J P Livermore, Gerhard Michael Bauer)*

STOKE D'ABERNON [Station Road; TQ1259], *Plough*: comfortably modernised old pub with well kept Watneys real ales and reasonably priced sensible bar food; big window seats, sizeable garden *(BB)*

SUTTON [TQ1046], *Volunteer*: friendly and fast service, most welcoming atmosphere, good choice of hot food and beer, and wide range of wines; superb winter log fire; big garden *(P G Rossington)*

THAMES DITTON [High Street; TQ1567], *George & Dragon*: good value bar food and welcoming atmosphere in tastefully refurbished pub *(Richard Sullivan)*; [Summer Road] *Olde Swan*: civilised black-panelled upper bar overlooking quiet Thames backwater, with good value bar food and restaurant; tables outside; unusual real ales; own moorings *(Simon Small, LYM)*

TILFORD [SU8743], *Barley Mow*: well kept Courage beer in efficiently run pub in lovely surroundings on large green *(C Elliott)*

WALTON-ON-THAMES [Manor Road; TQ1066], *Swan*: big well run Youngs pub on river *(Lesley Foote and Alan Carter)*; [Towpath] *Weir*: good cold buffet in clean and well kept busy pub overlooking Thames weir; good moorings *(Brian Frith)*

WEST BYFLEET [Old Woking Road; TQ0460], *Carafino*: interesting range of beers and bar food including lots of cheeses in lively spacious pub, popular with young people in the evening and business people at lunchtime *(N J Roberts)*

WEST CLANDON [TQ0452], *Onslow Arms*: stylish and softly lit thick-carpeted pub with quiet corners and reliable food including luxurious sandwiches *(LYM)*

WEYBRIDGE [Thames Street; TQ0764], *Lincoln Arms*: well kept local with good Adnams, Fullers and Greene King real ales, tasty bar food, very popular – especially since recent CAMRA award for sensitive refurbishment and attractive furnishings; excellent atmosphere *(Richard Younger-Ross, J Gooch, Capt F A Bland)*

WRECCLESHAM [Sandrock Hill Road; SU8245], *Sandrock*: well kept beer – especially from West Midlands breweries – in simply furnished pub; bar billiards *(David Symes)*

Sussex

The many Sussex pubs new to the Guide *in this edition include some that are charmingly unspoilt: the Fountain at Ashurst, with a marvellously companionable front bar, the Royal Oak in its little quiet hollow near Chilgrove, the Dunnings Mill on the edge of East Grinstead (the millstream still flows right underneath the bar – and they brew their own beer in a very traditional way), the Noah's Ark beside an interesting church in the secluded village of Lurgashall (good sandwiches), the thatched Gribble at Oving, the Mucky Duck in nice country at Tisman's Common, and two pubs that are excellent by any standards – the Shepherd & Dog just below the Downs at Fulking (hardly changed in the last 40 years, with good food) and the traditional Bull hidden away at Three Legged Cross near Ticehurst. It too has good food, and like the Shepherd & Dog, a fine garden. We have awarded both a star, even though this is their first appearance in the* Guide. *Another pub, though, completely new to us, struck us as our Find of the Year: the Three Horseshoes at Elsted, a charming set of traditionally furnished and beautifully kept rooms, with interesting food, a fine range of drinks and a very friendly welcome – we have awarded it two stars (very rare indeed for a newcomer to the book). Other new entries here that deserve a special mention include the unpretentious Anglesey Arms at Halnaker and the old White Hart at Selsfield (both have good food), the Black Rabbit for its fine position by the river just outside Arundel (in that town, the Swan is a good place to stay – or eat and drink), and the Star & Garter in East Dean (a friendly village pub with an attractive garden and lovely*

The Royal Oak, Wineham

surrounding countryside). Among the old guard of pubs which have graced these pages before, we should note that the owners of the Black Horse at Byworth (a fine old pub anyway, with the best garden here) have now left, while the Old House at Home in Chidham is evidently flourishing under its new owners. Food seems a stronger point than in the past at the Swan near Dallington (fine views), the Swan at Fittleworth (a place to stay, in a pretty spot) and the friendly Cat at West Hoathly (another very attractive village). Many Sussex pubs successfully combine good food with a distinctive and attractive old building, such as the Six Bells in Chiddingly (a low-beamed village pub with good value straightforward food and old-fashioned furnishings, but a jolly atmosphere and frequent live music); the Star in Old Heathfield, near Heathfield itself (big helpings, lovely puddings and a beautiful garden); the George & Dragon in Houghton and, under the same ownership, Lickfold Inn at Lickfold (civilised and well run Elizabethan or Tudor pubs with careful cooking and, at Lickfold, an enterprising if pricey range of real ales); the welcoming old Rose and Crown in Mayfield; the Black Horse at Nuthurst (a small-roomed family-run pub which readers return to again and again for its reliable food); the Chequers on its quiet country lane in Rowhook (generous helpings of home-cooked food in old-fashioned cosy bars); and the Horse & Groom at Rushlake Green (particularly nice for summer barbecues, but good honest bar meals too). Other pubs where character is the main thing are also generally, in their varying ways, worth thinking about for food: the smugglers' Market Cross and much grander and older Star, both in Alfriston; the notably friendly Black Horse below the Downs in Amberley (almost a museum of Downland life); the Blue Ship near Billingshurst (unspoilt and traditional, down a honeysuckle lane – excellent ham rolls); the outstanding Blackboys in the village of Blackboys (lots of little rooms, splendid garden, plenty of things to interest children); the Merrie Harriers in Cowbeech (an ex-farmhouse with a high curved settle by its inglenook fireplace); the traditional and lovingly kept Royal Oak near Midhurst (in attractive grounds, with a good choice of well kept real ales, all sorts of uncommon bottled beers, and lots of old-fashioned pub games); the Three Cups near Punnett's Town (home-pickled free-range eggs in an old-fashioned country pub which has just set up a useful children's games hut); the Mermaid in Rye (one of the country's most striking old inns, with a long smuggling history); the White Hart at Stopham (lovely riverside gardens outside this ancient pub, with an ambitious fish restaurant); and the Royal Oak at Wineham (a splendid traditional country pub). Fine surroundings for bracing winter walks or lazy summer days can be found at the Sussex Ox near Berwick (a splendid play garden for children, lots of Downland walks nearby – and interesting food all the year); the simple Hatch at Coleman's Hatch (well placed for walks in the Ashdown Forest); and the George & Dragon near Coolham (with a particularly attractive garden). The best choice of real ales is at the Richmond Arms in West Ashling, a friendly pub with interesting food to match its uncommon range of drinks.

ALFRISTON   TQ5103   Map 3
Market Cross ('The Smugglers Inn')

In the early nineteenth century this medieval pub was the home of Stanton Collins, a particularly bloodthirsty gangster who used to smuggle brandy at nearby Cuckmere Haven, and once hid eight of his gang up the chimney here. The low-beamed L-shaped bar is comfortably furnished, with Liberty print cushions on the window seats, Windsor chairs, some brass on the walls (which have quite a lot of nautical-looking white-painted panelling), a snugger little room leading off, and as a reminder of its smuggling history a couple of cutlasses hanging over the big inglenook fireplace. Bar food includes a good choice of freshly cut sandwiches (from 60p, double-deckers £1.50), cheese and onion flan (£2), basket meals such as cod (£2) or scampi (£2.30), gammon or trout (£3.75) and steaks (from nine-ounce rump, £4.25), and at lunchtime ploughman's with Cheddar (£1), pâté or Stilton (£1.10); but don't – like one unfortunate reader – arrive at ten minutes to two after a long drive, hoping for something to eat. Well kept Courage Best and Directors on handpump, and friendly service. There's a beer garden behind. The cliff walks south of here are superb, and if you're feeling lazier Old Clergy, a house in the village, is worth visiting for its fine Elizabethan furniture. *(Recommended by J Southern; more reports please)*

Courage · Licensee Mrs Maureen Ney · Real ale · Meals (not Sun lunchtime) and snacks · Public car park only fairly close · Open 10–2.30, 6–11

Star

The wooden pillar in the centre of this ancient inn's elegant bar was once a sanctuary post, putting people who were fleeing from the law under the instant protection of the Church. In 1516 someone rode a stolen horse here all the way from Lydd in Kent, to avoid prosecution (which could have brought the death penalty). The fireplace is Tudor, as are the massive beams supporting the white-painted oak ceiling boards. Handsome furnishings include a heavy oak refectory table with a big bowl of flowers, and antique Windsor armchairs worn to a fine polish. Food consists of soup (95p), sandwiches, ploughman's or pâté (£1.95), shell of prawns (£2.45), a mixed meat salad (£2.95) and home-made dishes of the day such as chicken casserole or steak and kidney pie (£3.25); there's also a separate restaurant. Bass and Badger Best on handpump. The striking red lion decorating the outside front corner is known by local people as Old Bill – probably a figurehead salvaged from a seventeenth-century Dutch shipwreck, like the one decorating the Red Lion in Martlesham (see Suffolk's Lucky Dip section). The rest of the fine brightly painted carving here is older, dating back more than 500 years to the time when this was a hostel for pilgrims going to the shrine of St Richard in Chichester. What looks like St George killing the dragon is actually St Michael killing a basilisk, and the man chewing a green rope is a complete enigma. The prancing stag is a subtle joke – actually the emblem of Trust House Forte, who own the comfortable hotel that's been built here, retaining the old inn as its front part. *(Recommended by C B M Gregory; more reports please)*

Free house · Licensee Peter Evans · Real ale · Meals (lunchtime, not Sun) and snacks (not Sun) · Children welcome · Open 10–2.30, 6–11 · Bedrooms tel Alfriston (0323) 870495; £37.95B/£56.90

AMBERLEY   TQ0212   Map 3
Black Horse

Off B2139

Readers have enjoyed a particularly friendly welcome in this village pub just below the Downs. The front bar is simply but comfortably furnished, with carpet over part of the old stone floor – which, as in some other pubs in this part of Sussex, is raised several feet above the level of the village street. Beams over its serving counter are festooned with sheep-bells, traps and shepherds' tools, and the walls are decorated with lots of old local prints and engravings. There are plenty of pictures too in the similar but more comfortable saloon bar. Food includes good home-made soup and sandwiches (toasted 95p, generously garnished prawn £1.60), ploughman's, giant sausages and chips (£2), fresh cod (£2.50), a good choice of salads, and their speciality prawn ploughman's (£2.65). Well kept Friary Meux and Ind Coope Burton on handpump; darts, cribbage and a fruit machine. There is also a popular bistro with a one-hour evening licensing extension. There are seats in the garden. The village is very pretty indeed, and is close to the River Arun, with a castle, and the nearby chalkpit industrial museum. There is a footpath through the Wild Brooks watermeadows (up the track on the right as you go along the lane opposite the pub). *Recommended by Mrs R Wilmot, Roger Entwistle, GL, SL, Peter Hitchcock)*

Friary Meux · Licensee Chris Acteson · Real ale · Meals and snacks · Children in eating area and bistro · Open 11–2.30, 6–11

ARUNDEL   TQ0107   Map 3
Black Rabbit

Mill Road; keep on and don't give up!

Included for its position, this busy pub is alone by the Arun, looking down the river and over the marshy water-meadows, now a bird-reserve, towards what is one of the best views of the castle. Cars are parked up and down the service lane between the pub and its riverside tables, so actually the best view is from here, outside. There are more tables under a verandah, lit at night by red fairground lights, and inside, a long bar with big windows is simply furnished– apart from a couple of nice hall-porter's chairs – with some red leatherette seats, and in winter has log fires at each end; Youngers Scotch and IPA on handpump, and a very wide choice of spirits and (from £2) cocktails. A roomy side snack bar, again with big windows, has captain's chairs around shiny wooden tables and is decorated with bird pictures. *(Recommended by L Kirkpatrick, Jane and Steve Edwards, Robert Mitchell)*

Free house · Real ale · Meals and snacks · Open 10.30–2.30, 6–11

Swan

High Street

A comfortable place to stay, this welcoming pub has a relaxed and casual local atmosphere in its spacious L-shaped Turkey-carpeted bar, which has red plush button-back banquettes and red velvet curtains. The good choice of well kept real ales consists of Badger Best and Tanglefoot, Everards Old Original, Harveys, King & Barnes Bitter and Festive and Ruddles County, all on handpump, and bar food includes soup (£1), sandwiches (from 95p), ploughman's (£1.25), garlic mushrooms (£1.50), basket meals from sausages (£1.70) to scampi or seafood (£3.60), bacon, sausages and eggs (£2.50), salads (from £2.50), steak sandwich (£2.95), grilled trout (£4.25), gammon (£4.75) and steaks (from eight-ounce rump £7.45 to 16-ounce rump £12.75). A comfortable dining-room leads off the bar. A fruit machine, and maybe piped music. *(Recommended by Dr A K Clarke, G Stevens)*

Free house · Licensees Diana and Ken Rowsell · Real ale · Meals and snacks Children in restaurant · Open 10.30–2.30, 6–11 · Bedrooms tel Arundel (0903) 882314; £25B/£30B

ASHURST TQ1716 Map 3

Fountain

B2135 N of Steyning

A charmingly unspoilt sixteenth-century pub is behind the Georgian façade here. It has scrubbed flagstones and a huge brick inglenook fireplace in the low-beamed room on the right as you go in, with a cushioned pew built right around two sides, a couple of high-backed wooden cottage armchairs by the fire, two antique polished trestle tables, brasses on the black mantelbeam, and a friendly pub dog. Well kept Flowers Original, Wethereds and Whitbreads Strong Country, Pompey Royal and Sam Whitbread tapped straight from the cask; sandwiches, and home-made hot dishes such as macaroni cheese or pizza (£1.50), cottage pie, turkey and ham pie or cauliflower cheese (£1.95) and spotted Dick with custard (85p). A bigger carpeted room (no dogs in this one) has spindleback chairs around its circular tables, a wood-burning stove, and darts, shove-ha'penny, dominoes, cribbage and a fruit machine. Service is very friendly and helpful. There are two garden areas, one with fruit-trees, roses, swings, a see-saw and a weekend barbecue counter with a tiled roof, the other with picnic-table sets on gravel by an attractive duckpond. *(Recommended by Jenny Newman)*

Whitbreads · Licensee Maurice Christopher Caine · Real ale · Snacks (not Sun) · Children in eating area · Open 11–2.30, 6–11 all year

nr BERWICK   TQ5105   Map 3
Sussex Ox

Milton Street; village signposted from A27, ¼ mile E of Alfriston roundabout

With country views all round, this pub has well spaced picnic-table sets on the big neat lawn which leads down to a good adventure playground with an elaborate climbing-frame, a Wendy house in the form of a log cabin as big as a castle, and swings. Inside, furnishings are attractively simple: low cushioned settles and sturdy kitchen chairs around the two or three scrubbed deal tables on a brick floor, a free-standing wood-burning stove, panelling painted cream, and shiny plaster and boarded ceiling. Bar food, with more concentration on the hot main dishes in the evening, includes home-made soup (60p), prawns and garlic mayonnaise (£1.10), ploughman's with good cheeses (£1.25), salads (from £1.50), good home-made pies such as steak and kidney (£2.50), chicken in butter, herbs and garlic (£2.50) and eight-ounce sirloin steak (£3.95). There are outdoor summer barbecues most Friday and Saturday evenings (85p–£3.95), with occasional special events such as a whole spit-roasted lamb, and in winter bistro meals on those evenings instead (£5.95). Well kept Harveys BB on handpump; darts, shove-ha'penny, table skittles, dominoes, cribbage, passe-temps and various board games. The big family room has TV and a cupboard of toys. There is fine Downland walking around here. *(Recommended by R R S Clarke and others)*

Free house · Licensee Dudley White · Real ale · Meals (not Sat or Sun lunchtime) and snacks · Children in family room · Open 10.30–2.30, 6–11 (7–10.30 in winter)

The Three Cups, nr Punnett's Town

nr BILLINGSHURST   TQ0925   Map 3
Blue Ship ★

The Haven; hamlet signposted off A29 just N of junction with A264, then follow signpost left towards Garlands and Okehurst

Idyllic on summer evenings, with people sitting out on benches by the tangle of honeysuckle round the door, or at the tree-shaded side tables, this remote and friendly country pub has an unspoilt front bar, served from a hatch at the back. Bar food includes stock-pot soup (85p), sandwiches made to order (from 65p), rolls filled with good home-made ham and salad (85p), home-made pâté (£1), ploughman's (from £1.25) and, from this last October, weekday hot dishes such as home-made steak and kidney pie (around £1.85). Well kept King & Barnes Bitter and Festive tapped from the cask. There is a small snug bar down a corridor at the back, and a plain and more brightly lit games room (with bar billiards, shove-ha'penny, cribbage and a fruit machine). *(Recommended by T Drake, Sarah Greening)*

King & Barnes · Licensee Michael Church · Real ale · Children welcome Snacks · Open 11–3, 6–11 (10.30–2.30, 6–10.30 in winter)

BLACKBOYS   TQ5220   Map 3
Blackboys ★ ★

B2192, S edge of village

Seats among flowers and shrubs in front of this partly black-weatherboarded fourteenth-century house overlook a pretty pond where ducklings bob about among yellow flag irises. Inside, there's a lovely series of old-fashioned small rooms, full of interesting odds and ends such as a stuffed red squirrel, a key collection hanging from beams, Spy cricketer caricatures and other more antique prints, a snug armchair by the inglenook fireplace, a collection of ancient bottles on a high shelf, and so forth. Waitress-served food includes home-made soup (£1), good sandwiches (from 95p), ploughman's with Cheddar, Stilton or giant sausage (£1.50), steak and kidney pie (£1.65), chilli con carne (£1.85), four-ounce sirloin steak in French bread (£2.05), spiced pork kebab (£2.10), salads (from £2.40) and lots of puddings; well kept Harveys PA and BB on handpump. There is also a separate restaurant. Darts, shove-ha'penny, table skittles, dominoes, cribbage, a fruit machine, space game and a juke box. Altogether, the pub stands in some 11 acres; the orchard behind, with rustic tables among apple-trees, has goats, friendly pigs, ponies, guinea-fowl, rabbits and even peacocks, and there is a big well equipped playroom in the barn. *(Recommended by G L Archer, A Saunders)*

Harveys · Licensee Patrick Russell · Real ale · Meals and snacks · Children welcome · Frequent jazz on summer evenings · Open 10–2.30, 6–11

BRIGHTON   TQ3105   Map 3
Royal Pavilion Tavern

Castle Square; between the actual Royal Pavilion and the bus station

Several different rooms opening into each other give this pub an attractively diverse feeling of varying old-fashioned styles – all recently contrived, but done well with some style, and worn in well now. A dimly candlelit panelled wine bar area has intimate alcoves, another clubbier part has comfortable armchairs, a winter fire and newspapers, a red velvet area has old theatre handbills and some interesting embroidered greetings cards, another part has heavy beams and nicely reproduced medieval plasterwork, and there's a real ale bar with Charrington IPA, Courage Directors, Harveys BB (and Old Ale in winter), King & Barnes and Springfield on handpump, and a fruit machine. There may be piped music. Bar food includes soup (50p), baked potato (75p), sandwiches (85p), ploughman's (from £1.25), pâté (£1.30), curry (£1.50 for a small helping, £2 for a big one), a lunchtime daily hot special (£2.15, not Sunday), quite a wide choice of salads, and grills such as plaice, liver and bacon, gammon, scampi (£3.25) and six-ounce sirloin steak (£3.85). Service is cheerful and helpful. *(Recommended by Andy Jones and the PA Club, Michael Sandy, Nina Blowes)*

Free house · Licensee A Zand · Real ale · Meals and snacks · Parking nearby can be difficult · Open 10.30–2.30, 5.30–11 all year

BYWORTH   SU9820   Map 3
Black Horse

Signposted from A283

As the early pages of this book were being printed, we heard that the Kings, who have made this pub so popular for its bistro-style food, have decided to give it up. But in any event there is a lot to please here. The pub was originally a fifteenth-century friary, and its garden is particularly attractive, dropping steeply down through a series of grassy terraces, each screened by banks of flowering shrubs (but still with a view across the valley to swelling woodland), with a bigger lawn at the bottom beside a small stream and a line of old willows. Inside has been furnished with austere restraint: stripped pews and scrubbed tables on bare floorboards, candles in bottles, and decoration confined to a collection of old sepia photographs in the back part, which has served as a small wine-bar-like restaurant. We don't yet know what will become of the food, which has run to a wide choice of unusual dishes such as egg and onion pâté, cassoulet or crispy savouries with hoi sin sauce, kidneys in sherry sauce and even Peking duck. Well kept Huntsman Royal Oak and Youngs Bitter and Special on handpump. *(Recommended by RIP, J P Berryman, A V Chute, Doug Kennedy, C H Cole, Susie Boulton; up-to-date reports please)*

Free house · Real ale · Meals and snacks · Children in eating area · Open 11–2.30, 6–11

CHIDDINGLY   TQ5414   Map 3
Six Bells ★

There is an unusually good, friendly atmosphere in this attractively simple and plainly furnished old-fashioned pub. Under its low beams there are scrubbed or polished tables, tall Windsor armchairs, pews, an antique box settle, some panelling and old engravings. The food is all home made, and customers are so keen on their favourites that it hasn't changed much over the last few years. It currently includes French onion soup (45p), cheesy garlic bread served hot with barbecue sauce (75p), shepherd's, steak and kidney or beef and vegetable pies (£1.25), ploughman's with cheese or mackerel pâté (£1.30), meat loaf or buttered crab and hot French bread (£1.30), locally smoked mackerel (£1.50), vegetarian or meaty lasagne (£1.35), chilli con carne or spicy prawns (£1.60) and spare ribs in barbecue sauce (£1.75), with generous banana splits, chocolate sundaes and other puddings (£1). The elaborately carved bar counter serves well kept King & Barnes Festive and Sussex and Courage Directors from handpump, with occasional guest beers such as Gales HSB; darts, dominoes, cribbage. There is a fine collection of enamelled advertising signs in the gents. There are some tables outside at the back, under a big Monterey cypress, beyond a goldfish pond. (Recommended by Dave Butler, Lesley Storey, Peter Hitchcock)

Free house · Licensee Paul Newman · Real ale · Meals and snacks (not Mon) Small children in lobby · Heavy rock, blues, reggae and pop live music Fri, Sat and Sun evenings · Open 10–2.30, 6–11 all year; closed Mon

CHIDHAM   SU7903   Map 2
Old House At Home
Cot Lane; turn off A27 at Barleycorn pub

New owners are running this relaxed and cheerful pub – for a long time part of a working farm – in the same fine old traditional way. As well as beers brewed here (Old House and Old Rectory), they keep a good range of other real ales, such as Badger Best, Bass, Palmers and Ringwood, and serve simple home-made food such as soup, ploughman's, pâté, cottage pie, lasagne, and curries and gammon (from £1.60). The bar has timbered white walls, low black joists in the white ceiling, long wall benches, tables and Windsor chairs on a green carpet, and a log fire in winter; sensibly placed darts, a fruit machine, and a juke box. Behind the house, which stands in a very quiet country lane, a sycamore-tree shelters a cluster of picnic-table sets, and there are two more on the front terrace. (Recommended by Jane English, Miss H R Morgan; up-to-date reports on the new regime please)

Own brew · Licensees D Haines and Mrs C A Lombardi · Real ale · Meals and snacks · Open 10.30–2.30, 6–11

CHILGROVE   SU8214   Map 2
Royal Oak
Hooksway, signposted off B2141 Petersfield–Chichester; OS Sheet 197 reference 814163

Almost alone down a track in a quiet partly wooded valley, this white cottage has a couple of very simply furnished rooms: low faded yellow ceiling, plain deal tables, sturdy leatherette wall benches, a brick floor in the lower room, some carpet in the upper one. But all the things that matter are here: two winter log fires, a friendly welcome, well kept real ales (Badger Best and Tanglefoot, Gibbs Mew Bishops Tipple, Hunstman Royal Oak, and Ringwood Best and Old Thumper on handpump), various country wines, and good value food. This includes soup, substantial ploughman's with fresh wholemeal bread (from £1.40), pâté (£1.60), cottage pie (£1.80), good venison pie (£2.10), salads (£2.50–£3.80) and prawn or beef curry (£2.80). There are rustic seats on a small and sunny front terrace, and on grass. Sensibly placed darts, shove-ha'penny. *(Recommended by Mrs A M Arnold, Steve and Carolyn Harvey)*

Free house · Licensee John Marshall · Real ale · Meals and snacks · Children welcome · Open 10.30–2.30, 6–11 all year

COLEMAN'S HATCH TQ4533 Map 3
Hatch

Turn off B2110 opposite church, or off B2026 at Coleman's Hatch signpost

This unpretentious and friendly pub stands alone among woods on the edge of the Ashdown Forest. The traditionally furnished low-ceilinged bar is partly panelled, with built-in benches, sensibly placed darts, dominoes, cribbage, and a fruit machine, and has some seats by an airy spread of windows. Bar food includes toasted sandwiches

The Swan, nr Dallington

(from 55p), cottage pie (£1.20), ploughman's (£1.25), pâté and ham, egg and chips (£1.60); well kept Harvey, BB and Fremlins on handpump. There are tables outside on a bluff of grass above the quiet lane. *(Recommended by Richard Gibbs)*

Free house · Licensee D R Hickman · Real ale · Snacks (lunchtime, not weekends) · Open 11–2.30, 6–11 all year

nr COOLHAM TQ1423 Map 3
George & Dragon
Dragons Green; pub signposted off A272 between Coolham and A24

The bar in this flower-ringed country cottage is small, snug and very cleanly kept, with unusually low and massive black beams (see if you can decide whether the date cut into one is 1677 or 1577), heavily timbered walls, simple chairs and rustic stools on the floor (which is partly woodblock, and partly polished tiles with a carpet), and a big inglenook fireplace with an early seventeenth-century grate. Bar food includes sandwiches, a choice of ploughman's (£1.20), turkey curry (£2), and home-made pies such as sausage and onion, turkey and mushroom and steak and kidney (£2.25), with a choice of summer salads and a good selection of puddings; well kept King & Barnes PA and Festive on handpump, with Old Ale in winter; darts, bar billiards, table skittles, shove-ha'penny, dominoes, cribbage, and a fruit machine, maybe piped music. The big lawn which stretches away behind is lovely in summer, with rustic tables and chairs well spaced among fruit-trees, shrubs and flowers, a big play caravan for children, and quite a few cats strolling around. *(Recommended by Paul Edwards, Gordon and Daphne)*

King & Barnes · Licensee John Jenner · Real ale · Meals and snacks (not Mon–Thurs evenings) · Children in eating area and caravan · Open 10.30–2.30, 6–11

COWBEECH TQ6114 Map 3
Merrie Harriers [*illustrated on page 659*]
Village signposted from A271

Good value bar food in this friendly ex-farmhouse includes freshly cut sandwiches, pâté (95p), avocado or melon (£1), egg and prawn mayonnaise (£1.30), salads from quiche (£2.25) to mixed meats (£3.25) or smoked salmon and prawn cornets (£4.75), a generous mixture of seafoods (£6.50), hot dishes such as steak and kidney pie or lasagne (£2.50), Dover sole (£5) and steak (£5.50), with a choice of sauté, baked potatoes or bubble and squeak (50p). The friendly panelled public bar still has something of the atmosphere of an old-fashioned farm parlour, with its curved high-backed settle by the brick inglenook fireplace, beams, pewter tankards hanging by the bar counter, pot plants in the window, and log fires in winter. The communicating lounge has spindleback chairs around the tables on its flowery carpet. Charrington IPA, Flowers Original and Fremlins on handpump; darts, shove-ha'penny. Outside the white clapboarded village house is a flower garden and a lawn with a swing and rustic seats. *(Recommended by Donald Clay, R R S Clarke)*

Free house · Licensees G M and B J Richards · Meals and snacks (not Sun)
Open 10.30–2.30, 6–11 (11–2.30, 7–10.30 in winter) · Two-bedroom
cottage in grounds to let tel Hailsham (0323) 833108

nr DALLINGTON   TQ6619   Map 3

Swan   [*illustrated on page 643*]

Wood's Corner; B2096, E of Dallington

Appetising bar food in this friendly country pub – which has terrific
views from behind – includes toasted sandwiches (from 90p), open
sandwiches (£1–£1.80), ploughman's (£1.80, with chicken
drumsticks £2.20), several pâtés (around £1.50), moules marinière or
whitebait (£1.50), ham and mushroom and various other filled
pancakes, moussaka, lasagne, chilli con carne or turkey and
mushroom pie (£2.95), salads such as cheese, turkey, beef or prawn
(£2.70–£4.20), and dishes of the day such as scampi (£3), poached
salmon (£3.50) or three lamb cutlets (£5.25). The low-beamed front
bar has an interesting collection of foreign car number plates, chiefly
from the United States and Canada but also from Iraq, Libya and
European countries. There are also vintage car photographs – the
licensee keeps a vintage sports car in one of the side sheds. A long
window seat overlooks the quiet road, and there are other wall seats
and Windsor chairs around the tables on the green carpet. Beards
(Harveys) BB on handpump; bar billiards, shove-ha'penny, maybe
piped music. On a clear day you can see right across the soft country
below this ridge all the way to Beachy Head, either from the big
picture window in a simply furnished back room, or from picnic-
table sets and slatted wood tables in the airy back flower garden
(quiet except for birdsong during the week). Don't imagine you can
stay the night here, from the words 'Accommodation for commercials
& cyclists' in faded but enormous letters on the tile-hung frontage –
it's just that they won't come off! Good woodland walks nearby,
especially in Dallington Forest. *(Recommended by BOB)*

Beards (brewed by Harveys) · Licensees David and Mary Melville-Ross
Real ale · Meals and snacks (not Sun) · Open 11–2.30, 6.30–11

EAST DEAN   SU9013   Map 2

Star & Garter

Village signposted from A286 and A285, N of Chichester

A well run and happy pub, this flint house looks down to the big,
peaceful village green and beyond to the attractive surrounding
Downland (it's close to the South Downs Way and welcomes
walkers). It has three rooms comfortably knocked together, with
captain's chairs, leatherette armchairs, some corn dollies, and local
oil paintings above the lower panelling. Bar food normally includes
home-made soup (60p), sandwiches (from 60p), ploughman's (from
£1.20), burgers (£1.50), prawn-burgers (£1.50), chicken (£1.60) and
scampi (£2.20), with daily specials (£1.75). On Goodwood race days
and bank holidays they do a lunchtime salad bar and barbecue
instead – occasionally with Country and Western singers and/or a
brass band – in a marquee in their pretty garden, which has rustic

seats and a swing by a long herbaceous border, a giant of an apple-tree, and a flower-ringed little pool. As the garden is completely walled in, it's good for families. Well kept Friary Meux and Ind Coope Burton on handpump; sensibly placed darts, shove-ha'penny, dominoes, cribbage, a fruit machine, and maybe piped music. *(Recommended by A G Thompson)*

Friary Meux (Ind Coope) · Licensee Leslie Frank Hellier · Real ale · Meals and snacks · Children in side rooms · Occasional live music · Open 10.30–2.30, 6–11

EAST GRINSTEAD   TQ3939   Map 3
Dunnings Mill

Dunnings Road; from town centre, at mini-island top of High Street, turn opposite Lloyds Bank towards half-timbered Clarendon House into right-hand bend; immediately turn left into Ship Street; Dunnings Road is at next mini-island, and pub is by stream at bottom of dip

Appealing to people who like back-to-basics traditional furnishings, this very low-ceilinged three-roomed sixteenth-century mill cottage, built right over the stream, has traditional long wall benches and cast-iron-framed tables, dim gas lighting, tiled floor, a heavy wooden cogged millwheel as the central table, and a pair of caryatids supporting one part of the ceiling. Bar food normally includes sandwiches, burgers, steak sandwiches, and daily specials, with sirloin steak (£4.50); on Sundays there's a three-course roast lunch (separate restaurant). They are once again brewing their own cheap Dunnings Bitter (using traditional open-vat methods), and also keep a wide range of other real ales – Flowers Original, Harveys, King & Barnes, Shepherd Neame and Youngs Special, with a changing guest beer, most on handpump, some tapped from the cask. There are picnic-table sets by a yew-tree on the front terrace, and behind the car park you may find geese and sheep by the big millpond. The stream is prettily landscaped, and there are National Trust woods nearby. Darts, bar billiards, dominoes, cribbage, and a fruit machine (with piped music in one area); there is a big functions room in a separate building. *(Recommended by Andy Jones and the PA Club; more reports please)*

Own brew · Licensees Brian and Linda Watson · Real ale · Meals and snacks Children welcome · Open 11–2.30, 6–11 all year

ELSTED   SU8119   Map 2
Three Horseshoes ★ ★

Village signposted from B2141 Chichester–Petersfield

Some readers told us that the pub reminded them in style of the Three Chimneys near Biddenden in Kent – a firm favourite of a great many readers, and when we finally found it ourselves we were very taken indeed with its friendly combination of simple traditional furnishings, enterprising food, and a fine range of interesting drinks. Though it's new to the *Guide* this year, we have straight away awarded it two stars, and put it among the best half-dozen pubs in the south east. Its four connecting rooms have rugs on ancient bricks, on tiles or on bare boards, there are low beams in a yellowing ceiling, antique high-backed settles, studded leather seats, oak benches and attractive tables, engravings and old photographs, flowery curtains in the small windows, and log fires – one fireplace is vast. Bar food includes generous ploughman's with a good choice of cheeses (£1.75), garlic mussels (£2.50), baked potatoes filled with interesting stuffings such as sausage and Cheddar or Stilton, celery and mayonnaise (£2.25–£2.85), tagliatelle provençale (£2.95), barbecued spare ribs (£3), cheesy mackerel bake or home-baked pies such as chicken and ham or steak and kidney (£3.45), pork cooked in cider (£3.65) and beef in red wine (£3.85), with puddings such as blackberry crumble (£1). On Sundays there's a cold lunchtime buffet, and a pretty little rustic dining-room with candles in brass holders on its plain wooden tables has a more elaborate menu. Well kept changing ales tapped from the cask included on our visit Badger Best, Ballards Best and Wassail, Bosham, Friary Meux, Fullers London Pride and Gales HSB, and they keep Inch's and Churchward's farm cider and country wines; a rack of newspapers, cheap local farm eggs. There are sunflowers and other flowers in front of the pretty tiled white house, and seats in a biggish garden with a colourful herbaceous border. *(Recommended by A Handford, Dave Butler, Steve and Carolyn Harvey)*

Free house · Real ale · Meals and snacks · Open 10.30–2.30, 6–11 all year

FITTLEWORTH   TQ0119 Map 3
Swan
Lower Street; B2138

This pretty tile-hung fifteenth-century inn's main bar is comfortably furnished with Windsor armchairs on the patterned carpet in front of its big inglenook fireplace, which has good log fires in winter. In summer, perhaps the nicest place to sit is at one of the white tables spaced well apart on the big back lawn, sheltered by flowering shrubs and a hedge sprawling with honeysuckle, and there are benches by the village lane in front. Bar food includes soup (90p), a wide choice of open French bread and other sandwiches (from 90p) such as home-cooked ham with Cheddar cheese, bacon and mushroom or fresh crab, generous ploughman's with a good selection of cheeses (£2.10), and hot dishes such as sardines in garlic (£1.95), cottage pie or curry (£2.50), steak and kidney pie (£3) and local trout (£4). Three-course meals are served in an attractive panelled room decorated with landscapes by Constable's brother George (£6.50 lunch, including Sundays, £7.95 dinner). During 1986 they hope to open a lunchtime Pie Shop serving seven different pies with elaborate salads (£3.95). Well kept Tamplins on handpump; piped music, and the smaller public bar has a fruit machine. There are good nearby walks in beech woods. *(Recommended by Mr and Mrs K Virgin and others; more reports please)*

Host (Watneys) · Real ale · Meals (lunchtime) and snacks · Children in eating area · Open 10–2.30, 6–11 · Bedrooms tel Fittleworth (079 882) 429; £20S/£30S

Pubs brewing their own beers are listed at the back of the book.

FULKING TQ2411 Map 3
Shepherd & Dog ★

From A281 Brighton—Henfield on N slope of Downs turn off at Poynings
signpost and continue past Poynings

One reader who came here first in 1946 reckons that the garden –
nestling so prettily below the 700-foot slope of the steep Downs – has
been much improved, but that inside, this charming traditional pub
hardly seems to have changed. Though it's a newcomer to the *Guide*,
you can see from the star award that this little slate-hung cottage
impressed us very much (we were lucky and caught it at a quiet time –
it can get very crowded as it's relatively small). The very warm low-
ceilinged bar has stout pegged rustic seats around little gateleg oak
tables, an antique cushioned oak settle, attractive bow window seats,
shepherds' crooks, harness, stuffed squirrels, mounted butterflies and
blue and white plates on its partly panelled walls, and a big log-filled
fireplace in one stripped wall hung with copper and brass. Good
food, all freshly made by a team of cheerful girls, includes sandwiches
(lunchtime, from 65p), various ploughman's (from £1.45 – widest
choice at lunchtime, including locally smoked salmon pâté), and,
particularly in the evening, hot dishes such as seafood Mornay
(£1.85), rack of lamb with apricot and red wine sauce or duck and
apple pancakes (£4.25), steak and mushroom pie, steak kebabs
(£4.25), duck and porterhouse steak, with puddings such as
raspberries and cream (75p) or summer fruit fool (95p). Tamplins or
Ushers Best and Websters Yorkshire on handpump, with (on our
visit) King & Barnes Sussex and Festive as guest beers; darts, shove-
ha'penny, dominoes, cribbage, toad in the hole; local produce
including honey and attractively priced smoked salmon to take away.
The garden has a series of prettily planted grassy terraces, some fairy-
lit, with an upper tree-sheltered play lawn with veteran farm
machinery, swings, see-saw and an old-lady-who-lived-in-a-shoe
playhouse. The stream running through washes into a big stone
trough where the shepherds bringing their flocks to sell at Findon
sheep fair used to clean up their merchandise – while having a nip of
the illicit liquor sold by one of the twin cottages which later became
this pub. (*Recommended by Sigrid and Peter Sobanski, G R Hall, S V Bishop
and others*)

*Phoenix (Watneys) · Licensee Antony Bradley-Hole · Real ale · Meals and
snacks (not Sun evening) · Open 10.30–2.30, 6–11 all year; closed evenings
25 and 26 Dec*

HALNAKER SU9008 Map 2
Anglesey Arms

A285 Chichester—Petworth

This very well run roadside pub remarkably combines a thoroughly
lively and friendly local atmosphere with good food. If you want to
eat in comfort, you must book: that gives you room in the right-hand
bar, where you can choose between stripped deal settles and wall
seats around candlelit stripped deal tables on the flagstones, with
modern paintings on the cream walls, or a rather more dining-

roomish carpeted back area. We hadn't booked, and though it was a busy Friday night so that all the tables in the bar side were full (two composers submerging one of them under piles of stave paper), they kindly made room for us to have a meal at the bar counter. The home-made food, in generous helpings, is simple but very satisfying, including soups such as cream of watercress (£1), sandwiches (from 60p), toasties (from 90p), ploughman's (£1.15), crab pâté (£1.50), omelettes (from £1.50), fry-ups (£2.25), spinach or courgette quiche (£2.75), giant prawns (£3.55), good dressed Selsey crab (£3.85), sirloin steak (£4) and fillet steak (£5). Well kept Friary Meux and Ind Coope Burton on handpump; dominoes, cribbage, a fruit machine and a sitting space game. There are picnic-table sets on the side grass, and white metal and plastic seats and tables in a sheltered back beer garden, by a fig-tree. *(Recommended by G A Wright, G P Hewitt)*

Friary Meux (Ind Coope) · Licensee Chris Houseman · Real ale · Meals – tel Chichester (0243) 773474 – and snacks · Children welcome · Open 10.30–2.30, 6–11; closed 25 Dec

The Cat, West Hoathly

nr HEATHFIELD   TQ5920   Map 3

Star

Old Heathfield; from B2096 coming from Heathfield, turn right at signpost to
Heathfield Church, Vines Cross and Horam, then right at T-junction and
follow lane round church to the left

The irregular stonework at the bottom of this beautifully placed pub
shows its great age: it dates from 1380 when it served pilgrims
following this high ridge across the Weald to Canterbury. The
modernised L-shaped bar has close-set sturdy rustic furniture on its
brown tweedy carpet, fine heavy black oak beams, some panelling,
window seats, and a couple of tables in the huge inglenook fireplace:
get there early if you want a place to eat. Generous helpings of
waitress-served food include good vegetable soup made with a rich
turkey stock (85p), ploughman's (from £1.50), home-baked ham and
eggs or three-egg omelette (£2.50), home-made quiche, turkey and
mushroom or steak and kidney pie with good pastry (£2.75), salads
(from £3.50) and tempting puddings such as bread and butter or
treacle tart drenched in rich cream (£1). Well kept Tamplins and
Websters Yorkshire on handpump, with a guest beer such as Gales
HSB, and good value wines by the bottle or litre. The very well kept
garden, with solid furniture among the bright, well planted flower
borders, or by the big fig-tree with its carpet of flowering balsam
underneath, is lovely in summer: on one side is the fine old pub, with
massive medieval sandstone blocks in its walls, and behind it the
graceful church spire; on the other, there are peaceful views over the
oak-lined fields that roll down from this ridge in the Weald.
*(Recommended by Dave Butler, BOB, Richard Gibbs; year after year, this pub
fails to return our fact-checking sheets, which we regret prevents us giving you
as full a description of the food choice as we would like – we'd be particularly
grateful for price details in readers' reports)*

*Phoenix (Watneys) · Licensee Roger Gilbert · Real ale · Meals and snacks (not
Mon evening) · Children allowed only if eating · Parking can be difficult (if so,
park beyond church and walk through churchyard) · Open 11–2.30, 6.30–11*

HOUGHTON   TQ0111   Map 3

George & Dragon

B2139

Partly thirteenth-century but mainly Elizabethan – and from outside
looking much as it did when Charles II stopped here while escaping
from the Battle of Worcester in 1651 – this well kept and comfortable
pub serves a wide choice of good food. Under the same ownership as
the entry which follows this, it does get crowded at weekends and
peak holiday times, and it's at quieter moments that you can best
enjoy its sympathetic modernisation: the big fireplace on your left as
you come in from the road, for example, with its handsome iron
fireback and clockwork device for turning a spit. Part of the open-
plan heavily beamed bar is set aside for diners, with Windsor chairs
around neat tables, and full table service in the evenings. The
food includes home-made soup (£1), smoked mackerel (£1.50), pâté
(£1.50), a range of salads such as home-baked ham (£3.75), nicely

rare beef (£3.95), egg with prawn or fresh crab (£4.50), and puddings, with lunchtime additions such as sandwiches (from 75p, smoked salmon £1.75), ploughman's (from £1.60), sausages and eggs (£2.50) and other hot dishes, and in the evening trout or wiener Schnitzel (£4.95), steaks (from eight-ounce rump, £6.50) and other grills. Well kept Harveys, King & Barnes and Youngs Special on handpump. Behind the half-timbered pub, tables and chairs on a terrace and on grass sloping down past a walnut-tree and wishing-well give lovely views over the Arun valley. You can join the South Downs from the village (turn left off the side road to Bury). *(Recommended by Mr and Mrs Raymond Watkins, Mrs A M Arnold, L Kirkpatrick, Mrs Betty Norman and others)*

Free house · Licensee Laurence Tyler · Real ale · Meals and lunchtime snacks Open 11–2.30, 6–11; closed 25 Dec

LICKFOLD   SU9225   Map 2
Lickfold Inn ★

Comfortable and stylishly restored, the bar of this Tudor pub is an elegant and relaxed place in which to eat sandwiches, ploughman's or whitebait (£1.65), baked potatoes in winter, steak and kidney pie and many other traditional English dishes (around £3), scampi (£3.30), or in the evening dishes such as fillet of sole Capri, pork Holstein or ragout of beef (all around £5). The more or less open-plan bar is divided into cosier areas by the huge central brick chimney (there are big log fires in winter), with some snug alcoves. There are heavy oak beams, handsomely moulded panelling, and some attractive furniture including Georgian settles – most of the seats are antique or well chosen to tone in. The building is timbered, with herringbone brickwork, and the bar floor repeats this herringbone pattern under its rugs. A good range of well kept real ales on handpump, such as Badger Best and Tanglefoot, Fullers ESB, Huntsman Royal Oak and Marstons Pedigree and Old Peculier. On Sundays there is a roast lunch. There are picnic-table sets under cocktail parasols on a lawn behind with a background of trees and birdsong, and the surrounding countryside is very attractive, with the National Trust woods of Black Down a couple of miles north and more woodland to the south. *(Recommended by Doug Kennedy; more reports please)*

Free house · Licensees C L and L J Tyler · Real ale · Meals (not Sun evening) and snacks · Children in restaurant · Open 11–2.30, 6.30–11 all year

LINDFIELD   TQ3425   Map 3
Bent Arms

98 High Street; B2028

Highly idiosyncratic, this entertaining series of rambling rooms is crowded with old metal pots and pans dangling from its beams, spinning-wheels, ships' telegraphs, heavy chandeliers, Victorian stained glass, a red lacquer grandfather clock, a stuffed bear, a wheel-mounted cannon from the Afghan Wars, and a fine medley of furniture from old-fashioned settles and sturdy dining-tables to elegantly Louis-Seize-style bar seats. Except in warm weather a model steam engine drives a spit in a vast open fireplace, roasting pork, beef, ham, chicken, duck or pheasant (lunchtime, not Sunday or Wednesday: from £1.25 for hot beef sandwich to £4.75 for venison or pheasant). Other bar food includes more sandwiches, chicken en croûte stuffed with cream cheese and mushrooms (£2.65), home-made rabbit, venison and pheasant pie (£3.95) and Dover sole (£6); well kept Courage Directors, Flowers Original, King & Barnes, Whitbreads Pompey Royal and Youngs on handpump; a fruit machine, maybe piped music. There's also a separate restaurant. There are seats in the garden, which has a recently discovered well. *(Recommended by Donald Mather, Philip Denison)*

Free house · Licensee Rita Hoyle · Real ale · Meals and snacks · Children in eating area and lounge · Open 10.30–2.30, 6–11 all year · Bedrooms tel Lindfield (044 47) 3146; £11.50/£20

LITLINGTON   TQ5201 Map 3
Plough & Harrow

The popular bustle in this attractively placed pub spreads from the original relatively small beamed and carpeted front bar (with its wall of mirrors giving an illusion of space) to the newer back dining area, done up as a dining-car and decorated with steam railway models, pictures and memorabilia (in the evenings tables can be booked here; particularly popular on Saturdays for the weekend special menu which includes halibut (£4.50) and roast duck (£5.50), as well as the charcoal-grilled steaks such as 10-ounce porterhouse (£5.75) or 16-ounce T-bone (£7) that are served on Tuesday to Thursday evenings too). Other food, served both inside and outside the comfortable lattice-windowed flint pub, includes soups such as game or lobster bisque (£1.10) and home-made turkey broth (£1.40), sandwiches (from 90p, with rare beef £1.25, crab £2, smoked salmon £2.25), ploughman's with Cheddar (£1.75), Stilton (£1.90) or home-cooked ham (£2), a good range of salads (from £2, including fresh crab £4.60), lasagne (£2.80), home-made steak and kidney pie (£2.95) and puddings such as fruit pie with cream (90p). Well kept Badger Best and Tanglefoot, Brunel, Harveys BB, and King & Barnes Festive on handpump, and a full wine list; darts, shove-ha'penny, dominoes, maybe piped music. You can sit on rustic seats by a mass of clematis on the lawn beside the big back car park: the view across the Cuckmere Valley to nearby Alfriston is a pretty one. *(Recommended by W J Wonham, J D Rodgers, Gwen and Peter Andrews, Stuart Perry; more reports please)*

Free house · Licensee Roger Taylor · Real ale · Meals and snacks; dining-room bookings tel Alfriston (0323) 870632 · Singer/guitarist/organist Fri · Open 11–2.30, 6.30–11 (7–10.30 in winter)

LURGASHALL   SU9327 Map 2
Noah's Ark

Village signposted from A283 N of Petworth; OS Sheet 186 reference 936272

This friendly and secluded pub stands opposite a tree-shaded churchyard, at the end of the cottagey village green; it's very pretty in summer, its yard bright with hanging baskets, cockerels in its private back garden and rustic seats and tables on the front grass, and the unusual church is well worth a look. Inside, two small bars – one with oak parquet, the other carpeted – have simple but attractive furnishings, warm winter fires (a big inglenook in the lounge on the left, which has sporting prints and comfortable chairs), and in summer they are decorated with freshly picked flowers. Bar food includes sandwiches (from £1, toasted £1.20, fresh crab £1.25), ploughman's (£1.25), lasagne or chilli con carne (£2.20), steak and kidney pie or gammon and egg (£2.25), plaice or scampi (£2.40), and salads (from £2.75, smoked salmon or crab £3.75), and they have a separate dining-room. Well kept Friary Meux and Ind Coope Burton; sensibly placed darts and bar billiards, also shove-ha'penny, dominoes, and cribbage. *(Recommended by Richard Gibbs)*

Friary Meux (Ind Coope) · Licensee Barton Swannell · Real ale · Meals and snacks (not Sun) · Children in dining-room · Open 10.30–2.30, 6–11

MAYFIELD   TQ5827   Map 3
Rose and Crown ★
Fletching Street; off A267 at NE end of village

Good bar food in this civilised low-beamed Tudor village pub is served in generous helpings. It varies from day to day, but might typically include in its wide choice – beside home-made soup (55p), ploughman's with a choice of cheeses (£1.15) and salads (£1.95) – dishes such as fresh sardines with mustard sauce (£1.75), fresh salmon or crab mousse or chicken curry mayonnaise (£1.85), home-made burgers or pancakes filled with seafood, savoury beef or crab with smoked haddock (£1.95), squid and prawn vinaigrette (£2.15) and T-bone steaks (£4.15); prices are low for this part of the world. The partly panelled, small, snug rooms have ceiling boards with coins

The Chequers, Rowhook

embedded in their glossy ochre paint, a big inglenook fireplace, flowery carpet, built-in wall benches, and an attractive bow window seat. Though most customers are regulars, giving a relaxed and casual atmosphere, strangers are made to feel very welcome. A small separate restaurant is open for bookings on Friday and Saturday evenings. Well kept Adnams Best, Everards Tiger and Old Original, and a quickly changing guest beer, on handpump; sensibly placed darts and bar billiards, also shove-ha'penny, dominoes and cribbage. You can sit outside at rustic wooden tables on the smallish lawn beside this pretty weatherboarded house, which used to be a village brewhouse. (*Recommended by R and S Bentley, A G Thompson, Donald Clay, BOB*)

Free house · Licensees Richard and Claudette Leet · Real ale · Meals and snacks (not Sun, nor Mon evening); restaurant bookings tel Mayfield (0435) 872200 Children in restaurant or eating area · Open 10.30–2.30, 6–11 all year; closed 25 Dec

nr MIDHURST   SU8821 Map 2
Royal Oak ★

A286 towards Chichester

Extensive stretches of grass running out to mature oak-trees and a pretty garden behind with views of the South Downs surround this old-fashioned, simple and lovingly kept pub. Its rambling rooms are small, with some very low shiny ceilings, stripped panelling, wall benches and Windsor chairs on the carpet, and a gleamingly polished copper hood over the main fireplace in the back bar. The welcoming hosts, very strong on tradition, have collected an unusually wide range of lesser-known bottled beers to go with the Ballards, Boddingtons (replaced in winter by King & Barnes Old Ale), King & Barnes Festive, Ringwood Old Thumper and Whitbreads Pompey Royal kept on handpump, and served through a hatch to the front bar. As in a few other pubs noted for the quality of their real ales, this one does sensibly use a very light touch of CO_2 to keep nasties out of the barrels just before they're sealed at night – a praiseworthy practice which doesn't affect the flavour of the beer or the development of its own natural yeasts, and which we wish was adopted by more pubs for real ales that aren't being drunk very quickly. The food includes sandwiches (from 65p), home-made soup (75p), ploughman's (from £1.25), pâté or crab pâté (£1.45), hot fresh sardines, chicken and chips (£1.75), salads (from £2.65, with home-cooked ham and home-made coleslaw), chicken in the house red wine, jugged pigeon, and grills (the only lunchtime main dishes) such as Barnsley chop (£4.75), steaks and Portsmouth-landed whole plaice or sole; the meat all comes fresh daily from a reliable local butcher. They will do vegetarian dishes with prior notice, and as the food is freshly cooked they warn of delays at busy times. Some tables can be booked in side rooms, one of them up a few steps. Darts, shove-ha'penny, dominoes, cribbage, nine men's morris, backgammon, shut the box, chess, draughts and Scrabble (and a fruit machine through by the door). On the Saturday before Goodwood Week they hold a vigorous festival of outdoor traditional games, and have some 20 or more additional real ales then. *(Recommended by Ceri and Beti Wyn Thomas, Doug Kennedy, Brian Frith and others)*

Free house · Licensee Andrew Chiverton · Real ale · Meals (not Sun) – tel Midhurst (073 081) 4611 – and snacks (not Sun evening) · Children in dining-room · Open 10.30–2.30, 6–11 (11–2.30, 6–10.30 in winter); opens 7 Mon and Tues; closed evenings 25 and 26 Dec (no food those days)

NUTHURST   TQ1926   Map 3

Black Horse ★

Village signposted from A281 SE of Horsham

The black-beamed bar of this welcoming family-run village pub – so popular with readers for its food and atmosphere – has room for just a couple of armed Windsor chairs and a built-in settle on the big Horsham flagstones in front of its inglenook fireplace; it opens out into other small carpeted rooms with more seats, where the walls are decorated with Victorian photographs and engravings. The food includes garlic bread (50p), various sandwiches, plain or toasted, garlic mushrooms on toast (£1.40), ploughman's (from £1.55), good home-made chilli con carne (£2.30), home-cooked ham and egg (£2.75), plaice (£2.85), quiche or fisherman's platter (£3.50), salads including smoked chicken and ham with new potatoes (£3.50) and eight-ounce fillet steak (£7.65), with home-made daily specials such as leek and potato, mushroom or Stilton soup, steak kebabs (£3.10) and – particularly popular with readers – seafood lasagne (£3.50). There is a good range of well kept ales on handpump: Badger Best and sometimes Tanglefoot, King & Barnes PA, Fullers London Pride, Marstons Pedigree and Whitbreads Pompey Royal. Many people have praised the quick, friendly service. You can sit outside in front, or in the attractive back garden by a little stream, and they now have barbecues on fine summer Sunday evenings. There are good woodland walks nearby. *(Recommended by Aubrey Saunders, J H DuBois, Mr and Mrs Raymond Watkins, J Dewhirst, M W Spolton, Tony Gayfer, Roy and Shirley Bentley and others)*

Free house · Licensee Marion Cheshire · Real ale · Meals and snacks (not Sun evening) · Children at licensee's discretion in dining-room · Folk music Sun evening · Open 11–2.30, 6–11

OVING   SU9005   Map 2

Gribble

Between A27 and A259 just E of Chichester, then signposted just off village road; OS Sheet 197 reference 900050

Named after Rosa Gribble who lived here for over 90 years, this still looks from outside like the archetype of an English country cottage, with its hump of a thatched roof, and the rustic seats out under its apple-trees. Inside bustles with cheerful business: it has been stripped down to its old heavy beams and timbered bare bricks, with wheelback chairs and cushioned pews around the old wooden country tables on its carpet, and a big log fire. On the left, a family room with more pews, and rugs on its oak parquet floor, has bar billiards, darts and a sitting space game; also shove-ha'penny, dominoes, cribbage, and a fruit machine. Well kept Badger Best, King & Barnes Sussex and Festive, a beer brewed for the pub, and Ringwood Old Thumper on handpump, with a guest beer such as the local Bosham Harvest; also Webber's farm cider, and country wines. Well presented bar food includes sandwiches, soup (75p), home-made burgers (£1.40), ploughman's (from £1.50), home-made cottage pie (£1.70), a choice of locally made pâtés (£1.85), ham and eggs, turkey and ham or steak and mushroom pie (£2.25), scampi (£2.80) and steaks, with daily specials such as local crab salad (£4.25). A small open-sided barn leads on to the garden. *(Recommended by W B Goldring, Mike Hallett)*

Free house · Licensee Paul Tanser · Real ale · Meals (not Sun, not Mon evening) and snacks (not Sun or Mon evening) · Children in family room · Folk music Sun evening · Open 11–2.30, 6–11

nr PUNNETT'S TOWN   TQ6220 Map 3
Three Cups   *[illustrated on page 639]*
B2096 towards Battle

This old-fashioned country pub has a welcoming low-beamed bar with comfortable old chairs on its partly carpeted woodblock floor, a large stone inglenook fireplace with a winter log fire, and brown panelling. It faces a spreading green with picnic-table sets, and there are more sheltered seats close by the building. Besides home-pickled free-range eggs, bar food includes sandwiches, rolls and toasties (from 85p), ploughman's (£1 – the only food sold on Sundays), home-made quiche, giant sausages, beefburgers and smoked mackerel (all £1.10). There are full salads with home-cooked meats (£1.75–£3) from June to September and in winter hot lunchtime casseroles and pies. Well kept Courage Best and Directors on handpump; darts, shove-ha'penny, dominoes and cribbage. There is an adventure play area behind the pub, with a pool-table and space games in a games hut. *(More reports please)*

Courage · Real ale · Meals (lunchtime, not Sun) and snacks (lunchtime in winter, evenings too in summer – not Sun) · Children in games hut · Open 11–2.30, 6–11

nr RINGMER   TQ4412 Map 3
Cock
A26, N of Ringmer turn-off

This snug old country pub has winter log fires in its inglenook fireplace, heavy beams, small Windsor chairs and a sturdy armchair on the patterned carpet, soft lighting, and a quiet golden labrador. There's a warmly friendly welcome and a very wide choice of good bar food, running from open sandwiches (around £1–£1.50) to quite a few main dishes, such as marinated lamb steak, at around the £6 mark. King & Barnes Festive, Ushers PA and Websters Yorkshire on handpump; eclectic and enjoyable piped music. The sizeable fairy-lit lawn is attractively planted with fruit-trees, shrubs, honeysuckle and clumps of old-fashioned flowers, and there are seats on a well placed terrace closer to the white weatherboarded house. *(Recommended by D L Johnson; more reports please)*

Phoenix (Watneys) · Licensee Brian Cole · Real ale · Meals (not Sun) and snacks (not Sun evening) · Children in restaurant · Open 10–2.30, 6–11

ROWHOOK   TQ1234   Map 3
Chequers ★   [*illustrated on page 653*]
Village signposted from A29 NW of Horsham

The snug front bar of this sheltered country pub has black beams in its white ceiling, and upholstered benches and stools around the tables on its flagstone floor; it is warmed in winter by an antique cast-iron stove in the inglenook fireplace. Up a step or two, a carpeted side dining-room with a very low ceiling has neatly ordered tables: popular for the home-cooked food which at lunchtime includes sandwiches, ploughman's (from £1.35), pâté (£1.65) and a changing range of casseroles and other hot dishes such as liver and onion (around £2.50), with puddings like cheesecake and chocolate fudge. In the evenings there are also such things as prawn dip, pizza (£2.15), scampi or home-cooked ham (£2.75), trout (£3) and fillet steak (£5.95). They do traditional roasts on Sundays (£2.85). Well kept Flowers Original, Whitbreads Strong Country, Pompey Royal and Sam Whitbread on handpump, served from the elaborately carved bar counter; darts, shove-ha'penny, dominoes, cribbage, maybe piped music. Sunny benches outside overlook the quiet country lane, and there are picnic-table sets under cocktail parasols on a crazy-paved terrace and in the big, peaceful side garden, among roses and flowering shrubs. *(Recommended by Ceri Thomas; more reports please)*

Whitbreads · Licensee Paul Barrs · Real ale · Meals and snacks (not Sun evening) · Children in dining-room · Open 11–2.30, 6–11

RUSHLAKE GREEN   TQ6218   Map 3
Horse & Groom
Village signposted from B2096

This friendly old country pub serves good bar food such as cream cheese pâté, tuna and beans or smoked mackerel pâté (£1.40), curried turkey snack (£1.50), home-made individual pies (from £2.75), fresh fish (from £3.25), a main-course mixture of hors d'oeuvre (£3.50), duck with black cherry and brandy sauce (£6.25) and an alcoholic peppered steak (£6.95), with home-made puddings (from around £1). It has comfortable modern upholstered high-backed settles in two snug carpeted rooms on the left of the central serving counter, and a more simply furnished beamed and timbered room on the right, with a log-effect gas fire in the big hearth; bar billiards and a fruit machine in here, also shove-ha'penny, dominoes, and cribbage. Well kept Harveys BB on handpump (as Beards). In summer, there are good value do-it-yourself barbecues: telephone half an hour or so ahead and they'll light one of half a dozen well spaced brick barbecues on a lawn sheltered by a neatly clipped beech hedge. There are more tables on another lawn in front. *(Recommended by A G Thompson, Donald Clay; more reports please)*

Beards (supplied by Harveys) · Licensees Anton and Elaine Levy · Real ale Meals and snacks (not Sun or Mon evenings); barbecues tel Rushlake Green (0435) 830320 · Children in bar on right · Open 11–2.30, 6–11 (12–2.30, 7–10.30 in winter)

RUSPER   TQ2037 Map 3
Plough

Village signposted from A24 and A264 N and NE of Horsham

This comfortably modernised seventeenth-century village pub has a fine collection of over 20 cheeses laid out neatly on white linen (£3 for any three, with help-yourself salads), and a wide collection of real ales on handpump – Adnams, Badger Best, Courage Directors, Fullers London Pride and ESB, King & Barnes Sussex (and Old Ale in winter), Ruddles County and Websters Yorkshire. There's a medley of well cushioned seats on the maroon carpet of the partly panelled very low-beamed bar, which has both an open log fire and a huge wood-burning stove. Other bar food includes sandwiches (from 75p), soup (75p), ploughman's (£1.50), sole or plaice (£2.50), and home-made fisherman's pie or steak and kidney pie (£2.75); there's a Sunday lunchtime shellfish bar (prawn or crab salads from £3). A small room at the end has a couple of space games and a fruit machine, and there may be piped music. There's an upstairs restaurant and family lounge. They have barbecues on fine Friday, Saturday and Sunday evenings; the back garden has a pond, fountain and old well, and there's a pretty front terrace. *(More reports please)*

Free house · Licensees Tony and Denise Cripps · Real ale · Meals and snacks (lunchtime) · Children in upstairs lounge and games room · Open 11–2.30, 6–11

RYE   TQ9220 Map 3
Mermaid ★

This black and white timbered Tudor inn, on a steep cobbled lane, looks extremely striking, and you can imagine the murderous Hawkhurst gang hauling kegs of smuggled rum up here, where they used to drink with their loaded pistols beside their tankards. (The ghost of a serving girl who loved one of the smugglers is said to be seen sometimes just before midnight). The inn is now a luxurious contrast – or is it a memorial – to those heady days, with panelled rooms, heavy timbering and wall frescoes, and at the back there's a fine old-fashioned bar with handsome antique seats (one of them carved in the form of a goat) around its timbered walls, a magnificently big fireplace with a halberd and pike mounted over it, eighteenth-century carvings of dancing putti, and a long-case clock. A picture of the room 60 years ago (when it was the Gentleman's Club Room) shows that it has hardly changed since. Home-made soup and ploughman's in here, with Fremlins and Wethereds, and since the last edition the local Cinque Ports Bitter, on handpump. The separate

restaurant serves dishes such as sea trout and Romney Marsh lamb.
There are seats on a small back terrace. A comfortable place to stay.
(Recommended by Lissa Halliday)

*Free house · Licensee M K Gregory · Real ale · Meals and snacks (lunchtime)
Open 11–2.30, 6–11 all year · Bedrooms tel Rye (0797) 223065; £20 (£29B)/
£36 (£50B)*

nr SCAYNE'S HILL   TQ3623 Map 3
Sloop

Freshfield Lock; from Scayne's Hill (on A272 E of Haywards Heath), follow
Church lane signpost, then Freshfield signposts

Freshfield Lock, beside which the pub stands, was a part of the
derelict Ouse Canal – you can still see its remains from the neat and
sheltered garden here, where the seating area has been extended since
our last edition. Inside, there are sofas and other comfortable
furniture in the long carpeted saloon bar (which often has pictures for
sale). Food consists of sandwiches with a good choice of fillings
including both rare and well done beef, plain or toasted (from 85p),
large Cheddar ploughman's (£1.50), and a changing menu chalked
up on a blackboard that might have salmon and prawn quiches
(£2.50), seafood Venice (£2.95), Avon trout (£3.50), battered scampi
(£3.95) and rump steak (£5.95) – this changes daily. Helpings are
generous to a fault. Well kept Harveys BB (as Beards) on handpump;
maybe piped music. The simpler, airier public bar has a small games
rom with sensibly placed darts, bar billiards, dominoes, cribbage, and
a fruit machine. The tile-hung old house, with benches in its old-
fashioned brick porch, is handy for the Bluebell steam railway and
not far from the great lakeside gardens of Sheffield Park.
*(Recommended by Peter Hart, Hazel Morgan, Mr and Mrs Raymond Watkins,
S V Bishop)*

*Beards (supplied by Harveys) · Licensee David Mills · Real ale · Meals and
snacks · Children in eating area and small games room · Open 10.30–2.30,
6–11 all year*

The Merrie Harriers, Cowbeech

SELSFIELD TQ3434 Map 3
White Hart

Ardingly Road; B2028 N of Haywards Heath, just S of junction with B2110 at Hartfield; close to West Hoathly (which is its postal address)

This old timbered and tiled building alone on a pretty tree-lined road stands just above a wooded combe which drops steeply away below the picnic-table sets on the lawn at the side. It's very popular for its food (filling up by noon at weekends), which includes sandwiches (from 55p), ploughman's (£1.10), a wide choice of good omelettes (from £1), lots of varieties of filled baked potatoes, and steaks including T-bone. The food, though freshly prepared, is quickly served. The pub has been made comfortable inside without spoiling the appeal of its black oak beams in a dark ochre ceiling, with some old black wooden-plank tables. There are a couple of very thick elm tables by the big log fire which serves to divide the bar into two areas. A good range of well kept real ales includes Adnams, Gales HSB, Harveys Sussex, King & Barnes Sussex and Ruddles Bitter or County. A big mossy bison's skull decorates a low roof by the car park, and a stuffed mongoose wrestles vigorously with a snake in the bar. Handy for Wakehurst Place and Ingwersen's alpine plants nursery. *(Recommended by GTM; more reports please)*

Free house · Licensee Ian Buchanan · Real ale · Meals and snacks · Children in eating area · Open 11.30–2.30, 6.30–10.30

STOPHAM TQ0218 Map 3
White Hart

A283 towards Pulborough

Outside this friendly old pub, a big lawn with well spaced tables has tree-lined grass walks down by the slow Arun and Rother rivers, where they meet at a graceful seven-arched bridge built in 1309 of the same warm honey-coloured stone as the pub itself. The three snug rooms of the simply furnished bar include one with a table and chairs tucked into a neatly converted inglenook fireplace; bar food consists of a good choice of sandwiches (from 80p, bacon and mushroom or fresh local crab £1.20, toasted 10p extra), home-made soup (80p), ploughman's with both ham and cheese (£1.50), bacon, sausage, egg and mushroom (£1.95), home-made fish pie (£2.25) and scampi (£2.50). Well kept Flowers Original and Whitbreads Strong Country on handpump; darts, shove-ha'penny, dominoes, cribbage, a fruit machine, maybe piped music. The beamed and candlelit restaurant specialises in fresh fish – they reckon that given 24 hours' notice they can get you any fish from anywhere in the world. *(More reports please)*

Whitbreads · Licensees Bill and Elizabeth Bryce · Real ale · Meals and snacks Children welcome · Open 11–2.30, 6–11

nr TICEHURST TQ6830 Map 3
Bull ★

Three Legged Cross; coming into Ticehurst from N on B2099, just before

Ticehurst village sign, turn left towards Maynards Pick Your Own beside corner house called Tollgate (though on our visit there was a signpost, the arm had been broken off)

Delightfuly tucked away and (at least on our visit) without an inn-sign, this fourteenth-century pub betrays its existence only by the cars parked outside, and the pleased anticipatory look of the people going in. Though it's been reorganised internally to make for better service, its several low-beamed rooms still have a fine feeling of the past, with heavy oak joined tables, kitchen seats, and flowery cushions on benches and settles. The floors are flagstone, brick or oak parquet, and there's a big central fireplace (which the soft grey tabby heads for). Good value lunchtime bar food includes home-made soup, sandwiches (from 60p), ploughman's (from £1.20), tasty kipper pâté (£1.35), maybe omelettes, a wide range of salads (from £2.30), and a changing hot dish such as chicken in cider or roast pork and rabbit (£2.35); service is friendly and generous. In the evenings, besides snacks, they do meals with starters such as avocado with crab (£1.65) and main courses such as dressed crab (£4.25), lemon sole en papillotes done with a dry vermouth and herb sauce (£5) or rack of lamb with garlic and rosemary (£5.75); everything is home cooked, and for evening dinners they appreciate booking. Well kept Harveys and Shepherd Neame Master Brew on handpump. The sheltered garden has old-fashioned seats, with fruit-trees, roses, and a pool by a young weeping willow – all very pretty, and quiet but for birdsong. *(Recommended by Susan Corker, Richard Gibbs, Gordon and Daphne, Patrick Stapley, RAB)*

Free house · Licensee Mrs Evelyn Moir · Real ale · Meals and snacks (not Sun, not Mon evening); dinners tel Ticehurst (0580) 200586 · Children in small dining-room · Open 10–2.30, 6–11

TILLINGTON   SU9621 Map 2
Horseguards

As the pub is perched on a stone embankment high over the lane opposite the church, the big black-panelled bow window seat in the beamed front bar gives a lovely view beyond the village to the Rother Valley. The comfortably refurbished bar is a friendly place and serves well kept King & Barnes Sussex, Festive and Mild from handpump, at low prices; good value simple bar food includes freshly cut sandwiches (from 45p, toasted from 50p), home-made soup (75p), a choice of ploughman's, home-made steak and kidney pie (£1.10) and a range of basket meals from sausage and chips (95p) to scampi (£2). Darts, dominoes, cribbage, a fruit machine; maybe piped music. Down a corridor is a small restaurant, with a choice of chicken, fish dishes, duck and steaks (main courses £1.75–£6.50), and home-made puddings. There's a terrace outside, and more tables and chairs in a garden behind. *(Recommended by RIP, Sarah Greening; more reports please)*

King & Barnes · Licensee Mike Wheller · Real ale · Meals (not Sun, not Tues evening) and snacks · Children in eating area and restaurant · Open 10.30–2.30, 6–11

If we know a pub does summer barbecues, we say so.

TISMAN'S COMMON   TQ0732   Map 3

Mucky Duck

Off A281 Horsham—Guildford; follow Loxwood 3 signpost by Fox Inn in
Bucks Green – don't turn off at Tisman's Common signpost!

This cheerful and well run country pub has a lively atmosphere, with
lots of young people in the evenings and well reproduced pop music.
For all that, it preserves old-fashioned virtues, too: prettily tile-hung
outside, with lots of beams inside, and country prints, horse brasses
and brass plates hanging among the black timbers on the white walls,
a big winter log fire, flagstones on the floor of the main part, and
brocaded seats in a quieter carpeted side area. Well kept Ballards
Best, King & Barnes and Ruddles County on handpump; good
straightforward hot dishes such as bangers and mash, fish and chips
and steaks; there is a separate pool-room. Outside there are robust
wood-and-concrete seats, with a climber, swings and a slide at the far
end of the grassy garden which is hedged off from the country road;
open-air drinkers are served from a hatch by the car park.
(Recommended by Peter Ney Bennett)

*Free house · Licensees John and Mary Sawyer · Meals and snacks · Open
12–2.30, 6–10.30*

WEST ASHLING   SU8107   Map 2

Richmond Arms

Mill Lane; from B2146 in village follow Hambrook signpost

All being well, by the time this *Guide* is published the enthusiastic
licensees will have had 300 different real ales on their 10 handpumps,
after just four years in this simple, out-of-the-way and very friendly
village pub. They also have Selborne Gold cider tapped from the cask,
and one of the best ranges of good foreign bottled beers in the south,
including all five Trappist beers, wild cherry beers from Belgium, and
some of the rarer German ales. Besides the three quickly changing
guest beers, they keep a fairly permanent range of Ballards Best and
Wassail, Boddingtons, Harveys XX Mild, King & Barnes Bitter and
Festive, and Timothy Taylors Landlord. The real food fits in well:
besides sandwiches (from £1, croque monsieur £1.50), ploughman's
(from £1.30), and steak sandwich (£2.95), there are vegetarian dishes
(from £1.50 for home-made cheese and nut pâté ploughman's),
quiche Lorraine (£1.95), local trout (£2.95) and puddings such as
bread and butter pudding (55p). They have local cockles (from mid-
May to early September), mussels, and more seafood as the summer
progresses. There are long wall benches, library chairs and black
tables around the central servery, with a fire in winter; bar billiards,
shove-ha'penny, dominoes, cribbage, and a fruit machine. You can sit
by the car park at picnic-table sets. *(Recommended by R H Inns,
N Wohlgemuth)*

*Free house · Licensees Roger and Julie Jackson · Real ale · Meals and snacks
(lunchtime, not Sun) · Children in family/bar billiards room · Folk music Mon
or Thurs, about fortnightly · Open 11–2.30, 6–11*

Waterside pubs are listed at the back of the book.

WEST HOATHLY   TQ3632   Map 3

Cat   [*illustrated on page 649*]

Village signposted between A22 and B2028 S of East Grinstead

Enterprising home-made food in this comfortably renovated old smugglers' pub includes stock-pot soup (75p), ploughman's (from £1.55), unusual pâtés such as tuna and apple, or cream cheese with peppers and toasted almonds, and good brandied duck served with geranium jelly (£1.50), mushrooms marinated in red wine, with melted Brie (£2.15), salads from a cold buffet counter (from £2.65), home-made lasagne (£2.65), cassoulet (£2.65), turkey with fried banana (£3.95) and sirloin steak (£4.95), with a decent choice of home-made puddings. The daily specials are always worth trying. A small dining-room does different evening menus in winter. The separate partly panelled rooms of the bar have now been opened into one, but keeping a traditional character and a cheerful and friendly atmosphere, thanks to the engaging landlord. There's some ancient carving round the massive central chimney. Harveys (as Beards) BB, XX Mild and in winter Old Ale on handpump. Seats among roses on a small sun-trap terrace look past big yew-trees to the church of this pretty hamlet, and the Bluebell steam railway terminus at Horsted Keynes isn't far away. (*Recommended by Philip Denison, Noel Giffard, A J Milman, Brian and Lil Jobson, Alan Franck, Ceri Thomas*)

Beards (supplied by Harveys) · Licensee Peter Balfour · Real ale · Meals (not Sun) and snacks (not Sun evening) · Children in dining-room and entrance lobby only (the pub isn't really suitable for small children) · Open 11–2.30, 6–10.30

WINEHAM   TQ2320   Map 3

Royal Oak ★   [*illustrated on page 634*]

Village signposted from A272 and B2116

Full of character, this handsome black and white timbered country pub has a well worn brick floor in front of its vast inglenook fireplace, and throughout, its furniture is fittingly simple and old-fashioned. Above the serving counter, the very low beams are decorated with ancient corkscrews, horseshoes, racing plates, tools and a coach horn. Excellently kept Whitbread Pompey Royal is tapped from casks in a still-room, on the way back through to the small snug; darts, shove-ha'penny, dominoes; toasted sandwiches (60p). There are rustic wooden tables on the grass by a well in front, and on a clear day you can just see Chanctonbury Ring from the window in the gents, far beyond the nearby meadows and oak-trees. (*Recommended by A G Thompson, Philip Gibson, Gordon and Daphne*)

Whitbreads · Licensees Robert and Timothy Peacock · Real ale · Snacks (not Sat evening or Sun) · Open 10.30–2.30, 6–10.30

Lucky Dip

Besides the fully inspected pubs, you might like to try these Lucky Dips recommended and described by readers (if you do, please send us reports):

ADVERSANE [TQ0723], *Blacksmiths Arms*: food includes a good selection of snacks and meals in a spacious old beamed pub *(Miss P M Gammon, DJ)*

ALCISTON [TQ5005], *Rose Cottage*: food good, wide choice, including afters, in most charming country pub with delightful atmosphere and cheerful service; attractive garden in pretty village below Downs; goat; children welcome *(W J Wonham, Stuart Perry)*

ANGMERING [TQ0704], *Lamb*: pleasant B&B accommodation in traditional pub *(Mr and Mrs A D Clayton)*

ANSTY [TQ2923], *Ansty Cross*: food, welcome and service good; pleasant fenced-off garden *(F J and M L Mahoney, B R Shiner)*

ARDINGLY [TQ3429], *Oak*: a very good selection of excellent salads and bar snacks in this genuine old pub; free house *(GHW)*

ARUNDEL [Queen Street; TQ0107], *General Abercrombie*: fine atmosphere; character pub nicely equipped with brass things; friendly staff, good value food *(Sigrid and Peter Sobanski, Jane and Steve Edwards)*; *Golden Goose*: food excellent in bar of pleasant pub *(A G Thompson)*; [Chichester Road] *White Swan*: good food, reasonable prices; efficient and friendly service *(A J Smith)*

ASHBURNHAM [Brown Bread Street; TQ6814], *Ash Tree*: food good, reasonable prices; cosy, warm atmosphere and very popular *(Mrs J M Heslep)*

BARCOMBE [TQ4114], *Anchor*: charming gardens, and boating on very peaceful river outside remote inn with small bar (sandwiches) and restaurant; bedrooms *(LYM)*

BERWICK [TQ5105], *Berwick*: excellent children's playground behind well run pub with attractive Perspex-roofed garden bar; decent choice of food and real ales *(R R S Clarke, LYM)*

BILLINGSHURST [High Street; TQ0925], *Olde Six Bells*: partly fourteenth-century flagstoned and timbered pub with well kept King & Barnes real ales, and food; inglenook fireplace, pretty roadside garden *(LYM)*

BINSTEAD [Binstead Lane; SU9806], *Black Horse*: friendly little pub in tiny hamlet, Gales beers tapped from the barrel and country wines, good lunchtime food; pleasant views from back garden *(Paul Edwards)*

BODIAM [TQ7825], *Curlew*: fish pie and moussaka very good, seafood pancakes superb, also steak and kidney pie; well kept Beards real ale; new owners *(John Townsend)*

BODLE STREET GREEN [TQ6514], *White Horse*: old pub with nice honest food *(Anon)*

BOREHAM STREET [TQ6611], *Bulls Head*: pleasant *(A G Thompson)*

BOSHAM [High Street; SU8003], *Anchor Bleu*: lovely sea views from waterside pub with low ceilings and open fires; readers report most enthusiastically out of season *(Helen Morgan, Mrs A M Arnold, Steve and Carolyn Harvey, LYM)*

BRIGHTON [St James's Street; TQ3105], *Bulldog*: 'Uncle Jim' Marley the owner of this free house keeps his extensive range of real ales extremely well *(MEO)*; [Black Lion Street] *Cricketers*: snug Victorian rooms downstairs, airy upstairs lunchtime buttery bar, partly covered courtyard *(W T Aird, A Saunders, LYM)*; [Marlborough Place] *King & Queen*: medieval-style main hall, straightforward food, lively jazz most evenings, and aviary in flagstoned courtyard *(Julian Grundy, LYM)*; [Upper Bedford Street] *Stag*: unassuming free house with extensive range of real ales and rare Belgian bottled beers *(MEO)*; [South Coast Road] *Telscombe Tavern*: really professionally run; excellent food and drink; prompt friendly efficient service – tables cleared fast; children welcomed if eating *(A J V Baker)*

BURPHAM [TQ0308], *George & Dragon*: lunchtime food popular in bar and restaurant of old pub, close to Norman church in quiet village with good walks and fine views over Arundel Castle *(Paul Edwards, Mrs A M Arnold, BB)*

BURWASH [TQ6724], *Bell*: small friendly inn opposite church in attractive village; simple bedrooms *(LYM)*; *Rose & Crown*: several beers and choice of food in heavily beamed and timbered pub *(BB)*

BURWASH COMMON [TQ6322], *Kicking Donkey*: food (sandwiches and so on) in country pub by cricket field with adventure playground; landlord plays organ *(Richard Gibbs)*

CHALVINGTON [TQ5109], *Yew Tree*: food is home cooked, served in friendly atmosphere; building seems about 200 years old with a cosy parlour, nice open log-filled fireplace and basic décor; small beer garden ideal in the summer; good Beards (Harveys); children allowed if accompanied by a parent *(P A Finlay)*
CHICHESTER [St Martins Street; SU8605], *Hole in the Wall*: food in bar and restaurant in pleasant panelled and beamed pub with old signs and actor photographs on walls, and stripped pine furnishings *(Martin Quinn, Mr and Mrs Harvey)*; [North Street] *Old Cross*: good food in town pub with decent range of beer; discreet piped music *(Richard Busby)*

nr CHICHESTER [SU8605], *Black Boy*: food in restaurant as well as snacks and wide choice of real ales in this beamed, atmospheric, friendly pub; always plenty of people, and children accepted; large garden with peacocks *(Frances Abbott)*
CHILGROVE [SU8214], *White Horse*: food (including home-cured ham and lobster), wine and ales good; a friendly welcome for weary walkers, man and dog; plenty of tables in garden *(M C Ryan, A G Thompson, Prof A N Black)*
COOKSBRIDGE [TQ3913], *Rainbow*: food and snacks good in clean, warm, welcoming Watneys pub with two comfortable bars *(D W Lloyd-Davies)*
COPTHORNE [TQ3139], *Abergavenney Arms*: modern, conservatively furnished main road pub with donkey paddock behind garden, popular for lunchtime food and well kept real ale; relaxed atmosphere *(Mrs A M Digges La Touche, BB)*
COUSLEYWOOD [TQ6533], *Old Vine*: food in bar good, also extensive menu and well cooked set-price meals in restaurant – part of delightful, popular, busy pub *(HRP, Sigrid and Peter Sobanski, F W and S M Sturch)*
CUCKFIELD [South Street; TQ3025], *Kings Head*: food tasty and reasonably priced, but no chips; bedrooms comfortable and good value *(M M Lindley)*; [A272] *White Harte*: popular medieval pub close to church, comfortably modernised; keen darts team; well kept Watneys real ales *(LYM)*
DALE HILL [TQ6930], *Cherry Tree*: very wide choice of food in comfortable bar *(H W Brearley)*
DELL QUAY [SU8302], *Crown & Anchor*: yacht harbour views from garden and bow window of modernised fifteenth-century pub on site of Roman quay; popular food *(BB)*
DEVIL'S DYKE [TQ2511], *Devil's Dyke*: staggering views night and day from busy touristy pub perched on Downs above Brighton *(Doug Kennedy, LYM)*
DITCHLING [TQ3215], *Black Bull*: especially excellent lunchtime sandwiches, with good beer, and attentive barmaids; civilised *(Dave Butler and others)*
EARTHAM [SU9409], *George*: food in bar good with friendly service without being obtrusive; wonderful log fires; pleasant restaurant open some days *(David Barnard-Smith)*
EAST HOATHLY [TQ5216], *Kings Head*: food included tasty coq au vin in warmly welcoming pub *(Mrs D M Edgerton)*
EASTBOURNE [Old Town; TV6199], *Crown*: allows dogs, very friendly; beer garden *(B R Shiner)*; [The Goffs, Old Town] *Lamb*: food good and excellent Harveys ales on handpump in interesting and historic pub with ancient beams, priesthole, secret passage to Old Parsonage and twelfth-century vaulted crypt used as a unique cellar – everything in the way of atmosphere and character *(Michael Parrott, Jeff Dixon)*; [Meads] *Pilot*: garden, good value reasonable snacks, efficient service *(B R Shiner)*; *Victoria*: spacious; B&B *(Bob Rendle)*
EASTDEAN [TV5597], *Tiger*: oasis of quiet, nestled opposite village green on road to Birling Gap; a few benches outside where you can watch the world go by – inside, the furniture is simple but the atmosphere convivial, still very much a farmers' pub *(C M Harnor, C B M Gregory)*
EWHURST GREEN [TQ7925], *White Dog*: popular food pub above Bodiam Castle with heated pool and other facilities for residents; but has been found closed recently *(LYM)*
FERRING [TQ0902], *Tudor Close*: food not cheap but excellent standard in converted sixteenth-century barn with magnificent fireplace; very lofty and spacious *(W J Wonham)*
FINDON [TQ1208], *Gun*: modernised pub with nice sheltered lawn and

efficiently served food, in quiet village below Cissbury Ring *(Mrs Betty Norman, LYM)*

GLYNDE [TQ4509], *Trevor Arms*: known for many years, and very pleasant for a drink *(A G Thompson)*

GUN HILL [TQ5614], *Gun*: friendly service; log fires, cosy warm atmosphere, well kept pub, lavish helpings of well cooked food with wide choice of cold buffet; Charrington IPA *(Mr and Mrs Raymond Watkins, Mrs J M Heslep, Gwen and Peter Andrews)*

HARTFIELD [TQ4735], *Anchor*: food includes wide choice of seafood in comfortable and clean pub with oak tables and padded bench seats *(R and S Bentley)*; *Haywaggon*: wide range of well presented bar snacks and real ales, welcoming staff, well run *(Cynthia and John Coppard)*

HASTINGS [Cornwallis Street; TQ8109], *Prince Albert*: excellent back-street Shepherd Neame pub, extremely friendly, with a large number of Sussex characters – place to spend many happy hours *(MEO)*

HEATHFIELD [Burwash Road; TQ5821], *Crown*: food at lunchtime consistently good; roomy; separate games bar *(W J Teer)*

HENFIELD [TQ2116], *Plough*: most interesting bar, with generous helpings of cheap food *(M A Radford)*

HERMITAGE [SU7505], *Sussex Brewery*: own brewery provides excellent ales at cottage-type pub rather like going into someone's living-room: very cosy and welcoming atmosphere, fairly plain furnishings, log fire; some snacks (sausages, pasties, rolls) *(Steve and Carolyn Harvey)*

nr HORSHAM [Plummer's Plain; TQ1730], *Wheatsheaf*: King & Barnes on handpump; wide range of hot and cold bar food; garden; isolated in pleasant wooded area on country road; cheerful atmosphere *(Tony Gayfer)*

HORSTED KEYNES [TQ3828], *Green Man*: nice atmosphere, good ploughman's, local real ale; about a mile from Bluebell Steam Railway centre *(J Barden)*

HURSTPIERPOINT [High Street; TQ2716], *New*: old-fashioned pub with charming traditional back room, bar billiards in panelled snug, simpler public bar, well kept Bass and Charrington IPA *(LYM)*

ICKLESHAM [TQ8816], *Queens Head*: good food and old world courtesy in pub with elegant décor; efficient service, most friendly atmosphere *(D A Irvine-Turner)*

ISFIELD [TQ4417], *Laughing Fish*: simple modernised village pub with robust food, lively atmosphere and well kept Beards real ales *(BB, Stuart Perry)*

KEYMER [TQ3115], *Greyhound*: interesting: big collection of mugs and jugs hang from ceiling; comfortable and excellent food lunchtime and evening *(P J Cornford)*

KINGSTON NEAR LEWES [TQ3908], *Juggs*: food includes very good ploughman's and choice of rough pâté, sausages and so on, and most enjoyable taramosalata, in excellent village pub; very popular, very busy at lunchtime *(M Boniface)*

LAMBS GREEN [TQ2136], *Lamb*: cosy plush bar with beams and open fire in friendly pub with wide choice of quickly served food and well kept Badger Best, Courage Directors, King & Barnes and Youngs Special on handpump; big glass-walled garden room *(BB, Philip J Gibson)*

LAUGHTON [TQ5013], *Roebuck*: good bar food in The Cabaret; Trumans beers, country wines; cabaret some evenings *(G M Denton)*

LEWES [TQ4110], *Lewes Arms*: small friendly local pub, in Harveys/Beards home town; among other attractions a dwyle flunking team perform occasionally – strangers quickly welcomed *(MEO)*; [High Street, St Anne's] *Pelham Arms*: food in bar (and restaurant) good value; pleasant atmosphere *(MMB)*

LINDFIELD [High Street; TQ3425], *Linden Tree*: looks more like a shop than a pub outside; spacious lounge-type bar with mix of ancient and modern furnishings; good value food, well kept wide range of real ales, open fire, very friendly family service *(A Saunders, Miss T A Ambrose, Dave Butler, Lesley Storey)*

MARK CROSS [TQ5831], *Mark Cross*: decent range of bar food at reasonable prices *(A J V Baker)*

MAYFIELD [Fletching Street; TQ5827], *Carpenters Arms*: pretty country village pub with old-fashioned charm and atmosphere, good food, and real ale *(Mrs G Rich)*

nr MAYFIELD [TQ5827], *Five Ashes*: food good (evening meals seven days a week); pleasant terrace *(VS)*

MIDHURST [North Street; SU8821], *Angel*: good Gales BBB and HSB; old oak beams, tapestry chairs, fireplaces; huge walled garden with metal tables at back; reasonably priced food in pleasant big restaurant; an atmospheric and friendly place to stay *(Doug Kennedy)*

NEW BRIDGE [TQ0625], *Limeburners Arms*: friendly old beamed pub with good simple lunchtime food and garden; caravan site nearby *(DJ)*

NEWICK [TQ4121], *Bull*: very pleasant pub *(A G Thompson)*

PEASE POTTAGE [TQ2533], *James' King*: attractive and quite roomy country pub with warm atmosphere *(S M Wines, Ceri and Beti Wyn Thomas)*

PETWORTH [Angel Street; SU9721], *Angel*: good value food in warm and comfortable medieval inn with pleasant décor and big open fire; real ale; bedrooms *(D J Penny, W B Goldring)*; *Red Lion*: freshly cooked food, friendly atmosphere, real ale *(HB)*

nr PETWORTH [SU9721], *Welldiggers*: low-ceilinged food pub very popular for its good value restaurant-style meals – hardly a place for just a drink now – and attractive lawns and terraces *(Miss P M Gammon, Mrs Betty Norman, LYM)*

PULBOROUGH [TQ0418], *Arun Hotel*: clean, nice dinners, good value seafood, choice of beers, lovely views and gardens *(John Warren)*; [Lower Street] *Oddfellows Arms*: friendly and efficient service in attractive sixteenth-century pub with excellent steaks and fish *(D J P Dutton)*; *Waters Edge*: very good *(A G Thompson)*

RINGLES CROSS [TQ4721], *Ringles Cross Inn*: useful and well kept roadside inn, good real ale, reliable food including steaks *(D R Crafts, BB)*

ROBERTSBRIDGE [TQ7323], *Seven Stars*: food in bar good from ploughman's to steaks, and small restaurant with log fire (Sunday lunch £4.50 with coffee); well furnished 1380 pub on site of twelfth-century monastery has plenty of settles and stools, sporting prints, hop bines on ceiling; good atmosphere, log fire) *(Heather Sharland)*

RODMELL [TQ4106], *The Holly*: good atmosphere and food *(M A Radford)*

RUSPER [Friday Street; TQ2037], *Royal Oak*: food tasty, King & Barnes beer kept well, homely, welcoming atmosphere *(Paul Friday)*; *Star*: food includes excellent toasted sandwiches in charming old pub with winter log fire *(VS)*

RYE [High Street; TQ9220], *George*: THF hotel with bar well patronised by locals, usual THF drinks, choice of bar snacks; very popular, very old; bedrooms *(Heather Sharland)*; [Gun Garden] *Ypres Castle*: recommended for its position (on town footpath near Ypres Tower) with front garden overlooking river mouth; ideal for people with children *(Gordon and Daphne)*

SALEHURST [TQ7424], *Salehurst Halt*: inn in pretty village by fourteenth-century church, with real ale and good food; opens noon, closed Tuesday; bedrooms *(Anon)*

SAYERS COMMON [TQ2618], *Duke of York*: food and snacks good, Watneys/Phoenix beers; relatively modern, very clean, warm and welcoming *(D W Lloyd-Davies)*

SEAFORD [TV4899], *Beachcomber*: friendly service, excellent value for money; homely and can take children; good food and beer *(Mrs J Koj, D R Crafts)*

SEDLESCOMBE [TQ7718], *Queens Head*: olde-world village pub in pretty setting with garden, and Fremlins on draught *(John Reynolds)*

SHARPTHORNE [Vinols Cross; TQ3732], *Vinols Cross*: Fullers and Badger beers in pub with tasty snacks *(J A H Townsend)*

SLAUGHAM [TQ2528], *Chequers*: food and drink good at reasonable prices, served with a smile; clean; nice garden, in beautiful village *(J A Price)*

SOUTH HARTING [SU7819], *Ship*: friendly atmosphere, log fires, decent choice of pub food including wide range of sandwiches in fine old pub with keys collection; garden seats, children welcome; near Uppark *(P J Brooks, Mrs A M Arnold and others)*

SOUTH STREET [TQ3918], *Horns Lodge*: popular with locals and travellers, has real ales, traditional games, big open fireplaces, low beams, window seats, meals and snacks; beer garden has sandpit and other things for kids *(Stuart Perry)*

STAPLEFIELD [TQ2728], *Jolly Tanner*: foreign money stuck on ceiling (for benefit of RNLI) in pub with delightful atmosphere, good bar food and garden, in picturesque village at the back of Nymans (National Trust woodland gardens) *(W J Wonham)*; *Victory*: food simple but sound in pleasant old beamed pub with tables by cricket green; good traditional cider *(Alan Franck)*

STEYNING [High Street; TQ1711], *Chequer*: friendly bar staff: two bars – locals bar with darts, snooker, electronic games, and saloon with grandfather clock and open fire giving cosy atmosphere; choice of handpumped beers and country wines, and a good selection of food *(Paul Edwards)*; *White Horse*: food includes wide choice of well presented dishes in attractive beamed building with nice friendly staff *(Miss P M Gammon)*

STOUGHTON [SU8011], *Hare & Hounds*: modernised Downland village pub with good value food, well kept Gales ales, pleasant staff, and seats on terrace *(N Wohlgemuth, BB)*

TICEHURST [TQ6920], *Cherry Tree*: immaculately clean, nice terrace garden, good service and food *(Colin and Cindy Warren)*

nr UCKFIELD [TQ4721], *Barley Mow*: food good and reasonably priced, with excellent fast service; well kept King & Barnes Festive *(S A Lovett)*

WARNHAM [TQ1533], *Greets*: pleasant country village pub with garden *(Beti and Ceri Wyn Thomas)*

WARNINGLID [TQ2426], *Rifleman*: pleasant service; tasty food, and wines reasonably priced, also scrumpy; collection of nineteenth-century military uniforms; most beautiful peaceful village *(J A Price, RN)*

WEST CHILTINGTON [Smock Alley: TQ0918], *Five Bells*: food now excellent – both snacks and full meals – in friendly, well managed pub of no great antiquity with good range of King & Barnes ales *(E C Goldring, Peter Harding)*

WEST FIRLE [TQ4607], *Ram*: simple locals' pub in quiet village, handy for Firle Place and Downs *(Stuart Perry, LYM)*

WHATLINGTON [TQ7518], *Royal Oak*: food is good value, pleasant service, in attractive country pub *(C D Bond)*

WILMINGTON [TQ5404], *Wilmington Arms*: food and service good in spacious, spotless bar with well kept beer and cheerful licensee; surrounded by beautiful countryside *(Gordon Leighton)*

WITHYHAM [TQ4935], *Dorset Arms*: unusual raised bar with Tudor fireplace and beams; well kept Harveys real ales, and home-made bar food *(Eirlys Roberts, LYM)*

Warwickshire *see* Midlands
West Midlands *see* Midlands

Wiltshire

This area seems to breed pubs of very considerable character, such as the recently restored George & Dragon in Potterne (an interesting fifteenth-century inn with a remarkable antique indoor shooting gallery); the charmingly untouched Horseshoe in the sleepy downland village of Ebbesbourne Wake, and the not dissimilar and equally unpretentious Red Lion in East Chisenbury (locals snugly talking over their garden problems); the Cross Guns at Avoncliff near Bradford-on-Avon (tucked away in remarkably unspoilt surroundings, with a fine riverside garden and a good choice of real ales); the charming thatched Weight for Age in Alvediston (a new name – it used to be the Crown – and new owners, concentrating firmly on its food, including good fresh fish); the delightful White Hart in Castle Combe, one of England's prettiest villages; the unspoilt and remote Compasses in Chicksgrove (with good food – also bedrooms); the Bear in Devizes (with a rambling old-fashioned lounge and always-available food – a nice place to stay); the Crown at Everleigh (a fine easy-going atmosphere in comfortable surroundings, with a big walled

The Old Bell, Malmesbury

garden, home cooking using fresh ingredients, and bedrooms); the romantic White Hart at Ford (another place to stay); the thatched Ivy in Heddington, with winter firelight flickering over its parquet floor; both entries in Lacock – the George (where new licensees are proudly conserving all its old features, even the treadle for the dog that worked the spit-roast), and the Red Lion with its collection of agricultural tools and odd bric-à-brac (both good for food, and the Red Lion has good value bed and breakfast); the heavily thatched Hatchet in Lower Chute; the civilised Old Bell by the abbey in Malmesbury (a comfortable place to stay, with painstaking new licensees); the Green Dragon in Market Lavington (with its individually selected furnishings, and worthwhile food); the heavy-beamed little Sun in Marlborough (again, reasonable food, and recently refurbished bedrooms); the Haunch of Venison in Salisbury (very atmospheric small rooms); and the smart Red Lion there, with its medieval restaurant and strange skeleton-bellringers clock. Besides those mentioned, pubs to pick out for food might include the Waggon & Horses in Beckhampton (lots of unusual sandwiches, among other imaginative dishes – and an interesting pub, near Avebury and Silbury Hill); the stylish old Lamb at Hindon (a place to stay); the Royal Oak at Great Wishford (a very wide choice of good value food, catering well for children too); the chintzy Suffolk Arms in Malmesbury; the very civilised Bell in Ramsbury, with its unusual pies; the Rose & Crown just outside Salisbury, with lovely views of the cathedral and comfortable bedrooms; and the Black Horse at Teffont Magna (steadily gaining ground – they've now re-opened their refurbished bedrooms). Two pubs deserving a special mention are the Green Dragon at Barford St Martin (a friendly old-fashioned pub with cheap bedroom accommodation) and the Cuckoo at Landford (a country pub surrounded by birds). Among the Lucky Dip entries at the end of the chapter, particularly interesting possibilities – in the running for inspection as potential main entries if further reports are confirmatory – include the George in Amesbury (good food, old coaching atmosphere), the Horse & Groom in Charlton (good food in interesting rustic building), the Lysley Arms near Chippenham (good food), the beamed Swan at Enford, the Malet Arms at Newton Toney and Victoria and Albert in Netherhampton (two good all-round old pubs), the Vine Tree at Norton (good food), the Benett Arms at Semley (a useful place to stay) and, especially, the Dove at Corton (an unexpected little bistro of a pub, with good food) and Royal Oak at Wootton Rivers (beamy thatched charm).

ALVEDISTON ST9723 Map 2

Weight for Age

Formerly the Crown, this thatched pub has new owners who are
nearing completion of some restoration work following a thatch fire
just before they moved in; they are adding a new kitchen and family
room (that will double up as an extra restaurant area in the evening).
Miss Allenby comes from The Warehouse restaurant in Poole, and
will be serving only fresh, home-cooked food here, with an accent in
the restaurant on seafood bought from her regular suppliers in Poole.
Bar food includes sandwiches (from 55p), baked potato with various
fillings (65p), home-made soup (75p), ploughman's with Stilton or
Cheddar (£1.10), home-made pâté (£1.50), avocado and crab
(£1.80), prawn open sandwich (£1.90), giant sausage (£2.10), moules
marinière or breaded plaice (£2.90), steak and kidney pie or chicken
curry (£3.40) and chicken Kiev (£3.85); puddings (£1.25) and a
children's menu (95p); fish dishes in the restaurant include Poole
plaice (£3.95), fillet of sole with a cream sauce or dressed crab cooked
with peppers and onions and topped with a cheese sauce (£5.45);
Sunday lunch is £3.75. Huntsman Dorchester on handpump; darts.
The two knocked-together beamed rooms, with an open fire at one
end, have deeply upholstered seats on the red patterned carpet, and
subdued lighting. The attractive garden, on different levels around a
thatched white well, and nicely broken up with shrubs and rockery
features among the neatly kept lawns, faces a farmyard with ponies
and other animals. *(Recommended by W H B Murdoch, DP, Gordon and
Daphne, Brian Frith; up-to-date reports please)*

*Free house · Licensees Miss Rachel Allenby and Lars Andersson · Real ale
Meals and snacks · Children welcome in separate family room · Open
11.30–2.30, 6.30–11*

BARFORD ST MARTIN SU1531 Map 2

Green Dragon

Junction of A30 with B3089

The original front bar in this friendly and comfortable inn, with its
dark squared oak panelling, cushioned wall benches, dark seats and
tables, and a big log fire in winter, is warmly welcoming. There is a
separate games bar with darts, shove-ha'penny, dominoes, a fruit
machine, juke box and pool which doubles as a spacious functions
room. Food is served in both bars and includes home-made soup
(60p), toasted sandwiches (75p), ploughman's (£1.20), special pot
meals (£1.60), local ham and egg (£1.65) and rump steak (£4.85);
well kept Badger Best, Hectors and Tanglefoot. The simple bedrooms
are good value. *(Recommended by R H Inns, Sandy Muirhead; more reports
please)*

*Badger · Licensee David Southgate · Real ale · Meals and snacks (residents only
Mon evenings) · Open 10.30–2.30, 6–11 · Bedrooms tel Salisbury (0722)
742242; £9.50/£19*

All *Guide* inspections are anonymous. Anyone claiming to be a *Good Pub Guide*
inspector is a fraud, and should be reported to us with a name and description.

BECKHAMPTON   SU0868   Map 2
Waggon and Horses

A4 Marlborough–Calne

In summer you can sit at picnic-table sets on the big front cobbles, among troughs of flowers, by the massive stone walls of the inn – a welcome sight to coachmen coming in from what was notorious as the coldest stretch of the old Bath road. This was the scene in *Pickwick Papers* for the bagman's tale about Tom Smart, the buxom widow licensee with a face as comfortable as the bar, and the talkative Spanish mahogany chair. Inside, the open-plan bar of this old thatched coaching-inn is cosy, with a roaring fire in winter, old-fashioned high-backed settles as well as the red cushioned Windsor chairs, leatherette stools, comfortably cushioned wall benches, and beams in the shiny ceiling where walls have been knocked through. A wide and imaginative choice of bar food includes filled rolls (70p), lots of sandwiches (80p), several more elaborate combination sandwiches such as ham, banana, cheese and pineapple, all grilled together (85p – named after Jeremy Tree, whose training stables are nearby), double-decker sandwiches (£1.20), an unspecified dish of the day which you have to order as a pig in a poke (£2.25), several variations on the ploughman's theme (£2.35), home-made steak and vegetable pie (£2.50), a good choice of salads (£2.75), grills such as half a chicken (£4.30), gammon or scampi (£4.60), eight-ounce sirloin steak (£4.95), and home-made puddings such as cheesecake, treacle sponge or passion cake (85p) – even a sweet toasted banana and fruit sandwich with ice cream (£1.10). Well kept Wadworths IPA, 6X, Farmers Glory and in winter Old Timer on handpump; dominoes, cribbage, fruit machine, maybe piped music. Silbury Hill, a prehistoric mound which took some 18 million manhours to build, is just towards Marlborough, and Avebury stone circle and the West Kennet long barrow are very close too. *(Recommended by Dr B W Marsden, A J Triggle, Dr A K Clarke)*

Wadworths · Licensee Jon Scholes · Real ale · Meals (not Mon evening or Sun lunchtime) and snacks (not Mon evening) · Open 11.30–2.30, 6.30–11; closed 25 Dec

nr BRADFORD-ON-AVON   ST8060   Map 2
Cross Guns ★

Avoncliff; pub is across footbridge from Avoncliff Station (first through road left, heading N from river on A363 in Bradford centre, and keep bearing left), and can also be reached down very steep and eventually unmade road signposted Avoncliff – keep straight on rather than turning left into village centre – from Westwood (which is signposted from B3109 and A366 W of Trowbridge); OS Sheet 173 reference 805600

Coming down into this remote hamlet gave us an uncanny feeling of stepping right into an early nineteenth-century landscape painting. This old-fashioned pub with good simple food is popular in summer for its floodlit and terraced gardens overlooking the wide River Avon and a maze of bridges, aqueducts (the Kennet and Avon Canal) and tracks winding through this quite narrow gorge, below steeply wooded hills and close to the Barton Farm Country Park. Inside the pub, candlelit at night, are rush-seated chairs around plain sturdy oak tables on the brightly patterned carpet, low seventeenth-century beams, stone walls, and a large ancient fireplace with a smoking chamber behind it – a cosy, chatty atmosphere in winter, but it may be crowded in summer. A good range of well kept real ales on handpump: Badger Bitter and Tanglefoot, Butcombe, Cross Guns IPA (brewed for the pub), Marstons Pedigree, Smiles, Wadworths 6X and Farmers Glory. Food includes a lunchtime buffet in summer (Tuesday–Saturday) as well as soup (£1.10), a chunk of bread with cheese and two fried eggs (£1.65), home-made lasagne and cottage pie (£2.75) and Maggie's Special – minced beef cooked with courgettes, cheese, tomatoes, onion, garlic and herbs (£2.75). Darts, dominoes, cribbage, cards, backgammon, chess, Monopoly and other board games; maybe piped music. (Recommended by Nick Dowson and Alison Hayward, Dr A K Clarke, Hugh Calvey)

Free house · Licensees Maggie and Wim Van Huizen · Real ale · Meals (Weds to Sat evenings) and snacks (lunchtime, not Mon, limited Sun) · Open 11– 2.30, 6.30–11 all year (opens 12 and 7 in winter); closed Mon lunchtime

CASTLE COMBE   ST8477 Map 2

White Hart ★

Village centre; signposted off B4039 Chippenham–Chipping Sodbury

Especially popular with visitors in summer, this friendly and cheerful family-run old stone pub is one of the most attractive buildings in a beautiful village. The flagstoned main bar's old-fashioned furnishings include a traditional black wall bench built in to the stone mullioned window, an antique elm table as well as Windsor chairs, and in winter there's a big log fire in the elegant stone fireplace. An appetisingly laid out cold buffet counter includes ploughman's (£1), ham salad (£2) and good turkey and ham pie or beef salad (£1.95), all with good crusty bread, and there is soup (70p), hot pizza (95p) and toasted sandwiches. In winter, hot daily specials (£2.15) include chilli con carne with rice and garlic bread, baked ham, casseroles and pies. Badger Best, Huntsman Royal Oak, Marstons Pedigree, Moles, Theakstons Best and Whitbreads West Country on handpump, with a good range of country wines, cocktails, and in appropriate weather mulled wine, buttered rum or toddy; darts, shove-ha'penny, dominoes, cribbage. A carpeted room leads off the main bar, similarly furnished and decorated with some copper and brass, and there's a family room, with more seats in a small central covered courtyard. You can also sit outside in the garden. (Recommended by Peter Dilnot, Philip Denison)

Free house · Licensee C E Wheeler · Real ale · Meals (not Sat or Sun) and snacks · Children in family room and covered courtyard · Occasional folk singing · Parking nearby may be difficult; village car park is up steep hill Open 10–2.30, 6–10.30; closed evening 25 Dec

---

People named as recommenders after the main entries have told us that they feel the pub should be included. But they have not written the report – we have, after anonymous on-the-spot inspections.

CHICKSGROVE   ST9629 Map 2

Compasses ★

From A30 5½ miles W of B3089 junction, take lane on N side signposted
Sutton Mandeville, Sutton Row, then first left (small signs point the way to the
pub, but at the pub itself, in Lower Chicksgrove, there may be no inn sign –
look out for the car park; OS Sheet 184 reference 974294

This unspoilt country inn is a friendly place, with old bottles hanging
from beams above the roughly timbered bar counter, farm tools on
the partly stripped stone walls, and high-backed wooden settles
forming snug booths around the tables on the mainly flagstone floor.
The very popular and wide choice of good home-cooked bar food
includes soup with croûtons (60p), sandwiches (from 70p), open
prawn sandwich (£1.50), filled baked potatoes (from £1.10),
hamburger (£1.35), ploughman's with a choice of eight cheeses (from
£1.50), omelettes (from £1.50), clam fries or steak sandwich (£1.75),
sausage, cheese and egg (£1.80), chicken (£1.95), home-made steak
pie (£2.25), grilled ham or veal (£2.50), and steaks (from £4.95).
Well-kept Halls Harvest, Ind Coope Burton and Wadworths 6X on
handpump; darts, shove-ha'penny, table skittles, dominoes and
cribbage. A separate restaurant serves main dishes such as Stilton and
port mousse, steak and oyster pie and game casserole. There is a big
garden to sit in, as well as the flagstoned farm courtyard (the lane
carries very little traffic). *(Recommended by Paul Edwards, Bob and Val
Collman, Roy McIsaac, R H Inns)*

*Free house · Licensee Alan Poulton · Real ale · Meals and snacks (not Tues)
Children welcome · Open 10–2.30, 6–11; closed Tues lunchtime · Bedrooms*
tel *Fovant* (072 270) 318; £8/£16

CHILMARK   ST9632 Map 2

Black Dog

B3089

The friendly and neighbourly carpeted lounge bar in this comfortably
modernised fifteenth-century pub has rush-seated armchairs,
equestrian plates on the walls, horse brasses on the beams, a big
fireplace with logs burning in winter and more brass in summer, and
piped music. In another bar the plaster has been stripped back so that
you can see fossil ammonites in the stone (from Chilmark quarry –
the same stone as Salisbury Cathedral). Bar food includes soup (from
55p), sandwiches (from 80p), ploughman's (from £1.40), liver pâté
(£1.50), plaice (£2.20), ham or chicken salad (£2.40), beef salad
(£2.60) and scampi (£2.60). Well kept Courage Best and Directors
and Simonds on handpump, and in summer a wine and strawberry
cup; maybe piped music; sensibly placed darts, popular with people
from the big RAF camp beyond the village (marked as open country
on the latest Ordnance Survey map), cribbage and a fruit machine. A
separate restaurant serves main dishes such as veal escalope (£3.50),
poached salmon (£3.75) and steaks (from £4.75). There are white
tables and chairs on the prettily daisy-covered lawn, well screened by
the tiled house from any road noise. The village, off the main road, is
most attractive. *(Recommended by Robert L Scott, N F Mackley)*

Courage · Licensee Geoffrey Price-Harris · Real ale · Meals and snacks
Children welcome · Open 10–2.30, 6–11

DEVIZES   SU0061   Map 2
Bear

Market Place

The main bar of this imposing stone building rambles through the
central hall: friendly and companionable, with groups of seats
including one or two easy chairs around oak occasional tables, fresh
flowers here and there, old prints on the walls, and big logs on the fire
in winter. A simply furnished grill and snack room is named after the
portrait painter Thomas Lawrence whose father was the landlord
here in the 1770s; it is specially useful as it continues serving until the
bar closes. At lunchtime this has buffet service (you can take food
through into the bar), with salads (from £2.25) and hot dishes such as
ham and asparagus or leek and bacon in cheese sauce, casseroles
made with real ale, home-made raised pies (£2.95) such as veal and
ham or pork and tarragon, and a Devizes pie (£3.25) that they have
resurrected from a recipe in an 1836 cookery book, *Good Things in
England*. In the evening it reverts to a waitress-served grill room
(using charcoal), with most of the lunchtime food as well as decent
grills such as mustard and honey chops (£2.45), a generous mixed
grill (£3.25) and steaks (from £5.45). There is a special children's
menu (not after 8pm). Quick snacks such as sandwiches,
ploughman's (from £1.20), rolls and sausages are served from the
bar, with a wider choice ordered from the Lawrence Room waitress
in the evening. There is a separate restaurant, with an à la carte menu
changing weekly – the full choice is served the previous Saturday
evening as a table d'hôte meal for £9.50; also Sunday roast lunches
(the breakfasts in here, incidentally, give a choice of four different
teas as well as dishes such as kidneys and bacon). Freshly ground
coffee and well kept Wadworths IPA and 6X on handpump; it's
brewed in the town, and from the brewery you can get it in splendid
old-fashioned half-gallon earthenware jars. This old-fashioned inn
used to be one of England's great coaching-inns; it's a nice place to
stay and some of the rooms have four-poster beds. *(More reports please)*

*Wadworths · Licensee W K Dickenson · Real ale · Meals and snacks · Children
in eating area · Occasional bar piano music · Bedrooms tel Devizes (0380)
2444; £22 (£26B)/£30 (£36B) · Open 10–2.30, 6–11; closed evening 25 Dec*

EAST CHISENBURY   SU1452   Map 2
Red Lion

Village signposted from A342 Upavon–Everleigh, and from
A345 Upavon–Amesbury in Enford

This old-fashioned inn has a long wooden-ceilinged room with
leatherette benches built against its walls, and the bar servery houses
a curious collection of enigmatic objects. It's the place to come for
gardening advice, and certainly we found the locals who had made
themselves comfortable on the old-fashioned high-backed settles
drawn up snugly around the fire – and made us very welcome there –

were full of gardening talk. The friendly licensees keep their Whitbreads Strong Country well – it's tapped straight from the cask; bread, cheese and pickles (40p); darts. Outside, there are swings and a seesaw by the tables on the lawn. *(Recommended by Dr A K Clarke, Gordon and Daphne)*

Whitbreads · Licensees Mr and Mrs Coombs · Real ale · Snacks (not Sun) · Open 11–2.30, 6.30–11

EBBESBOURNE WAKE ST9824 Map 2
Horseshoe

This homely old-fashioned Downland village pub has such a warmly welcoming atmosphere that it's difficult to leave. The carpeted and beautifully kept public bar is a friendly parlour, its beams crowded with lanterns, farm tools and other bric-à-brac – even the fruit machine is crowned with a rotary knife grinder, and there's an antique kitchen range in the big chimney embrasure. The tables are usually decorated with fresh flowers from the most attractive little garden, where seats look out over the small, steep sleepy valley of the River Ebble. Well kept Wadworths 6X drawn straight from the row of casks behind the bar; darts. *(Recommended by Gordon and Daphne; more reports please)*

Free house · Licensees Tom and Gladys Bath · Real ale · Open 11–2.30, 6.30–10.45 (opens noon Tues; closes 11.10 Fri and Sat)

EVERLEIGH SU2054 Map 2
Crown

The warm and chatty lounge bar in this seventeenth-century country inn with its striking twin eighteenth-century wings has a family rather than a formal atmosphere, with a splendidly easy mix of customers, and friendly service. The décor is clean and light, with sporting prints on the walls, lots of polished copper, fresh flowers, log fires in winter, and a mixture of upright rush-seated chairs, big Windsor armchairs, little easy chairs and the variety of other seats you might find in the corners of a country house. Food is all home cooked and relies heavily on fresh vegetables and local meat (the ham is home cooked): it might include good rare beef sandwiches, soup (90p, French onion soup £1.40), ploughman's with well chosen cheeses and granary bread (£1.40), goose egg and chips (£1.80), four-ounce burger (£2.40), home-barbecued spare ribs or calamari with tagliatelli (£2.80) and oak-smoked prawns and granary bread (£2.90). There is also a small restaurant. The downstairs public bar (the one for muddy boots) has darts, pool, bar billiards, snooker, shove-ha'penny, dominoes, cribbage, a fruit machine, space game, juke box and background music – none of it audible in the lounge; a family room has a piano and games. Well kept Wadworths IPA and 6X on handpump. The extensive walled garden (safe for children) has animals and geese, and the inn's extensive stables are now used by the trainer Richard Hannon. Dry-fly fishing for residents. *(Recommended by Arthur Roome; more reports please)*

Free house · Licensees Jim and Andrew Earle · Real ale · Meals and snacks Children welcome · Open 11–2.30, 6–11 · Bedrooms tel Collingbourne Ducis (026 485) 223; £15 (£16B)/£25 (£28B)

FORD   ST8374   Map 2
White Hart

A420 Chippenham–Bristol; follow Colerne sign at E side of village to find pub

In summer you can drink outside at the front of this L-shaped stone building partly covered with ivy; there is another terrace behind, by a stone bridge over the By Brook, and for residents a secluded swimming-pool. The cosy old bar of the friendly small inn has a romantic atmosphere in the evenings – gentle lighting, music soft enough not to drown the tick of the clock, small pictures and a few advertising mirrors on the walls, heavy black beams supporting the white-painted boards of the ceiling, and in winter the warmth of a big log-burning stove in the old stone fireplace. Bar food includes sandwiches, home-made soup (85p), home-made pâté (£1.50), hot turkey sandwich with gravy (£1.50) game hot-pot (£1.75) and home-cooked ham (£2.75). Well kept Archers Village, Badger Best, Fullers ESB, Marstons Pedigree and Wadworths 6X on handpump; shove-ha'penny, dominoes, fruit machine. The separate restaurant, lit by brass and copper lanterns, does a five-course £8.75 dinner with main courses such as venison, beef bourguignonne and seafood provençale, and beside it is a buttery serving salads and hot dishes such as those served in the bar. A nice place to stay, but if you want to check in outside pub hours you should make advance arrangements. *(Recommended by Sally Filby and others)*

Free house · Licensee Ken Gardner · Real ale · Meals and snacks · Children in buttery and restaurant · Open 11–2.30, 6–10.30 · Bedrooms tel Castle Combe (0249) 782213; £25B/£36B

GREAT WISHFORD   SU0735   Map 2
Royal Oak

In village, which is signposted from A36

This village pub has pleased readers from far and wide with its unusually large choice of food. It includes sandwiches (85p), six varieties of ploughman's (from £1.55), a range of filled jacket potatoes and pizzas (around £2), Wiltshire ham and eggs (£2.65), pies baked to order with a dozen different fillings, such as steak and kidney or steak and oyster (£3.65), vegetarian dishes, such as aubergine and courgette moussaka and mushroom lasagne (£3), Avon trout, Scotch salmon and halibut (£4.50) and steaks with wine and cream sauces (£5.85); puddings include raspberry and peach crumble, treacle roly-poly, bread and butter pudding, spotted dick and lots of ice creams and sorbets, all home made (95p). A small separate restaurant is open on Wednesday to Saturday evenings. The main front bar has cushioned pews, small seats and some easy chairs on its brown carpet, beams, and in winter a log fire at each end. There is a cheery family area just behind, with sturdy bleached wood tables: children can get smaller (and cheaper) helpings from the main menu or choose from their own special menu. Besides a good choice of some 20 reasonably priced wines by the glass and others by the bottle, there is well kept Ushers Best and Founders on handpump, and they do a number of cocktails. Darts, shove-ha'penny, cribbage, maybe piped music. The garden behind this flint house, with its massive Virginia creeper, has swings; and you can go home with a jar or two of Mrs Fisher's home-made jam, marmalade or chutney, or some home-made meringues. *(Recommended by A K Triggle, Professor A N Black, Peter Harding, Dr A K Clarke, Martyn Quinn, Gwen and Peter Andrews)*

Ushers (Watneys) · Licensees Colin and Katie Fisher · Real ale · Meals and snacks · Children in family area and restaurant · Open 10.30–2.30, 6–10.30 (opens 7 in winter); closed 25 Dec

HEDDINGTON ST9966 Map 2
Ivy

Follow village signs from A4 via Quemerford (E fringe of Calne), or A3102 S of Calne

You can sit on the lawn of this quaint and friendly black and white thatched country pub, which has a good view of the Downs, where the Battle of Roundway was fought in 1643, or under hanging baskets by the quiet lane in front. The low-beamed bar has benches built against the timbered magnolia walls, Windsor chairs and sturdy country seats on the woodblock floor, and, in winter, a huge fire in the stone inglenook fireplace. Cheap bar snacks include filled rolls (from 40p), hot pasties (50p) and ploughman's (£1), egg and chips (£1); Wadworths IPA and 6X tapped from casks behind the bar; darts, shove-ha'penny, dominoes, cribbage, and a fruit machine. There is a separate children's room at the back. *(Recommended by Dr A K Clarke; more reports please)*

Wadworths · Licensee S R Alexander · Real ale · Snacks · Children welcome · Open 11–2.30, 6–10.30

HINDON ST9132 Map 2
Lamb

B3089 Wilton–Mere

This solidly built old inn has a well cared for feel, what with flowers, freshly waxed furniture and friendly staff. The varied choice of bar food includes a very popular curry which comes with six side dishes (£2.50, poppadum 20p extra), soup (60p), sandwiches (60p–£1.25 for smoked salmon), toasties (70p–85p), home-made pâté (£1.25), home-cooked ham, thin-sliced good rare beef and other salads (£2.25), and, when it's available, fresh salmon (£3.50), with puddings including a good fruit pie (75p–85p). They keep Stilton well. There is also a separate restaurant. Well kept Wadworths Devizes and 6X on handpump; shove-ha'penny. The friendly carpeted bar has attractive old settles in quiet alcoves, and decent hand-made tables. This road is a good alternative to the main routes west. *(Recommended by Roy McIsaac, J S Evans, AH, S V Bishop, Mr and Mrs N G W Edwardes)*

*Free house · Licensee Christopher John Nell · Real ale · Children in restaurant
Open 10.30–2.30, 6–11 · Bedrooms tel Hindon (074 789) 225; £15 (£17B)/
£30 (£34B)*

LACOCK   ST9168   Map 2

George

The big central fireplace in this friendly old pub has a three-feet
treadwheel set in to its outer breast, originally for a dog to drive the
turnspit. There are flagstones just by the bar, but carpet elsewhere,
the stone mullioned windows have seats, and the low beamed ceiling
and upright timbers in the place of knocked-through walls make for
snug corners. The new licensee serves lunchtime bar food which
includes sandwiches (40p–70p), ploughman's (£1.35), jumbo
sausage or pâté (£1.50), home-made steak or cottage pie, filled baked
potatoes (£2.25), ham salad (£2.50) and in the evenings grills such as
trout or gammon (£4.25) and eight-ounce sirloin steak (£5.75). Well
kept Wadworths IPA, 6X, and in winter Old Timer, on handpump;
unobtrusive piped music; darts, cribbage and a fruit machine in the
smaller public bar. Very popular at weekends. A bench outside looks
over the main street in this lovely village. Lacock Abbey and the Fox
Talbot museum are close by. *(Recommended by R S Varney, Gordon and
Daphne, Alan Franck, Iain C Baillie)*

*Wadworths · Licensee John Glass · Real ale · Meals and snacks · Children in
eating area · Open 10–2.30, 6–10.30*

Red Lion

High Street; village signposted off A350 S of Chippenham

The friendly bar of this tall red brick Georgian inn has been knocked
through into one and is divided into separate areas by the various cart
shafts, yokes and other old farm implements which decorate it;
there's old-fashioned furniture, with Turkey rugs on the partly
flagstoned floor, branding irons hanging from the high ceiling, and
plates, oil paintings and Morland prints, more tools, and stuffed birds
and animals on the partly panelled walls. A log fire burns brightly on
cool days in a great central stone chimney. A fixed choice of good
home-made bar food in the evening includes soup (£1.20), duck liver
terrine with pickled damsons (£1.90), prawns (£2.20), good fresh
salads in season (from £3.60), hot dishes such as beef and vegetable
pie (£3.90), stuffed fillet of pork with apricots and almonds (£5.25)
and T-bone steak (£6.75); puddings include a giant meringue with
cream and chocolate sauce and a changing hot pudding (£1.20);
lunchtime food is cheaper as the service is less formal. Wadworths
IPA, 6X, Farmers Glory and in winter Old Timer on handpump;
darts, cribbage and billiards. A separate restaurant is open on Friday
and Saturday evenings. Good value bed and breakfast, and they serve
morning coffee from 10am. *(Recommended by Peter Dilnot, Mrs A M
Arnold, Stephen and June Clark, Alan Franck, M E Lawrence, Philip Denison,
Paul Fisher)*

Wadworths · Licensee John Levis · Real ale · Meals and snacks · Children in eating area · Occasional folk music, pianist, jazz · Open 10–2.30, 6–10.30; closed 25 Dec · Bedrooms tel Lacock (024 973) 456; £20/£27(£32B)

LANDFORD   SU2519 Map 2
Cuckoo

Village signposted down B3079 off A36 Salisbury–Southampton; take first right turn towards Redlynch

The front lawn of this friendly country pub, not far from that unlikely sounding pair of villages, Lover and Bohemia, is patrolled by bantam cocks, and there are peacocks and rabbits in a pen at the side; a big play area has swings and a slide. It's surrounded by copses and birdsong, and from it there are walks through the fields and woods to Redlynch. The little front parlour has a stuffed cuckoo behind the bar, rustic seats and spindle-back chairs on its carpet, lots of bird pictures on the papered walls, and a log fire in winter. Two other rooms lead off, one with sensibly placed darts, dominoes, cribbage and a juke box. Well kept Badger Best and Wadworths 6X are tapped from casks in a cool lower back room; food is confined to ploughman's (£1.20). *(More reports please)*

Free house · Licensees Joy and Richard Morton · Real ale · Snacks (lunchtime) Occasional folk music · Open 11–2.30, 7–11

LOWER CHUTE   SU3153 Map 2
Hatchet

Inside this well kept Downland village pub there's a miscellany of cushioned wheelback or captain's chairs ranged neatly around oak tables, and in winter big logs crackle in front of a splendid seventeenth-century fireback in the huge fireplace. You may have to duck to avoid the low beams. Well kept Ballards Wassail, Bass and Wadworths IPA and 6X on handpump. Bar food includes a choice of ploughman's with home-baked bread (from £1.30), Stilton soup (£1.50), cheese herbies (£1.50) and changing home-cooked main dishes such as kedgeree (£2.50), steak and kidney pie or fish pie (£3.25), steak in red wine or beef in beer (£3.75) and T-bone or fillet steak (£7.50) and Scotch salmon salad (£4); barbecues in summer; more dining space is to be provided in an extension from the end bar; darts and shove-ha'penny. There are seats out on a crazy-paved terrace by the front car park and on the side grass. *(Recommended by R H Inns, Gordon and Daphne; more reports please)*

Free house · Licensee Mrs Jacki Chapman · Real ale · Children in eating area Open 11–2.30, 6–10.30

MALMESBURY   ST9287 Map 2
Old Bell [*illustrated on page 670*]

Abbey Row; beside abbey, on Bristol–Tetbury road

The garden behind this creeper-covered old gabled building, parts of which date back 700 years, is attractive and very old-fashioned, with crazy paving, a clipped box knot garden, lawn, herbaceous border, rose garden, and some of those stone toadstools that used to be anti-rat devices for hay-ricks. There are also seats in front of the inn among prettily planted stone troughs, looking out to where an early medieval monk called Elmer, who had fitted himself out with wings, flew a couple of hundred yards from the top of the abbey tower, but broke both legs when he crash-landed. There are traditional high-backed settles on the polished oak floor of the high-beamed bar, which has harness hanging on its cream walls and an unusually large mirror above its open fire; the view of the churchyard and abbey from the stone-mullioned windows is attractive. A comfortable lounge, traditionally furnished, is decorated with Edwardian pictures. The new owners have introduced a different bar menu that includes sandwiches (from 70p, toasties from 90p), home-made soup (£1), ploughman's (£1.40), home-made chicken liver pâté (£1.50), various omelettes (£1.75), cottage pie or Wiltshire ham and egg (£1.90), smoked trout salad (£1.95),venison and port pie (£2.45) and steaks (£4.85). Ushers Best and Wadworths 6X on handpump; darts, dominoes, cribbage, maybe piped music. There is a separate restaurant. A nice place to stay. *(Recommended by D J Fawthrop, Dr A K Clarke)*

Free house · Licensee Harry Spengler · Real ale · Meals and snacks · Children in lounge · Open 10.30–2.30, 6.30–11; closes 10.30 in winter · Bedrooms tel Malmesbury (066 62) 2344; £22 (£36B)/£38 (£44B)

Suffolk Arms

Tetbury Hill; B4014 towards Tetbury, on edge of town

The bar here has been knocked through in quite an imaginative way, leaving a big square room around the stairs, which climb up apparently unsupported, and using a stone pillar to support the beams. There are soft red lights among the copper saucepans and warming-pans on the stripped stone walls, and the comfortable seats include a chintz-cushioned antique settle, sofa and easy chairs as well as captain's chairs and low Windsor armchairs. Bar food includes sandwiches, pâté, garlic mushrooms, sausage and baked potatoes, cottage pie, steak and kidney pie, smokies and daily specials such as chicken sauté (main dishes around £3); there is also a separate restaurant. Well kept Archers Village on handpump, relatively cheap. There are seats on the neat lawns outside this Virginia creeper-covered stone house. *(Recommended by E G Parish, Harry Blood)*

Free house · Licensee Cliff Johnson · Real ale · Meals (not Sun) and snacks (not Sun evening) · Children in eating area · Open 10.30–2.30, 6–11

MARKET LAVINGTON   SU0154   Map 2

Green Dragon

High Street; B3098 towards Upavon

The rambling bar of this small inn has a series of interestingly furnished areas, from old kitchen chairs through smart dining-room chairs to massive boxy settles; from fancy Victorian wallpaper to stripped deal panelling; from corn dollies to a mobile; from a Spy cartoon of Sir Henry Irving through photographs of the town in the old days to Highland views. Bar food includes home-cooked and locally bought meat and vegetables (when not grown in their garden); home-made soup (70p), sandwiches (from 70p), filled crusty rolls (from 95p), ploughman's (£1.25), sausage and eggs (£1.75), pork chop (£2.25), lamb chops or chicken (£2.50), salads (from £2.60), mixed cold meats or a large mixed grill (£2.85) with specials such as liver and bacon, shepherd's pie or home-made polony (£1.80), and, for pudding, cheesecake or apricot mousse (70p). There is also a separate restaurant (must book). Wadworths IPA, 6X, Farmers Glory and in winter Old Times on handpump; bar billiards and darts in a raised, communicating section, also shove-ha'penny, dominoes and cribbage; maybe piped music. There's a garden fenced off behind the car park. *(Recommended by Helen Woodeson; more reports please)*

Wadworths · Licensees Gordon and Elaine Godbolt · Real ale · Meals and snacks (not Sun) · Children in restaurant if over 14 · Open 10–2.30, 6–10.30

MARLBOROUGH   SU1869 Map 2
Sun

High Street

The dimly lit bar of this quaint little inn has brasses and harness hanging above the log fire, benches built in to the black panelling, an antique settle with a very high back but a very low seat, heavy sloping beams, and a window looking out on the busy street – so effectively silenced by the massive old walls that you can hear the clock ticking. A lounge bar on the other side of the entrance, though comfortable, has less atmosphere. Good bar food includes a wide choice of sandwiches on white or brown bread (70p, toasted 85p), ploughman's (£1.30, with ham £1.70), home-made pâté (£1.50), pizzas (£1.40), three-egg omelettes (from £1.45), good hot puffed prawns on toast, a choice of salads (from £2.40), locally smoked trout (£2.65), prawns with a good freshly made garlic mayonnaise (£3.20), chicken fillets with tomato and garlic dip or grilled gammon with egg or pineapple (£3.65) and sirloin steak (£5.25), with various puddings (from 75p), and a weekday lunchtime special such as lasagne, braised liver, or lamb and apricot pie (£1.85); there are good bar nibbles on Sundays which include pork crackling. Ushers PA, Best and Founders on handpump; darts, shove-ha'penny, dominoes, cribbage. There is a back room which is usually free for children. You can sit outside on a small sheltered back courtyard. Comfortably modernised bedrooms. *(Recommended by Dr A K Clarke, P T Young)*

Ushers · Licensees Geoff and Nicola Hickson · Real ale · Meals and snacks (not Tues evening) · Children in family room · Open 10.30–2.30, 6–11 · Bedrooms tel Marlborough (0672) 52081; £14/£22

MERE   ST8132 Map 2
Old Ship

B3095, off A303

This venerable building was first licensed early in the eighteenth century for the London—Exeter coaches, and it has some distinguished furnishings, including a handsome elm staircase. Its old-fashioned bars are comfortable and welcoming – one of them small and snug. The bar that passers-by are most likely to find is the one on the other side of the coach entry: lively and spacious, with some armour above the big log fire, navy hat-ribands, railed curtains making booths around the button-back red leatherette banquettes, and darts, pool, bar billiards, shove-ha'penny, dominoes, cribbage, a fruit machine and juke box. There's an attractive high-backed traditional settle by the serving counter, which has Badger Best and Tanglefoot on handpump under light blanket pressure. Pleasantly served bar food includes soup (85p), freshly cut sandwiches (90p), baked potatoes (from 75p), ploughman's (from £1.50), cold roast beef (£1.90), home-made cottage pie (£2.10), chicken curry (£2.50), salads (£2.50), good steak and kidney pie (£2.80) and puddings such as home-made fruit pie (90p). *(Recommended by S V Bishop, N F Mackley)*

Badger · Licensee P L Johnson · Meals and snacks · Children in area partly set aside for them · Open 10.30–2.30, 6–11 · Bedrooms tel Mere (0747) 860258; £21.50(£25B)/£33(£38B)

POTTERNE ST9958 Map 2
George & Dragon
A360 beside Worton turn-off

Since the last edition of the *Guide*, this thatched late fifteenth-century village inn has been extensively restored, and the old beamed ceiling and fireplace of the original hall have been exposed. They've kept most of the old bench seating and have added country-style tables to match. But the pub's most interesting feature is still its indoor .22 shooting gallery; so far as we know, it's unique. A hatch beyond the pool-room opens on to a 25-yard shoulder-high tube, broad enough at its mouth to rest your elbows in, but narrowing to not much more than the width of the target. The small bull is an electric bell-push, which rings when hit. After your nine shots (two for practice), you pull a rope which lifts a brush from a whitewash bucket to whiten the target for the next marksman. Well kept Wadworths IPA and 6X on handpump. Bar food is home made and the lunchtime menu includes soup (75p), sandwiches and a changing selection of specials, steak and kidney pie (£1.95) being a favourite. The evening menu ranges from a good local ham salad (£2.50) to mixed grill or steak (£5.25). A separate room has darts, pool, shove-ha'penny, dominoes, cribbage and a fruit machine; a full skittle alley in the old stables. There's a pleasant garden and a sun-trap yard with a grapevine. *(Recommended by Helen Woodeson; more reports please)*

Wadworths · Licensee Roger Smith · Real ale · Meals and snacks (not Tues) Children in breakfast room · Open 11–2.30, 6.30–11 · Bedrooms tel Devizes (0380) 2139; £8B/£16B

Bedroom prices normally include full English breakfast, VAT and any inclusive service charge that we know of. Prices before the '/' are for single rooms, after for two people in double or twin; B denotes a private bath, S a private shower.

RAMSBURY   SU2771 Map 2
Bell

Village signposted off B4192 (still shown as A419 on many maps) NW of
Hungerford, or from A4 W of Hungerford

The bar of this civilised and friendly inn is relaxed and welcoming,
with two sunny bay windows (one with Victorian stained-glass
panels) facing the stump of the great elm that still commands the
quiet main street. There are simple, comfortable furnishings, log fires,
some attractive embroidery samplers, and an eighteenth-century wall
painting. Good bar food includes home-made soup (75p), a choice of
home-made pâtés (£1.45), ploughman's (£1.45), a daily hot dish such
as kedgeree or guinea-fowl casserole, and a choice of at least six of
their wide repertoire of speciality pies (£2.15 to £2.50), such as
Coronation (chicken in a mild curry sauce on broccoli with a crispy
breadcrumb top), pigeon and port pie with mushrooms, button
onions and cranberries, foie poie (liver, bacon and onions with sliced
potato) and Windsor (tuna fish, tomatoes, sweetcorn and hard-boiled
egg). There are other dishes, too, such as moussaka (£2.15) and
omelettes (prawn and asparagus £2.75), with home-made puddings
(£1.10). Food is served with salad (75p), not vegetables. There is also
a separate restaurant. Well kept Wadworths IPA and 6X on
handpump, and some decent wines; occasional piped music. Games
have been restricted to a board put up for people to try their hand at
the *Daily Express* Target competition. Roads lead from this quiet
village into Downland on all sides. *(Recommended by M E Lawrence,
Peter Dyer)*

*Free house · Licensee Michael Benjamin · Real ale · Meals and snacks (not Sat
evening) · Children in room between bar and restaurant · Open 10–2.30, 6–11*

SALISBURY   SU1429 Map 2
*The pubs mentioned here – except for the last, out at East Harnham –
are all within a short stroll of one another. The Old George, which
used to be one of the finest old inns – Shakespeare probably
performed in its yard – has now been rebuilt as a shopping arcade,
but it's still very well worth visiting for its façade and for the upstairs
coffee shop which gives some idea of what it was like inside.*

Haunch of Venison ★

The chief attraction in this friendly and cheerful pub – sometimes
very crowded – is the atmosphere of the ancient building itself. The
small and cosy main bar has stout red cushioned oak benches built in
to its timbered walls, massive beams in the ochre ceiling, a black and
white tiled floor, and an old-fashioned – and as far as we know
unique – pewter bar counter with a rare set of antique taps for
gravity-fed spirits and liqueurs. There is also well kept Courage Best
and Directors on handpump. An upper panelled room has a splendid
fireplace that dates back some 600 years to when this was the church
house for St Thomas's just behind. It has antique settles and a carved
seat around several small tables. Bar food includes sandwiches,

ploughman's (£1.25–£1.30), shepherd's pie (£1.10), a daily special (£1.25) and steak and kidney or game pie (£1.25) – this last includes venison, which always figures in their cooking in some form. At lunchtime the lower part of the separate restaurant is given over to bar snacks (if you want the three-course lunch at £5.50, you should book; telephone Salisbury (0722) 22024); in the evenings the whole restaurant is devoted to more serious eating, with a three-course menu at £8.75 and à la carte working out at around £12–£15 a head with wine. *(Recommended by Martyn Quinn, Paul Edwards, Jill Woolford, Antony Lewis Furreddu)*

Courage · Licensees Antony and Victoria Leroy · Real ale · Meals (lunchtime) and snacks (not Sun evening) · Children in eating area and restaurant · Nearby parking may be difficult · Open 10–2.30, 6–11

King's Arms

St John Street; the main one-way street entering city centre from S

The fireplaces in this creaky old inn with Tudor timbering are of the same Chilmark stone as the cathedral, so may be as old as it. The dark-panelled bars have red leatherette benches built around their walls, Windsor armchairs, darts, shove-ha'penny, dominoes, cribbage, a fruit machine and maybe piped music. The panelling in the heavily beamed restaurant, which has snug high-backed settles, is considerably older, as is that in the pleasantly old-fashioned residents' lounge upstairs. Well kept Ushers PA, Best and Founders on handpump or tapped from the cask; freshly cut sandwiches and pâté, basket meals (from £1.20), hot daily specials (£1.65) and salads from a buffet counter (from around £2.05), with fixed-price meals from the restaurant (for example, roast beef, a starter and pudding at £7.15). Car parking (welcome in this city) free by arrangement with the neighbouring White Hart. A nice place to stay. *(Recommended by Jill Woolford, Roy McIsaac)*

Ushers · Licensees Tim and Diana Wright · Real ale · Meals and snacks Children welcome · Open 11–2.30, 6–11 · Bedrooms tel Salisbury (0722) 27629; £20(£21B)/£31(£36.23B)

Red Lion

Milford Street

There's a nicely old-fashioned glass loggia sheltering a row of cushioned Windsor armchairs in the sheltered and creeper-hung courtyard which is dotted with quite a pride of cheery red lions. The stylishly medieval restaurant of this expansively renovated grand coaching-inn is as old as it looks – there's a tradition that this part of the hotel housed the draughtsmen who worked on the cathedral. Beside it, the spacious hall has sedate, old-fashioned furniture, and some curiosities such as the elaborate gothick long-case clock with little skeletons ringing bells to mark the hours. In here, a smartly dressed waitress will, if you like, bring your drink from the much livelier and busier bar – sometimes too busy for you to find space on the comfortable button-back banquettes below the coaching prints on its timbered walls. There's also another relatively quiet communicating room, with antique settles and small leather armchairs. Lunchtime bar food includes good value sandwiches (from 60p), soup (60p), ploughman's (90p), and hot dishes such as turkey fricassée and steak and kidney pie (£1.50). Well kept Bass, Ushers Best and Gibbs Mew Wiltshire on handpump. A nice place to stay. *(More reports please)*

Free house · Licensee Michael Maidment · Real ale · Meals and snacks (lunchtime) · Children in eating areas · Nearby daytime parking may be difficult · Open 11–2.30, 6–11 · Bedrooms tel Salisbury (0722) 23334; £22(£31B)/£35(£48B)

Rose & Crown

Harnham Road; at southernmost ring road roundabout (towards A354 and A338) an unclassified road – *not* to city centre – leads to the pub

The neatly kept and flower-filled lawns that run down to the River Avon have a fine view of the cathedral rising gracefully from the watermeadows, and the original building is roughly the same age as the nearby bridge, built in 1444 to take the Exeter road. The inn used to be quite a notorious tavern, with a cockpit and bare-knuckle prize-fights, but was elegantly restored between the wars and has since been carefully and comfortably extended, so that you can stay either in the beamed and timbered rooms of the original building or in a smart modern extension. Many of the rooms, like the picture-window extension, share the lovely view. The bar is friendly and comfortable, with neat and efficient service: an open fire, beams and timbers in ochre plasterwork, tapestry-upholstered settles, and as decoration a few gin-traps, big stuffed trout and chub, and silver platters. Popular bar food includes sandwiches, ploughman's (£1.25), pâté (£1.40), liver and bacon, chicken in a basket (£2.15), steak and kidney or chicken and ham pie, deep-fried fish and scampi, with a good cold food bar at lunchtime in summer, including rare roast beef, Wiltshire pie and help-yourself salads (£2.75). Bass and Hancocks HB on handpump; darts, dominoes, cribbage, fruit machine, space game, maybe piped music. *(Recommended by Roy McIsaac, Carolyn West, A J Milman, N M Williamson)*

Free house · Licensee Dale Naug · Real ale · Meals and snacks · Children in eating area and restaurant · Open 10.30–2.30, 6–10.30 · Bedrooms tel Salisbury (0722) 27908; £58.45B

TEFFONT MAGNA   ST9832 Map 2
Black Horse

B3089

One of the main attractions of this attractive and friendly old stone village inn is the food: it includes sandwiches cut to order (85p–£1.30 for prawn), home-made soup (90p), ploughman's with Cheddar, Stilton, or home-made pâté (£1.40), salads (£2.65), home-made lasagne or steak and kidney pie (£2.65), home-cooked Wiltshire ham and egg (£2.65), plaice stuffed with prawns and mushrooms or local trout (£3) and sirloin steak (£6), with a choice of home-made puddings such as meringues, fruit sponges and crumbles and fools (from 90p), and frequent specials, such as stew with dumplings or pigeon pie. They try to use fresh local ingredients as much as possible, so in season there may be strawberries and raspberries, rhubarb sponge or baked home-grown apples. There's a separate restaurant; Sunday roast lunches (£3.60). Well kept Bass, Ushers Best and Founders on handpump, and quite a few whiskies. The comfortable lounge has lots of tables, Windsor chairs and recently made traditional-style settles. In the winter, when it's less busy and the log fire in the huge fireplace has been lit, they bring out some deeply stuffed armchairs. The public bar has darts, shove-ha'penny, table skittles and dominoes. Outside by the corner of the road there is a very well kept garden with flowers by neat low stone walls and tables on immaculate patches of grass, and meals can be served at tables on a sheltered terrace behind the pub. (*Recommended by S V Bishop, Susan Pritchard*)

Ushers · Licensees Colin and Jacqui Carter · Real ale · Meals and snacks (not Mon evening) · Children in village bar · Open 10.30–2.30, 6.30–11 Bedrooms tel Teffont (072 276) 251; £12.50/£20

Lucky Dip

Besides the fully inspected pubs, you might like to try these Lucky Dips recommended and described by readers (if you do, please send us reports):

ALDERBURY [SU1827], *Green Dragon*: much-modernised fifteenth-century village pub used by Dickens as Mrs Pugin's Blue Dragon in *Martin Chuzzlewit*, Courage real ales (*LYM*)

AMESBURY [SU1541], *George*: lounge bar with nice old settles, unusual chairs made with interwoven leather, and lots of character, in old coaching-inn with good bar food – the goulash soup's a meal in itself (*Gordon and Daphne, Jon Reed*)

ANSTY [ST9526], *Maypole*: food and beer good in cosy pub next to 80-feet maypole which is still used (*John Morrow*)

AVEBURY [SU0969], *Red Lion*: much-modernised comfortable thatched pub listed for its position right in the heart of the stone circles; Whitbreads real ales, steakhouse (*Dr A K Clarke, LYM*)

BECKINGTON [ST8051], *Woolpack*: good food, service and beer, pleasantly decorated (*Mark Spurlock*)

BERWICK ST JOHN [ST9323], *Talbot*: stone village pub in Ebble valley, single big low-beamed bar with window seats, inglenook with bread ovens and old settle, well kept Badger Best (*Gordon & Daphne*)

BIDDESTONE [ST8773], *Biddestone Arms*: pretty and friendly pub with lots of points of interest in slightly remote village (*Dr A K Clarke*); *White Horse*: good village pub on green of attractive village (*Dr A K Clarke*)

BLUNSDEN [SU1593], *Cold Harbour*: good food with some unusual dishes, good beer, efficient service (*M J Brightmore*)

BRADFORD ON AVON [ST8261], *Bunch of Grapes*: good value home-made food in friendly town pub (*Brian Barefoot*); *Swan*: good food in comfortably modernised bar of old inn; bedrooms (*LYM*); [Frome Road] *Three Horseshoes*: good food (not Tuesday), attractive small restaurant area, Trumans and Ushers real ale, in modernised old pub with seats outside (*R S Varney*)

BROAD HINTON [SU1076], *Bell*: food good – very large helpings – good service and a well kept cellar (*M J Brightmore*)); *Crown*: big open-plan bar with well kept Bass, Huntsman Dorchester and Royal Oak and Wadworths 6X, good home-cooked bar meals, help-yourself salad bar and restaurant section, cheerful piped music, unusual gilded inn sign; bedrooms *(Derek Webber, Ian Meharg, BB)*

CASTLE EATON [High Street; SU1495], *Red Lion*: free house with grassy banks leading to River Thames; wide choice of reasonably priced bar snacks, real ale *(P M Taylor)*

CHARLTON [SU1156], *Horse & Groom*: good freshly cooked food in restaurant part of smart roadside rustic pub (closed Monday lunchtime) with well kept real ale and nice blend of customers *(David Surridge, Mr and Mrs J L T Godfrey, Dr A K Clarke)*

CHIPPENHAM [New Road; ST9173], *Little George*: imposing town centre pub with food and good beer *(Dr A K Clarke)*

nr CHIPPENHAM [Pewsham; ST9173], *Lysley Arms*: long knocked-through bar with walk-around fire, candles in bottles, discreet piped classical music, very popular freshly cooked food, well kept Bass, bedrooms *(Derek Webber, Mr and Mrs D Dodd, BB)*

CHOLDERTON [SU2242], *Crown*: externally pretty, with good beer – a pleasant summer pub *(Dr A K Clarke)*

COLLINGBOURNE DUCIS [SU2453], *Last Straw*: well modernised pub with lots of homely features including huge collection of *Country Life* magazines *(Dr A K Clarke)*

CORSHAM [High Street; ST8670], *Pack Horse*: interesting old pub in historic town, doors salvaged from a bank, lots of atmosphere *(Dr A K Clarke)*

CORTON [ST9340], *Dove*: friendly and charming pub with unusually good food in bar and restaurant – especially good salad trolley and excellent puddings; garden; no food Sunday evening or Monday *(R A Gibbons, Dr A K Clarke, Mrs A Cotterill-Davies, Tom and Ann Lowth)*

CRUDWELL [ST9592], *Plough*: delightful Cotswold pub on busy road – useful journey break *(Dr A K Clarke)*

nr DAUNTSEY [ST9782], *Peterborough Arms*: a wide range of good beer, friendly landlord *(Dr A K Clarke)*

DEVIZES [Hare & Hounds Street; SU0061], *Hare & Hounds*: good beer from the wood; grand atmosphere; good company; friendly bar staff *(R W Tennant)*; [Maryport Street] *Three Crowns*: friendly town pub with well kept local Wadworths real ales, George 1 backsword blade (recently found hidden in inn's ex-stables) decorating one hessian wall, seats in small sheltered yard *(Dr A K Clarke, BB)*; [Northgate Street] *White Lion*: homely pub with good beer – right by Wadworths brewery *(Dr A K Clarke)*

DINTON [SU0131], *Penruddocke Arms*: spacious and comfortable country pub with good real ales, country wines, and range of bar food *(Mrs Ella Crawford, LYM)*

EASTERTON [SU0155], *Royal Oak*: always good and now much improved, with a great local social conscience *(Dr A K Clarke)*

ENFORD [SU1351], *Swan*: lovely well modernised thatched and beamed village pub, sloping ceiling behind bar, friendly landlord, well kept beer, separate dining-room, good choice of food; rare old gallows sign still spans road *(Gordon and Daphne, Dr A K Clarke)*

FARLEIGH WICK [ST8064], *Fox & Hounds*: good food in recently extended and refurnished pub with Ushers Founders on handpump *(R G Tennant)*

FONTHILL GIFFORD [ST9232], *Beckford Arms*: unspoilt inn in rural surroundings, good beer and food, peaceful friendly atmosphere; big Chilmark stone fireplaces *(R H Inns)*

GREAT DURNFORD [SU1338], *Black Horse*: bar meals and sandwiches; one bar, three rooms and games area (darts); brasses, open fire *(Martyn Quinn)*

HANNINGTON [SU1793], *Jolly Tar*: recently renovated free house with mock-Tudor beams in village setting, separate grill bar, bar food, real ale *(P M Taylor)*

HIGHWORTH [SU2092], *Saracens Head*: good simple food in comfortable interesting bar with warm welcome (and a mysterious central column); Arkells real ales *(Ian Meharg)*

HILPERTON [ST8659], *Kings Arms*: well restored, a good lunchtime stop-off with food bar *(Dr A K Clarke)*

HOLT [ST8662], *Old Ham Tree*: Wadworths 6X and good lunchtime food in friendly pub with character *(James D M Forbes)*

HORNINGSHAM [ST8141], *Bath Arms*: well kept real ales including Bass, good food, warm welcome; bedrooms *(Philip Turner)*

KILMINGTON [ST7736], *Red Lion*: lovely cool stone-built pub with friendly staff and excellent beer *(Dr A K Clarke)*

nr LACOCK [Bowden Hill, Bewley Common; ST9168], *Rising Sun*: one-room traditional cottage pub with far views from back terrace, well kept Gibbs Mew Salisbury and Wadworths IPA and 6X tapped in back room *(LYM; up-to-date reports please))*

LAVERSTOCK [Duck Lane; SU1631], *Duck*: very friendly, well appointed estate pub with good beer and lots of attractions *(Dr A K Clarke)*

LITTLE BEDWYN [SU2966], *Harrow*: a delicate pub just a little off the beaten track, a sort of 'nouvelle cuisine' type of pub – the parallel increased by its French cider *(Dr A K Clarke)*

LOWER WOODFORD [SU1235], *Wheatsheaf*: friendly country pub, covered in ivy, with oak beams, good food and Badger beer in its two rooms (which can get full); stuffed badger on wall *(Carolyn West)*

LUCKINGTON [ST8383], *Old Royal Ship*: really friendly village local with interesting American pudding list for lunch *(Dr A K Clarke)*

MARLBOROUGH [High Street; SU1869], *Royal Oak*: food served in bar as well as larger restaurant; one of the new generation of bistro-type pubs with wickerwork chairs and little tables *(Dr A K Clarke)*; [High Street] *Wellington Arms*: food great in warm and traditional pub with well considered choice of beers, very friendly owners and nice clientele *(Gordon W Priest Jr)*

MARTON [SU2860], *Nags Head*: well kept Bass and Wadworths 6X, good value food, big garden surrounded by countryside *(Elaine and Gavin Walkingshaw)*

MERE [ST8132], *Butt of Sherry*: small and friendly, well kept Ushers Best, home-cooked ham in sandwiches, other food includes ploughman's, ham and eggs, chilli con carne, quiche, etc; tables in small back court *(Hope Chenhalls)*

NETHERHAMPTON [SU1029], *Victoria & Albert*: cosy thatched village pub not far from Salisbury (popular with army officers), good simple snacks, open fires in low beamed bars, interesting brass ornaments, good service, big well kept garden *(Gordon and Daphne, Paul and Jane Davis)*

NEWTON TONEY [SU2140], *Malet Arms*: good atmosphere, friendly staff, good range of food and well kept Wadworths 6X *(Sue White, Tim Kinning, Dr A K Clarke)*

NORTON [ST8884], *Vine Tree*: friendly quiet pub, good real ales including Flowers and Wadworths 6X, good food especially puddings, traditional Sunday lunch (best to book at weekends and holidays) *(Peter Dilnot, N W Charles)*

NUNTON [SU1526], *Radnor Arms*: friendly village pub with good bar snacks, comfortable, garden, in pleasant area *(Martyn Quinn)*

PEWSEY [North Street; SU1560], *Royal Oak*: seventeenth-century, Wadworths real ale, attractive lounge, good food in bar and dining-room *(Arthur Roome)*

QUEMERFORD [SU0069], *Talbot*: comfortably renovated pub with seats in garden, popular for its food *(Anon)*

RODE [ST8153], *Red Lion*: good food, garden *(Mr and Mrs D Dodd)*

SALISBURY [New Street; SU1429], *New Inn*: creaky beamed and timbered ancient pub with good choice of simple food and Badger beers *(BB)*; *Pheasant*: friendly well modernised old pub with open fires and well kept Courage real ales *(Carolyn West, Mark Spurlock, BB)*

SANDY LANE [ST9668], *George*: neat stone pub with well kept Wadworths real ales, good buffet lunches, swings and climbing-frame on lawn *(Dr A K Clarke)*

SEEND [ST9461], *Barge*: simple canalside pub rebuilt after 1981 fire, well kept Wadworths real ales (OS Sheet 173 reference 930616) *(Dr A K Clarke, Alan Bickley, LYM)*; *Bell*: typical friendly local *(A J Triggle)*

SEMINGTON [ST8960], *Somerset Arms*: spacious roadside pub with good beer and range of bar food, friendly staff *(Dr A K Clarke)*

SEMLEY [ST8926], *Benett Arms*: hospitable and friendly inn in quiet village, good food in bar and restaurant, real ales including Gibbs Mew, more character than outside would suggest, comfortable bedrooms in modern wing *(N W Charles, P Harrison)*

SHAW [Folly Lane; ST8965], *Golden Fleece*: friendly landlord and good lunchtime snacks in nice little roadside pub *(Dr A K Clarke)*

SHERSTON [ST8585], *Rattlebone*: much renovated but keeps character, with thick stone walls and open fires; well kept beer *(Dr A K Clarke)*

SOUTH NEWTON [SU0834], *Bell*: friendly old-world pub with good food in bar and restaurant, Badger Best, big garden (coaches welcome), welcoming golden retriever called Sean, close to pretty River Wylye *(Lorna Mackinnon)*

STAPLEFORD [SU0637], *Pelican*: big roadside pub with good beer and good atmosphere *(Dr A K Clarke)*

STIBB GREEN [SU2363], *Three Horseshoes*: small old pub devoid of gimmicks; good beer, two huge open fires, young landlord and friendly customers *(Dr A K Clarke)*

STOURTON [Church Lawn; ST7734], *Spread Eagle*: included as being just right for its surroundings in this beautiful National Trust village by entrance to Stourhead Gardens; homely, roaring fires, plain unpretentious furnishings; Bass real ale; bedrooms *(S V Bishop)*

STRATFORD SUB CASTLE [SU1232], *Old Castle*: quite a big friendly pub with pool-table and a fox's head, big children's play area *(Carolyn West)*

SUTTON BENGER [ST9478], *Old Bell*: food good, at reasonable prices (home-made soups, delicious rare beef sandwiches, for instance), and good draught beer in well run pub; also restaurant *(P F and T Dilnot)*

TISBURY [High Street; ST9429], *Boot*: homely, with beer tapped from the cask *(Dr A K Clarke)*

TOLLARD ROYAL [ST9417], *King John*: Wadworths 6X very well kept in quietly lit bars and restaurant, welcoming barmaid, seats outside *(Gwen and Peter Andrews)*

TROWBRIDGE [Frome Road; ST8557], *Black Horse*: well renovated, possibly a little more up-market than most pubs here *(Dr A K Clarke)*; [Dursley Road] *Dursley Arms*: most surprising Ushers estate pub, successfully done up *(Dr A K Clarke)*

nr TROWBRIDGE [The Strand, A361 towards Devizes; ST8557], *Lamb*: included in last edition for charming series of corridors and separate rooms, food and real ale, but under new management and completely refurbished *(A J Triggle, LYM; up-to-date reports on the new regime please)*

UPAVON [SU1355], *Antelope*: food in bar good, well kept beers and friendly service *(A J Triggle)*

UPPER CHUTE [SU2954], *Cross Keys*: attractive pub with animal paintings, nice young licensees, real ale, views from garden *(Gordon and Daphne)*

WANBOROUGH [SU2083], *Harrow*: food and beer good, open fires and good service in two interesting bars *(Ian Meharg)*; [Upper Wanborough] *Shepherds Rest*: food at lunchtime good, good beer and cider, good friendly service *(Ian Meharg)*

WESTBROOK [ST9565], *Westbrook Inn*: good value food and well kept Ushers in recently renovated roadside pub with marathon-runner landlord *(Alan Bickley)*

WESTWOOD [ST8059], *New*: good home cooking in friendly, clean and characterful village pub, Ushers real ale *(K R Harris)*

WINGFIELD [ST8256], *Poplars*: friendly pub with well kept Wadworths real ale and own cricket pitch *(Dr A K Clarke, LYM)*

WOOTTON BASSETT [Wood Street; SU0682], *Five Bells*: small and friendly simple back street local with attractive atmosphere, space game kept out at the back *(Dr A K Clarke)*

WOOTTON RIVERS [SU1963], *Royal Oak*: rambling thatched and beamed country pub with good range of low-priced food and well kept Wadworths real ale, friendly landlord, children welcome, lovely village setting, no fruit machines *(M C Dickson, Gordon and Daphne, Anthony Fernau)*

WROUGHTON [SU1480], *White Hart*: bar food and Wadworths real ales in spacious lounge with old stone fireplace, lively public bar and skittle alley; handy for M4 junction 16 *(LYM)*

WYLYE [SU0037], *Bell*: good bar snacks in delightful pub in peaceful village; quick friendly service *(Mrs Joan Harris)*

Yorkshire

There are so many very good pubs in this area, combining in an inimitable Yorkshire way extreme hospitality with solid honest and unassuming quality and value, that to keep this introductory note from getting almost as long as the book itself we'll confine it mainly to introducing some of the newcomers to this edition of the Guide. Of these new entries, many are in or near exceptionally fine countryside, including several that are also good for food: the civilised Red Lion at Burnsall, a nice place to stay, the very convivial Horse Shoe with its lovely garden by the Esk in Egton Bridge, the pleasantly clubby Feathers on Helmsley's market square (it's run by the Feathers family), the snug small-roomed Fountaine in its unusual village setting at Linton in Craven (new owners already getting a reputation for good value simple snacks), the lively old Milburn Arms at Rosedale Abbey, and the cheerful Stone House Inn on its windy plateau at Thruscross. Among the newcomers, the Plough at Fadmoor probably serves the best evening meals (during the week it doesn't open at lunchtime). Other new entries in fine positions include the idiosyncratic George virtually alone in its delightful spot by the river at Hubberholme in upper Wharfedale (back in these pages by, as they say, popular demand), not far from it the White Lion at Cray (a very engaging little traditional pub by a steep stream), the decidedly unpretentious Old Hill Inn just below Ingleborough in Chapel le Dale, the Horseshoe at Levisham (an attractive village setting in moorland walking country, not far from the steam railway), the snug Laurel at

The Fauconberg Arms, Coxwold

Robin Hood's Bay and the Royal at Runswick Bay (difficult to argue the toss between these two different types of seaside pub), the White Horse looking down on Rosedale Abbey, and the Castle Hill up on its pinnacle above Almondbury, with a view that makes even the big towns look romantic. Marked character is the main point at some other new entries: the Anne Arms in Sutton (for its flamboyant collections of brightly coloured china), the Old Hall in Heckmondwike (an artful conversion of Joseph Priestley's fourteenth-century home, with very pleasant service), the small-roomed White Swan in Wighill (the splendid settled-in feeling of having been run by the same family for very many years – well kept beer here), the Lendal Cellars in York (an entertaining conversion of ancient cellars), the quite unspoilt and interesting small-roomed Griffin in Barkisland, and the friendly Bruce Arms in West Tanfield. Among pubs retained from last year's edition, five seem to have been gaining ground in readers' affections: the Angel in Hetton, for its combination of good, often enterprising food and careful stylish décor with an old-fashioned Dales village pub; Whitelocks in Leeds, for its vividly alive atmosphere in a meticulously kept mid-Victorian environment; the big Green Tree at Hatfield Woodhouse for its fine relaxed atmosphere and consistently high standards; the old Blacksmiths Arms in the attractive village of Lastingham; and the Malt Shovel at Oswaldkirk, a splendid old house in the hands of a landlord who has firm ideas about what an inn should be – judging by our postbag, many readers agree with him.

ALDBOROUGH (N Yorks)   SE4166   Map 7

Ship

Village signposted from B6265 just S of Boroughbridge, close to A1

Good value home-made food fills this ancient and friendly pub with mouthwatering lunchtime smells – and with lots of regular customers. Besides a daily hot special such as beef casserole (£1.75), the food includes soup (60p), excellent barm cake sandwiches (from 60p, bacon and egg 75p), ploughman's (£1), local gammon and egg (£2.80 – their most popular dish) and eight-ounce rump steak (£3.50), with a big bowl of first-class chips for just 30p. On Sundays there's an eat-as-much-as-you-can buffet, hot and cold dishes (£2.75, children £1.50). The busy main bar has heavy black beams, a coal fire in its stone inglenook fireplace, sentimental engravings on the walls, old-fashioned seats around heavy cast-iron tables, and latticed window seats looking across the lane to the fourteenth-century village church. A quieter back room decorated with ship pictures has plenty more tables, with a buffet bar and waitress service. Well kept Tetleys on handpump; darts, shove-ha'penny, dominoes, cribbage, a fruit machine, maybe piped music in one bar; summer seats on the spacious grass behind. The bedrooms are comfortably equipped. The

Roman town for which the village is famous is mainly up beyond the church. *(Recommended by Tim Halstead, D W Roberts, Philip Asquith, Keith Myers, Paul West)*

Free house · Licensee Edgar John Morgan · Real ale · Meals and snacks Children welcome · Open 11.30–2.30, 6.45–11 all year · Bedrooms tel Boroughbridge (090 12) 2749; £13B/£24B

ALMONDBURY (W Yorks)   SE1615   Map 7
Castle Hill

Village signposted from A629/A642 just E of Huddersfield; follow Castle Hill signs, turn left into Lumb Lane then bear left – the last bit is steep and narrow

Remarkable views over Huddersfield and its surrounding moors single out this pub, quite isolated on the rough grass site of a neolithic hill fort; a tower built beside it to commemorate Queen Victoria's 1899 Jubilee is a landmark serving by daylight to guide you to the pub from miles away. Inside, it's busy on fine weekends, often quiet otherwise. The partly ply-panelled bar rambles around, with views on every side. As you go in, the part on the left dates from 1852, and the more modern areas blend in well: there are lots of coal fires, attractive settles as well as other seats, heavy well polished cast-iron tables and old gateleg tables, and a splendid antique cast-iron coat stand. Bar food includes soup (60p), sandwiches (70p, steak sandwich £1.50), home-made meat and potato pie, chilli con carne with pitta bread or cheese and onion flan (£1.60) and scampi (£2.50), with a popular Sunday lunch (£3.50). Well kept Timothy Taylors Best and Landlord and Tetleys on handpump, from the long copper-topped stone serving counter; a juke box, fruit machine and on our visit piped Country and Western. The friendly golden labrador is called Ben. *(Recommended by Tim Halstead, Peter and Carolyn Clark, Philip Asquith, Jon Dewhirst, Keith Myers, J R Glover, Paul West)*

Free house · Licensee Mr Bassett · Real ale · Meals and snacks (not Sun–Tues evenings) · Open 11–3, 5–10.30

AUSTWICK (N Yorks)   SD7668   Map 7
Game Cock

The cosy and friendly back bar of this prettily placed village inn is straightforwardly furnished, with well made built-in wall benches and plain wooden tables, beams above, and a few cockfighting prints on the butter-coloured walls. Its sensible lino and mat flooring show its popularity with climbers and walkers – crags and screes rise above the green pastures around this quiet village of rose-covered stone houses, which is in the Dales National Park and close to the Three Peaks. There are some seats in a sheltered front sun loggia and outside the inn, and there is a more softly comfortable lounge. With very welcoming service, the wide range of wholesome bar food includes sandwiches (from 85p), egg or pork pie and chips (85p), ploughman's (£1.40), home-made minced beef pie (£1.80), Cumberland sausage (£1.95), home-made steak and kidney pie (£2.25), gammon and egg (£2.45), seafood platter (£2.95) and sirloin steak (£4.85), with salads (from £2.40) and puddings (85p), and good meals in the separate restaurant – there are special rates including dinner for residents, as well as for stays longer than two nights. Well kept Thwaites on handpump; darts and dominoes in the evening. *(Recommended by MGBD, T I Muntz)*

Thwaites · Real ale · Meals and snacks · Children in restaurant · Open 11–3, 6–11 · Bedrooms tel Clapham (046 85) 226; £14/£28

BARKISLAND (W Yorks)   SE0520   Map 7
Griffin ★
Stainland Road

Awarded a star for its charming old-fashioned warmth and for the unspoilt layout of its separate rooms, this moorland village pub has as a bonus well kept Burtonwood Best on handpump and good value traditional snacks. These include baked potatoes (from 45p), freshly made soups such as a rich cream of cauliflower (65p), pork pie with mushy peas (65p), massive generously filled teacakes (from 60p) with good home-cooked beef and salad 75p) and ploughman's or home-made meat and potato pie with red cabbage (£1); chilli con carne (£1.50) on Friday evening, lasagne or roast topside of beef (£1.50) on Sunday. Our favourite room is the cosy oak-beamed parlour on the right, with old oak settle, cushioned built-in wall seat, small red upholstered chairs, lots of little electric bell-pushes as well as brass bells (for service in the old days), plates on a high shelf and pottery in a corner cupboard, embroidered samplers on the walls, a mullioned window, and a cast-iron open range with Staffordshire pottery dogs mounting guard on its side ovens. It was in this room that General Fairfax is said to have been shot, on his way to Brighouses. Other rooms opening off the good clear space around the bar include a lively tap-room, with darts, dominoes, cribbage, a fruit machine and a juke box. On our visit classical music wafted through from the kitchen, with an occasional obbligato accompaniment from a vocal Burmese cat – there's also a friendly black labrador called Sally. *(Recommended by Jon Dewhirst)*

Free house · Licensee Bryan Sharratt · Real ale · Meals and snacks · Children welcome · Open 12–2, 6.20–10.30 (supper extension to 11.30)

BINGLEY (W Yorks)   SE1039   Map 7
Brown Cow
Ireland Bridge; B6429, just W of junction with A650

The popular food in the well kept and spacious open-plan main bar here includes home-made soup (70p), sandwiches (from 85p), steak and kidney pie (£2.85), big T-bone steaks (£3.65), and roasts – they specialise in a large Yorkshire pudding served either with beef or with stew and Yorkshire sausage (from £2.25); home-made puddings. The room is divided by large pillars and the natural shapes of the original rooms into smaller areas – two of them with tables set neatly for people eating. It is carpeted and quite smart, with comfortable easy chairs and captain's chairs around the black tables, some panelling, lots of pictures and some brass on the walls, a high shelf of toby jugs under the dark ceiling, and a large brown cow's head. There is also a

695

separate restaurant. Well kept Timothy Taylors Best, Golden Best and Landlord on handpump; dominoes or cribbage on request, a fruit machine, and piped music. In fine summer weather they have barbecues on a sheltered corner terrace behind, with tables and chairs – some of them sturdy pews – below a steep bluebell wood. The stone bridge over the River Aire is very pretty. *(Recommended by Mr and Mrs Michael Parrott, Tim Halstead, Philip Asquith, Keith Myers, Paul West, Mark Waddington)*

Timothy Taylors · Licensee Brian Sampson · Real ale · Meals (not Sun–Tues evenings) and snacks (not Sun or Mon evenings) · Children in eating area and small snug · Traditional jazz Mon · Open 11–3, 7–10.30; closed evening 1st Weds in Aug (Bingley Show Day night) · Bedrooms in adjoining cottages tel Bradford (0274) 569482; £16.95S/£29.50S

BRADFORD (W Yorks)   SE1633 Map 7
Cock & Bottle

93 Barkerend Road, Bradford 3; A658 by junction with Otley Road

A full-blooded place, this is thoroughly lively and down-to- earth, and attracts all sorts. The most striking thing about its small and friendly rooms is their well preserved Victorian décor, with heavily carved woodwork, deep-cut and etched windows and mirrors enriched with silver and gold leaf patterns, stained glass, enamel intaglios, and heavy traditional furniture. There's an open fire in the public bar, and the saloon opens into a couple of little snugs, and a rather larger carpeted music room. Good value lunchtime snacks consist of freshly heated butties with chips (35p), bacon (40p), burger, sausage and onion or steak canadien (45p), and burgers or steak canadien with chips (80p), sausage and egg (90p) and a quarter chicken (£1); particularly well kept Tetleys Bitter and Mild on handpump. Darts, dominoes, a fruit machine and a juke box. Though close to the city centre, parking is easy. *(Recommended by Tim Halstead, Philip Asquith, Keith Myers, Paul West, Maria Glot)*

Tetleys (now one of their Heritage Inns) · Licensee Terry Breakwell · Real ale Meals and snacks (lunchtime, not Sat or Sun) · Children in snugs · Old-fashioned stomping piano sing-along Weds, Fri, Sat and Sun, also Sun lunchtime · Open 11–3, 5.50–10.30

BUCKDEN (N Yorks)   SD9477 Map 7
Buck ★

B6160

The extended and modernised bar of this old stone inn – in a glorious setting in upper Wharfedale – has upholstered built-in wall banquettes and square stools around shiny dark brown tables on its patterned red carpet, with the wall by its big log fire (where the plump little black cat likes to sit) stripped back to bare stone and the others left buttery cream, decorated with local pictures, the mounted head of a roebuck, and bunches of fresh flowers even in the depths of winter. It's more or less open-plan, but given the feeling of separate areas by a trelliswork divider, and by the distinct flagstone-floored area, with hunting prints and willow-pattern plates, down by the serving counter. Service is quick and friendly; food includes home-made soup (75p), sandwiches (£1), toasties (£1.25), sausage, egg and bacon (£1.75), ploughman's (£1.95), a choice of omelettes (£2), steak sandwich (£2.25), salads (from £2.50), home-made steak and kidney pie (£2.75), pork chop or local trout (£3.50) and sirloin steak (£5.80); there is also a separate evening restaurant. Well kept Theakstons Best, XB, Old Peculier and Mild and Youngers Scotch on handpump; darts and dominoes, maybe piped music. Seats on the terrace and beyond the sloping car park in the shelter of a great sycamore have good views of the moors which surround this solid stone village inn. The bedrooms, recently refurbished, are comfortable and well equipped: a nice place to stay. *(Recommended by H E Emson, Dr R F Fletcher, J Dewhirst, Tim Halstead, Philip Asquith, Keith Myers, Paul West, J A Catton, H Davies and Mr and Mrs H Mirfin; more reports please)*

Free house · Licensee John Robinson ; Real ale · Meals and snacks · Children in eating areas · Open 11–3, 6–11 · Bedrooms tel Kettlewell (075 676) 227; £15/£30 (£34B)

BURNSALL (N Yorks)   SE0361 Map 7

Red Lion

B6160 S of Grassington, on Ilkley road

White tables on the cobbles in front of this pretty stone-built inn look over the quiet road to the village green (which has a tall maypole) running along the banks of the River Wharfe. The lively main bar, very popular indeed at peak holiday times, stretches quite a long way back, with rugs on the floor, Windsor armchairs, flowery-cushioned sturdy seats built in to the attractively panelled walls, and steps up past a solid-fuel stove to a back area with sensibly placed darts (dominoes players are active up here, too). Decorations include pictures of the local fell races. There's a coal fire in the cosy carpeted front lounge bar, which is served from the same copper-topped counter through an old-fashioned small-paned glass partition. Well kept Timothy Taylors Landlord and Tetleys on handpump, and good bar food – the ham salad is strongly tipped, and you may be lucky enough to get free Yorkshire puddings if they are surplus from the restaurant (which is also popular). *(Recommended by Tim Halstead, Eileen Broadbent, Philip Asquith, A J Williamson, Keith Myers, Paul West and others)*

Free house · Licensee Leslie Warnett · Real ale · Meals and snacks (lunchtime, not Sun) · Children in lounge · Open 11–3, 6–11 · Bedrooms tel Burnsall (075 672) 204; £17B/£34B

CADEBY (S Yorks)   SE5100 Map 7

Cadeby Inn

3 miles from A1(M) at junction with A630; going towards Conisbrough take first right turn signposted Sprotbrough, then follow Cadeby signposts

The cheerful serving bar of this stone ex-farmhouse is in the main lounge at the back – stone, dark boards, joists and skylighting, furnished with plush stools around wooden tables and a high-backed settle made in the traditional style to fit around one alcove. It's decorated with more and more house plants, a stuffed fox and pheasant, some silver tankards, and in cool weather there's a fire in the big stone fireplace. Quiet and peaceful at lunchtime, it's usually busy in the evenings and at weekends – especially when the Morgan Car Club meets here; but even then you can find peace and quiet in the front sitting-room. On the way through to it there's a fruit machine (they also have darts, shove-ha'penny, dominoes and cribbage, and there may be piped music). Bar food includes soup (45p), sandwiches (from 55p lunchtime), home-made steak and kidney pie (£1.55, lunctime), seafood platter (£1.75), gammon with two eggs (£2.25), a lunchtime cold table (£2.25) and good value steaks (from eight-ounce sirloin £3.20); they do traditional Sunday lunches (£2.95). Well kept Sam Smiths OB and Tetleys on handpump, attractively priced. There are seats in the front beer garden, and in summer they have barbecues out here. (Recommended by ILP, M D Hare; more reports please)

Free house · Licensee Walter William Ward · Real ale · Meals and snacks Children in small front lounge · Open 11–3, 6–10.30

CHAPEL LE DALE (W Yorks)   SD7477   Map 7
Old Hill Inn

B6255 1¾ miles S of junction with B6479

This friendly and unpretentious moorland inn isn't the place to expect neat table settings and smart menus; its real appeal is to people in off Ingleborough or one of the many other fine walks, scrambles and climbs all around (or even from the pot-holes which abound here – like Weathercote Cave which swallows up quite a big waterfall, regurgitating it after goodness knows what convolutions a mile or so further on). With peat-cutting tools on the stonework above the big open fire in its cosy if haphazardly furnished back parlour (there's a pool-table in here), and lots of simple seating in the big bare-boarded front bar, it bustles with life in season, and is an absolute haven for outdoors people on a cold evening – when it still serves soup or hot drinks close to closing time. Well kept Theakstons Best and Old Peculier on handpump, maybe a guest real ale. (Recommended by Jon Dewhirst)

Free house · Real ale · Snacks ·Open 11–3, 6–11 all year · Bedrooms tel Ingleton (0468) 41256; £11/£22

COXWOLD (N Yorks)   SE5377   Map 7
Fauconberg Arms ★   [illustrated on page 692]

Smart and civilised, this well kept old stone inn is however pleasantly free from pretentions – a friendly welcome for everyone. It has pleased some of our most discriminating readers so much that we are this year encouraged to award it a star. The comfortably furnished beamed lounge bar has two cosy knocked-together rooms, with matting on their flagstones, Windsor armchairs, cushioned antique oak settles including one that's handsomely carved and another curved to fit the attractive bay window, an oak porter's chair, brasses on one beam and a good log fire in the unusual arched stone fireplace (in summer there may be fresh flowers there instead). Efficiently served bar snacks include excellent home-made soup (85p) and sandwiches such as salami and beetroot, roast ham or beef and cheese and tomato (95p), with a cottage cheese, celery, nuts and apple special (£1). Good full meals with generous helpings of main courses such as liver with Dubonnet sauce, devilled kidneys or savoury baked sole (around £6–£7) are served in the separate restaurant (not Sunday evening or Monday; it can be very busy at Sunday lunchtime). Well kept Tetleys, Theakstons and Youngers Scotch on handpump. The locals' spacious back public bar has darts, a fruit machine, space game and maybe piped music. The inn is handsomely set in a broad, quiet village street with tubs of flowers on its grass or cobbled verges, and is close to Shandy Hall, the home of Laurence Stern the novelist. Its bedrooms are charming and cottagey. *(Recommended by Eileen Broadbent, Simon Wilmot-Smith, Tim Halstead, Philip Asquith, Keith Myers, Paul West, G M Heath, Neil and Sue Coley)*

Free house · Licensee Richard Goodall · Snacks · Open 10.30–2.30, 6–11; bedrooms closed 2 weeks each Feb and Oct · Bedrooms tel Coxwold (034 76) 214; £18 (£20S)/£28 (£30S)

CRAY (N Yorks)   SD9379 Map 7

White Lion ★

It was such a rare fine evening on our visit that the landlord suggested we took our drinks out to sit on one of the flat limestone slabs in the shallow stream which tumbles down opposite this friendly little stone-built country pub. Inside, the cosy bar – the highest in Wharfedale, 1,100 feet up by Buckden Pike – is traditionally furnished with country kitchen chairs and a fabric-covered settle on the flagstone floor, and is decorated with shelves of china, racks of pipes, iron tools and so forth, with a high beam-and-plank ceiling. Well kept Theakstons Best, Youngers No 3, McEwans and Goose Eye on handpump, with regular guest beers. Bar food – the snacks at lunchtime only – includes sandwiches (70p), pie and peas (85p), hot crusty ham roll (£1.15), ploughman's (£1.60), beef curry (£2.25), beef in Old Peculier casserole (£2.75) and ham and eggs (£3.25); bar billiards, dominoes, ring the bull. There are picnic-table sets in a pretty little garden above the very quiet, steep lane, and of course the surrounding hill country is superb. *(Recommended by Jon Dewhirst, Tim Halstead, Philip Asquith, Keith Myers, Paul West)*

Free house · Licensees David and Rachel Hird · Real ale · Snacks (lunchtime) and meals · Children welcome if kept under supervision · Open 11–3, 5.30ish–11; closed Mon in winter

CRAYKE (N Yorks)   SE5670 Map 7

Durham Ox

Though it can be almost too quiet at lunchtime on a winter weekday, at other times this stylish old inn is very popular for its bar food, such as soup served with croûtons (£1.10), lasagne (£2.55), ploughman's with Stilton and Wensleydale or with pâté, home-made cottage pie or steak and kidney pie (around £3.25), savoury kebabs (£3.50) and sirloin steak (£5.25). There is a separate restaurant. The lounge bar is old-fashioned, with pictures and old local photographs on its dark green walls, a high shelf of plates, interestingly satirical carvings in its panelling (birds hanging a fox, say), and antique seats and settles around venerable tables on the partly carpeted flagstone and tiling floor. There's an enormous inglenook fireplace at one end. Some of the panelling divides off a bustling public area with a lively atmosphere, more old-fashioned furnishings, and darts, dominoes, a fruit machine, space game and juke box; there may be background music. Well kept Camerons Lion and Tetleys on handpump. The inn faces the village church at the far end of a broad grass-edged street lined with attractive brick houses. (Recommended by Flt Lt A Darroch Harkness, Theresa Lister, W A Rinaldi-Butcher and others)

Free house · Licensee J T Horsley-Scott · Real ale · Meals and snacks (not Mon evening) · Children in restaurant · Open 10.30–2.30, 6.30–11 · Bedrooms tel Easingwold (0347) 21506; £10.50/£21

CRIDLING STUBBS (N Yorks)   SE5221   Map 7
Ancient Shepherd

4 miles from M62 junction 33: S of A1, first left signposted Cridling Stubbs; 3½ miles from M62 junction 34: S on A19, first right; pub signposted from village

This carefully decorated pub has comfortable seats, a décor of soft browns, and sentimental engravings on the walls; it is handy for the motorway, but a really welcome respite from it. Good bar food, which changes monthly, might include home-made soup (£1), ploughman's (£1.95), pizza (£2.50), tortellini (£2.55), cottage cheese with pineapple, prawns and peppers (£2.65), a good mixed seafood platter (£2.80), and gammon, steak, black pudding and sausage mixed grill (£3.25). There is also a separate restaurant, with a weekly changing menu (not Saturday lunchtime, Sunday or Monday – booking advised). The serving bar is in an attractive flagstoned hall, with soft lighting and stone pillars: well kept Timothy Taylors Best and Tetleys on handpump, also draught cider. The service is friendly. The public bar has darts, dominoes, cribbage and a fruit machine. (Recommended by D A Angless, M J Connor)

Free house · Licensees David and Carole Craven · Real ale · Meals and snacks (not Sat lunchtime, not Sun or Mon); restaurant bookings tel Knottingley (0977) 83316 · Children in eating area and restaurant · Open 12–2, 7–11.30, closed lunchtime Sat and Mon

EAST LAYTON (N Yorks)   NZ1609   Map 10
Fox Hall Inn

A66

Good value food in the panelled bar of this tall roadside inn includes sandwiches (from 40p), soup, pizza (£1.60), salads (from £1.60), haddock (£1.80), pork or lamb chop (£1.90), gammon and pineapple (£1.90), home-made steak pie or lemon sole (£1.95) and rump or sirloin steak (from £4.20), with puddings (from 50p); a separate restaurant is open in the evening. The panelled bar has settles built in to make cosy booths around the tables, and the back part is more open, with a big south-facing window. It's decorated with Victorian prints and etchings, and a high shelf of plates. There are dominoes, cribbage and sensibly placed darts, maybe piped music. Down the nearby lane to Ravensworth (which climbs to fine views of the rolling countryside) is a ruined medieval castle. Be careful entering or leaving the pub's car park, as some of the traffic on this road is dangerously fast. The bedrooms are comfortable. *(Recommended by Patrick Stapley, Richard Gibbs, Colin Heather)*

Free house · Licensee John Jackson · Meals and snacks · Children in eating area and restaurant · Open 10.30–3, 6–11 · Bedrooms tel Darlington (0325) 718262; £10.50 (£11.50B)/£20 (£21B)

EGTON BRIDGE (N Yorks)   NZ8105   Map 10

Horse Shoe ★

Village signposted from A171 W of Whitby; via Grosmont from A169 S of Whitby

A really relaxed and convivial atmosphere, with welcoming local regulars, makes this inn's bar particularly attractive. A couple of cats drowse in front of the log fire, there are high-backed built-in winged settles, wall seats and spindleback chairs around the modern oak tables, and the walls are decorated with a big stuffed trout (caught near here in 1913), a fine old print of a storm off Ramsgate and other pictures. Good fresh food includes beef and vegetable or chicken and vegetable soup (70p), well made sandwiches (from 70p, newly caught prawns £1), cottage pie (on its own, £1.30), pâté (£1.65), ploughman's (£1.95), a wide choice of dishes such as good home-made steak and kidney pie, garlic prawns, and lasagne (all around £2.35), salads (from £2.35) and some more expensive ones such as sirloin steak (£4.25). Very well kept Theakstons XB and Old Peculier on handpump (most unusually, the cellarwork is all done by a 20-year-old girl); darts, dominoes, maybe piped music. There are comfortable seats and tables on a quiet terrace and lawn outside the stone house, by a little stream with ducks and geese; a footbridge over this leads to the tree-sheltered residents' lawn which runs down to the River Esk. These gardens are pretty and well kept – idyllic in summer with the water tinkling past the stepping-stones. *(Recommended by Dr R Wright, Eileen Broadbent, Peter Thurgood, H B Smith)*

Free house · Licensee Mrs Mary Swinglehurst · Real ale · Meals and snacks Open 11–3, 6.30–11 (11–2.30, 6.30–10.30 in winter) · Bedrooms tel Whitby (0947) 85245; £12.50/£25 (not over Christmas and New Year)

Postgate

This is one of the prettiest parts of the moors, down in the steep twisty valley of the lovely River Esk – used by the British Rail Esk Valley line, which links at nearby Grosmont with the magnificent private North Yorkshire Moors line. Inside, the friendly carpeted lounge bar has Windsor chairs, upholstered modern settles and seats in a sunny window, with a high shelf of silver cups and bottles, though in summer the obvious place to sit is on the terrace. Bar food includes soup, sandwiches, ploughman's with crusty French bread (from £1.65), home-made steak and kidney pie or quarter chicken (£1.95), breaded scampi (£2.30), mixed meats salad (£2.50), gammon (£3.20) and sirloin steak (£4.25), also children's dishes; there is a separate restaurant, where they do a traditional Sunday lunch. Camerons Lion and Strongarm on handpump, kept under a light blanket of CO_2, and draught cider; the public bar has darts, dominoes and a juke box. The inn is named after Father Nicholas Postgate, hanged, drawn and quartered at York 300 years ago for baptising a child into the Roman Catholic Church. *(Recommended by Tim Halstead, Philip Asquith, Keith Myers, Paul West, G M Heath and others)*

Camerons · Licensee Anthony Wells · Real ale · Meals and snacks · Children in restaurant · Open 10.30–3, 6.30–11 all year · Bedrooms tel Whitby (0947) 85241; £11B/£19B

FADMOOR (N Yorks)   SE6789 Map 10
Plough

It's the food which really matters here – quite exceptional quality for a pub, though there's nothing high-falutin' about the atmosphere (which is notably friendly and relaxed) or furnishings. The front bar, which overlooks the village green, has wheelback chairs and some small Windsor armchairs around its heavy cast-iron-framed tables; it's mainly carpeted, with tiles by the serving counter (they have Camerons Strongarm on electric pump), black beams supporting the ceiling of narrow white planks, a small log fire and darts. The comfortable old-fashioned dining-room leads off behind, with a wide choice of excellent food such as plump king prawns with parsleyed garlic bread, smoked salmon mousseline with sorrel sauce, duck with lemon preserve in a port sauce, perfect vegetables – often unusual (baby turnips in sauce, an interesting salad of white cabbage with onion and garlic), and home-made walnut ice cream with plum preserve or hot chocolate sauce. Booking is essential. On Saturdays and Sundays there are snacks such as soup (55p), smoked salmon pâté (£1.50), two-cheese ploughman's (£1.60) or beef and vegetable pie (£2), to eat in the bar or dining-room. There is a notable wine list. *(Recommended by K A Chappell, Heather Sharland)*

Free house · Licensee Kathlyn Brown · Real ale · Restaurant meals (Tues to Sat evenings) tel Kirkbymoorside (0751) 31515 and bar snacks (Sat, Sun and bank hol lunchtimes) · Open 7–10.30 (also weekend and bank hol lunchtimes, opening at noon); closed normal weekday lunchtimes

GARGRAVE (N Yorks)   SD9354 Map 7
Anchor

A65 W of village

The comfortably refurbished and carpeted open-plan main bar of this extended canalside pub rambles around a central servery which has Timothy Taylors, Tetleys and Youngers Scotch on handpump. Bar food includes soup (70p), sandwiches (from 80p), ploughman's with two cheeses (£1.75), salads (from £2.50), and a very wide choice of hot dishes from sausage, egg and chips (£1.50), burgers (from £1.60) or a selection of three-egg omelettes (£1.75) to big mixed grills and steaks (around £6.50). Puddings include home-made cheesecake (£1), and there are children's dishes such as beefburger (£1). A separate restaurant has big windows overlooking the canal. Various more or less segregated areas have darts, pool, dominoes, cribbage, a fruit machine, space game, and a juke box, and there is piped music. A family room with amusements such as table football and space games opens on to a terrace which in turn leads to a play area with lots of swings and so forth. And there are tables on the grass by the Leeds and Liverpool Canal. There is a modern bedroom wing. *(Recommended by J A Catton, Sue and Len Beattie)*

Free house · Licensee Roland Feather · Real ale · Meals and snacks · Children in family room · Open 11—3, 5.30—11 (6—10.30 in winter) · Bedrooms tel Gargrave (075 678) 666; £20B/£30B

GOOSE EYE (W Yorks)   SE0340 Map 7
Turkey

On high back road between Haworth and Sutton-in-Craven, and signposted from back roads W of Keighley; OS Sheet 104 reference 028406

We are not certain about the present circumstances of this pub: since hearing that it was up for sale at the time we were going to press, we've been unable to reach it by letter or telephone. It's well worth finding, so we hope that all is well with it. In an interesting tucked-away ex-milling village at the bottom of a steep valley with high-walled lanes, it is simply but enterprisingly furnished — with barrel tops set in to its concrete floor, soft beige button-back banquettes built in to its various snug alcoves, and a good old-fashioned copper-topped bar counter to direct attention to the beers brewed here: Goose Eye, and Goose Eye Special. They also keep Thwaites Bitter and Mild and Websters Yorkshire on handpump. The simple bar food has been good value, and it gets very busy when there is a weekend function on at the Mint Bar nightclub across the road (in a smartly converted old mill building) though it's quiet at lunchtime. A separate games area has darts, various space games, a juke box and a fruit machine. *(Recommended by M Elwood, Jack Davey, Maria Glot)*

Own brew · Real ale · Meals and snacks · Live music Fri and Sat · Open 11—3, 6—10.30

GREAT AYTON (N Yorks)   NZ5611 Map 10
Royal Oak

High Green; off A173 — follow village signs

The main dark-panelled bar of this friendly inn is pleasantly old-fashioned, with a good local atmosphere. It has sturdy settles — some of them antiques — and wheelback chairs around its traditional cast-iron-framed tables, an inglenook fireplace (big enough to hold two of the tables), thick butter-coloured plaster on the humpy stone walls, beams supporting wide white ceiling planks, and bow windows looking out on the square of elegant houses around the village green —

some Georgian, some older, either bare stone or rendered in grey or (like the inn) white. An adjoining longer room is set with more tables for the bar food, which includes hot beef baps (70p), soup (70p), macaroni cheese with ham (95p), a curry snack (£1.35), braised sausages (£1.65), reliably fresh salads (from £1.80), curried mixed meats (£2.10), good braised pork chops and chicken and mushroom pie (around £2.25); there is a separate restaurant. The public bar has darts, dominoes and a fruit machine, and there may be piped music. *(Recommended by A Driver, Jean Hellier)*

Scottish & Newcastle · Licensee Derek Monaghan · Meals (lunchtime) and snacks (not Sun evening) · Children welcome · Open 11–3, 6–11 (closes 10.30 Mon and Tues in winter) · Bedrooms tel Great Ayton (0642) 722361; £16 (£18B)/£24 (£26B)

GRENOSIDE (S Yorks)   SK3394 Map 7
Cow and Calf

Skew Hill Lane off A61 N from Sheffield; at traffic lights turn left following Oughtibridge, Grenoside Hospital sign

3 miles from M11 junction 35; on A629 towards Chapeltown, turn left to Ecclesfield on first minor road; at A6135 T-junction turn right, then shortly at multiple junction with B6087 go straight ahead on minor road to Grenoside

This old stone farmhouse – which still has wandering hens and offstage animal noises – has been handsomely converted, with several interconnecting rooms all in sight of the well-manned bar counter, some pieces of harness and so forth, a few dog or farmyard pictures on the plain white walls (just bare stone in one back room). There are well made high settles against the walls, and the atmosphere is welcoming and in the evenings quite smart. Bar food includes sandwiches (around 50p) and at lunchtime home-made pie with two vegetables and chips (£1.20), fish (£1.40), gammon (£1.95) and steak (£3.85). Like the food, the well kept Sam Smiths on electric pump is attractively priced. Dominoes, cribbage, fruit machine, maybe piped music. There is a family area opposite the main entrance, and a shop catering for children outside in the farmyard. *(Recommended by Jane English; more reports please)*

Sam Smiths · Licensee Geoffrey Hopkin · Real ale · Meals (lunchtime, not Sat or Sun) and snacks · Children in family area · Open 11–3, 5.30–11 all year

GRISTHORPE (N Yorks)   TA0982 Map 10
Bull

Village signposted just off A165 Scarborough–Filey

Very useful for an area not abounding in good pubs, this low-beamed old place has had its big open-plan main bar comfortably refurbished with cushioned wall banquettes and stools, and is decorated with lots of sporting pictures and village scenes. Well kept Youngers Scotch and No 3; good value sandwiches and other food including soup, hot dishes such as steak and kidney pie, a lunchtime cold buffet, and puddings – also a separate dining-room. A more or less segregated games area has darts, fruit machines and a juke box. You can walk through the attractive older part of the village to a disued railway station, and there are magnificent sea cliffs a mile or so away on the other side of the main road. *(Recommended by Lee Goulding; more reports please)*

Youngers · Real ale · Meals and snacks · Children in dining-room Open 10.30–2.30, 6–10.30

HARDEN (W Yorks)   SE0838 Map 7
Malt Shovel

Follow Wilsden signpost from B6429

By a bridge over Harden Beck, this handsome low building of dark stone has a friendly three-room bar, with red plush seats built in to its walls – some of them panelled – brass funnels, kettles and the like hanging from the black beams, horse brasses on leather harness, and stone mullioned windows. Bar food includes sandwiches (from 65p), ploughman's (£1.40), steak and kidney pie (£2.70) and salads (from £2.85); well kept Tetleys Bitter and Mild on handpump; dominoes, cribbage. From the other side of the bridge you can walk upstream beside the river. *(Recommended by Mark Waddington, Tim Halstead)*

Tetleys · Licensee Ivor Robinson · Real ale · Meals and snacks · Open 11.30–3, 5.30–10.30

HAROME (N Yorks)   SE6582 Map 10
Star ★   *[illustrated on page 725]*

2 miles south of A170, near Helmsley

The atmosphere in this charming little thatched pub is very civilised, and some readers with wide experience of Yorkshire pubs rate this one as among the very best. It is decidedly stylish with classical music, chintz-cushioned settles and wall benches, lighting by lamps hanging between the very low beams, foxes' masks, and an attractively tiled

The Bruce Arms, West Tanfield

old cooking-range opposite an elegant solid-fuel stove. Bar food consists of tasty home-made soup, cheese and biscuits, and a wide range of sandwiches including chicken or prawn curry, smoked trout pâté and crab, besides good roast beef, ham, egg and cress, smoked salmon and so forth (the prices are high, but readers reckon the quality justifies them; there is also a separate restaurant (closed January). Well kept Camerons Lion, Theakstons Best and Old Peculier and Vaux Samson on handpump; darts, dominoes, cribbage. In summer there are seats and tables outside on a sheltered front flagstoned terrace, with more in an attractive garden behind the building. *(Recommended by Mr and Mrs G D Amos, Dr D B Fox, Tim Halstead, Philip Asquith, Keith Myers, Paul West)*

Free house · Licensee Peter Gascoigne-Mullett · Real ale · Snacks (lunchtime) Children in coffee loft · Open 11.30–2.30, 6–10.30; restaurant closed Jan

HATFIELD WOODHOUSE (S Yorks)   SE6808   Map 7
Green Tree

1 mile from M18 junction 5: on A18/A614 towards Bawtry

This very popular, well kept and comfortably modernised old pub has plenty of room in its spacious series of connecting open-plan rooms and alcoves, with brown leatherette seats and Windsor chairs around the tables spread out on its expanse of Turkey carpet. Good bar food includes sandwiches (from 65p), soup (70p), ploughman's (£1.45), salads such as quiche Lorraine (£1.75) or cold meats (£1.95), good lasagne (£1.95), fresh haddock or plaice from Grimsby (£2.35), home-made rabbit pie (£1.95) and steak and kidney pie (£2.35), steaks (£4.95), and puddings such as cherry and apple pie (65p). They do a seafood buffet on Friday and Saturday evenings, serving cockles, mussels, whelks and prawns; there is also a separate restaurant. Well kept Darleys Thorne and Mild on handpump; maybe piped music. A large ballroom is available for functions. *(Recommended by Richard Cole, ILP, Dr Tony Clarke)*

Darleys · Licensee Trevor Hagan · Real ale · Meals and snacks · Children in eating area and restaurant · Open 11–3, 6–10.30

HEATH (W Yorks)   SE3519   Map 7
King's Arms

Village signposted from A655 Wakefield–Normanton – or more directly, turn off opposite Horse & Groom

The gaslit dark-panelled bars of this unusual pub have plain wooden stools and settles built in to the walls – intentionally quite without frills. Outside, sunny benches face a neat green, with imposing stone houses standing apart – in time, almost as well as in space – on the other sides. This is surrounded by over 100 acres of rough common where gipsy horses wander, and as you come to the edges of that you suddenly look down on giant power station cooling towers and sprawling industry. The pub, quiet on weekday lunchtimes, is very

---

Children welcome means the pub says it lets children inside without any special restrictions.

popular for an evening outing. Well kept Tetleys and Theakstons on hand-taps; dominoes; note that there's no food. *(Recommended by Tim Halstead, Philip Asquith, Keith Myers, Paul West)*

Free house · Licensee David Kerr · Real ale · Open 11.30–3, 6.30–11 all year

HECKMONDWIKE (W Yorks)   SE2223 Map 7
Old Hall

New Hall Road; B6117 between A62 and A638

A fine old manor sensitively restored, by an open space above the town: it's partly knocked through inside, showing lots of oak beams and timbers, stripped old stone or brick walls, and latticed mullioned windows. It dates from 1470 and was the home of the Nonconformist scientist Joseph Priestley. The central part has a high ornate plaster ceiling, and snug low-ceilinged alcoves lead off this – with an upper gallery room under the pitched roof, looking down on the main area through timbering 'windows'. Comfortable furnishings include cushioned oak pews and red plush seats, some with oak backs, on a sweep of Turkey carpet (there are flagstones by the serving counter). Service has that nice Yorkshire blend of smart efficiency with warmly interested friendliness, and Tetleys Bitter and Mild, Websters Yorkshire and Wilsons Original on handpump are well kept. Weekday happy hour 5.30–6.30; fruit machines, sitting space game, piped music. The food is very popular locally. *(Recommended by Tim Halstead, Philip Asquith, Keith Myers, Paul West)*

Tetleys · Licensee G M Baynes · Real ale · Meals and snacks · Children in eating area, restaurant and side room · Jazz Tues · Open 11–3, 5.30–11 all year

HELMSLEY (N Yorks)   SE6184 Map 10
Feathers

Market Square

Though the main inn (with its own comfortable lounge bar) is a handsomely solid three-storey stone block, the friendly adjoining pub part is much lower and a good deal older, with heavy medieval beams in its two cosy rooms, a big log fire in the stone inglenook fireplace, some dark panelling and a venerable wall carving of a dragon-faced bird in a grape vine, and unusual cast-iron-framed tables topped by weighty slabs of oak and walnut. Good value food includes lots of changing specials such as beef curry or potato, vegetable and cheese casserole (£1.75), Greek Feta cheese salad (£2), chilli con carne (£2.50), mussels in garlic (£2.75) and jugged hare (£3), as well as a wide basic choice from sandwiches (80p and up), soup (85p) and ploughman's (£1.75) to home-made steak pie (£3.75) and 12-ounce sirloin steak (£6.50); well kept Theakstons XB on handpump; darts, dominoes, a fruit machine, and a juke box. There's an attractive back garden. This is a pleasant and relaxing town, close to Rievaulx Abbey (well worth an hour's visit). *(Recommended by Fergus Bastock)*

Free house · Licensees Jack, Lance and Andrew Feather · Real ale · Meals and snacks · Open 10.30–2.30, 6–10.30 (open for coffee from 10am); closed evening 25 Dec · Bedrooms tel Helmsley (0439) 70275; £16 (£19B)/£32 (£38B)

HETTON (N Yorks)   SD9558   Map 7

Angel ★

The good food in this friendly and attractively decorated Dales village pub does include substantial sandwiches (from £1), but it concentrates on bistro-style cooking, with soups such as cream of onion or maybe carrot with basil or provençale fish with croûtons (£1.60), a rich and creamy smoked salmon mousse or excellent pork and chicken liver terrine (£1.70), tasty salad niçoise (£1.70), steak and kidney pie (£2.75), lamb cutlets with béarnaise butter (£3.75) and eight-ounce sirloin steak (£4.50), with home-made puddings such as hot sticky toffee (£1.25). Daily specials may include Scotch langoustines (£4.25) or Scotch salmon with home-made mayonnaise (£4.65), with richer winter dishes such as chine of pork (with better chips and side salad than most), or prize sausages with red cabbage. A separate restaurant serves a good value roast Sunday lunch (£7.25), and evening dinners (£10.50, not Sunday), where the main courses might include baked sea bass or rack of lamb with raspberry vinegar gravy. The rambling bar has lots of alcoves made cosy with Laura Ashley cushions, log fires in a big stone fireplace, some beams and standing timbers, Ronald Searle wine snob cartoons above the low panelling, and in one side room little silvery plush armchairs on a Turkey carpet. The old tap-room has recently been turned into extra table space as well as a small snug. Well kept Theakstons Bitter, XB and Old Peculier, Timothy Taylors Landlord and Youngers Scotch; darts, dominoes, a fruit machine. Sturdy wooden benches and tables are built on to the cobbles outside this pretty house, in the little village which is very much quieter than nearby Grassington. *(Recommended by Do and Kenneth Hummer, Miss S Rodgers, Ian Clay, Paul Denham, Valerie Patten, David Symes, Miss S Rodgers, Dr H B Cardwell, Tim Halstead, Philip Asquith, Keith Myers, Paul West, Dr P H Walker, Dennis Royles, N CHodgsons)*

Free house · Licensee Denis Watkins · Real ale · Meals and snacks · Children welcome · Open 11.30–2.30, 6.30–11

HUBBERHOLME (N Yorks)   SD9178   Map 10

George

Village signposted from Buckden; about 1 mile NW

In a lovely remote part of the Dales, this ancient inn looks down over a swirly stretch of the River Wharfe rattling over the rocks by a bridge – it has fishing rights in the river, and a centuries-long association with the church on the other side (about the only other building here now). It's an idiosyncratic place, very appealing indeed to some readers, and has heavy beams, some stripped stone, warm winter fires (a huge cauldron swings on its pot-arm in the big stone hearth), and it does bar food such as big French bread filled with cheese, beef, ham or bacon (£1.20), ploughman's (£1.50), pâté (£1.65), and hot dishes including steak and kidney or chicken and

---

If you're interested in real ale, the CAMRA *Good Beer Guide* – no relation to us – lists thousands of pubs where you can get it.

ham pie, pork chop, and chicken (£2.35); they do much of the
cooking on an Aga, and there's a separate restaurant. Well kept
Youngers Scotch on handpump; darts, dominoes, cribbage. Behind, a
few seats look up past swings to the moors, which rise all around.
(Recommended by Tim Halstead, J Dewhirst, Trevor Williams, Lynda Brown)

*Free house · Licensee John Fredrick · Real ale · Meals and snacks · Children in
eating area · Open 11.30–3, 6–11 · Bedrooms tel Kettlewell (075 676) 223;
£14.50 (£14.50B)/£21 (£21B)*

LANGDALE (N Yorks)   SE9491 Map 10
Moorcock

Best reached from A170 at East Ayton (signposted Forge Valley, just E of
bridge), or A171 via Hackness.

This quite unspoilt village pub, in a beautiful valley, has as its bar a
neat little parlour in a whitewashed stone terraced cottage, with
simple old settles around a scrubbed table and one or two calendars
on the wall. The beer is poured in a back room and brought out on a
tray, and you can have tea or coffee and biscuits if you wish. You can
expect a cheery welcome, with a warm fire even – or especially –
when the weather makes it unlikely that there'll be many other
customers (we remember some time ago turning up in grim weather
to hear that we were the first customers all week). The landlady's
family have kept the pub open for wayfarers on this lonely road over
the moors since the turn of the century. Sandwiches (60p–70p) are
freshly cut. *(Recommended by Trevor Williams, Tim Halstead, Philip
Asquith, Keith Myers, Paul West, R K Whitehead)*

*Free house · Licensee Maud Martindale · Evening snacks (not Sun) · Children
welcome · Open 10.30–2.30, 6–10.30; bar closed for drinks Sun*

LASTINGHAM (N Yorks)   SE7391 Map 10
Blacksmiths Arms

Well placed for some of the best scenery on the North Yorkshire
Moors, this neat stone village inn has a comfortable oak-beamed bar,
with Windsor chairs and traditional built-in wooden wall seats well
cushioned in Liberty prints. Good simple bar food includes soup
(85p), sandwiches (90p), ploughman's (£1.65, lunchtime), sausage
and chips (£1.90), chicken (£2.20), salads (£2.70), ham and eggs
(£3.60), eight-ounce sirloin steak (£4.80, evening) and home-made
apple pie (90p). A simply furnished dining area opens off the main
bar, with excellent traditional Sunday roasts. Well kept Tetleys Bitter
and Mild, and Theakstons Best and Old Peculier, on handpump;
darts, dominoes, maybe piped music. The inn nestles under the yews
of the steep churchyard. Two hundred years ago it was the church's
curate who kept this inn, saying he needed the money to eke out his
stipend and feed his 13 children, and you can imagine them all
warming themselves around the attractive cooking range, with its
swinging pot-yards. There is lovely countryside all around here,
below Spaunton Moor, with tracks through Cropton Forest.
(Recommended by John Hosker, Trevor Williams, Jane English, Frank

Cummins, Heather Sharland, Ian Clay, Tim Halstead, Philip Asquith, Keith Myers, Paul West, J M Tansey and others)

Free house · Licensee Rodney Taylor · Real ale · Meals and snacks · Children in dining area · Open 11–2.30, 6.30–10.30 (opens 7.30 in winter); closed winter weekday lunchtimes · Bedrooms tel Lastingham (075 15) 247; £18/£30

LEDSHAM (W Yorks) SE4529 Map 7
Chequers

The new owners of this pleasant pub are proving as welcoming and friendly as the old, and there have been few signs of change here. Its small individually decorated rooms open off an old-fashioned little central panelled-in servery, and there are lots of cosy alcoves, low beams, and log fires. Bar food includes soup (60p), sandwiches (from 75p), ploughman's (£1.40), hot dishes such as lasagne (£2), steak pie (£2.50) and the good ham and eggs that have always been so popular here (£2.80), with salads such as dressed crab (£3.75); they now have Theakstons and Youngers Scotch on handpump. A sheltered two-level terrace behind the creeper-covered stone village house has tables among roses. *(Recommended by Richard Thompson, Tim Halstead, Philip Asquith, Keith Myers, Paul West)*

Free house · Licensee G M Wraith · Real ale · Meals and snacks (lunchtime, not Sun) · Children in one room away from bar · Open 11.30–3, 5.30–10.30; closed Sun

LEEDS (W Yorks) SE3033 Map 7
Fox & Newt

9 Burley Road, Leeds 3; at junction with Rutland Street

Attractively done up as an old-fashioned tavern, this is popular for the beers it brews on the premises (if he's available and not too busy, the licensee will show you round his brewery). The house beers are Burley, Old Willow and Festival; they also keep Clarks and Whitbreads Castle Eden, and perhaps a guest bitter. You can order by the four-pint jugs if you want; service is friendly and efficient. The cheerful bar, full of green, red and gold paintwork, has leatherette seats built in to the dark panelling of the lower part of the walls (there's dark red embossed Anaglypta above) and dimpled copper-topped cast-iron tables on the bare floorboards of its main room, with one or two steps up to a snugger area behind a wooden balcony. Reasonably priced bar food includes sandwiches and steak sandwiches, and filled baked potato (50p), quiche with coleslaw (75p), barbecued spare ribs (£1.70) and lasagne (£1.75), with cold pies and French bread sandwiches on Saturdays, and on Sundays either roast beef with Yorkshire pudding or gammon, bacon, Cumberland sausage, black pudding and egg with fried bread (£1.85). Well reproduced pop music and a fruit machine; and there's a working nickelodeon (the pianola's last stand against the emerging juke box – complete with internal drums, triangles and so forth). *(Recommended by Bryan Shiner, D J Winter, Tim Halstead, Philip Asquith, Keith Myers, Paul West)*

Own brew/Whitbreads · Licensee Mark Guy · Real ale · Meals (lunchtime, not Sat) and snacks (lunchtime, not Sun) · Open 11–3, 5.30–10.30

Garden Gate

Whitfield Place, Hunslet; leaving Leeds centre on A61, turn right at traffic lights signposted Hunslet Centre P, Belle Isle 1½, Middleton 3, park in the public car park on your right, and walk through – the pub is obvious

Because it's surrounded by a modern development, the marvellously preserved Victorian layout and décor of this lively and down-to-earth pub seem specially striking. The building itself is a handsome one, and inside, a high, cool corridor with tiled floor and panelled in mahogany and deep-cut glass – with a service-hatch if you just want to stand there and drink – opens into four old-fashioned rooms, with sturdy leatherette seats, and lots of mahogany and glass screens. The finest room is the one on the left as you enter, with a mosaic floor and a lovely free-flowing design of tiles coloured in subtle tones of buff, cream and icy green: the bar counter itself, its front made of elaborately shaped and bowed tiles, is the masterpiece. Others might have men (we saw no women here) playing dominoes or talking sport (it has two Rugby League teams), if they're not watching it on the big colour TV. We found the best kept Tetleys Bitter and Mild we've come across here, on handpump – the brewery is just up the Hunslet Road. Ham or cheese salad sandwiches (40p); darts, dominoes and a juke box. *(Recommended by Barrie Pepper, Tim Halstead, Philip Asquith, Keith Myers, Paul West)*

Tetleys (Ind Coope) · Licensee Lawrence Graham · Real ale · Snacks · Open 11–3, 5.30–10.30

Whitelocks ★

Turks Head Yard; gunnel (or alley) off Briggate, opposite Debenham's and Littlewoods; park in shoppers' car park and walk

This splendidly preserved city-centre tavern, with its bustling lively atmosphere, hasn't changed much since 1886, when the building – much older than that, and first licensed as the Turks Head in 1715 – was rebuilt in this form. Everything you see here now as antique was actually the height of modernity then; this was the first place in the city to have electricity. Its fine bar counter, decorated with polychrome tiles, stretches down a very long old-fashioned narrow room. The heavy copper-topped cast-iron tables and red button-back banquettes squeezed along the side opposite the bar quickly fill up at lunchtimes, as do those in the waitress-served restaurant area further along – here the tables are in old-fashioned booths with spiral brass pillars. There are some grand advertising mirrors and stained-glass windows, and it's nice to see hams hanging over the food counter. The quickly and cheerfully served lunchtime bar food includes soup (40p), sandwiches (from 60p), with succulent big meat ones cut straight from home-cooked joints, in white or granary bread (from £1.20), black pudding, mushy peas and bubble and squeak (each 30p), Scotch eggs (50p), sausage and mash (£1.15) and meat and potato pie (£1.20), fresh salads, and jam roly-poly or fruit pie (50p);

711

besides soup and sandwiches, they do Yorkshire puddings (50p with onion gravy, £1 with fillings) and steak and potato pie (£1.20) in the evening. There's also a separate restaurant (not Sundays), with main courses such as omelettes (£2.50), roast beef (£3.80) and steaks (from eight-ounce rump, £4.65, to 16-ounce T-bone, £6.95). Well kept Youngers IPA, Scotch and No 3. At the end of the long narrow yard (where one of our readers remembers getting into trouble in the 1930s, after a cricket match, for trying to roll barrels down it) they have a cheerful pastiche of a Dickensian Victorian tavern. *(Recommended by S V Bishop, Tim Halstead, Dr A K Clarke, Andrew Barnett, ILP, Ian Clay, Philip Asquith, Barrie Pepper, Keith Myers, Paul West)*

Youngers · Licensee Christopher Paul Morris · Real ale · Meals and snacks Children in restaurant · Open 11–3, 5.30–10.30; no late extension Fri

LEVISHAM (N Yorks)   SE8391   Map 10
Horseshoe

Pub and village signposted from A169 N of Pickering

Steam trains of the North Yorkshire Moors Railway stop at the village twice a day each way in spring and autumn, and four times in summer: the pub looks down the broad grass-edged village road to the moors beyond, and is included chiefly for its position in fine walking country. Simple bar food includes soup (60p), French bread sandwiches (from £1.15, sirloin steak £2.35), ploughman's (£1.70), pâté (£1.75), four-ounce burger or ham and mushroom pizza (£2), plaice (£2.25), home-made cottage pie (£1.30), goulash (£2.45), scampi (£2.50) and home-made steak and kidney pie (£2.50); well kept Tetleys Bitter and Mild and Theakstons Best on handpump. There are small red plush settees and built-in banquettes around glossy dark wooden tables on the Turkey carpet, a log fire in a stone fireplace, bar billiards, occasional darts, and dominoes; and a simply furnished warm sun-lounge. *(Recommended by Jane English)*

Free house · Licensee Roy Hayton · Real ale · Meals and snacks · Open 10.30–2.30, 6–10.30 · Bedrooms tel Pickering (0751) 60240; £12 (£12B)/£26 (£26B)

LINTON (W Yorks)   SE3947   Map 7
Windmill

Leaving Wetherby W on A661, fork left just before hospital and bear left; also signposted from A659, leaving Collingham towards Harewood

Though we understand that this old stone village pub may be changing hands, we are keeping it in for the charm – much enjoyed by readers – of its carefully restored small rooms. Walls have been stripped back to the bare stone, there are polished antique oak settles around copper-topped cast-iron tables, pots hanging from the oak beams, a high shelf for plates, and a grandfather clock. It is very neatly kept, and has had a decidedly civilised yet trendy atmosphere. The food has been popular for its imaginative use of ingredients, and there has been well kept Youngers Scotch and No 3 on handpump. *(Recommended by Simon Reevell; more up-to-date reports please)*

Free house · Real ale · Meals and snacks (see above) · Open 5.30–10

LINTON IN CRAVEN (N Yorks)   SD9962   Map 7

Fountaine

Named not after a fountain but after the local lad who made his pile
in the Great Plague (contracting in London to bury the bodies), this
neat and tidy traditional pub looks down across a peaceful and
charming green by a stream crossed by a pack-horse bridge, with the
Hospital Chapel founded by Richard Fountaine on one side. It's cosy
inside, with copper-topped tables, high-backed settles forming a
square snug around the big open fireplace, and a series of little rooms
opening off including one for children with a nine-foot-long stuffed
lion called Thomas. Under good new management, it serves a snack
basket of chips (40p), freshly cut sandwiches (from 60p),
ploughman's (£1.50), salads such as beef or ham (£2.10), very good
steak and kidney pie (£2.95) and puddings such as apple pie with
cream (80p); well kept Theakstons and Timothy Taylors Landlord on
handpump; cards, dominoes, ring the bull, fruit machine, maybe
piped music. (Recommended by Ian Clay, Derrick Turner, David Symes;
more reports please)

Free house · Licensee Jean Parkinson · Real ale · Meals and snacks (not Sun
evening) · Children in lion's room · Open 11.30–3, 7–11

LITTON (N Yorks)   SD9074   Map 7

Queens Arms

Dating from the seventeenth century, this friendly and attractively
refurbished country inn is in a lovely spot – a sheltered valley with the
moors rising all around. A track behind the pub leads over Ackerley
Moor to Buckden, and the quiet lane through the valley leads on to
Pen-y-ghent. Food in the simple, homely bars, which are warmed by
open coal fires in cool weather, includes dishes such as soup (70p),
sandwiches (from 80p), home-made meat and potato pie with peas
(90p), pâté (£1.10), ploughman's (£1.80), thick pork sausages with
apple sauce and stuffing (£1.90), cold ham or beef with vegetables
and chips (£2), scampi (£2.50), ham and eggs (£2.90), steaks (£5.50)
and salads with home-cooked ham or chicken (£2.50); at lunchtime
there may be only one or two hot dishes. Well kept Youngers Scotch
on handpump; darts, dominoes, cribbage, maybe piped music. The
bedrooms are clean and neat, and the breakfasts excellent.
(Recommended by Tim Halstead, Philip Asquith, Keith Myers, Paul West,
Robert Anderson)

Free house · Licensee Freda Brook · Real ale · Meals (evening) and snacks
Children welcome · Open 11–3, 6–11 · Bedrooms tel Arncliffe (075 677) 208;
£11/£22

MARTON CUM GRAFTON (N Yorks)   SE4265   Map 7

Olde Punch Bowl

Village signposted from A1 3 miles N of A59

This comfortable and well run pub, convenient for the A1 and with
friendly licensees, serves generous helpings of fresh food, with the

lunchtime choice including home-made soup (65p), sandwiches (from 50p), ploughman's (£1.20), salads (from £1.50), and hot dishes such as liver and onion (£1.55), omelettes or shepherd's pie (£1.75), lamb chops (£1.80), steak and kidney pie (£2.10) and chicken or gammon and egg (£2.50), with fresh vegetables. Main dishes are served only in the dining-room, where evening meals include main courses such as breaded scampi (£2.75), grilled salmon steak (£4.75) and steaks (from £4.40), as well as the dishes of the day. The pub's core dates from the sixteenth century, and the heavy beams in the open-plan lounge bar's newly painted ceilings, timber uprights and varying ceiling heights preserve the snug sense of individual rooms. Windsor chairs are set neatly around groups of tables on an expanse of Turkey carpet. Well kept John Smiths and Tetleys on handpump; maybe piped music; pool, dominoes, pin-table, fruit machine, space game and a juke box in the public bar. The large car park has a Caravan Club licence. (Recommended by Doug Kennedy, J S McCallum, John Oddey, Philip Whitney)

Free house · Licensees Allan and Glennis Broadbent · Real ale · Meals (not Mon) and snacks (not Mon evening) · Children welcome · Open 12–2, 7–11

MASHAM (N Yorks)   SE2381   Map 10
White Bear
Signposted off A6108 opposite turn into town centre

Theakstons' home-based pub, it's part of their old stone headquarters buildings – the brewery itself is on the other side of the town. The popular and traditionally furnished public bar has the best of the collections of stuffed animals (a polar bear, as well as squirrels and foxes), foreign banknotes, harness, pottery, and copper brewing implements. There's a much bigger, more comfortable lounge, with a Turkey carpet. Well kept Theakstons Best, Mild and Old Peculier on handpump; lunchtime snacks such as ploughman's, sandwiches, stuffed jacket potatoes; shove-ha'penny, dominoes, cribbage; maybe piped music. In summer there are seats out in the yard. Masham has an attractive, broad market square shaded by trees; in July there's a traction engine rally. (Recommended by Eileen Broadbent, Dr Andrew Herxheimer, Barrie Pepper, D W Roberts, Tim Halstead, P T Young; more reports please)

Real ale · Licensee Neil Cutts · Snacks (lunchtime) · Children welcome · Folk music (weekends) · Open 10.30–3, 6–11

nr MIDGLEY (W Yorks)   SE0326   Map 7
Mount Skip
Village signposted from Hebden Bridge; or from A646 W of Halifax go straight through village, keeping on high road

The ground falls away so steeply and so far below this high pub that on a clear day the mill towns and moorland opposite take on a toy-town quality; and at night the sodium street lamps down there are reduced to the little strings of twinkling gold that otherwise one sees only from an aeroplane. There's a warm coal fire in the briskly modernised bar, which has windows well placed for the view, copper-topped tables and so forth. Simple food includes good home-made soup such as mushroom (40p), sandwiches (50p), steak canadien (95p), plaice (£1), chicken (£1.40) or scampi (£1.45), with daily specials such as rabbit or meat pie (£1). An upstairs restaurant serves main meals with dishes such as chops (£3.75) or eight-ounce sirloin steak (£4). They do Sunday teas up here, and in summer high teas too. Well kept Timothy Taylors Bitter, Landlord, Golden Best and Dark Mild on handpump; darts, pool, dominoes, a fruit machine, maybe piped music – and an electric organ for anyone who wants to play it. There are benches outside for the view, and high walks nearby on Midgley Moor and Crow Hill. *(Recommended by Sue and Len Beattie, Tim Halstead, Philip Asquith, Keith Myers, Paul West, Brian and Anna Marsden; more reports please)*

Timothy Taylors · Licensees Bill and Sandra Barnes · Real ale · Meals (evening, upstairs) and snacks · Children welcome · Open 11.30–3,6–11 (opens 12 and 7 in winter)

MOULTON (N Yorks)   NZ2404 Map 10
Black Bull

Just E of A1, 1 mile S of Scotch Corner

Remarkable for its locality, this stylish place owes it abundance of character to its owner, a wine importer who took it over a good few years ago and has since converted and extended it into a series of different rooms ranging from the snug beamed bar with its traditional high-backed settles, copper-topped bar counter and tables and log fire, to a handsome curvaceous conservatory, an elegant Brighton Belle Pullman dining-car serving excellent meals, and what for most of its customers has now become its heart – the chrome-and-glass no-bookings fish restaurant (you won't get food from the bar counter staff, so you shouldn't be shy of searching out someone to take your order for snacks such as cream of asparagus soup, lightly smoked salmon sandwiches, Welsh rarebit, perhaps rare local Swaledale cheese). It has the well heeled atmosphere of a comfortable club and regular customers are prominent. *(Recommended by A Ning, The Countess Peel)*

Free house · Licensee George Pagendam · Meals and snacks (lunchtime, not Sun) · Children welcome · Open 12–2.30, 6–10.30; closed Christmas week, and food side closed Sun

NUNNINGTON (N Yorks)   SE6779 Map 7
Royal Oak

Church Street; at back of village, which is signposted from A170 and B1257

Pleasantly furnished and popular for its food, this old house has had one of its walls stripped back to the bare stone to display a fine collection of antique farm tools, and its high black beams are strung with earthenware flagons, copper jugs and lots of antique keys. The furniture on the Turkey carpet has an attractively individual and hand-picked look, with kitchen and country dining-chairs or a long

715

pew around the sturdy tables; there's a lectern in one corner, and a white-faced stuffed barn owl sits on one of the mantelpieces (there are open fires in winter). Bar food includes sandwiches (from 70p), home-made soup (70p), pâté, salami and peach salad (£1.40), ploughman's with several cheeses (£1.70 – the chutneys are good), chicken, pork and ham pie (£1.95), roast chicken (£2.65) and sirloin steak (£5.25). Theakstons beers kept under top pressure; darts, dominoes, and on our visit piped country and western music. *(Recommended by W A Rinaldi-Butcher)*

Free house · Licensee P J Handley · Meals and snacks (not Mon lunchtime) Children welcome · Open 11–2.30, 6.30–10.30; closed Mon lunchtime

OSWALDKIRK (N Yorks)   SE6279 Map 7

Malt Shovel ★ ★

Village signposted off B1363/B1257, S of Helmsley

This unusual old inn used to be the manor house, and though the public rooms aren't in the least awesome, the handsome staircase and upper landing do give an idea of its previous importance. There's plenty of sitting space in the various beamed rooms, which include old-fashioned furnishings and are decorated with shire horse pictures, old clay pipes, miners' lamps, and lots of colour photographs. The back lounge opens on to spacious lawns around an old-fashioned box knot-garden, and the lively front bar, which has a vast fireplace (and a good fire in winter), has darts, shove-ha'penny, and dominoes; there may be piped music (and there's occasionally loud live entertainment – check on this beforehand if you're thinking of staying and don't want to be up late). A high point is the good home-cooked bar food: soup (90p), granary bread open sandwiches (including ham cooked with oranges and honey, £1.25), fresh cauliflower with walnuts, tomatoes and cheese sauce (£1.75), salmon and cucumber mousse (£1.80), curried chicken and pickles in a cottage loaf (£2.85), fresh salads (from £3), whiting fillets with crabmeat and Mornay sauce (£3.40), game pie (£3.50), liver with a honey and lemon sauce (£3.95) and steaks (from 10-ounce sirloin, £6.50); vegetables are all fresh. The restaurant has similarly good food. Well kept Sam Smiths on handpump, and traditional cocktails. *(Recommended by Heather Sharland, Tim Halstead, M E Lawrence, Philip Asquith, CJB, H E Emson, Keith Myers, G M Heath, Paul West, James and Anne Clinch, Mark Pickthall)*

Sam Smiths · Licensee Ian Pickering · Real ale · Meals and snacks (not Mon evenings, except bank hols) · Children welcome · Open 11–2.30, 6.30–10.30 · Three bedrooms tel Ampleforth (043 93) 461; £11/£22

RAMSGILL (N Yorks)   SE1271 Map 7

Yorke Arms

This fine inn was the shooting-lodge of the Yorke family's Gouthwaite Hall, which now lies drowned under the nearby reservoir named after it. Behind its warm stone façade – stately but not too grand – are comfortable sofas and easy chairs, as well as some fine older oak furniture including splendid Jacobean carved seats and a great dresser laden with pewter. With the sun streaming in through the mullioned windows, this is a fine place to sit with a pot of coffee (good value) before setting off on the right-of-way track that leads along the hill behind the reservoir, also a bird sanctuary, or perhaps up the narrow, steep and splendid moors road to Masham. Bar food, all home made, includes soup (80p), cottage pie or quiche Lorraine (£1.20), game pie or chilli con carne (£2), and fruit pie with cream (75p), and the comfortable old-fashioned dining-room serves main dishes such as roast local goose and Nidderdale lamb. The inn's public rooms are open throughout the day for tea and coffee. Dominoes and cribbage available. A nice place to stay, handy for the moors, and close to the bird-sanctuary reservoir. *(Recommended by Tim Halstead, Neil and Sue Coley and others)*

Free house · Licensee J S Ralston · Snacks · Children welcome · Open 10.30–2.30, 5.30–11 · Bedrooms tel Harrogate (0423) 75243; £21 (£23B)/ £42 (£44B)

REETH (N Yorks) SE0399 Map 10
Black Bull

B6270

As we went to press, good reports were coming in on the new management at this big white coaching-inn, which dominates the wide sloping green of this Swaledale village and looks across it over to the great swell of Marrick Moor. You can sit out here under the handsome wrought-iron sign and in cold weather the beamed L-shaped bar, with two cheery fires and high-backed wall benches, is snug and friendly. Service is now quick even at busy times, and good value bar food includes soup (50p), sandwiches (from 65p), home-made pâté (90p), ploughman's with a choice of local cheeses (£1), home-made cottage pie (£1.75), chilli con carne (£1.85), and home-made steak and kidney pie or home-roasted ham salad (£2); there is also a separate restaurant, and a comfortable lounge bar. Well kept Theakstons XB and Old Peculier on handpump; darts, pool, bar billiards, dominoes, cribbage, a fruit machine and a juke box. The hotel has its own fishing on the Swale, and the bedrooms are comfortable. *(Recommended by Trevor Williams, Jon Dewhirst, Ian Clay, Eileen Broadbent, D W Roberts, Colin Heather)*

Free house · Licensee R E Sykes · Real ale · Meals and snacks · Children welcome (not after 8.30) · Open 11–3, 6–11 · Bedrooms tel Richmond (0748) 84213; £13.95/£27.90

RIPPONDEN (W Yorks) SE0419 Map 7
Old Bridge ★

Priest Lane; from A58, best approach is Elland Road (opposite Golden Lion), park opposite the church in pub's car park and walk back over ancient hump-backed bridge

This carefully restored medieval house has over the 15 years it has been in the same hands built up a relaxed and welcoming atmosphere in its three communicating rooms, each on a slightly different level. But this year one welcome change is that they have brought the old handpumps back into use, now serving well kept Timothy Taylors and Youngers Scotch. The bar has comfortable rush-seated chairs, oak settles built in to the window recesses of the thick stone walls, antique oak tables, a few well chosen pictures and a big wood-burning stove. You can see the fine structure of the old building – ceilings have been removed to show the pitched timbered roof, and the plasterwork is stripped away just here and there to expose the handsome masonry. On weekday lunchtimes a popular cold meat buffet always has a joint of rare beef, as well as spiced ham, quiche, Scotch eggs and so on (£4.50, with salads). In the evenings, and at lunchtime on Saturdays, good filling snacks include mushrooms with garlic mayonnaise (£1.25), Stilton kromeskis (£1.30), chicken and ham vol-au-vent (£1.50), and minced beef with red and green peppers in a red wine, fennel and tomato sauce or fisherman's pie (£2.50). They will cut fresh sandwiches. The pub is associated with a good restaurant across the very pretty medieval bridge over the little River Ryburn. *(Recommended by Tim Halstead, William Meadon, Richard Steel, Ian Clay, Sue and Len Beattie)*

Free house · Licensee Ian Beaumont · Real ale · Snacks (not Sat evening or Sun) Children in eating area, lunchtime · Open 11.30–3, 5.30–11 all year

ROBIN HOOD'S BAY (N Yorks)   NZ9505   Map 10
Laurel

This cosy little white pub is right in the heart of a picturesque fishing village, wedged tightly in to a steep jumble of waterfront fishermen's cottages. Snug inside, it has a good local atmosphere in its friendly beamed main bar, which is decorated with old local photographs, Victorian prints and brasses. Good value bar food includes sandwiches, ploughman's (£1.35), sausage, egg and chips (£1.40), fresh haddock (£1.75), steak pie (£1.85), scallops in cream sauce (£1.95), scampi (£2.30) and prawn parcels (£2.50); well kept Camerons Bitter and Strongarm on handpump, with changing guest beers; darts, shove-ha'penny, table skittles, dominoes, cribbage, maybe piped music. *(Recommended by Eileen Broadbent)*

Free house · Licensee Martin Robert Tucker · Real ale · Meals and snacks (lunchtime) · Children in snug bar · Open 11.30–3, 7–11 all year

ROSEDALE ABBEY (N Yorks)   SE7395   Map 10
Milburn Arms

The easiest road to the village is through Cropton from Wrelton, off the A170 W of Pickering

The spacious and well run open-plan bar of this comfortable eighteenth-century stone inn is popular for its good value food, such as watercress soup (70p), rare roast beef bun (90p), home-made chicken liver pâté (£1.50), black pudding with fried apple and onions (£1.65), pork and ale casserole (£2.25), lemon sole (£2.50), a choice of salads from the cold table (from £2.50, with fresh lobster from May to September from £5.90), home-made steak and kidney pie (£2.95), fresh halibut (£3.50) and sirloin steak (£4.95), with children's dishes such as pizza and beans (90p). One reader was delighted to find not a single chip or scampi in sight, and the hotel restaurant is highly praised by readers, too: the welcoming licensees know their wines (and indeed come from that trade). In the bar, a snug area by the log fire has black beams in its bowed cream ceiling, sentimental engravings (*The Poor Poet, The Pensionist*) by Karl Spitzweg, and Liberty-print wall banquettes, grey plush stools and captain's chairs around cast-iron-framed tables. The rest of the room is furnished in much the same style – partly carpeted, partly woodblock floor. Well kept Camerons Lion, Tetleys Mild, Theakstons Best and XB and Youngers Scotch on handpump, and Stowford Press cider; lots of malt whiskies, and cocktails; maybe unobtrusive piped classical music (though none on our own visit); sensibly placed darts, with pool-table, shove-ha'penny, dominoes, cribbage and a fruit machine in a separate new balconied area with more tables, up a few steps; seats outside. The quiet village is surrounded by splendid steep moorland. *(Recommended by Frank Cummins, P L Dale, D and J W, Ian Clay)*

Free house · Licensees Stephen and Frances Colling · Real ale · Meals and snacks · Children in eating area and new balconied area · Occasional Fri jazz or folk rock · Open 11.30–2.30, 6–10.30 · Bedrooms tel Lastingham (075 15) 312; £19 (£23.50B)/£28 (£35B)

White Horse

Above village, 300 yards up Rosedale Chimney Bank – the exhilarating 1-in-3 moorland road over Spaunton Moor to Hutton-le-Hole

Views from the picnic-table sets on the stone front terrace are marvellous – almost as good from the bar, which has a fine collection of china pub tankards hanging above its serving counter, several fox masks, a stuffed heron and peregrine falcon, and various antlers, horns and a bearskin on the stone walls. This friendly beamed room is furnished with red plush cushioned pews salvaged from a church in Wakefield (where the licensees come from), captain's chairs and wooden tables, and the very wide choice of popular home-cooked food often uses ingredients from the inn's 10 acres. It includes open meat sandwiches (£1.60), ploughman's (£1.70 – both these lunchtimes only), mussels in red rather than white wine (£1.80), lasagne (£2.60), steak and kidney or local rabbit pie (£3.40), salads (from £3.40), local game pie or wood-pigeon breasts in game sauce (£3.60) and eight-ounce sirloin steak (£4.95), with children's dishes such as fish fingers (£1.65). Well kept Camerons Lion and Tetleys on handpump, and a good choice of malt whiskies; dominoes, a fruit machine, piped background music. *(Recommended by D and J W)*

Free house · Licensees David and Angela Wilcock · Real ale · Meals and snacks Children if eating (to 8.30) · Open 12–2.30, 6–10.30 (and from 10am for coffee) · Bedrooms tel Lastingham (075 15) 239; £24.50B/£37B

RUNSWICK BAY (N Yorks)   NZ8217 Map 10

Royal

The terrace of this seaside inn and its big-windowed modernised front bar have lovely views down over the village to the sea and the arms of the steep, attractive bay – on a fine summer's day it buzzes with life. At any time there's a cheerful atmosphere inside, and the back bar has nautical bits and pieces, including local lifeboat photographs – also darts back here, and dominoes, cribbage, a fruit machine, maybe piped music. Bar food includes sandwiches, local sausages and chips (£1.70), fresh Whitby cod (£2.50) and in winter home-made soups and curries; well kept John Smiths on handpump. They unfortunately no longer have bedrooms (which were comfortable, and you had enormous breakfasts). *(Recommended by G M Heath, Peter Walker, Ian Clay)*

Free house · Licensee Alan King · Real ale · Meals (weekend lunchtimes) and snacks (lunchtime) · Children in small bar · Open 11–3, 6–11 (12–3, 7–11 in winter)

SETTLE (N Yorks)   SD8264   Map 7
Golden Lion

A65

This is the only coaching-inn we've come across which still has horses stabled in its coachyard, and inside, the lounge bar – a spacious entrance hall – has a surprisingly grand staircase sweeping down through the elegantly beamed high ceiling. There are well spaced easy chairs, sofas, an imposing antique carved settle, and big Windsor armchairs around the gateleg tables, a long-case clock made in Skipton, hunting prints and stags' heads on the partly oak-panelled walls, and a reconstructed inglenook fireplace with an unusual broad chimney-arch. Bar food includes sandwiches (from 50p), soup (65p), home-made pâté (£1.20), home-made meat and potato pie (£1.65), cod (£1.85), home-made steak and kidney pie (£2.25), lamb cutlets (£2.50), gammon and pineapple (£2.65) and roast beef with Yorkshire pudding (£2.85), with children's dishes such as fish fingers. At lunchtime you can have these dishes in the restaurant, which in the evenings has charcoal grills such as kebab (£4.75), steaks (from £4.65) and fresh trout (£5) or salmon (£5.75). Well kept Thwaites Bitter and Mild on handpump, and a good collection of whiskies. The lively public bar has darts, pool, shove-ha'penny, dominoes, cribbage, a fruit machine, space games and a good juke box. Though pets are welcome dogs must be kept on a lead – partly so as not to ruffle the inn's resident cats. *(Recommended by Tim Halstead, Philip Asquith, Keith Myers, Paul West; more reports please)*

Thwaites · Licensees Joan and Bernard Houghton · Real ale · Meals and snacks Children welcome · Open 11–3, 5.30–11 · Bedrooms tel Settle (072 92) 2203; £11/£22

SICKLINGHALL (N Yorks)   SE3648   Map 7
Scotts Arms

Busy and cheerful, with a welcoming atmosphere, the open-plan main bar of this stone village pub keeps some sense of its original rooms with stubs of the old dividing walls left, and seats built in to cosy little alcoves cut in to the main walls. Besides a big inglenook fireplace, there's a curious sort of double-decker fireplace with its upper hearth intricately carved. Bar food includes sandwiches, good home-made hot dishes such as lasagne, chilli con carne, beef curry and steak and kidney pie (all around £2), and chicken, haddock, scampi and so forth; there's also a separate restaurant. Particularly well kept Tetleys Bitter and Mild, Timothy Taylors and Theakstons Best on handpump; darts, dominoes and a fruit machine, and down steps a separate room has pool, space game and another fruit machine. There are tables outside in summer. *(Recommended by Tim Halstead, Andrew Williamson, Philip Asquith, Keith Myers, Paul West)*

Free house · Licensee Richard Wyatt · Real ale · Meals (not Sun lunchtime) and snacks · Children welcome · Open 11–3, 5.30–11

SOUTH ANSTON (S Yorks)   SK5183   Map 7
Loyal Trooper

3 miles from M1 junction 31; village signposted off A57 towards Worksop; pub on Sheffield Road

The main lounge bar of this village pub is a small, friendly room, with Windsor chairs, leatherette seats and leather-cushioned settles by its swirly-plastered walls, which are decorated with brass toasting forks and elaborately worked brass spoons. The oak-panelled serving counter has well kept Tetleys on handpump, and sells cocktails as well as quite a good choice of whiskies. Leading off is another comfortable lounge, set with tables at lunchtime for the bar food, which includes chip butties (35p), freshly made sandwiches (65p – these are the only snacks served at weekends), soup (60p), sausage and onion or four-ounce hamburger (70p), ploughman's (£1.70), salads (£1.70), quiche Lorraine (£1.70), home-made pie (£1.95), gammon with egg or pineapple (£1.95) and sirloin steak (£3.45), with children's dishes such as giant sausage or fish fingers (£1.20). A big and lively public bar has darts, dominoes, cribbage, and a fruit machine in a side lobby. There is a big functions room upstairs, and there is a terrace with tables and cocktail parasols. *(Recommended by M J Hensman)*

Tetleys (Ind Coope) · Licensee Brian Beecroft · Real ale · Meals (lunchtime, not Sun) and snacks (lunchtime) · Children in second lounge · Open 11.30–3, 6–10.30

SOWERBY BRIDGE (W Yorks)   SE0623   Map 7
Moorings

Off Bolton Brow (A58) opposite Ashtree

The atmosphere of this pleasantly converted ex-canal warehouse is quite unusual: the very high ceiling and big windows make for a calm and airy ambience, and it's attractively furnished with tile-top tables, rush-seated stools and fabric-covered seats built against the stripped stone walls (which are decorated with old waterways maps and modern canal pictures). It overlooks the basin where the Calder and Hebble Canal joins the Rochdale Canal, and other old canal buildings here are now crafts workshops and shops. Big openings lead to a family room alongside, similarly furnished and with the same charming view, and there's an upstairs restaurant (Tuesday to Saturday evenings). Bar food includes a lunchtime help-yourself buffet (£2.25–£3.50, depending on which meat you choose), and home-made soup (55p), granary cob sandwiches (from 65p – a good choice such as salami, mature Cheddar, prawn and crab), bacon chop or Cumberland sausage and egg (£2), steak pie, pork goulash, or chicken Kiev (£2.25), and in the evening a charcoal-grilled home-made burger (£3.25). Besides well kept Clarks (from Wakefield) and Youngers Scotch, IPA and No 3, there is a range of some three dozen bottled and canned beers from the Continent (particularly Belgian bottle-conditioned real ales), USA, Australia and Singapore, reasonably priced house wines, and cocktails – including children's specials. Dominoes, soft piped music. There are tables out on a terrace with grass and small trees. (*Recommended by Sue and Len Beattie, A E Uttley, M N Stead, A L Armstrong and others*)

Free house · Licensees Ian Clay and Ed Parker · Real ale · Meals and snacks Children in side room · Open 12–3, 6.30–11 all year; closed 25 Dec

STARBOTTON (N Yorks)   SE9574   Map 7
Fox & Hounds ★

When we last saw this beautifully placed Dales pub it was just getting a refreshing lick of paint from the family who have now taken it over – and who are running it in very much the same way as before. It's snug and welcoming, with a big stone fireplace (and enormous fire in winter) in the small bar, old copper lamps and oil cans hanging from the high beams that support rough unpainted ceiling boards, an antique settle and other solid old-fashioned furniture. An inner room has wheelback chairs and a Gothick chest on its flagstone floor, irons and cooking-pots decorating its beams, flowery curtains hanging from a heavy wooden rail, and a stuffed fox. Good value bar food includes home-made soup (65p), sandwiches (80p), home-made steak and kidney or game pie (£2.95) and trout with almonds (£3.40); well kept Theakstons Best and Old Peculier and Youngers Scotch on handpump; darts, dominoes, maybe piped music. There are sturdy tables and benches in a sheltered corner outside the pretty stone-slab-roofed inn; here you can look out to the hills all around this little hamlet, and listen to the swifts and curlews. (*Recommended by Trevor Williams, Tim Halstead, Philip Asquith, D M Potts, Keith Myers, Paul West and others*)

Free house · Licensees Ann Wilkinson and family · Real ale · Meals and snacks Children in eating area · Open 11–3, 6–11 (11–2.30, 7–10.30 in winter) Bedrooms tel Kettlewell (075 676) 269; £10.50/£21

SUTTON (S Yorks)   SE5512   Map 7
Anne Arms ★

From A1 just S of Barnsdale Bar service area follow Askern, Campsall signpost; Sutton signposted right from Campsall

Memorable for its profuse ornamentation: a throng of toby jugs collected over many years; lots of colourful five-litre and smaller Bavarian drinking steins; oak dressers filled with brightly coloured plates; fruit plates embossed with life-size red apples; latticed glass cases filled with china shepherdesses and the like; wooden figures popping out of a Swiss clock when it chimes the quarter-hours; and a separate room filled with brass and copper. Everything is of a piece with this: goldfish tanks, chintz stools and cushioned seats on the Turkey carpet, 1930s piped music, and a platoon of painted gnomes guarding the rustic tables (there are lots of these) outside this creeper-covered stone house. Good value food includes stuffed ham, gammon, lasagne, quiche or rabbit pie (£1.65), a help-yourself salad buffet, and the trifles, gateaux and meringues that you sort of expect here; friendly efficient service; very popular, particularly with older people. *(Recommended by Richard Cole)*

Free house · Licensee Jonathan Richardson Simm · Meals and snacks · Children in buffet room/snug · Open 10.30–3, 6–10.30

SUTTON HOWGRAVE (N Yorks)　　SE3279　Map 7
White Dog
Village signposted from B6267 about 1 mile W of junction with A1

There are flowers on the polished tables of this pretty village cottage's two main rooms, which are furnished with comfortably cushioned Windsor chairs. There is an open kitchen range on one side of the black-beamed bar, with a welcoming fire in cool weather. Good bar lunches include sandwiches (from 65p), home-made soup (95p), omelettes (from £1.50), pâté (£1.95), seafood hot-pot or chilli con carne (£2.25), game pie (£3.50) and sirloin steak (£5.50). A small evening dining-room with a supper licensing extension (bookings only) serves meals with main dishes such as chicken breasts stuffed with prawns and crabmeat or game pie (£6.95) and steaks (from £6.75). The pub stands at the end of this little farming hamlet, by a peaceful green with field maples and sycamores. Its upper windows are almost hidden in summer by the flowers in its window-boxes, though the jungly Russian vine we mentioned in the last edition has had a setback (with mice gnawing its roots). There are picnic-table sets among flowerbeds on the grass beside it. *(Recommended by D W Roberts, D A Angless)*

Free house · Licensees Pat and Basil Bagnall · Meals and snacks (lunchtime, not Mon); dining-room bookings tel Melmerby (076 584) 404 · Open 12–2.30, 7–10.30; closed Sun evening, Mon, and 1st half Feb

TADCASTER (N Yorks)　　SE4843　Map 7
Angel & White Horse
Bridge Street

The pub's coachyard is the stables for the Sam Smiths team of dappled grey shire horses – from the bar you can see Barrel, Hogshead, Bitter and Sovereign peering out of their stalls across the neat yard. With the Old Brewery itself within rolling distance – they do brewery tours at arranged times: Tadcaster (0937) 832225 – the Sam Smiths on handpump here is well kept and reasonably priced. An open-plan series of rooms opens off the servery: naturally darkening oak panelling in the main back part, with well made cushioned seats built against it, oak stools, Windsor armchairs and an open fire with an oil painting of a dappled grey shire horse above it. Good value bar food includes soup, sandwiches, Yorkshire pudding with onion gravy, Welsh rarebit, shepherd's pie, beef casserole, local recipes such as rabbit pie or bacon and egg pie, and a help-yourself salad bar; juke box, and collect four. There is also a separate restaurant. *(Recommended by J S McCallum, Thelma Cowlishaw, ILP, Tim Halstead; up-to-date reports on the new management please)*

Sam Smiths · Meals and snacks · No nearby daytime parking · Open 10.30–3, 6–10.30

TAN HILL (N Yorks)   NY8907   Map 10
Tan Hill

Unclassified moorland road from Keld to Reeth, N of B6720 (on boundary with Durham)

Isolated in its glorious moorland setting, this – at 1,732 feet – is England's highest inn. Grouse and blackcock calling, water tumbling, but otherwise no sound except in the brief summer tourist season and perhaps during the nearby hill sheep fair in May. It has been through several hands in the last few years, and unfortunately the ex-editor of the Campaign for Real Ale's excellent *Good Beer Guide*, who bought it in 1984, has now had to give it up – we are keeping it in as a main entry for its outstanding position, and hope for good news of it from readers. It is simply furnished, with wooden chairs and some panel-backed and cushioned stone walls seats; darts, pool, dominoes, cribbage, a fruit machine and a juke box. *(Recommended by H E Emson; more reports please)*

Free house · Real ale · Meals and snacks · Children have been welcome · Open 11–3, 6–10.30 · Bedrooms tel Teesdale (0833) 28246; around £10/£16

THRUSCROSS (N Yorks)   SE1558   Map 7
Stone House Inn

Village signposted from A59 Harrogate–Skipton at Blubberhouses, or off B6265 Grassington–Pateley Bridge at Greenhow Hill; OS Sheet 104 reference 159587

The two communicating bar rooms of this cheerful moorland pub have cushioned built-in settles, dark squared panelling, lots of brass blowlamps, old conserve jars, ginger-beer bottles and so forth on a high shelf, a stuffed stoat and black-faced sheep's head; one side has a flowery carpet and wood-burning stove, the other flagstones and an old-fashioned kitchen range (with a couple of cats dozing by it on our visit). Popular bar food using fresh ingredients includes sandwiches (from 70p), soup (75p), pâté (£1.60), ploughman's (£1.75), local sausage with hot mustard sauce (£2.45), steak and kidney pie, fresh grilled sardines or seafood platter (£2.75), and sirloin minute steak (£3.45); there is a separate restaurant where dinner can be booked Monday to Saturday. Well kept Theakstons Best, XB and Old Peculier and Youngers No 3 on handpump; piped music. Tables outside in front are sheltered by attractive stone bays planted with geraniums and other flowers. *(Recommended by B Priestley, I J Clay)*

Free house · Licensees Ian and Amanda Taylor · Real ale · Meals and snacks (not Sun evening); restaurant bookings tel Blubberhouses (094 388) 226 · Children in eating area and restaurant · Open 10.30–3, 6–11

WATH-IN-NIDDERDALE (N Yorks)   SE1467   Map 7

Sportsman's Arms

To get the best of the young chef's excellent cooking in this friendly country inn, you should really stay overnight and enjoy a leisurely dinner – perhaps including hot avocado with mushrooms or warmed chicken liver pâté in a reduced glazed raspberry vinegar sauce, then pink and tender duck in a fig and orange sauce or lightly cooked local river trout with fresh lime and capers (main courses are mostly around £7.50 – not cheap, but delicious and served with style). Vegetables are particularly good. There's a very sensible and extensive wine list, and service is attentive. Bar lunches, much simpler, are good too, though not cheap: home-made soup, Cheddar and red Leicester ploughman's or chicken liver pâté (£1.90), bacon, egg, sausage and black pudding (£3.10, not Sundays), locally caught trout sauté or smoked (around £3.25) and sirloin steak (£5.50, not Sundays), with specials such as rarebit cooked with bacon as well as cheese, or chicken hot-pot. Tetleys, Theakstons Best and Youngers Scotch are kept under pressure. The comfortable blond-panelled bar has big gamebird prints on Madras cotton wallhangings, and dominoes and maybe piped music. There's a quiet lounge with easy chairs. The old-fashioned bedrooms are comfortable, and this is a nice peaceful place to stay, with owls hooting at night, and in the morning perhaps a short walk through the wood behind the inn up to the sheep pastures above Gouthwaite Reservoir. *(Recommended by W A Rinaldi-Butcher, D A Angless and others)*

Free house · Licensee J R Carter · Meals and snacks (lunchtime) · Children welcome · Open 12–2.30, 7–11 · Bedrooms tel Harrogate (0423) 711306; £16/£32

The Star, Harome

WELBURN (N Yorks)   SE7268   Map 7
Crown & Cushion

Village signposted from A64 York–Malton

Close to Castle Howard, this old stone inn in a quiet village has been popular for its bar food, such as sandwiches (from 70p), soup (85p), ploughman's (£1.65), pâté (£1.75), steak and kidney pie (£1.95), salads (from £2.20), half a chicken (£3.20), lamb cutlets (£3.45) and eight-ounce sirloin steak (£5.20), with daily specials such as chilli con carne (£2.45) or plaice (£3.20). The two connecting rooms of the lounge have tapestried small settles, stools and wheelback chairs around wooden tables on a patterned red carpet, little pictures between strips of black wood on the cream walls, high shelves of plates, and open fires in winter. Well kept Camerons Lion and Strongarm on handpump; darts, a juke box and fruit machine in the public bar; comfortable bedrooms. As we went to press we learned that the licensees were planning to leave at around the time this book is published – it seems unlikely that there will be any major changes in such a well established local inn, and we hope for good news from readers! *(Recommended by BHP, PLC; up-to-date reports please)*

Camerons · Real ale · Meals and snacks (may be limited Tues) · Children if eating (lunchtime) · Bedrooms tel Whitwell-on-the-Hill (065 381) 304; £12/£24

WENTWORTH (S Yorks)   SK3898   Map 7
Rockingham Arms

B6090; 3 miles from M1 junction 36; village signposted from A6135; can also be reached from junction 35 via Thorpe

The comfortable and neatly kept main bar of this popular country inn, its partly stripped stone walls decorated with hunting photographs and prints, has Windsor chairs around copper-topped tables. A quieter little room with small pictures on its walls opens off this. Bar food includes sandwiches (50p), ploughman's (85p), shepherd's pie (£1), steak pie (£1.85) and steaks – sirloin (£3) or rump (£4.35); well kept Clarks and Theakstons Best and Old Peculier on handpump; dominoes, cribbage, and a space game. The big lawn is attractive in summer, with its own bowling green, and towards the end of the week The Barn is popular and lively: black paintwork and whitewashed walls, high eaves, and neat barn stalls to make for some intimacy around the tables – but the main point here is the jazz (Wednesday), country and western (Thursday) and folk music (Friday). *(More reports please)*

Free house · Licensee Cyril Ayscough · Real ale · Meals and snacks (lunchtime, not Sat or Sun) · Open 11–3, 6–10.30 · Bedrooms tel Barnsley (0226) 742075; £10 (£15B)/£20 (£28B)

WEST TANFIELD (N Yorks)   SE2678   Map 7
Bruce Arms   [*illustrated on page 705*]

A6108 (a quiet road) N of Ripon

There's a relaxed family atmosphere in the two cosy and intimate bars of this unspoilt and attractive old village inn. The front bar has unusual open stone bread ovens beside its log fire, a cushioned curved-back antique settle, a carved oak armchair, red plush cushioned Jacobean-style seats (perhaps with the retriever – called Bruce – sitting on one), and spindleback chairs around rustic tables; the back room is more or less similar, with a stuffed owl. Cheap bar food includes pasties (50p), sandwiches (from 60p, bacon and egg 75p), home-made soup (60p), burger (60p), shepherd's pie (£1), ploughman's (£1.20), chicken and mushroom or steak and onion pie (£1.80), grilled ham and eggs (£3.50) and steaks (from sirloin, £3.50); well kept Theakstons Best and Old Peculier on handpump; darts, dominoes, cribbage, a juke box and space game, and – sharing a lobby with an attractive pew that has fine carved finials – a fruit machine. Tables on a flagstoned side terrace are sheltered by roses and flowering shrubs, with a splendid pear-tree trained against the inn's wall. The back stables are still in use. *(Recommended by Tim Halstead, Philip Asquith, Keith Myers, Paul West)*

Free house · Licensee J I Airth · Real ale · Meals and snacks · Open 10.30– 2.30, 5.30–11; closed Mon lunchtime except bank hols · Bedrooms tel Bedale (0677) 70325; £12/£22

WIDDOP (W Yorks)   SD9333 Map 7
Pack Horse

The Ridge; from A646 on W side of Hebden Bridge, turn off at Heptonstall signpost (as it's a sharp turn coming out of Hebden Bridge road, signposts direct you around a turning circle), then follow Slack and Widdop signposts; can also be reached from Nelson and Colne, on high, pretty road; OS Sheet 103 reference 952317

High on the moors and miles from anywhere, this traditional pub's central bar still has regular customers clustered around it, as well as the many hikers (who are asked to leave boots and packs outside) – the Pennine Way passes quite close by. The walls are decorated with duck and hunting prints, and photographs and engineering drawings of Enoch Tempest's remarkable three-feet-gauge Dawson City railway that was built for the construction of the Wallshaw Dean Reservoir a bit north of here. There are heavy curly-armed settles, plush (but not plushy) seats, captain's chairs and stools around cast-iron-framed tables, stripped stone walls and panelling, and some window seats looking out over the moors. There are open fires in winter. Good straightforward bar food includes wholemeal bread sandwiches (from 65p, double-deckers from £1.20, open sandwiches with crusty bread from £1.30), beefburger (£1.50), ploughman's with ham and cheese (£1.75), lasagne (£1.80), salads (from £2.25), steak and kidney pie (£2.75), steak sandwich (£2.70) and steaks (from eight-ounce sirloin, £4.25), with summer weekday specials – be prepared for a wait on summer weekends when it's crowded. Well kept Thwaites and Youngers on handpump, and some good malt whiskies – including Macallan (they have a collection of old Macallan advertisements). There are seats outside. *(Recommended by Sue and Len Beattie, Ian Clay)*

Free house · Licensee Peter Jackson · Real ale · Meals and snacks (not Mon evenings in winter) · Children welcome · Open 12–2.30, 7–11 (7.30–11 in winter); closed winter weekday lunchtimes except Christmas week

WIGHILL (N Yorks)   SE4746   Map 7
White Swan ★

Village signposted from Tadcaster; also easily reached from A1 Wetherby bypass – take Thorpe Arch Trading Estate turnoff, then follow Wighill signposts; OS Sheet 105 reference 476468

The central bar area of this welcoming and unspoilt village pub serves a small lobby with a carved two-seat oak settle, and three or four separate rooms attractively furnished by this family over the half-century that they've kept the pub. At the back, for instance, there's a very deep square-sided Second Empire cane sofa (in need of recaning), leather bucket seats and a curly-armed mahogany settle, small sporting prints and a dark oil painting, a long-case clock and – as in all the other rooms – a coal fire. The bar snacks are good value: well filled sandwiches (from 50p), ploughman's with a choice of cheeses (£1.20 – 30p extra for two cheeses), giant crusty-bread sandwiches (£1.50), and salads (up to £3), with soup on cold winter days. But they firmly see the food as being subsidiary to their well kept Stones and Theakstons Best, XB and Old Peculier on handpump; piped radio; frog machine (non-gambling fruit machine) in the family room; a dignified but friendly dog (mainly golden labrador) called Wooster. There are picnic-table sets in the sheltered back yard, by the old stable-block. *(Recommended by Tim Halstead, Philip Asquith, Keith Myers, Paul West)*

Free house · Licensee Peter Swale · Real ale · Snacks (lunchtime) · Children in rooms without bars if with adults (not after 8pm) · Open 12–3, 6–10.30

YORK (N Yorks)   SE5951   Map 7
Black Swan

Peaseholme Green; inner ring road, E side of centre; the inn has a good car park

One of the city's most interesting buildings, this was built over 500 years ago for a family of rich merchants who included York's Lord Mayor and, later, Queen Elizabeth's jeweller. It was quite plain and plastered until complete restoration before the last war revealed the splendid jettied and timbered façade and original lead-latticed windows in the twin gables. Though the furnishings in the well kept bars are by no means as old, there's a good atmosphere here, and unusually for a city pub it has two open fires going in winter. Points of interest include the fine staircase and an upstairs room fully panelled in oak, with an antique tiled fireplace. Bar food includes baked potatoes (from 60p, with home-made curry £1), soup (60p), sandwiches in white or granary bread (from 60p, toasted from 80p), chip butty (70p), beefburger or hot bacon sandwich, ham and egg pie, ploughman's with ham and cheese (£1.60) and daily specials such as steamed beef pudding (£2.20); Bass on handpump, under a light CO_2 blanket; dominoes, fruit machine, maybe piped music. There is a separate restaurant. *(Recommended by S V Bishop, Tim Halstead, Philip Asquith, Keith Myers, Paul West, P T Young)*

Bass · Licensee Robert Atkinson · Meals and snacks (lunchtime) · Children welcome · Folk night Thurs · Open 11–3, 5.30–11 all year · Bedrooms tel York (0904) 25236; £25/£30

King's Arms

King's Staithe; left bank of Ouse just below Ouse Bridge; in the evening you should be able to get a parking space right outside, turning down off Clifford Street; otherwise there's a ¼-mile walk

On its cobbled riverside terrace, this ancient pub gets flooded so often that its 'cellar' is above ground in an adjacent building which used to be a mortuary (hence, perhaps, the ghost which credulous customers say they've seen). The pub has a flagstoned floor, bowed black beams, bare brick and stone walls, and good thick cushions on the stone window seats that look out over the river. Attractively priced Sam Smiths on handpump; good value bar food includes sandwiches, ploughman's or pâté (from £1.40), garlic mushrooms (£1.50), savoury quiche, steak and kidney pie, curry (£1.75), a daily special (£1.75–£2) and salads (£1.90); a fruit machine, space game and a juke box. In such a fine spot by the river, it does get crowded in summer. *(Recommended by Lee Goulding, Ian Clay, Jane English, A Darrock Harkness, P T Young, Nick Dawson, Alison Hayward)*

Sam Smiths · Licensee I Winterbottom · Real ale · Meals and snacks (not Sat evening) · Open 11–3, 5.30–11 all year

Lendal Cellars

Corner of Lendal and St Helen's Square; evening parking easy, daytime parking a walk away

One of the handsome conversions with which Whitbreads have been impressing us this last year or so: broad-vaulted medieval cellars carefully spotlit to show the brickwork, a floor of stone setts, simple hand-crafted-looking wooden tables and a clutch of old casks, in a network of interconnecting alcoves with steps down to a lower area. It's warmly heated and well kept. Whitbreads Trophy on handpump, and fresh coffee or tea by the pot; a lunchtime food bar serving pâté (£1.20), ploughman's (£1.25), home-made quiche (£1.65), shepherd's pie (£1.70), chilli con carne (£1.75), ham or beef salad (£1.95) and home-made lasagne (£2.25); on our visit loudish well reproduced funky music. Fairly empty early on a weekday evening, it really needs the crowds which frequent it at lunchtime or later on to give it atmosphere. You go in past a lifesize figure of an injudicious wine-taster, sleeping it off in a hammock. *(Recommended by Fergus Bastock)*

Whitbreads · Licensee Patrick Fitzgerald · Real ale · Meals and snacks (lunchtime) · Open 11–3, 5.30–11 all year

We checked prices with the pubs as we went to press in summer 1985. They should hold until around spring 1986, when our experience suggests that you can expect an increase of around 10p in the £.

Olde Starr

Stonegate; pedestrians-only street in centre, far from car parks

Off one of York's prettiest old streets, this pub has a Victorian layout and a lively atmosphere; its courtyard tables have a view of the minster. A 'gallows' sign stretches right across the street (we know of only two or three others: they were generally banned when coach and waggon loads became so high that they were obstructed). The little courtyard is a lively place on a summer's day, and up above the chimneys and tiled roofs of York's medieval Shambles you can see the minster's towers. Inside, beamed rooms ramble happily around with some little oak Victorian settles and heavy cast-iron tables, a recreated oil-lamp-style panelled Victorian parlour bar, and a stained-glass hatch servery with a copper-topped bar counter; well kept Camerons Best on electric pump. Food from a separate snack counter includes soup (60p), sandwiches (70p), ploughman's (£1.50), burgers (from £1.50), shepherd's pie (£1.60), a hot daily special (from £1.75), salads (from £2.25), eight-ounce sirloin steak (£3.95) and home-made fruit pie (60p), with a Sunday roast. A games room has darts, dominoes, cribbage, and a fruit machine, and there may be piped music. (*Recommended by Martyn Quinn, Tim Halstead, Barrie Pepper, Philip Asquith, Eirlys Roberts, Keith Myers, Paul West*)

Camerons · Licensee R W Koetsier · Real ale · Meals and snacks (lunchtime) Children in parlour bar and games room · Open 11–3, 5.30–11 all year

Red Lion

Merchantgate; not marked on the usual miniguide map: between Fossgate and Piccadilly; nearest day-time parking probably at museum, but parking outside easy at night

This pretty timbered house is inside attractively stripped back to Tudor brickwork in some places; there's a relaxed atmosphere, with its rambling little low-beamed rooms simply furnished, now with green velour seats against the part-panelling, old cast-iron-framed tables, some big Windsor armchairs, an old-fashioned kitchen range in one room, a coal-effect fire in a nice arched brick hearth in another. There are quite a few early photographs of the pub. Besides snacks and sandwiches, they do meals in the summer season only. John Smiths on handpump; good juke box (or piped music), darts, dominoes and a fruit machine. Outside, there's one of the few city pub gardens around here. (*Recommended by Tim Halstead, Philip Asquith, Keith Myers, Paul West*)

Imperial Inns (Courage) · Licensee N O Bailey · Meals and snacks · Open 11–3, 5.30–11 all year

---

Lucky Dip

Besides the fully inspected pubs, you might like to try these Lucky Dips recommended and described by readers (if you do, please send us reports):

ADDINGHAM [SE0749], *Craven Heifer*: food varied, with a reasonable and interesting choice – also arrives quickly with attentive waitress; good beer –

Websters Yorkshire, Tetleys; comfortable, lots of seats and well looked after by welcoming staff *(John and Pam Mason)*

APPLETREEWICK [SE0560], *Craven Arms*: friendly atmosphere in clean pub with good food and drink *(Dr and Mrs M Ferguson, Catherine Roffe)*; New: interesting and unusual – a no-smoking pub *(Bob Rendle, A Saunders, Derrick Turner, LYM)*

ARNCLIFFE [SD9473], *Falcon*: simple family-run inn charmingly set on moorland village green, near fine walking country; Youngers real ale, bar snacks; bedrooms *(LYM, Janet Williams, Susie Boulton)*

ASKRIGG [SD9591], *Crown*: food good value in comfortably but not indulgently modernised Dales pub with fair Youngers Scotch on handpump *(J Dewhirst)*; [Market Square] *Kings Arms*: food and service first class; bedrooms good value *(Mr and Mrs E A W Long, Mr and Mrs J R Tooke, J and R Gunning)*

ASKWITH [SD1648], *Black Horse*: food in attached restaurant good; bar menu reasonably good; well appointed and pleasant service; in a beautiful spot *(T F Redman)*

AUSTERFIELD [SK6694], *Austerfield Manor*: new purpose-built pub with very mixed clientele; old people and younger business women at lunch, young parents early evening and young couples late evening; masses of room, built-in food bars, restaurant upstairs; well cooked food *(ILP)*

AYSGARTH [SE0088], *Palmer Flatt*: modernised moorland village inn with several bars, from ancient flagstoned monastic room at back to bustling modern games room; fishing rights, campsite, close to Aysgarth waterfalls and carriage museum; bedrooms *(LYM)*

BAILDON [Prod Lane; SE1539], *Old Glen House*: friendly free house with three bars; stone walls and pitched black and white beams, big fireplace, copper-topped bar; conservatory family room, terrace restaurant; tea-room open outside licensing hours; summer evening barbecues *(J A C Edwards)*

BAINBRIDGE [SD9390], *Rose & Crown*: comfortable inn attractively placed in moorland village, but up for sale as we went to press *(LYM, Anon)*

BARDSEY [SE3643], *Bingley Arms*: food good with wide choice; well kept Tetleys beer; historic building with terraced gardens *(Dr and Mrs M Ferguson)*

BARKISLAND [SE0520], *Fleece*: decent choice of well kept real ales in comfortable pub on moors edge; food includes Tuesday spit-roasts, traditional jazz on Sunday afternoons, and disco-bar – open till small hours *((BB, Peter and Carolyn Clarke)*

BIRSTALL [SE2226], *Black Bull*: pleasant if unspectacular, with wood panelling and generally tasteful decorations *(Tim Halstead)*

BLAKELEY RIDGE [SE6996], *Lion*: old stone inn with lovely moorland views, popular with walkers and hikers; restaurant (good Sunday lunch) and bedrooms *(Doug Kennedy)*

BOLTON PERCY [SE5341], *Crown*: good food with cook-your-own steaks on some evenings in attractive terraced garden; excellent village pub with period interior, lively atmosphere, decent beer *(Michael Powell)*

BRADFORD [Low Moor; SE1633], *British Queen*: interesting, attractive old pub *(Maria Glot)*; [Preston Stret] *Fighting Cock*: basic pub with huge choice of real ales and ciders – in a run-down area but no fear of muggers; gets packed in the evenings *(J A C Edwards)*; [Kent Street] *Jacobs Well*: small but (at lunchtime) busy Tetleys house with well kept ale and good bar snacks – preserved while all around has been knocked down *(J A C Edwards)*; [Oak Avenue, Manningham] *Oakleigh*: high-ceilinged Victorian mansion; real ale *(Maria Glot)*; [Manningham Lane] *Royal Standard*: classic Victorian façade, ornate etched glass, tiled-floor mosaic entrance, mirrors; full of potential *(Maria Glot, Tim Halstead)*

BROUGHTON [SD9351], *Bull*: imaginative bar snacks and friendly service in well run pub, comfortable and smartly modernised; restaurant *(LYM, Dr P H Walker)*

BYLAND ABBEY [SE5579], *Abbey*: though not smart – austere, almost spooky – looked interesting; opposite abbey *(Patrick Stapley)*

CALDER GROVE [SE3116], *Navigation*: canalside garden and simple food, ¼ mile from M1 junction 39 *(John DuBois, LYM)*

CARLTON [SE0684], *Foresters Arms*: flagstoned bar with open fire, old gnarled settles and tables, friendly service; good Youngers on handpump, good value food in restaurant (doubles as afternoon tea-room *(Jon Dewhirst)*

CLOUGHTON [TA0194], *Blacksmiths Arms*: a real pub, owned by Duchy of Lancaster; busy, spruce; food cooked to order so hot and fresh *(Eileen Broadbent)*

COLLINGHAM [SE3946], *Old Star*: friendly pub with cheerful staff, well kept Theakstons and Whitbreads on handpump, good bar snacks, restaurant *(Simon Reevell)*

CONSTABLE BURTON [SE1791], *Wyvill Arms*: fine stone farmhouse converted to pub, run by active, cheerful young people; elegantly painted plaster ceiling in one room, beams elsewhere, warm log fires; good beer, wide choice of bar meals; restaurant *(Anon)*

DEWSBURY [Eightlands], [SE2523], *Eightlands Well*: converted recently to a pub and well decorated; jolly atmosphere with live entertainment; pub lunches, real ale; terrace *(Margaret Harrison)*

DONCASTER [Frenchgate; SE5703], *White Swan*: excellent Wards Sheffield Best; lively, friendly town centre pub with tallest tap-room bar in UK; snacks *(S Gee)*

EASINGWOLD [Market Place; SE5270], *George*: home-made bar food – steak and kidney pie, chicken ham and mushroom pie, real chips; good beer; bedrooms *(Anon)*

EAST AYTON]Main Street; TA0085], *Denison Arms*: food (with daily specials) and handpumped Camerons real ale good; Country and Western music on Friday evening and piano sing-along on Wednesday and Saturday evenings *(Mike Haworth, Chris Openshaw, Dave McMillan)*

EAST MARTON [SD9051], *Cross Keys*: interesting old-fashioned furnishings and good range of well kept ales in pub quite close to Leeds and Liverpool Canal *(LYM, Dr H B Cardwell, Sue and Len Beattie)*

EAST WITTON [SE1586], *Blue Lion*: almost unique, like walking into a time-warp; beer served on a tray from a back kitchen, old settles and chairs in the single room, very friendly landlord; always quiet (no music, no food), serves only handpulled Theakstons Mild *(Jon Dewhirst)*; *Coverbridge*: friendly and genuine old wayside pub with a homely atmosphere and well cooked substantial bar meals; children welcome *(Anon)*

EDENTHORPE [Thorne Road; SE6206], *Ridgewood*: high standard of beer including real ale; bar snacks; ideal local *(M Connor)*

EGTON [NZ8106], *Horseshoe*: warm welcome and open fire in low-beamed moorland village pub popular for fried food and grills *(LYM, Ian Clay)*

ESCRICK [SE6343], *Black Bull*: Inexpensive varied bar snacks – especially salads; well kept beer *(D C Turner)*

ESHOLT [Main Street; SE1840], *Commercial Inn*: pleasant pub in attractive village; exterior used for The Woolpack in the *Emmerdale Farm* TV series *(Maria Glot, Tim Halstead)*

FELIXKIRK [SE4785], *Carpenters Arms*: tasty food in friendly pub; good atmosphere (and occasional visits from James Herriott) *(Jenny Newman)*

FOLLIFOOT [SE3452], *Lascelles Arms*: pub which has kept its individuality, pleasantly located in village of character *(Philip Asquith)*; *Ratcliffe Arms*: somewhat tarted up and perhaps best avoided at busy times, but a nice pub in attractive village *(Keith Myers)*

FULNECK [Bankhouse Lane; SE2132], *Bankhouse*: popular pub with copper and brass, on site of eighteenth-century Moravian settlement and Moravian HQ in England; well kept Youngers *(Paul West)*

GAYLES [NZ1207], *Bay Horse*: simply furnished farm pub with lovely views but uncertain opening times *(BB)*

GOOSE EYE [SE0340], *Goose Eye Mint Bar*: brews its own beer; smart; with separate restaurant; opens fairly late *(Maria Glot)*

GRANGE MOOR [SE2216], *Kaye Arms*: food includes imaginative bar snacks; friendly waitress service; immaculate pub *(D G Bland)*

GREAT OUSEBURN [SE4562],*Three Horseshoes*: food includes huge inexpensive steaks, served till late, in friendly pub (used as local by RAF officers from Linton-on-Ouse) in quiet, scenic village *(A Darroch Harkness)*

GREENHOW HILL [SE1164], *Miners Arms*: food tasty and varied – juicy sandwiches; children's portions; separate eating area for children/families; friendly landlord, well kept beer; bedrooms *(John and Pam Mason)*

HALIFAX [SE0924], *Shears*: unique for its setting at bottom of satanic mill valley; reasonably tasteful decoration, worth a visit if nearby (for pub location see OS Sheet 104 reference 097241) *(Tim Halstead)*

HARDEN [SE0838], *Malt Shovel*: nice food in this welcoming sixteenth-century pub with open fires and real ale on handpump; children welcome; bedrooms *(K S McCallum)*

HARDROW [SD8791], *Green Dragon*: pub has garden access to Britain's highest single-drop waterfall; bedrooms *(Ian Clay, LYM)*

HARROGATE [Montpellier Gardens; SE3155], *Drum & Monkey*: food reasonably priced and very popular in small Edwardian-style pub which is essentially a very good seafood restaurant; extremely busy *(Anon)*

nr HARROGATE [Pannal; SE3155], *Platform One*: converted railway station, almost unique in that station itself is still in use on main Leeds–Harrogate line (for pub location see OS Sheet 104 reference 307514) *(Philip Asquith)*; [Whinney Lane, Pannal] *Squinting Cat*: popular and lively old pub with well kept Tetleys; rather trendy (for pub location see O S Sheet 104 reference 296517) *(Keith Myers, Roger Entwistle)*

HARTOFT END [SE7593], *Blacksmiths Arms*: friendly, well run old moorland pub with good bar snacks, and outstanding Sunday lunch with traditional roast beef *(Anon)*

HAWORTH [West Lane; SE0337], *Old White Lion*: friendly welcome in pleasant bar with character; good food in dining-room; comfortable bedrooms *(L W Thomas)*

HEPTONSTALL [SD9827], *White Lion*: quiet stone pub in steep and very attractive moorside village; grills, Duttons real ale; simple bedrooms *(LYM)*

HORNBY [NZ3505], *Grange Arms*: friendly local with fairly priced food and good Theakstons on handpump; bar and lounge/dining-room with open coal/log fire, darts; no music *(E J Coates, Jon Dewhirst)*

HORTON IN RIBBLESDALE [SD8172], *Crown*: remote pub, handy for Pennine Way; food with good choice and reasonable prices; excellent beer; bedrooms *(K W Lomas, Wayne Rossiter, Jeff Cousins)*

HOVINGHAM [SE6775], *Worsley Arms*: food in back bar at lunchtime recommended, particularly pâté and pies – though this is really a hotel; bedrooms *(W A Rinaldi-Butcher)*

HUDDERSFIELD [Lockwood; SE1416], *Shoulder of Mutton*: classic West Riding town pub, with three small rooms; one for darts, dominoes and other games, upstairs pool-room, central bar with Golden Oldies juke box; wide range of real ales; nicely placed at end of small cobbled street *(Jon Dewhirst)*

HUDSWELL [NZ1400], *George & Dragon*: food includes good home-cooked bar meals; small country pub atmosphere with excellent service, darts and dominoes; garden overlooks Swale valley; Richmond Folk Club here *(J R Glover)*

ILKLEY [Skipton Road; SE1147], *Listers Arms*: decent beers and friendly service in solid inn with basement nightclub; bedrooms *(F G Barnard, Mark Buxton, LYM)*; [19 Church Street] *Sangster's Wine Bar*: good food and quality wines at moderate prices *(Dr H B Cardwell)*

KETTLEWELL [SD9772], *Bluebell*: well kept real ales, bar food and restaurant in simply furnished Wharfedale village inn with knocked-through bar; being sold last year; bedrooms *(LYM, David Symes, Anon)*; *Kings Head*: lively and cheerful, Youngers real ales, pool-table; near church; bedrooms *(David Symes, BB)*; *Racehorses*: quiet and sedate open-plan hotel bar, comfortable and well furnished, serves well kept Tetleys, Websters, Moorhouses and Youngers real ales; bedrooms *(BB, David Symes)*

KILNHURST [SK4697], *Ship*: food at reasonable prices, lunchtime and evenings *(R Merrills)*

KIRKBYMOORSIDE [SE6987], *Black Swan*: picturesque and lively, wide choice of bar snacks, Camerons real ale, open all day Wednesday; bedrooms simple *(LYM)*

733

LANGTHWAITE [NZ0003], *Red Lion*: useful walkers' pub, and cosy; pleasant surroundings near river in Dales village; beers include Old Peculier and Newcastle Original; reasonable food, friendly landlord; seats outside; no machines *(Philip Blaxill, Trevor Williams)*

LEEDS [Arkwright Street, Armley Road; SE3033], *Albion*: well restored, fine building *(Tim Halstead)*; [North Street] *Eagle*: pub-goers' pub which was popular for its wide range of real ales – now Sam Smiths alone, but just as well kept as ever; live music some nights, attracts students *(LYM, Tim Halstead, J A C Edwards, D W Roberts)*; [Town Street] *Nags Head*: cheerful local with well kept Sam Smiths and good value robust food; on the way to Harewood *(Alan Carter and Lesley Foote, LYM)*; *Town Hall Tavern*: popular at lunchtime with lawyers and barristers; comfortable and civilised; good beer, especially Castle Eden *(David Symes)*; [Kirkstall Road] *Vesper Gate*: sturdy stone pub overlooking the abbey; recently refurbished; family room, separate restaurant, quiet patio at rear; well kept handpumped Bass beers *(Lee Goulding)*; *Victoria*: grand Victorian pub, renovated and restored; court visitors by day, concert-goers at night; Tetleys *(Paul West)*

LEYBURN [Market Place; SE1191], *Golden Lion*: friendly village pub with no pretentions; fair range of home-made bar lunches with generous helpings at reasonable prices; bedrooms *(Peter Walker)*; *Sandpiper*: warm friendly atmosphere, well stocked bar at reasonable prices, good, sometimes unorthodox bar meals; a few yards from market square *(Anon)*

LOCKTON [SE8490], *Fox & Rabbit*: bustling family pub on fast moors road; well kept Camerons real ales, good value simple food, children's room and seats outside or in sun-lounge *(LYM)*

LONG MARSTON [SE5051], *Sun*: Sam Smiths pub; well kept real ale, always in wooden barrels; wide choice of bar food, also at weekends *(D W Roberts)*

LONG PRESTON [SD8358], *Boars Head*: extremely friendly welcome in big pub with lots of plates on textured wallpaper, and fish tanks in lounge; bar snacks, good Youngers Scotch on handpump *(Sue and Len Beattie)*

LUDDENDEN [SE0426], *Lord Nelson*: cheerful modernised eighteenth-century local with interesting features, where Branwell Brontë borrowed books; in attractive very steep village *(LYM)*

MEXBOROUGH [SE4800], *Ferry Boat*: old-fashioned with some traditional furnishings, lively and friendly atmosphere, quite near canal *(LYM)*

NEWHOLM [NZ8611], *Beehive*: long, low, snug pub with seats on grass terrace; good value food, well kept beer *(C B M Gregory, Patrick Walker, Peter Walker, H B Smith, LYM)*

NEWTON-ON-OUSE [SE5160], *Dawnay Arms*: friendly and welcoming, with quick and tasty bar food, good restaurant; fine site next to the Ouse *(A Darroch Harkness, Alasdair Humphrey)*

NORTH RIGTON [SE0748], *Square & Compass*: wide range of food in large portions; plush and comfortable bar; beer on handpumps Tetley-Walkers and Youngers Scotch; children if quiet *(John and Pam Mason)*

OTLEY [Bondgate; SE2045], *Junction*: bustling real ale pub with surprisingly interesting interior, in market town with lots of other pubs (for pub location see OS Sheet 104 reference 204454) *(Tim Halstead)*; *Spite*: used to be The Roebuck; food recommended *(Philip Asquith)*

OXENHOPE [SE0335], *Waggon & Horses*: good ploughman's in moorland pub; fleeces on stone walls *(LYM)*

PICKERING [18 Birdgate; SE7984], *Black Swan*: warm and friendly with sparkling brass and copper; generous servings of food with good meat at reasonable prices *(Eileen Broadbent)*; [Westgate] *Sun*: small locals' pub, handpulled Tetleys; friendly welcome *(Andrew Armstrong)*

QUEENSBURY [SE1030], *Old Raggalds*: good, interesting, and has restaurant; children's room *(Maria Glot)*

RICHMOND [Market Place; NZ1801], *Castle Tavern*: Victorian décor with stuffed birds; food in bar at lunchtime recommended – includes pheasant and pigeon *(C Worsick)*

RIPPONDEN [SE0419], *Royal Hotel*: good food in spacious well run pub hotel with comfortable bars, decent beer, willing service *(P J Taylor)*

ROBIN HOOD'S BAY [Station Road; NZ9505], *Victoria*: food reasonably priced from a relatively wide menu; warm welcome, pleasant, well kept; bedrooms *(Roger Bellingham)*

ROECLIFFE [SE3766], *Crown*: fine ales, good bar lunches and restaurant in exceptional family-run village pub *(John Renwick)*

ROTHERHAM [Broom Lane; SK4393], *The Limes*: lunchtime snacks, well kept Youngers real ales and free nuts in plush bar of quiet suburban hotel; separate restaurant; bedrooms cheapish for area *(BB, Alan Thompson)*

SAXTON [SE4736], *Greyhound*: was small and unspoiled, with winter coal fires in bar, snug and tap-room – no games, machines, juke boxes; new manager fairly recently *(D W Roberts)*

SCAMMONDEN RESERVOIR [SE0215], *Lower Royal George*: food simple and good value; keg Stones beer; near lovely walks and riding on Pennine moors *(Jack Davey)*

SCARBOROUGH [Cambridge Terrace; TA0489], *Cask*: decent choice of real ales in lively conversion of big Victorian house *(LYM)*

SETTLE [SD8264], *Royal Oak*: food tasty and cheap; excellent service, good beer *(K W Lomas)*

SHEFFIELD [Handsworth Road; SK3687], *Cross Keys*: ancient and friendly pub inside churchyard; well kept real ales and open fires *(LYM)*; [23 Alma Street] *Fat Cat*: food has wholefood bias; good choice of real ales and traditional cider, in pub with no-smoking lounge *(Amanda Priestley, Gillian Back)*; [Division Street] *Frog & Parrot*: food at lunchtime recommended in this mock-Edwardian city pub with two good home brews in its range of beers, and traditional pianists *(M J Hensman, J Hilditch)*; [Ringinglow Road] *Hammer & Pincers*: food at lunchtime good in newly decorated pub with summer barbecues and pleasant garden for children *(A J Dobson)*; [Cambridge Street] *Henry's*: food good all day in up-market central pub; busy in the evening *(A J Dobson)*; [Orchard Street] *Museum Hotel*: decent range of real ales, popular with university students *(Wayne Rossiter)*; *Red Deer*: excellent for beer drinkers and darts players *(N P Stocks)*; [Church Street] *Stone House*: plush, well kept pub with clever pastiche of Dickensian cobbled shopping-square in central courtyard; can be very crowded *(R K Whitehead, LYM)*; [Glossop Road] *West End*: food and salad bar at lunchtime good; decent Tetleys, interesting Victorian décor; trendy *(A J Dobson, M E Lindley)*

SICKLINGHALL [SE3648], *Scotts Arms*: friendly Yorkshire atmosphere, well kept real ale on handpump, good bar snacks; pool-table, fruit machines, juke box (for pub location see OS Sheet 104 reference 363485) *(Andrew Williamson)*

SLINGSBY [SE7075], *Grapes*: food good value for money; real beer and real cider; children welcome *(GKS)*

SOWERBY BRIDGE [SE0623], *Ashtree*: friendly service in smart sand-blasted mansion; real ale, draught cider; emphasis on restaurant which serves English and authentic Indonesian cooking *(Tim Halstead, S N Segal)*

SPOFFORTH [SE3651], *Railway*: small out-of-the-way Sam Smiths pub with well kept beer; wartime vintage handpumps *(D S Smith)*

STAINFORTH [SD8267], *Craven Heifer*: friendly three-roomed village pub with good Thwaites beer; nice beer garden by stream *(Jon Dewhirst, David Symes)*

STAITHES [NZ7818], *Cod & Lobster*: superb waterside setting in unspoilt fishing village under sandstone cliff *(Ian Clay, LYM)*

STANBURY [SE0137], *Old Silent*: popular moorland village inn near Haworth, small rooms packed with bric-à-brac; real ale, bar meals; bedrooms *(Ian Clay, Tim Halstead, J R Geoghegan, Sue and Len Beattie, LYM)*

STAVELEY [SE3663], *Royal Oak*: charming and welcoming country pub; food home cooked, specialising in pâtés *(Mrs Gina Sancken Fox)*

SWINTON [Rockingham Road; SK4599], *Kings Head*: well run comfortable pub; food includes high-quality lunches at low prices *(R Merrills)*

TERRINGTON [SE6571], *Bay Horse*: good food in nice village inn run by welcoming landlady; bedrooms *(Patrick Wood)*

THORNER [Main Street; SE3840], *Fox*: well kept pub in attractive village with fresh flowers, gleaming brasses, and darts in tap-room; good bar snacks made by landlady; sandwiches in the evening; no food on Sunday *(Mrs B Badger)*

THORNTON WATLASS [SE2486], *Buck*: old, unspoilt village pub on the green (it acts as cricket boundary); good food and dining-room *(David Gaunt)*

THRESHFIELD [SD9763], *Old Hall*: quiet and comfortable village pub, with good Taylors real ale *(David Symes, Keith Myers)*

TONG [SE2230], *Greyhound*: pleasant pub in attractive Georgian village centre *(Keith Myers)*

WAKEFIELD [Westgate; SE3321], *Henry Boons*: lively pub which brews own beer; also good guest beers and bottled beers from other countries; enjoyable pub lunches *(Margaret Harrison)*

WENSLEY [SE0989], *Three Horseshoes*: beautifully kept village pub; exceptionally welcoming landlord and wife, good beer quickly served; light snacks available (not sampled) *(J Dewhirst, Anon)*

WENTWORTH [SK3898], *George & Dragon*: wide choice of bar food, and home-made jams for sale in homely and welcoming village pub *(LYM)*

WEST WITTON [SE0688], *Wensleydale Heifer*: attractive eighteenth-century pub with imaginative well cooked bar food and good beer *(Anon)*

WICKERSLEY [SK4891], *Three Horseshoes*: pleasant, neat mock-Tudor suburban pub with friendly atmosphere; well kept Bass *(Alan Thompson)*

WIGGLESWORTH [SD8157], *Plough*: good food in bar and in charming restaurant, with wide range of salads and hot dishes; excellent Hartleys bitter; friendly service; comfortable bedrooms *(D C Turner)*

WRELTON [SE7786], *Huntsman*: friendly restaurant/pub (not a place for just a drink, so excluded on that ground from main entries) with big helpings of really good enterprising food *(BB, Roger Bach and Melissa Campbell, James and Anne Clinch, Eileen Broadbent)*

YORK [Terry Avenue; SE5951], *Barge*: genuine barge afloat on Ouse; deck-house furnished as pub, hold as disco *(LYM)*; [Blossom Street] *Bay Horse*: lots of nooks and alcoves in rambling rooms of Victorian pub *(Nick Dowson, Alison Hayward, LYM)*; [29 Bootham] *Bootham Tavern*: good Tetleys pub *(Barrie Pepper)*; *Lowther*: good John Smiths bitter on handpump, and reasonably priced lunches *(R Merrills)*; [24 Marygate] *Minster*: quiet pub overlooking ruins of St Mary's Abbey on edge of city; choice of real ales; two well furnished small lounges, darts in little front bar *(F S Bastock, Barrie Pepper)*; [Walmgate] *Spread Eagle*: massive choice of some 17 real ales *(F J Bastock)*; [26 High Petergate] *York Arms*: good Sam Smiths pub near minster (and within strolling distance of the Olde Starre – see main entry) *(Barrie Pepper)*

London

London

The London chapter is divided into Central, North, South, West and East. In London, there are – as you can see from the size of the Lucky Dip section at the end of the chapter – innumerable pubs that are averagely good (and might deserve a full mention if they were in the countryside) without perhaps being outstanding. So, to save readers chasing through the traffic, we have in general tended to pick as main entries pubs that are either in the main parts of central London or close to some special attraction outside the centre. However, a few pubs would stand out anywhere and, depending on your tastes, would certainly repay a special expedition. These include the intricately Edwardian Black Friar (Central), with such a wealth of marble and bronze relief that it's hard to believe so much time and money could ever have been spent on decorating a pub, the George in Southwark (South),

The Nag's Head, Kinnerton Street, SW1

London's only surviving galleried coaching-inn, the bustling up-and-down-stairs Olde Cheshire Cheese in its little court off Fleet Street (Central), Hollands (East) for a taste of simple but truly Victorian pub-going (it can hardly have changed in the 150 years that it's been run by successive generations of the Holland family). Among pubs that make the most of one of London's best assets – the River Thames – two with the finest river views are the Founders Arms looking across to St Paul's Cathedral and the Angel facing Tower Bridge in one direction and the Pool of London in the other (both South). For views, though, you could hardly better the stylish setting of the bar perched on the top of the St George's Hotel (Central). Other good riverside pubs include the Bulls Head with good jazz every day, the eighteenth-century Mayflower beside the jetty from which the Pilgrim Fathers set sail, the Ship with a big waterside terrace (barbecues in summer and a working Thames sailing barge moored there in winter – all these are South); the very popular London Apprentice, the rambling Bulls Head, the little Dove (which lots of customers still know as the Doves even though it's been singular since 1948), and the homely and easy-going White Swan (all these are in the West section); or the friendly and snug Grapes and noisily touristy Prospect of Whitby (in the East section). Another good waterside pub – with a big terrace by a mooring basin of the Regent's Canal – is the Waterside (North), an entertaining pastiche of a big barn-like country tavern. If you're looking for something more genuinely close to a country pub, but within easy reach of the centre, you also have to head north, to either the Clifton (a really relaxed rural style of place, with a feeling almost of being in someone's home) or the little mews-cottage Compton Arms (a good range of real ales). Unusual pubs in the Central section include the old-fashioned Antelope, the handsomely refurbished and very comfortable Chiswell Vaults (good food in cellar surroundings), the very Chelsea Cross Keys (which inspired a TV series and has a nice little garden), the Grenadier (lively little old-fashioned pub tucked away in a stylish mews with its own gate-porter; new licensees this year), Henry J Bean's (a well done new cross between a pub and an open-all-day hamburger joint, with easily the best central London pub garden), the very well kept Lamb (with its Victorian snob-screens still intact), the Dickensian Lamb & Flag (good cheeses here), the Museum Tavern (for its good home cooking and wide range of real ales in Bloomsbury surroundings), the Olde Mitre in a curious, almost private City enclave, the Orange Brewery (for a stylish mock-up of a Victorian pub, brewing its own beer), the Princess Louise (the real thing – high-Victorian decoration, a good range of real ales and good food), the Punch & Judy (couldn't be better placed for the Covent Garden pedestrian precinct), the Red Lion in Duke of York Street (crowded, but one of London's prettiest little Victorian pubs, perfectly preserved), and the stylish Red Lion in Waverton Street (with a nice terrace outside, and good food). In North London, there's the wide range of real ales in the well restored, sumptuous Victorian Crockers, the little panelled rooms of the Flask, the handsomely redecorated Freemasons Arms with its good garden by Hampstead Heath, the gas-lit Holly Bush tucked away in Hampstead Village's nicest part, or the flamboyantly decorated Island Queen (good, unusual food). In the South, the basic under-the-arches Hole in the Wall has a wide range of real ales, the Olde Windmill (a spacious pub on Clapham Common) has very good value accommodation, the Orange Tree has a theatre upstairs and good food downstairs, the Prince of Orange has good jazz, the Market Porter has its own beer in unpretentious surroundings, and the Phoenix & Firkin is a fine new restoration of a railway station converted into a pub. It's one of David Bruce's small but growing chain of similar pubs brewing their own beer, all with Firkin in their name; our full report on another of these (the Ferret & Firkin, one of the Guide's two locals) will give a good idea of what you can expect at the others. In West London there's the smart Scarsdale Arms and the handsomely old-fashioned Windsor Castle (a fine terrace garden – no children are allowed here, though). In East London, the well kept and friendly Grave Maurice has reliably good value food. In general, London pub prices for both food and drink tend to be the highest in the country, and food is far less often a really special attraction than it is in the country.

As before, we have followed the general trend of readers' reports and some specific comments by adding only a few exceptional London pubs to the main entries so that we could concentrate our inspection energies in other areas where readers are crying out for news of more good pubs. However, the massive Lucky Dip section includes so many possibilities that there should be plenty of pub interest, even beyond the main entries, within easy reach of most parts of London. And we'd be particularly grateful for more readers' reports of any of these Lucky Dips so that we can narrow down the very wide choice of possibilities to a much firmer and smaller core of potential main entries that genuinely deserve inspection. If, faced with all that small print, you don't know where to start, here are a few suggestions: the atmospheric and old-fashioned City of York with its incredibly long bar and little panelled alcoves, in the centre (WC1); the well renovated Anerley Arms (SE20), the low-beamed Hand in Hand on its broad green

741

(SW19), and the well restored White Cross in Richmond (all South); and in the East, the Victorian-pastiche Dickens Inn on St Katharine's Dock (E1), and the MV Medina, an ex-Scottish Islands ferry moored in another part of the Docks (E14).

CENTRAL LONDON

Covering W1, W2, WC1, WC2, SW1, SW3, EC1, EC2, EC3 and EC4 postal districts

Parking throughout this area is metered during the day, and generally in short supply then; we mention difficulty only if evening parking is a problem too

Antelope (Belgravia) Map 13

Eaton Terrace, SW1

It's quiet and relaxed at lunchtime in this pretty and pleasantly old-fashioned pub not far from Sloane Square. There's been a bit of a change-around since our last edition, with the lunchtime food bar moved into what used to the back snug and given a smart tiling background – the old settles from that area have been moved out to the front part to join more modern but still traditional ones there. And the fruit machine has been moved right out into what used to be the side food room. So on balance the atmosphere stays much as ever, with the same gathering liveliness as evening draws on that must have pleased Augustus John, who was a regular here. Even in the evenings you can usually find a seat somewhere. Well kept Benskins and Ind Coope Burton on handpump; the food counter serves generous helpings of ploughman's, pâté or creamy taramosalata with granary bread (£1.50), quiche, and hot dishes such as shepherd's pie (£1.85), and there is an upstairs wine bar. There are a couple of long seats outside in the quiet street. *(Recommended by Janet Williams, W T Aird)*

Benskins · Licensee Anthony Kirkman · Real ale · Meals and snacks (not Sat evening, not Sun) · Open 11–3, 5.30–11 all year

Audley (Mayfair) Map 13

41 Mount Street, W1

The big Victorian saloon of this smart and very well kept pub has heavily ornamented polished mahogany panelling climbing to its high red ceiling, with some decorative white plasterwork and crystal chandeliers. Furnishings are in character: button-back red leatherette banquettes, plenty of traditional cast-iron-framed tables, and high chairs along the bar counter. Its big windows give an airy feel, and it has a calm, relaxing atmosphere. Given the surroundings, the generous helpings of good meat, and the detailed attention of the traditionally dressed chef who fills your order from one end of the long bar counter, the prices are fair: a wide range of sandwiches – cheese (from £1.10, Derby sage £1.35), beef (£2), prawn (£2.85) – and fresh salads with these meats and cheeses (£5–£6.50); also double-decker and open sandwiches. There's a separate English restaurant upstairs (closed Sunday lunchtime), and a wine bar downstairs where you can play traditional games like nine men's morris, chess and backgammon. Well kept Youngers IPA, Watneys Stag and Websters Yorkshire on handpump; fruit machines, dignified piped music. This handsome terracotta-faced building has benches on the pavement outside. *(Recommended by W T Aird, Miss K Elwell, John Thirlwell)*

Watneys · Licensee Christopher Plumpton · Real ale · Meals and snacks (no hot food Sat or Sun lunchtimes) · Children in restaurant · Open 11–3, 5.30–11 all year

Black Friar (City) Map 13

174 Queen Victoria Street, EC4

This pub has the most individual and finely worked Edwardian bronze and marble décor that we have found in London, and some would say that it's the best-preserved art nouveau on this scale in any building anywhere. It includes big bas-relief friezes of jolly Dominican monks done by Henry Poole set into richly coloured Florentine marble walls, an opulent marble-pillared inglenook fireplace, a low vaulted mosaic ceiling, gleaming mirrors, seats built in to rich golden marble recesses, and tongue-in-cheek verbal embellishments such as 'Finery Is Foolery'. The best of it – and your best chance of a seat – is in the carpeted back room. Since last year they've got rid of all the games machines and extended the range of well kept real ales on handpump, which now covers Adnams, Bass, Charles Wells Eagle and Morrells. All food is now home cooked, including sandwiches, big filled rolls (some of which may still be available in the evening), shepherd's pie (£1.20), lasagne or moussaka (£1.40), beef and ale pie (£1.50), scampi in a basket (£2), lamb curry (£2.30) and plaice (£2.50). There's a wide forecourt in front by the approach to Blackfriar's Bridge. *(Recommended by W T Aird)*

Free house · Licensee Douglas Walls · Real ale · Meals (lunchtime, not Sat or Sun) and snacks (lunchtime, not Sun) · Open 11.30–3, 5.30–9.30; closed Sat evening and Sun

Buckingham Arms (Westminster) Map 13

62 Petty France, SW1

This friendly and cheerful pub close to the Passport Office has comfortable seats on a Turkey carpet in the lounge bar, a few reproduction old engravings of the area, and bar food such as cauliflower cheese (£1.20), ploughman's (£1.75), cottage pie (£1.75), steak and kidney pie (£1.85), spicy giant sausage (£1.92), ham and chips (£2.40) and beefburgers (£2.70); Youngs Bitter, Special and light John's on handpump; fruit machine. An unusual feature here is the long side corridor, bare bricks and tiles, with a chest-high ledge for glasses and plates running down its whole length – useful extra space when the lunchtime rush is on. *(Recommended by H E Emson, Wayne Rossiter, David Symes)*

Youngs · Licensee J Mountiain · Real ale · Meals and snacks (lunchtime, not Sun) · Open 11–3, 5.30–11 all year

Bunch of Grapes (Mayfair) Map 13

Shepherd Market, W1 [*illustrated on page 773*]

In a lively pedestrian precinct, this pub is attractively decorated with stuffed fish, old photographs and prints, a grandfather clock, elaborate net curtains in the big windows that reach up to its high red ceiling, button-back red leatherette banquettes built around the walls, red plush stools on the carpet, and swivelling bar stools with built-in footrests around the serving bar. There is a cosy and relaxed little dining area, quite sheltered from the much busier main part of the pub, past the counter where a traditionally dressed chef cuts good beef, turkey, ham or fresh-cooked salmon for salads (£6.10 for an unlimited quantity). Other bar food includes shepherd's pie (£2.80), beef salad or smoked salmon salad (£2.80). Well kept Arkells, Brakspears, Ind Coope Burton and Wethereds on handpump; fruit machine, juke box, maybe piped pop music. (*Recommended by H E Emson, John Thirlwell*)

Free house · Licensees A F Wigram and P L Jacobs · Real ale · Meals (lunchtime, not Sun) and snacks (not Sun) · Children in restaurant Open 11–3, 5.30–11 all year

Chiswell Vaults ★ (City) Map 13

Chiswell Street, EC1

This being Whitbread's old City cellars, the Wethereds on handpump is well kept – as it ought to be – and wine by the glass is good value. The spacious, rambling cellar bar has a comfortable lounge area; it's nicely lit, well heated in winter, not stuffy in summer, and it's divided by low sweeping arches, steps, partitions and balustrades. It's well run and has a good range of cold food such as a half-pint of prawns (£1), pâté (£1.25), pork and egg or chicken and ham pie, roast beef and gammon (all £1.50), prawn and crabmeat (£2.50) as well as a wide selection of cheeses (from 90p), with some cold puddings; helpings are generous. A separate dining area with kind waitresses has hot dishes such as lamb curry (a service charge and a small cover charge in here). Close to the Barbican Centre. (*Recommended by Hope Chenhalls, Michael Quine, John Thirlwell*)

Whitbreads · Licensee Chris Burford · Real ale · Meals and snacks · Children in eating area and restaurant · Open 11–3, 5.30–8.30; closed Sat and Sun

Cross Keys (Chelsea) Map 12

Lawrence Street, SW3

This friendly pub has a very lively atmosphere in the evenings as it's a popular meeting place, but it's a relaxing place for lunch. Bar food is good value and includes sandwiches (from 70p), ploughman's (£1) and filled baked potatoes (80p–£1), and there are hot dishes such as home-made steak and kidney pie, sweet and sour pork, spare ribs and curry or chilli (all £1.80). Well kept Courage Best and Directors on handpump; service is cheerful and efficient even when the pub fills up in the evenings; and you know it's time to leave when the barman comes round shouting 'Come on now, folks; Freddie's beddies' as he collects the glasses. At lunchtime, though, there's space to take in its old-fashioned décor of high ceilings, military prints on the red or khaki walls, and the walk-round island serving counter. Dominoes, cribbage and fruit machine. There are tables in a pretty little sunny back courtyard, and on warm summer evenings people tend to overflow into the Cheyne Walk gardens by the Thames. *(Recommended by W T Aird, Patrick Stapley and RAB, Richard Gibbs)*

Courage · Licensees Arthur and Jean Goodall · Real ale · Meals and snacks (not Sun) · Open 11–3, 5.30–11 all year

George (West End) Map 13

55 Great Portland Street, W1

Saved from nondescript refurbishment by a campaigning group which owed a lot to its BBC regulars – including the poets Dylan Thomas and Louis MacNeice – this solid place has heavy mahogany panelling, deeply engraved mirrors, etched windows, equestrian prints, comfortable green plush high chairs at the bar and captain's chairs around traditional cast-iron-framed tables. There's a good choice of real ales such as Adnams, Eldridge Pope Royal Oak, Felinfoel Double Dragon, Greene King IPA and Abbot and Charles Wells Bombardier and a monthly guest ale on handpump. Bar food includes sandwiches (70p), ploughman's (from £1.30), salads (from £1.70) and at lunchtime hot meals such as a three-egg omelette (from £1.50), home-made steak pie (£2.85), chicken (£2.75) or scampi (£3.30); fruit machine. *(Recommended by Stuart Baker, G Berneck)*

Free house · Licensee T C Thomas · Real ale · Meals and snacks · Open 11–3, 5.30–11

The Spaniards, Spaniards Road, NW3

Grenadier (Belgravia) Map 13

Wilton Row, SW1; the turning off Wilton Crescent looks prohibitive, but the barrier and watchman are there to keep out cars; walk straight past – the pub is just around the corner

This tucked-away little pub is proud of its connection with Wellington, whose officers used to use it as their mess. The front bar buzzes with life as it fills with a remarkable cross-section of easy-mixing customers. Besides the well kept Ruddles County, Combes (Watneys London brew) and Stag and Websters Yorkshire on handpump from the rare pewter-topped bar counter, the new licensee or Tom the very long-standing head barman will shake you a most special Bloody Mary; in fact on Sunday mornings the food counter is turned into a Bloody Mary manufactory (see if you can help them beat their current record – as we went to press it had crept up to 127). A corner snack counter serves very reasonably priced lunchtime food such as French bread and cheese (50p), sandwiches (from 70p), quiche (70p), ploughman's or pâté (90p) and steak and kidney pie (£1.10). In the evenings bar food is limited to giant sausages (25p), though the intimate back restaurant – two small candlelit rooms – is open lunchtime and evening seven days a week (to book telephone 01-235 3074). There's a red, white and blue sentry box outside, where tables on a raised area overlook the quiet cobbled mews. *(Recommended by Tim Bracey, Joel Dobris, A Saunders)*

Watneys · Licensee Alan Taylor · Real ale · Bar meals and snacks (lunchtime, not Sun) · Children in restaurant · Open 11–3, 5.30–11 all year; closed 25–26 Dec

Guinea (Mayfair) Map 13

30 Bruton Place, W1

This simple little mews pub has just been undergoing refurbishments, which we hope won't spoil its charming villagey atmosphere. Good value bar food includes generously filled sandwiches, though it's the steak pies (£2) that are popular; well kept Youngs Bitter and Special on handpump, and mulled wine in winter. The Thames Flood Barrier might well have been inspired by the way the twice-daily tidal flood of smartly dressed customers is somehow gently checked from overcrowding the bar itself, but instead flows happily out into the quiet mews. There's also a big back grill-room where a garden used to be. *(Recommended by Rodney Collins, John Thirlwell)*

Youngs · Licensee Victor Ledger · Real ale · Meals (lunchtime only, not Sat or Sun) and snacks (lunchtime only, not Sun) · Children in restaurant · Open 11–3, 5.30–11 all year; closed Sun

Hand & Shears (City) Map 13

Middle Street, EC1

The old-fashioned island bar counter in this sixteenth-century Smithfield pub is surrounded by a series of little rooms divided by panelling partitions – it's one of the least spoilt pubs in London, with lanterns hanging from the brown ceiling, Victorian and other cartoons on the walls, and a thoroughly lively mixture of market traders and porters, city analysts and printers, and of course doctors (always quick to find a good pub), all providing an excellent atmosphere. Well kept Courage Best and Directors on handpump, relatively reasonably priced for the area; sandwiches, filled rolls. Known locally as the Fist & Clippers, the Flemish and French cloth traders used to stay here for the clothing trade's St Bartholomew's Fair in August – finally abolished in 1855 because it had become simply an excuse for making a tremendous midnight din. *(Recommended by W T Aird)*

Courage · Licensee John Latimer · Real ale · Snacks · Open 11.30–3, 5–11 all year; closed Sat, Sun and bank hols

Henry J Bean's (Chelsea – where else?) Map 13

195–197 King's Road, SW3

This pub has been very successfully converted by a gifted American catering entrepreneur, Bob Payton, into something that might send shivers up the spine of a really stern traditionalist but seems to us great fun. The décor (though not the atmosphere – that's trendier, but not dauntingly over-young – with late 1970s funky music) is late 1950s American. Big blond claw-foot wooden tables with high stools – spaced well apart – furnish the main part, which is airily high-ceilinged and has a polished woodstrip floor, and there are two or three low steps up into a railed-off carpeted area with pale plum button-back banquettes and more tables. It's decorated with a copious and interesting collection of old enamel advertising placards. The long bar counter is manned by neat slicked-hair barmen, backed by tall mirrored shelves housing an excellent collection of whiskies. An interesting range of beers (no real ales) includes several Americans, and you can have them served by the jug, as well as with slugs of this and that, in small or outsize glasses; there are American as well as good French house wines, and of course they do cocktails. You order food from the barman, and the till transmits the order to a grill area (some electronic inflexibility here: the till can say you want your burger well done, but it evidently can't say you want it without a bun); when it's ready video screens show your number – the last three digits on your receipt. The food includes deep-fried potato skins with sour cream (from £1.75), hot dog (£2.75), salads (£2.95), chilli con carne (£2.95) and burgers (£3.55). A cream-tiled area with bentwood chairs opens through tall glass French windows into a really big crazy-paved back courtyard, with sturdy seats and tables under plane and lime trees among well tended green pergolas and old streetlamps, and a central fountain playing around a tall flame.

Watneys · Licensees Gavin Williams and Steven Gee · Meals and snacks Children in dining-room · Open 11.30–3, 5.30–11 all year; closed 25 Dec and 1 Jan

---

Children welcome means the pub says it lets children inside without any special restriction. If it allows them in, but to restricted areas such as an eating area or family room, we specify this. Places with separate restaurants usually let children use them, and hotels usually let them into public areas such as lounges.

Lamb ★ (Bloomsbury) Map 13

94 Lamb's Conduit Street, WC1

Cosy, with space to overhear journalists' gossip in the evenings, it quickly fills up at lunchtime – but at any time you can enjoy the cut-glass swivelling 'snob screens' all the way around the U-shaped bar counter, masses of sepia photographs on ochre panelling of 1890s actresses and traditional cast-iron-framed tables with neat brass rails around the rim, though (you can see we're paranoiac about our drink) we find that makes us worry even more about tipping our glass of well kept Youngs Bitter or Special over the edge. Bar food includes a good range of snacks such as filled rolls (from 45p), sandwiches (from 55p), pasties (80p) and ploughman's (from £1.20), as well as lunchtime hot dishes such as cauliflower cheese (90p), cottage pie or steak and kidney pie with two vegetables (£1.90), and daily specials such as lasagne or a casserole (£1.60–£1.90). There are slatted wooden seats in a little courtyard (no children allowed here), beyond the quiet room which is down a couple of steps at the back – past what one reader reckons is the cleanest gents' in London. (*Recommended by Joel Dobris, John Thirlwell*)

Youngs · Licensee A G Corrigall · Real ale · Meals (lunchtime) and snacks Open 11–3, 5.30–11 all year

Lamb & Flag (Covent Garden) Map 13

Rose Street, WC2; off Garrick Street

The back room, with its low ceiling, high-backed black settles and a number of dark paintings on its yellowing walls, used to be known as the Bucket of Blood in Regency days, from the bare-knuckle prize-fights held here. It's much as it was when Dickens described the Middle Temple lawyers who haunted it in the days when he was working nearby in Catherine Street. Now, it's mainly publishers and local office workers jammed in at lunchtime, particularly in the narrow black-panelled passage along the saloon bar counter, and though in the evenings it's much easier to find a seat it can be crowded then too – more and more so, as Covent Garden (for which this is handy) becomes increasingly popular for outings. Bar food concentrates on a particularly good selection of cheeses, with ham and pâtés, served with hot bread or French bread (£1.40–£1.75), with lunchtime hot dishes such as pasty, mash and beans, steak and kidney pie, salt beef or chilli con carne (all £2). Well kept Courage Best and Directors on handpump. Darts in the small front public bar. You can drink outside in the courtyard, close to where Dryden was nearly beaten to death by hired thugs when he'd been a shade too witty at someone else's expense. (*Recommended by R Raimi, R A Hutson, Chris Miller, W T Aird*)

Courage · Licensee A Zimmerman · Real ale · Meals (lunchtime only) and snacks · Open 11–3, 5.30–11 all year; closed 25 Dec

---

Food details, prices, timing and so on refer to bar food, not to a separate restaurant if there is one.

Museum Tavern (Bloomsbury) Map 13

Museum Street, WC1

This popular pub has always been a temptation for people staggering out of the British Museum (which is just opposite) and even Karl Marx is fondly supposed to have had the odd glass here after it had shut him out for the night. There's a touch of Bloomsbury, with gas lamps above the tables outside, old-fashioned high-backed benches around the traditional cast-iron pub tables inside, and old advertising mirrors between the wooden pillars behind the bar. Good bar food includes sandwiches, ploughman's with a choice of cheeses and a changing choice of five main dishes such as shepherd's pie, steak and kidney pie, stuffed peppers and chilli con carne (all £2.50); mini grills in the evening. A good choice of real ales on handpump might include Greene King IPA and Abbot, Brakspears, Everards, Ruddles County, and Websters Yorkshire, and there is a wide range of wines by the glass; fruit machine, maybe piped music. Afternoon cream teas are served from 3.45 to 5pm (not Sunday). The new licensees and their staff speak five languages between them to help foreign visitors. *(Recommended by J Dobris, H E Emson, John Thirlwell, Roger Bellingham)*

Free house · Licensees Peter and Jean Jones · Real ale · Meals and snacks Children in eating area · Open 11–3, 5.30–11 all year

Nag's Head (Belgravia) Map 13

53 Kinnerton Street, SW1 [*illustrated on page 739*]

A friendly welcome and good value home-cooked food in this pub attractively placed in a quiet mews. Sandwiches (hot salt beef £1.50, smoked salmon £2) and changing daily specials such as shepherd's pie (£1.75), fisherman's pie or Hungarian goulash (£2.25), beefburgers (£2.50) and roast beef with Yorkshire pudding (£3.50); other dishes include bacon and peanut-butter quiche, leek, bacon and tomato pie, and spinach quiche; they also offer freshly squeezed orange juice and freshly ground coffee. The games have been cleared out to make way for comfortable seats in the back room – down steps from the little old-fashioned front area, with its low ceiling, panelling, and old cooking-range with wood-effect gas fire. Benskins and Ind Coope Burton on handpump. The pub is attractively placed in a quiet mews. *(Recommended by M W, Tim Bracey, G Berneck, W T Aird, Richard Gibbs)*

Benskins (Ind Coope) · Licensees Kevin and Kate Moran · Real ale · Meals and snacks (not Sun) · Children in eating area · Open 11–3, 5.30–11 all year

Olde Cheshire Cheese (City) Map 13

Wine Office Court; off 145 Fleet Street, EC4

The vaulted cellars of this interesting pub survived the Great Fire of London, and its pies and meat puddings have been an institution for a long time (served in the old-fashioned restaurant). The small rooms, up and down stairs, have sawdust on bare boards, bare wooden benches built in to the walls, and on the ground floor high beams, crackly old black varnish, Victorian paintings on the dark brown

749

walls, and a big open fire in winter. Congreve, Pope, Voltaire, Thackeray, Dickens, Conan Doyle, Yeats and perhaps Dr Johnson used to eat and drink here, and the bustling mixture of tourists, lawyers and journalists, squeezing up and down the panelled stairway or spilling out into the narrow courtyard, somehow suits it very well. Well kept Marstons Pedigree and Merrie Monk on handpump; snacks like filled rolls. *(Recommended by Stephan Carney)*

Free house · Licensee Leslie Kerly · Real ale · Open 11.30–3, 5–9; closed Sat and Sun

Old Mitre (City) Map 13

Ely Place, EC1; there's also an entrance beside 8 Hatton Garden

With its quaint courtyard façade and small rooms panelled in dark oak, jugs hanging from the beams, antique settles and big vases of flowers, this carefully rebuilt pub carries the name of a predecessor built in 1547 to serve people working in the palace of the Bishop of Ely, who ruled this part of London absolutely. In theory, police still have to get permission to enter the court, and only recent fire regulations have ended the tradition of the beadle locking up the entrance gates with the cry of 'Past ten o'clock and all's well'. Bar snacks include Scotch eggs and pork pies (45p), pork sausages (22p), ham or cheese rolls (45p), and a good selection of plain or toasted sandwiches such as ham, salmon and cucumber, egg mayonnaise (50p), turkey and roast beef (65p); there is also French bread with Cheddar cheese (50p) or Camembert (60p); well kept Friary Meux and Ind Coope Burton on handpump, reasonably priced for the area. There are some seats with pot plants and jasmine in the narrow yard between the pub and St Ethelreda's church, which is the only one in London to have switched back to Roman Catholicism since the Reformation. *(Recommended by Stephan Carney)*

Taylor-Walkers (Ind Coope) · Licensee Frederick Rix · Real ale · Snacks (not Sat or Sun) · Open 11–3, 5.30–11 all year; closed Sat, Sun and bank hols

Old Wine Shades (City) Map 13

6 Martin Lane, EC4

As this is one of very few buildings in the City to have escaped the Great Fire of 1666, its heavy black beams and dark panelling are older than most things you'll see nearby. Old prints, subdued lighting, dignified alcoves, antique tables and old-fashioned high-backed settles underline the atmosphere, though in fact the lunchtime bustle, with this as a background, makes a very lively picture; it's quiet in the evenings. They keep a good range of wines (the pub is under the same ownership as El Vino's); bar lunches include sandwiches (from 80p, home-cooked topside of beef £1.10), jacket potato filled with cheese (£1), various pies and quiche (from £1.30), pâté (£1.50) and French bread with a choice of seven cheeses (mostly £1.50). They insist on collar, tie, jacket and trousers for men, and no jeans or jump suits for women. *(Recommended by R Raimi, RAB)*

Free house · Licensees Victor Little and Christopher Mitchell · Meals and snacks (lunchtime) · Open 11.30–3, 5–8; closed Sat, Sun and bank hols

Orange Brewery (Pimlico) Map 13

37 Pimlico Road, SW1

Beer is brewed in the cellars of this attractive and welcoming Victorian-style pub; it includes SW1, a stronger SW2, and Celebration, and they usually have a couple of guest beers on handpump as well. At one side there's a cheery Pie Shop with lots of sepia photographs on the dark stained plank-panelling, plain wooden tables and chairs on pretty black and white tiles, and a shelf full of old flagons and jugs above the counter where they serve sandwiches, including hot beef or pork (£1.60), ploughman's (£1.40), daily hot dishes such as lasagne, steak and kidney pie, goulash and chicken chasseur (£2.60) with puddings such as fruit pie with cream. The bar servery, in another room, has solid armed seats and armchairs around its high ochre walls, which are decorated with more sepia photographs, some decorative Victorian plates, and a stuffed fox above a nicely tiled fireplace. A fruit machine, maybe piped music. There are seats outside facing a little concreted-over green beyond the quite busy street. *(Recommended by R H Inns, Timothy Errock)*

Own brew · Licensee W J Fletcher · Real ale · Meals and snacks · Open 11–3, 5.30–11 all year

The Red Lion, Waverton Street, W1

Pheasant & Firkin (Finsbury) Map 13

166 Goswell Road, EC1

One of David Bruce's attractively done back-to-basics refurbishments, serving beers brewed on the premises, others from small breweries, and Murphys stout. Smaller than some, it tends to get crowded; charming lady licensees. See Ferret & Firkin, West London, for fuller details. *(Recommended by J Dobris, M P Egan)*

Princess Louise (Holborn) Map 13

208 High Holborn, WC1

The upstairs bar of this elaborately Victorian pub was undergoing some redecoration as we went to press, and there were plans for a wider range of food here. The big open-plan downstairs bar has a flamboyant old-fashioned décor of etched and gilt mirrors, brightly coloured and fruity-shaped tiles, a high, deeply moulded brown plaster ceiling, an enormous island bar stretching down the middle, and green plush seats and banquettes. Food from a separate serving counter includes giant sausage (60p), filled rolls (65p), sandwiches (80p), ploughman's (£1.10), generous helpings of potato and other salads with quiche (£2.20), or with meat or poacher's pie (£2.75), and a hot dish of the day (£2.75). A good, unusual range of real ales on handpump might include Chudleys, Darleys Thorne, Greene King IPA and Abbot, Ruddles County, Sam Smiths, Vaux Bitter and Samson, and Wards, and upstairs they have a wider range of wines by the glass than usual – including champagne. Fruit machine. *(Recommended by Sheila Keen, John Thirlwell, G E Judd, M I Constable)*

Free house · Licensees I M Phillips and D A Curtis · Real ale · Meals (not Sun, not Sat evening) and snacks (not Sun evening) · Jazz Sat and Sun evening Open 11–3, 5.30–11 all year

Punch & Judy (Covent Garden) Map 13

The Market, WC2

The relatively small upstairs bar – usually the quieter of the two – has a balcony overlooking the spacious piazza of the Covent Garden pedestrian complex, where acrobats, mimers, tumblers, jugglers and musicians are usually performing. Though it's much larger, the bare brick cellar is usually much more crowded: knots of trendily dressed young people standing on the flagstones in the main section, sitting in the relative peace of a series of barrel-vaulted bays at the back, or at the front with a view of the pub's courtyard below the galleries of smart shops that have taken over this imaginatively converted flower, fruit and vegetable market. Good piped pop music, fruit machine. Bar food includes ploughman's, quiche, filled jacket potato, sweet and sour pork, and chicken, ham and mushroom cheesecake (hot food in the cellar only); Courage Best and Directors on handpump are served in half-gallon jugs if you want. *(Recommended by Roger Bellingham, William Meadon and Richard Steel)*

Courage · Licensee Trevor Mitchell · Real ale · Meals (not Sat and Sun evenings, not after 8) · Open 11–3, 5.30–10.45

Red Lion (Mayfair) Map 13

Waverton Street, W1 [*illustrated on page 751*]

The L-shaped bar of this stylish Mayfair pub is so small and local-feeling that it almost has the atmosphere of a civilised country pub, with old photographs and London prints below the high shelf of china on its dark-panelled walls, and small winged settles on the partly carpeted scrubbed floorboards. Don't expect country prices, though – you are after all paying for Mayfair property values as well as for the neat skills of the man in a butcher's boater and apron who serves good food, which includes ploughman's, generous rare beef sandwiches, salads and specials such as dressed crab or salmon. Unusually for the area, food is served morning and evening seven days a week, and in winter includes hot dishes. Well kept Combes (Watneys' new London brew), Manns IPA, Ruddles County, Watneys Stag and Websters Yorkshire on handpump. There's a small separate restaurant (bookings 01-499 1307). Though the pub itself can get crowded at lunchtime, it has cut-away barrel seats among the bay trees under its front awning – unusually peaceful for London, as it's at the end of a quiet cul-de-sac. *(Recommended by H E Emson, John Thirlwell)*

Watneys · Licensee David Butterfield · Real ale · Meals and snacks · Children in restaurant · Open 11–3, 5.30–11 all year

Red Lion (St James's) Map 13

2 Duke of York Street, SW1

A sparkling little mid-Victorian tavern: the *Architectural Review* has called this 'a perfect example of a small Victorian gin palace at its best', and you can find no better in London. You are quite surrounded by deeply cut patterned mirrors set into the rosewood and mahogany walls, so that at night the small brass and crystal chandeliers set thousands of reflections twinkling. It tends to be very busy indeed at lunchtime, and is often crowded in the early evening too. Well kept Taylor-Walkers Best and Ind Coope Burton on handpump; even when it is full, bar service is quick, and they're good at catching your eye over bar-proppers' shoulders. Bar food, which is cheap for the area and home made, includes cheese and onion pie (48p), Scotch eggs (55p), sandwiches (from 65p), shepherd's pie (£1.35), steak and kidney pie (£1.50), fish and chips (Friday only, £1.70) and roast pork or roast beef and Yorkshire pudding (£1.80); fruit machine. The elegant little spiral staircase leads to the kitchens and private quarters. *(Recommended by W T Aird)*

Taylor-Walkers (Ind Coope) · Licensees Roy and Corinne Hamlin · Real ale Meals (lunchtime, not Sat or Sun) and snacks (not Sun evening) · Open 11–3, 5.30–11 all year; closed Sun evening

---

In next year's edition we hope to include a few really interesting, attractive, unusual or just plain odd bars abroad. If you know any, please tell us about them as evocatively as possible. No stamp needed if posted in the UK to *The Good Pub Guide*, FREEPOST, London SW10 0BR.

St George's Hotel (West End) Map 13

Langham Place, W1

As we said in the last edition of the *Guide*, this is by no means a pub, but it remains our favourite place in London for a stylish, relaxed drink. Walk in at the door, and a non-stop lift in the far corner of the lobby whisks you up to a spacious modern fourteenth-floor lounge, with great picture windows looking westwards over and far beyond London. Comfortable small armchairs are well spaced between the white marble walls. There's usually a pianist at the grand piano (not Sunday), and always plenty of room. Uniformed but warmly friendly bar staff mix proper cocktails, bring your drinks to your low gilt and marble table, and make sure that your dishes of free nuts and little biscuits are always topped up. If you get there early enough they may give you little freshly grilled cocktail sausages wrapped in bacon, too. They don't expect you to pay until you leave: given the surroundings and service, you obviously can't expect normal pub prices, though a bottled beer, say, shouldn't cost you more than about £1 here. Bar food includes sandwiches (from £1.40), toasted chicken and cheese sandwich (£1.65), open fish or cold meat sandwich (£2.50), steak sandwich (£2.75), Parma ham and melon salad (£5.20), beef Stroganoff or spiced seafood (£5.75), and dressed crab (£5.50). There's also a separate restaurant on this floor. (*Recommended by BOB*)

Free house (THF) · Licensee Peter Mereweather · Meals and snacks · Children welcome · Open 10.30–3, 5.30–11 all year; closed 24 Dec (noon)–27 Dec Bedrooms tel 01-580 0111; £66B/£88B (much cheaper weekend rates)

Victoria (Bayswater) Map 13

Strathearn Place, W2

The downstairs bar here has just been reopened by the pub's new licensee as an attractive Dickensian tavern – a lot of it original, like the little alcoves in the mahogany panelled wall, tiled with Dickens scenes, for you to put your drinks; there's even a mock-up of the Old Curiosity Shop, and they will be serving food such as winkles and cockles as well as a selection of sandwiches. There's a charming little replica of the bar from the Gaiety Theatre upstairs (though it's not always open) – all gilt and red velvet, with a sky-and-clouds painted ceiling and posters advertising George Edwardes' theatrical company. The atmosphere is relaxed and friendly. Well kept Bass and Charrington IPA on handpump; a smartly manned food counter serves good freshly cut sandwiches in white or brown bread, quiche Lorraine (£1.80), salt beef and suet, steak and kidney pie or chicken and ham pie (£2.50) and beef bourguignonne (£2.60); fruit machine. There are picnic-table sets outside by the pavement. (*Recommended by C B M Gregory*)

Charringtons · Licensee Liam Byrne · Real ale · Meals and snacks (not Sun) Open 11–3, 5.30–11 all year

---

Pubs with particularly interesting histories, or in unusually interesting buildings, are listed at the back of the book.

NORTH LONDON

Parking in this area is not a special problem, unless we say so

Clifton (St John's Wood) Map 12

96 Clifton Hill, NW8

This – remarkably – keeps a quiet and countrified atmosphere in a part of London where you would have thought that such a good pub would quickly get trampled under foot in the rush to get to its bar. But rushing is the last thing you'd think of in this calm series of high-ceilinged rooms, with attractively stripped doors, panelling and other woodwork, Edwardian and Victorian engravings and 1920s comic prints on its elegant wallpaper, unusual art-nouveau wall-lamps, cast-iron tables and fine brass and glass ceiling-lights. Careful placing of wooden balustrades and one or two steps from one level to another keeps the idea of small rooms without destroying the pleasant airiness of what is actually quite a spacious place. Though it's mostly bare-boarded (there's a carpet on the homely flight of stairs leading up to the private quarters), this does seem almost like a private house. But it's been a pub a long time; Edward VII and Lily Langtree used to come here, and there are quite a few prints of both of them (one signed by the king and his son – who became George V). Now, the dignitaries you see here are more likely to be actors and musicians. Good bar food includes crab and cheese tartlets, pâté, crudities and smoked mackerel mousse (all around £1.50), steak and oyster pie, spinach and mushroom pancakes, chicken and sweetcorn pie and chicken Marengo (£3.30–£3.45), with salads (around £3.25) and some wrapped sandwiches. Well kept Taylor-Walker and Ind Coope Burton on handpump; cribbage; fruit machine. There are some tables in a back courtyard, and more attractive marble-topped ones on a very leafy front terrace (one is in a roofed porch). *(Recommended by John Thirlwell, Hugh Morgan, Arnold Pearce)*

Taylor-Walker · Licensee John Murtagh · Real ale · Meals and snacks Children in eating area · Open 11–3, 5.30–11 all year

Compton Arms (Canonbury) Map 12

4 Compton Avenue, off Canonbury Lane, N1

Remarkable to find this villagey little pub here: small and cheerful rooms, simply furnished with wood and leatherette, hidden away up a mews (far less grand than the address sounds). There are low ceilings, little local pictures on the walls, and really friendly service – and that extends to free snacks at Sunday lunchtime. Cheap freshly cooked food includes sandwiches (from 65p, steak £1), ploughman's (from £1.50), burgers, sausages, garlic mushrooms (£1.50) and dishes of the day (£1.65). The unusual range of well kept real ales includes Adnams Southwold and Extra, Arkells, Greene King Abbot, Sam Smiths OB and guests such as James Paine; dominoes, cribbage, chess. A quiet little crazy-paved back terrace has benches around cask

There are report forms at the back of the book.

tables under a big sycamore tree (its shade doesn't seem to stop the passion flower blooming). *(Recommended by Roger Protz)*

Free house · Licensee Pat Benson · Real ale · Meals (lunchtime, not Sun) and snacks (not Sat evening or Sun) · Open 11–3, 5.30–11 all year

Crockers ★ (Maida Vale) Map 13

24 Aberdeen Place, NW8

Previously known as the Crown, this imposing place is reverting to a name closer to its Victorian nick-name, Crocker's Folly, after its builder's optimistic blunder: miscalculating where the entrance to Marylebone Station would be, he built it on the grand scale to cash in on floods of customers from the new railway – missing them by half a mile or so. The main room has a sweeping marble bar counter, marble pillars supporting arches inlaid with bronze reliefs, the most elaborately moulded ceiling of any pub we have seen in London, and a vast pillared marble fireplace (with a log-effect gas fire). A row of great arched and glazed mahogany doors opens into a similarly ornate but more spacious room. Another less opulent room has bar billiards, darts, two fruit machines and three space games. Vaux of Sunderland, who recently bought this and its sister pub in Central London, the Princess Louise (see entry), have left it as a free house, keeping the good range of well kept real ales on handpump: Bass, Chudleys (from nearby, in Maida Vale) Lords, Greene King Abbot, Ruddles County, Sam Smiths, Vaux Bitter and Samson and Wards, which can be served in quart pots (10p off). Bar food includes home-made soup (95p), prawns in curry-flavoured sauce (£1.60), chilli con carne or four-ounce beefburger (£1.90), chicken with barbecue sauce (£3.50) and steaks (from five-ounce sirloin £3.75), and there are Sunday roast lunches. *(Recommended by G Berneck, Geoffrey Normile, David Symes, John Thirlwell)*

Free house (see above) · Licensees David and Joan Curtis · Real ale · Meals and snacks · Children in eating area · Theatre, music hall and live music planned Daytime parking meters · Open 11–3, 5.30–11 all year

Flask (Highgate) Map 12

77 Highgate West Hill, N6

The small partly panelled rooms in the original part of this old tavern have little wooden armchairs and a high-backed carved settle, copper jugs hanging from the beams, an open fire, and a sash-windowed bar counter – so that you have to stoop below the sashes to see the barman. Quiet at lunchtime in the week, it gets very busy in the evenings and at weekends. There are steps up to the more spacious tile-floored extension, which has Windsor chairs, low settles, and tables for the food: bread and cheese, sandwiches, big sausages, filled rolls, salads, quiche or vegetarian pie, and (except Sunday) shepherd's pie; Taylor-Walkers and Ind Coope Burton on handpump. A separate restaurant does full meals (under £5). There are sturdy wooden tables outside by the flowering cherry trees, with one or two protected by a wood-pillared porch decorated with hanging baskets of geraniums and petunias. In this pub one of Hogarth's rowdy friends clobbered a regular with his tankard, **and Hogarth himself nearly got** clobbered back for sketching the result. *(Recommended by John Thirlwell, Hazel Morgan, G. Berneck)*

Ind Coope · Licensee Mrs Gillian Light · Real ale · Meals (lunchtime, not Sat or Sun) and snacks · Children in restaurant · Open 11–3, 5.30–11 all year

Freemasons Arms (Hampstead) Map 12

Downshire Hill, NW3

The garden here, across the road from Hampstead Heath, is great for families, as it's quite fenced off from the road. It has a series of crazy-paved areas with heavy wooden seats and tables, divided by roses and patches of grass, and in summer is usually full of children and dogs. A terrace down by the pub itself has a fountain and goldfish-pool; there's an upper terrace here too. The 90-year-old skittle alley has just been extensively refurbished (one of only three left in London) and the pub has the only existing lawn billiards court left in England. Inside has been stylishly redecorated: the inner lounge has cane-look chairs around the well spaced tables on its patterned blue carpet, Wedgwood plaques and large and elegant modern prints of flamingoes and flowers on the walls, a big brass and wicker ceiling fan, and a coal-effect gas fire. There are plenty of seats including leather Chesterfields in the outer lounge, too, which now leads through to what used to be the public bar but has also been comfortably refurnished – with a new bridge out into the garden. The new licensee has extended the bar food to include jacket potatoes with a variety of fillings, as well as three daily specials such as liver Stroganoff or cider sausage (£2.65), barbecued spare ribs (£2.70), Jamaican-style beef casserole (£2.80) and salads; Springfield (relatively reasonably priced for London), Bass and Charringtons IPA on handpump (by the jug if you want – two, three or four pints), sangria in summer and mulled wine in winter; fruit machine and piped pop music. *(More reports please)*

Bass Charringtons · Licensee Martin Wainwright · Real ale · Meals and snacks Open 11–3, 5.30–11 all year

Holly Bush (Hampstead) Map 12

Holly Mount, NW3

This old-fashioned pub, tucked away in a quiet corner of one of the prettiest old parts of Hampstead Village, has hardly changed in the twenty years that we've known it, though the new licensee is planning to reupholster the seating: real gas lamps, a dark and sagging ceiling, seats built in to bays against the brown and cream panelled walls (which are decorated with old advertisements and a few hanging plates), and partly glazed partitions dividing it into small areas. The back room has an embossed red ceiling, panelled and etched glass alcoves, and ochre-painted brick walls covered with small prints and plates; subdued electric lighting and an intimate atmosphere. This part's named after the painter George Romney: the present tavern was built in 1802 on the site of his stables. In between the two bars home-cooked food is served by the new licensee including sandwiches and a selection of hot and cold daily dishes; evening basket meals and a traditional Sunday lunch. Well kept Benskins and Ind Coope Burton on handpump, with draught cider; fruit machine, space game. There are seats on the pavement by the quiet cul-de-sac.

Benskins/Taylor-Walker (Ind Coope) · Licensee Peter Dures · Real ale · Meals and snacks · Children in coffee room off bar · Jazz Sun evenings · Nearby parking quite a squeeze · Open 11–3, 5.30–11 all year

Island Queen (Islington) Map 13

Noel Road, N1

One reason for the popularity of this idiosyncratically decorated pub, close to the antique shops of Camden Passage, is its good choice of freshly made and often unusual food, such as leek and potato soup, mushroom and tomato quiche or ploughman's (£1.10), crab and spinach flan or freshly made beefburgers (£1.35), ratatouille and French bread (£1.75), prawn, spinach and potato or red Malaysian chicken curries (£2.20), stir-fried beef and broccoli in oyster sauce (£2.60) and steak and kidney pie (£2.75). Above the bar float grotesque over-lifesize monstrous caricatures of an angelic Prince and Princess of Wales, Ronald Reagan as a tartan mule (we always thought it was meant to be Lionel Blair until they put us right), and Mrs Thatcher as a long and sinuous blue dragon. There are big mirrors with simulated green palms and jungle vegetation stuck over them, and an open coal fire in cool weather; otherwise furnishings are simple. At lunchtime during the week it's very quiet and spacious, with its airy big windows, but at weekend lunchtimes it's packed with trendily dishevelled regular customers – often with children or grandchildren – and in the evenings, when the juke box with its good collection of nostalgic 1960s and 1970s records is turned up, it can get quite lively. The upstairs restaurant, available for private functions, serves roast Sunday lunch (£7.50, bookings only: 01-359 7586). Well kept Bass, Charringtons IPA and (very reasonably priced for London) Springfield on handpump; pool in a back room, and two space games. There are tables in front of the creeper-covered pub, by the quiet street. *(Recommended by Sue Hanson, René Wiesner, Hugh Paget, Beti Wyn Thomas)*

Charringtons · Licensees J D Evans and G Foster · Real ale · Meals (not Sun evening) and snacks (not Sun) · Daytime parking metered · Open 11–3, 5.30–11 all year

Spaniards (Hampstead) Map 12

Spaniards Lane, NW3 [*illustrated on page 745*]

A Hampstead Heath landmark for generations, with the old tollhouse opposite (for what used to be the Bishop of London's great country park here) making a bottleneck twist in the main road over the Heath, this pub, built in 1585, has some nice touches, like barmen in hunting pink, candle-shaped lamps in pink shades, a couple of fruit machines alongside the genuine antique winged settles, open fires and snug little alcoves in its several low-ceilinged oak-panelled rooms. In the evenings the building's own character yields to the lively, crowded atmosphere brought by its **droves of regular customers**. The new licensee serves home-cooked, good value food that changes daily: giant sausages (50p), filled rolls (£1), quiche (£1.25), ploughman's pie (£1.35), macaroni milanese (£2.50), chicken provençale (£3) and lamb kebabs (£3.50). In cool weather they make hot toddies. During the 1780 Gordon Riots the innkeeper cunningly gave so much free drink to the mob on its way to burn down Lord Mansfield's Kenwood House that by the time the Horse Guards got here the rioters were lying drunk and incapable on the floor. The attractive sheltered garden has slatted wooden tables and chairs on a crazy-paved terrace which opens on to a flagstoned walk around a small lawn, with roses, a side arbour of wistaria and clematis, and an aviary. *(Recommended by Jimmy Georgiou, Guy Atkins)*

Charringtons · Licensee G M Culver · Meals and snacks · Children in eating area · Open 11–3, 5.30–11 all year

Waterside (King's Cross) Map 13

82 York Way, N1

Behind the smart new shiny brick façade is a very well done pastiche of a country pub, with genuinely old stripped timbers in white plaster, lots of dimly lit alcoves, stripped brickwork, latticed windows, milkmaid's yokes, spinning wheels, horse brasses and so on, with plenty of rustic tables and wooden benches. Outside, there's a spacious well kept terrace looking over Battlebridge Basin, where barges from the Regent's Canal tie up. A girl in an apron serves food such as ploughman's (from £1.75), a biggish spread of salads (from £2.85), dishes of the day such as liver and bacon, pork chop and beef and mushroom casserole (about £3.50), and roast beef (£4.85). Well kept Bass, Charringtons IPA, Fullers London Pride and ESB and Sam Smiths OB and Museum on handpump (quite pricey), and quite a few wines by the bottle; somewhat muzzy piped pop music. A very enjoyable place, crowded with young business people at lunchtime. *(Recommended by Jack Davey, J R Grocott)*

Free house · Licensees Natalie Rachael Hurst and David John Sykes · Real ale Meals and snacks · Open 11–3, 5.30–11 all year

SOUTH LONDON

Anchor (South Bank) Map 13

Bankside, SE1; Southwark Bridge end

This is probably the 'little alehouse on the Bankside' where Pepys went to watch the Great Fire: 'one entire arch of fire above a mile long, the churches, houses, and all on fire at once, a horrid noise the flames made, and the cracking of houses at their ruine.' He had persuaded the king to order houses pulled down as a firebreak in the path of the flames, but when at last he'd found the Lord Mayor (who would have to put the order into effect), 'he cried like a fainting woman, "Lord, what can I do? I am spent! People will not obey me. The fire overtakes us faster than we can do it."' The pub (except when tourist coaches arrive) is still an atmospheric place, with its several black-panelled little rooms, up and down stairs, creaky boards and beams, and old-fashioned high-backed settles as well as sturdy leatherette chairs. Bar food includes ploughman's with a good choice of cheeses (£1.20), pies and cold meats (80p–£2.75) with salads, and lunchtime hot dishes such as casseroles, curries, lasagne, cottage pie and steak and kidney pie (£1.80). There is also a big restaurant upstairs. Well kept Courage Best and Directors on handpump, reasonably priced for the area; fruit machine and space game. The present building, carefully restored in the 1960s, dates from about 1750, when it was rebuilt to replace the earlier tavern. *(Recommended by RW, Tim, Sue and John Kemp)*

Courage · Licensees Frank and Glyn Smith · Real ale · Meals (lunchtime) and snacks · Children in restaurant and Globe Room · Open 11.30–3, 5.30–11 all year

Angel (Bermondsey) Map 12

Bermondsey Wall East, SE16

This friendly riverside pub has perhaps the finest Thames view. The bare-boarded lanternlit balcony, built on timber piles sunk into the river bed, has a sweeping view up to and beyond Tower Bridge on the left and down over the Pool of London on the right. The inside has now been made open-plan, and is comfortably furnished, with captain's chairs around tables by the river windows. Bar food includes Cornish pasties (85p), giant sausage and roll (£1.15), pâté or cheese ploughman's (£1.40), various pies with salad (£2.80) and at lunchtime a hot dish of the day such as liver and onions, cottage pie, chicken casserole or steak and kidney pie (£2.60); well kept Courage Best and Directors on handpump. There is an upstairs restaurant, with big windows for the view, strong on seafood starters and fish and including other main dishes such as rack of lamb (£8.50) and steaks (£8.75), with a roast lunch (£9) on Sunday (restaurant closed Saturday lunchtime and Sunday evening; to book telephone 01-237 3608). *(Recommended by Dave Hoy)*

Courage · Licensee Richard Barrell · Real ale · Meals (lunchtime) and snacks (not Sun evening) · Children in restaurant · Open 12–3, 5.30–11 all year

Bulls Head (Barnes) Map 12

373 Lonsdale Road, SW13

Top-class modern jazz groups every evening, and weekend lunchtime big band sessions (practice on Saturday, concert on Sunday), are the draw to this well run and comfortable riverside pub. Though admission to the well equipped music room is £2 to £3, the sound is perfectly clear – if not authentically loud – in the adjoining lounge bar. This is well carpeted, with solid seats upholstered in a sort of candlewick material – very comfortable. Alcoves open off the main area around the efficient island servery, which has well kept Youngs Bitter and Special on handpump, reasonably priced for London. Bar lunches include soup with crusty bread (95p), sandwiches (from 95p), filled French bread, hot roast meat sandwiches, a pasta dish of the day (£2.10), home-baked pies (£2.20–£2.50) and at lunchtime a carvery of home-roasted joints (from £2.60 for a big helping); fruit machine, and darts in the public bar. Across the road, you can sit on the flood wall by the Thames. *(Recommended by RAB, Patrick Stapley)*

Youngs · Real ale · Meals and snacks · Jazz nightly and weekend lunchtimes Nearby parking may be difficult · Open 11–3, 5.30–11 all year; closed 25 Dec

Founders Arms (Southwark) Map 13

Bankside, SE1; through new housing at end of Hopton Street

This stylish new riverside pub looks across to St Paul's Cathedral. It has a superb position and makes the most of it, with almost unobstructed glass walls facing the Thames: the view is the reason for coming. Its pale green plush banquettes and free-standing elbowrest screens are cunningly placed to allow for the best view and still divide the spacious carpeted bar into friendly-sized areas. Bar food includes

The George, off Borough High Street, SE1

large filled baps (90p–£1), home-made pâtés, cold meats or pies with a wide choice of salads; also a separate restaurant; well kept Youngs Bitter and Special on handpump; dominoes, cribbage and fruit machine. A spacious terrace with white tables on herringbone brick looks out on the water and leads into the attractively planted new Bankside river walks. *(Recommended by D Kennedy, G S Whittet)*

Youngs · Licensees D A Irvine-Turner and C P W Read · Real ale · Meals (not Sat lunchtime or Sun evening) and snacks · Children in restaurant only · Open 11–3, 5.30–11 all year

Fox & Firkin (Lewisham) Map 12

316 Lewisham High Street, SE13

One of David Bruce's own-brew pubs with a choice of other real ales in a large uncluttered bar, and a speaker's pulpit if you get that Hyde Park Corner feeling; see Ferret & Firkin, West London, for further details. *(Recommended by N W McArthur, Stephen Locke)*

George ★ (Southwark) Map 13

Off 77 Borough High Street, SE1 *[illustrated on page 761]*

This is the only galleried coaching-inn left in London, and it's worth repeating the potted history that we included in the last edition of the *Guide*. When it was rebuilt in 1676 after the fire that destroyed most of Southwark (stopped only by the massive new building of St Thomas's Hospital), the building went round three sides of the courtyard. It was bought in the early nineteenth century, and well protected, by the trustees of neighbouring Guy's Hospital, but eventually sold to a predecessor of London and North Eastern Railways, who in the words of E V Lucas 'mercilessly reduced' it in 1889 to build railway sheds. Eventually LNER gave the surviving structure to the National Trust, who have kept it well and simply and very much on the lines of the inns where jugglers, acrobats, conjurers, animal-trainers, musicians and even Shakespeare's strolling players would have performed when Southwark was London's entertainment centre – as Thomas Decker said: 'a continuous ale-house, not a shop to be seen between red-lattice and red-lattice: no workers, but all drinkers'. The yard has been cobbled since our last edition and cars are not allowed in any more. The coachloads of tourists who come here really get their money's worth. The row of ground-floor rooms and bars all have square-latticed windows looking out to the yard, with bare floorboards, black beams, some panelling, old-fashioned built-in settles, plain oak or elm tables, a 1797 'Act of Parliament' clock, dimpled glass lantern-lamps and so forth – the bar closest to the main road is perhaps the most natural and pub-like. Well kept Wethereds, Flowers Original, Greene King IPA and Abbot are served from an ancient beer engine that looks like a cash register; steak and kidney pies and pasties in this end bar, and at the far end (where the staff are adept at coping with people who can't speak English) lots of

---

Places with gardens or terraces usually let children sit there – we note in the text the very very few exceptions that don't.

cheeses, salads, cold meats, rollmops, smoked mackerel, as well as hot dishes such as sausage and beans (95p) or steak and kidney pie or pork in cider (£1.75). A splendid central staircase goes up to a series of dining-rooms, which have posh menus and various degrees of smartness from stripped deal to darkly polished tables, and to a gaslit balcony. *(Recommended by Stephan Carney, Eirlys Roberts, Lesley Foote, Alan Carter, William Meadon and Richard Steel)*

Whitbreads · Licensee John Hall · Real ale · Meals and snacks · Nearby daytime parking difficult · Open 11–3, 5.30–11 all year

Green Man (Putney) Map 12

Wildcroft Road, SW15

This friendly old pub on the edge of Putney Heath has lots of seating and a swing, slide and see-saw among the flowering shrubs and trees on the good-sized lawn behind, and there are also tables outside on sheltered colonnaded side terraces. The pub used to be a haunt of ruthless young highwaymen like Jerry Avershawe, hanged at Kennington in 1795, as well as the rather pitiful footpads (the old equivalent of muggers) like Will Brown and Joseph Whitlock who were hanged after they'd stolen a baker's boy's silver buckle and a ha'penny: now it's altogether more cheerful, with a cosy green-carpeted main bar opening into a quiet sitting-room. Bar food includes sandwiches, lasagne, curry, chilli con carne or moussaka (£1.80), plaice (£2), chicken (£2.20) and sirloin steak (£3.95); they will be doing help-yourself barbecues soon; well kept Youngs Bitter and Special on handpump, reasonably priced for London; ring the bull, cribbage and dominoes as well as sensibly placed darts and a fruit machine. *(Recommended by Jimmy Georgiou, Lesley Foote, Alan Carter)*

Youngs · Licensee Douglas Ord · Real ale · Meals and snacks · Open 11–3, 5.30–11 all year

Hole in the Wall (Waterloo) Map 13

Mepham Street, SE1

The main bar's dark brown brick ceiling is in fact a railway arch virtually underneath Waterloo Station. Every so often things shake as a train rumbles over: it's not just your imagination, aided by the good range of well kept real ales on handpump – Adnams, Brakspears SB, Burke's Best and Original, Godsons Black Horse, Ruddles County and Youngs Special, reasonably priced for the area. They also keep Murphys stout as well as Guinness. A good range of amusements includes a jukebox, two fruit machines and two space games, and the furnishings are very basic. Bar food includes filled rolls (80p), pizzas or beefburgers (85p), ploughman's (£1), two giant sausages with chips and peas (£1.50), salads such as quiche (from £1.75), chilli con carne, chicken and ham pie or steak and kidney pie (£1.75). A smaller front bar is rather smarter. *(Recommended by Peter Hart, David Symes)*

Free house · Licensee Ulick Burke · Real ale · Meals and snacks · Weekday daytime parking difficult · Open 11–3, 5.30–11 all year; closed 25 Dec

Market Porter   (Southwark)   Map 13

9 Stoney Street, SE1

This lively and popular pub brews its own beer. The main part of the long U-shaped bar has rough wooden ceiling beams with beer barrels balanced on them, a heavy wooden bar counter with a beamed gantry, red-cushioned bar stools, a real fire with stuffed animals in glass cabinets on the mantelpiece, several mounted stags' heads and 1920s-style wall lamps. There's a fruit machine and pinball table here. Red-cushioned captain's chairs sit on the patterned dark red carpet, and at one end there is a glass cabinet for food, which includes sausage and bread (80p), grilled chop in a toasted bun (£1), pasty and beans (£1.40) and salads with beef, ham or game pie (£2). There's a small separate room which is partly panelled, with leaded glass windows and a couple of tables; darts in a sensibly segregated area in another small room. *(Recommended by Patrick Stapley and RAB)*

Own brew · Licensee Peter Conlan · Real ale · Meals and snacks · Open 11–3, 5.30–11 all year

Mayflower   (Rotherhithe)   Map 12

117 Rotherhithe Street, SE16

The wooden jetty outside this friendly and carefully restored eighteenth-century pub feels very close to the Thames of days gone by, with its heavy piles plunging down into the water, high old warehouse buildings on either side, and lighters swinging on their moorings. The pub, known until recently as the Spreadeagle & Crown, took its new name in honour of the Pilgrim Fathers' ship that sailed from here in 1611, and one side room has a set of pictures showing the way it would have been built; there's a model of the ship, too. The main bar is old-fashioned, with black ceiling beams, latticed windows, and high-backed winged settles around its tables. A food counter serves reasonably priced ready-made filled rolls, ploughman's or pâté, baked potatoes with a choice of fillings in winter, and salads or hot dishes (steaks as well as casseroles). At lunchtime you can eat these upstairs or in the bar; in the evenings the upstairs becomes a waitress-service restaurant. Well kept Bass and Charringtons IPA on handpump; fruit machine. *(Recommended by Dave Hoy, Dr A K Clarke)*

Charringtons · Licensee Amanda Munro · Real ale · Meals (not Sun evening) and snacks (not Sun) · Open 11–3, 5.30–11 all year

Olde Windmill   (Clapham)   Map 12

Clapham Common South Side, SW4

Who says London hotels are expensive? Try the prices in this Victorian inn's comfortably modern bedroom wing. On Clapham Common, it's a nice pub, too. The front room, under its fancy plaster ceiling, is dominated by the substantial and heavily manned bar counter – even so, it can be difficult to reach late on a summer Saturday, as it then seems to serve not just the pub but half the Common too. Further in, the main room is spacious and domed, with clusters of orange leatherette seats, sofas and small armchairs around elegant black tables, and big prints of Dutch windmill pictures on the flowery black and brown wallpaper. Ploughman's, macaroni cheese, cottage pie, chilli con carne or ham salad, clam fries, curry and rice and lunchtime grills from an efficiently manned food counter in this inner room (main dishes from around £2.40); well kept Youngs Bitter, Special and John's London Lager on handpump, quite cheap; fruit machines. There are picnic tables in courtyards at each side, one with a colonnaded end shelter and tubs of shrubs. *(Recommended by Lesley Foote, Alan Carter, Bryan Shiner, Jimmy Georgiou)*

Youngs · Licensee Michael Tobin · Real ale · Meals and snacks (not Sun) Open 11–3, 5.30–11 all year · Bedrooms tel 01-673 4578; £22.50S/£27S

Orange Tree   (Richmond) Map 12

45 Kew Road

The Orange Tree Fringe Theatre upstairs carries on a long-standing tradition: the big courtly paintings of the seven ages of man by Henry Stacy Marks in the main bar were presented to the Green Room theatre club here in 1921. This spacious open-plan room is popular, with comfortable seats on the carpet that spreads around its efficient central servery, big coaching and Dickens prints, and an unusual embossed ceiling pattern of fruit and foliage. At lunchtime there's a full range of sandwiches, ploughman's and so forth upstairs; at lunchtime and in the evening, good food is also served in a wine-bar-like basement – soft lighting, simple tables on a tiled floor, old stripped brickwork walls. It includes chicken and mushroom or steak and kidney pie (£2.80), navarin of lamb (£3.20), duck in orange (£3.40), and a good choice of salads. There are good value Sunday roast lunches (£3.45). Well kept Youngs Bitter and Special on handpump, relatively reasonably priced for London; darts, dominoes, fruit machine. *(Recommended by N M Williamson, C J Darkens, Beti Wyn Thomas)*

Youngs · Licensees Don and Chris Murphy · Real ale · Meals and snacks Children in downstairs restaurant · Nearby parking difficult · Open 11–3, 5.30–11 all year

Phoenix & Firkin   (Denmark Hill) Map 12

5 Windsor Walk, SE5

Recently well restored fire-gutted Victorian Denmark Hill Railway Station, converted into the latest of David Bruce's own-brew pubs; the bars span four working railway lines. For more details see Ferret & Firkin, West London.

Prince of Orange   (Rotherhithe) Map 12

118 Lower Road, SE16

This popular pub is East London's premier jazz spot, with different acts and styles every night and weekend lunchtimes. The large L-shaped open-plan bar has a central stage at one end with, below it, orange plastic chairs and wooden kitchen ones set around low dark wood tables; the ceiling and walls are decorated with posters of forthcoming acts, some neon signs and photographs of various groups. Two small rooms lead off: you can either stand at the bar in one or eat at tables in the other; the walls here are completely covered with old photographs, including some old 1930s jazz sessions at Abbey Road Studios. Food is simple but good and includes toasted sandwiches (75p), pizzas (£1.20) and chilli con carne or burgers (£1.60). Trumans on handpump; spirits with a splash of mixer (£1). It's a cheerful place for listening to music. *(Recommended by PM, RAB)*

Trumans · Licensee John Payne · Real ale · Meals and snacks · Open 11–3, 5.30–12 all year

Rose & Crown (Wimbledon) Map 12

55 High Street, SW19

Close to Wimbledon Common, this comfortably modernised ex-coaching-inn has lots of tables outside in the long courtyard with a trellis of roses and honeysuckle along one side and a little verandah at the far end. The rambling main bar, which used to be the poet Swinburne's local, has a full set of Hogarth's proverb engravings on its silky golden walls, comfortable brown leatherette seats in friendly carpeted alcoves, and a relaxed background babble of conversation. The separate buttery bar has sandwiches, home-made pies and Scotch eggs, sausages, baked potatoes, various quiches (£1.20), lasagne (£1.20), cauliflower cheese, macaroni cheese or fish pie (£1.50) and chilli con carne (£1.60); well kept Youngs Bitter and Special on handpump; dominoes, cribbage. *(Recommended by Peter Hart, Mike Muston, Dave Butler and Les Storey, Helen Ridley)*

Youngs · Licensee A D Hughes · Real ale · Meals and snacks · Children in buttery bar · Open 11–3, 5–11 all year

Ship (Wandsworth) Map 12

41 Jews Row, SW18

Since the last edition, a Thames barge has been acquired by the pub and moored alongside its spacious riverside terrace as a sort of floating annexe, although she sails along the East and South Coasts during the summer months. Partly cobbled and partly concrete, the terrace spreads over a wide area and is divided into sections by low planted walls; one part even has a bower of runner bean plants. The tables have good sturdy seats and are well spaced out. In the evenings, and at weekend lunchtimes, a substantial charcoal barbecue counter out here does good home-made hamburgers and three sausages (£2.85), whole leg of lamb for four or five (£17.50) and spit-roast beef, all imaginatively garnished. Other bar food includes fresh tomato, basil and mint soup (90p), baked potatoes, club sandwich and seafood lasagne (£1.95) and beef in Guinness (£2.25). It's well away from traffic. The house itself (which is too far from the water to

---

If we know a pub does summer barbecues, we say so.

have a river view) is plain, with a comfortably relaxed atmosphere:
the bar opening on to the terrace has a harmonium and easy chairs
and sofas, and the public bar has sensibly placed darts, and a fruit
machine and juke box. Well kept Youngs Bitter and Special on
handpump. *(Recommended by Jimmy Georgiou, David Potter, Alan Franck)*

*Youngs · Licensee Charles Gotto · Real ale · Meals and snacks · You may have
to park some way away · Open 11–3, 5.30–11 all year*

White Swan   (Richmond) Map 12

Old Palace Lane

The atmosphere in this popular little pub is more like that of a
country local than a busy London pub – at 8.30pm still quiet enough
for someone on a comfortable red-cushioned settle to be reading his
paper undisturbed. The bar is open-plan but is almost S-shaped and
so doesn't give the feeling of one big room. Copper pots hang from
the dark beamed ceiling, and there are old prints of London on the
walls, along with one wall of old china plates. Captain's chairs, dark
wood tables and red velveteen banquettes are set on the red patterned
carpet and around the open brick fireplace. Food at lunchtimes is
served from a glass cabinet displaying cold meats, quiches and salads.
Well kept Courage Best and Directors on handpump; fruit machine.
Outside there is a paved garden with climbing plants, flowering tubs,
flower beds and wooden tables and benches. Summer evening
barbecues include sausage and onion in a roll (80p), spare ribs
(£2.75) and eight-ounce rump steak (£4.50): best to get there by 9pm
if you want a table. *(Recommended by RAB)*

Courage · Real ale · Meals and snacks · Open 11–3, 5.30–11 all year

WEST LONDON

Anglesea Arms   (Chelsea) Map 13

15 Selwood Terrace, SW7

With Adnams, Brakspears Special, Fullers London Pride and ESB,
Greene King Abbot, Sam Smiths and Youngs Special well kept on
handpump, this welcoming pub gets very busy in the evenings and at
weekends, when even the outside terrace (which has seats and tables)
tends to overflow into the quiet side street. It's had a thorough
refurbishment and is under new licensees since the last edition, and at
lunchtime seems spacious and airy inside, with steps down to a lower
side area. A quick-service food counter has ploughman's with
Cheddar, Brie, Stilton or pâté (£1.60), Buckingham pie and assorted
salads (£2.50) and steak and kidney pie (£2.95). *(Recommended by W T
Aird, RAB, Amanda Barford; up-to-date reports please)*

*Free house · Licensees Norah Marden and T W Simpson · Real ale · Meals
(lunchtime, not Sun) and snacks (not Sun) · Daytime parking metered · Open
11–3, 5.30–11 all year*

Prices of main dishes usually include vegetables or a side salad.

767

Bulls Head (Chiswick) Map 12

Strand-on-the-Green, W4

This riverside pub rambles about up and down steps and through black-panelled alcoves, and its traditional furnishings include benches built in to the simple panellings and so forth. Small windows look past attractively planted hanging flower baskets to the river just beyond the narrow towpath (where you can take your Combes, Watneys Stag, or Websters Yorkshire, well kept on handpump). There's a pleasant, relaxed atmosphere, and it's not too crowded even on fine evenings – except perhaps at weekends. A separate lunchtime food bar serves reasonably priced ploughman's, chicken curry, lasagne, moussaka, chilli con carne, shepherd's pie, steak and mushroom pie and salads (main dishes around £1.95–£2.20). A games room at the back has bar billiards, darts and a fruit machine. The original building here, then an inn, served as Cromwell's HQ several times during the Civil War, and it was here that Moll Cutpurse overheard Cromwell talking to Fairfax about the troops' pay money coming by horse from Hounslow and got her gang to capture the moneybags. (Recommended by RAB and Patrick Stapley)

Watneys · Real ale · Meals and snacks (lunchtime) · Open 11–3, 5.30–10.30

Dove ★ (Hammersmith) Map 12

19 Upper Mall, W6

Customers as different as Coleridge and Captain Marryat have enjoyed a drink at this intimate and old-fashioned riverside tavern. Its three small rooms are quite unspoilt, with bare floorboards, low beams, black panelling, old-fashioned wooden settles and similar seats, and some Thames photographs and prints. Its small suntrap terrace with a grapevine is open in summer but enclosed in winter and looks directly out on the Thames reach just above Hammersmith Bridge and across to the playing-fields on the far side. There's a tradition that James Thomson (who wrote 'Rule, Britannia') wrote the final part ('Winter') of his less well-known 'The Seasons' in an upper room here, dying of a fever he had caught on a trip from here to Kew in bad weather. The lunchtime buffet bar has a spread of several different meats, pies, good pâtés, cheeses and salads (most £1.10–£1.75), and there are five home-made hot specials such as shepherd's pie (£2.15) and perhaps juicy roast beef; there are cold snacks in the evening. Well kept Fullers London Pride and ESB on handpump. (Recommended by Tim, Sue and John Kemp)

Fullers · Licensee Brian Lovrey · Real ale · Meals (lunchtime) and snacks Open 11–3, 5.30–11 all year

Eel Pie (Twickenham) Map 12

9 Church Street

Since the last edition the food in this popular pub is served upstairs, though you can take it down to the simply furnished bar and eat it there; main dishes include seafood platter, cheesey cottage pie,

chicken Kashmir, creole jambalaya, barbecue pork and a range of
salads (all around £2.50). But for many, the chief draw is the well
kept range of real ales on handpump: Badger Best and Tanglefoot,
Flowers Original, Godsons Black Horse, Websters Yorkshire,
Wethereds and Youngs Special. A good, lively atmosphere; darts,
dominoes, cribbage and a fruit machine, maybe piped music; a bench
out on the pavement. *(Recommended by D J Penny, N M Williamson, C J
Darkens)*

*Badger · Manager D Wright · Real ale · Meals and snacks (lunchtime, not Sun)
Children welcome · Open 11–3, 5.30–11 all year*

Ferret & Firkin   (Fulham) Map 12

Lots Road, SW10

Just around the corner from the *Guide*'s office, this is one of the best
of David Bruce's small chain of pubs brewing their own beer on the
premises. It's a simple conversion of an old pub that had been
disused, with bare floorboards not even sealed, but furnishings well
made from good wood. The main wall is curved, with tall airy
windows, and sturdy seats form booths around tables along it,
leaving plenty of standing room in front of the long bar counter –
which is itself curved to match the front wall. Fittings such as the
slowly circulating colonial-style ceiling fans and punning
advertisements for the beers put an old-fashioned streak in the
atmosphere, but the main ingredient is the relaxed feeling you get
from the easy-going crowd of customers – most youngish but
otherwise a very mixed bag indeed. The beers include ones named
along the lines of the pub (here, Ferret, Stoat, an occasionally brewed
much lighter Weasel Water or superstrong Balloonatic), always a
strong Dogbolter, and usually a Bruce's. With 24 hours' notice you
can collect a bulk supply. There are also two or three guest beers from
other breweries. Bar food includes home-made giant sausages (50p),
heftily filled giant meat-and-salad rolls (£1), quiche (£1.25), Stilton
ploughman's (£1.50) and hot dishes (from £1.50). There's usually a
pianist on duty, and there are seats out on the pavement. Sister pubs
we'd recommend in London follow much the same pattern as this, so
have not been described in detail. *(Recommended by James Cane, Patrick
Stapley and RAB, and others)*

*Own brew · Proprietor David Bruce · Real ale · Meals and snacks · Daytime
parking metered (although traffic wardens have been very rare) · Open 11–3,
5.30–11 all year*

Frog & Firkin   (Notting Hill) Map 12

41 Tavistock Crescent, W11

See preceding entry; has a pianist and an unusual hat collection.
*(Recommended by J Barden, Nicholas Dowson; more reports on this one,
please)*

Planning a day in the country? At the back of the book is a list of pubs in really
attractive scenery.

London Apprentice (Isleworth) Map 12

Church Street

Picturesque and spaciously comfortable riverside pub near Syon House. There's a very long L-shaped bar with tapestry-style covered wall benches and stools on the brown patterned carpet and lots of dark wood veneered tables. At one end there are darts, bar billiards and a fruit machine, and at the other a separate room with partly panelled walls, wheel-back chairs and a glass food cabinet; various ploughman's (£1.40 for cheese, £1.60 for pâté) and a help-yourself selection of freshly made salads (from £2.60 for mackerel or veal or ham and egg pie to £3.40 for prawn and mayonnaise). There's a separate restaurant upstairs. Watneys Stag and Combes on handpump. It's popular with young people, and the staff are young and friendly. Outside there's a pretty terrace overlooking the river, with garden furniture and hanging baskets and tubs full of bright flowers. As it's signposted from the main road it can get very crowded in summer. *(Recommended by RAB, J R Grocott, W T Aird, R K Whitehead)*

Watneys · Licensee Anthony Cain · Real ale · Meals (lunchtimes) and snacks Children in eating area · Open 11–3, 6–11

Scarsdale Arms (Kensington) Map 12

23A Edwardes Square, W8

With gas lighting inside as well as out by the pretty flower-hung terrace under its tall plane tree, this old-fashioned pub is quiet at lunchtime but tends to get packed in the evening when it's got the feel of being at the top of the trend. The spacious bar has cushioned wooden benches built in to the cream walls, stuffed squirrels and a gazelle's head, shelves of blue and white plates behind the food counter, bare floorboards, a dark, high ceiling, big etched windows, and open coal fires in winter. Bar food includes giant sausage in French bread (90p), pâté and French bread (£1.50), beef or ham salad or pies (£2.20), and in the evening griddle chops (£3.50) and steaks (£5); there's also a Sunday carvery. Well kept Watneys Stag, Websters Yorkshire and Wilsons on handpump, and a separate back serving counter which to some extent concentrates on cocktails, Pimms and so forth. *(Recommended by RAB)*

Watneys · Licensee Joe Chambers · Real ale · Meals and snacks (not Sun) Children in eating area · Parking nearby can be difficult (there's a car park in Earls Court Road) · Open 11–3, 5.30–11 all year; closed 25 and 26 Dec

White Swan ★ (Twickenham) Map 12

Riverside

A weekday lunchtime when you've plenty of time to spare is when this old riverside pub is at its best. Lunch is a leisurely, almost clubby affair, maybe with the menu not emerging until one o'clock and a meal itself not until nearer two. The food is simple but good value: home-made soup and changing hot dishes such as good beef hot-pot or steak and kidney pie that's good even to the crust (hot dishes from around £2.20–£3.95). Snacks include filled rolls, ploughman's and pâté (£1.75). There are homely country pictures on the faded walls, open log fires in winter, and maybe old-fashioned music, with simple scrubbed tables to eat at, and a big semi-communal one in the back room. Well kept Combes, Manns IPA, Watneys Stag and Websters Yorkshire on handpump, good genuine Beaujolais, and mulled wine in winter and on cold nights; darts, shove-ha'penny, dominoes, fruit machine. Service, like the atmosphere, is very relaxed. At weekends and in the evenings it's much more crowded. The picturesque seventeenth-century house is built on a platform well above ground level, with steep steps up to the door and the sheltered terrace, which is full of tubs and baskets of flowers; even its cellar is raised above ground as insurance against the flood tides that wash right up to the house. As a result the little riverside lawn across the lane tends to be rather muddy sometimes – it's got a peaceful view over a quiet stretch of the Thames, to country meadows on its far bank past the tip of Eel Pie Island. There are often Saturday evening barbecues out here. It's a short stroll to the imposing Palladian Marble Hill House in its grand Thames-side park (built for a mistress of George II) and Orleans House Gallery. (*Recommended by D J Penny, J P Berryman, G Berneck, Guy Atkins, H E Emson, B R Shiner, C J Darkens, RAB*)

Watneys · Licensee Shirley Sutton · Real ale · Meals (lunchtime) and snacks (not Sun) · Children in dining-room · Open 11–3, 6–11 all year

Windsor Castle ★   (Holland Park/Kensington) Map 12

114 Campden Hill Road, W8

Everything about this well kept pub is old-fashioned: its series of little rooms with dark panelling and wooden partitions, sturdy built-in elm benches, time-smoked ceilings and soft lighting; its absolute freedom from fruit machines, piped music and so on; its friendly personal attention; even a snug little pre-war-style dining-room opening off the bar. Bar food includes cheese and biscuits or French bread (from 60p), a good choice of sandwiches (from 80p) including a chip butty (80p), toasted sandwiches (from 90p) and even a bargain eight-ounce steak sandwich (£2.80), pâté (£1.10), ham and egg pie (£2.40), salads (from £2.40), ham or beef or quiche Lorraine and chips (£2.20), gammon and egg (£2.50), eight-ounce rump steak (£4.20) and home-made fruit pie (65p); well kept Bass and Charringtons IPA on handpump, reasonably priced by London standards. A special summer feature is the big tree-shaded back terrace – note that, unusually, no children are allowed here – which is quite roomy, with lots of sturdy teak seats and tables on flagstones, knee-high stone walls (eminently sittable-on), high ivy-covered sheltering walls, and soft shade from a sweeping low-branched plane tree, a lime and a flowering cherry. A bar counter serves the terrace directly, as does a separate food stall. Usually fairly quiet at lunchtime, the pub is often packed in the evenings. (*Recommended by Dr A K Clarke, Patrick Curry, C B M Gregory*)

Charringtons · Licensee Anthony James Owen · Real ale · Meals and snacks (not Sun evening) · Daytime parking metered · Open 11–3, 5.30–11 all year

---

Food details, prices, timing and so on refer to bar food, not to a separate restaurant if there is one.

EAST LONDON

Grapes (Limehouse) Map 12

76 Narrow Street, E14

Whistler used to come here to paint, and as this little pub is off the tourist track it is one of the friendliest and most genuine of any on the river. The glass-roofed back balcony is one of the most sheltered places for a riverside drink, and there's an attractive little restaurant upstairs. There are lots of prints, often of actors, on the partly panelled walls of the long narrow bar. Bar food, with prices unchanged since last year, includes filled sandwiches (from 70p), ploughman's or pâté (£1), Irish stew (£2.40), prawn curry (£2.50) and fish and seafood pie (£2.70). Well kept Ind Coope Burton and Friary Meux and Taylor-Walker Bitter on handpump. Dickens used this pub as the basis of his 'Six Jolly Fellowship Porters' in *Our Mutual Friend*, on the strength of its grim reputation for losing its best customers to the anatomists: when they were insensibly drunk, people would row them out into the Thames, tip them in, then fish them out when drowned and sell them as raw material for anatomy experiments.

Taylor-Walker (Ind Coope) · Licensee Frank Johnson · Real ale · Meals (not Sat or Sun or Mon evening) and snacks (not Sat evening or Sun) · Open 11–2.30, 5–11 all year; closed 25 Dec

Grave Maurice (Whitechapel) Map 12

269 Whitechapel Road, E1

Readers who have known this pub for many years say it has hardly changed; it's kept very neatly, well run by Mrs H, and has a good friendly atmosphere. Opposite London Hospital and much used by the younger medical staff, it has a long and quietly comfortable lounge bar edged by high-backed soft red seats forming booths around long, rather narrow tables, with green leatherette bucket seats in the middle. Its good value and quickly served bar food includes filled rolls and sandwiches, ploughman's, casseroles and summer salads, and there is a lunchtime restaurant. Well kept Trumans Bitter and Best on handpump; maybe piped music. *(Recommended by Michael Dempsey, Barry Smith)*

Trumans (Watneys) · Licensee Alan Hodges · Real ale · Meals and snacks Open 11–2.30, 5–11 all year

Hollands (Stepney) Map 12

9 Exmouth Street, E1

Set on the edge of a modern housing estate and just off the busy Commercial Road, this little pub is a real surprise. It's not changed much since Queen Victoria was young, when a Mr Holland was running it then too – the present landlord's great-grandfather. Its decorations are all original Victorian. There are two cosy bars: the lounge bar, on two levels and separated from the main bar by an arched doorway and heavy velvet curtains, has panelled and velveteen-cushioned bench seats, old sepia photographs, a red tiled floor, brass pots hanging from the ceiling and a big Victorian fireplace with large china ornaments on the mantelpiece. The main bar is dimly lit with an ochre-painted and panelled ceiling, fairy lights hung along the cornice, *Vanity Fair* pictures, Victorian cartoons and photographs and a clutter of trumpets, glass and brass ornaments hanging from the ceiling; the heavy bar counter has swivelling etched and cut glass snob screens, and antique mirrors. It's a friendly oasis of well kept calm, handed carefully down to us over four generations – we wish there were more like this! Bar food includes sandwiches, baked potatoes (30p), ploughman's (70p), pâté (80p), hot flans with salad (£1.26) and hot specials in winter; Fremlins on handpump; darts, cribbage. *(Recommended by RAB, Michael Dempsey, R J Watkins)*

Free house · Licensee J C Holland · Real ale · Meals and snacks (lunchtimes, but snacks available in the evening with advance warning) · Open 11–12.30, 5–11 all year

The Bunch of Grapes, Shepherd Market, W1

Prospect of Whitby (Wapping) Map 12

Wapping Wall, E1

This famous pub is very much an entertainment and should be seen as that. But it also has superb river views (appreciated by Turner), and an attractive flagstoned courtyard overlooking the river and the warehouses on the far bank. Inside, there are plenty of beams, panelling and flagstones, a pianola and rollicking groups of live musicians, and coachloads of foreign visitors lapping up the stories about Judge Jeffreys dining here, his appetite whetted by the sight of his executed victims' corpses hanging in chains from the piles outside. Well kept Combes, Ruddles County, Watneys Stag and Websters Yorkshire on handpump; giant sausage in French bread (90p), pasty (95p), ploughman's (£1.45), jumbo sausage (£1.50), fresh salads (from £1.70) and a hot dish such as beef Mexican (£2.60); there's also a separate river-view restaurant upstairs (about £30 for two). Fruit machine; piped music when it isn't live. *(Recommended by Michael Dempsey)*

Watneys · Licensee T Chapman · Real ale · Meals and snacks · Children in eating areas · Guitar and vocalist Mon–Fri evening, Irish folk band Sat and Sun lunchtime and evening · Open 11–3, 5.30–11 all year; closed 25 Dec

---

Lucky Dip

Besides the fully inspected pubs, you might like to try these Lucky Dips recommended by readers (if you do, please send us reports). We have split them into the main areas used for the full reports – Central, North and so on. Within each area the Lucky Dips are listed by postal district, ending with Greater London suburbs on the edge of that area.

CENTRAL

EC1

Empress of Russia [362 St Johns Street]: unspoilt with undeniable character, two separate bars, well kept Wethereds and (though a Whitbreads house) Greene King Abbot too: a minute from Sadlers Wells – the orchestra drinks here (always a recommendation!). Old Sadlers Wells prints on wall, folk club upstairs, splendid Stilton with big hunk of bread for under 60p *(Roger Protz)*
King of Diamonds [Greville Street]: good modern pub in centre of London's diamond market; rooftop terrace outside, upstairs wine bar and downstairs Ring Bar lavishly decorated with sporting photographs and posters (both these bookable for private parties); also good ground-floor Middle Bar *(Frank Arnold)*
Oakley Arms [32 Hall Street]: good atmosphere, friendly customers *(K Mitchell)*
Old Red Lion [418 St John Street]: hearty good value freshly cooked food such as stuffed hearts, kippers with French bread, liver, and roast beef or lamb, fresh sandwiches, good Bass and Charringtons IPA *(Jack Davey)*
One Tun [Saffron Hill]: food in good upstairs restaurant, evening snacks, oak-panelled walls give a homely atmosphere, several different beers *(Frank Arnold)*
Surprise [Bowling Green Lane]: food good – and lots of it; good welcome, cheerful wicker furniture, green and white paintwork combined wine bar and bar inside; Ind Coope Bitter and Burton *(M Quine)*
Three Compasses [Cow Cross Street]: modern pub, pseudo-Victorian inside with panelling, wooden floor, carpeted snug area beyond bar; Trumans Best and Samson on handpump, good bar food, live jazz Saturday night and Sunday

lunchtime; popular with rag trade and Clerkenwell jewellers and metalworkers. There has been a pub here since 1723 *(P T Young)*

EC2

Dirty Dick's [Bishopsgate]: lively barrel-vaulted cellar with good loud pop music, traditional-style ground floor with good range of real ales and cheerfully served lunchtime food, upstairs wine bar *(LYM)*

Kings Arms [Wormwood Street]: neat and efficiently run City pub with lively atmospheric downstairs bar and good food *(David Surridge)*

Windmill [Tabernacle Street]: multiple choice of beers; very comfortable pub *(David Symes)*

EC3

Hoop & Grapes [47 Aldgate High Street]: enjoyable big pub where east meets City – quite enjoyed it really! *(Dr A K Clarke)*

EC4

Bouncing Banker [Cousin Lane]: good river views from balcony, plenty of lunchtime seating, real ale, lively atmosphere *(MHG)*

Olde Watling [Watling Street]: well kept Bass and Charringtons IPA in heavy-beamed and timbered pub built by Wren in 1662 as a site commissariat for his new St Paul's Cathedral *(Stephan Carney, LYM)*

Pavilions End [24 Watling Street]: food very good and a good range of real ales including Boddingtons; done out as a cricket pavilion with good lunchtime 'City' atmosphere and bright 'cricket' décor *(A W Wells)*

SW1

Albert [Victoria Street]: *Standard*'s Pub of the Year 1984: ornate Victorian exterior dwarfed by glassy skyscrapers, comfortable well kept, efficiently served food, crowded at lunchtime *(BB)*

Bag o' Nails [6 Buckingham Palace Road]: comfortable and tastefully furnished and decorated L-shaped bar, handy for Queen's Gallery and Royal Mews (open Wednesday and Thursday afternoon); excellent reasonably priced hot or cold lunches *(FA)*

Barley Mow [104 Horseferry Road]: lively and spacious, well decorated in restful reds and greens, real plants as well as real ale, both well cared for. Grand piano played, no piped music. Appetising food bar, real ales *(Peter Hart)*

George IV [Montpelier Street]: lively pub, good lunchtime food, well kept beers *(Chris Grundy)*

Gloucester [187 Sloane Street]: good food with excellent truly polite service at a sensible price; a real pleasure to visit *(Roger Bloye)*

Red Lion [Crown Passage]: well run local with splendid atmosphere for such a built-up area; gets crowded *(David Surridge)*

St Stephens Tavern [Parliament Street]: MPs' pub with elaborately old-fashioned bar all etched glass and mahogany, basement food bar, upstairs restaurant *(LYM)*

Star [Belgrave Mews West]: popular Georgian mews pub, Fullers, quite smart upstairs, can get crowded *(W T Aird, LYM)*

Two Chairmen [1 Warwick House Street]: tiny single bar pub near Trafalgar Square: quaint little retreat from the bustle outside *(Dr A K Clarke)*

Westminster Arms [9 Storeys Gate]: two-floor friendly pub with excellent choice of real ales, some food, basement wine bar, can get crowded *(W R Rossiter, LYM)*

SW3

Admiral Codrington [17 Mossop Street]: warm, inviting, good varied food *(W T Aird)*

Black Lion [Old Church Street]: quiet small local, gentle calm atmosphere *(W T Aird)*

Cadogan Arms [298 King's Road]: rough timber baulks, red-bulbed lanterns, impression of intimacy, well kept Combes and Watneys Stag, friendly atmosphere, Chef & Brewer food in waitress-service area *(Mrs L Griffiths, BB)*

Crown & Sceptre [132 Brompton Road]: food good (lasagne, pizza, pies, sandwiches, strawberries and cream, cake), good choice of drinks, handy for Harrods *(Gerhard Michael Bauer)*

Kings [Cheyne Walk]: views of Thames and houseboats from bright refurbished cocktail bar *(BB)*

Kings Head & Eight Bells [50 Cheyne Walk]: roomy, pleasing subdued music, views of Thames, tasteful décor, not crowded on our visit, good variety of food *(Robert L Scott, RFD)*

Man in the Moon [392 King's Road]: attractive and roomy pub with interesting tiles, popular for lunch, theatre downstairs *(Mrs L Griffiths, W T Aird, LYM)*

Phoenix [Smith Street]: clean, friendly atmosphere and service, good food at excellent prices; well run pub *(J Madley)*

Queens Elm [Fulham Road]: good atmosphere in two-bar Chelsea local *(W T Aird)*

Roebuck [King's Road]: attractive neighbourhood pub *(Mrs L Griffiths)*

Trafalgar [King's Road]: smart and spacious old-style renovation, neatly well kept, good bar layout including food display, Charringtons *(S R Collins, BB)*

W1

Angel [Marylebone High Street]: well kept two-storey Sam Smiths pub, lively at lunchtime, quieter in the evening *(LYM)*

Blue Posts [28 Rupert Street]: busy well staffed bar, good beer and proper cocktails including hot drinks in winter, good buffet (did blue blazers and buttered rum) *(W T Aird, BB)*

Bricklayers Arms [Gresse Street]: busy two-level executive pub; lounge bar with modern décor, settees, coffee tables; public bar has darts, fruit machine. Well kept Sam Smiths on handpump. Packed at lunchtime, but comfortable and relaxing *(C Rosling, Stuart Baker)*

Coach & Horses [Romilly Street]: one of the busiest and most popular pubs here, partly because prices aren't very West End; good buffet lunch *(W T Aird)*

Cockney Pride [Piccadilly Circus]: flamboyantly splendid, lives up to its name; marvellous pastiche of old-world London tavern even down to the music *(Frank Arnold)*

Devonshire Arms [21a Devonshire Street]: decorously friendly and comfortable Edwardian pub with bar food and upstairs dining-room *(LYM)*

Dog & Duck [18 Bateman Street]: real Soho pub with splendid decorative tilework in its cosy and friendly little bar, well kept Taylor-Walkers *(Jon Dewhirst, LYM)*

Dover Castle [Weymouth Mews]: food good and atmosphere pleasant (but beer's pricey) *(W T Aird, Dr A K Clarke)*

Duke of Wellington [94A Crawford Street]: nice cosy little pub with lovely collection of duke's-head ornaments; more villagey in style than a London pub, very pleasant landlord; lunchtime food *(Rosemary and Brian Wilmot)*

Duke of York [47 Rathbone Street]: well kept Bass and Charringtons IPA in old-fashioned welcoming local with popular and reasonably priced lunchtime home cooking *(LYM)*

King Charles II [18 Kingly Street]: popular and ornate *(Stephan Carney)*

Kings Arms [2 Shepherd Market]: stripped-down décor of bare wood and concrete with dimly lit galleried upper floor, well kept real ale, good value pub food, attractive atmosphere – most unlikely find behind Piccadilly *(Dr A K Clarke, BB)*

Red Lion [Kingly Street]: smartly modernised and relaxing two-storey pub with well kept Sam Smiths and upstairs food bar *(Michael Sandy, W T Aird, LYM)*

Rose & Crown [2 Old Park Lane]: charming little pub in quiet nook off Piccadilly; sporting trophies on the walls and liquors in miniature casks give a gamey atmosphere *(Frank Arnold)*

Star & Garter [Poland Street]: very friendly little Soho local with well kept Courage Best and Directors *(Stephan Carney, W T Aird, LYM)*

Westmorland Arms [34 George Street]: deeply comfortable and welcoming, Tolly beers, food bar *(LYM)*

W2

Kings Head [33 Moscow Road]: big well furnished pub with good beer and lively clientele. Chess! *(Dr A K Clarke)*

Swan [66 Bayswater Road]: courtyard with tree-shaded tables outside old pub looking across busy road to Kensington Gardens; well kept Watneys real ales, busy food bar *(LYM)*

WC1

City of York [22 High Holborn]: splendid long bar — longest in the country — tuns and casks over the counter, little nooks for confidential lunches, with good real ales from the north, food, friendly service, relaxing even though very popular *(J S Evans, G S Whittett, Anthony Hooper, Maria Tedeschi, Michael Sandy, H L McDougall)*

Friend at Hand [4 Herbrand Street]: pleasant, good sandwiches, Ruddles County; mentioned in one of the songs in *Cats (J Dobris)*

Queen's Larder [Queen Square]: friendly, with charming upstairs dining-room overlooking square *(W T Aird, LYM)*

Sun [63 Lamb's Conduit Street]: food in bar good, and very interesting cellar tour (have to book — quite expensive, but lots of free sampling!) *(Joel Dobris)*

WC2

Devereux [Devereux Court]: atmospheric panelled bar with barristers and office workers, well kept Courage Best and Directors, good reasonably priced bar food *(Hugh and Richard Fowler)*

Nags Head [Floral Street]: well kept McMullens real ale and efficient staff in busy central pub, ideal meeting place, good cheap food *(David Surridge, Kevin Lyne, Tony Lewis, Anne Dabbadie)*

Salisbury [90 St Martins Lane]: floridly decorated with red velvet, well preserved glass and mirrors, flamboyantly theatrical; good value food, close to theatres and antiquarian bookshops *(W T Aird, BB)*

Seven Stars [53 Carey Street]: lovely pub whatever one's criteria, but much too small even for those plucking up their courage on their way to the bankruptcy court and for those who've dropped in to fight despondency and despair on their way back! *(W T Aird)*

Sherlock Holmes [10 Northumberland Street]: lots of convincing Sherlock Holmes memorabilia in well run pub with quick lunchtime food counter *(BB)*

White Swan [14 New Row]: small pillared front bar crowded at lunchtime with publishing people, real public-bar atmosphere in roomier seventeenth-century panelled back part, food *(BB)*

NORTH

N1

Malt & Hops [33 Caledonian Road]: slightly basic but comfortable enough with unusual range of good beer *(David Symes)*

Marquess Tavern [Canonbury Street]: large Youngs pub with comfortably plush domed back room, front bar with attractively stripped half-panelling, relaxed atmosphere, good value food including salads, toasted sandwiches and hot dish of the day, well kept real ales *(W Fitzgerald, Roger Protz, BB)*

Wharfdale [Wharfdale Road]: food (hot and cold) good in waterside pub overlooking canal *(Guy Atkins)*

N2

Clissold Arms [Fortis Green]: well kept Courage Best and Directors, bars cool even in summer *(Jack Davey)*

N6

Prince of Wales [Highgate High Street]: olde worlde, with friendly staff, good jazz twice a week, pub food *(Patrick Stapley, David Wiseman)*

Red Lion & Sun [25 North Road]: great favourite where lords mingle happily with lollipop men, teachers, musicians, choral societies, punks. David and Tina the genial licensees serve good Bass, good choice of lunchtime food, very friendly atmosphere, no music *(David Gutmann)*

N7

Flounder & Firkin [54 Holloway Road]: opened March 1985, David Bruce's seventh London pub, £250,000 development of an ex-Allied Breweries pub previously the Highgate Brewery Tap on the site of Willoughbys Brewery (1815–1914); brewery can be viewed through portholes in floor. Huge tropical aquarium, Whale ale, etc, fish pie *(Anon)*

Tufnell Park Tavern [Tufnell Park Road]: music! Live jazz several nights a week, including local heroes, the Crouch End All Stars, in big roomy pub that fills up for them. Staff cope with courtesy and efficiency; food includes pizza *(Hazel Morgan)*

N8

Dicks Bar [61 Tottenham Lane]: free house with excellent range of real ales including Arkells BBB, Kingsdown, Gales HSB, Sam Smiths, Godsons Black Horse, Old Tom, Everards Old Original, good solid generous helpings of food, happy atmosphere *(John, Tim and Andrew Kemp, Sue Weil, Odile Roudet)*

New Priory [169 Priory Road]: was a used-car showroom, but pleasantly converted, with wide range of real ales such as Greene King, Marstons Pedigree; buffet bar food good *(Simon White)*

N12

Moss Hall [283 Ballards Lane]: now a Fullers pub, good atmosphere, reasonably priced lunchtime food, friendly staff, relaxing atmosphere *(David Gutmann)*

N16

Marler [Stoke Newington High Street]: newish free house, tastefully done out in stained woods. Good choices of bottled and draught beers, cheapish Westons cider. Best early week! *(Martin Patrick Egan)*

N17

Bell & Hare [724 Tottenham High Road]: tastefully renovated, 1930s style saloon bar, Whitbreads and Flowers *(Martin Patrick Egan)*

N20

Cavalier [Russell Lane]: spacious, friendly and comfortable; good value lunchtime food; sheltered garden; children welcome *(Barbara Hill)*

Griffin [1,262 High Road, Whetstone]: inviting and friendly, with unusual brickwork and domed ceiling in back room, good food weekday lunchtimes; next to original Wet Stone Garden *(T G W Carrington)*

N21

Salisbury [Hoppers Road]: good food both lunchtime and evening, well kept Bass *(Dr John Nixon)*

NW1

Camden Stores [25 Parkway]: food at lunchtime good in this big modernised pub – a somewhat surprisingly high-class establishment in a run-down part of London *(Dr A K Clarke)*

Lock [35 Chalk Farm Road]: large downstairs bar with fruit machine, big cold food counter (also hot food), Bass and Charringtons IPA, back terrace and smaller first-floor front roof-garden *(Norman and Lucy Bishop, Colin Thomas, BB)*

Moriarty's [Marylebone Road]: amazingly, there are quite a lot of regulars even though you have to buy a ticket in this Underground Railway bar – these can be fascinating, this is perhaps the best *(Dr A K Clarke)*

Prince Albert [Princess Road]: friendly well run local, comfortable and relaxing, generous helpings of food, small well kept garden *(Geoffrey Normile, LYM)*

Prince George of Cumberland [195 Albany Street]: food good in well refurbished pub *(Dr A K Clarke)*

Russell Arms [1 Lidlington Place]: friendly service in well decorated pub with upstairs and basement as well as ground floor *(S R Collins)*

Spread Eagle [59 Parkway]: good cosy Youngs pub with three bars, old pictures on walls, handy for Regent's Park *(J R Grocott)*

Victoria & Albert Bars [Marylebone Station]: more like a theatre bar than a station bar, with huge range of real ales – would that all BR bars were as tasteful as this! *(Dr A K Clarke)*

Volunteer [245 Baker Street]: plush and black-panelled, bar food, restaurant and wine bar too, close to Regent's Park *(Roger Bellingham, LYM)*

NW2

Hogs Grunt [108 Cricklewood Lane]: music – usually jazz funk – in expensive but lively pub with nice atmosphere *(J Cunningham)*

NW3

Flask [14 Flask Walk]: snug Hampstead local, with well kept Youngs; popular with actors and artists for 300 years *(N W McArthur, BB)*

George [250 Haverstock Hill]: lots of character; back bar has lots of cosy alcoves and a good mixed crowd of customers *(Keith Garley)*

Horse & Groom [68 Heath Street]: food available from a varied menu (lunchtimes, not Sunday) and well kept real ales; no music or fruit machines; comfortable. Evening 1930s-style cocktail bar; genial landlord *(FS)*

Jack Straws Castle [North End Way]: lots of separate eating areas including attractive spacious upstairs dining-room, wide choice of food; good garden on edge of Heath – highest spot in London *(Guy Atkins)*

King of Bohemia [10 Hampstead High Street]: sound, straightforward pub, friendly service, reliable reasonably priced English food, Whitbreads beers, no music *(Nigel Williamson)*

Old Bull & Bush [North End Way]: lively pub on traffic-busy hill, interesting history – and the home of that famous song *(J Cunningham, LYM)*

Roebuck [15 Pond Street]: cosy and pleasant pub with plenty of young people *(Geoffrey Normile)*

Washington [50 Englands Lane]: spacious bar with elegant Victorian mirrors, well kept real ales, fresh and appetising bar food *(Anon)*

NW4

Chequers [Church End]: very lively pub with lots of old 1960s and 1970s records on juke box, usually on at full volume *(J Cunningham)*

Load of Hay [Brent Street]: recent bar extension has not spoilt this cosy discreet pub *(J Cunningham)*

White Bear [56 The Burroughs]: plainly furnished pub with cheap well kept beer *(J Cunningham)*

NW7

Rising Sun [Highwood Hill]: lovely unspoilt country pub in heart of suburbs; comfortable lounge, simple public bar *(J Cunningham)*

NW8

Heroes of Alma [11 Alma Square]: good value freshly cooked food and well kept Ruddles, Watneys and Websters Yorkshire real ales in friendly little Victorian pub with tables outside *(Robin Fuller, LYM)*

Lords Tavern [St Johns Wood Road]: good food counter and well kept real ales in attractively mocked-up pubby interior, tables outside *(BB)*

Rossetti [23 Queens Grove]: smart modern Italianate pub with garden, terrace and restaurant; bar food includes salads, pies, pâtés, some cheese and pizzas *(John Thirlwell, LYM)*

NW9

Upper Welsh Harp [Broadway, West Hendon]: good weekend Irish entertainment, excellent beers including best Guinness in London *(J Cunningham)*

BARNET

Gate at Arkley [Barnet Road]: pleasant well kept pub with pretty summer rose garden, big open fire in winter, good choice of whiskies, real ales, good lunchtime sandwiches, salads and daily hot specials *(BOB)*

Green Dragon [St Albans Road]: tastefully refurbished pub with real ale, garden with barbecues in summer and space for children – a pleasant break on the long journey from Barnet to Bentley Heath! *(Joslin Lewis)*

King William IV: good well kept local, popular with young people *(Helen Ridley)*

Mitre [High Street]: small-roomed friendly tavern with Dickens connections, well kept Benskins and Ind Coope Burton *(Helen Ridley, LYM)*

ENFIELD

Pied Bull [Bullsmoor Lane]: good beer and bar food in nicely carpeted rural Whitbreads pub with old-world feel, well kept Wethereds, good value lunchtime food, helpful staff; gardens front and back *(Brian Lee, Charlie Salt)*

FORTY HILL

Old Park Heights: excellent Rayments real ale in non-smoking bar of plush hotel; first exclusively non-smoking bar in London; bedrooms *(Bob Rendle)*

HARROW

Castle: one of London's better suburban pubs: very busy, lots of atmosphere. No food *(Paul A Smith, Ian Clay)*

Kings Head [High Street]: very popular spacious local, comfortable, wide range of real ales, good bar food, several bars, large garden with summer barbecues *(S Trowbridge, R K Whitehead, W R Rossiter)*

HARROW WEALD

Case is Altered [Old Redding]: opposite Grims Dyke: magnificent country views from windows and tables outside; good food, well kept Benskins and Ind Coope Burton. Popular with riders, golfers, ramblers, young people. Said to be the original pub of this name *(J R Grocott)*

PINNER

Queens Head [High Street]: old timbered pub in attractive village, one long bar with log fire at each end, well kept Benskins and Ind Coope Burton, good lunchtime home-made steak and kidney pie, chicken curry, sandwiches, sausages *(Tim Bracey)*

PONDERS END

Boundary House [Hertford Road]: Whitbreads house, excellent Wethereds and bottled English ale (rather rare around here), fine licensees *(MEO)*

Horse & Dray [Alma Road]: out-of-the-way newly renovated estate pub, well run as family pub, Whitbreads and bottled English ale *(Martin Patrick Egan)*

TOTTERIDGE

Orange Tree [Totteridge Village]: spacious pub by duckpond, plush décor, separate restaurant *(J Cunningham, LYM)*

SOUTH

SE1

Albert Arms [1 Gladstone Street]: splendidly redecorated and commanding exterior, set off against bleak cliffs of modern glass. Packed inside on weekday lunchtimes, quiet otherwise. Fair range of pub food *(Anon)*

Doggetts Coat & Badge [Upper Ground]: magnificent Thames views from comfortable three-level modern pub handy for South Bank arts complex *(BB)*

Goose & Firkin [47 Borough Road]: good own-brew pub, simply furnished with rough wooden tables; the Dogbolter takes some drinking! Good value simple food *(William Meadon, Richard Steel, Paula Beever)*

Loose Vine [2 St Thomas Street]: good food, friendly. Upstairs room *(Eirlys Roberts)*

Mudlark [Montague Close]: modern repro-pub near Glaziers Hall – very busy, a bit trendy but enjoyable *(Dr A K Clarke)*

Prince William Henry [216 Blackfriars Road]: comfortable modern estate pub with well kept Youngs beers and quick pleasant service *(N W McArthur, BB)*

SE3

Black Prince: one of the best pubs in this part of London *(Stephen Locke)*

Hare & Billet [1a Eliot Cottages]: comfortably furnished Whitbreads pub looking up to the common and pond, pleasant for a quiet weekday lunch; separate wine bar *(BB)*

SE9

Greyhound (86 Eltham High Street]: food and beer good and inexpensive in nice seventeenth-century pub, friendly and picturesque, with nice old furnishings and separate games room; a great rarity here, one forgets one is in suburbia *(Simon Evans)*

SE11

Cricketers [Kennington Oval]: music pub with different groups each night in purpose-built room, good atmosphere *(Lissa Halliday)*

SE13

Royal Oak [Boone Street]: comfortable, friendly, mainly locals. Courage Best and Directors on handpump *(Dave Hoy)*

SE19

Conquering Hero [262 Beulah Hill]: very friendly staff and very good atmosphere in Courage pub with complete cross-section of society *(A W Wells)*

SE20

Anerley Arms [Ridsdale Road]: outstanding renovation of historic pub. One of earliest Sam Smiths pubs in London, excellent real ale, pictures of nearby canal and railway, old poster for this pub and its adjacent pleasure garden; good beer and food *(Philip Daniell, Dave Hoy)*

SE21

Crown & Greyhound [College Road]: food very good (especially help-yourself salads), served in renovated billiards room with ample seating at cottage-style tables; good pub atmosphere, excellent service from young staff *(Heather Sharland, E G Parish)*

SW8

Royal Albert [St Stephen's Terrace]: good, reasonable snacks *(Mick and Neil)*

Surprise [Southville]: friendly Youngs pub, good games, reasonably priced snacks, in dead-end by small park *(Lesley Foote, Alan Carter, Jon and Ros MacKenzie)*

SW14

Victoria [West Temple, Sheen]: very pleasant atmosphere, good and reasonably priced food *(Peter Mason)*

SW15

Dukes Head [8 Lower Richmond Road]: good food, good view of river, good Youngs beer, civilised atmosphere – always very busy; good live music *(Martin Linton, Doug Kennedy, Patrick Stapley, RAB, M Fegan)*

Quill [22 Charlwood Road]: good locals' pub, well decorated, extremely amiable landlord *(Marilynne Blyth)*

SW17

Leather Bottle [538 Garratt Lane]: nice garden, good Youngs beer, good atmosphere, friendly landlords. Can get crowded in the evening *(Martin Linton, David Potter)*

Tooting Tavern [196 Tooting High Street]: food and beer good in very friendly and lively pub, always crowded in the evenings *(Maureen Barrett)*

SW18
County Arms [345 Trinity Road]: good Victorian decor, generally friendly service, good value filled rolls and other bar snacks. Relaxed at weekday lunchtimes, though slightly odd (quivering whining dog an evident regular, too vocal). Crowded weekends; public grass area outside by dual carriageway is nice when it's sunny. Well kept Youngs real ales *(Alan Franck, BB)*

SW19
Fox & Grapes [Camp Road]: Courage pub within a few yards of Wimbledon Common (ideal for afternoon walks) and close to Cannizaro House (grounds nice to wander in); high-ceilinged bar on right is attractively lit and decorated, carpeted, with lots of tables and chairs; bar on left is down steps – smaller, lower-ceilinged, softer lighting. Lunchtime sandwiches, rarely crowded though one of the best pubs in the area *(Mike Muston)*
Hand in Hand [6 Crooked Billet]: food at lunchtime good in charming Youngs pub set back from the green (where you can take your drinks in summer); rambling low-beamed bar with wooden seats at front, comfortable seats and carpeting behind, with back restaurant *(Mike Muston, Alex Clay)*
Princess Royal [25 Abbey Road]: family-run Courage house with good food and well kept beer, very nice saloon and decent public bar *(James Bryan)*
Trafalgar [23 High Path]: very good beer (Best, HSB, Festive) and good value home-made food at lunchtime – short menu *(M P Kerschbaum)*

BECKENHAM
Jolly Woodman (Chancery Lane): food and atmosphere good in unspoilt local, Bass, Charringtons IPA and Highgate well kept *(M K Jackson)*

BEXLEY
Rising Sun [Vicarage Lane]: very friendly, Courage Best and Directors, customers mostly keep their horses in the lane next to the pub – lots of pictures of their animals and pets on the walls *(Peter Vanson)*

BEXLEYHEATH
Crook Log: pleasant suburban pub with choice of good value lunchtime food from sandwiches to light meals; well kept Bass and Charringtons IPA on handpump *(Debbie and Ian Trotman)*

BROMLEY
Oak [Widmore Road]: for those who don't like noise of juke box or gambling machines, but do like perfectly served Flowers, Fremlins Tusker and Wethereds. Service, décor and food all good *(M K Jackson)*

CARSHALTON
Coach & Horses [High Street]: good friendly atmosphere in old-fashioned High-Street pub with barbecue and well kept real ale – cellar cooled by underground stream *(R B Entwistle)*
Racehorse [17 West Street]: food in restaurant and bar (lunchtime and evening) exceptionally good, well kept Courage real ale, well run pub *(M P Kerschbaum)*

CHEAM
Red Lion: amusing Australian landlord; good food, busy *(Marilynne Blyth)*

CHISELHURST
Tigers Head [Manor Park Road]: good well cooked food, very reasonably priced. Pleasant and helpful manager. Always busy *(Mr and Mrs J M Ross)*

COULSDON
Fox [Old Coulsdon]: friendly and well run *(Mike Muston)*

CROYDON
Royal Standard [Old Town]: friendly, basic pub with cheap wholesome food; good garden area opposite, under flyover *(Roger Entwistle)*

DOWNE
George & Dragon [High Street]: exceptionally good bar snacks and well kept beer *(AA)*
Queens Head: good food and drink, pleasant surroundings. Interesting lounge bar, and adjacent rooms are cosy on a cold night *(Alan Franck)*

KEW
Coach & Horses [Kew Green]: opposite Kew Gardens, friendly, well kept, overlooking Green, three open-plan bar areas merge, good lunchtime bar food, well kept Youngs, separate restaurant; bedrooms *(S G Revill, Thomas Clayton)*
Rose & Crown [Kew Green]: well placed, well kept beer, good food, relaxing atmosphere *(N W McArthur, R K Whitehead)*

KINGSTON
Bishop out of Residence: lively, well run and comfortable pub, good beer *(Lesley Foote and Alan Carter)*

MITCHAM
Bull: good atmosphere, well kept beer *(Lesley Foote and Alan Carter)*

RICHMOND
Angel & Crown [5 Church Court]: music some sessions. Very friendly, lively Fullers pub *(Beti Wyn Thomas)*
Cricketers [The Green]: between town and green: lovely for summer drink, watching the cricket or the fair. Well kept Bass and Charringtons IPA *(Lesley Taylor, John Light)*
Rose of York [Petersham Road]: food reasonably priced and pleasant, served from enormously long bar: salads, quiches, pâté, chilli con carne and very good Sunday lunch carvery. Well refurbished by Sam Smiths, their beer well kept *(Doug Kennedy)*
White Cross [Cholmondeley Walk]: good lunchtime carvery, well kept Youngs beers, acceptable wines, good buffet lunchtime and evening, well run by new licensees; won a Richmond Society conservation award for quality of restoration *(Nigel Williamson, Lesley Taylor, John Light)*

THAMES DITTON
Albany [Queens Road]: food includes a big selection of hot and cold, home-made, tastefully prepared dishes and salads – ample portions and averagely priced; well proportioned bars overlook the Thames; large car park *(A B Stenhouse)*

WEST

SW7
Merrie Go Down [Ashburn Place]: good pub-in-a-hotel, lots of local memorabilia on walls, well kept Scottish real ale; bedrooms *(Dr A K Clarke)*

SW10
Fox & Pheasant [1 Billing Road]: cosy old-fashioned back-street pub with welcoming local atmosphere *(BB)*

W4

City Barge [27 Strand on the Green]: attractively placed riverside pub, partly fifteenth century and previously a main entry for its snug old-fashioned charm, but recently refurbished and extensively modernised by Courage *(LYM)*
Crown & Anchor [374 Chiswick High Road]: Youngs, open plan and comfortable, bar food, upstairs restaurant; very pleasant *(C Elliott)*

W5

Fox & Goose [Hanger Lane]: long bar counter. Friendly but not pushy, well kept Fullers beers, good range of food with lunchtime restaurant *(N W McArthur)*
Grange [Elm Grove Road]: a find for the area. Recently decorated: small public bar; High Bar with individual lounge chairs; main bar opening into attractive conservatory then garden. Food lunchtime and evening (salads, quiches, baked potatoes, etc). Websters, Watneys London, Stag on handpump *(S G Revill)*
Red Lion [South Ealing Road]: food at lunchtimes is simple but good, like home-made burgers; hand pumped Fullers served in the single bar which is often crowded at lunchtime and early evening, but always friendly; small local used by the BBC staff from the studios across the Green; wooden settles and old wood panelling and lots of photographs from the studios' old film days; benches outside for the nicer weather *(Gerald Newman)*

W6

Black Lion [2 South Black Lion Lane]: well kept simple local carefully refurbished by Fullers, with good friendly service and atmosphere, not far from Thames, spacious garden; children welcome *(GD, D S Smith, BB)*
Old Ship [25 Upper Mall]: spacious riverside pub, comfortably modernised, with big well kept terrace, bar food and well kept Watneys real ales *(Tim, Sue and John Kemp, LYM)*

W8

Churchill Arms [9 Kensington Church Street]: nicely panelled pub with lots of prime ministers on the walls, well kept Fullers ESB *(Dr A K Clarke)*
Devonshire Arms [37 Marloes Road]: lots of good-natured bustle in big pub with real heart, opposite St Mary Abbots Hospital *(Dr A K Clarke)*
Elephant & Castle [40 Holland Street]: lovely little local behind Kensington Town Hall, well kept beer and good atmosphere *(Dr A K Clarke)*
Prince of Wales [8 Kensington Church Street]: most interesting décor, especially the little country kitchen at the back; seemed to be full of policemen *(Dr A K Clarke)*

W9

Truscott Arms [55 Shirland Road]: plush and pleasant. Ten well-kept beers (range varies): wallboards list the membership of the rather dubious '10 Club' who have drunk a pint from each handpump in one session, under rigorous rules; some good jazz *(G Bernecker, David Symes)*
Warwick Castle [6 Warwick Place]: unspoilt straightforward high-ceilinged Victorian pub with good sandwiches and well kept Bass and Charringtons IPA, close to Little Venice *(LYM)*

W10

Narrow Boat [346 Ladbroke Grove]: small Fullers pub serving good London Pride; also ESB and Mild. Friendly, can be cramped evenings if not warm enough for canalside terrace — large paved area at water level. Inside decorated with interesting narrow-boat objects. Comfortable. Wholesome simple food at lunchtime very reasonably priced *(John Brundrett)*

W11

Ladbroke Arms [54 Ladbroke Road]: food includes good salads and hot dish of day in recently refurbished small Victorian pub with sunny, flowery

forecourt, Ruddles and Websters Yorkshire on handpump, crowded with locals at weekends and business people during the week – and policemen at all times *(P T Young)*
Prince of Wales [Portland Road, Pottery Lane]: big, pleasant Victorian pub with saloon and public bars, mixture of locals (especially weekends) and builders; normal pub food (sausages, steak pie, cottage pie, macaroni cheese, ham and turkey salads, sandwiches and buns; Hellman's mayonnaise); Charringtons IPA and Bitter on handpump; big north-east-facing courtyard gets some lunchtime sun *(P T Young)*

W14

Colton Arms [187 Greyhound Road]: huge settle, dark wood, very local, friendly: more like a village or small town pub than a London one; small but very pretty back garden; nicely decorated; ring bell for service; good beer *(Patrick Stapley, RAB, Lesley Foote, Alan Carter)*
Three Kings [171 North End Road]: big free house which calls itself 'The World Centre for Real Ale', a multitude of real ales and handpumps, masses of seating, superb choice of lunchtime food; piped music *(J A C Edwards)*
Ballot Box [Horsenden Lane]: very popular and busy recently refurbished Ind Coope pub *(S Trowbridge)*

BRENTFORD

Express Hotel [Kew Bridge Road]: no longer a hotel, but with the atmosphere of a small one. Family business, well kept beer (free house). Ornamental back garden: you'd think you were miles from the busy road and adjacent railway *(Win Caldwell)*

CRANFORD

Queens Head [123 High Street]: Fullers pub opposite site of (former) Heston Airport, not far from Heathrow; lounge once a barn, with excellent photographs of ancient aircraft alongside the bar; interesting real ales *(J R Grocott)*

CROXLEY GREEN

Artichoke [The Green]: food in bar and well kept Trumans (Sampsons), Websters and Yorkshire bitter; double-fronted pub on village green, recently, and skilfully, restored with beams, open fires, gas lighting and a parrot! Friendly atmosphere, dogs allowed *(John and Denise Keable)*

HAMPTON

White Hart [70 High Street]: attractive L-shaped bar, links with Dickens and Garrick; eight real ales on handpump, constantly changing; very good atmosphere *(Martin Drew, Richard Barber)*

HAMPTON COURT

Cardinal Wolsey [The Green]: on day of French-English Rugby match at Twickenham, lots of French eating here – and food didn't disappoint them; excellent genial service *(Derek Keen)*

HAMPTON HILL

Windmill [80 Windmill Road]: Bass and lunchtime food always good in small and friendly pub *(C Leach, B W Beesley)*

HAMPTON WICK

White Hart [Kingston Bridge]: spacious old-fashioned Fullers pub close to Thames, big curving bar, old-fashioned fireplace – ideal for Sunday lunchtime diversion *(D S Smith)*

HAREFIELD

Plough: wide range of beers including Archers and Ruddles; pool, darts *(W R Rossiter)*

White Horse [Church Hill]: period pub with excellent range of Ind Coope beers, superb choice of lunchtime food, sociable atmosphere *(G P Dobson)*

HOUNSLOW

Chariot [Hounslow High Street]: only pub with a bus stop inside along with underground railway signalling apparatus. Real Fullers ale, good selection of food *(J R Grocott)*

Ruby Tuesday [Staines Road]: excellent choice of beers and good food, surprisingly good décor, pleasant to eat and drink, overseas visitors quite surprised *(David Regan)*

ISLEWORTH

Rising Sun [4 London Road]: friendly staff and service, good atmosphere, good food well and freshly cooked, well served *(Timothy Errock)*

OSTERLEY

Hare & Hounds [Windmill Lane]: opposite Osterley Park; well kept Fullers, food at lunchtime, big beer garden – in warm weather one of the best pubs in area; very popular *(David Ellis, S V Bishop)*

SIPSON

Plough [Sipson Road]: period pub with good range of Watneys beers, wide choice of lunchtime food, sociable atmosphere *(G P Dobson)*

TWICKENHAM

Cabbage Patch [London Road]: good atmosphere, good food including full evening meals; children welcome; music occasionally (local folk club) *(Mr and Mrs R Ellis)*

Duke of Cambridge [Kneller Road]: food good value in pleasant Georgian pub opposite Kneller Hall Royal Military School of Music; welcoming licensees *(Renate Brandt)*

Pope's Grotto [Cross Deep]: spacious and well run Youngs pub, comfortable, with well kept real ale, a good range of food, summer weekend barbecues; opposite riverside gardens *(Leslie Cottage, Lesley Foote, Alan Carter, LYM)*

EAST

E1

Dickens Inn [St Katharine's Way]: big simple pub – Victorian pastiche – by rapidly developing dockside, sawdust floor, wooden benches and chairs give simple uncomplicated atmosphere, good food, wide range of beers, seats outside for view of waterfront and Tower Bridge *(William Meadon, Richard Steel, Michael Dempsey, Aubrey Saunders)*

Golden Heart [110 Commercial Street]: mixed, friendly well run little pub, convenient for Hawksmoor's Christchurch Spitalfields and the developing arts centre *(Michael Dempsey)*

Jack the Ripper: popular. Convenient for Christchurch Spitalfields *(Michael Dempsey)*

Thomas Neale [39 Watney Street Market]: very surprising shop conversion *(Michael Dempsey)*

Town of Ramsgate [62 Wapping High Street]: smashing little friendly panelled pub with real riverside atmosphere *(Dr A K Clarke)*

E2

Marksman [254 Hackney Road]: own-brew pub, wide range of real ales. Excellent. Near Museum of Childhood *(Michael Dempsey)*

Needle Gun: has a big garden. Good *(Michael Dempsey)*

E3

Hand & Flower [72a Parnell Road]: near Roman Road Market. Good *(Michael Dempsey)*

Palm Tree [Palm Street]: well run local; as Mile End Park (which has occasional festivals and events) develops this may develop a canalside garden and provide family refreshments *(Michael Dempsey)*

Pearly King [94 Bromley High Street]: excellent *(Michael Dempsey)*

Royal Cricketers [210 Old Ford Road]: excellent, with canal terrace. Close to Museum of Childhood *(Michael Dempsey)*

Royal Hotel [Grove Road]: backs on to Victoria Park (good for boating in summer), and has occasional theatre *(Michael Dempsey)*

Widows Son [75 Devons Road]: excellent, with collection of Good Friday fossilised hot cross buns dating back many years *(Michael Dempsey)*

E4

Fountain [Lea Valley Road]: Ind Coope pub, very nice inside. Good beer and service, not too dear *(Martin Patrick Egan)*

E5

Fountain [211 Lower Clapton Road]: very friendly and well kept *(Leslie Cottage)*

E6

Boleyn [1 Barking Road]: big Victorian gin palace with huge displays of etched glass, marvellous carved ceiling. Lunchtime food. Taylor-Walker real ale. *(MHG)*

Le Pub [West Ham Lane]: food good value in very comfortable Charringtons pub – no under-25s, and smart dress required *(Eric Stephens)*

Two Puddings [Stratford High Street]: food good with good Guinness, evening entertainment; quaint – if saucy – pub sign; no under-21s, smart dress required *(Eric Stephens)*

E8

Albion [33 Albion Drive]: excellent Shepherd Neame on draught. Best early in week: packed late week *(Martin Patrick Egan)*

L & A Bar [64 Clarissa Street]: very clean, low light level and background music *(Martin Patrick Egan)*

Lady Diana [Forest Road]: small local pub with wide choice of well kept real ales including Youngs, Fullers, Greene King Abbot, Adnams. Relaxed, friendly atmosphere, good service. Lunchtime meals, darts, shove-ha'penny, fruit machine *(W Fitzgerald)*

E9

Royal [Grove Road]: good friendly local – big, well renovated bar. Occasional theatre upstairs. Friendly staff, excellent Trumans beer *(IW)*

E10

Auctioneers (596 Lea Bridge Road): home-brew pub selling good Legover, Evil and several others (not brewed on the premises); music usually unobtrusive *(Martin Patrick Egan, MEO)*

E11

Eagle [76 Holly Bush Hill]: excellent: big, with garden *(Michael Dempsey)*

E14

Five Bells & Blade Bone [27 Three Colt Street]: nice little pub, near National Museum of Labour History *(Michael Dempsey)*

MV Medina [Canary Wharf]: ex-Scottish Islands ferry moored near Limehouse TV studios, excellent restaurant (Italian staff), good bar snacks, young atmosphere, tables on quay *(Barry Smith)*

Queens Head [8 Flamborough Street]: mixed Youngs pub in beautiful restored

Georgian square with fine porticoed villa and Rose and Hawthorn Cottages, near National Museum of Labour History *(Michael Dempsey)*
Watermans Arms [1 Glengarnock Avenue]: comfortable and popular, by Island Gardens *(Michael Dempsey)*

E15
King Edward VII [47 Broadway]: 'The Prussia' – excellent Bass/Charringtons pub *(Michael Dempsey)*
Manby Arms [19 Water Lane]: has purpose-built children's room, and is good *(Michael Dempsey)*
Yorkshire Grey [High Street, Stratford]: noisy and cheerful, attractive staff, cheap food *(N W McArthur)*

EC3
Hoop and Grapes [47 Aldgate High Street]: scheduled ancient monument, thought to be London's oldest licensed building; saved at last minute from bulldozer and convenient for Petticoat Lane or Whitechapel Art Gallery *(Michael Dempsey)*

Scotland

Scotland

A great many of the Scottish pubs included as main entries owe part of their charm to their position. Often enough, on a road through beautiful scenery, you come to a particularly special spot, or an interesting fishing village, say – and there's a little inn. By the sea or on sea lochs there are the little fishermen's Sun at Anstruther, the Ardentinny Hotel in the hamlet of that name on Loch Long, the comfortable Loch Melfort Hotel at Arduaine (looking out to sea, with a marvellous woodland garden), the Ardvasar Hotel at Ardvasar (with good food) looking across the Sound of Sleat, the Fisherman's Tavern at Broughty Ferry (just round the corner from a fine view of the Tay bridges), the Old Inn at Carbost (sharing its sea loch with the Talisker Distillery), the Cramond Inn at Cramond (good food), the Crinan Hotel at Crinan (spectacaular sea views, and good food), the Old Chain Pier at Newhaven on the outskirts of Edinburgh (cantilevered out over the Firth of Forth), the friendly little Ship on the harbour at Elie, the Crown and Anchor at Findhorn, the stately Georgian Argyll Arms in Inveraray, the engaging Steam Packet with its big windows looking out on the sheltered haven of Isle of Whithorn, the welcoming Gaelic-speaking Hotel Eilean Iarmain at Isle Ornsay with its gorgeous views over the water to the mainland mountains, the friendly Anchor overlooking the yachting basin at Kippford,

The Riverside, Canonbie

the interesting and well run Udny Arms, just a walk over the dunes from the sea at Newburgh, the Plockton Hotel among the palm trees in its quiet West Coast inlet at Plockton, the lively Crown right on the harbour at Portpatrick, the Hawes Inn, R L Stevenson's Kidnapped inn at Queensferry, the Sconser Lodge at Sconser – included chiefly for its terrific water's-edge position, with grand mountains just behind, the civilised Creggans Inn in extensive grounds at Strachur (good food again), the atmospheric Stein Inn at Stein (very lively of an evening), and the Lookout overlooking the marina at Troon. Inland, the Kenmore Hotel at Kenmore has its own jetty on the Tay and still preserves the poem Burns wrote on its wall when he was so impressed by the surrounding scenery, the Loch Tummel Hotel has a grand view over its loch, the Inverbeg Inn at Luss has a jetty on Loch Lomond, the Tibbie Shiels Inn is alone by beautiful St Mary's Loch, and the Letterfinlay Lodge Hotel near Spean Bridge has extensive grounds running down to Loch Lochy. Other pubs and inns in fine surroundings include the remote highland Achnasheen Hotel at Achnasheen, the Sheep Heid in the pretty village of Duddingston just below Arthur's Seat, outside Edinburgh, the Lewiston Arms at Lewiston, handy for Loch Ness and Glen Coiltie, the Grant Arms in Monymusk, the Gordon Arms down towards the Borders, at Mountbenger, the Killiecrankie Hotel in extensive grounds at the north end of the Killiekrankie Pass near Pitlochry (good food), and the Crook Inn at Tweedsmuir (again, good food). Other places with good food include the civilised Riverside Inn in Canonbie (decorated with great charm), Findlay's in Cupar, the Horseshoe at Eddleston (popular for outings from Edinburgh), the stylish Nivingston House (a country house hotel at Cleish), the interesting Murray Arms at Gatehouse of Fleet (for its lunchtime buffet), the comfortable and old-fashioned Tweeddale Arms in Gifford, the Old Howgate Inn at Howgate (a remarkable choice of open sandwiches), the elegant Victorian Clifton Hotel in Nairn (our highest-rated Scottish entry), and the Skeabost House Hotel at Skeabost Bridge (good lunchtime buffet in fine surroundings), while many others that we mention in the text have food that won't disappoint you, though it's less ambitious or unusual. For sheer character, you might enjoy Gabriels in Aberdeen (a soaring converted chapel), the Globe in Dumfries (parts of it hardly changed since it was Burns' favourite drinking-place – and it's still particularly welcoming), the Café Royal Circle Bar and Guildford Arms, neighbours in Edinburgh, for their sumptuous Victorian décor, the Kings Arms in Girvan for its odd cocktail-bar serving counter like a giant golfball with a bite out of it, the old-fashioned kilt-wearing atmosphere of the

Inverarnan Inn at Inverarnan just north of Loch Lomond, the friendly and ancient George Inn at Moniaive and Habbie's Howe Hotel at Nine Mile Burn near Penicuik, and – because it's so very different – the airy Victoria Café in St Andrews. On the drinks side, the friendly and well run Ferryhill House Hotel in Aberdeen, the smart Pot Still and cheaper Outside Inn, both in Glasgow, and the Whyteside Hotel in Polmont each has several hundred malt whiskies to choose from, while the smart new Bon Accord and cheaper Overflow (both in Glasgow) both have a particularly wide range of real ales. The Athletic Arms in Edinburgh deserves a special mention for its remarkably well kept beer. Beer prices in general are round about the British average in Scotland, perhaps a trifle higher – and tend to rise the further north you go.

ABERDEEN (Grampian)   NJ9305 Map 11
Ferryhill House Hotel
Bon Accord St (bottom end)

This friendly small hotel has three main pluses: the biggest choice of malt whiskies and real ales in the region, a good range of food (and a choice of places to eat it), and prices that haven't been much affected by Aberdeen's oil money. The half-dozen real ales are kept in immaculate condition: McEwans 80/–, Maclays 80/–, Youngers IPA and No 3, and the local Devanha XB (a rich, golden full-flavoured bitter), all on air pressure tall founts, and Devanha XXX (a dark, slightly sweetish Scotch ale) on handpump; bar food includes sandwiches, a good cold table (£4), pâté (£2), a bar lunch of soup followed by a choice of dishes such as beef curry or breaded veal escalope with cheese sauce (£3.30), and main dishes up to steaks; fruit machine, maybe piped music. A separate restaurant serves main courses such as roast beef (£6) and rump steak (£6.50). There are big golfing cartoons on the high white walls of the attractive and comfortable main bar, which has red plush corduroy seats on a swirly patterned carpet and airy bow windows overlooking the lawns. The central lounge hall has lots more seating, and there's also a softly lit cocktail bar with button-backed leatherette seats around dimpled copper tables. There are plenty of well spaced tables outside on the grass, which is edged by neatly kept flower beds and sheltered by lime trees. *(Recommended by MRS)*

Free house · Licensee Douglas Snowie · Real ale · Meals and snacks (lunchtime, not Sun) · Children in eating area and lounge hall · Open 11–11 all year; closed 2.30–5 Sat · Bedrooms tel Aberdeen (0224) 590867; £18 (£26B)/£36 (£38B)

Gabriels
Dee Street

Walk in when it's quiet and at first glance you might feel you'd got the address from *Crockford's Clerical Directory* instead of the *Guide*: very high, steeply vaulted ceiling, putti and other statuary in the tall lancet windows, heavy altar rail, rich sombre colours. But the well reproduced music in this converted chapel gives the game away – less than heavenly, as one reader says. And the centrepiece is decidedly unchurchly: a showy octagonal bar counter full of blue tilework and fancy mouldings, under a sort of arched glass canopy with a couple of big colonial fans whirling. Bar food includes soup (45p), filled baked potatoes (£1.50), burgers (from £1.90), scampi or home-made chicken and mushroom pie (£2.75) and salads (£2.75). There are some good big mirrors and Scottish genre paintings above the comfortable seats and gilt or cast-iron tables. Fruit machine. The back exit takes you down a sombre, arras-hung gallery of curious mirror-reflecting photographic portraits, framed and lit as if they were oil paintings, and leads to the management's new venture – a nightclub on which they've spent £400,000, including £100,000 on sound equipment, video and lasers. *(Recommended by W T Aird)*

Free house · Licensee Mr Stuart · Snacks · Nearby parking metered Open 11–2.30, 5–12 all year

Prince of Wales

7 St Nicholas Lane

Some say this basic bar is the best pub in Aberdeen; it's certainly got the longest serving counter, and its lunchtime food has for generations been famous for good value. The Dickensianly narrow and fusty cobbled alley that twists right underneath Union Street sets the right mood: don't expect to be cossetted in here. Groups of girls on their own evidently feel confident that this isn't a strictly male preserve in the old-fashioned Scottish way, and after the sympathetic refurbishments which have been afoot here they may now feel happier about plonking their coats down on the floor. There are leatherette seats and other chairs in small bays around cast-iron-framed pub tables. A changing range of real ales might typically include well kept Lorimers 80/– and Theakstons Best on handpump, and Old Peculiar, Heriot 80/– and Youngers No 3 on air pressure tall founts; the staff are most friendly and welcoming. The food includes thick soup, pies, bridie-cakes, well filled rolls, stovies, and main dishes such as chilli con carne or cod baked in cheese sauce (around £1.50). Sensibly placed darts, fruit machine. *(Recommended by W T Aird, Miss S Stearn)*

Free house · Licensee Peter Birnie · Real ale · Meals (lunchtime, not Sun) and snacks (lunchtime) · Impromptu folk music Weds and Sat · No nearby parking Open 11–11 all year

ABERLADY (Lothian)   NT4679 Map 11
Waggon

A198, Edinburgh side

On a clear day you can see right over to Fife from the big windows of this old inn's unusual octagonal back extension. The Firth of Forth is a glimmer of silver beyond the extensive salt flats that stretch out behind the tables that shelter outside. This back part is now really the heart of the well run and friendly inn: an airy room, with high spoked beams radiating from a central post, and comfortable, Spanish-style seats around varnished pale-wood tables. It extends through to the old part of the house, which has kept its orginal shape and character, with pointed arched front windows and a coach entry (drive through for parking – carefully if your car is big). What used to be the front bar is now a charming family room. Bar food includes cold meats and Grosvenor pie (£1.30), chicken curry, pizza or chipsteak (£2.25), scampi or salmon with prawn sauce (£4.75) and steak (£5.50); well kept McEwans 80/– on air pressure. There is a separate upstairs restaurant. *(Recommended by W T Aird)*

Free house · Licensee Graham Young · Real ale · Meals and snacks · Children in restaurant or family room · Open 11–2.30, 5–11 all year

ABOYNE (Grampian)   NO5298 Map 11
Boat
Charlestown Road; follow South Deeside signposts from A93

Generous helpings of good simple food and the friendly welcome have won plenty of friends for this old inn that used to serve the Dee ferry it's named for (there's a bridge now). The simply furnished lounge bar is shaped a bit like a dumb-bell: two rooms, with the bar counter running down a narrower linking section (where there's a fruit machine). It has beige leatherette table-tops matching the button-back seats, plain white walls, a red patterned carpet, and a cosy fire, and the food includes sandwiches (75p), cock-a-leekie soup, omelettes (£2.10), pizza or haddock (£2.50), ham salad (£3.20), mixed grill (£3.60), rump steak (£4.20) and home made meringues; there may be piped music. Drybroughs 80/– on air pressure, also draught cider (not so common around here). There's also a restaurant. The public bar has darts, pool, dominoes, a space game and juke box. Grand, partly forested hills rise around this relatively broad stretch of the Dee valley. *(More reports please)*

Free house · Licensee Victor Sang · Real ale · Meals and snacks · Children in eating area and restaurant · Open 11–2.30, 5–11 all year · Bedrooms tel Aboyne (0339) 2137; £13 (£15B)/£26 (£30B)

ACHNASHEEN (Highland)   NH2669 Map 11
Achnasheen Hotel
A832

This is a lovely spot: a cluster of one or two houses alone with the inn in a windswept and grandly bleak broad valley, with heather and rough pasture on the hills that sweep away on all sides. The bar is warm, simply but comfortably furnished, and softly decorated; food in here includes pies, bridies and sausage rolls (48p), soup (55p), sandwiches (65p), toasted sandwiches (75p), pie or bridie with vegetables or sausage and egg (£1.85), salads or gammon steak (£2.75) and trout (£2.95), with a daily hot special such as beef stew or pie (£2.85). There is a separate restaurant. The public side has darts, pool, dominoes, cribbage, a fruit machine and juke box. Three trains a day run past on the single-track line that runs right across this splendid, lonely part of Scotland from Inverness to the Kyle of Lochalsh, and the hotel itself runs its own minibus sightseeing tours and three-day packages with free minibussing thrown in – the road is largely single-track, too.

Scottish & Newcastle · Licensee Sid Abraham · Meals and snacks · Open 11–11; closed 1 Jan · Children welcome · Bedrooms tel Achnasheen (044 588) 243; £15.50 (£18B)/£29 (£34B)

ANSTRUTHER (Fife)   NO5704 Map 11

Smugglers Inn

High Street

The upstairs bar of this friendly old inn rambles about attractively, with easy chairs and winged settles as well as the wheel-back chairs on its red patterned carpet, and beams and some of its walls stripped back to bare stone. Downstairs – apart from some uncommon bird-of-paradise wallpaper – is more simply furnished: pool-table, dominoes and juke box. Good straightforward bar food includes sandwiches (from 60p), lots of pizzas (from £1.35), fried local haddock (£1.95), curried chicken or gammon and pineapple (£2.25) and fresh local crab salad (£2.50), and in the evenings a wider choice of main courses runs up to sirloin steak (£4.85). There is also a separate restaurant. Behind the house is a gravel and flagstones terrace, with tables among rose bushes, just above a little creek which winds between stone walls out to the seashore. In summer there are sometimes barbecues out here. *(Recommended by Alastair Campbell)*

Free house · Licensees Mr and Mrs M McSharry · Meals and snacks · Children welcome if eating · Open 11–11 all year · Bedrooms tel Anstruther (0333) 310506; £15 (£16B)/£30 (£32B)

Sun [*illustrated on page 818*]

East Shore

Come out of here in a rush and you'd tumble into the sea: this friendly old fisherman's tavern is right on the harbourside, looking out to the working fishing boats, and red-and-white lightship removed from its North Carr station and now open for visits at the nearby pier, and the boats that do trips out to the Isle of May. It's also next door to the Scottish Fisheries Museum, which has a salt-water aquarium. As you'd expect, seafood finds its way on to the menu too – especially good dressed locally caught crabs; also toasties and pizzas; well kept McEwans 70/– and 80/– on handpump. The simply furnished bar has some stripped panelling on its cream-painted stone walls, comfortable seats, and beams in the ceiling, and a side music room has a well lit pool-table and juke box; also darts, dominoes, cribbage, chess and fruit machine. A teak bench under the pillared balcony that gives access to the top floor of this picturesque white house looks out on the harbourside bustle. *(Recommended by BOB)*

Free house · Licensee William Findlay · Snacks · Live music Fri and Sat, every evening in July and Aug · Open 11am–midnight all year

ARDENTINNY (Strathclyde)   NS1887 Map 11

Ardentinny Hotel

Harry Lauder used to live at nearby Glenbranter, and besides big
photographs of the man himself on the light-coloured panelling of the
sprucely decorated tiled-floor bar there's a big reproduction of his
song *O'er The Hill To Ardentinny*. There are lovely views from here
across Loch Long to the pier at Coulport – about a mile over the
water, but more than 65 miles by road (unless you take the hill
tracks). The comfortable little lounge bar – again, a modern décor
here – shares the view. Though it's popular, the inn's enough out of
the way to avoid crowds even in August, when its garden, also
overlooking the sea loch, is a pleasant place to sit. Good value bar
food includes soup (90p), pâté with oatcakes (£1.35), toasted
sandwiches (85p), ploughman's (£1.65), savoury omelettes (£1.75),
salads (from £2.55), scampi (£2.95) and steaks (from £5.75), with
daily specials such as chicken fricassée (£1.95) or lasagne (£2.95). A
separate restaurant is open for full evening meals. The hotel has a
courtesy boat for guests, moorings for those with boats, and can
arrange fishing or deerstalking. It is well placed for the Younger
Botanic Garden at Benmore. *(Recommended by Jack Taylor)*

*Free house · Licensee John Horn · Meals and snacks · Children welcome · Open
12–3, 5.30–11; closed Nov–15 Mar · Bedrooms tel Ardentinny (036 981) 209;
£19.50B/£34B*

ARDUAINE (Strathclyde)   NM7911 Map 11

Loch Melfort Hotel

Breathtaking views of islets and further islands, set in an expressive
sea that seems to change mood with every slightest shift of the clouds
or turn of the sun, are given pride of place in the airy, non-residents'
bar of this comfortable hotel. There's a pair of powerful marine
glasses by the big picture window, and one wall is papered with
nautical charts – Mr Tindal has been Commodore of the Royal
Highland Yacht Club – and in summer the hotel is popular with
yachtsmen (not to mention windsurfers). Comfortable modern
fabric-and-wood easy chairs cluster around light oak tables, and
there's a freestanding wood-burning stove. Local seafood salads are a
strong point, with giant prawns (£2.30), succulent crabs, salmon or
smoked trout (around £3.50), and there are toasted sandwiches (70p)
and roast beef salads (£2.75); a separate restaurant is open for
dinner. Wooden seats on the front terrace are a step away from the
rocky foreshore, backed by grass and wild flowers, and the
neighbouring Arduaine woodland gardens, at their best from late
April to early June, are magnificent. Quiet and comfortable, this is a
nice place to stay, with seaview bedrooms in a modern wing (some in
the older-fashioned main house are cheaper). *(Recommended by
Fl Lt A Darroch Harkness)*

*Free house · Licensees Colin and Jane Tindal · Snacks · Children welcome
Open 11–2.30, 5–11 all year; closed weekdays in winter · Bedrooms tel
Kilmelford (085 22) 233; £20 (£25B)/£36 (£42B)*

ARDVASAR (Isle of Skye)   NG6203   Map 11

Ardvasar Hotel

Just past Armadale pier where the summer car ferries from Mallaig dock, this is our most southern entry on the island: well placed for exploring the Sleat peninsula whose landscapes are more gently picturesque and fuller of wildlife than the stern grandeur to the north. It's a comfortably modernised eighteenth-century inn, with friendly and obliging young owners who serve good fresh food in the dining room – including local fish and shellfish. The bars look out across the Sound of Sleat to the fierce Knoydart mountains: the cleanly decorated Hideout bar has leatherette seats around dimpled copper coffee-tables, a tartan carpet, and Highland dress prints on fabric-and-wood walls; the locally popular public bar has stripped pews and kitchen chairs. Home-cooked bar food varies day by day, and on a typical day might include tomato and scallop soup (60p), sweet-cured herring (75p), liver pâté (£1), haddock (£2.40), steak pie (£2.50) and roast pork with apple and almonds (£2.75). We found the biggest TV we'd ever seen in a room off the comfortable hotel lounge, which has armchairs around its open fire. Not far from the Clan Donald centre; and the far side of the peninsula, by Tarskavaig, Tokavaig and Ord, has some of the most dramatic summer sunsets in Scotland – over the jagged Cuillin peaks, with the islands of Canna and Rhum off to your left. (*Recommended by Helen Woodeson*)

Free house · Licensees Bill and Gretta Fowler · Real ale · Meals and snacks Children in eating area · Occasional winter ceilidhs · Open 11–11; closed 25 Dec, 1–3 Jan · Bedrooms tel Ardvasar (047 14) 223; £14.50 (£18B)/ £26 (£30B)

BIELDSIDE (Grampian)   NJ8702   Map 11

Water Wheel

North Deeside Road; W edge of village, A93 W of Aberdeen

This used to be a watermill, with the attractive name of Murtle Mill. The restoration has been civilised and understated: the old paddlewheel almost camouflaged in a rockery out by the terrace, and just a few good photographs of other mill-wheels gently touching is the theme in the main Paddle Bar. This is a spacious open-plan area of armed seats and cushioned banquettes built up behind with thin wooden balusters to divide it into sections around the many black tables, with walls either bare stone or white-painted. Good value reliable food is the main draw in here: sandwiches to order, soup (65p), steak pie or salads (£3.65), trout (£3.85), two fillets of Aberdeen-landed haddock (£2.85), mixed grill (£4.20). Well kept McEwans 80/– on handpump; gentle piped pop music. There's more of a cocktail-bar effect in the softly-lit Yorkshire Bar, with big film-star photographs on stripped stone walls, red plush button-back banquettes on its patterned red carpet, and darts. Soft sofas and easy chairs are grouped around a colour TV in the entrance lounge, which has a fruit machine. (*Recommended by MRM*)

Free house · Licensees John and Thelma Quinn · Real ale · Meals and snacks Open 11–2.30, 5–11 all year.

BLANEFIELD (Central)   NS5579 Map 11
Carbeth Inn
West Carbeth; A809 Glasgow–Drymen, just S of junction with B821

Cheerful and unpretentious, this well kept and popular country pub below the Kilpatrick Hills has an old-fashioned bar with a stone and tile floor, cushioned booths built from brown wood under a high frieze of tartan curtain (with a big colour TV peeping out), heavy cast-iron-framed tables, and a high ceiling of the same brown planking. A stag's head is mounted on the bare stone wall above an open fire – there's a wood-burning stove at the opposite end. Generous helpings of good value bar food – with good chips – include filled rolls (from 40p, hot bacon 50p), filled baked potatoes (95p), scampi (£2.40) and sirloin steak, with children's dishes such as fish fingers (£1.20); there's a pleasant pannelled family room. Well kept McEwans 80/– from air pressure tall founts; sensibly placed darts, loud juke box, fruit machine. A rather smarter carpeted bar (the Ptarmigan) was closed on our visit; there are lots of rustic benches and tables on the front terrace. (Recommended by Ian Baillie)

Free house · Real ale · Meals and snacks · Children in family room Open 11–2.30, 5–11 all year

BROUGHTY FERRY (Tayside)   NO4630 Map 11
Fisherman's Tavern
12 Fort Street; turning off shore road

Just round the corner from the lifeboat station (from where the lifeboat *Mona* was lost with all hands in the Tay storm of December 1959), this small-roomed, rambling pub is well known for its wide range of real ales, in good condition. It has the feel of an easy-going fishermen's tavern – yet it's neatly well kept, and the friendly service is thoroughly professional. Soft red leatherette seats are built into the wide-pannelled walls of the inter-communicating rooms, which also have round stools and small café-style chairs under their shiny, low, butter-coloured ceiling, and over this last year there's been some decorating and carpeting. A cosy little snug with red-fringed lamps on red-papered walls leads off the standing-room lobby by the entrance. Well kept Greenmantle, McEwans 80/–, Maclays 80/– and Theakstons Best and Old Peculier on handpump, and Youngers No 3 and a guest beer, changed weekly, on tall-fount air pressure; a goodish choice of whiskies, including distinguished single malts, on the dispensing optics. Bar food consists of filled rolls, pies, bridies and sausage rolls (44p), and hot dishes served without vegetables, such as lasagne or cottage pie (from 75p); darts, dominoes, cribbage, two fruit machines. The nearby seafront gives a good view of the two long, low Tay bridges. (Recommended by William Meadon, Richard Steel, Brian Kirkaldy, Alan Docherty)

Free house · Licensee Robert Paterson · Real ale · Snacks (lunchtime) · Scottish traditional music Weds · Open 11–2.30, 5–11 all year

---

If we know a pub has a no-smoking area, we say so.

CABRACH (Grampian)   NJ3827   Map 11

Grouse

A941

This family pub, open all day, is a handy stop on a good route
through the Grampians from Braemar to Dufftown, the 'whisky
toon': A93 North from Braemar, then left on B976, left on A939,
right on B973, left on A97, left on B9002, left on A941. The pub has
a big airy cafeteria, open all day from 9am, serving all home-cooked
food including soup, hot filled rolls (around 55p), sandwiches (from
55p), home-baked scones and cakes with home-made jam, farm
cheese with oatcakes, steak pie or mince and tatties (£1.60) and
various salads (from £1.60). The bar proper is simply furnished with
red leatherette wall benches and café-style seats, and has pool, space
games, fruit machines and well reproduced pop music. Opening off
on the left is a tourist shop with Highland woollens and gifts –
especially an enormous choice of miniature whisky bottles. The
scenery around this quiet isolated house is gently hilly.

*Free house · Licensee Ian McBain · Meals and snacks · Children in family area
Various Scottish dance bands and country and western groups Sat and Sun
Apr–Oct · Open 11–11, food from 9am; closed Nov–Mar · Bedrooms tel
Cabrach (046 689) 200; £5.50 (£6.50B)/£14 (£16B)*

CANONBIE (Dumfries and Galloway)   NY3976   Map 9

Riverside ★★ *[illustrated on page 791]*

Follow village signposts from A7

A charming welcome, attractive and sensitively chosen furnishings,
immaculate housekeeping and the carefully prepared and often
imaginative food – good in both bar and restaurant – earn this
civilised inn its second star. We are by no means alone in giving it
special praise; in recent years it has been chosen by both our sister
publication *The Good Hotel Guide* and the AA as Inn of the Year.
The bar has open fires in winter: relaxing and comfortable knocked-
through rooms decorated with stuffed moorhens, red squirrel, barn
owl, mounted butterflies, local photographs and prints. In summer
the tables here, with easy chairs as well as the wooden country seats,
can get quite full, and it's then pleasant to go out to the picnic-table
sets under the trees on the front grass. Over the road – quiet now,
since the A7 bypass has been opened – a public playground runs
down to the River Esk (the inn can arrange fishing permits). Readers
particularly enjoy the discreetly served bar food, which includes
sandwiches, unusual home-made soups such as apple, fish and
tomato or chilled avocado (75p), home-potted venison (£1.75),
ploughman's with Cumberland farmhouse cheese or Stilton, chicken
liver or smoked mackerel pâté (all £1.75), a choice of meat salads that
might include roast duck, excellent cider-baked ham and rare roast
beef (£2.95), pink trout or home-cured ham and eggs (£3.95), and
home-made puddings such as yoghurt, ice cream or rhubarb and
orange Brown Betty (95p). Well kept Marstons on handpump,
reasonably priced. The separate restaurant serves grander dishes such
as delicate pigeon breast in wine, maize-fed chicken stuffed with

oysters and bacon, or fresh local salmon cooked in a variety of sympathetic ways, and is strong on carefully cooked fresh vegetables and home-made puddings: good value. The clean and comfortable rooms all have colour TV, and breakfasts are epicurean. *(Recommended by C N Gregory)*

Free house· Licensees Robert and Susan Phillips · Real ale · Meals and snacks (not Sun lunchtime) · Children welcome · Open 11–2.30, 6.30–11 all year; closed Sun lunchtime · Bedrooms tel Canonbie (054 15) 295; £28B/£38B

CARBOST (Isle of Skye)   NG3732 Map 11
Old Inn
This is the Carbost on B8009, in the W of the central part of the island

A warmly convivial local atmosphere envelops you in the simply furnished bar of this recently reopened old white-painted stone inn, tucked down beside the sea loch near the Talisker distillery – that malt whisky, peatily robust, seems to taste even better here so close to its home. There are red leatherette settles, benches and seats around this clean bare-boarded room, which on our visit had a big bowl of flowers on the mantelpiece above the peat fire. The bar meals – sandwiches, ploughman's (£1.75), pie and beans (£1.90), haddock (£2.40), scampi (£2.90) or a dish of the day (from £2.50) – are popular, and served in helpings robust enough for climbers down from the fiercely jagged peaks of the Cuillin Hills; darts (in winter), dominoes, cribbage and piped music (on our visit scarcely noticeable under the happy hum of evening conversation). *(Recommended by Alan Franck)*

Free house · Mrs Deirdre Cooper · Meals and snacks · Children welcome Open 11–2.30, 5–11 all year · Bedrooms tel Carbost (047 842) 205; £9l/£18

The Murray Arms, Gatehouse of Fleet

CASTLECARY (Central)   NS7878   Map 11

Castlecary House Hotel

Handily placed between Glasgow and Stirling on the spinal route north, this hotel has a cheerful, open-plan main bar which is open all day (except on Sunday afternoons, when they serve high teas instead). It's roomy, with a central fireplace and a series of snug banquette-alcoves around the walls (which have some attractive sporting prints). There is a sensibly segregated pool-table and fruit machine, as well as a juke box, and you can play dominoes. A small panelled room opens off the main area, and at the front of the building there's a comfortable little lounge with gentle piped music. Well kept Belhaven 80/–, Castlecary Heavy (brewed for them by Heriot), Greenmantle and Theakstons Best on handpump; good value simple food includes lentil broth (35p), sandwiches, sausage, egg and chips or hamburger (£1.10), haddock in breadcrumbs or home-made steak pie (£1.70), ploughman's (£1.30), roast chicken or sweet and sour pork (£1.80), chicken and mushroom pie or Irish stew (£1.75), salads (£1.95) and puddings (80p). A separate restaurant is open for dinners. (Recommended by Tim Halstead, Les Weston)

Free house · Licensee M Johnston · Real ale · Meals and snacks · Children in eating area · Open 11–11 all year · Bedrooms tel Banknock (0324) 840233; £14/£22B

CLEISH (Tayside)   NT0998   Map 11

Nivingston House

1½ miles from M90 junction 5; follow B9097 W until village signpost, then almost immediately inn is signposted

We have known this plushy comfortable country house hotel for a good long time: interesting bar snacks – with nary a chip in sight – have included good home-made soup (£1.10), home-made chicken, sherry and orange pâté with oatcakes and salad (£2.60), ploughman's (£2.60), toasted French bread with ham and prawns cooked in white wine with garlic and tomato and topped with cheese (£3.35), tagliatelle with garlic, or venison burger in a sesame bun (£2.95), home-smoked trout with caper and horseradish sauce (£3.25), and steak sandwich (£4.65). Recently there have been moves towards full dining-room lunches instead. The cosy shades-of-red L-shaped bar has softly upholstered seats against sumptuous lotus-plant wallpaper, and looks out over a lawn sweeping down to shrubs and trees, with hills in the distance; there are picnic-table sets below the gravel drive. Belhaven 80/– on handpump, other guest ales and some unusual bottled beers. A comfortable place to stay. (Recommended by S V Bishop)

Free house · Licensee Allan Deeson · Real ales · Meals and snacks · Children welcome · Open 11.30–2.30, 5.30–11 all year · Bedrooms tel Cleish Hills (057 75) 216; £32.50B/£48.50B

Real ale to us means beer which has matured naturally in its cask – it is not pressurised and has not been filtered.

CRAMOND (Lothian)   NT1876 Map 11
Cramond Inn
Cramond Glebe Road

Friendly and welcoming, this old white pub in an attractively
renovated fishing village by the Firth of Forth serves home-cooked
bar food such as soup (65p), game pâté (85p), cold ham, tongue or
raised pie salads (£1.95), fresh sea trout when it's available (£2.25),
daily hot dishes such as steak and kidney pie or pork, mushroom and
cider casserole (£2.20), and freshly made apple pie (80p) in the neatly
refurbished lounge bar, which has cloth-upholstered modern
armchairs on its Turkey carpet. The partly panelled restaurant
(booking advisable), with seats at a more informal serving counter,
concentrates to some extent on seafood such as crab soup (£1.20),
whitebait (£2), Arbroath smokie (£2.25), smoked salmon mousse
(£2.40), sole Mornay (£3.95) and grilled or poached salmon (£4.25).
Well kept Lorimers 80/– under air pressure; friendly, willing service.
The water is only a short walk down through the steep, smartly
renovated white cottages of the village, and the pub's car park has
some fine views out over the Forth; there are seats and tables on a
small side terrace. (Recommended by David Fearnley)

Free house · Licensees Sam Proudfoot · Real ale · Meals tel Edinburgh (031)
336 2035 – and snacks (lunchtime) · Children in dining area · Open 11.30–
2.30, 5–11 all year; closed Sun in winter

CRAMOND BRIDGE (Lothian)   NT1875 Map 11
Cramond Brig
A90

This substantial roadside pub on the main trunk road north serves
good straightforward food at any time of day: soup (40p), giant
sausage (£1.40), haddock (£1.60), steak and kidney pie (£1.90), and
salads with meat pie, pâté or meats; well kept McEwans 80/– under
air pressure, served by neatly white-shirted bar staff. It's a good stop
for families, with a roomy and comfortable area set aside for them off
the main lounge: spacious and open-plan, with plenty of comfortable
button-back banquettes, leatherette seats and stools, big bay
windows and high ceilings. There is a separate downstairs restaurant.
(Recommended by W T Aird)

Scottish & Newcastle · Real ale · Meals and snacks · Children in family room
Open 11–11 all year

CRINAN (Strathclyde)   NR7894 Map 11
Crinan Hotel

Largely rebuilt after a fire some eight years ago, this inn now
combines stylish modern comfort with its mouthwateringly attractive
position (where the Crinan Canal opens into the Atlantic, with
fishing boats and yachts wandering out towards the Hebrides). A
picture window in the cocktail bar looks down on the bustle at the
neat black-and-white entrance locks to the canal: comfortable seats

in the cosy carpeted back part are welcome to yachtsmen tired from beating up the Sound of Jura, while the seats in the tiled front part keep us armchair boatmen in the thick of things – the latest coastal waters forecast is chalked on a blackboard and the décor includes model boats in glass cases, sea drawings and paintings, and a nautical chest of drawers. There is a simpler public bar, and a side terrace with seats outside. Good bar food might include cream of broccoli or Jerusalem artichoke soup (90p), grilled fresh local herring in oatmeal (£2.95), omelette filled with avocado pear (£3), local clams wrapped in bacon (£3.50), Tarbert herring, Arbroath smokie, savoury flans such as leek and Cheddar or Stilton and onion (£3.25), or Tay salmon (£5.95), with puddings such as apricot and sultana russe. You can get sandwiches from their coffee shop. The seafood restaurant on the top floor has a lovely sea and islands view, as does the smart evening bar up here (jacket and tie needed). A nice, comfortable place to stay.

Free house · Licensee N A Ryan · Meals and snacks (lunchtime) · Children welcome · Open 11–11 all year; closed Nov-mid March · Bedrooms tel Crinan (054 683) 235; £31.50B/£50B

CUPAR (Fife)   NO3714 Map 11
Findlay's
43 Bonnygate; A91, just W of centre

There's an almost Continental feel about this small, well kept bar-restaurant. Yes, it has a bar counter, with bar stools and well kept Belhaven 80/– and Maclays 70/– on handpump. But the relaxed and civilised atmosphere is a very far cry indeed from the Scottish drinking-house of a few years ago – and indeed of today, in many places. It's quietly busy, with ladies drifting in from the shops to ease into the dark brown corduroy cushioned seats built into stripped wide-plank full panelling. There are wheel-back chairs around hand-picked antique tables on a Bokhara-style carpet, bird prints, old photographs of the town and rather muffled piped music. Good value bar food includes home-made soup (75p), and lunchtime main dishes such as ham or chicken salad (£2.20), chicken casserole or baked haddock with egg and parsley sauce (£2.25), and a daily special (£2.10), with rather a wider choice of main meals in the evening including sweet-cure herring as a starter (£1.25) and sole with prawns (£3.75) or venison casserole (£5.25). *(Recommended by E Munn)*

Free house · Licensee Mrs J M Findlay · Real ale · Meals (not Sun) and snacks (lunchtime, not Sun) · Children in area partly set aside · Open 11–2.30, 5.30–11 all year; closed Sun, and 25 Dec, 1–3 Jan

DALBEATTIE (Dumfries and Galloway)   NX8361 Map 9
Pheasant
1 Maxwell Street

Not so very unlike the English style of pub, this friendly inn has recently turned its comfortable upstairs lounge bar, overlooking a main crossroads of this peaceful town, into a lounge-restaurant, with a relaxing atmosphere and piped music: it serves food until 10pm –

late for the area. Below is a lively bar with darts, pool, dominoes, fruit machine, space game and juke box, and there's a disco on Friday, Saturday and Sunday night. Bar food includes sandwiches, starters from soup (40p) upwards, and at lunchtime main dishes such as pizza (£1.70), fish (£2) or steak pie (£2.15), with omelettes (£2.50), lasagne (£3.50) and kebabs or steaks (from £5) in the evening. *(Recommended by William Meadon, Richard Steel, W T Aird)*

Free house · Licensee Christine McGimpsey · Meals and snacks · Children welcome · Open 11–2.30, 5.30–12 all year · Bedrooms tel Dalbeattie (0556) 610345; £11.50(£13B)/£23(£26B)

DUMFRIES (Dumfries and Galloway)   NX9776 Map 9
Globe ★

High St; up a narrow entry at S end of street, between Timpson Shoes and J Kerr Little (butcher), opposite Marks & Spencer

If you like the poems of Robert Burns, this friendly tavern is a must; and even if the shaky strains of *Auld Lang Syne* leave you cold you might start being converted just by the atmosphere here – surely not much changed since he wrote that 'the Globe Tavern here . . . for these many years has been my Howff' (a Scots word meaning a regular haunt). These words (from a letter now in the J Pierpoint Morgan Library in New York) are shown in facsimile on the wall of the simple old-fashioned dark-panelled Snug Bar, where you'll be made notably welcome – maybe with a pint of McEwans 80/– from handpump, very reasonably priced. Off to the left the room Burns used most often has been carefully preserved ever since as an evocative little museum devoted to him, and upstairs one bedroom has two window panes with verses scratched by diamond in his handwriting (though not the touching verse he wrote for Anna Park the barmaid here, who had his child). There's a big plain public bar at the back, with dominoes, a fruit machine and maybe piped music. Good value simple bar food includes home-made soup (35p), filled rolls (30p), steak and kidney pie or beef olives (£1.75), quiche and salads, and apple pie (45p); there is also a separate restaurant. *(Recommended by William Meadon, Richard Steel, HKR, W T Aird)*

Free house · Licensee Mrs Maureen McKerrow · Real ale · Meals and snacks (lunchtime, not Sun) · Children in restaurant · Nearby daytime parking difficult; car park 5 mins away · Open 11–11

EDDLESTON (Borders)   NT2447 Map 9
Horseshoe

A703 Peebles–Penicuik

Big windows shaped like horseshoes tell you from the outside that this is no ordinary Scottish roadside tavern, and inside you'll find soft lighting, gentle piped music, comfortable green leatherette banquettes, a patterned carpet, open fire, claymores, Lionel Edwards hunting prints and a Highland cattle oil painting on the walls, and a wide range of good bar food including soup (65p), Stilton soup (95p), sandwiches (from 80p), lasagne (£1.70), ploughman's (£1.85), haddock (£2.20), shepherd's pie (£2.40), steak sandwich (£3.05), gammon (£3.55) and sirloin steak (£5.95). There is also a popular separate restaurant. Belhaven 70/–, Greenmantle, McEwans 80/– and Theakstons Best on air-pressure tall founts, and a good choice of spirits (served in generous ¼ gill measures); a welcoming, friendly atmosphere. *(Recommended by Mark Medcalf)*

Free house· Licensee C A McIntosh Reid · Real ale · Meals and snacks Children in eating area · Open 11.30–2.30, 5–11 all year; closed 25 Dec, 1 Jan

EDINBURGH (Lothian)   NT2574 Map11

Edinburgh has the widest choice of good pubs in Scotland, and indeed scores over all other British cities for the way that so many pubs worth visiting are strung so closely together. The two main areas for finding good pubs here, both main entries and Lucky Dips, are around Rose Street (just behind Princes Street in the New Town) and along or just off the top part of the Royal Mile in the Old Town.

Abbotsford ★

Rose Street; E end, beside South St David Street

A decorous Edinburgh institution, not much changed since the first three decades of this century when our grandfather lunched here most weekdays: friendly dark-uniformed waitresses seem to step straight out of those days, when they come to you on your leather-cushioned bench at one of the long deeply polished old tables which line the tall severely classical panelled walls, to take your order for good value hot dishes. These might include curried chicken or haggis and bashed neeps (mashed turnips) (£1.75), shepherd's pie or liver and bacon (£2.05), lamb cutlets or gammon (£2.15), haddock (£2.25) or sirloin steak (£3.35), and there's a cold buffet (£1.85–£2.25). Well kept Greenmantle and Heriot 80/– on handpump from the heavily panelled Victorian island serving counter, under the high elaborate plaster ceiling; fruit machine, tucked well away. The separate upstairs restaurant is open lunchtimes and evenings. *(Recommended by Ian M Baillie, W T Aird)*

Free house · Licensee John Grant · Real ale · Meals (lunchtime only, not Sun) Open 11–2.30, 5–11 all year; closed Sun

Athletic Arms

Angle Park Terrace; on corner of Kilmarnock Road (A71)

Two separate readers with wide experience of Scottish pubs both independently claim that the Diggers or Gravediggers – as this basic bustling pub is known – serves the best pint in Edinburgh, and perhaps in Britain. A team of red-jacketed barmen work hard at the gleaming row of tall air-pressure founts to keep the throng of mainly young and very thirsty customers supplied with McEwans 80/– in tip-top condition: as you come in, hold up a number of fingers to show how many pints you want, and by the time you work your way through to the bar they should be waiting for you. No frills here: a few roomlets partitioned in glossy grey wood open off the central island servery, lighting and furnishings are utilitarian, and a side room is crowded with enthusiastic dominoes players. *(Recommended by Karen Love, Andrew McKeand, C B M Gregory, Bob Rendle)*

Scottish & Newcastle · Licensee T W Innes · Real ales · Open 11–2.30, 5–11 all year

Bannermans Bar

212 Cowgate

This warren of small rooms burrows deep under some of the Old Town's tallest buildings, with musty, brick barrel-vaulted ceilings in the back part, flagstone floors, massive bare stone walls, and a medley of old settles, pews and settees around barrels, red-painted tables and one long mahogany table. A monumental disused marble-topped bar counter stands idle in one alcove, as if waiting in the wings (which are liberally decorated with fringe-theatre handbills) as an understudy for the one in the panelled main front room. Well kept Archibald Arrols 70/– and Ind Coope Burton on handpump, an interesting choice of reasonably priced salads at lunchtime and filled rolls in the evening (when it's sometimes bustling). *(Recommended by Andrew McKeand)*

Tennents (Ind Coope) · Real ale · Meals (lunchtime, not Sun) and snacks Open 11–2.30, 5.30–11 all year

Beehive

18–20 Grassmarket

The range of well kept real ales here – McEwans 70/– and 80/–, Theakstons Best and Old Peculier and Youngers No 3, from air pressure tall founts – is uncommonly wide for Scotland, but this is no basic beer-drinkers' tavern. It's civilised and well kept, with comfortable leatherette-cushioned wrought-iron seats and some button-back banquettes on the tartan carpet of its two rooms, which are linked by arches with wrought-iron balustrades. There are 1890s prints of Edinburgh on the green and gilt patterned wallpaper, under a high, terracotta-coloured ceiling. The atmosphere is cheerful and lively, and good value bar food – usefully served from noon until 6pm – includes soup, sandwiches, beef, honey-baked ham, quiche or pork pie salads, and hot dishes such as curry, gammon, Cumberland sausage, steak and kidney pie, haddock and haggis with bashed neeps (sensibly, all these main courses are the same price – £1.95). Fruit machine, maybe piped music. There is a restaurant upstairs. The pub has a fine location, in a broad handsome street below the back of the Castle. *(Recommended by Dr A K Clarke, Alasdair Humphery)*

Scottish & Newcastle · Licensee Alan Noble · Real ale · Meals and snacks (lunchtime, not Sun) · Children over 8 in restaurant · Open 11–midnight all year; closed 1 Jan

---

Bedroom prices normally include full English breakfast, VAT and any inclusive service charge that we know of.

Bennets Bar

8 Leven Street; leaving centre southwards, follow Biggar, A702 signpost

This splendid Victorian set-piece has all sorts of treasures: the arched
and mahogany-pillared mirrors surrounded by tilework cherubs,
stately Roman warriors, nubile Florentines, art nouveau stained
glass, a fancy maroon ceiling supported by high elaborately moulded
beams, red leather seats curving handsomely around the marble
tables – an Offenbach or Franz Lehar pub, if Bannermans (see above)
is more Samuel Beckett. The people here are often fun to watch, too.
The splendid long bar counter serves the pub's own blend of whisky
from the barrel, as well as well kept McEwans 70/– and 80/– under
air pressure. Bar food includes sandwiches, mince pie (45p), lentil
soup (45p), macaroni cheese (£1.40), baked potato with cheese and
sweetcorn (£1.50), omelettes (£1.60), chilli con carne with baked
potato (£1.80) and seafood salad (£2.65). *(Recommended by
Lee Goulding, Dr A K Clarke, W T Aird, Paul Edwards, Alan Docherty)*

*Free house · Licensee Cameron Farquharson · Real ale · Meals (lunchtime, not
Sun) and snacks (not Sun) · Open 11–midnight all year; closed 25 Dec, 1 Jan*

Café Royal Circle Bar

West Register Street

This handsome pub started life as a showroom for the latest thing in
Victorian gas and plumbing fittings – hence the striking series of
vastly detailed Doulton tilework portraits of Watt, Faraday,
Stephenson, Caxton, Benjamin Franklin and Robert Peel (known
then as much for introducing calico printing as for his bobbies).
Perhaps you'd need their ingenuity to fathom what obscure tidal
mechanism governs the good atmosphere here: you sometimes find
the pub uncrowdedly relaxed, and sometimes – as one reader puts it –
can feel it really moving. Well kept McEwans 80/– and Youngers
Scotch, IPA and No 3 from air pressure tall founts on the big island
serving counter, which is surrounded by a sea of marble and which
this last year has been graced by a new bar gantry, in style with the
rest of the room, made from hand-carved walnut. Bar food includes
soup (40p), pies and filled rolls (40p–60p) and salads (60p a helping),
with a hot dish of the day; fruit machine. A smart separate Oyster Bar
specialises, as you'd guess, in fish and shellfish, and is open lunchtime
and evening (not Sundays). *(Recommended by Lee Goulding,
Dr A K Clarke, W T Aird, Alan Docherty, Paul Edwards)*

*Free house · Licensee Robert King-Clark · Real ales · Snacks (lunchtime, not
Sun) · Open 11–11 all year; closed Sun, except during Festival*

Guildford Arms

West Register Street

What is it that gives a theatrical feel to so many Edinburgh pubs?
Perhaps that Edinburgh penchant for enjoying seeing what other
people are up to – especially easy to indulge here, where a snug little
gallery bar gives a dress-circle view of the main one (notice the lovely

old mirror, decorated with two tigers, on the way up). Under this gallery a little cavern of arched alcoves (where the fruit machine lives) leads off the well preserved Victorian main bar. Its chief glory is the crusty plasterwork, carefully painted in many colours, with lots of mahogany, scrolly gilt wallpaper, big original advertising mirrors and heavy swagged velvet curtains for the arched windows. Well kept Lorimers 80/– on handpump, and McEwans 80/– and Youngers No 3 on air pressure tall founts, scrupulously professional service. *(Recommended by Karen Love, W T Aird, Russell Fox)*

Free house · Licensee D M Stewart · Real ale · Meals and snacks (lunchtime, not Sat or Sun) · Open 11–11 all year

Jolly Judge

James Court; by 495 Lawnmarket

Tuck down off the Royal Mile into a close surrounded by tall narrow-windowed buildings, then down steps into this snug tavern: the fruits and flowers painted on the low beam-and-board ceiling are typical of sixteenth-century Scottish houses, and a 1787 engraving commemorates Burns' triumphant stay in nearby Lady Stair's Close that January. The atmosphere is cosy and relaxed, with captain's chairs around the cast-iron-framed tables on the carpet, and quickly served small pies (40p–50p), sandwiches, pâtés, pizzas (£1.10), Scotch egg, ham or quiche salad and lasagne, cannelloni or enchiladas (all around £1.85). Well kept Ind Coope Burton on handpump. *(Recommended by Lee Goulding, Richard Gibbs, Patrick Stapley)*

Free house · Licensee Gordon de Vries · Real ale · Meals (lunchtime) and snacks · Children welcome · Open 11–11.30

Old Chain Pier

Newhaven; Trinity Crescent (off Starbank Road)

This attractively converted old pier building is partly cantilevered out from the harbour wall to overhang the water, and behind the serving counter the wall is mostly glass – so the friendly bar staff in the foreground are silhouetted against a marvellous spread of the Firth of Forth, with Newhaven pier over to your right, the Fife hills straight ahead in the distance, and on the left in summer, sunsets. Inside is fun, too, with good piped music (pop in the evening), and up steps a snug dimly lit gallery with old photographs, engravings and *Illustrated* covers on the red walls. Well kept Pentland 70/– and 80/– on handpump; home made soup (40p), pâté or prawn cocktail (90p), haggis (£1.80), goulash, haddock, chicken chasseur and salads (all £1.90); fruit machine, juke box. *(Recommended by C B M Gregory)*

Drybroughs (Watneys) · Real ale · Meals and snacks (not Sun) · Children in gallery (lunchtime only) · Folk singer Tues evening · Open 11–11 all year

---

Looking for ideas for a country day out? We list pubs in really attractive scenery at the back of the book – and there are separate lists for waterside pubs, ones with a really good garden, and ones with lovely views.

Peacock

Newhaven; Lindsay Road

The back room of this well kept pub is brightly decorated with trellises and plants to seem like a conservatory (it leads on out to a garden), and the main lounge is plushly comfortable, with lots of ply panelling and cosy seats. The photographs on the wall give some idea of what Newhaven used to be like before the new development (named after the pub) and other modern changes set in here, and it's not so long since this 200-year-old place was a down-to-earth fishermen's pub. Its food still includes quite a lot of fish, such as mussels (95p), dressed crab (£1.60), mussel salad (£1.95), rollmop salad (£2.20), their special haddock and chips (£2.25), grilled trout (£2.75) and scampi provençale (£3.70), but there's also a wide choice of steaks (from £3.95) and other dishes, and there's a separate restaurant. Well kept McEwans 80/– under air pressure; fruit machine in a side lobby. (Recommended by W T Aird)

Free house · Licensee Peter Carnie · Real ale · Meals and lunchtime snacks
Children in family room · Open 11–2.30, 5–11 all year

Sheep Heid

Duddingston; Causeway

The main room of this old-fashioned ex-coaching-inn has a Turkey carpet, seats built against the walls below Highland prints, some reproduction panelling, anda fine rounded bar counter, and in a side room tables are given some privacy by elegant, partly glazed screens dividing them. A good mix of people, and an easy going atmosphere even when it's full. The garden behind is a pretty place, with a goldfish pond and fountain, and clematis and hanging baskets on the sheltering stone walls of the house and its skittle alley – as far as we know this is the only pub in Scotland that plays alley skittles. Barbecues are held outside in fine weather. Indoors, food includes filled rolls (40p–45p), soup (50p), haggis (95p), haddock (£2.05), dishes of the day such as liver and bacon, curry or roast beef, and a lunchtime cold buffet (£2.30). They hope to do Sunday lunches. There's also a restaurant upstairs. To ask for the pub's own beer (on handpump – actually Heriot), you need to know that it's pronounced Sheep Heed; dominoes, a fruit machine. The pub is in a lovely little village; getting here is a pleasant expedition, past Holyrood house, Arthur's Seat and the little nature reserve around Duddingston Loch. (Recommended by Lee Goulding, W T Aird)

Tennents (Bass) · Licensee Mrs C A Thomson · Real ale · Snacks (lunchtime, not Sun) and meals · Children welcome · Open 11–11 all year; closed Sun

Tilted Wig

1 Cumberland Street (Dundonald Street end)

This civilised pub's unusual décor includes rose and fruit wallpaper on the ceiling, shiny grainy ply panelling, black and white floor and red plastic-topped (but solid) tables. As we went to press they were opening a food servery in the back bar, to make Mrs Crossan's cooking more accessible, and changes in the type of food are possible, but typically there have been sandwiches (50p–60p), pâté (£1.10) and main dishes such as steak and kidney pie or meat salad (£2.20). Steps outside lead down to an attractive little sunken terrace garden which is floodlit at night (any space outside is a rarity for Edinburgh pubs), and there are tables in front by the pavement of this back street. The pub is very popular with advocates, young and old. Well kept Maclays 70/– and 80/– under air pressure from tall founts and Theakstons Best on handpump, and well made Bloody Marys. *(Recommended by J Dobris, C B M Gregory, W T Aird)*

Free house · Licensee Patrick Crossan · Real ale · Meals and snacks (lunchtime, not Sun) · Children in eating area by special arrangement · Open 11–11 all year; closed Sun (though Sun opening under consideration), 25–26 Dec, 1–2 Jan

EILEAN IARMAIN (Isle of Skye)   NG6912 Map 11

see ISLE ORNSAY

ELIE (Fife)   NO4900 Map 11
Ship
Harbour

Right by the water, this friendly old pub has a nautical atmosphere, with winged high-backed button-back leather seats against the partly panelled walls, beams in an ochre ceiling, and a cosy, carpeted back room. Well kept Belhaven 70/– on handpump; a welcoming, lively atmosphere, particularly at weekends. Outside, there are sturdy seats and timber-baulk benches on a sandy grass terrace by the low sea wall, looking over to the pier and the old stone fish warehouse on the left, the little town on the right, and a grassy headland opposite. At low tide the bay is mostly sand, with oyster-catchers and gulls shrilling over the water's edge. *(Recommended by MRM)*

Free house · Real ale · Snacks · Open 11–2.30, 5.30–11 all year

FINDHORN (Grampian)   NJ0464 Map 11
Crown and Anchor
Coming into Findhorn, keep left at signpost off to beach and car park

The cheerful but comfortable lounge bar of this old inn – very close to the water, where Highlanders would have stayed before taking ship for Edinburgh or even London – has lots of pictures, and there are old photographs of the area on the walls of the public bar, with lively atmosphere, games (darts, dominoes, cribbage, fruit machine and space game) and an unusually big arched fireplace. The water still plays a big part in life at the inn, and people staying have the use of its boats; sandy beaches are only a few moments' stroll away. Bar food, usefully served all day up to 9.45pm includes soup (35p), filled rolls and toasties (from 35p), burger (70p), ploughman's (£1.50), pizza

(£1.80), haddock or chipsteak (£2.20) and chicken fillet (£2.30); there's also a separate restaurant. They do half-price helpings for children and keep a high chair. Well kept Devanha XXX, Heriot 80/– and Maclays 80/– on handpump, two guest beers such as Gibbs Mew Bishops Tipple and Sam Smiths OB; also draught ciders (rare around here). They keep unusual strong foreign bottled beers, and have a good choice of spirits as well as some Highland country wines. *(Recommended by I D G Mackie, Robin Leake)*

Free house · Licensees Robin Graham and Gay Robertson · Real ale · Meals and snacks · Children in eating area · Folk, early 60s and jazz music Sun evening · Open 11–11 all year (Fri and Sat closing 11.45) · Bedrooms tel Findhorn (030 93) 2243; £12.50B/£22B

GATEHOUSE OF FLEET (Dumfries and Galloway) NX55 Map 9
Murray Arms [*illustrated on page 801*]

A big lunchtime buffet, attractively set out in an airy room with Scottish landscape prints on its dark blue walls, serves a good range of salads (£3) beside other bar food such as filled baked potatoes (from 60p), sandwiches (70p), toasties (75p), ploughman's (£1.40), pâté (£1.70) and hot dishes of the day (£2.30–£2.85). In the evenings there's a wider choice of hot dishes such as garlic mushrooms (£1.30), locally caught herring (£1.70 – Dorothy Sayers wrote *Five Red Herrings* in the town) or haddock (£1.86) and scampi (£2.95). The bar has well kept Greenmantle on handpump and Youngers No 3 on an air pressure tall fount, and opens into a room with an antique box settle, comfortable easy chairs, Thorburn game bird prints and Victorian coaching prints, and various other sitting areas include the quietly old-fashioned front Burns Room (he composed *Scots Wha' Hae* riding here over the hills from Kenmure Castle in July 1793). The quite separate public bar has darts, dominoes, a fruit machine and juke box, and a sunny (well, sometimes) sheltered side courtyard has a tea-room opening off the side. With its striking tower, this carefully rebuilt inn dates back to the seventeenth century, and was originally called the Gatehouse (the town took its name from the inn), incorporating the 1661 tollhouse for the road. *(Recommended by W T Aird)*

Free house · Licensee Mrs Elizabeth Murray-Usher · Real ale · Meals and snacks · Children in eating areas · Open 11–2.30, 5–11 all year · Bedrooms tel Gatehouse (055 74) 207; £20(£23B)/£40(£46B)

GIFFORD (Lothian)   NT5368 Map 11
Tweeddale Arms
High Street

Across the corridor from the very snug and cosy little lounge bar is a calmly beautiful hotel lounge: chintzy easy chairs, antique tables and paintings, chinoiserie chairs, an oriental rug on one wall, a splendid corner sofa, magazines on a table – a lovely place to sit over a long drink. The public bar has darts, and lunchtime bar food which varies from day to day might include good lentil soup (55p), sandwiches (from 70p), pâté and oatcakes (£1), fried fresh-caught haddock (£1.20), minced beef collops or beef stew (£2) and cold meat salad (£2.10); service is good. There is also a separate gracious dining-room, opening on to a walled garden with white tables among roses, good for dinner in the evening. The old white inn faces an attractive long wooded green and the avenue to Yester House (Goblin Hall from Scott's *Marmion* is supposed to be a thirteenth-century ruin in the grounds, with an underground chamber). The village is surrounded by wooded hills: the B6355 southwards from here over the Lammermuirs, and its right fork through Longformacus, are both fine empty moors roads. *(Recommended by S V Bishop, W T Aird)*

Free house · Licensee Chris Crook · Meals and snacks (lunchtime) · Children welcome · Open 11–11 all year · Bedrooms tel Gifford (062 081) 240; £13.50 (£15B)/£26(£29B)

GIRVAN (Strathclyde)   NX1897 Map 9

Kings Arms

12 Dalrymple Street; A79 in centre

The most thorough-going golfing theme of any we have seen distinguishes the cocktail bar of this long-established hotel, used by the Editor's family since the 1920s. Its specially woven carpet has a pattern of golfballs, putters, greens and bunkers, the walls are printed with lifesize black and white pictures of famous golfers, and its glory is the serving counter – a giant floor-to-ceiling golfball with the barmaid inside it. Soft piped music in here; the spacious lounge bar, with blue plush button-back banquettes in bays around dimpled copper tables, has a good juke box and fruit machine. Bar food, varying daily, includes hot dogs (35p), sandwiches, soup such as potato broth (45p), chilli con carne or lasagne (95p), home-made curries (£1.95), home-baked pies (£2.20) and salads such as home-cooked roast beef (£2.50); Heriot 80/– on handpump; coffee (served too in the central comfortable hotel lounge). *(Recommended by W T Aird)*

Free house · Licensee John Morton · Real ale · Meals and snacks · Children welcome · Open 11–1am all year · Bedrooms tel Girvan (0465) 3322; £16 (£18B)/£25.50(£27.50B)

GLASGOW (Strathclyde)   NS5865 Map 11

Bon Accord

153 North Street

Since our last edition they've opened a wine-bar-style restaurant here, with a cold table (£2.20), cheap three-course lunches, and evening meals with main courses costing around £3.80. But the main focus of attention is still the remarkably wide range of well kept real ales served here in a stylishly neat and simple newly refurbished pub. They usually include Belhaven 80/–, Greenmantle, Ind Coope Burton, Marstons Burton, Pedigree, Merrie Monk and Owd Rodger and Theakstons XB and Old Peculier on handpump, with McEwans 70/–,

813

Maclays 60/–, 70/– and 80/–, and Youngers No 3 on air pressure tall founts, and there may be a couple of other guest beers. There are quite a few malt whiskies, too. The red hessian walls are decorated with beer trays, and there are padded leatherette seats built in, and little rounded-back chairs on the floor – which is partly carpeted, partly new quarry tiles. One side has quiet booth seating, and there is a fruit machine and space game in a back lobby (a TV in the bar may be on for sport). The atmosphere is clean and relaxed. Quite a wide choice of bar food includes home-made soup (40p), snacks such as Scotch pie (90p), ploughman's with Cheddar, Stilton or Edam (from £1.10), Lorne sausage, egg, bacon and black pudding (£1.60), American-style cheeseburger (£1.60) and a daily special such as veal escalope or steak pie. There's a functions room and restaurant. *(Recommended by J E Bainbridge)*

Free house · Licensee Dharam Vir Chopra · Real ale · Children in restaurant Daytime parking restricted · Open 11–11 all year

Outside Inn

1256 Argyle Street; corner with Radnor Street

The very wide choice of malt whiskies – some 230, with off sales as well as bar sales – is the chief draw to this bar, simply furnished with plain leatherette seats on a dark red carpet. It also has attractively priced Belhaven 60/–, 70/–, 80/– and Greenmantle, on handpump. Bar food includes sandwiches (between 3pm and 8pm), home-made soup (40p), filled baked potatoes (55p–80p), salads (from £1.50), lasagne or tuna (£1.70), home-made four ounce beefburgers (£1.75–£1.85), gammon steak (£1.95) and beef curry with pitta bread (£2); darts, a fruit machine, juke box and space game. *(Recommended by R E Leake)*

Belhaven · Licensee Ron Baxter · Real ale · Meals (not Sun) and snacks (afternoon) · Open 11–11 all year

Overflow

67 Old Dumbarton Road

The good range of well kept real ales, mostly on handpump, in this cheerful and easy-going pub includes Belhaven 80/–, and 90/–, Greenmantle, Heriot 80/–, Maclays 60/– and 80/–, Marstons Pedigree, Theakstons Best and Old Peculier, and – unusually for Scotland – farm ciders. The high-ceilinged room has leatherette seats forming booths around the tables, and high-backed bar seats around the central servery; there are small engravings of old Glasgow on the dark brown hessian walls. Bar food includes soup (45p), pies (45p), beefburgers (around 90p), ploughman's, beef and onion or steak and onion pie and a wide range of salads (from £1.50); piped music. *(Recommended by R E Leake)*

Free house · Licensee Andrew Main · Real ale · Meals and snacks (lunchtime) Open 11–11 all year

---

We say if we or readers have seen dogs or cats in a pub.

Pot Still

154 Hope Street

The name implies a special interest in malt whiskies, and indeed they do have a tremendous range – helpfully documented – of several hundred, including several different versions of the great single malts in different ages and strengths, far more vatted malts than we knew of (these are blends, but malts only – no grain whisky), and a changing, attractively priced malt-of-the-month. They sell by the bottle as well as the glass. The well run split-level pub (no jeans allowed, and the white shirted barmen wear black bow-ties) is attractively decorated, with photographs of old Glasgow on red hessian walls, an elaborately plastered high red ceiling, and seating in neat booths around tables. Bar food includes home-made soup (50p), filled rolls, sandwiches and toasties (55p–70p), hamburgers (from 85p), double-decker sandwiches (£1.25), ploughman's (£1.40), cod or moussaka (£1.40), steak sandwich (£1.55), and ham, turkey or roast beef salad (£1.85); Heriot 80/– on handpump and Maclays 80/– on air pressure. (*Recommended by Ian Baillie*)

Free house · Licensee Paul Waterson · Real ale · Meals and snacks (not Sun) Open 11–12 all year; closed Sun

GLENDEVON (Tayside)   NN9904 Map 11
Tormaukin

A823

On what is arguably the most attractive north–south route through this part of Scotland, this comfortable and well run inn serves very good bar food such as melon (£1.30), a mild but distinctive home-made pâté (£1.40), good grilled rainbow trout (£3.25) and minute steak (£4.25), and well kept cheeses; they serve soup, cold meat and other salads and coffee throughout the day. The softly lit bar has red plush seats against stripped stone and partly panelled walls, and there's Ind Coope Burton on handpump and a good choice of malt whiskies, and gentle piped music. Even when it's very crowded, it stays relaxing. There is also a busy dining-room. The bedrooms are well equipped, and there are said to be 90 golf courses within an hour's drive – there's certainly some glorious countryside. (*Recommended by Gwen and Peter Andrews*)

Free house · Licensee Ann Dracup · Real ale · Meals and snacks · Children welcome up to 7pm · Open 11–11 all year; closed 25 Dec, 1 Jan · Bedrooms tel Glendevon (025 982) 252; £25B/£35B

GULLANE (Lothian)   NT4882 Map 11
Golf

Main Street; A198

Good bar snacks in this small, friendly and quite golf-fixated hotel include filled rolls (40p), sandwiches (50p), home-made soup (50p), filled baked potatoes (from 70p), ploughman's (£1.25), Scotch pie (£1.40), pizza or hamburger (£1.60), home-made pie (£1.80) and scampi or salads (£2) – what's more, they are served from noon until 10pm. An evening restaurant does three-course dinners (£6). The lounge has dimpled copper tables and banquettes, with piped music, there are some seats in the back garden, and the simple public bar has darts, pool, dominoes, cribbage, skittles, a fruit machine, space game and juke box. Well kept McEwans 80/– on air-pressure tall fount. *(Recommended by L N Goulding, C B M Gregory)*

McEwans · Licensee Thomas Saddler · Real ale · Meals and snacks · Children in eating area · Open 11–11 all year · Bedrooms tel Gullane (0620) 843259; £11.50(£12.50B)/£23(£25B)

HOWGATE (Lothian)   NT2458 Map 11
Old Howgate Inn

Since our last edition there's been a change of licensee at this civilised and interesting food pub (it's under the same ownership as the Horseshoe at Eddleston – see above), but things seem to be going on very much as before. The special thing here is sandwiches – a very wide range of Danish-style open ones. To get the full range, go through to the tiled dining-room which has high seats at a neat bar counter as well as banquettes and armed seats around old tables. They are presented prettily, as well as tasting good, and range from home-made chicken liver pâté (£1.30), through tongue, ham or roast pork with poached apple rings and crisped onions (£2.20) to smoked trout with spinach pâté (£3.15), steak tartare with prawns (£3.25) or fresh lobster with asparagus and lemon mayonnaise (£4.60). There's other food too, including soups (around £1.20), Danish cheeses (around £2) and more substantial dishes, mainly Danish, including hot ones. The bar, which now has Belhaven 80/–, Greenmantle, McEwans 80/– and Theakstons Best on handpump, as well as frozen akvavit, does smaller versions of the sandwiches – ones you can pick up in your fingers without risking them nose-diving into your drink. This room is airy and pretty, white panelled, with a stone fireplace, tiled floor, red plush window seats and nests of oak stools. There are a couple of civilised sitting-rooms, with comfortable easy chairs and orange-red hessian walls. There are some slat wood tables on a small back lawn, edged with potentilla and herbaceous borders. *(More reports please)*

Free house · Licensee M McIntosh Reid · Real ale · Snacks · Children in restaurant · Open 11–2.30, 5–11; closed 25 Dec, 1 Jan

INVERARAY (Strathclyde)   NN0908 Map 11
Argyll Arms

The lounge bar of this stately and old-fashioned West Highland hotel has elaborate plaster mouldings around the ceiling, and tall velvet-curtained windows looking out to Loch Fyne. A spacious front conservatory has a good loch view, and the well run building generally reflects the simple grandeur aimed at by Robert Mylne when he was designing this stylish Georgian lochside town for the

Duke of Argyll. A good choice of bar food includes soup (60p), sweet-cure herring in sherry (£1.30), house game liver pâté with oatcakes or ploughmans (£1.90), open sandwiches (from £1.90), home-made haggis burger (£2.45), fillet of haddock or fried venison liver in red wine (£2.75), cold meat salads (£3.50) and sirloin steak (£5.25); also a separate restaurant. McEwans 80/– real ale, and a good choice of malt whiskies. The public bar has pool, dominoes, a fruit machine and juke box. A nice place to stay, well very run, with a fine landlord who is an excellent conversationalist. It's handy for the woodland garden at Crarae and well placed for other West Coast gardens. *(Recommended by W T Aird)*

Free house · Licensee Niall Iain MacLean · Real ale · Meals and snacks Children welcome · Young pipers and dancers Weds evening, occasional accordionist Tues evening · Open 11–11 all year · Bedrooms tel Inveraray (0499) 2466; £13.50(£19.50B)/£27(£39B)

INVERARNAN (Central)   NN3118   Map 11

Inverarnan Inn

A82 N of Loch Lomond

The friendly bar of this early eighteenth-century house conjures up the days when it was a drovers' inn: it's a long room with log fires in big fireplaces at each end, black winged settles with green tartan cushions and deer-skins slung over their backs, stripped stone or butter-coloured plaster walls, small windows, red candles in Drambuie bottles if not candlesticks, cupboards of pewter and china, bagpipes, a horse-collar and a gun among the Highland paintings, and a stuffed golden eagle on the bar counter. The barman wears a kilt, and on our visit there was piped Scottish traditional music. Broth (50p), toasted sandwiches (from 60p) and ploughman's or pâté (£1) are served all day; at mealtimes there is also food such as hamburgers (£1.90), breaded haddock (£2.25), herring in oatmeal (£2.50), pork chop (£3) and salmon steak (£4.25). Lots of sporting trophies, horns and so forth hang on the high walls of the central hall. There are tables and cocktail parasols in a field beside the house (also on a small back terrace), with a stream running behind. *(Recommended by Richard Glover)*

Free house · Meals and snacks · Open 11–11 all year

ISLE OF WHITHORN (Dumfries and Galloway)
NX4736   Map 9

Steam Packet

In a lovely spot on the edge of a fine natural harbour, this friendly, recently refurbished inn has big picture windows looking out on the yachts and inshore fishing boats. The low-ceilinged bar has two rooms: on the left, green leatherette stools around cast-iron-framed tables on big stone tiles, an open fire in the bare stone wall; on the right, plush button-back banquettes, brown carpet, boat pictures. There may be piped music. Good value bar food includes home-made soup (35p), filled rolls (from 50p), a hot dish of the day (£1.25), burger (£1.25), fresh fish (£1.75), cold meat salads (from £2, good rare beef £2.15) and scampi (£2.50). It may be served in the lower beamed living-room, which has excellent colour wildlife photographs and a big model steam packet boat on the white walls, rugs on its wooden floor, and a solid-fuel stove (there's also an upstairs restaurant). Lots of boat trips (usually 1½ to 4 hours) from the harbour; in the rocky grass by the harbour mouth are the remains of St Ninian's Kirk. The inn's five bedrooms are comfortable and well equipped; a nice place to stay. *(Recommended by W T Aird, David Tomlinson)*

Free house · Licensees John and Sarah Scoular · Meals and snacks · Children welcome · Occasional folk music · Open 11–11 · Bedrooms tel Whithorn (098 85) 334; £12.50B/£25B

ISLE ORNSAY (Isle of Skye)   NG6912 Map 11
Hotel Eilean Iarmain ★
Signposted off A851 Broadford–Armadale

Gaelic is spoken by this friendly inn's staff and many of its customers – even the drinks price list and, with translations, the menus are in Gaelic – but everyone quickly makes the veriest Sassenach feel at home in the busy bar. This is big and cheerful, with good tongue-and-groove panelling on walls and ceiling, brass lamps and a brass-

The Sun, Anstruther

mounted ceiling fan, leatherette wall seats and light wooden chairs, a huge mirror over its open fire, and a swooping stable-stall-like wooden divider that gives it a two-room feel. Good bar food at lunchtime includes sandwiches (55p), home-made soup (60p), smoked mussels (£1.30), scampi (£2.50), salads such as ham (£2.30) or salmon (£3) and one or two hot dishes such as sausage stew (£1.70) or roast meat (around £2). In the evening there's more concentration on main dishes such as locally caught fish with chips (£2.50) and salmon or steak (£5.50), with dinners in the pretty dining-room. This has a lovely sea view past the little island of Ornsay itself and the lighthouse on Sionnach (you can walk over the sands at low tide). Well kept McEwans 80/– from an air-pressure tall fount; darts and pool. A nice place to stay (some of the simple bedrooms are in a cottage opposite), in an attractive part of Skye – less austere than the central mountains – where you will probably see red deer, and maybe otters and seals. *(Recommended by W T Aird)*

Free house · Licensee Iain Noble · Real ale · Meals and snacks · Children welcome · Local folk music Fri · Open 11–11; closed 1 Jan · Bedrooms £13/ £26

KENMORE (Tayside)   NN7745 Map 11
Kenmore Hotel

Pencilled on the wall above the fireplace of the residents' lounge in this comfortable old inn, in Burns' own unmistakable handwriting, is his long poem 'Admiring Nature in her wildest grace' – a tribute to the beauty of the area. This front part of the inn is quietly old-fashioned, with armchairs and sofas, a lounge where children are allowed, and a separate restaurant. Further back is the friendly Archie's Bar, with salmon fishing photographs and old prints above the seats in its series of snug alcoves; it looks down to the River Tay and beyond to Drummond Hill. Bar food includes home-made soup (95p), sandwiches, ploughman's or pâté (£1.75), omelettes or a dish of the day (£2.50) and scampi (£3.50). In a different building behind there's the high-roofed Boar's Head, a barn bar with white-painted stone walls, darts, shove-ha'penny, dominoes, cribbage, a colour TV, lots of rustic-style tables. A steep upper garden has seats among its grass paths and shrubs, and the lower back lawn stretches down to the hotel's jetty on the Tay. The hotel has good salmon and trout fishing. A nice place to stay. *(More reports please)*

Free house · Licensee T Finlayson · Real ale · Buffet lunches and snacks Children welcome · Open 11–2.30, 5–11 all year · Bedrooms tel Kenmore (088 73) 205; £22B/£44B

KILLEARN (Central)   NS5285 Map 11
Old Mill
A875

We have it on good authority that there are usually fine views of the Campsie Fells from behind this quietly friendly old village pub – on our visit all was clouds, and we were glad to scuttle in to the warmth of the open fire in the stone fireplace. There are wheel-back chairs and cushioned built-in settles around the dark tables on a brown patterned carpet, with rustic beams in the swirly white ceiling of the main room, and a snug little side room leading off. Bar food includes rolls (from 50p, steak sandwich 75p), home-made soups (75p), cheese and oatcakes (75p), steak roll (75p), ploughman's (£1.50), omelettes or burgers (£1.50), pâté (£1.75), haddock (£1.75) and scampi (£2.75); on our visit, piped pop music; fruit machine in the lobby, also dominoes. *(Recommended by J R Glover)*

Free house · Licensee John Greenshields · Meals and snacks (lunchtime) Children in eating area · Open 11–2.30, 5–11 all year (open all day Sat and bank hol Mons)

KIPPFORD (Dumfries and Galloway)   NX85 Map 9
Anchor

Overlooking the broad yachting inlet and the peaceful hills beyond, this friendly waterfront white inn has a big picture window in the cocktail bar to make the most of the view. Its most atmospheric bar is at the back: simply furnished, with nautical prints and a few boat trip advertisements on its warm brown panelled walls (the ceiling's panelled too), a coal fire, and built-in red leatherette seats, some of them forming quite high booths around sturdy wooden tables – there's a view from this part too. There may be piped music. Freshly cooked bar food includes haddock (£1.80), bacon, egg and tomato quiche (£1.95), and trout (£2.60), with sandwiches or filled rolls (from 45p), and salads with sea trout (£2.25) and Solway salmon (£3.20) when they're available; children's dishes start from fish fingers (75p). Well kept McEwans 80/– from air pressure tall fount; and a back games room with two well lit pool-tables, a fruit machine, space games and juke box. There's a restaurant for occasional use. *(Recommended by W T Aird, Janet Williams)*

Free house · Licensee Cliff Henderson · Real ale · Meals and snacks · Children welcome · Occasional live music Fri and Sat · Open 11–2.30, 5–11 all year Bedrooms tel Kippford (055 662) 205; £10.50/£21

KIRKCUDBRIGHT (Dumfries and Galloway) NX6850 Map 9
Selkirk Arms
Old High Street

Much modernised, this well kept place has been a hotel since 1777, and its simple high-ceilinged lounge bar is comfortable and friendly, with soft red leatherette seats on a red patterned carpet, big turtle shells on the partly panelled walls, and the arms of the various local towns above its fireplace. It opens broadly into a table-service dining-room, but bar food is served too: soup (50p), sandwiches (from 60p), ploughman's (£1.50), grilled sausages or hot pies (£1.85), smoked trout or scampi (£2.25). In the evening there are basket meals (around £2.25), and, besides the restaurant, also in the evening there is a steak bar. Talking of food, there's a tradition that Burns composed the Selkirk Grace –

> *Some hae meat and canna eat,*
> *And some wad eat that want it,*
> *But we hae meat and we can eat,*
> *Sae let the Lord be thanket*

– while staying here, though to some it seems more likely that he did so while staying at St Mary's Isle with Lord Daer, Selkirk's son. There's a clubby and popular locals' front bar. The spacious and sheltered back garden has white tables and chairs: the live music is out here in summer if it's fine. The hotel has salmon and trout fishing on the Dee. *(Recommended by W T Aird)*

Free house · Licensee David Armstrong · Meals and snacks · Open 11–2.30, 5.30–11 all year · Guitar/singer Tues in summer · Bedrooms tel Kirkcudbright (0557) 30402; £14.75(£17.50B)/£29.50(£35B)

LAUDER (Borders)   NT5347 Map 11
Black Bull
A68

The bar of this 300-year-old inn has a tack-room theme, with lots of harness on walls of wood planking, and photographs and championship certificates of a wide variety of pedigree animals (not just the bulls you'd expect from the name, but also sheep and even the championship dachshunds which Mrs Cook used to breed). The bar opens from a narrow entrance part into a more spacious area with tables set for the food. This includes a wide choice of dishes such as soup (40p), ham, egg or hamburger rolls (65p), ploughman's or club sandwiches (£1), steak roll (£1.60), chicken and chips (£2.45), bacon, sausage and egg (£3.20), grilled gammon (£3.75) and sirloin steak (£4.50), or you can have a steak pie meal with coffee (£2.50 for two courses, £3.50 for three). There is also a cold buffet (£3.95, including starters and pudding or cheese). There's a separate Georgian dining-room, handsome and high ceilinged. *(Recommended by S V Bishop)*

Free house · Licensee Jean Cook · Meals and snacks · Children and dogs welcome · Open 11–11 all year · Bedrooms tel Lauder (057 82) 208; £12.50 (£14.50B)/£18.50(£22.50B)

Eagle
A68

The lounge bar of this old inn has a serving counter like an Elizabethan four-poster, and newly upholstered seats around its dimpled copper tables; there may be piped music. Bar food includes home-made soup (40p), pies and pasties (40p), lamb, beef or ham sandwiches (from 65p, toasties from 75p), breaded haddock (£2.20), gammon or chicken drumsticks (£2.50), turkey breast (£3) and sirloin steak (£4.75), with a selection of salads (£2.75). The locals' public bar has darts, pool, dominoes, cribbage, a fruit machine and

---

Pubs with outstanding views are listed at the back of the book.

juke box. Behind the inn there are tables in the old stables yard, which has cut-down barrels as flower planters – there are summer barbecues here. The bedrooms are comfortable and well equipped. *(More reports please)*

Free house · Licensee Ron Dick · Meals and snacks · Children welcome · Open 11–11 all year · Bedrooms tel Lauder (057 82) 426; £11.50/£23S

LEWISTON (Highland)   NH5029 · Map 11

Lewiston Arms

Village signposted from A82 just S of Drumnadrochit

There is a neat garden outside the comfortable and well kept lounge bar here: flower borders, fruit trees, a lawn and even a loggia to sit in on almost-warm days. A locals' public bar is friendly and plainly furnished, with darts, dominoes, a fruit machine, space game and juke box. Bar food includes home-made soup (70p), ploughman's or open sandwiches (£1.25), pâté with salad and crusty bread (£1.50), grilled garlic prawns (£1.75), lasagne (£2.50) and scampi (£3.50), with puddings (from 60p); Youngers No 3 on tall fount. A small dining-room opens off the lounge. A mile or two down the A82 are the ruins of Urquhart Castle, and Loch Ness. And from the end of the village lane there are pretty walks into wooded Glen Coiltie. *(Recommended by W T Aird)*

Free house · Licensee N J Quinn · Meals and snacks · Children welcome · Open 11–2.30, 5–11 all year; closes 1am Thurs and Fri · Bedrooms tel Drumnadrochit (045 62) 225; £11/£22

LOANS (Strathclyde)   NS3431 Map 9

Dallam Tower Hotel

Old Loans Road; from S end of Loans turn up hill, following Dundonald (B730) signpost

In spite of the imposing name, this is actually a friendly family-run house, not big. A big bay window in the airy lounge gives a splendid view over the fields and the village to the Firth of Clyde, and on a clear day to the Isle of Arran some 20 miles away. This spacious room is attractively furnished with pale wood rounded-seat captain's chairs and button-back built-in brown leatherette seats on the geometric brown carpet, big photographs of Clydeside in the old days on the walls, and a greenish ceiling. Tables are set for bar food, which includes soup (45p), pâté (£1.25), farm chicken with bacon (£2.60), pork chops or gammon (£2.75), lamb cutlets (£3.10), scampi (£3.40) and a cold buffet (£2.90), with other grills such as a mixed farmhouse grill (£3.60) and minute steak (£4.60) in the evening (when there's a restaurant – must book at weekends). At lunchtime there are more hot dishes such as spaghetti bolognese or chilli con carne (£2.40), with children's dishes such as beefburgers (80p). Well kept Greenmantle and Lorimers 70/– and 80/– on handpump, and guest beers (you can order Lorimers in 34-pint polypins on Mondays and collect on Wednesdays); sit-down space games, dominoes and on our visit soft piped pop music, with a fruit machine and another space game in an outer lobby. There's a terrace outside, from which spacious terraced lawns step down to trees and rhododendrons. *(Recommended by C Elliott)*

Free house · Licensee Mrs Elizabeth Lindsay · Real ale · Meals · Children welcome · Open 11–2.30, 5–12 all year · Bedrooms tel Troon (0292) 312511; £25B/£35B

LOCH TUMMEL (Tayside) NN8460 Map 11
Loch Tummel Hotel
B8019

This old stone inn, with big windows to make the most of the view, looks out over Loch Tummel and to the wooded mountains beyond. It stands quite a way above the loch (there is a way down). Its long bar has white-painted walls, a sturdy white beam supporting the black joists and creaky boards of the simple upstairs restaurant, which is closed in the winter, and a big free-standing wood-burning stove. There are whitewood rush-seat chairs and red leatherette seats around the black tables, where bar food ranges from home-made soup with home-made wholemeal bread (60p) or ploughman's lunch and home-made pâté to local sirloin steaks (£5.25), fresh salmon and trout when available, and Sunday curries and roasts; McEwans 80/–

The Stein Inn, Stein

on air pressure tall fount; piped music. A games bar has pool, darts, dominoes, Scrabble, a fruit machine and an antique piano. *(Recommended by Mr and Mrs G and C Rowlands; more reports please)*

Free house · Licensee Ronald Spinner · Real ale · Meals and snacks · Children welcome · Open 11am–midnight · Bedrooms tel Tummel Bridge (088 24) 272; £15(£18B)/£24(£30B)

LUSS (Strathclyde)   NS3593   Map 11
Inverbeg Inn
A82 about 3 miles N of village

The big lounge of this neat and good-humoured inn has lots of close-set dark brown cord easy chairs, sofas and armed seats in the carpeted lounge bar, which has lots of gilt-framed landscapes, a big *Monarch of the Glen* and spaniel and game-bird prints above the varnished part-panelling. There's a big bay window. In here, very polite and busy waitresses serve a wide range of bar food from 9am to 11pm, including home-made soup (75p), filled baked potatoes (from 75p), sandwiches (70p), bacon roll (80p), toasties (from 90p), pizza (£2.20), ploughman's (£1.95), pâté (£2.60), salads (from £2.60), American-style beefburger (£2.75), shepherd's pie (£3.75), gammon (£4), lamb chops (£4.60), game pie (£5.20) and eight-ounce sirloin steak (£6.30). Well kept Strathalbyn 70/– on handpump. A separate restaurant is open in the evening. The simply furnished public bar has pool, dominoes, cribbage, a juke box, television, fruit machine and space game. In summer the Loch Lomond ferry to Rowardennan below Ben Lomond calls three times a day at the inn's jetty (over the road), and you can hire boats here too. *(More reports please)*

Free house · Licensee Jack Bisset · Meals and snacks all day · Children welcome Open 11–12 all year; closed 25 Dec · Bedrooms tel Luss (043 686) 678; £20/£34(£40B)

MELROSE (Borders)   NT5434   Map 10
Burts Hotel
A6091

> *If thou wouldst view fair Melrose aright,*
> *Go visit it by the pale moonlight;*
> *For the gay beams of lightsome day*
> *Gilt, but to flout, the ruins grey.*

Scott, in his *Lay of the Last Minstrel*, was talking about the Abbey, and if you do take his advice – it is lovely by moonlight – this comfortable old inn would be an appropriate place to stay. Its spacious, comfortably refurbished L-shaped lounge bar has Scottish prints on its walls, and Windsor armchairs around the tables on its Turkey carpet. There may be background music. A good range of waitressed-served bar food includes soup such as Scotch broth or good lentil soup (80p), sandwiches, chicken liver pâté or smoked mackerel pâté (£1.50), prawns with bacon and mushrooms in garlic (£1.80), good fried haddock (£2.10), chicken in a basket (£2.50) and sirloin steak (£5), with lunchtime additions such as ploughman's

(£1.30), cold meats with salad (£2.20), steak and mushroom pie
(£2.30) and perhaps fresh dressed crab, and in the evening extra
dishes such as home-made beefburgers (£2.80) and ham and chicken
salad (£3.30). There's also a spacious separate restaurant which looks
over a well tended garden (with tables out in summer). Belhaven 80/–
on handpump. Nearby Priorswood is a garden that specialises in
flowers grown for drying. Melrose has perhaps the quietest and most
villagey atmosphere of all the Scottish Border towns: a good place to
stay. (Recommended by S V Bishop, I D G Mackie)

*Free house · Licensees Graham and Anne Henderson · Real ale · Meals and
snacks · Children welcome · Open 11–2.30, 5–11 all year · Bedrooms tel
Melrose (089 682) 2285; £16(£18B)/£30(£34B)*

MOFFAT (Dumfries and Galloway)   NT0905 Map 9
Black Bull

A choice of three different bars here includes the tiled-floor lounge
bar with coaching notices and prints on its walls, and benches along
the row of tables where they serve food such as soup, sandwiches,
filled rolls (65p), pâté, sweetcorn, salads such as quiche, cheese and
pineapple, beef, ham or chicken, and hot dishes such as shepherd's
pie, cheese and potato hot-pot, fish pie, macaroni and haggis (main
dishes are around £1.60–£2), with cheesecake, fruit pie, waffles and
other puddings. There's also a separate restaurant. A smart, softly lit
plush cocktail bar, with a pink ceiling, plum-coloured walls and soft
piped music, has a very good choice of malt whiskies, and a fruit
machine and space game in a side room. Across a small courtyard,
another bar has red panelling covered with metal station plates and
other railway memorabilia, benches built in to these panelled walls,
darts, and well kept Greenmantle on handpump and Youngers IPA
and No 3 on air pressure tall founts. They have dominoes here. You'd
have to go to Moscow now to see the inn's famous Burns window:
when young Deborah Davies rode by with her mother, Burns
scratched on the pane his answer to the question:

> *Why had she been formed so well*
> *And Mrs D so big?*
> *Ask why God made the gem so small*
> *And why so huge the granite?*
> *Because God meant mankind should set*
> *That higher value on it.*

*Free house · Licensee Mrs H Poynton · Real ale · Meals and snacks (not Sun
evening; no food Jan–Easter) · Children welcome · Open 11–11 all year
Bedrooms tel Moffatt (0683) 20206; £13/£26*

MONIAIVE (Dumfries and Galloway)   NX7790 Map 9
George

The delightful little flagstoned bar of this seventeenth-century white
stone Covenanters' inn has good antique Tam O'Shanter engravings
on its butter-coloured timber walls, high winged black settles

upholstered with tartan carpet, some small seats made from conical straight-sided kegs, open fires in winter, and dark butter-coloured ceiling-planks. A wide choice of good bar food includes freshly cut sandwiches, tasty home made soup, haddock (£1.80), steak and kidney pie (£2.10), a good ham and mushroom omelette with excellent mashed potatoes, salads with home cooked tongue or smoked ham, chicken curry (£2.75) and maybe fresh Solway salmon. The atmosphere is warm and friendly, and service charming; darts, dominoes, cribbage, fruit machine, space game and juke box away in the public bar. A separate restaurant is open on Friday to Sunday evenings and for Sunday roast lunch, and has piped music. This is a pretty, very peaceful village, surrounded by pasture hills. *(Recommended by Mark Medcalf)*

Free house · Licensee John Michael Wassmer · Meals and snacks · Children welcome · Open 11–2.30, 5–11 all year · Bedrooms tel Moniaive (084 82) 203; £9/£18

MONYMUSK (Grampian)   NJ6815 Map 11
Grant Arms
Inn and village signposted from B993 SW of Kemnay

This handsome eighteenth-century stone inn has – until this last year – been in the hands of the Grant family, and its lounge bar is carpeted in Grant hunting green tartan. It's now been taken over by new landlords, who will be gradually refurbishing it, taking care not to affect the general style of its comfortable green leatherette seats and bar stools and fawn plush armchairs, log fire in the stub wall which divides it into two areas, and high shelf of china above the dark panelling. Bar food includes quiche Lorraine or rough pâté (£1.25), five-ounce burgers (from £1.75), haddock fillet (£2.85), butterfly pork chop (£3.95) and sirloin steak (£4.95); Heriot 80/– on handpump. There is a separate restaurant. In the past there's been a friendly atmosphere, with a good mixture of local people and visitors (often staying for the fishing – they have about ten miles of trout and salmon water on the River Don). The simpler public bar has darts, dominoes, fruit machine and space game. North of the village – spick and span in its estate colours of dark red woodwork and natural stone – the gently rolling wooded pastures soon give way to grander hills. *(Recommended by S V Bishop; up to date reports on the new management please)*

Free house · Licensee Colin Hart · Real ale · Meals and snacks · Children welcome · Open 11–2.30, 5–11 all year · Bedrooms tel Monymusk (046 77) 226; £19/£35(£37)

MOUNTBENGER (Borders)   NT3125 Map 9
Gordon Arms
Junction of A708 and B709

A welcome sight from either of the two lonely moorland roads which cross here: both roads take you through attractive scenery, and the B road in particular is very grand – indeed, it forms part of a splendid empty moorland route between the A74 and Edinburgh (from Lockerbie, B723/B709/B7062/A703/A6094). Bar food includes sandwiches, beefburger roll with chips (£1.20), ploughman's or pizza (£1.60), sausage, egg and chips (£2), haddock (£2.40), a choice of salads (£3), home-made steak and kidney pie (£2.90) and breaded scampi (£3.40), with very popular fresh trout from a nearby fish farm (£2.90); well kept Greenmantle on handpump (brewed in Broughton, near Peebles). There is also a separate restaurant. Since our last edition a new games room has been opened with darts, pool, dominoes and fruit machine. The cosy public bar has a fire in cold weather, and an interesting set of photographs of blackface rams from local hill farms. A local 'shepherd song' in honour of the present landlord is pinned up by the bar. A hundred and fifty years ago another shepherd poet, James Hogg, the 'Ettrick Shepherd', recommended that this very inn should keep its licence, which Sir Walter Scott, in his capacity as a justice and who also knew the inn, subsequently granted. There's also a lounge bar. High teas – a speciality here – can be served in the late afternoon.

Free house · Licensees W M and M P Rowe · Real ale · Meals and snacks Children in eating area · Occasional accordionist Fri or Sat · Open 11–11 all year · Bedrooms tel Yarrow (0750) 2222; £12/£21

NAIRN (Highland)   NH8856 Map 11
Clifton Hotel ★★
Viewfield Street; coming from Inverness on A96, turn left at roundabout just below Tourist Office into Marine Road, which runs into Seafield Street, with Viewfield Street a left turn

Our highest-rated Scottish entry – and the only one which is also licensed as a theatre, staging recitals, concerts and plays during the winter – this substantial Victorian house is sumptuously decorated, and bar lunches benefit from fresh ingredients and good cooking which has earned the stylish restaurant high praise: there are good thick soups, sandwiches with home-cooked meats, and perhaps more important dishes such as fresh oysters, good local sea fish and trout or salmon. For these, the best place to eat is in the little Green Room (lunch only), with antique silver, linen napkins and Wedgwood plates (booking advisable). The deeply comfortable lounge bar has easy chairs on its thick carpets and rugs, attractive prints on handsome red Victorian wallpaper, an antique cast-iron stove, a sonorously vast Victorian clock, and vases of flowers form the well kept walled garden. The catholic collection of spirits goes well beyond the good range of malts to include, for example, a choice of Russian and Polish vodkas. On clear days you can see the Highland mountains beyond the broad Moray Firth (there are good sandy beaches here). A nice place to stay.

Free house · Licensee J Gordon Macintyre · Meals and snacks (lunchtime) Children welcome · Open 11–2.30, 6–11.30; closed Nov–March · Bedrooms tel Nairn (0667) 53119; £28B/£40B

Pubs with attractive or unusually big gardens are listed at the back of the book.

NEWBURGH (Grampian)   NJ9925   Map 11

Udny Arms

Behind this attractively converted house there are lots of white tables on the sheltered back lawn, and from this a private footbridge crosses the little Foveran Burn to the nine-hole golf links, the dunes and the sandy beach along the Ythan estuary. Inside, a thoughtfully furnished lounge bar has nicely cushioned stripped pine seats and wooden chairs around plain wooden tables on its grey carpet, bird prints, salmon flies and a pictorial map of the River Dee on the cream walls, and stuffed salmon above the bar counter, which serves well kept Alice, Alford and McEwans 80/– from handpump. A sun lounge has green basket chairs around glass-topped wicker tables, and the back public bar is now a café bar serving snacks and real ale; dominoes, cribbage and table games such as Scrabble. Food might include cream of vegetable soup (75p), chicory with Stilton dip (£1.50), pâté (£1.75), ploughman's (£2.25), chilli con carne (£2.75), haddock in mushroom and cheese sauce (£2.95), savoury beef pancakes or casseroled pork in sweet cider and apples (£3) and grilled sirloin steak (£6.50), with a sticky toffee pudding (£1.25). In the afternoon they serve tea and shortbread. Service is friendly and obliging, and the inn is very well kept. The Garden Suite, across the yard, is used as a restaurant on Sunday lunchtimes (£8.50). A comfortable place to stay, with three good golf courses and Pitmedden Gardens nearby. (Recommended by T C Bidie)

Free house · Licensee Mrs V McKinlay · Real ale · Meals and lunchtime snacks Children welcome · Open 11–2.30, 5.30–11 all year · Bedrooms tel Newburgh (Aberdeen) (035 86) 444; £34B/£48B

NEWTON STEWART (Dumfries and Galloway)
NX4165   Map 9

Black Bull

Queen Street; A714; main street into town from A75 roundabout

The cheerful and well kept bar of this popular and recently renovated town pub has brown button-back leatherette seats in booths with wrought-iron screens, and lots of horse brasses on the white walls (given a half-timbered look with strips of black wood). Good value bar food includes soup (40p), sandwiches (45p), hamburgers (£1.75), salads (from £1.95), chicken escalope or scampi (£2.35) and eight-ounce sirloin steaks (£4.25); tea (25p a head) as well as coffee; dominoes, cribbage, fruit machine and juke box or piped music, with pool in an inner room. There's also a plusher cocktail bar, open on weekend evenings (till 1am on Friday night). White tables under cocktail parasols in the sheltered back courtyard of this white-painted old stone building look out to the pine woods on Larg Hill, beyond the River Cree. Fishing and shooting can be arranged in advance for residents. (Recommended by Maureen Guthrie)

Free house · Licensees Jim and Dee Harper · Meals (lunchtime, not Sun) and snacks (not Sun lunch) · Children welcome · Live music most Tues and Fri Open 11–11 · Bedrooms tel Newton Stewart (0671) 2054; £12 (£12B)/ £20 (£20B)

nr PENICUIK (Lothian)   NT2360   Map 11
Habbie's Howe
Nine Mile Burn; signposted off A702

The little public bar of this attractive old coaching-inn has a heavy beam in the shiny ochre ceiling, a high shelf of china and brass, and old-fashioned high-backed settles with copper-topped tables by the open fire. It opens into a lounge converted from the stables: heavy rustic tables stand in 'stalls' with a hayrack overhead, some harness hangs on the roughly plastered crushed-raspberry walls, and the black beams that support the white ceiling boards are decorated with horses' bits. There may be piped music (and if not, the clock chimes very melodiously). The atmosphere's welcoming and friendly. Bar food includes home-made soup (from 50p), sandwiches (from 55p), toasties (75p), a choice of cheeses (95p), home-made pâté (£1.40), prawns (£1.45), herrings (£1.50), home-made quiche or smoked salmon (£1.80), scampi (£2.60) and a cold meat platter with salad or chips (£2.70). A separate restaurant, open all week in summer, is open Friday to Sunday in winter, and serves traditional high teas. Dominoes, cribbage. The inn incorporates the remains of a twelfth-century mead mill. *(Recommended by C B M Gregory)*

Free house · Licensees Jimmy and Jean Watson · Meals and snacks (not Mon–Thurs evening) · Children in dining area and restaurant · Open 12–2.30, 5–11; Sunday opening 12.30–2.30, 6.30–11 · Bedrooms tel Penicuik (0968) 76969; £9.50/£17

nr PITLOCHRY (Tayside)   NN9458   Map 11
Killiecrankie Hotel
Killiecrankie signposted from A9 N of Pitlochry

Now that the trunk-road bypass is complete, leaving this country house hotel in peace, Mr Hattersley Smith is a changed man – as he says, no longer dazzled by drivers' clenched white knuckles gleaming through a haze of asbestos brake-lining dust. The bar iself, which has dimpled copper tables and light armed chairs and opens into a front sun-lounge extension, has acquired a ptarmigan in its white winter plumage and a sparrowhawk to go with the other stuffed birds, as well as a red squirrel holding some nuts, and has been recarpeted in a quiet oatmeal colour. Thre are also good wildlife photographs in here – if you haven't been lucky enough to see a red squirrel or a roe buck in the spacious grounds, which back on to the hills and include a putting-course and a croquet lawn. At lunchtime bar food can be served either in here or more restfully in the dining-room (which also has a picture-window front extension); it becomes a full restaurant in the evening. The food (available until 10pm – unusually late for the area) is good, and strong on local cooking, including good fresh soups such as chicken and watercress, mushroom and walnut and carrot and orange (from 70p), egg and prawn cocktail (£1.85), sandwiches (from 65p, through home-cooked ham, 80p, to smoked salmon, £1.65), Buckie haddock (£2.40), good Tay trout, either freshly smoked and very succulent, served with freshly made horseradish sauce (£2.30) or grilled (£3.95), lunchtime salads (from

£1.80) and evening steaks (£5.25). Reasonably priced wines include an excellent 1982 Pouilly–Fuissé shipped by Peter Thompson of Perth, and service is charming. The views of the mountain pass are splendid. *(Recommended by J C Aitkenhead, J M Cooley)*

Free house · Licensees Duncan and Jennifer Hattersley Smith · Meals and snacks · Dogs and well behaved children welcome · Open 12–2.30, 6–11; closed mid-Oct–Easter · Bedrooms tel Pitlochry (0796) 3220; £17 (£19B)/£34 (£36B)

PLOCKTON (Highland)   NG8033 Map 11
Plockton Hotel
Village signposted from A87 near Kyle of Lochalsh

This lovely sheltered village, strung out among palm trees along the seashore and looking across Loch Carron to rugged mountains, is owned by the National Trust for Scotland. The inn is part of a long, low terrace of stone-built houses. The lounge bar, on the right as you go in, is comfortably furnished with green leatherette seats around neat Regency-style tables on a tartan carpet; it's partly panelled (with a ship model set into the woodwork), partly bare stone, with an open fire and window seats looking out to the boats on the water. Bar food includes home-made soup (55p), filled rolls such as egg (55p) or bacon (70p), home-made pâté, ploughman's (£1.90), deep-fried haddock (£2.50), home-made steak and kidney pie (£3), home-baked ham salad (£3.25) and fresh local prawns or salmon (£5), with some vegetarian dishes; there's a good collection of whiskies (this is one of the select handful of pubs which keep the Royal Household whisky). There may be piped music, and the public bar has darts, pool, shove-ha'penny, dominoes and cribbage. *(Recommended by W T Aird)*

Free house · Licensee Mrs L M Peacock · Meals and snacks · Children welcome Open 11–11 · Bedrooms tel Plockton (059 984) 274; £10/£20

POLMONT (Central)   NS9378 Map 9
Whyteside Hotel
Under a mile from M9, junction 7; A803 towards Polmont, then left into Gilston Crescent

The two room areas of the extensive open-plan bar that spreads out from this well run and friendly Victorian house are comfortably furnished with soft green leatherette banquettes and wheel-back chairs around dark tables. There is a very pleasant atmosphere – the relaxed feel of lots of people quietly enjoying themselves. They stock over 300 whiskies but aren't narrow-minded: there are also over a dozen different gins, sixteen rums, lots of vodkas, over sixty different bottled beers and well kept Archibald Arrols 70/– and Ind Coope Burton on handpump. Bar food includes soup (80p), baked potatoes (from 80p), pâté (£1), toasties (£1.50), beefburger (£1.80), pizza (£2.30), cold meat salads (£2.40) and sirloin steak (£5.25), with two or more daily hot specials (£2.20) such as lasagne or home-made steak pie; there is also a separate charcoal-grill restaurant. Darts, dominoes, cribbage, maybe piped music. Goats graze outside, and a discreet housing estate spreads beyond. *(Recommended by T D Sneddon)*

Free house · Licensee Barbara Batchelor · Real ale · Meals and snacks
Children in eating area (not after 7.30) and restaurant · Organ music Tues and
Thurs · Open 11.30–2.30, 5–11 all year; closed 1 Jan · Bedrooms tel Polmont
(0324) 712394; £18S/£25S

PORTPATRICK (Dumfries and Galloway)   NX0154 Map 9

Crown ★

One of the nicest pubs in Scotland: on the harbourfront of this quiet
village, it has a rambling old-fashioned bar with lots of little nooks,
crannies, and alcoves – full of atmosphere and bustle, yet almost
always with somewhere to sit even when it's crowded. Interesting
furniture includes a carved settle with barking dogs as its arms and an
antique wicker-backed armchair; the partly panelled butter-coloured
walls are decorated with a stag's head (over the coal fire), old mirrors
with landscapes painted in their side panels, and shelves of old bottles
above the bar counter. Bar food includes sandwiches (from 50p),
open sandwiches (from 60p, local crab £1.75), home-made soup
(65p), ploughman's (£1.50), haddock (£1.75), salads (£2.10), cod
fillet (£3), breaded local scallops (£3.75) and lobster (£8) – much of
the fish and shellfish is caught by the landlady's son Robert, who is in
charge of the cooking. Piped music (on our visit Bobby Womack and
the Rolling Stones); sensibly placed darts in the separate public bar,
also dominoes, and a fruit machine. An airy and very attractively
decorated 1930s-ish dining room opens into a sheltered back garden.
Seats outside in front – served by hatch in the front lobby – make the
most of the evening sun. A nice place to stay. *(Recommended by W T
Aird, T A V Meikle)*

McEwans/Youngers · Licensee Mrs Mollie Campbell · Meals (not Sun evening)
and snacks · Children in eating area and dining room · Open 11–2.30, 5–11 all
year · Bedrooms tel Portpatrick (077 681) 261; £16B/£28B

QUEENSFERRY (Lothian)   NT1278 Map 11

Hawes Inn

This waterside inn's spacious and comfortable lounge bar has a fine
view of the Forth stretching out between the massively practical
railway bridge and the elegant supercilious road bridge. An efficient
food counter serves sandwiches, filled rolls, and at lunchtime soup,
casseroles or stews and pies, and salads running up to dressed crab; in
the evenings hot dishes are basket meals instead. Archibald Arrols
70/– and Ind Coope Burton on handpump. There's a separate
restaurant in the quieter, older part of the inn, where there's still
something of the atmosphere that made the inn so appealing to R L
Stevenson (he used it as a setting in *Kidnapped*, and may even have
been moved to start writing the book while staying here). The small
public bar has darts and a fruit machine. A back lawn with hedges
and roses has white tables. *(Recommended by S V Bishop, Mark Medcalf)*

Ind Coope · Licensee Miss E P S Reid · Meals (lunchtime) and snacks
Children in dining-room and family room · Open 11–11 all year · Bedrooms
tel Edinburgh (031) 331 1990; £22/£33

ST ANDREWS (Fife)   NO5161   Map 11

Victoria Café

St Mary's Place; corner of Bell Street

Not exactly a pub, but quiet pubby in an airy way: the big upstairs room has stripped panelling, tall green walls and a darker green ceiling, and bentwood chairs around marble-topped cast-iron tables on an oak floor. There are potted plants, brass single-globe lamps and a colonial ceiling fan; on our visit, quite well reproduced piped modern jazz. It opens on to a sunny roof terrace with three or four tables. Bar food is served throughout the day. McEwans 80/– from an air-pressure tall fount, and good value fruit juices. A rather elegant oval room with waitress service is used as a family room. *(Recommended by Alastair Campbell)*

Maclays · Licensee Peter Dickson · Real ale · Meals and snacks · Children in oval room · Variable live music about twice a month · Open 11–11; closes midnight Thurs, Fri and Sat

ST BOSWELLS (Borders)   NT5931   Map 10

Buccleuch Arms

A68 just S of Newtown St Boswells

The bar in this Victorian sandstone inn has pink plush seats and banquettes in elevant curves, velvet curtains and reproduction Georgian-style panelling. It serves well kept Greenmantle on handpump, and there are dishes of nuts and other nibbles on the bar; there may be piped music. Bar food includes soup (50p), sandwiches, chicken liver and ham pâté (95p), turkey and ham salad (£2.50), pizza or herring in oatmeal (£2.50), steak and kidney pie (£2.75) and sirloin steak (£4.75), with puddings such as cherry tart (80p); there's also a separate restaurant. The lively public bar has darts, pool, dominoes, fruit machine, space game and juke box. *(Recommended by S V Bishop)*

Free house · Licensees Mrs N Johnston and Mrs L Stevenson · Real ale · Meals and snacks · Children welcome · Open 11–2.30, 5–11 all year · Bedrooms tel St Boswells (0835) 22243; £13 (£19.25B)/£25.50 (£35.20B)

ST MARY'S LOCH (Borders)   NT2422   Map 9

Tibbie Shiels Inn

The Southern Upland Way, a long-distance foot path, passes this remote old inn. The loch is beautiful, and fishing is free to residents. A simple but comfortable modern side extension lets you eat your waitress-served bar food looking out over the water: sandwiches (from 50p), home-made soups, ploughman's (£1.30), chops (from £1.85), home-baked steak pie (£2), scampi (£2), trout (£2.45) and salmon salad (£2.85), and home-made fruit pie. There are home-baked scones and biscuits at high tea (£3.25) in the restaurant, which is open for dinner (from £5). The back bar, in the original old stone part of the building, is cosy, with well cushioned black wall benches or leatherette armed chairs and a photograph of the redoubtable

Tibbie Shiels herself. Her name, after she'd married the mole-catcher who originally lived here, was really Isabella Richardson, but she'd been in service with the family of James Hogg, the shepherd poet and writer of Ettrick, and all Hogg's literary friends who followed her here – Scott, Stevenson, Carlyle, and others – knew her by her maiden name. Her comment on Hogg himself, whose grey statue is above the inn, was: 'He was a gey sensible man, for a' the nonsense he wrat.'

Free house · Licensees Shanks and Hildegard Fleming · Meals and snacks Children welcome · Open 11–11 · Bedrooms tel Selkirk (0750) 42231; £10.50/£21

SCONSER (Isle of Skye) · NG5132 Map 11
Sconser Lodge
A850 Portree–Broadford

Included for its waterside position and splendid views across to the Island of Raasay and the mountainous mainland beyond, this hotel has a lively locals' bar which quickly welcomes passing strangers. It's simply furnished, with brown upholstered small armchairs on the carpet, a TV, and a great spread of window looking out across the water. A side room has pool and darts. Handy for the Red Hills (easier walking than the Cuillins, rising directly behind the hotel); and the little Raasay car ferry runs three or four times a day from a pier just down the road (bookings form Mr Nicholson the Ferrymaster, of Churchton House on Raasay).

Free house · Licensee J W Baker · Real ale · Meals and snacks · Children welcome · Open 11am–12pm (noon–11 in winter) · Bedrooms tel Sligachan (047 852) 333; £13/£25(£28B)

SKEABOST (Isle of Skye) NG4148 Map 11
Skeabost House Hotel
A850 NW of Portree, 1½ miles past junction with A856

This very civilised small hotel in pleasant grounds at the head of Loch Snizort serves popular lunches in a spacious and airy lounge. The food, from an attractively laid out buffet table, includes soup (65p), sandwiches (£1), vegetarian salad (£2.15), a hot dish of the day (£2.40–£3), cold meat salads (£3.10) and local salmon (£3.60); note that service stops at 1.30. The adjacent high-ceilinged bar has red brocade seats on its thick red carpet – some in a big bay window which overlooks a terrace (with picnic-table sets) and the well kept lawn. This doubles as a putting-course and runs down to the loch, bright with bluebells on its far side. A fine panelled billiards room leads off the stately hall, and the restaurant serves good set dinners. The grounds include an attractive bog-and-water garden under overhanging rocks and rhododendrons, and the hotel has fishing on the Snizort, perhaps Skye's best salmon river. A nice place to stay. The village Post Office here has particularly good value Harris wool sweaters, blankets, tweeds and wools. *(Recommended by Joyce Walker)*

Free house · Licensee Iain McNab · Snacks (lunchtime) and meals · Open 11–2.30, 5–11; public bar closed Sun; closed Nov–Easter · Bedrooms tel Skeabost Bridge (047 032) 202; £16 (£22B)/£36 (£44B) nr SPEAN BRIDGE (Highland)   NN2281 Map 11

Letterfinlay Lodge Hotel

7 miles N of Spean Bridge on A82

The lunchtime buffet in this decorous family-run inn looking down over Loch Lochy includes home-made soup (75p), a wide choice of salads such as quiche, lamb, beef, pork, venison and salmon, and hot dishes such as roast beef or steak and kidney pie (all main courses are £3.50). The big main bar has a long glass wall giving a splendid view over to the forests on the far side of the loch, and comfortable brown plush seats clustered around dark tables, and communicates on the one hand with a games area (pool, darts, dominoes, cribbage and space game) and on the other with an elegantly panelled small cocktail bar with its black-bow-tied barman, button-back leather seats, old prints, a chart of the Caledonian Canal, and piped music. A couple of white tables under cocktail umbrellas on the side gravel might be a good starting-point for a stroll down through the rhododendrons to the waterside. Fishing and perhaps deerstalking can be arranged. It's essential to book if you want dinner in the smartish restaurant (open 7–9). A good place to stay. *(Recommended by Gwen and Peter Andrews, Caroline Curry)*

Free house · Licensee Ian Forsyth · Meals and snacks (lunchtime) · Children welcome · Open all day · Bedrooms tel Invergloy (039 784) 222; £12.50 (£14B)/£25 (£28B)

STEIN (Isle of Skye)   NG2656 Map 11

Stein Inn   ★ *[illustrated on page 823]*

Waternish; B886, off A850 Dunvegan – Portree; OS Sheet 23 map reference 263564

One of Skye's liveliest and most attractive pubs, this splendid little inn stands just above a sheltered inlet on the island's west side – perfect for the glorious sunsets you get this far north (towards 10.30 or 11 in high summer). The bar is traditionally furnished: flagstones by the serving counter, country chairs around good solid tables, partly panelled bare stone walls, some roped cork floats hanging from the beam-and-plank ceiling, a really hot peat fire in the stone fireplace (which is set with seashells). Piped Scottish music – live folk singing on many evenings, which seems to get livelier as the night wears on. Bar food includes locally caught fish and shellfish (there's also a separate dining-room); there's a fine choice of malt whiskies. On one wall is a copy of the original plan for this village; the inn was opened in 1787 as part of the British Fisheries undertaking which planned this as a great fishing centre – but not long afterwards the herring migrations shifted away from these coasts. Dinghies can be hired here. *(Recommended by Patrick Stapley, Richard Gibbs, Derek Cooper, Janet Williams, Robert Aitken)*

Free house · Meals and snacks · Frequent live folk music · Open 11–11 Bedrooms tel Waternish (047 083) 208; £8.50/£17

Pubs in outstandingly attractive surroundings are listed at the back of the book.

STIRLING (Central)   NS7993 Map 11
Settle Inn

91 St Mary's Wynd; from Wallace Memorial in centre, go up Baker Street and keep right at the top

Stirling's oldest inn, built in 1733 and handsomely restored, it has a great arched stone fireplace in its lower room (with two curling stones in front of the actual hearth), black beams and brown panelling, some stripped bare stone, and Windsor chairs and wall benches around the tables; up steps, another room has a barrel-vaulted ceiling of big interlocking stone blocks and more of the simple furnishings, with old local landscape prints including a big Clark print of Stirling Castle (to compare with the aerial photograph downstairs). Bar food includes ready-filled rolls, bridies, Scotch pie, pizza, sausage rolls and pasties, with some quick-served hot dishes such as cottage pie, lasagne, moussaka and beef in ale casserole. The well kept Belhaven 70/– and 80/– on handpump is served in twenty-four-ounce lined glasses (a splendid way of avoiding the short measure which is almost inevitable with the usual brim twenty-ounce glasses, and which in other pubs loses you so much that you are actually paying an average of seven per cent more than you think for your beer!). Dominoes, cribbage, fruit machine and juke box, and a giant colour TV used for special sporting events and the like. *(Recommended by Russell Fox)*

Belhaven · Licensee Andrew Morrison · Real ale · Snacks (not after 7pm) Open 11–11 all year; closes 11.30pm Fri and Sat; closed 25 Dec, 1–2 Jan

STRACHUR (Strathclyde)   NN0901 Map 11
Creggans ★

A815 N of village

On fine days the white tables in front of this elegant inn have a good view of the loch and the hills on the far side (a quiet road runs between, but is partly screened by the hedge at the edge of the lawn). Perhaps best of all is the bench across the road, close to the spot where Queen Mary of Scots landed on 26 July 1563. The lounge bar is at the back: attractively furnished with comfortable tweedy bucket seats on its beige carpet, and eighteenth-century caricature drawings on its apricot hessian walls. The varnished boards of the ceiling add an appropriate nautical touch. There may be discreet piped music. A side room has similarly well chosen furniture and big early-nineteenth-century prints of Scottish landscapes by Clark. The lively locals' public bar, furnished simply, (with pool, darts, dominoes, a fruit machine and space game) looks out over Loch Fyne, as does the separate restaurant (which has a good range of wines, often distinguished). Good bar food includes home-made soup (80p), bacon roll (85p), toasted sandwiches (£1), home-made burgers, including a venison one (£1.85–£1.90), a choice of home-made pâtés and terrines (£2.10), sweet pickled herring (£2.35), omelettes (£2.70) spiced beef open sandwiches (£2.80), locally smoked trout (£3.45), cold meat salads (£3.85–£4.30), local plaice or trout (prices on request), lamb cutlets (£4.20), and perhaps local oysters (£5.50 the half-dozen) or langoustines (£6). McEwans 80/– on handpump (actually rather cheaply for the area), and a good selection of malt whiskies. *(More reports please)*

Free house · Licensee Sir Fitzroy Maclean Bt, manageress Mrs Laura Huggins Meals and snacks · Children welcome (but no babies at dinner) · Open 11–midnight (Thurs and Fri to 1am) all year · Bedrooms tel Strachur (036 986) 279; £23.50 (£27B)/£37 (£51B)

THORNHILL (Central)   NS6699 Map 11
Lion & Unicorn
A873

This is one of very few inns north of Yorkshire to have its own bowling green – it can be booked for private functions. The two communicating rooms of this friendly old-fashioned inn – which has been in business now for about 300 years – include one that's carpeted, with small easy chairs around dimpled copper tables, and stripped stone walls, and another (to our mind, more fun) with leather-cushioned pews, settees and antique oak tables on bare floorboards, and flowery wallpaper. Bar food includes sandwiches (from 80p), toasties (£1), ploughman's (£1.60), roast chicken (£2.75), scampi (£4.25) and twelve-ounce sirloin steak (£5.25); well kept Greenmantle on handpump, and a good range of spirits. Booking is recommended for the separate restaurant. The public bar has darts, dominoes, space games and a fruit machine. Though they do have bedrooms (see below), they feel that the restaurant keeps them too busy to want to 'push' the bedroom side of the business. *(Recommended by G R Brown)*

Free house · Licensee John Cosgrove · Real ale · Meals and snacks · Children welcome · Open 11–3, 5–11 all year · Bedrooms tel Thornhill (078 685) 204; £10.50/£21 (£24B)

THORNHILL (Dumfries and Galloway)
NX8795 Map 9
Buccleuch & Queensberry Hotel

This substantial red sandstone inn, built for the Duke of Buccleuch in 1845, has access to salmon fishing on the River Nith; this borders valley is green, rich with lushly leafy trees, and sheltered by plump hills. Bar food includes sandwiches, ploughman's, macaroni cheese, haddock, cottage pie, lasagne and steak and kidney pie, with more grills in the evening, and a high teas session from 5pm to 8pm. The dignified lounge bar has high beams, a mounted stag's head, comfortable brown button-back banquettes forming cosy booths around dark tables, and perhaps discreet piped music; there's also a separate restaurant. The livelier public bar has darts, dominoes, fruit machine and juke box. *(More reports please)*

Free house · Licensee George H Balharrie · Meals and snacks (lunchtime, high teas and Fri–Sun suppers) · Children welcome · Open 11–2.30, 5–11 all year Bedrooms tel Thornhill (0848) 30215; £14 (£17.50B)/£26 (£30B)

TROON (Strathclyde)   NS3230 Map 9

The Lookout

Troon Marina, Harbour Road; from centre, go into Temple Hill and keep
bearing right

A real find, this: it looks like a yachting clubhouse, but isn't. Up the
steps in the new, blocky building is a stylish first-floor bar with
wicker and bentwood chairs and comfortable grey-blue plush
banquettes around low tables on a royal blue carpet, a dark powder-
blue high ceiling, and good big colour yachting pictures on the grey
walls. Big windows give a lovely view out over the crowded yachts of
the marina to the sea and the coast beyond. Food is served in a
separate room away from the bar and includes a range of starters
(65p–£1.50) and several main course dishes (£1.10–£6.25); seafood
is a speciality. Well kept Greenmantle, Strathalbyn and Theakstons
on air-pressure tall founts, good espresso coffee, and a fruit machine
and (on our visit) well reproduced salsa music; a separate pool-room.
The wooden balcony-terrace outside (a bit breezy sometimes) has a
do-it-yourself gas barbecue, and in the marina you can arrange
sailing, windsurfing and waterskiing. *(Recommended by W T Aird)*

*Free house · Licensee W M Bickerton · Real ale · Meals and snacks · Children
in eating area and special area for them · Strolling mandolin and guitar in
restaurant Fri–Sun · Open 11–11; closes midnight Thurs, Fri and Sat*

TWEEDSMUIR (Borders)   NT0924 Map 9

Crook

A701 a mile N of village

The back bar of this friendly inn, once a drovers' halt on this lonely
and beautiful Borders road, has knobby and irregularly paved
flagstones, photographs of sheep and of fishing on the ochre plaster
walls, tartan cushions on its rustic seats, and well kept Greenmantle
on handpump (also bottled beer from Traquair House). One very
thick wall, partly knocked through, has a big hearth with a good fire
in winter. It open into an airy and spacious lounge with comfortable
chairs around low tables on a tartan carpet, and beyond that is a sun
lounge. Bar food includes soup (70p), home-made pâté (£1.25),
ploughman's (£1.95), smoked trout mousse (£1.75), bridie (£2.50),
home-made beefburger (£2.20), scampi (£3.20) and home-made
steak and kidney pie (£3.95); home-made puddings include trifle
(80p) and fruit pie and cream (90p). A separate room has darts, pool,
dominoes, cribbage, a fruit machine and space game. There are tables
on the grass outside, with a climbing-frame and slide, and across the
road the inn has an attractive garden, sheltered by oak trees. There
are grand hills, some forested, all around. *(Recommended by W T Aird)*

*Free house · Licensee C M Masraff · Real ale · Meals and snacks · Children in
eating area (not bar) · Open 11–2.30, 5–11 all year; closed 25 and 26 Dec
Bedrooms tel Tweedsmuir (089 97) 272; £24 (£26B)/£40 (£44B)*

If you see that cars parked in the lane outside a country pub have their lights on
at night, leave yours on too: it's a sign that the police check up there.

TWYNHOLM (Dumfries and Galloway)   NX6654   Map 9

Burnbank Hotel

Village signposted just off A75 Castle Douglas–Gatehouse of Fleet; in village centre turn down Burn Brae

Warmly friendly, this unpretentious inn by Auchengassel Burn on the edge of the village serves good value freshly cooked simple bar snacks, sandwiches and meals, using local produce. There are comfortable button-back banquettes and little green leatherette armchairs around rustic wooden tables in the airy carpeted lounge; the separate public bar has a fruit machine. Even in the dining-room meals are cheap: soup (40p), haddock (£1.70), steak pie (£2.20), scampi or gammon (£2.75) and sirloin steak (£3.95), with tea by the pot (28p) as well as coffee. There are tables outside, with cocktail parasols, on the front terrace and in the beer garden by the burn. The countryside around is pretty, with the tidal sands of the Dee estuary a couple of miles away, and plenty of golf, boating, fishing and shooting. (Recommended by Maureen Guthrie)

Free house · Licensee John Paton · Meals and snacks · Open 11–2.30, 6.30–11 all year; closed Mon lunchtime · Bedrooms tel Twynholm (055 76) 244; £8/£16

WEEM (Tayside)   NN8449   Map 11

Aileen Chraggan

B846

Recently extended, the comfortable modern lounge bar of this friendly inn has enormously thick and soft plum-coloured banquettes against its walls, which have Bruce Bairnsfather First World War cartoons on the red and gold Regency striped wallpaper. Big picture windows look out across the flat ground between here and the Tay to the mountains beyond that sweep up to Ben Lawers, and the separate restaurant shares this same view. Bar food includes soup (65p), home-made pâté (£1.20), lasagne (£1.75), omelettes (from £2.15), salads (from £2.25 – fresh Tay salmon when it's available £4.25), chicken casserole with mushrooms and bacon (£3.85), beef casserole (£4) and sirloin steak (£5.95), with a hot pudding (£1.20) and various ice creams. They are hoping to introduce a new seafood menu at weekends. There are tables on the large terrace outside.

Free house · Licensee Alistair Gillespie · Meals · Children welcome Open 11–11; closed 25 and 26 Dec, 1–3 Jan, and maybe for lunch on day of Tay raft race (middle Sun in June) · Bedrooms tel Aberfeldy (0887) 20346; £15/£30

Lucky Dip

Besides the fully inspected pubs, you might like to try these Lucky Dips recommended and described by readers (if you do, please send us reports):

ABERDEEN [Union Street; NJ9305], *Grill Bar*: old fine bar with well kept mirrors and panelling *(W T Aird)*

ALLOWAY [NS3318], *Burns Monument*: comfortable hotel lounge which tends to be overcome by American tourists in summer – Burns' birthplace is nearby *(Colin McLaren)*

ALTNAHARRA [NC5635], *Altnaharra*: fishing bar on shores of Loch Naver: well equipped bar with good snacks, first-rate coffee and friendly staff *(Gwen and Peter Andrews)*

ARDFERN [NM8004], *Galley of Lorne*: old inn in lovely setting, interestingly decorated: battle scenes, shelves of china, stone floors. Good bar food in long single bar with pool and fruit machine at back, some garden; modern hotel accommodation behind, also restaurant; bedrooms *(Patrick Stapley and Richard Gibbs)*

AULTGUISH [NH3570], *Aultguish Inn*: isolated highland inn near Loch Glascarnoch, bar food; children welcome; bedrooms *(W T Aird, LYM)*

AVIEMORE [High Street; NH8912], *Mr Sirs*: pop videos shown all day (they'll show your favourite), frequent live music, and 10-minute bell when all drinks 20p! *(M G McKenzie)*

[Main Road] *Winking Owl*: good bar food, restaurant *(Michael Hyde)*

AYR [8 Dunure Road, Doonfoot; NS3321], *Balgarth Hotel*: free house with good value bar lunches in stately lounge bar; bedrooms *(Colin McLaren)*

BALLATER [NO3695], *Tullich Lodge Hotel*: good food in hotel bar at lunchtime; all the best gossip in Scotland to be had in the bar; bedrooms *(S V Bishop)*

BALLINLUIG [NN9853], *Ballinluig Inn*: friendly and efficient service, good food and bedrooms (reasonably priced) *(J Parkinson)*

BEATTOCK [NT0802], *Old Brig*: varied menu of good and interesting food, moderate prices, drinkable red wine by glass. Style rather bare and Scottish, gravely courteous service *(Mrs Betty Barnes, S V Bishop)*

BOTHWELL [27 Hamilton Road; NS7058], *Cricklewood*: friendly staff in popular pub with variety of good bar meals at reasonable prices, choice of real ales; bedrooms; children welcome in dining-room attached to bar *(Derek Shackleton)*

BROADFORD [NG6423], *Broadford*: comfortable modern furnishings in lounge bar of inn in well placed village; also public bar and restaurant; bedrooms *(BB, W T Aird)*

BRODICK [NS0136], *Ormidale*: stone nineteenth-century pub, small side bar with tartan carpet, cheerful fire, well kept real ale, good bar snacks, space game and fruit machine, back disco, seats in garden with sea view; bedrooms *(Patrick Stapley, Richard Gibbs)*

CARINISH [NF8159], *Carinish*: cosy biggish public bar with white slat walls, also small saloon *(Patrick Stapley and Richard Gibbs)*

CHIRNSIDE [NT8757], *Waterloo Arms*: good bar food in comfortable homely bar and lounge with Belhaven real ale on electric pump *(M Medcalf)*

CONNEL [NM9133], *Falls of Lora*: splendid Victorian pile, lovely view over Loch Etive, partly modernised: antlers, high rooms, modern central log fire, forty or fifty whiskies, reasonably priced good bar snacks, friendly service; bedrooms *(Jenny Woolf)*

CONON BRIDGE [NH5455], *Conon*: comfortably refurbished lounge bar with golden oldies juke box, lively public bar, straightforward bar meals, McEwans 80/–, restaurant; bedrooms; children welcome *(LYM)*; *Drouthy Duck*: good home cooked food, friendly service, pleasant ambience *(Kieran Byron)*

CRAIGNURE [NM7136], *Craignure*: one of Scotland's few real inns; bedrooms *(Stephen Brough)*

CREAGORRY [NF7948], *Creagorry*: good pub; bedrooms *(T N de Bray)*

CRIEFF [47 High Street; NN8691], *Star*: good fresh fish, and liver casserole, McEwans 80/–; friendly service; bedrooms *(Russell A Fox)*

DIRLETON [NT5184], *Castle*: impressive stone-clad pub in quiet, picturesque village; panelled public bar, fine bar mirrors, local pictures, pool-room with fruit machine; McEwans 80/–. Friendly atmosphere, good lunchtime food, piped music; bedrooms *(L N Goulding)*

DRUMMORE [NX1336], *Queens*: simple public bar in coastal village inn with bar food and late fish suppers, pool-room; not far from Logan Gardens *(BB, W T Aird)*

DRYMEN [NS4788], *Salmon Leap*: pubby L-shaped beamed bar, plusher lounge, wide range of food, restaurant, open all day; children welcome; bedrooms *(LYM, R K Whitehead)*

DULNAIN BRIDGE [NH9925], *Muckrach Lodge*: bar lunches with good sandwiches in spacious bar of Victorian ex-shooting-lodge in lovely valley, popular restaurant with enterprising menu at night. Fishing, shooting; bedrooms *(Roger Hemingway, Anon)*

DUMFRIES [English Street; NX9776], *Cairndale*: comfortable and substantial red sandstone hotel with Rotary Club lunches and plush hotel cocktail bar; bedrooms *(BB, W T Aird)*

DUNBAR [163 High Street; NT6070], *Castle*: tartan decor pub in pretty town. Food good – especially soup and salad; hospitable publican *(Mark Medcalf)*

DUNDEE [16 Victoria Road; NO4030], *Ladywell Tavern*: no-frills small town pub, open all day, with well kept McEwans 80/– and Youngers No 3, lively friendly atmosphere, sometimes crowded. Quickly served bar food *(BB, William Meadon and Richard Steel, Russell A Fox, Alan Docherty, Bryan Kirkaldy, Lee Goulding)*

DUNFERMLINE [NT0987], *Dander*: small, cheery pub *(Bob Rendle)*; [Kirkgate] *Old*: open all day, over 100 whiskies and well kept Youngers IPA in panelled main bar, games room, lunchtime meals and snacks – the abbey and palace ruins, close by, are well worth seeing *(LYM)*

EDINBURGH [39 Rose Street; NT2574], *39*: delightful solid bar, friendly staff; busy, though always room to squeeze in; some lunch snacks *(W T Aird)*; [Rose Street] *Auld Hundred*: dark pub, partitioned into small alcoves, yesteryear atmosphere, informal friendly service, top bar restricted to diners at lunchtime. Good Alloa; very full at Festival time *(Gwen and Peter Andrews)*; [20 Great King Street] *Claret Jug*: clubby atmosphere with Chesterfields, good beer on tap, good salads at lunchtime. Generally young people (sometimes a bit Sloane-ish) *(Mark Medcalf)*; [142 Dundas Street] *Clarks Bar*: good beer in old-style traditional Scottish pub *(J M Tansey)*; [Rose Street] *Daddy Milne's*: has been a great writers' and poets' pub – Hugh McDiarmid, Sorley McLean, Hector MacIvor, Norman McCaig, painter Peter Westwater etc *(W T Aird)*; [Lawnmarket] *Deacon Brodie's*: especially for history-minded tourists: commemorates highwayman town councillor hanged on scaffold he designed *(C B M Gregory)*; [Hanover Street] *Edinburgh Wine Bar*: well kept locally brewed Leith; good food all times, reasonably priced, good atmosphere with no music, wide variety of customers *(Andrew McKeand)*; [Candlemakers Row] *Greyfriars Bobby*: especially for US tourists who know their Walt Disney: commemorates dog who stayed by his master's grave at city's expense for years, tartan carpet etc *(C B M Gregory)*; [26–28 Shandwick Place] *Grosvenor*: friendly service, 80/– real ale, good lunchtime meals at reasonable prices, open all day and on Sunday *(Russell Fox)*; [Fleshmarket Place] *Jinglin' Geordie*: small, unusual furnishings, great atmosphere *(C B M Gregory)*; [Jamaica Street West] *Kay's Bar*: cosy plush mock-up of Victorian tavern, good choice of real ales, food, open all day *(LYM)*; [Rose Street] *Kenilworth*: beautiful elegant Victorian decoration; business lunchers *(W T Aird)*; [30 Wrights Houses] *Olde Golf Tavern*: old golf prints, good lunch food; good big bar, little cocktail bar, upstairs restaurant *(C B M Gregory, W T Aird)*; [200 Rose Street] *Scotts*: restrained modernisation, subdued lighting, old-fashioned, efficient service, good beer *(LYM, W T Aird)*; [Drummond Street] *Stewart's Bar*: easy-going traditional bar, open all day, very busy; good value sandwiches, Belhaven 80/– and Youngers IPA, blends own whisky *(LYM)*; [Thistle Street] *World*: old-fashioned pub with ¼ gill spirits measures *(Anon)*

FOCHABERS [NJ3458], *Gordon Arms*: real ale, snacks and meals in comfortable bars of town inn which can arrange stalking and fishing for residents; bedrooms *(LYM, W T Aird, I D G Mackie)*

FORT WILLIAM [NN1174], *Nevis Bank Hotel*: haunt of thirsty climbers from Ben Nevis; Youngers IPA and No 3 on draught *(D J Fisher)*

FORTINGALL [NN7347], *Fortingall Hotel*: enjoyable help-yourself cold buffet, stalker's lunch, good coffee. Light small bar, well stocked, equally welcoming to residents and non-residents; garden; bedrooms *(Gwen and Peter Andrews)*

FOYERS [NH4921], *Foyers*: local angling photos and press cuttings in public bar; well kept Alice real ale; staff will talk about Loch Ness Monster if asked; bedrooms *(M G McKenzie)*

GAIRLOCH [NB8077], *Old Inn*: friendly place with malt whiskies; good food; if you catch the local fish they'll cook it for you; bedrooms *(Martyn Quinn)*

by GARVE [NH3961], *Inchbae Lodge*: good home cooking and friendly efficient service, attractive decor *(Mrs A M Marker)*

GATEHOUSE OF FLEET [High Street; NX5956], *Angel*: friendly and welcoming service and locals; bedrooms *(Paul Atkins)*

GLASGOW [183 Hope Street; NS5865], *Annie's Bath House*: smart bar with youthful staff *(LYM)*; [17/19 Drury Street] *Horseshoe*: classic big Victorian bar (if a bit tatty), fine mirrors and friendly service *(Dr A K Clarke)*; [61 Renfield Street] *Maltman*: innovative food in good variety in the Pot Still's sister pub (see main entry). Downstairs coffee lounge open from 8am, no-smoking bar and more orthodox lounge bar; pleasing decor, Heriot 80/– *(Ian M Baillie)*; [80 Dumbarton Road] *Reid's*: decoratively interesting, a watering hole rather than a family pub; good bar snacks *(Dr A K Clarke)*; [Highburgh Road] *Rock*: few pubs are improved by modernisation/renovation, but this one is. Two comfortable, attractive lounge bars; good selection of lunchtime food at reasonable prices; Youngers No 3 and Strathalbyn real ales *(Ian M Baillie)*; [Old Dumbarton Road] *Stirling Castle*: good choice of food at competitive prices in well-run bar *(Niall Hamilton)*; [Byre Road] *Tennents*: recently redecorated in and out; good plain food and Heriot 80/– *(W T Aird, Ian M Baillie)*; [Bridge Gate] *Victoria*: unprepossessing outside, but with a cosy and attractive little bar with a recently expanded lounge; good Maclays 70/– and readily available snacks; beloved by folk fraternity *(Ian M Baillie)*

GLENFARG [NO1310], *Bein Inn*: excellent bar meals and atmosphere in 500-year-old wayside ex-drovers' inn – free house; bedrooms *(C B M Gregory)*

GLENLUCE [NX1957], *Judge's Lodging*: worth a look *(W T Aird)*; *King's Arms*: known as the Auld King's Airms – worth going to; bedrooms *(W T Aird)*

GRANTOWN-ON-SPEY [NJ0328], *Craiglynne Hotel*: nice pleasant bar, efficient good-natured service, quite a pubby atmosphere; restaurant; bedrooms *(W T Aird)*

HAMILTON [18 Campbell Street; NS7255], *George*: relaxed and friendly pub with good bar meals and well kept Maclays; very pleasant staff and landlord is in the 'mein host' mould *(R D J Maclean)*

INVERARAY [NN0908], *George*: trendily refurbished Georgian inn, bar food, McEwans 80/–, restaurant, open all day; bedrooms; children welcome *(LYM)*

INVERKEITHING [NT1383], *Volunteer*: good welcome *(Bob Rendle)*

INVERMORISTON [NH4117], *Glenmoriston Arms*: lots of malt whiskies in cosy lounge of inn not far from Loch Ness, fishing and stalking by arrangement; also cheery stables bar; bedrooms *(LYM, Martyn Quinn)*

INVERNESS [NH6645], *Clachnaharry*: lots of character, public bar in very old original building; outstanding view; good range of draught beers, whisky etc, popular food, good service, garden tables. Open all day, closes midnight Thurs and Fri (closes 3–6.30 Sun) *(J Gilchrist, Duncan Allan)*; [Stoneyfield] *Coach House*: very friendly. Attractive site, views and period building. Food in bar and separate restaurant; bedrooms *(HKR)*; [Academy Street] *Phoenix*: truly Scottish traditional bar, full of history – ask to see murals in back bar. Landlord very helpful to visitors. Used by brickies and solicitors *(Peter Coleman)*

ISLE OF WHITHORN [NX4736], *Queens Arms*: friendly lounge with popular bar food, pool-room, public bar, just up street from harbour; open all day; bedrooms *(BB, W T Aird)*

JOHNSTONE [NS4263], *Masonic Arms*: well kept comfortable local with good Greenmantle and McEwans 80/– real ale and bar snacks. Courteous, attentive staff *(M J McGlone)*

KILDONAN [NS0231], *Breadalbane*: bar is very much part of hotel with restaurant and sun lounge leading off, good sea view, interesting series of postcards of hotel in early part of century; bedrooms *(Patrick Stapley, Richard Gibbs)*

KILDONAN [NS0421], *Kildonan*: seafront hotel with seats on lawn overlooking sea, panelled bar with Edwardian feel divided into two by modern stone fireplace; piano, pool, McEwans; bedrooms *(Patrick Stapley, Richard Gibbs)*

nr Killin [NN5732], *Ardeonaig Hotel*: good bar food and coffee; bedrooms *(Dr T B Brewin)*

KILMELFORD [NM8412], *Cuilfail Hotel*: recently restored and re-opened cosy beam and plaster bar with open fire. Attractive rustic garden with shrubs and mature trees, seats – running down to a burn, lots of rhododendrons and daffodils in spring. Interesting, well cooked food; bedrooms *(Robert Aitken, Patrick Stapley and Richard Gibbs)*

KILMORY [NR9521], *Lagg*: darts, juke box, fruit machine and stone fireplace in fairly recent purpose-built long rectangular popular bar separate from inn, set in wooded area. Good carvery, palm trees in gardens with stream where you can drink out; bedrooms *(Patrick Stapley and Richard Gibbs, C B M Gregory)*

KIPPEN [NS6594], *Cross Keys*: comfortably refurbished lounge with stuffed birds, McEwans 80/– and waitress-served bar food; militaria in public bar; bedrooms *(LYM)*; *Crown*: really pubby, good varied bar food and restaurant *(R B W Bolland)*

KIRKCUDBRIGHT [116 High Street; NX5851], *Gordon House Hotel*: food good, wide choice, inexpensive, in both bar and formal restaurant. Well kept Ind Coope Burton; bedrooms *(John Bird)*

KYLE OF LOCHALSH [NG7527], *Lochalsh*: comfortable lounge looking across to Skye in solid well kept hotel by ferry pier; open all day; bedrooms *(W T Aird)*

nr LAIRG [NC4123], *Overscaig*: bars rather dark but lovely sun lounge with good views to hills beyond Loch Shin; comfortable chairs outside. Substantial bar snacks. Friendly landlord. Free fishing in Loch Shin, Loch Ghriam and Loch Merkland (famous for brown trout); open all day; bedrooms *(Gwen and Peter Andrews)*

LAMLASH [NS0231], *Old Pier Tavern*: straightforward pub, part of seafront hotel, with pool, darts, fruit machine and juke box – mainly young people and popular with locals; bedrooms *(Patrick Stapley, Richard Gibbs)*

LECKMELM [NH1690], *Tir Alluin*: 100-year-old family home, converted into country-house hotel with bar, well stocked with malts, liqueurs, Tio Pepe in prime condition. Quiet, warm welcome, efficient pleasant staff, unobtrusive colour TV; bedrooms *(Gwen and Peter Andrews)*

LERWICK [HU4741], *Queens*: friendly pub on Sound of Bressay. Food from restaurant. Over 25 different whiskies; bedrooms, many overlooking sea *(HKR)*

LINLITHGOW [High Street; NS9976], *Four Marys*: a tribute to Mary Queen of Scots (born in Linlithgow) in fine setting with beautiful old furniture and good décor. Friendly staff, good beer and wine selection at competitive prices *(Alan Coleman)*

LOANS [NS3431], *Bruce*: big modernised lounge with dimpled copper tables, wooden lanterns, piped music; friendly and well kept, open all day; Friday singalong *(BB, Gordon Kennedy)*

LOCH BROOM [NH1392], *Altnaharrie Inn*: well kept, cosily furnished, with fine loch views. Good range of open sandwiches and interesting meals including crawfish/langoustines. Efficient service. Return ferry 4 times a day. Golden eagle in area; bedrooms and self-catering chalet *(C J Richardson)*

LOCH ECK [NS1495], *Whistlefield*: charmingly isolated seventeenth-century inn above loch, interesting bric-a-brac in bar; bedrooms *(LYM)*

LOCHEARNHEAD [NN3404], *Craigroyston*: pleasant small hotel, attractive bar overlooking loch; meeting place for dinghy sailors, windsurfers – friendly, good snacks; bedrooms *(W T Aird)*

NEWARTHILL [NS7859], *Cottage*: friendly good service in comfortable and discreet pub with wide choice of food and drink *(Michael McCormick)*

NEWTON STEWART [NX4165], *Bruce*: nice place to stay; comfortable bedrooms *(W T Aird); Crown*: convivial pub; nearby Glen Trool has some of the finest countryside in Britain; bedrooms *(W T Aird)*

OBAN [NM8630], *Argyll*: bar nice size for either joining in or staying separate; run as part of hotel but both bar and barman have distinct character *(W T Aird)*; [George Street] *Rowan Tree*: small bar with limited range of drinks; bedrooms at realistic prices *(W T Aird)*

PEAT INN [NO4509], *Peat Inn*: informal elegance in small cosy areas with tapestry, heavy dark chairs, ornate carved sideboards, silver plate, fresh roses, lacy tablecloths, Laura Ashley-ish waitresses; interesting and good food *(Mr and Mrs T M Tompkins)*

PEEBLES [High Street; NT2540], *Tontine*: pleasant bars; bedrooms *(W T Aird)*

PITSCOTTIE [NO4113], *Pitscottie*: friendly family pub with good value food; local lunchtime favourite, deserted in evenings *(Dr S G Bauer)*

POLLACHAR [NF7546], *Pollachar*: simple one-bar pub with nautical flavour, maps and so forth on walls, nice atmosphere *(Patrick Stapley and Richard Gibbs)*

POOLEWE [N68580], *Poolewe*: eighteenth-century inn in lovely west coast village, close to the remarkable Inverewe Gardens (best May to early June); bedrooms *(AVML)*

PORT APPIN [NM9045], *Airds Hotel*: friendly and comfortable inn with lovely shoreside position and good food; has been a main entry in previous editions but is closing its pub side to become solely a hotel/restaurant; bedrooms *(LYM, W T Aird)*

PORTPATRICK [NX0154], *Portpatrick*: large hotel with heated pool, tennis, on cliff overlooking harbour; bedrooms comfortable *(W T Aird, BB); Fernhill*: lounge bar with views over the harbour; good lunchtime food *(T A V Meikle)*

PORTWILLIAM [NX3343], *Monreith Arms*: good roomy bar with good range of drinks *(W T Aird)*

RATHO [NT1370], *Bridge*: good food and service, good value; does canal-boat evenings *(Mrs Browning)*

RODEL [NG0481], *Rodel*: pub with wonderful atmosphere, very local, friendly, cold, Scottish decrepit; bedrooms *(Richard Gibbs, Patrick Stapley, Sue Cunningham)*

SELKIRK [NT4728], *Queens Head*: open-plan beamed lounge bar with freshly cooked food, Archibald Arrols 70/– on handpump, log fires; open all day *(LYM)*

SHIEL BRIDGE [NG9318], *Shiel Bridge*: hotel bar well suited to travellers, including families; fair comfort, better than usual bar lunch; bedrooms *(W T Aird)*

SLIGACHAN [NG4432], *Sligachan*: marvellously placed walkers' and climbers' inn, remote in central Skye, with basic public bar and plusher more sedate hotel bar; bedrooms *(W T Aird, BB, Alan Franck)*

ST ANDREWS [Grange Road; NO5116], *Grange*: in splendid setting with good atmosphere; run by two former St Andrews University students. Good food at reasonable prices – plus two or three dishes each night from adjoining restaurant *(Dr S G Bauer)*

STIRLING [Easter Cornton Road, Causewayhead; NS7993], *Birds and the Bees*: dark ex-byre, bare stone walls, Youngers IPA and McEwans 80/–, boules; open all day; children welcome *(LYM)*; [Castle Wynd] *Portcullis*: mid-eighteenth century building set only 100 yards from the castle, with stone walls, original stone roof, open fire, sociable retired landlord; comfortable seating and décor. Occasional folk singing and ceilidhs. Good home-cooked bar snacks and restaurant; bedrooms *(Richard Glover)*

STORNOWAY [NS4233], *County*: wood-panelled lounge, Alice Ales (from Inverness) on handpump; meeting place for local clubs; bedrooms *(D J Fisher)*

STRUY [NH3939], *Struy*: small inn serving a good real ale called Alice Ale *(A J Eardley)*

TARBERT [NR8467], *West Loch*: pierside inn with bar lunches 12–2 and afternoon teas; bedrooms; children welcome *(Anon)*

TOBERMORY [NM5055], *Macdonald Arms*: attractive bar overlooking harbour, not large, comfortable, log fire, always pleasant landlord and supporting staff; more than 100 malts; bedrooms *(W T Aird)*; *Western Isles*: large hotel in a superb position on cliff top over the harbour with panoramic views over the sound of Mull; pleasant pubby bar; bedrooms *(Robert Aitken, W T Aird)*

TONGUE [NO5957], *Ben Loyal*: convivial lively atmosphere, welcoming to campers, locals and residents. Large choice of malts, generously long bar menu, plenty of room at the tables; bedrooms *(Gwen and Peter Andrews)*

UDDINGSTON [60 Old Mill Road; NS6960], *Rowan Tree*: was warmly welcoming old-fashioned town tavern with well kept real ales and very generous snacks, notable for Edwardian décor, but found closed in early 1985; news please *(LYM)*

WEST LINTON [High Street; NT1551], *Linton Hotel*: good food – including Sunday lunchtime; good Greenmantle and Tennents Heriot 80/– *(Russell Fox)*

WHITING BAY [Eden Lodge Hotel; NS0426], *Shurig Bar*: stone building around 100 years old on sea front with lively basement bar full of locals, darts, space game, fruit machine, still has cramped, jostling atmosphere at 11.30 pm; bedrooms *(Patrick Stapley, Richard Gibbs)*

Wales

Wales

The great majority of pubs we've included here stand in or close to attractive scenery. Up in the hills and mountains, there's the Halfway Inn perched over the Vale of Rheidol at Pisgah near Aberystwyth (with a wide choice of real ales, lots of character, and good robust food), the Dinorben Arms at Bodfari (one of our two highest-rated pubs in Wales, with lots of cleverly designed areas, good views, and an excellent value lunchtime buffet), the friendly Welsh-speaking Sportsmans Arms up on the moors near Bylchau, the Slaters Arms tucked into its steep valley at Corris, the Dolfor Inn at Dolfor (both have good simple food), the Tyn-y-Groes by Snowdonia forests near Ganllwyd, the comfortable Hand and the interestingly furnished West Arms at Llanarmon D C in the hills of Clwyd, the Pen-y-Gwryd at Nant Gwynant near Llanberis, right in the heart of Snowdonia and a cradle of mountaineering (with good robust food), the very civilised Glansevern Arms Hotel alone near the headwaters of the Wye above Llangurig, the friendly and old-fashioned Harp on its hill at Old Radnor (good food), and the Red Lion at Penderyn, full of character and close to hill walks. By the waterside there's the friendly Harbourmaster at Aberaeron (on the pretty harbour, with good seafood), the Sailors Safety under the dunes in its remote cove by Dinas Head (good food and a splendid atmosphere), the Boat in an unsurpassed spot on the River Dee at Erbistock, the Ship at Fishguard (an old fishermen's pub, down by the old harbour), the old-fashioned Swan looking over the beach at Little Haven, the Gazelle near Menai Bridge, looking over the straits to Snowdonia, the

The Hand Hotel, Llanarmon Dyffryn Ceiriog

lively Captains Wife near Penarth, with something for everyone and good value straightforward food, and the Stately George III at Penmaenpool, with a gracious upstairs bar and a simpler summer bar downstairs. Pubs with unusual character (and not already mentioned) include the Olde Bull's Head in Beaumaris, with its antique furnishings (good straightforward food), the Joiners Arms at Bishopston on the Gower (lots of real ales), the Bear at Crickhowell (a civilised old lounge, with particularly good bar food), the quite unspoilt cottagey Dyffryn Arms in Cwm Gwaun (a lovely valley inland from Fishguard), the Blue Anchor at East Aberthaw (very old, with lots of little rooms, a good collection of real ales, and good home cooking), the Fishguard Arms (a cosy little terraced pub in Fishguard with an excellent atmosphere), the remarkable Prince of Wales in Kenfig (a long history, keeping old-fashioned virtues very much alive), the old White Lion in Llanelian-yn-Rhos (with a snug old front bar, and good simple food), the Leyland Arms in Llanelidan (a most unusual little farmyard pub, beautifully kept, with good food), the Skirrid at Llanfihangel Crucorney (Wales's oldest pub, with a macabre history but a friendly atmosphere), the Red Lion in Llangynidr (old and traditional, with good straightforward food), the Welcome to Town in Llanrhidian (an unspoilt village pub on the Gower, above the Loughor tidal flats), the Maenan Abbey Hotel near Llanrwst (a stately neo-medieval place, in charming gardens, with good food), the Abbey Hotel in Llanthony (part of a remote and glorious ruined Norman priory, with good lunchtime bar food and evening restaurant meals – our other top-rated Welsh entry), the bouncy Trewern Arms in the interesting village of Nevern, and the rambling 600-year-old Groes at Ty'n-y-Groes. Pubs with specially good food that we have not already mentioned include the Walnut Tree at Llandewi Skirrid (marvellous food – perhaps the best of any pub in Britain), the Queens Head in a little village near Llandudno Junction and the Crown at Llwyndafydd (both for careful use of local ingredients), the Bridge at Llangwm (a choice between its smart new food extension or a very snug and pubby older part), the Fox at Penllyn (especially for fish), and the Wolfe at Wolf's Castle. Many other Welsh pubs not picked out in this shortlist do reliable straightforward food, or particularly good simple snacks. The Star in Talybont-on-Usk has a splendid combination of a very wide range of real ales with an excellent atmosphere and good honest food.

The Lleyn Peninsula (where we have not found any pubs to include) and the District of Ceredigion (between Cardigan and the mouth of the River Dovey, where we do have some) are dry on Sundays. Pubs there are not allowed to open on

Sundays, though hotels can sell drinks to their residents and may stay open for meals (readers report that there may be some blurring of the distinction between these two supposedly separate activities). We mention in the text any pubs that do close on Sundays.

ABERAERON (Dyfed)   SN4462   Map 6
Harbourmaster
Quay Parade

Right on the picture-book harbour, this attractively unpretentious pub serves good seafood in its upstairs restaurant, and even in the bar does crab sandwiches, mussels or cockles in garlic butter (£1.45), cod or plaice (£1.95), scampi (£2.45), king prawn tails in garlic butter or prawns with curry mayonnaise (£2.55), and seafood platter (£3.65), alongside other sandwiches (from 65p), home-made soup (85p) and ploughman's (£1.70). The separate restaurant has main courses such as fresh skate with black butter, poached fresh salmon and jugged hare (around £5.50–£6.50). The friendly bar's still used by the fishing-boat skippers, and some nights you may find them having a sing-song. It has green button-back banquettes built against the walls, which are darkly panelled, with good local sea photographs under a higher shelf of china. As it's not big, it can get crowded. Well kept Flowers IPA on handpump. In summer it's pleasant to sit outside on the harbour wall – very pretty, with the yachts below and the neat row of houses opposite, all attractively painted in different bright colours. (Recommended by Philip Denison; more reports please)

Free house · Licensees M B Mackay and family · Real ale · Meals – bookings tel Aberaeron (0545) 570351 – and snacks (not Sun) · Children welcome · Open 11–3, 5.30–11 all year; closed Sun

nr ABERYSTWYTH (Dyfed)   SN5882   Map 6
Black Lion
Llanbadarn Fawr; set back from main road in village one-way system, signposted off A44 just E of Aberystwyth

The high-ceilinged front rooms of this cheerful and well run local are simply furnished with leatherette wall benches and old-fashioned cast-iron pub tables; there are darts in a sensibly segregated alcove, dominoes, cribbage and a juke box. A separate big back lounge (usually opened later) has tartan-upholstered seats around neat tables on wall-to-wall carpeting, and maybe piped music. Through a row of white arches are sensibly placed darts, pool, a juke box, fruit machine and space game. Good value simple food includes soup (45p), sandwiches, burgers, pasties or pizzas (50p), filled baked potatoes (60p), ploughman's (£1.25), salads (from £1.50, dressed crab £2.25), ham and egg (£1.50), and chicken, plaice, cottage pie, moussaka, lasagne and so forth (£2). Well kept Banks's Mild and Bitter on

---

Pubs in outstandingly attractive surroundings are listed at the back of the book.

electric pump. The big sheltered garden behind is useful in summer for its children's swings, sandpits, rides and games such as swing-ball, and on fine evenings there are cook-it-yourself barbecues, with a well lit dance square. (*Recommended by Beti Wyn Thomas*)

Banks's · Licensee Brian Carter · Real ale · Meals and snacks (not Sun) Children in eating area · Open 11–3, 5.30–11 all year; closed Sun

Halfway Inn ★ [*illustrated on page 885*]

Pisgah; on A4120 towards Devil's Bridge, 5¾ miles E of junction with A487

The heart of this lively and out-of-the-way pub is the imposing row of casks – such as Burtonwood, Felinfoel, Gwynedd Cwrw Môn, Marston's Pedigree, Theakstons Best and Wadworths 6X, with a cask or two of farm cider and perry – which you tap yourself; there are detailed instructions, and you're then trusted to leave the right money. The exact choice varies widely within the three dozen or so different brands that they can get delivered, and two or three are on handpump. Altogether, they usually have about a dozen different ones at a time. This last year they've proved the catholicity of their taste by converting part at the back into a wine bar, with a choice of about 30 different reasonably priced wines – but the atmosphere stays that of a pub, cheerful and relaxed, helped by the pub's determined stand against electronics, piped music and so forth. There are bare stone walls, stripped ceiling beams, and stripped deal tables and settles on the flagstones, with Windsor chairs and upholstered settles in a neat heavily beamed back lounge/dining-room. Bar food is genuine and positively anti-chip. The wide choice includes French bread sandwiches, rich thick soup (90p), quiche Lorraine with salad (£1.98), giant Cornish pasty (£2.20), chilli con carne or chicken and mushroom pie (£2.25), various pizzas (evening) or steak and kidney pie (£2.45), and daily specials such as faggots or roast beef. Darts, dominoes, cribbage. There are fine views of the Vale of Rheidol and the gentle pasture hills and forests beyond it, from the bar itself and from picnic-table sets with cocktail parasols above the quiet road; people are welcome to picnic out here, and very public-spiritedly they have now started to terrace and landscape their grounds to provide free parking and picnic space to anyone visiting this lovely spot – whether or not they use the pub (there is already free overnight camping for their customers). There is a children's play area, and they organise various special events such as sheep shearing and vintage motor-cycle rallies. As this is close to the Devil's Bridge and on a popular route for outings, it can get almost swamped by visitors – including coaches – in summer, so get here early if you want to eat. *Recommended by C Byron, Beti Wyn Thomas, Philip Denison*)

Free house · Licensee Keith Mees · Real ale · Meals and snacks (not Sun) · Well behaved children in back lounge/dining-room until 9pm · Occasional folk groups · Open 12–3, 6–11 all year; closed Sun

---

All main entries have been inspected anonymously by the Editor. We accept no payment for inclusion, no advertising, and no sponsorship from the drinks industry – or from anyone else.

BEAUMARIS (Anglesey)   SH6076 Map 6
Olde Bull's Head ★
Castle Street

The rambling bar of this friendly inn has antique chairs and tables, ancient settles hardly higher than milking stools, leather-cushioned window seats, the town's ducking stool (the winged oak armchair in the snug alcove at the far end), copper and china jugs hanging from the oak beams in the low ochre ceiling, and quite a collection of cutlasses on one wall. Bar food includes soup (75p), sandwiches served in a basket with some salads including duck, crab or Welsh beef (95p), home-made fish, sausage, cottage or Florentine pies (85p–95p), lasagne (£1.35), ploughman's (£1.40) and prawns in a shell (£1.85), with salads (from £2.20, fresh salmon £3.50); there is a good separate dining-room with waitress service, and the residents' lounge is very comfortable. Bass on handpump is well kept. Parts of this inn go back some 500 years, and in 1645 it was commandeered by General Mytton when he captured the Royalist castle for the Parliamentarians; the brass water clock over the bar fireplace dates from 1695. Outside, the entrance to the attractive courtyard is closed by the biggest single hinged door in Britain. A comfortable place to stay, with excellent breakfasts. *(Recommended by Miss Brenda Wright, Pamela and Merlyn Horswell, Mr and Mrs R Houghton, R J Harvey)*

Free house · Licensee Mrs D M Barnett · Real ale · Meals (lunchtime, not Sun) and snacks (lunchtime) · Children in eating area · Open 11–3.30, 6–10.30 Bedrooms tel Beaumaris (0248) 810329; £13.50 (£14B)/£27 (£28B)

BISHOPSTON (West Glamorgan)   SS5789 Map 6
Joiners Arms
Village signposted from B4436

On the Gower Peninsula, this neatly kept beamed pub has Buckleys Best, Felinfoel Double Dragon, Marstons Pedigree and Worthington Dark Mild on handpump, served in good condition from the copper-topped stone bar counter that straddles the two communicating bars. It's been attractively restored, with red quarry-tiles in both front and back bars, comfortable traditional furnishings, some walls stripped back to the bare stone, and an unusual spiral iron staircase in the front bar as well as a massive stove, strong as a safe, set in to the chimney. Good value bar food includes ready-filled rolls, pies, quiche and fish. The atmosphere is good whether it's empty (weekday lunchtimes, say) or full of enthusiastic young customers. *(Recommended by Michael Sandy)*

Free house · Licensee B Miles · Real ale · Snacks · Open 11.30–3.30, 5.30–10.30

In next year's edition, as well as star ratings we hope to use a special rating to show pubs that either have specially good food or are specially nice to stay at. Please tell us if you think any pub – in the *Guide* or not – deserves one of these 'Food Awards' or 'Stay Awards'. No stamp needed: *The Good Pub Guide*, FREEPOST, London SW10 0BR.

BODFARI (Clwyd)   SJ0970 Map 6

Dinorben Arms ★ ★

From A541 in village, follow Tremeirchion 3 signpost

This thoughtfully extended pub makes the most of its splendid hill
views. Carefully landscaped and attractively planted brick-floored
terraces rambling around the pub (which is perched quite high above
the quiet lane) are brightly planted with boxes and hanging baskets of
summer flowers, and give some very snugly sheltered corners where
you can find old-fashioned winged settles as well as the many neat
black and white wooden seats and tables – and even a small pool.
There is a light and airy garden room out by the terraces, particularly
suitable for children and their parents – indeed, designed for them. In
the main part of the pub there are several different neatly kept areas
on two floors. Furnishings include comfortably cushioned seats and
older-fashioned settles on the carpet of the three downstairs rooms,
which have old beams with tankards and flagons hanging from them,
tapestry-look wallpaper, high shelves of china and open fires in
winter; there may be piped music. Lunchtime bar food includes soup,
filled French bread (85p), and an excellent value smorgasbord
counter which includes three hot dishes as well as at least half a dozen
cold meats, some ten fish dishes, and a couple of dozen salads (as
much as you like for £5; children under ten £3). In the evenings there
is a quick-service starters and puddings counter by the ancient glass-
covered well in the main bar servery, with a wide choice including
home made soused herrings, hot potted shrimps, pâté, whitebait and
several salamis and smoked meats (most things around £1.55). You
can order main courses from the bar, including home-made steak and
kidney pie or chicken and mushroom pie (£2.75), fish (£2.75–£4.35),
three-egg omelettes (from £2.30), trout (£3.50), salads (£3.10–£4.25)
and steaks (£6.95 for a sixteen-ounce T-bone), with several daily
specials such as salmon mayonnaise or fried scallops (£4.75) and
chicken à la crème (£5.25). There is a wide choice of liqueur coffees.
Alternatively, you can eat in an upstairs carvery (Wednesday to
Saturday evenings), with table service (£9). Border Traditional and
Wilsons on handpump, and a good range of whiskies. There is a
swing in a grassy play area by the car parks that are cut into the steep
hillside – children enjoy coming here very much. *(Recommended by Sue
and Len Beattie, Dennis Royles, C F Walling, Mrs K Clapp)*

*Free house · Licensee Gilbert Hopwood · Real ale · Meals and snacks
Children in garden room and restaurant · Open 12–3.30, 6–11 all year;
closed 25 Dec*

BYLCHAU (Clwyd)   SH9863 Map 6

Sportsmans Arms (Tafarn yr Heliwr)

A543 3 miles S of village

The highest pub in Wales – and the local for mountain people from
miles around – this is surrounded by splendidly lonely hills, with a
good view of the moors and the growing forests around Brenig
reservoir (which has sailing and is well laid out for walking –
including archaeological trails). Good value bar food includes home-

made pâté and shrimps in garlic or moules marinière (£1.95, in season), specials including home-made pies or lasagne (£2.70), and fresh grilled herring fillets with mustard sauce (£3.25), and regular hot dishes such as generous ham and eggs (£3.90) and eight-ounce sirloin steak with creamy blue cheese sauce (£6.30); they do a traditional three-course lunch on Sundays (£4.95 adults, £3.50 children – filled rolls then as the alternative). There's a welcoming atmosphere in this lively bar, which has photographs showing it in its winter plumage (snowed up) and an attractive mural of a dog working sheep in the hills, and is comfortably furnished with some old-fashioned high-backed settles as well as Windsor chairs, and a massive wood-burning stove plus an open log fire. Most of the regular customers are Welsh speaking, and there is Welsh singing at weekends. Lees Best and Best Dark Mild on handpump; darts, pool, fruit machine. *(Recommended by Michael Main; more reports please)*

Lees · Licensee Ioan Aled Evans · Real ale · Meals and lunchtime snacks Children in eating area · Organist Sat · Open 11–3, 7–11 (12–3, 7–10.30 in winter); closed Tues lunchtime in winter

CAREW (Dyfed)   SN0403   Map 6
Carew Inn [*illustrated on page 864*]
A4075 just off A477

Carew Castle, an imposing eleventh-century ruin above the estuary of the River Carew, is in the meadow opposite this friendly country pub, and in summer the unusual village watermill, with its millpond filled by the rising tide, is open for visits. Old-fashioned benches in the sunny back courtyard face a splendid Celtic cross, and others by the flowers in front look down the lane to the river. There are swings and a slide for children in the garden. The recently panelled public bar is simply furnished with a high-backed box settle and another lower settle, and there is a comfortable parlour. Sensibly placed darts, dominoes and cribbage, with television in a separate room. Snacks such as sandwiches, plain or toasted (55p), and ploughman's with cheese or home-made pâté (£1.20); well kept Worthington BB on handpump. *(Recommended by Janet Williams; more reports please)*

Free house · Licensee Barbara Trainer · Real ale · Snacks (not Sun evening) Children in lounge lunchtime · Occasional guitarist · Open 11–2.30, 5–11 all year

CARNO (Powys)   SN9696   Map 6
Aleppo Merchant
A470 Newtown–Machynlleth

Popular freshly cooked food in this comfortable and friendly pub at lunchtime includes soup (65p), toasted sandwiches (from 75p), ploughman's or pâté (£1.25), ravioli or cannelloni (£1.40), whitebait (£1.50), three-egg omelettes (from £2.25), open prawn sandwich (£2), ham and egg (£2.65) and entrecôte steak (£6). In the evening they do a wide choice, including starters from soup (95p) to lobster bisque with a touch of brandy (£2), main courses such as scampi

(£3.35), grilled bacon chop with egg or pineapple (£4) and fillet steak (£6), with a cold table (from £2) and lots of puddings (£1.25); a separate restaurant is open in the evening (not Sundays). The licensees and the well kept Tetleys – rare around here – from handpump bring a touch of warm northern friendliness to the old inn (named after the ship of the seafarer who retired to open it in 1632). The small front lounge has red plush button-back banquettes against the walls (mostly cream painted, but one is stripped back to the bare stone), copper-topped tables, and some copper utensils hanging from the stripped beams. Opening off here is an even more comfortable room, with sofas and easy chairs, and there may be soft piped music. A public bar has snooker, darts, dominoes, a fruit machine and juke box. *(Recommended by Mr and Mrs E Reading; more reports please)*

Free house · Licensees Mr and Mrs Walter Twomey · Real ale · Meals and snacks · Children in eating area · Open 11–2.30, 6–11 · Bedrooms tel Carno (055 14) 210; £14.50/£24

CILGERRAN (Dyfed)   SN1943   Map 6
Pendre
Village signposted from A478

This fourteenth-century pub has massive bare flagstones, old settles and an antique fruit machine, and the thick walls have been stripped back to bare stone above the panelling, like those of the carpeted lounge, which has high-backed settles; there's a modern fruit machine too, a juke box in the public bar, and darts in a recently converted side area. Bar food includes rolls and sandwiches (from 60p), smoked mackerel (£1.25), ploughman's (£1.50), basket meals (from £1.55), pasty (£1.60), steak and kidney pie (£1.75), cod or gammon (£2.50) and Teifi sea trout or salmon (£4.50). Ansells SDB, Worthington BB and Felinfoel Double Dragon on handpump. More elaborate evening meals can be booked ahead (ring Cardigan (0239) 614223 before lunchtime), with starters such as salmon quenelles, and main courses such as veal escalope in a white wine and artichoke sauce or lamb noisettes Reform. Outside, the beer garden includes an enclosed play area for small children. This end of the village is top of the town (what the pub's Welsh name means); at the other there's a well organised local wildlife park and a romantic ruined castle on a crag over the River Teifi (which has coracle races on the Saturday before the August bank holiday). *(Recommended by Elizabeth St George)*

Free house · Licensee Tony Harris · Real ale · Meals and snacks · Children in eating area · Open 11–3, 6–11 all year

CORRIS (Gwynedd)   SH7608   Map 6
Slaters Arms
Village signposted off A487 Machynlleth-Dolgellau

This friendly and well run village pub has a big black inglenook fireplace holding a couple of chairs, some high-backed antique settles (one very long in the back room), local photographs on the faded gilt wallpaper, and unusual coloured mouldings of black grapes on the ceiling cornices. Cheap bar food includes baked potatoes (30p, with cheese 40p), pork pies (37p), toasted sandwiches or hot pies (55p), ploughman's (£1.10), lasagne and beef curry (£1.40), with low-priced and well kept Banks's Bitter and Mild from meter-type electric pumps; darts, dominoes, cribbage, fruit machine. The terraced hamlet, in a narrow valley village so bound up with slate that even the manhole covers are made of it, has slate crafts workshops here as well as a slate mining museum. Further up-stream there are tracks into the steep Dovey Forest, and towards Machynlleth the Centre for Alternative Technology makes an interesting visit. *(Recommended by R B Entwistle)*

Banks's · Licensee Peter Cruikshank · Real ale · Snacks · Open 11–3, 6–10.30

CRICKHOWELL (Powys)   SO2118   Map 6
Bear

Brecon Road; A40

This friendly old coaching-inn has a civilised lounge bar with leather easy chairs, a big sofa, handsome cushioned antique settles and lots of smaller plush-seated bentwood armchairs, a window seat looking down on the old market square, a big log fireplace, a fine old oak dresser with pewter mugs and brass platters, a grandfather clock, old prints including a contemporary one of Brunel's experimental ss *Great Britain,* and heavy beams and rugs on its parquet floor. Good bar food includes sandwiches, ploughman's, home-made pâté (£1.20), pear and Stilton cocotte (£1.50), open cottage cheese and fruit sandwich (£1.65), avocado pear filled with seafood (£2.40), and more elaborate dishes from the separate restaurant such as home-made curry (£3.25), rabbit casserole (£3.60), turkey americaine (£4.50), salmon and prawn béchamel pie (£4.85) and trout stuffed with smoked trout wrapped in bacon; well kept Bass on handpump, and civilised touches like the decanter of peppermint water. The upstairs residents' lounge – bare stone, high rafters, antique furniture and somnolently friendly dogs – is interesting. The charming and

The Griffin Inn, Llyswen

855

attractively floodlit back lawn has old-fashioned seats among the high shrubs around it. (*Recommended by Philip Denison, Pamela and Merlyn Horswell, SJS, Janet Williams, Helen Woodeson, Tim and Ann Bracey, M J Muston*)

Free house · Licensee Mrs Laura Hindmarsh · Real ale · Meals and snacks Children in family bar · Open 11–3, 6–11 all year; closed evening 25 Dec Bedrooms tel Crickhowell (0873) 810408; £18.40 (£22.43B)/£28.75 (£31.63B)

CROSS INN (Dyfed)   SN5464 Map 6

Rhos yr Hafod

Junction of B4577 with B4337, E of Aberaeron (*not* the Cross Inn near Newport)

This friendly pub has some high-backed antique settles among the wheel-back chairs on the red and black tiled floor of its front room, some antique pictures on the partly panelled walls, an ancient built-in cupboard of china facing the bar servery, and open fires in winter; most of the regular customers are Welsh speaking. There are also carpeted back rooms, with some easy chairs; it's hard to believe that parts of the pub were once stables. Bar food is popular and includes sandwiches (from 50p), a basket of chips (50p), ploughman's (from £1.25), pizza (£1.50), home-made pâté (£1.65), and cottage pie or chicken and chips (£1.80), with occasional specials such as half a lobster with crusty bread and salad (£4.50); there are some cheap children's dishes. Well kept Bass and Hancocks HB on handpump. The restaurant upstairs is quite smart. Outside, there are picnic-table sets on the back grass. (*Recommended by Richard and Nia Hall Williams; more reports please*)

Free house · Real ale · Meals and snacks · Children in eating area · Open 11–3, 5.30–11 all year; closed Sun

CWM GWAUN (Dyfed)   SN0035 Map 6

Dyffryn Arms

Pontfaen; Cwm Gwaun and Pontfaen are signposted from B4313 E of Fishguard

There are stripped settles and kitchen chairs on the red and black tiled floor of this delightfully unspoilt cottage pub. The small room is served from a little hatch where well kept Bass or Ind Coope Burton is tapped straight from the cask into jugs, and on our visit they were playing draughts – though tip-it is apparently the usual game here. Freshly cut sandwiches. The pub stands in a hamlet by a remarkably narrow road through this beautiful oak-wood valley, quiet but for birdsong and the noise of a little stream. (*Recommended by SJS*)

Free house · Licensee Bessie Davies · Real ale · Snacks · Children in separate room · Open 11–3, 5.30–11 all year

Sunday opening in Wales is 12–2 and 7–10.30; but pubs in Ceredigion (Cardigan to the mouth of the Dovey) and the Lleyn Peninsula are not allowed to open at all on that day.

DEFYNNOG (Powys)   SN9228   Map 6
Lion

A4067 just S of Sennybridge

Carefully restored, the bar of this roadside pub has some high-backed
built-in settles as well as the wheel-back chairs around its dimpled
copper tables, and a few pewter mugs hanging from beams in the high
cream ceiling. Home-cooked bar food includes spicy and garlicky
sausage rolls (85p), beef and onion pie (75p), chicken and mushroom
pie (£1.40), ham and chips (£2.40) and scampi (£2.60); they have
Bass, Hook Norton Best (unusual around here) and Wem on
handpump, well kept; darts, table skittles. There's a good
atmosphere, thanks to the enthusiastic attitude of the couple who run
it. Unusually, you step down into the bar from the road (where there
is still an old mounting block for horses). *(Recommended by K P Leach;
more reports please)*

*Free house · Licensee S Woolhouse · Real ale · Meals and snacks · Children
welcome · Open 12–3, 7–11 (has been closed Weds, but we understand they
are now open then – to check tel Sennybridge (087 482) 391*

DENBIGH (Clwyd)   SJ0666   Map 6
Bull

Hall Square, in town centre

The rambling bar of this largely sixteenth-century inn has lofty
beams, one massive stone fireplace, some seventeenth-century settles
and leather armchairs among the newer seats, and a good country-
town atmosphere. Perhaps the inn's oldest feature is the natural well
by the back entrance, which is thought to date back many more
centuries than the building itself. Bar food includes soup (50p),
sandwiches (from 50p, with a chip butty 40p), pâté (95p),
ploughman's (£1.30), bacon and egg or home-made steak and kidney
pie (£1.50), pizzas (from £1.70), omelettes (from £1.75), salads (from
£1.95), scampi (£2), trout (£2.25), two lamb chops (£2.50) and
steaks (from eight-ounce sirloin, £4.75); there's also a handsome
panelled restaurant. There is a fruit machine in the reception area,
and another room has a pool-table. The gloved hand you can see
carved in the oak of the Elizabethan staircase sweeping up from the
bar is the crest of Robert Myddelton who built the house, and whose
son Sir Hugh Myddelton organised the New River, London's first
proper water supply. *(More reports please)*

*Free house · Licensees Les and Dot Palmer · Real ale · Meals and snacks
Children welcome · Open 11–3, 5.30–11 all year (and open all day Weds)
Bedrooms tel Denbigh (074 571) 2582; £13.75 (£15.25B)/£26.50 (£28B)*

Real ale to us means beer that has matured naturally in its cask – not pressurised
or filtered. We name all real ales stocked. We usually name ales preserved under
a light blanket of carbon dioxide too, though purists – pointing out that this
stops the natural yeasts developing – would disagree (most people – including us
– can't tell the difference!).

DINAS (Dyfed)   SN0139   Map 6

Sailors Safety ★ [illustrated on page 868]

From A487 in Dinas Cross follow Bryn-henllan ½, Pwll Gwaelod 1 signpost

Tucked behind protective dunes in its isolated cove, this pub has been here since the sixteenth century, and is well worth visiting for its marvellous position and intrinsic character. It's full of life even on a quiet day – let alone when the sun comes out in summer (or when it's submerged under TV crews on the track of drugs smugglers). The atmosphere owes a great deal to its enthusiastic owners – a pub well worth a special trip. There are scrubbed deal tables on the red tiled floor, and steamer benches against the partly bare stone walls of one red-lit alcove. Nets with lobster pots and seashells hang from the pyramidal green ceiling, with fairy lights strung below them, and big silver plate platters on the walls. The elaborately carved bar counter intricately inlaid with curlicues of brass was made for the pub in 1922. There may be piped music. Good bar food includes a choice of sandwiches (from 65p, crab £1.35, triple-decker prawn £2.20), lasagne, chilli con carne or moussaka (£1.50), whitebait (£1.60, with chips and salad £3), ploughman's (£2.15), plaice or scampi (£2.65), trout (£4.25) and steak au poivre (£5.65); also crab, lobster and sea trout when local supplies are available. In winter there is a separate restaurant (bookings only; telephone Dinas Cross (034 86) 207; in deepest winter it might be wise to telephone anyway in case they decide to take an annual day's holiday then). In summer an adjoining café is open throughout the day. Well kept Felinfoel Double Dragon tapped from the cask, and a range of cocktails – conventional ones, as well as their own Submarine, Lighthouse, Seaspray and Bladder Wrack; a pool-table, pin-table, and fruit machine, juke box and space game. There are inspiriting walks around the cliffs of Dinas Head and along the Coast Path, and the valley behind, which is common land, has free camping. (Recommended by Janet Williams, Alan Franck, Beti Wyn Thomas)

Free house · Licensees Philippa Brown and Patricia Bell · Real ale · Meals and snacks · Children in dining area · Occasional live music · Caravan and small chalet to let · Open 11–3, 6–11 all year

DINAS MAWDDWY (Gwynedd)   SH8615   Map 6

Llew Coch (Red Lion)

Off A470; follow village signpost

The main bar of this friendly old village inn sparkles with hundreds of horse brasses on its beams and its copper-topped serving counter; by contrast, one table is so worn that it looks like driftwood. There are darts in here, and a good side games room (with an antique settle) has pool, darts, a pin-table, shove-ha'penny, dominoes, cribbage, a space game and fruit machine. There is another old high-backed settle by the serving hatch in the tiled entry, where there is another fruit machine. Bar food includes soup (55p), sandwiches, beefburger (£1.40), smoked mackerel salad (£1.45), home-made meat pie (£1.75), salad with trout or salmon (£2.85) from the River Dovey, which runs behind the inn; well kept Bass on handpump. There is also a separate restaurant. The menu is rather more limited in the evenings and on Sundays. On Saturday evenings when the music gets going there's a fine lively atmosphere, and at quieter times it's a relaxing break from the long journeys that the trunk road bypassing the village involves for most people using it. Outside, there are tables on the corner of the village street, which is in a quiet valley below plunging fir forests on the south edge of Snowdonia: the lane past the pub leads up to a steep, wild pass which used to be haunted by the murderous red-headed brigands of Mawddwy. *(Recommended by Annie Taylor, Richard and Nia Hall Williams, Beti Wyn Thomas)*

Free house · Licenseee Chris Rowlands · Real ale · Meals and snacks · Children in eating area, restaurant and games room · Organist Sat evening (sometimes Fri) · Open 10.30–3, 6–10.30 · Bedrooms tel Dinas Mawddwy (065 04) 247; £8.50/£17

The Boat, Erbistock

DINAS POWIS (South Glamorgan)   ST1571   Map 6

Star

Station Road

The carefully refurbished main bar of this cheerful village pub has
stone walls, heavy Elizabethan beams decorated with horse brasses
and copper, a little arched door opening on to the foot of a narrow
spiral staircase, a grandfather clock that chimes the hour, and an
open fire. The back bar has comfortable settles on its quarry-tiled
floor, and home-cooked food is served in a peaceful panelled side
room which now opens (during the evening) into another room
beyond. It includes sandwiches, home-made soup (60p), ploughman's
with Cheddar (£1.20), pâté or Stilton (£1.50), home-made pies such
as steak and kidney, cottage pie cooked with herbs, garlic and red
wine, and fish pie (from £2), scampi (£2.30), and gammon, eggs and
chips (£2.75). Reasonably priced Brains Bitter, SA and Dark (mild)
well kept on handpump. Since the last edition they've opened up a
back terrace with tables under cocktail parasols. *(Recommended by
Dr P M Smith)*

*Brains · Licensee John Pagler · Real ale · Meals (lunchtime, not Sun) and snacks
(not Sun) · Children in eating area · Traditional jazz Sun lunchtime and Thurs,
piano Mon · Open 11.30–3.30, 5.30–11 all year*

DOLFOR (Powys)   SO1187   Map 6

Dolfor Inn

Pub signposted up hill from A483 about 4 miles S of Newtown

By the summer of 1986 this smartly refurbished white pub high in the
hills should have a new bedroom wing ready. In the spacious lounge
there are red cloth banquettes built all around the fresh white walls,
dimpled copper tables on the patterned carpet, and reproduction
advertising mirrors; the communicating room by the serving bar has
more individual seats under its exposed sixteenth-century oak beams.
Good bar food includes filled rolls, local sausages (£1.50), salads
(from £2), gammon and egg or pineapple (£3.50), steak and kidney
pie (£3.50), steaks (from sirloin, £4.20), and puddings such as apple
pie (80p) or raspberry meringue (£1); Tetleys on handpump. Service
is welcoming and efficient. Opposite the pub, which is over 1,000 feet
high, a path leads into the hills. *(Recommended by Mrs M H Lord,
Pat and Malcolm Rudlin)*

*Free house · Licensee Barry Wardle · Real ale · Meals and snacks · Children
welcome · Open 11.30–2.30, 6.30–11 all year · Bedrooms planned (see above)*
tel *Newtown (0686) 26531*

Most pubs in this book sell wine by the glass. We mention wines only if they are a
cut above the average.

Meal times tend to vary from day to day and with season, depending on how
busy the pub hopes to be. We don't specify them as our experience shows you
can't rely on them. Avoid the disappointment of arriving just after the kitchen's
closed by sticking to normal eating times for whatever area the pub is in.

EAST ABERTHAW (South Glamorgan)   ST0367 Map 6

Blue Anchor ★

B4265

The stone-floored front bar of this many-roomed thatched house (which dates from 1380 and has been very carefully preserved) is a welcoming place, with antique settles built in to the massive bare stone walls, some Windsor chairs on the other side of the old tables, and an excellent array of real ales on handpump or tapped from the cask: Brains Red Dragon and SA, Flowers IPA, Marstons Pedigree, Robinsons Best, and Wadworths 6X, and maybe guest beers such as Marstons Owd Rodger or Theakstons Old Peculier, kept in good condition at a controlled temperature. Other rooms wriggle round behind this central servery: carpeted, with snug settles carefully built in to make the most of the many low-beamed alcoves, low-stooping doors between, and coal fires in winter. Good bar food includes baked potatoes (40p), soup, pasties and pies (50p), ploughman's with cheese or pâté (from £1), sausage and mash or faggots and peas (£1.60), cottage pie or steak and kidney pie (£1.60), beef curry (£1.70), meat salads (from £1.80), and salads with fresh crab (£2) or salmon (£2.25). Darts, fruit machine. There are rustic seats by barrels of flowers against the sunny front wall of the creeper-covered house, and wooden benches by stone tables on a newer terrace. Though the area is dominated by the vast power station and the cement works a little further inland, there is a path to the shingly flats of the estuary. *(Recommended by E D Hurford, Lawrence Mountjoy, Richard and Nia Hall Williams, Del Fletcher)*

Free house · Licensee W J G Coleman · Real ale · Meals (lunchtime, not Sun) and snacks · Children in area away from bar, daytime · Open 11.30–3.30, 5.30–11 all year

The West Arms, Llanarmon Dyffryn Ceiriog

EGLWYSBACH (Gwynedd)   SH8070 Map 6

Bee

Village signposted form A470 Llandudno–Llanrwst

Convenient for the gardens of Bodnant, just further north along the
road, this well run village pub has copper pans and jugs hanging from
its high brown joists, brass guns and platters gleaming on the cream
walls above the built-in red leatherette wall seats, and a bubbling
goldfish aquarium. Bar food might include sandwiches, home-made
soup (60p), cheese and tomato pizza (£1.40), roast chicken (£2),
lasagne (£2.25) and home-made rhubarb tart with cream (60p);
they've now switched to Ansells Bitter and Mild on handpump;
sensibly placed darts, dominoes, fruit machine and juke box, maybe
colour TV or piped music. There are rustic seats outside the house,
built of stone and unusually faced with mosaic of flat granite chips.
(Recommended by GSC)

*Free house · Licensee J T Rowlands · Real ale · Meals and snacks (not winter
evenings) · Children welcome (lunchtime) · Singer and guitarist Weds · Open
11–3, 6–11 (12–3, 7–10.30 in winter)*

ERBISTOCK (Clwyd)   SJ3542 Map 7

Boat ★   *[illustrated on page 859]*

Village signposted from A539 W of Overton, then pub signposted

If you can, try to visit this pub at times other than during summer
weekends or other probably busy periods (such as Bangor race days):
its star is earned largely by the marvellous tranquillity of its superb
setting, alone by Erbistock church on a sleepy bend of the River Dee.
The air is alive with the song of thrushes, blackbirds, wrens and
chaffinches in the steep wood on the far bank, ducks and grebes and
maybe a heron potter about on the river, and on the pub's side there
are charming informal up-and-down lawns, attractively planted with
flowers. Out here, a gravel terrace by a weeping ash has old-
fashioned dark wooden seats and metal tables with cocktail parasols,
and behind the pub – prettily decorated with hanging baskets – is a
natural sandstone cliff garden full of bright colour. There is a small
bar inside, with oak tripod talbes on its crazy-paved flagstones,
spindle-back chairs and a fire in the open-grate kitchen range, but
most of the building is given over to food, which includes soup (90p),
ploughman's, pâté or hot smoked mackerel (£1.90), roast poussin
(£3.15), grilled trout (£3.20) and a good cold buffet which might
include fresh local salmon (£4.95); the puddings are enterprising
(90p). There's a comfortable beamed dining-room with plush seats
around more antique oak tables, and small windows overlooking the
Dee; an adjoining more spacious building, where food is served from
April to September, has more plush seats and bigger windows. If you

---

Most of the big breweries now work through regional operating companies that
have different names. If a pub is tied to one of these regional companies, we put
the parent company's name in brackets in the details at the end of each main
entry.

want an evening meal – when people dress smartly and the cooking is more elaborate – it would be wise to book (telephone Bangor-on-Dee (0978) 780143). There may be piped music. *(Recommended by T A Pritchard, P J Taylor, B W Williams, Margaret Winter, William Meadon, Richard Steel)*

Free house · Licensee Mrs H G Mostyn · Meals and snacks (lunchtime, and in summer Fri-Sat evenings) · Open 11–3, 6–11

FISHGUARD (Dyfed)   SM9537   Map 6
Fishguard Arms

24 Main Street; A487 just E of central roundabout

This tiny terraced pub is friendly and relaxed; a cosy front bar with sturdy wooden chairs around scrubbed tables on a rubber composition floor, lots of rugby photographs on the cream walls, a very high bar counter ideal for propping elbows and, neatly painted on the ceiling, a detailed record of how its beer prices have changed since 1981. Their well kept ales, tapped into a jug straight from the cask, are Felinfoel Double Dragon, Marstons Pedigree and Worthington BB; snacks are baked potatoes (40p), steak and kidney pies (55p) and pizza (75p). The tiled entry corridor leads to a back room with a piano, coal fire and darts, shove-ha'penny, table skittles, dominoes and cribbage. *(Recommended by P A King)*

Free house · Licensee Heather Phillips · Real ale · Snacks · No nearby daytime parking (but easy at night) · Impromptu piano and accordian music · Open 11–3, 6–11 all year

Ship

Lower Town; A487 towards Newport, close to harbour

The long narrow bar of this dimly lit fisherman's pub has nets with scallop shells strung from low joists among the softly lit crystal lampshades, and sea photographs, mostly local, on its vertical panelling. There are barrel tables, well padded wall benches and some easy chairs. Well kept Worthington BB and Mild are tapped in a back room; television, fruit machine in the main bar. This old harbour, all low stone houses and narrow walks, was the setting for Richard Burton's 1971 version of Dylan Thomas's *Under Milk Wood*. *(Recommended by BOB)*

Free house · Licensee M George · Real ale · Open 11–3, 6.30–11 all year

GANLLWYD (Gwynedd)   SH7224   Map 6
Tyn-y-groes

A 470 S of village

This fine old Snowdonia inn is owned by the National Trust. The comfortably refurbished and partly panelled lounge, decorated with old maps of Wales and so forth, has a splendid view from its little arched windows of the Coed-y-Brenin forests rising above the Mawddach Valley (where the hotel has 1½ miles of salmon and sea trout fishing), and has some 100 malt whiskies to choose from, besides Wilsons on handpump; there may be piped music. Besides sandwiches, snacks, salads and hot dishes in the bar, the restaurant, with a lot of pictures and a big gilded mirror, does traditional Sunday lunches as well as meals throughout the week. The public bar has darts, dominoes and cribbage. There are seats in a narrow sun lounge, and white tables out by the main road. A goldmine at Gwynfynydd – which you can walk to along the river, through the Coed-y-Brenin forest on the opposite side of the road – dug up about £25 million-worth before it closed in 1917, and has recently been re-opened; there are lots of other hill and forest walks from here. *(Recommended by Anne Morris, Prof G M and Dr G S Stephenson; more reports please)*

Free house · Licensees John and Jean King · Real ale · Meals and snacks Children welcome · Open 10.30–3, 6–10.30 · Bedrooms tel Ganllwyd (034 140) 275; £12.50/£23

KENFIG (Mid Glamorgan)   SS8383   Map 6

Prince of Wales ★

2¼ miles from M4 junction 37; A4229 towards Porthcawl, then right when dual carriageway narrows, on bend, signposted Maudlam, Kenfig

This fine pub, on a ridge slightly above the dunes, has been fittingly restored since the last edition: the outside rendering which disguised its great age has been stripped away so that the original stonework

The Carew Inn, Carew

shows, and the windows have all been restored to their original style. It used to be a Guildhall, and you can still ask to see the old aldermen's mace, kept in the upper room (where – we think uniquely – there is still a weekly Sunday School). The pub's many virtues include good value simple home-made food, using fresh and sometimes home-produced ingredients, such as pasties (35p), sandwiches and rolls filled to order (from 50p: all the meat is home-roasted), home-made faggots (small 50p, large 95p), lasagne (85p), steak and onion pie (90p), ploughman's (£1.20), and in winter substantial hot dishes such as cawl (lamb stew) and laver-bread with bacon. There is a good range of well kept real ales: Bass, Marstons Pedigree tapped from the cask, and Worthington Dark Mild and Youngers IPA on handpump, with Worthington BB available either way. The main room has a splendid old-fashioned tavern atmosphere, with its heavy settles and red leatherette seats around a double rank of cast-iron-framed tables, a red ceiling, stripped stone walls with snug little windows, and an open fire, and a side piano room has been recently refurbished, using salvaged original material so as to give a stone fireplace, timber wall cladding and quarry-tiles. Dominoes and cribbage. In the twelfth-century Kenfig was an important port, with a castle and a sanctuary church, but drifting sand was a problem, and in 1607 storm-blown dunes virtually submerged it – the pub's about all that's left above them. *(More reports please)*

Free house · Licensee Jeremy Evans · Real ale · Meals and snacks Spontaneous music in side room · Open 11.30–4, 6–11 all year; closed evening 25 Dec

nr LAMPETER (Dyfed)   SN6748   Map 6
Tafarn Jem
A482 beyond Cwmann towards Pumpsaint

The simply furnished public bar of this isolated, friendly pub has a big picture window making the most of the view over the steep valley below these gold-bearing hills. There is a small lounge, without the view. Bar food includes filled rolls (40p), pasty (60p), burgers (from 65p), ploughman's (£1.40), sausages, egg and chips (£1.50), gammon (£2.35) and rump steak (£4.85), with puddings such as apple pie (60p), and there is a separate restaurant. Well kept Buckleys Bitter and Mild, with another real ale such as Felinfoel Double Dragon or Worthington BB changing every month or so. Darts, pool, dominoes, cribbage, juke box, fruit machine and space game. Seats on the small back terrace, sheltered by the building, share the view. *(Recommended by Beti Wyn Thomas)*

Free house · Licensees Paul and Mary Mayes · Real ale · Meals and snacks Children welcome · Open 10.30–3, 5.30–11 all year

---

Stars after the name of a pub show that it has exceptional quality. But they don't mean extra comfort – and though some pubs get stars for special food quality, it isn't necessarily a food thing either. The full report on each pub should make clear what special quality has earned the star rating.

nr LISVANE (South Glamorgan)   ST1883 Map 6

Ty Mawr Arms

From central Lisvane follow Mill Road into Graig Road and continue into the country

There are several smart and comfortable rooms here, recently redecorated: the main bar has blue plush button-back banquettes and stools on its carpet, black beams, rapiers on the walls, and a snug panelled alcove by the stone hearth. A communicating room has elegant cabriole stools and red plush banquettes against its red walls, and an elaborate black and gilt fireplace; another comfortable room leads off from here. Robinsons Best, Courage Directors and Marstons Pedigree on handpump; briskly served food such as filled rolls (65p), soup (75p), ploughman's (£1.70), a buffet including hot dishes such as chicken curry, lasagne, steak and kidney pie as well as cold salads (£2–£2.50), and a choice of omelettes (£2.25); also a separate restaurant; a couple of fruit machines, maybe piped music. In summer this is a pleasant spot, with white tables and chairs on a front terrace, and steps down to a lawn bordered by flowers, roses and tall hedges, with a big aviary of pheasants and geese. The road past the pub (which is gated) leads on to Rudry Common and Cefn Onn country park. (*Recommended by Ceri and Beti Wyn Thomas, Del Fletcher*)

Free house · Real ale · Meals and snacks (lunchtime, not Sun) · Children welcome · Open 11.30–3, 5.30–10.30 (opens 6 in winter)

LITTLE HAVEN (Dyfed)   SM8512 Map 6

Swan

Village signposted on narrow steep roads from B4341 and B4327

This old-fashioned fishing-village pub is attractive chiefly for its position. Seats in a bay window and outside the sea wall – just the right height for sitting on – give lovely views across the sheltered cove, with sailing dinghies now rather than fishing boats drawn up on to the sand. The two communicating rooms are traditionally furnished with high-backed settles and Windsor chairs, and have old Pembrokeshire prints on their partly stripped stone walls. Home-made bar food includes soup, ploughman's, pies, pâtés, lasagne, smoked trout and fresh dressed crab, and there's a separate restaurant (open Wednesday to Saturday; to book telephone Broad Haven (043 783) 256). Handpumps on the heavily panelled bar counter serve well kept Bass and Worthington BB. (*Recommended by John Paulett; more reports please*)

Free house · Licensee Peter Seward-Jones · Real ale · Children in restaurant Meals and snacks (lunchtime) · Open 11–3, 6–11 all year

LLANARMON DYFFRYN CEIRIOG (Clwyd) SJ1633 Map 6

Hand *[illustrated on page 847]*

Our very comfortable bedroom looked out on a bank of daffodils, with just the sleepy sounds of sheep and birds drifting down from the hillside pastures beyond the post-and-rails fence. Indeed, we recommend this inn primarily as a place to stay; hospitable welcome, old-fashioned service (they bring your morning tea), nice breakfasts (pats of real butter decorated with knife-cuts, none of your beastly packet stuff), good dining-room evening meals varying each day with freshly cooked local ingredients (lamb chops, trout, kidneys in red wine, steak, lots of vegetables, puddings such as Norwegian cream, interesting cheeses – £9.95 for three courses), and of course the lovely scenery of this favoured valley. Residents have the use of a tennis court, and there's trout fishing in the River Ceiriog. Winged armchairs and Victorian settees face the log fire in the main black-beamed bar, which has some hunting prints on its walls, and a couple of other comfortable rooms lead off; one, with the reception desk, has old flagstones and an attractive cast-iron open range. Bar food includes soup (95p), sandwiches (from £1), pizza or burgers (£1.95), omelettes (£2.25), salads (from £2.25), ham and eggs (£2.75), scampi (£3.25) and local trout (£3.75); at lunchtime in summer, apart from soup, this is replaced by a cold buffet (£2.75). A generous point is half prices for elderly people as well as children. There are traditional rustic seats and tables outside on a crazy-paved terrace in front and on a sheltered side terrace decorated with flower-beds and a heather scree. The village is very quiet, virtually a dead-end. *(Recommended by Gerald Newman and others)*

Free house · Licensees Tim and Carolyn Alexander · Open 11–3, 6–11 Bedrooms tel Llanarmon Dyffryn Ceiriog (069 176) 666; £26.50B/£42B

West Arms [*illustrated on page 861*]

This village inn, a popular evening meeting place for people from round about in the lovely Berwyn hills, has charming furnishings in its airy lounge bar, including an elaborately carved confessional stall as well as comfortably upholstered armchairs, sofas and some antique settles among the lighter wooden armchairs under its heavy beams, nice tables, and open log fires. There are deeply comfortable easy chairs in the snug little cocktail bar, and a roomy traditional public bar (with darts). There's also a cosy front lounge hall with an inglenook fireplace and seats including a winged armchair and a finely polished antique settle. A wide choice of bar food includes soup (75p), sandwiches (from 75p), ploughman's (£1.85), meat salads (£2.25), gammon and trout (£3.75), and there is a separate restaurant. They also serve morning coffee and afternoon teas. There are sheltered seats on a verandah, with tables on a flower-edged granite-chip courtyard, and more on the neat lawn running down to the River Ceiriog where the hotel has fishing (free for residents). *(Recommended by R J Harvey; more reports please)*

Free house · Licensees Arnold and Jean Edge and family · Meals and snacks (not Sun evening) · Children welcome · Open 11–3, 6.30–11 · Bedrooms tel Llanarmon Dyffryn Ceiriog (069 176) 665; £17 (£18.50B)/£34 (£37B)

Bedroom prices are for high summer. Even then you may get reductions for more than one night, or (outside tourist areas) weekends. Special rates in winter are common, and many inns cut bedroom prices if you have a full evening meal.

LLANARMON-YN-IAL (Clwyd)   SJ1956 Map 6

Raven

B5431

The heavy-beamed public bar of this simple and friendly inn has an old inglenook fireplace converted into a snug sitting space, Windsor armchairs and a leatherette cushioned settle. At the other end two window seats look on to the front lawn (where there are tables and chairs), and there are more seats around copper tables on herringbone brick tiles. There may be piped music. Bar food includes sandwiches, salads in season, chicken, scampi and grills, and there are cheap evening meals for residents. Well kept and reasonably priced Burtonwood and Dark Mild on handpump; darts, dominoes and fruit machine. The Welsh prince Gruffydd ap Llewelyn is buried in the village church. The village is surrounded by low hills, and there is a track up to Offa's Dyke Path which is only about a mile away. *(More reports please)*

Burtonwood · Licensee Ian Robinson · Real ale · Meals and snacks · Children welcome · Open 11.30–3, 6–11 all year · Bedrooms tel *Llanarmon-yn-Ial (082 43) 787; £8/£16*

The Sailors Safety, Dinas

LLANARTHNEY (Dyfed) SN5320 Map 6

Golden Grove Arms

B4300

The front bar of this neatly kept inn has an unusually imposing black bar counter, old-fashioned chairs and settles around heavy traditional cast-iron-framed tables on a dark quarry-tiled floor, one wall stripped to bare stone, and a ceiling stripped to show bare boards above the high beams; there may be soft piped music. A carpeted back lounge has comfortable seats upholstered to match the Liberty-print curtains, and a small public bar has darts, dominoes and a fruit machine. Good bar food includes home-made soup, sandwiches, ploughman's, and changing main dishes such as steak and kidney pie or home-cured ham (£2.95), fresh oysters or civet of venison pie (£3.75), pigeon breasts cooked in Beaujolais (£3.95), prawns with garlic butter (£4), grilled local trout (£3.10), and lightly smoked local sea trout (£4.75). There is also a separate restaurant. You can often get fresh salmon and local beef for your freezer here. There are tables on a small terrace in the big back yard, sheltered by an extensive range of old stable and store buildings, with more on a side lawn. Fishing and shooting can be arranged. This road is a good, fast alternative to the A40. *(Recommended by J Hayes)*

Free house · Licensee Simon Buckley · Meals and snacks (not Sun evening or Mon) · Children welcome · Occasional jazz or classical music · Open 11.30–3, 6–11 all year; closed Sun evening and Mon lunchtime · Bedrooms tel Dryslwyn (055 84) 551; £13/£19

LLANBEDR-Y-CENNIN (Gwynedd)   SH7669 Map 6

Olde Bull ★

Village signposted from B5106

There are lovely views over the Vale of Conwy and the mountains beyond from here, so it's good to have the newly extended terrace behind this lively and friendly sixteenth-century inn. Its two knocked-together rooms are crowded with gaily striped stools and older settles, including antique or elaborately carved ones; there are heavy beams, two log fires (one in a big inglenook fireplace), and photographs, brass ornaments and Prussian spiked helmets on the walls. The popular bar food, all home cooked, relies heavily on local ingredients and includes baked potato (45p), burger (55p), soup (55p), sandwiches (from 60p), toasted sandwiches (from 89p, egg and bacon £1.25), excellent home-made bacon and egg flan (£1.15) or steak and kidney pie (£1.25), home-made pasta bolognese (£1.78), salads (from £1.98), steaks (from ten-ounce sirloin at £4.98), and a daily hot special such as braised steak and onions (£2.10). Well kept Lees Bitter and Mild on handpump; darts, dominoes, cribbage and a fruit machine, maybe piped music. A separate dining-room, with

---

Please tell us if the décor, atmosphere, food or drink at a pub is different from our description. We rely on readers' reports to keep us up to date. No stamp needed: *The Good Pub Guide*, FREEPOST, London SW10 0BR.

beams salvaged from a wrecked Spanish Armada ship, has much the same grills as are available in the bar (in some cases larger helpings at slightly higher prices). The great garden of Bodnant is fairly close. Dogs (except for guide dogs) have to be left in cars. *(Recommended by R F Warner, William Meadon, Richard Steel, Dennis Royles, Dr B W Marsden)*

Lees · Licensees Phillipe and Brenda de Ville Forte · Real ale · Meals and snacks Well behaved children welcome · Electric organ and Welsh singing Fri evening Open 11.30–3, 6.30–11 · Bedrooms tel Dolgarrog (049 269) 508; £10/£20

nr LLANBERIS (Gwynedd)   SH5860   Map 6

Pen-y-Gwryd

Nant Gwynant; at junction of A498 and A4086, ie across mountains from Llanberis

The slate-floored climbers' bar, like a log cabin, is a mountain rescue post, and this inn, isolated among high peaks, has been a training base for generations of mountaineers, including the team that climbed Everest in 1953. The residents' panelled smoke-room is full of mementoes of famous climbs and climbers (ordinary customers are welcome to have a look). At lunchtime, there are good robust helpings of home-made food such as sandwiches, ploughman's using home-baked French bread (£1.60), quiche Lorraine (£1.80), cold meat or pâté salad (£1.80), and a home-made pie of the day such as steak and kidney, duck and vegetable or chicken and mushroom pie (£2); places to eat it include a snug little room with built-in wall benches and sturdy country chairs on its Turkey carpet, and a view over a lake to precipitous Moel-siabod. The dining-room serves good value five-course evening meals, (£8.63) with a choice of changing main courses such as roast lamb or steak and kidney pie, and puddings such as baked jam roll. Besides the pressurised beer, they have sherry from their own solera in Puerto Santa Maria; darts, pool, shove-ha'penny, and ping pong, for residents (who have a cosy and comfortable sitting-room). *(Recommended by G H Theaker, Len Beattie)*

Free house · Licensees Mr and Mrs C B Briggs · Bar meals and snacks (lunchtime) · Children welcome · Open 11–3, 6–10.30; closed 2nd week Nov to New Year, open weekends only Jan to early Mar · Bedrooms tel Llanberis (0286) 870211; £12.53 (£13.68B)/£25.07 (£27.37B)

LLANDEWI SKIRRID (Gwent)   SO3416   Map 6

Walnut Tree ★

B4521

The good food in this stylish Italian-run pub outclasses what restaurants in the area can produce, and that's what people come here for – from Wales and much further. The choice is very wide indeed. About twenty first courses range from minestrone soup or artichoke vinaigrette (£2.50) through tenerelli, a filling and piping hot lasagne bolognese, or delicious cold trout in vermouth and orange (around £3), home-cured beef, crispy crab pancakes, bavarois of smoked salmon, carpaccio (slivers of raw beef fillet with a spicy dip) and scallops (around £4.50), to a mountain of fresh shellfish and seafood (£10 or so). Main courses – even more choice, and most around £8 – include Barbary duck with figs and strawberries, rabbit, a saffron-flavoured Mediterranean fish casserole, good fish such as sea bass, turbot, Dover sole and salmon served in various ways, curried prawns, venison steak with apple and blackberries, and quails roasted with sage. There are lots of puddings (around £2), and an unusual range of Italian cheeses. The pub imports its own Italian wines. If our star system depended on food quality (which of course it doesn't), this would certainly get three. Though practically everyone here is eating, we still count it firmly as a pub for two good reasons which do not apply to some places where food comes first. First, the tables in the pub part cannot be booked, though the food served is exactly the same as in the separate restaurant (to book telephone Abergavenny (0873) 2797), and the atmosphere is pleasantly relaxed. Secondly, if you do want just a drink they treat you as well as if you're having a full meal, and put out free nuts and gherkins for you on the small bar counter, where there are a handful of traditional cast-iron-framed tables with polished settles and kitchen chairs on the flagstones, and pewter plates and advertising mirrors on the white walls above stripped panelling. The bigger lounge is carpeted in brown, with rush-seat Italianate chairs, the same tables as the other room, and a few pictures on airy white walls. There are a few white cast-iron tables by the fuchsias in front of this plain white house by the car park. In the evening a separate restaurant serves a more formal dinner. *(Recommended by B K and R S Levy, Janet Williams, Sian Reen, and many other readers)*

Free house · Licensees Franco and Ann Taruschio · Meals (not Sun, not Mon lunchtime) · Children in eating area · Open 12–3, 7–11 all year

LLANDRINDOD WELLS (Powys)   SO0561   Map 6
Llanerch
Waterloo Road; from centre, head for station

Down a drive through a sizeable orchard, this sixteenth-century inn has a lively, friendly atmosphere. Its main bar is a big, square carpeted room, and now has partly glazed partitions forming alcoves with old-fashioned settles under the beams in its dark ceiling, and a big stone fireplace full of copper and glass. Two communicating lounges with button-back banquettes lead out to a back terrace and garden, where there's summer outdoor bar and food service and a play area. Good lunchtime bar food includes home-made soup such as Radnor broth (65p), sandwiches (65p), baked potatoes (from 80p), ploughman's with cheese or pâté (£1.40), home-made steak and kidney pie (£2.25), sirloin steak or mixed grill (£4.50), and good

---

People don't usually tip bar staff (though this is different in a really smart hotel, say). If you want to thank a bar man – he is dealing with a really large party, say, or has shown special friendliness – offer him a drink.

value daily specials such as a tasty liver casserole served with a roll of bacon and good chips (£2). Similar food is available in the evening, in bar or restaurant. Well kept Bass, Flowers IPA, and Robinsons Best on handpump; a separate pool-room, with darts, dominoes, cribbage, fruit machine, piped music. *(Recommended by John Bush, S G S Houghton)*

Free house · Licensee Kenneth Leach · Real ale · Meals and snacks · Children welcome · Open 11–3, 6–11 all year · Bedrooms tel Llandrindod Wells (0597) 2086; £11 (£13.50B)/£20 (£25B)

nr LLANDUDNO JUNCTION (Gwynedd)   SH7883   Map 6

Queens Head

Glanwydden; heading towards Llandudno on A546 from Colwyn Bay, turn left into Llanrhos Road as you enter the Penrhyn Bay speed limit; Glanwydden signposted as first left turn off this

Unusually carefully prepared food and outstanding service have delighted several readers who've found their way to this friendly and comfortable village pub. The choice includes brown bread sandwiches (90p), home-made soup such as celery (80p), a bacon and cheese open roll (£1.70), and lots of seafood prepared and presented with subtlety, including Arbroath smokies (£2.50), Anglesey mussels in garlic butter (£2.50), mushrooms stuffed with crabmeat (£2.75), prawns in garlic butter (£3.20), seafood vol-au-vent or fresh crab salad (£3.50), fresh trout with prawn stuffing (£3.95), local plaice (£4.50) and Conwy salmon (£5.95), as well as a wide range of other dishes such as prettily arranged salads (from £2.25), lasagne (£2.95), gammon (£3.95) and sirloin steak (£5.50). There are good puddings such as rum and raisin flan. Well kept Ind Coope and Burton and Tetleys on handpump, and good coffee. The lounge bar, divided into two by a partly knocked through wall, has brown plush wall banquettes and Windsor chairs around the neat black tables on its patterned carpet, Spanish-look beams, log fires in winter, and soft piped music. There is also a small quarry-tiled public bar. Tables on a corner by the car park catch the evening sun. *(Recommended by Sue and Len Beattie, M A Watts, Mrs M R Sprawson, Mrs K Clapp)*

Free house · Licensees Robert and Sally Cureton · Real ale · Meals and snacks (not Sun evening) · Children in area away from serving bar · Open 11–3, 7–11

LLANELIAN-YN-RHOS (Clwyd)   SH8676   Map 6

White Lion

Village signposted from A5830 (still shown as B5383 on most maps) and B5381 S of Colwyn Bay

The original front bar of this friendly old village pub has a snug Turkey-carpeted area by a big log fire, with antique high-backed settles, one of them angled around against draughts from the door behind it, lots of toby jugs on the handsome beams, and a barometer among the pictorial plates on the butter-coloured walls. There are flagstones out by the serving counter, which has well kept Bass on handpump. Bar food includes soup (65p), sandwiches (from 65p), black pudding (£1.40), ploughman's (from £1.60), chicken (£2.25), a choice of pizzas (from £2), cold meat salads (around £4) and sirloin steak (£5.65). There are broad steps up to a dining-room with Windsor chairs around neat tables (and for decoration an antique one-arm bandit in the corner). Dominoes, maybe piped music. Outside, there are rustic seats and tables under cocktail parasols in a sheltered corner of the courtyard which the pub shares with the church (and which is used for parking). There are lovely views of the surrounding pasture hills from this quiet village. *(Recommended by D J Bleasdale, C F Walling; more reports please)*

Free house · Licensees Robert and Mary Doyle · Real ale · Meals and snacks Children welcome · Open 11–3, 5.30–11

LLANELIDAN (Clwyd)   SJ1150   Map 6
Leyland Arms
Village signposted from A494 S of Ruthin; pub on B5429 just E of village; OS sheet 116 reference 110505

This unusual hidden-away country pub serves good food such as home-made soup (£1.10), ploughman's (at lunchtimes), home-made chicken liver pâté (£1.50), seafood pancakes or fresh Parkgate shrimps (£2.25), curries (£3.25), gammon steaks off the bone (£3.75), fresh salmon salad (£5), duck or steak (£5.50) and sole meunière (£6.95). The bread is home made. The pub is housed in what used to be a farm dairy, in a stable and cottage yard behind what was once the village inn: itself a striking twin-gabled early-nineteenth-century gothick house, standing alone by the church, some way from the village itself. The pub has modern settles around dimpled copper tables in the small carpeted room by the servery, which has Burtonwood Bitter and Mild on handpump and mugs hanging from its beams; darts, dominoes. A rather larger room has wheel-back chairs around neat dark tables decorated with little bunches of fresh flowers. Booking would be wise if you want a meal (Clawdd Newydd (082 45) 207). There are rustic seats on the grass by the open side of the old yard, absolutely quiet except for swallows swooping around the church tower and the distant cackling of geese in the village. *(Recommended by A A Worthington, Margaret Winter, Ernest Lee)*

Free house · Licensee Jenny Street · Real ale · Snacks (lunchtime) and meals Children in eating area · Open 12–3, 7–11 all year

LLANFIHANGEL CRUCORNEY (Gwent)   SO3321   Map 6
Skirrid
Village signposted off A465

Parts of this gaunt dark brown stone building may date from 1110 — the earliest record of an inn on this site, making it the oldest pub in Wales and among the oldest in Britain. There are settles and stripped deal tables on the flagstones of the high-ceilinged bar, walls have been stripped back to show ancient stonework, and a wood-burning stove sticks out in front of the stone hearth. A wide choice of home-cooked bar food includes sandwiches or filled rolls, soup (80p), ploughman's with three cheeses (£2), pâté (£2.45), poached eggs with asparagus and cress sauce, grilled (£2.95), home-made cottage pie (£3.25), vegetable crumble (£3.20), fisherman's pie or lasagne (£3.40), tripe and onions (£3.80) and wild rabbit casserole (£4.45). A separate restaurant has a midnight supper licence. Well kept Felinfoel, Robinsons, Sam Smiths OB and Wadworths 6X on handpump. Since its earliest days the inn doubled as the area's courthouse, and to the seventeenth-century – when formal courts and prisons took over – nearly 200 people had been hanged here, evidently from the beam above the foot of the stairs that had become the traditional scaffold. If you look closely, you can detect marks on it that may have been worn by the ropes. A crazy-paved back terrace has old white seats and tables, and there are more rustic ones on a small sloping back lawn. *(Recommended by Julian Lloyd Webber, SJS, Janet Williams, M J Muston)*

Free house · Licensee David Foster · Real ale · Meals and snacks · Children in eating area · Open 11–3, 6–11 all year (opens 7 in winter) · One bedroom tel Crucorney (087 382) 258; £30B

LLANFRYNACH (Powys)   SO0725   Map 6
White Swan
Village signposted from B4558

The quietly lit rambling lounge bar of this secluded pub has a long line of neat tables by the front windows with red leatherette benches built in to the partly stripped stone walls and Windsor chairs on the flagstones, a big log fire in winter, and piped classical music; further back there are snugger alcoves. The food here has quite a reputation, with light dishes (around £1.25–£2) such as soup, smoked fish in cream sauce, liver or smoked mackerel pâté and whitebait, snacks (around £2–£3) such as filled pancakes, lasagne, curry, chicken and ratatouille or vegetable goulash, and more expensive main dishes (from around £5) such as Welsh lamb casserole, steak or chicken pie and grilled steaks. Brains and Flowers IPA on handpump; a separate games room with pool, bar billiards and space game. The picturesque black and white stone pub, long and low, faces the churchyard across a very quiet village lane. In summer the sheltered back courtyard is attractive, with white tables and chairs around stone tables, a bower of roses and climbing shrubs, and a view out over the quiet paddocks. *(Recommended by G A Hawkes, G Berneck)*

Free house · Licensee David Bell · Real ale · Meals and snacks (not Mon) Children welcome · Open 12–3, 6–11 all year; closed Mon lunchtime (except bank hols)

LLANGATTOCK (Powys)   SO2117   Map 6
Vine Tree
Village signposted from Crickhowell centre

Close to the splendid old stone bridge over the River Usk – with Crickhowell's bathing place just over the bridge – this friendly pub is

popular for straightforward food such as soup (80p), freshly cut
sandwiches (from 75p, prawn £1.50), ploughman's or liver pâté
(£1.65), plaice (£2.40), salads (from £2.50), home-cooked ham
(£2.95), grilled rainbow trout (£3.60), pork chops (£4.50) and
twelve-ounce sirloin steak (£5.50). The back part of the bar is partly
set aside as a dining area, with Windsor chairs and an upholstered
wall seat around scrubbed deal tables, and plates and antique
engravings of Highland cattle on its walls. In the front part there are
soft leatherette seats, lots of china jugs hanging from the beams, some
of the wall stripped back to the thick stone masonry, and brass
ornaments around the open fireplace. Well kept Flowers Original on
handpump; fruit machine, juke box, piped music. There are a few
white tables under cocktail umbrellas in front looking over to the
bridge. *(Recommended by M D Vaughan, SJS; more reports please)*

*Whitbreads · Licensees Roger and Joan Sutton · Real ale · Meals and snacks
Children welcome · Open 10.30–3, 6–11 all year*

nr LLANGURIG (Powys)   SN9179   Map 6
Glansevern Arms Hotel
Pant Mawr; A44 Aberystwyth road, 4½ miles W of Llangurig; OS Sheets 135
or 136 reference 847824

Quite alone 1,050 feet up in the upper Wye Valley, this hospitable
and civilised inn has a marvellous setting with steep hills and forests
rising on both sides. When we arrived (by car, alas), the only
customers on a wild evening with remarkable Turneresque weather
sweeping up the pass from a distant stormy sea, we were asked if
we'd walked over the hills – and this is a marvellous base for anyone
who enjoys the outdoors. Its cosy bar has cushioned antique stripped
settles and captain's chairs, an open fire, china mugs on its high
beams, and well kept Bass and Worthington Dark Mild on
handpump – which you may be lucky enough to have served in a
silver tankard. There are several good malt whiskies. Bar snacks
consist of home-made soup (55p) with home-baked and roasted meat
and other sandwiches (75p). The comfortable residents' lounge has
an excellent supply of books, and the five-course meals (must book)
are good value at £10. The outside lavatories are an object lesson:
sparkling clean, commodious, warm, well equipped. A nice,
comfortable place to stay. *(Recommended by R B Entwistle)*

*Free house · Licensee W T O Edwards · Real ale · Meals · Open 10.30–2.30,
6.30–11; closed for meals and accommodation Christmas week · Bedrooms tel
Llangurig (055 15) 240; £17.50B/£27.50B*

LLANGWM (Gwent)   SO4200   Map 6
Bridge
B4235 S of Raglan

There are two quite distinct halves to this unusual pub: the new
dining extension, and the original beamed and tiled-floor pubby core.
Vivid attention to detail marks both sides – the licensees really do
keep their eyes open to make sure customers are having a good time.

It's food that attracts people from a long way away, and in the bar that means sandwiches (from 50p), pies, pasties, filled baked potatoes, curry, chilli con carne or the like. But it's at its best in the airy extension, where a blackboard choice of nearly 30 dishes (most £4–£6.50) might include bresaola, lightly smoked prawns, dressed crab with prawns, salmon, smoked trout, Indonesian pork salad, liver in peach and brandy sauce, pork griskin, lasagne and kidneys and bacon, with a salad cold cabinet. To get a seat in this simple fairly bright room, you have to get there really early. It has richly varnished pews making four booths, each around a couple of tables, a few round cast-iron-framed tables, some enamelled advertising signs, house plants and fresh flowers, and Staffordshire china dogs and a stuffed great crested grebe on the wooden overmantel. By contrast, the bar area – where the locals and the longer-standing customers head for – has all sorts of dark nooks and crannies, a hare hanging from one of its many beams, foxes' brushes, a badger skin and a stag's head over the stone fireplace, traditional furnishings including an antique oak settle. Well kept Bass on handpump in here, and a segregated carpeted area with darts, a well lit pool-table, sitting space game and fruit machine (also dominoes and cribbage). There are some seats outside, including a couple of picnic-table sets on a crazy-paved terrace by a little wooden stream below the car park.
(Recommended by Julian Proudman, Mr and Mrs G D Amos, C A Davies)

Free house · Licensees Bob and Jane Evans · Real ale · Meals and snacks · Open 11–3, 6.15–11 all year

LLANGYFELACH (West Glamorgan)   SS6498   Map 6
Plough & Harrow

¼ mile from M4 junction 46, westbound carriageway only: on B4489; also 2 miles from junction 47, via A48

The spacious and smoothly comfortable lounge bar of this well kept pub has plush button back banquettes in big bays and elegant gilt-legged plush chairs and stools around cast-iron-framed round tables. There's a good view over the fields, beyond the car park, from the extended back part, where a food counter serves generously filled rolls, salads, and hot dishes such as plaice (£2.50), gammon and egg or scampi (£3.25). Fruit machine, gentle piped music. The military-looking detached tower of the church nearby is unusual.
(Recommended by Michael Sandy)

Free house · Licensee John Holland Lewis · Meals and snacks · Open 11.30–3.30, 6–10.30

LLANGYNIDR (Powys)   SO1519   Map 6
Coach & Horses
B4558

This friendly and well run Brecon Beacons pub has a spacious Turkey-carpeted lounge with small armchairs and comfortable banquettes against the stripped stone walls, and in winter a big open fire. An efficient food counter serves sandwiches when the staff have time (from 60p), and ploughman's (£1.75), lots of salads (£3), with home-made hot dishes such as chicken curry (£2.75) and chicken and ham or steak and kidney pie (£3.25). In the evenings they also do main dishes such as sole bonne femme or beef bourguignonne (£5.20) and sirloin steak (£6.25). Well kept Bass and Hancocks on handpump, with guest beers such as Wadworths 6X; darts, pool, dominoes, cribbage, fruit machine, juke box and quoits. Across the road a well fenced lawn runs down to a lock on the narrow Monmouth and Brecon Canal, with plenty of tables; there are moorings here. *(Recommended by SJS, Janet Williams)*

Free house · Licensee Stuart Lancaster · Real ale · Meals and snacks · Children welcome · Occasional impromptu folk music · Open 11–3, 6–11 all year (opens an hour later in winter)

Red Lion

Upper village, off B4558

This charming creeper-covered sixteenth-century inn has an old-fashioned lounge bar with lots of fox-brown leather armchairs and antique settles with red plush cushions, seats in the flowery-curtained bay window overlooking the neat garden, a grandfather clock and a good yachting picture; the ceiling's a flushed pink. An inner room with a wood-burning stove has chairs neatly ranked around its papered walls. The well staffed bar counter serves well kept Brains and Flowers IPA and Original from handpump, and there's a good range of well presented bar snacks, with full meals served in a dining-room, its walls stripped back to the old masonry. *(Recommended by G H Theaker; more reports please)*

Free house · Licensees R J and K V Latham · Real ale · Meals and snacks Open 11–3, 6–11 all year · Bedrooms tel Bwlch (0874) 730223; £24

LLANRHIDIAN (West Glamorgan)   SS4992 Map 6
Welcome to Town

Village signposted from B4295

This low and ancient white village pub has two friendly little beamed rooms inside, both served by the same small counter: on the left sturdy small settles form booths around tables, and there is another much older traditional settle against the flowery brown wallpaper; on the right, there are wheelback chairs around tables on a Turkey carpet. Well kept Marstons Pedigree tapped straight from the cask; filled rolls, Cornish pasties and pies; a back room with pool, dominoes, cribbage and a fruit machine. Two long benches on the little partly sunken front terrace face a prehistoric standing stone on the steeply sloping daisy-covered village green, and beyond that the tower of the church peeping up over elders and fruit trees. Down below the village, the marshy foreshore of the Loughor Estuary and the cockle sands beyond are as interesting as indeed they look from up here. *(More reports please)*

Free house · Licensees B H Watters and P M Cottle · Real ale · Open 12–3.30, 6–10.30 (opens 7 in winter); closed Weds and Fri lunchtime in winter nr LLANRWST (Gwynedd)   SH8062 Map 6

Maenan Abbey Hotel

Maenan; A470 towards Colwyn Bay, 2½ miles N

Solidly stone-built in 1850 as a medieval-style country house, with
steep gables and a battlemented tower, this hotel has a serenely
comfortable back lounge. This room has brocaded dining-chairs
around drop-leaf tables on a Turkey carpet, lots of potted plants in
the big stone-mullioned windows that look out on tall conifers and a
calm copper beech, and silky flowered wallpaper, with a log fire in an
elegant fireplace and landscape plates on a high shelf. A more
spacious front bar has Windsor chairs around the tables on its oak
parquet floor, and more big windows; faint piped music. There is a
calm, relaxing atmosphere. An unusually wide choice of good bar
food includes soup (75p), well garnished sandwiches such as rare beef
or dressed crab (85p), deep-fried mushrooms (£1.25), filled baked
potatoes (from £1.50), salads (from £1.55), chicken, bacon, sausage
and chicken liver kebabs (£2.95), deep-fried crab rolls or pork chop
with sherry and apricot sauce (£3.50), lambs' kidneys (£2.95) and
omelettes or lamb chops with honey and mint sauce (£3.25), besides
anything from the wide choice of dishes on the menu of the separate
restaurant, including its three-course lunch (£4.95). Bass on
handpump. Outside, there are well spaced picnic-table sets on side
terraces and out on the main lawn, among old topiary yew chess-
pawns; on another lawn, by a shrub-planted garden wall, there are
good swings and a children's palisade-castle. *(Recommended by
D J Bleasdale; more reports please)*

*Free house · Licensee Michael Kerridge · Real ale · Meals and snacks · Children
in eating area and family room · Organist and Welsh singing Sat · Open 11–3,
6–11 · Bedrooms tel Dolgarrog (049 269) 247; £18B/£30B*

LLANTHONY (Gwent)   SO2928 Map 6

Abbey Hotel ★ ★

The setting is more beautiful than that of any other pub in Britain; the
inn is surrounded by the graceful ruins of a Norman priory, with
lawns among the broken arches and beyond them the soft Welsh
border hills – very remote and peaceful. The bar is down a few steps
from the ruins, in a pair of low vaulted cellars, with high-backed
settles and Windsor chairs on its flagstone floor (part is carpeted as a
lunchtime eating area). Well kept Brains, Flowers IPA and Original
and Ruddles County tapped from casks behind the small serving
plank; they also serve Welsh whisky. Though there's been a change of
licensees since our last edition, readers agree that the atmosphere
hasn't changed, and most have reported favourably on the simple
food, which as before includes ploughman's with mature Cheddar or
Stilton in home-baked granary rolls, toasted sandwiches, quiches and
other home-baked dishes, and what the Abbey has (incongruously)
long been known for – good home-made hamburgers, either meat or
nut (most snacks around £2–£3). In the evenings good, imaginative
food in robust helpings is served in the small restaurant, which has
simple, old-fashioned furniture under its vaulted ceiling (and, like the

bedrooms, has to be booked a long way ahead). The priory was founded in 1108 by the queen's chaplain and William de Lacy, who had been the warlord in charge of Hereford, but tiring of military power retired with 40 monks to the seclusion of this remote valley. The cellar bar itself is a crypt dating from about 1175. The inn is part of the prior's house, bought and restored in 1811 by Walter Savage Landor. There are seats outside a front loggia. A nice place to stay. *(Recommended by Philip Denison, Robert Aitken, J H du Bois, Graham Simpson, Dr and Mrs R Neville, Annie Taylor, Martin Jones, M J Muston)*

Free house · Licensee I T Prentice · Real ale · Meals and snacks (not Tues to Sat evenings) · Children welcome · Folk music Mon · Open 11–3, 6–10; closed Jan and Feb · Bedrooms tel Crucorney (087 382) 487; £15/£25 (note that they get booked up many weekends ahead)

LLWYNDAFYDD (Dyfed)   SN3755 Map 6
Crown

Hard to find (but worth the effort): coming S from New Quay on A486, both the first two right turns eventually lead to the village; the side roads N from A487 between junctions with B4321 and A486 also come within signpost distance; OS Sheet 145 reference 371555

The main bar of this attractive country pub has a good warm atmosphere, with its red plush button-back built-in wall banquettes around smooth copper-topped tables, a window seat looking down the garden, a big wood-burning stove, and – beyond the island serving counter – walls stripped back to the bare stone (the pub was largely rebuilt in the early eighteenth century). For this area, they keep an unusually good range of real ale on handpump: Bass, Flowers IPA and Original, Ind Coope Burton, Tetleys and Worthington BB. Good home-made bar food includes sandwiches, soup (90p), pâté (£1.40), ploughman's (£1.95), omelettes (£2.25), quiche or large pizzas (£2.50), lasagne (£3.20), steak and kidney or Welsh lamb pie (£3.30), gammon (£4.40) and sirloin steak (£5.95), besides vegetarian dishes and a good choice of salads, and home-made ice creams and puddings. Vegetables may come from their own garden, and fish and shellfish are caught locally. On the left as you come in, a family room, with walls mostly stripped to bare stone, has plenty of tables and comfortable seats, and beyond that is a restaurant. There are darts, dominoes, cribbage and piped music in the bar, and a pool-room behind it has a fruit machine. Tall trees shelter this hamlet, and the pub's garden is prettily planted with shrubs and flowers around a small pool where they keep trout; there are picnic-table sets on a terrace above it, and a play area with a slide and rides. The narrow road around the corner from the pub leads to a cove with caves by National Trust cliffs. *(Recommended by Mrs P Hides; more reports please)*

Free house · Licensees Mr and Mrs R W Chitson and Mr and Mrs P K Lloyd Real ale · Meals and snacks (not Sun) · Children in family and games rooms Open 11–3, 5.30–11 all year; closed Sun

---

Sunday opening is 12–2 and 7–10.30 in all Welsh pubs allowed to open on that day (we mention in the text the few that aren't).

LLYSWEN (Powys)   SO1337   Map 6
Boat

On B4350, turning off A470 towards Builth Wells

This simple pub is included for its garden overlooking the Wye. Over a pretty stone wall you can look down into what is here quite a ravine, where the river flows under the high stone road bridge, and beyond to forested Brechfa Hill – a path leads up to an ancient ring fort settlement on its top. There are tables out here, among roses, flowering shrubs and trees. Inside the small white house is a light and airy public bar with café seats and sensibly placed darts, and a simple but comfortable saloon with bar billiards, space game and juke box.

Free house · Licensee M P Richards · Open 11–3, 6–11 all year

Griffin *[illustrated on page 855]*

A470, village centre

The food in this small and friendly inn depends partly on the luck that its customers have had in the famous nearby salmon pools of the River Wye – most days after Easter you should find it on the menu, but at any time of the year there's a fishing-inn atmosphere in the pleasant and welcoming Fishermen's Bar, with its old fishing tackle and flies. There are comfortable upholstered stools, big Windsor armchairs and leatherette wall benches around the low tables, and a good log fire in its stone hearth (the old bread oven beside it now has little model monks carousing in it). The heavy beams are decorated with horse brasses and long leathers with heart-shaped brass studs. Popular bar food includes home-made soup (95p), good sandwiches served with a small salad, such as sugar-baked ham (£1.10) and salmon or crab (£1.50), salads (from £2), kebabs (£2), rabbit or beef and pigeon pies (£2.25), boiled bacon with parsley sauce (£2.50), and fresh trout or salmon (£2.75). A separate restaurant is open in the evenings. Well kept Brains Best and Flowers IPA and Original on handpump; quoits played. Given notice, the inn can arrange Wye salmon and other fishing. *(Recommended by Miss A M Burton, Beti Wyn Thomas; more reports please)*

Free house · Licensees Richard and Di Stockton · Real ale · Meals (not Sun) and snacks (not Sun evening) · Children welcome · Open 11–3, 6–11 all year Bedrooms tel Llyswen (087 485) 241; £14.95B/£27.90B

MAENTWROG (Gwynedd)   SH6741   Map 6
Grapes

A496; village signposted from A470

This seems to be the friendliest pub in this part of Wales – and is certainly the most heavily endowed with pitch-pine, salvaged avidly by the landlord for panelling and furnishing his bars. They are now full of pine pews, settles, pillars and carving. The atmosphere is cheerful and lively, and there's a good log fire in winter. A wide choice of good value home-made bar food includes sandwiches and toasted sandwiches (from 55p) and ploughman's (from £1.50 – both these at lunchtime only), steak sandwich or cod (£1.50), salads (from £2), cottage pie or liver and onions (£2.50), spare ribs, curry, hot chilli con carne or home-made steak and kidney pie (£2.75), generous gammon steak or ten-ounce rump steak (£4.50) and roast duck (£5). Well kept Bass and Mitchells & Butlers Mild on handpump, and a range of cocktails (including one called Grapes of Wrath). Darts, fruit machine and juke box in the public bar. The separate restaurant, stripped back to the bare slate and silvery granite, with intimate lighting and oil paintings, has a big open fireplace which in winter may be used for spit-roasting joints (both bars have open log fires in winter, too). There are seats on a verandah overlooking the walled garden, which has a fountain on the lawn. The bedrooms have colour TVs, central heating and (if you didn't guess) stripped pine furniture. *(Recommended by William Meadon, Richard Steel, R A Corbett, David Stanley, Michael Main, G H Theaker)*

Free house · Licensee Brian Tarbox · Real ale · Meals and lunchtime snacks Children in restaurant · Open 11–3, 6–10.30 (closes 11 Fri and Sat summer only) · Bedrooms tel Maentwrog (076 685) 208; £10/£20 (£20S)

nr MENAI BRIDGE (Anglesey)   SH5572   Map 6

Gazelle

Glyngarth; A545, half way towards Beaumaris

Right on the straits, this popular inn is often very busy indeed with yachtsmen – even outside the first half of August, when there is a regatta here. Its lively main bar has big picture windows for the views over the straits to the mountains of Snowdonia, and leading off are smaller rooms with easy chairs, antique settles, quieter alcoves and some interesting features such as the ornate Welsh dresser or the carved grotesque fireplace. The inn is well kept, with helpful staff. Bar food includes soup (75p), freshly cut sandwiches (75p), steak canadien with chips (£2.25), fresh cod or plaice (£2.75), ploughman's (£2.95), home-roast beef, home-made steak pie or cheese flan (£2.95), various salads (from £2.95), and sirloin steak (£6), with a choice of home-made puddings (from 95p); Robinsons Best on handpump; fruit machine, space game and maybe piped music. There are now two restaurants, one upstairs and one down; open for dinner every evening, with main courses such as grilled trout (£5.95) and steaks (from £6.95), and Sunday roast lunch (£5.50). An attractive garden climbs steeply behind, with paths and steps zigzagging up and seats dotted around among the aromatic Mediterranean-seeming plants; you can also sit on the stone wall of the old ferry jetty, above the rocky shore. Fishing can be arranged. A nice place to stay. *(Recommended by Pamela and Merlyn Horswell)*

Robinsons · Licensees Kenneth and Barbara Moulton · Real ale · Meals and snacks · Children in areas away from serving bar · Open 11–3.30, 6–10.30 (closes 11 Fri and Sat summer only) · Bedrooms tel Menai Bridge (0248) 713364; £18 (£19B)/£28 (£35B)

People named as recommenders after the main entries have told us that they feel the pub should be included. But they have not written the report – we have, after anonymous on-the-spot inspections.

MONTGOMERY (Powys)   SO2296   Map 6

Dragon

At the top of the steep, quiet town, below the ruined Norman castle,
this hotel has a friendly carpeted lounge bar with a window seat
looking down to the market square and the old town hall (which has a
very sweet-toned clock bell), tapestried stools and wall benches around
dimpled copper tables, game bird and old England prints, and willow-
pattern plates on a high shelf by the colonial ceiling fan. It has had
Three Tuns on handpump (see entry for Bishop's Castle in Shropshire),
and serves coffee; there may be piped music. Lunchtime bar food
includes soup (70p), sandwiches with home cooked meats (from 95p)
and ploughman's (£1.40), and a grill-room is open every lunchtime
and evening except Sunday evening. Residents have the use of a
swimming-pool. (*Recommended by Gordon and Daphne; more reports
please*)

*Free house · Licensee Roland Milnes-Burgan · Real ale · Snacks (lunchtime)
Children in area partly set aside · Open 11–2.30, 6.30–11 · Bedrooms tel
Montgomery (068 681) 476; £17.25S/£27.60B*

NEVERN (Dyfed)   SN0840   Map 6

Trewern Arms ★

B4582

A lively pub that a lot of readers find their way to, this relaxed and
cheerful place is close to a medieval bridge crossing the River Nyfer.
The comfortable lounge bar overlooks a garden with tables among
shrubs and small trees, but there's more atmosphere in the entertaining
front bar, with stone walls and floor, plush banquettes in the corners,
one or two traditional high-backed settles, and high rafters hung with
nets, ships' lamps, shepherds' crooks and cauldrons. Good value bar
food includes toasted sandwiches, ploughman's (£1.15), chicken, cod
or plaice with chips (£1.70), whole dressed crab salad (£2.75),
vegetarian dishes (from £2.75), eight-ounce sirloin steak (£4.10) and
when it's available locally caught sea trout; there are children's dishes
such as beefburger served with chips or waffles (85p); well kept
Flowers IPA and Original on handpump; quiet pop music. There is a
separate evening restaurant. A games room behind the public bar has
sensibly placed darts, pool, a juke box, and a couple of fruit machines
and space games. A music/functions room has a wooden dance floor let
into its slate flagstones: it opens on to the back lawn. The churchyard
over the river has a notable Celtic cross – and, even more remarkable, a
grove of ancient yew trees that bleed tears of something which looks
remarkably like blood unless the priest is Welsh-speaking.
(*Recommended by Philip Denison, SJS, Beti and Ceri Thomas, Janet Williams,
John and Marlene Paulett*)

*Free house · Licensees Tony and Vivienne Robinson · Real ale · Meals and snacks
· Children in eating area, restaurant and games room · Occasional music (with
licence extension until 1am) · Open 11–3, 5.30–11 all year
Bedrooms tel Newport (0239) 820395; £7/£14*

NEWCASTLE EMLYN (Dyfed)   SN3040 Map 6

Pelican

Sycamore Street; A475

This carefully preserved old inn has low black beams in the white ceiling, long settles and some panelling. Good value bar food includes sandwiches (from 50p), ploughman's (from £1.25), game pie in wine (£2.20), salmon pie (£2.30) and smoked pork or lamb chops from the nearby Cenarth smokery (£2.30); there is also a small separate low-beamed restaurant. Well kept Ansells Bitter and Mild and Ind Coope Burton on handpump; darts, a pool-room, a fruit machine and juke box. The bedrooms are in an adjoining cottage, which can also be let for self-catering. The inn – like the Aleppo Merchant at Carno in mid Wales – was built in the seventeenth century by a retired sea captain who named it after his old ship (which had carried pilgrims to America in around 1645). When Thomas Rowlandson stayed at this 'decent inn' on his 1797 Welsh sketching tour, he drew for a later engraving the dog in a ceiling-height treadmill that worked the roasting spit in the fireplace here; attractively tiled, it still has its side bread oven (but not the treadmill or the treadmill dog – they still welcome pets here, though). *(Recommended by PEF)*

Free house · Licensee Marjorie Robson · Real ale · Meals and snacks · Children in back lounge · Open 11–3, 5.30–11 all year, all day Friday and bank hol weekends · Bedrooms tel Newcastle Emlyn (0239) 710606; £7.50B/£15B

NEWPORT (Dyfed)   SN0539 Map 6

Golden Lion ★

East Street; A487 on E edge of Newport

This warmly welcoming seventeenth-century inn's knocked-through bar has a long and imposing art nouveau bar counter (with well kept Felinfoel and Ushers Founders on handpump) and bustles with life in the holiday season. Good home cooked food served here includes sandwiches (from 50p), ploughman's, winter soups, pâté or whitebait (£1–£1.20), garlic mushrooms (£1.20), spaghetti bolognese or meat and mushroom pie (£2.20), chilli con carne (£1.95), plaice (£2.30), lamb chop or gammon (£2.75), chicken paprika (£2.75), steak (from £4) and sometimes lobster (£5); there's also a separate restaurant. The bar is furnished with distinctive antique settles, sturdy bare benches built against the stripped stone walls, and comfortable easy chairs; shove-ha'penny, dominoes, darts and a fruit machine, maybe piped music. It's decorated with old local photographs, but perhaps its most interesting feature is the floor, as it's partly made from seashells. A children's bar – into which adults overflow when things

---

In next year's edition we hope to pick out pubs that are specially nice to stay at, alongside the star ratings. Please tell us if you think any pub – in the *Guide* or not – deserves a 'Stay Award'. No stamp needed: *The Good Pub Guide*, FREEPOST, London SW10 0BR.

are really busy – has pool, bar billiards, space game and juke box. The inn has a sauna, spa pool and solarium, and you can sit outside. It's close to sandy beaches and lovely cliff walks. A nice place to stay; bedrooms are in a modern back block. *(Recommended by Michael and Alison Sandy, Janet Williams, Beti and Ceri Thomas, SJS, P A King, Richard and Nia Hall Williams, M Mathews, Peter Walker)*

Free house · Licensees Glyn and Penny Rees · Real ale · Meals and snacks Children welcome · Open 11–3, 5.30–11 all year; bar closed alternate Suns, Oct–spring bank hol · Bedrooms tel Newport (0239) 820321; £10S (£10B)/ £18S (£18B)

NOTTAGE (Mid Glamorgan)   SS8178   Map 6
Rose and Crown

2 miles from M4 junction 37; A4229 towards Porthcawl, then follow Nottage, Rest Bay signpost

In a village within strolling distance of the coast yet very handy for the M4, this smartly kept old inn has three bar rooms divided by thick stone walls; the two on the left have slate flagstones with some carpet, seats with red plush cushions, some beams, shiny smooth copper-topped tables, one or two old-fashioned though recently made high-backed settles, and log-effect gas fire in a huge open fireplace decorated with black kettles and a big black urn with a brass tap. The room on the right has wheelback chairs around tables on its fitted carpet, and beyond that is the restaurant. The efficient bar counter has dozens of triplicated spirits bottles on optics to cope with even the busiest holiday evening rush. Bar food includes home-made soup (65p), ploughman's with warmed bread (£1.30), home-cooked ham and beef for sandwiches (70p) and salads (£2.60, served with baked potato), and hot dishes such as cauliflower cheese and baked potato (£1.75), scampi (£2.20), grilled gammon (£2.60), home-made pies (£2.60), prawn curry (£3.20); also children's dishes (£1.25). There's a separate carvery (three courses £5.95, children £3.75). Well kept Ushers Best and Founders on handpump; fruit machine and gentle piped music. The bedrooms are comfortable and well equipped, and breakfasts are good. *(Recommended by T P Lovesey; more reports please)*

Wessex Host (Watneys) · Licensee J R Mullett · Real ale · Meals (not Fri–Sun evenings) and snacks (not Fri or Sat evenings) · Children welcome · Open 11.30–4, 7–11 all year · Bedrooms tel Porthcawl (065 671) 4849; £17B/£27B

OLD RADNOR (Powys)   SO2559   Map 6
Harp ★

Village signposted from A44 between B4355 and B4362

This brown stone inn, alone with a fifteenth-century turreted church on a peaceful hill above the Lugg valley, is so welcoming and so idyllically placed that readers booking for a single night have found themselves staying for several. The cosy old-fashioned lounge bar, with lovely views, has library chairs and some cushioned high-backed settles, one of them a curved antique, and a Turkey rug on its varnished floorboards. The slate-floored public bar is similarly traditional, with sensibly placed darts, dominoes and cribbage, and there is a simple Welsh dining-room. Good value bar food includes filled crusty rolls (50p), baked potatoes (from 50p), cheese or pâté ploughman's (95p), macaroni cheese or omelettes (£1.50), curries (from £2.25), steak (£4.50), and several daily specials such as lentils au gratin with a wholemeal roll (£1.60), Tandoori chicken (£2) and beef bourguignonne (£3.50); there are children's dishes (£1), and they do special curry lunches on Sundays. Restaurant main courses might include lamb cutlets or home cooked pork in cider. Benches outside under an oak tree look out over the Radnor Forest, and they play quoits here. A nice place to stay, with scrupulously clean and comfortable bedrooms (and a choir of sheep to lull you to sleep). *(Recommended by Julian Lloyd Webber, Michael and Peggy Rowley, DNC, Michael and Alison Sandy, Stephen Locke, C F Walling, Robert and Hazel Yates)*

Free house · Licensees John and Mavis English · Meals and snacks (not Tues lunchtime) · Children welcome · Open 11.30–3, 6.30–11 all year (opens 7 in winter); closed Tues lunchtime · Bedrooms tel New Radnor (054 421) 655; £16.50B/£27B

nr PENARTH (South Glamorgan)   ST1871   Map 6

Captains Wife ★

Beach Road, Swanbridge, which is signposted off B4267 at Penarth end of Sully

This entertaining seaside pub has exposed stone walls and Turkey rugs and carpets on its broad bare boards, and relatively quiet areas

The Halfway Inn, nr Aberystwyth

at either end: one with an antique settle and red plush chairs by an old tiled-surround kitchen range, the other with a high-backed curved settle and more plush seats by an antique trestle table under a high raftered ceiling. You should be able to find a seat in here even when it's really busy in summer, and it's got a good long serving counter with well kept Brains SA and Flowers Original on handpump. Leading back from here is a more cosily comfortable area, with Liberty-print seats in snug booths under a shiny red-painted plank ceiling. Bar food includes filled rolls (40p), a generous ploughman's (£1.95), and at lunchtime a cold buffet spread out on a big refectory table, where you can order hot dishes too (around £1.50 to £3.50). Upstairs, with a gallery overlooking the raftered-ceiling end of the main bar, is a charcoal-grill steak bar serving beefburgers and kebabs as well as fillet steaks (£6.50), with puddings such as liqueur pancakes (£1.95). Outside, there is a large and attractive flagstoned back courtyard, with heavy varnished seats and tables, which used to be the stable yard of the former manor house. It's surrounded by low white buildings, one of them a bistro with a garden room. There's a splendid view of grassy Sully Island and the sea from the front terrace by the sea wall. (Recommended by DROL, H L McDougall, Michael Quine, Dr P M Smith)

Free house · Licensees S G and E P Jenkins · Real ale · Snacks (not Sun lunchtime) and meals · Children in eating areas · Open 11.30–3.30, 5.30–11 all year; closed evening 25 Dec

PENDERYN (Mid Glamorgan)   SN9408 Map 6

Red Lion

At Lamb Inn on A4059, turn up hill and keep left at T-junction

This old stone pub, hand-in-hand with an isolated church 950 feet up in the hills, looks out over sheep pastures and down the valley beyond a quarry; there are plenty of sturdy seats and tables out here, some cleverly built in to the wall and fence over the pasture that drops steeply away below. Inside there is a log fire in one enormous fireplace, a coal fire in another, and the connecting rooms have dark beams hung with ale flagons, an antique settle and another with a punched-wood back, plates on the walls (some of which are bare stone), a good range of real ales, and a lively, friendly atmosphere. Going back down the hill, if you keep straight on across the main road at the Lamb you come to the forests of Cwm Tâf, where there are forest walks. (Recommended by Lawrence Mountjoy; more reports please)

Free house · Real ale · Open 12–3, 6–11 all year

PENLLYN (South Glamorgan)   SS9776 Map 6

Fox

Village signposted from A48

This simple but stylishly kept village pub has a remarkably wide and frequently changing range of good food. There is some specialisation in fresh fish, such as charcoal-grilled sardines, seafood pâté, Welsh smoked salmon, poached salmon or sole, lemon sole stuffed with prawns and served with cream and sherry sauce, charcoal grilled trout or sole, Pembroke lobster, grilled garlicky giant prawns, and large mixed cold seafood platter. Other food might include typically pâté, deep-fried Camembert with gooseberries, tagliatelle, chicken breast cooked with red peppers, mushrooms, cream and white wine, home baked ham, pork tenderloin in a slightly curried pineapple and almond sauce, and steaks (from twelve-ounce sirloin to a twenty-four-ounce T-bone). Besides soup (£1.15) and ploughman's with three cheeses (£1.95), you should in general allow for starters costing around £2–£2.50 (with some rather more, such as fresh Pembroke crab at £3.75), main courses around £6–£7, and puddings around £1.60 – or opt for the more limited three-course set menu (£9.95 including coffee). The bar has a Turkey-style Axminster rug and close-set but elegant metal-legged tables on its dark flagstones, with flowery-cushioned seats built against the walls; it's an airy room, with white paintwork, big windows and high ceilings. Well kept Bass and Hancocks HB on handpump; darts, shut-the-box, dominoes, cribbage, and boules on Sunday lunchtimes – and they have managed to muster a cricket team. A separate restaurant which has a broadly similar but somewhat grander choice, is open in the evenings from Monday to Saturday. There is a front terrace under a fairy-lit yew tree, where tables are now neatly laid with tablecloths. *(Recommended by Col G D Stafford, Gordon Mair, Pat and Jeremy Temple, Michael Quine, A J Goater)*

Free house · Licensees Michael and Barbara Taylor · Real ale · Meals and snacks (lunchtime, not Sun) · Children in eating area · Open 12–3, 6.30–11 all year; closed Sun and 25–27 Dec

PENMAENPOOL (Gwynedd)   SH6918   Map 6

George III

Just off A493

An invigorating mixture of styles in this elegant seventeenth-century white waterside inn includes a very lively summer cellar bar with heavy beams, flagstones and rough stone walls, with – by complete contrast – a civilised and comfortable upstairs bar, opening on to a balcony giving fine views across the Mawddach Estuary to the forested hills beyond. This upper room has easy chairs, oak settles and antique oak tables, and a beamed ceiling, old prints and maps on the walls, a bar counter made from an oak Welsh dresser, and piped classical music. Home-made lunchtime food here (not Sundays) includes soup with garlic bread (75p), farmhouse cheese and biscuits (95p), pâté (£1.30), steak and kidney pie (£2.45), roast spare rib (£2.55), smoked pink trout (£3.15) and fresh local lobster salad (£5); there is also a separate evening restaurant. The upstairs residents' lounge has armchairs in front of a big inglenook fireplace and looks into a lush little conservatory with sub-tropical epidendrums, dendrobiums and other orchids. The downstairs bar, with long green leatherette seats around its plain varnished tables, has a self-service cold buffet (from £2.10); also pizza (£1) and toasted sandwiches, lunchtime and evening. Border Bitter and Old Master under top

pressure; darts, shove-ha'penny, dominoes and a mute space game.
Benches on slate flagstones in front, some protected by the balcony of
the upper bar, face the estuary and the nearby toll bridge, and catch
the evening sun. A nice place to stay. *(Recommended by
Col G D Stafford, Philip Denison)*

*Free house · Licensee Gail Hall · Meals and snacks (see above) · Children in
restaurant · Open 10.30–3, 6–10.30; closed Christmas and New Year
Bedrooms tel Dolgellau (0341) 422525; £15.50 (£26B)/£31 (£45B)*

PONT-AR-GOTHI (Dyfed)   SN5021   Map 6
Cothi Bridge Hotel
A40

The bow windows of this hotel's comfortable and neatly kept lounge
bar look out on the clear River Cothi (where the hotel can arrange
salmon fishing), and on summer evenings tables along the streamside
are well placed to catch the last of the sun. Popular bar food here
includes freshly cut sandwiches (from 70p, with local salmon £1.50
when it's available), and there might also be Welsh broth (80p),
home-made pâté with Cumberland sauce (£1.80), fried mushrooms
stuffed with Stilton or giant sausage (£2), lasagne (£2.25), home-
made seafood pie (£2.20) and sirloin steak (£6.75). The room has
plush stools and button-back seats against red and gold striped
wallpaper, with a flowery carpet, and maybe piped music. Well kept
Felinfoel Double Dragon on handpump. There is a popular separate
restaurant. *(Recommended by A B Garside; more reports please)*

*Free house · Licensee Terry Davison · Real ale · Meals and snacks (not Sun
lunchtime) · Children welcome · Open 11–3, 5.30–11 · Bedrooms tel
Nantgaredig (026 788) 251; £17 (£21B)/£29 (£31B)*

RHOSMAEN (Dyfed)   SN6424   Map 6
Plough
A40

Big windows in the comfortable and deeply cushioned back lounge
look out over sheep pastures, and this room is popular for bar food
such as sandwiches (from 50p), pâté (75p), ploughman's (£1.10),
beefburger (£1.30), lasagne (£1.70), chicken (£2.10), scampi (£3) and
steak (£6.40), with salads from cheese or Scotch egg (£1.35) to ham
(£2.25); a good choice of puddings includes a light fluffy meringue,
creamy cheesecake and apple and calvados pancake. There may be
piped music. A smaller glazed-tiled front bar, with a fire in one
exposed stone wall, has cushioned Windsor chairs and one attractive
old cushioned settle; there's darts and a fruit machine. A separate
restaurant concentrates on fish from trout to sole bonne femme and
grills from pork or lamb chop to fillet steak, and has a half-hour

supper licensing extension. There are some stone tables and seats on the grass behind the car park. *(Recommended by Richard and Nia Hall Williams)*

Free house · Licensees G L and D R Rocca · Meals and snacks (not Sun) Children in eating area · Open 11–3, 5.30–11 all year; closed Sun, 1st week Nov and 25 Dec

RUDRY (Mid Glamorgan)   ST1986 Map 6
Maenllwyd
Village signposted from A468

This knobby stone house with its heavily studded oak door dates back some 500 years, and its lounge bar is comfortably furnished, with some old settles at one end, and leatherette upholstered small casks or unusual ace-of-spade chairs on the red carpet over its stone floor. Its low black oak beams are decorated with martingale and other unusual bits for horses, and there is a fruit machine, and maybe piped music. A higher-ceilinged back room has neatly carved modern settles around its tables, and the spacious new back restaurant, with a midnight supper licence, has main dishes such as trout (£5.50) and a wide choice of steaks (from £5.85). The popular bar food includes soup (65p), pâté (£1), smoked mackerel (£1.30), home-made steak and kidney or chicken and ham pie (£1.95), spaghetti bolognese (£1.95), trout (£2.50), chicken curry (£2.50), gammon and egg (£2.90) and eight-ounce sirloin steak (£4.85), with home-made apple pie (60p); Whitbreads Traditional on handpump is well kept, and there are quite a few wines by the glass. The road on towards Caerphilly takes you to the ferny and partly wooded hills of Rudry Common, a nice place for strolling. *(Recommended by Beti Wyn Thomas)*

Free house · Licensee Neville Johnson · Real ale · Meals and snacks (not Sun lunchtime) · Children welcome 12–2 only, restaurant any time · Open 11.30–4, 6–11 all year

ST HILARY (South Glamorgan)   ST0173 Map 6
Bush
Village signposted from A48 E of Cowbridge

Tucked away behind the village church, this thatched pub has a comfortable low-beamed lounge bar, its walls stripped to the old stone, with Windsor chairs around copper-topped tables on the carpet. The public bar has old settles and pews on flagstones, with darts, bar billiards, shove-ha'penny, table skittles and dominoes in a room leading off. Bar food includes dishes such as Welsh lamb cutlets and perhaps laver-bread, along with sandwiches, ploughman's, chicken, and so forth; well kept Bass, Hancocks HB and Worthington BB on handpump, and farm cider. There is a separate restaurant. There are white tables and chairs in front, and more under cocktail parasols in the back garden. *(Recommended by Beti Wyn Thomas)*

Welsh Brewers (Bass) · Licensee Derry Trott · Real ale · Meals and snacks Children welcome · Open 11.30–3, 6–11 all year

SHIRENEWTON (Gwent)   ST4893   Map 6

Tredegar Arms

Village signposted off B4235 just W of Chepstow

The affable ex-RAF landlord of this village pub will try to get at least a grin out of you, if not a guffaw. The carpeted main bar area has cushioned library chairs and Windsor chairs around wood-effect tables, and the stripped stone walls are decorated with horse brasses and etched metal reproductions of grave rubbings – there's a good cosily contented atmosphere, helped along a bit by the little black and white cat. A wide choice of bar food includes soup (70p), pâté (85p), ploughman's (£1.35), filled baked potatoes (from £1.55), ham and egg, lasagne, chilli con carne and so forth (around £1.85–£2), scampi (£2.35), home-made steak and Guinness pie (£2.60) and puddings such as chocolate-fudge sponge (80p). Well kept Smiles, Ushers Best and Founders and Wadworths 6X on handpump, and several dozen malt whiskies; maybe piped Tchaikovsky or Beethoven; pool, sensibly placed darts and fruit machine in the public bar. There are seats in front, and on a small and attractive sheltered back terrace, with pots of bright annuals. *(Recommended by Doug Kennedy, Julian Proudman)*

Free house · Licensees David and Jean Roberts · Real ale · Meals and snacks (not Sun evening) · Open 11–3, 6.30–11 all year

TALYBONT (Dyfed)   SN6589   Map 6

Black Lion

A487

This substantial stone inn has a comfortable back lounge with cushioned Windsor chairs around copper tables and red plush stools by the serving counter; blue and white plates decorate the shelf below the red ceiling. Bar food includes plain or toasted sandwiches (from 55p), home-made soup (80p), smoked mackerel (£1.30), ploughman's or pâté (£1.40), salads (from £1.40), plaice or chicken (£2.25), scampi (£3.10), grilled gammon (£3.25) and rump steak (£3.50), with a children's menu (from 75p) and a daily hot special in winter, such as steak and kidney pie; also a popular separate restaurant. A small front public bar has darts, dominoes and cribbage, and in another room there is a juke box and fruit machine; Bass on handpump. There are picnic-table sets under cocktail parasols on the sheltered and walled back lawn, with a couple more in front by the village green. *(Recommended by Beti Wyn Thomas)*

Bass · Licensees Chris and Hilda Reynolds · Real ale · Meals and snacks (not Sun) · Children welcome · Open 11–3, 5.50–11 all year; closed Sun Bedrooms tel Talybont (097 086) 335; £11/£20

Bedroom prices normally include full English breakfast, VAT and any inclusive service charge that we know of. Prices before the '/' are for single rooms, after for two people in double or twin; B denotes private bath, S a private shower. If there is no '/', the prices are only for twin or double rooms (as far as we know there are no singles).

TALYBONT-ON-USK (Powys)   SO1122   Map 6
Star
B4558

This fine village pub keeps about a dozen real ales, rotating the choice
through a pool (if that's the right word) of some 80 different
possibilities as each cask empties. A typical selection might be
Archers, Baileys, Bass, Everards Old Original, Felinfoel, Fullers ESB,
Hook Norton Best, Marstons Pedigree, Robinsons Best, Smiles,
Theakstons Old Peculier, Wadworths 6X, Wem and Youngers Scotch
or No 3; idiosyncratically, the only permanent fixture is Spaten, from
Germany. There are two ciders on handpump, too. The rambling
rooms radiating from the busy central servery seem in winter to have
almost as many open fires as there are ales, and include a plain and
brightly lit public bar, with darts, fruit machine and space game;
opposite that a partly panelled quarry-tiled area with bentwood
chairs and plain tables; and a neater carpeted area more or less
remote from the serving counter. There is a juke box and another
fruit machine; also dominoes and cribbage. Bar food includes filled
rolls and sandwiches (from 50p), filled baked potato (90p), pasty or
pie (£1.60), chicken or curry (£2.50), scampi (£2.80) and vegetarian
dishes (from £2). You can sit outside, and the village, with both the
Usk and the Monmouth and Brecon Canal running through, is
surrounded by the hills of the Brecon Beacons National Park.
*(Recommended by G A Hawkes, G Leonard, Tim and Ann Bracey; more
reports please in view of the change of licensee)*

*Free house · Licensee Mrs J Coakham · Real ale · Meals and snacks (not Mon
or Tues) · Children welcome · Open 11–3, 6–11 all year*

TAL-Y-CAFN (Gwynedd)   SH7972   Map 6
Tal-y-cafn
A470

The well run lounge bar of this roadside inn has deeply cushioned
bucket seats around the low tables on its Turkey carpet, settles in an
enormous inglenook fireplace, fairy lights along the beams, and piped
music. Bar food, mostly prepared here, includes soup, sandwiches,
pâté (£1.25), ploughman's (£1.50), good home-made pizzas (from
£2.20), plaice (£2.10), lasagne, steak and kidney pie, turkey, quiche
or roast pork (£2.25), gammon and egg or haddock in prawn and
cheese sauce (£2.50), scampi (£2.60) and salads; Greenalls on
handpump. There is a fruit machine and space game in a side room.
The well hedged lawn, out past an aviary with an African Grey
parrot, has rustic tables and seats by a rose border, and may be
patrolled by an amiable Great Dane. The great gardens of Bodnant
are just across the road. *(Recommended by Ron Salmon,
Beti Wyn Thomas)*

*Greenalls · Licensee Garry Beard · Meals and snacks · Children in side lounge
Organ Sat in summer · Open 12–3, 6.30–11 (12–3, 7–10.30 in winter)
Bedrooms tel Tynygroes (049 267) 203; £8.50/£17*

THREE COCKS (Powys)   SO1737   Map 6

(called Aberllynfi on some maps)

Old Barn

A438/A4079 junction

This long and spacious converted barn has high rafters and stripped stone walls, with a raised games area at one end (where young people congregate around pool, juke box, sensibly placed darts, fruit machine – also dominoes and cribbage), and a much quieter area of neat tables and Windsor chairs under lowered beams at the other, and rustic tables along the long stone serving counter between. Bar food includes hefty sandwiches (from 65p), home-made soup (80p), ploughman's with Cheddar or Stilton (£1.80), and hot dishes from cottage pie to steaks, with a choice of salads and some children's dishes. Well kept Hancocks HB on handpump. Outside, there's a big play area on the grass behind the car park of this well converted barn, with a tractor, sand pit, challenging climbing-frame and quite a few other things. There are picnic-table sets back here, and more tables on the side terrace, where barbecues are held on fine Friday evenings. *(More reports please)*

Welsh Brewers (Bass) · Licensee Janet Long · Real ale · Meals and snacks Children in eating area · Disco Mon evening · Open 11–3, 6–11 all year (opens noon and 7 in winter)

TREMEIRCHION (Clwyd)   SJ0873   Map 6

Salusbury Arms

Off B5429 up lane towards church

Readers have found a warm welcome in this spick-and-span pub. It has thickly cushioned cane seats on the richly patterned carpet of the oak-beamed lower lounge bar, which has dark green velvet curtains and a baize-faced bar counter – and was once the stables (parts of the building date back 700 years). The upper room is similar but smaller. There may be piped music; there's a civilised, relaxed atmosphere, and they keep dominoes. Bar food includes sandwiches (from 55p), soup such as chunky mushroom (55p), shepherd's pie (£1.85), steak and mushroom pie or lamb cutlets (£1.30), good chicken curry (£2.25), grilled trout (£2.65) and seafood platter (£3.25), with puddings such as apple pie and cream; they've now got Youngers Scotch on handpump. A separate restaurant is open in the evening (not Sundays). The flower garden in front of this pretty shuttered cottage is very well kept, and there are seats around marble-topped tables on a terrace by the back lawn, which is neatly edged with flower and shrub borders and has a fish-pool and cascades. *(Recommended by Sue and Len Beattie, G W Crowther)*

Free house · Licensees Jack and Margaret Poole · Real ale · Meals and snacks (not Sun evening, except party bookings) · Children welcome · Country and western Weds and Sat, organist sing-song Sun evening · Open 11–3.30, 6–11 all year; closed winter weekday lunchtimes, except festive season

TY'N-Y-GROES (Gwynedd)   SH7672 Map 6

Groes

B5106 N of village

The pub dates back some 600 years, and its warren of bars weave among thick stone walls and a quirkily-balustered old staircase, and under low beams. There is a fine antique fireback built in to one wall, a big wood-burning stove in one formidable fireplace, and an interesting mixture of seats from antique settles and an old sofa to neat low cane chairs and wicker bucket seats. There may be piped music. One area has Windsor chairs and tables set out for the food, which includes sandwiches (from 65p), soup (65p), burgers and pizzas, main dishes such as chicken, scampi, steak and kidney pie or gammon (around £2.50–£3), and grills (around £4.50–£5.50); there's also a separate restaurant. Sensibly placed darts, pool, dominoes, a juke box, fruit machine and two space games. There are rustic tables and chairs on the grass behind, and more by the road in front have a good view of the wide River Conwy. *(Recommended by William Meadon, Richard Steel, G M Bauer; more reports please)*

Free house · Licensee R Williams · Meals and snacks (not lunchtime in winter) Children in room away from bar servery · Open 12–3, 7–11; closed weekday lunchtimes in winter

WOLF'S CASTLE (Dyfed)   SM9526 Map 6

Wolfe

A40

With a warm welcome even for parties with quite a few children, this well kept and efficiently run inn has a good choice of places in which to eat the good value food, served efficiently by brisk but friendly waitresses. There's a comfortable red-carpeted lounge, with cheerful background music; a simpler tiled-floor public bar; the restaurant proper, with a fuller menu; a garden room, or conservatory-restaurant; and, outside the slate-roofed stone house, white tables and chairs in a hollow, part terrace and part grass, sheltered by banks of shrubs, ash and sycamore trees and surrounded by an arbour of roses and hanging baskets. The main choice of bar food includes sandwiches cut to order, soup (75p), ploughman's (£1.45), a wide choice of salads (from £1.50), pâté (£1.75), smoked trout pâté (£1.95), locally smoked trout (£2.35), chicken chasseur (£3.35), gammon and egg (£4.35), sirloin steak (from £5.60) and a dish of the day such as roast duck, fresh Dover sole, chicken Kiev, perhaps local salmon, dressed crab or fresh lobster. Puddings, all home made, include gateaux, syllabubs, roulades, meringues and profiteroles (£1.15). Felinfoel Double Dragon on handpump; darts, dominoes, fruit machine. Eight miles from Fishguard and the Irish ferry, the pub is a handy lunch stop for people arriving on the boat, which gets in just before lunch, and for those planning to board the one leaving at 2.30. *(Recommended by Elizabeth St George, SJS, L V Nutton)*

Free house · Licensees Fritz and Judith Neumann · Real ale · Meals and snacks (not Sun evening or Mon) · Children welcome · Open 11–3, 6–11 all year; closed 25–26 Dec, Mon lunchtime Oct–Whitsun

Lucky Dip

Besides the fully inspected pubs, you might like to try these Lucky Dips recommended and described by readers (if you do, please send us reports):

ABERBARGOED [ST1699], *Neuadd Wen*: friendly, personal service, good reasonably priced bar meals and snacks; good for lunches *(R W Lewis)*

ABERGAVENNY [Flannel Street; SO3014], *Hen & Chickens*: freshly made lunchtime sandwiches, well kept Bass; mixed clientele *(Pamela and Merlyn Horswell)*

ABERYSTWYTH [Queens Road; SN5882], *Boars Head*: cheerful back lounge and lively front pool-room, freshly cooked bar food, well kept Felinfoel, restaurant, beer garden. Popular with students in termtime; bedrooms July–September *(BB, Ashley Finch)*; [Terrace Road] *Central Hotel*: bustling town pub with welcoming atmosphere, old-fashioned lounge, bright public bar, freshly cooked bar food, restaurant *(Mrs Bevan Jones, Mrs H Davies, D H Hides, BB)*

AMMANFORD [Station Road, Tir-y-dail; SN6212], *Great Western*: friendly pub, mainly Welsh-speaking locals, Buckleys real ale, good food and efficient service; convenient for Central Wales railway service *(E O Stephens)*

BALA [High Street; SH9336], *Olde Bulls Head*: food and Whitbreads real ale in comfortably refurbished bar of oldest inn here; bedrooms *(LYM)*; [High Street] *Plas Coch*: friendly atmosphere in big well furnished bar, comfortable and 'country elegant'; wide choice of lunchtime bar snacks; bedrooms *(P J Taylor)*

BARRY [Dobbins Road; ST1168], *Glenbrook*: friendly well furnished pub. Good real ale and good value food; wide variety of wine *(P Dawson)*

BEAUMARIS [Castle Street; SH6076], *Liverpool Arms*: well maintained and run family hotel; good value food; bar broken up by screens, giving cosy feel; bedrooms *(John Colclough, D C Goodwin, John Lindley, Robert Ashton, Mrs E Rose, Capt A Richards, T Lloyd-Williams, K Humphries, Capt E Lindley-Jones)*

BEDDGELERT [SH5948] *Prince Llewellyn*: attractive small inn named after the prince who killed his legendary hound Gelert with his sword nearby; bedrooms *(Janet Williams)*; *Saracens Head*: imaginative bar food – baked potatoes, kebabs, etc. Pleasant staff; bedrooms *(GSC)*

BETWYS-Y-COED [SH7956], *Ty Gwyn*: beamed and carpeted bar with some bare stone walls in pub surrounded by mountains; good food, attractive dining-room, relaxed atmosphere, well decorated bedrooms *(Philip Denison, G M Bauer)*

BODEDERN [SH3281], *Crown*: friendly and welcoming pub, beer consistently good, big helpings of good food at reasonable prices *(A Musgrove)*

BOSHERSTON [SR9694], *St Govan's Inn*: big broken-up one-room pub, popular with locals and cliff-climbers and near coastguard houses and lily-ponds. Hard-working friendly staff. Fresh cooked simple food, children welcomed; bedrooms *(Michael Quine)*

BRECHFA [SN5230], *Foresters Arms*: fresh, clean and welcoming, good meal in restaurant, nice surroundings; bedrooms *(Anne Atkinson)*

BRIDGEND [Coychurch Road; SS9079], *Haywain*: friendly and tastefully renovated old farmhouse, warm and comfortable; good choice of hot and cold bar food, reasonable prices; well kept Courage Directors *(Gordon Mair)*

BWLCH [SO1522], *Farmers*: free house under new management: range of exotic and well presented bar meals, choice of beers, nice décor *(G H Theaker)*

CAIO [SN6739], *Brunant Arms*: friendly welcome. Good range of well kept beers, and good bar food at modest prices *(Alan Massam)*

CANTON [ST1576], *Romilly*: friendly local with well kept Brains real ales and huge back bar *(Beti Wyn Thomas)*

CAPEL GARMON [SH8255], *White Horse*: pub in superb spot with Snowdonia views, near Iron Age fort. Good bar meals; restaurant. Open fire in saloon bar; public bar has juke box, electronic darts scorer *(Robert McArthur)*

CARDIFF [Cowbridge Road East; ST1877], *Victoria Park*: friendly staff and customers in local with Brains Bitter, SA and Dark real ale and reasonably priced good food *(E O Stephens)*

CARDIGAN [Pendre; SN1746], *Bell Hotel*: good bar food, especially curry, reasonably priced. Friendly landlord; bedrooms *(P A King)*

CARMARTHEN [Tanerdy; SN4120], *Welsh Guardsman*: well kept, large interesting pub with variety of hot meals and bar snacks and Sunday carvery. Tables on grass in summer, restaurant *(Anon)*

CHIRK [SJ2938], *Hand*: old beamed pub with atmosphere. Food served in a buttery and restaurant with a good range of bar snacks, friendly service and Border beer; bedrooms *(G H Theaker)*

CILYCWM [SN7540], *White Hall*: food and décor good in pub with nice landlord, reasonable beer and fantastic surroundings *(Simon Rees)*

COLWYN BAY [Chapel Street, Mochdre; SH8578], *Mountain View*: friendly family-fun pub, renovated in 1983, with Burtonwood ales, good choice of cocktails and good value fresh home cooked bar meals *(A J Anderton)*

CRESSWELL [Cresswell Quay; SN0406], *Cresselly Arms*: good beer and very good atmosphere, in great surroundings *(Simon Rees)*

nr CRICKHOWELL [SO2118], *Nantyffin Cider Mill*: converted cider mill: small well decorated bar with good atmosphere, real ale, good choice of unusual bar food, restaurant *(RJD, G H Theaker, G Archer)*

FAIRBOURNE [SH6213], *Fairbourne*: comfortable pub with good food and convivial landlord; fudge pork scratchings a speciality; bedrooms *(Roger Entwistle)*

GLASBURY-ON-WYE [SO1739], *Harp*: friendly well run pub with nice view over River Wye, well used by locals and visitors, welcoming landlord; separate games bar, good range of bar food; bedrooms *(Jonathan Rowe)*; *Maesllwch Arms*: simple inn doing canoe holidays, real ales, farmhouse cider; bedrooms *(LYM)*

GROSMONT [SO4024], *Angel*: very simple village local in attractive steep village; welcoming, cheap snacks and cheap Whitbreads real ale *(Janet Williams, BOB)*

nr GROSMONT [SO4024], *Cupids Hill*: tiny homely pub alone on very steep hill. Bottled beers only, old settles by fire, low white ceiling; table skittles, dominoes, cribbage. OS Sheet 161 reference 407254 *(BOB)*

HAY ON WYE [Lion Street; SO2342], *Old Black Lion*: friendly town inn with popular filled pancakes and other bar food; children welcome; bedrooms *(LYM, PLC, Mr and Mrs G D Amos)*

HUNDLETON [SM9600], *Highgate*: large well equipped welcoming pub with restaurant, more suburban than rural in character; good Ushers real ale and draught Guinness; attractive bar menu *(JAB, Eric Owen Stephens)*

ILLSTON [SS5590], *Fox & Goose*: well worth a visit *(Michael Cooke)*

JAMESTON [SS0599], *Swanlake*: good pub near spectacular Manorbier Castle *(Janet Williams)*

JOHNSTON [SM9310], *Vine*: friendly pub renovated from ruin; good pub food, well kept real ale, draught Guinness; children in lounge if eating *(Eric Owen Stephens)*

LISVANE [ST1883], *Griffin*: food includes good steaks; cheery service in recently refurbished Whitbreads pub *(S Y Craig)*

LLANBEDR [SH5827], *Victoria*: food reasonable and fairly cheap, good Robinsons beer. Spacious garden by river *(Wilma Langhorne)*

LLANBEDROG [Bryn-y-Gro; SH3332], *Ship*: friendly atmosphere, good Burtonwood real ale; small local bar and spacious family bar, wide range of good value food *(Ken Leach, D O'Neill, A E Jones)*

LLANCARFAN [ST0570], *Fox & Hounds*: comfortably modernised old pub with choice of real ales, bar food, evening restaurant and attractive crazy-paved terrace *(LYM)*

LLANDAFF [ST1578], *Butchers Arms*: small cosy front bar; big well kept back bar *(Beti Wyn Thomas, Janet Williams, Julian Proudman)*; [Cardiff Road] *Maltsters Arms*: cheerful and spacious downstairs bar, easy chairs upstairs, well kept Brains real ales and quickly served food *(LYM, Beti Wyn Thomas, Del Fletcher)*

LLANDISSILIO [SN1221], *Bush*: efficient and friendly, with generous helpings of cold duck or fried scampi and chips, good salads, wine and puddings *(Peter J Dyer)*

LLANDOVERY [SN7634], *White Swan*: friendly bar staff, good atmosphere and real ales; open all day on market day *(Simon Rees)*

LLANDUDNO [SH7883], *Kings Head*: good food in spotlessly clean bar, good choice of beer; pleasant atmosphere, efficient staff *(A R Griffith, Brenda Wright)*

LLANEDEYRN [ST2182] *Holly Bush*: new and pleasant Brains pub for Llanedeyrn and Pentwyn estates *(Beti Wyn Thomas)*

nr LLANEGWAD [SN5321], *Halfway House*: good service and food at low prices *(Mr and Mrs J Fenn)*

LLANGATTOCK LINGOED [SO3620], *Hunters Moon*: thirteenth-century beamed and flagstoned pub near Offa's Dyke, with civilised atmosphere and good food, in remote village. Closed all day Tuesday *(BB)*

LLANGEINOR [SS9187], *Llangeinor Arms*: old pub beside ancient village church; panoramic view to Bristol Channel and West Country coast beyond. Fair choice of reasonably priced food in bar; conservatory and terrace *(Gordon Mair)*

LLANGENNY [SO2417], *Green Dragon*: food includes well presented range of bar snacks in pleasant country pub; range of real ale *(G H Theaker)*

LLANGORSE [SO1327], *Red Lion*: village inn well placed for Brecon Beacons and Black Mountains; bedrooms *(G A Hawkes)*

LLANGURIG [SN9179], *Blue Bell*: cheerful simple country inn; bedrooms *(Beti Wyn Thomas, LYM)*

LLANISHEN [SO4803], *Carpenters Arms*: food includes good home-made soups and pâtés; well kept Butcombe and Hook Norton; old cottage décor *(Mr and Mrs G D Amos)*

LLANNEFYDD [SH9871], *Hawk and Buckle*: remarkable views from bedrooms of cleanly run and comfortably modernised hill-village inn, good menu in both restaurant and bar; bedrooms *(LYM, Mr and Mrs J W Reeves, M J Reeves)*

LLANRHIDIAN [SS4992], *North Gower*: spacious mock-timbered pub with reasonably priced food, Buckleys and Felinfoel real ales, good views, restaurant, garden *(LYM, Sean Brady, C D Webb, W F C Bayliss)*

LLANSANNAN [SH9466], *Red Lion*: old-fashioned front parlour with antique furnishings in friendly hill-village local; well kept Lees real ale, simple food *(LYM)*

LLANSANTFFRAID YM MECHAIN [SJ2221], *Lion*: good food in bar and restaurant reasonably priced; two big comfortable bars, open fire, friendly character landlord *(Brian Huggett)*

LLANTWIT MAJOR [SS9668], *Old Swan*: unusual medieval building housing straightforward pub with lively public bar and busy juke box; also restaurant *(LYM)*

LLANVIHANGEL GOBION [SO3509], *Chart House*: smoothly modernised with nautical memorabilia and soothing piped music, good food in popular restaurant, distant hill views *(BB, Cdr D H Jones)*

LLANWDDYN [SJ0219], *Lake Vyrnwy Hotel*: old-fashioned, welcoming, with good English food; bedrooms *(Margaret H Winter)*

LLANWNEN [SN5346], *Fish & Anchor*: friendly pub in attractive countryside with good home-cooked food at reasonable prices and well kept Buckleys Best; short lunchtime opening *(BB, G Cross, S M Davies)*

LLANYNYS [SJ1063], *Cerrigllwydion Arms*: food good; dining-room and bars pleasantly decorated with welcoming landlord *(Mrs Sheila Lewis)*

LLYSFAEN [Llysfaen Road; SH8978], *Semaphore*: friendly free house with splendid sea view, good beer and menu, wide range of spirits *(A J Anderton)*

MACHYNLLETH [SH7501], *Red Lion*: good real ale and real locals, bar snacks, separate room with coin-slot pool-table which children can use *(Christopher Corke)*

MILTON [SN0303], *Milton Brewery*: good simple food in comfortable stone-walled ex-brewery with seats outside; children in games area *(Anon)*

MONMOUTH [SO5113], *Kings Head*: plush and quite stylish pub, bar has fine plasterwork with seventeenth-century moulded head of Charles I over fireplace. Food, including afternoon tea; bedrooms *(Helen Woodeson)*

MONTGOMERY [SO2296], *Cottage*: good bar meals and Sunday lunches; clean and attractive *(HSY)*

MORGANSTOWN [ST1281], *Ty Nant*: pleasant place to visit *(Beti Wyn Thomas)*

NANNERCH [ST1669], *Rising Sun*: good bar food and restaurant (booking recommended), with excellent service and evening à la carte menu. Friendly owners *(Mrs F Hall)*

NEWGALE [SM8422], *Duke of Edinburgh*: good food, real ale and friendly service. Public bar like modernised cowboy ranch; bedrooms *(Sheila Lewis, Rex Haigh)*

NEWPORT [SN0539], *Castle*: good food, big helpings, wide variety; friendly, clean, well decorated; bedrooms *(Anon)*

OLD COLWYN [SH8678], *Plough*: good beer and warm, friendly staff and locals in clean pub with small selection of lunchtime food *(A J Anderton)*

OLDWALLS [SS4891], *Greyhound*: good atmosphere with open fire; good bar food, including oysters done several different ways; good draught Bass *(Dave Parkins)*

OYSTERMOUTH [SS6188], *White Rose*: friendly and efficient service in busy town-centre pub with good range of beers and wide choice of reasonably priced good bar meals; small but crowded terrace where children are welcome *(Mr and Mrs Ager)*

PAINSCASTLE [SO1646], *Maesllwch Arms*: friendly old village inn up in hills with comfortable lounge bar and restaurant; owners who won high praise for food left last year – more reports please; bedrooms *(LYM, D A Lloyd)*

PEMBROKE DOCK [Melville Street; SM9603], *Navy Inn*: good steaks and fish. Friendly, efficient staff, draught Guinness. Close to Irish ferry terminal *(E O Stephens)*

PEMBROKE FERRY [SM9603], *Ferry*: riverside pub. Real ale and draught Guinness. Bar snacks, Sunday carvery lunch and restaurant. Friendly staff. Children welcome lunchtime *(E O Stephens)*

PENCOED [Coychurch Road; SS9581], *Maerdy*: well kept real ale, friendly service in well run pub restaurant; bedrooms *(R Owen)*

PENTRAETH [SH5278], *Bull*: good bar food including home-made Italian dishes. Baby Bull eating house specialises in Italian food and traditional dishes, steaks, home-made pies *(Mrs J M Reverter)*

PENTRECAGAL [SN3340], *Pensarnau Arms*: good home-made food, quickly prepared and served, and at a reasonable cost. Wide variety of real ales. Attractive and well run, with friendly atmosphere *(JC, MHS, C J Dutton, John Evans)*

nr PONTERWYD [SN7581], *Dyffryn Castell*: friendly inn alone in dramatic mountain valley, comfortable lounge bar, food, Bank's real ale; bedrooms *(LYM, R F Warner, Beti Wyn Thomas, Philip Denison)*

PRESTEIGNE [SO3265], *Radnorshire Arms*: picturesque rambling timbered THF inn with food in panelled bar, Bass, well spaced tables on sheltered lawn; bedrooms *(LYM, Pamela and Merlyn Horswell)*

PWLLMEYRIC [ST5192], *New*: welcoming friendly roadside pub with games and well kept Bass *(Dr A K Clarke)*

RAGLAN [SO4108], *Beaufort Arms*: extensively rebuilt and usually busy: enjoyable restaurant meals, Sunday lunches and bar snacks; bedrooms (Pamela and Merlyn Horswell, Helen Woodeson)

RHIWBINA [ST1581], *Deri Arms*: spacious pub of unusual design *(Beti Wyn Thomas)*

RHYDOWEN [SN4445], *Alltrodyn Arms*: friendly main-road pub with good Marstons (also Buckleys and Welsh Brewers) and good range of lunchtime food, tables in garden *(SJS)*

ROSEBUSH [SN0729], *Preseli*: interesting pub in ex-slate quarry village *(Janet Williams)*

SKEWEN [SS7297], *Crown*: good pub – worth a visit *(G J Harries)*

SOLVA [SM8024], *Ship*: food delicious – home-made soup and chicken pie, very fresh salad and vegetables, reasonably priced; cosy atmosphere and good beer *(C Byron)*

SOUTHERNDOWN [SS8873], *Three Golden Cups*: near coast and locally popular for meals, views to Devon when it's clear; bedrooms *(LYM)*

ST BRIDES MAJOR [SS8974], *Farmers Arms*: friendly and spacious old pub opposite village pond, attractive inside. Restaurant meals as well as good bar food *(Gordon Mair)*

ST DAVIDS [SM7525], *Farmers Arms*: cheerfully busy pub in holiday area *(Dr A K Clarke)*

ST DOGMAELS [SN1645], *Ferry*: popular waterside family pub, simply furnished *(LYM)*; *White Hart*: friendly welcome and good locally made Welsh pasties, good beer; cosy and dark inside, with a few roadside tables *(SJS)*

ST MELLONS [TT2281], *Bluebell*: picturesque pub with good atmosphere; good food and service *(Linda Thomas)*

TAL-Y-BONT [SH7669], *Y Bedol*: country pub with summer flower boxes and tubs, winter open fire in lounge. Unusual dishes and seafood besides usual bar food, at very reasonable prices, lunchtime and evening. Garden with tables *(Sandra Walker)*

TALYCOED [SO4115], *Halfway House*: friendly relaxed pub in hilly farmland, stone fireplaces, flagstones, plain wood furniture. Felinfoel DD, Bass, good ploughman's, hot home-made pies, seats outside *(Doug Kennedy)*

TEGRYN [SN2233], *Butchers Arms*: said to be the highest pub in Pembrokeshire; picturesque view; good Buckleys bitter and bar snacks; also has small but good restaurant *(EH)*

TEMPLETON [SN1111], *Boars Head*: clean, spacious, friendly atmosphere. Good value food seven days a week, well kept beer *(Miss S Herbert, David Ferguson)*

TENBY [SN1300], *Five Arches*: good beer, bar, service, snacks and comfort, pleasant Scottish owner *(G Keen)*

TINTERN [SO5301], *Anchor*: cheerful pub by ferry slipway, good value bar lunches and evening snacks. Good choice in restaurant with excellent steaks *(L Welch)*; [Devauden Road] *Cherry Tree*: good location in wooded valley, old-fashioned decorations, friendly landlord *(P A Woolley)*; *Moon & Sixpence*: unusual décor with goldfish pond in stone surround in lounge; good value home-made food, separate restaurant *(Alan Stevens, Jane English)*; *Rose & Crown*: good food from the French chef in rather touristy pub opposite Tintern Abbey; bedrooms *(Roger Entwistle)*

TREMADOG [SH5640], *Golden Fleece*: old stone pub with good atmosphere. Fine range of bar snacks and a restaurant during season; draught Bass, Guinness and Stones *(G H Theaker)*

VALLEY [SH2979], *Bull*: good food *(Mrs J M Reverter)*

WHITEBROOK [SO5406], *Crown*: wide range of good and unusual food in comfortable no-smoking dining-room. Friendly welcome; bedrooms *(A J Goater)*

Overseas *Lucky Dip*

This section includes readers' reports on pubs in the Scillies, Isle of Man, Channel Islands and the Republic of Ireland. We'd be grateful for more reports on places to drink abroad – of course, in countries which don't have proper pubs or inns, these are likely to be different in character. But the same general principle applies: they should be places that strangers would enjoy going to for almost any reason – the more memorable the better! We're very grateful to the readers named for the entries for their pioneering explorations.

Scilly Isles

HUGH TOWN [The Quay], *Mermaid:* friendly staff and good beer in busy downstairs bar of very old pub crammed with ships' figureheads, model ships, other maritime and local memorabilia; pool-table, quieter upstairs bar with view over harbour has reasonably priced food including outstanding salads and puddings (*Pat Bromley, Peter and Rose Flower*)

ST AGNES, *Turks Head:* friendly welcome in tiny old pub overlooking Porth Conger and islands; large but cheap snacks, Ushers beer; cosy furnishings (*John Morrow, Peter and Rose Flower*)

Isle of Man

ANDREAS [Jurby Road], *Grosvenor:* high-quality restaurant and good lounge bar makes this one of the most comfortable pubs on the island (*Dr A K Clarke*)

BALLASALLA [Airport Road], *Whitestone:* nicely done up, with a lot of style and frendly staff (*Dr A K Clarke*)

DOUGLAS [North Quay], *Bridge:* really friendly little quayside pub with bags of atmosphere, well worth a visit; there's a barmaid known as The Glamorous Granny – and she is! (*Dr A K Clarke*)

LAXEY [Tram Station], *Mines Tavern:* bar is an old railway carriage, and there's a big outside drinking area; pub at one of the main stations on the electric railway, near the famous wheel (*Dr A K Clarke*)

PEEL [Station Place], *Creek:* well kept pub, with unusually young landlord for the Isle of Man; very friendly, with enviable location by the harbour (*Dr A K Clarke*)

Channel Islands

JERSEY

GREVE DE LECQ, *Prince of Wales:* new hotel with big lounge, children's room, aviary and splendid bay views from one of its two big terraces; popular but spacious (*Howard Gascoyne*)

Jersey Airport, *Horizon Bar:* smart and comfortable, with good service, excellent views over airport and to distant Guernsey; adjoining restaurant; children welcome *(Howard Gascoyne)*

St Aubin [le Boulevard], *Old Court House:* lovely old partly seventeenth-century inn with three bars full of character, nautical décor, cosy and comfortable; old well in central bar (where children are allowed); harbour views from front terrace; restaurant; bedrooms *(Howard Gascoyne)*

St Brelade [le Boulevard], *La Marquanderie:* food emphasised – spit-roast lunches – in pleasant comfortable old granite pub/restaurant with friendly service; separate children's 'cabin' *(Howard Gascoyne);* [Portelet Bay], *Old Portelet:* seventeenth-century granite farmhouse with seven bars; antiques, spacious in parts with lots of character; Bass on handpump, meals; children in games room (pin-ball, space games); attractive garden *(Howard Gascoyne);* [Onaisne Bay], *Old Smugglers:* good food and well kept Bass on handpump in lovely old pub, originally two fishermen's cottages (name refers to Second World War smuggling); snug, cosy and well run, in pleasant spot near beach and slipway; children in central lounge *(Howard Gascoyne)*

St Helier [Esplanade], *Bristol:* comfortable upstairs children's lounge with good views over St Aubins Bay and Elizabeth Castle, a cross between playroom with slide and toys and ordinary lounge; bar itself rather plain; hotel *(Howard Gascoyne);* [The Quay], *La Folie:* authentic nautical pub dating from eighteenth century; three smallish bars (children allowed in two) with wind speed indicators and other nautical hardware, charts and notices, sailors, fishermen and dockers; keg beers served from curious tall fonts; fresh fish sometimes sold from terrace *(Howard Gascoyne)*

St Peters [St Peters Mill], *Windmill:* pleasant pub, built around old windmill: big bars resembling barns, with sacks, farm tools and milk-churns, and millwheel serving as bar counter; bar snacks, restaurant; children in gallery; big terrace *(Howard Gascoyne)*

Trinity, *Fishermans Bar:* smallish bar with covered terrace in lovely setting overlooking harbour; friendly and welcoming inside, fishing nets cover walls; national hill-climb championships held nearby *(Howard Gascoyne); Trinity Arms:* splendid farmhouse type of pub: two big friendly bars, heavy ceiling timbers, stone floors; space games in lobby where children are allowed; seats outside *(Howard Gascoyne)*

GUERNSEY

St Peter Port, *La Frégate:* rated as the best inn the recommender had ever stayed in; fabulous harbour views from good restaurant; bedrooms *(S G Pickles); Ship & Crown:* interesting pub, serving really nice and woody local Pony Ale; comfortable seats but busy (used by lots of day-trippers) *(Lesley Foote and Alan Carter)*

St Sampsons, *English & Guernsey:* massive pub with lots of different bars, skittles room, children's room with Disney wallpaper, piped music; popular *(Lesley Foote and Alan Carter); Pony:* lots of bars to choose from (including what's reputed to be the best-decorated lounge on the island, but perhaps a bit twee), one with a juke box, two with tvs; good value simple food *(Lesley Foote and Alan Carter)*

SARK

SARK, *Mermaid:* open every day except Sunday 8am to 11pm, with Bobby Bitter from Guernsey, excellent ploughman's too big to finish; talking pool-table ('quit talking and start chalking') *(Lesley Foote and Alan Carter)*

Ireland

DUBLIN

[Duke Street], *Bailey:* very attractive and comfortable, greater range of food than in most Dublin pubs; 'vurry vurry historic' as an American told recommender, with lots of exhibits to prove it *(W T Aird)*

[Molesworth Street], *Boswells:* a hotel bar with all the atmosphere of a good pub; close to the Dáil, so very political with representatives and journalists; good service; bedrooms comfortable *(W T Aird)*

[College Street], *College Mooney:* very pleasant, with two lounges and entertaining customers (not all from Trinity College Dublin) *(W T Aird)*

[Lower Bagott Street], *Doheny & Nesbitt:* highly recommended, unpretentious, basic, decidedly Irish – genuinely welcoming though not for the old lady from Surbiton or ex-Army chap from Woking or Esher; sandwiches, cold meats, coffee *(W T Aird)*

[Duke Street], *Doug Byrnes:* the Moral Pub from *Ulysses* and popular with folk who have 'a book on the way'; comfortable, lots of private corners; friendly and efficient service, sandwiches, modicum of simple hot dishes, wines by glass *(W T Aird)*; *Duke Lounge:* very comfortable up-to-date lounge – used to be lovely for a snipe (Irish for a quarter bottle) of champagne at noon when it was affordable 10 or so years ago; professional friendly service, wines by glass, coffee, sandwiches and rolls *(W T Aird)*

[Poolby Street], *John Mulligans:* John F Kennedy drank here; licensed for about 200 years, interesting building, uncompromisingly Irish, warmly welcoming; sandwiches, coffee *(W T Aird)*

[South George Street], *Long Hall:* great Irish pub with décor from the real days of pub design: long narrowish main bar leading to cosy lounge, then back by long mahogany hall; not for anyone wanting breweryised conformity *(W T Aird)*

[Christchurch Place], *Lord Edward:* original downstairs bar and more recent comfortable upstairs bar; soup, salads and other lunchtime snacks; handy for St Patrick's Cathedral and Dublin Castle *(W T Aird)*

[Talbot Street], *Malloys:* traditional public bar and modern cocktail bar with interesting show of modern Irish paintings; used to open very early on weekdays (around 7am) *(W T Aird)*

[Stillorgan Road], *Montrose:* comfortable and well appointed hotel lounge bar; roomy, good service and grill room; bedrooms *(W T Aird)*

[1 Chatham Street], *Neary's:* highly recommended: traditional Irish pub of the best sort plus a touch of smartness, especially upstairs; marble-topped bar counter, mahogany and brass; good snacks including oysters in season, coffee, professional service on the formal side *(W T Aird)*

[Marlborough Street], *O'Farnells:* said to be Dublin's smallest pub – hence the name *(W T Aird)*

[Exchequer Street], *Old Stand:* very highly recommended: splendid service in two big lounge bars – not unlike those of an English pub, but clientele unmistakably and indefatigably Irish; good range of food, including hot dishes 12 to 2 and 6 to 9pm; friendly staff, warm and pubby atmosphere especially in the evenings; named afer the Old Stand at Lansdowne Road where the Rugby Internationals are played *(W T Aird)*

[Middle Abbey Street], *Oval:* badly damaged in Easter Rising 1916, rebuilt 1918, and named after Gurney's Cricket Ground; agreeable upstairs lounge and downstairs public bar *(W T Aird)*

[Fleet Street], *Pearl:* great convivial journalists' and writers' pub, well designed, very comfortable and friendly; photographs of writers and publishers *(W T Aird)*

[Lower Abbey Street], *Plough:* good pre-theatre drinking in great rendez-vous with more than one bar *(W T Aird)*

[Kildare Street], *Powers Royal:* comfortable, willing service; mainly political regulars, as close to the Dáil; bedrooms *(W T Aird)*

[Upper Baggot Street], *Searsons;* two comfortable old front bars and very restful big back lounge; nine pictures of the river gods of Ireland; good salads, sandwiches, very efficient service; wines by bottle or glass, coffee; highly recommended *(W T Aird)*

[South King Street], *Sinnots:* typical theatre pub, splendid atmosphere, original glass and woodwork; simple foods, professional service *(W T Aird)*

[Harry Street], *Zodiac;* comfortably modernised old bar, signs of zodiac upstairs, modest but better than usual snack menu *(W T Aird)*

ADARE, *Dunraven Arms:* lovely bar overlooking beautiful garden, almost like an Engliah pub *(W T Aird)*

CAHERDANIEL, *Daniel O'Connels Bar:* typical locals' bar in same building as shop, mainly Gaelic speaking but mixture of languages depending on season *(Martyn Quinn)*

nr CAHERDANIEL, *Scariff:* good view of Atlantic and coastline from friendly modern pub with bar snacks; popular in summer *(Martyn Quinn)*

CORK, *Oyster Bar and Tavern:* lovely bar on way in, and good straightforward restaurant; would take a lot of beating for real honest-to-God Irish drinking *(W T Aird); Two Cygnets:* splendid basic bar *(W T Aird)*

DALKEY, *Sportsmans:* good pub – a nice summer's-evening jaunt to Dalkey all the better for a drink here *(W T Aird)*

ENNIS (O'Connell Street), *Brogans:* excellent pub, often crowded but service always brisk; good food in bar and restaurant *(Barrie Pepper)*

ENNISCORTHY, *Antique:* close to an English inn – very popular *(Martyn Quinn)*

GAP OF DUNLOE, *Kate Kearneys Cottage:* good Guinness and magnificent Killarney lakes scenery; local history; bit of a tourist spot: the ponies wait to take you up the steep track; also has a souvenir shop *(Martyn Quinn)*

SNEEM, *Blue Bull:* typical friendly Irish bar with two rooms, smooth Guinness and good (but expensive) restaurant; pleasant village *(Martyn Quinn)*

STILLORGAN, *Leopardstown:* several good bars, upstairs grill room; very crowded on race days, and grill room probably needs booking on weekend and summer evenings *(W T Aird)*; *Stillorgan:* modernised coaching-inn on Bray road; panelling, coloured lanterns, pleasant atmosphere; lunchtime light snacks *(W T Aird)*

Special interest lists

Pubs with gardens

The pubs listed here have bigger or more beautiful gardens, grounds or terraces than are usual for their areas. Note that in a town or city this might be very much more modest than the sort of garden that would deserve a listing in the countryside.

BERKSHIRE
Aldworth, Bell
Chaddleworth, Ibex
Cookham, Kings Arms
Hampstead Norreys, New Inn
Hungerford, Bear
Hurley, Dew Drop
Littlewick Green, Shire Horse
Sonning on Thames, White Hart
Streatley, Swan
Wickham, Five Bells
Winkfield, White Hart
Woolhampton, Rowbarge

BUCKINGHAM-SHIRE
Bledlow, Lions of Bledlow
Denham, Swan
Dunsmore, Fox
Fawley, Walnut Tree
Fingest, Chequers
Hambleden, Stag & Huntsman
Hawridge Common, Full Moon
Marsh Gibbon, Greyhound
Northend, White Hart
Penn, Crown
Skirmett, Old Crown
Stony Stratford, Cock
The Lee, Cock & Rabbit; Old Swan

CAMBRIDGESHIRE AND BEDFORD-SHIRE
Clayhithe, Bridge Hotel
Elsworth, George & Dragon
Eltisley, Leeds Arms
Fowlmere, Chequers
Great Chishill, Pheasant
Hexton, Live & Let Live

Horningsea, Plough & Fleece
Madingley, Three Horseshoes
Ridgmont, Rose & Crown
Sandy, Locomotive
Southill, White Horse
Swavesey, Trinity Foot
Tempsford, Anchor
Wansford, Haycock
Whittlesford, Tickell Arms

CHESHIRE
Brereton Green, Bears Head
Goostrey, Olde Red Lion
Lower Peover, Bells of Peover
Wildboarclough, Crag

CORNWALL
Helford, Shipwrights Arms
Manaccan, New Inn
Philleigh, Roseland
Trebarwith, Mill House

CUMBRIA
Barbon, Barbon Inn
Bassenthwaite, Pheasant
Eskdale Green, Bower House
Rydal, Glen Rothay Hotel
Warwick-on-Eden, Queens Arms

DERBYSHIRE AND STAFFORDSHIRE
Bamford, Marquis of Granby
Birch Vale, Sycamore
Buxton, Bull i'th'Thorn
Clifton Campville, Green Man
Kinver, Whittington

Little Bridgeford, Worston Mill
Melbourne, John Thompson
Rowsley, Peacock
Ticknall, Chequers

DEVON
Broadhembury, Drewe Arms
Dartington, Cott
Doddiscombsleigh, Nobody Inn
Exminster, Turf Hotel
Haytor Vale, Rock
Horndon, Elephants Nest
Lee, Grampus
Newton Abbot, Two Mile Oak
Sidford, Blue Ball
Sidmouth, Bowd
South Zeal, Oxenham Arms
Torbryan, Old Church House
Welcombe, Old Smithy

DORSET
Chedington, Winyard's Gap Inn
Christchurch, Fishermans Haunt
Lytchett Minster, Bakers Arms
Marshwood, Bottle
Nettlecombe, Marquis of Lorne
Shave Cross, Shave Cross
Stoke Abbott, New Inn
Tarrant Monkton, Langton Arms

DURHAM
Belford, Blue Bell
Blanchland, Lord Crewe Arms
Chollerford, George Hotel

Egglescliffe, Blue Bell
Longhorsley, Linden Pub
Ulgham, Forge

ESSEX
Castle Hedingham, Bell
Coggeshall, Compasses; Fleece
Great Henny, Swan
Woodham Walter, Cats

GLOUCESTER-SHIRE
Ampney Crucis, Crown of Crucis
Chaceley Stock, Yew Tree
Ewen, Wild Duck
Fossebridge, Fossebridge Inn
Great Rissington, Lamb
Kingscote, Hunters Hall
Lechlade, Trout
Minchinhampton, Old Lodge
North Nibley, New Inn
Redbrook, Boat
Southrop, Swan
Withington, Mill Inn

HAMPSHIRE
Fawley, Jolly Sailor
Linwood, High Corner
Liphook, Passfield Oak
Longparish, Plough
Ovington, Bush
Petersfield, White Horse
Steep, Harrow

HEREFORD AND WORCESTER
Bretforton, Fleece
Broadway, Lygon Arms
Ewyas Harold, Trout
Fownhope, Green Man
Sellack, Loughpool
Weatheroak Hill, Coach & Horses
Woolhope, Butchers Arms

HERTFORDSHIRE
Amwell, Elephant & Castle
Ayot St Lawrence, Brocket Arms
Chipping, Countryman
Chorleywood, Garden Gate
Colney Heath, Crooked Billet

Flaunden, Green Dragon
Kings Langley, Eagle
Newgate Street Village, Coach & Horses
Sarratt, Boot
St Albans, Barley Mow
Walkern, White Lion
Wheathampstead, Wicked Lady

ISLE OF WIGHT
Chale, Clarendon (Wight Mouse)
Niton, Buddle

KENT
Aldington, Walnut Tree
Benover, Woolpack
Biddenden, Three Chimneys
Bough Beech, Wheatsheaf
Brasted, Stanhope Arms
Chiddingstone, Castle
Cobham, Leather Bottle
Dargate, Dove
Plaxtol, Golding Hop
Smarden, Bell

LANCASHIRE
Burnley, Coal Clough House
Chorley, Railway
Darwen, Old Rosins
Lancaster, Howe Ghyll
Standish, Crown
Uppermill, Cross Keys
Whitewell, Inn at Whitewell

LEICESTERSHIRE, LINCOLNSHIRE AND NOTTINGHAM-SHIRE
Barrow on Soar, Riverside
Drakeholes, Griff Inn
Exton, Fox & Hounds
Newton, Red Lion
Nottingham, Three Wheatsheaves
Old Dalby, Crown
South Luffenham, Boot & Shoe
Stamford, George of Stamford
Upton, French Horn

MIDLANDS
Ashby St Ledgers, Old Coach House

Berkswell, Bear
Edge Hill, Castle
Farnborough, Butchers Arms
Priors Marston, Holly Bush
Shrewley, Durham Ox
Studley, Old Washford Mill
Weedon, Narrow Boat

NORFOLK
Hethersett, Kings Head
Letheringsett, Kings Head

OXFORDSHIRE
Burford, Lamb
Chinnor, Sir Charles Napier
Clifton Hampden, Barley Mow
Faringdon, Crown
Fyfield, White Hart
Maidensgrove, Five Horseshoes
Minster Lovell, Old Swan
Moulsford, Beetle & Wedge
Newbridge, Rose Revived
Noke, Plough
Oxford, Perch
Radcot, Swan
Shipton-under-Wychwood, Shaven Crown
South Leigh, Mason Arms
South Stoke, Perch & Pike
Stanton Harcourt, Harcourt Arms

SHROPSHIRE
Bishop's Castle, Three Tuns
Claverley, Crown

SOMERSET AND AVON
Ashcott, Ashcott
Bath, Crystal Palace
Monksilver, Notley Arms
Tintinhull, Crown & Victoria
Tormarton, Compass

SUFFOLK
Badingham, White Horse

Blythburgh, White Hart
Brandeston, Queens Head
Hoxne, Swan
Lavenham, Swan
Laxfield, Kings Head
Walberswick, Bell
Wenhaston, Star

SURREY
Addlestone, White Hart
Bletchingley, William IV
Chipstead, Well House
Compton, Withies
East Clandon, Queens Head
Ewhurst, Windmill
Forest Green, Parrot
Horley, Olde Six Bells
Laleham, Three Horseshoes
Newdigate, Surrey Oaks
Outwood, Bell
Pyrford Lock, Anchor
Warlingham, White Lion
Worplesdon, Jolly Farmer
Wotton, Wotton Hatch

SUSSEX
Berwick, Sussex Ox
Blackboys, Blackboys
Byworth, Black Horse
Coolham, George & Dragon
East Dean, Star & Garter
Elsted, Three Horseshoes
Fittleworth, Swan
Fulking, Shepherd & Dog
Heathfield, Star
Houghton, George & Dragon
Midhurst, Royal Oak
Ringmer, Cock
Rowhook, Chequers
Rushlake Green, Horse & Groom
Stopham, White Hart
Wineham, Royal Oak

WILTSHIRE
Alvediston, Weight for Age

Bradford-on-Avon, Cross Guns
Chicksgrove, Compasses
Chilmark, Black Dog
Everleigh, Crown
Landford, Cuckoo
Malmesbury, Old Bell
Salisbury, Rose & Crown

YORKSHIRE
Egton Bridge, Horse Shoe
Gargrave, Anchor
Wentworth, Rockingham Arms

LONDON, CENTRAL
Cross Keys, SW3
Henry J Bean's, SW3
Red Lion, W1

LONDON, EAST
Prospect of Whitby, E1

LONDON, NORTH
Waterside Inn, N1
Flask, N6
Freemasons Arms, NW3
Spaniards, NW3

LONDON, SOUTH
Founders Arms, SE1
Green Man, SW15
Ship, SW18
Rose & Crown, SW19
White Swan, Richmond

LONDON, WEST
Dove, W6
Scarsdale Arms, W8
Windsor Castle, W8
White Swan, Twickenham

SCOTLAND
Aberdeen, Ferryhill House
Arduaine, Loch Melfort Hotel
Cleish, Nivingston House
Edinburgh, Tilted Wig
Gifford, Tweeddale Arms

Kirkcudbright, Selkirk Arms
Lewiston, Lewiston Arms
Loans, Dallam Tower
Nairn, Clifton
Newburgh, Udny Arms
Pitlochry, Killiecrankie Hotel
Skeabost, Skeabost House Hotel
Spean Bridge, Letterfinlay Lodge Hotel
Strachur, Creggans
Thornhill, Lion & Unicorn
Tweedsmuir, Crook

WALES
Aberystwyth, Halfway Inn
Bodfari, Dinorben Arms
Crickhowell, Bear
Dinas, Sailors Safety
Lisvane, Ty Mawr Arms
Llanarmon DC, West Arms
Llandrindod Wells, Llanerch
Llanfrynach, White Swan
Llangynidr, Coach & Horses
Llanrwst, Maenan Abbey
Llanthony, Abbey
Llwyndafydd, Crown
Llyswen, Boat
Menai Bridge, Gazelle
Nevern, Trewern Arms
Old Radnor, Harp
Pont-ar-Gothi, Cothi Bridge Hotel
St Hilary, Bush
Tal-y-Cafn, Tal-y-Cafn
Talybont, Black Lion
Three Cocks, Old Barn
Tremeirchion, Salusbury Arms
Ty'n-y-Groes, Groes
Wolf's Castle, Wolfe

Waterside pubs

The pubs listed here are right beside the sea, a sizeable river, canal, lake or loch that contributes significantly to their attraction.

BERKSHIRE
Great Shefford, Swan
Hungerford, Bear
Kintbury, Dundas Arms
Newbury, Old Waggon & Horses
Sonning on Thames, White Hart
Streatley, Swan
Woolhampton, Rowbarge

BUCKINGHAM-SHIRE
Chalfont St Peter, Greyhound

CAMBRIDGESHIRE AND BEDFORD-SHIRE
Cambridge, Fort St George
Clayhithe, Bridge Hotel
Holywell, Olde Ferry Boat
Needingworth, Pike & Eel
Tempsford, Anchor
Wansford, Haycock

CHESHIRE
Audlem, Shroppie Fly
Tiverton, Shady Oak
Warrington, Ferry

CORNWALL
Bodinnick, Old Ferry
Falmouth, Chain Locker (Marine Restaurant)
Helford, Shipwrights Arms
Malpas, Heron
Mylor Bridge, Pandora
Polkerris, Rashleigh Inn
Polperro, Blue Peter
Port Gaverne, Port Gaverne Hotel
Porthleven, Ship
Portmellon Cove, Rising Sun
St Mawes, Rising Sun

CUMBRIA
Ravenstonedale, Kings Head Hotel
Sandside, Ship

DERBYSHIRE AND STAFFORDSHIRE
Bamford, Marquis of Granby
Cheddleton, Boat
Consall, Black Lion
Rowsley, Peacock
Stone, Star

DEVON
Burgh Island, Pilchard
Exeter, Double Locks
Exminster, Turf Hotel
Lynmouth, Rising Sun
Salcombe, Ferry
Topsham, Passage; Steam Packet
Tuckenhay, Maltsters Arms

DORSET
Chideock, Anchor
Lyme Regis, Pilot Boat

DURHAM AND NORTHUMBER-LAND
Chollerford, George Hotel
Egglescliffe, Blue Bell
Saltburn-by-the-Sea, Ship

ESSEX
Burnham-on-Crouch, White Harte
Great Henny, Swan

GLOUCESTER-SHIRE
Chaceley Stock, Yew Tree
Fossebridge, Fossebridge Inn
Great Barrington, Fox
Lechlade, Trout
Redbrook, Boat
Withington, Mill Inn

HAMPSHIRE
Bursledon, Jolly Sailor
Fawley, Jolly Sailor
Langstone, Royal Oak
Ovington, Bush
Portsmouth, Still & West

HEREFORD AND WORCESTER
Elmley Castle, Old Mill
Upton upon Severn, Swan

HERTFORDSHIRE
Boxmoor, Fishery
London Colney, Green Dragon

ISLE OF WIGHT
Shanklin, Fishermans Cottage Club
Ventnor, Mill Bay

KENT
Conyer Quay, Ship
Plaxtol, Golding Hop
Wye, Tickled Trout

LANCASHIRE
Clitheroe, Hodder Bridge Hotel
Garstang, Th'owd Tithebarn
Heaton with Oxcliffe, Golden Ball
Lancaster, Water Witch
Manchester, Mark Addy
Whitewell, Inn at Whitewell

LEICESTERSHIRE, LINCOLNSHIRE AND NOTTINGHAM-SHIRE
Barrow on Soar, Riverside

MIDLANDS
Northampton, Britannia
Stoke Bruerne, Boat
Studley, Old Washford Mill
Weedon, Narrow Boat

NORFOLK
Coltishall, Rising Sun
Norwich, Ferryboat
Surlingham, Ferry House
Sutton, Sutton Staithe

907

OXFORDSHIRE
Godstow, Trout
Goring, Leatherne
  Bottle
Moulsford, Beetle &
  Wedge
Newbridge, Maybush;
  Rose Revived
Oxford, Perch
Radcot, Swan

SHROPSHIRE
Llanyblodwel, Horse
  Shoe

SOMERSET AND
  AVON
Bristol, Pump House
Porlock Weir, Ship

SUFFOLK
Aldeburgh, Cross Keys
Chelmondiston, Butt &
  Oyster
Orford, Jolly Sailor
Ramsholt, Ramsholt
  Arms
Southwold, Harbour
  Inn

SURREY
Addlestone, White Hart
Horley, Olde Six Bells
Pyrford Lock, Anchor
Staines, Swan

SUSSEX
Arundel, Black Rabbit
Blackboys, Blackboys
Stopham, White Hart

WILTSHIRE
Bradford-on-Avon,
  Cross Guns

Salisbury, Rose &
  Crown

YORKSHIRE
Gargrave, Anchor
Sowerby Bridge,
  Moorings
York, Kings Arms

LONDON, EAST
Prospect of Whitby, E1
Grapes, E14

LONDON, NORTH
Narrow Boat, N1
Waterside Inn, N1

LONDON, SOUTH
Anchor, SE1
Founders Arms, SE1
Angel, SE16
Mayflower, SE16
Bulls Head, SW13
Ship, SW18

LONDON, WEST
London Apprentice,
  Isleworth
Bulls Head, W4
Dove, W6
White Swan,
  Twickenham

SCOTLAND
Anstruther, Sun Tavern
Ardentinny, Ardentinny
  Hotel
Arduaine, Loch Melfort
  Hotel
Carbost, Old Inn
Crinan, Crinan Hotel
Edinburgh, Old Chain
  Pier
Elie, Ship

Findhorn, Crown &
  Anchor
Inverary, Argyll Arms
Isle of Whithorn, Steam
  Packet
Isle Ornsay, Hotel
  Eilean Iarmain
Kenmore, Kenmore
  Hotel
Kippford, Anchor
Luss, Inverbeg
Plockton, Plockton
  Hotel
Portpatrick, Crown
Queensferry, Hawes
Sconser, Sconser Lodge
  Hotel
Skeabost, Skeabost
  House Hotel
Spean Bridge,
  Letterfinlay Lodge
  Hotel
St Mary's Loch, Tibbie
  Shiels Inn
Stein, Stein Inn
Strachur, Creggans
Troon, Look Out

WALES
Aberaeron,
  Harbourmaster
Dinas, Sailors Safety
Erbistock, Boat
Little Haven, Swan
Llangynidr, Coach &
  Horses
Llyswen, Boat
Menai Bridge, Gazelle
Nevern, Trewern Arms
Penarth, Captains Wife
Penmaenpool, George III
Pont-ar-Gothi, Cothi
  Bridge Hotel

Pubs in attractive surroundings

These pubs are in particularly attractive or interesting places – lovely
countryside, charming villages, occasionally notable town
surroundings. Waterside pubs are listed again here only if their other
surroundings are special, too.

BERKSHIRE
Aldworth, Bell
Frilsham, Pot Kiln
Hurley, Dew Drop
Littlewick Green,
  Cricketers

BUCKINGHAM-
  SHIRE
Bledlow, Lions of
  Bledlow
Botley, Five Bells
Downley, Le De Spencer
Dunsmore, Fox
Hambleden, Stag &
  Huntsman

Hawridge Common,
  Full Moon
Ibstone, Fox
Little Hampden, Rising
  Sun
Littleworth Common,
  Jolly Woodman
Northend, White Hart
Skirmett, Kings Arms
Turville, Bull & Butcher

CAMBRIDGESHIRE AND BEDFORDSHIRE
Barrington, Royal Oak
Dullingham, Kings Head
Grantchester, Green Man; Red Lion
Hexton, Live & Let Live
Studham, Red Lion

CHESHIRE
Barthomley, White Lion
Lower Peover, Bells of Peover
nr Macclesfield, Cat & Fiddle
Swettenham, Swettenham Arms
Wildboarclough, Crag

CORNWALL
Boscastle, Cobweb
Chapel Amble, Maltsters Arms
Lamorna, Lamorna Wink
Morwenstow, Bush
Pillaton, Weary Friar
Polperro, Blue Peter
St Dominick, Who'd Have Thought It
St Kew, St Kew Inn
Trebarwith, Mill House

CUMBRIA
Bassenthwaite, Pheasant
Boot, Burnmoor
Cartmel, Kings Arms
Elterwater, Britannia
Far Sawrey, Sawrey Hotel
Hawkshead, Drunken Duck
Langdale, Old Dungeon Ghyll
Little Langdale, Three Shires
Loweswater, Kirkstile Inn
Melmerby, Shepherds
Scales, White Horse
Wasdale Head, Wasdale Head Inn

DERBYSHIRE AND STAFFORDSHIRE
Consall, Black Lion
Edale, Old Nags Head
Flash, Travellers Rest
Little Hucklow, Old Bulls Head
Over Haddon, Lathkil

Rowarth, Little Mill

DEVON
Burgh Island, Pilchard
Exminster, Turf Hotel
Haytor Vale, Rock
Holne, Church House
Horndon, Elephants Nest
Knowstone, Masons Arms
Lee, Grampus
Lydford, Castle Inn
Lynmouth, Rising Sun
Meavy, Royal Oak
North Bovey, Ring of Bells
Peter Tavy, Peter Tavy
Rattery, Church House
Stokenham, Tradesmans Arms

DORSET
Askerswell, Spyway
Chedington, Winyard's Gap Inn
Marshwood, Bottle
Milton Abbas, Hambro Arms
Powerstock, Three Horseshoes
Worth Matravers, Square & Compass

DURHAM
Bamburgh, Lord Crewe Arms
Blanchland, Lord Crewe Arms
Craster, Jolly Fisherman
Eggleston, Three Tuns
Etal, Black Bull
High Force, High Force Hotel
Moorsholm, Jolly Sailor
Romaldkirk, Rose and Crown

ESSEX
Belchamp St Paul, Half Moon
Purleigh, Bell

GLOUCESTER-SHIRE
Bledington, Kings Head
Great Rissington, Lamb
Minchinhampton, Old Lodge
North Nibley, New Inn
Painswick, Royal Oak
Snowshill, Snowshill Arms

St Briavels, George

HAMPSHIRE
Bucklers Hard, Master Builders House
Fritham, Royal Oak
Hamble, Olde Whyte Harte
Linwood, High Corner
Liphook, Passfield Oak
Ovington, Bush
Petersfield, White Horse
Tangley, Cricketers
Vernham Dean, Boot
Winchester, Eclipse

HEREFORD AND WORCESTER
Ewyas Harold, Trout
Sellack, Loughpool
Woolhope, Butchers Arms

HERTFORDSHIRE
Chipperfield, Two Brewers
Chorleywood, Garden Gate
Frithsden, Alford Arms
Harpenden, Three Horseshoes
Sarratt, Cock
St Albans, Fighting Cocks
Westmill, Sword in Hand

HUMBERSIDE
North Newbald, Tiger

ISLE OF WIGHT
Chale, Clarendon (Wight Mouse)

KENT
Boughton Aluph, Flying Horse
Chiddingstone, Castle
Chilham, White Horse
Cobham, Leather Bottle
Luddenham, Mounted Rifleman
Luddesdown, Golden Lion
Sole Street, Compasses

LANCASHIRE
Blacko, Moorcock
Blackstone Edge, White House
Denshaw, Rams Head
Marple, Romper

Middleton, Tandle Hill
  Tavern
Slaidburn, Hark to
  Bounty
Uppermill, Church Inn;
  Cross Keys
Whitewell, Inn at
  Whitewell

**LEICESTERSHIRE,
LINCOLNSHIRE
AND
NOTTINGHAM-
SHIRE**
Exton, Fox & Hounds
Hallaton, Bewicke Arms
Maplebeck, Beehive

MIDLANDS
Edge Hill, Castle
Kingswinford, Glynne
  Arms
Priors Marston, Holly
  Bush
Stratford upon Avon,
  Dirty Duck/Black
  Swan
Tanworth-in-Arden,
  Bell

NORFOLK
Blickling,
  Buckinghamshire
  Arms
Brancaster Staithe, Jolly
  Sailors
Heydon, Earle Arms
Sutton, Sutton Staithe
Thornham, Lifeboat

OXFORDSHIRE
Chinnor, Sir Charles
  Napier
Clifton Hampden,
  Barley Mow
Cropredy, Red Lion
Great Tew, Falkland
  Arms
Hailey, King William IV
Letcombe Regis,
  Sparrow
Maidensgrove, Five
  Horseshoes
Minster Lovell, Old
  Swan
Oxford, Turf Tavern
Pishill, Crown
Satwell, Lamb
Shipton-under-
  Wychwood, Shaven
  Crown
Stoke Row, Crooked
  Billet

Swinbrook, Swan

SHROPSHIRE
Bridgnorth,
  Railwaymans Arms
Cardington, Royal Oak
Claverley, Crown
Llanfairwaterdine, Red
  Lion

**SOMERSET AND
AVON**
Appley, Globe
Ashill, Square &
  Compass
Huish Champflower,
  Castle
Priddy, Hunters Lodge
Simonsbath, Exmoor
  Forest
Stogumber, White
  Horse
Winsford, Royal Oak

SUFFOLK
Blythburgh, White Hart
Chelworth, Peacock
Dunwich, Ship
Felixstowe Ferry, Ferry
  Boat
Long Melford, Bull
Ramsholt, Ramsholt
  Arms
Sutton, Plough
Walberswick, Bell

SURREY
Abinger Common,
  Abinger Hatch
Blackbrook, Plough
Cobham, Cricketers
Ewhurst, Windmill
Forest Green, Parrot
Ockley, Punch Bowl
Outwood, Bell
Reigate Heath,
  Skimmington Castle
Shere, White Horse

SUSSEX
Amberley, Black Horse
Berwick, Sussex Ox
Billinghurst, Blue Ship
Chilgrove, Royal Oak
Coleman's Hatch,
  Hatch
Dallington, Swan
East Dean, Star &
  Garter
Fulking, Shepherd &
  Dog
Heathfield, Star
Lickfold, Lickfold Inn

Lurgashall, Noah's Ark
West Hoathly, Cat
Wineham, Royal Oak

WILTSHIRE
Alvediston, Weight for
  Age
Bradford-on-Avon,
  Cross Guns
Castle Combe, White
  Hart
Ebbesbourne Wake,
  Horseshoe
Landford, Cuckoo
Malmesbury, Old Bell

YORKSHIRE
Buckden, Buck
Burnsall, Red Lion
Chapel le Dale, Old Hill
Cray, White Lion
Heath, Kings Arms
Hubberholme, George
Langdale End, Moor
  Cock
Lastingham,
  Blacksmiths Arms
Levisham, Horse Shoe
Linton in Craven,
  Fountaine
Litton, Queens Arms
Midgley, Mount Skip
Ramsgill, Yorke Arms
Robin Hood's Bay,
  Laurel
Rosedale Abbey,
  Milburn Arms; White
  Horse
Starbotton, Fox &
  Hounds
Sutton Howgrave,
  White Dog
Tan Hill, Tan Hill Inn
Thruscross, Stone
  House Inn
Wath-in-Nidderdale,
  Sportsmans Arms
Widdop, Pack Horse

**LONDON,
CENTRAL**
Punch & Judy, WC2

LONDON, NORTH
Freemasons Arms, NW3
Spaniards, NW3

LONDON, SOUTH
Rose & Crown, Kew
Olde Windmill, SW4
Green Man, SW15

SCOTLAND
Achnasheen, Achnasheen Hotel
Arduaine, Loch Melfort Hotel
Crinan, Crinan Hotel
Edinburgh, Sheep Heid
Kenmore, Kenmore Hotel
Loch Tummel, Loch Tummel Hotel
Luss, Inverbeg
Mountbenger, Gordon Arms
Pitlochry, Killiecrankie Hotel
St Mary's Loch, Tibbie Shiels Inn

Strachur, Creggans
Tweedsmuir, Crook

WALES
Aberystwyth, Halfway Inn
Bylchau, Sportsmans Arms
Carew, Carew Inn
Corris, Slaters Arms
Cwm Gwaun, Dyffryn Arms
Dinas, Sailors Safety
Erbistock, Boat
Fishguard, Ship
Ganllwyd, Tyn-y-Groes
Llanarmon DC, Hand Hotel; West Arms

Llanbedr-y-Cennin, Olde Bull
Llanberis, Pen-y-Gwryd
Llanelidan, Leyland Arms
Llangurig, Glansevern Arms
Llanrhidian, Welcome to Town
Llanthony, Abbey
Maentwrog, Grapes
Old Radnor, Harp
Penderyn, Red Lion
Penmaenpool, George III

Pubs with good views

These pubs are listed for their particularly good views, either from inside the building or from a garden or terrace. Waterside pubs are listed again here only if their view is exceptional in its own right.

BERKSHIRE
Chieveley, Blue Boar

BUCKINGHAM-SHIRE
Great Brickhill, Old Red Lion
Penn, Crown

CHESHIRE
Langley, Hanging Gate
Mow Cop, Cheshire View
nr Macclesfield, Cat & Fiddle
Overton, Ring of Bells
Rainow, Highwayman
Tiverton, Shady Oak

CUMBRIA
Cartmel Fell, Masons Arms
Hawkshead, Drunken Duck
Keswick, Swinside
Langdale, Old Dungeon Ghyll
Loweswater, Kirkstile Inn
Sandside, Ship
Wasdale Head, Wasdale Head Inn

DERBYSHIRE AND STAFFORDSHIRE
Flash, Travellers Rest
Foolow, Barrel

Over Haddon, Lathkil

DEVON
Burgh Island, Pilchard
Hennock, Palk Arms
Westleigh, Westleigh Inn

DORSET
Chedington, Winyard's Gap Inn
Kingston, Scott Arms
Worth Matravers, Square & Compass

DURHAM
Eggleston, Three Tuns
North Shields, Wooden Doll
Seahouses, Olde Ship

ESSEX
Purleigh, Bell

ISLE OF WIGHT
Niton, Buddle

KENT
Goudhurst, Star & Eagle
Penshurst, Spotted Dog

LANCASHIRE
Blacko, Moorcock
Blackstone Edge, White House
Darwen, Old Rosins

Marple, Romper
Tockholes, Black Bull
Uppermill, Cross Keys

MIDLANDS
Long Buckby, Buckby Lion

SHROPSHIRE
Bishop's Castle, Three Tuns

SUFFOLK
Levington, Ship

SURREY
Ewhurst, Windmill

SUSSEX
Dallington, Swan
Houghton, George & Dragon

WILTSHIRE
Salisbury, Rose & Crown

YORKSHIRE
Almondbury, Castle Hill
Litton, Queens Arms
Midgley, Mount Skip
Rosedale Abbey, White Horse
Runswick Bay, Royal
Tan Hill, Tan Hill Inn

LONDON,
  CENTRAL
St George's Hotel, W1

LONDON, SOUTH
Angel, SE16
Founders Arms, SE1

SCOTLAND
Ardentinny, Ardentinny
  Hotel
Ardvasar, Ardvasar
  Hotel
Crinan, Crinan Hotel
Edinburgh, Old Chain
  Pier

Isle Ornsay, Hotel
  Eilean Iarmain
Loans, Dallam Tower
Loch Tummel, Loch
  Tummel Hotel
Nairn, Clifton
Pitlochry, Killiecrankie
  Hotel
Sconser, Sconser Lodge
  Hotel
St Mary's Loch, Tibbie
  Shiels Inn
Strachur, Creggans
Troon, Look Out
Weem, Ailean Chraggan

WALES
Aberystwyth, Halfway
  Inn
Bodfari, Dinorben Arms
Bylchau, Sportsmans
  Arms
Ganllwyd, Tyn-y-groes
Lampeter, Tafarn Jem
Llanbedr-y-Cennin,
  Olde Bull
Llanberis, Pen-y-Gwryd
Old Radnor, Harp
Penmaenpool, George III
Ty'n-y-groes, Groes

Pubs in interesting buildings

Pubs and inns are listed here for the interest or beauty of their building
– something really out of the ordinary to look at, or occasionally a
building that's got a very interesting historical background.

BERKSHIRE
Cookham, Bel & The
  Dragon

BUCKINGHAM-
SHIRE
Forty Green, Royal
  Standard of England

CORNWALL
Morwenstow, Bush

DERBYSHIRE AND
  STAFFORDSHIRE
Buxton, Bull i'th'Thorn

DEVON
Dartmouth, Cherub
Rattery, Church House
Sourton, Highwayman
South Zeal, Oxenham
  Arms

DURHAM AND
NORTHUMBER-
LAND
Blanchland, Lord Crewe
  Arms

HAMPSHIRE
Beauworth, Milbury's
Bursledon, Fox &
  Hounds
Southampton, Red Lion

HEREFORD AND
WORCESTER
Bretforton, Fleece
Broadway, Lygon Arms

HUMBERSIDE
Hull, Olde White Harte

KENT
Goudhurst, Star &
  Eagle

LANCASHIRE
Garstang, Th'owd
  Tithebarn
Liverpool, Philharmonic

LEICESTERSHIRE,
LINCOLNSHIRE
AND
NOTTINGHAM-
SHIRE
Grantham, Angel &
  Royal
Nottingham, Olde Trip
  to Jerusalem
Stamford, George of
  Stamford

MIDLANDS
Birmingham, Bartons
  Arms
Kingswinford, Glynne
  Arms

NORFOLK
Scole, Scole Inn

OXFORDSHIRE
Fyfield, White Hart

SHROPSHIRE
Ludlow, Feathers

SOMERSET AND
AVON
Glastonbury, George &
  Pilgrims
Norton St Philip,
  George

SURREY
Chiddingfold, Crown
Shere, White Horse

SUSSEX
Alfriston, Star
Rye, Mermaid

WILTSHIRE
Salisbury, Haunch of
  Venison

LONDON,
CENTRAL
Black Friar, EC4

LONDON, EAST
Hollands, E1

LONDON, NORTH
Crockers, NW8

LONDON, SOUTH
George, SE1
Phoenix & Firkin, SE5

SCOTLAND
Dumfries, Globe
Edinburgh, Bennets Bar
Edinburgh, Cafe Royal
  Circle Bar

Edinburgh, Guildford
  Arms

WALES
Llanfihangel Crucorney,
  Skirrid
Llanthony, Abbey

Pubs that brew their own beer

These pubs brew their own beer on the premises; many others not
listed have individual beer brewed specially for them (but not on the
premises). We mention these in the text.

BUCKINGHAM-
  SHIRE
Marsh Gibbon,
  Greyhound

CHESHIRE
Mow Cop, Mow Cop

CORNWALL
Helston, Blue Anchor

DERBYSHIRE AND
  STAFFORDSHIRE
Melbourne, John
  Thompson

DEVON
Newton St Cyres, Beer
  Engine

ESSEX
Gestingthorpe, Pheasant

HANTS
West Tisted, Pig &
  Whistle

HEREFORD AND
  WORCESTER
Upton upon Severn,
  Olde Anchor

HERTFORDSHIRE
Barley, Fox and Hounds
Frithsden, Alford Arms

MIDLANDS
Netherton, Old Swan
Studley, Old Washford
  Mill

SOMERSET AND
  AVON
Bristol, Fleece & Firkin

SUSSEX
Chidham, Old House At
  Home
East Grinstead,
  Dunnings Mill

YORKSHIRE
Goose Eye, Turkey
Leeds, Fox & Newt

LONDON,
  CENTRAL
Pheasant & Firkin, EC1
Orange Brewery, SW1

LONDON, SOUTH
Market Porter, SE1
Phoenix & Firkin, SE5
Fox & Firkin, SE13

LONDON, WEST
Ferret & Firkin, SW10
Frog & Firkin, W11

Bars open all day (at least in summer)

SCOTLAND
Aberdeen, Ferryhill
  House
Achnasheen,
  Achnasheen Hotel
Anstruther, Smugglers;
  Sun Tavern
Ardvasar, Ardvasar
  Hotel
Cabrach, Grouse
Castlecary, Castlecary
  House Hotel
Cramond Bridge,
  Cramond Brig
Crinan, Crinan Hotel
Dumfries, Globe
Edinburgh, Beehive;
  Bennets Bar; Café
  Royal Circle Bar; Jolly
  Judge; Old Chain
  Pier; Sheep Heid;
  Tilted Wig

Findhorn, Crown &
  Anchor
Gifford, Tweeddale
  Arms
Girvan, Kings Arms
Glasgow, Outside Inn;
  Overflow; Pot Still
Glendevon, Tormaukin
Gullane, Golf
Inveraray, Argyll Arms
Inverarnan, Inverarnan
  Inn
Isle of Whithorn, Steam
  Packet
Isle Ornsay, Hotel
  Eilean Iarmain
Lauder, Black Bull;
  Eagle
Loch Tummel, Loch
  Tummel Hotel
Luss, Inverbeg
Moffat, Black Bull

Mountbenger, Gordon
  Arms
Plockton, Plockton
  Hotel
Queensferry, Hawes
Sconser, Sconser Lodge
  Hotel
Spean Bridge,
  Letterfinlay Lodge
  Hotel
St Andrews, Victoria
  Cafe
St Mary's Loch, Tibbie
  Shiels Inn
Stein, Stein Inn
Strachur, Creggans
Stranraer, George
Troon, Look Out
Weem, Ailean Chraggan

WALES
Denbigh, Bull

Pubs close to motorway junctions

The number at the start of each line is the number of the junction. Detailed directions are given in the main entry for each pub. In this section, to help you find the pubs quickly before you're past the junction, we give the name of the chapter where you'll find them.

M1
5: Northampton (Midlands) 3¾ miles
8: Boxmoor (Herts) 3½ miles
13: Ridgmont (Cambs) 2 miles
15: Stoke Bruerne (Midlands) 3¾ miles
16: Weedon (Midlands) 3 miles
18: Ashby St Ledgers (Midlands) 4 miles
24: Kegworth (Leics) 1 mile
31: South Anston (Yorks) 3 miles
35: Grenoside (Yorks) 3 miles
36: Wentworth (Yorks) 3 miles

M18
5: Hatfield Woodhouse (Yorks) 2 miles

M2
1: Cobham (Kent) 2½ miles
3: Aylesford (Kent) 3 miles
6: Luddenham (Kent) 3½ miles

M20
2: Wrotham (Kent) 1¾ miles

M23
9: Horley (Surrey) 3 miles

M25
6: Bletchingley (Surrey) 3 miles
6: Bletchingley (Surrey) 3 miles
8: Reigate Heath (Surrey) 3 miles

M27
1: Fritham (Hants) 4 miles
8: Hamble (Hants) 3 miles

M4
9: Littlewick Green (Berks) 3¾ miles
9: Bray (Berks) 1¾ miles
9: Littlewick Green (Berks) 3 miles
10: Binfield (Berks) 4½ miles
13: Chieveley (Berks) 3½ miles
14: Wickham (Berks) 3 miles
14: Hungerford (Berks) 3 miles
14: Great Shefford (Berks) 2 miles
37: Kenfig (Wales) 2¼ miles
37: Nottage (Wales) 2 miles
46: Llangyfelach (Wales) ¼ mile

M40
1: Denham (Bucks) ¾ mile
2: Forty Green (Bucks) 3½ miles
2: Littleworth Common (Bucks) 2 miles
5: Bolter End (Bucks) 4 miles
5: Ibstone (Bucks) 1 mile
6: Cuxham (Oxon) 4 miles

M45
1: Dunchurch (Midlands) 1⅓ miles

M5
6: Claines (H&W) 3 miles
27: Burlescombe (Devon) 4 miles

27: Sampford Peverell (Devon) 1 mile
28: Cullompton (Devon) ½ mile
28: Broadhembury (Devon) 5 miles
30: Woodbury Salterton (Devon) 3½ miles
30: Exeter (Devon) 4 miles
30: Topsham (Devon) 2 miles
30: Topsham (Devon) 2¼ miles

M55
1: Broughton (Lancs) 3½ miles

M56
10: Little Leigh (Cheshire) 4½ miles
12: Overton (Cheshire) 2 miles

M6
6: Birmingham (Midlands) 2 miles
14: Seighford (Derbys) 3 miles
14: Little Bridgeford (Derbys) 2½ miles
14: Sandon Bank (Derbys) 4½ miles
15: Whitmore (Derbys) 3 miles
17: Brereton Green (Cheshire) 2 miles
19: Plumley (Cheshire) 2½ miles
27: Standish (Lancs) 4 miles
31: Balderstone (Lancs) 2 miles
40: Stainton (Cumbria) 3 miles
40: Penrith (Cumbria) 1 mile
40: Tirril (Cumbria) 3½ miles
40: Askham (Cumbria) 4½ miles
40: Askham (Cumbria) 4½ miles
43: Warwick-on-Eden (Cumbria) 2 miles

M62
20: Rochdale (Lancs)
    3 miles
22: Denshaw (Lancs)
    2 miles
34: Cridling Stubbs
    (Yorks) 3½ miles

M9
 4: Polmont (Scotland)
    ¾ mile

M90
 5: Cleish (Scotland)
    1½ miles

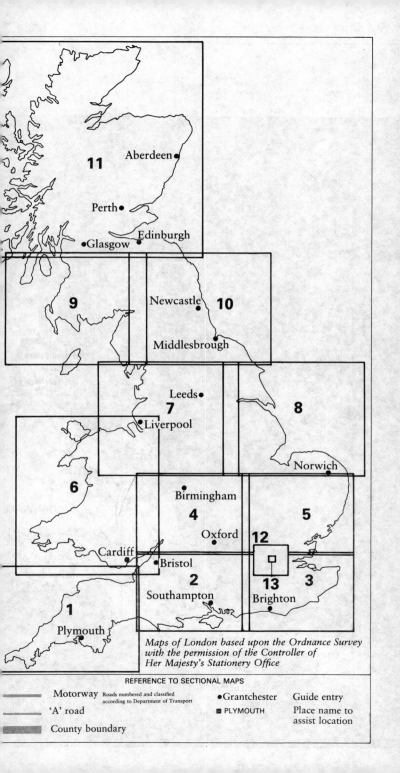

11
Aberdeen •

Perth •

• Glasgow • Edinburgh

9

10
Newcastle •

Middlesbrough •

Leeds •
7
• Liverpool

8

6

Norwich •

Birmingham •
4

5

Oxford •
12

Cardiff •
• Bristol

2
Southampton •

13
Brighton •

3

1
Plymouth •

Maps of London based upon the Ordnance Survey with the permission of the Controller of Her Majesty's Stationery Office

REFERENCE TO SECTIONAL MAPS

Motorway Roads numbered and classified according to Department of Transport   • Grantchester   Guide entry

'A' road   ▣ PLYMOUTH   Place name to assist location

County boundary

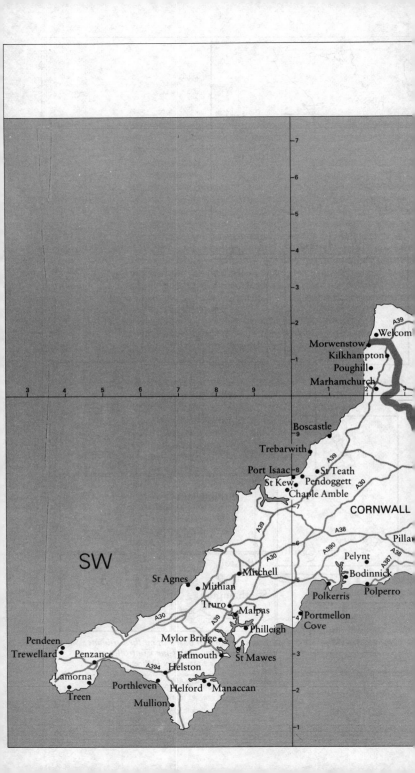

SW

CORNWALL

Welcom
Morwenstow
Kilkhampton
Poughill
Marhamchurch

Boscastle
Trebarwith
Port Isaac
St Kew
Pendoggett
Chaple Amble

St Teath

Pilla

Pelynt
Bodinnick
Polperro
Polkerris
Portmellon
Cove

Mitchell
St Agnes
Mithian
Truro
Malpas
Philleigh
Mylor Bridge
Pendeen
Trewellard
Penzance
Falmouth
St Mawes
Helston
Lamorna
Porthleven
Helford
Manaccan
Treen
Mullion

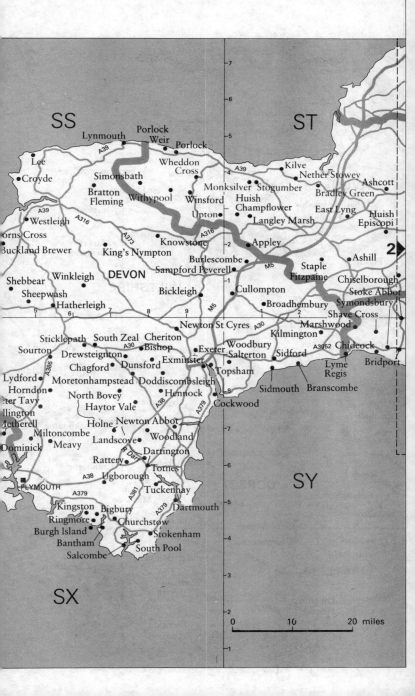

MAP 1

SS

ST

SX

SY

Lynmouth
Porlock
Weir
Porlock
Lee
Croyde
Wheddon
Cross
Kilve
Nether Stowey
Ashcott
Simonsbath
Monksilver
Stogumber
Bradley Green
Bratton
Fleming
Withypool
Winsford
Huish
Champflower
East Lyng
Huish
Episcopi
Westleigh
Upton
Langley Marsh
orns Cross
Knowstone
Appley
Ashill
uckland Brewer
King's Nympton
Burlescombe
Staple
Fitzpaine
Chiselborough
Shebbear
Winkleigh
DEVON
Sampford Peverell
Stoke Abbot
Sheepwash
Bickleigh
Cullompton
Symondsbury
Hatherleigh
Broadhembury
Shave Cross
Newton St Cyres
Marshwood
Sticklepath
South Zeal
Cheriton
Kilmington
Chidcock
Sourton
Drewsteignton
Bishop
Woodbury
Salterton
Sidford
Bridport
Exeter
Lydford
Chagford
Dunsford
Exminster
Topsham
Lyme
Regis
Horndon
Moretonhampstead
Doddiscombsleigh
Sidmouth
Branscombe
er Tavy
North Bovey
Hennock
llington
Haytor Vale
Cockwood
etherell
Holne
Newton Abbot
Miltoncombe
Landscove
Woodland
Dominick
Meavy
Dartington
Rattery
Totnes
SY
Ugborough
Tuckenhay
PLYMOUTH
Kingston
Bigbury
Dartmouth
Ringmore
Churchstow
Burgh Island
Stokenham
Bantham
South Pool
Salcombe

0   10   20 miles

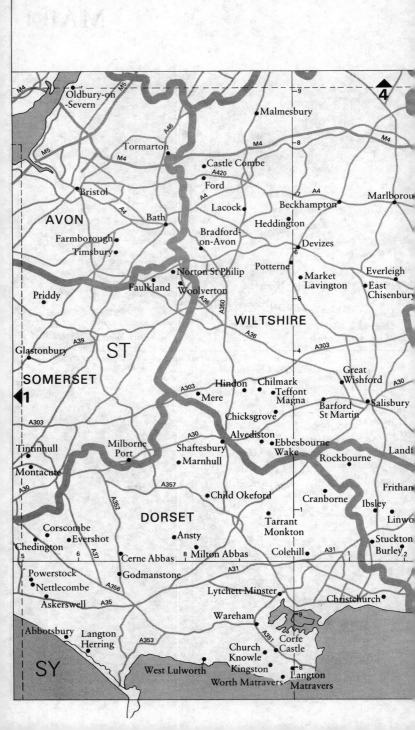

MAP 2

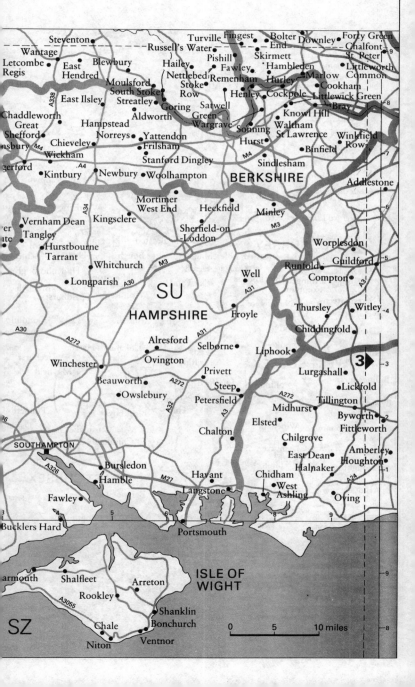

Steventon • Wantage • Letcombe Regis • East Hendred • Blewbury • Russell's Water • Turville • Fingest • Bolter End • Downley • Forty Green • Chalfont St Peter • Littleworth Common

Hailey • Pishill • Skirmett • Hambleden • Cookham
Nettlebed • Fawley • Remenham • Hurley • Marlow • Littlewick Green
Moulsford • Stoke Row • Henley • Cockpole • Bray
South Stoke • Satwell • Knowl Hill
East Ilsley • Streatley • Goring • Green • Wargrave • Waltham St Lawrence • Winkfield Row
Chaddleworth • Aldworth • Sonning • Binfield
Great Shefford • Hampstead Norreys • Yattendon • Hurst • Sindlesham
nsbury • Chieveley • Frilsham
Wickham • Stanford Dingley • **BERKSHIRE**
gerford • Kintbury • Newbury • Woolhampton • Addlestone

Mortimer West End • Heckfield • Minley
Vernham Dean • Kingsclere • Worplesdon • Guildford
Tangley • Sherfield-on-Loddon • Runfold • Compton
Hurstbourne Tarrant • Well
Whitchurch • **SU**
Longparish • Thursley • Witley
HAMPSHIRE • Froyle • Chiddingfold
Alresford • Selborne • Liphook • **3** • Lurgashall
Winchester • Ovington • Privett • Lickfold
Beauworth • Steep • Tillington • Byworth
Owslebury • Petersfield • Midhurst • Fittleworth
Chalton • Elsted • Chilgrove • Amberley • Houghton
SOUTHAMPTON • East Dean • Halnaker • Oving
Bursledon • Havant • Chidham
Hamble • Langstone • West Ashling
Fawley • Portsmouth
Bucklers Hard

ISLE OF WIGHT
armouth • Shalfleet • Arreton
Rookley • Shanklin
SZ • Chale • Bonchurch
Niton • Ventnor

0   5   10 miles

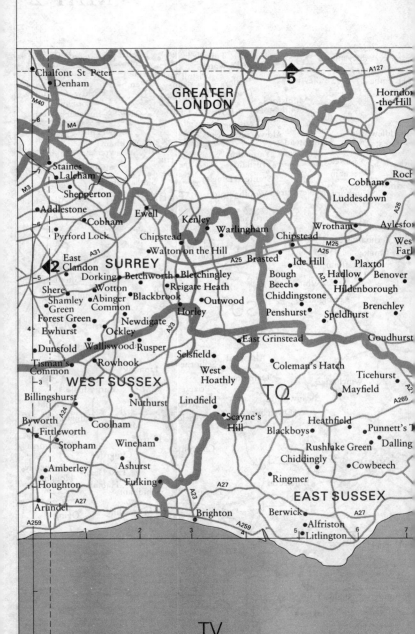

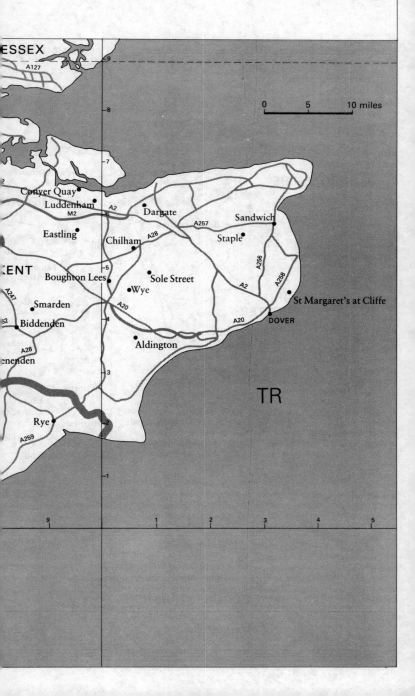

MAP 3

ESSEX

A127

0   5   10 miles

Conyer Quay
Luddenham   A2   Dargate
M2
Eastling   Chilham   A28   Sandwich
Staple
KENT
Boughton Lees   A256
Sole Street   A258
Smarden   Wye   A2   St Margaret's at Cliffe
A20
Biddenden   A20   DOVER
A28
enenden   Aldington

Rye
A259

TR

9   1   2   3   4   5

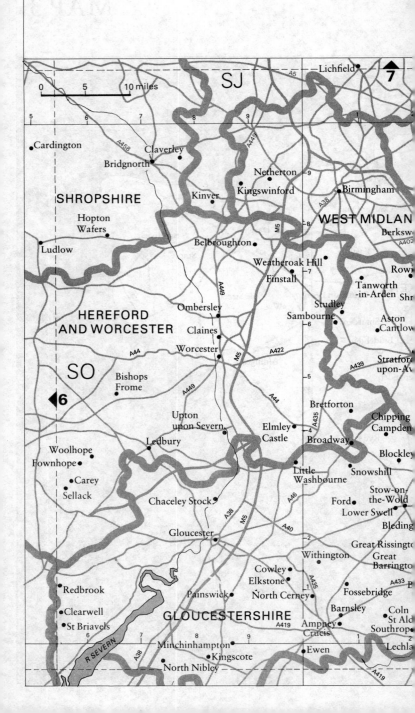

MAP 3

SJ
7

Lichfield
A5

0 5 10 miles

Cardington
A458
Claverley
Bridgnorth
Netherton
Kinver Kingswinford
Birmingham
SHROPSHIRE
Hopton
Wafers
WEST MIDLAN
Berksw
A402
Ludlow
Belbroughton
Weatheroak Hill
Finstall
Row
Tanworth
-in-Arden Shr
Ombersley
Studley
Sambourne
Aston
Cantlow
HEREFORD
AND WORCESTER
Claines
Worcester
A44
SO
Bishops
Frome
A449
Stratfore
upon-Av
A439
A422
6
Bretforton
A435
Chipping
Campden
Upton
upon Severn
Ledbury
Elmley
Castle
Broadway
Blockley
Woolhope
Fownhope
Carey
Sellack
Little
Washbourne
Snowshill
Stow-on-
the-Wold
Ford
Lower Swell
Chaceley Stock
A46
Bleding
Gloucester
M5
A40
Great Rissingto
Withington
Great
Barringto
Cowley
Elkstone
A435
Fossebridge
A433
Redbrook
Painswick
North Cerney
Barnsley
Coln
St Ald
Clearwell
St Briavels
GLOUCESTERSHIRE
A419
Ampney
Crucis
Southrop
R SEVERN
A38
Minchinhampton
Kingscote
North Nibley
Ewen
Lechla
A419

MAP 4

SK

LEICESTERSHIRE

Ratby• •Leicester

South
Luffenham
Wing• •

•Sheepy 4 Sutton Cheney
Magna

A47 8 9

A5

A6

Hallaton•

East Langton•

A6

A43

Twywell•
Titchmarsh•
Keyston•

ENTRY

NORTHAMPTONSHIRE

Dunchurch• Ashby
St Ledgers•

•Long Buckby

Melchbourne•

WARWICKSHIRE

M1

Southam•

Weedon
Badby• Gayton•

Northampton•

5

Priors Marston•

A381

SP

A5

Stoke
Bruerne•

Turvey•

Farnborough•
Edge Hill•

Towcester•

•Cropredy
•Great Bourton

Marston
St Lawrence•

A43

Astwood•

Biddenham•

M1
A422

Stony
Stratford•
Akeley•

A421

Ridgmont•

Bloxham•
•Adderbury

A316

Long Compton• Barford St Michael•

•Great Tew

Great
Brickhill•

Woburn•

A5

M1

Chipping
Norton•

•Steeple
Aston

A413

•Marsh
Gibbon

Dunstable•

Charlbury•

OXFORDSHIRE

BUCKINGHAMSHIRE

pton-upon-Wychwood

brook
•Minster Lovell
uth Leigh• Wytham•
Stanton•
Harcourt
Newbridge•
Fyfield•
adcot
ringdon
rnham

Murcott•

•Noke

•Godstow

OXFORD

Cumnor•

A40

Studham•

Dunsmore•
Litttle
Hampden•

Hawridge Frithsden•
Common•

A329

Chinnor•

Bledlow•

The
Lee•

Flaunden•
Botley•

5 6 7 8 9

Clifton Hampden•

Cuxham• Ibstone•
2
Northend•
Turville•

West
Wycombe•
Fingest• •Downley
•Bolter End

Amersham•

Penn•
Forty Green•

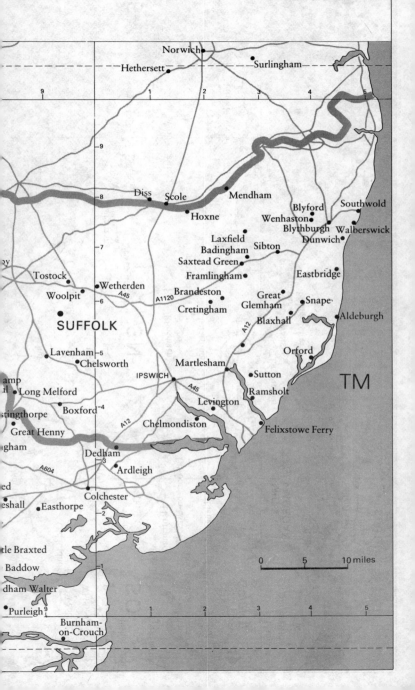

MAP 5

Norwich
Hethersett   Surlingham

9   1   2   3   4   5

—9

Diss   Scole   Mendham   Blyford   Southwold
—8   Hoxne   Wenhaston
     Blythburgh   Walberswick
    Laxfield   Dunwich
   Badingham   Sibton
Tostock   Wetherden   Saxtead Green
     Framlingham   Eastbridge
Woolpit   A45   A1120   Brandeston
—6   Cretingham   Great   Snape
     Glemham
SUFFOLK   Blaxhall   Aldeburgh
     A12

Lavenham—5   Orford
  Chelsworth   Martlesham
amp   IPSWICH   Sutton
il   Long Melford   A45   Ramsholt
   Boxford—4   Levington
stingthorpe   A12
  Great Henny   Chelmondiston   Felixstowe Ferry
gham
   Dedham
  A604 —3
    Ardleigh

ed   Colchester
eshall   Easthorpe
—2

tle Braxted

Baddow

dham Walter

Purleigh 9   Burnham-
     on-Crouch

0   5   10 miles

TM

1   2   3   4   5

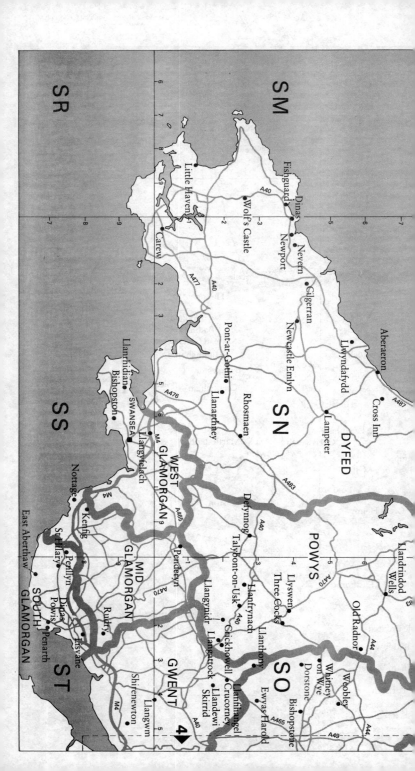

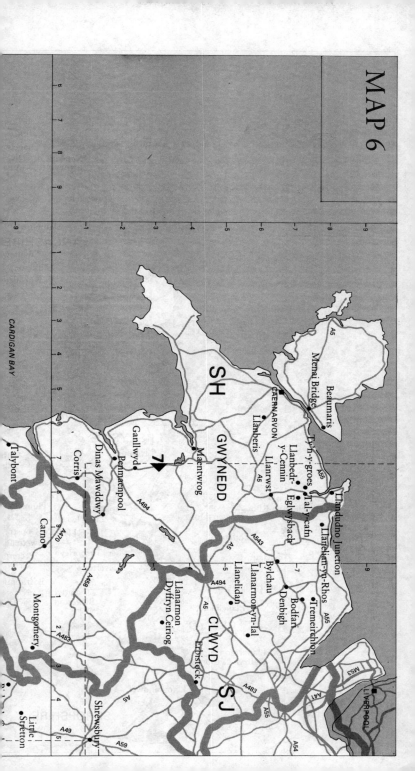

MAP 6

CARDIGAN BAY

SH

GWYNEDD

CLWYD

SJ

Beaumaris
Menai Bridge
Llandudno Junction
Tyn-y-groes
CAERNARVON
Llanberis
Llanbedr-y-Cennin
Llanrwst
Tal-y-cafn
Eglwysbach
Llanrhos
Llanelian-yn-Rhos
Tremeirchion
Maentwrog
Ganllwyd
Penmaenpool
Dinas Mawddwy
Corris
Talybont
Carno
A494
A470
A458
Montgomery
Llanarmon Dyffryn Ceiriog
A5
A543
A494
Bodfari
Denbigh
Bylchau
Llanarmon-yn-Ial
Llanelidan
 Erbistock
A483
A55
Shrewsbury
Little Stretton
A49
A59
A54
A41
M53
LIVERPOOL
A483

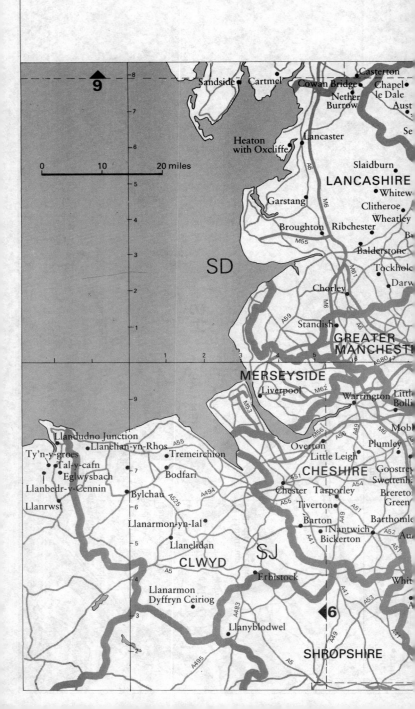

MAP 7

10

8▶

4▼

Buckden
Starbotton

Masham
West Tanfield
Sutton
Howgrave

Oswaldkirk • Nunnington

Coxwold

...ton
Craven

Ramsgill

Wath-in-
Nidderdale

Aldborough

Crayke

Welburn

Burnsall

Marton
cum Grafton

Sledmere

...ton

Gargrave   Thruscross

NORTH
YORKSHIRE

Millington

Sicklinghall

Wighill

York

Sutton
upon Derwent

Allerthorpe

HUMBERSIDE

A59

A650   Bingley

A65

WEST
YORKSHIRE

A64

Tadcaster

Ellerton

SE

Goose Eye   Harden

Bradford

Leeds

Ledsham

A163

...o

Widdop

Sowerby
Bridge

A62

Heath

Cridling Stubbs

Midgley

...kstone
...dge

Ripponden
Barkisland

Heckmondwike

M62

A19

M62

M62

...dale

Almondsbury

Sutton

Hatfield
Woodhouse

M180

...am

Denshaw
Delph

Uppermill

SOUTH
YORKSHIRE

Cadeby

A1

M18

...leton
...ridge

A616

1   4   5   6   7   8   9

...hester

Marple
...port

Rowarth

Grenoside

Wentworth

M18

M1

A631

Birch Vale   Edale

SHEFFIELD

A57

South
Anston

Blyth

Drakeholes

Bamford
Hathersage

...ow

Little
Hucklow

Foolow

...Macclesfield   Litton   Wardlow

Buxton   A6

Millthorpe

A57

A1

Langley
...worth   Wildboarclough

Beeley

M1

NOTTINGHAMSHIRE

A46

...o

Flash

Over
Haddon

Rowsley

Maplebeck

Newark

...lleton
...sall

Hope

Hartington

Ravenshead

Southwell   Upton

Cauldon

A523

DERBYSHIRE

Lambley

A46

TOKE

A52

A52

A50

SK

Nottingham

Grantham

...stone

Sandonbank

Hose

...ttle
...dgeford

Newborough   Melbourne

Kegworth
West Leake

...ford   Abbots
Bromley

Burton
on Trent   Ticknall

Wilson

A138

Old
Dalby

...AFFORDSHIRE

A60

Barrow
on Soar

A6

A606

Stretton

A34

Clifton Campville

A50

Langham   Exton

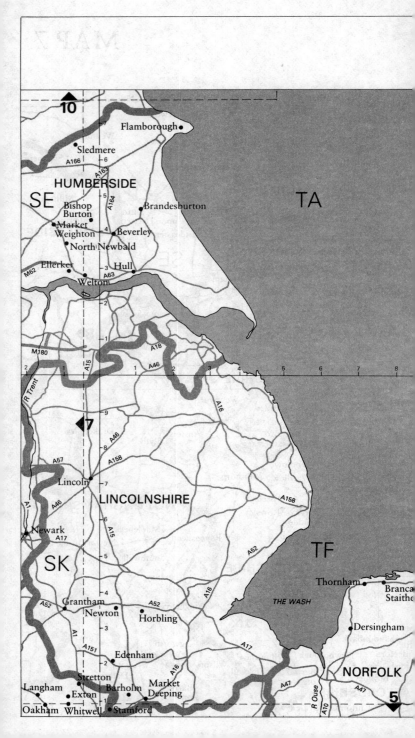

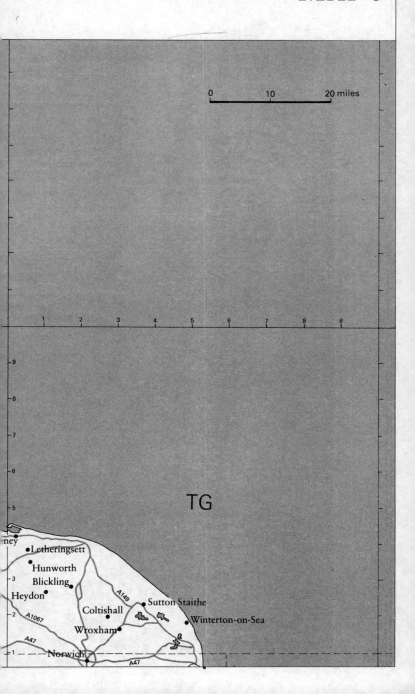

MAP 8

0   10   20 miles

1   2   3   4   5   6   7   8   9

-9

-8

-7

-6

-5

TG

ney
• Letheringsett
• Hunworth
-3 Blickling•
Heydon•
                              •Sutton Staithe
Coltishall
-2 A1067   •Winterton-on-Sea
    Wroxham•
A47
-1 Norwich
        A47

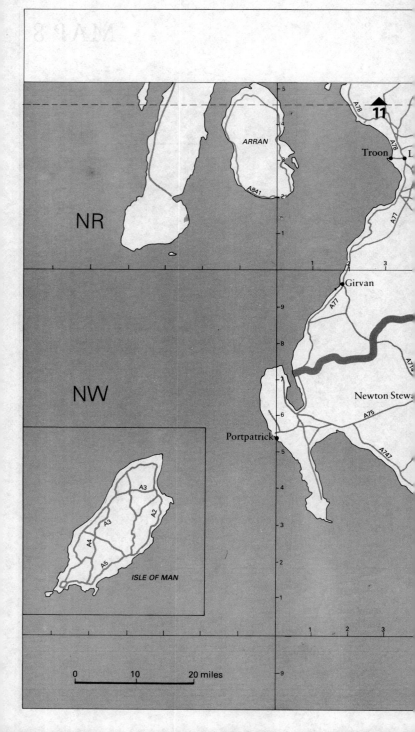

MAP 8

NR

NW

ARRAN

A841

Troon

A78

A78

A77

11

Girvan

A77

A714

Newton Stew

A75

A747

Portpatrick

A3

A3

A2

A4

A5

ISLE OF MAN

0   10   20 miles

MAP 9

Eddleston
Lauder

BORDERS

Melrose

STRATHCLYDE

Mountbenger

Tweedsmuir
St Mary's Loch

NT

Moffat

Moniaive
Thornhill

**DUMFRIES
AND
GALLOWAY**

10▶

Canonbie

Warwick on Eden
CARLISLE
Talkin

Faugh

atehouse
f Fleet
Dalbeattie
Kippford
NY

Twynholm

Kirkcudbright

CUMBRIA

Bassenthwaite
Lake
Penrith

Scales Stainton
Eaglesfield
Tirril

Loweswater
Keswick
Askham

Whithorn

NX
Buttermere

Wasdale Head
Langdale Grasmere
Little
Langdale Elterwater
Boot
Troutbeck
Hawkshead
Bowness-on
Eskdale
-Windermere
Green
Far Sawrey
KENDAL
Near Sawrey

SD Lowick
Cartmel Fell
Green
Levens

SC
7▼
Heversham

Cartmel

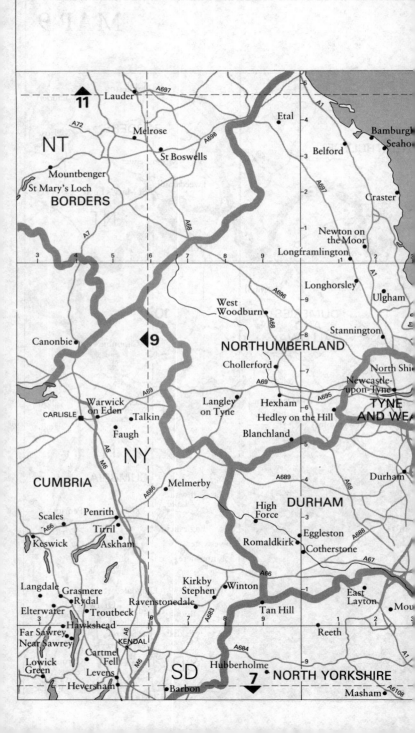

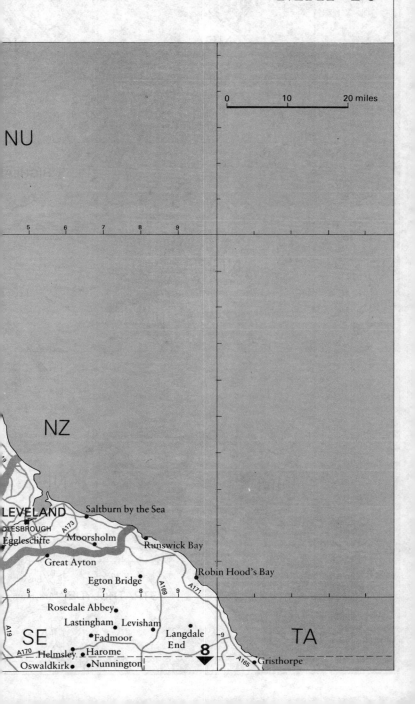

MAP 10

0   10   20 miles

NU

NZ

LEVELAND   Saltburn by the Sea
DLESBROUGH
Egglescliffe   Moorsholm   Runswick Bay

Great Ayton

Egton Bridge   Robin Hood's Bay

Rosedale Abbey
Lastingham Levisham
SE   Fadmoor   Langdale   TA
End
Helmsley Harome   Gristhorpe
Oswaldkirk Nunnington

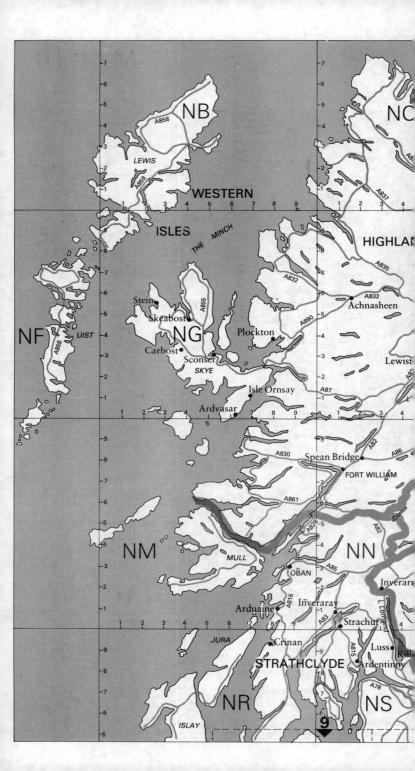

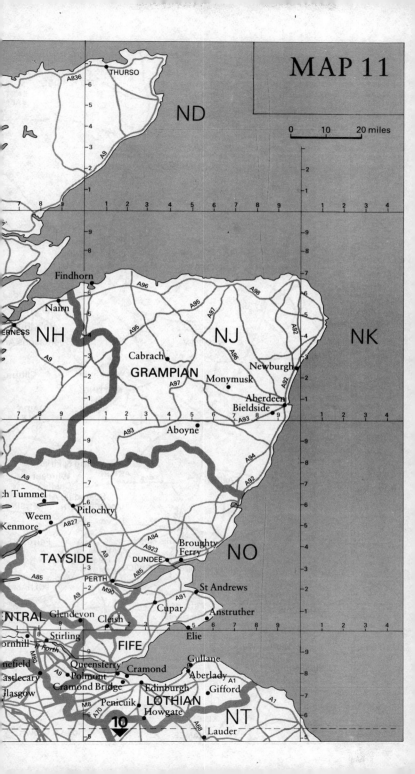

MAP 11

0   10   20 miles

THURSO

ND

NK

NJ

NH

Findhorn

Nairn

ERNESS

A96

A95

A97

Cabrach

GRAMPIAN

Monymusk

Newburgh

Aberdeen

Bieldside

A93

Aboyne

A94

A92

ch Tummel

A9

Weem

Pitlochry

Kenmore

A827

A94

A923

Broughty
Ferry

TAYSIDE

A9

DUNDEE

NO

A85

A85

PERTH

M90

St Andrews

A9

A91

Cupar

Glendevon

Cleish

Anstruther

NTRAL

Stirling

Elie

ornhill

R Forth

FIFE

Gullane

nefield

Queensferry

Cramond

Aberlady

astlecary

Polmont

A1

Gifford

lasgow

Cramond Bridge

Edinburgh

M8

Penicuik

LOTHIAN

A70

Howgate

NT

10

Lauder

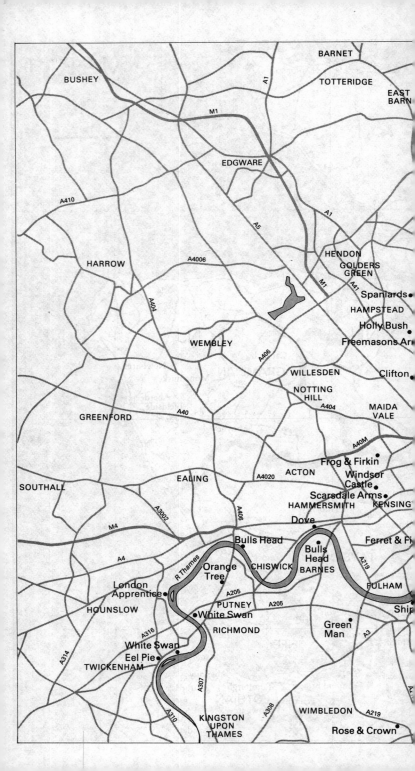

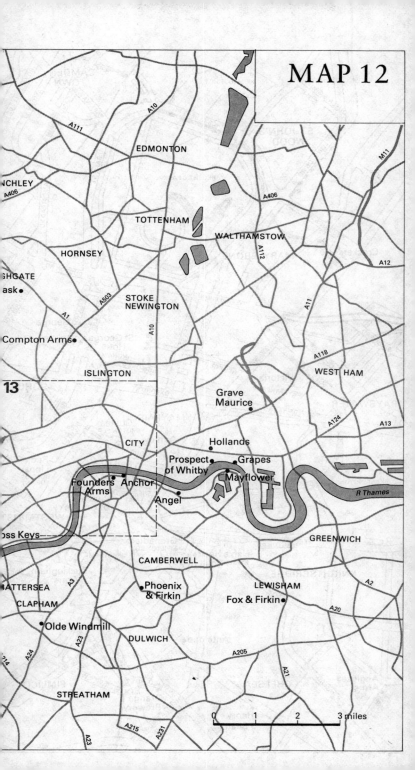

MAP 12

A111

A10

EDMONTON

NCHLEY

A406

A406

A11

M11

TOTTENHAM

WALTHAMSTOW

HORNSEY

A112

A12

GHATE

ask●

A503

STOKE
NEWINGTON

A10

A118

WEST HAM

Compton Arms●

A1

ISLINGTON

13

Grave
Maurice●

A124

A13

CITY

Hollands●

Prospect
of Whitby●

Grapes●

Founders
Arms●

Anchor●

Mayflower

R Thames

Angel●

ss Keys

GREENWICH

CAMBERWELL

ATTERSEA

A3

Phoenix
& Firkin●

LEWISHAM

A2

CLAPHAM

Fox & Firkin●

A20

●Olde Windmill

A23

DULWICH

A205

A21

714

A24

STREATHAM

A215   A231

A23

0   1   2   3 miles

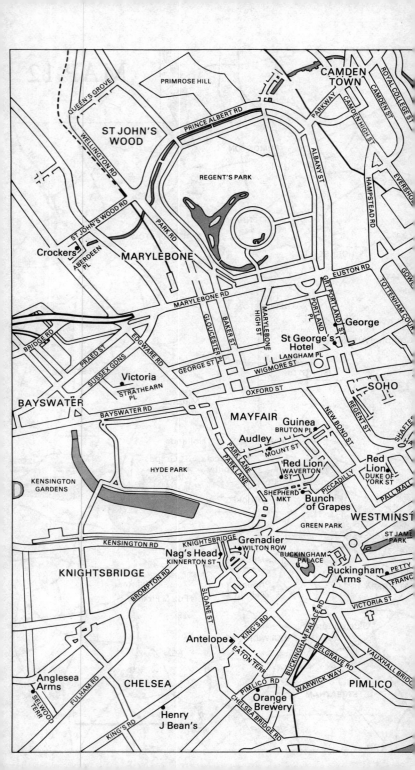

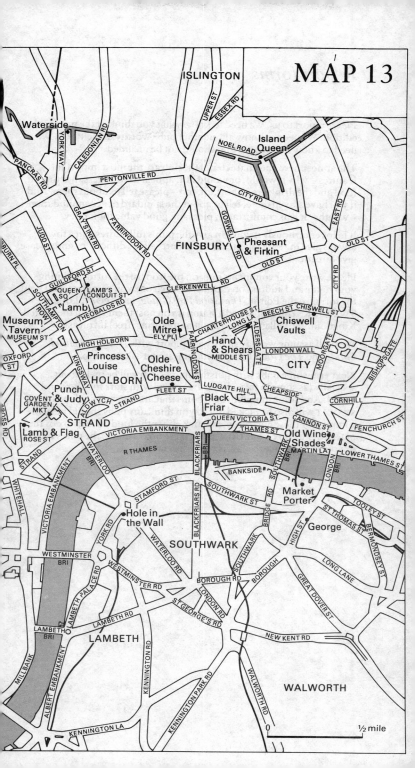

MAP 13

ISLINGTON

Waterside

Island Queen

NOEL ROAD

UPPER ST

ESSEX RD

YORK WAY

CALEDONIAN RD

PANCRAS RD

PENTONVILLE RD

CITY RD

EAST RD

GOSWELL RD

FARRINGDON RD

GRAY'S INN RD

JUDD ST

Pheasant & Firkin

FINSBURY

OLD ST

OLD ST

CITY RD

CLERKENWELL RD

GUILDFORD ST

QUEEN SQ

LAMB'S CONDUIT ST

Lamb

SOUTHAMPTON ROW

THEOBALDS RD

Museum Tavern

MUSEUM ST

OXFORD ST

HIGH HOLBORN

KINGSWAY

Princess Louise

HOLBORN

Punch & Judy

COVENT GARDEN MKT

ALDWYCH

STRAND

STRAND

Lamb & Flag

ROSE ST

CHARING CROSS RD

WHITEHALL

WESTMINSTER BRI

Olde Mitre

ELY PL

Olde Cheshire Cheese

FLEET ST

CHARTERHOUSE ST

LONG LA

Hand & Shears

MIDDLE ST

ALDERSGATE

BEECH ST

CHISWELL ST

Chiswell Vaults

LONDON WALL

CITY

MOORGATE

BISHOPSGATE

LUDGATE HILL

CHEAPSIDE

CORNHILL

Black Friar

QUEEN VICTORIA ST

CANNON ST

FENCHURCH ST

THAMES ST

Old Wine Shades

MARTIN LA

LOWER THAMES ST

VICTORIA EMBANKMENT

WATERLOO BRI

R THAMES

BLACKFRIARS

BLACKFRIARS BRI

BANKSIDE

SOUTHWARK BRI

LONDON BRI

STAMFORD ST

SOUTHWARK ST

Market Porter

TOOLEY ST

Hole in the Wall

WATERLOO RD

BLACKFRIARS RD

SOUTHWARK ST

BRIDGE RD

SOUTHWARK

HIGH ST

George

ST THOMAS ST

BERMONDSEY ST

YORK RD

WESTMINSTER BRI

WESTMINSTER RD

BOROUGH RD

LONDON RD

SOUTHWARK BRIDGE RD

BOROUGH

LONG LANE

GREAT DOVER ST

LAMBETH BRI

LAMBETH PALACE RD

LAMBETH RD

ST GEORGE'S RD

LAMBETH

KENNINGTON RD

NEW KENT RD

WALWORTH

MILLBANK

ALBERT EMBANKMENT

KENNINGTON LA

KENNINGTON PARK RD

WALWORTH RD

0

½ mile

Report forms

Please report to us. We need to know what you think of the pubs in this edition. We need to know about other pubs worthy of inclusion. We need to know about ones that should not be included.

The atmosphere and character of the pub are the most important features – why it would, or would not, appeal to strangers. But the bar food and the drink are important, too – please tell us about them. And if you have stayed there, tell us about the standard of accommodation – whether it was comfortable, pleasant, good value for money.

It helps enormously if you can give the pub's full address: in a town, always give the street name; in the country, if it's difficult to find, please give directions.

Please write your comments only on the front of the forms, printing your name and address on the back of each one you complete, and send the forms to the Editor, *The Good Pub Guide*, FREEPOST, London SW10 0BR. You don't need a stamp if you post them within the United Kingdom. We will gladly send you more forms (free) if you ask.

We shall assume we may share your report with *The Good Hotel Guide* and *The Good Food Guide* unless you ask us not to.

Next year some pubs with outstanding FOOD will be picked out specially (as some in this edition are picked with stars for all-round merit). And some inns with bedrooms that are outstandingly NICE TO STAY AT will also be picked out. If you think any pubs should be in the running for these awards, please tick either the food award box or the place-to-stay box – but DON'T tick these boxes unless the pub's food, or appeal as a place to stay, is really special.

REPORT on _____ *(pub's name)*

Pub's address: _____

_____

☐ YES should be included;
    deserves FOOD award ☐
    PLACE-TO-STAY award ☐
    (you may print my name/initials as a recommender)
☐ NO this pub should not be included
Please tick the YES or NO box to show your verdict

Reasons and descriptive comments:

PLEASE GIVE YOUR OWN NAME AND ADDRESS ON THE BACK OF THIS FORM

1

REPORT on _____ *(pub's name)*

Pub's address: _____

_____

☐ YES should be included;
    deserves FOOD award ☐
    PLACE-TO-STAY award ☐
    (you may print my name/initials as a recommender)
☐ NO this pub should not be included
Please tick the YES or NO box to show your verdict

Reasons and descriptive comments:

PLEASE GIVE YOUR OWN NAME AND ADDRESS ON THE BACK OF THIS FORM

2

REPORT on _____ *(pub's name)*

Pub's address: _____

_____

☐ YES should be included;
    deserves FOOD award ☐
    PLACE-TO-STAY award ☐
    (you may print my name/initials as a recommender)
☐ NO this pub should not be included
Please tick the YES or NO box to show your verdict

Reasons and descriptive comments:

PLEASE GIVE YOUR OWN NAME AND ADDRESS ON THE BACK OF THIS FORM

Your own name and address *(block capitals please)*

Your own name and address *(block capitals please)*

Your own name and address *(block capitals please)*

REPORT on _____ *(pub's name)*

Pub's address: _____

☐ YES should be included;
    deserves FOOD award ☐
    PLACE-TO-STAY award ☐
    (you may print my name/initials as a recommender)
☐ NO this pub should not be included
Please tick the YES *or* NO *box to show your verdict*

Reasons and descriptive comments:

PLEASE GIVE YOUR OWN NAME AND ADDRESS ON THE BACK OF THIS FORM

7

REPORT on _____ *(pub's name)*

Pub's address: _____

☐ YES should be included;
    deserves FOOD award ☐
    PLACE-TO-STAY award ☐
    (you may print my name/initials as a recommender)
☐ NO this pub should not be included
Please tick the YES *or* NO *box to show your verdict*

Reasons and descriptive comments:

PLEASE GIVE YOUR OWN NAME AND ADDRESS ON THE BACK OF THIS FORM

8

REPORT on _____ *(pub's name)*

Pub's address: _____

☐ YES should be included;
    deserves FOOD award ☐
    PLACE-TO-STAY award ☐
    (you may print my name/initials as a recommender)
☐ NO this pub should not be included
Please tick the YES *or* NO *box to show your verdict*

Reasons and descriptive comments:

PLEASE GIVE YOUR OWN NAME AND ADDRESS ON THE BACK OF THIS FORM

9

Your own name and address *(block capitals please)*

Your own name and address *(block capitals please)*

Your own name and address *(block capitals please)*

REPORT on _____ *(pub's name)*

Pub's address: _____

_____

☐ YES should be included;
     deserves FOOD award ☐
     PLACE-TO-STAY award ☐
     (you may print my name/initials as a recommender)
☐ NO this pub should not be included
Please tick the YES *or* NO *box to show your verdict*

Reasons and descriptive comments:

PLEASE GIVE YOUR OWN NAME AND ADDRESS ON THE BACK OF THIS FORM

10

....

REPORT on _____ *(pub's name)*

Pub's address: _____

_____

☐ YES should be included;
     deserves FOOD award ☐
     PLACE-TO-STAY award ☐
     (you may print my name/initials as a recommender)
☐ NO this pub should not be included
Please tick the YES *or* NO *box to show your verdict*

Reasons and descriptive comments:

PLEASE GIVE YOUR OWN NAME AND ADDRESS ON THE BACK OF THIS FORM

11

....

REPORT on _____ *(pub's name)*

Pub's address: _____

_____

☐ YES should be included;
     deserves FOOD award ☐
     PLACE-TO-STAY award ☐
     (you may print my name/initials as a recommender)
☐ NO this pub should not be included
Please tick the YES *or* NO *box to show your verdict*

Reasons and descriptive comments:

PLEASE GIVE YOUR OWN NAME AND ADDRESS ON THE BACK OF THIS FORM

12

Your own name and address *(block capitals please)*

Your own name and address *(block capitals please)*

Your own name and address *(block capitals please)*

REPORT on

(pub's name)

Pub's address:

☐ YES should be included;
    deserves FOOD award ☐
    PLACE-TO-STAY award ☐
    (you may print my name/initials as a recommender)
☐ NO this pub should not be included
Please tick the YES *or* NO *box to show your verdict*

Reasons and descriptive comments:

PLEASE GIVE YOUR OWN NAME AND ADDRESS ON THE BACK OF THIS FORM

13

....

REPORT on

(pub's name)

Pub's address:

☐ YES should be included;
    deserves FOOD award ☐
    PLACE-TO-STAY award ☐
    (you may print my name/initials as a recommender)
☐ NO this pub should not be included
Please tick the YES *or* NO *box to show your verdict*

Reasons and descriptive comments:

PLEASE GIVE YOUR OWN NAME AND ADDRESS ON THE BACK OF THIS FORM

14

....

REPORT on

(pub's name)

Pub's address:

☐ YES should be included;
    deserves FOOD award ☐
    PLACE-TO-STAY award ☐
    (you may print my name/initials as a recommender)
☐ NO this pub should not be included
Please tick the YES *or* NO *box to show your verdict*

Reasons and descriptive comments:

PLEASE GIVE YOUR OWN NAME AND ADDRESS ON THE BACK OF THIS FORM

15

Your own name and address *(block capitals please)*

Your own name and address *(block capitals please)*

Your own name and address *(block capitals please)*

REPORT on _____ (pub's name)

Pub's address: _____

_____

☐ YES should be included;
    deserves FOOD award ☐
    PLACE-TO-STAY award ☐
    (you may print my name/initials as a recommender)
☐ NO this pub should not be included
Please tick the YES *or* NO *box to show your verdict*

Reasons and descriptive comments:

16

REPORT on _____ (pub's name)

Pub's address: _____

_____

☐ YES should be included;
    deserves FOOD award ☐
    PLACE-TO-STAY award ☐
    (you may print my name/initials as a recommender)
☐ NO this pub should not be included
Please tick the YES *or* NO *box to show your verdict*

Reasons and descriptive comments:

17

REPORT on _____ (pub's name)

Pub's address: _____

_____

☐ YES should be included;
    deserves FOOD award ☐
    PLACE-TO-STAY award ☐
    (you may print my name/initials as a recommender)
☐ NO this pub should not be included
Please tick the YES *or* NO *box to show your verdict*

Reasons and descriptive comments:

18

Your own name and address *(block capitals please)*

Your own name and address *(block capitals please)*

Your own name and address *(block capitals please)*

REPORTon   *(pub's name)*

Pub's address:

☐ YES should be included;
     deserves FOOD award ☐
     PLACE-TO-STAY award ☐
     (you may print my name/initials as a recommender)
☐ NO this pub should not be included
Please tick the YES *or* NO *box to show your verdict*

Reasons and descriptive comments:

PLEASE GIVE YOUR OWN NAME AND ADDRESS ON THE BACK OF THIS FORM

19
....

REPORTon   *(pub's name)*

Pub's address:

☐ YES should be included;
     deserves FOOD award ☐
     PLACE-TO-STAY award ☐
     (you may print my name/initials as a recommender)
☐ NO this pub should not be included
Please tick the YES *or* NO *box to show your verdict*

Reasons and descriptive comments:

PLEASE GIVE YOUR OWN NAME AND ADDRESS ON THE BACK OF THIS FORM

20
....

REPORTon   *(pub's name)*

Pub's address:

☐ YES should be included;
     deserves FOOD award ☐
     PLACE-TO-STAY award ☐
     (you may print my name/initials as a recommender)
☐ NO this pub should not be included
Please tick the YES *or* NO *box to show your verdict*

Reasons and descriptive comments:

PLEASE GIVE YOUR OWN NAME AND ADDRESS ON THE BACK OF THIS FORM

21

Your own name and address *(block capitals please)*

Your own name and address *(block capitals please)*

Your own name and address *(block capitals please)*

REPORT on _____ *(pub's name)*

Pub's address: _____

☐ YES should be included;
     deserves FOOD award ☐
     PLACE-TO-STAY award ☐
     (you may print my name/initials as a recommender)
☐ NO this pub should not be included
Please tick the YES or NO box to show your verdict

Reasons and descriptive comments:

PLEASE GIVE YOUR OWN NAME AND ADDRESS ON THE BACK OF THIS FORM

22

....

REPORT on _____ *(pub's name)*

Pub's address: _____

☐ YES should be included;
     deserves FOOD award ☐
     PLACE-TO-STAY award ☐
     (you may print my name/initials as a recommender)
☐ NO this pub should not be included
Please tick the YES or NO box to show your verdict

Reasons and descriptive comments:

PLEASE GIVE YOUR OWN NAME AND ADDRESS ON THE BACK OF THIS FORM

23

....

REPORT on _____ *(pub's name)*

Pub's address: _____

☐ YES should be included;
     deserves FOOD award ☐
     PLACE-TO-STAY award ☐
     (you may print my name/initials as a recommender)
☐ NO this pub should not be included
Please tick the YES or NO box to show your verdict

Reasons and descriptive comments:

PLEASE GIVE YOUR OWN NAME AND ADDRESS ON THE BACK OF THIS FORM

24

Your own name and address *(block capitals please)*

Your own name and address *(block capitals please)*

Your own name and address *(block capitals please)*